Engineering Design and Graphics with SolidWorks®

Engineering Design and Graphics with SolidWorks®

James D. Bethune
Boston University

Prentice Hall
Boston Columbus Indianapolis New York San Francisco Upper Saddle River
Amsterdam Cape Town Dubai London Madrid Milan Munich Paris Montreal Toronto
Delhi Mexico City Sao Paulo Sydney Hong Kong Seoul Singapore Taipei Tokyo

Editor in Chief: Vernon Anthony
Acquisitions Editor: Jill Jones-Renger
Editorial Assistant: Doug Greive
Director of Marketing: David Gesell
Marketing Manager: Kara Clark
Senior Marketing Coordinator: Alicia Wozniak
Senior Managing Editor: JoEllen Gohr
Associate Managing Editor: Alexandrina Wolf
Project Manager: Louise Sette
Senior Operations Supervisor: Pat Tonneman
Operations Specialist: Deidra Schwartz
Senior Art Director: Jayne Conte
Cover Designer: Bruce Kenselaar
Cover Art: James D. Bethune
Full-Service Project Management: Lisa S. Garboski, bookworks publishing services
Composition: Aptara®, Inc.
Printer/Binder: Edwards Brothers
Cover Printer: Coral Graphic Services, Inc.
Text Font: Times New Roman

Disclaimer:
The publication is designed to provide tutorial information about the SolidWorks computer program. Every effort has been made to make this publication complete and as accurate as possible. The reader is expressly cautioned to use any and all precautions necessary, and to take appropriate steps to avoid hazards, when engaging in the activities described herein.

Neither the author nor the publisher makes any representations or warranties of any kind, with respect to the materials set forth in this publication, express or implied, including without limitation any warranties of fitness for a particular purpose or merchantability. Nor shall the author or the publisher be liable for any special, consequential or exemplary damages resulting, in whole or in part, directly or indirectly, from the reader's use of, or reliance upon, this material or subsequent revisions of this material.

Library of Congress Control Number: 2009921889

10 9 8 7 6 5 4 3

Prentice Hall
is an imprint of

www.pearsonhighered.com

ISBN-10: 0-13-502429-3
ISBN-13: 978-0-13-502429-4

Preface

This book shows and explains how to use SolidWorks to create engineering drawings and designs. Emphasis is placed on creating engineering drawings including dimensions and tolerances and the use of standard parts and tools. Each chapter contains step-by-step sample problems that show how to apply the concepts presented in the chapter.

The book contains hundreds of projects of various degrees of difficulty specifically designed to reinforce the chapter's content. The idea is that students learn best by doing. In response to reviewers' requests, some more difficult projects have been included.

Chapter 1 and 2 show how to set up a Part Document and how to use the SolidWorks **Sketch** tools. **Sketch** tools are used to create 2D Part Documents that can then be extruded into 3D solid models. The two chapters include 42 projects using both inches and millimeters for students to use for practice in applying the various **Sketch** tools.

Chapter 3 shows how to use the **Features** tools. **Features** tools are used to create and modify 3D solid models. In addition, reference planes are covered, and examples of how to edit existing models are given.

Chapter 4 explains how to create and interpret orthographic views. Views are created using third-angle projection in compliance with ANSI standards and conventions. Also included are section views, auxiliary views, and broken views. Several of the projects require that a 3D solid model be drawn from a given set of orthographic views to help students develop visualization skills.

Chapter 5 explains how to create assembly drawings using the **Assembly** tools (**Mate**, exploded **View**) and how to document assemblies using the Drawing Documents tools. Topics include assembled 3D solid models, exploded isometric drawings, and bills of materials. Assembly numbers and part numbers are discussed. Both the **Animate Collapse/Explode** and **Motion Study** tools are demonstrated.

Chapter 6 shows how to create and design with threads and fasteners. Both ANSI Inch and ANSI Metric threads are covered. The **Design Library** is presented, and examples are used to show how to select and size screws and other fasteners for assembled parts.

Chapter 7 covers dimensioning and is in compliance with ANSI standards and conventions. There are extensive visual examples of dimensioned shapes and features that serve as references for various dimensioning applications.

Chapter 8 covers tolerances. Both linear and geometric tolerances are included. This is often a difficult area to understand, so there are many examples of how to apply and how to interpret the various types of tolerances.

Chapter 9 covers gears, pulleys, and belts. The chapter relies heavily on the **Design Library**. The chapter does not deal with the forces present in gears, pulleys, and belts but rather deals with their selection and modification for incorporation into drawings. Motion Studies are also included.

Chapter 10 explains bearings and fit tolerances. The **Design Library** is used to create bearing drawings, and examples show how to select the correct interference tolerance between bearings and housing, and clearance tolerances between bearings and shafts.

Chapter 11 shows how to draw cams and springs. Displacement drawings are defined. The chapter shows how to add hubs and keyways to cams and then insert the cams into assembly drawings. Motion Studies are also included.

The **Appendix** includes fit tables for use with projects in the text. Clearance, locational, and interference fits are included for both inch and millimeter values.

ONLINE RESOURCES

To access supplementary materials online, instructors need to request an instructor access code. Go to **www.pearson-highered.com/irc,** where you can register for an instructor access code. Within 48 hours after registering, you will receive a confirming e-mail, including an instructor access code. Once you have received your code, go to the site and log on for full instructions on downloading the materials you wish to use.

ACKNOWLEDGMENTS

I would like to acknowledge the reviewers of this text: Peggy Condon-Vance, Penn State Berks; Lisa Richter, Macomb Community College; Julie Korfhage, Clackamas Community College; Max P. Gassman, Iowa State University; Paul E. Lienard, Northeastern University; and Hossein Hemati, Mira Costa College.

Thanks to the editor Jill Jones-Renger. A special thanks to Lisa Garboski who made sense out of a very rough manuscript. Thanks to my family David, Maria, Randy, Lisa, Hannah, Will, Madison, Jack, Luke, Sam and Ben.

A special thanks to Cheryl.

James D. Bethune
Boston University

Contents

Chapter 3—Features 93

Chapter 4—Orthographic Views 153

Chapter 5—Assemblies 201

Chapter 6—Threads and Fasteners 245

Chapter 7—Dimensioning 285

Engineering Design and Graphics with SolidWorks®

Introduction

I-1 A PERSONAL HISTORY OF CAD

The first devices created to assist in creating engineering drawings that I remember were introduced in the mid-sixties. The devices were plotters used to draw loft lines—more specifically, the contour of an aircraft wing. Up to that time wing contours were created by loftsmen, who worked on very large tables, at least 10 feet by 20 feet, and had to literally crawl around the table on their knees. They created line shapes using a long, thin plastic extrusion shaped like an H called a ***spline***. The spline was held in place by weights with hooks mounted in them called ***ducks***. The hooks were inserted into the spline and positioned to create the required contour. A line was then carefully traced along the spline to create the contour. Drawing using this procedure was slow and tedious.

To give you some idea of the speed and effectiveness of these early devices consider Figure I-1. The shape is created by first defining 24 equally spaced points on a circle and then joining each point with every other point using only straight lines. It would take about four hours to draw the shape by hand, using ink. It would take about six hours to draw the shape using an early plotter with punch card inputs. In defense of the plotter, the plotted drawing was more accurate than the hand drawing. There were no error messages at the time, so if an error occurred the machine simply stopped. If often required two people working together to examine each punch card to find the error.

In the late seventies I attended a course in how to use Unigraphics. The computer used to drive the system was huge, taking up an entire room. The room was climate controlled and had special lighting.

The cursor was controlled using ***thumbscrews***, which were two wheels located in the workstation's desktop positioned at 90° to each other. One wheel was turned using the thumb, the other the index finger. The thumbscrews positioned the cursor, and inputs were entered from the keyboard or by pushing buttons on a control box located on the desktop. Again, there were no error messages. Unigraphics worked in only two dimensions and did not use color. At that time the acronym CAD meant computer-aided drafting.

An example of how these early systems worked is found in drawing a fillet. First, a square corner was drawn using straight lines, then an arc was created tangent to the corner. The line segment that extended beyond the fillet was then erased. It was often difficult to locate the tangency between the straight lines and the fillet arc, as there was no tangency constraint. It was not unusual to have to try many times to erase the line segment.

There was resistance at that time to the "new" technology. Many draftspersons simply refused to learn the new systems that they saw as slow, cumbersome, and impersonal. There was a great deal of pride among draftspersons in creating accurate, carefully crafted engineering drawing, and the new machine seemed to disregard that skill. The machines

This drawing was created by hand using ink. Note the slight error at the center point.

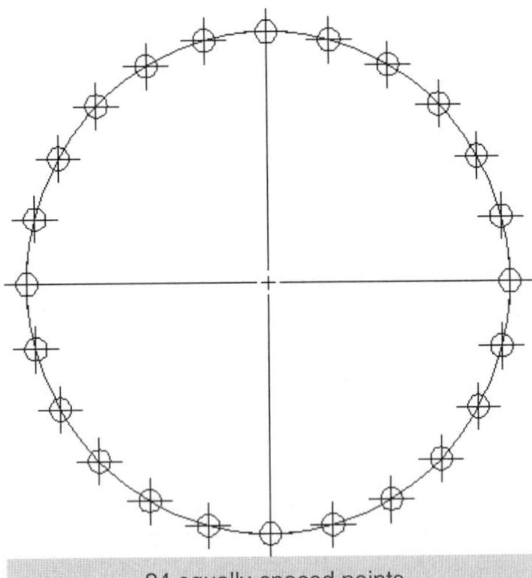

24 equally-spaced points

Connect each point with every other point using a straight line.

Figure I-1

required a different set of skills and a different way of thinking that seemed threatening to many.

While working as a consultant I heard a draftsman say "Hey, I'm going to retire in about five years, so I'm not interested in learning this stuff." (He didn't really say stuff).

In the mid-eighties I used a system called Catia. Catia had some three-dimensional capability and could be programmed. For example, a graduate student at Boston University created a Catia program that could create a flat pattern for simple sheet metal parts. The computers were still very large and required special rooms with controlled environments.

The real breakthrough in CAD which now meant came with the introduction of PCs. The first CAD (computer-aided design) software I used was AutoCAD Release 9.0. It was two-dimensional and had no color, but shapes could easily be erased and edited. In about 1990 AutoCAD Release 11 included an add-on option called AME that created three-dimensional (3D) models. Until the release of the AME add-on, 3D shapes were generated using surfaces. For example a box shape was created by joining six surfaces—one for each face of the box. These were not solid models but did appear three-dimensional. The AME add-on generated solid 3D models. Many of the 3D shapes were based on ***primitives***, that is, basic 3D shapes such as a box, a wedge, and a sphere.

The 3D models could be used to generate limited orthographic views. Hidden and centerlines were not included. Often, additional lines had to be added to complete the generated views.

As the power of PCs increased, the capabilities of the CAD programs grew. Autodesk introduced an add-on program called Mechanical Desktop that could transition more easily from 3D models to orthographic views. It was, for me, the start of real 3D designing.

By the late nineties parametric modelers, such as SolidWorks, became available and improved with each new release. SolidWorks allows the designer to work in three dimensions. Parts can easily be edited, and information about the documents can easily be transferred electronically to the shop. SolidWorks can generate complete orthographic views directly from the solid model.

So, what is the future of CAD programs? A very rough prediction is that there will be no more paper; that is, designs will be transmitted directly from the designer's computer to the manufacturing machines. Future CAD programs will be able to identify errors such as part interference and signal the designer about the error. Animation capabilities will greatly increase, so that future designers will be able actually to test their designs and see how they work. Regardless of what the future brings, we have come a long way from T-squares and triangles to solid modelers such as SolidWorks. SolidWorks is a vast improvement.

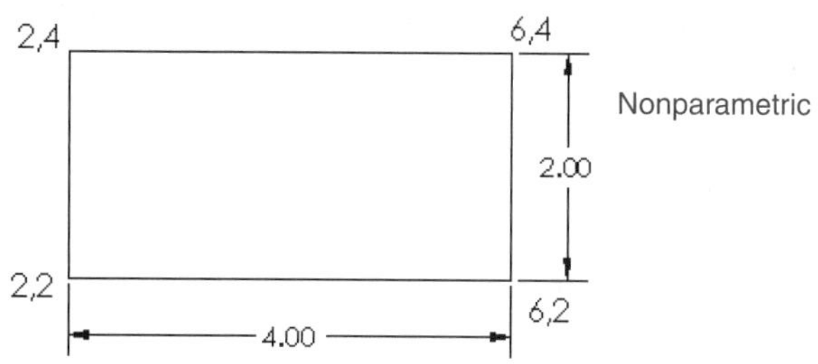

Rectangle defined using coordinate points.

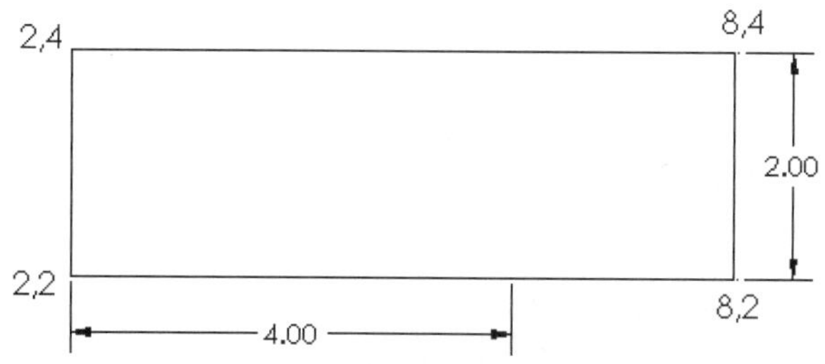

When the coordinates are changed, the dimensions are not.

Figure I-2

I-2 PARAMETRIC MODELERS

SolidWorks is a ***parametric modeler***; that is, the dimensions drive the shapes. To understand this concept, look at the 2 × 4 rectangle shown in Figure I-2. The rectangle was drawn using a nonparametric program. The rectangle was defined using coordinate points. The dimensions were added after the rectangle was drawn. If the coordinate points are edited to create a 2 × 6 rectangle, the 4.00 dimension remains in place. The dimension is independent of the rectangle.

Figure I-3 shows a 2 × 4 rectangle drawn using SolidWorks. The rectangle was defined using the dimensions, not coordinate points. Because SolidWorks is a parametric modeler, changing the dimensions changes the shape. Double-clicking the 4.00 dimension and entering a value of 6.00 changes the shape to a 2 × 6 rectangle.

Because parametric modelers are dimension driven, the way an object is dimensioned affects how its shape changes when edited. Figure I-4 shows a 2 × 2 square with a Ø1.00 circle. The circle is located using horizontal and vertical dimensions from the lower right corner of the square. If the 2.00 horizontal dimension is changed to 4.00, the hole will move to the right side of the object following the locating dimensions based on the lower right corner. If the hole's location is dimensioned from the upper left corner, and the horizontal dimension is changed to 4.00, the hole remains in the same location, because the edges that affect the hole's locating dimensions have not been changed.

I-3 AN OVERVIEW OF SOLIDWORKS

SolidWorks is a very user friendly program. Objects are initially created as sketches on one of three planes (XY, YZ, and XZ) then sized and developed into solid objects. Figure I-5 shows a rectangle sketched on the top plane (XY). It has no dimensions. Dimensions, thickness, and features will be added to this sketch to create a solid model.

Figure I-5 also shows the same rectangular sketch located on the top plane but viewed from a different orientation. The orientation (isometric) gives the appearance of three dimensions, but at this stage of the drawing, it is still two-dimensional.

Figure I-6 shows an object created using SolidWorks. Note that the object has highlights, that is, as if a light were shining on the object. This helps create a more realistic view.

SolidWorks has nine standard view orientations. See Figure I-6. Note the difference in axis references for each of these views.

Objects may be rotated into any orientation by holding down the mouse button and moving the cursor. This is called a ***custom*** orientation.

SolidWorks tools are listed in toolboxes located along the top of the drawing screen and in pull-down menus under the headings at the top of the screen. Figure I-7 shows the **Circle** tool listed in two different locations.

You can create you own custom menus that include those tools you use the most. This is recommended for your own computer, that is, a computer that only you use. It is not recommended for a lab setting where computers are shared with others.

The area on the left side of the screen is called the **Properties Manager**, and it contains a list of all the tools and sketches used to create the object. See Figure I-8. The **Extrude1** tool has been accessed with a left mouse click. The plus sign in the box to the left of the name changes from a plus sign to a minus sign. The cursor is then located on the **(-) Sketch1** heading. Note the circle at the top of the part. The initial sketch that was extruded is highlighted on the part. The **Properties Manager** will be used later to edit drawings.

You will notice that the lines in the drawing change colors as you work on a part. Line color is used to indicate the status of the line. When you first draw a line it is blue, meaning it is not completely defined. You have drawn a line, but not specified a length. When you select the line to define its length (using the **Smart Dimension** tool) it turns red, indicating that the cursor has identified the line. As you define the length of the line it turns green, indicating that it has been selected and is being edited. The length first appears blue again meaning that it is not completely defined. When the length is completely defined and the OK check mark (close dialog check mark) located in the upper left of the

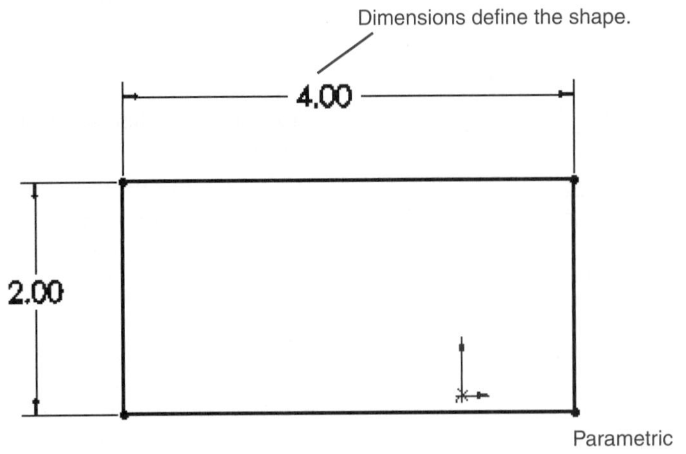
Dimensions define the shape.
4.00
2.00
Parametric

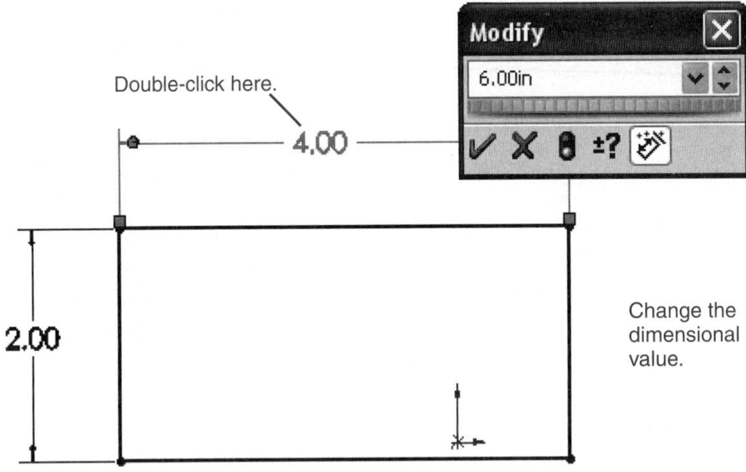
Modify
6.00in
Double-click here.
4.00
2.00
Change the dimensional value.

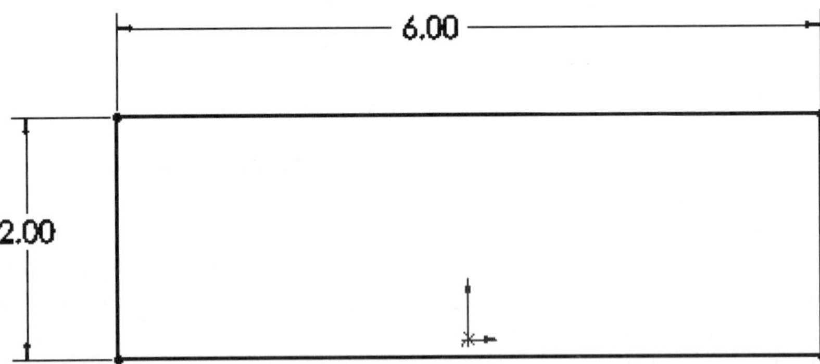
New dimension changes the rectangle's shape.
6.00
2.00

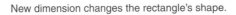

Figure I-3

Panel Control is clicked, the line turns black, indicating it is completely defined.

As stated previously SolidWorks is a very user friendly program and can be used to produce spectacular drawings. However, remember that drawings must not only look good but must also function as manufacturing instructions, so they must also be accurate and easy to understand. Overall, SolidWorks is a fun program to use. Let's get started.

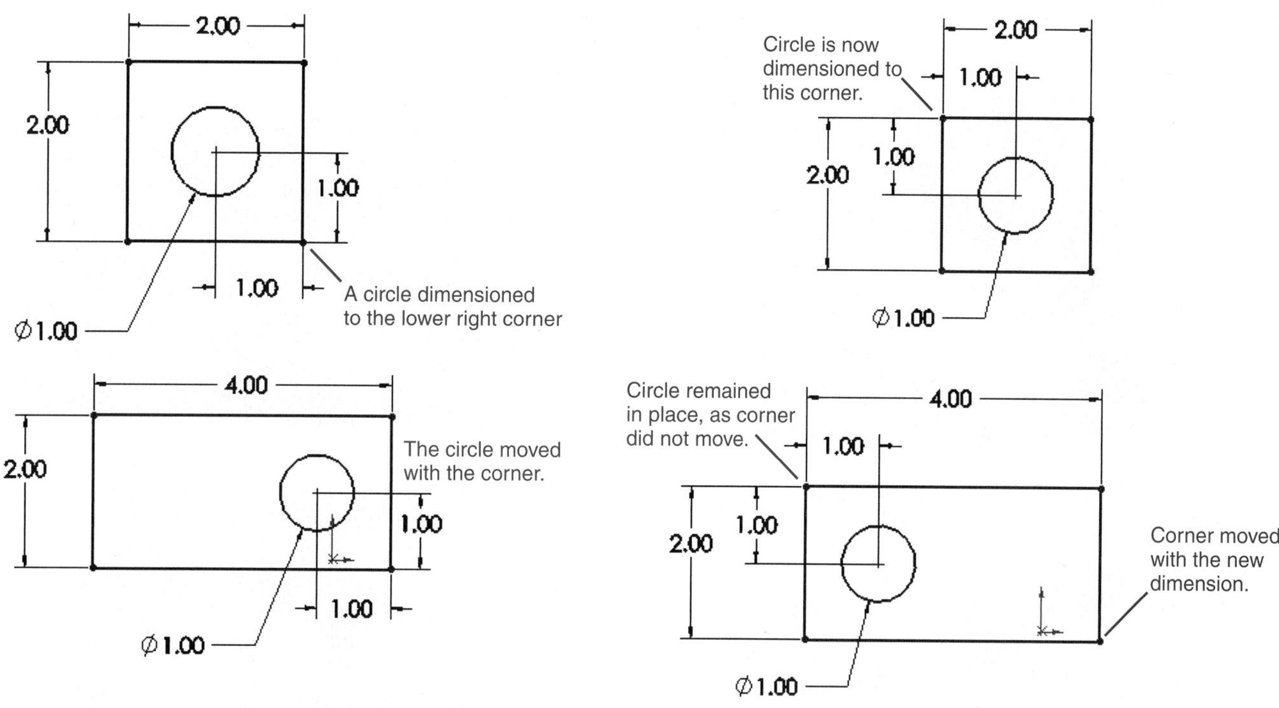
2.00
2.00
1.00
1.00
A circle dimensioned
to the lower right corner
∅1.00
Circle is now
dimensioned to
this corner.
2.00
1.00
1.00
2.00
∅1.00
4.00
2.00
The circle moved
with the corner.
1.00
1.00
∅1.00
Circle remained
in place, as corner
did not move.
4.00
1.00
1.00
2.00
Corner moved
with the new
dimension.
∅1.00

Figure I-4

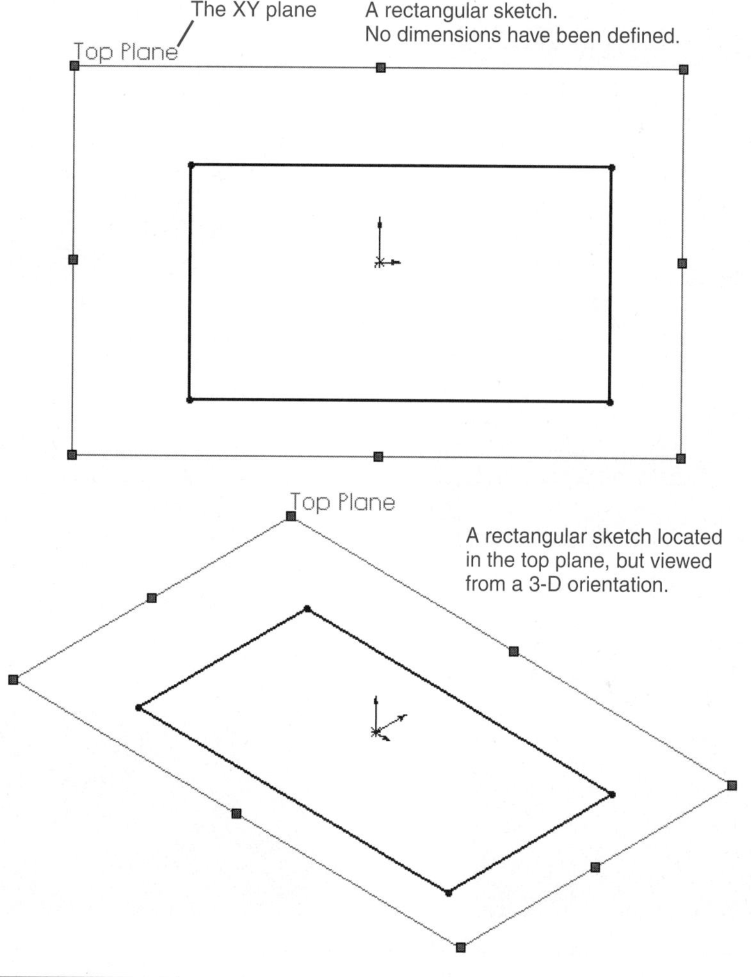
The XY plane
Top Plane
A rectangular sketch.
No dimensions have been defined.
Top Plane
A rectangular sketch located
in the top plane, but viewed
from a 3-D orientation.

Figure I-5

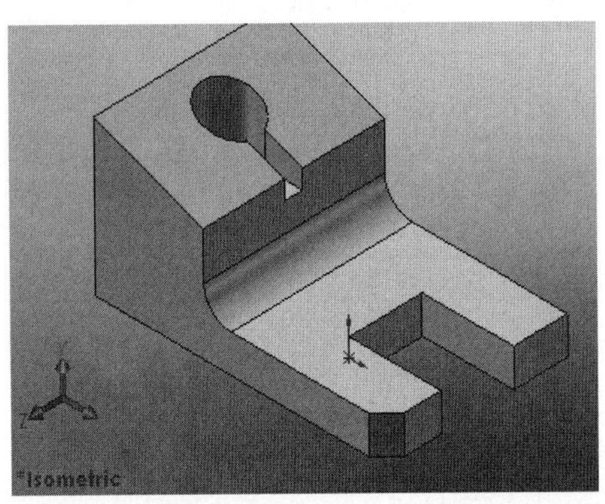
*Isometric

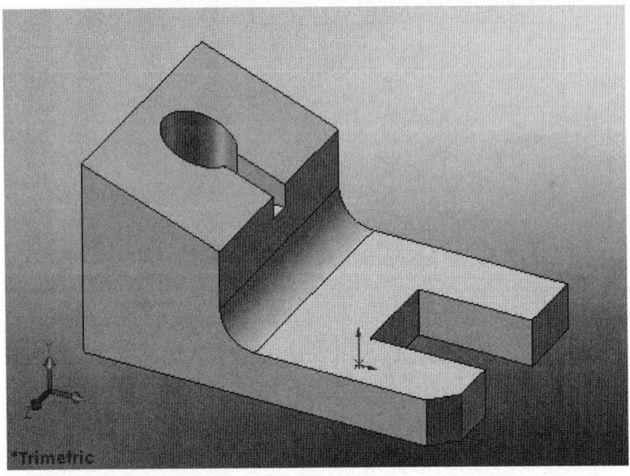
*Trimetric

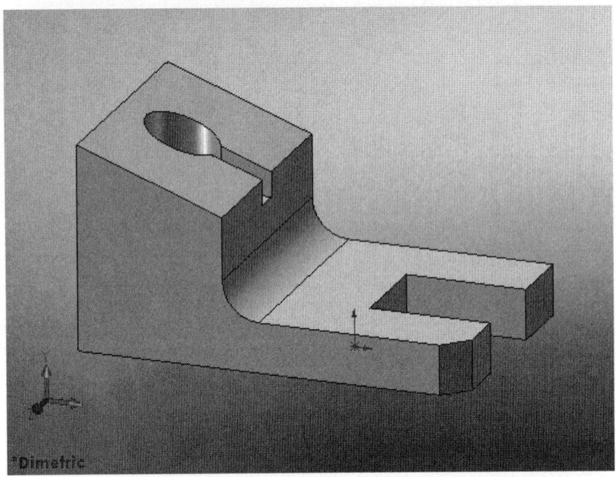
*Dimetric

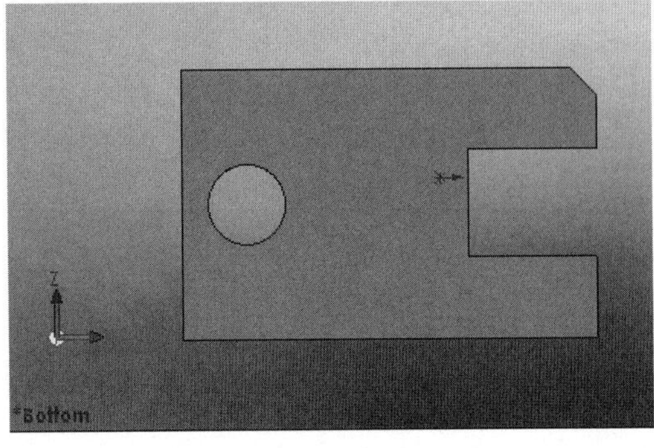
*Bottom

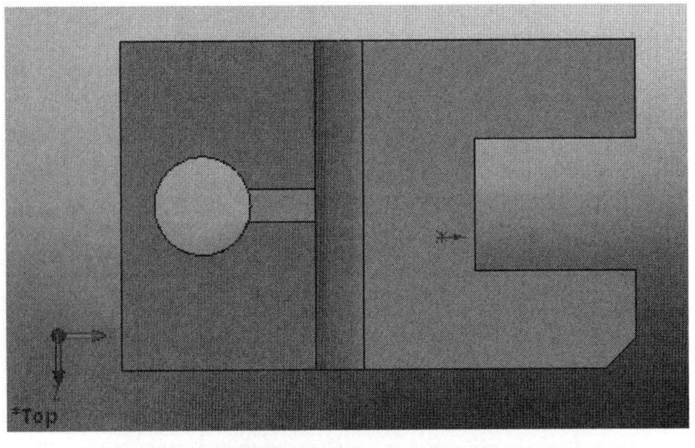
*Top

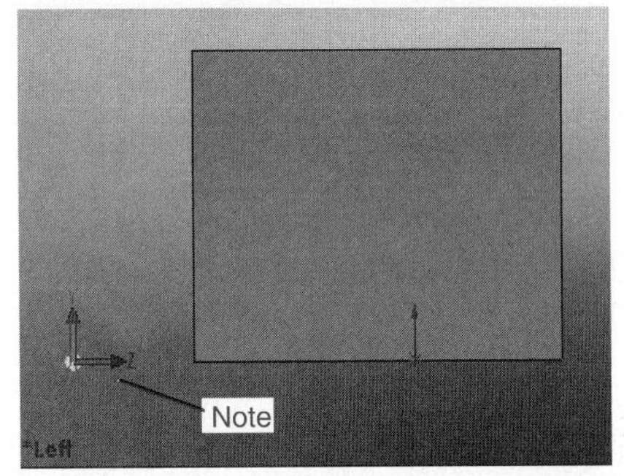
Note
*Left

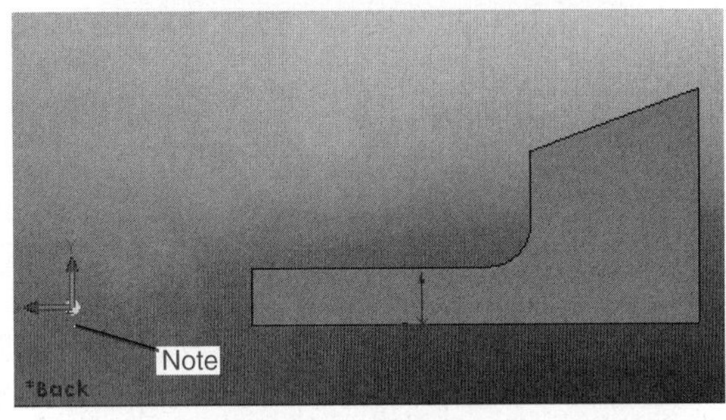
Note
*Back

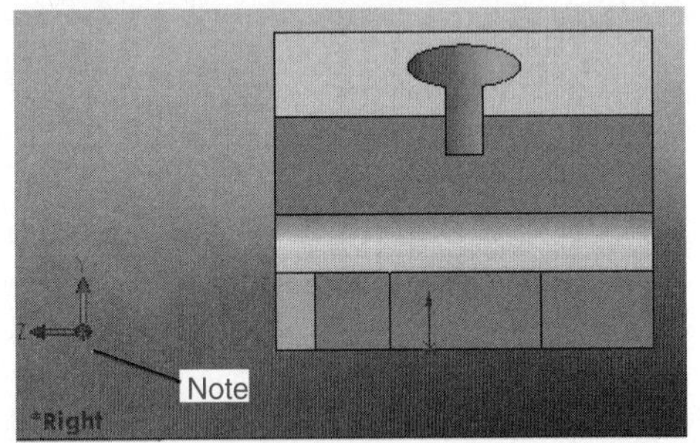
Note
*Right

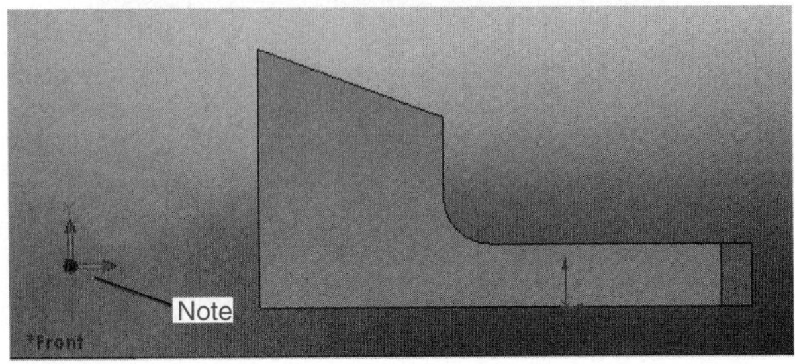
Note
*Front

Figure I-6

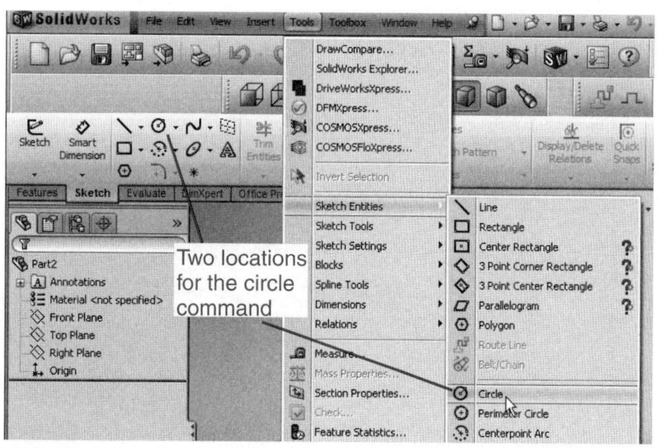

Figure I-7

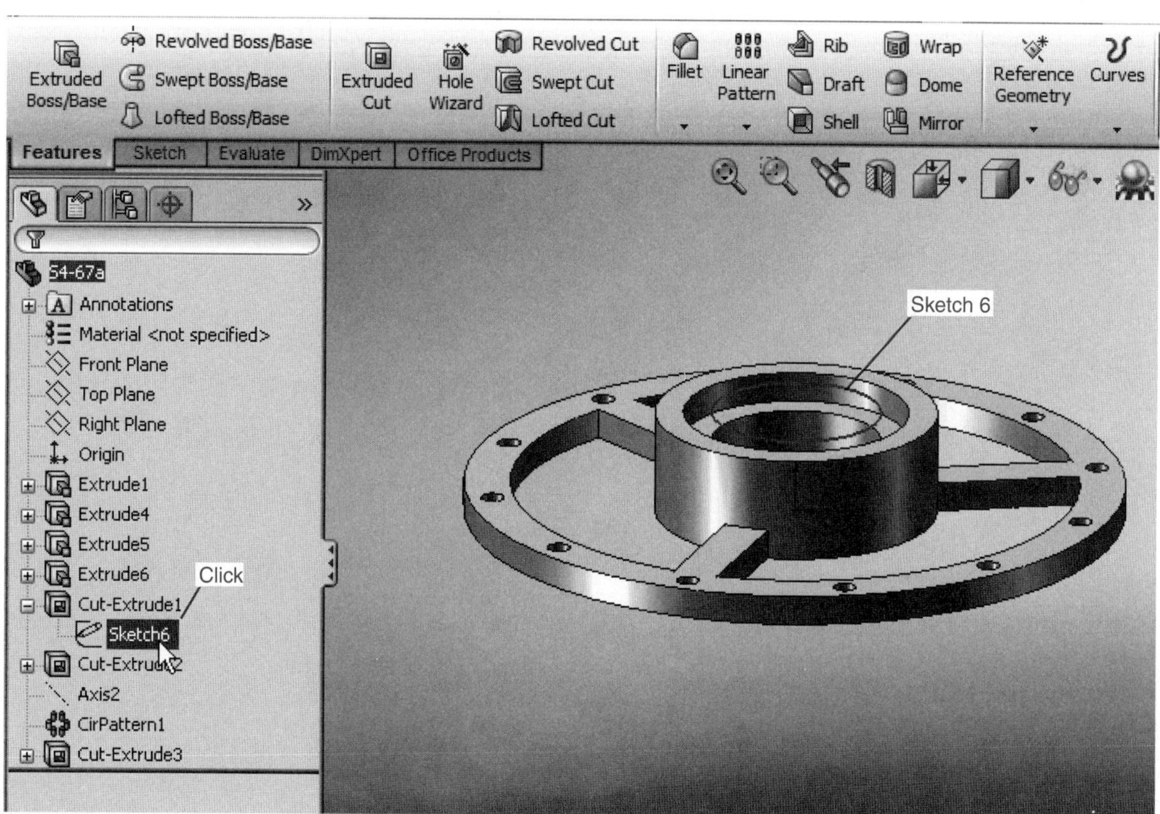

Figure I-8

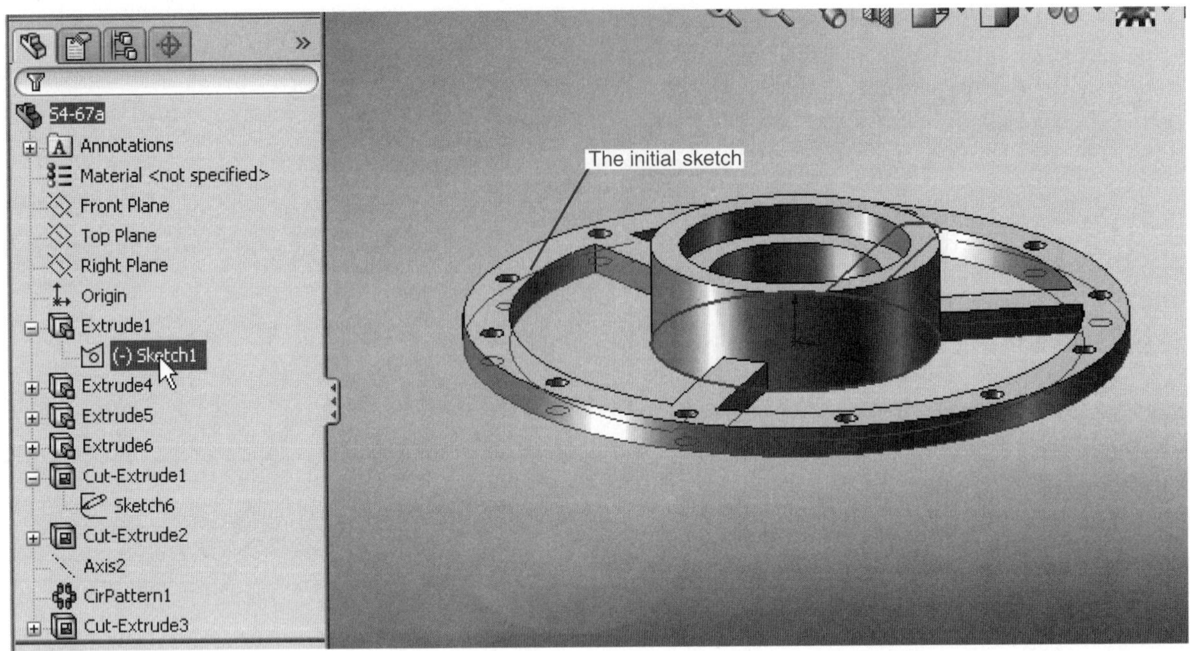

Figure I-8 ***(continued)***

CHAPTER 1

Getting Started

Objectives

- Learn how to create a sketch.
- Learn how to create a file/part.
- Learn how to create a solid model.
- Learn how to edit and modify a sketch.
- Learn how to draw angular and circular shapes.
- Learn how to draw holes.
- Learn how to use the Sketch tools.
- Change units of a part.

1-1 INTRODUCTION

This chapter presents a step-by-step introduction to SolidWorks 2008. The objective is to have first-time users access SolidWorks and be able to start drawing shapes within a few minutes. The use of the tools initially presented in Chapter 1 will be expanded in Chapters 2 and 3.

1-2 SKETCHING A LINE

Figure 1-1 shows the opening SolidWorks screen. This screen should appear when you first access the SolidWorks program. Move the cursor to the icon in the upper left corner of the screen located under the heading **Files**. This is the **New** tool. It is used to create a new drawing.

1. Click the **New** tool.

The **New SolidWorks Document** dialog box will appear. See Figure 1-2.

2. Click the **Advanced** box located in the lower left corner of the box.

> **TIP**
>
> The **Advanced** tool access box may not appear after your first use. SolidWorks will go directly to the **New SolidWorks Document** box. The **Novice** box can be used to return to the **New SolidWorks Document** box if needed.

The next **New SolidWorks Document** dialog box will appear. See Figure 1-3. SolidWorks can generate three different types of drawings: **Part**, **Assembly**, and **Drawing** documents. Individual parts are drawn using the **Part** document. This section will use **Part** documents. **Assembly** and **Drawing** documents will be covered in later chapters.

3. Click the **Part** tool, then click **OK**.

The initial screen display will appear. See Figure 1-4. This screen shows the components of a new **Part** document,

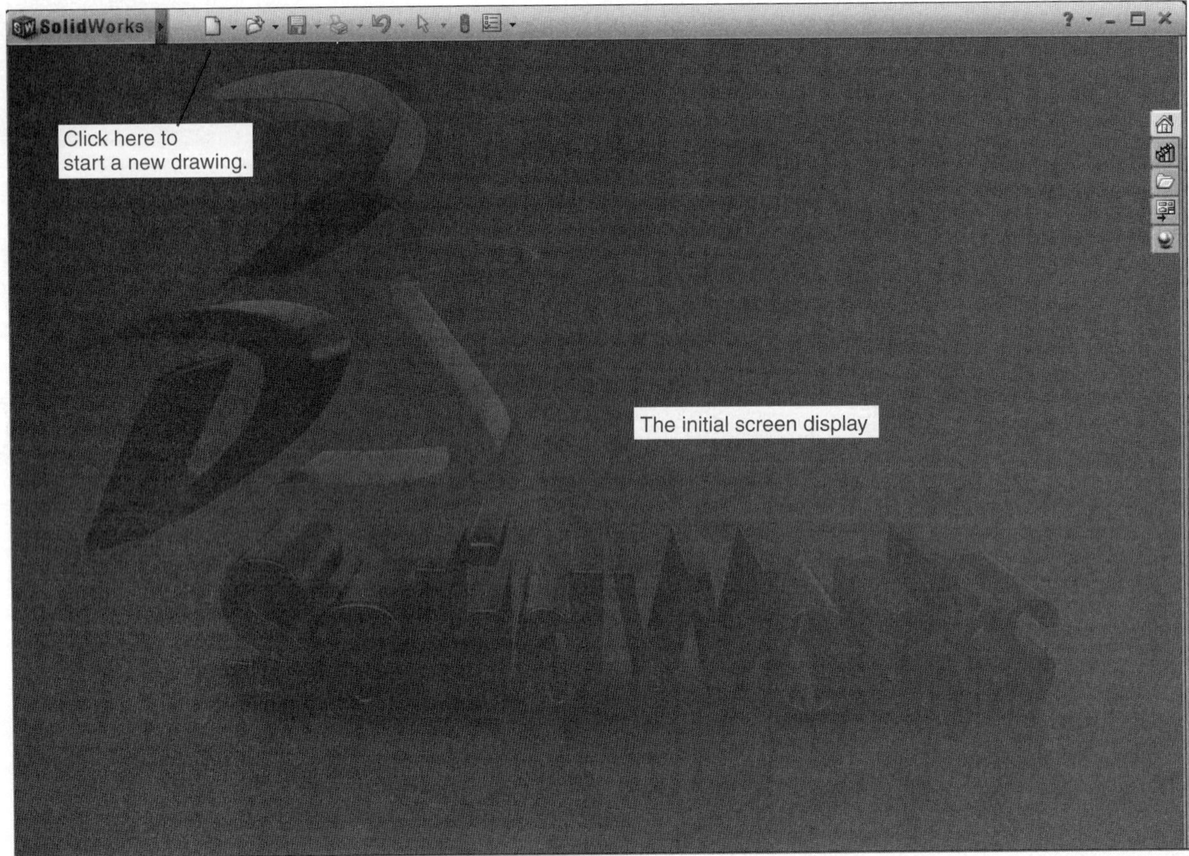

Figure 1-1

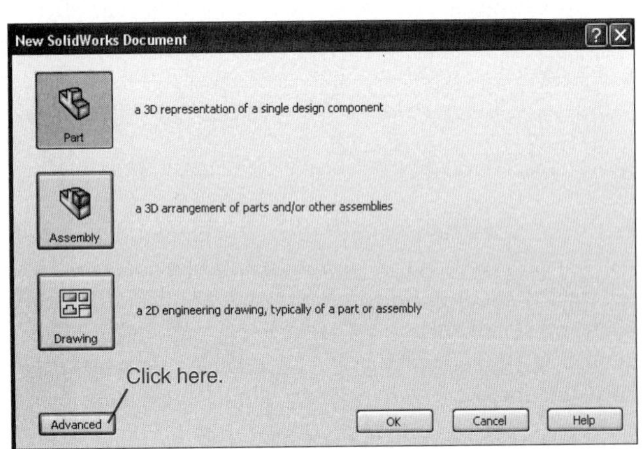

Figure 1-2

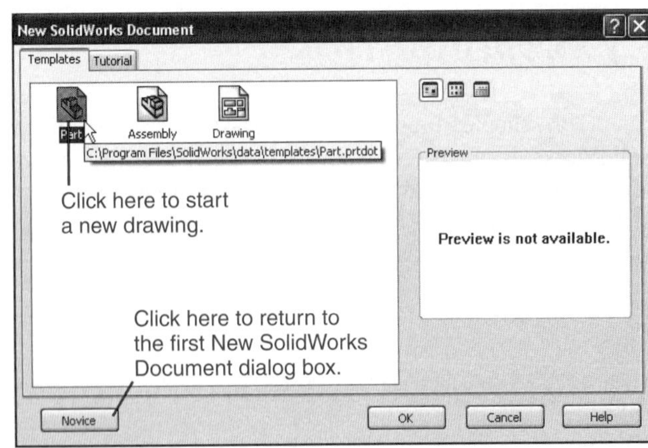

Figure 1-3

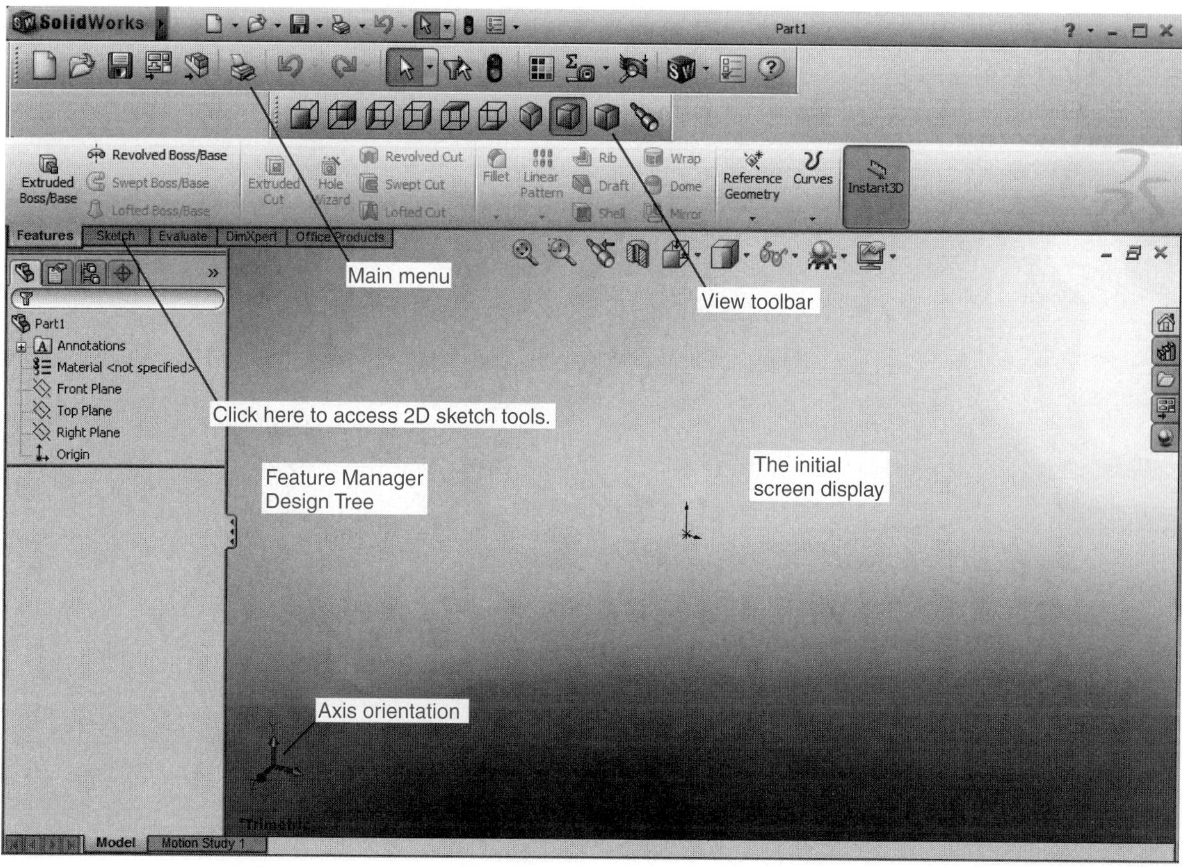

Figure 1-4

which includes toolbars, the **Command Manager,** main menu headings, the **Features Manager**, and the axis orientation icon.

4. Click the **Sketch** tool located on the **Command Manager**.
5. Click the **Front Plane** tool located on the **Features Manager**.

A reference plane will appear. See Figure 1-5. The plane appears in a trimetric orientation but will be automatically oriented normal (at right angles to) the selected view once sketching begins. There are three basic sketching planes: front, top, and right side. These views correspond to the three basic orthographic views that will be covered in Chapter 4.

6. Click the **Sketch** tool again.

A grouping of 2D sketching tools will appear on the **Command Manager**. See Figure 1-6.

7. Click the **Line** tool.

The front plane will rotate normal to a 2D sketching mode. Figure 1-7 shows the default screen display in the sketching environment.

> ***Note:***
> The triangular-shaped area in the upper right corner of the drawing screen indicates that the document is in sketch mode.

8. Locate the cursor in the drawing area, and select a starting point for the line.
9. Click the left mouse button to start the line, and move the cursor horizontally across the screen. Determine an endpoint for the line and again click the mouse button. Click the green check mark on the **Features Manager**, press the **<Esc>** key, or right-click the mouse and click the **Select** option to end the **Line** tool.

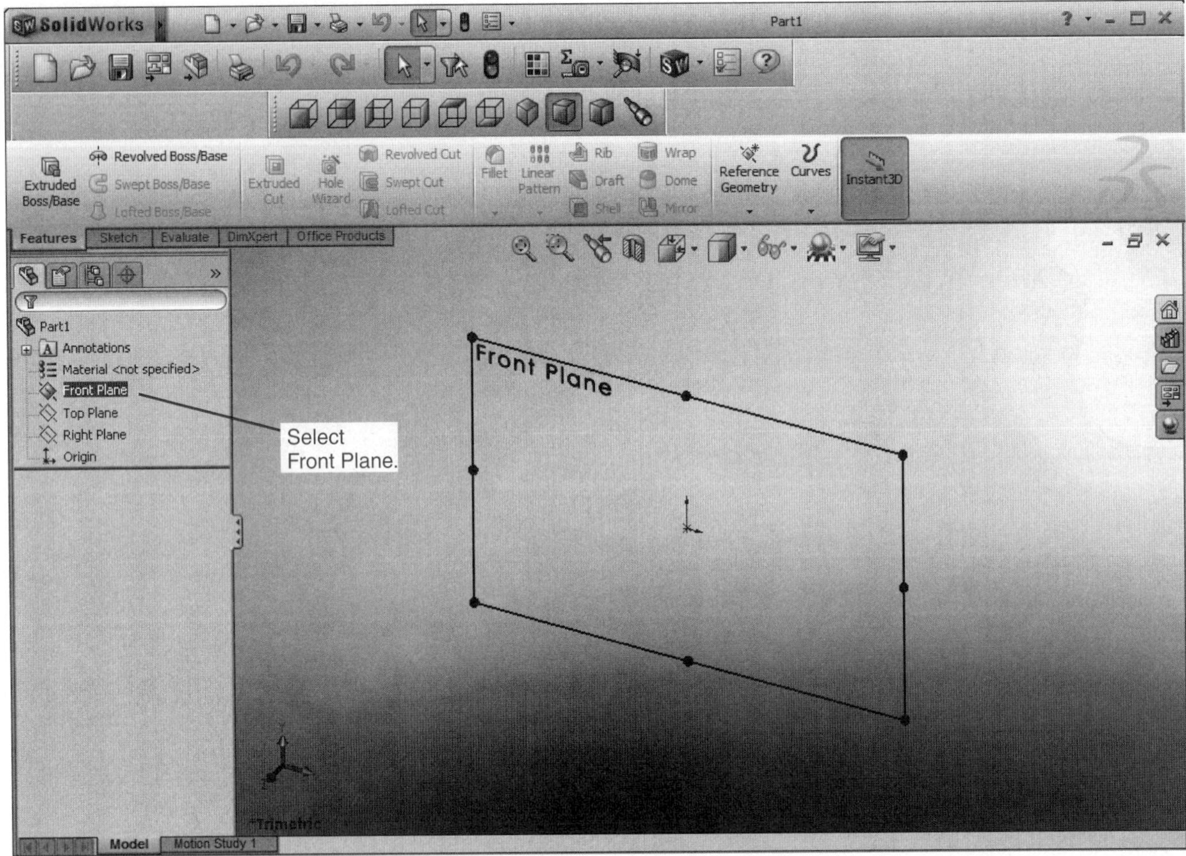

Figure 1-5

TIP

Lines can also be drawn by selecting a starting point and holding the left mouse button down as the cursor is moved. The end of the line is defined by releasing the mouse button.

Note:

As you sketch, the line will change colors. The colors help you determine the status of the line. When you initially draw a line it will be green, meaning it has not been dimensioned. If you press the **<Esc>** key or start a continuing line, the line will turn blue, indicating that you have accepted the sketched length. If you pass the cursor over an existing line, the line will turn red, indicating that the line is activated and may be edited. If you click the **Smart Dimension** tool and move the cursor to a line, the line will initially turn red and be identified, then green when it is clicked, indicating it can be modified.
Text will appear as you draw the line indicating the length of the line and its angle. Make the line about 4 in. long at 180°. See Figure 1-8.

Note:

The examples given in this chapter are dimensioned in inches. To change units,

1. Click the **Tools** heading at the top of the screen and select **Options**.
2. Click the **Document Properties** tab, then **Units**, and select the desired **Unit system** radio button.
3. Click **OK**.

See Section 1-9 for a more detailed expalanation.

TIP

This drawing is a sketch, so exact dimensions are not required. The **Smart Dimension** tool will be used to define an exact length for the line.

The small shaded square with the horizontal bar across it indicates that the line is a horizontal line.

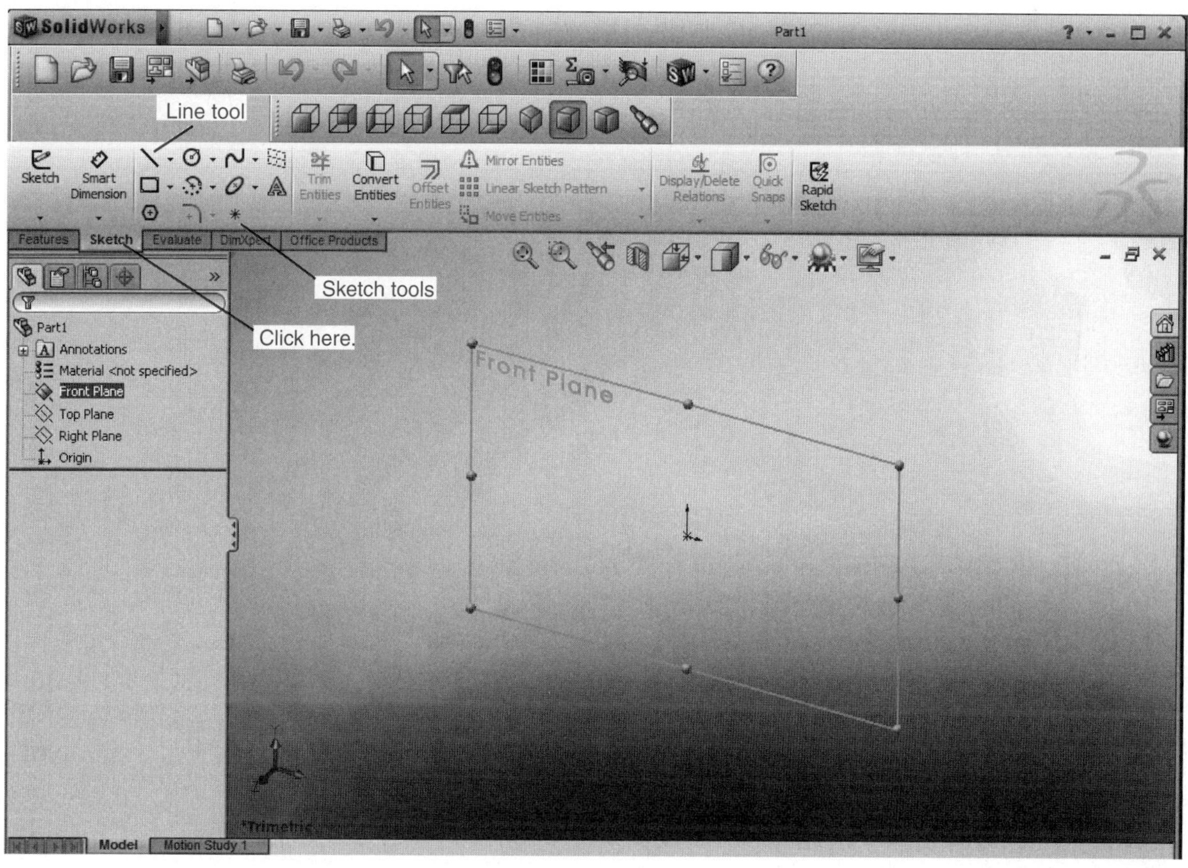

Figure 1-6

1-3 MODIFYING A LINE

The line created in Figure 1-8 is a sketched line; that is, it has an approximate length. We will now define an exact length for the line.

1. Click the **Smart Dimension** tool in the **Sketch** group on the **Command Manager**.

   See Figure 1-8.

2. Click on the line and move the cursor upward away from the line.
3. Determine a location for the line's dimension and click the mouse.

   The **Modify** dialog box will appear. See Figure 1-9.

4. Enter a dimension value of **4.00** and click the check mark in the lower left of the **Modify** dialog box.

> **TIP**
>
> The dimension for the line is in inches. The units can be changed to millimeters. Millimeters will be applied in a later example.

The line's length will be defined as 4.00 in. The line's length will be modified to this length. See Figure 1-10.

5. Click an open area of the drawing screen or press the **<Esc>** key.

The line is now drawn and sized (dimensioned). We will now close the drawing and create another drawing.

6. Select the **File** heading on the main menu.

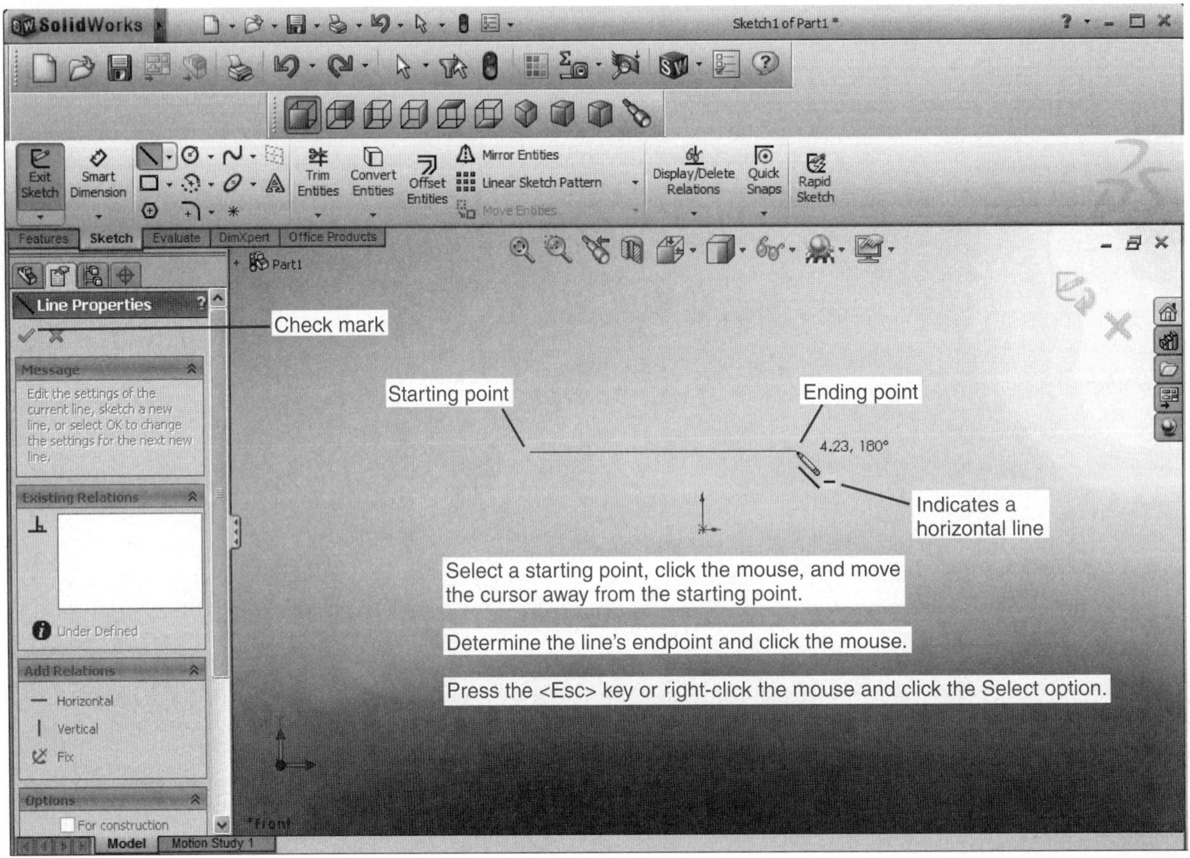

Figure 1-7

A series of commands will cascade down. See Figure 1-11.

7. Select the **Close** tool.

A dialog box will appear on the screen. See Figure 1-12.

8. Select the **No** option unless you want to save the line.

1-4 THE RECTANGLE TOOL

Start a new **Part** document file as defined in Section 1-2. Click the **Sketch** group on the **Command Manager** to display the **Sketch** tools. Select **Front Plane** from the **Features Manager**. See Figure 1-13.

1. Click the **Rectangle** tool in the **Sketch** group on the **Command Manager**.
2. Use the **Corner Rectangle** tool to sketch a rectangle by clicking a selected starting point, dragging the cursor down and across the screen, and selecting an endpoint for the rectangle by releasing the mouse button.

See Figure 1-14.

3. Click the **Smart Dimension** tool and create a **3.00 × 5.00-in**. rectangle. See Figures 1-15, 1-16, and 1-17.
4. Click the OK check mark on the **Features Manager**, or right-click the mouse and click the **Select** option.
5. Access the **View** toolbar, usually located at the top of the screen.

The **View** toolbar defines 10 different orientations that can be applied to the screen.

6. Select **Isometric**.

The rectangle will change to an isometric orientation. See Figure 1-19. Now, we will extend the first shape to create a solid feature.

Creating a Solid

1. Click the **Features** tool on the **Command Manager**.

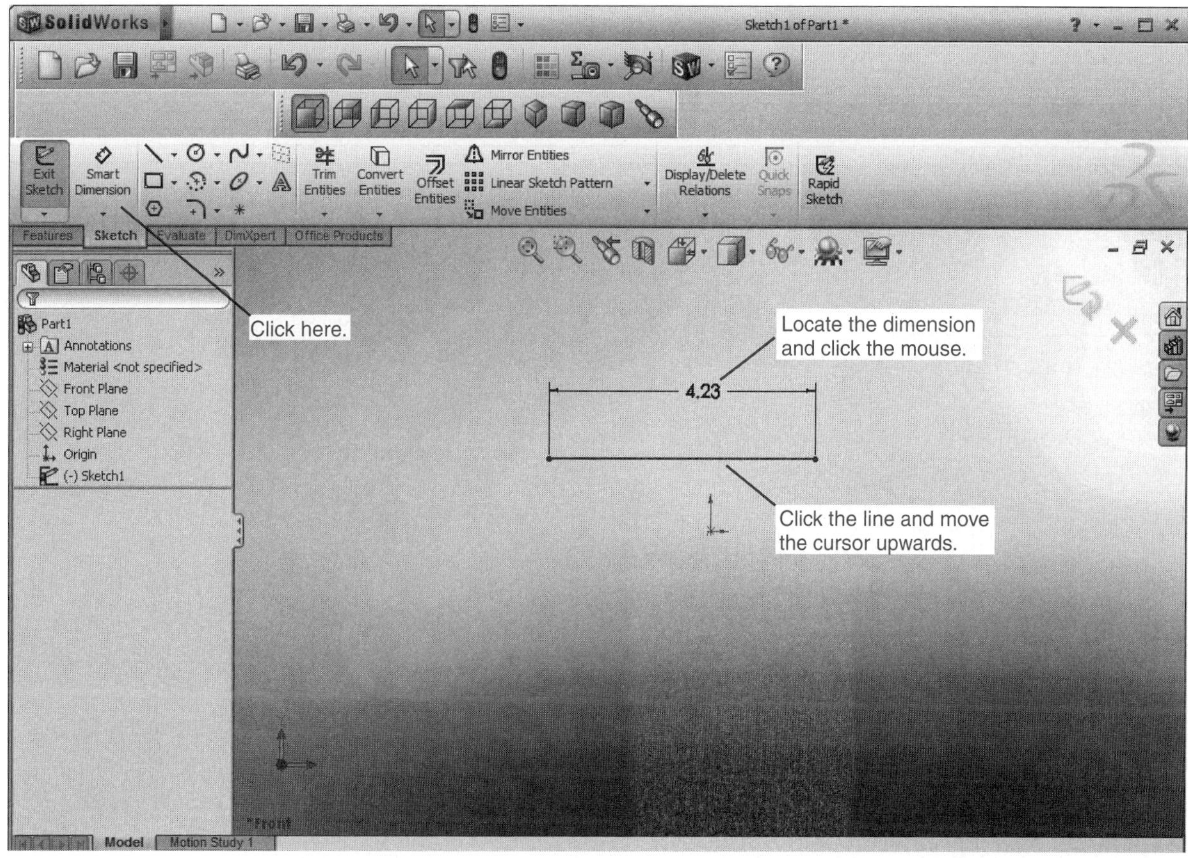
Click here.
Locate the dimension and click the mouse.
4.23
Click the line and move the cursor upwards.

Figure 1-8

The tools on the **Command Manager** will change from **Sketch** tools to **Features** tools. See Figure 1-20. The **Features** tools are used to convert sketches into solid models. The **Features** tools will be covered in detail in Chapter 3.

2. Click the **Extrude Boss/Base** tool.

The **Features Manager** will change to display the **Extrude Properties Manager**. See Figure 1-21.

3. Define the rectangle's thickness as **0.50 in**.

TIP

As the arrows to the right of the thickness definition are clicked the thickness values change, and the thickness of the rectangle also changes in real time. You may also click and drag the arrow shown in the rectangle to change the thickness.

4. Click the OK check mark.

Note:
The rectangle can also be transitioned to a solid model by right-clicking the mouse. A list of options will appear. Click the **OK** tool. See Figure 1-22.

Figure 1-23 shows the finished rectangle. The rectangle has been used to create a 3D solid model. The shape is now a rectangular prism.

1-5 DRAWING A SHAPE WITH 90° ANGLES

Figure 1-24 shows an object that includes only right (90°) angles.

1. Start a new **Part** document as explained in Section 1–2.
2. Select **Front Plane** from the **Features Manager**.
3. Select the **Sketch** group and access the **Line** tool.
4. Sketch the shape with horizontal and vertical lines. Approximate the dimensions.

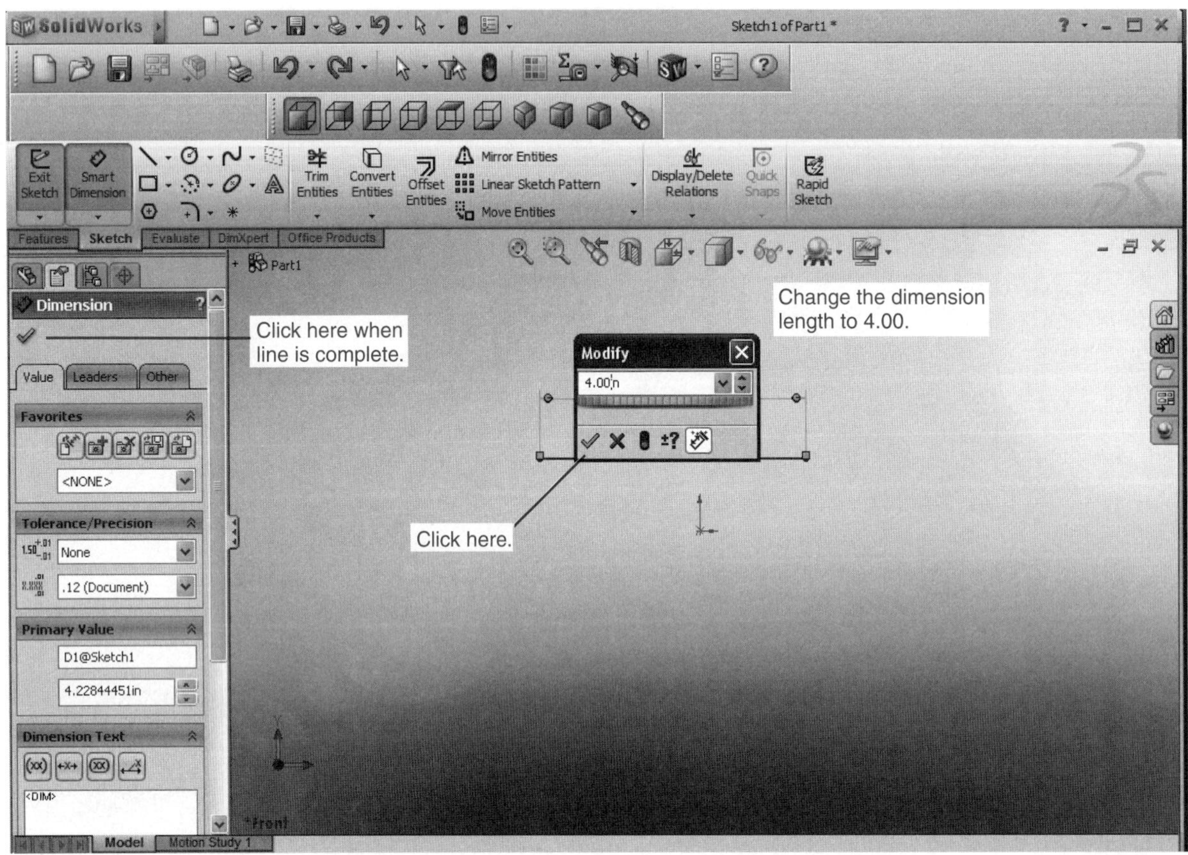

Figure 1-9

> **TIP**
>
> Note that as you sketch lines other lines and icons appear on the screen to tell you if you are aligned with a point or parallel or perpendicular to other lines.

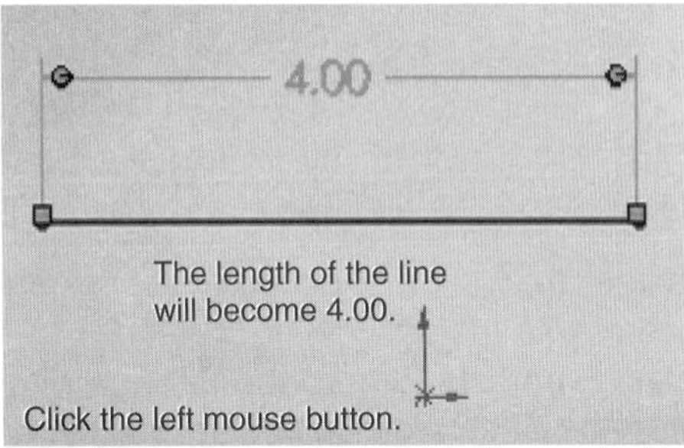

Figure 1-10

See Figure 1-25.

5. Use the **Smart Dimension** tool and size the object as shown in Figure 1-25.
6. Select the check mark in the **Line Properties Manager** and select the **Isometric** option from the selection flyout adjacent to the axis orientation icon. See Figure 1-18.
7. Right-click the mouse and click the **Select** option.
8. Click the **Features** tool, then the **Extrude Boss/Base** tool.

The screen orientation will automatically change to a three-dimensional orientation.

9. Set the object's thickness for **0.60 in**. Move the cursor into the drawing area and right-click the mouse.

See Figure 1-26.

10. Click the **OK** option in the menu that appears.

The object should look like the one shown in Figure 1-24.

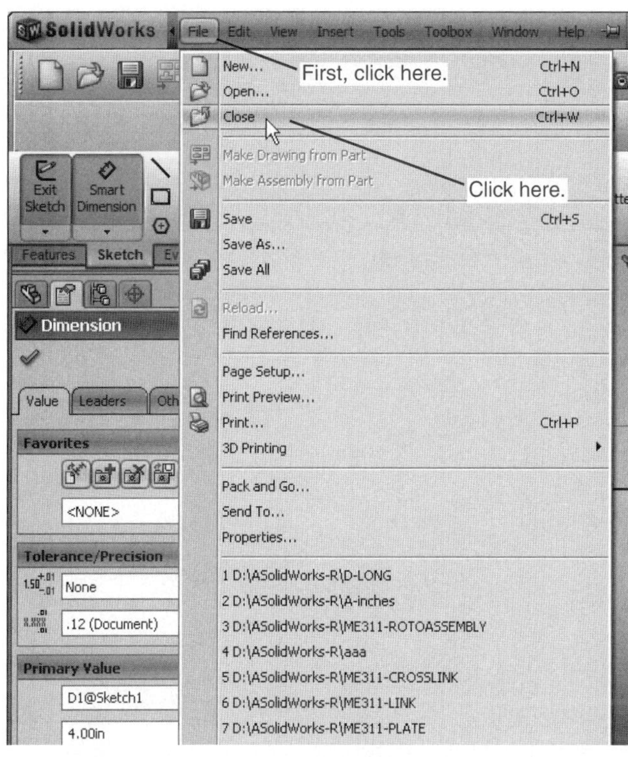

Figure 1-11

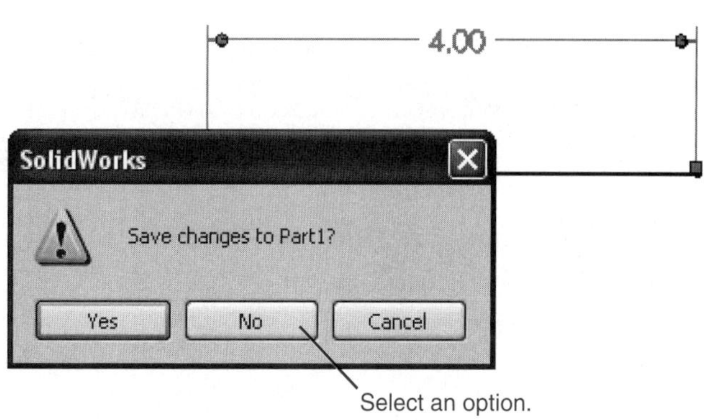

Figure 1-12

1-6 EDITING A SKETCH

It is possible to edit an existing shape using SolidWorks without resketching the object. For example, the shape created in the last section can be edited to change both the dimensions and the thickness. We will first change the depth of the cutout from 1.50 to 1.25 in. This procedure is called ***editing a sketch***. In the next section we will change the thickness of the object from 0.60 to 0.40 in. This is called ***editing a feature***. In general, changes to shapes created using the tools included in the **Sketch** group will be called *editing a sketch*, and shapes made using the tools included in the **Features** group will be called *editing a feature*. The **Features Manager** has recorded all the operations used to define the object. Click on the plus sign next to a feature to see the operations associated with that feature.

To Change the Dimensions

1. Right-click the mouse on the drawing screen. A listing of tools will appear.

   See Figure 1-27.

2. Select the **Edit Sketch** tool.
3. Double-click the 1.50 vertical dimension on the cutout.

   See Figure 1-28. The **Modify** dialog box will appear.

4. Dimension the vertical distance again using a value of **1.25** (the distance was 1.50).
5. Click the OK check mark.

   See Figures 1-29 and 1-30.

6. Double-click the second 1.50 dimension and change it to **1.25** so that the top surfaces align.
7. Click the OK check mark in the **Modify** dialog box to upgrade the dimension.

See Figures 1-31 and 1-32. These figures show the modified sketches. Click the **Exit Sketch** tool or the **Exit Sketch** icon in the triangular-shaped area in the upper right corner of the drawing screen to save the changes and upgrade the 3D feature. Figure 1-33 shows the edited object.

1-7 EDITING A FEATURE

This section will show how to change the extruded thickness of the feature from 0.60 to 0.40 in.

1. With the object on the screen, right-click the mouse button.

   A selection of tools will appear. See Figure 1-34.

2. Select the **Edit Feature** tool.

   Tools listed in the **Features** group require the **Edit Feature** tool to edit.

3. The **Extrude2 Properties Manager** will appear on the left side of the screen.

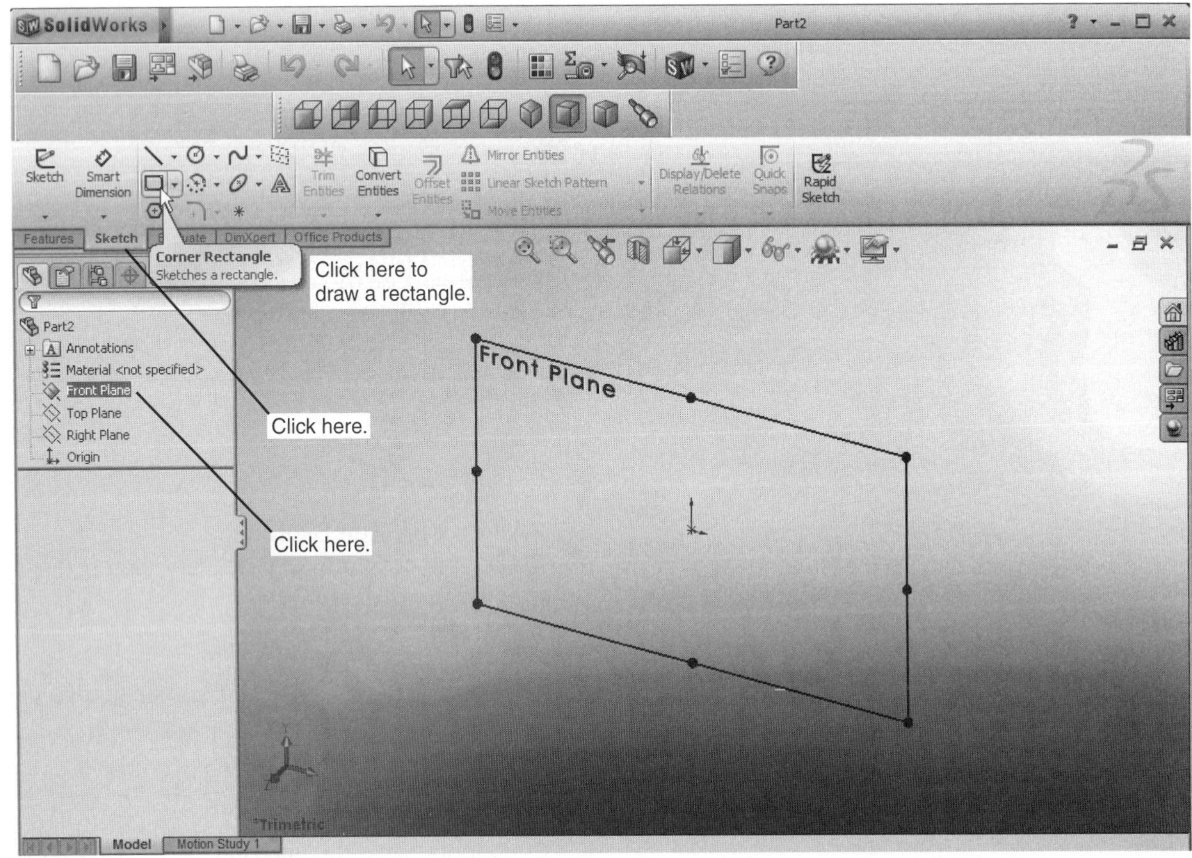

Figure 1-13

See Figure 1-35.

4. Change the thickness value from 0.60 in. to **0.40 in**., then click the green check mark to save and update the object.

Figure 1-36 shows the edited object.

1-8 THE CIRCLE AND SMART DIMENSION TOOLS

In this section we will create an object that includes angular corners and holes. It will be drawn in the top plane.

1. Start a new drawing using the procedures presented in Section 1-2.
2. Select the **Top Plane** orientation from the **Features Manager**.
3. Select the **Sketch** group icon on the **Command Manager**.

See Figure 1-37.

4. Select the **Line** tool and approximately sketch the shape shown in Figure 1-38.
5. Right-click the mouse and click the **Select** tool or click the check mark in the **Line Properties Manager**.

See Figure 1-39.

6. Select the **Smart Dimension** tool and dimension the overall width of the part to be **5.00 in**. and the top horizontal line to be **2.25 in**.

See Figure 1-40.

7. Continue dimensioning the other lines of the object as shown.
8. Continue dimensioning the second angular measurement as shown.

To create an angular dimension, click an angular line and then click an adjacent line. Move the cursor away from the lines. The dimension will appear. Insert the dimension as shown in Figure 1-41.

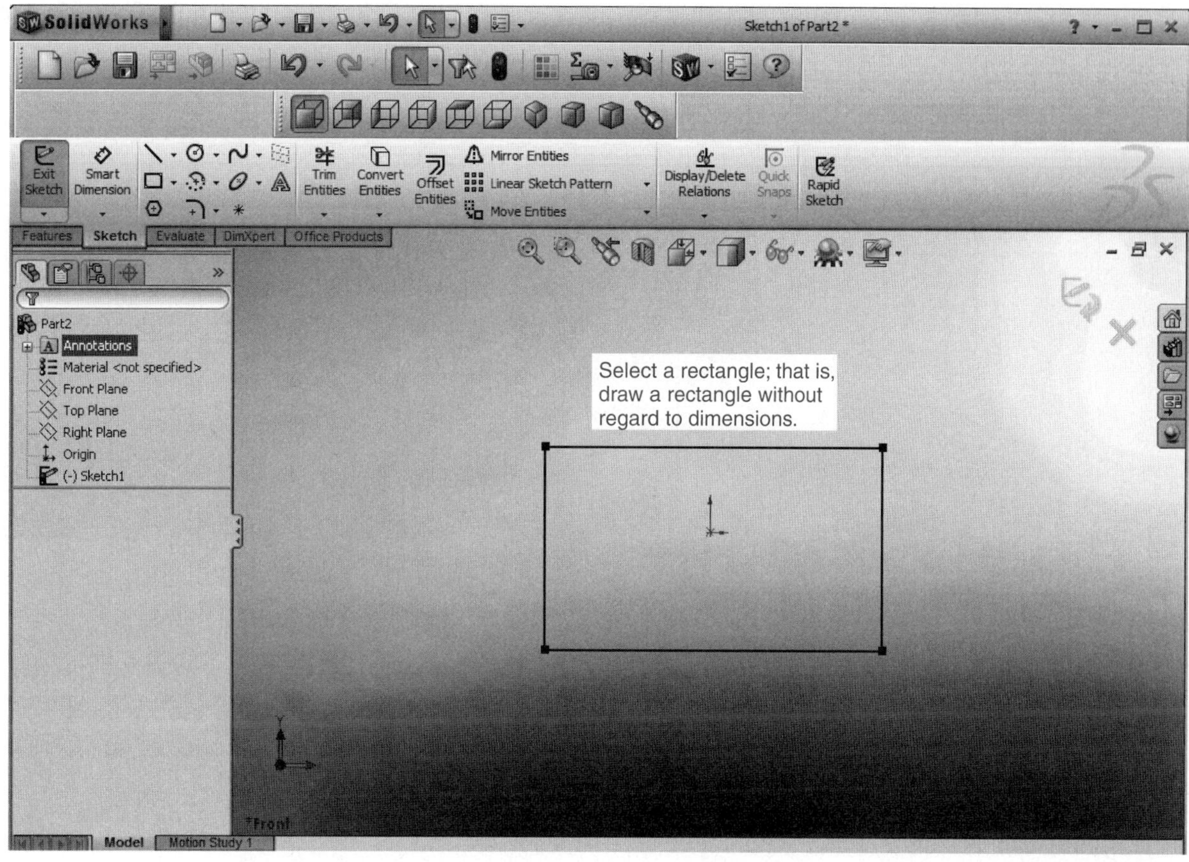
Select a rectangle; that is, draw a rectangle without regard to dimensions.

Figure 1-14

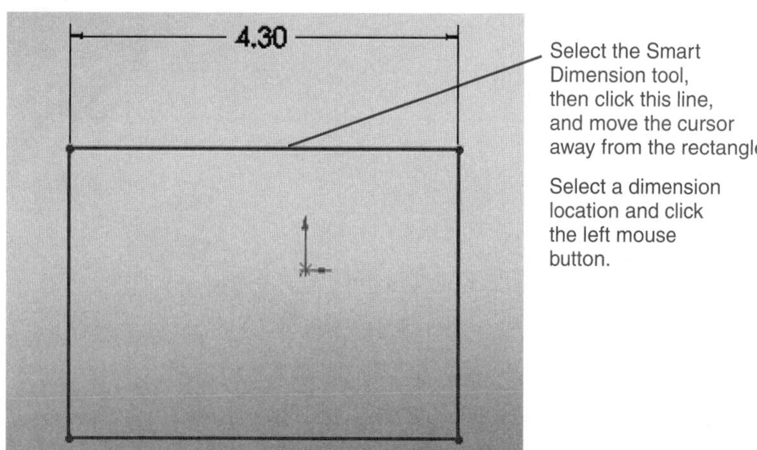
4.30
Select the Smart Dimension tool, then click this line, and move the cursor away from the rectangle.
Select a dimension location and click the left mouse button.

Figure 1-15

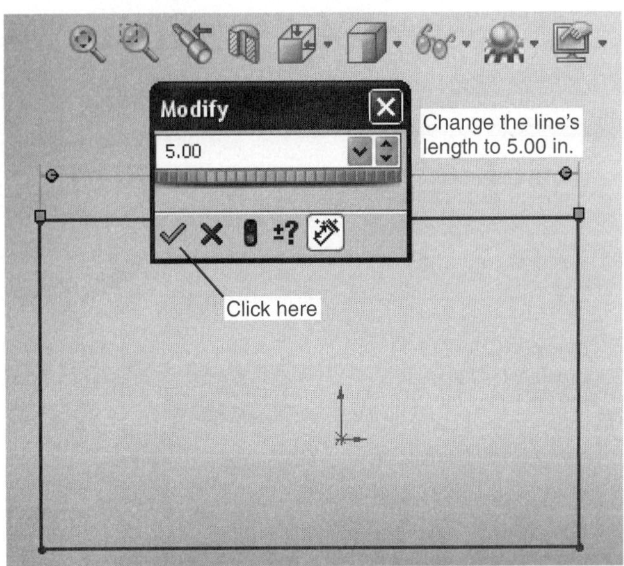

Figure 1-16

TIP

Move the cursor around the screen and note how different angular values appear.

1. Select the **Features** group on the **Command Manager** and then the **Extrude Boss/Base** tool.

The drawing's orientation will automatically change to three dimensional (trimetric).

2. Extrude the object to a thickness of **0.50 in**.
3. Click the OK check mark in the **Extrude Properties Manager** to change the figure into a solid object.

See Figure 1-42.

To Add a Hole

A hole is created in an object by first sketching a circle on a new sketch plane. The circle is then cut out of the object using the **Extrude Cut** tool, creating a hole.

> *Note:*
> Remember that a circle is a two-dimensional shape, and a hole is a three-dimensional shape.

1. Click the top surface of the object.

The surface will change colors, indicating that it has been selected.

2. Right-click the mouse and select the **Sketch** tool.

See Figure 1-43.

3. Use the **Circle** tool of the **Sketch** group on the **Command Manager** and draw a Ø0.25 circle. Use the **Smart Dimension** tool and locate the circle 0.75 from two edges as shown.

See Figures 1-44 and 1-45.

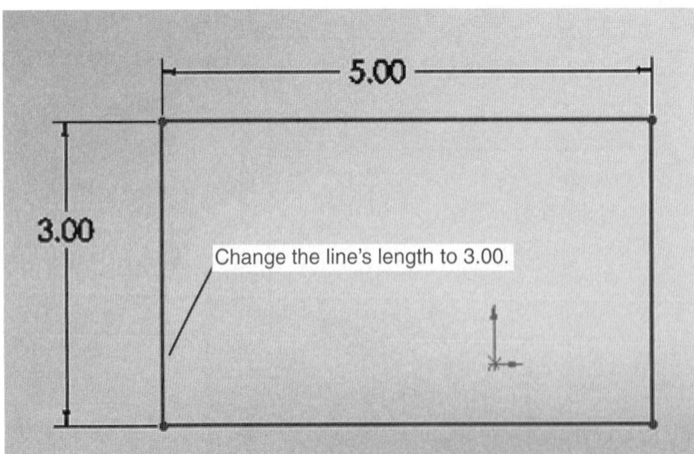

Figure 1-17

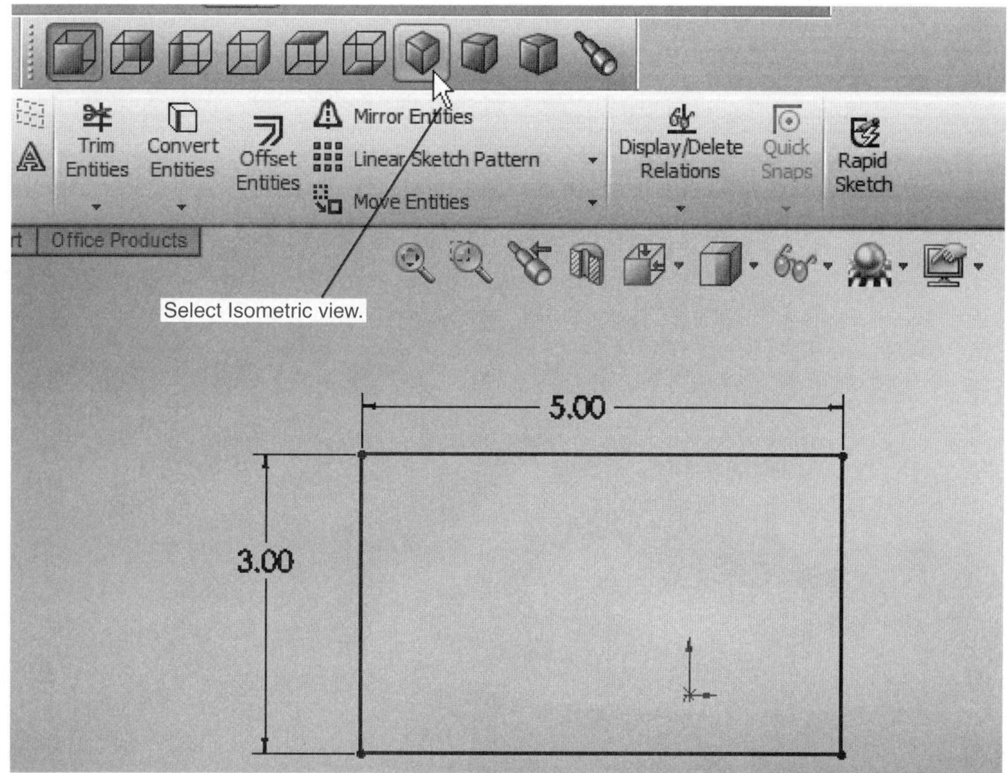

Figure 1-18

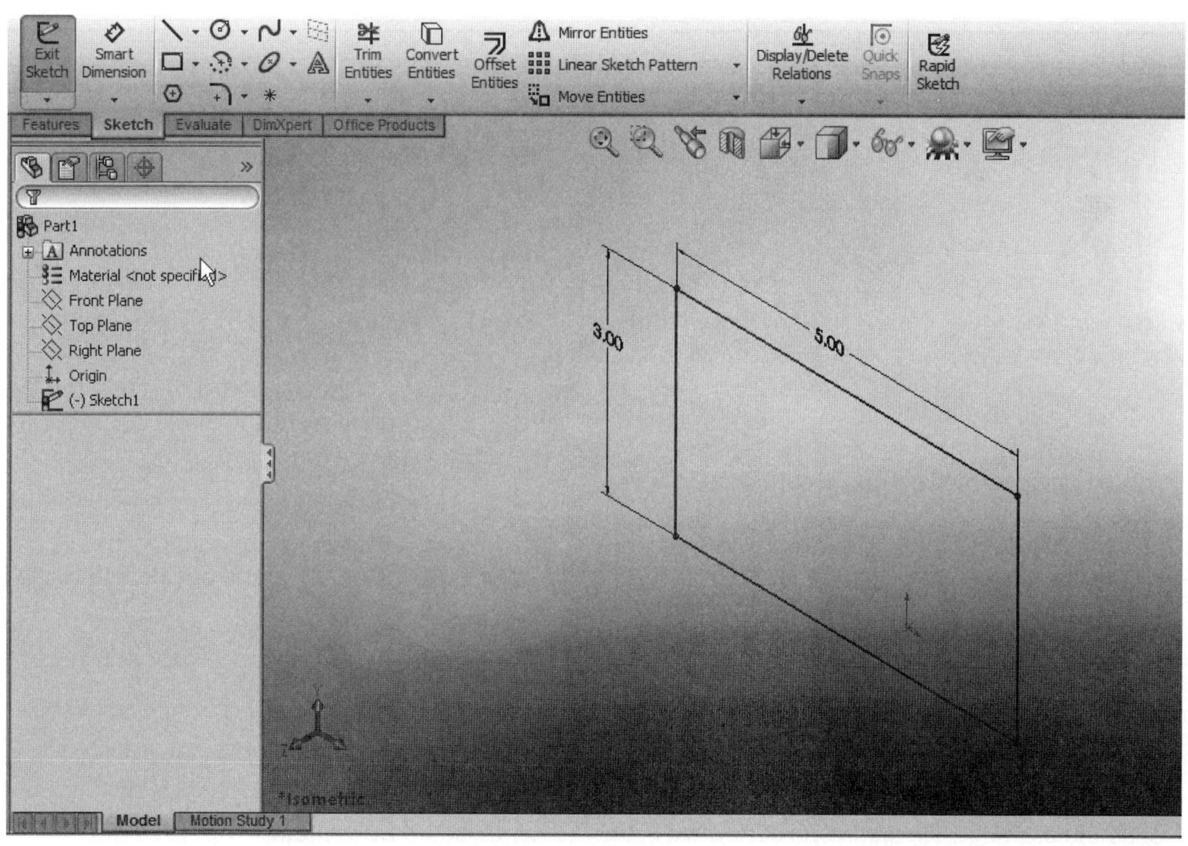

Figure 1-19

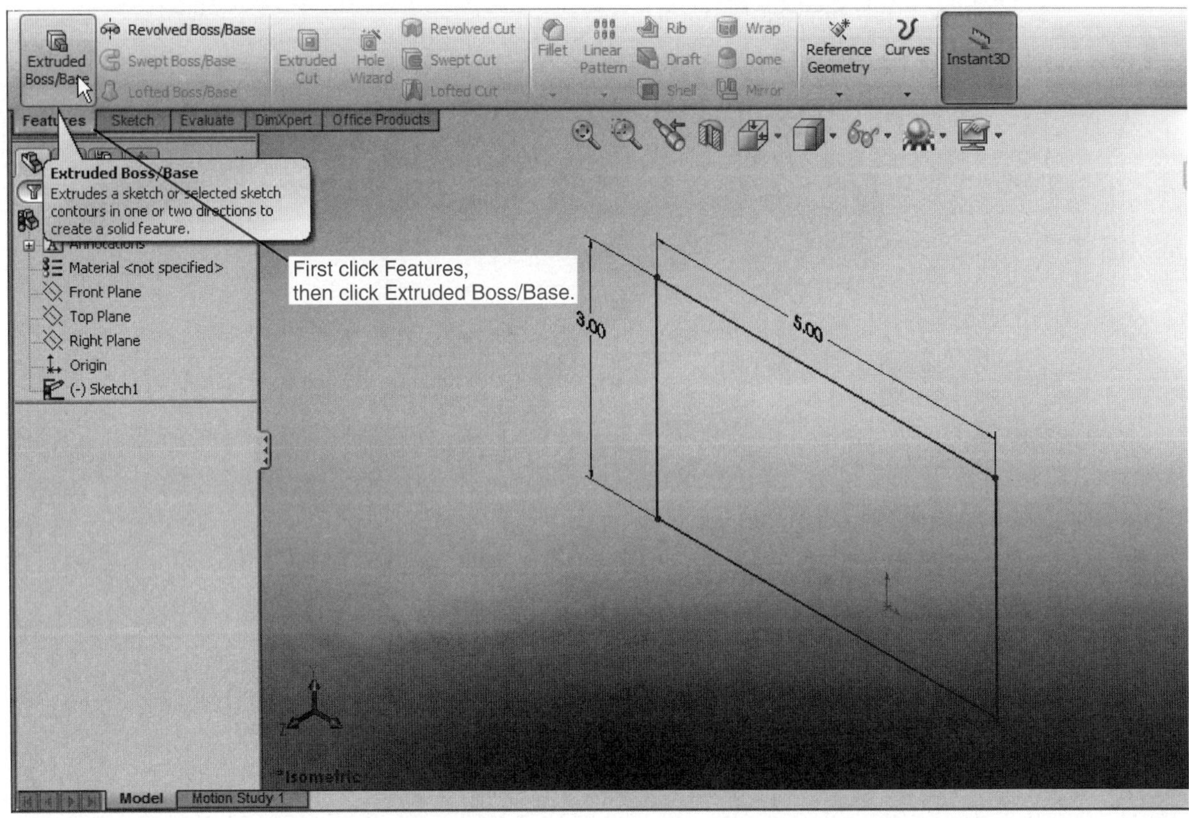

Figure 1-20

4. Click the **Features** group on the **Command Manager** and then select the **Extruded Cut** tool.

   See Figure 1-46.

5. Click the circle. A preview of the extruded cut will show on the object.
6. Click the OK check mark in the **Properties Manager**.

   See Figure 1-47. Figure 1-48 shows the resulting hole in the object.

7. Click the **File** heading at the top left of the screen.

   A series of tools will cascade down.

8. Click the **Save As** tool.
9. Define the drawing's file name and click **Save**.

1-9 SETTING UNITS ON THE DOCUMENT OPTIONS

The default settings for drawing units may be modified using the **Document Properties** dialog box. In this section we will define the drawing units as millimeters.

1. Start a new **Part** document.
2. Click **Tools** on the menu bar located at the top of the screen.

   A series of tools will cascade down. See Figure 1-49.

3. Click **Options**.

   The **Document Properties - Units** dialog box will appear. See Figure 1-50.

4. Click the **Document Properties** tab.

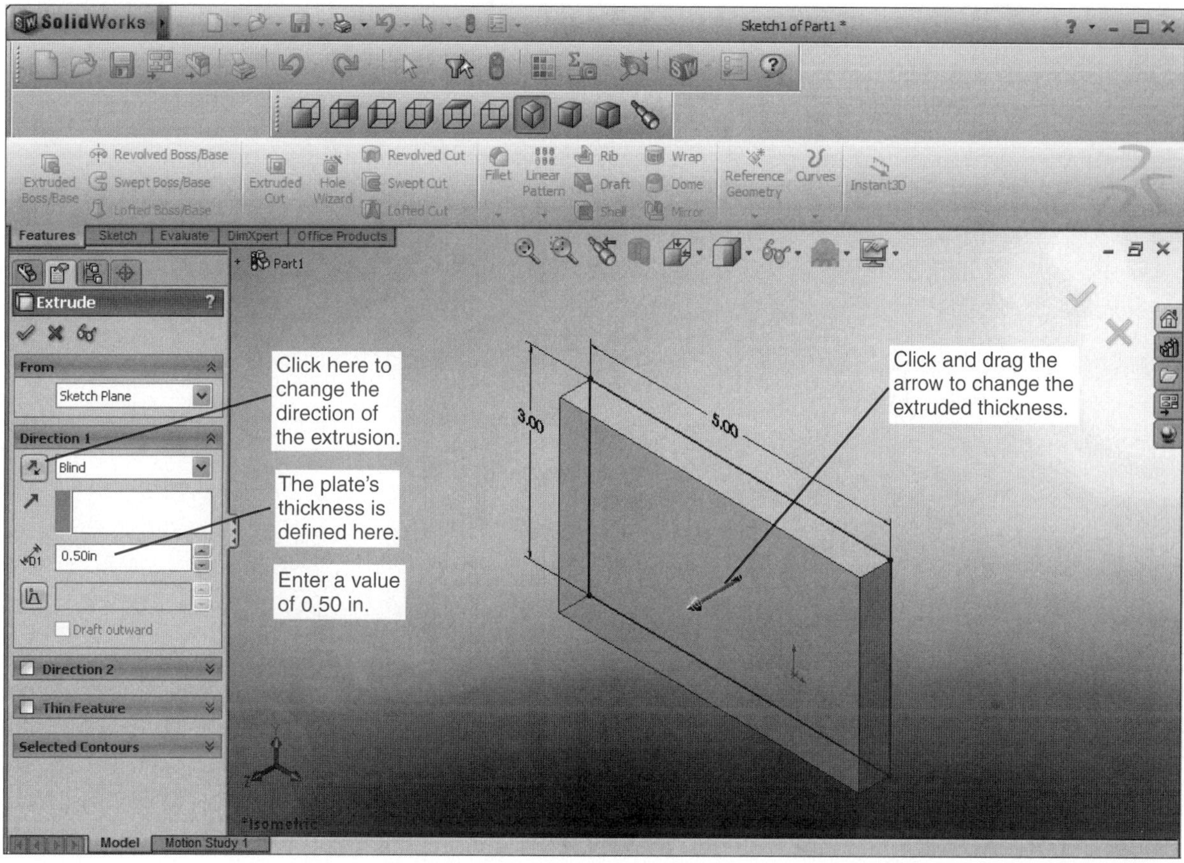

Figure 1-21

5. Click **Units** in the left column.

   The **Units** dialog box will appear.

6. Click the **MMGS (millimeter, gram, second**) tool listed in the **Unit system** box.
7. Click **OK**.

   The drawing units are now calibrated to millimeters.

8. Return to the drawing screen and proceed with the following section.

TIP

In SolidWorks the positive direction is the counter-clockwise direction.

1-10 THE CENTERPOINT ARC AND TANGENT ARC TOOLS

To Use the Tangent Arc Tool

Use the **Part** document started in the previous section. Select the top plane. Select the **Sketch** group from the **Command Manager**.

1. Select the **Line** tool and draw two lines **80 mm** long, **50 mm** apart, and parallel to each other. Assure that the line's starting points are vertically aligned.

   See Figure 1-51. Use the **Smart Dimension** tool to locate and size the lines.

2. Click the **Tangent Arc** tool.
3. Click the left end of the upper 80-mm line.

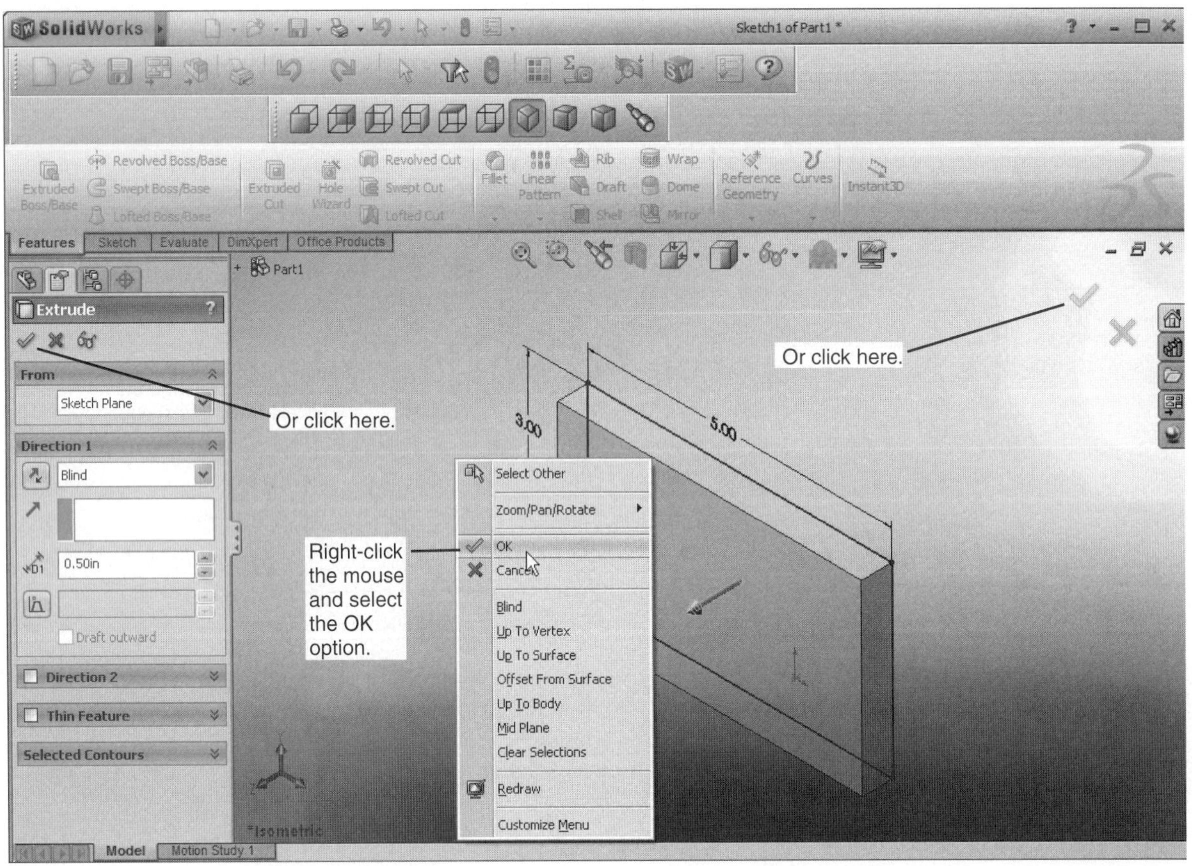

Figure 1-22

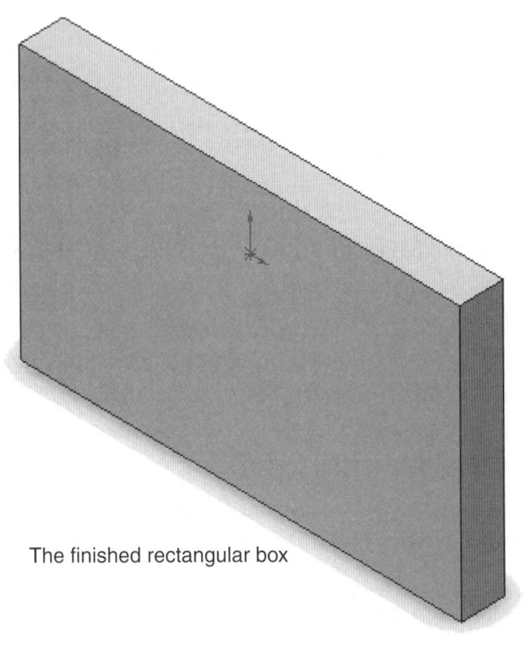

Figure 1-23

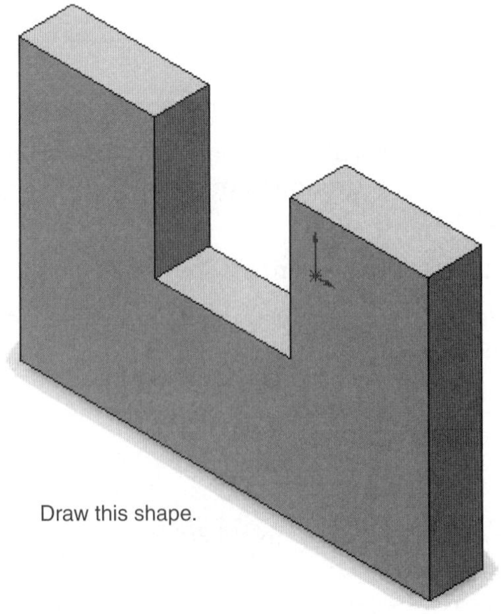

Draw this shape.

Figure 1-24

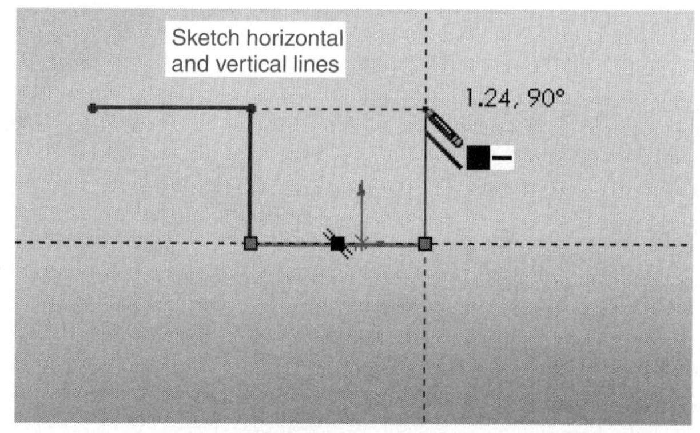
Sketch horizontal
and vertical lines
1.24, 90°

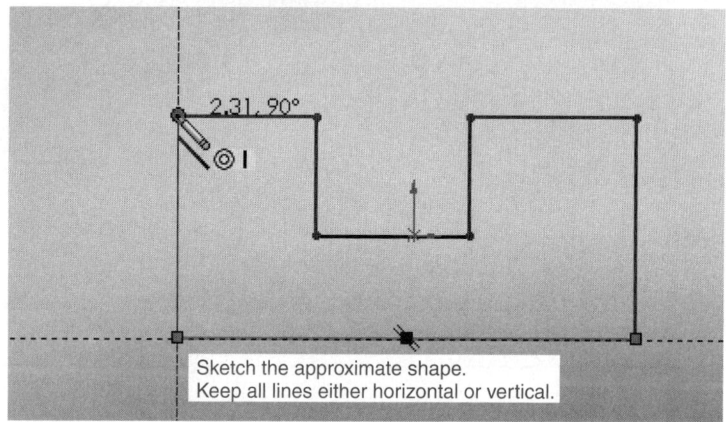
2.31, 90°
Sketch the approximate shape.
Keep all lines either horizontal or vertical.

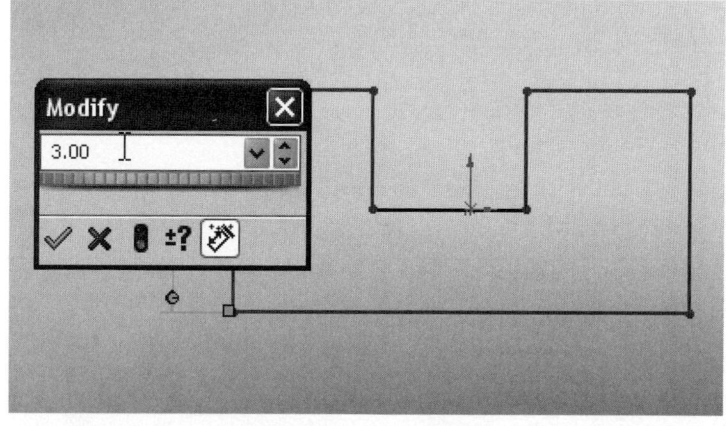
Modify
3.00

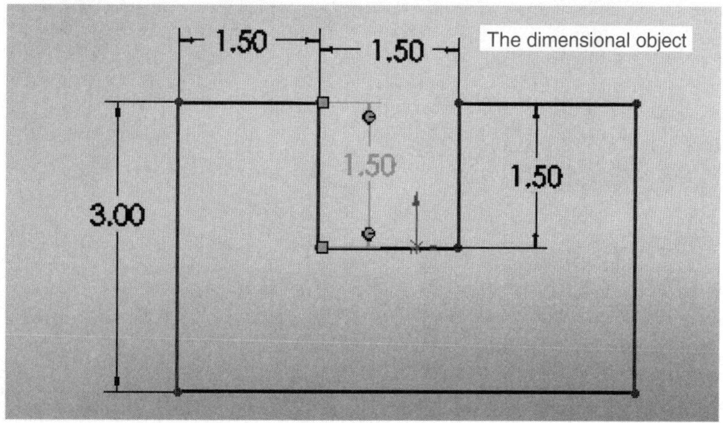
1.50
1.50
The dimensional object
3.00
1.50
1.50

Figure 1-25

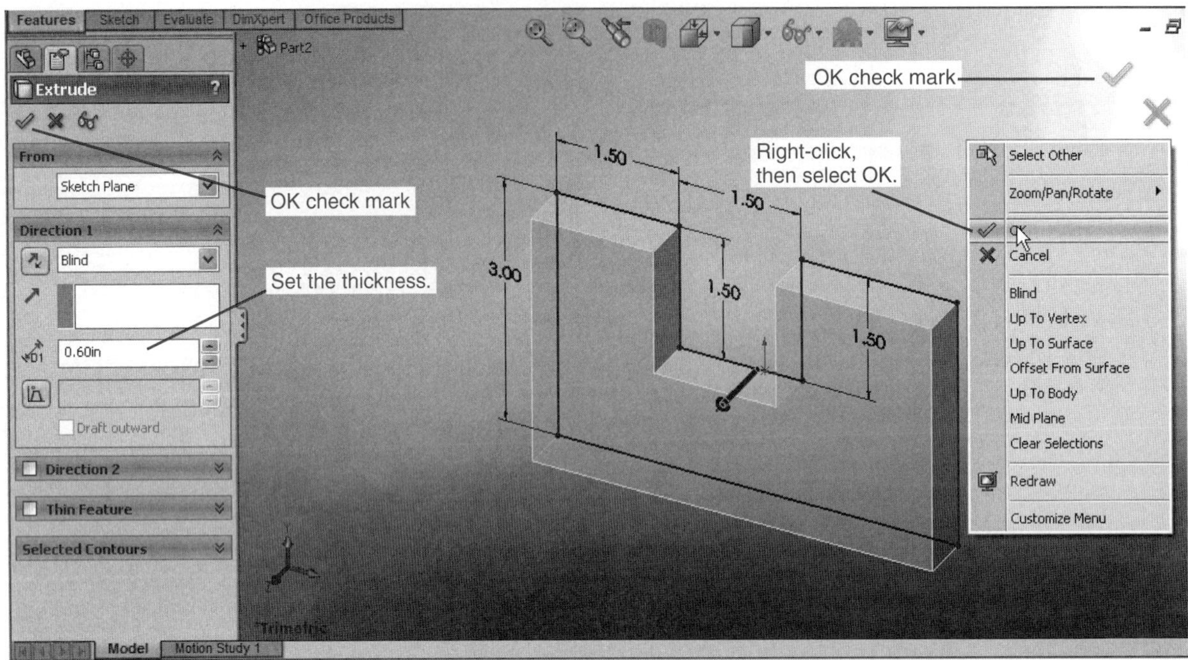

Figure 1-26

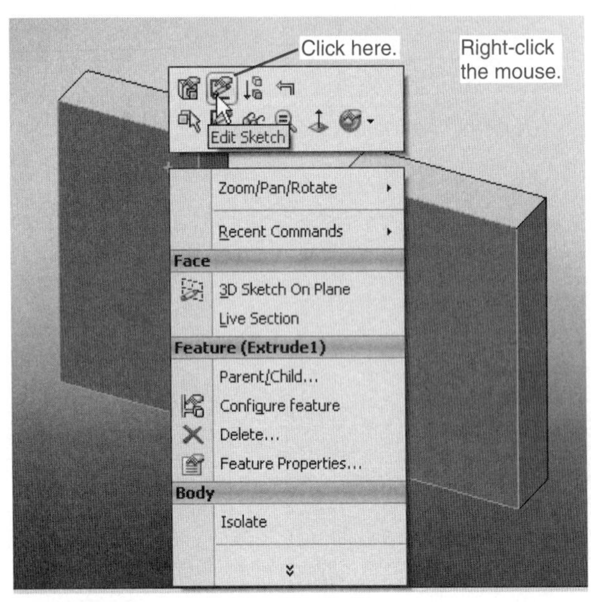

Figure 1-27

Figure 1-28

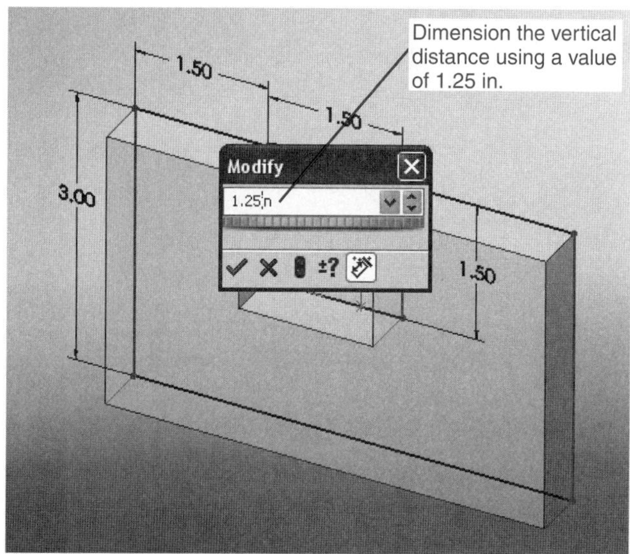

Figure 1-29

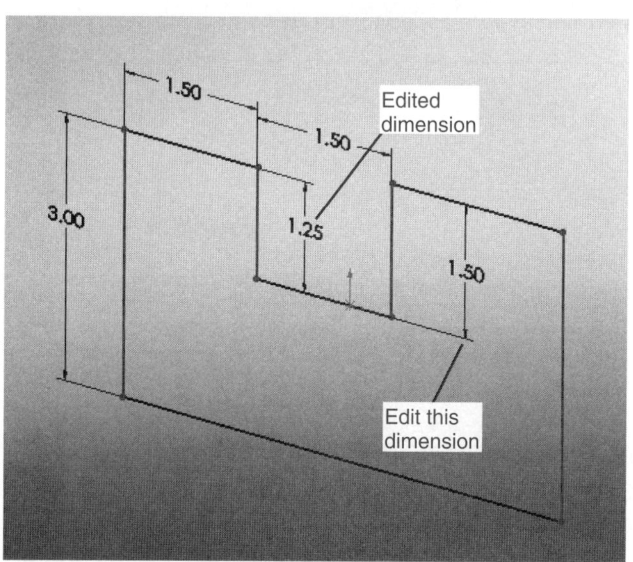

Figure 1-30

The ends of the lines are defined by colored circles. Circles will change to red and grow larger when they are selected. See Figure 1-52.

4. Move the cursor along the approximate path of the arc down to the left endpoint of the lower 80-mm line. Click the endpoint.
5. Right-click the mouse and click the **Select** option or click the check mark in the **Arc Properties Manager**.

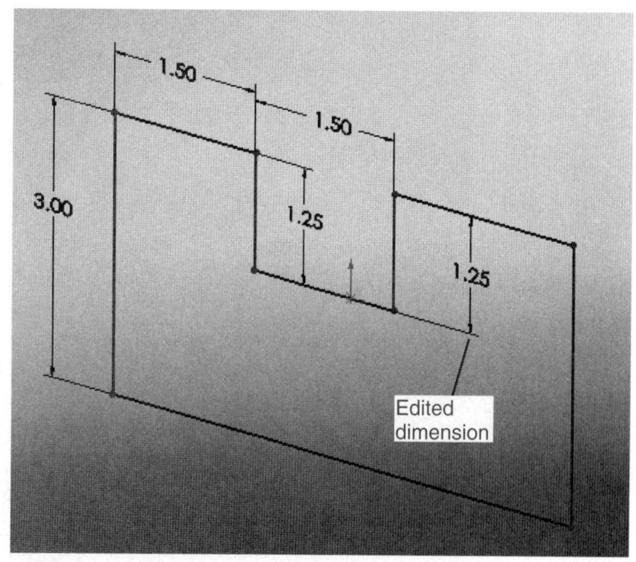

Figure 1-31

The Centerpoint Arc Tool

1. Click the **Centerpoint Arc** tool.
2. Locate the center point for the arc.

See Figure 1-53. The center point for the arc can be located by moving the cursor to the approximate midpoint between the ends of the two parallel lines. Dotted lines will project from the left arc's center point and the line's endpoint when the cursor is aligned with the points.

3. Click the center point.
4. Move the cursor to the endpoint of the lower 80-mm line and click the endpoint.
5. Move the cursor upward and click the right endpoint of the upper 80-mm line.

See Figure 1-54.

6. Right-click the mouse and click the **Select** option or click the check mark in the **Arc Properties Manager**.

1-11 EXTRUDING AN OBJECT

1. Click the arrow to the right of the axis orientation icon at the lower left of the screen.
2. Click the **Features** group on the **Command Manager** and select the **Extruded Boss/Base** tool.

See Figure 1-55.

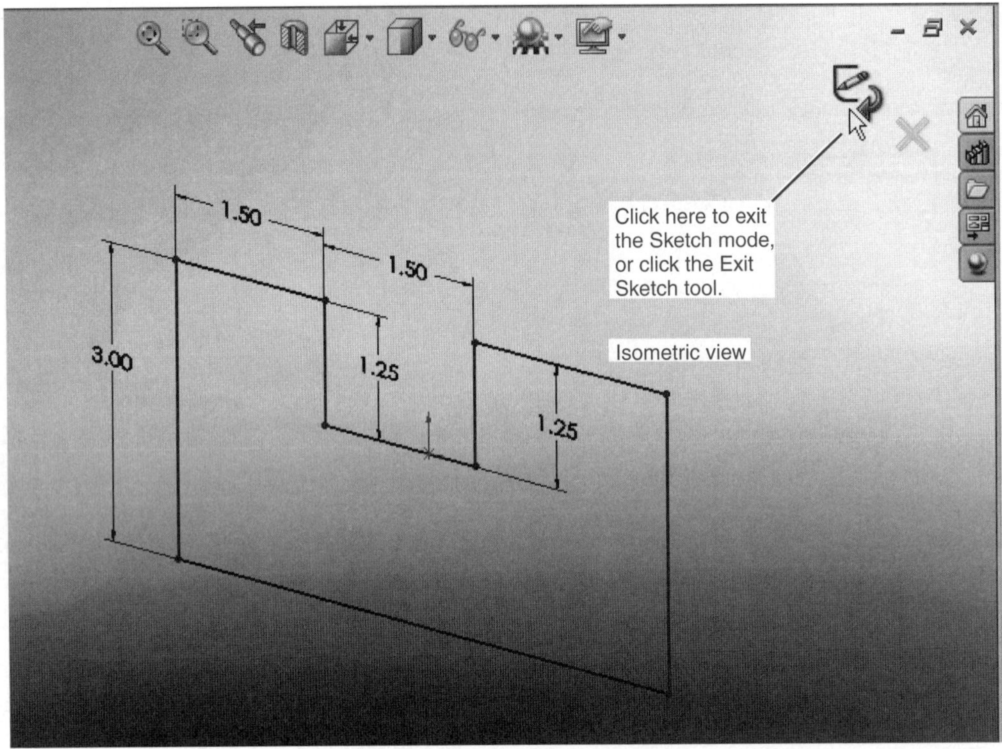

Figure 1-32

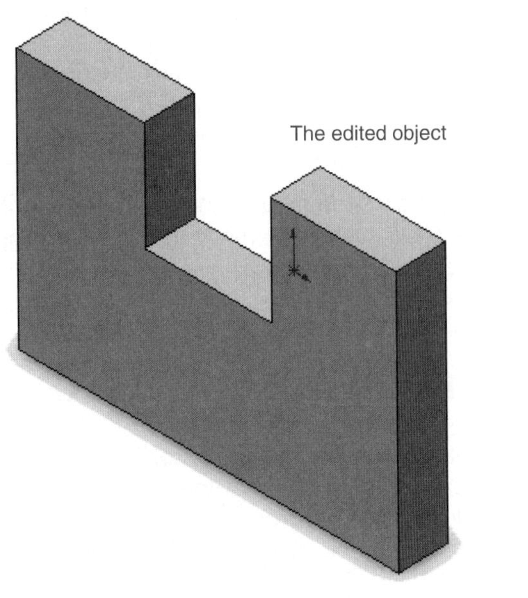

Figure 1-33

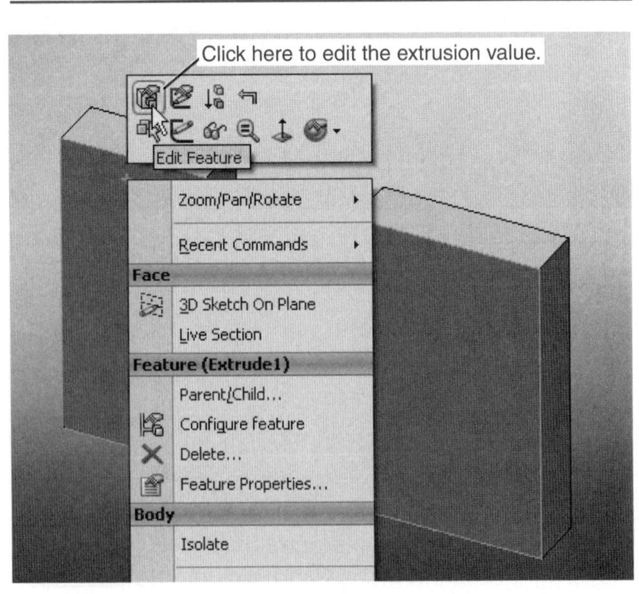

Figure 1-34

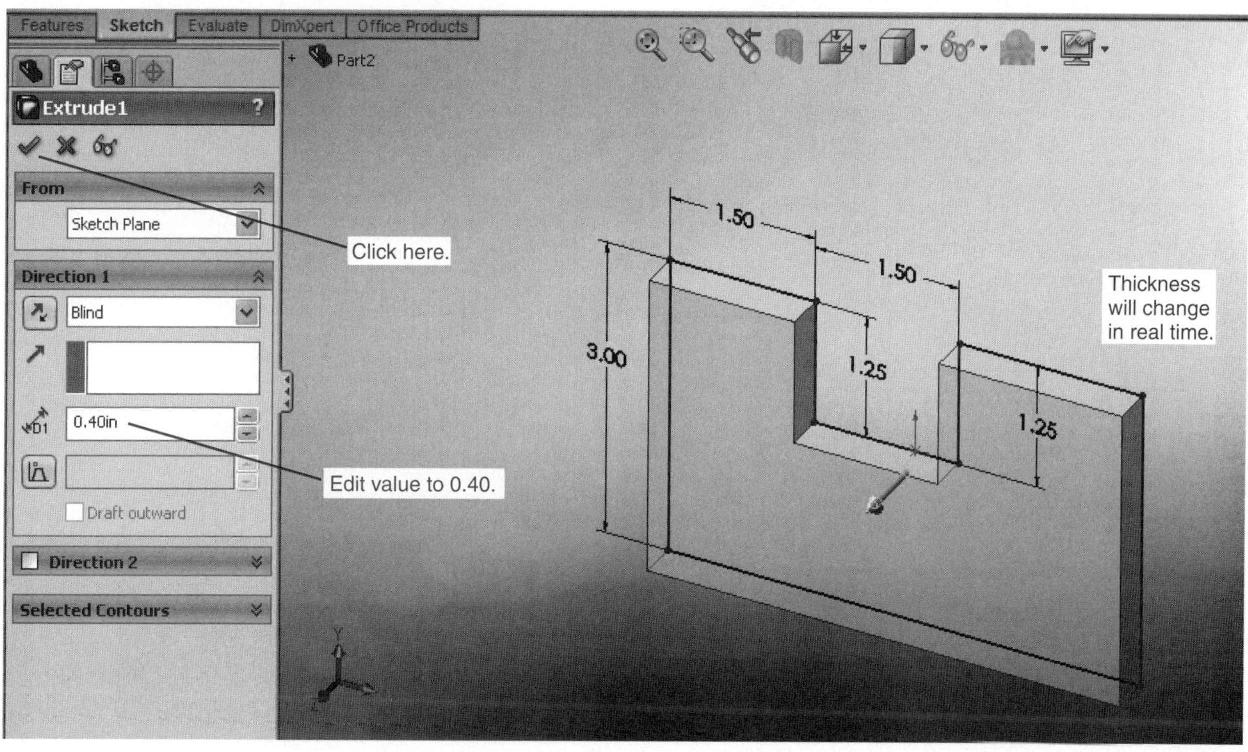

Figure 1-35

3. Set the depth of the extrusion as **20 mm**.
4. Click the OK check mark in the **Extrude Properties Manager** to complete the extrusion.

See Figures 1-56 and 1-57.

To Add Holes to the Object

1. Click the top surface of the object, then right-click the mouse.
2. Select the **Sketch** tool.

See Figure 1-58. This command allows you to create 2D shapes on the top surface.

3. Use the **Circle** tool and sketch a circle. Locate the center point of the circle on the center point of the arc used to define the left end of the object. Size the circle to **Ø20.0 mm** using the **Circle Properties Manager**.

See Figure 1-59.

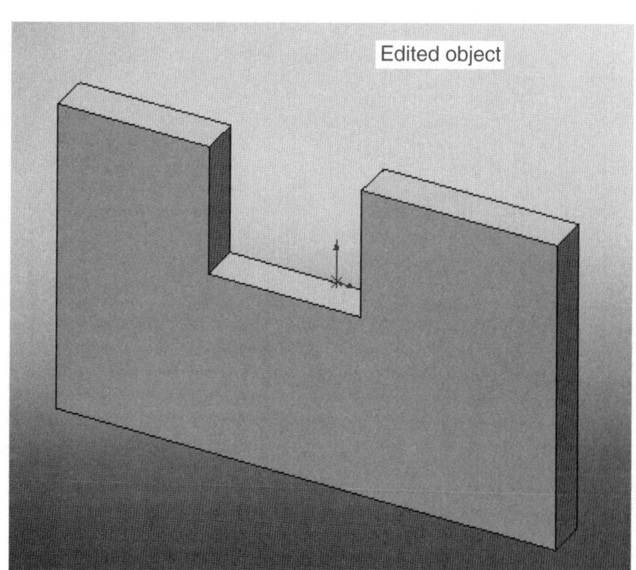

Figure 1-36

> **TIP**
>
> The center point for the arc can be found by moving the cursor in the general area of the arc's center point. A circle will appear with a center point when the cursor is located directly over the arc's center point.

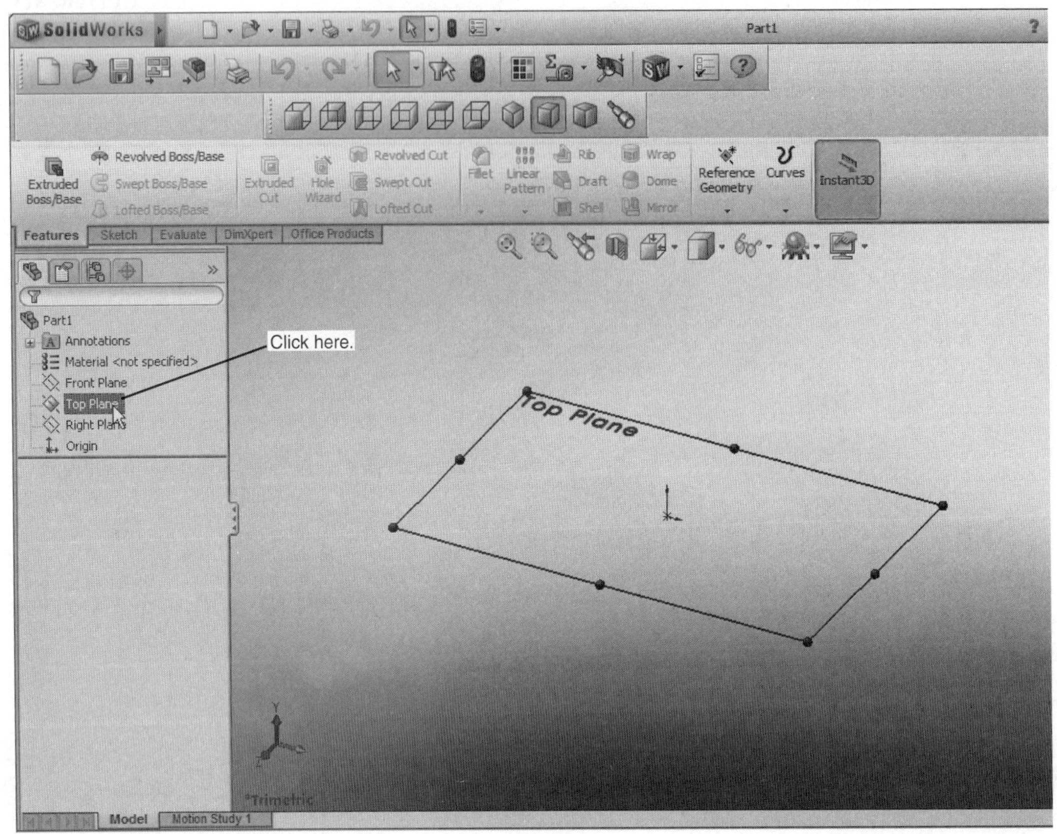

Figure 1-37

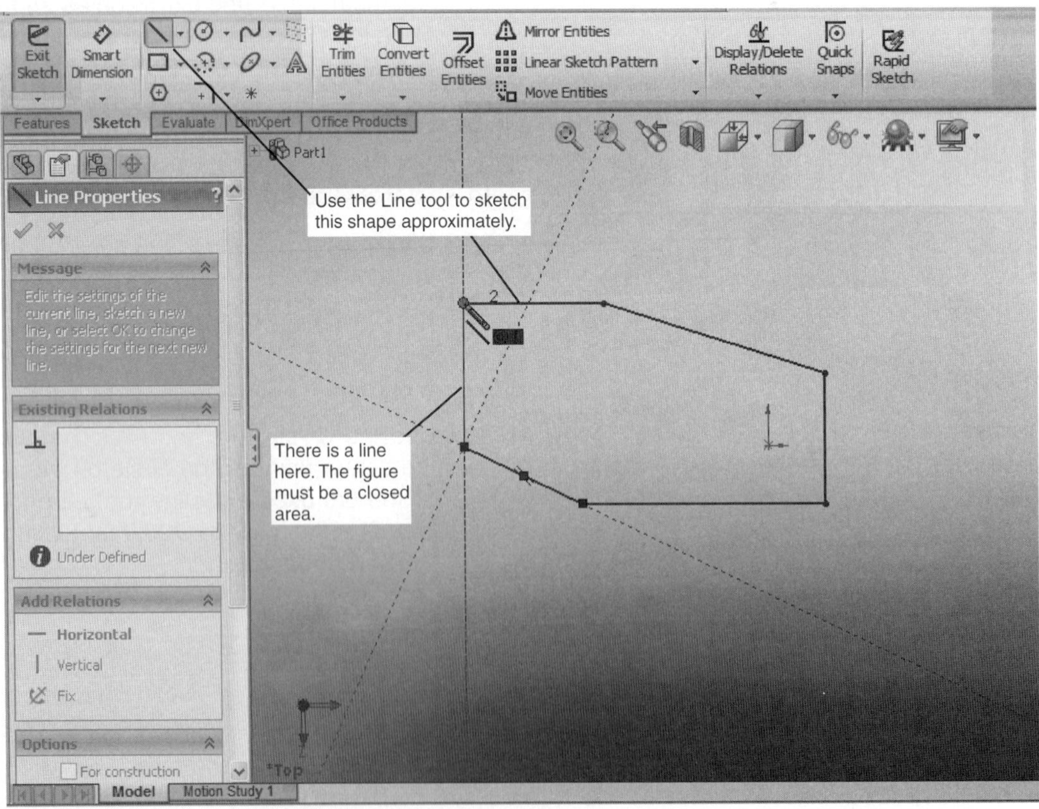

Figure 1-38

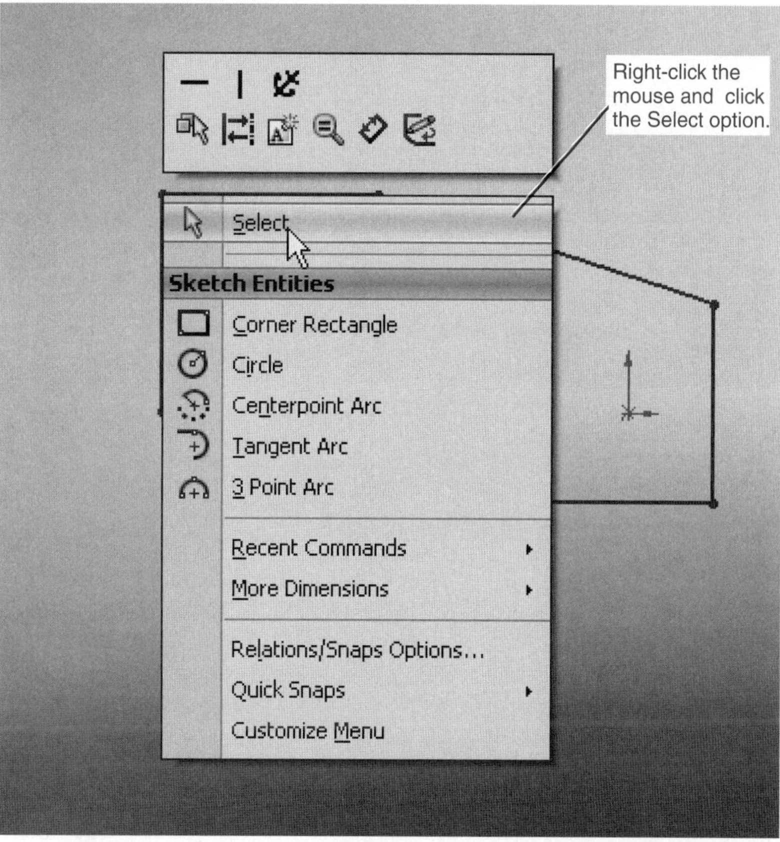

Figure 1-39

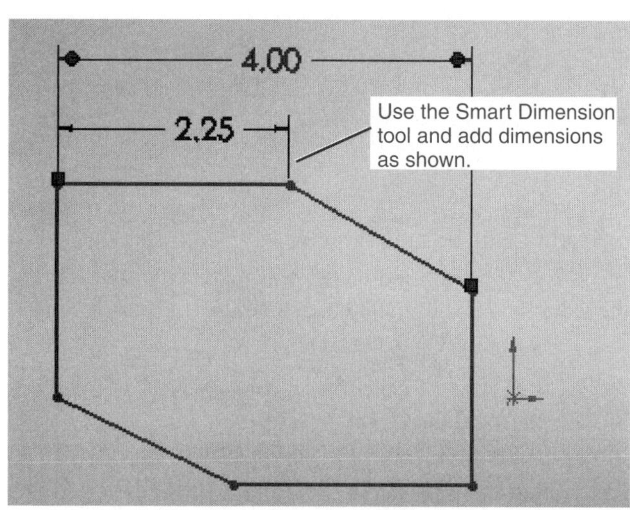

Figure 1-40

4. Locate the center point on the right end of the object for a second Ø20.0-mm circle and draw a circle.

The center point for the second circle can be located using the first center point and the endpoint of the lower 80-mm line. See Figure 1-60.

To Create Holes

1. Click the **Features** group, then the **Extruded Cut** tool.
2. Cut out the circles to form holes by clicking the check mark in the **Cut-Extrude Properties Manager**.

   See Figure 1-61.

To Create a Slot

1. Use the **Sketch** tool to create a sketching plane on the top surface of the object.
2. Select the **Rectangle** tool.
3. Sketch a rectangle on the top surface of the object.

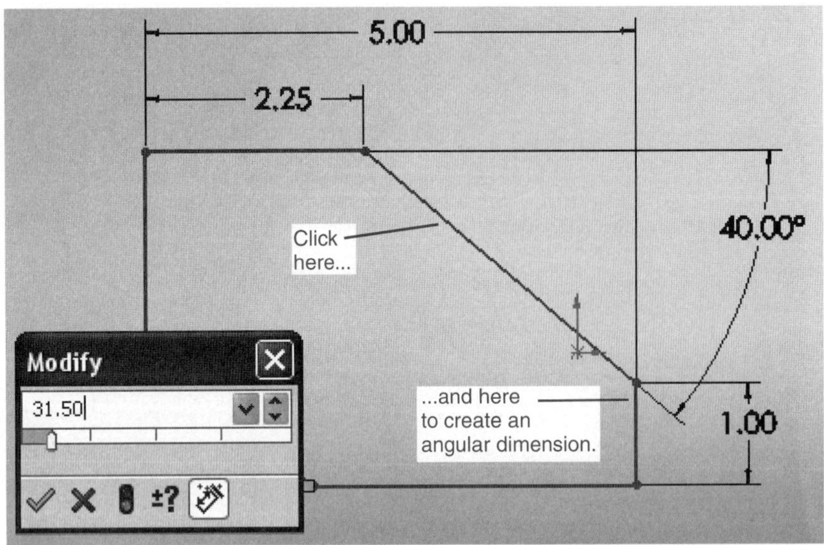

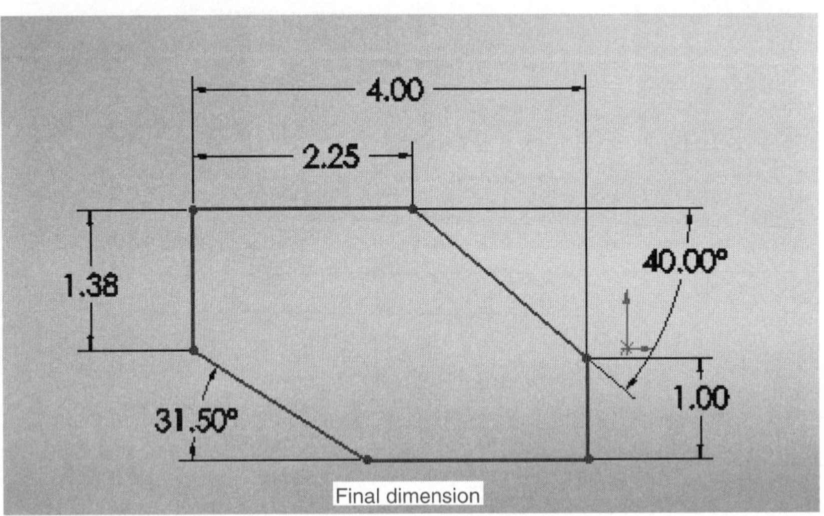

Figure 1-41

> **TIP**
>
> The edges of the part will highlight when touched by the cursor. Make sure that the rectangle goes from one edge of the part to the other.

See Figure 1-62.

4. Use the **Smart Dimension** tool to size and locate the rectangle as indicated in Figure 1-63.

The 30 locating dimension is taken from the edge of the slot to the end of the 80 edge line.

See Figure 1-63.

5. Click the **Features** group and select the **Extruded Cut** tool.
6. Set the slot depth for **10.00 mm**.
7. Click the check mark in the **Cut-Extrude Properties Manager**.
8. **Save** or **Exit** the drawing.

Figure 1-64 shows the finished object.

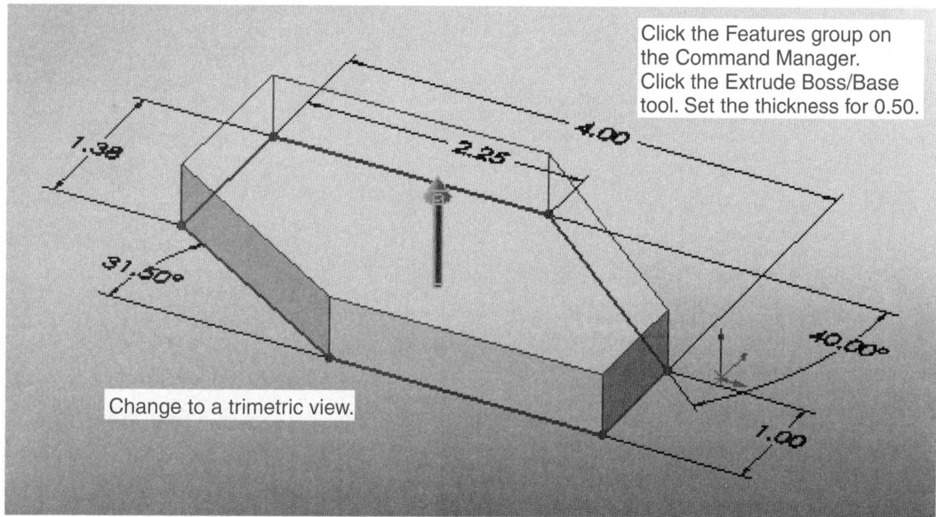
Click the Features group on the Command Manager.
Click the Extrude Boss/Base tool. Set the thickness for 0.50.
4.00
2.25
1.38
31.50°
40.00°
1.00
Change to a trimetric view.

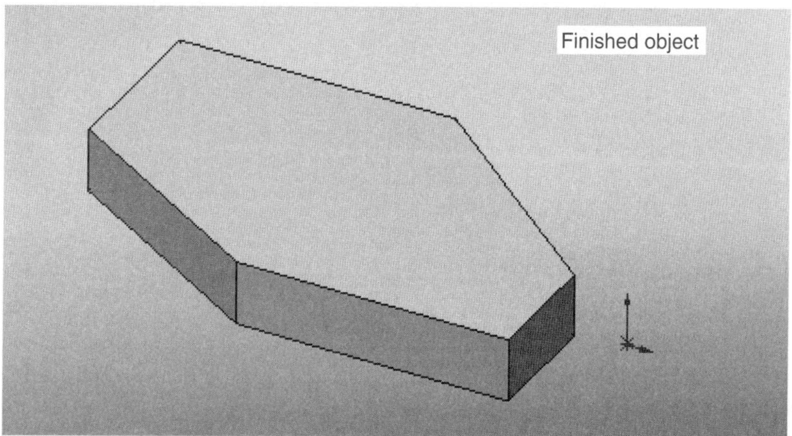
Finished object

Figure 1-42

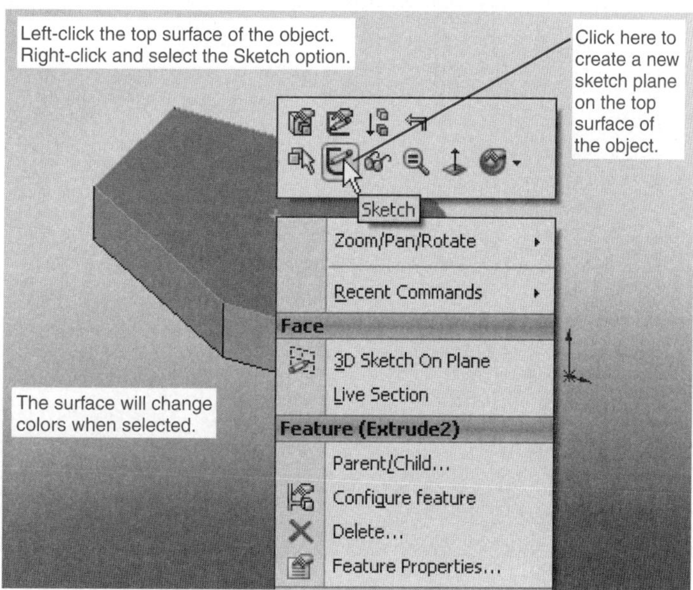
Left-click the top surface of the object.
Right-click and select the Sketch option.
Click here to create a new sketch plane on the top surface of the object.
Sketch
Zoom/Pan/Rotate
Recent Commands
Face
3D Sketch On Plane
Live Section
Feature (Extrude2)
Parent/Child...
Configure feature
Delete...
Feature Properties...
The surface will change colors when selected.

Figure 1-43

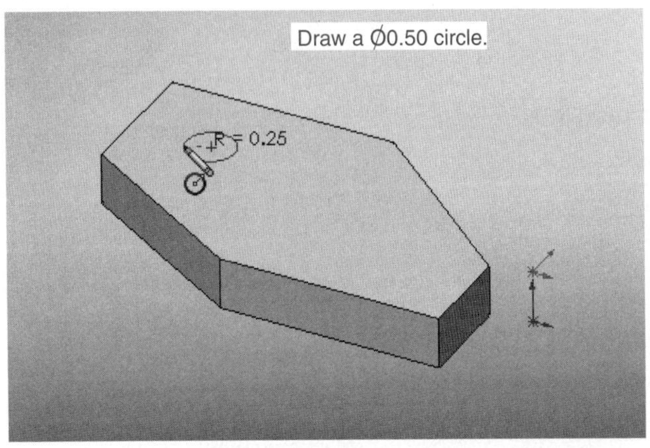

Figure 1-44

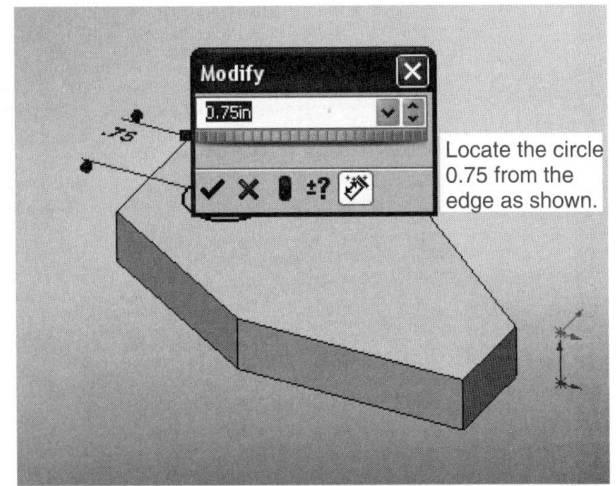

Figure 1-45

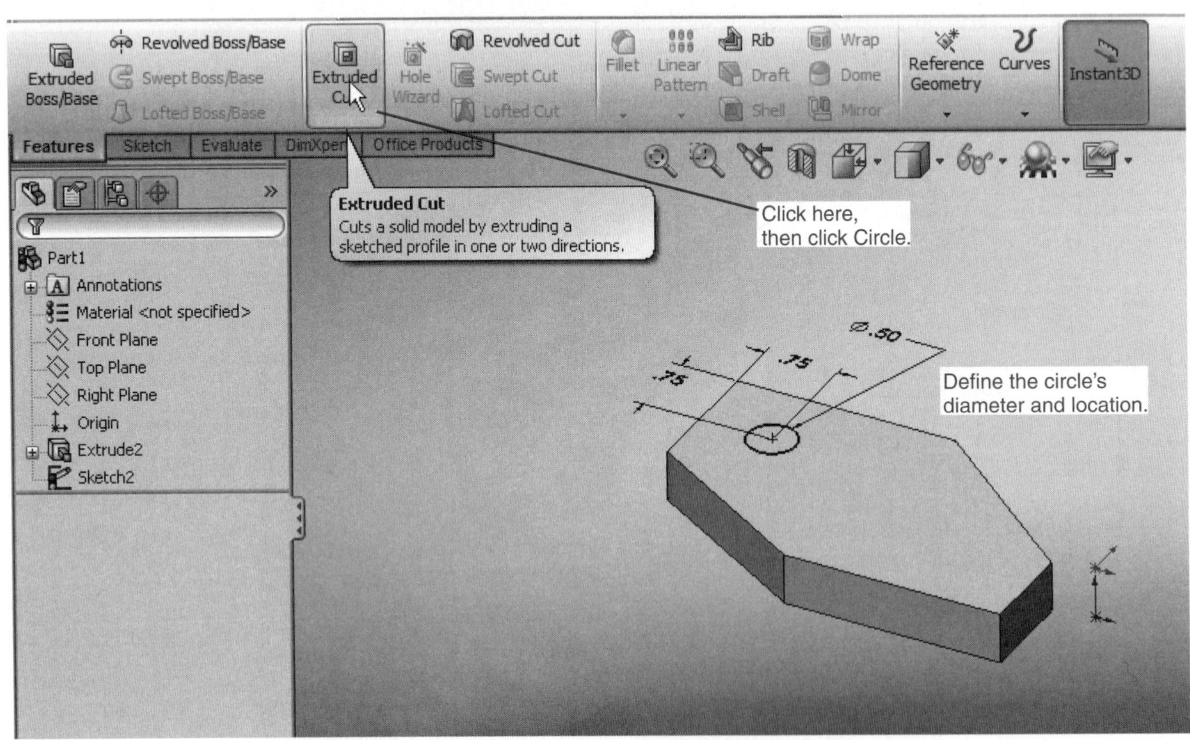

Figure 1-46

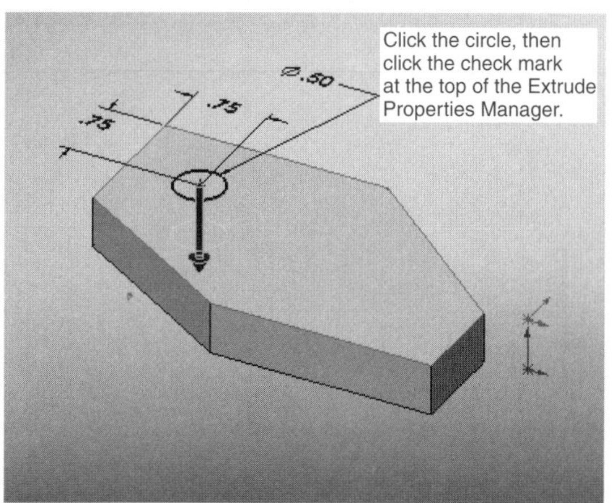
Click the circle, then click the check mark at the top of the Extrude Properties Manager.
Ø.50
.75
.75

Figure 1-47

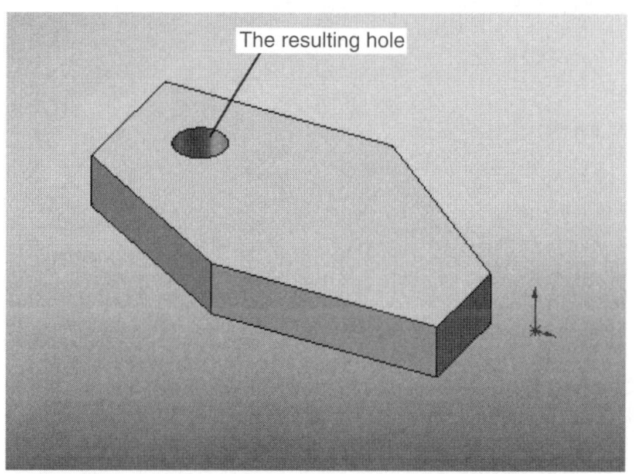
The resulting hole

Figure 1-48

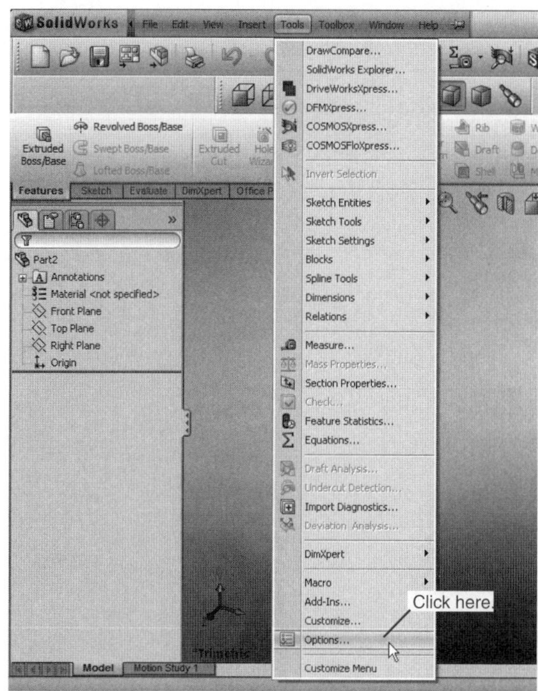
Click here.

Figure 1-49

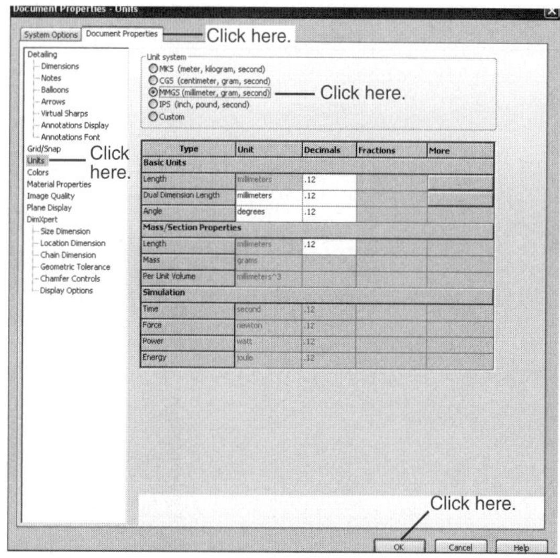
Click here.
Click here.
Click here.
Click here.

Figure 1-50

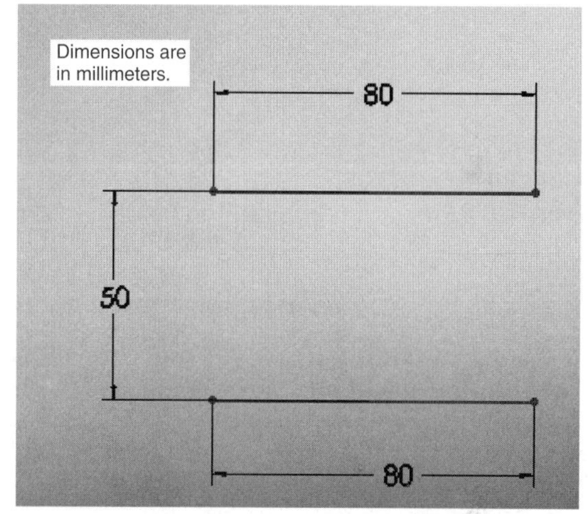
Dimensions are in millimeters.
80
50
80

Figure 1-51

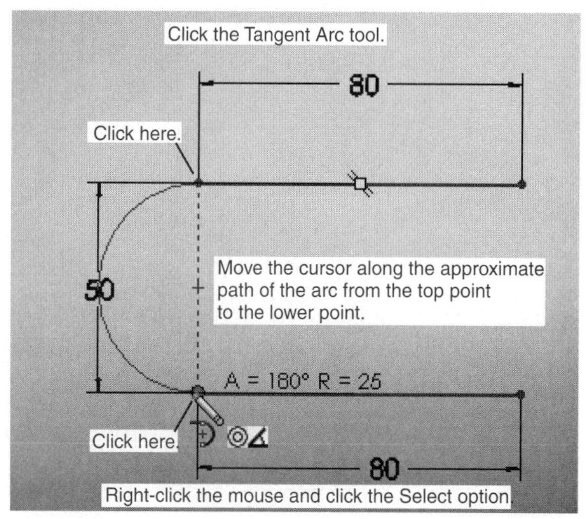
Click the Tangent Arc tool.
80
Click here.
Move the cursor along the approximate path of the arc from the top point to the lower point.
50
A = 180° R = 25
Click here.
80
Right-click the mouse and click the Select option.

Figure 1-52

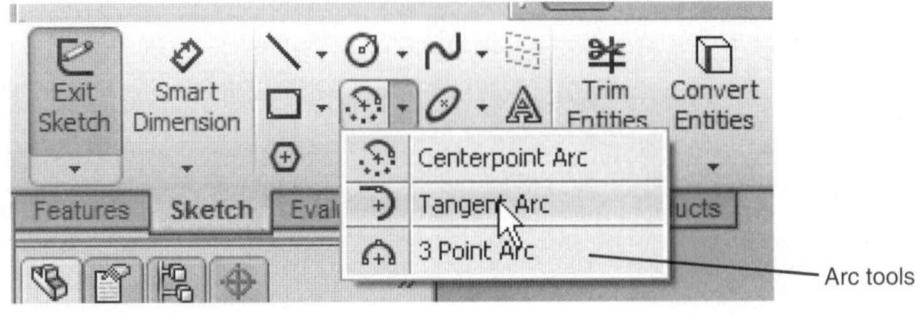

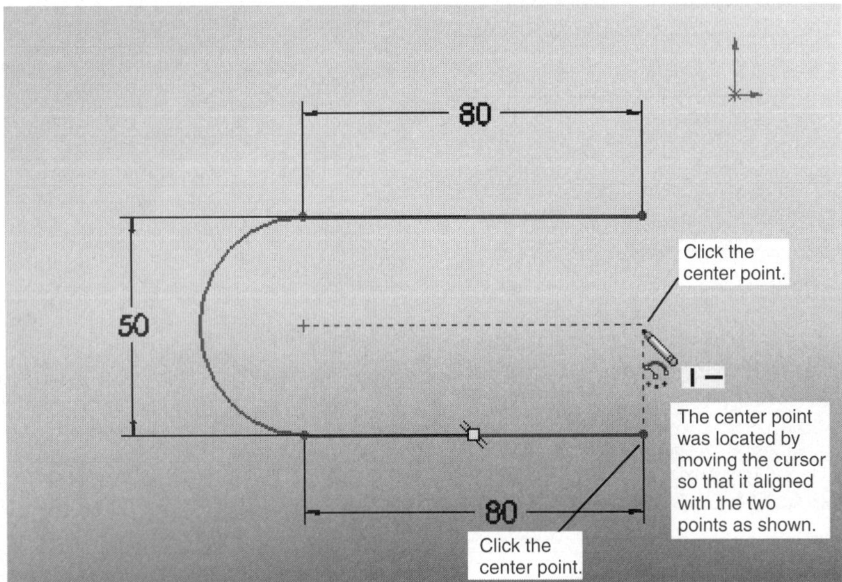

Figure 1-53

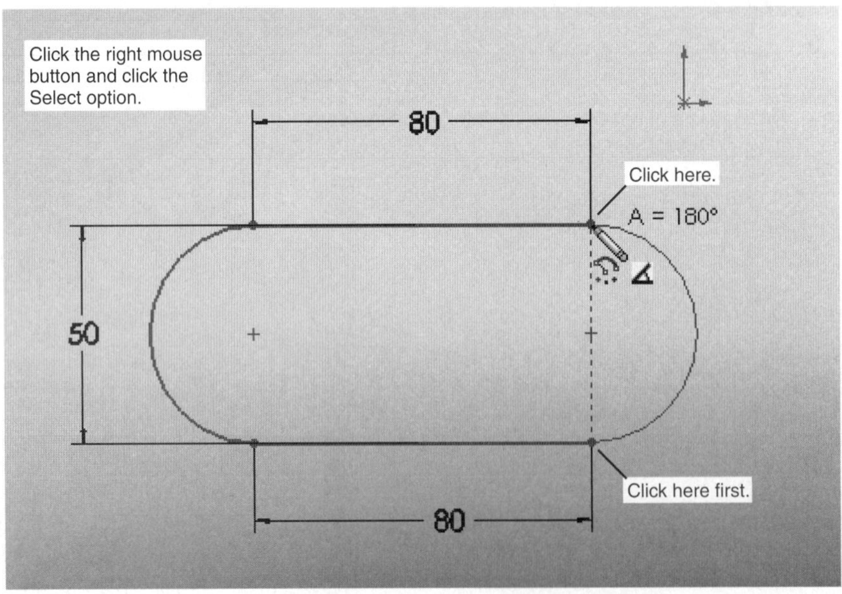

Figure 1-54

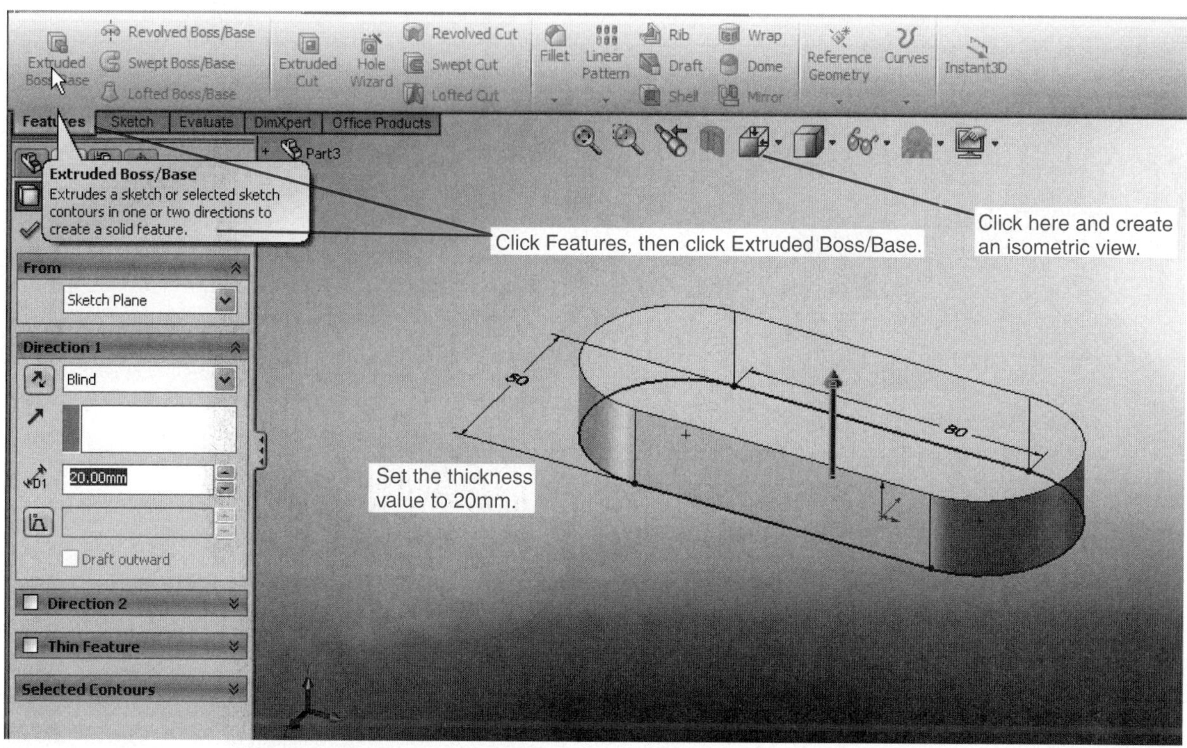

Figure 1-55

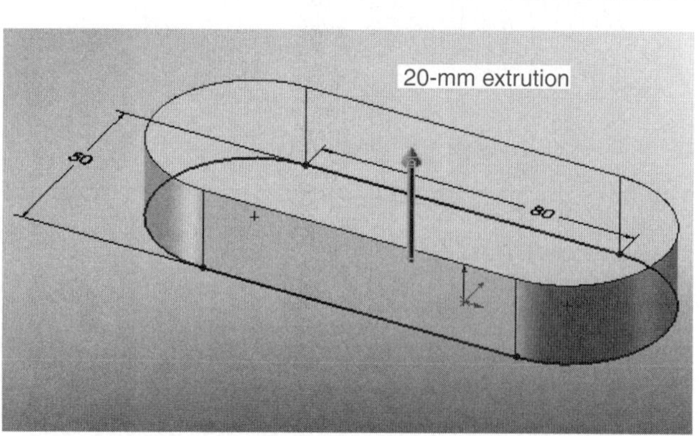

Figure 1-56

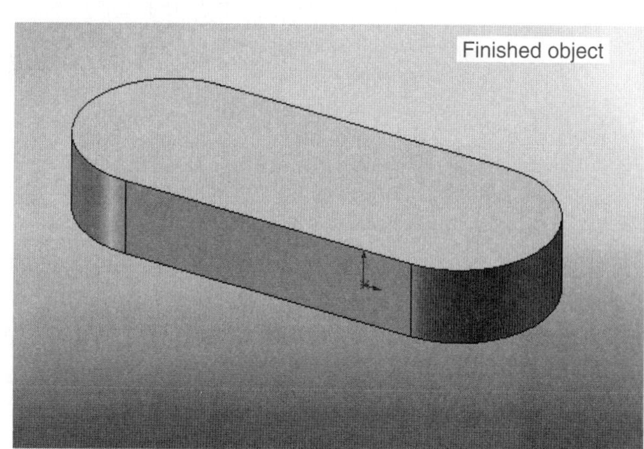

Figure 1-57

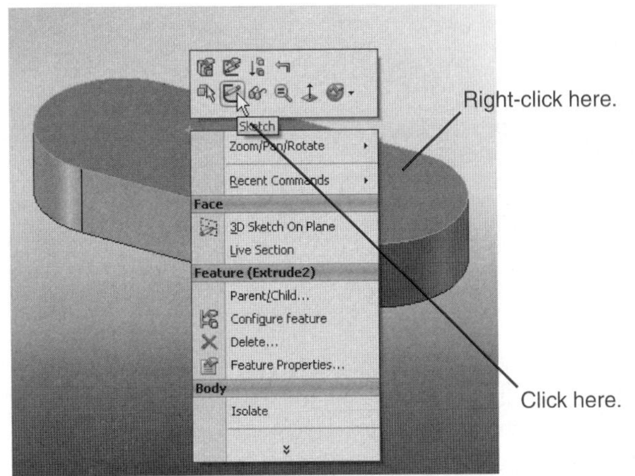

Figure 1-58

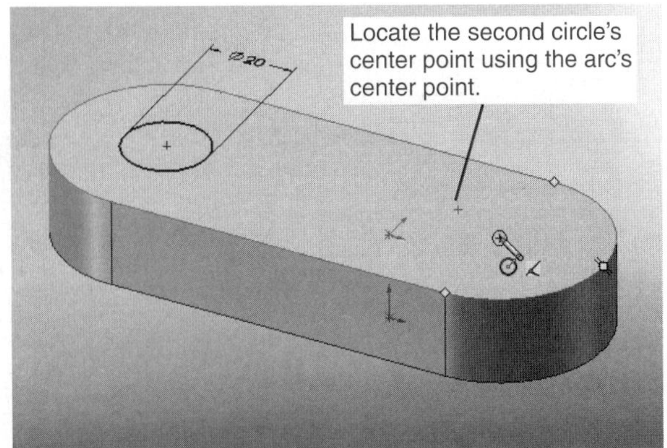

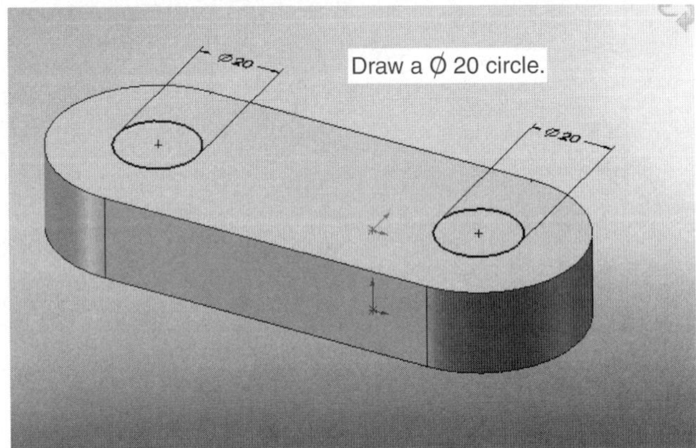

Figure 1-60

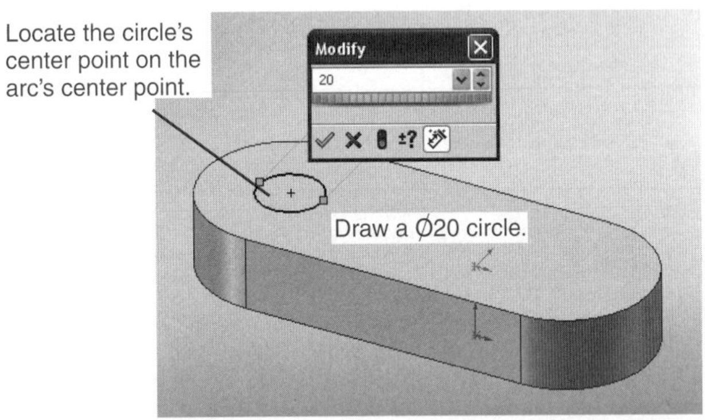

Figure 1-59

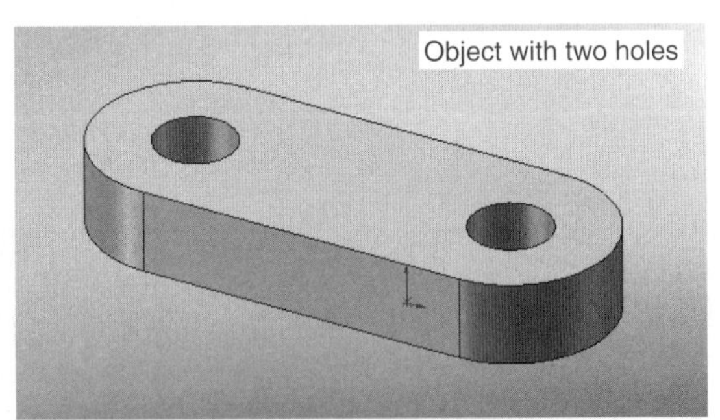

Figure 1-61

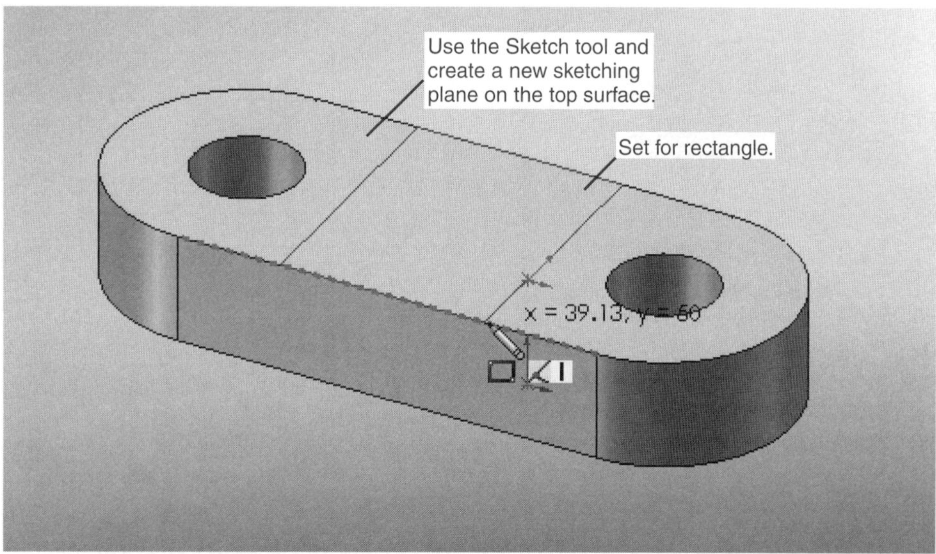

Figure 1-62

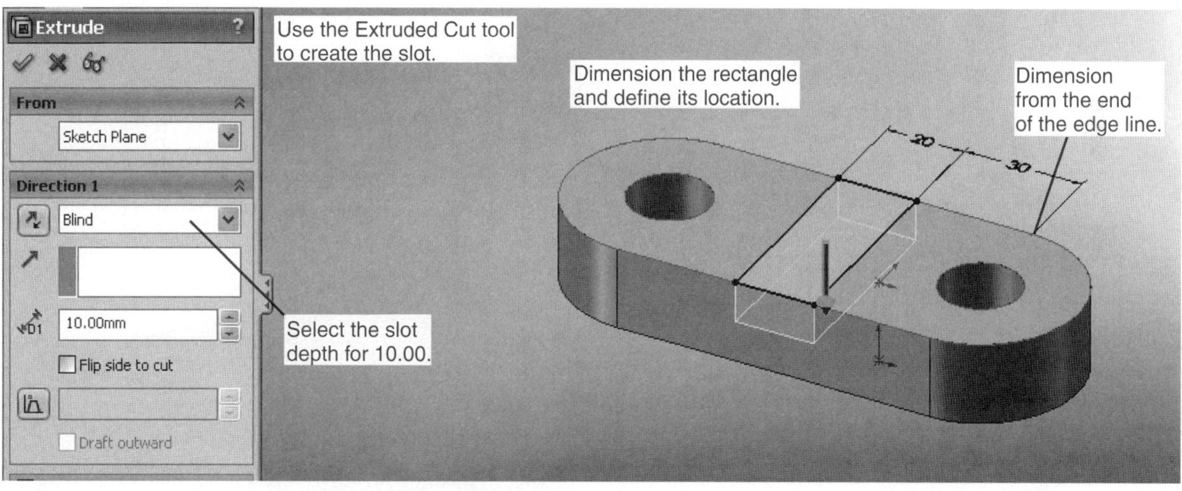

Figure 1-63

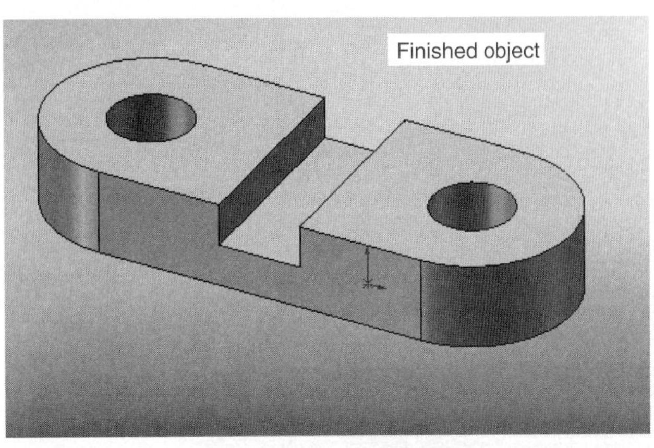

Figure 1-64

1-12 PROJECTS

Sketch the shapes shown in Figures P1-1 through Figure P1-18. Create 3D models using the specified thickness values.

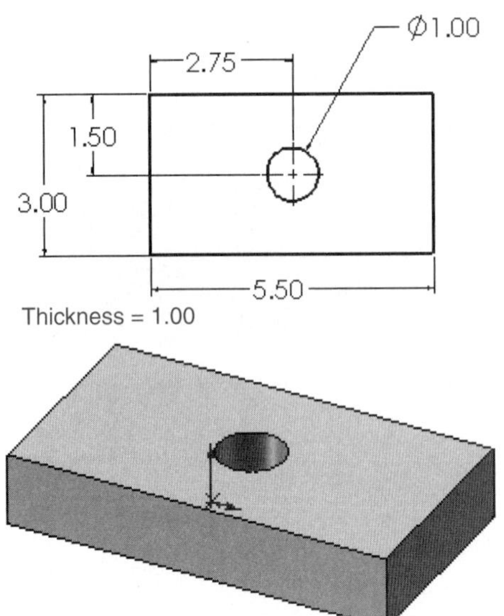

Figure P1-1 INCHES

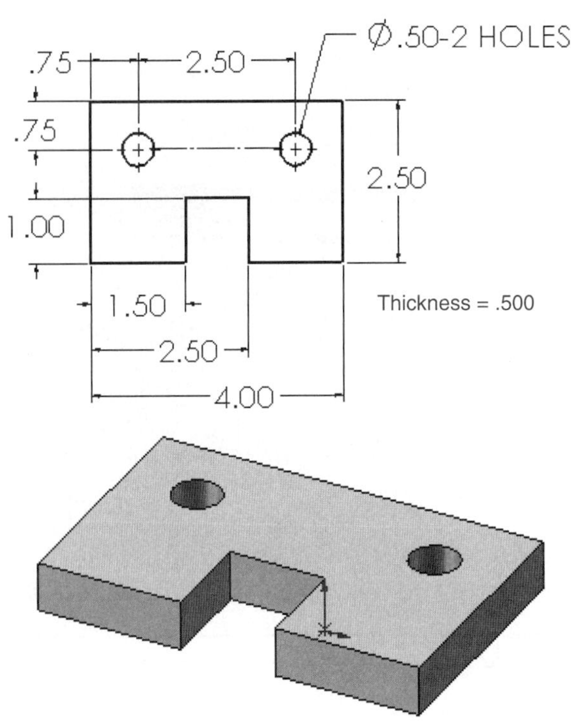

Figure P1-2 INCHES

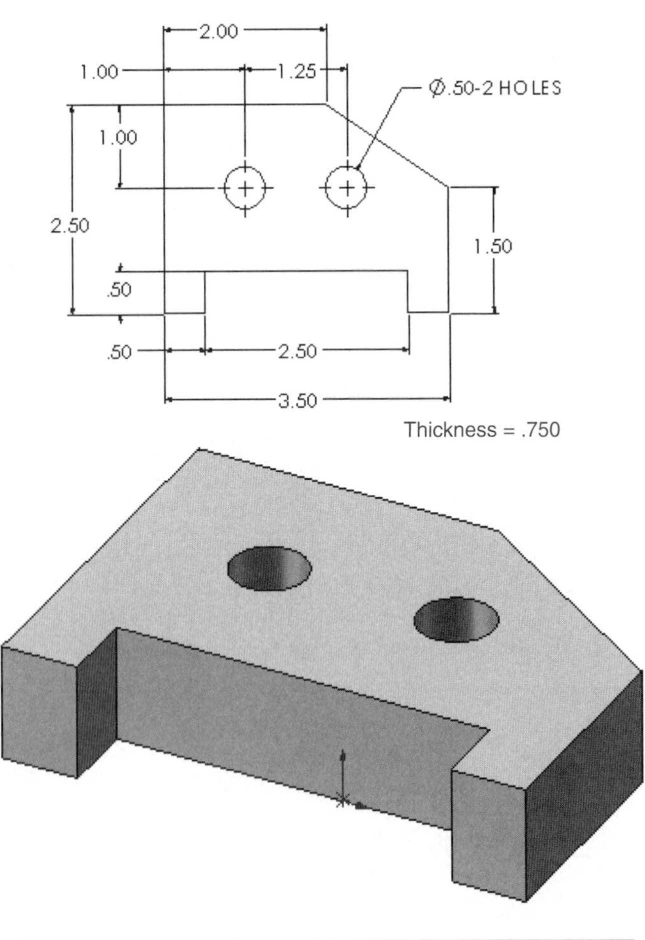

Figure P1-3 INCHES

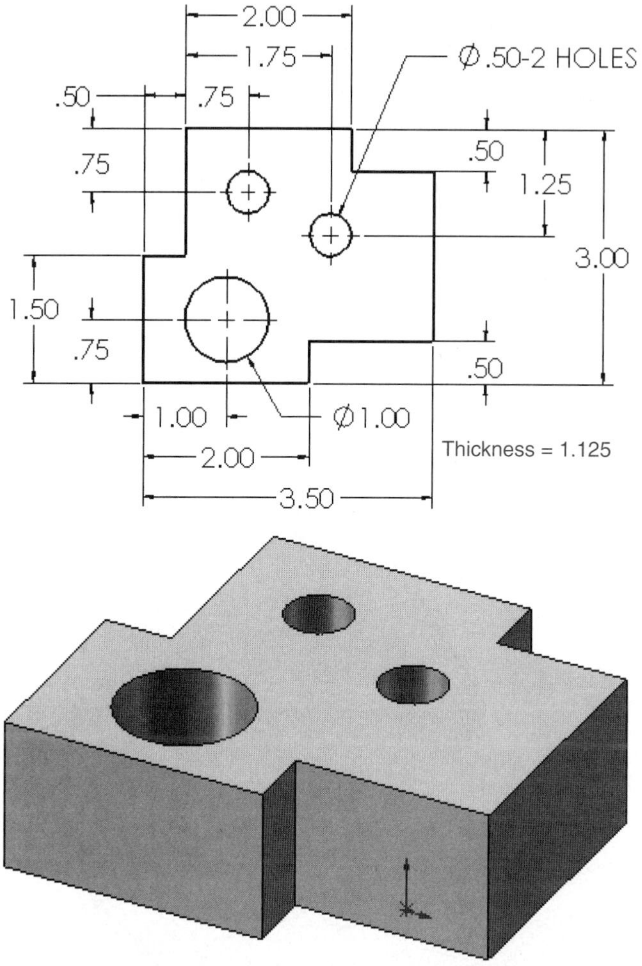

Figure P1-4 INCHES

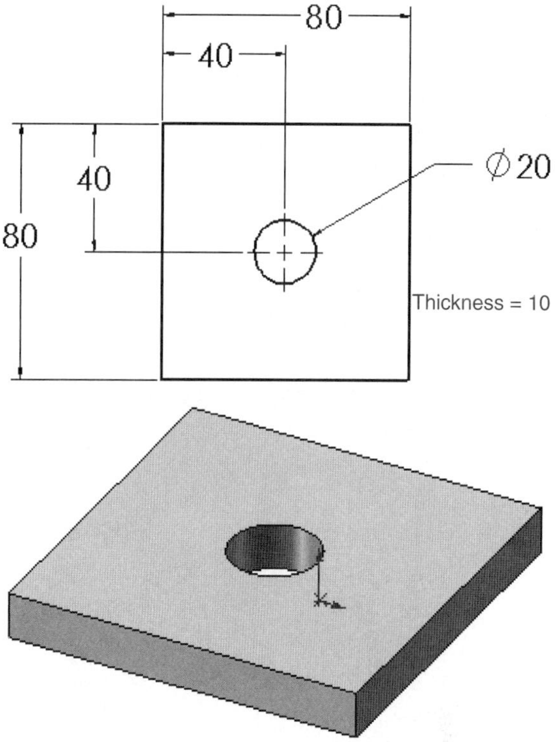

Figure P1-5 MILLIMETERS

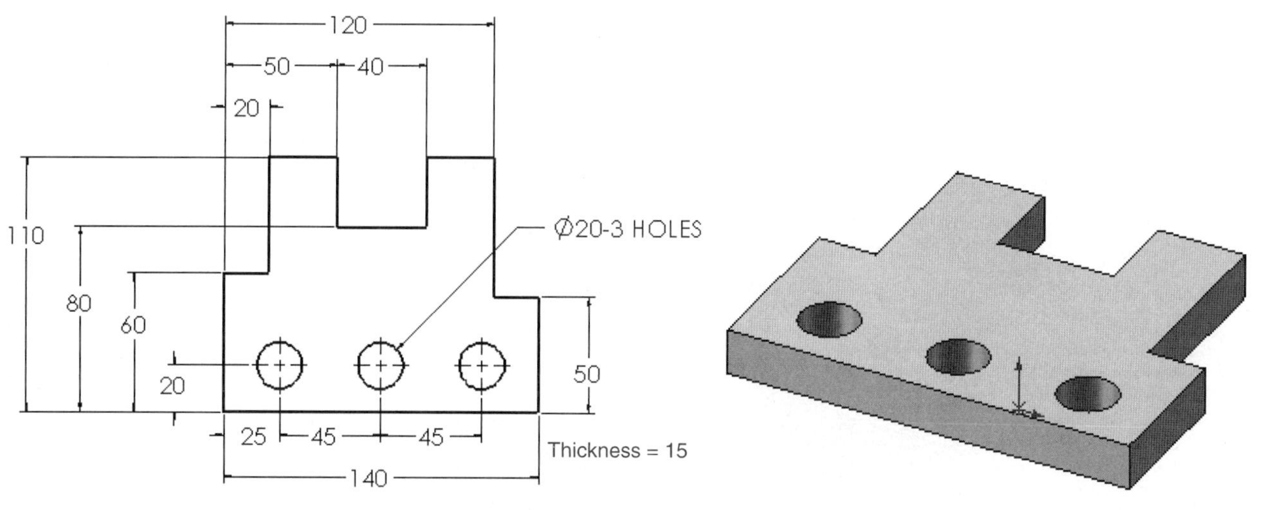

Figure P1-6 MILLIMETERS

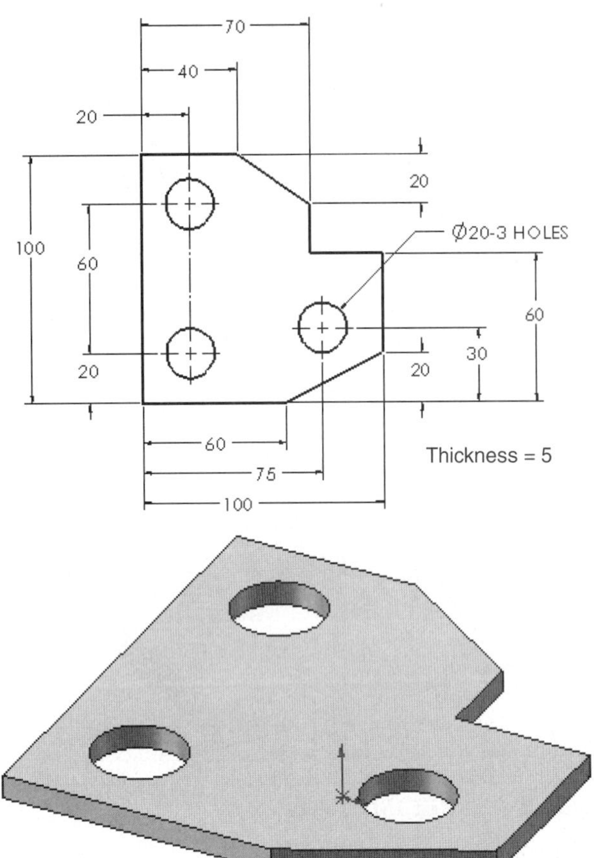

Figure P1-7 MILLIMETERS

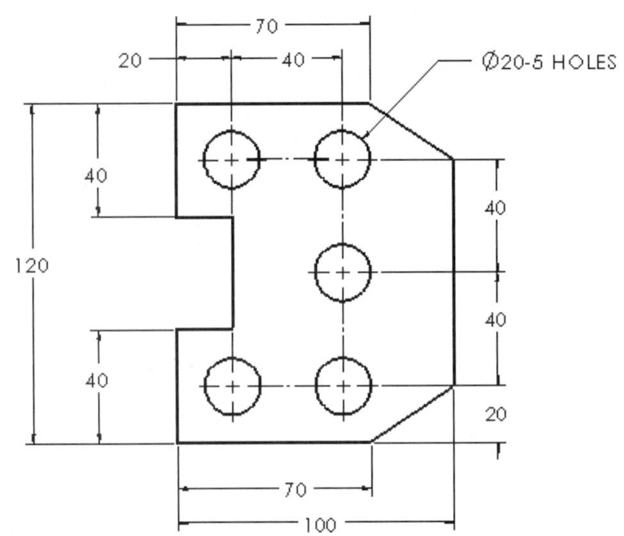

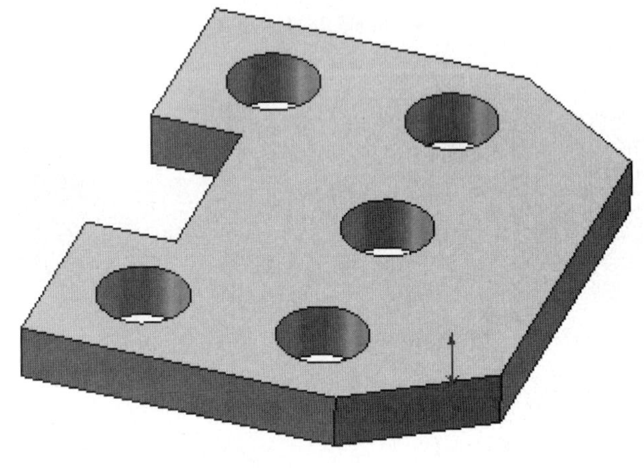

Figure P1-8 MILLIMETERS

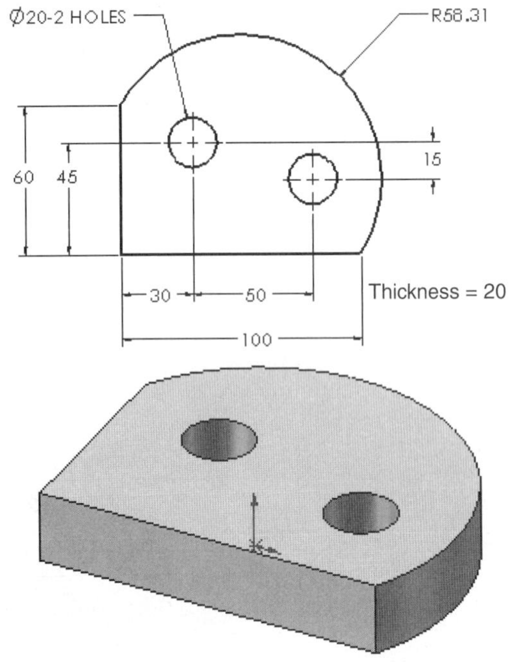

Figure P1-9 MILLIMETERS

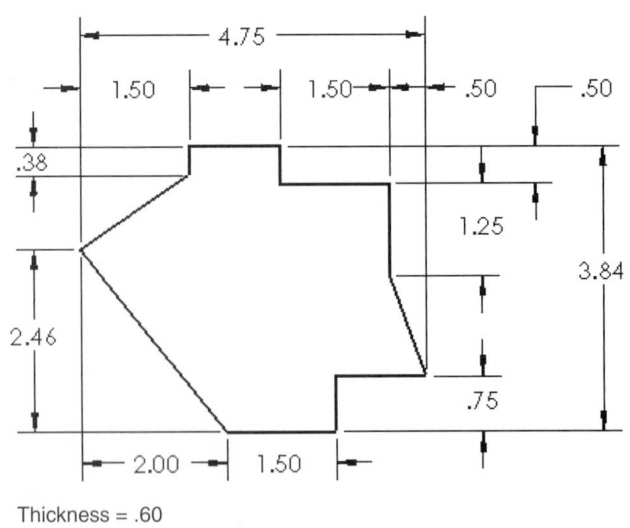

Figure P1-10 INCHES

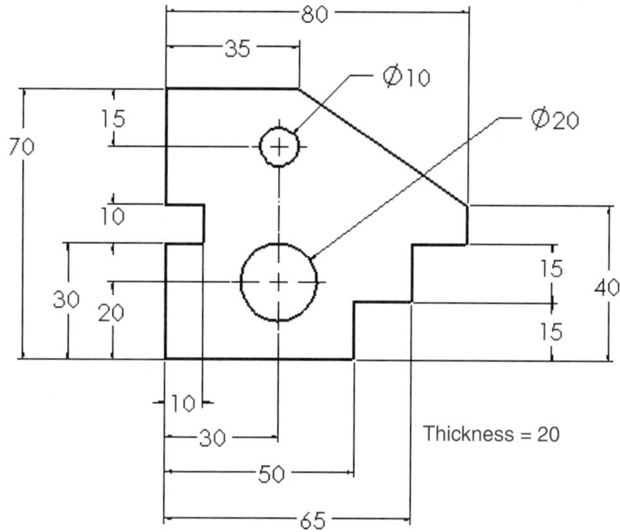

Figure P1-11 MILLIMETERS

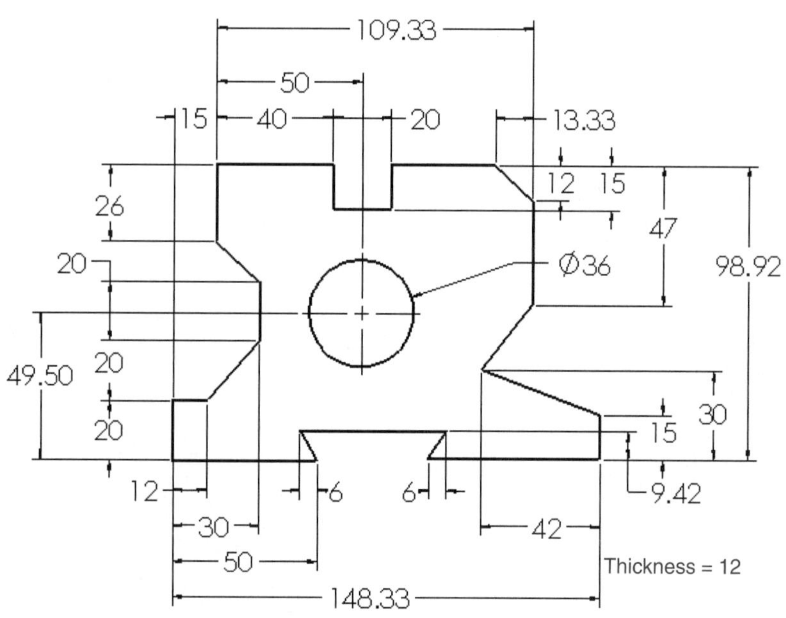

Figure P1-12 MILLIMETERS

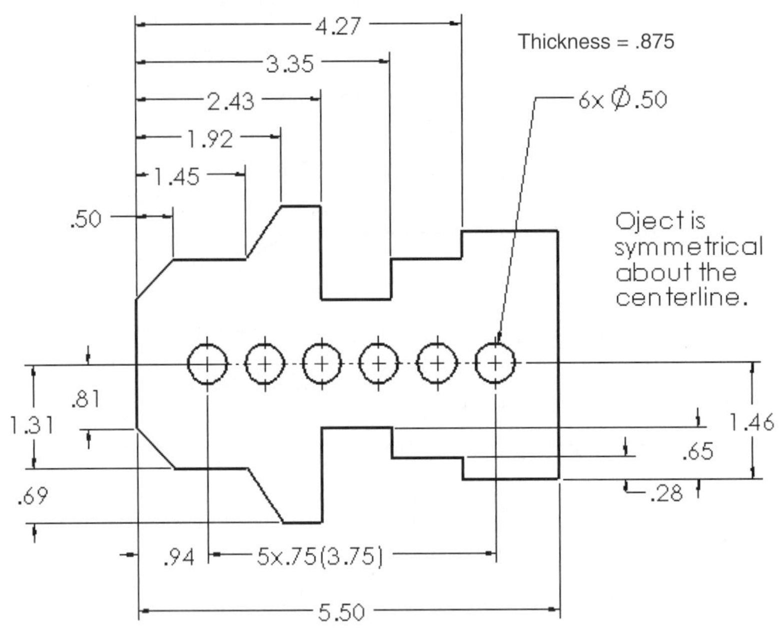

Figure P1-13 INCHES

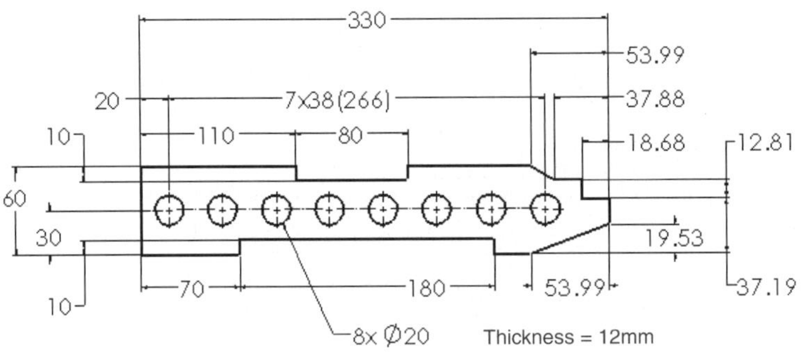

Figure P1-14 MILLIMETERS

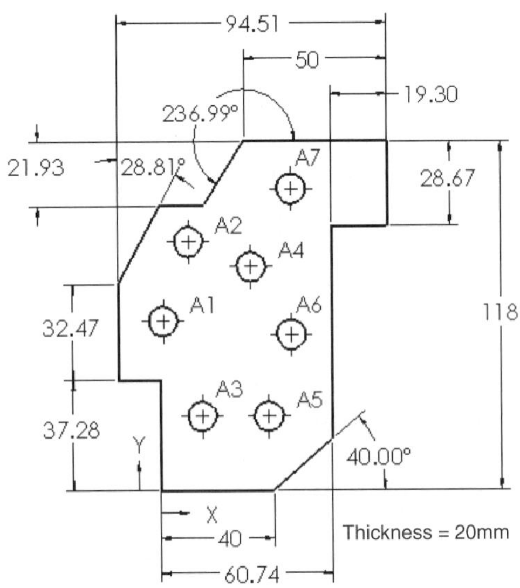

TAG	X LOC	Y LOC	SIZE
A1	1.22	57.14	Ø10
A2	10.27	84.04	Ø10
A3	15	25	Ø10
A4	32.38	75.51	Ø10
A5	38.51	25	Ø10
A6	46.50	52.61	Ø10
A7	46.50	101.88	Ø10

Figure P1-15 MILLIMETERS

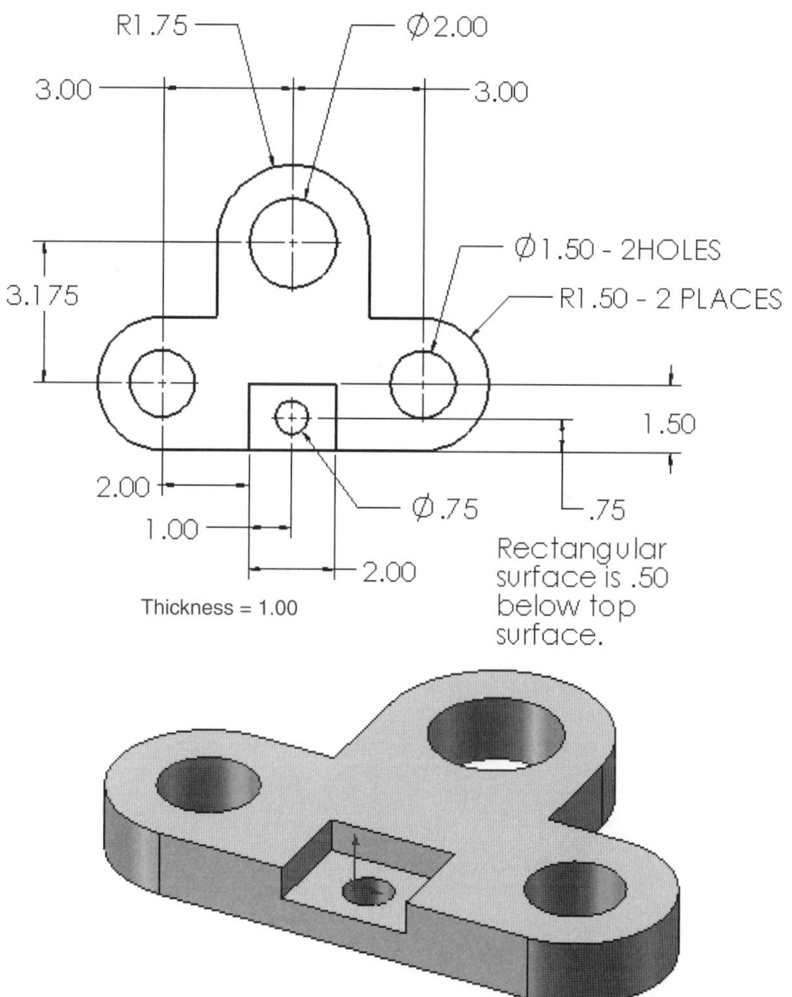

Figure P1-16 INCHES

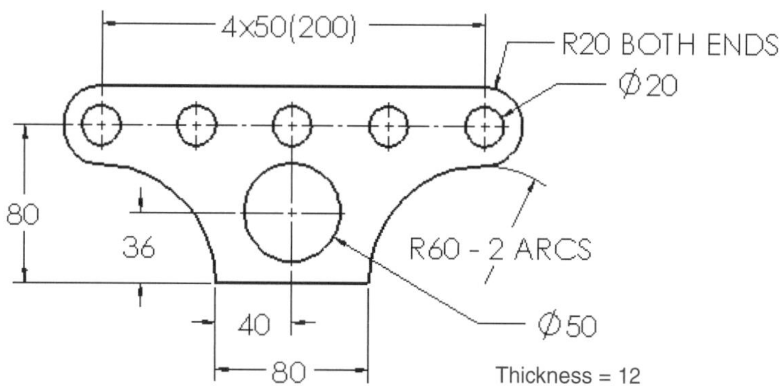

Figure P1-17 MILLIMETERS

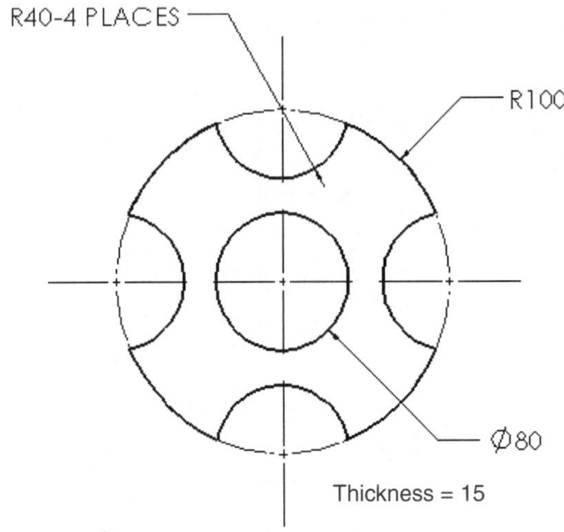

Figure P1-18 MILLIMETERS

C H A P T E R 2

Sketch Entities and Tools

Objectives

- Learn about the **Sketch Entities** tools.
- Learn about the **Sketch Tools.**
- Use the **Sketch Tools** together to create shapes and parts.

2-1 INTRODUCTION

Figure 2-1 shows the **Sketch Entities** toolbar, and Figure 2-2 shows part of the **Sketch** toolbar. The **Sketch Entities** toolbar is accessed by clicking the **Tools** heading at the top of the screen. The **Sketch** tool is already on the **Part** document screen.

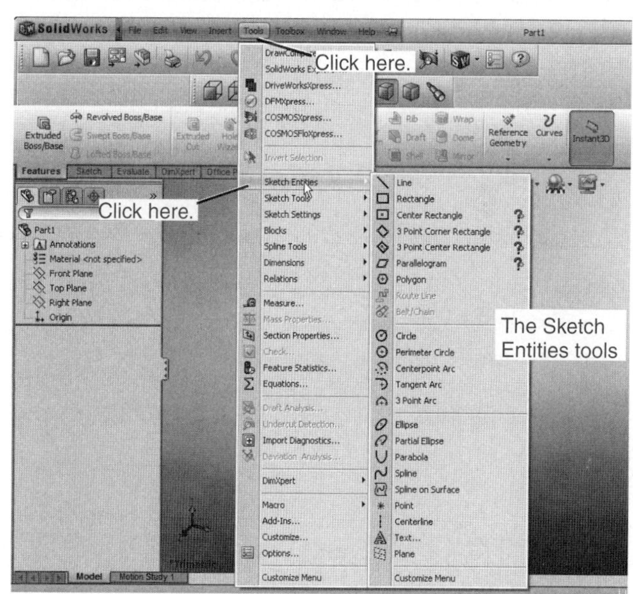

Figure 2-1

2-2 3 POINT ARC

Figure 2-3 shows three randomly located points. They were created using the **Point** tool.

1. Start a new **Part** document, click the **Sketch** group on the **Command Manager,** and select **Top Plane** from the **Features Manager.**

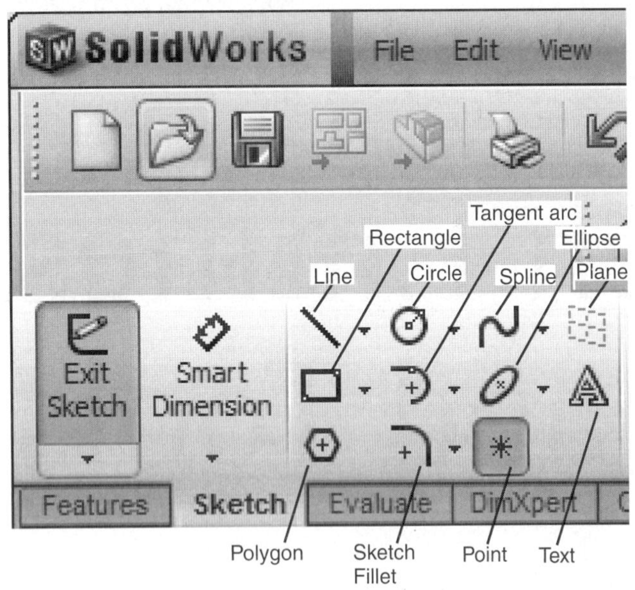

Figure 2-2

2. Use the **Point** tool and randomly locate three points approximately as shown.
3. Click the **3 Point Arc** tool and select three points to define an arc.

> *Note:*
> An alternative method for creating a 3 point arc is to start a new **Part** document, select the **Sketch** group **Manager**, select the **Front** view, then click the **3 Point Arc** tool on the **Command Manager.** This tool will simultaneously construct an arc as the three points are selected.

> **TIP**
> Try clicking the points in different sequences and seeing the different arcs that are created.

4. Right-click the mouse and click the **Select** option, or click the check mark in the **Arc Properties Manager.**

> *Note:*
> The **Arc Properties Manager** on the left side of the screen can be used to edit the location and size of the arc.

2-3 SKETCH FILLET AND UNDO TOOLS

Figure 2-4 shows a 2.50 × 5.00-in. rectangle. It was created using the **Rectangle** tool and sized using the **Smart Dimension** tool. See Section 1-4.

1. Start a new **Part** document, select the **Sketch** tool, and click the **Top Plane** option.
2. Use the **Rectangle** tool and create a **2.50 × 5.00-in.** rectangle. Use the **Smart Dimension** tool to size the rectangle.
3. Click the **Sketch Fillet** tool on the **Sketch** group on the **Command Manager.**

The **Sketch Fillet** options will appear in the **Sketch Fillet Properties Manager** on the left side of the drawing screen.

4. Set the radius value for the fillet for **0.50in.**

See Figure 2-5.

> **TIP**
> The scroll arrows to the right of the radius value box can be used to change the radius value, or a new value may be typed in.

5. Click the left vertical line, then click the top horizontal line.

A preview of the fillet will appear between the two lines.

6. Add an **R = 0.50in.** fillet to the upper right corner of the rectangle by selecting the top horizontal line and the right vertical line.
7. Reset the **Fillet Parameters** to **0.25in.** and add fillets to the two bottom corners of the rectangle.
8. Click the check mark in the **Sketch Fillet Properties Manager.**

See Figure 2-6.

9. Click the **Undo** tool and remove the four fillets.
10. Click the **Sketch Fillet** tool, define the radius as 1.24, and create four fillets as shown.
11. Close **(Save)** the document.

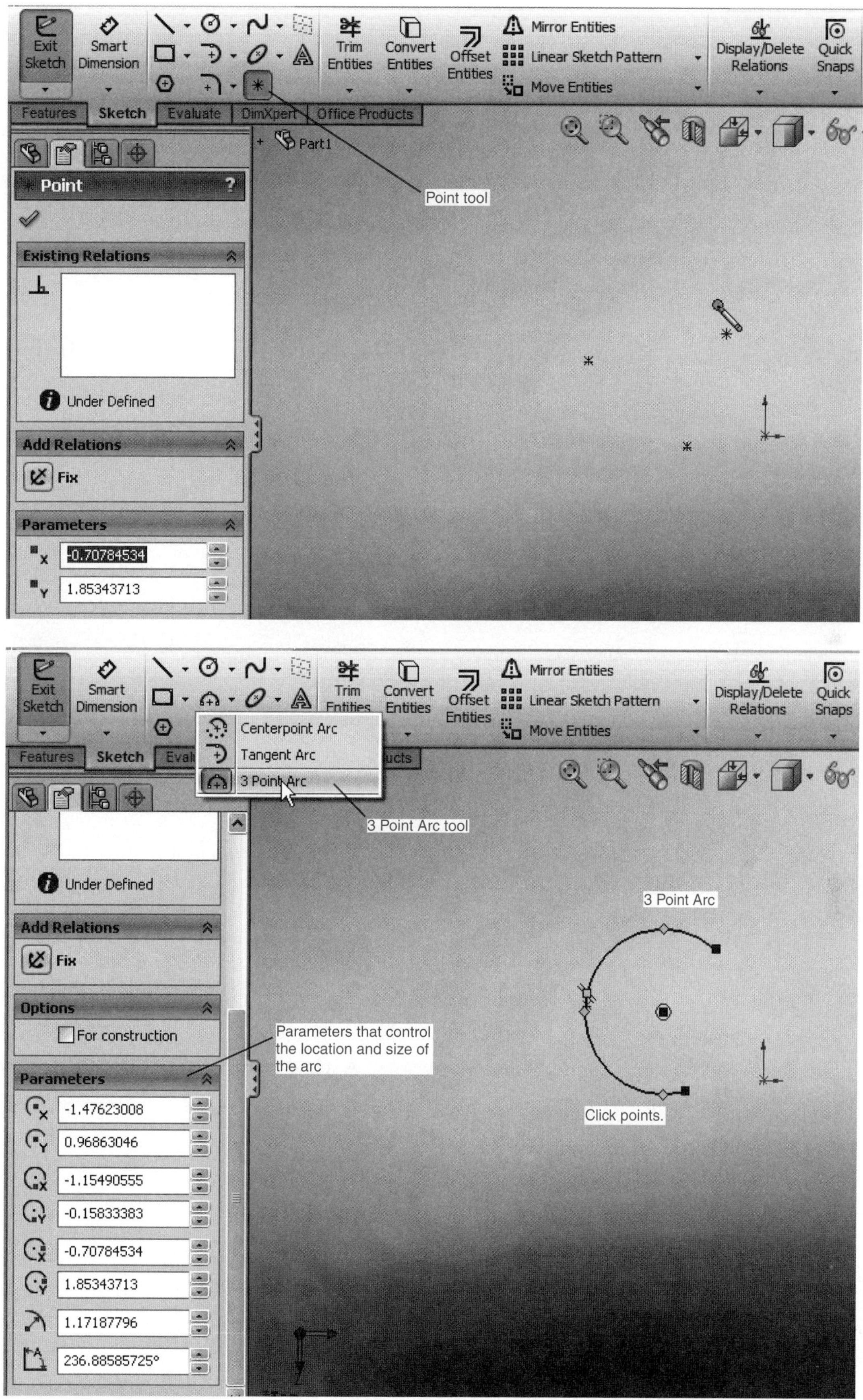
Exit Sketch
Smart Dimension
Trim Entities
Convert Entities
Offset Entities
Mirror Entities
Linear Sketch Pattern
Move Entities
Display/Delete Relations
Quick Snaps
Features
Sketch
Evaluate
DimXpert
Office Products
Part1
Point
Point tool
Existing Relations
Under Defined
Add Relations
Fix
Parameters
-0.70784534
1.85343713
Centerpoint Arc
Tangent Arc
3 Point Arc
3 Point Arc tool
3 Point Arc
Options
For construction
Parameters that control the location and size of the arc
Click points.
-1.47623008
0.96863046
-1.15490555
-0.15833383
-0.70784534
1.85343713
1.17187796
236.88585725°

Figure 2-3

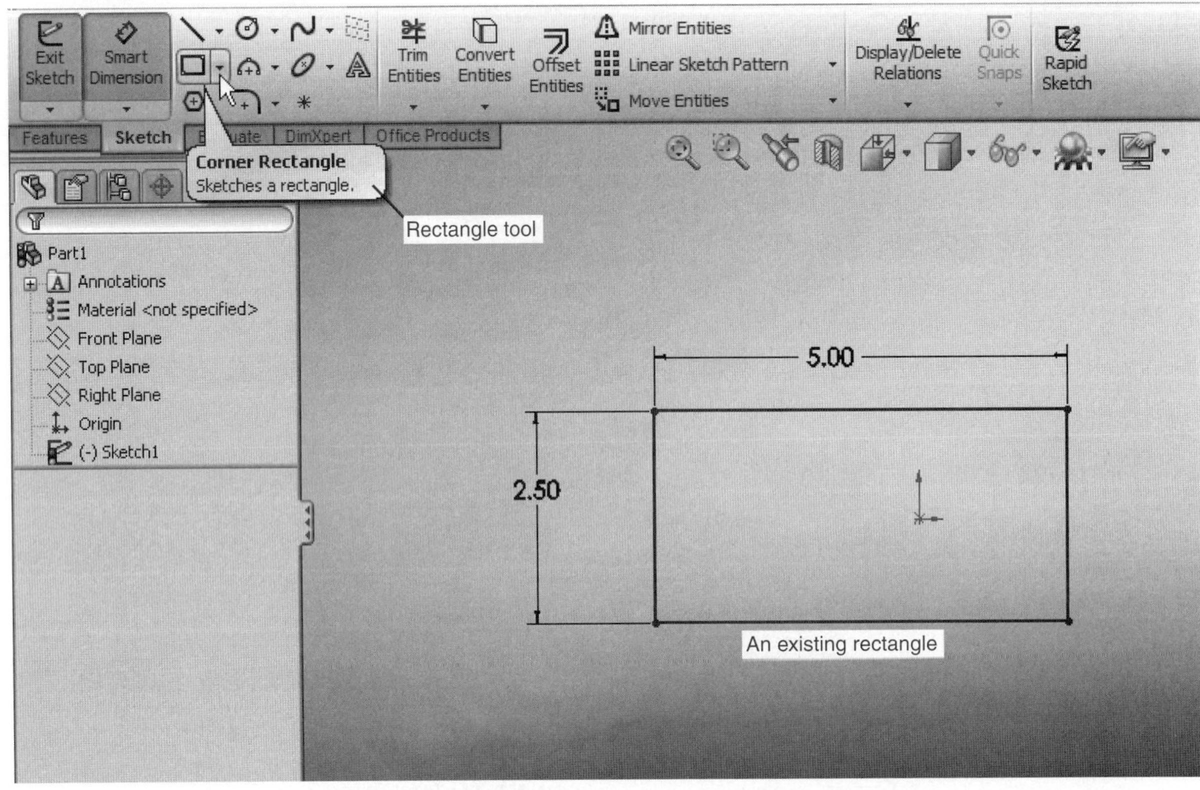

Figure 2-4

Figure 2-7 shows the original 2.50 × 5.00-in. rectangle modified using the **Sketch** tool to create a rounded shape with radii of 1.24.

2-4 SPLINE

Figure 2-8 shows a spline.

1. Start a new **Part** document, click the **Sketch** tool, and click the **Top Plane** option.
2. Click the **Spline** tool.
3. Select a starting point for the spline and click the point.
4. Select other points and extend the spline.
5. When the spline is complete, right-click the mouse and click the **Select** option or select the check mark in the **Spline Properties Manager.**

A spline may be edited by moving any one of its defining points.

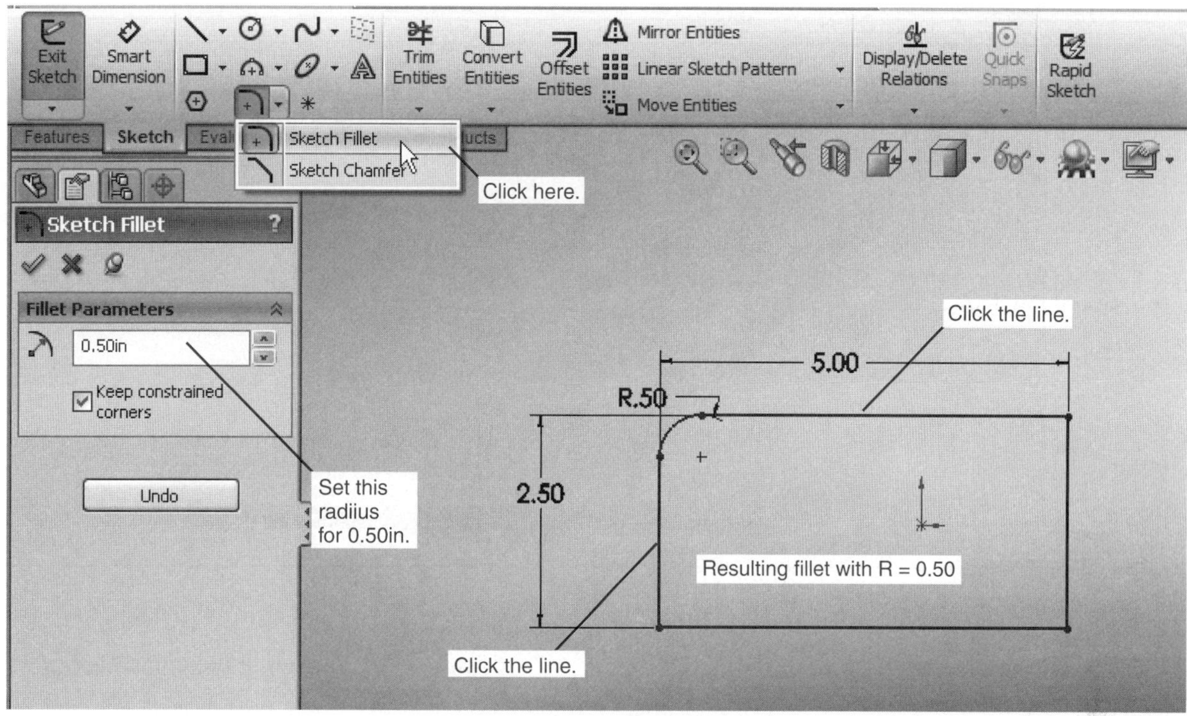

Figure 2-5

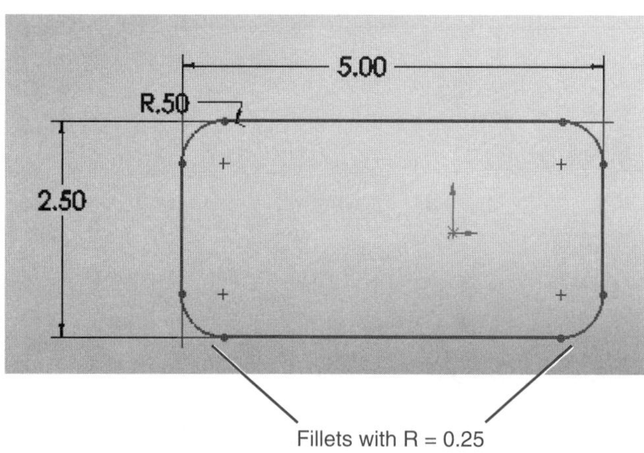

Figure 2-6

To Edit a Spline

1. Click and hold one of the defining points and drag the point to a new location and release the mouse button.

The point's parameters will be listed in the **Parameters** box. See Figure 2-8. These values will change as the point is moved. Point values may be entered directly into the **Parameters** box. Click the check mark in the **Point Properties Manager** to apply the entered values to the spines's points.

2-5 POLYGON

The **Polygon** tool is accessed by clicking **Tools** on the main menu (top of the screen), clicking **Sketch Entities** on the drop-down menu, then selecting the **Polygon** tool. See Figure 2-1.

1. Start a new **Part** document, click the **Sketch** tool, and click the **Top Plane** option.
2. Select the **Polygon** tool.
3. Under the **Polygon Properties Manager** define the number of sides as six.
4. Select a center point for the polygon by clicking the left mouse button.
5. Drag the cursor away from the center point to create the polygon.

A set of angular coordinate values will appear next to the cursor as it is moved. The values will define the distance from the center point to the edge line.

The example shown was created by dragging the cursor horizontally to the right.

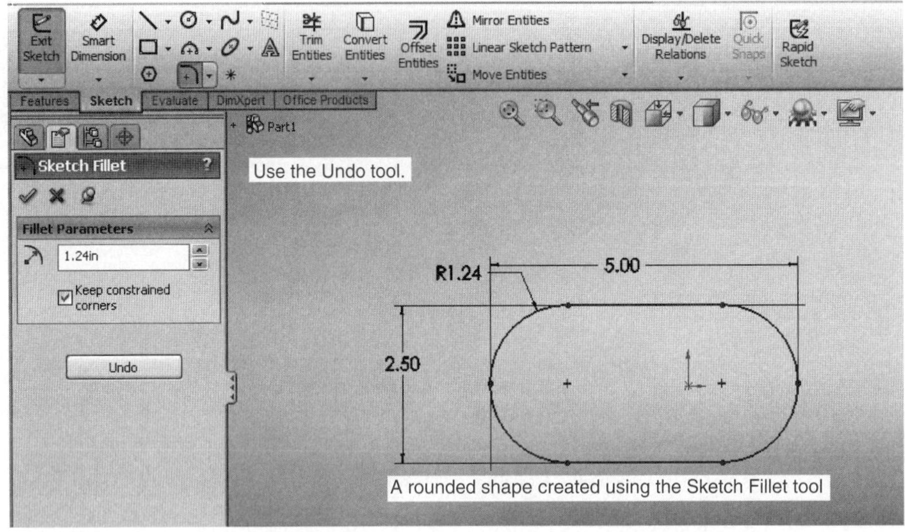

Figure 2-7

> **TIP**
>
> SolidWorks defines a horizontal line to the right as 0°. The counterclockwise direction is the positive direction.

6. Use either the parameter values or the **Smart Dimension** tool to size the polygon.
7. Click the OK check mark to complete the polygon construction.

The 3.00 in. dimension shown in Figure 2-9 is the distance *across the flats* of the hexagon. The distance along one of the sides is called the *edge distance,* and the distance across the hexagon from one corner to another is called the *corner distance.*

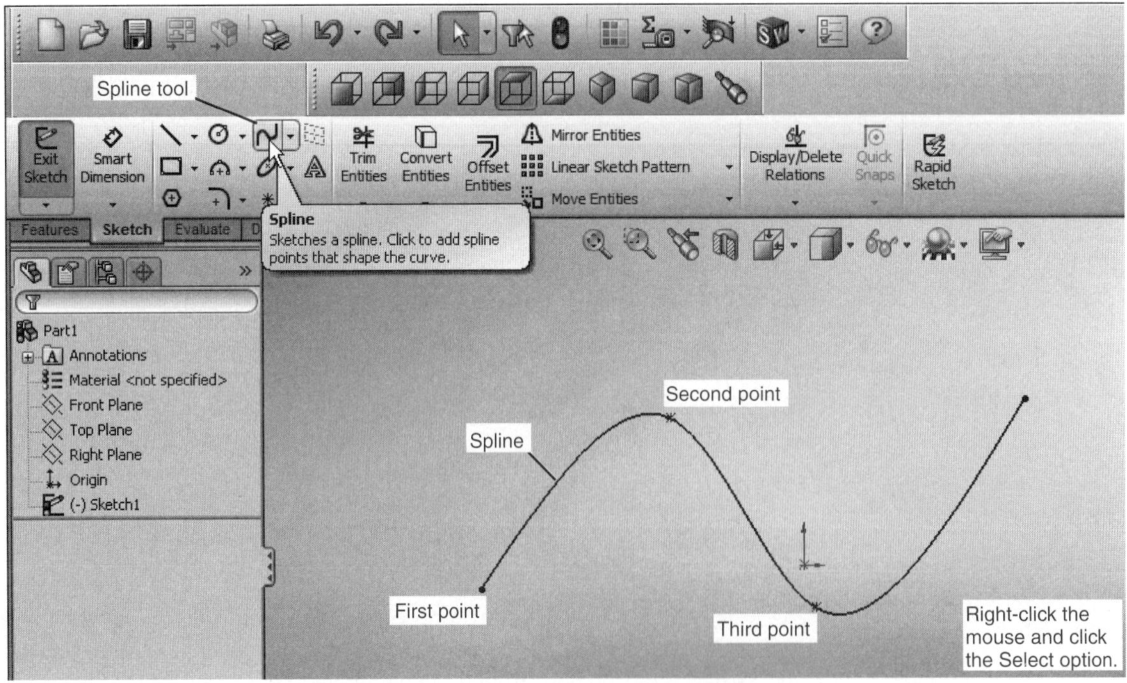

Figure 2-8

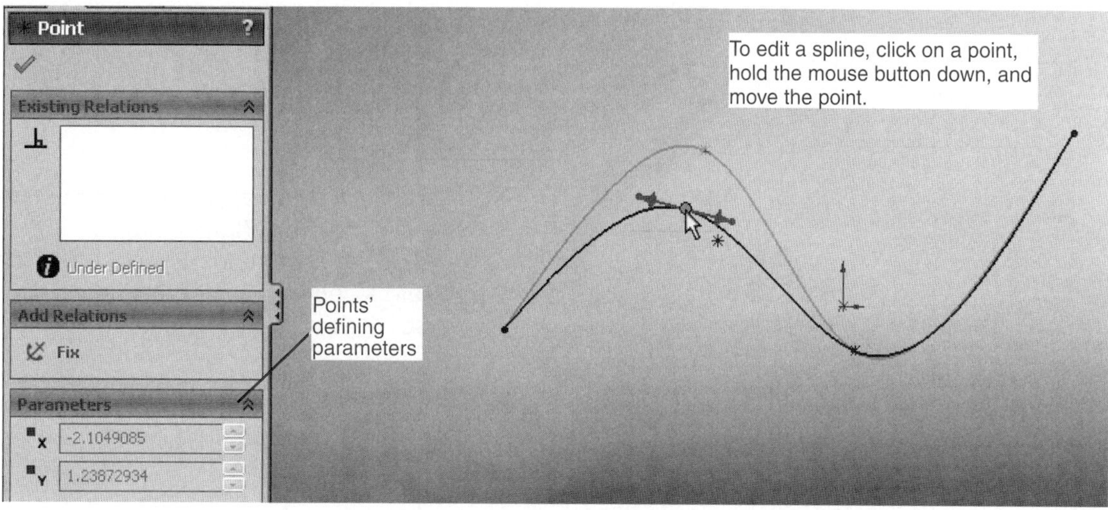

Figure 2-8 ***(continued)***

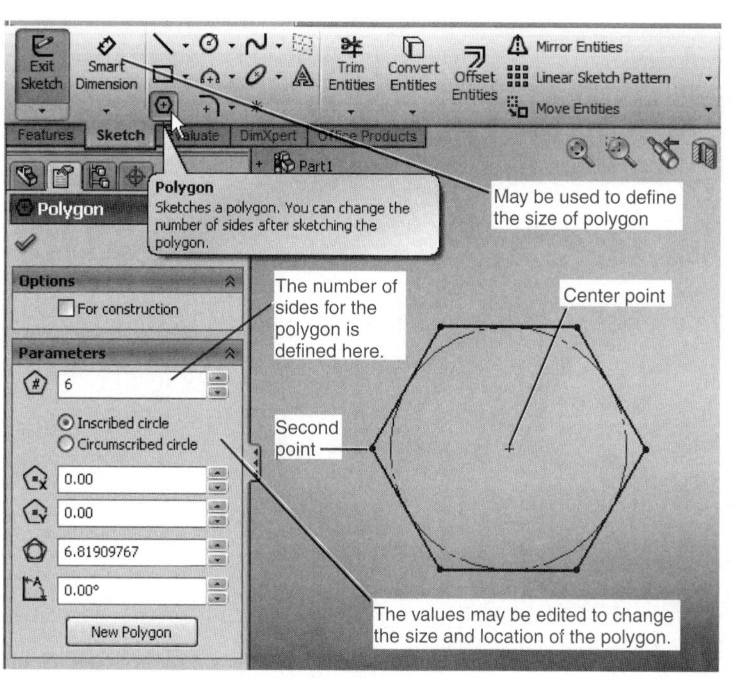

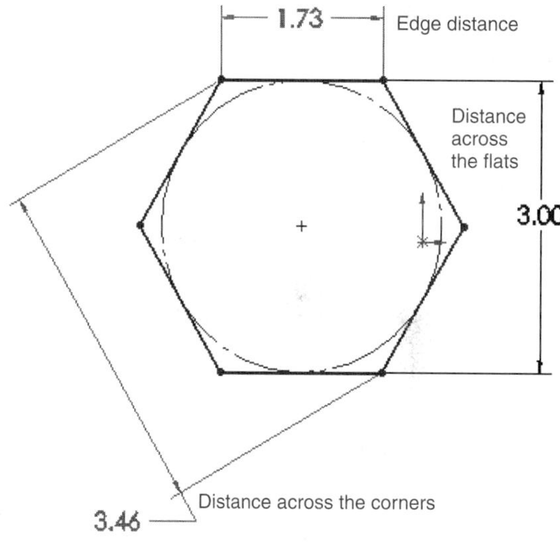

Finished polygon

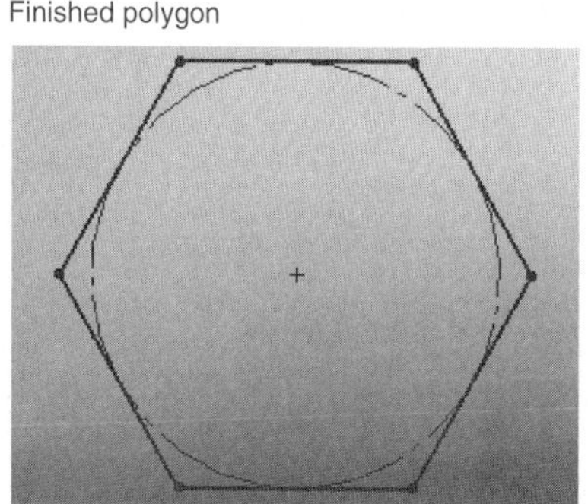

Figure 2-9

2-6 ELLIPSE

The **Ellipse** tool is located on the **Sketch** toolbar. See Figure 2-2.

Ellipses are defined by their major and minor axes. See Figure 2-10.

1. Start a new **Part** document, click the **Sketch** tool, and click the **Top Plane** option.
2. Access the **Ellipse** tool from the **Sketch** toolbar.
3. Locate a center point for the ellipse and drag the cursor horizontally away from the center point.

Values for the major and minor axes will appear as the cursor is moved. The initial values will be equal, as the first part of the ellipse construction is a circle. See Figure 2-11.

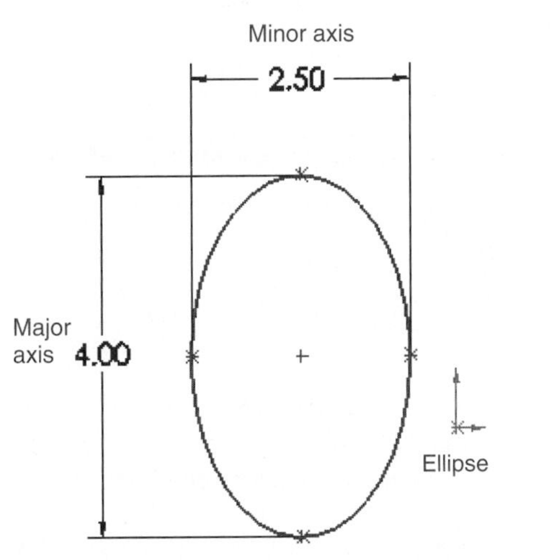

Figure 2-10

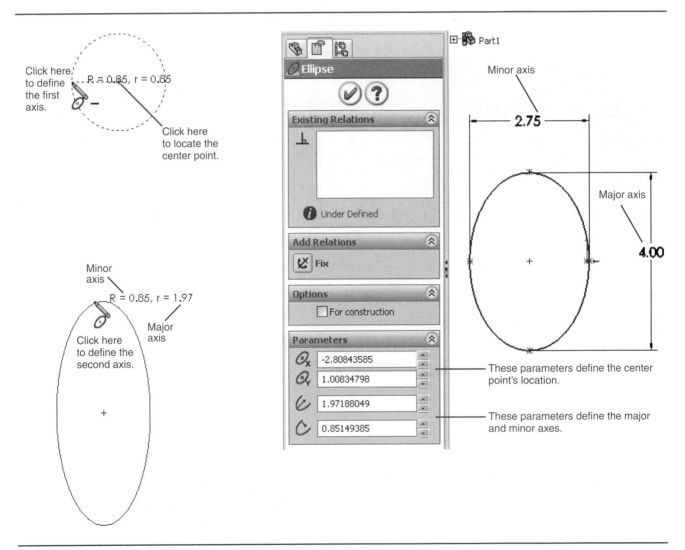

Click here to define the first axis.
R = 0.85, r = 0.85
Click here to locate the center point.
Minor axis
R = 0.85, r = 1.97
Major axis
Click here to define the second axis.
Part1
Ellipse
Existing Relations
Under Defined
Add Relations
Fix
Options
For construction
Parameters
-2.80843585
1.00834798
1.97188049
0.85149385
These parameters define the center point's location.
These parameters define the major and minor axes.
Minor axis
2.75
Major axis
4.00

Figure 2-11

4. Locate the first point for the ellipse; click the mouse.
5. Locate the second point along the second axis; click the mouse.

The finished size of the ellipse may be defined using either the parameter values in the **Ellipse Properties Manager** or the **Smart Dimension** tool.

6. Define the major and minor axes for the ellipse.
7. Click the OK check mark.

2-7 PARABOLA

A ***parabola*** is the loci of points such that the distance between a fixed point, the ***focus,*** and a fixed line, the ***directrix***, are always equal. See Figure 2-12.

The **Parabola** tool is a flyout from the **Ellipse** tool on the **Sketch** toolbar.

1. Start a new **Parts** document, click the **Sketch** tool, and select the **Top Plane** option.
2. Access the **Parabola** tool from the **Sketch** toolbar.
3. Select a location for the focus point.

In this example the 0,0,0 coordinate point, or origin, was selected as the focus point. See Figure 2-12. The directrix was added to the illustration to help you understand how the parabolic shape is generated. The directrix will not appear during the SolidWorks construction.

4. Select a point away from the locus; click the mouse.
5. Select the left endpoint for the parabola.
6. Select the other endpoint for the parabola.

The **Parameters** section of the **Parabola Properties Manager** can be used to change the location of the focus point and the orientation of the parabola. The parabola may also be sized using the **Smart Dimension** tool.

7. Click the OK check mark.

2-8 OFFSET

The **Offset** tool is used to draw entities parallel to existing entities. Figure 2-13 shows an existing line. The **Offset** tool is used to draw a line parallel to the exisiting line and of equal length.

1. Start a new **Part** document, click the **Sketch** group on the **Command Manager,** and click the **Top Plane** option.
2. Draw a random line on the screen using the **Line** tool.
3. Access the **Offset Entities** tool.

The **Offset** tool is located on the **Sketch** toolbar.

> ***Note:***
> You can also access the **Offset** tool by clicking the **Offset Entities** tool directly from the **Sketch** group.

4. Define the distance between the existing line and the offset line by entering the distance into the **Offset Entities Properties Manager.**

> ***Note:***
> As the arrows to the right of the defining offset value box are clicked, the offset line will move in real time to reflect the increase or decrease in the offset distances.

An arrow will appear on the existing line indicating the default direction of the offset. You can change the direction of the offset by moving the mouse to either side of the line or by checking the **Reverse** box in the Offset Entities **Properties Manager.**

5. Click the side of the line where the offset line is to be located.
6. Click the OK check mark.

Entities other than lines may be offset. Figure 2-14 shows an offset circle and an offset rectangle.

2-9 TRIM

The **Trim** tool is used to remove unwanted entities from existing sketches.

Figure 2-15 shows an existing configuration consisting of a circle, a rectangle, and a line. The **Trim** tool will be used to remove a segment of the line from within the circle and the rectangle.

1. Start a new **Part** document, click the **Sketch** group, and select the **Top Plane** option.
2. Draw a line, a circle, and a rectangle approximately as shown. Exact sizes are not required.
3. Access the **Trim** tool.

The **Trim** tool can be accessed by using the **Trim** tool directly from the **Sketch** group.

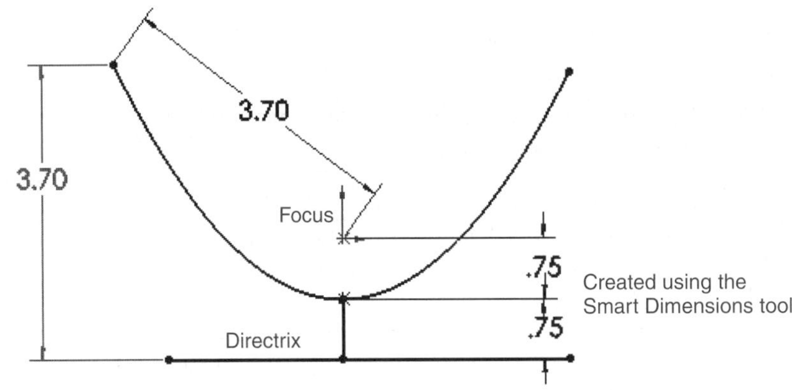
3.70
3.70
Focus
.75
.75
Created using the
Smart Dimensions tool
Directrix

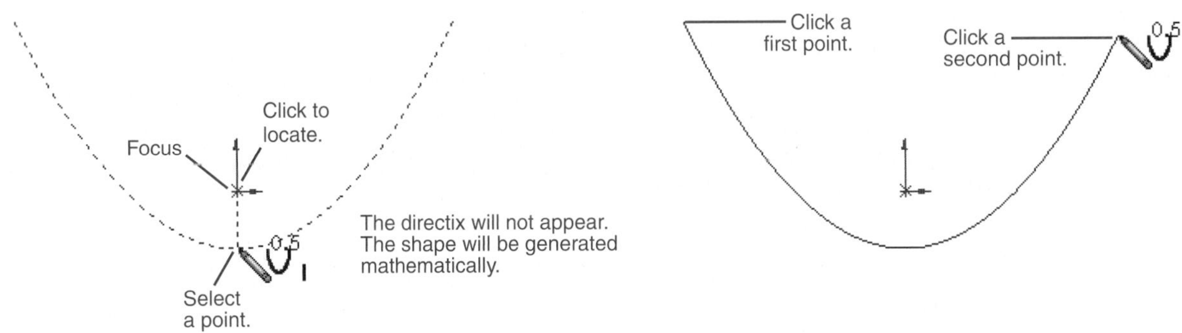
Focus
Click to
locate.
Select
a point.
The directix will not appear.
The shape will be generated
mathematically.
Click a
first point.
Click a
second point.

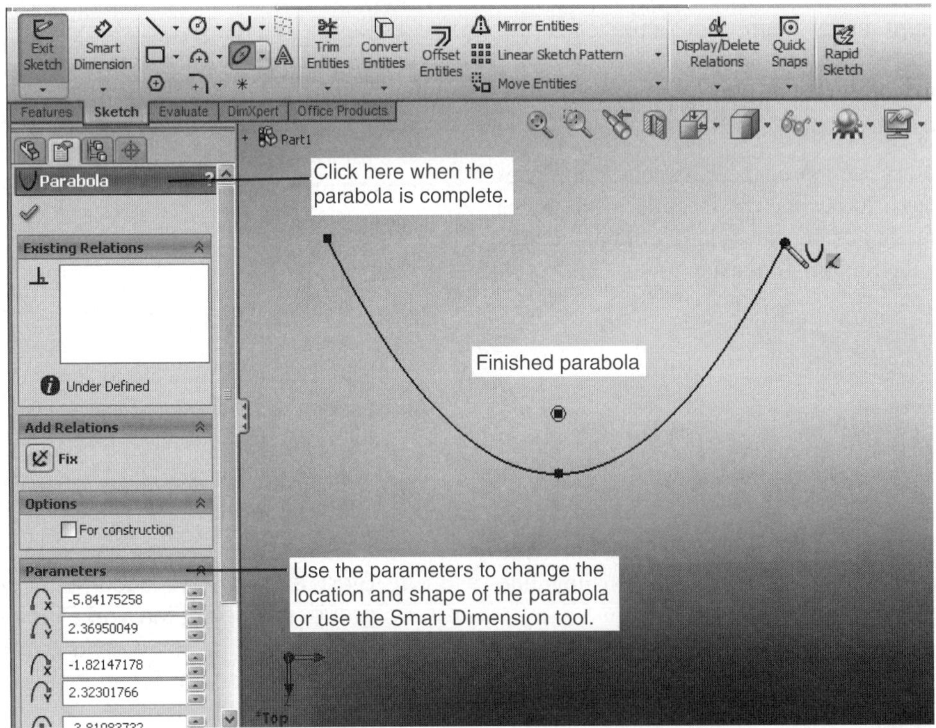
Exit Sketch
Smart Dimension
Trim Entities
Convert Entities
Offset Entities
Mirror Entities
Linear Sketch Pattern
Move Entities
Display/Delete Relations
Quick Snaps
Rapid Sketch
Features
Sketch
Evaluate
DimXpert
Office Products
Part1
Parabola
Click here when the
parabola is complete.
Existing Relations
Under Defined
Add Relations
Fix
Options
For construction
Parameters
-5.84175258
2.36950049
-1.82147178
2.32301766
Finished parabola
Use the parameters to change the
location and shape of the parabola
or use the Smart Dimension tool.

Figure 2-12

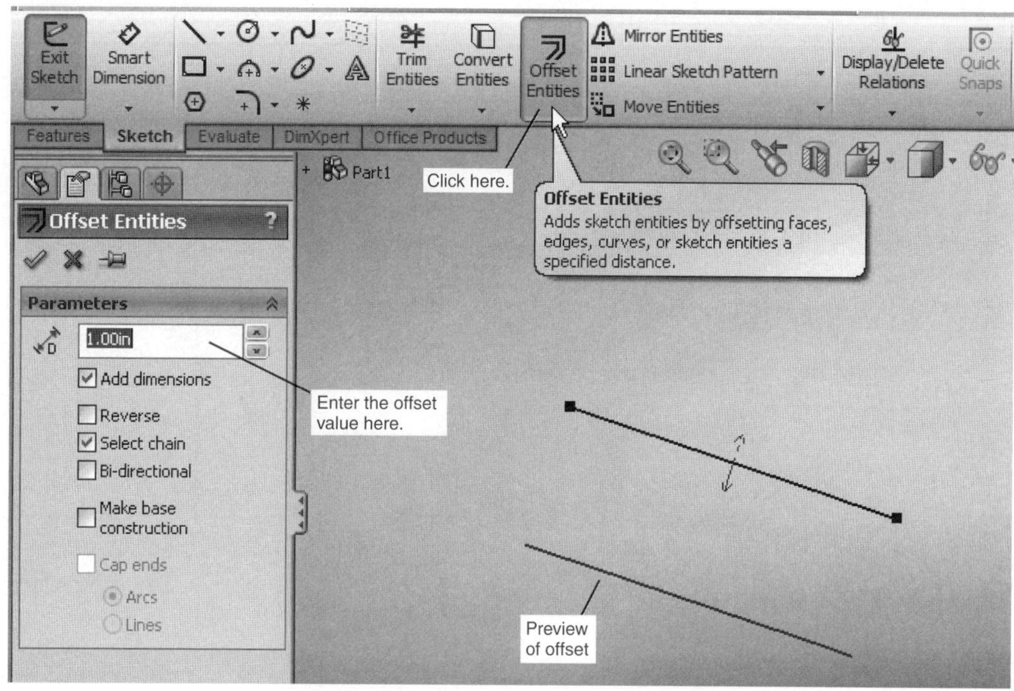

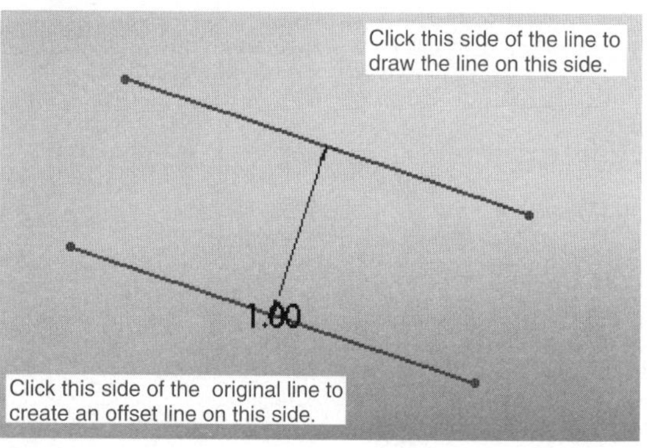

Figure 2-13

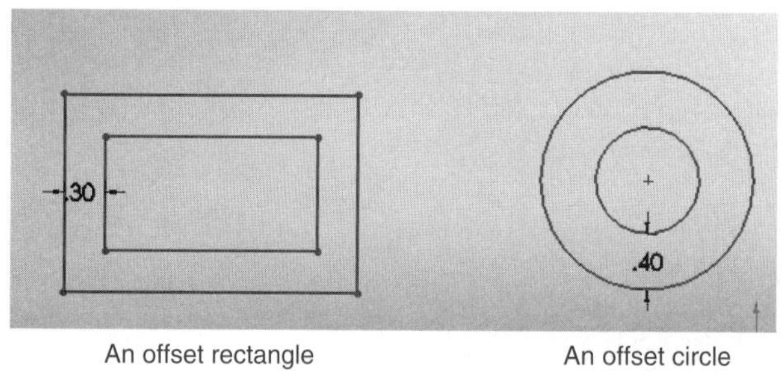

An offset rectangle An offset circle

Figure 2-14

4. Move the cursor to the line segment within the circle; click the line.

The segment will change colors when selected. The line segment will be removed when clicked.

5. Select the line segment within the rectangle; click the segment.
6. Click the OK check mark.

2-10 EXTEND

The **Extend** tool is used to extend existing lines and entities to new lengths or to other sketch entities.

Figure 2-16 shows a 1.50 × 4.00-in. rectangle. This example shows how to extend the rectangle so that it measures 1.5 × 5.5 in.

1. Start a new **Part** document, click the **Sketch** group, and select the **Top Plane** option.
2. Draw a **1.5 × 4.00-in.** rectangle.

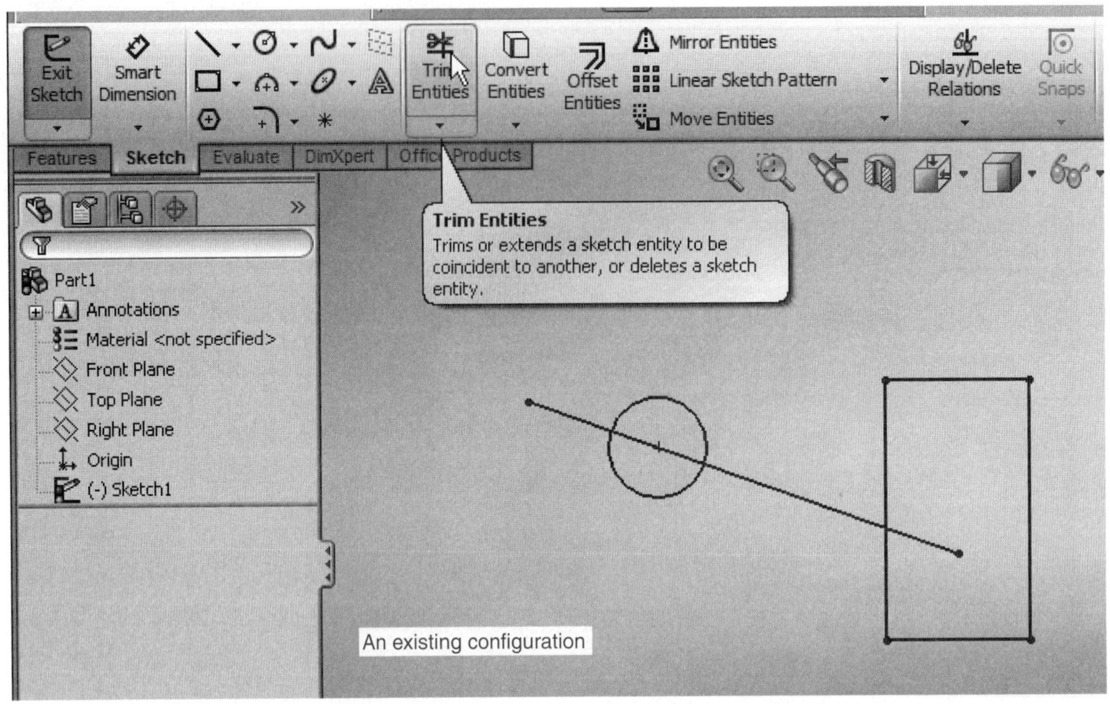
Exit Sketch
Smart Dimension
Trim Entities
Convert Entities
Offset Entities
Mirror Entities
Linear Sketch Pattern
Move Entities
Display/Delete Relations
Quick Snaps
Features
Sketch
Evaluate
DimXpert
Office Products
Part1
Annotations
Material <not specified>
Front Plane
Top Plane
Right Plane
Origin
(-) Sketch1
Trim Entities
Trims or extends a sketch entity to be coincident to another, or deletes a sketch entity.
An existing configuration

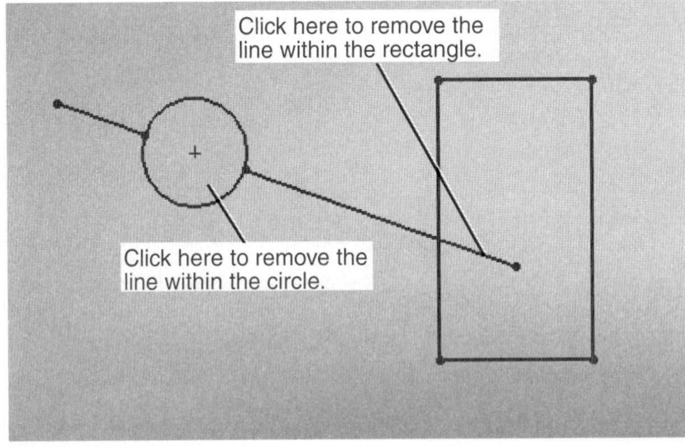
Click here to remove the line within the rectangle.
Click here to remove the line within the circle.

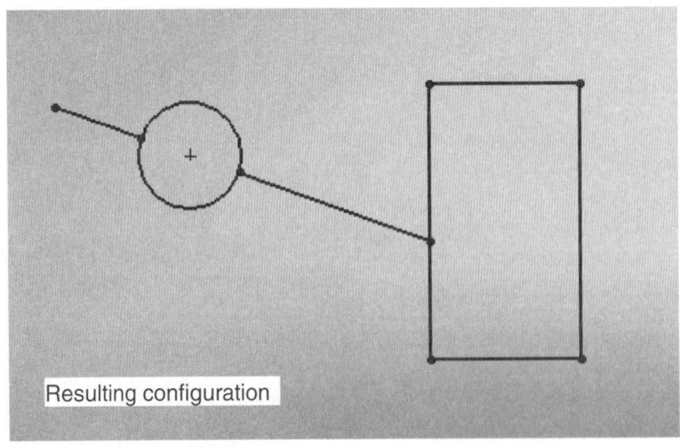
Resulting configuration

Figure 2-15

3. Draw a line parallel to the right vertical line of the rectangle. Locate the line **5.5 in.** from the left vertical line of the rectangle.
4. Access the **Extend** tool.

The **Extend** tool is a flyout from the **Trim Entities** tool located on the **Sketch** toolbar. The cursor will include the **Extend** icon as long as the **Extend** tool is active.

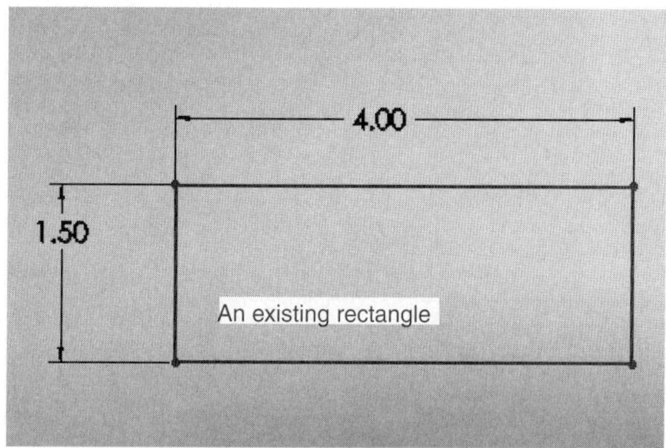

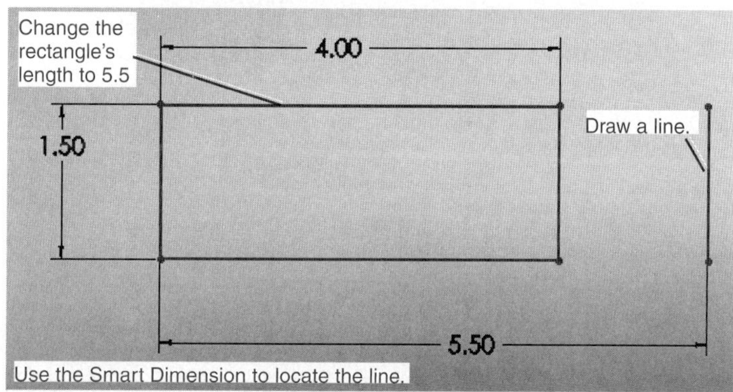

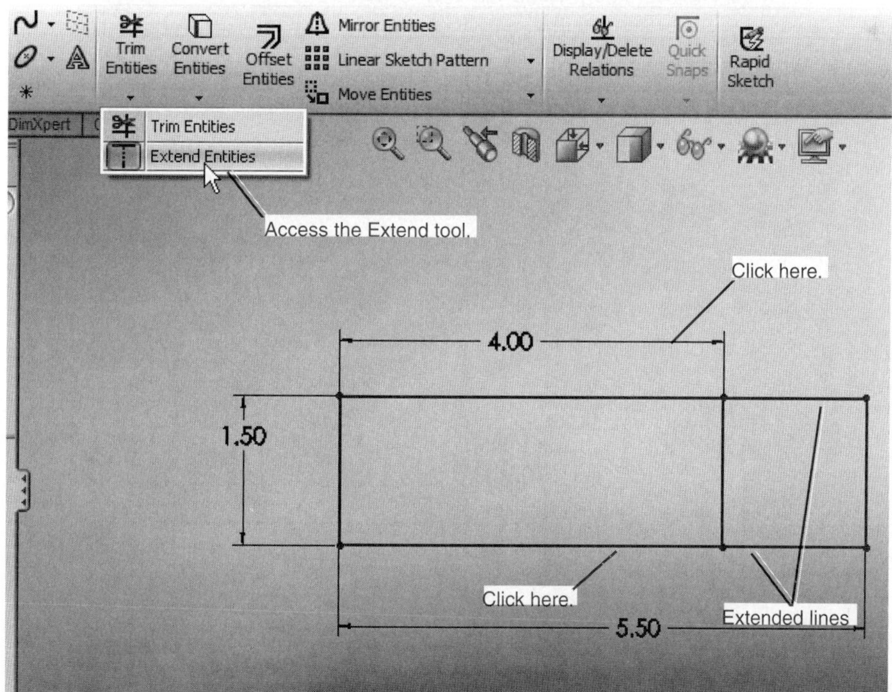

Figure 2-16

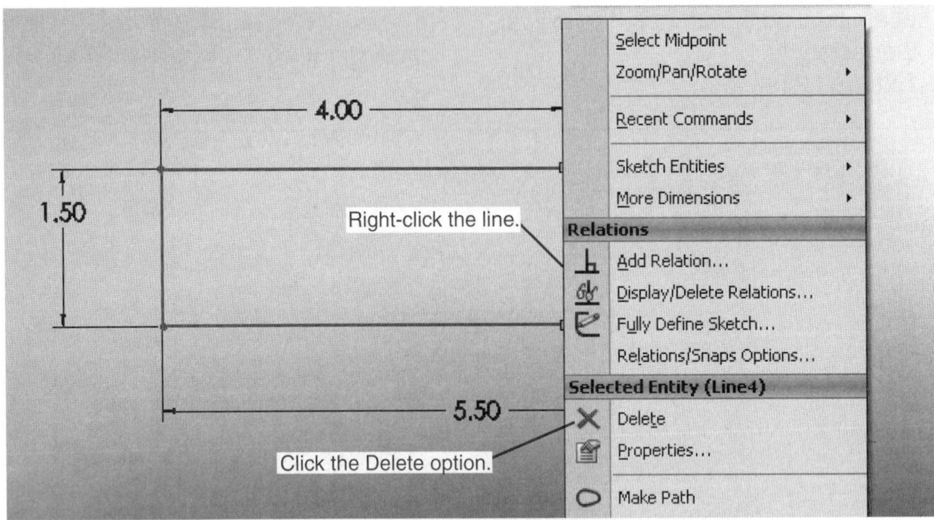

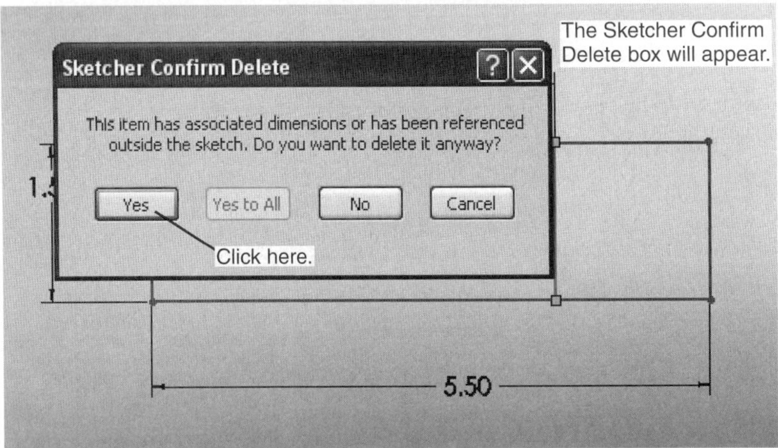

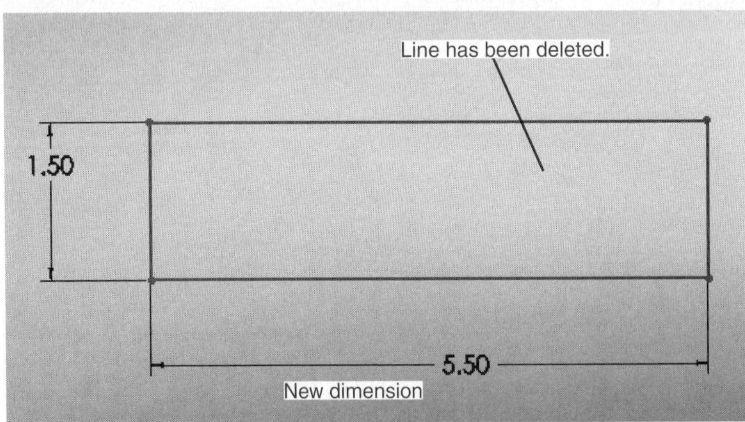

Figure 2-16 *(continued)*

5. Click the top horizontal line in the rectangle.

   The extended line will appear automatically.

6. Click the lower horizontal line in the rectangle.
7. Right-click the mouse and click the **Select** option.
8. Right-click the vertical line located 4.00 in. from the left vertical line.

   A list of options will appear.

9. Click the **Delete** option.

The **Sketcher Confirm Delete** box will appear.

10. Select the **Yes** button.
11. Click the OK check mark.

2-11 SPLIT ENTITIES

The **Split Entities** tool is used to trim away internal segments of an existing entity or to split an entity into two or more new entities by specifying split points.

Figure 2-17 shows the rectangle created in the last section. Remove a 1.00-in. segment from the top horizontal line so that the left end of the segment is 2.00 in. from the left side of the rectangle. If you have already created a 1.50 × 5.50-in. rectangle, proceed to step 3.

1. Start a new **Part** document, click the **Sketch** group, and select the **Top Plane** option.
2. Draw the shape shown in Figure 2-17.
3. Access the **Split Entities** tool.

The **Split Entities** tool is accessed by clicking the **Tools** heading on the main menu, clicking **Sketch Tools,** then selecting the **Split Entities** tool.

4. Click two random points on the top horizontal line.

As the line is clicked, points will appear. Locate the points approximately **2.00 in.** and **3.00 in.** from the left vertical line of the rectangle.

5. Right-click the segment between these two points and select the **Delete** option.

The line segment will disappear.

6. Use the **Smart Dimension** tool to size and locate the opening in the line.
7. Click the OK check mark.

2-12 JOG LINE

The **Jog Line** tool is used to create a rectangular shape (jog) in a line.

Figure 2-18 shows an existing line. This section will show how to add jogs to the line.

1. Start a new **Part** document, click the **Sketch** group, and select the **Top Plane** option.
2. Draw a random horizontal line on the screen.
3. Access the **Jog Line** tool.

The **Jog Line** tool is located on the **Explode Sketch** toolbar. To access the **Explode Sketch** toolbar click the **View** heading at the top of the **Part** document screen, click **Toolbars,** and select the **Explode Sketch** tool.

4. Click a point on the line and move the cursor away from the point as shown.

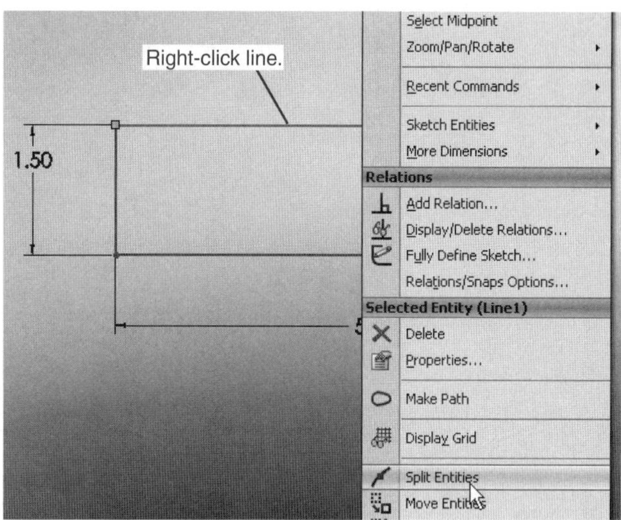

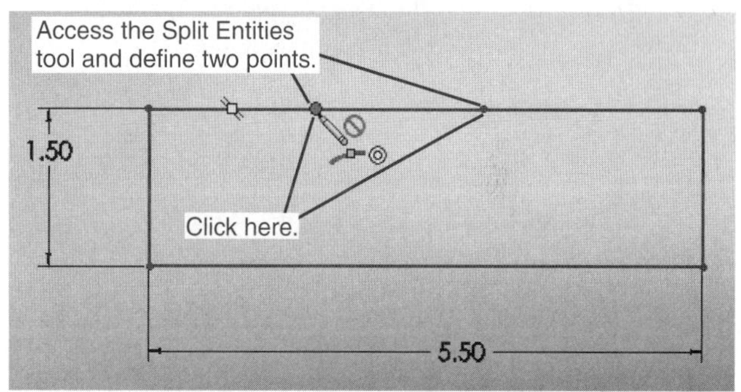

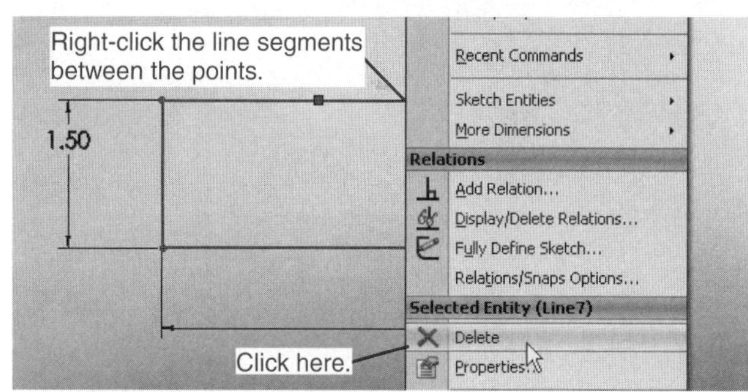

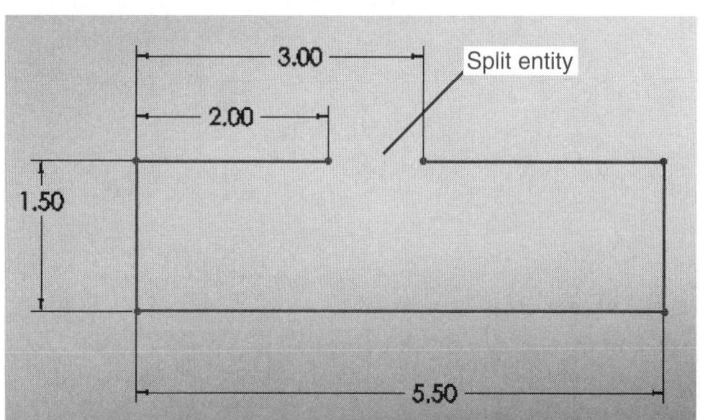

Figure 2-17

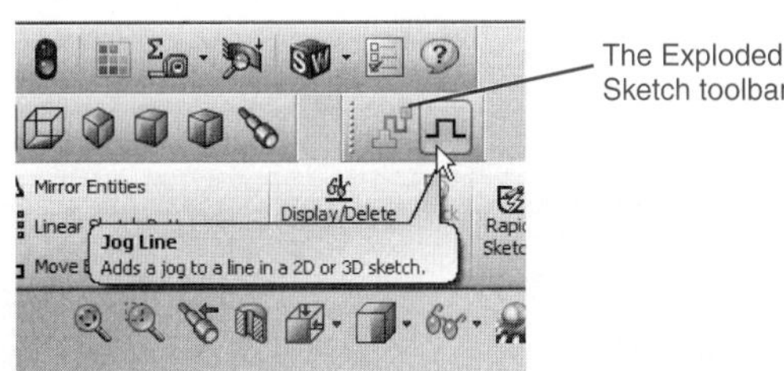

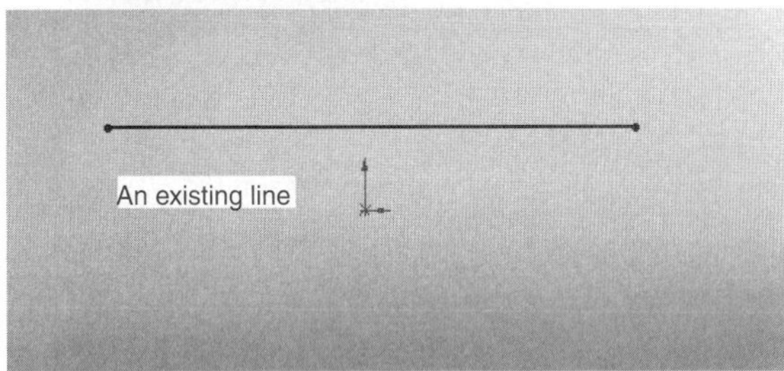

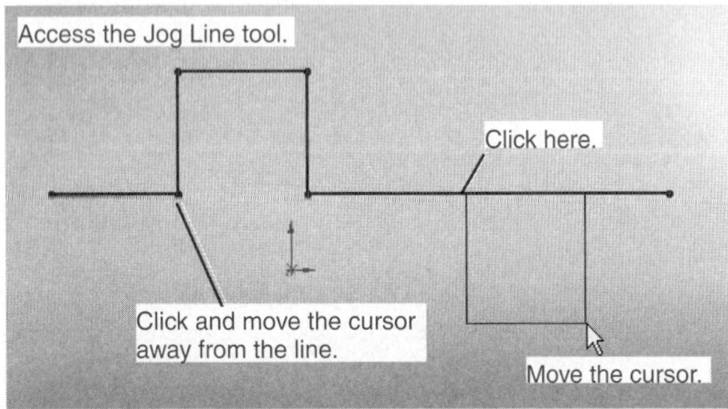

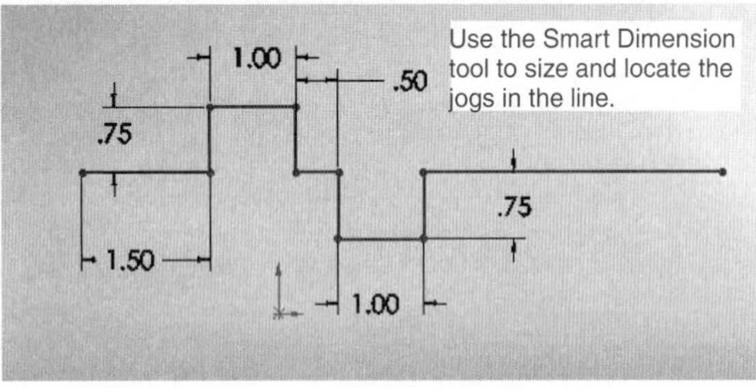

Figure 2-18

This will create a rectangular shape in the direction of the intended jog.

5. Click and move the cursor to create a second jog as shown.
6. Use the **Smart Dimension** tool to size and locate the jogs.
7. Click the OK check mark.

Sample Problem Using the Jog Line Tool

Figure 2-19 shows how the **Jog Line** tool can be used to help shape entities. Two cutouts are added to a 2.00 × 4.00-in. rectangle using the **Jog Line** tool.

Draw the shape shown in Figure 2-19.

1. Draw a **2.00 × 4.00-in.** rectangle in the top plane.
2. Use the **Jog Line** tool to create slots at each end of the object.
3. Use the **Smart Dimension** tool to size and locate the slots.

See Section 1-4.

4. Click the **Features** group on the **Command Manager** and select the **Extruded Boss/Base** tool.
5. Define the thickness by entering a value of **0.50in.** in the **Extrude Properties Manager.**
6. Use the **Fillet** tool in the **Features** group and add 0.50-in. radii fillets by clicking the vertical lines as shown.
7. Click the OK check mark to complete the object.

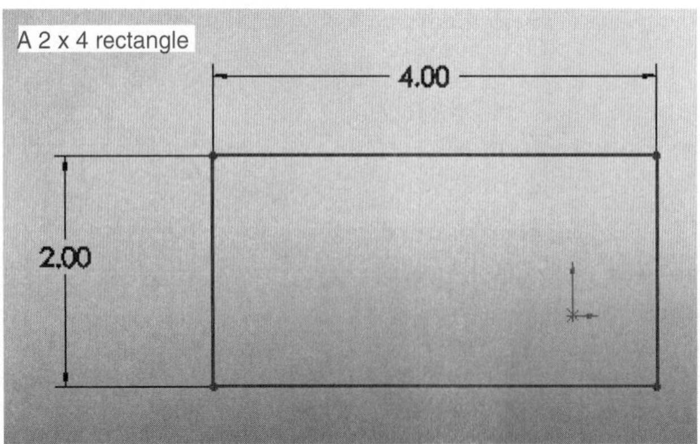

Figure 2-19

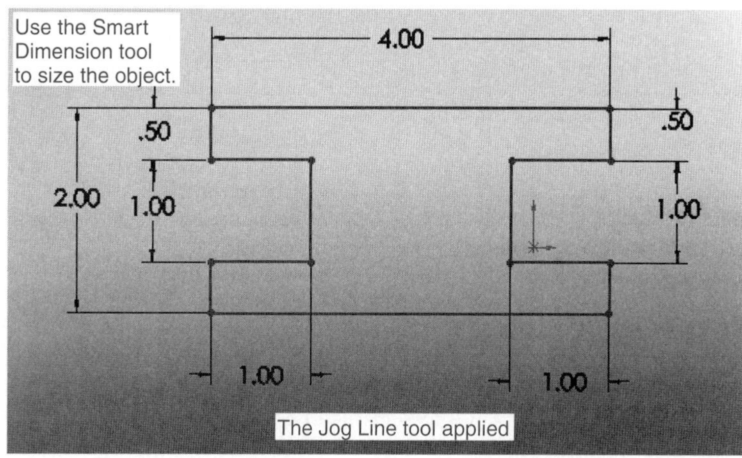
Use the Smart
Dimension tool
to size the object.
4.00
.50
.50
2.00
1.00
1.00
1.00
1.00
The Jog Line tool applied

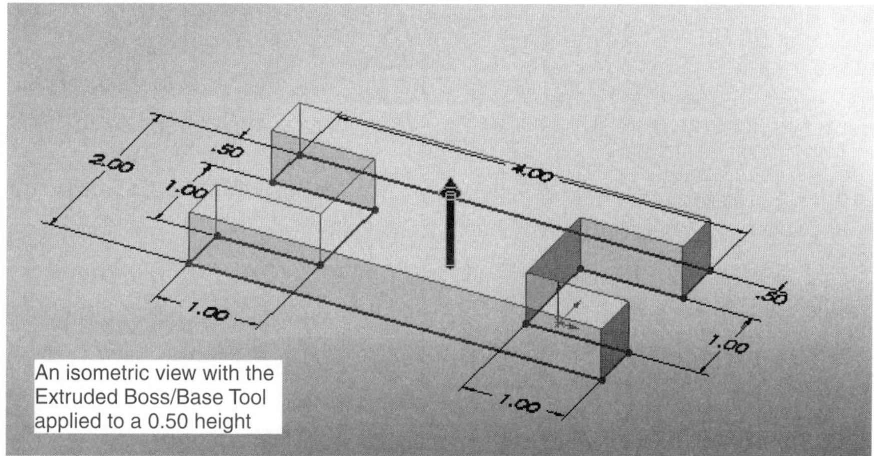
2.00
.50
1.00
4.00
1.00
.50
1.00
1.00
An isometric view with the
Extruded Boss/Base Tool
applied to a 0.50 height

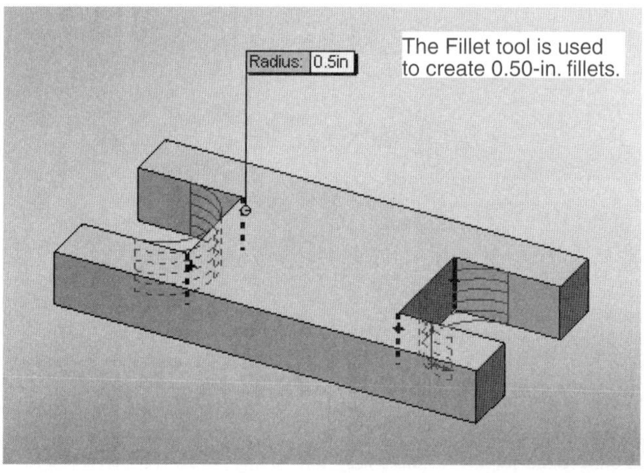
Radius: 0.5in
The Fillet tool is used
to create 0.50-in. fillets.

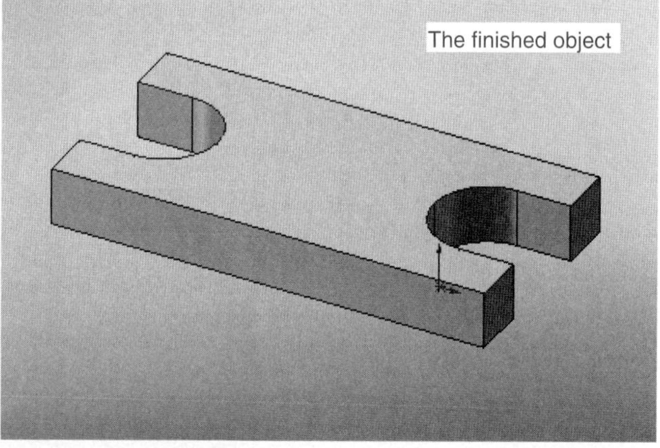
The finished object

Figure 2-19 *(continued)*

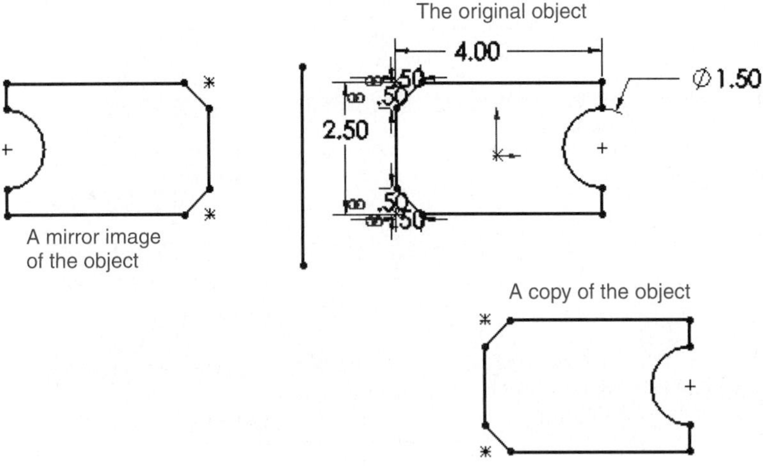

Figure 2-20

2-13 MIRROR ENTITIES

The **Mirror Entities** tool is used to create a mirror image of an entity. A mirror image is different from a copy of an image. Figure 2-20 shows both a mirror image and a copy of the same entity. Note the differences.

1. Start a new **Part** document, click the **Sketch** group, and select the **Top Plane** option.
2. Draw the shape and vertical line shown in Figure 2-21.
3. Access the **Mirror Entities** tool.

The **Mirror Entities** tool is located on the **Sketch** toolbar.

4. Window the object, but do not include the vertical line in the window.

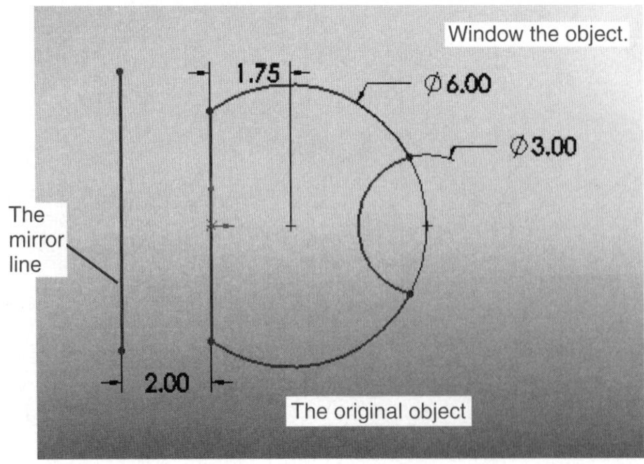

Figure 2-21

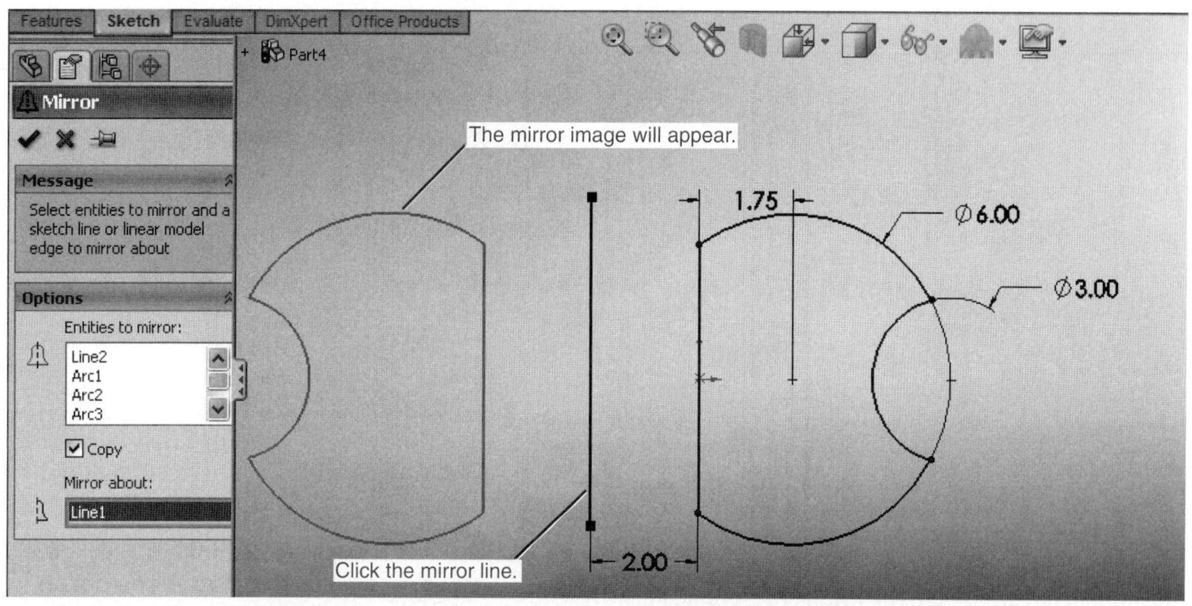

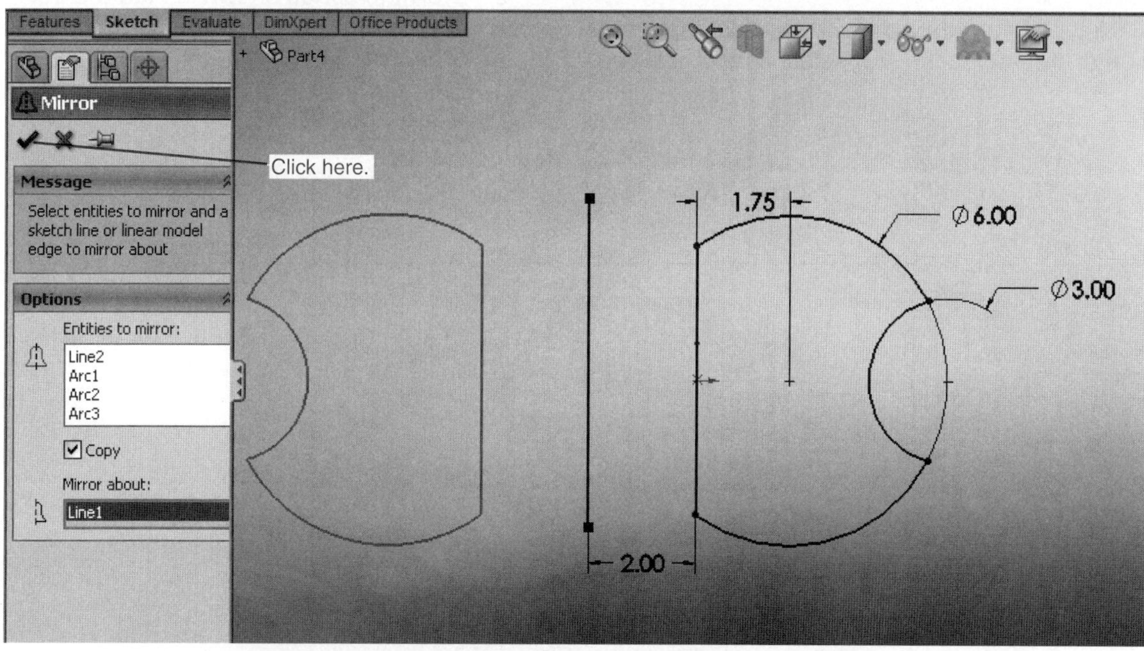

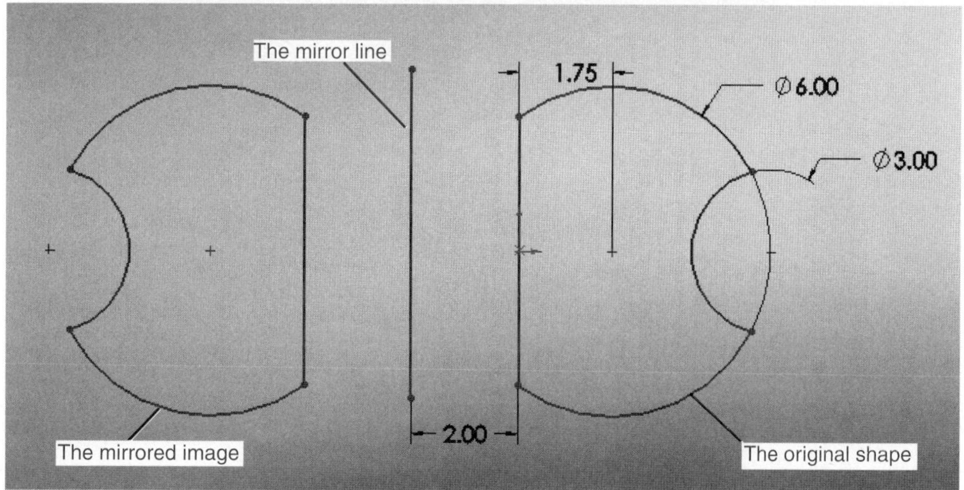

Figure 2-21 *(continued)*

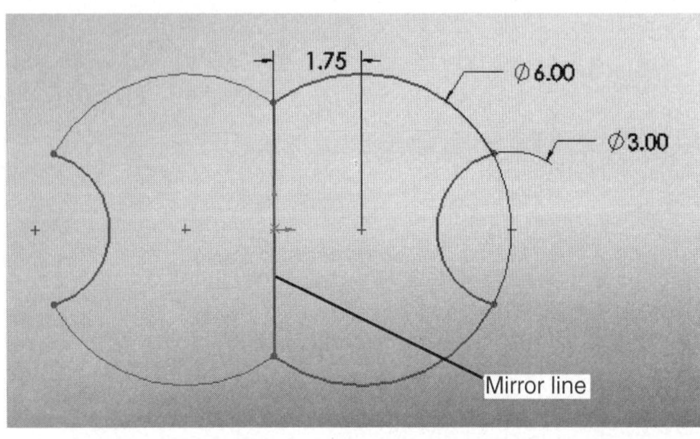

Figure 2-22

A listing of the selected entities will appear in the **Options** rollout box of the **Mirror Properties Manager.**

5. Click the **Mirror about:** box to highlight the selection of the mirror line and select the vertical line.

The vertical line will be used as the mirror line. The mirrored will appear as a preview in yellow. See Figure 2-21.

6. Click the OK check mark, or right-click the mouse and click **OK.**

Lines within an object can be used as mirror lines. Figure 2-22 shows the object in the previous figure mirrored about its own edge line.

2-14 MOVE ENTITIES

The **Move Entities** tool is used to relocate entities. See Figure 2-23.

1. Start a new **part** document, click the **Sketch** group, and select the **Top Plane** option.
2. Draw the shape shown in Figure 2-23.
3. Access the **Move Entities** tool located on the **Sketch** toolbar.

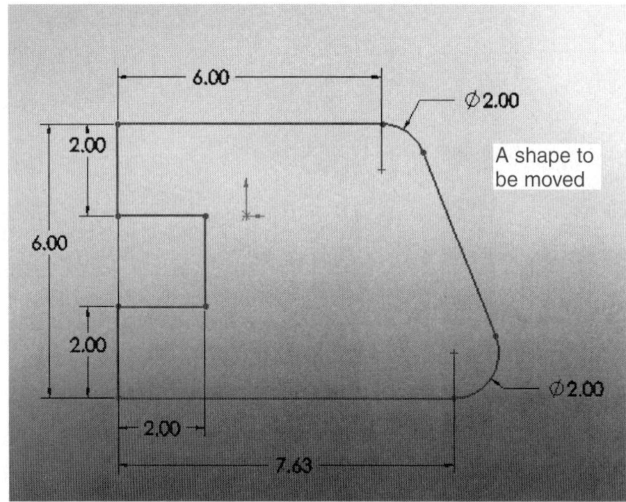

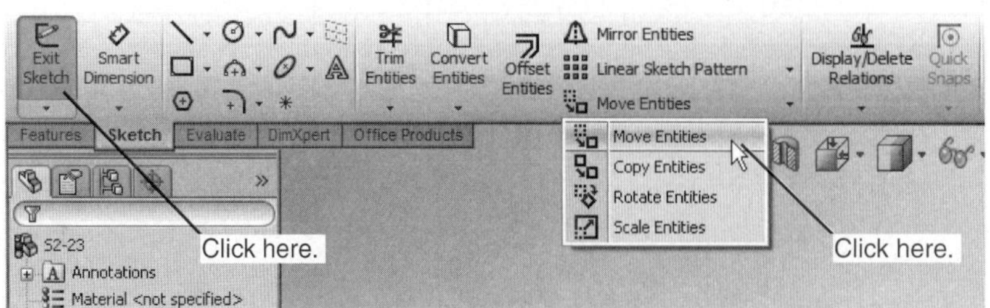

Figure 2-23

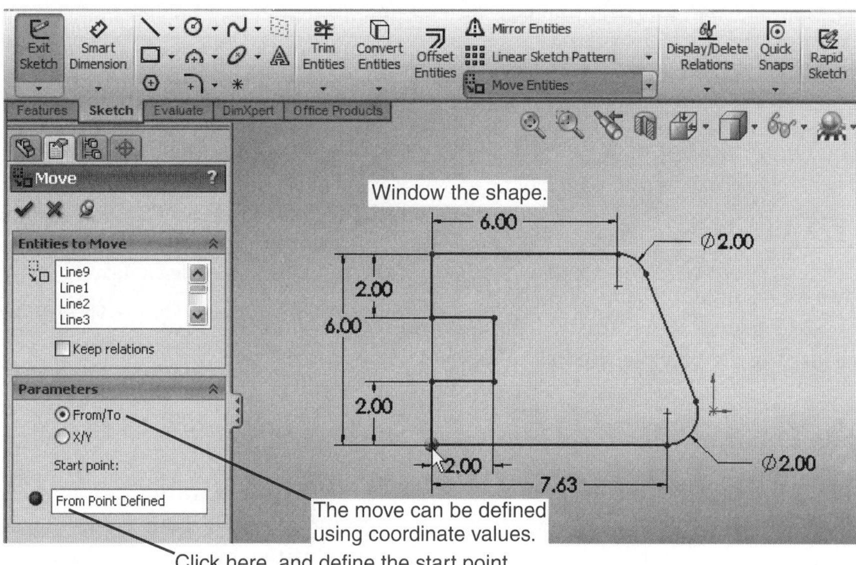

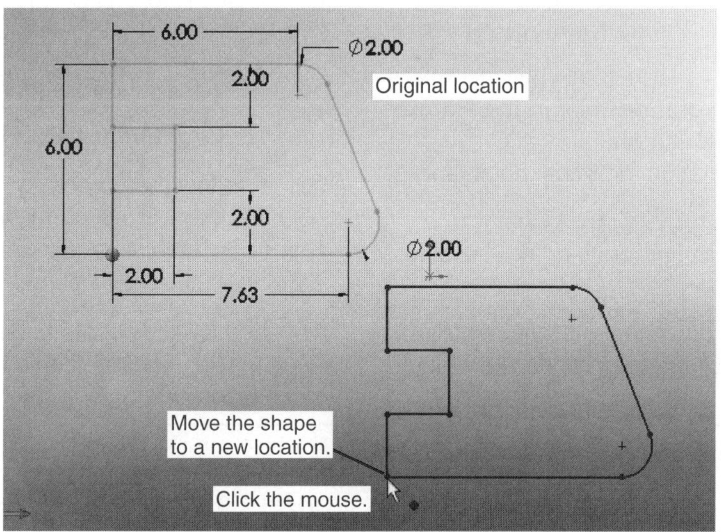

Figure 2-23 ***(continued)***

The **Move Entities** tool is accessed by clicking the **Tools** heading in the main menu, clicking **Sketch Tools,** and selecting the **Move Entities** tool. See Figure 2-2.

4. Window the object to be moved.
5. Click the **Start point:** selection area in the **Parameters** rollout box.

All the sketch entities will be displayed in the rollout box.

6. Select a start point by clicking a point. This point will become the base point.

Any point on the screen can be used as a base point. In this example the lower left corner of the object was selected.

> ***Note:***
> The start point does not have to be on the object. Any point on the drawing screen can be used.

> ***Note:***
> A move can also be defined using X,Y coordinate values.

7. Move the base point to a new location and click the mouse.

Notice that the blue outline of the object in its original position will remain, and the moved object will appear in green.

8. Once the object is in the new location, right-click the mouse and select **OK.**

2-15 ROTATE ENTITIES

The **Rotate Entities** tool is used to change the orientation of a sketched entity. See Figure 2-24. Figure 2-24 shows the same object that was used in the previous section on the **Mirror Entities** tool.

1. Access the **Rotate Entities** tool.

The **Rotate Entities** tool is a flyout from the **Move Entities** tool on the **Sketch** toolbar.

2. Window the object.

A listing of all the sketch entities windowed will appear in the rollout box in the **Rotate Entities Properties Manager.**

3. Click the **Center of rotation:** box in the **Rotate Entities Properties Manager.**
4. Select a point of rotation or base point about which the sketch will rotate.

In this example the lower left corner of the object was selected.

5. Drag (click and hold down the left mouse button) the cursor away from object to rotate the object.

The object will rotate as the object is moved. The angle of rotation will appear in the **angle selection** box in the **Rotate Entities Properties Manager.**

6. Click the OK check mark.

> *Note:*
> The angle of rotation may also be defined by entering angular values in the **Parameters** box in the **Properties Manager** and clicking the check mark at the top of the **Rotate Entities Properties Manager** box.

2-16 COPY ENTITIES

The **Copy Entities** tool is used to create a duplicate of an entity. See Figure 2-25. The difference between the **Move Entities** tool and the **Copy Entities** tool is that the **Copy Entities** tool retains the original object in its original location and adds a new drawing of the object. The **Move Entities** tool relocates the original object.

1. Access the **Copy Entities** tool.

The **Copy Entities** tool is located on the **Sketch** toolbar.

2. Window the object.
3. Click the **Start point** box in the **Parameters** box to define the base point.
4. Select the base point by clicking on a point.

In this example the lower left corner of the objected was selected as the base point.

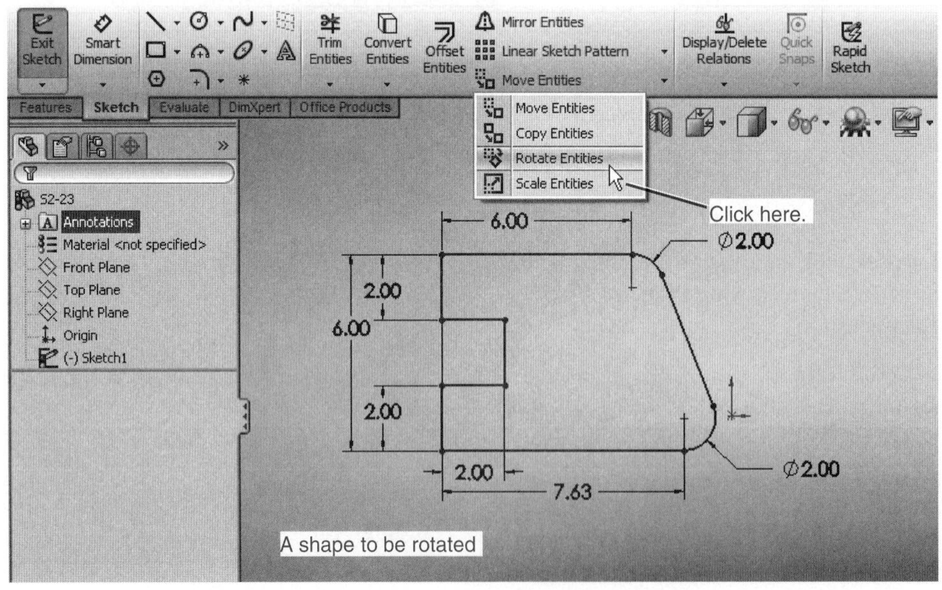

Figure 2-24

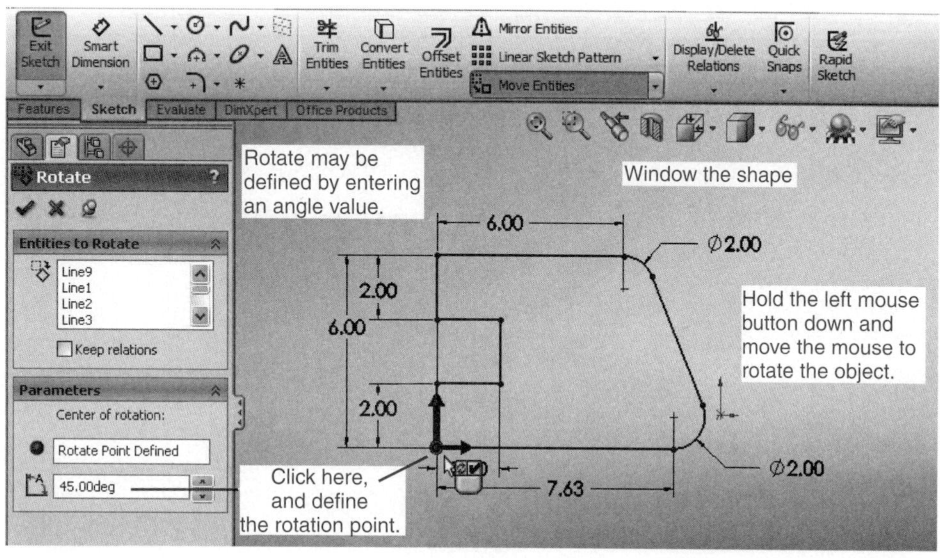

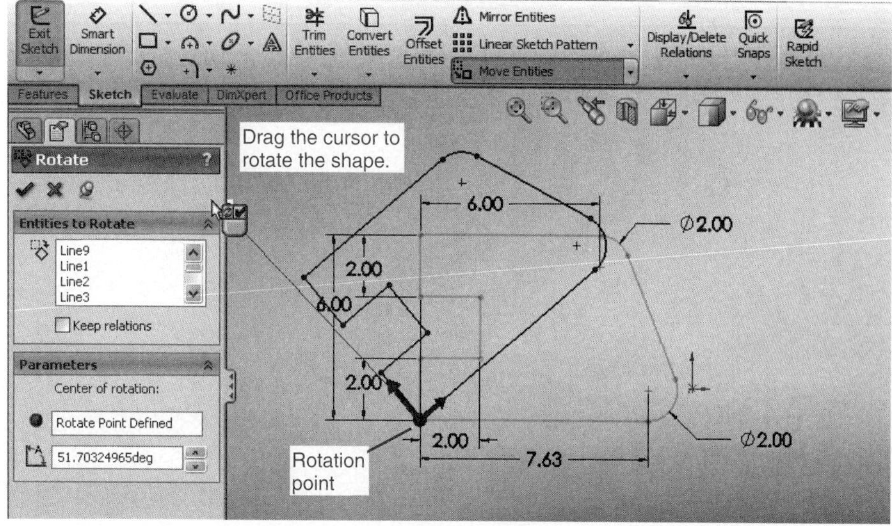

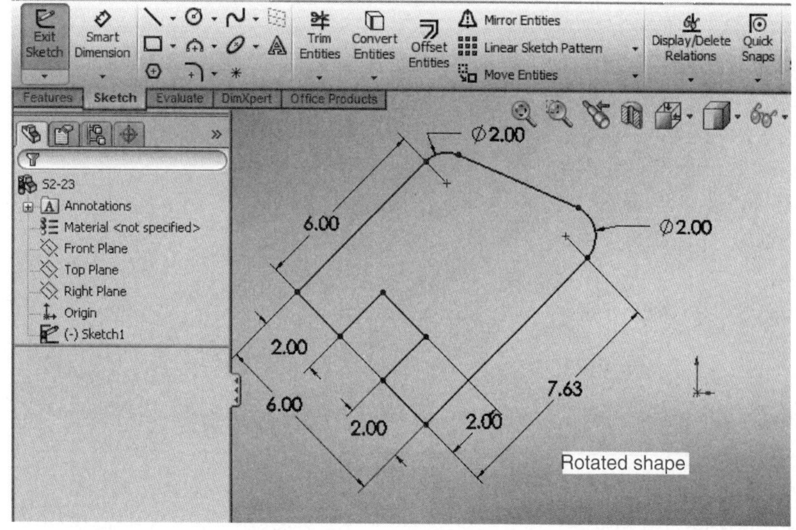

Figure 2-24 *(continued)*

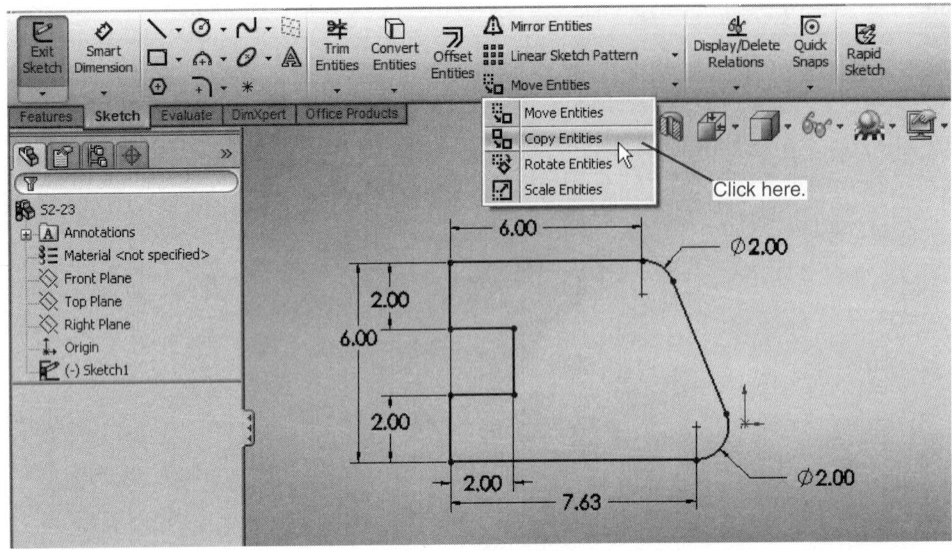

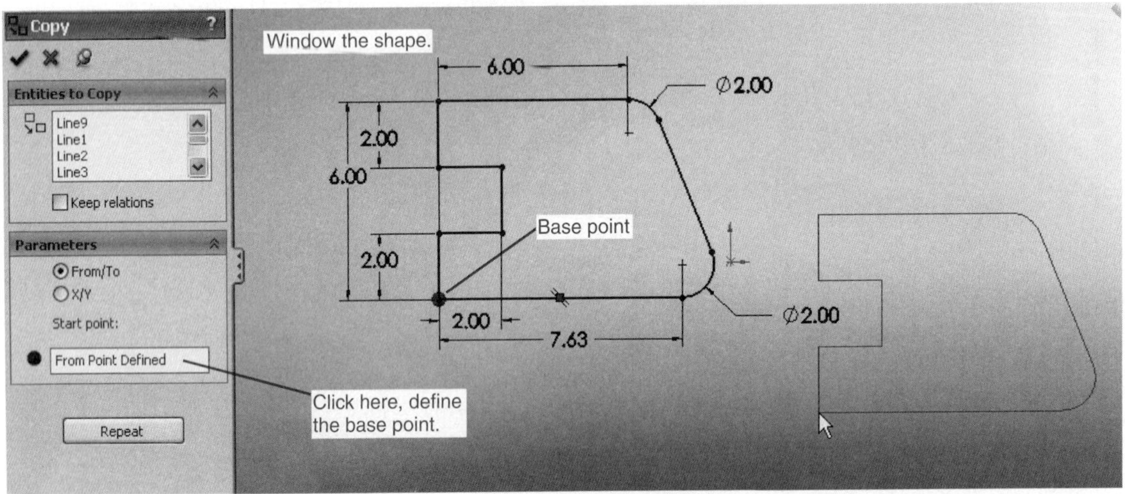

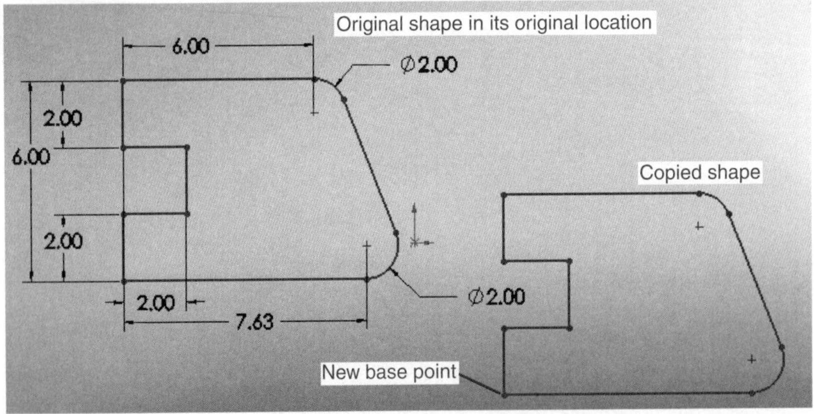

Figure 2-25

5. Move the cursor away from the object.

The preview of the object will be shown in yellow, and the original object will appear in green.

6. Determine the new location for the copy and click the mouse.
7. Click the OK check mark.

2-17 SCALE ENTITIES

The **Scale Entities** tool is used to change the overall size of an entity while maintaining the proportions of the original object. The **Scale Entities** tool includes a **Copy** option. If the **Copy** option is selected, when a scaled drawing is made, the original object will be retained. If the **Copy** option is off (no check mark) when a scaled drawing is made, the original object will be deleted.

Using Scale Entities with Copy On

See Figure 2-26.

1. Access the **Scale Entities** tool.

The **Scale Entities** tool is a flyout from the **Move Entities** tool located on the **Sketch** toolbar.

2. Window the object.
3. Define the scale factor and the number of copies to be made in the appropriate boxes in the **Scale Entities Properties Manager.**
4. Assure that the **Copy** option is on (there is a check mark in the **Copy** box).
5. Click on **Scale about:** in the **Parameters** box.
6. Select a scale point.

In this example the lower left corner of the object was selected.

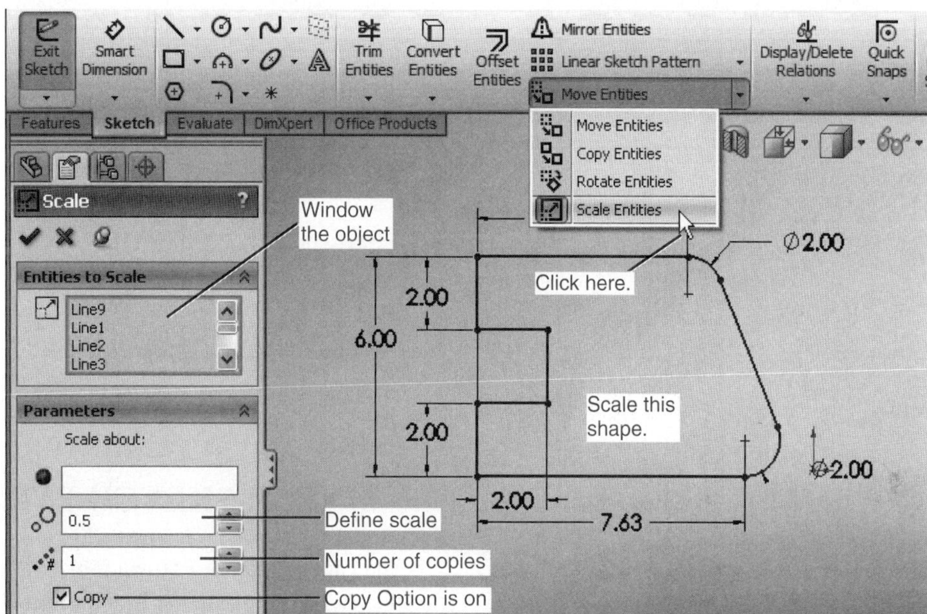

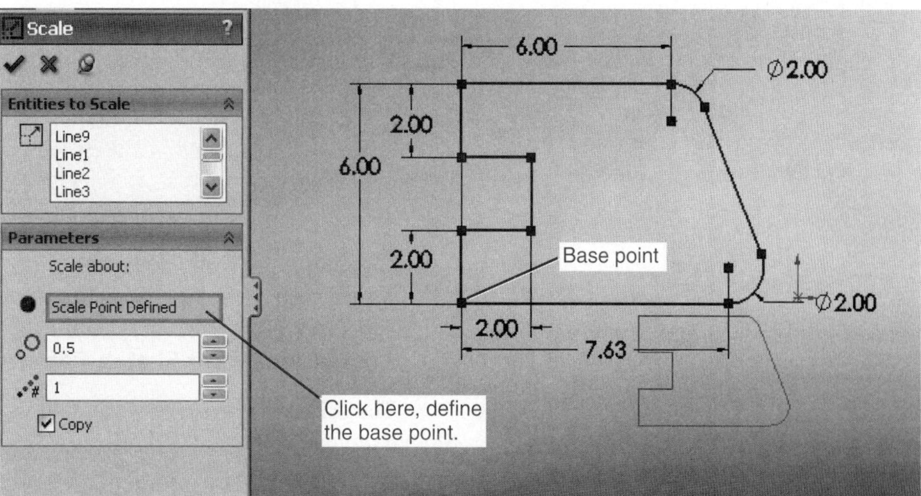

Figure 2-26

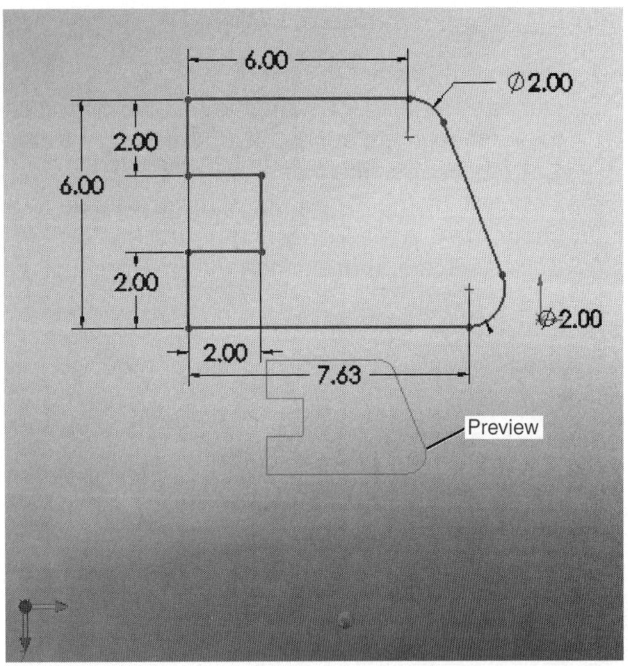

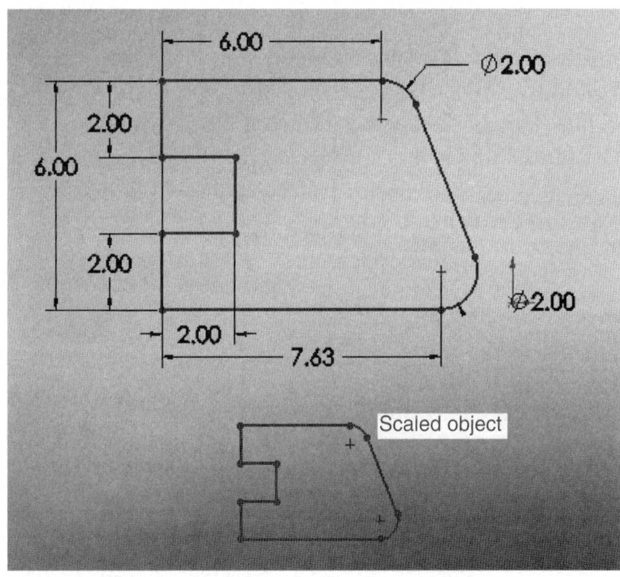

Figure 2-26 *(continued)*

7. Right-click the mouse.

   The scaled object will appear.

8. Separate the original object and the scaled object.

   In this example the **Move Entities** tool was used to separate the original and the scaled objects.

9. Click the check mark.

2-18 CENTERLINE

Centerlines are used to help define the center of entities. The **Centerline** tool is a flyout from the **Line** tool on the **Sketch** toolbar.

See Figure 2-27.

1. Draw a **2.00 × 4.00** rectangle.

   Draw the rectangle offset from the origin as shown.

2. Draw a centerline diagonally across the rectangle.
3. Click the origin.
4. Hold down the **<Ctrl>** key, click the centerline, and release the **<Ctrl>** key.

   The **Select Entities** dialog box will appear.

5. Click the **Midpoint** option in the Add Relations box.

   The centerline will be centered on the origin.

2-19 LINEAR SKETCH PATTERN

The **Linear Sketch Pattern** tool is used to create patterns of sketched entites in the X and Y directions. Figure 2-28 shows a square. In this section a 3 × 3 linear pattern will be created from the square.

> **Note:**
> A row is defined as a pattern in the horizontal direction, and a column is a pattern in the vertical direction.

1. Start a new **Part** document, click the **Sketch** group, and select the **Top Plane** option.
2. Draw a **1.00 × 1.00-in.** square as shown.
3. Access the **Linear Sketch Pattern** tool.

   The **Linear Sketch Pattern** tool is located on the **Sketch** toolbar.

4. Define the distance between the squares in the pattern.

The distance between the squares is measured from the lower left corner of the original square to the lower left corner of the next square. In this example a distance of 2.00 in. was specified.

5. Define the number of squares in a row of the pattern.

This example requires three squares in a row of the pattern (X-direction).

The **Linear Sketch Pattern** tool will automatically ask for the definition of the X-axis direction.

6. Define the X-axis by clicking the lower horizontal line of the square.

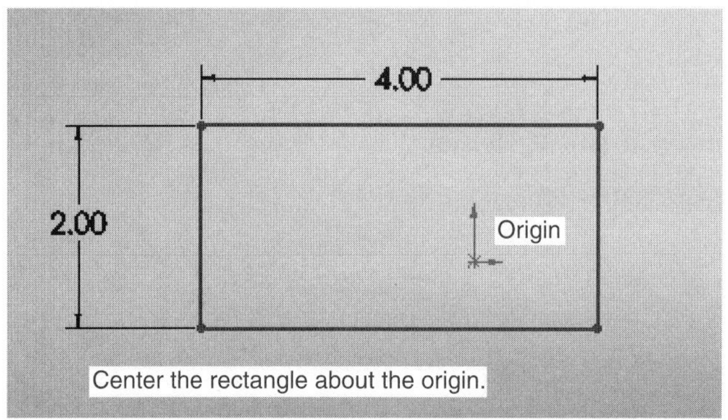

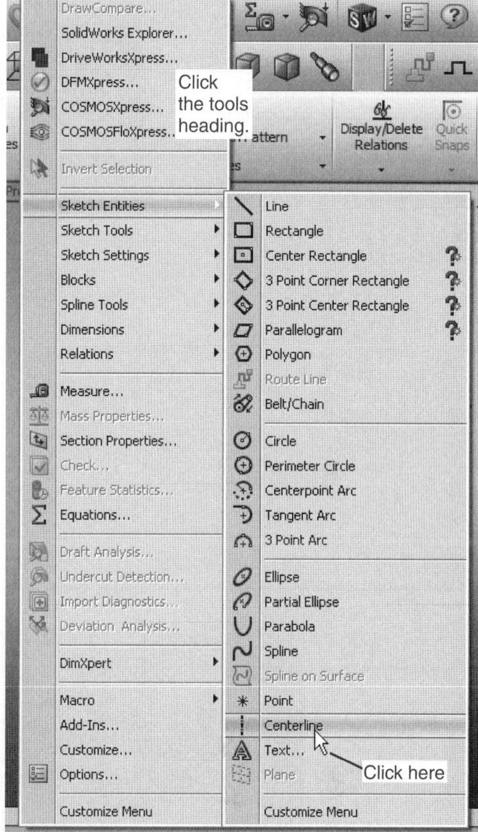

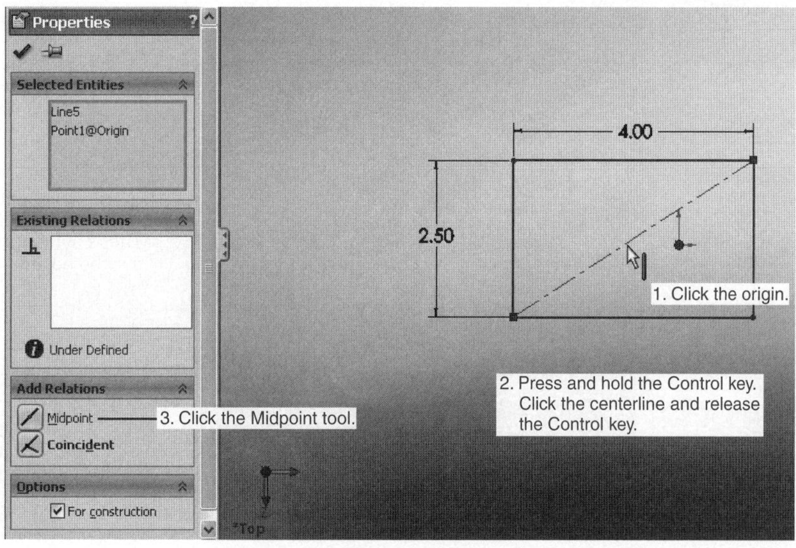

Figure 2-27

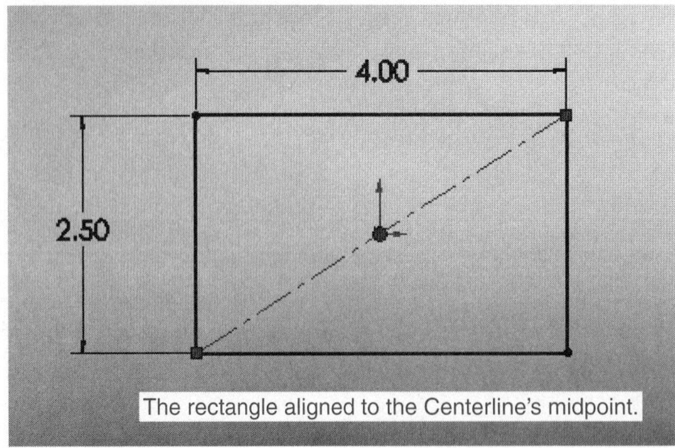

Figure 2-27 ***(continued)***

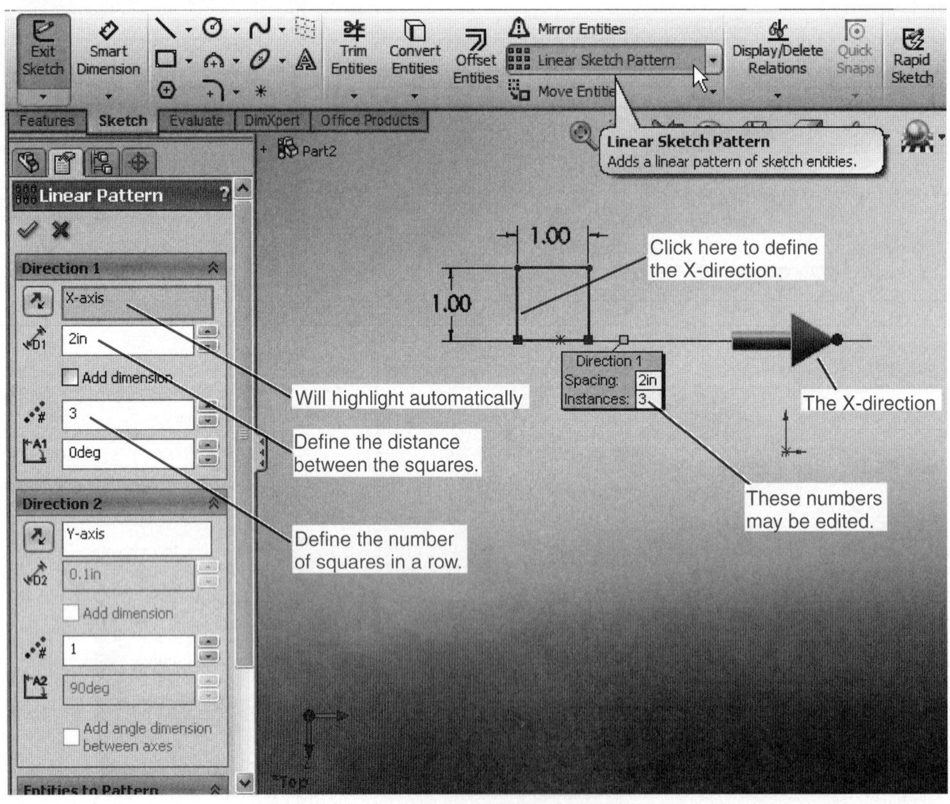

Figure 2-28

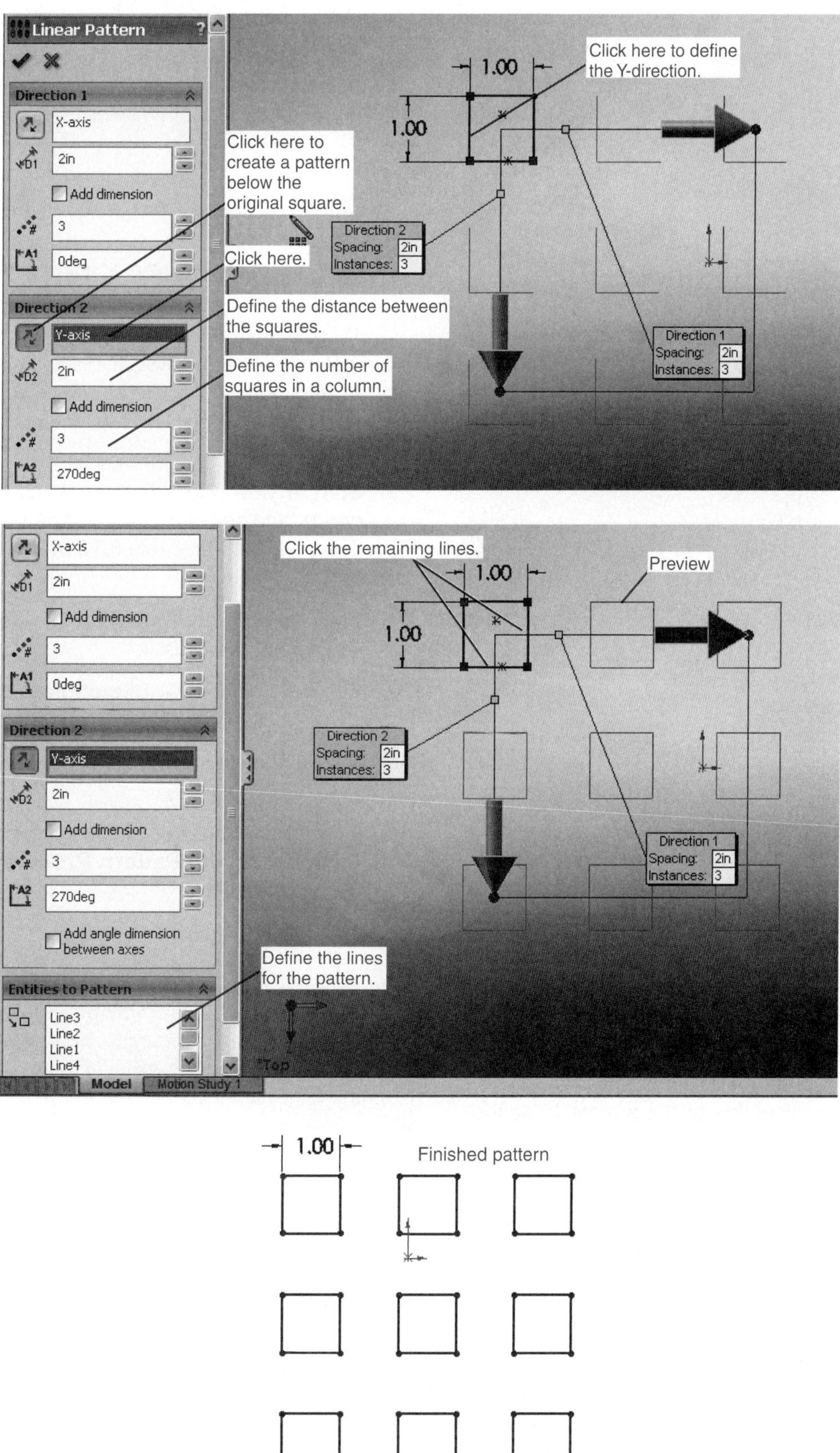

Figure 2-28 *(continued)*

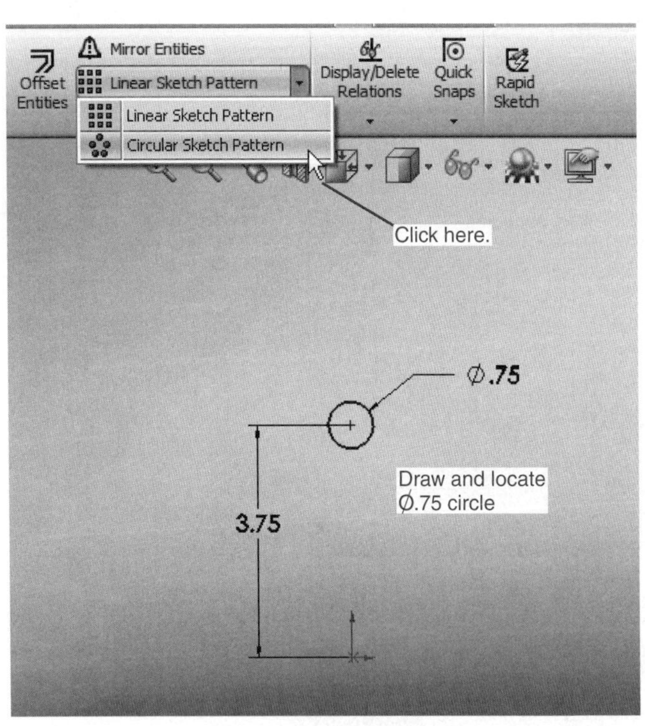

Figure 2-29

A large directional arrow will appear indicating the X-direction.

7. Click the Y-axis box
8. Click the direction arrow to the left of the Y-axis box.

Clicking this arrow box will define the Y-direction as downward toward the bottom of the screen.

9. Define the distance between the boxes and the number of boxes in the column.
10. Click the left vertical line of the square to define the Y-direction.

A larger arrow will appear defining the Y-direction.

11. Click the **Entities to Pattern** box in the **Linear Sketch Pattern Properties Manager** and click the remaining lines of the square.

> *Note:*
> A preview of the pattern will appear on the screen.

12. Click the OK check mark.

> **TIP**
> If you edit the dimensions of a pattern formed using the **Linear Sketch Pattern** tool, SolidWorks will readjust the size of the sketch entity and pattern entities.

2-20 CIRCULAR SKETCH PATTERN

The **Circular Sketch Pattern** tool is used to create patterns about a center point such as a bolt circle. See Figure 2-29. In this example a Ø0.75-in. circle will be patterned about a center point located 3.75 in. from the center point of the circle.

1. Start a new **Part** document, click the **Sketch** group, and select the **Top Plane** option.
2. Draw a **Ø0.75-in**. circle **3.75 in.** from the screen's origin.

In this example the origin was used for convenience; any starting point can be used.

3. Access the **Circular Sketch Pattern** tool.

The **Circular Sketch Pattern** tool is a flyout from the **Linear Sketch Pattern** tool located on the **Sketch** toolbar.

4. Enter the number of entities in the pattern in the **Circular Sketch Pattern Properties Manager.**
5. Click the circle.

> *Note:*
> The circle used in this example contains only one entity. More complex sketches would require all lines in the entity to be identified.

6. Click the OK check mark.

2-21 SAMPLE PROBLEM SP2-1

Any shape can be used to create a circular pattern. Figure 2-30 shows a slot shape located within a large circle. A circular pattern can be created using the slot shape.

1. Draw the circle and slot shown in Figure 2-30.
2. Access the **Circular Sketch Pattern** tool.

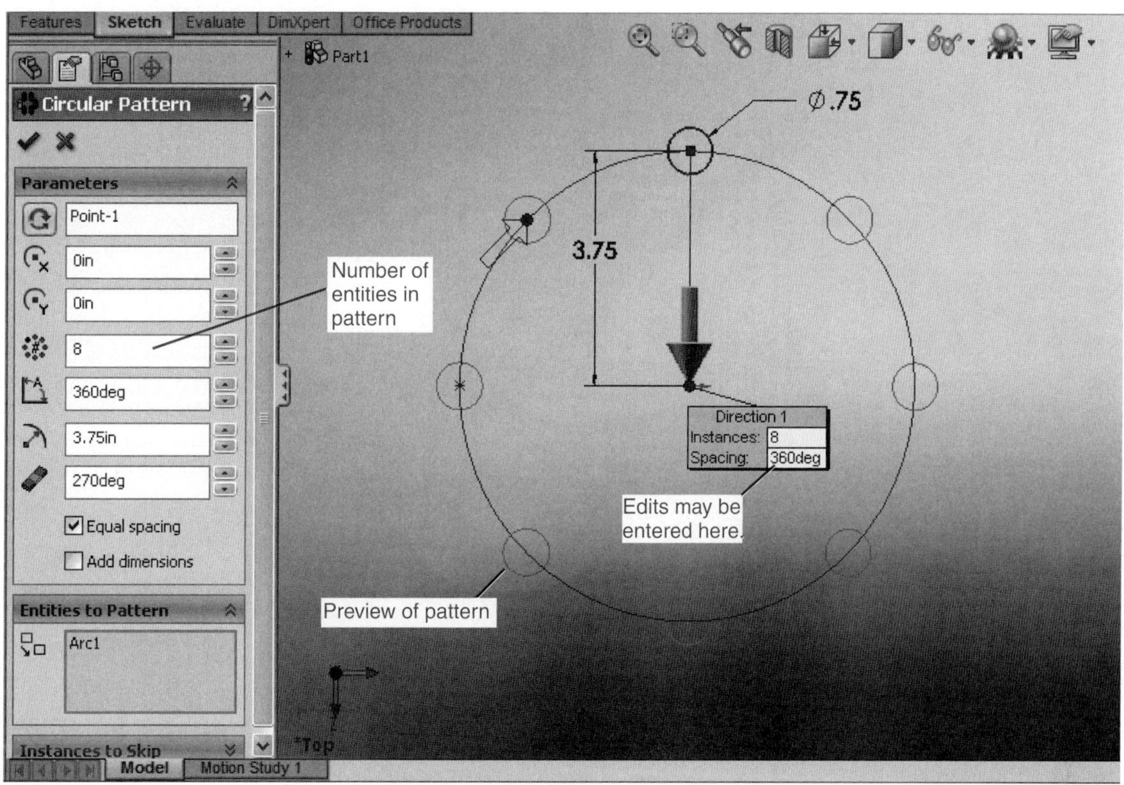

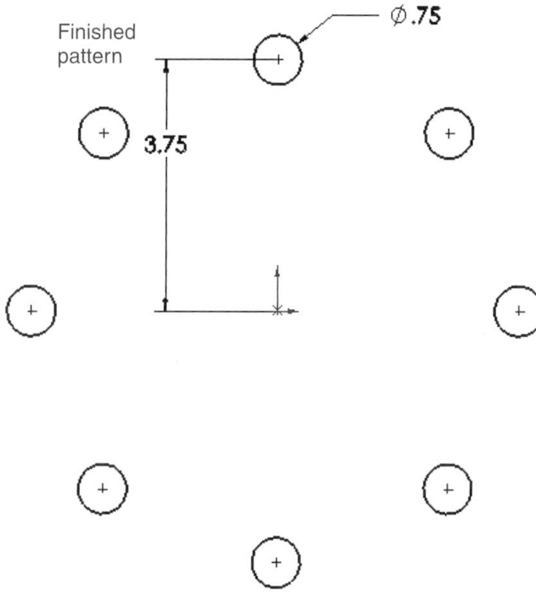

Figure 2-29 *(continued)*

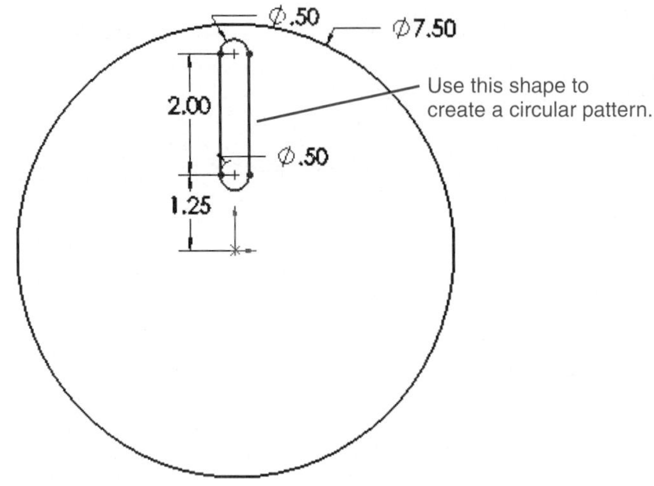

Ø.50
Ø7.50
Use this shape to create a circular pattern.
2.00
Ø.50
1.25

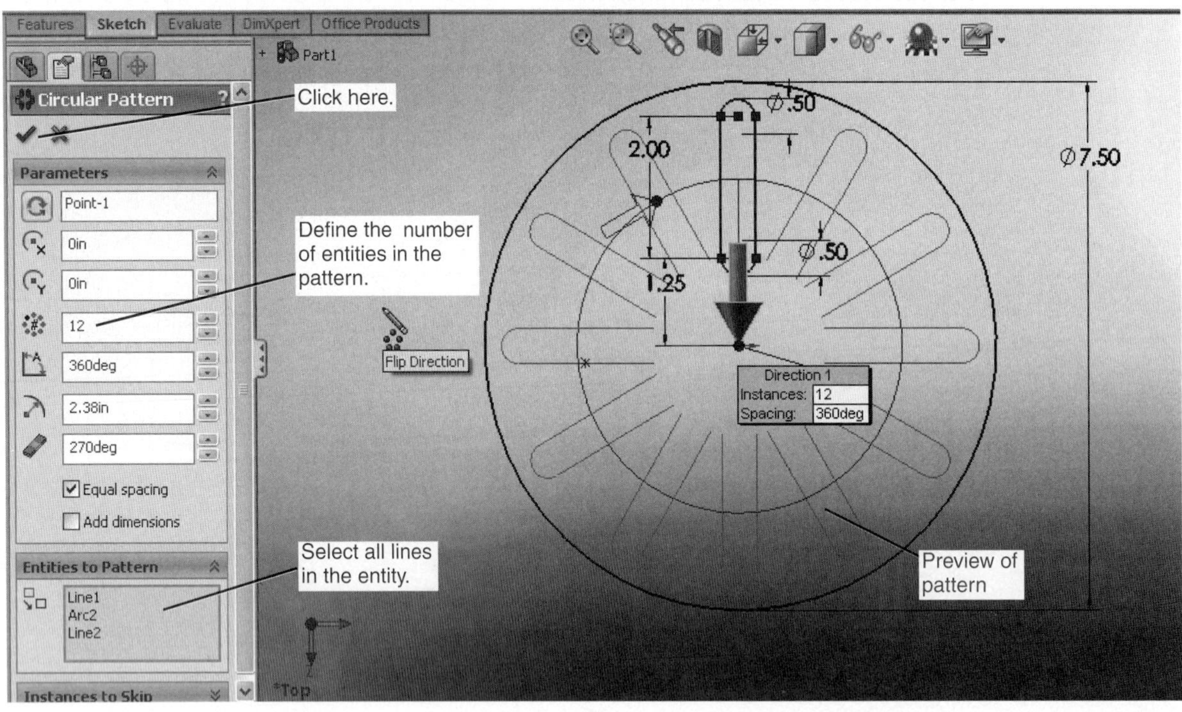

Features
Sketch
Evaluate
DimXpert
Office Products
Part1
Circular Pattern
Click here.
Parameters
Point-1
0in
0in
12
360deg
2.38in
270deg
Equal spacing
Add dimensions
Define the number of entities in the pattern.
Flip Direction
Entities to Pattern
Line1
Arc2
Line2
Select all lines in the entity.
Instances to Skip
*Top
Ø.50
2.00
Ø.50
1.25
Ø7.50
Direction 1
Instances: 12
Spacing: 360deg
Preview of pattern

Figure 2-30

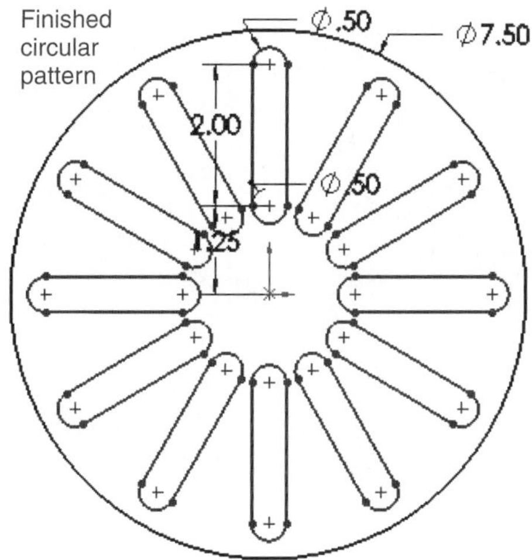

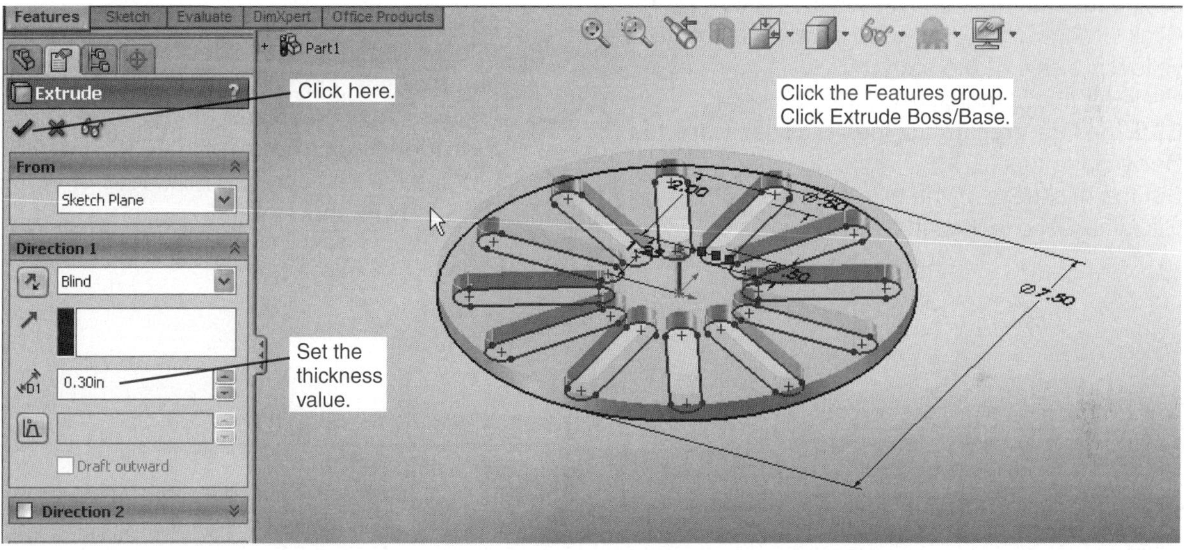

Figure 2-30 *(continued)*

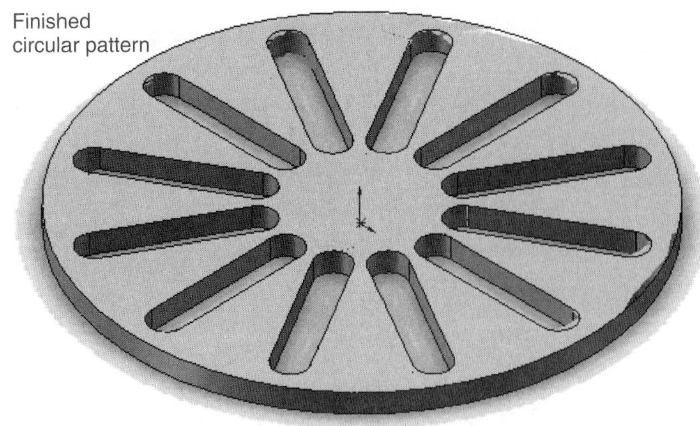

Figure 2-30 *(continued)*

See Section 2-20.

3. Click the **Entities to Pattern** box and enter all the entities that define the slot.
4. Define the number of entities in the pattern as **12.**
5. Click a point on the drawing screen to create a yellow preview of the pattern.
6. Click the check mark.
7. Click the **Features** group, then click the **Extruded Boss/Base** tool.
8. Set the thickness of the extrusion for **0.30.**
9. Click the OK check mark.

> **TIP**
>
> Do not overdefine the shapes and contours to be included in a circular pattern, as this may make the tool inoperable.

2-22 SAMPLE PROBLEM SP2-2

Figure 2-31 shows a shape that includes fillets. The shape is initially drawn square, that is, with 90° corners, then the fillets are added.

1. Start a new **Part** document and sketch the T-shape.
2. Use the **Smart Dimension** tool and size the part.
3. Click the **Fillet** tool, set the **Fillet Parameters** for **0.25in** and add the external fillets.
4. Sketch, locate, and size the **1.00 × 1.50** rectangle as shown.
5. Use the **Fillet** tool and add **0.25** fillets to the rectangle.
6. Use the **Circle** tool and draw two **Ø0.50** circles **2.00** apart, **1.50** from the left edge as shown.
7. Use the **Line** tool and draw two horizontal lines tangent to the two circles.
8. Use the **Trim** tool and delete the internal portions of the cirlces, creating a slot as shown.
9. Access the **Features** tools and click the **Extruded Boss/Base** tool.
10. Extrude the T-shape to a thickness of **0.375in.**
11. Click the OK check mark.

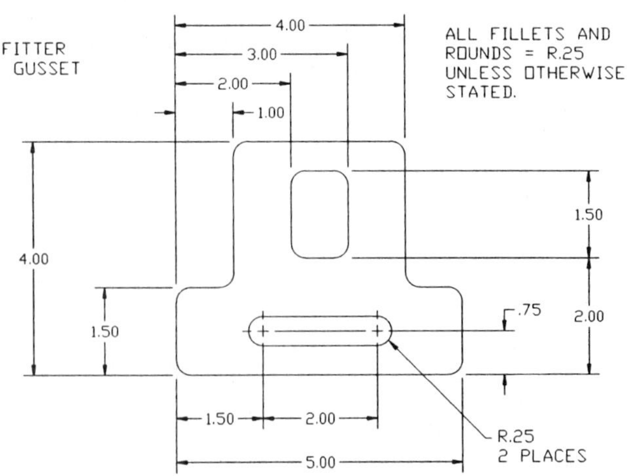

Figure 2-31

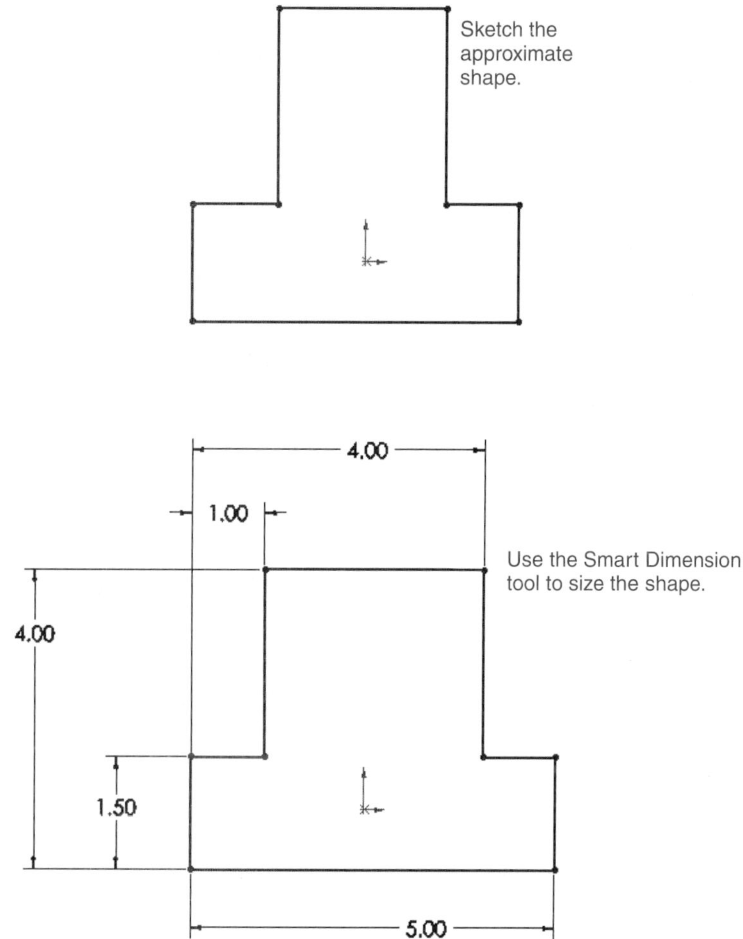

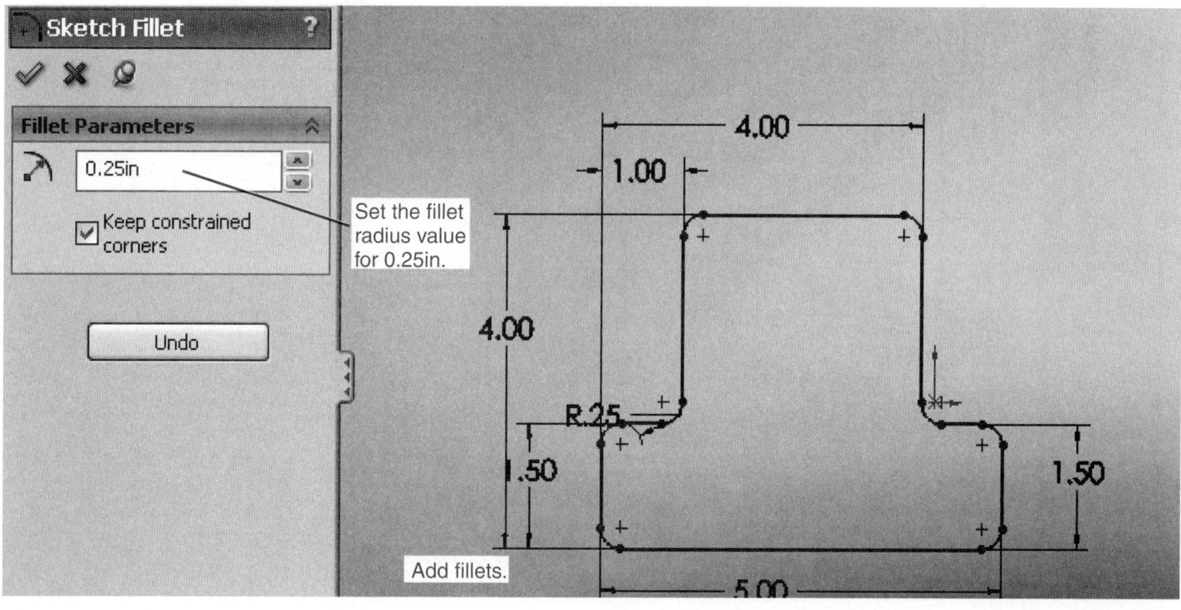

Figure 2-31 *(continued)*

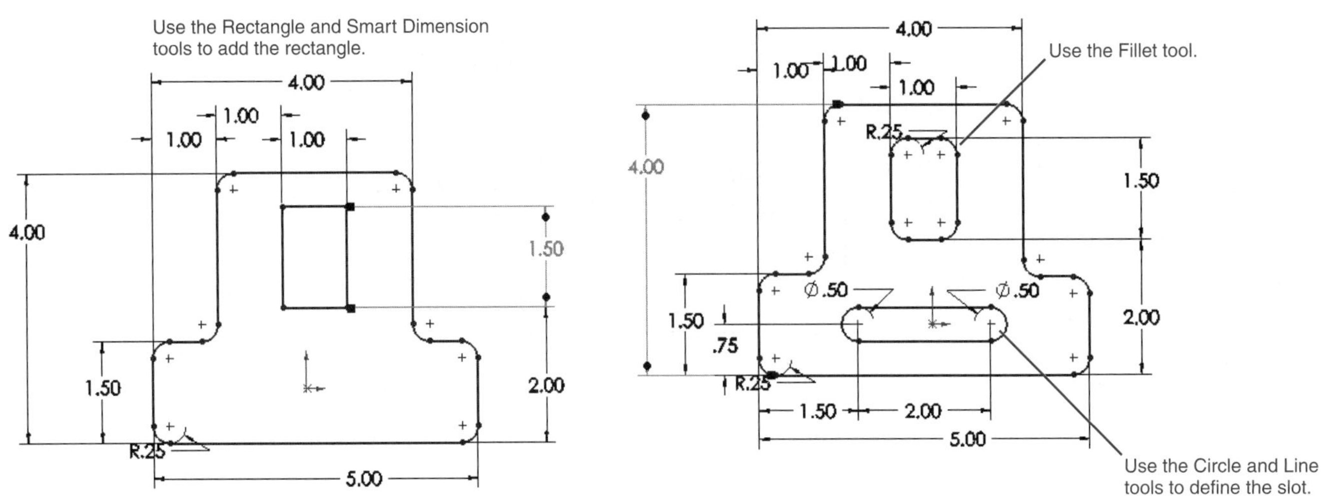

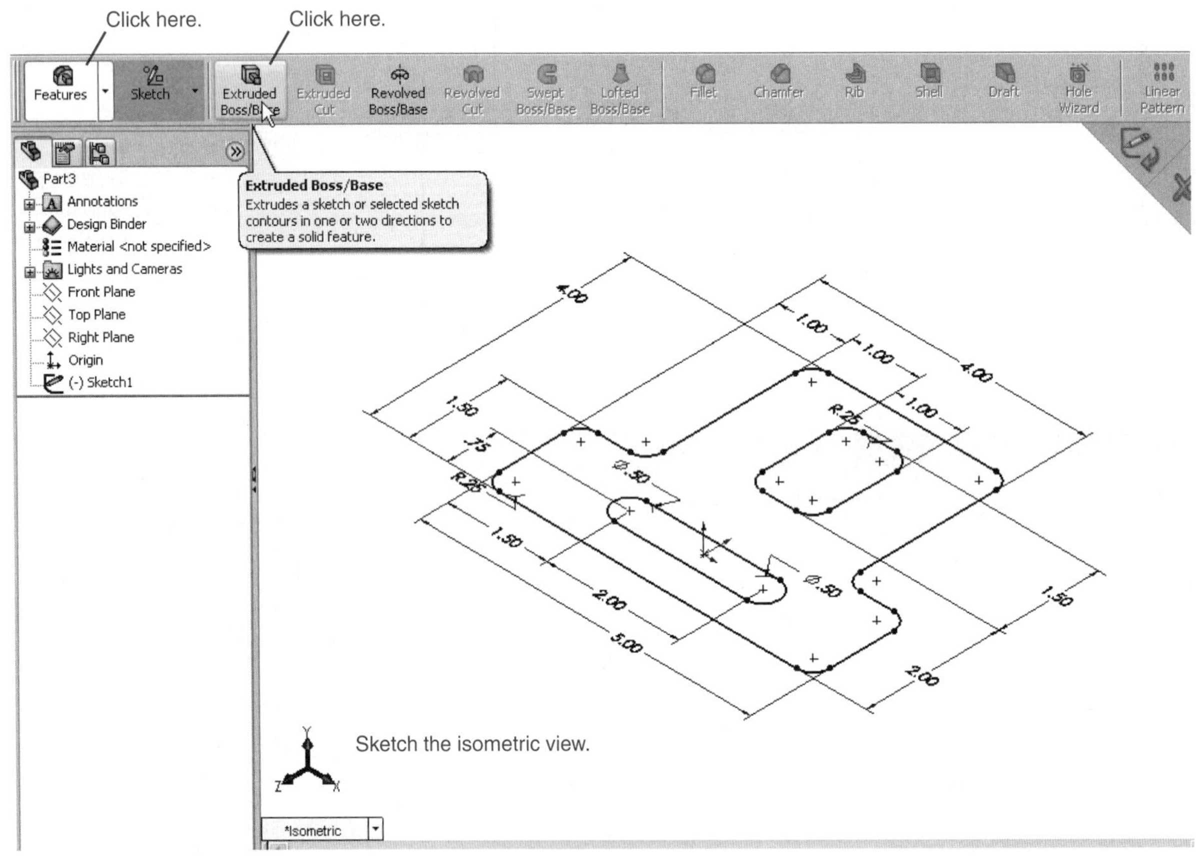

Figure 2-31 ***(continued)***

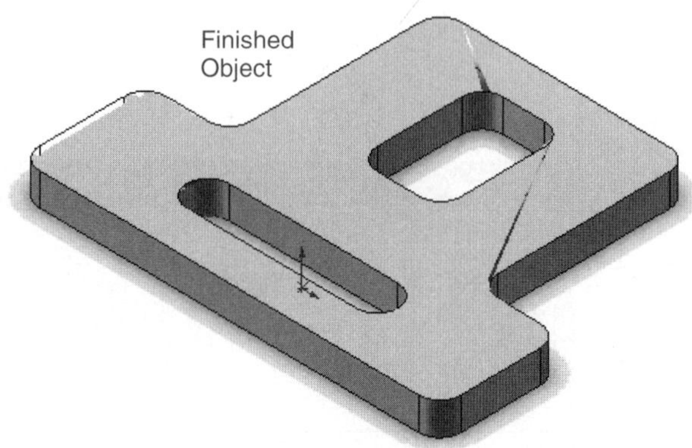

Figure 2-31 *(continued)*

2-23 TEXT

The **Text** tool is used to add text to a **part** document. See Figure 2-32.

1. Create a new **Part** document.
2. Click the **Tools** heading, click **Sketch Entities,** and click the **Text** tool. See Figure 2-1.
3. Click the **Text** box in the **Text Properties Manager** and type the text required.

The text will appear on the screen.

To Change the Font and Size of Text

1. Make sure that the **Use document font** box in the **Text Properties Manager** is off; that is, there is no check mark in the box.
2. Click the **Font** box.

The **Choose Font** dialog box will appear.

3. Select the desired font and height.

It is best to avoid fonts that are too stylistic. Simple block-type letters are best for engineering drawings.

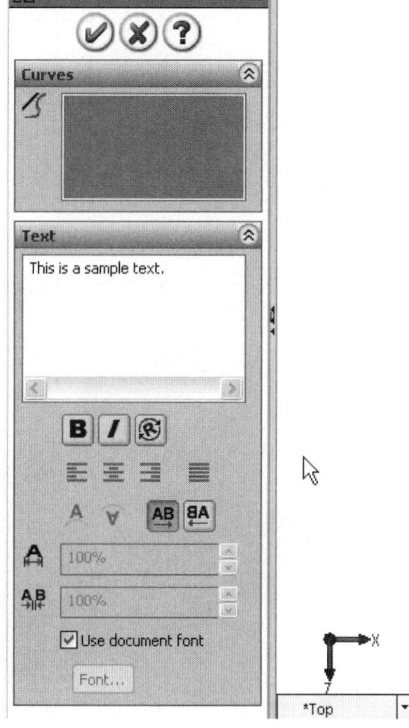

Figure 2-32

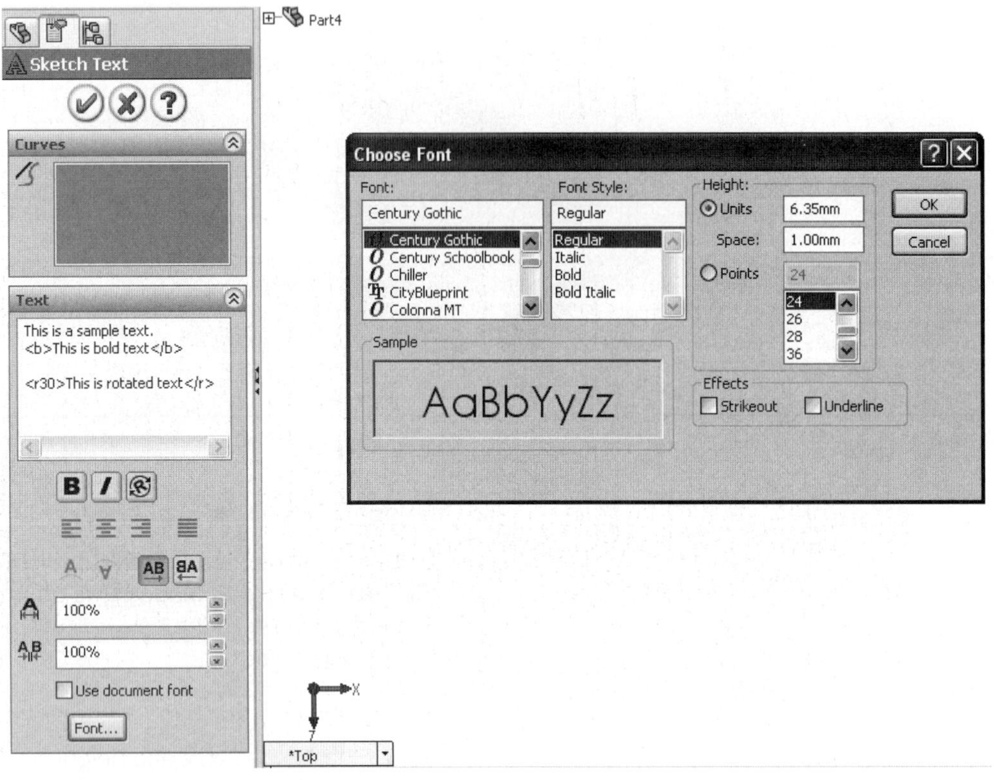

Figure 2-33

> ***Note:***
> The default font for SolidWorks is Century Gothic.

2-24 PROJECTS

Project 2-1:

Redraw the objects in Figures P2-1 through P-24 using the given dimensions. Create solid models of the objects using the specified thicknesses.

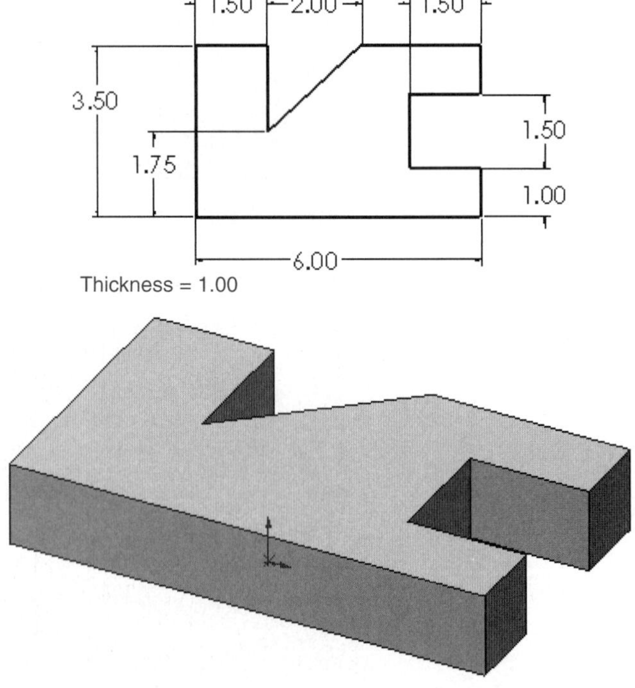

Figure P2-1 INCHES

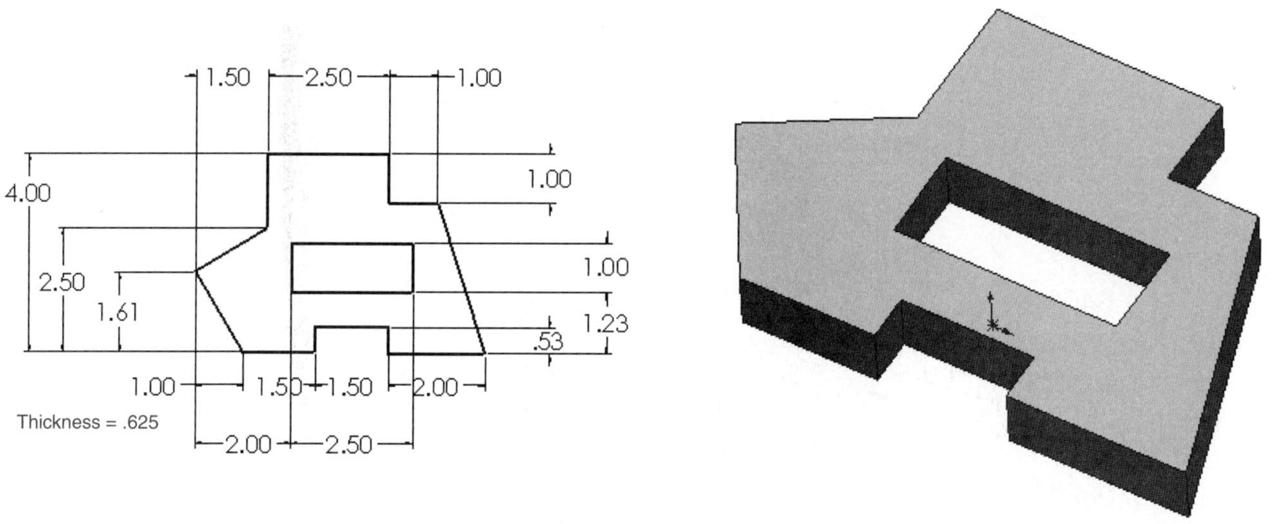

Figure P2-2 INCHES

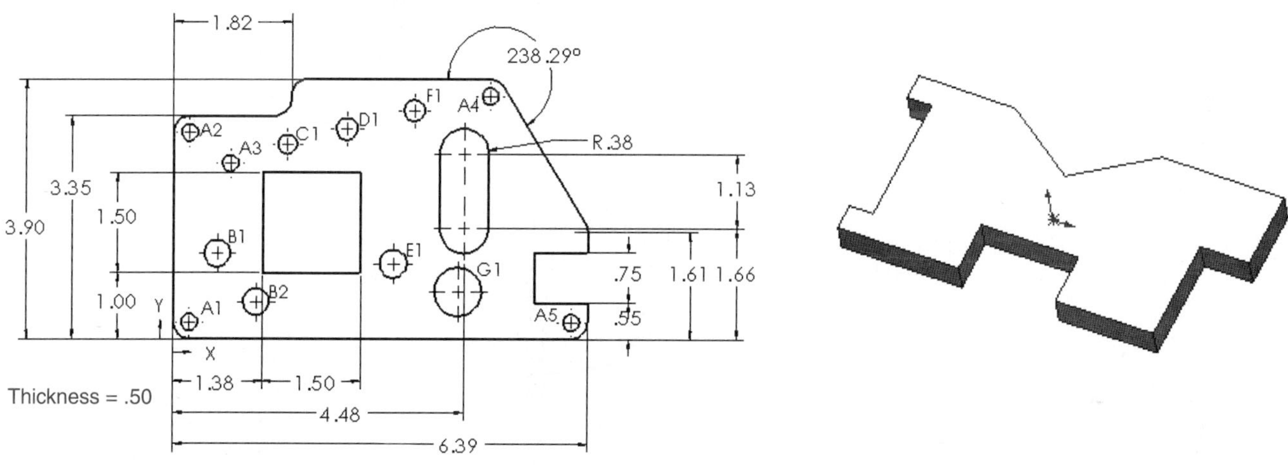

Figure P2-3 MILLIMETERS

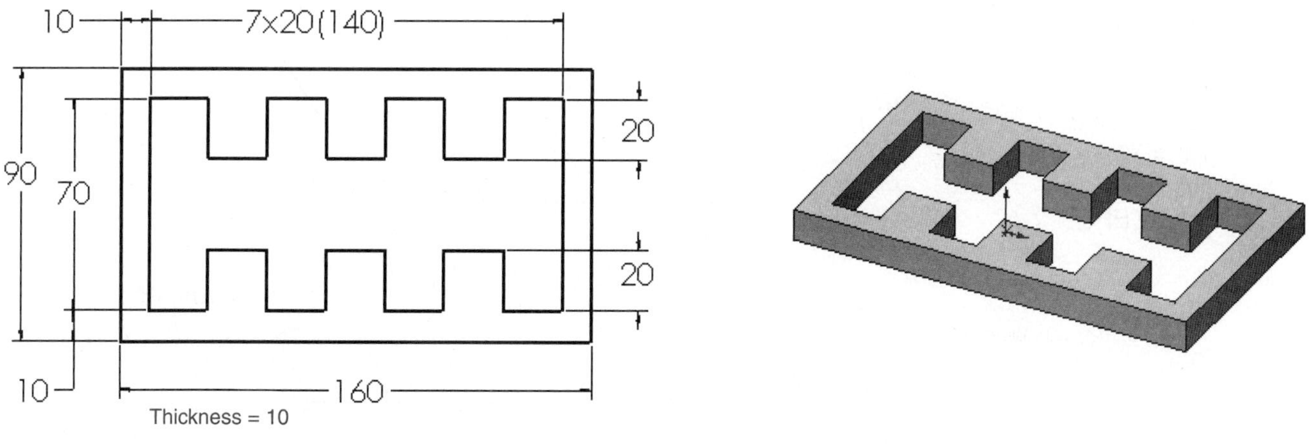

Figure P2-4 MILLIMETERS

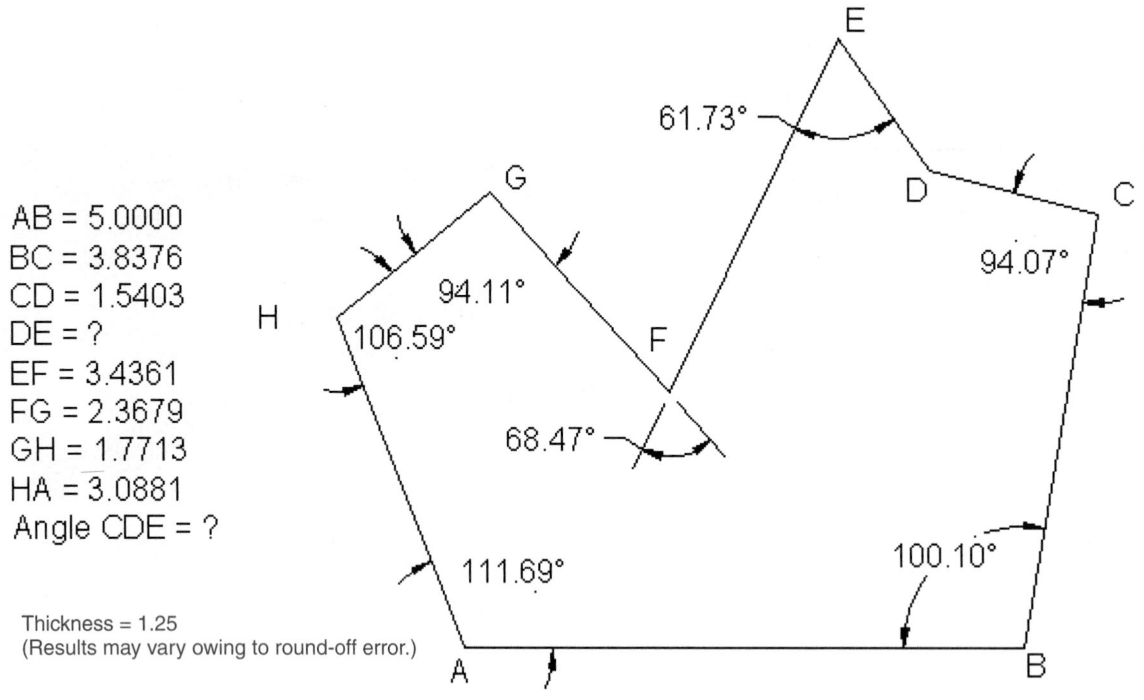

Figure P2-5 INCHES

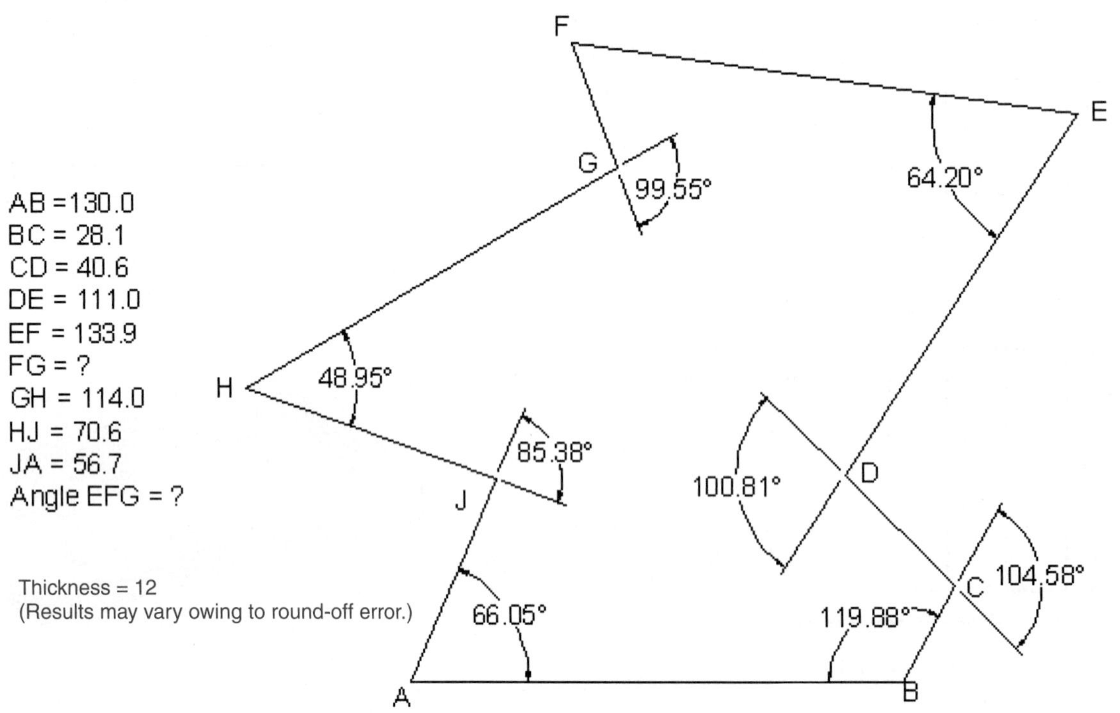

Figure P2-6 MILLIMETERS

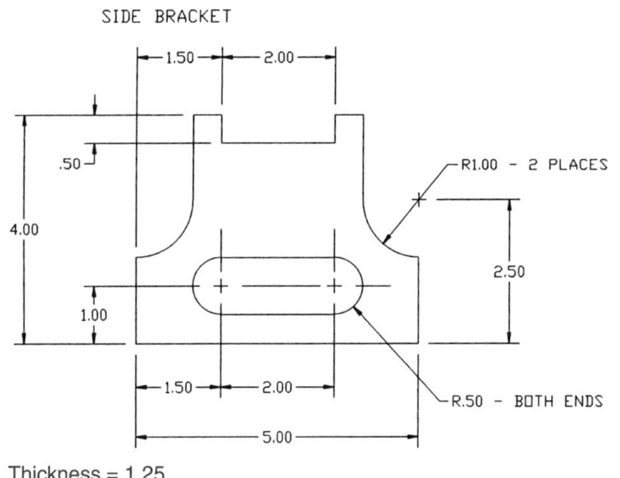

Figure P2-7 INCHES

FITTER GUSSET

4.00

3.00

2.00

1.00

ALL FILLETS AND ROUNDS = R.25 UNLESS OTHERWISE STATED.

1.50

4.00

.75

2.00

1.50

Thickness = .375

1.50

2.00

5.00

R.25
2 PLACES

Figure P2-9 INCHES

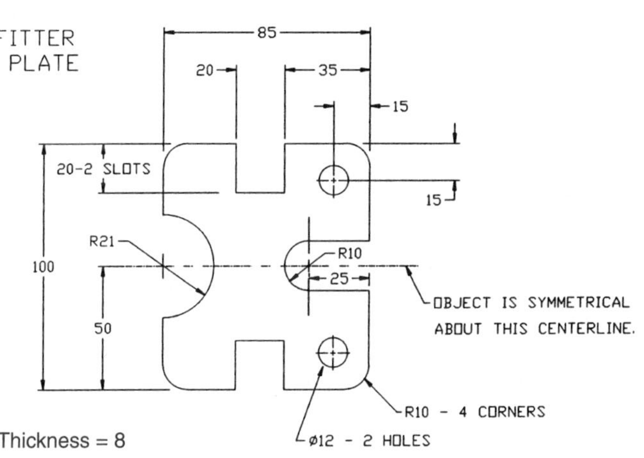

Figure P2-8 MILLIMETERS

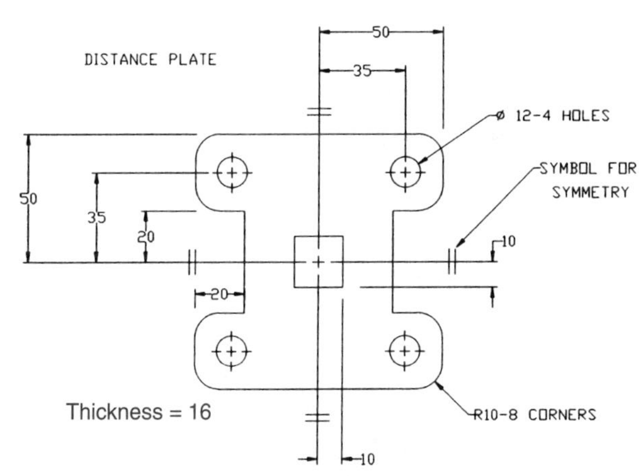

Figure P2-10 MILLIMETERS

TOP FILTER

Ø20 - 8 HOLES
EQUALLY
SPACED

Ø120

40 SQ

180

Thickness = 6

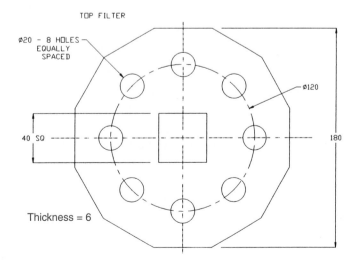

Figure P2-11 MILLIMETERS

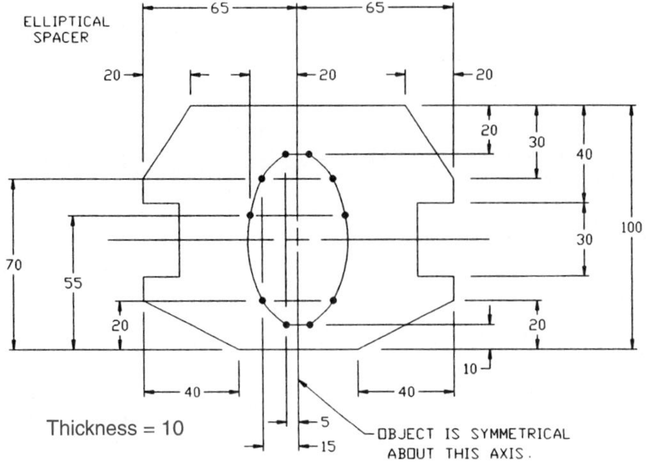

Figure P2-12 MILLIMETERS

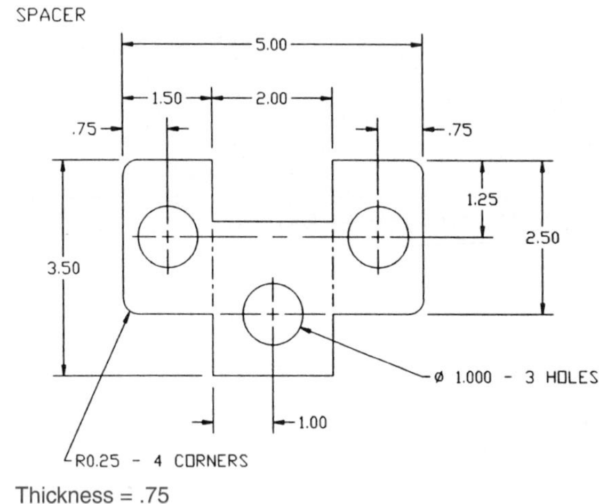

Figure P2-13 INCHES

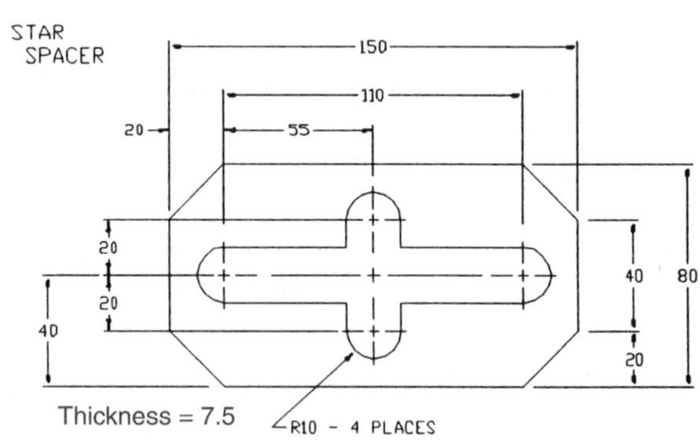

Figure P2-14 MILLIMETERS

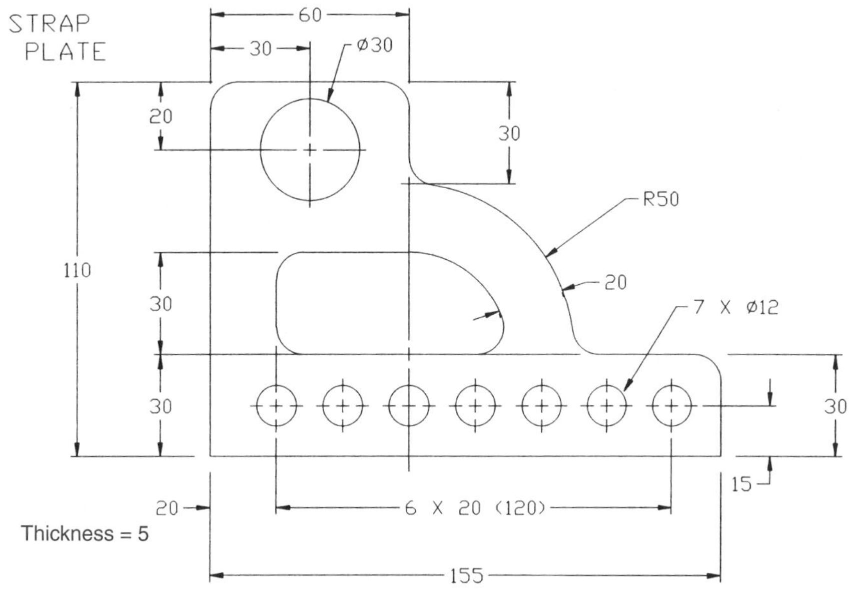

Figure P2-15 MILLIMETERS

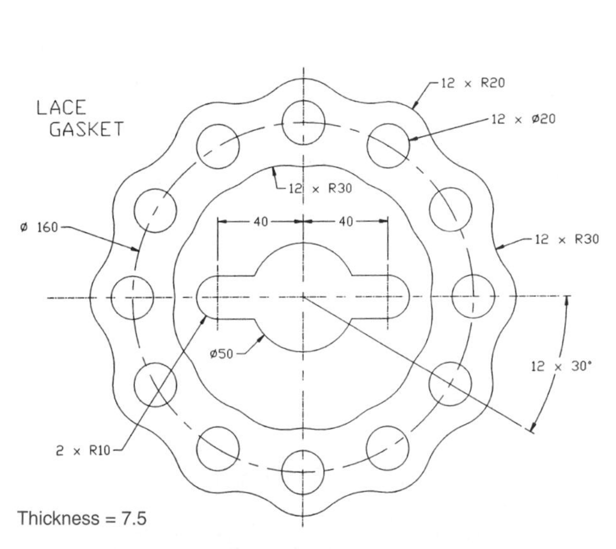

Figure P2-16 MILLIMETERS

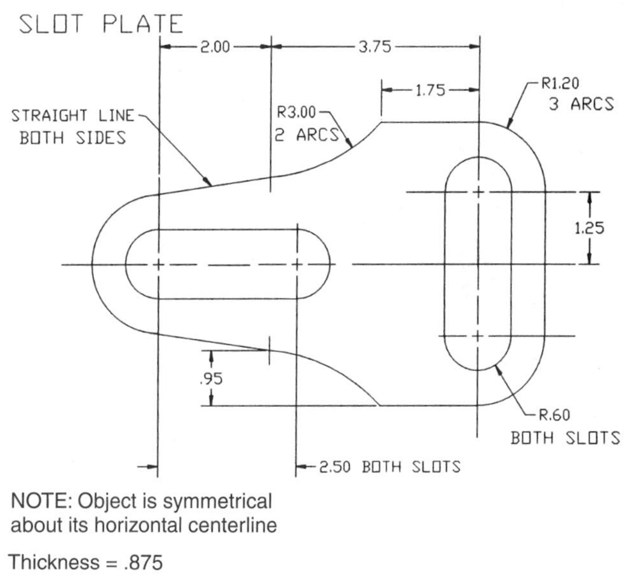

Figure P2-17 INCHES

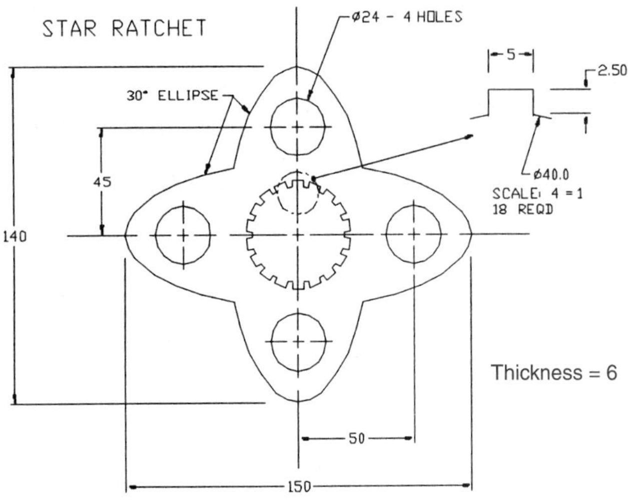

Figure P2-18 MILLIMETERS

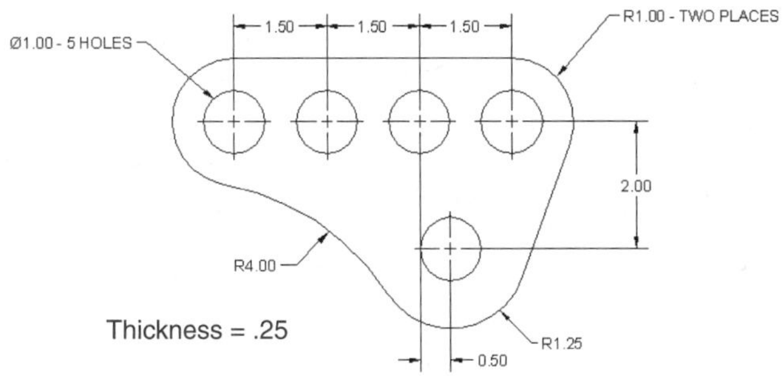

Figure P2-20 INCHES

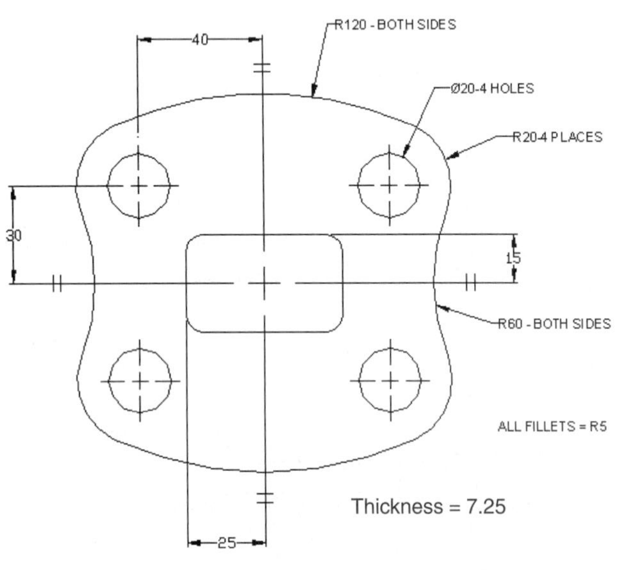

Figure P2-19 MILLIMETERS

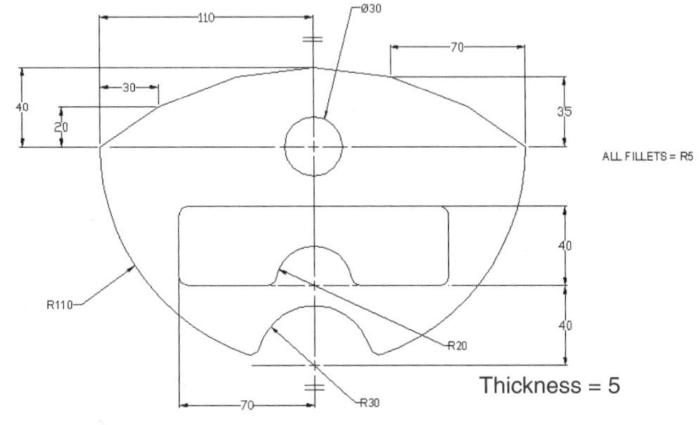

Figure P2-21 MILLIMETERS

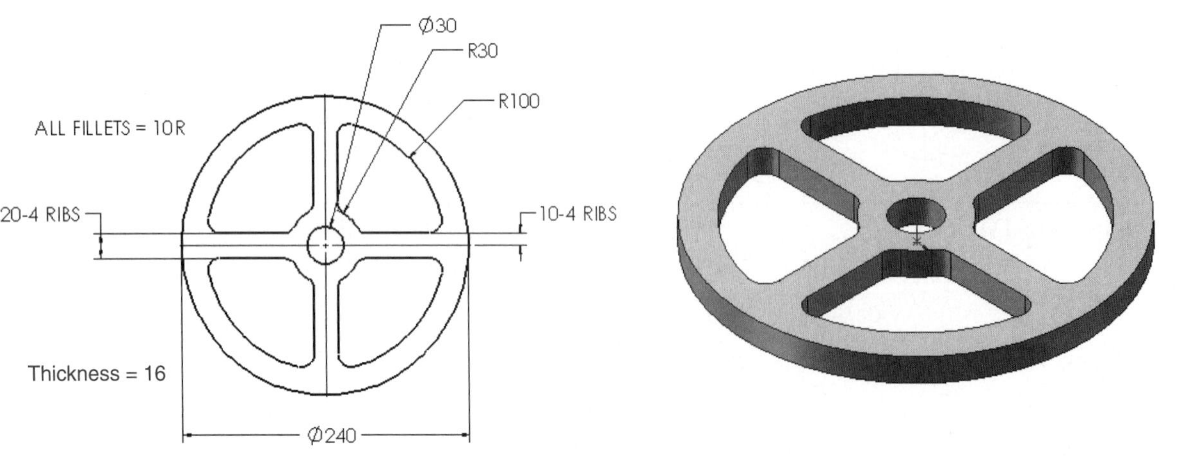

Figure P2-22 MILLIMETERS

All FILLETS AND ROUNDS = R.25

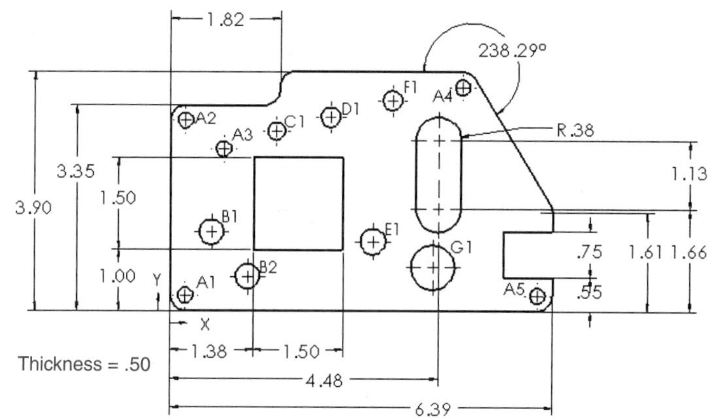

TAG	X LOC	Y LOC	SIZE
A1	.25	.25	Ø.25
A2	.25	3.10	Ø.25
A3	.88	2.64	Ø.25
A4	4.88	3.65	Ø.25
A5	6.14	.25	Ø.25
B1	.68	1.29	Ø.40
B2	1.28	.56	Ø.40
C1	1.76	2.92	Ø.29
D1	2.66	3.16	Ø.33
E1	3.38	1.13	Ø.42
F1	3.71	3.43	Ø.32
G1	4.39	.71	Ø.73

Figure P2-23 INCHES

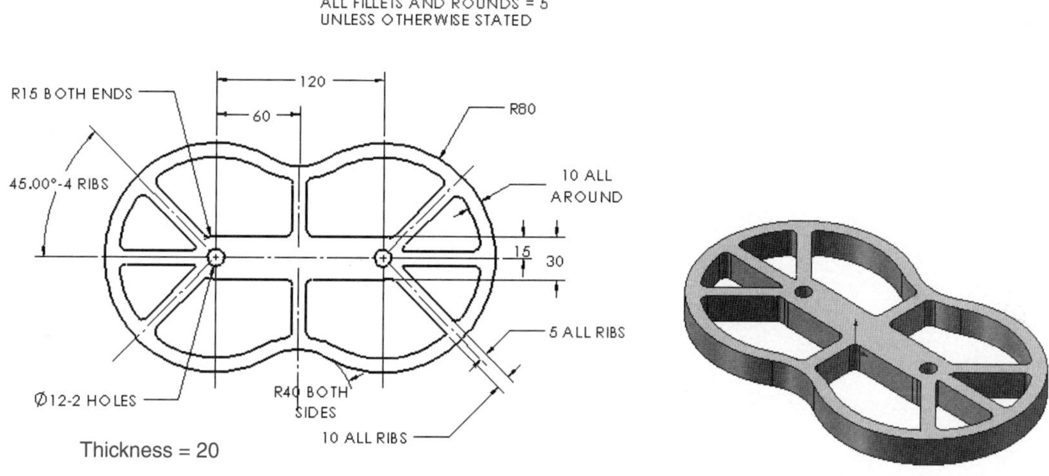

Figure P2-24 MILLIMETERS

CHAPTER 3

Features

Objectives

- Learn about the **Features** tools.
- Learn how to draw 3D objects.
- Learn how to use **Features** tools to create objects.
- Work with millimeter dimensions.

3-1 INTRODUCTION

This chapter introduces the **Features** tools. Several examples are included that show how to apply the tools to create objects.

3-2 EXTRUDED BOSS/BASE

The **Extruded Boss/Base** tool is used to add thickness or height to an existing 2D sketch. The examples presented use metric dimensions.

To Work with Dimensions in Millimeters

1. Click the **Tools** heading at the top of the drawing screen.

   See Figure 3-1.

2. Click the **Options** . . . tool.

   The **Document Properties** box will appear.

3. Click the **Document Properties** tab.
4. Click **Units.**
5. Click the **MMGS (millimeter, gram, second)** button.
6. Click **OK.**

   The system is now calibrated for millimeters.

To Use the Extruded Boss/Base Tool

1. Start a new drawing and draw a **60 × 100** rectangle in the top plane.

   See Figure 3-2.

2. Add the **Standard View** toolbar to your screen and click the **Isometric** icon.
3. Click the **Features** tool.
4. Click the **Extruded Boss/Base** tool.

   The **Extrude Properties Manager** will appear.

5. Define the extrusion height as **40.00mm.**

   A real-time preview will appear.

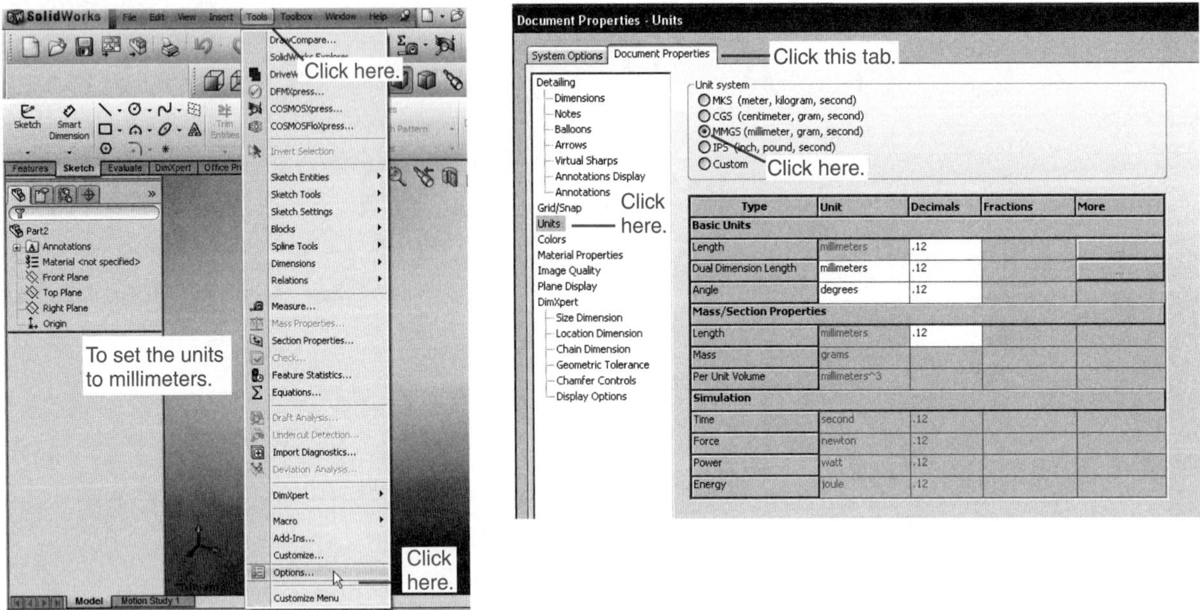

Figure 3-1

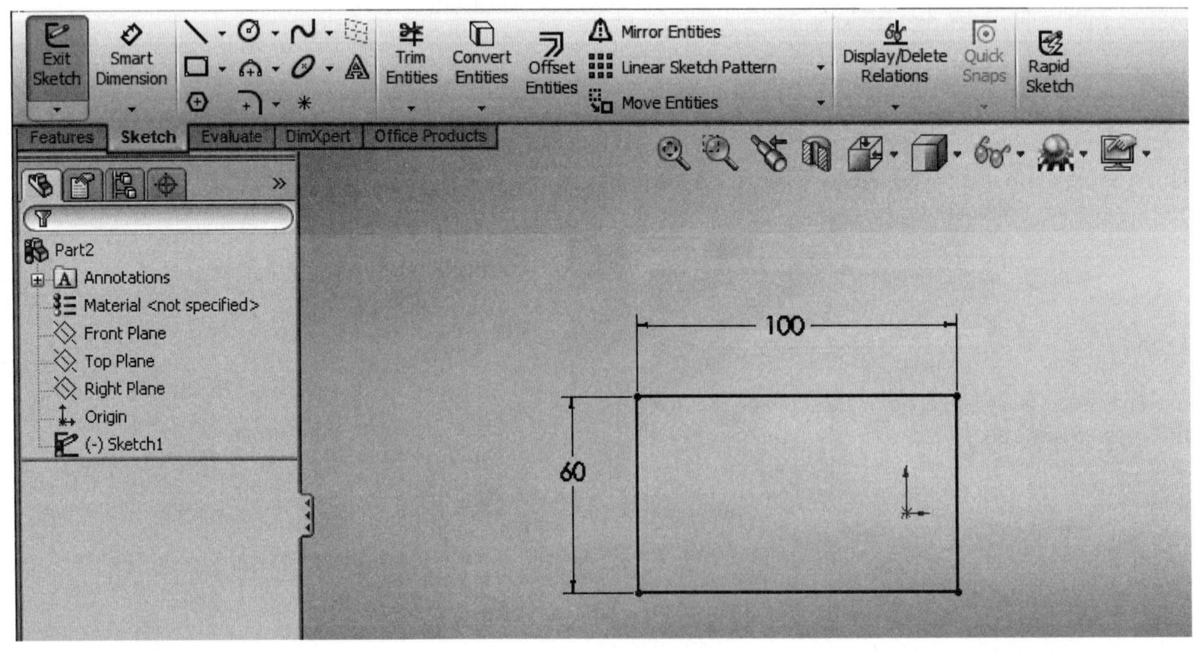

Figure 3-2

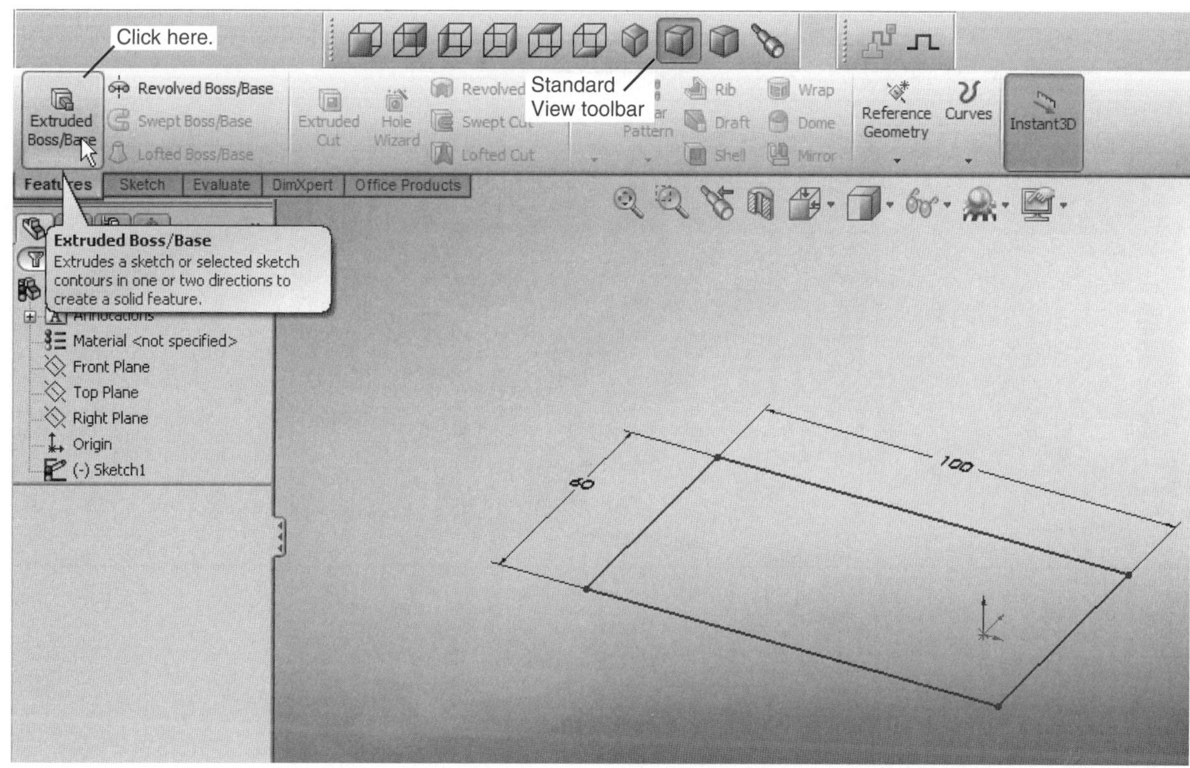

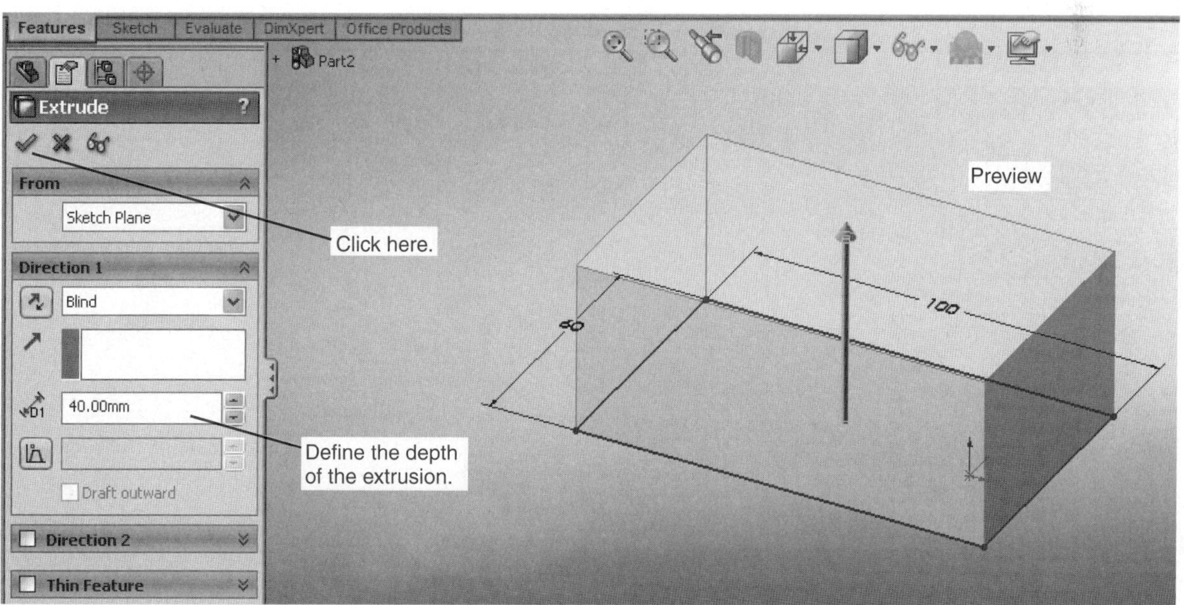

Figure 3-2 ***(continued)***

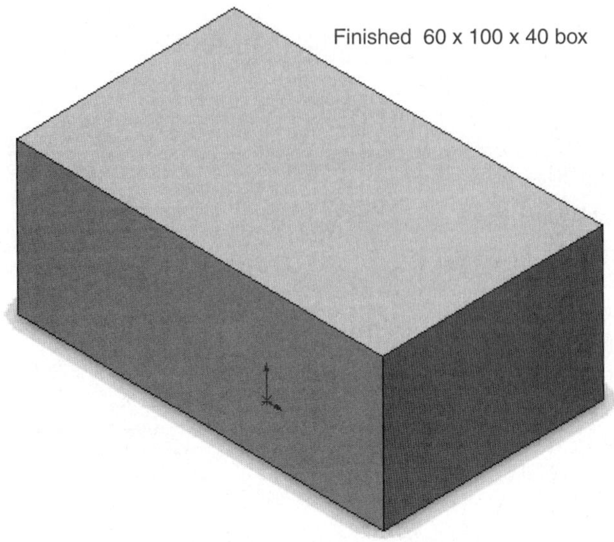

Figure 3-2 *(continued)*

> **TIP**
>
> The extrusion depth may be defined by entering a value or by using the arrows at the right of the **Depth** box.

6. Click the OK check mark at the top of the **Extrude Properties Manager.**

The preceding example has perpendicular sides. The **Extrude** tool may also be used to create tapered sides. See Figure 3-3 and Figure 3-4. Tapered sides are called ***draft sides.***

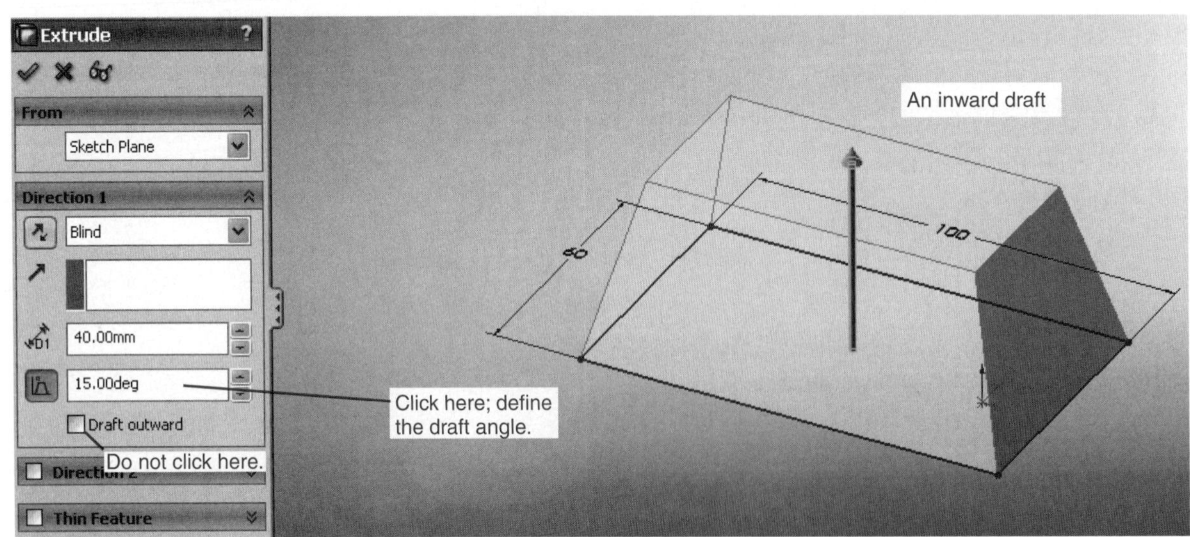

Figure 3-3

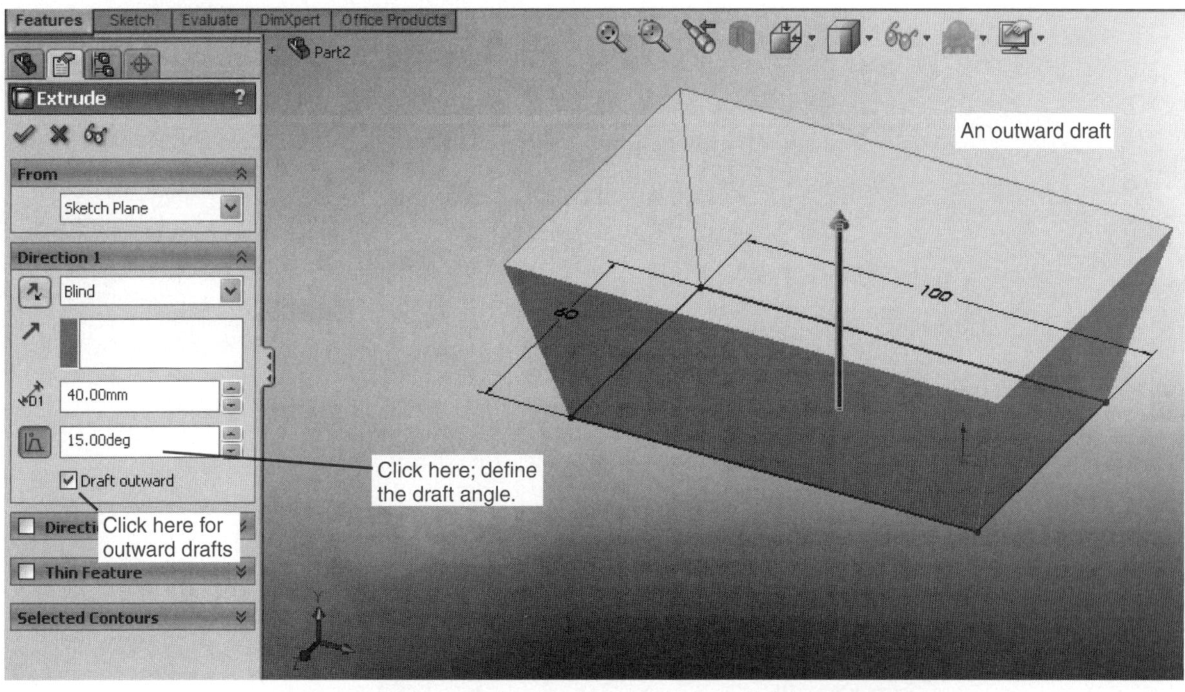

Figure 3-4

To Create Inward Draft Sides

1. Draw a **60 × 100** rectangle, click the **Features** tool, and click the **Extruded Boss/Base** tool.

   The **Extrude Properties Manager** will appear.

2. Click the **Draft On/Off** box.
3. Enter the draft angle value.

   In this example a **15°** value was entered. See Figure 3–3.

4. Click the OK check mark at the top of the **Extrude Properties Manager** to complete the object.

   The draft shown in Figure 3-3 is an inward draft.

To Create an Outward Draft

1. Repeat the same procedure, but this time check the **Draft outward** box.

   See Figure 3-4.

3-3 SAMPLE PROBLEM SP3-1

This section shows how to draw a solid 3D model of an L-bracket using the **Extrude** tool.

1. Draw a **60 × 100** rectangle and extrude it to a depth of **20mm.**

   See Figure 3-5.

2. Locate the cursor on the top surface of the box and right-click the mouse. Select the **Sketch** tool.

   The 2D sketch tools will return to the top of the screen.

3. Use the **Rectangle** tool to draw a rectangle on the top surface of the box. Use the upper left corner of the box as one corner of the rectangle.

> ***Note:***
> The corner points and edge lines will change colors when they are activated.

4. Select the **Smart Dimension** tool and size the rectangle to **20 × 100.**
5. Click the **Features** tool, then select the **Extruded Boss/Base** tool.
6. Select the **20 × 100** rectangle to extrude to a depth of **40.00mm.**
7. Click the OK check mark in the **Extrude Properties Manager.**

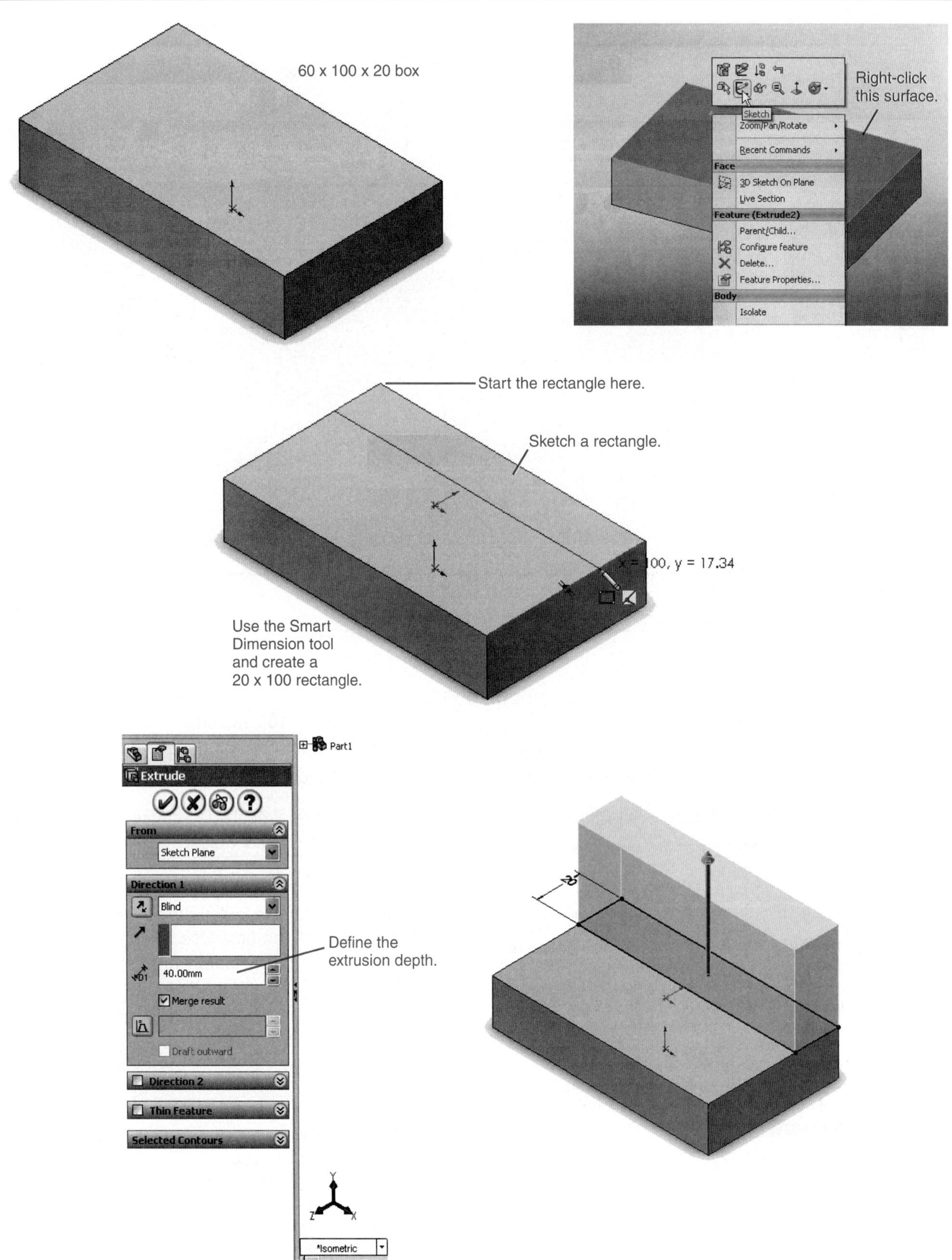
60 x 100 x 20 box
Right-click this surface.
Sketch
Zoom/Pan/Rotate
Recent Commands
Face
3D Sketch On Plane
Live Section
Feature (Extrude2)
Parent/Child...
Configure feature
Delete...
Feature Properties...
Body
Isolate
Start the rectangle here.
Sketch a rectangle.
x = 100, y = 17.34
Use the Smart Dimension tool and create a 20 x 100 rectangle.
Part1
Extrude
From
Sketch Plane
Direction 1
Blind
40.00mm
Merge result
Draft outward
Direction 2
Thin Feature
Selected Contours
Define the extrusion depth.
*Isometric

Figure 3-5

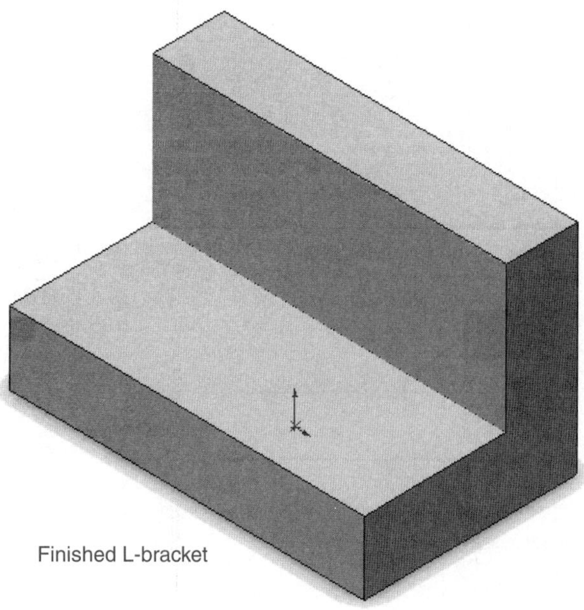

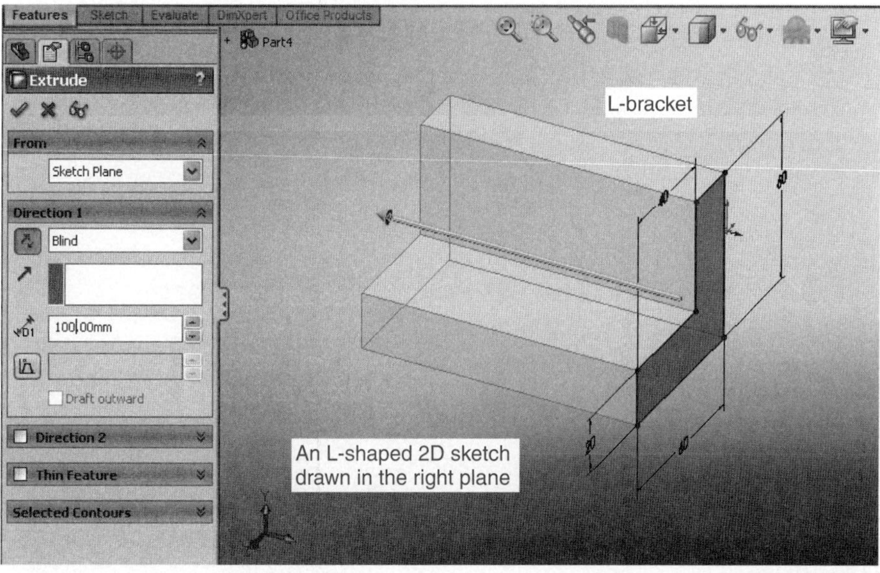

Figure 3-5 *(continued)*

3-4 EXTRUDED CUT

This section will add a cutout to the L-bracket using the **Extruded Cut** tool. See Figure 3-6.

1. Locate the cursor on the lower front horizontal surface and right-click the mouse.
2. Click the **Sketch** option.
3. Use the **Rectangle** and **Smart Dimension** tools to draw a rectangle as shown.
4. Click the **Features** tool, then click the **Extruded Cut** tool.
5. Click the OK check mark in the **Cut-Extrude Properties Manager.**

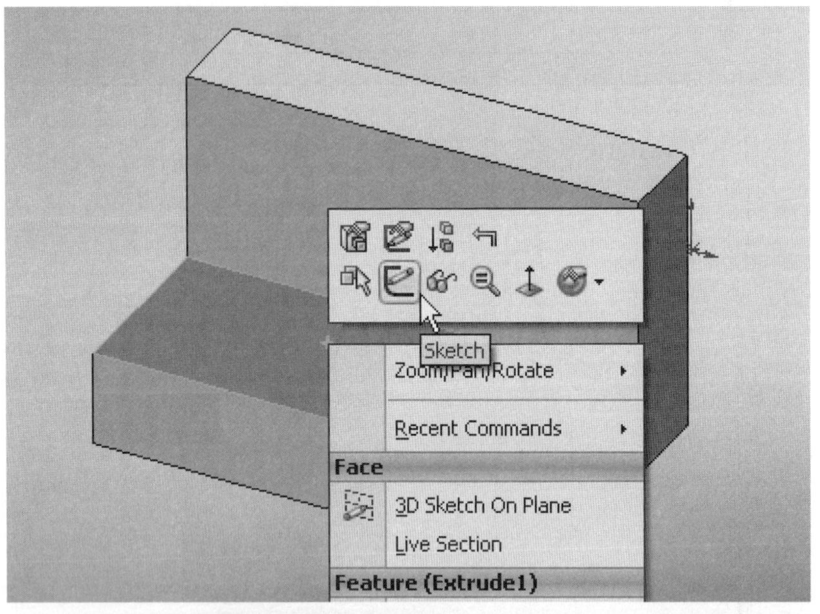
Sketch
Zoom/Pan/Rotate
Recent Commands
Face
3D Sketch On Plane
Live Section
Feature (Extrude1)

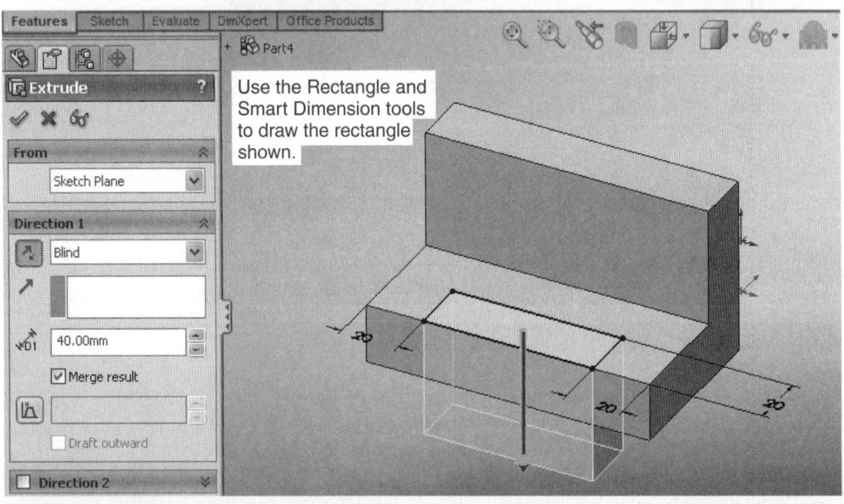
Use the Rectangle and Smart Dimension tools to draw the rectangle shown.
Features
Sketch
Evaluate
DimXpert
Office Products
Part4
Extrude
From
Sketch Plane
Direction 1
Blind
40.00mm
Merge result
Draft outward
Direction 2
20
20
20

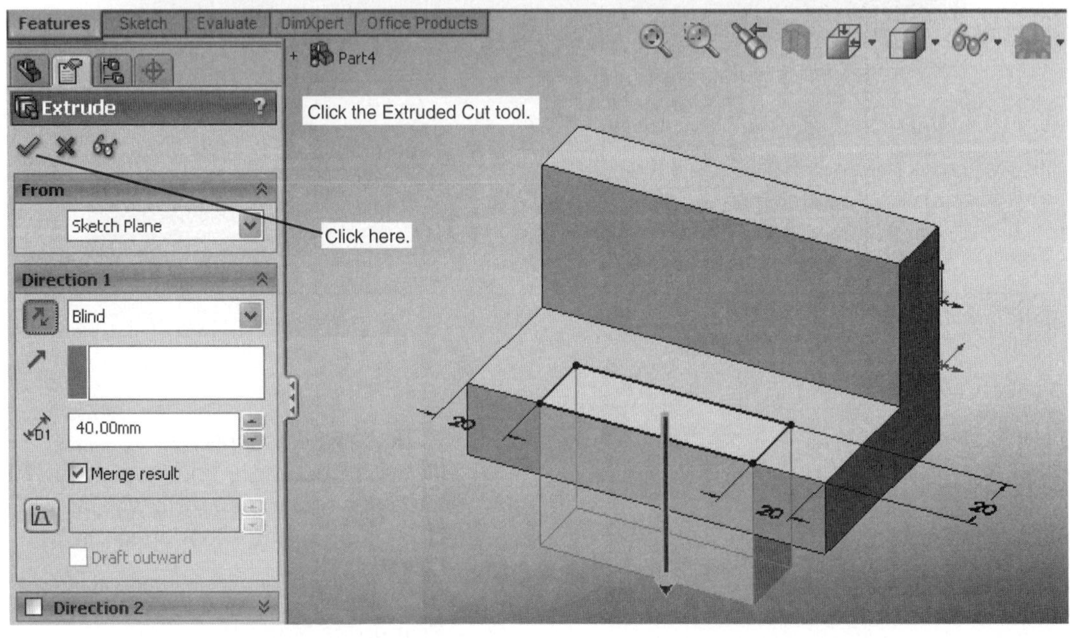
Click the Extruded Cut tool.
Click here.
Features
Sketch
Evaluate
DimXpert
Office Products
Part4
Extrude
From
Sketch Plane
Direction 1
Blind
40.00mm
Merge result
Draft outward
Direction 2
20
20
20

Figure 3-6

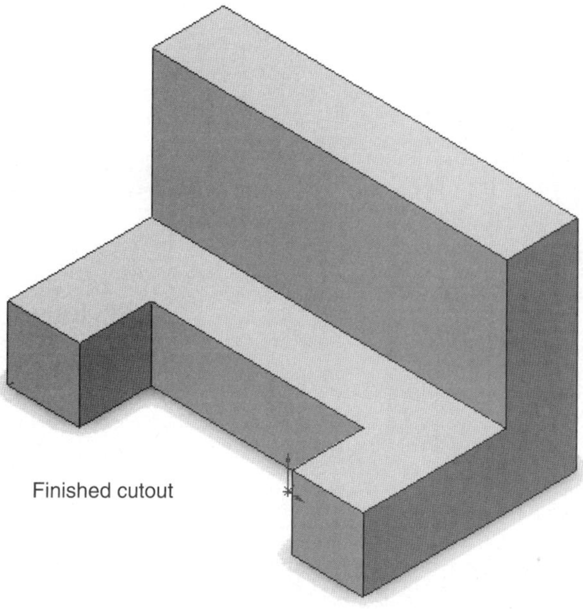

Figure 3-6 ***(continued)***

3-5 HOLE WIZARD

This section will add a hole to the L-bracket using the **Hole Wizard.** See Figure 3-7.

1. Click the **Features** tool, then click the **Hole Wizard** tool.
2. Click the front face as shown.
3. Select the type of hole, for example, clear, counterbore, or threaded.

In this example a clear hole was selected. SolidWorks calls this option **Hole.**

4. Select the **Standard** units.

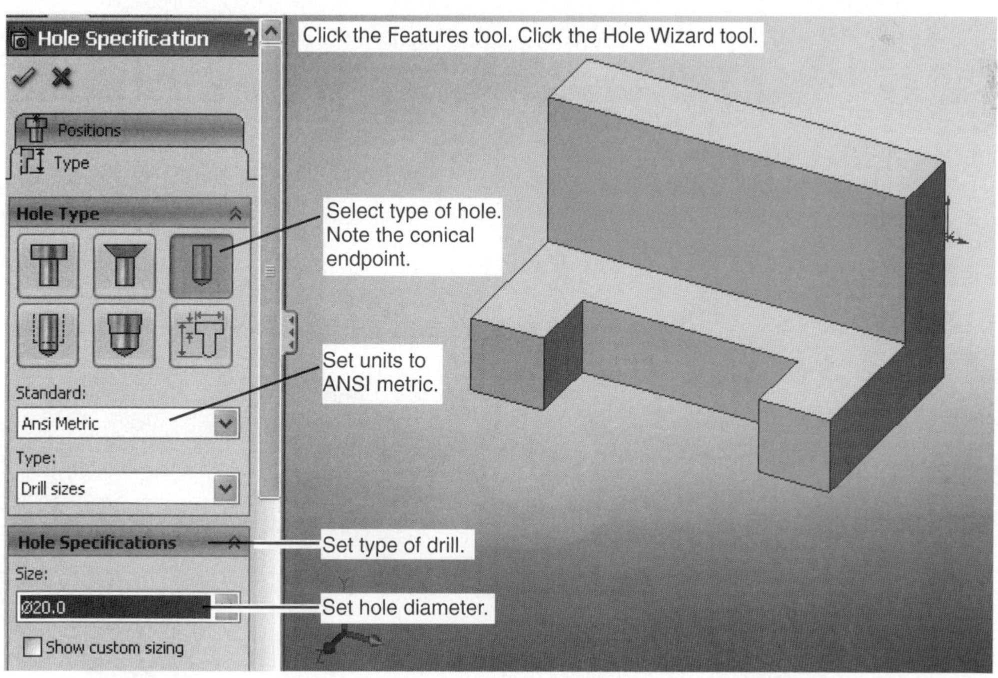

Figure 3-7

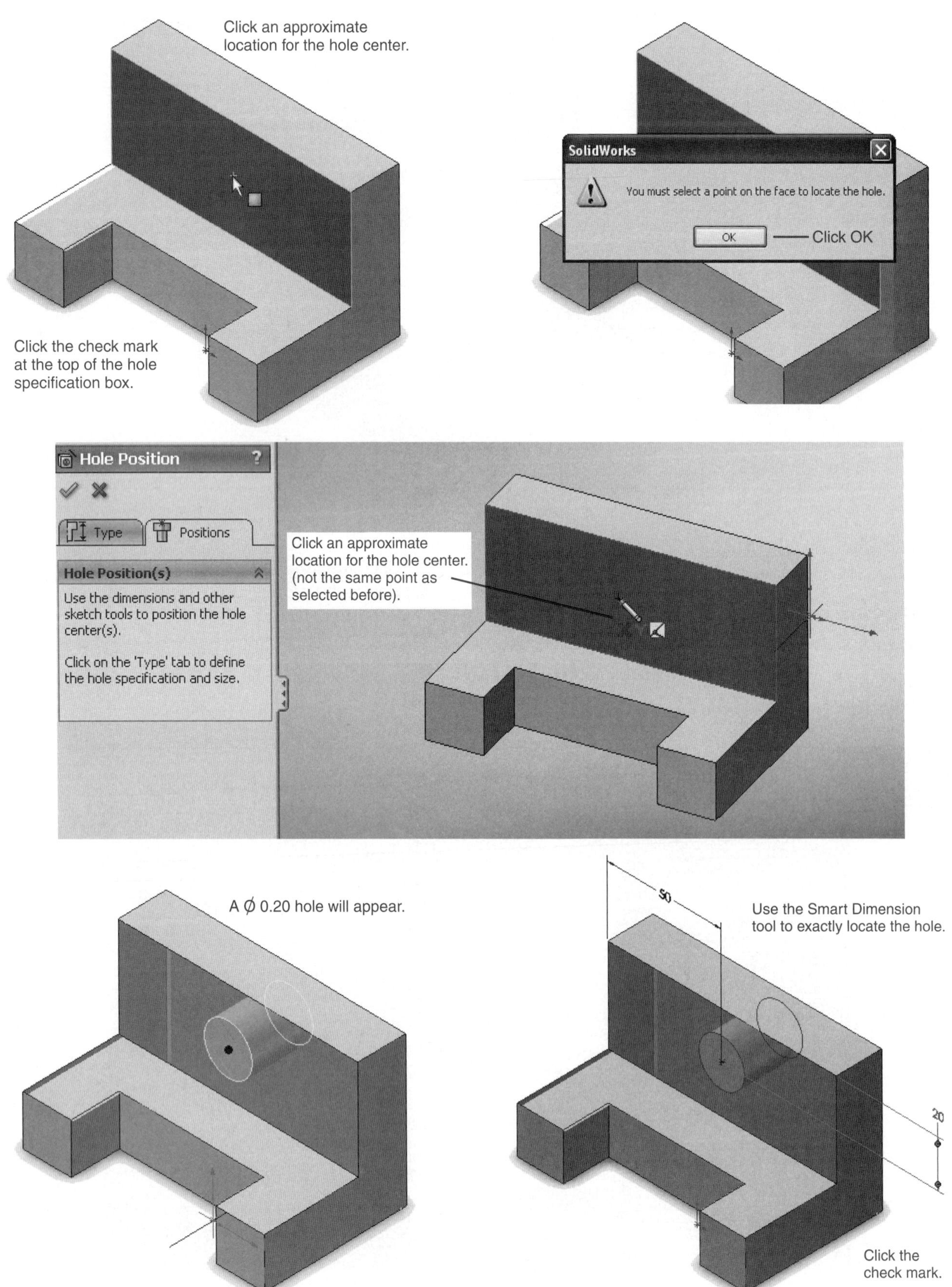
Click an approximate
location for the hole center.
Click the check mark
at the top of the hole
specification box.
SolidWorks
You must select a point on the face to locate the hole.
OK
Click OK
Hole Position
Type
Positions
Hole Position(s)
Use the dimensions and other
sketch tools to position the hole
center(s).
Click on the 'Type' tab to define
the hole specification and size.
Click an approximate
location for the hole center.
(not the same point as
selected before).
A ∅ 0.20 hole will appear.
.50
Use the Smart Dimension
tool to exactly locate the hole.
.20
Click the
check mark.

Figure 3-7 *(continued)*

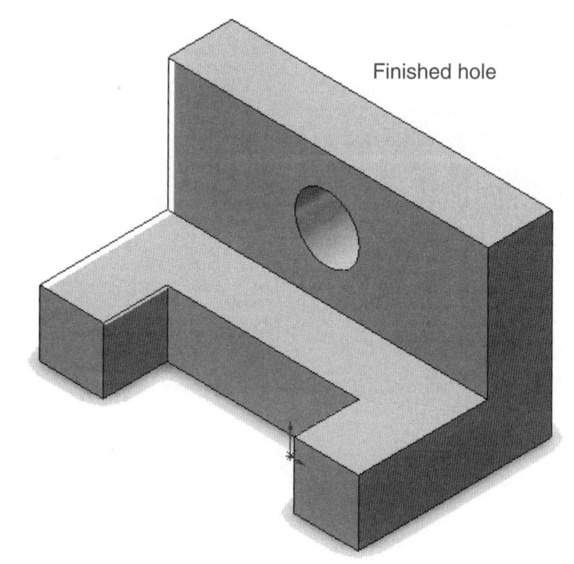
Finished hole

Figure 3-7 *(continued)*

In this example **Ansi Metric** was selected. ANSI is the American National Standards Institute, which publishes standards that will be covered in detail in the chapter on orthographic views and dimensions and tolerances.

5. Define the diameter of the hole.

   In this example a diameter of **20.0mm** was selected.

6. Click an approximate center point location for the hole.
7. Click the OK check mark.

   A dialog box will appear.

8. Click **OK** in the dialog box.
9. Again click an approximate location for the hole's center point.

> **TIP**
>
> Do not click the same point as was defined in step 6.

A preview of the hole will appear.

10. Use the **Smart Dimension** tool to locate the hole's center point.
11. Click the OK check mark.

    The hole will be added to the L-bracket.

12. Save the L-bracket, as it will be used in later sections.

The hole created in Figure 3-7 is a ***through hole,*** that is, it goes completely through the object. Holes that do not go completely though are called ***blind holes.*** Note that the **Hole Specification Properties Manager** shows a conical point at the bottom of the hole. Holes created using an extruded cut circle will not have this conical endpoint. Blind holes created using a drill should include the conical point. For this reason, blind holes should, with a few exceptions, be created using the **Hole Wizard** tool.

3-6 A SECOND METHOD OF CREATING A HOLE

Holes may also be created using the **Circle** tool and then applying the **Extruded Cut** tool. Figure 3-8 shows a 40 × 160 × 10 object. Add four **Ø20** holes.

1. Draw a **40 × 160 × 10** object.
2. Right-click the mouse and select the **Sketch** tool. Use the **Circle** tool and draw a circle. Use the **Smart Dimension** tool to size and locate the circle.
3. Add three more **Ø20** circles.

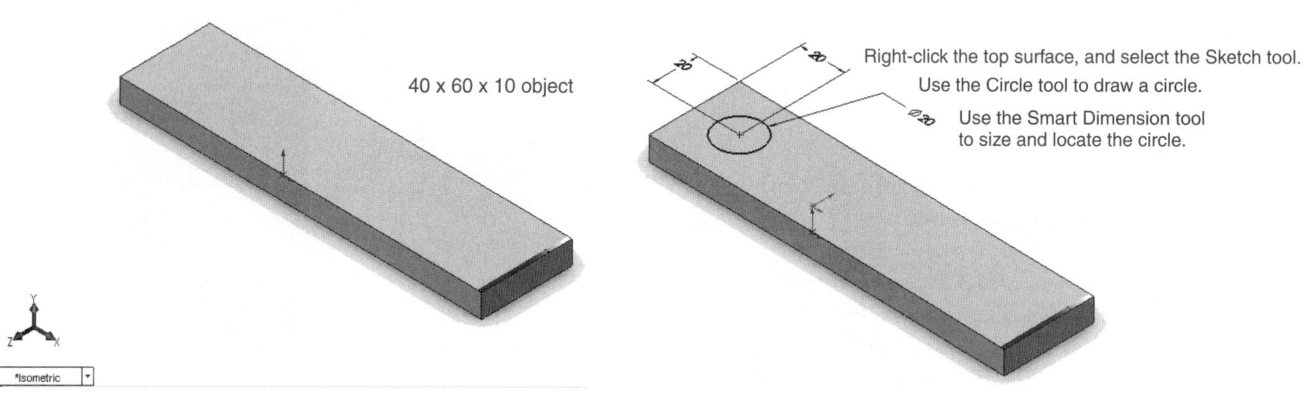
40 x 60 x 10 object
*Isometric
20
20
Ø20
Right-click the top surface, and select the Sketch tool.
Use the Circle tool to draw a circle.
Use the Smart Dimension tool to size and locate the circle.

Figure 3-8

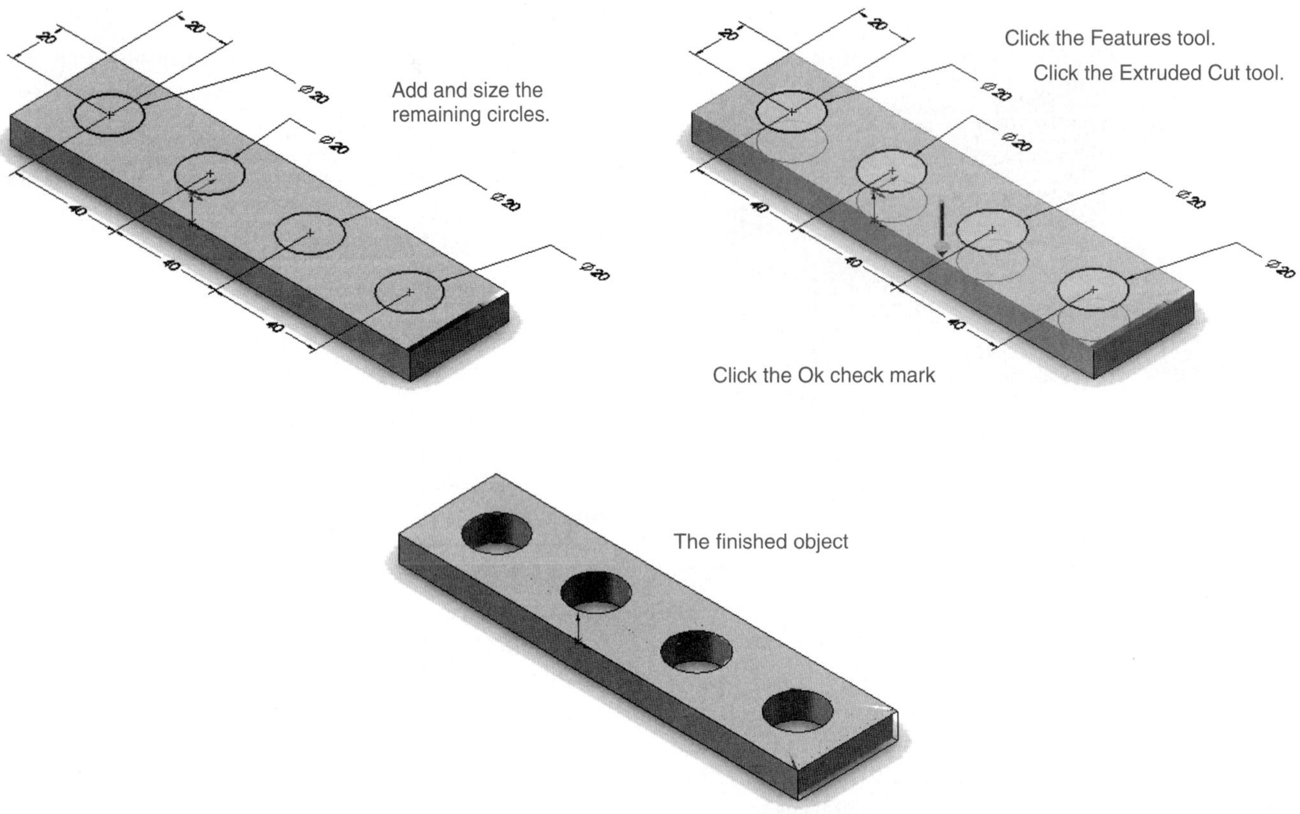

Add and size the remaining circles.
Click the Features tool.
Click the Extruded Cut tool.
Click the Ok check mark
The finished object

Figure 3-8 *(continued)*

4. Click the **Features** tool, then click the **Extruded Cut** tool.

   A preview of the hole will appear.

5. Set the cut depth for **10** or greater.
6. Click the OK check mark.

> **TIP**
>
> The same four-hole pattern can be created using the **Linear Sketch Pattern** tool.

3-7 FILLET

A ***fillet*** is a rounded corner. Specifically, convex corners are called ***rounds,*** and concave corners are called *fillets,* but in general, all rounded corners are called *fillets.*

SolidWorks can draw four types of fillets: constant radius, variable radius, face fillets, and full round fillets. Figure 3-9 shows the L-bracket used to demonstrate the previous **Features** tools. It will be used in this section to demonstrate fillet tools.

1. Open the L-bracket drawing.

If the L-bracket was not saved after the previous section, use the dimensions and procedures specified to re-create the object.

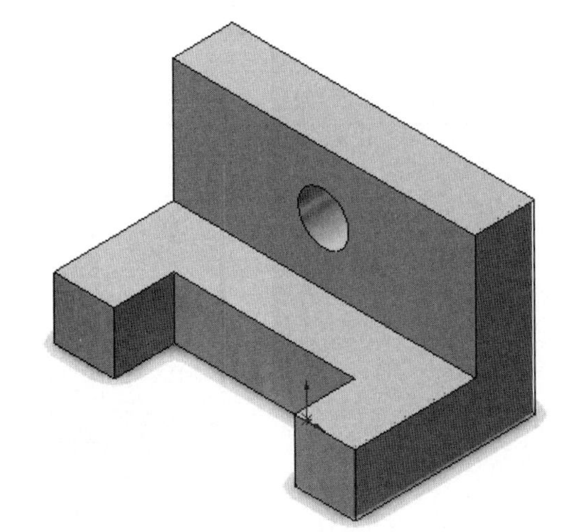

Figure 3-9

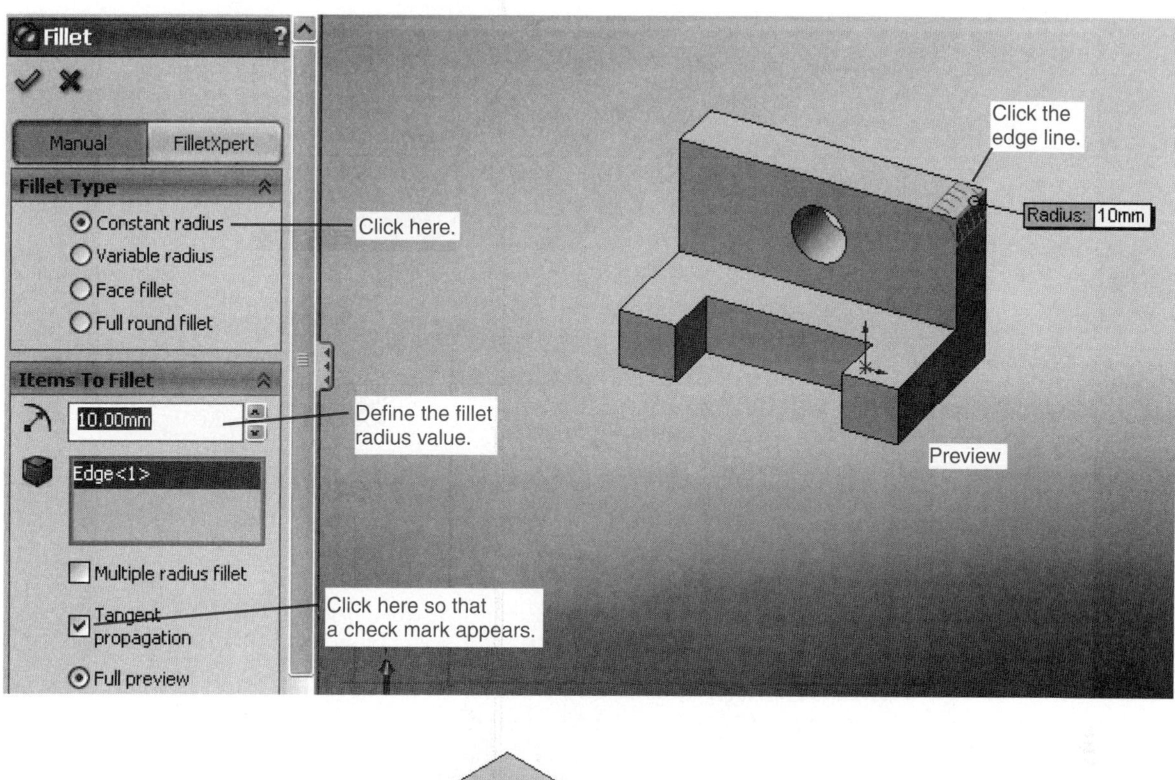

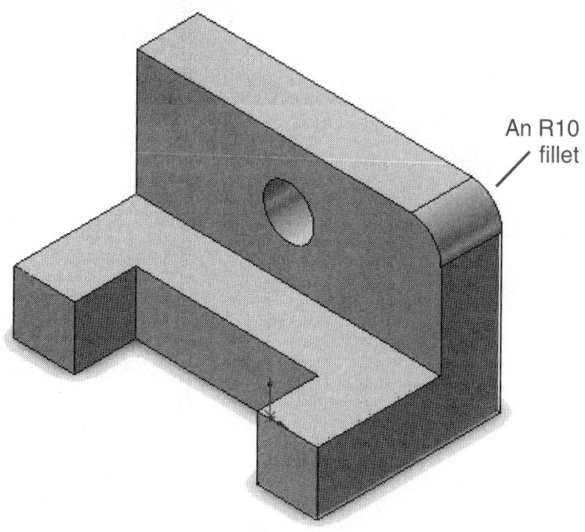

Figure 3-9 *(continued)*

2. Click the **Fillet** tool.
3. Select **Constant radius** in the **Fillet Type** box and define the fillet's radius as **10.00mm.** Click the **Full preview** button.
4. Click the upper right edge line of the object,

A preview of the fillet will appear.

5. Click the OK check mark.

To Create a Fillet with a Variable Radius

See Figure 3-10.

1. Click the **Fillet** tool.
2. Click the **Variable radius** button.
3. Click the edge line shown in Figure 3-10.

Two boxes will appear on the screen, one at each end of the edge line.

4. Click the word **Unassigned** in the left box and enter a value of **15.**
5. Click the word **Unassigned** in the right box and enter a value of **5.**
6. Click the OK check mark.

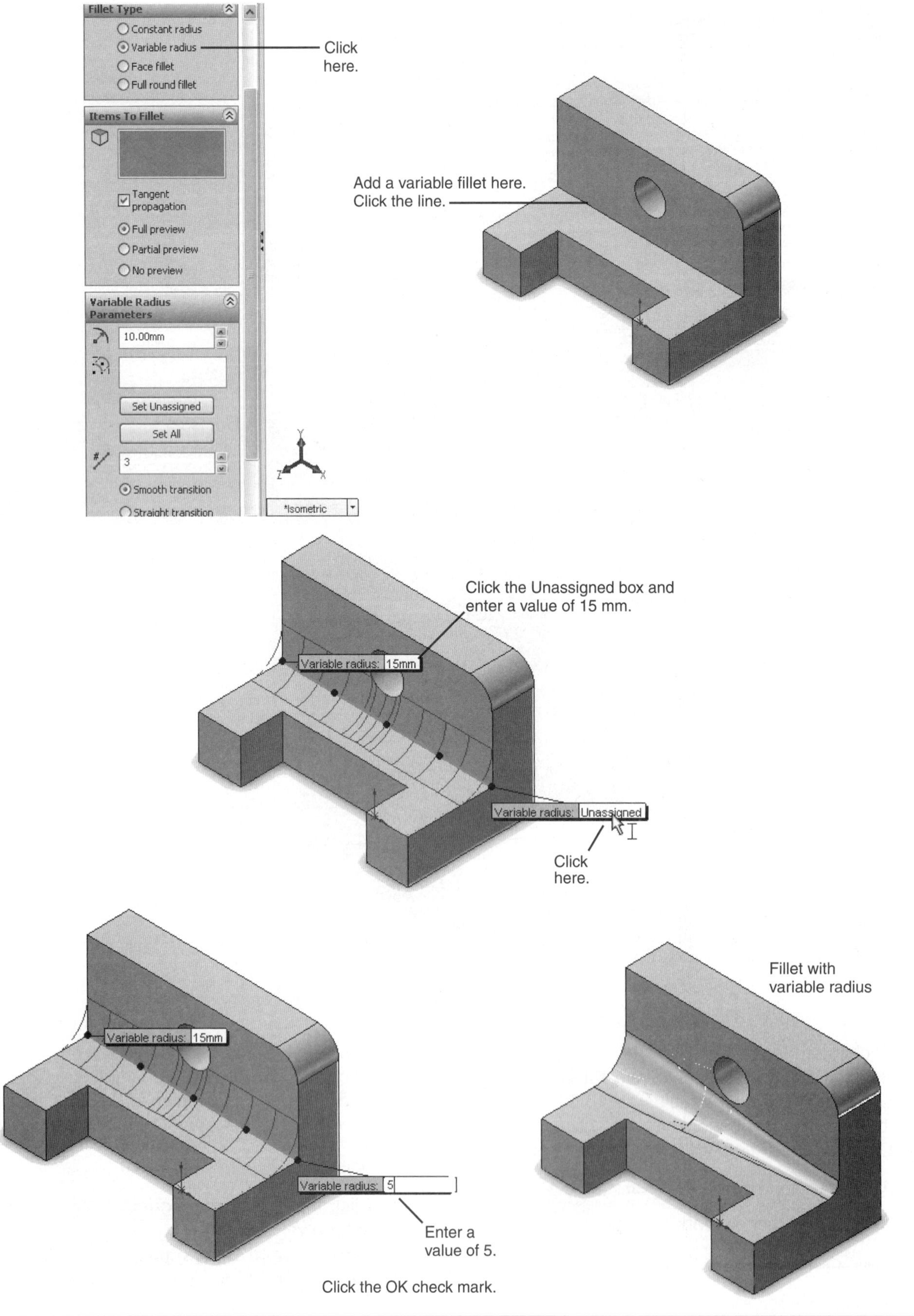
Fillet Type
Constant radius
Variable radius
Face fillet
Full round fillet
Click here.
Items To Fillet
Tangent propagation
Full preview
Partial preview
No preview
Variable Radius Parameters
10.00mm
Set Unassigned
Set All
3
Smooth transition
Straight transition
*Isometric
Add a variable fillet here. Click the line.
Click the Unassigned box and enter a value of 15 mm.
Variable radius: 15mm
Variable radius: Unassigned
Click here.
Variable radius: 15mm
Variable radius: 5
Enter a value of 5.
Click the OK check mark.
Fillet with variable radius

Figure 3-10

To Create a Fillet Using the Face Fillet Option

The **Face fillet** option draws a fillet between two faces (surfaces), whereas **Fillet** uses an edge between two surfaces to draw a fillet.

See Figure 3-11.

1. Click the **Fillet** tool.
2. Click the **Face fillet** option.

Two boxes will appear in **Items to Fillet** box. They will be used to define the two faces of the fillet.

3. Define the fillet radius as **10.00mm.**
4. Define **Face 1** as shown.

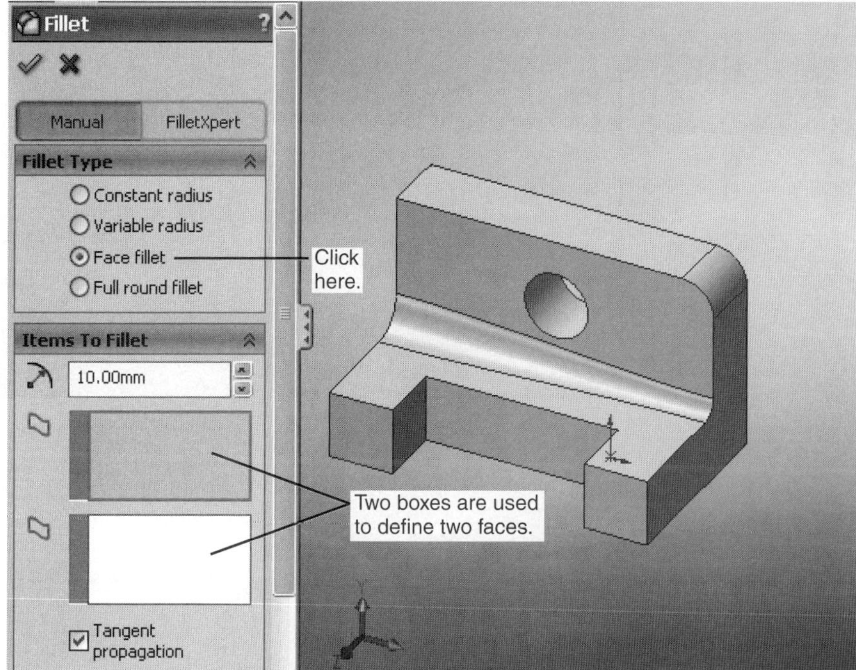

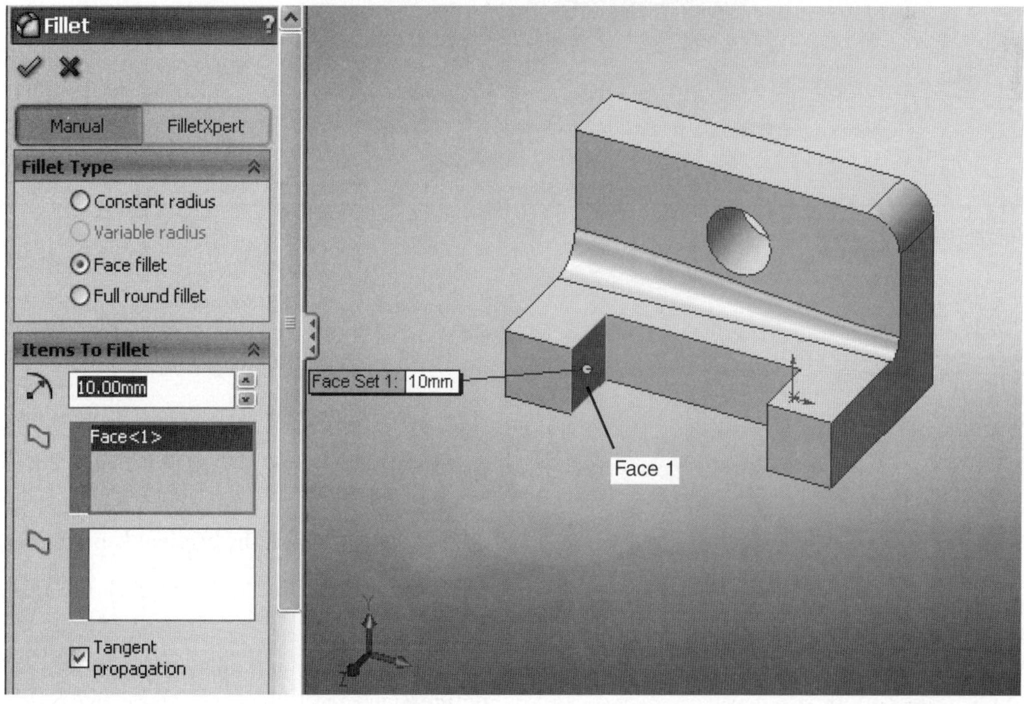

Figure 3-11

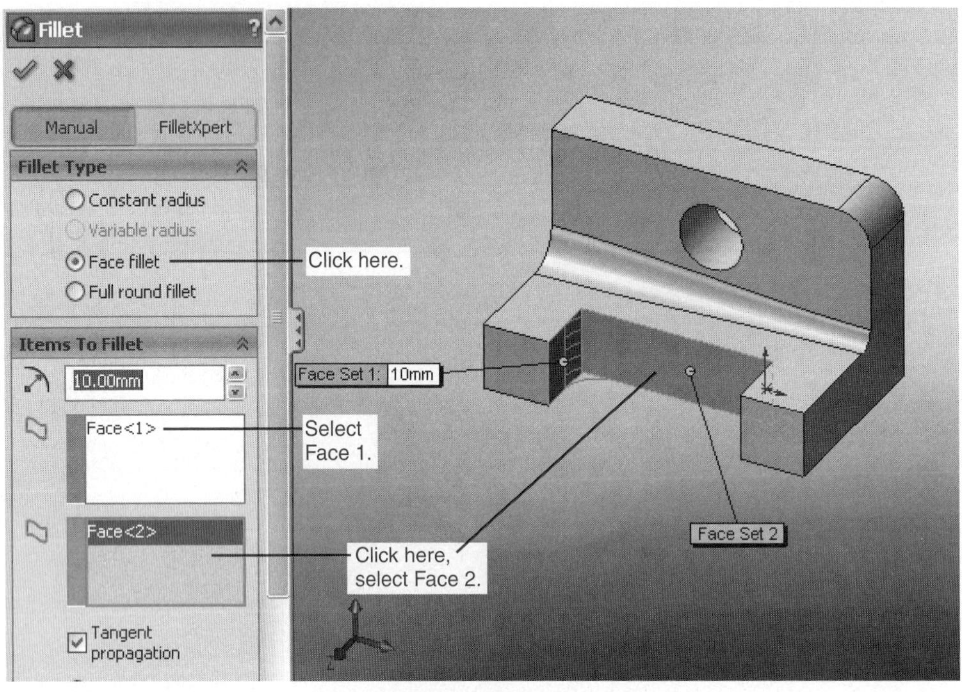

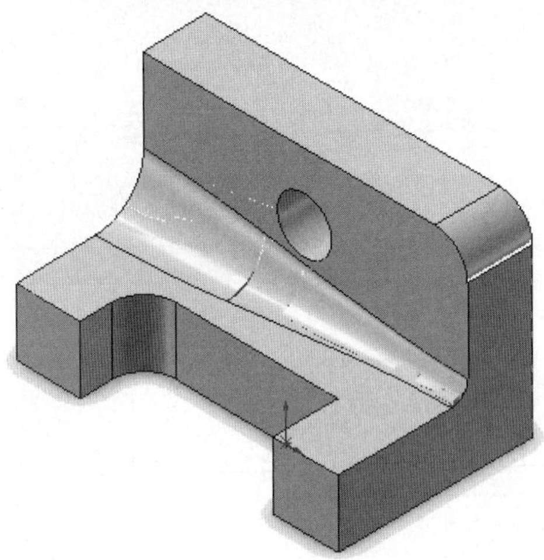

Figure 3-11 ***(continued)***

> ***Note:***
> The top box in the **Items to Fillet** box will be shaded, indicating that it is ready for an input.

5. Click the lower box in the **Items to Fillet** box (it will change colors) and define **Face 2** by clicking the surface as shown.
6. Click the OK check mark.

To Create a Fillet Using the Full Round Fillet Option

See Figure 3-12.

1. Use the **Undo** tool and remove the fillets created previously.

   This will return the original L-bracket shape.

2. Click the **Fillet** tool and click the **Full round fillet** button.

   Three boxes will appear. These boxes will be used to define Side Face 1, the Center Face, and Side Face 2.

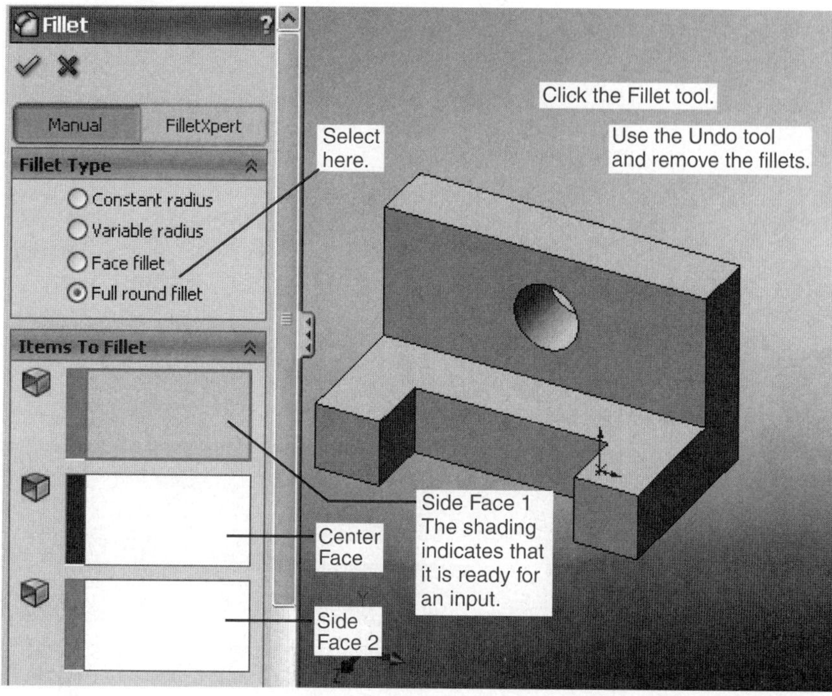

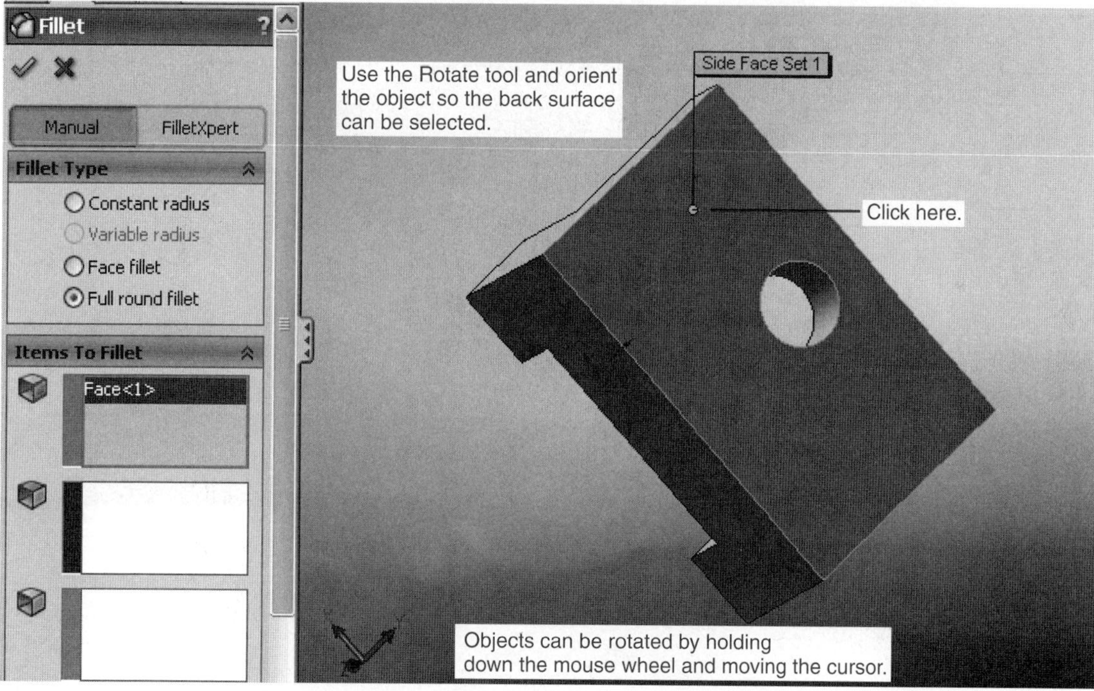

Figure 3-12

In this example, the default fillet radius value of **10** will be used.

3. Use the **Rotate** tool and orient the object so that the back surface can be selected.

> **TIP**
>
> Objects can be rotated by holding down the mouse wheel and moving the cursor.

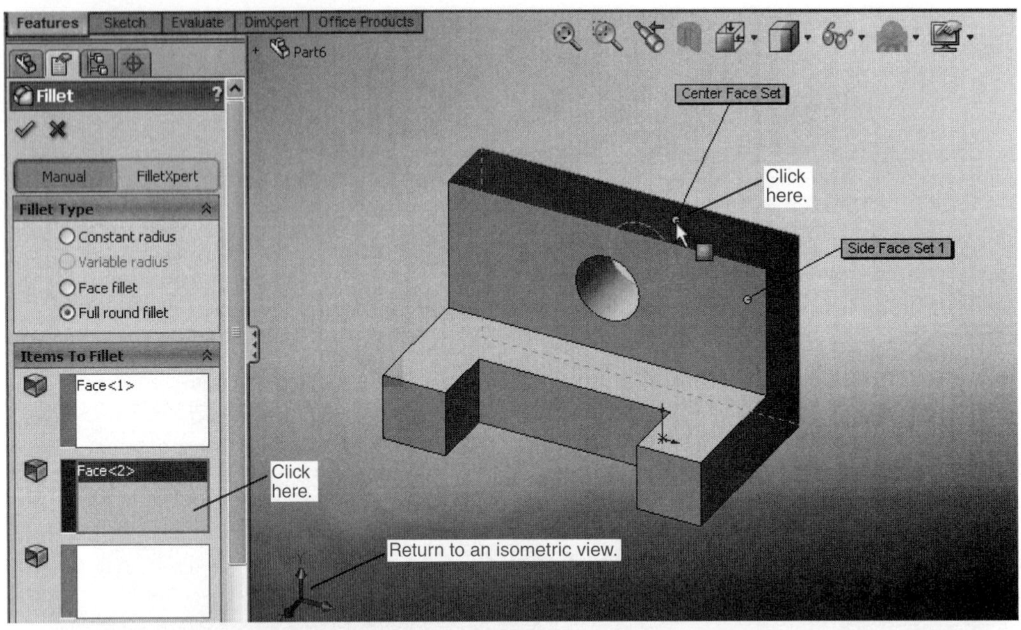

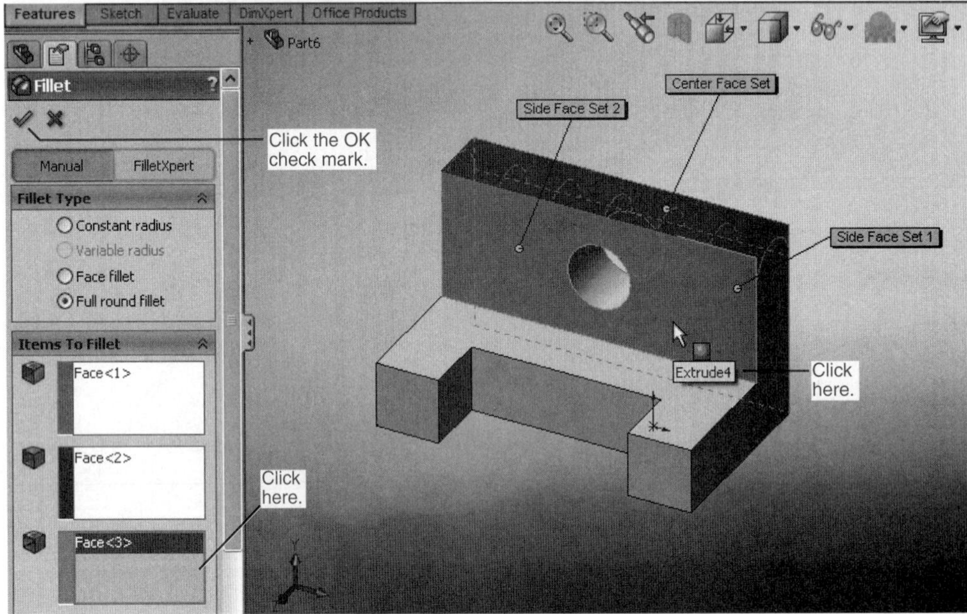

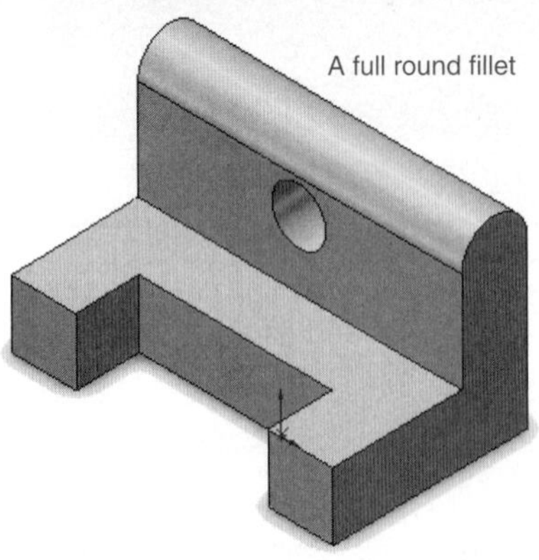

Figure 3-12 ***(continued)***

4. Click the back surface.

   The back surface is defined as **Side Face 1.**

5. Reorient the object to an isometric view.
6. Click the middle box in the **Items to Fillet** box and click the top surface of the object.

   The top surface is defined as the **Center Face.**

7. Click the lower of the three boxes in the **Items to Fillet** box and click the front surface of the object as shown.

The front surface is defined as **Side Face 2.** A preview of the fillet will appear.

8. Click the OK check mark.

3-8 CHAMFER

A ***chamfer*** is a slanted surface added to a corner of an object. Chamfers are usually manufactured at 45° but may be made at any angle. Chamfers are defined using either an angle and a distance (5 × 45°) or by two distances (5 × 5). A vertex chamfer may also be defined.

To Define a Chamfer Using an Angle and a Distance

See Figure 3-13.

1. Use the **Undo** tool and remove the fillet created in the last section.
2. Click the **Chamfer** tool.

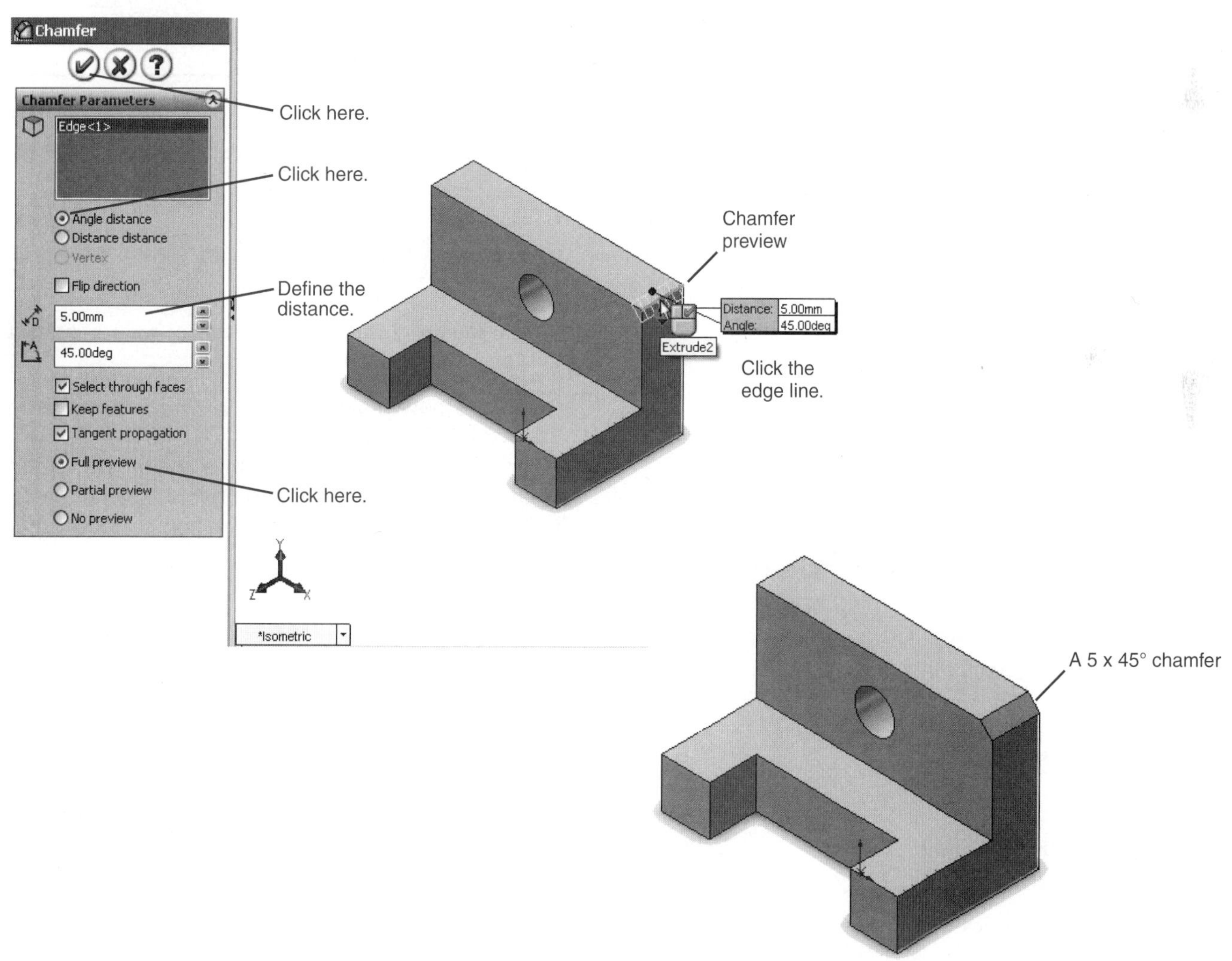

Figure 3-13

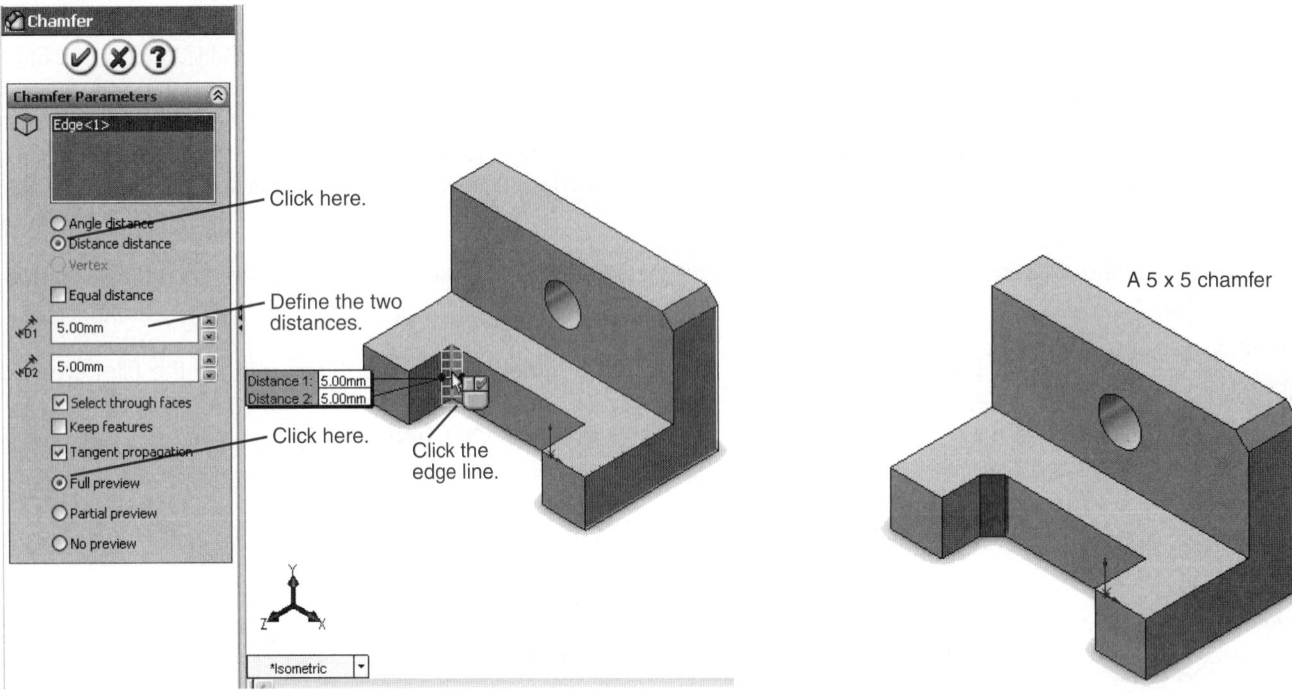

Figure 3-14

3. Click the **Angle distance** button.
4. Define the chamfer distance as **5** and accept the **45°** default value.
5. Click the top side edge line as shown.
6. Click the OK check mark.

To Define a Chamfer Using Two Distances

See Figure 3-14.

1. Click the **Chamfer** tool.
2. Click the **Distance distance** button.
3. Define the two distances as **5.00mm** each.

In this example the two distances are equal. Distances of different lengths may be used.

4. Click the inside vertical line as shown.
5. Click the OK check mark.

To Define a Vertex Chamfer

See Figure 3-15.

1. Click the **Chamfer** tool.
2. Click the **Vertex** button.

Three distance boxes will appear.

3. Define the three distances.

In this example three equal distances of **5.00mm** were used. The three distances need not be equal.

4. Click the lower top corner point as shown.
5. Click the OK check mark.

3-9 REVOLVED BOSS/BASE

The **Revolved Boss/Base** tool rotates a contour about an axis line. See Figure 3-16.

1. Start a new drawing, click the **Sketch** tool, and click the **Top Plane** option.
2. Use the **Sketch** tools to draw a line on the screen and then draw a 2D shape next to the line.
3. Change the drawing's orientation to **Isometric.**

Approximate the shape shown.

4. Click the **Features** tool, then click the **Revolved Boss/Base** tool.
5. Click the **Selected Contours** box, then click the contour on the screen.

> ***Note:***
> If the **Selected Contours** box is already shaded, it means that it has been activated automatically. Click the contour directly.

6. Click the axis box at the top of the **Revolve Parameters Properties Manager.**
7. Click the axis line on the screen

A preview of the revolved object will appear.

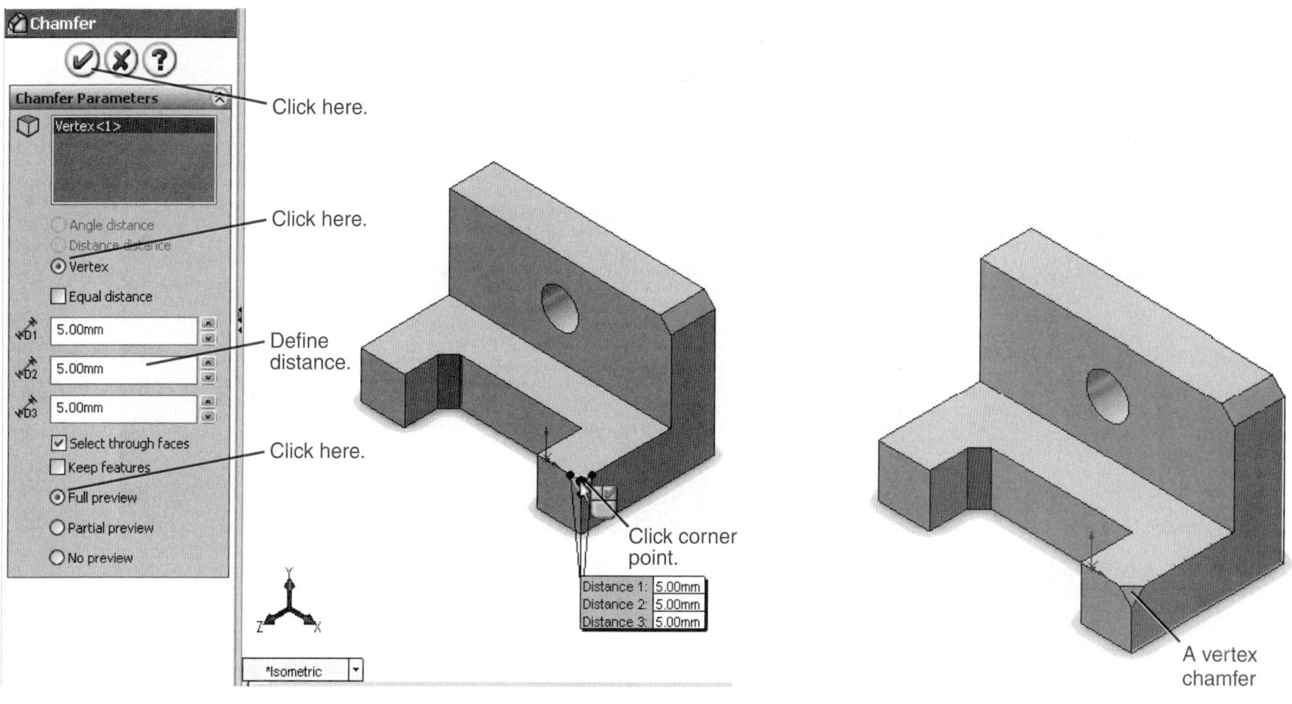

Figure 3-15

8. Click the OK check mark.

Figure 3-17 shows an example of a sphere created using the Revolve tool.

3-10 REVOLVED CUT

The Revolved Cut tool is used to cut revolved sections out of objects. Figure 3-18 shows a 60 × 100 × 40 box. Create a new sketch plane (**Sketch**) on the top surface of the box and use the **Centerpoint Arc** tool to draw an arc of radius **40** centered about the lower corner of the top surface as shown.

1. Click the **Revolved Cut** tool.
2. Click the **Selected Contours** box and select the area within the arc as the contour.
3. Click the **Axis of Revolution** box.
4. Click the top line as shown identifying the axis of revolution.

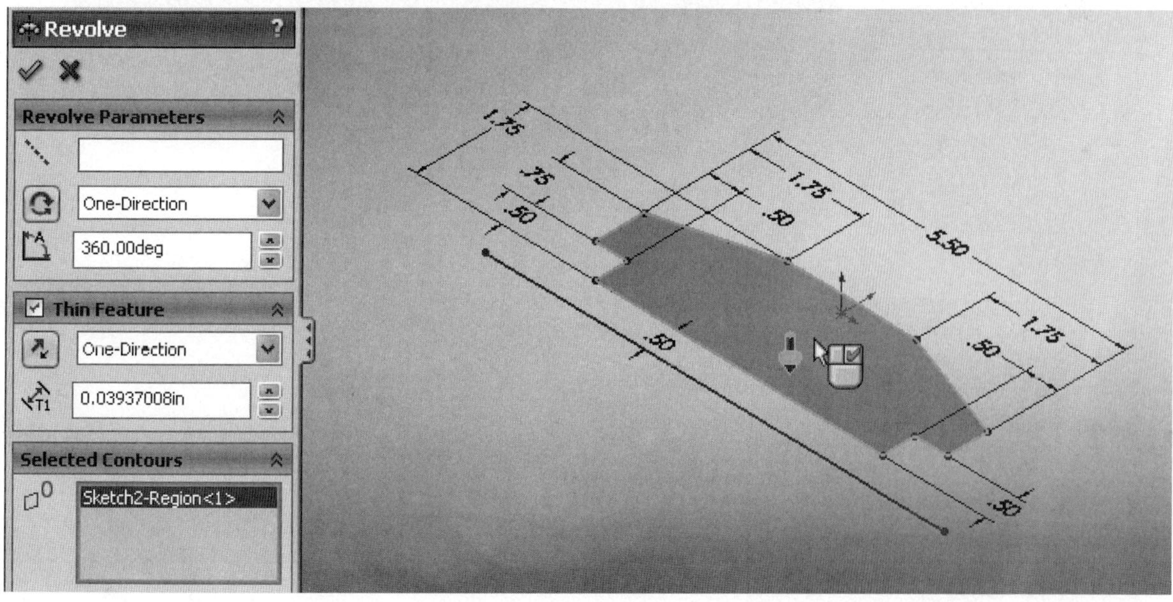

Figure 3-16

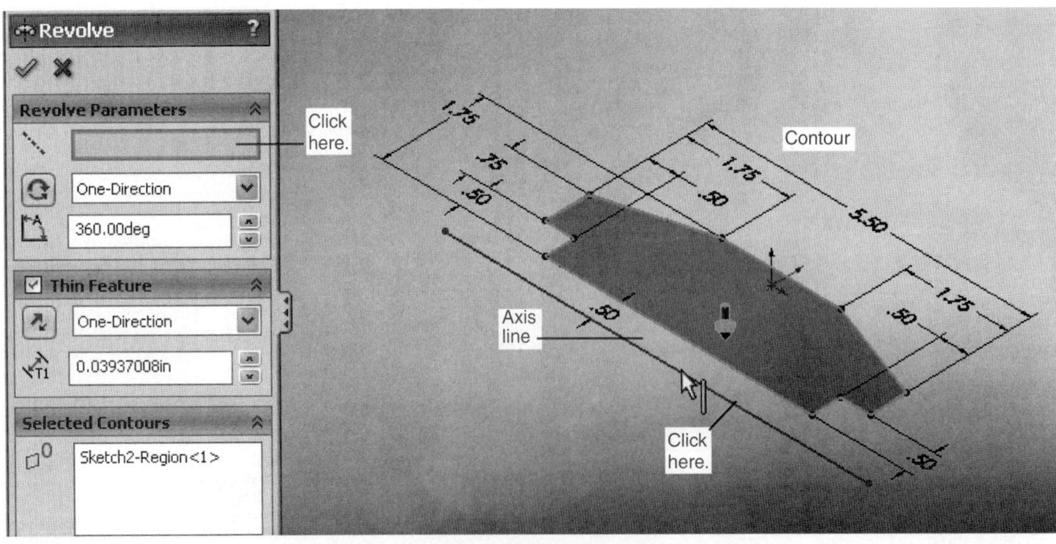

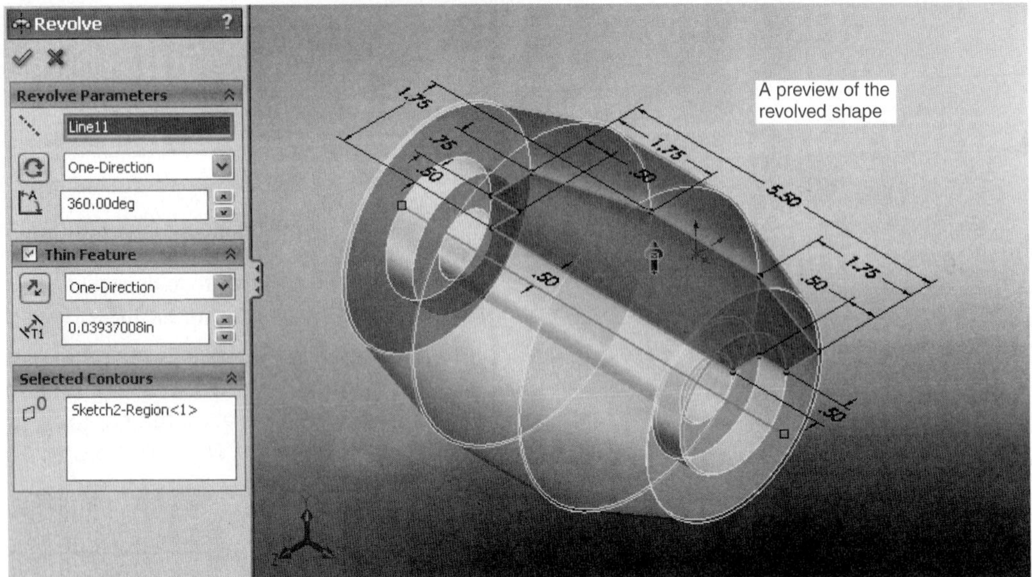

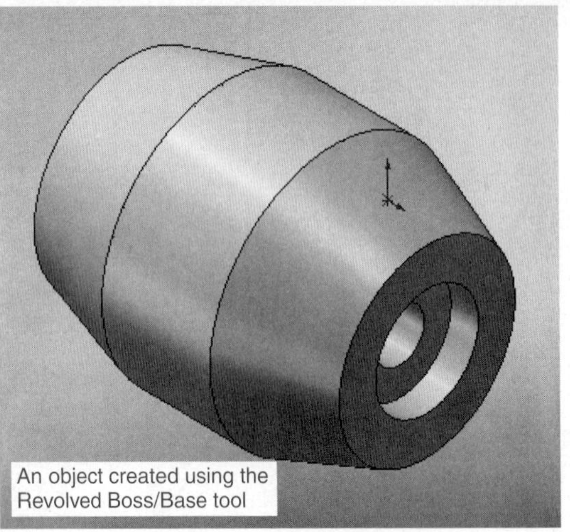

Figure 3-16 ***(continued)***

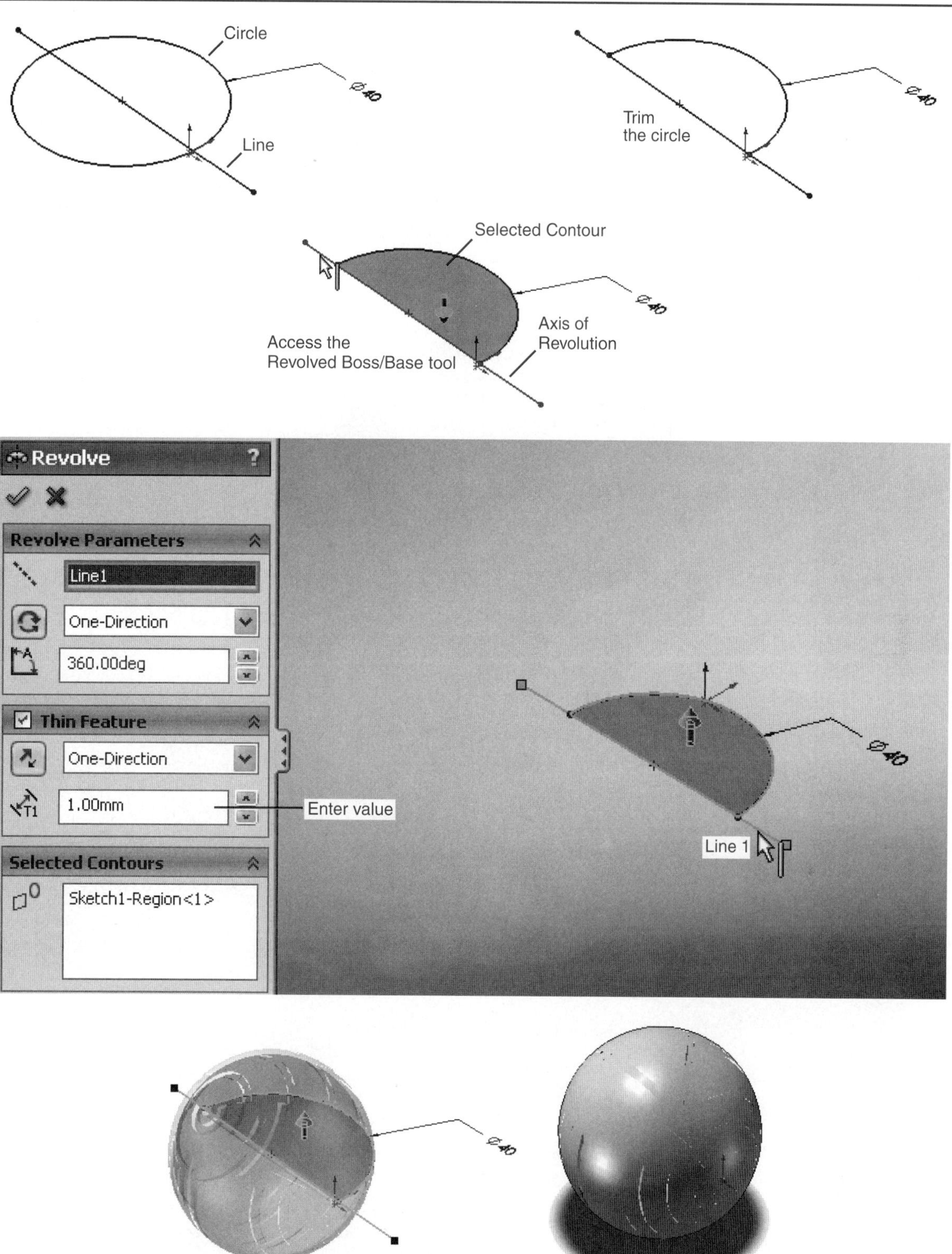

Circle
Ø40
Line
Trim
the circle
Ø40
Selected Contour
Ø40
Access the
Revolved Boss/Base tool
Axis of
Revolution
Revolve
Revolve Parameters
Line1
One-Direction
360.00deg
Thin Feature
One-Direction
1.00mm
Enter value
Selected Contours
Sketch1-Region<1>
Ø40
Line 1
Ø40
If necessary, click the Reverse Direction box
in the Thin Feature box.
Click the OK check mark.

Figure 3-17

5. Set the **Direction Thickness** for **5.**
6. Click the **Reverse Direction** box.
7. Click the OK check mark.

   The **Bodies to keep** dialog box will appear.

8. Click **Select bodies** in the **Bodies to keep** dialog box.
9. Click **Body 1.**
10. Click **OK.**

3-11 REFERENCE PLANES

Reference planes are planes that are not part of an existing object. Up to now if we needed a new sketch plane, we selected an existing plane on the object. Consider the Ø3.0 × 3.50 cylinder shown in Figure 3-19. The cylinder was drawn with its base on the top plane. How do we create a hole through the rounded sides of the cylinder? If we right-click the rounded surface, no **Sketch** tool will appear.

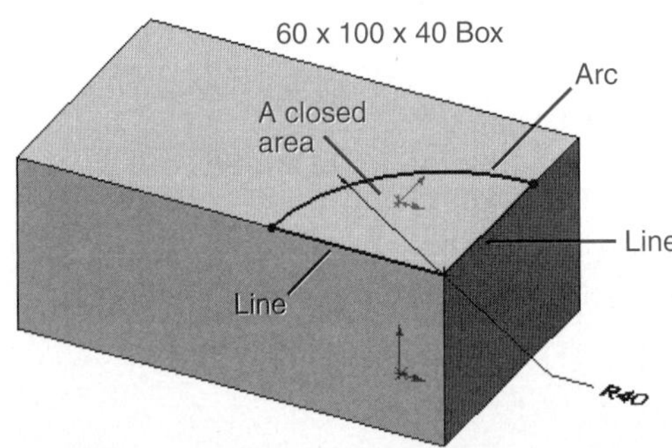

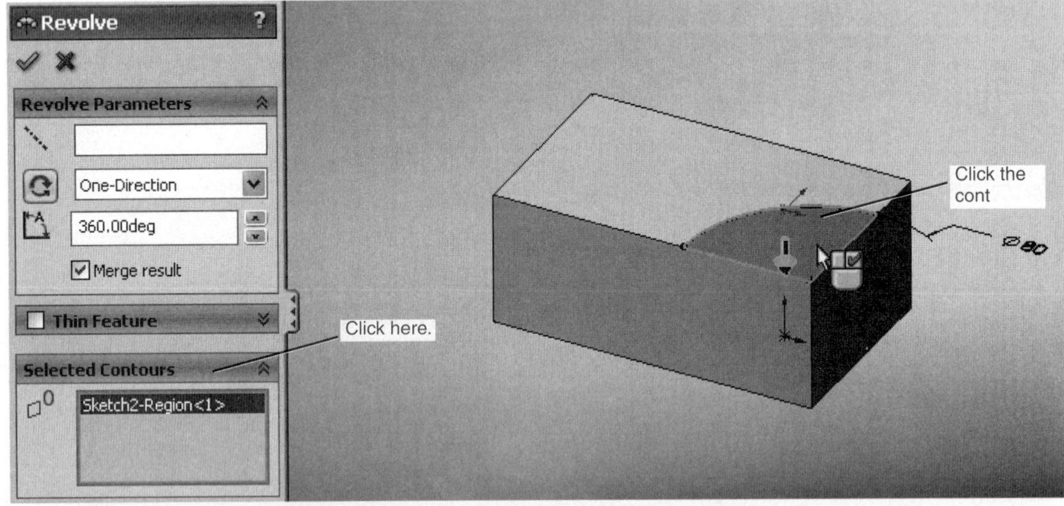

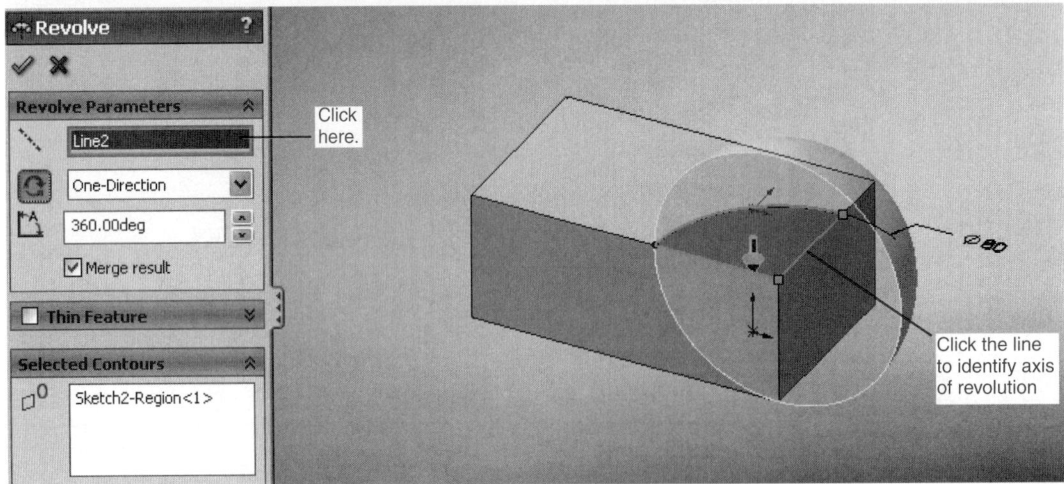

Figure 3-18

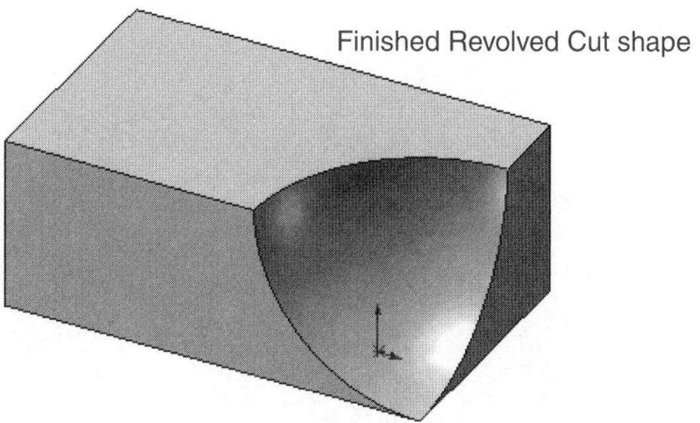

Figure 3-18 *(continued)*

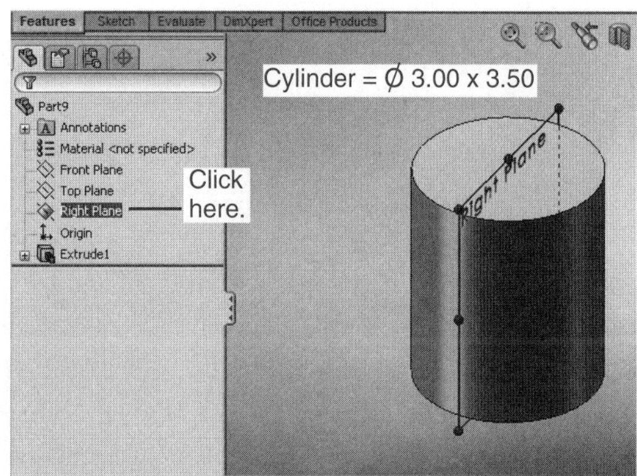

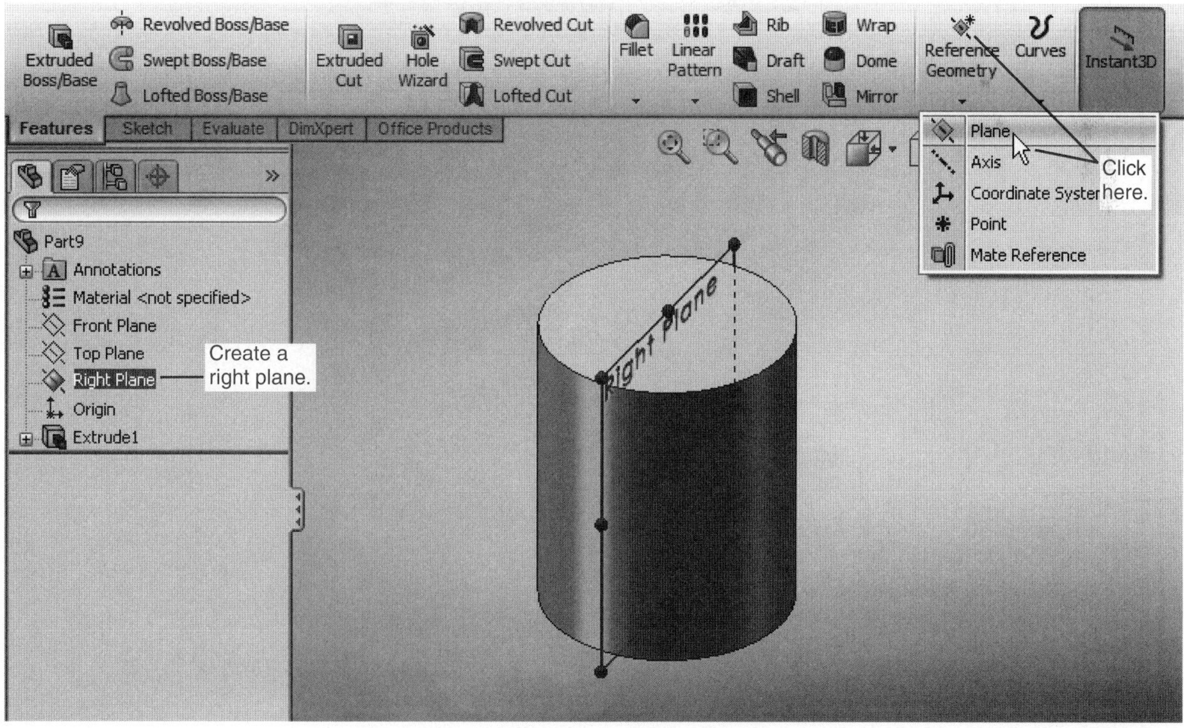

Figure 3-19

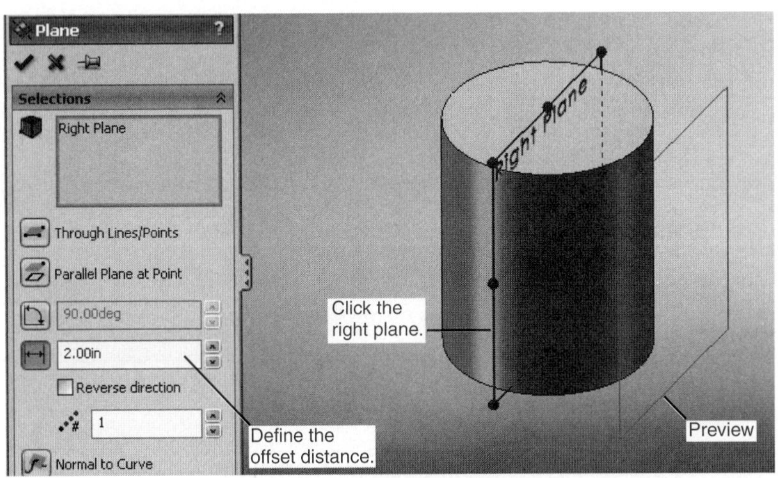

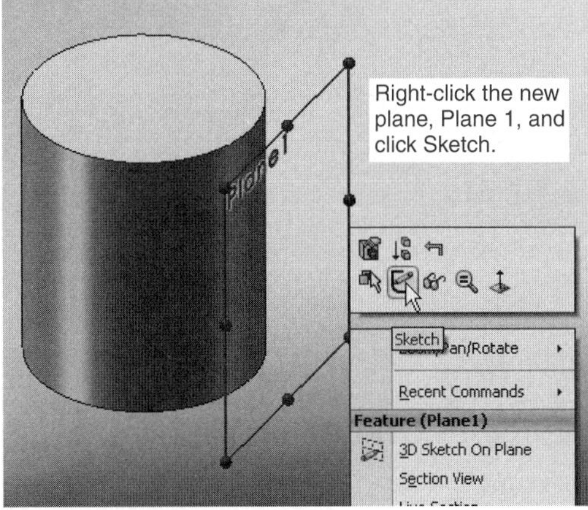

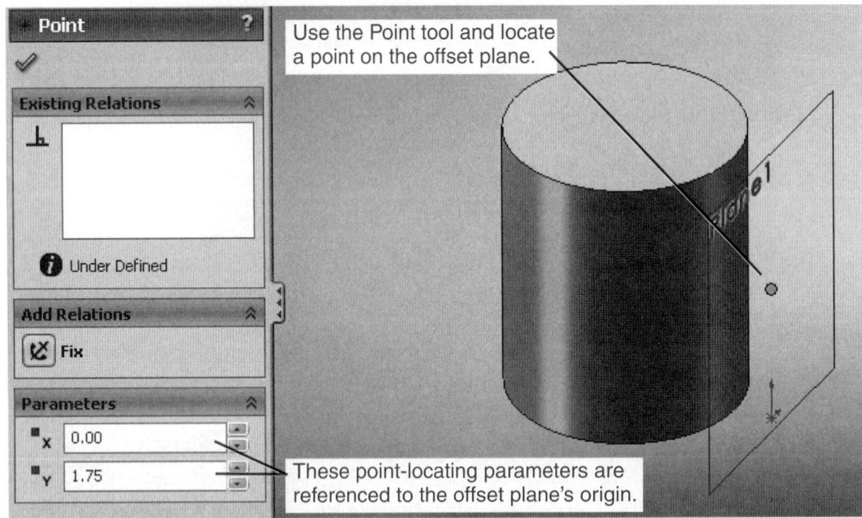

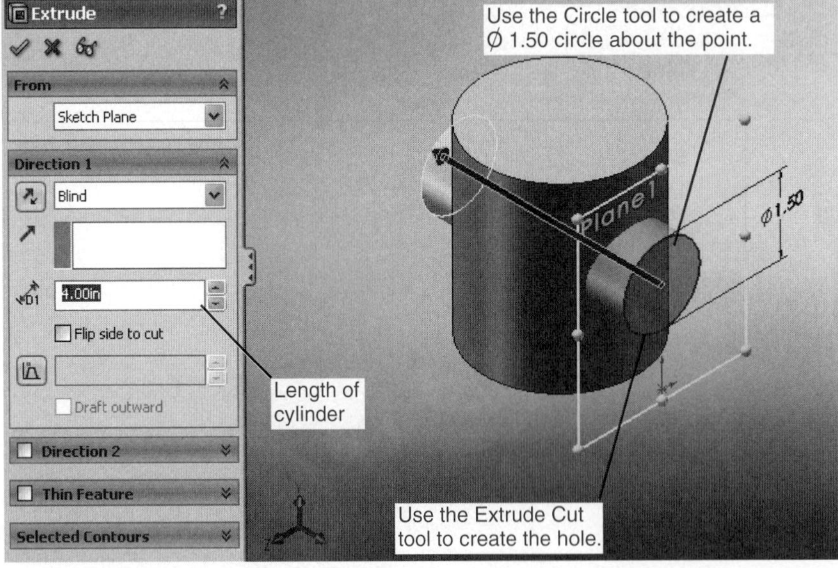

Figure 3-19 ***(continued)***

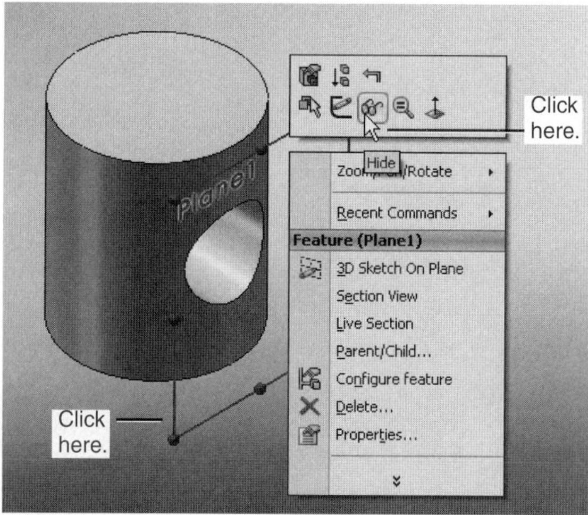

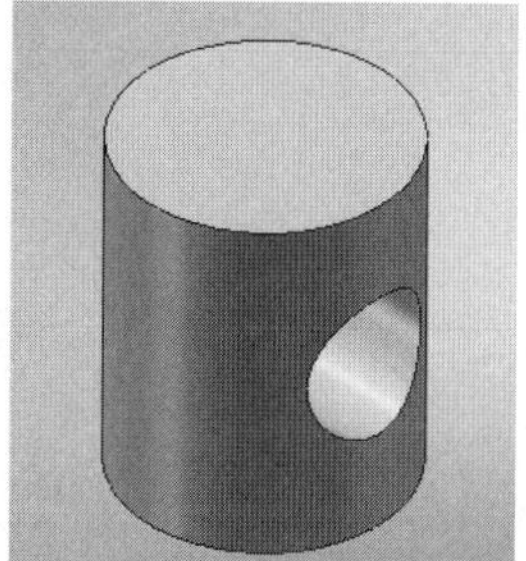
The finished cylinder with a hole

Figure 3-19 *(continued)*

To Create a Reference Plane

1. Click the **Right Plane** tool.
2. Right-click the **Right Plane** tool and click the **Show** tool to assure that the right plane is visible.
3. Click the **Reference** tool located in the **Features** group and select the **Plane** option.

The **Plane** box will appear. See Figure 3-19.

4. Set the offset distance for **2.00.**
5. Click one of the lines that show the right plane.
6. Click the OK check mark.

The new reference plane is defined as **Plane 1.**

7. Right-click **Plane 1** and click the **Insert Sketch** tool.
8. Use the **Point** tool and locate a point at **X = 0.00, Y = 1.75** on Plane 1.
9. Click the **Circle** tool and draw a **Ø1.50** circle on Plane 1 using the defined point.
10. Click the **Features** tool and click the **Extruded Cut** tool.
11. Define the length of the cutting cylinder as **4.00** to assure that it passes completely through the Ø3.00 cylinder.
12. Click the OK check mark.
13. Hide Plane 1 and the right plane by right-clicking on the planes and selecting the **Hide** option.

3-12 LOFTED BOSS/BASE

The **Lofted Boss/Base** tool is used to create a shape between two planes, each of which contains a defined shape. Before drawing a lofted shape we must first draw two shapes on two different planes. In this example a square is lofted to a circle. See Figure 3-20.

1. Set the **Units** for millimeters and access a top plane.
2. Right-click the **Top Plane** heading and click the **Show** option.
3. Click the **Features** tool and click the **Reference** tool. Select the **Plane** option. (See Figure 3-19.) The **Plane** box will appear.
4. Click the existing top plane.
5. Set the distance between the planes for **60mm.**
6. Click the OK check mark.

A new plane, **Plane 1,** will appear.

7. Right-click one of the outline lines of the top plane and select the **Sketch** option.

The view orientation will automatically change to a top view.

8. Sketch an approximate square about the origin. Right-click the mouse and click the **Select** option.

The **Centerline** line and **Line Properties** tools will be used to center the square about the origin.

9. Access the **Centerline** tool (located with the **Sketch** tools) and draw a centerline diagonally across the approximate square. Right-click the mouse and click the **Select** option.
10. Click the origin.
11. Click and hold the **<Ctrl>** key, and click the diagonal centerline. Release the **<Ctrl>** key.
12. Click the **Midpoint** option in the **Add Relations** box.

The midpoint of the diagonal centerline will align with the origin.

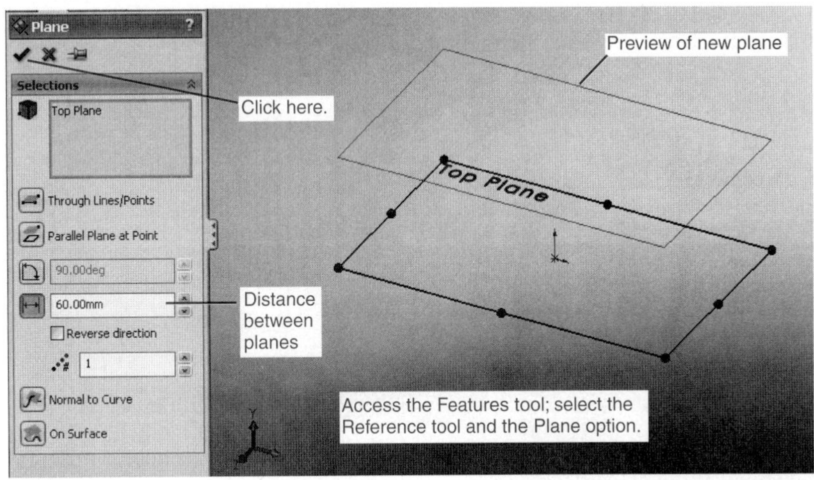

Plane
Selections
Top Plane
Through Lines/Points
Parallel Plane at Point
90.00deg
60.00mm
Reverse direction
1
Normal to Curve
On Surface
Preview of new plane
Click here.
Top Plane
Distance between planes
Access the Features tool; select the Reference tool and the Plane option.

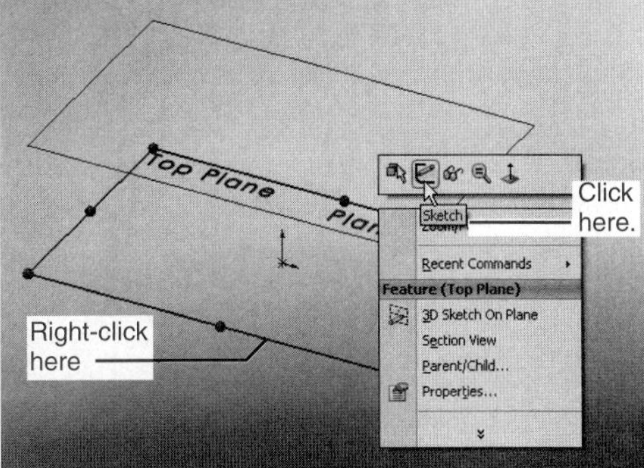

Top Plane
Click here.
Sketch
Recent Commands
Feature (Top Plane)
3D Sketch On Plane
Section View
Parent/Child...
Properties...
Right-click here

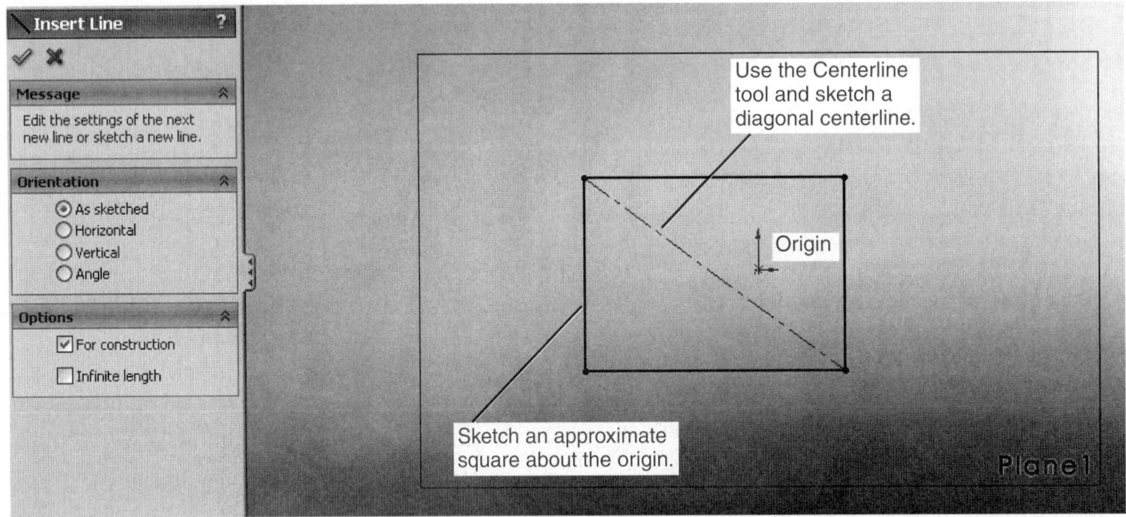

Insert Line
Message
Edit the settings of the next new line or sketch a new line.
Orientation
As sketched
Horizontal
Vertical
Angle
Options
For construction
Infinite length
Use the Centerline tool and sketch a diagonal centerline.
Origin
Sketch an approximate square about the origin.
Plane1

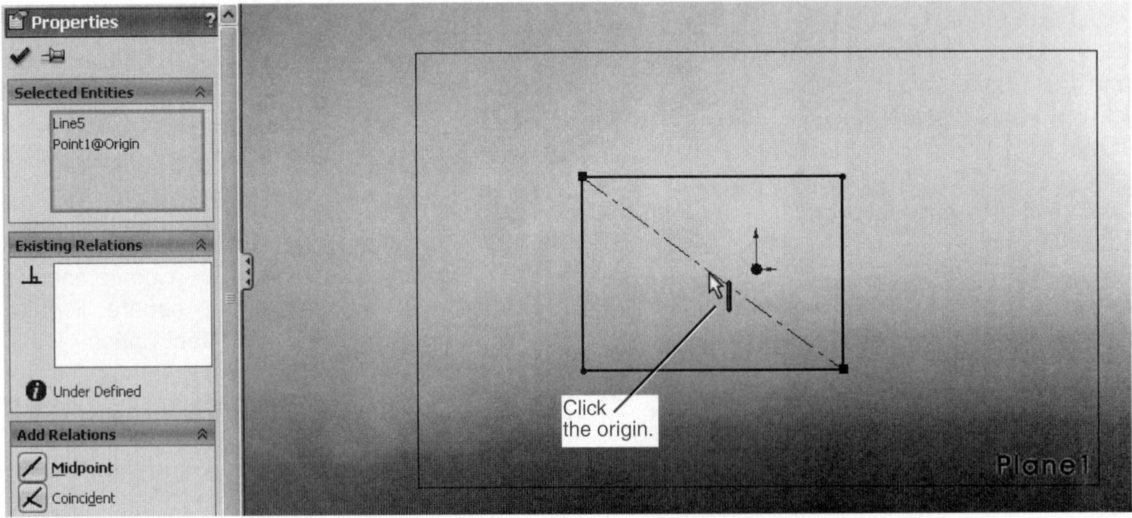

Properties
Selected Entities
Line5
Point1@Origin
Existing Relations
Under Defined
Add Relations
Midpoint
Coincident
Click the origin.
Plane1

Figure 3-20

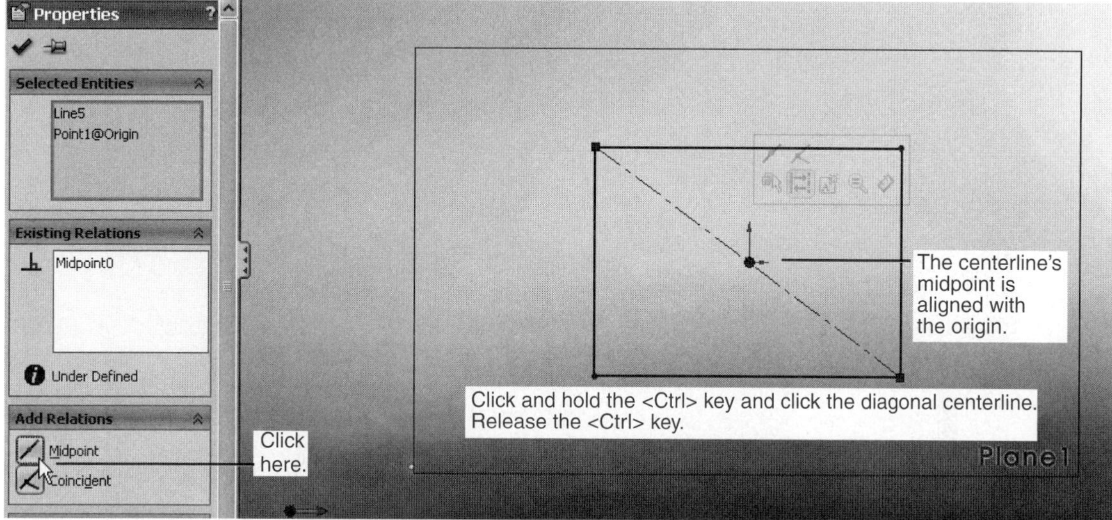

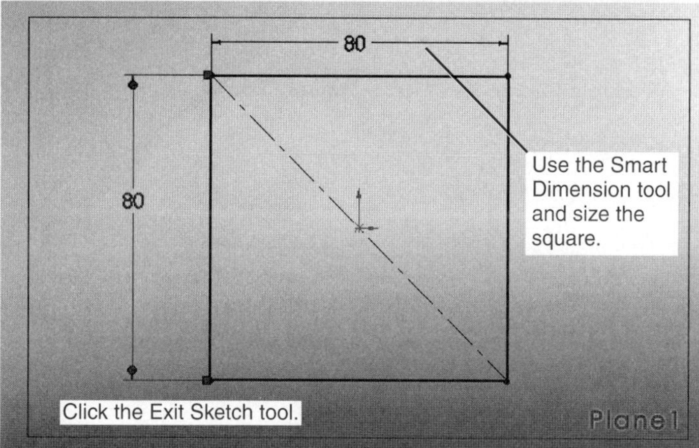

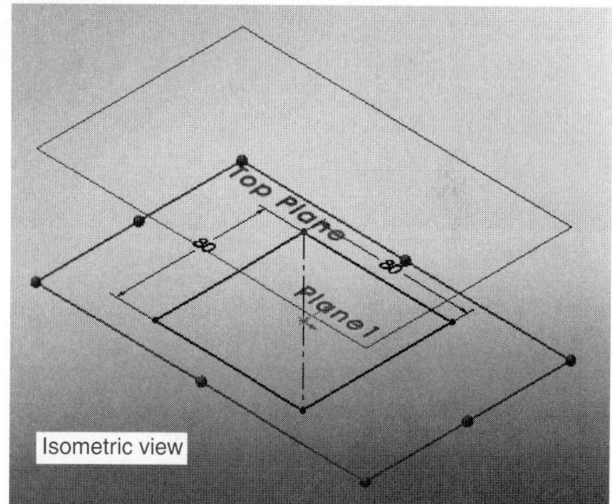

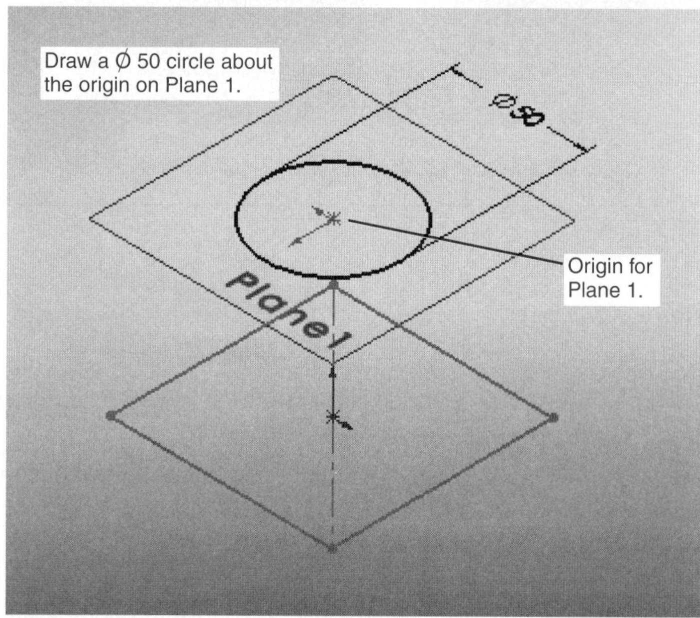

Figure 3-20 *(continued)*

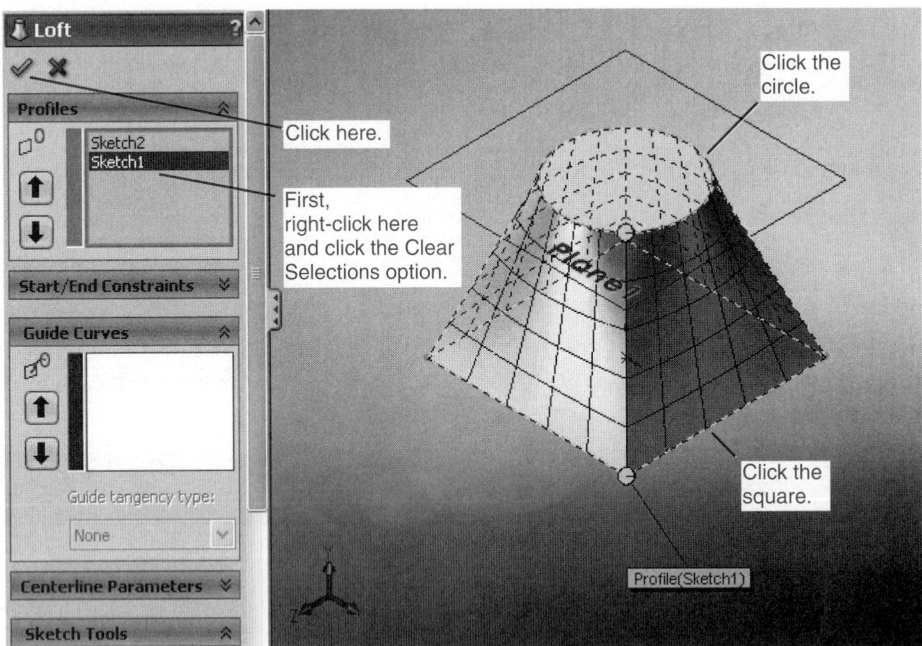

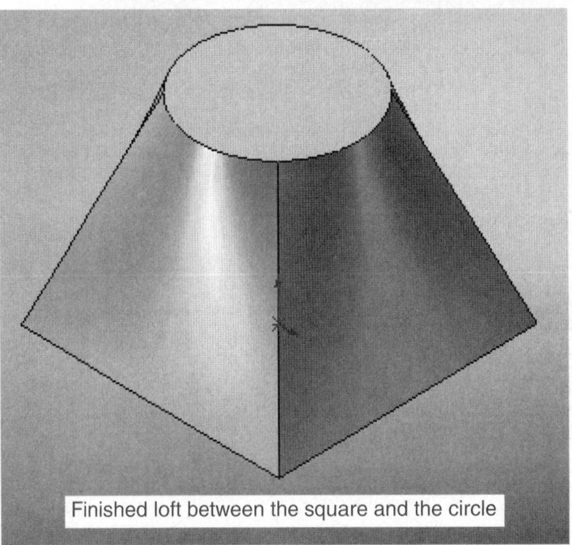

Finished loft between the square and the circle

Figure 3-20 *(continued)*

13. Use the **Smart Dimension** tool and size the square.

    In this example, dimensions of **80** were used.

14. Change the view orientation to **Isometric.**
15. Exit the sketch.

> **TIP**
>
> You can exit a sketch either by clicking the **Exit Sketch** tool on the **Sketch** toolbar or by clicking the **Exit Sketch** tool in the upper right corner of the drawing screen.

16. Right-click the **Plane 1** heading and click the **Sketch** option.

A new origin will appear on Plane 1. We can now sketch on Plane 1.

17. Sketch a circle about the origin in Plane 1. Use the **Smart Dimension** tool and size the circle to **Ø50.**
18. Right-click the mouse and click the **Select** option. Click the **Exit Sketch** tool.

    The **Lofted Boss/Base** tool can now be applied.

19. Click the **Features** tool and click the **Lofted Boss/Base** tool.

Top Plane
Ø.50
2.50
Origin

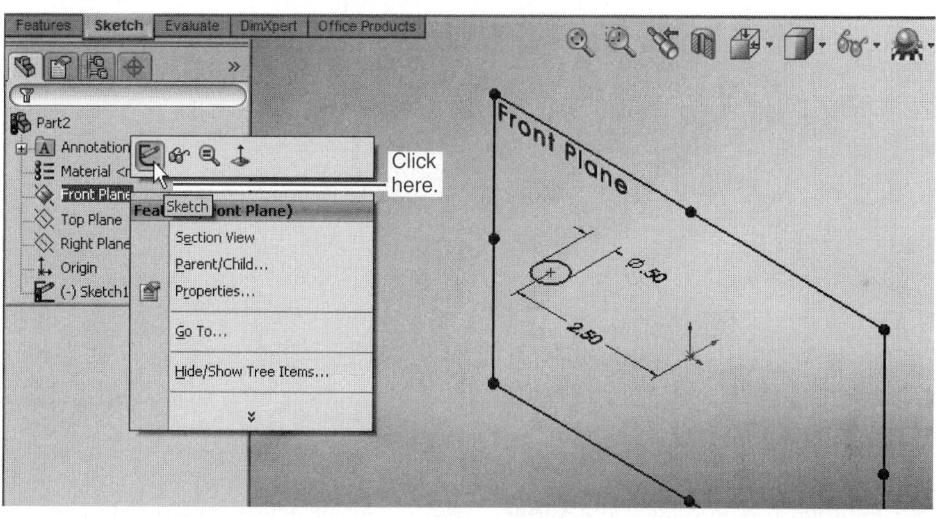
Features
Sketch
Evaluate
DimXpert
Office Products
Part2
Annotations
Material
Front Plane
Top Plane
Right Plane
Origin
(-) Sketch1
Sketch
ont Plane)
Section View
Parent/Child...
Properties...
Go To...
Hide/Show Tree Items...
Click here.
Front Plane
Ø.50
2.50

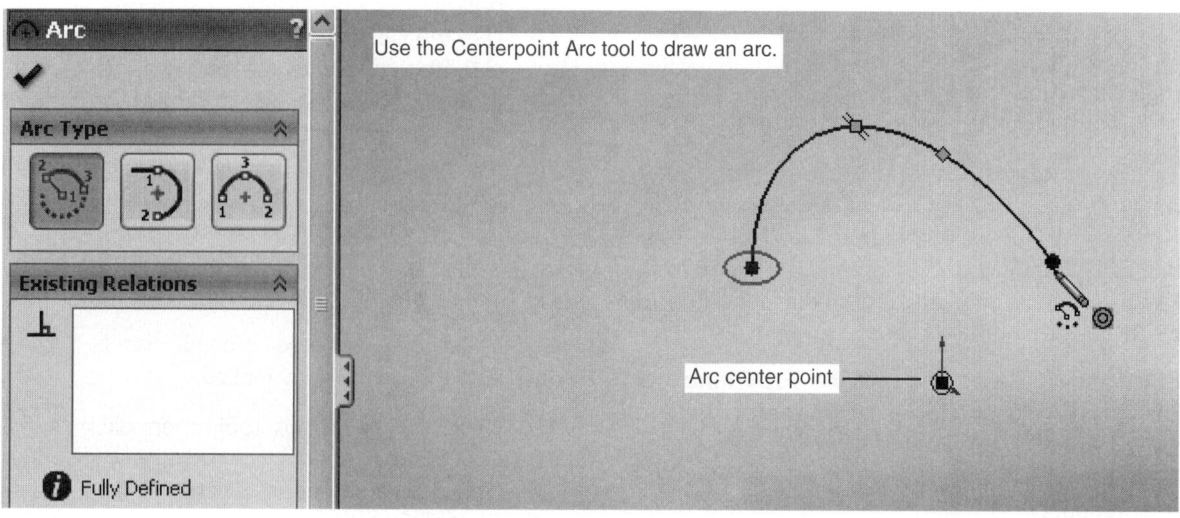
Arc
Arc Type
Existing Relations
Fully Defined
Use the Centerpoint Arc tool to draw an arc.
Arc center point

Figure 3-21

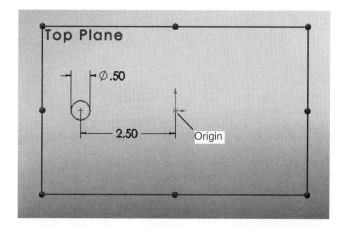

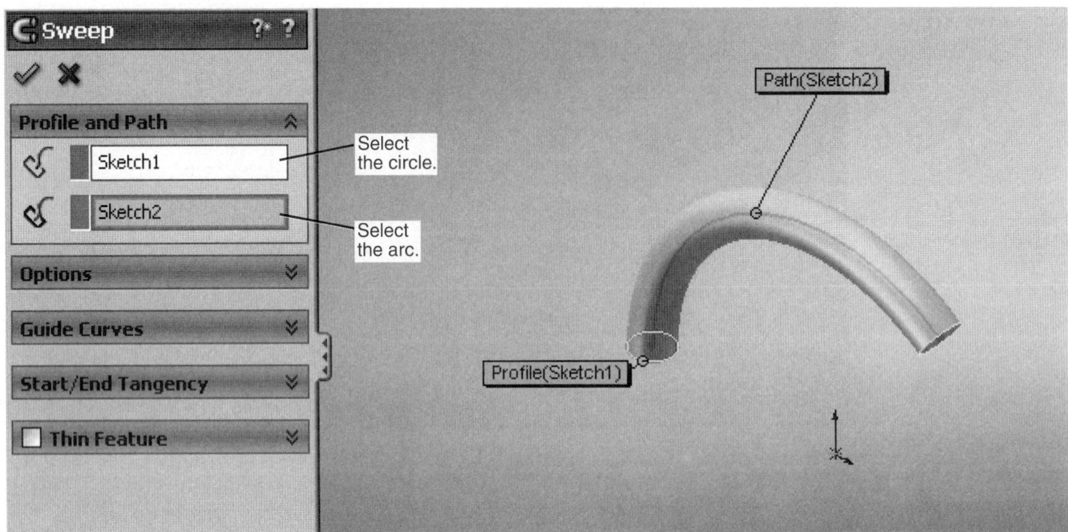

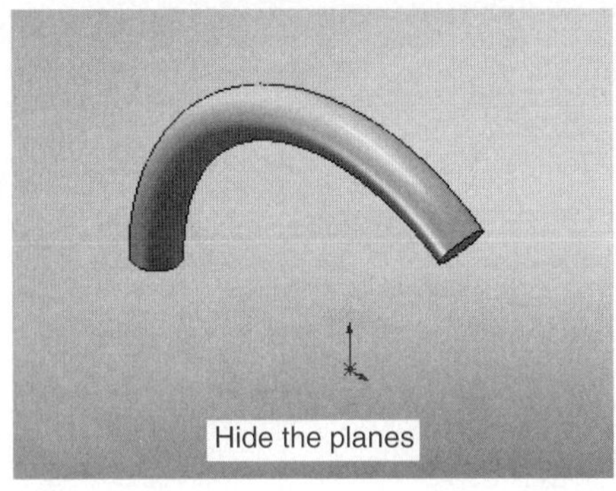

Figure 3-21 *(continued)*

20. Right-click the **Profiles** box and click the **Clear Selections** option.
21. Click the square, then click the circle.
22. Click the OK check mark. Hide the planes.

3-13 SWEPT BOSS/BASE

The **Swept Boss/Base** tool is used to sweep a profile along a path line. As with the **Lofted Boss/Base** tool, existing shapes must be present before the **Swept Boss/Base** tool can be applied. In this example, a Ø0.50 circle will be swept along an arc with a 2.50 radius for 120°. See Figure 3-21.

1. Start a new drawing and click the **Top Plane** tool. Use the **Circle** and **Smart Dimension** tools to draw a **Ø0.50** circle **2.50** from the origin.
2. Change the drawing screen to an isometric orientation.
3. Right-click the mouse and click the **Select** option.
4. Click the **Exit Sketch** tool.

We are now going to create a new sketch on a different sketch plane, so we must exit the top plane.

5. Right-click **Front Plane** and click the **Sketch** option.
6. Use the **Centerpoint Arc** tool to draw an arc with a **2.50** radius with the origin as its center point through 120°. Click the origin, expand the arc until it intersects with the circle's center point, click the center point, and move the cursor until the arc is approximately 120°. Define the arc's length as **120°** in the **Parameters** box.
7. Click the OK check mark.
8. Click the **Exit Sketch** tool.

This completes the second sketch. The **Swept Boss/Base** tool can now be applied.

9. Click the **Features** tool, then click the **Swept Boss/Base** tool.
10. Select the circle as **Sketch 1** and the arc as **Sketch 2.**
11. Click the OK check mark.

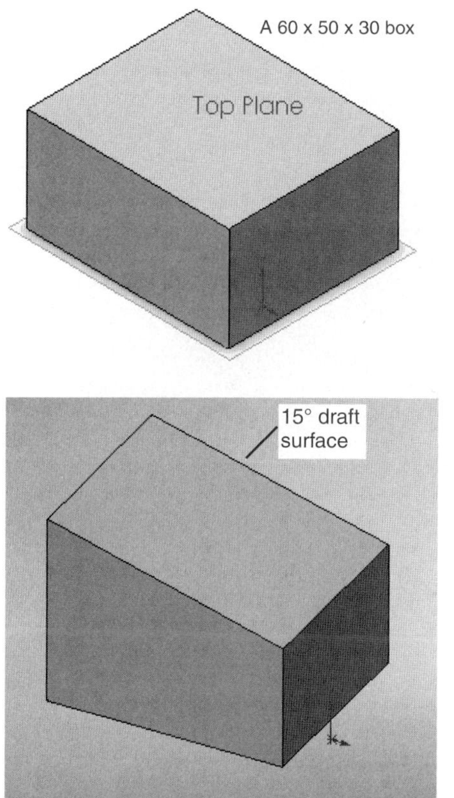

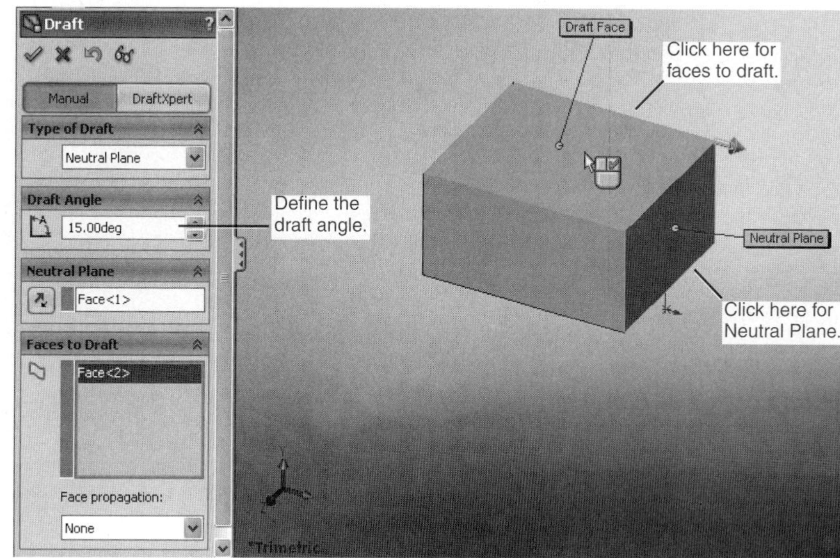

Figure 3-22

3-14 DRAFT

The **Draft** tool is used to create slanted surfaces. See Figure 3-22, which shows a 60 × 50 × 30 box. In this example a 15° slanted surface will be added to the top surface.

1. Click the **Draft** tool.
2. Select the **Neutral Plane** by clicking the right vertical face of the box.
3. Define the **Draft Angle** as **15°.**
4. Select the draft face by clicking the top surface of the box.

The draft angle will be applied to the draft face relative to the 90° angle between the two faces.

5. Click the OK check mark.

Figure 3-23 shows a slanted surface created by making the top surface the neutral plane and the front surface the draft plane.

3-15 LINEAR SKETCH PATTERN

The **Linear Sketch Pattern** tool is used to create rectangular patterns based on a given object.

Figure 3-24 shows a 15 × 20 × 10 box located on an 80 × 170 × 5 base. The box is located 10 from each edge of the base as shown.

1. Click the **Linear Sketch Pattern** tool.

> ***Note:***
> The box should be selected automatically, but if is not, use the **Features to Pattern** tool to select the box.

2. Define **Direction 1** by clicking the back top line as shown.
3. Define the spacing as **30.00.**

Spacing is the distance between two of the objects in the pattern as measured from the same point on each object, for example, the distance from the lower front corner on one object to the lower front corner of the next object.

4. Define the number of columns in the pattern.
5. Define **Direction 2,** the spacing for **Direction 2,** and the number of rows in the pattern.

A preview of the pattern will appear.

6. Click the OK check mark.

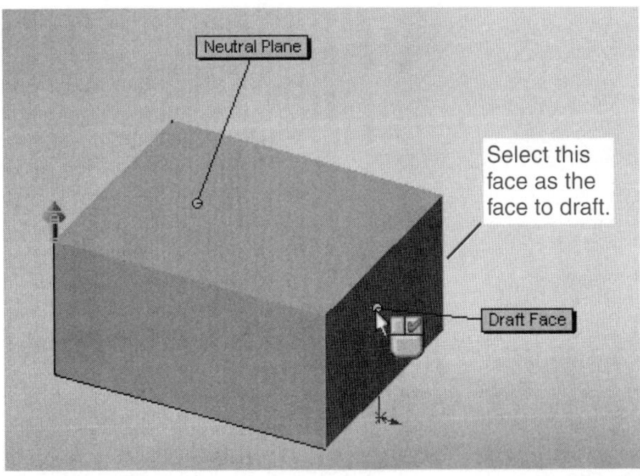

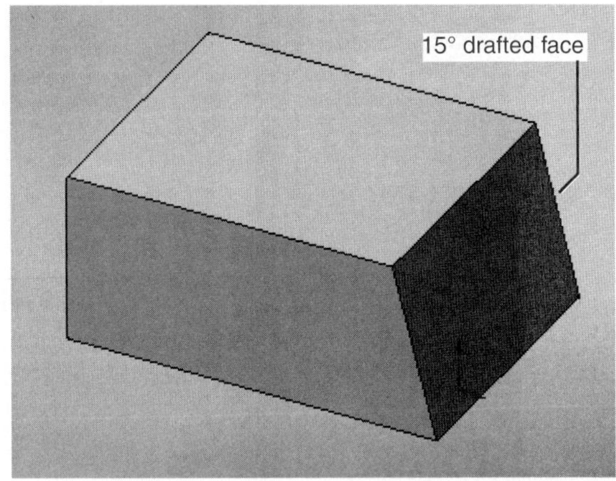

Figure 3-23

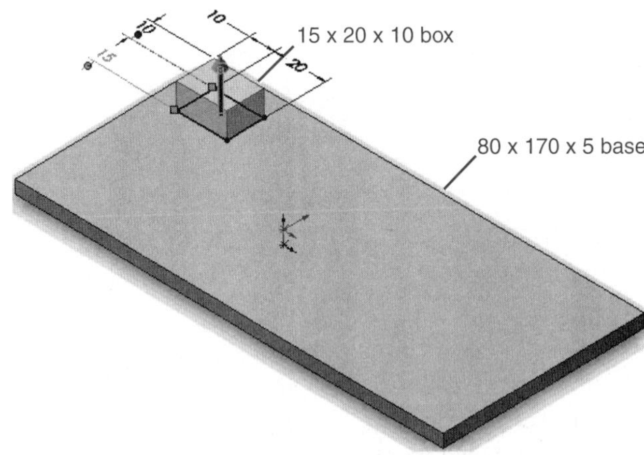

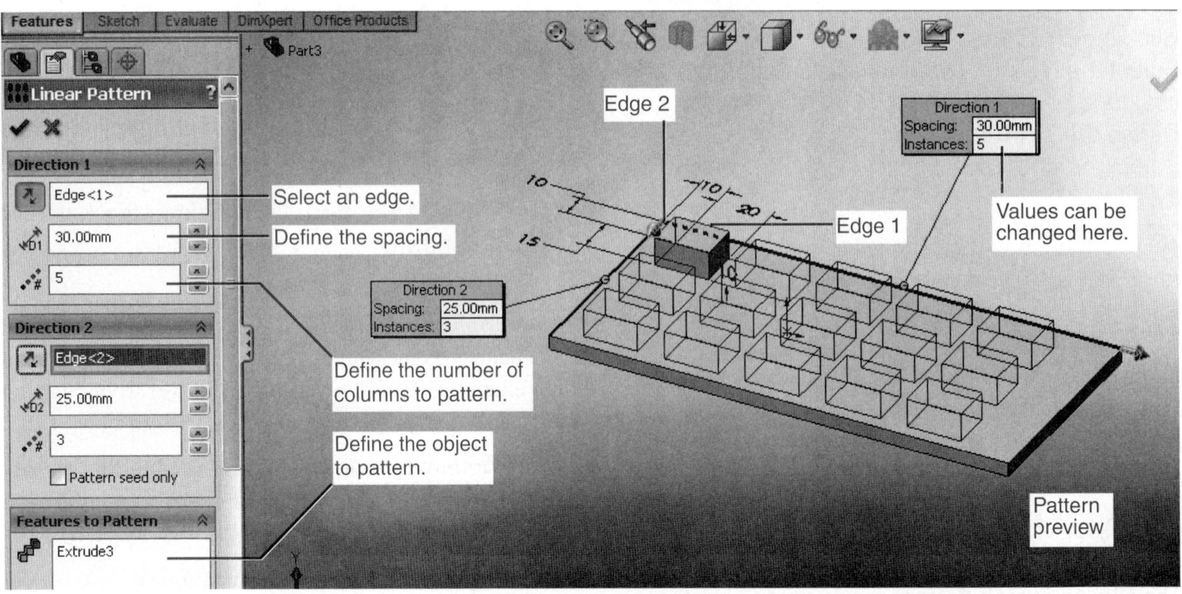

Figure 3-24

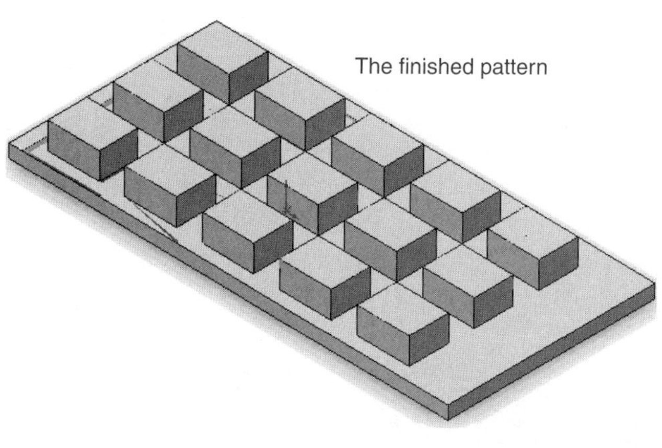

Figure 3-24 *(continued)*

3-16 CIRCULAR SKETCH PATTERN

The **Circular Sketch Pattern** tool is used to create circular patterns about an origin. See Figure 3-25.

1. Create a **Ø160** × **10** cylinder.
2. Create a **Ø30** hole centered about the Ø160 cylinder's origin.
3. Define an axis for the Ø30 hole by accessing the **Reference** tool in the **Features** tools and then clicking the **Axis** option.
4. Click the **Cylindrical/Conical Face** option in the **Axis Properties Manager** and click the inside surface of the Ø30 hole.

   An axis should appear in the center of the hole.

5. Right-click the top surface of the cylinder and click the **Sketch** option.
6. Sketch a **Ø20** circle **60** from the surface's center point.

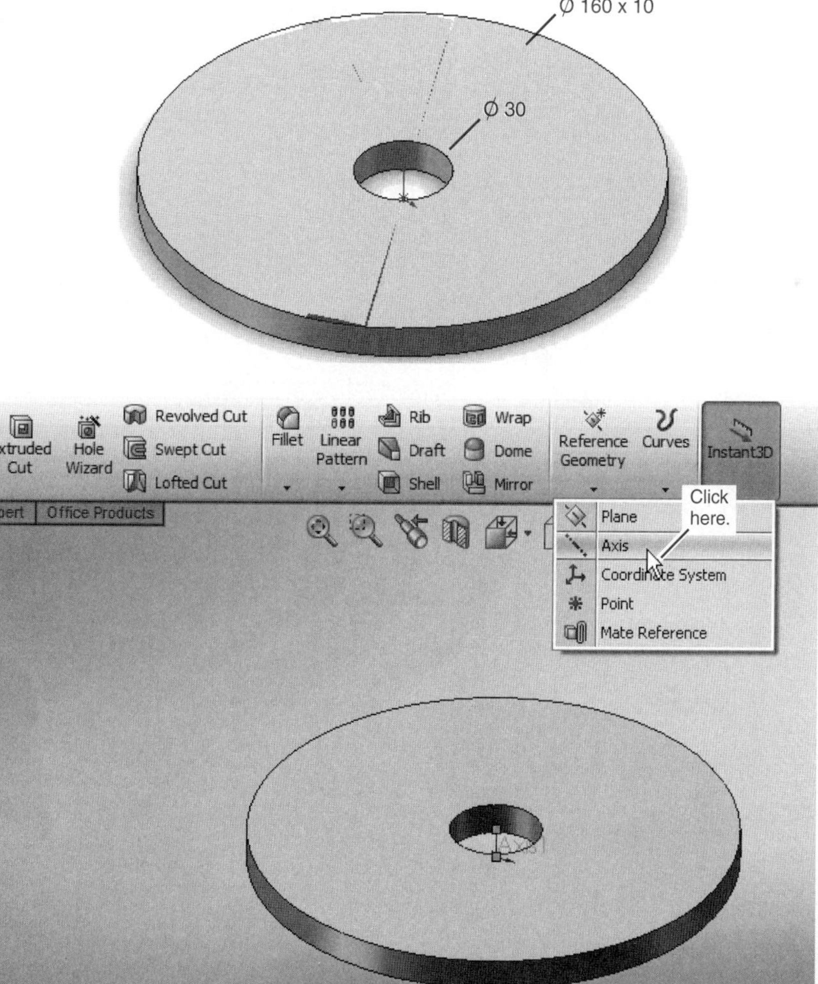

Figure 3-25

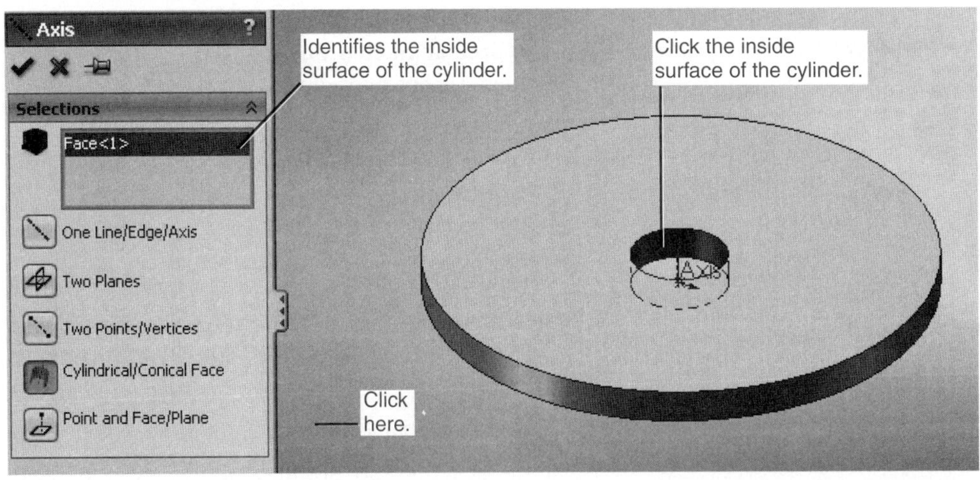

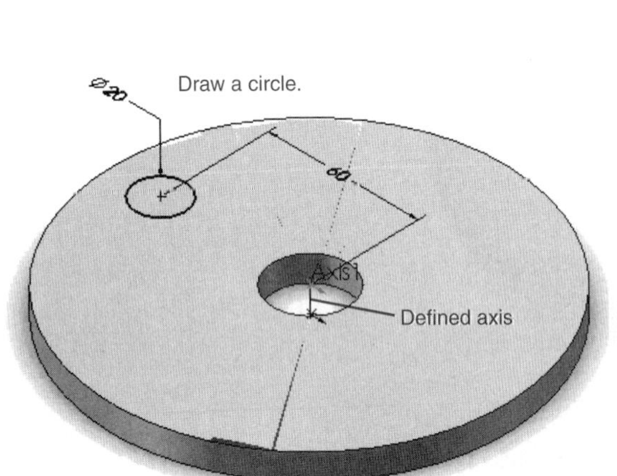

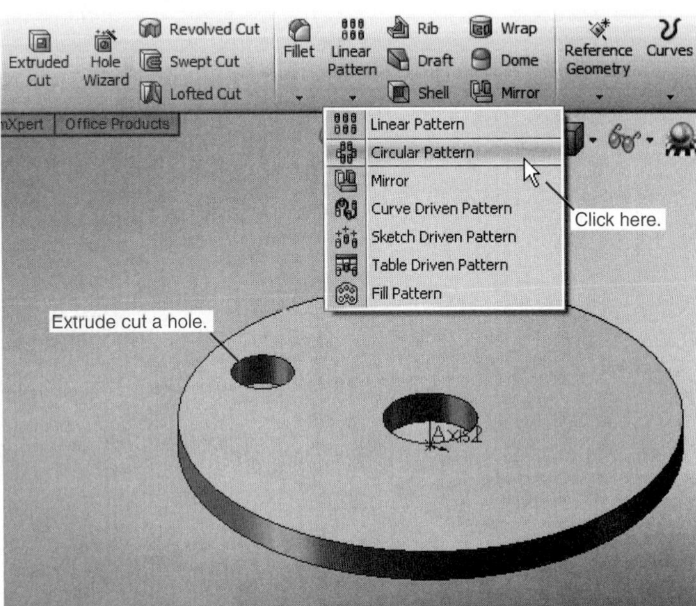

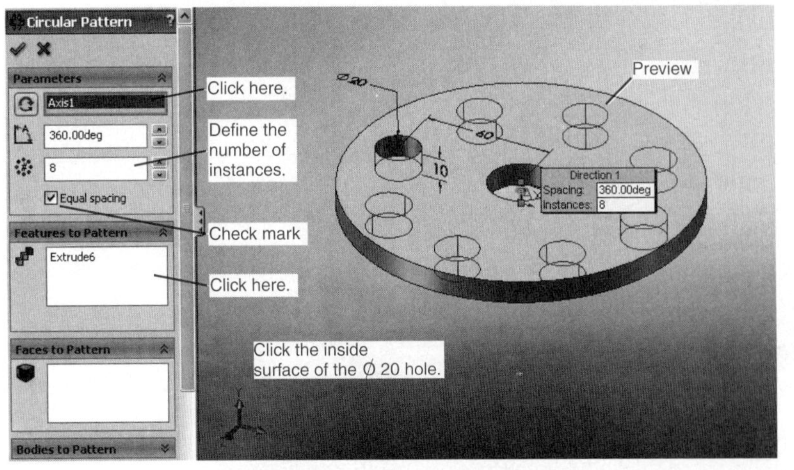

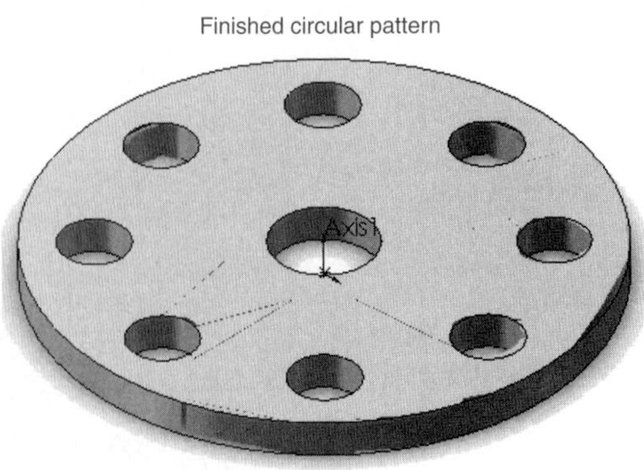

Figure 3-25 ***(continued)***

7. Access the **Features** tools and select the **Circular Pattern** tool.
8. Define the **Number of features** in the pattern for **8**, click the **Equal spacing** option, select the axis of the Ø30 hole as the axis and the Ø20 hole as the **Features to Pattern.**

   A preview will appear.
9. Click the OK check mark.

3-17 MIRROR

The **Mirror** tool is used to create mirror images of features. A mirror image is not the same as a copy. In this section we will mirror the object shown in Figure 3-26.

1. Access the **Features** tools, and click the **Mirror** tool.
2. Click the **Features to Mirror** box, then window the entire object.

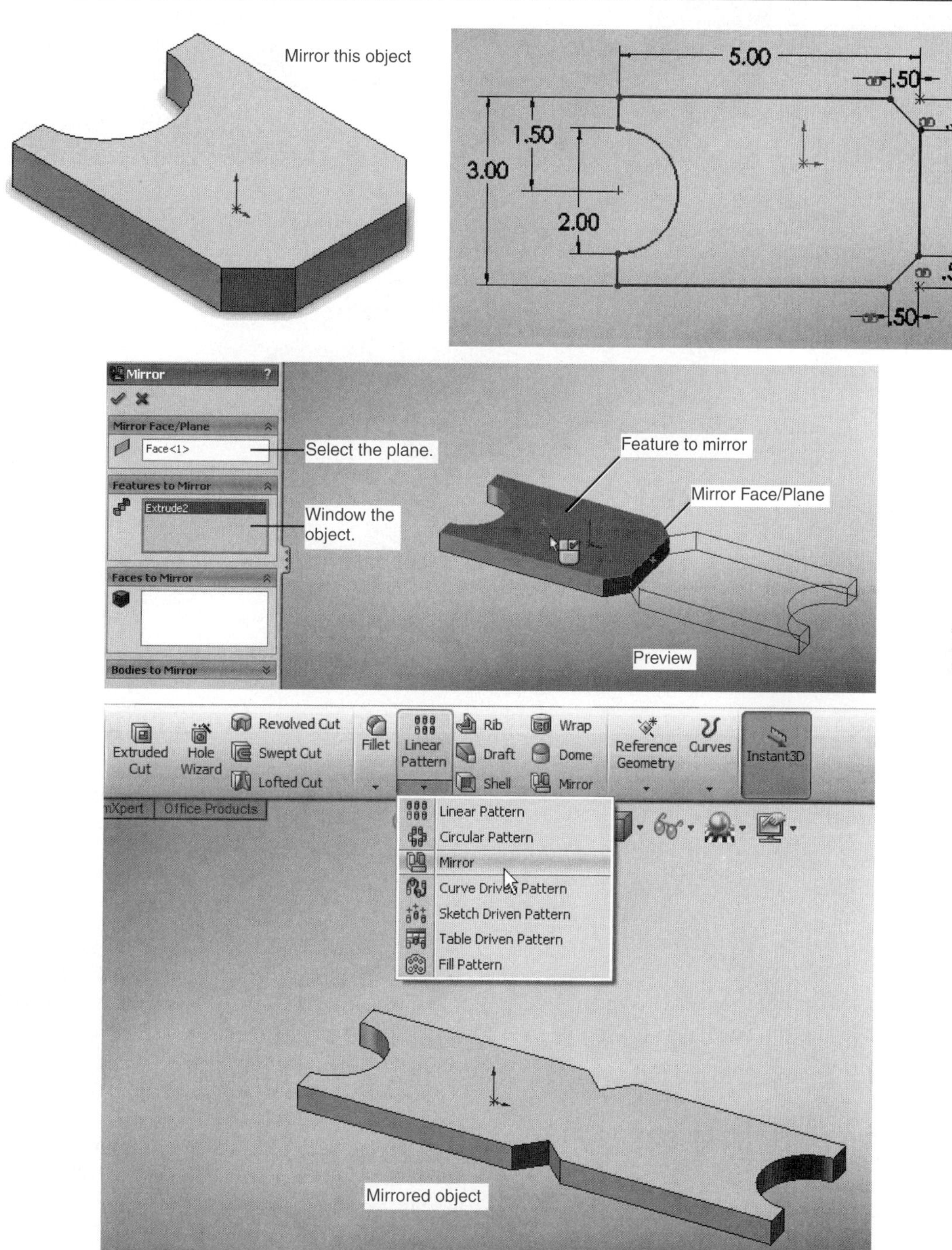

Figure 3-26

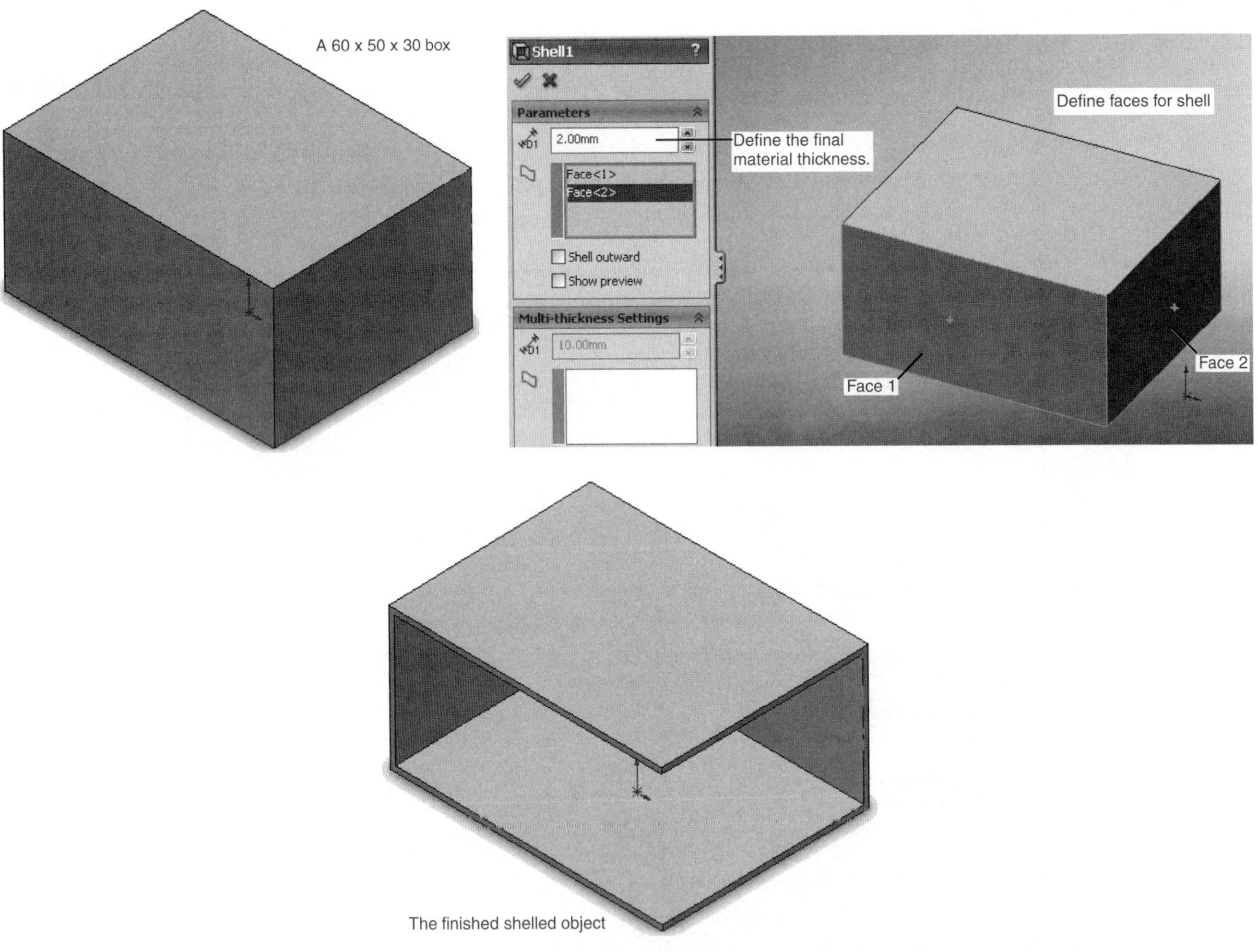

Figure 3-27

3. Click the **Mirror Face/Plane** box, then click the right edge plane as shown.

   A preview will appear.

4. Click the OK check mark.

3-18 SHELL

The **Shell** tool is used to hollow out an existing object, making it into a thin-walled object. See Figure 3-27.

1. Draw a 60 × 50 × 30 box. Use the top plane and an isometric orientation.
2. Access the **Features** tools, and click the **Shell** tool.
3. Define the final material thickness.

   In this example a value of **2.00** was entered.

4. Define the faces to be shelled. Click the **Faces to Remove** box, click the left front face and then the right front face as shown.
5. Click the OK check mark.

3-19 EDITING FEATURES

SolidWorks allows you to edit existing models. This is a very powerful feature in that you can easily make changes to a completed model without having to redraw the entire model.

> **TIP**
>
> The **Edit Sketch** tool is used to edit shapes created using the **Sketch** tools such as holes. The **Edit Features** tool is used to edit shapes created using the **Features** tools such as a cut or extrusion.

Figure 3-28 shows the L-bracket originally created in Sections 3-4 through 3-7. The finished object may be edited. In this example, the hole's diameter and the size of the cutout will be changed.

To Edit the Hole

See Figure 3-29.

1. Right-click the **Ø20.0** hole callout in the **Features Manager** on the left side of the drawing screen and select the **Edit Feature** option.

TIP

The hole will be highlighted when selected.

The **Hole Specification Properties Manager** will appear.

2. Select a new hole diameter.

   In this example **Ø24** was selected.

3. Click the OK check mark.

To Edit the Cutout

See Figure 3-30.

1. Right-click the **Cut-Extrude 1** callout in the **Features Manager** box on the left side of the drawing screen, and select the **Edit Sketch** option.

   The cutout will be highlighted when selected.
   The sketch used to define the cutout will appear.

2. Double-click the two **20** dimensions that define the length of the cutout and change their value to **30.**
3. Click the OK check mark.
4. Click the **Exit Sketch** tool.

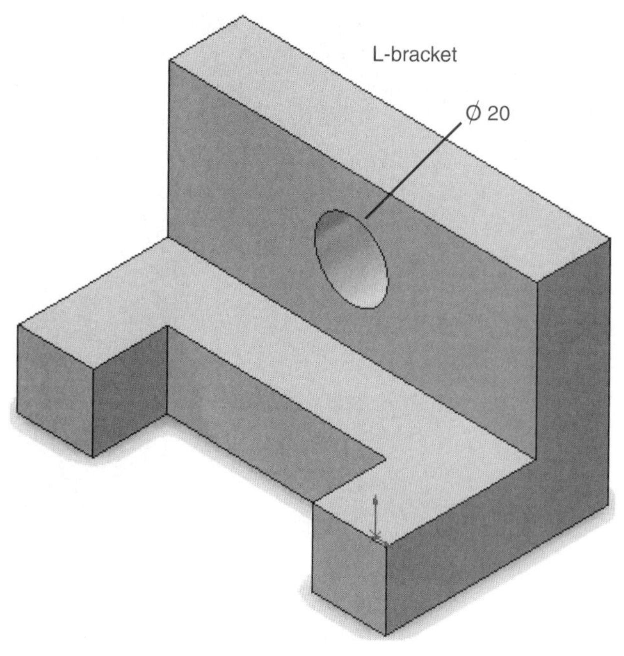

Figure 3-28

3-20 SAMPLE PROBLEMS SP3-1

Figure 3-31 shows a cylindrical object with a slanted surface, a cutout, and a blind hole. Figure 3-32 shows how to draw the object. The procedures presented in Figure 3-32 represent one of several possible ways to create the object.

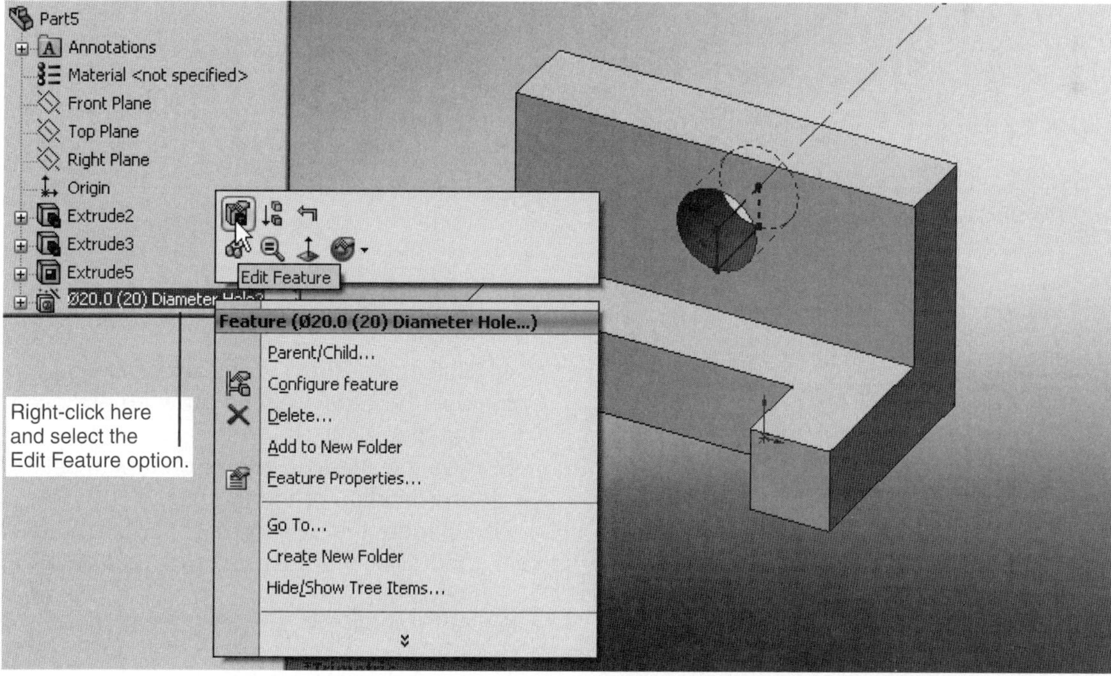

Figure 3-29

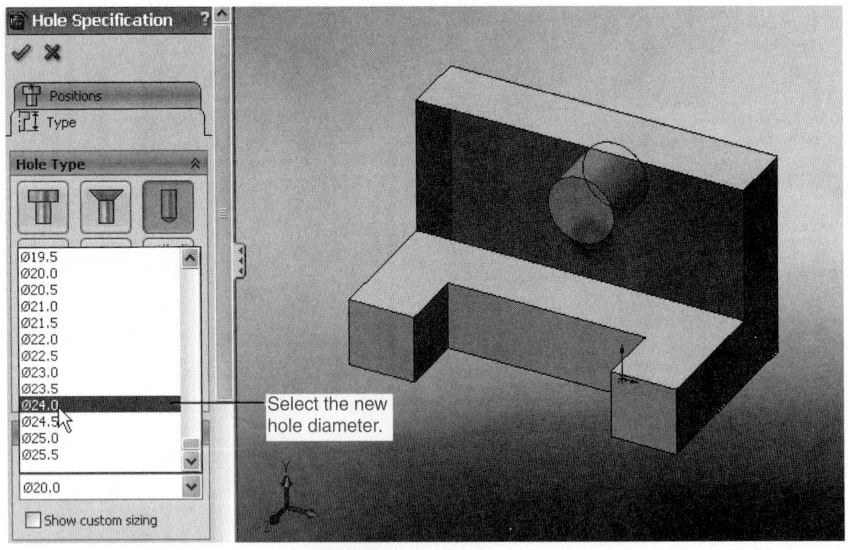

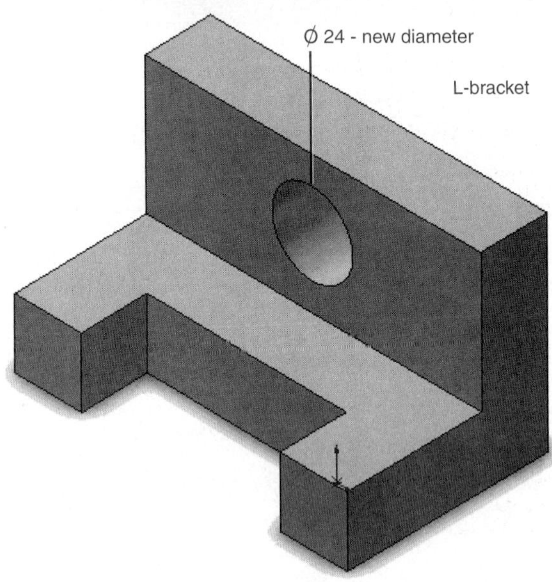

Figure 3-29 *(continued)*

To Draw a Cylinder

1. Start a new **Part** document.
2. Define the units as **millimeters** and access the top plane.
3. Draw a **Ø58** circle and extrude it to **60.**

To Create a Slanted Surface on the Cylinder

1. Click the **Right Plane** tool, access the **Reference** tool in the **Features** tools, and click the **Plane** option.
2. Define the offset plane distance in the **Plane Properties Manager** as **30,** and click the check mark.
3. Right-click the offset plane and select the **Sketch** option.
4. Select the **Right Plane** orientation.
5. Use the **Line** tool and draw an enclosed triangular shape.
6. Use the **Smart Dimension** tool to define the size and location of the triangle.
7. Change the drawing's orientation to **Dimetric** and click the **Extrude Cut** tool in the **Features** tools.
8. Set the length of the cut to **60.00mm** and click the check mark.
9. Right-click the offset plane and click the **Hide** option.

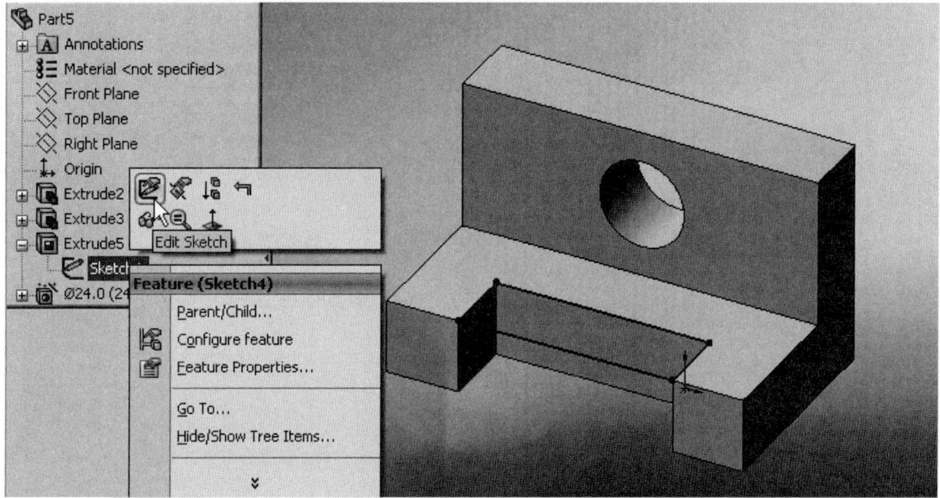
Part5
Annotations
Material <not specified>
Front Plane
Top Plane
Right Plane
Origin
Extrude2
Extrude3
Extrude5
Edit Sketch
Feature (Sketch4)
Parent/Child...
Configure feature
Feature Properties...
Go To...
Hide/Show Tree Items...

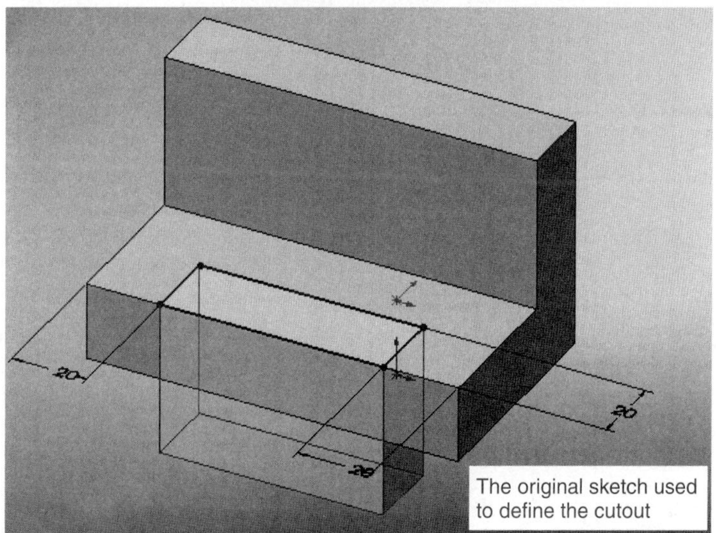
20
20
20
The original sketch used to define the cutout

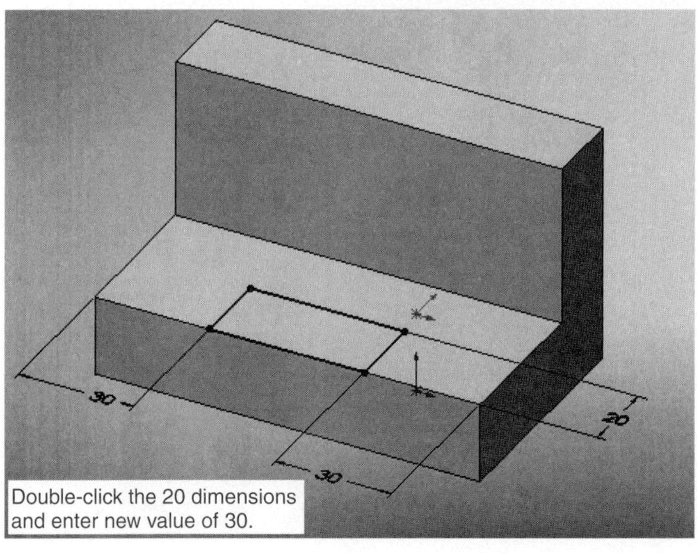
30
20
30
Double-click the 20 dimensions and enter new value of 30.

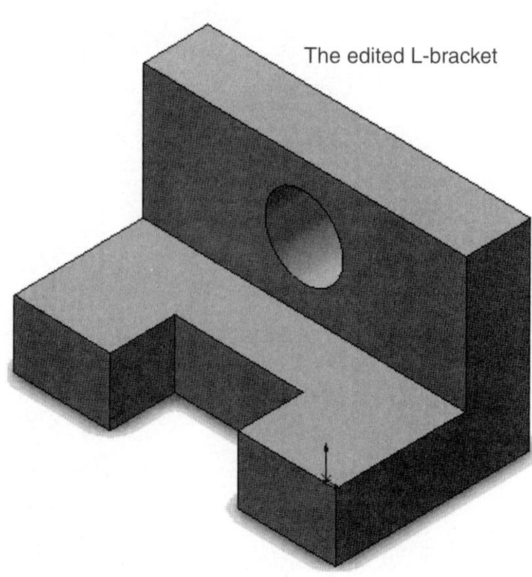
The edited L-bracket

Figure 3-30

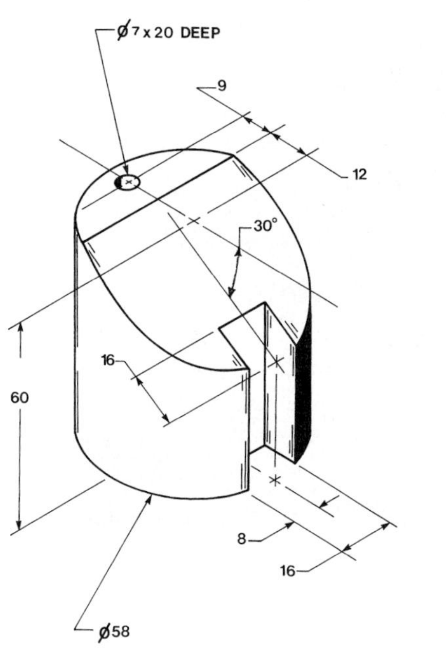

Figure 3-31

To Add the Vertical Slot

See Figure 3-33.`

1. Right-click the slanted surface and click the **Sketch** tool.
2. Click the **Custom** tool next to the axis orientation icon and click **Normal to view.**
3. Draw a vertical line through the origin. Start the line on the edge of the slanted surface.
4. Use the **Rectangle** tool on the **Sketch** toolbar and draw an **8 × 16** rectangle as shown. Use the **Smart Dimension** tool to size the rectangle.
5. Draw a second **8 × 16** rectangle as shown.
6. Change the drawing orientation to a dlmetric view.
7. Exit the sketch.
8. Click the **Top Plane** tool and use the **Reference** tool on the **Features** toolbar and create an offset top plane **60** from the base of the cylinder.

> ***Note:***
> The **Extruded Cut** tool will extrude a shape perpendicular to the plane of the shape. In this example the plane is slanted, so the extrusion would not be vertical, as required. The rectangle is projected into the top offset plane and the extrusion tool applied there.

9. Change the drawing orientation to the top view.
10. Sketch a rectangle on the offset plane over the projected view of the 16 × 16 rectangle on the slanted plane.
11. Change the drawing orientation to a dimetric view.
12. Use the **Extruded Cut** tool on the **Features** toolbar to cut out the slot.
13. Hide the 60 offset plane and hide the 16 × 16 rectangle on the slanted surface.
14. Click the check mark.

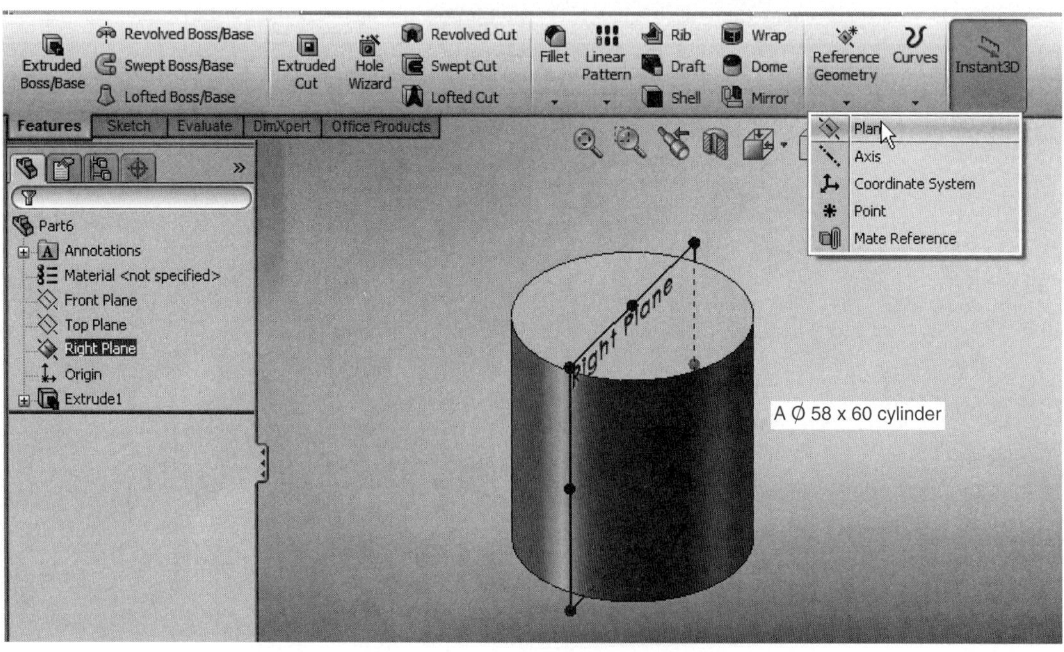

Figure 3-32

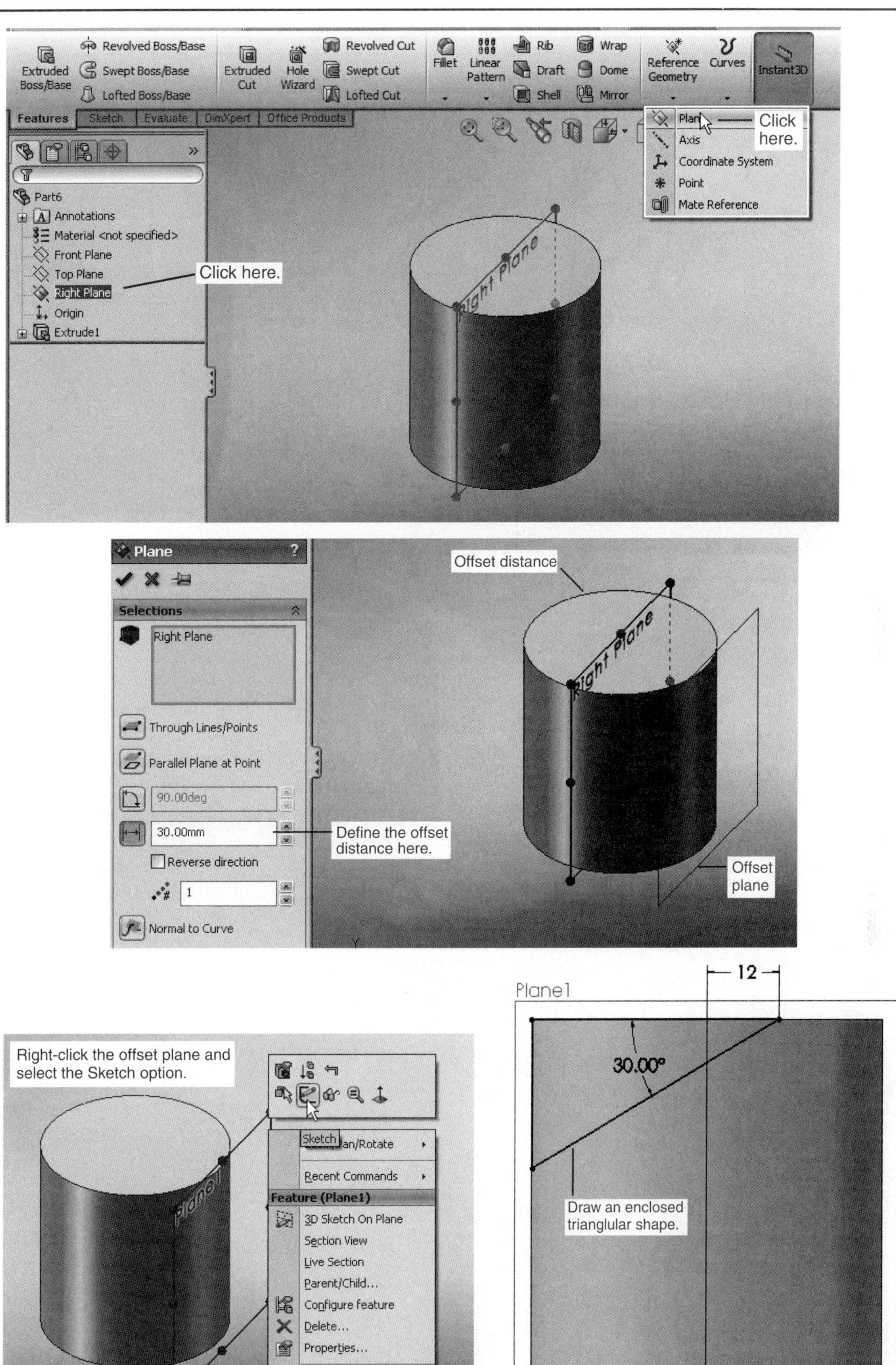

Figure 3-32 ***(continued)***

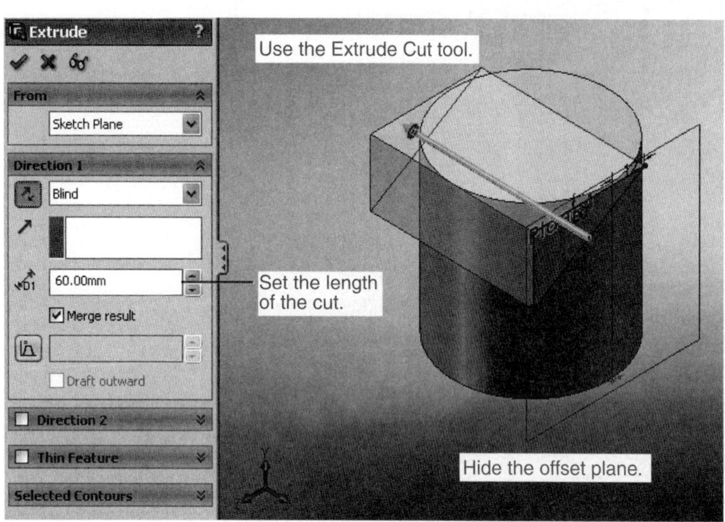

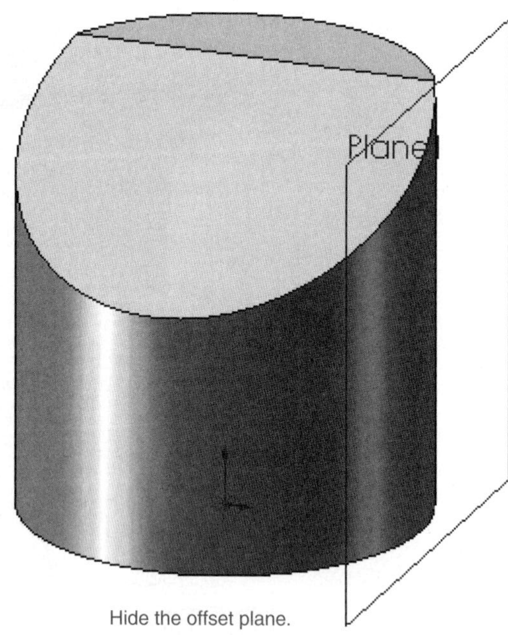

Figure 3-32 *(continued)*

To Add the Ø8 Hole

See Figure 3-34.

1. Use the **Point** tool and sketch a point on the flat portion of the top surface. Use the origin to center the point.
2. Use the **Smart Dimension** tool and locate the point according to the given dimensions.
3. Exit the sketch.

> ***Note:***
> There are two ways to draw blind holes (holes that do not go all the way through): draw a circle and use the **Extruded Cut** tool to remove material, or use the **Hole Wizard.** In this example the **Hole Wizard** tool is used because it will generate a conical-shaped bottom to the hole. Conical-shaped hole bottoms result from using a twist drill, which has a conical-shaped cutting end.

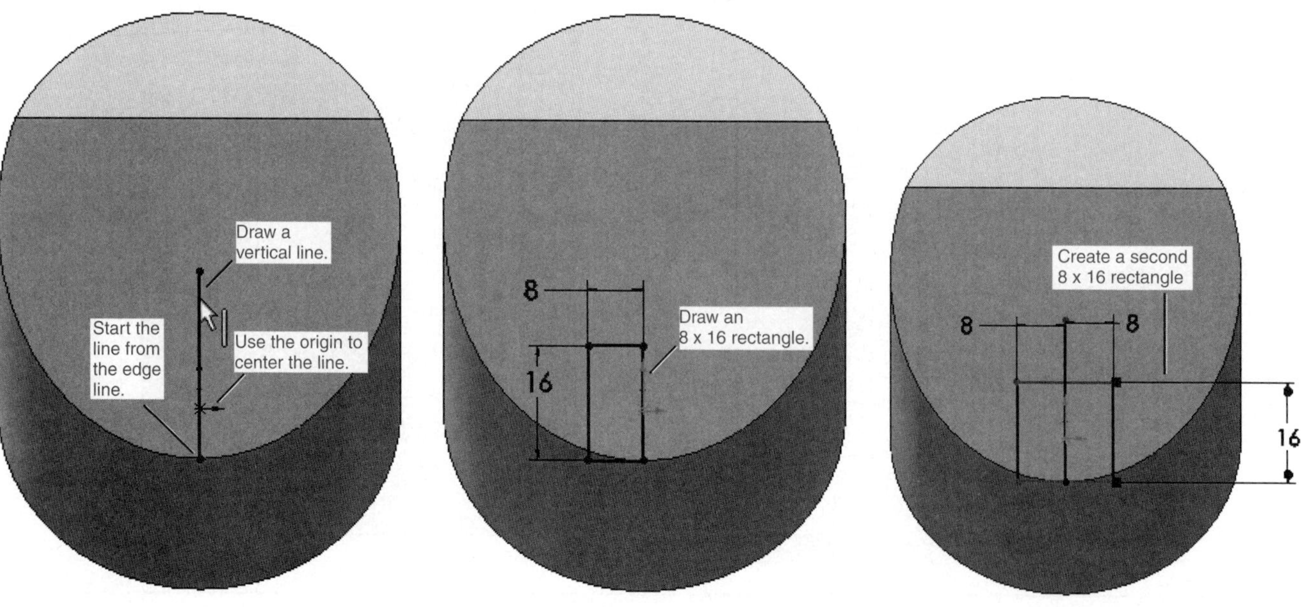

Figure 3-33

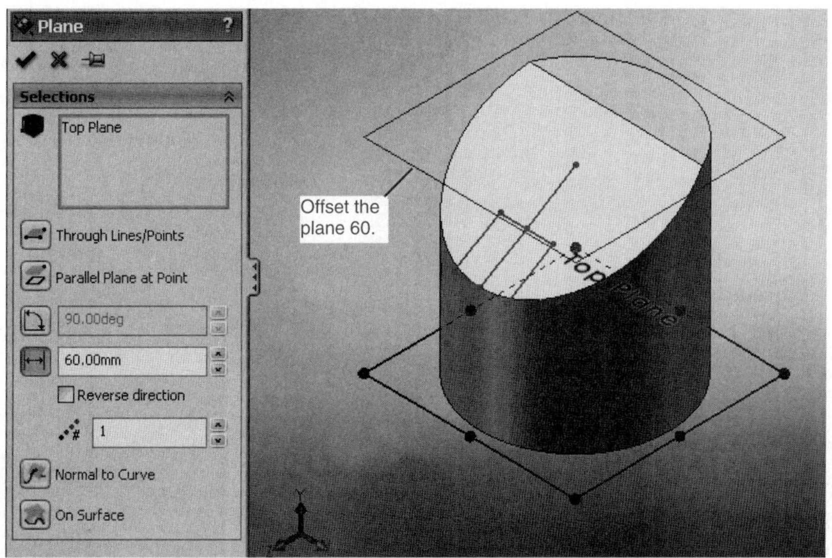

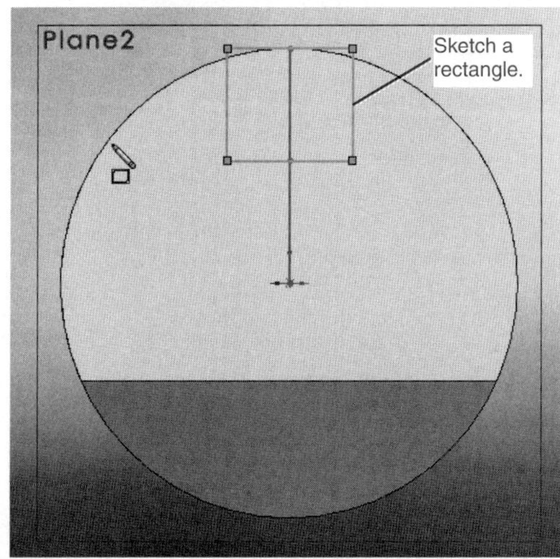

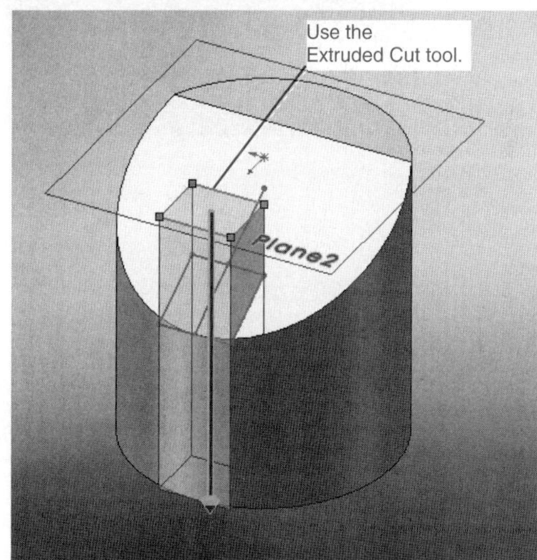

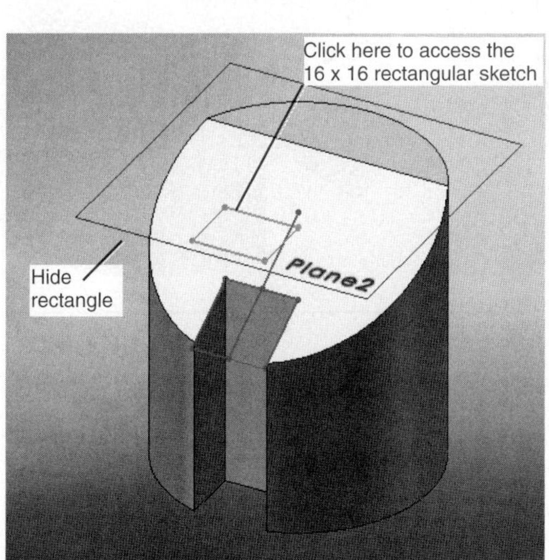

Figure 3-33 ***(continued)***

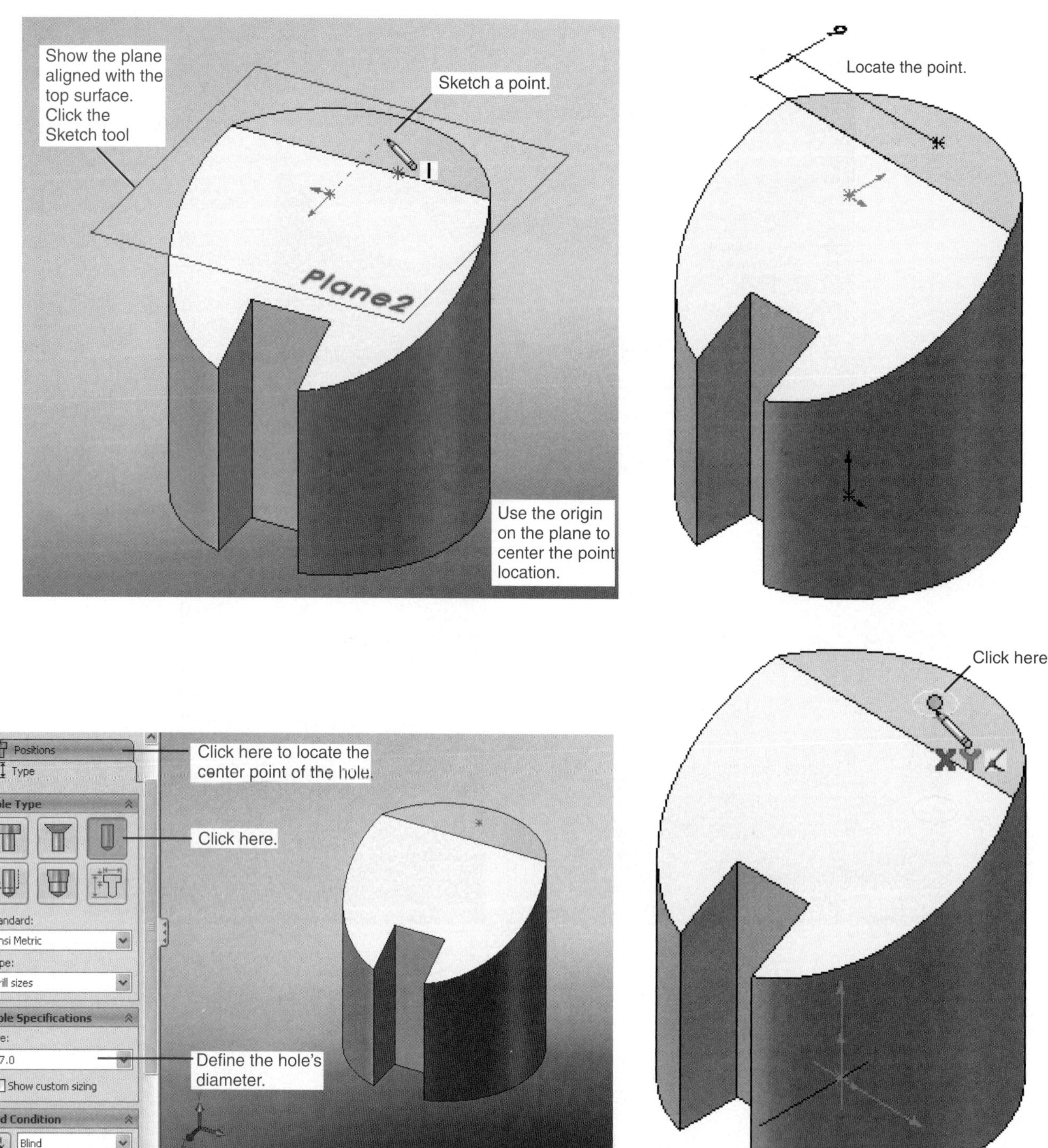

Figure 3-34

4. Click the **Hole Wizard** tool on the **Features** toolbar.
5. Click the **Hole** option and define the hole's diameter and depth.
6. Click the **Positions** tab in the **Hole Specification Properties Manager**.
7. Click the point.
8. Click the check mark.
9. Change the drawing orientation and verify that the hole has a conical-shaped bottom.

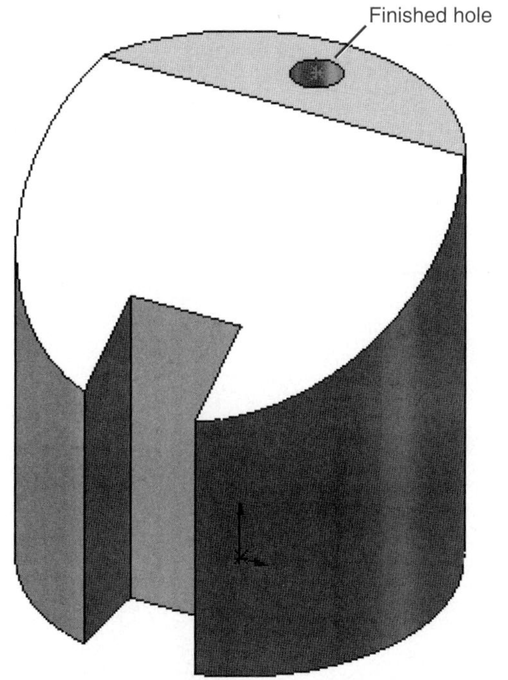

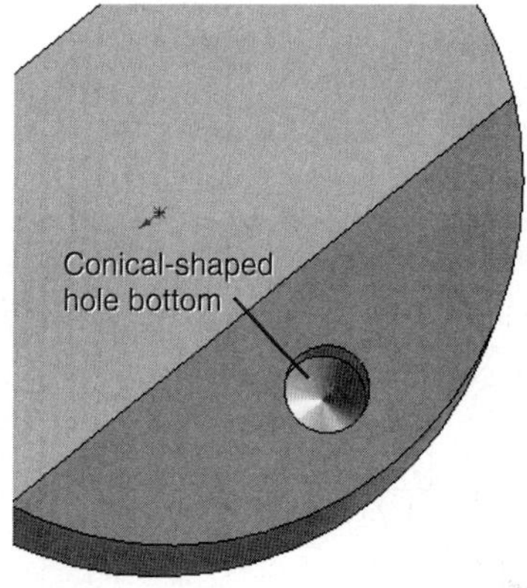

Figure 3-34 *(continued)*

3-21 SAMPLE PROBLEM SP3-2

Figure 3-35 shows a dimensioned object. In this example we will start with the middle section of the object. See Figure 3-36.

1. Sketch a profile using the right plane based on the given dimensions.
2. Use the **Extruded Boss/Base** tool to add thickness to the profile.
3. Right-click the right surface of the object and select the **Sketch** option.
4. Use the **Rectangle** tool and draw a rectangle based on the given dimensions. Align the corners of the rectangle with the corners of the object.
5. Use the **Extruded Boss/Base** tool and extrude the rectangle **20** to the right.
6. Reorient the object and draw a rectangle on the left surface of the object.
7. Use the **Extruded Boss/Base** tool and extrude the rectangle **20** to the left.
8. Create a sketch plane on the right side of the object and draw a rectangle based on the given dimensions as shown.
9. Use the **Extruded Cut** tool on the **Features** toolbar and cut out the rectangle over the length of the object.

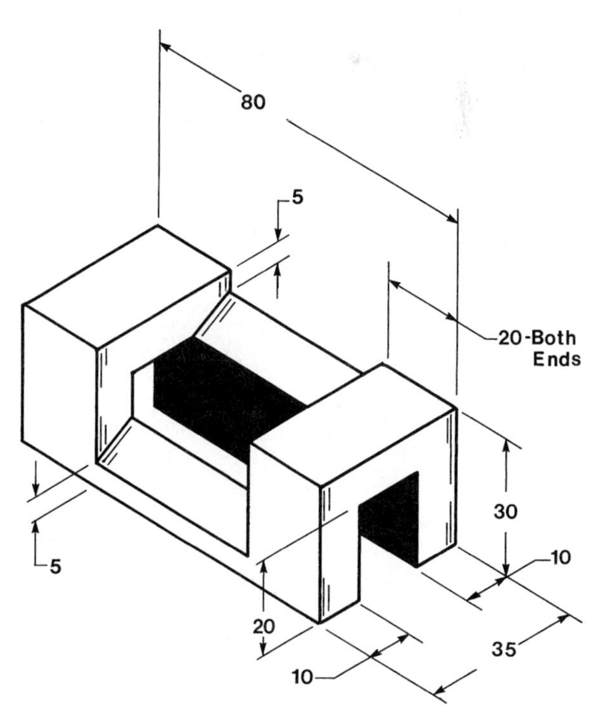

Figure 3-35

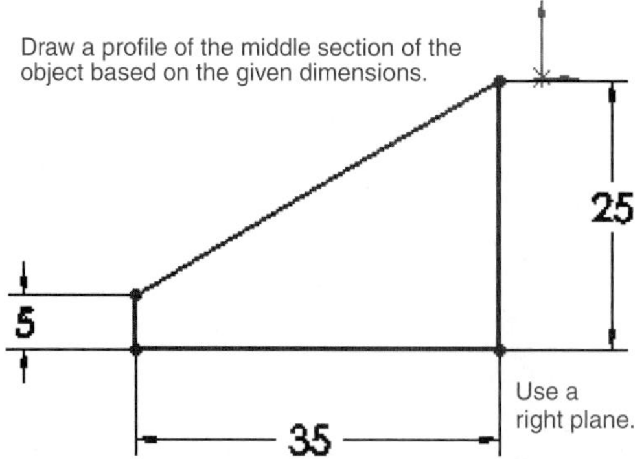
Draw a profile of the middle section of the object based on the given dimensions.
25
5
35
Use a right plane.

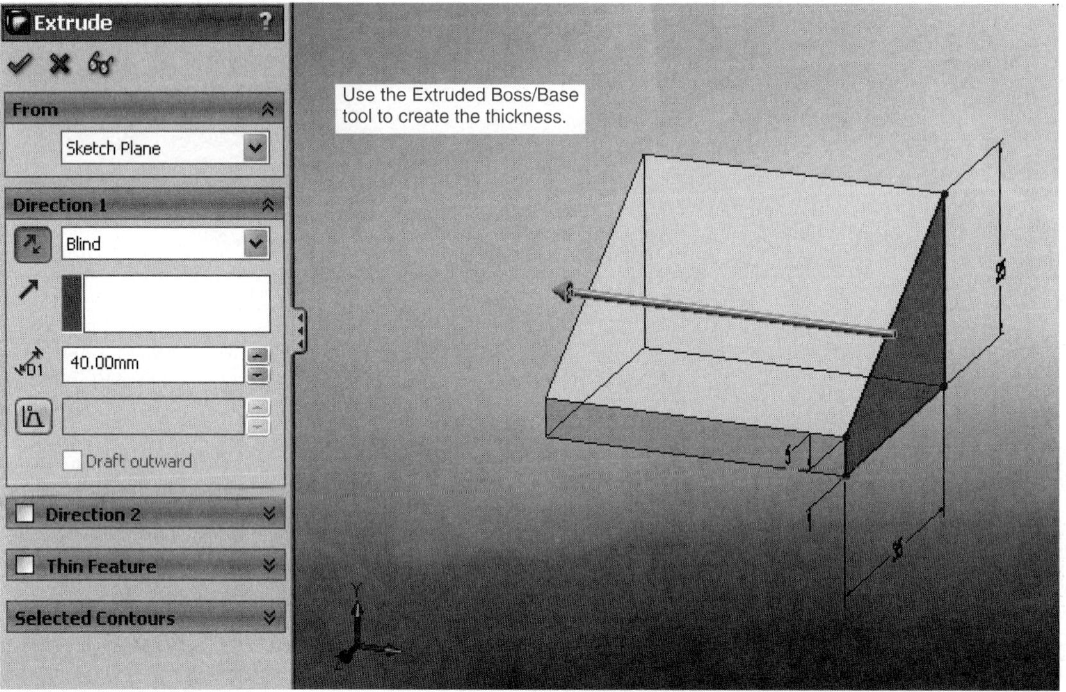
Extrude
From
Sketch Plane
Direction 1
Blind
40.00mm
Draft outward
Direction 2
Thin Feature
Selected Contours
Use the Extruded Boss/Base tool to create the thickness.

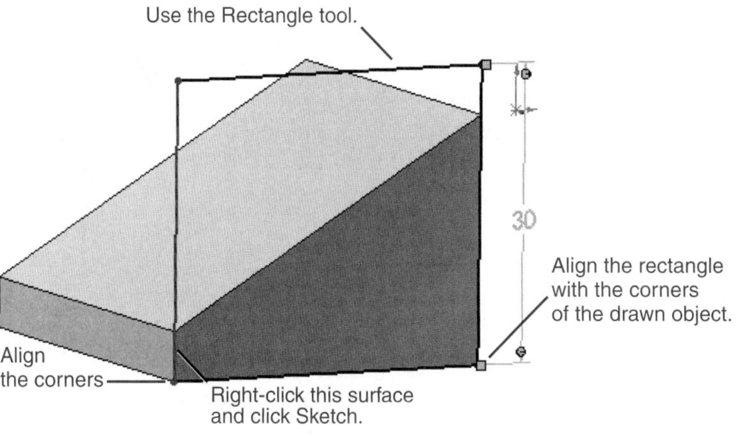
Use the Rectangle tool.
30
Align the rectangle with the corners of the drawn object.
Align the corners
Right-click this surface and click Sketch.

Figure 3-36

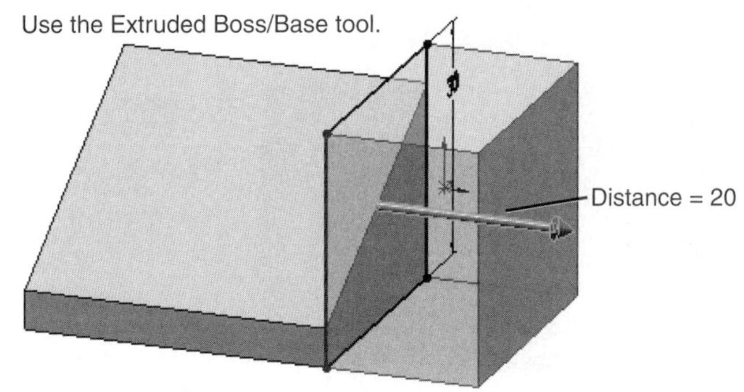
Use the Extruded Boss/Base tool.
Distance = 20

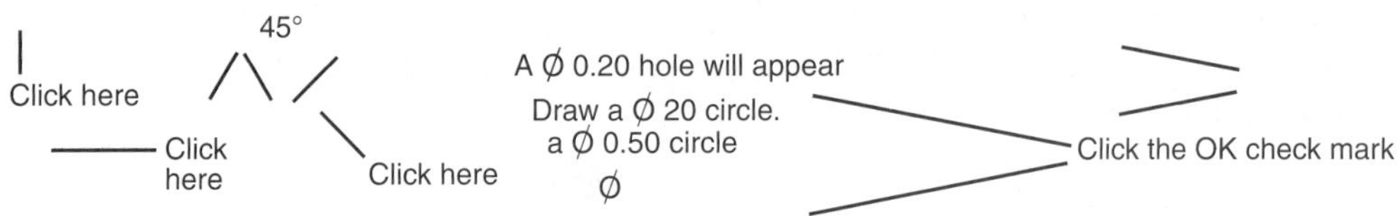
45°
Click here
Click here
Click here
A Ø 0.20 hole will appear
Draw a Ø 20 circle.
a Ø 0.50 circle
Ø
Click the OK check mark

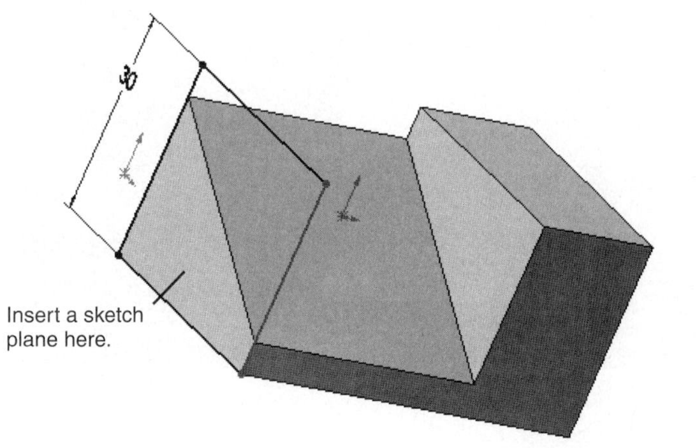
Insert a sketch plane here.

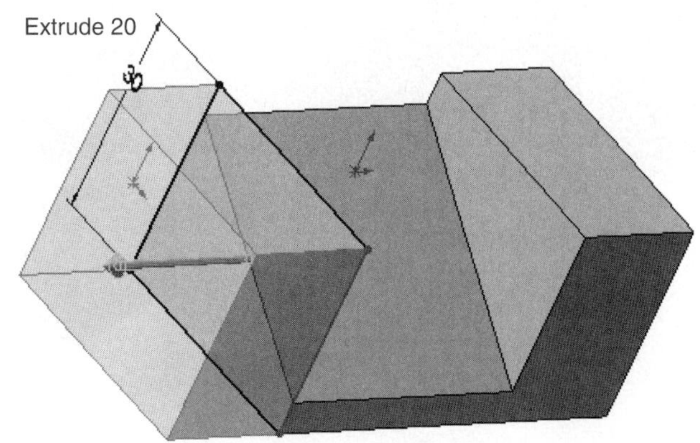
Extrude 20

Figure 3-36 ***(continued)***

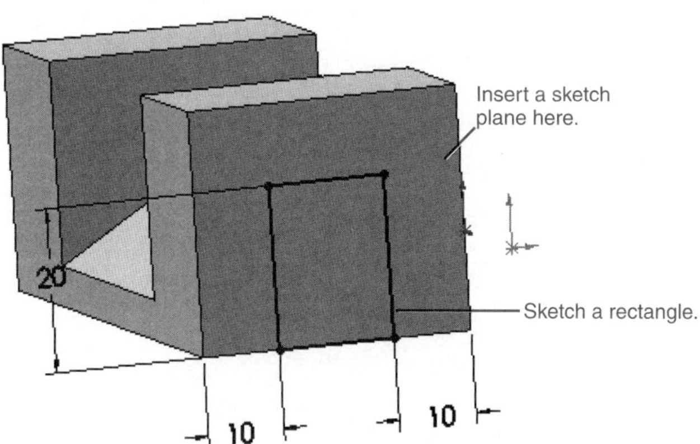

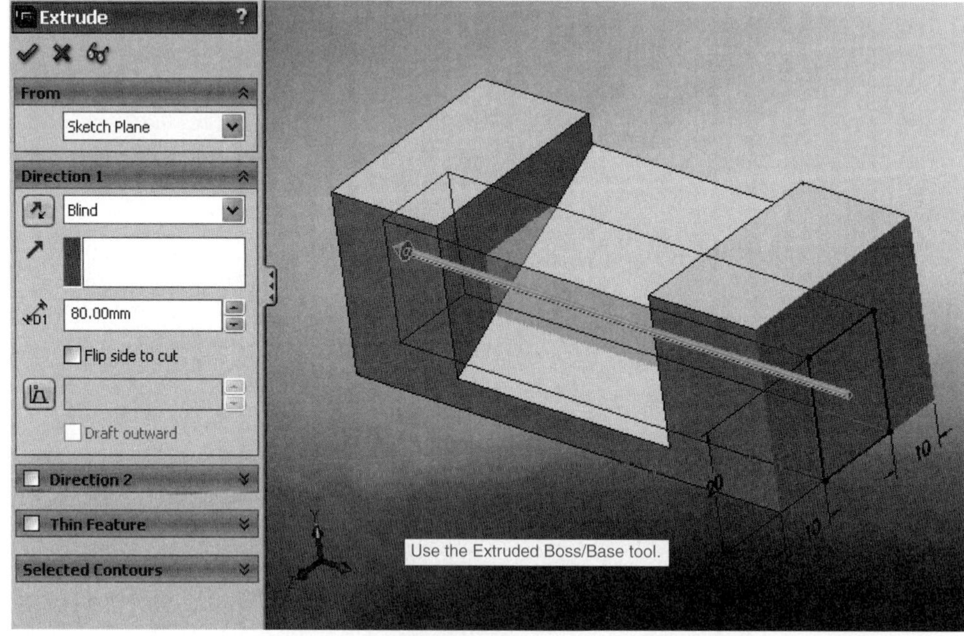

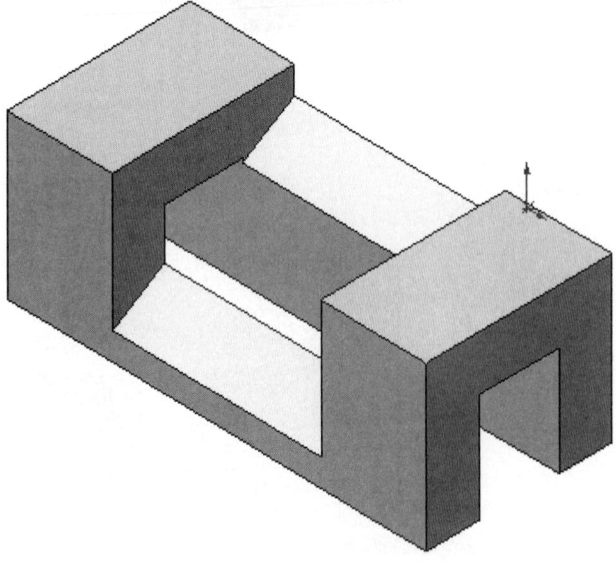

Figure 3-36 *(continued)*

3-23 PROJECTS

Project 3-1:

Redraw the following objects as solid models based on the given dimensions. Make all models from mild steel.

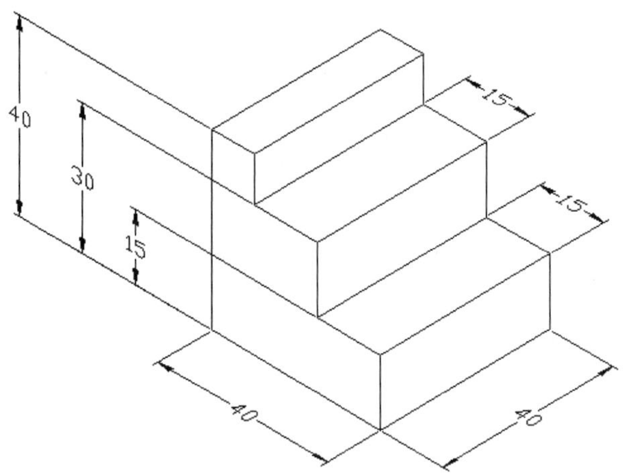

Figure P3-1 MILLIMETERS

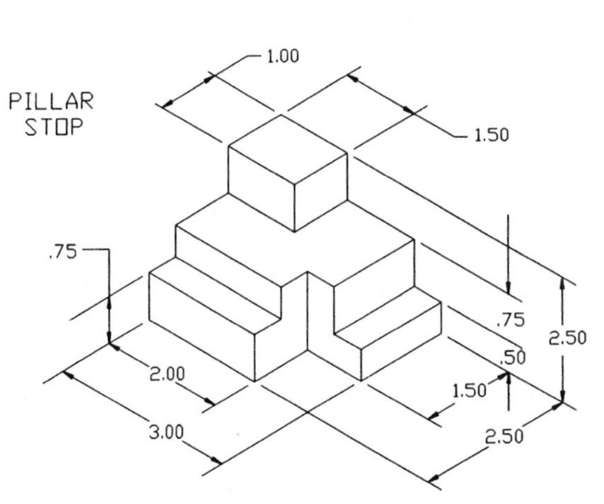

Figure P3-2 INCHES

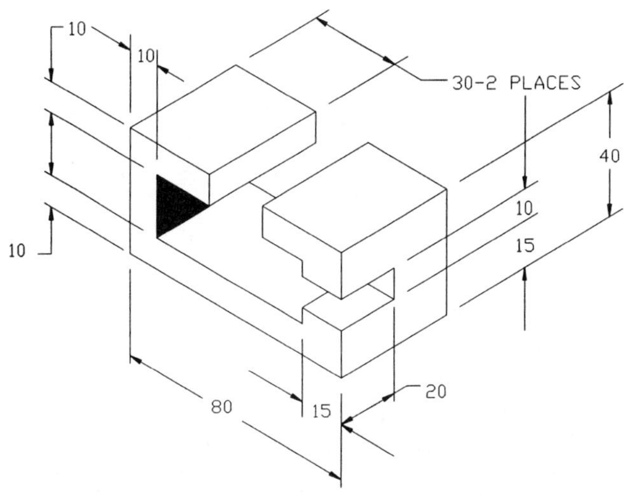

Figure P3-3 MILLIMETERS

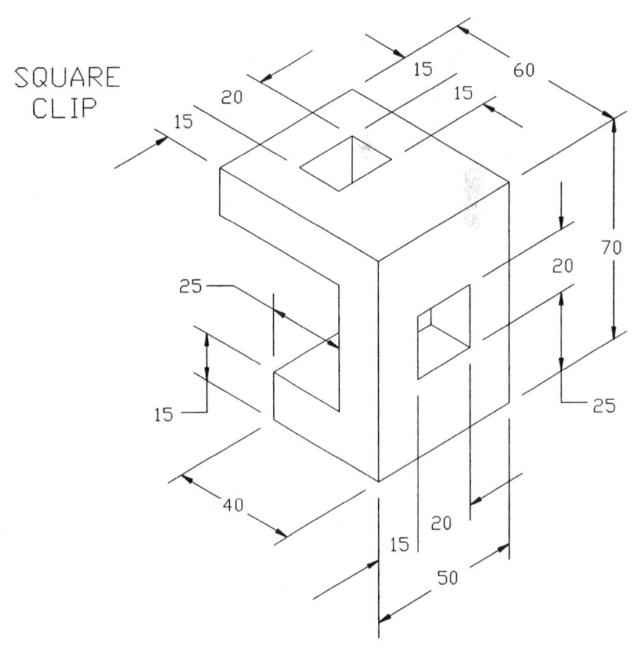

Figure P3-4 MILLIMETERS

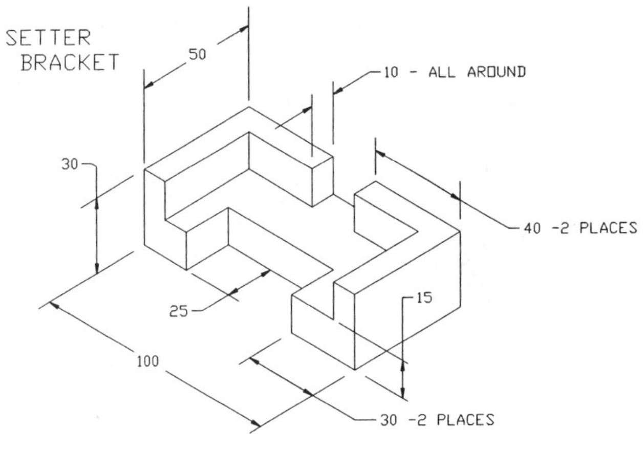

Figure P3-5 MILLIMETERS

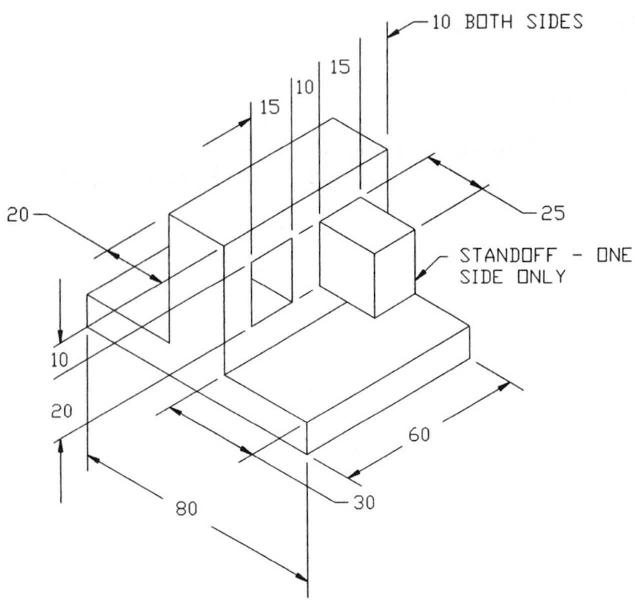

Figure P3-8 MILLIMETERS

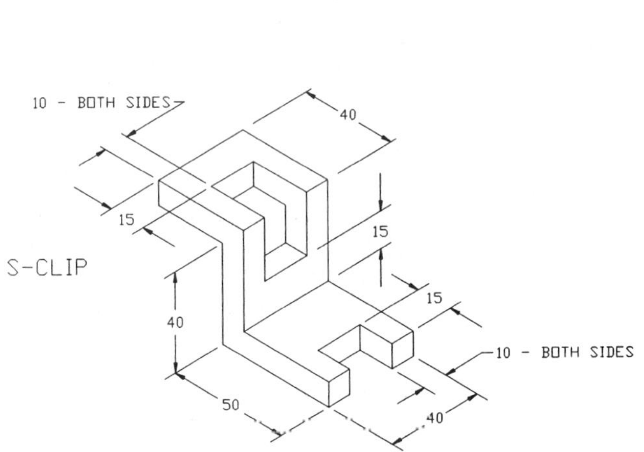

Figure P3-6 MILLIMETERS

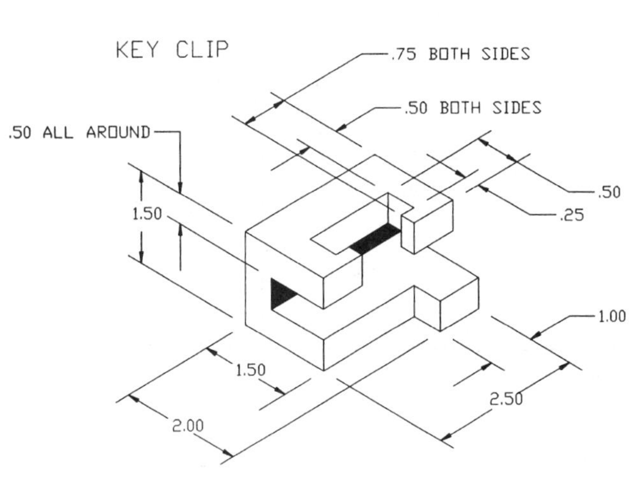

Figure P3-7 INCHES

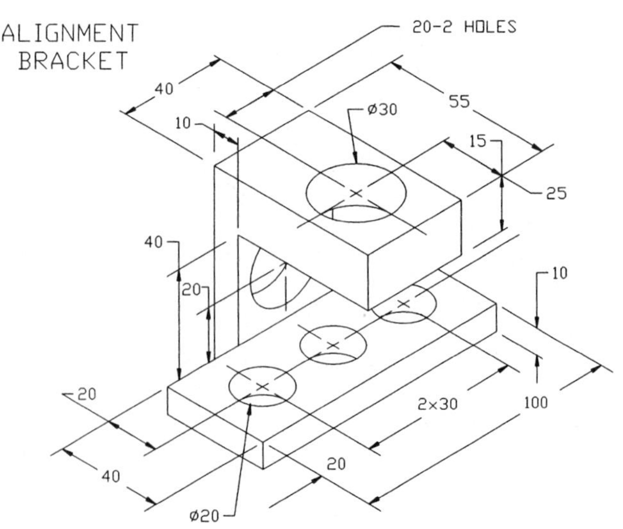

Figure P3-9 MILLIMETERS

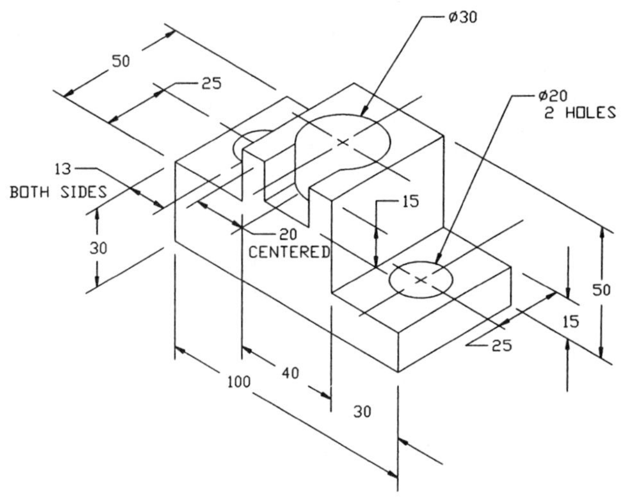

Figure P3-10 MILLIMETERS

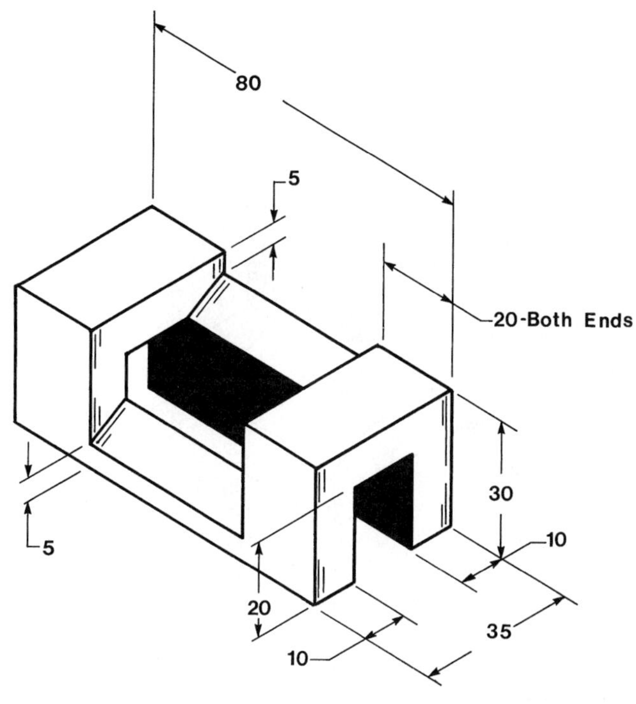

Figure P3-13 MILLIMETERS

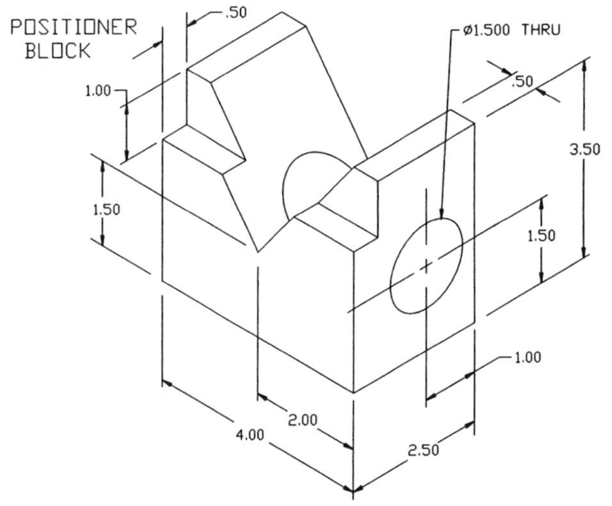

Figure P3-11 INCHES

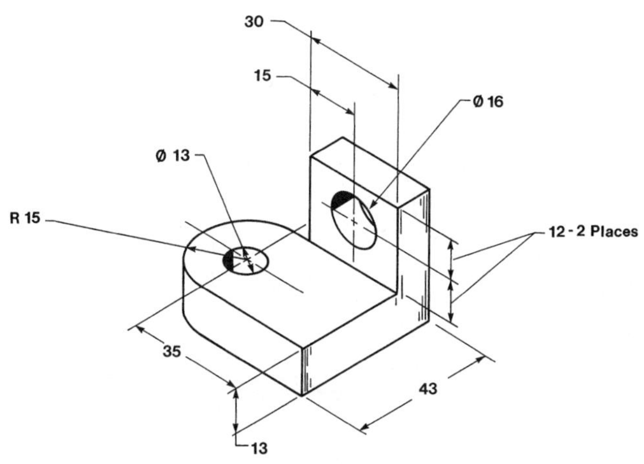

Figure P3-12 MILLIMETERS

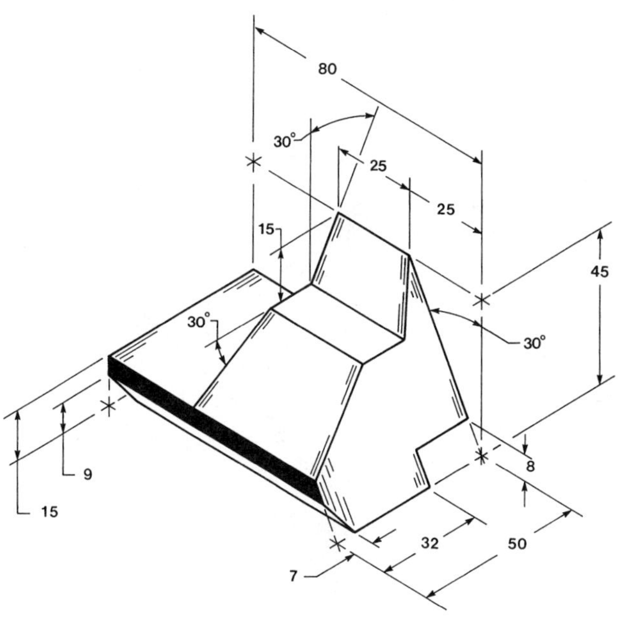

Figure P3-14 MILLIMETERS

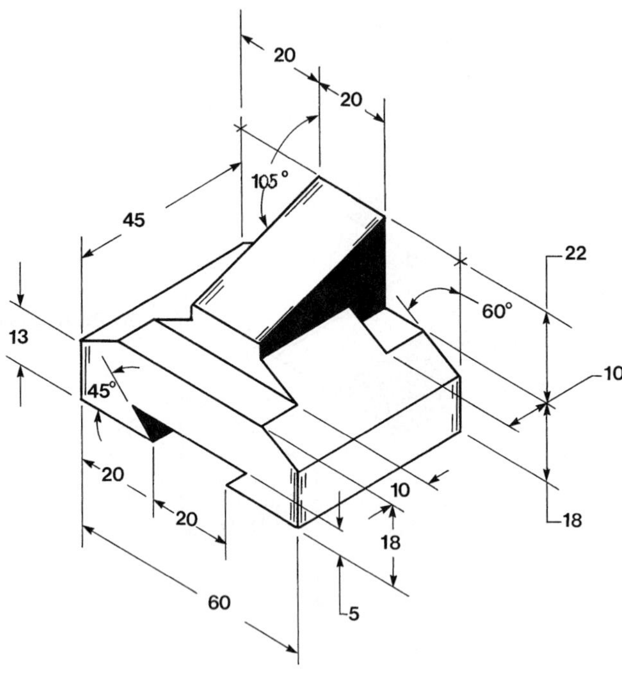

Figure P3-15 MILLIMETERS

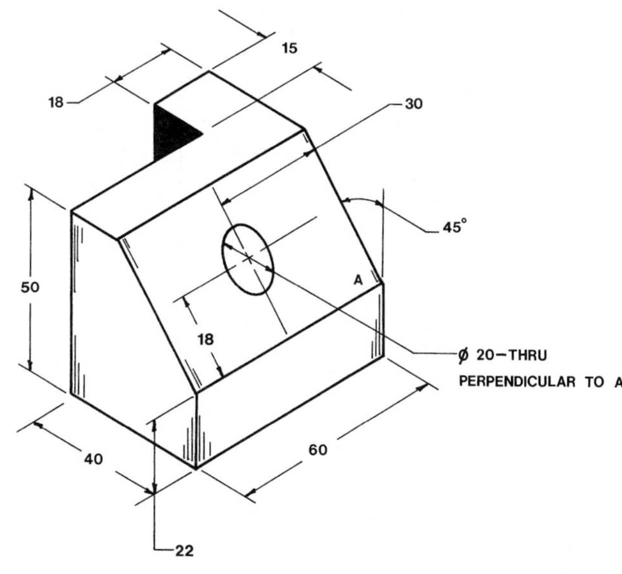

Figure P3-17 MILLIMETERS

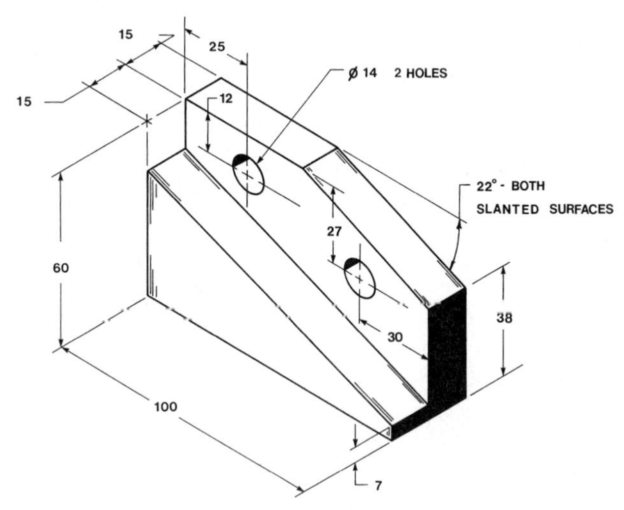

Figure P3-18 MILLIMETERS

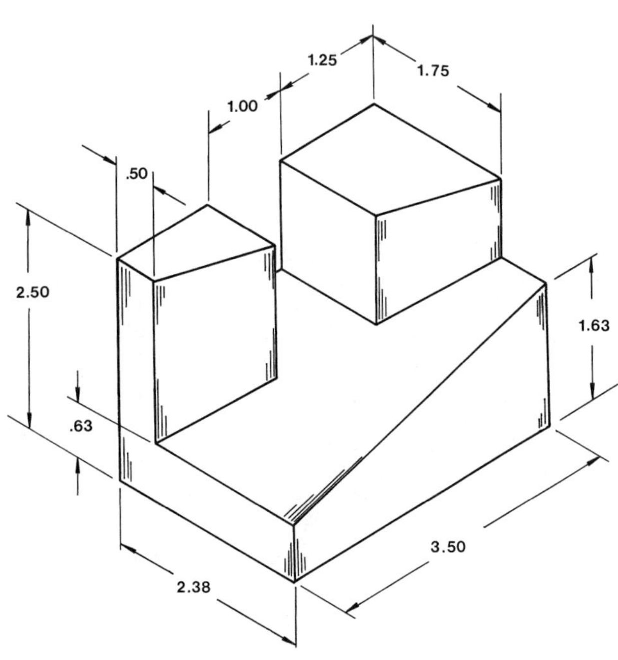

Figure P3-16 INCHES

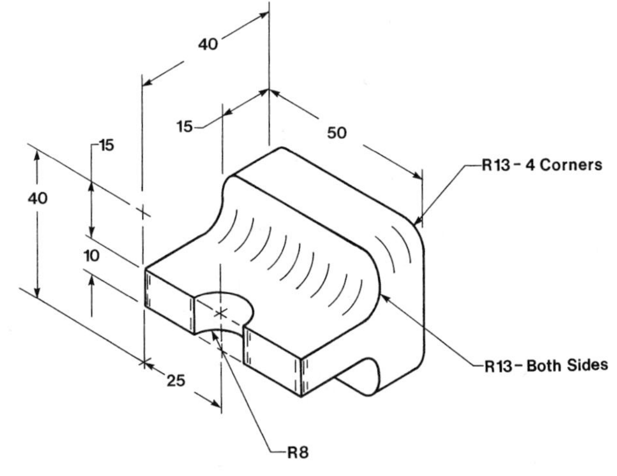

Figure P3-19 MILLIMETERS

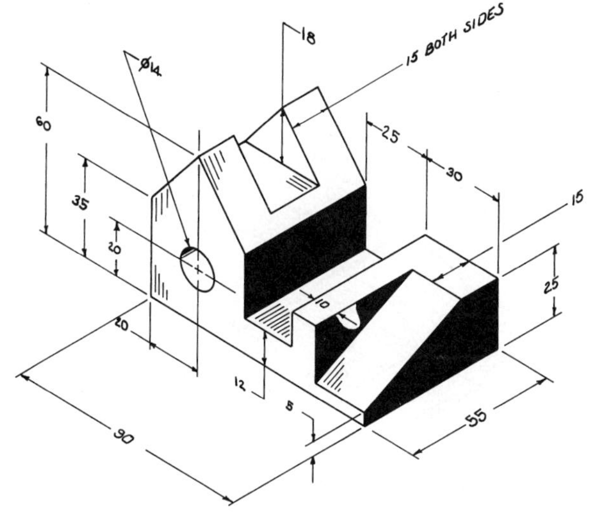

Figure P3-20 MILLIMETERS

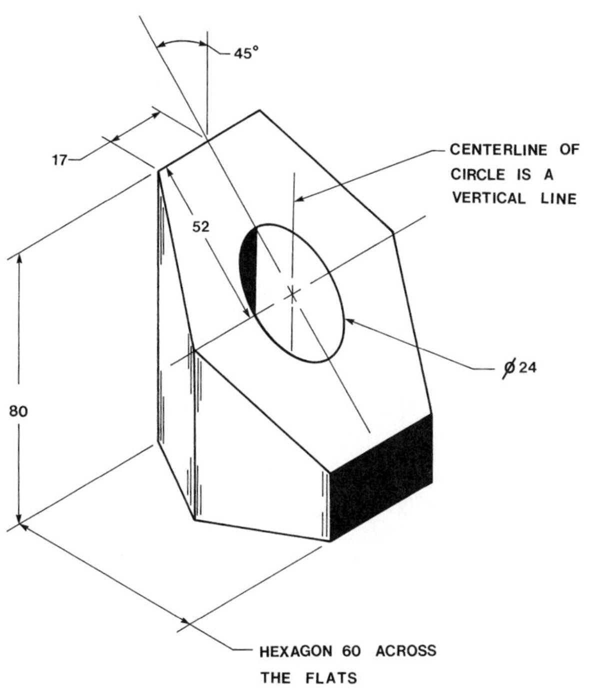

Figure P3-21 MILLIMETERS

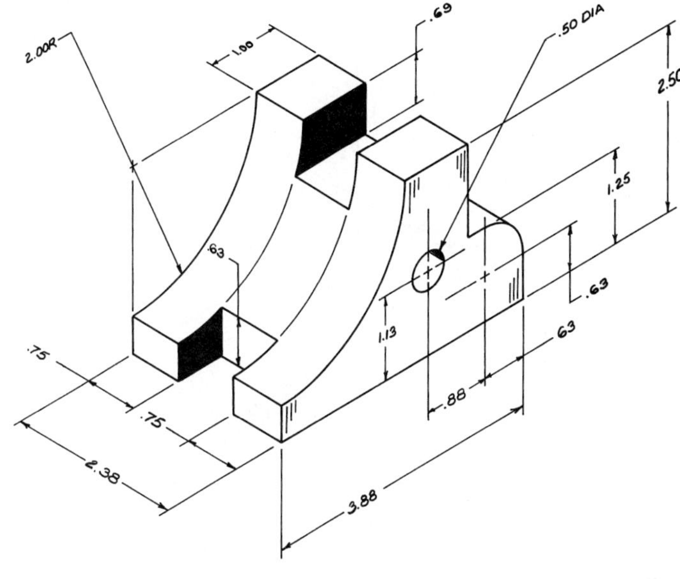

Figure P3-22 INCHES

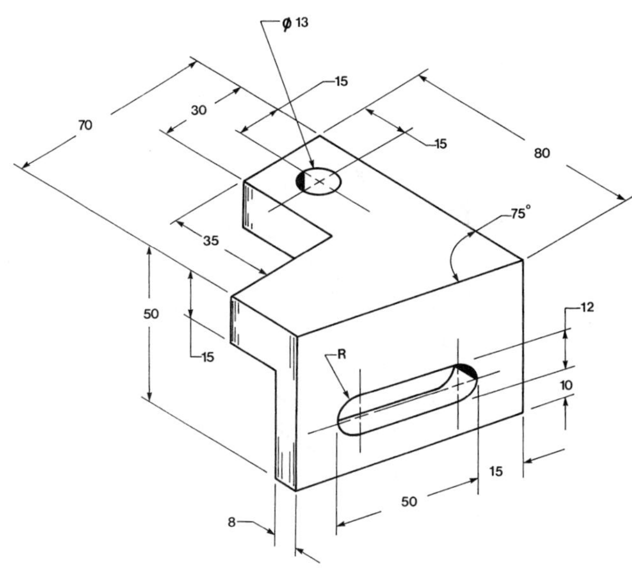

Figure P3-23 MILLIMETERS

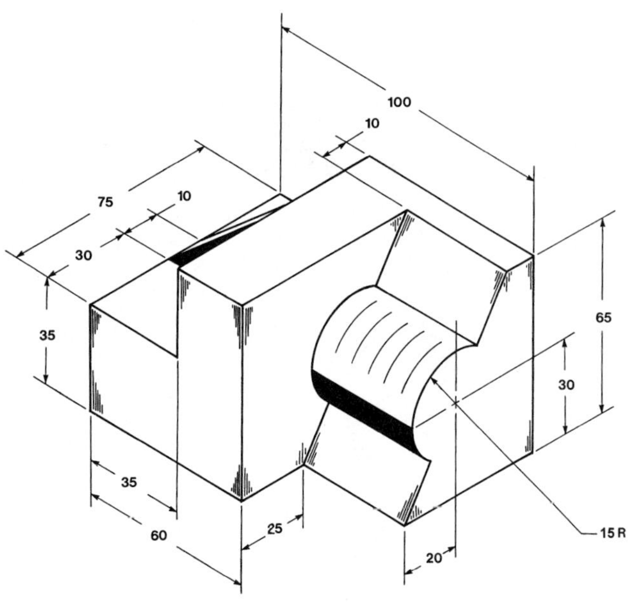

Figure P3-24 MILLIMETERS

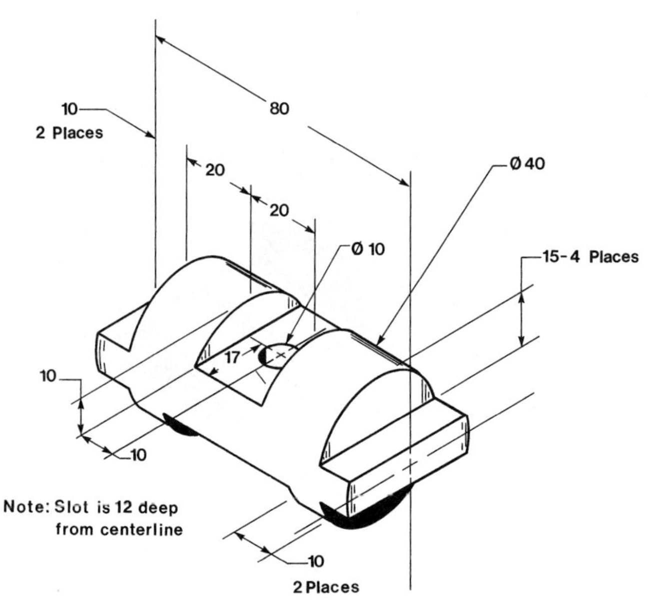

Figure P3-26 MILLIMETERS

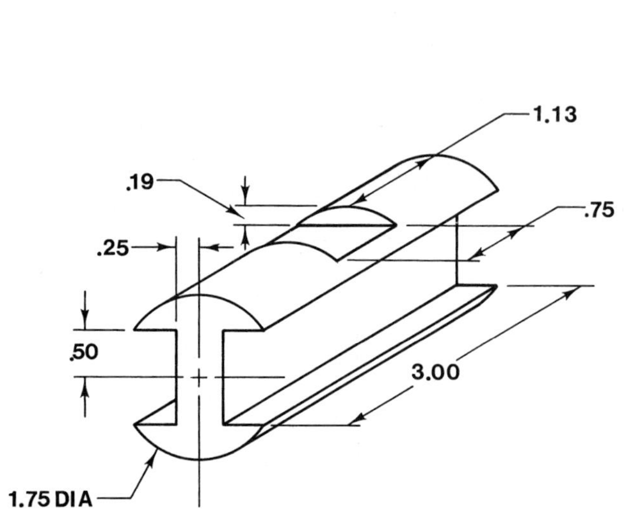

Figure P3-25 INCHES (SCALE: 4=1)

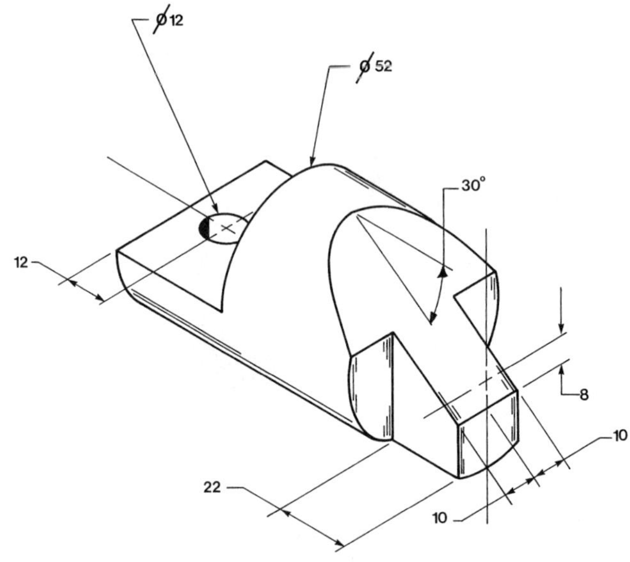

Figure P3-27 MILLIMETERS

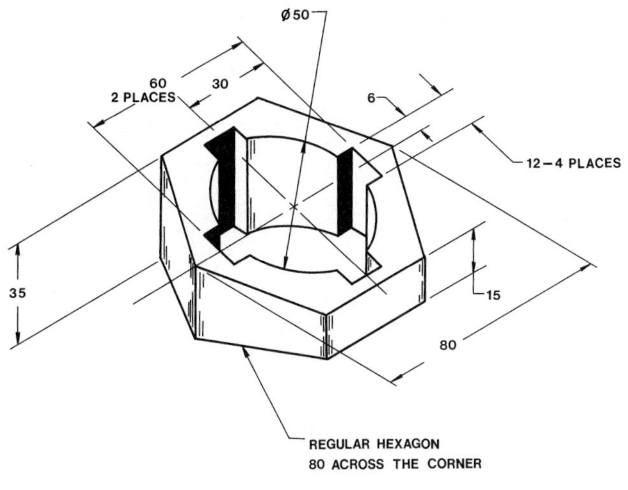

Figure P3-28 MILLIMETERS

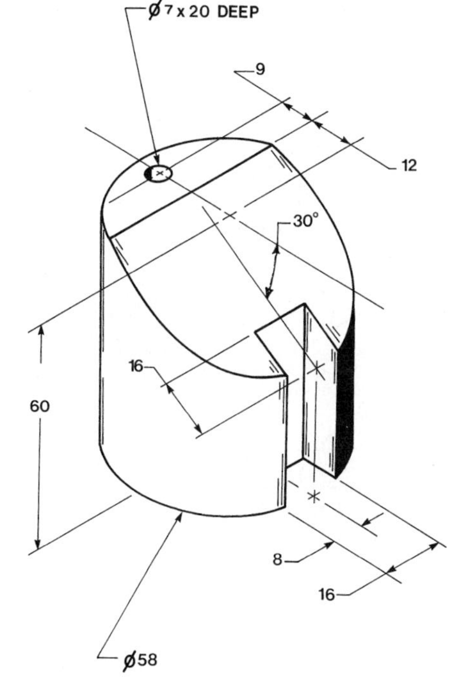

Figure P3-30 MILLIMETERS (SCALE: 2=1)

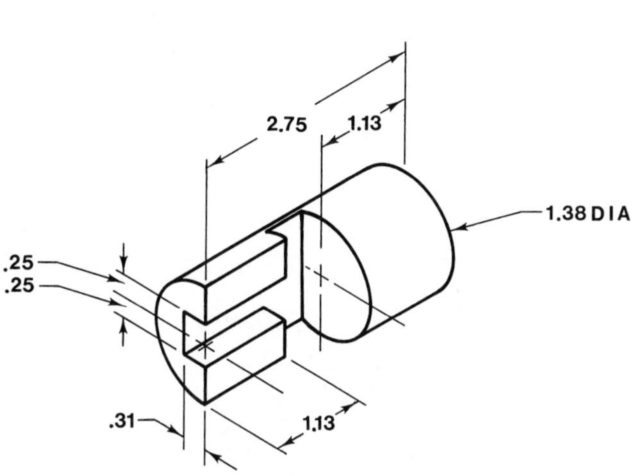

Figure P3-29 INCHES (SCALE: 4=1)

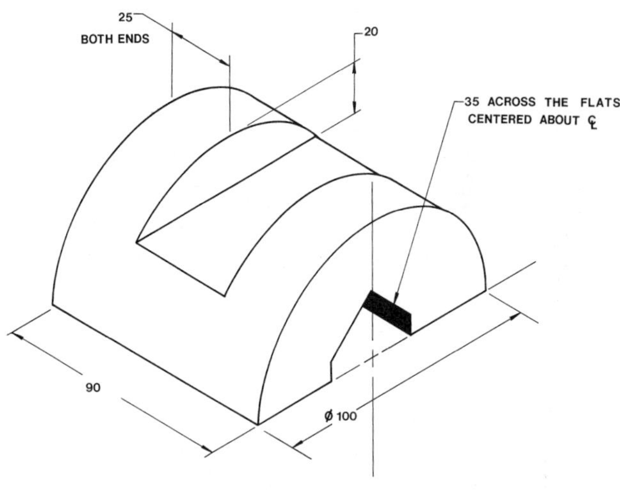

Figure P3-31 MILLIMETERS

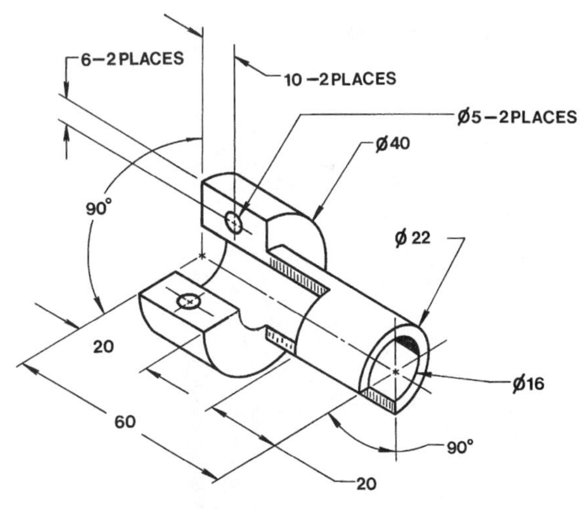

Figure P3-32 MILLIMETERS

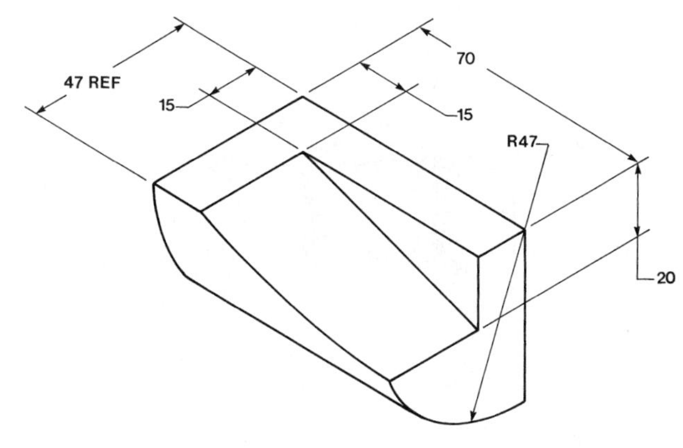

Figure P3-35 MILLIMETERS

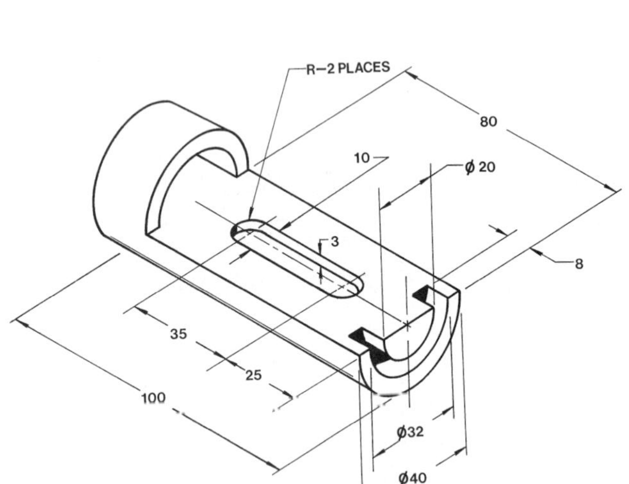

Figure P3-33 MILLIMETERS

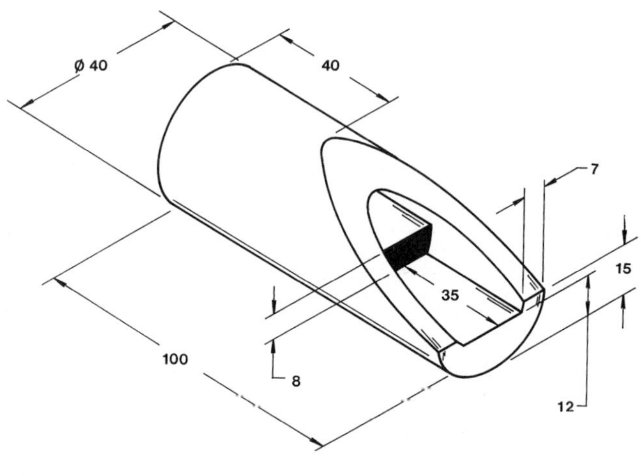

Figure P3-36 MILLIMETERS

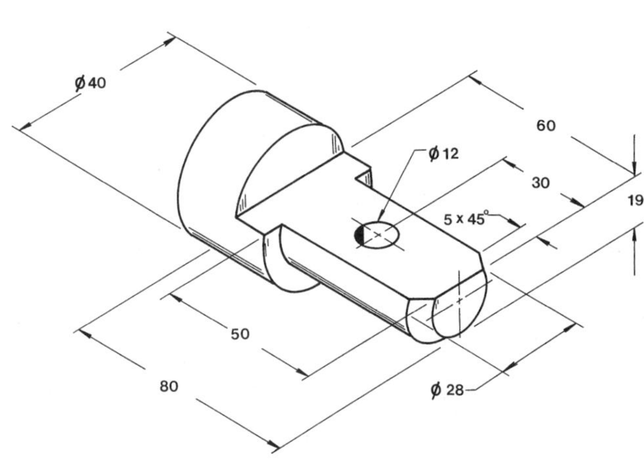

Figure P3-34 MILLIMETERS

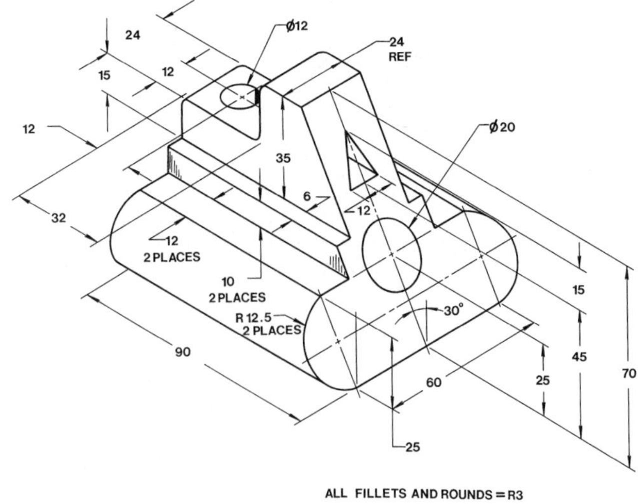

Figure P3-37 MILLIMETERS

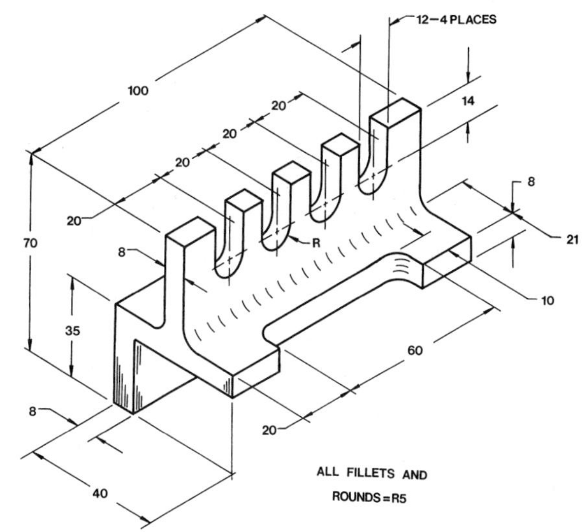

Figure P3-38 MILLIMETERS

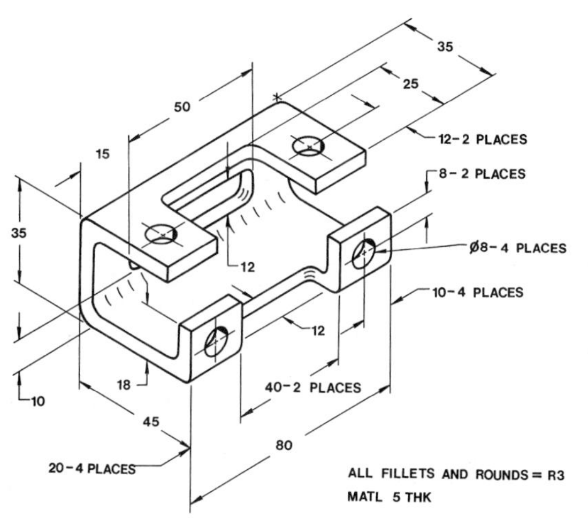

Figure P3-39 MILLIMETERS (CONSIDER A SHELL)

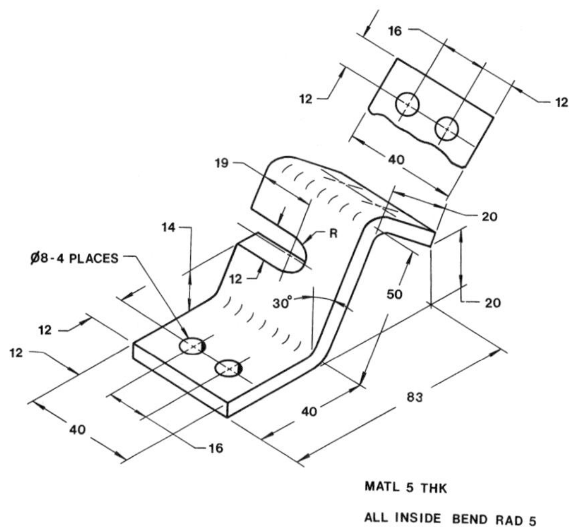

Figure P3-40 MILLIMETERS

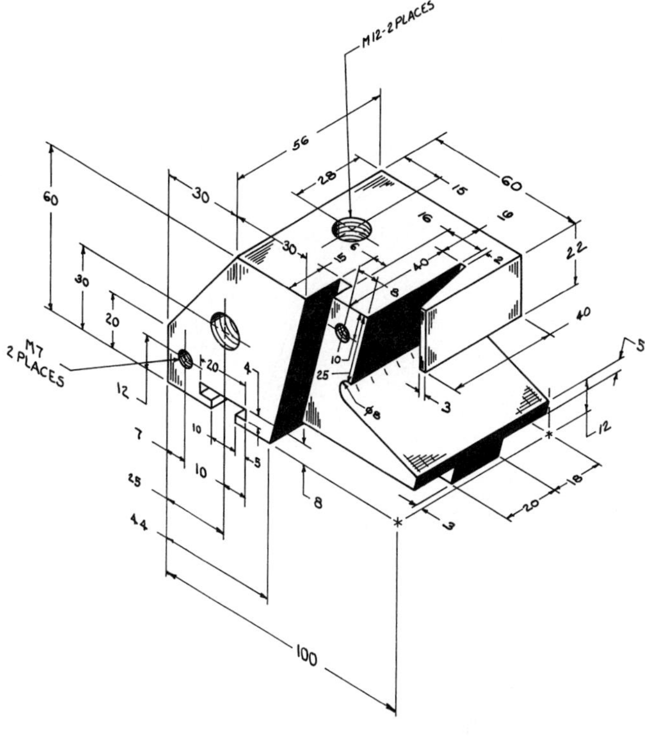

Figure P3-41 MILLIMETERS

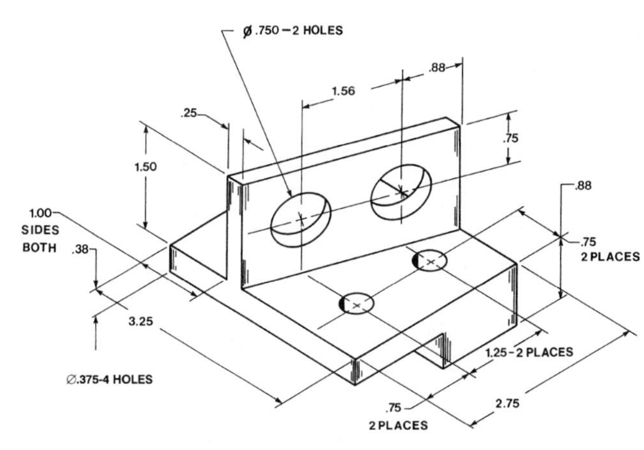

Figure P3-42 INCHES

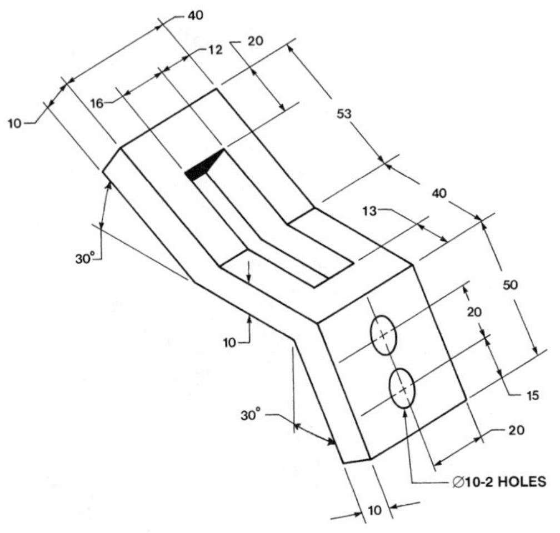

Figure P3-43 MILLIMETERS

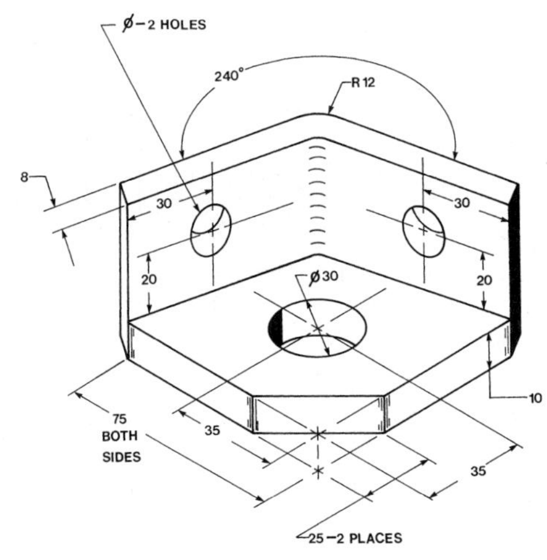

Figure P3-46 MILLIMETERS

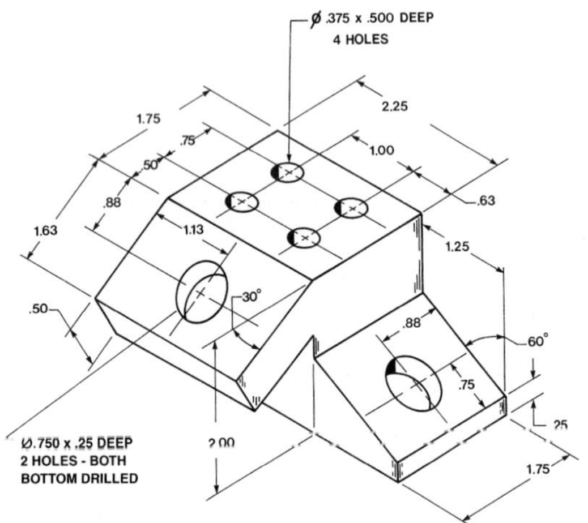

Figure P3-44 INCHES

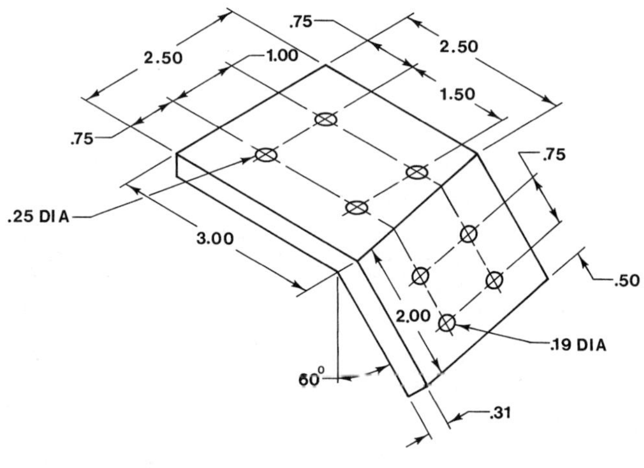

Figure P3-47 INCHES

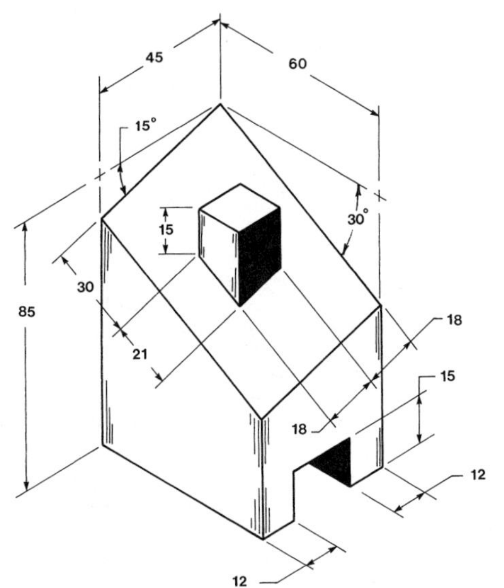

Figure P3-45 MILLIMETERS

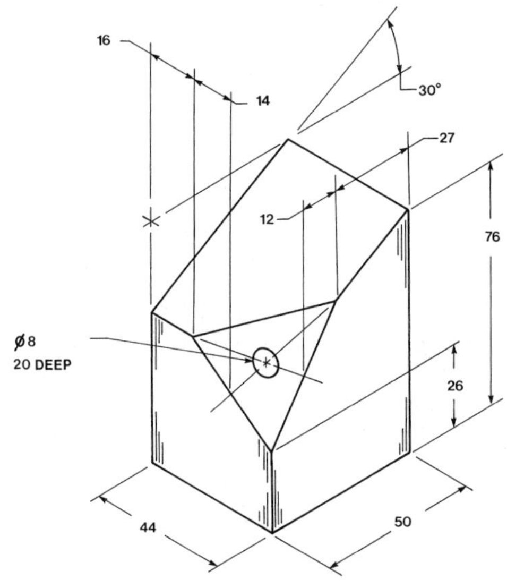

Figure P3-48 MILLIMETERS

CHAPTER 

Orthographic Views

Objectives

- Introduce orthographic views.
- Learn ANSI standards and conventions.
- Learn how to draw sectional and auxiliary views.

4-1 INTRODUCTION

Orthographic views may be created directly from 3D SolidWorks, models. ***Orthographic views*** are two-dimensional views used to define a three-dimensional model. Unless the model is of uniform thickness, more than one orthographic view is necessary to define the model's shape. Standard practice calls for three orthographic views: a front, top, and right side view, although more or fewer views may be used as needed.

Modern machines can work directly from the information generated when a solid 3D model is created, so the need for orthographic views—blueprints—is not as critical as it once was; however, there are still many drawings in existence that are used for production and reference. The ability to create and read orthographic views remains an important engineering skill.

This chapter presents orthographic views using third-angle projection in accordance with ANSI standards. ISO first-angle projections are also presented.

4-2 FUNDAMENTALS OF ORTHOGRAPHIC VIEWS

Figure 4-1 shows an object with its front, top, and right-side orthographic views projected from the object. The views are two-dimensional, so they show no depth. Note that in the projected right plane there are three rectangles. There is no way to determine which of the three is closest and which is farthest away if only the right-side view is considered. All views must be studied to analyze the shape of the object.

Figure 4-2 shows three orthographic views of a book. After the views are projected they are positioned as shown. The positioning of views relative to one another is critical. The views must be aligned and positioned as shown.

Normal Surfaces

Normal surfaces are surfaces that are at 90° to each other. Figures 4-3, 4-4, and 4-5 show objects that include only normal surfaces and their orthographic views.

Hidden Lines

Hidden lines are used to show surfaces that are not directly visible. All surfaces must be shown in all views. If an edge or surface is blocked from view by another feature, it is drawn using a hidden line. Figures 4-6 and 4-7 show objects that require hidden lines in their orthographic views.

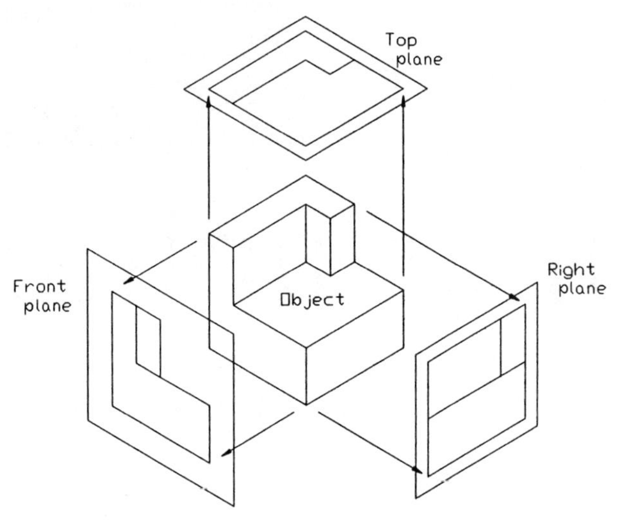

Figure 4-1

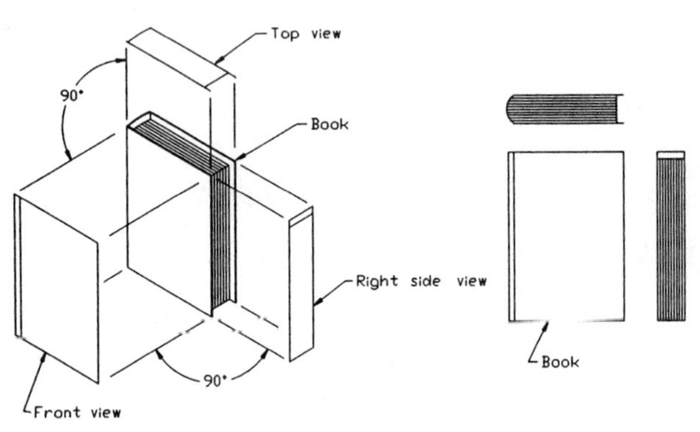

Figure 4-2

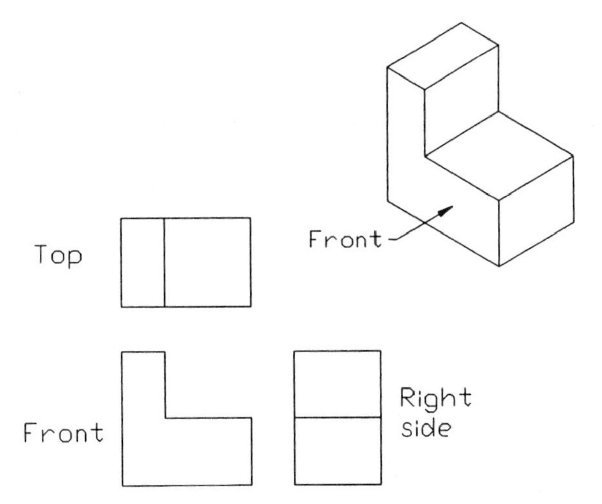

Figure 4-3

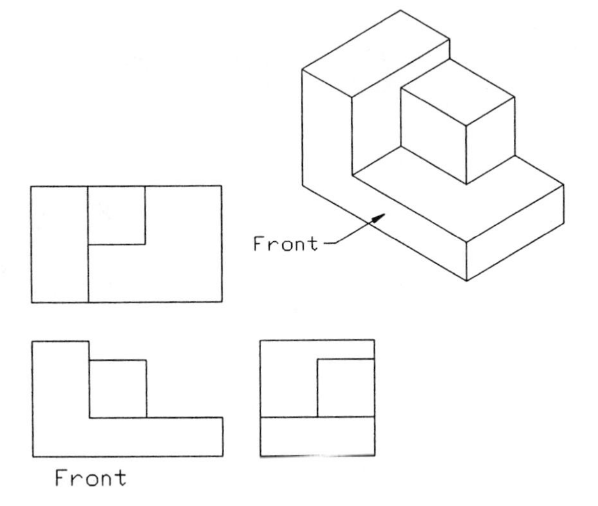

Figure 4-4

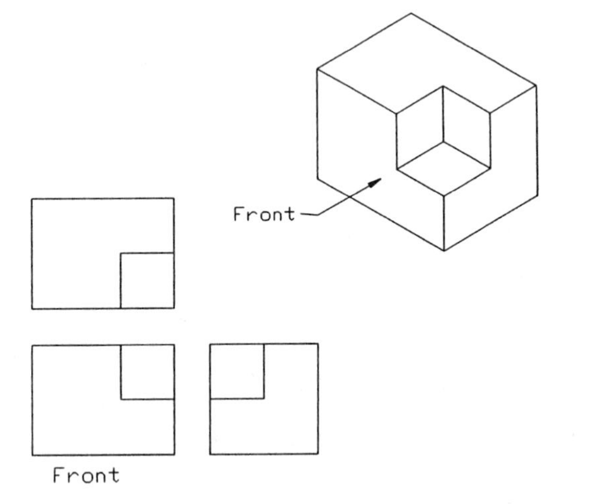

Figure 4-5

Figure 4-8 shows an object that contains an edge line, A-B. In the top view, line A-B is partially hidden and partially visible. The hidden portion of the line is drawn using a hidden-line pattern, and the visible portion of the line is drawn using a solid line.

Figures 4-9 and 4-10 show objects that require hidden lines in their orthographic views.

Precedence of Lines

It is not unusual for one type of line to be drawn over another type of line. Figure 4-11 shows two examples of overlap by different types of lines. Lines are shown on the views in a prescribed order of precedence. A solid line (object or continuous) takes precedence over a hidden line, and a hidden line takes precedence over a centerline.

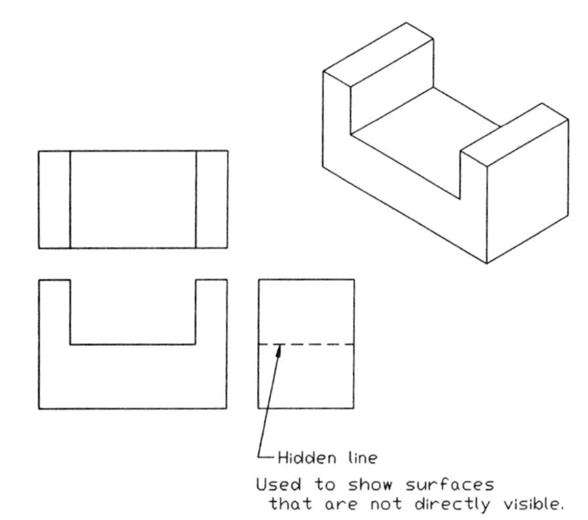

Figure 4-6

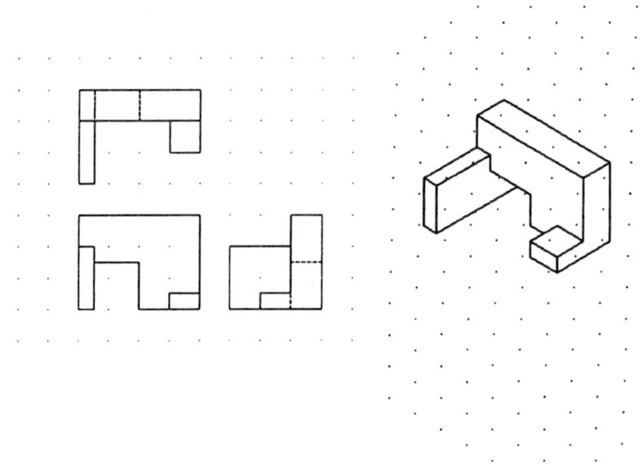

Figure 4-7

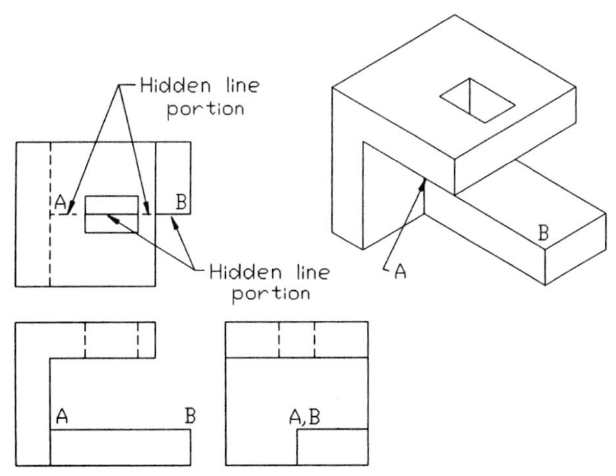

Figure 4-8

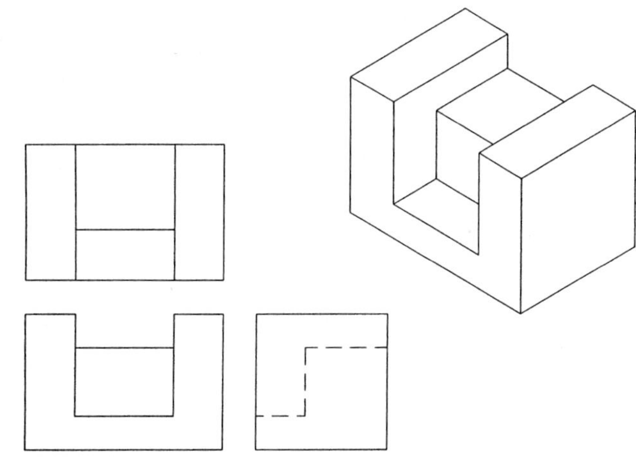

Figure 4-9

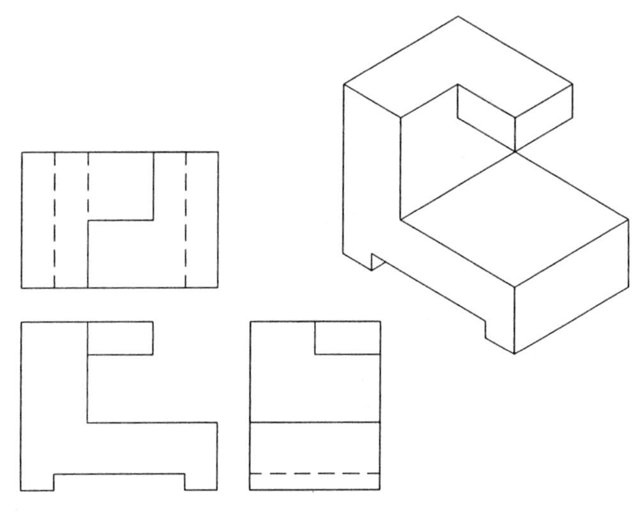

Figure 4-10

Slanted Surfaces

Slanted surfaces are surfaces drawn at an angle to each other. Figure 4-12 shows an object that contains two slanted surfaces. Surface ABCD appears as a rectangle in both the top and front views. Neither rectangle represents the true shape of the surface. Each is smaller that the actual surface. Also, none of the views show enough of the object to enable the viewer to accurately define the shape of the object. The views must be used together for a correct understanding of the object's shape.

Figures 4-13 and 4-14 show objects that include slanted surfaces. Projection lines have been included to emphasize the importance of correct view location. Information is projected between the front and top views using vertical lines and between the front and side views using horizontal lines.

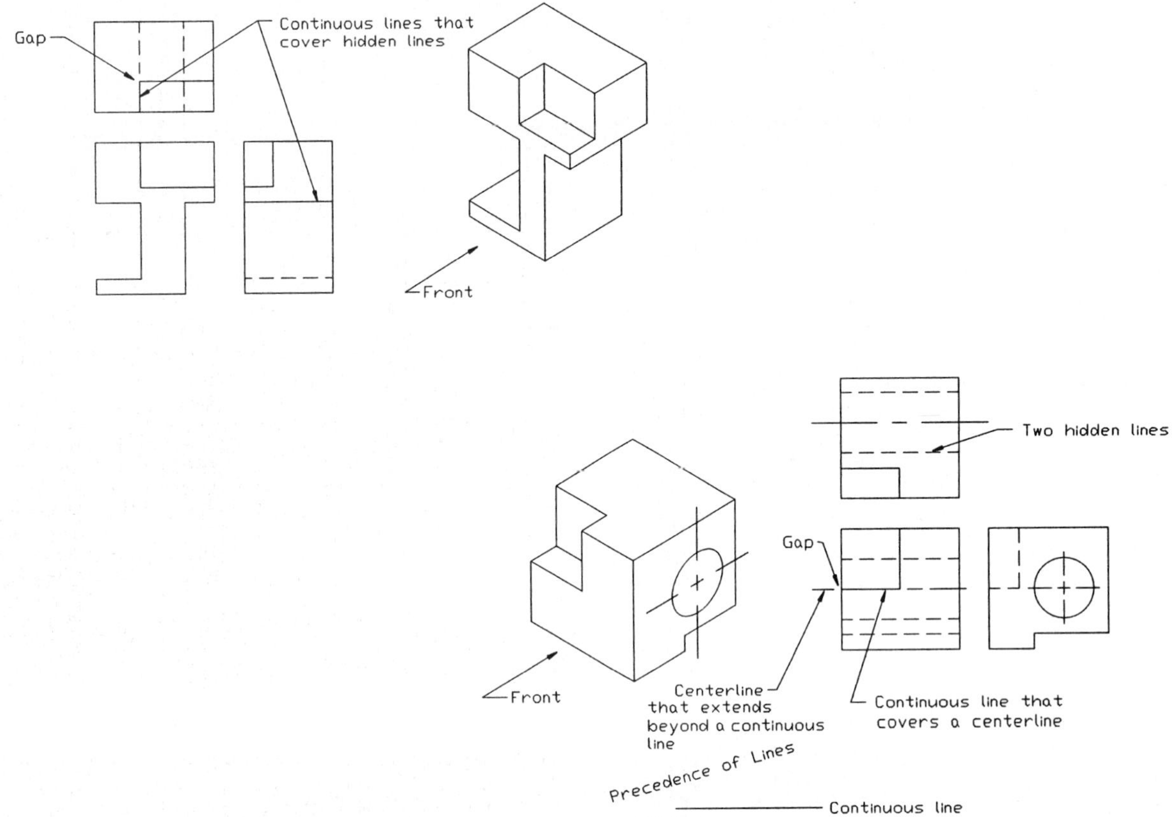

Figure 4-11

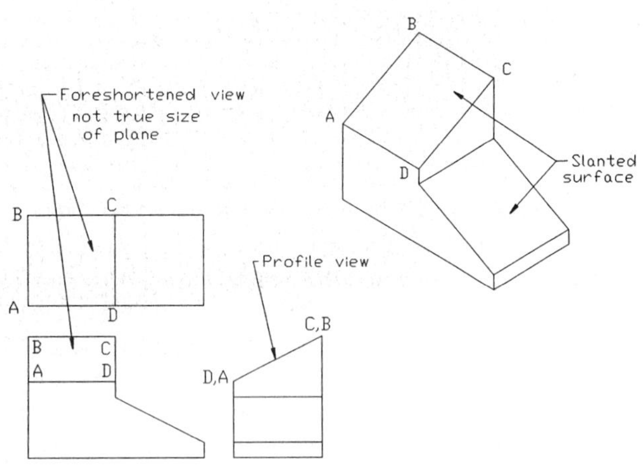

Figure 4-12

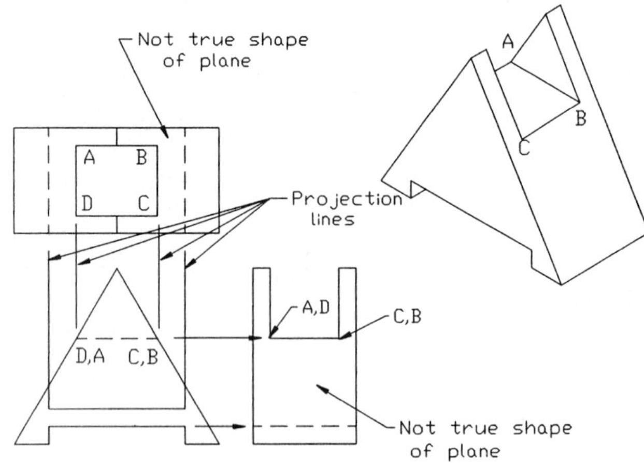

Figure 4-13

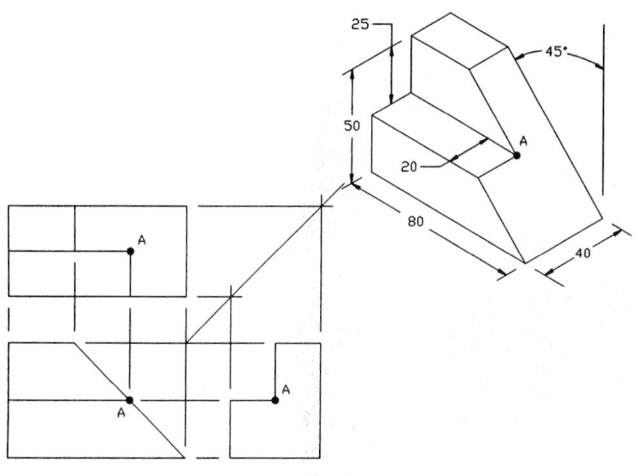

Figure 4-14

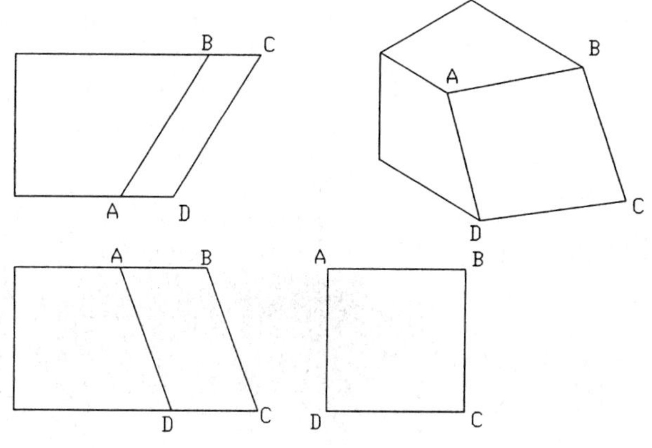

Figure 4-16

Compound Lines

A ***compound line*** is formed when two slanted surfaces intersect. Figure 4-15 shows an object that includes a compound line.

Oblique Surfaces

An ***oblique surface*** is a surface that is slanted in two different directions. Figures 4-16 and 4-17 show objects that include oblique surfaces.

Rounded Surfaces

Figure 4-18 shows an object with two rounded surfaces. Note that as with slanted surfaces, an individual view is insufficient to define the shape of a surface. More than one view is needed to accurately define the surface's shape.

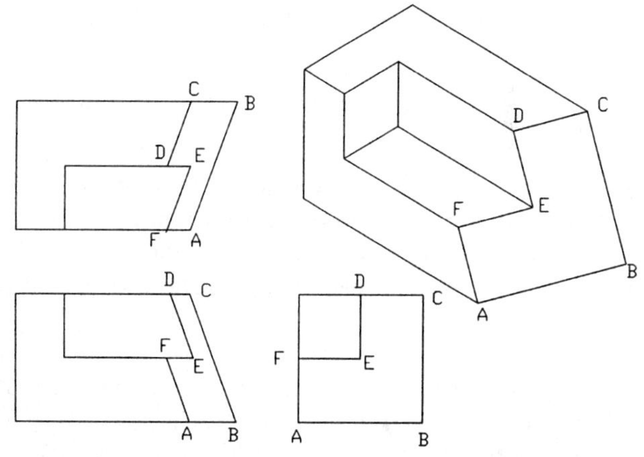

Figure 4-17

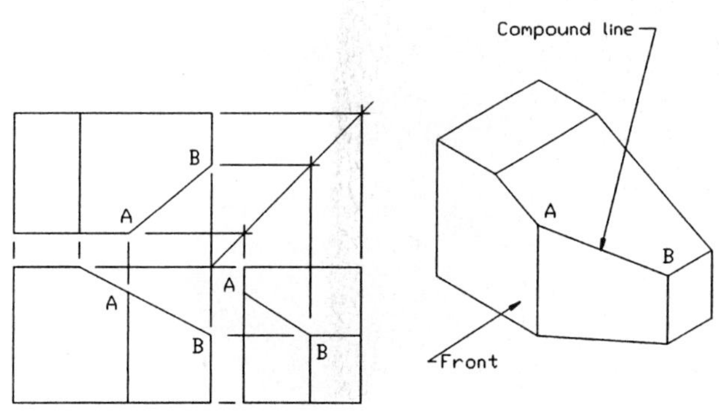

Figure 4-15

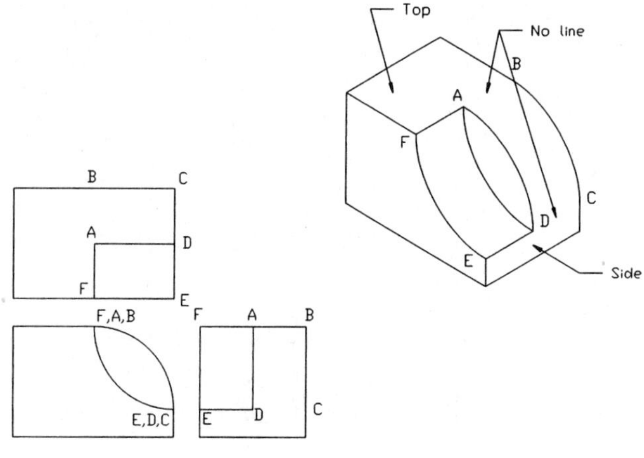

Figure 4-18

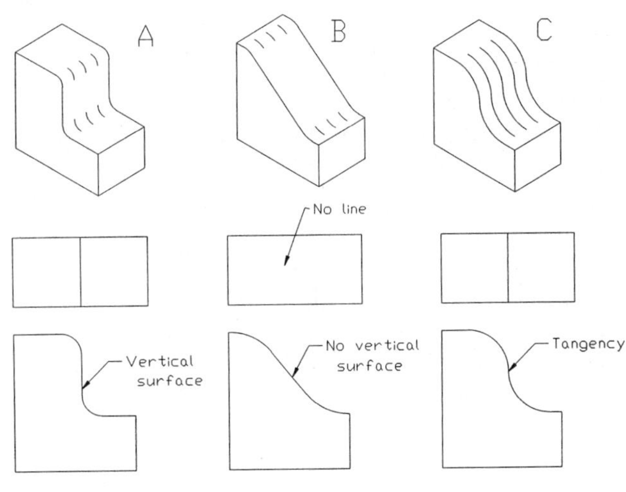

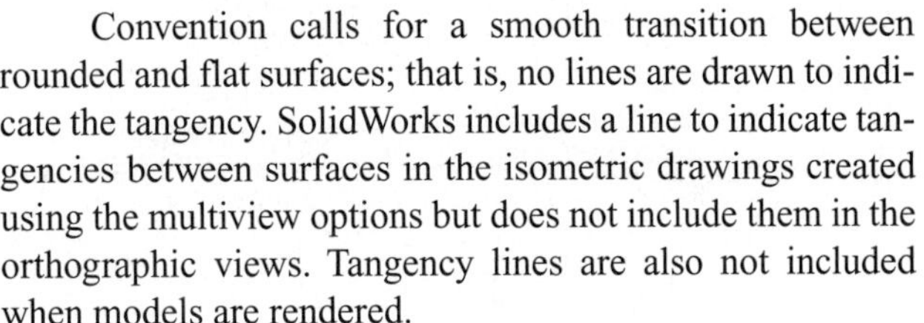

Figure 4-19

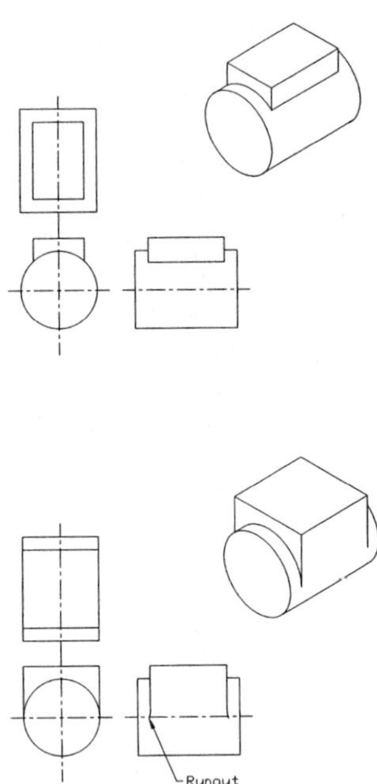

Figure 4-21

Convention calls for a smooth transition between rounded and flat surfaces; that is, no lines are drawn to indicate the tangency. SolidWorks includes a line to indicate tangencies between surfaces in the isometric drawings created using the multiview options but does not include them in the orthographic views. Tangency lines are also not included when models are rendered.

Figure 4-19 shows the drawing conventions for including lines for rounded surfaces. If a surface includes no vertical portions or no tangency, no line is included.

Figure 4-20 shows an object that includes two tangencies. Each is represented by a line. Note in Figure 4-20 that SolidWorks will add tangent lines to the 3D model. These lines will not appear in the orthographic views.

Figure 4-21 shows two objects with similar configurations; however, the boxlike portion of the lower object blends into the rounded portion exactly on its widest point, so no line is required.

4-3 DRAWING ORTHOGRAPHIC VIEWS USING SOLIDWORKS

SolidWorks creates orthographic views using the **Drawing** tools found on the **New SolidWorks Document** box. See Figure 4-22.

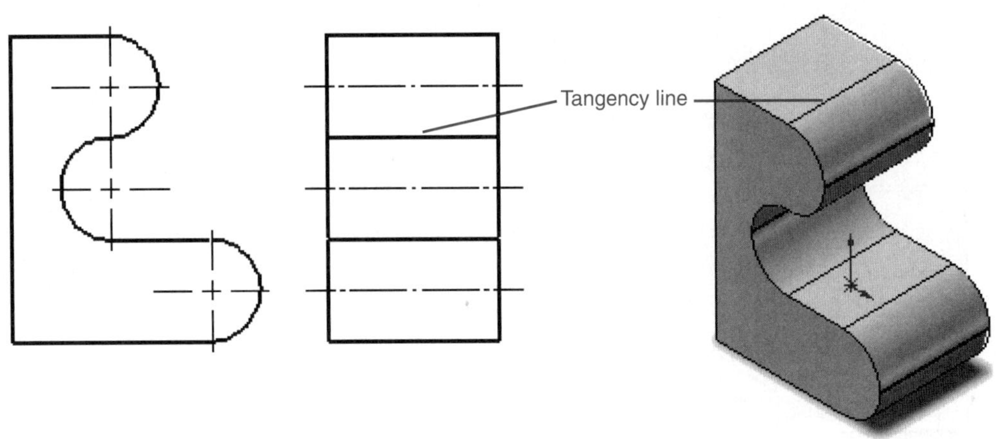

Figure 4-20

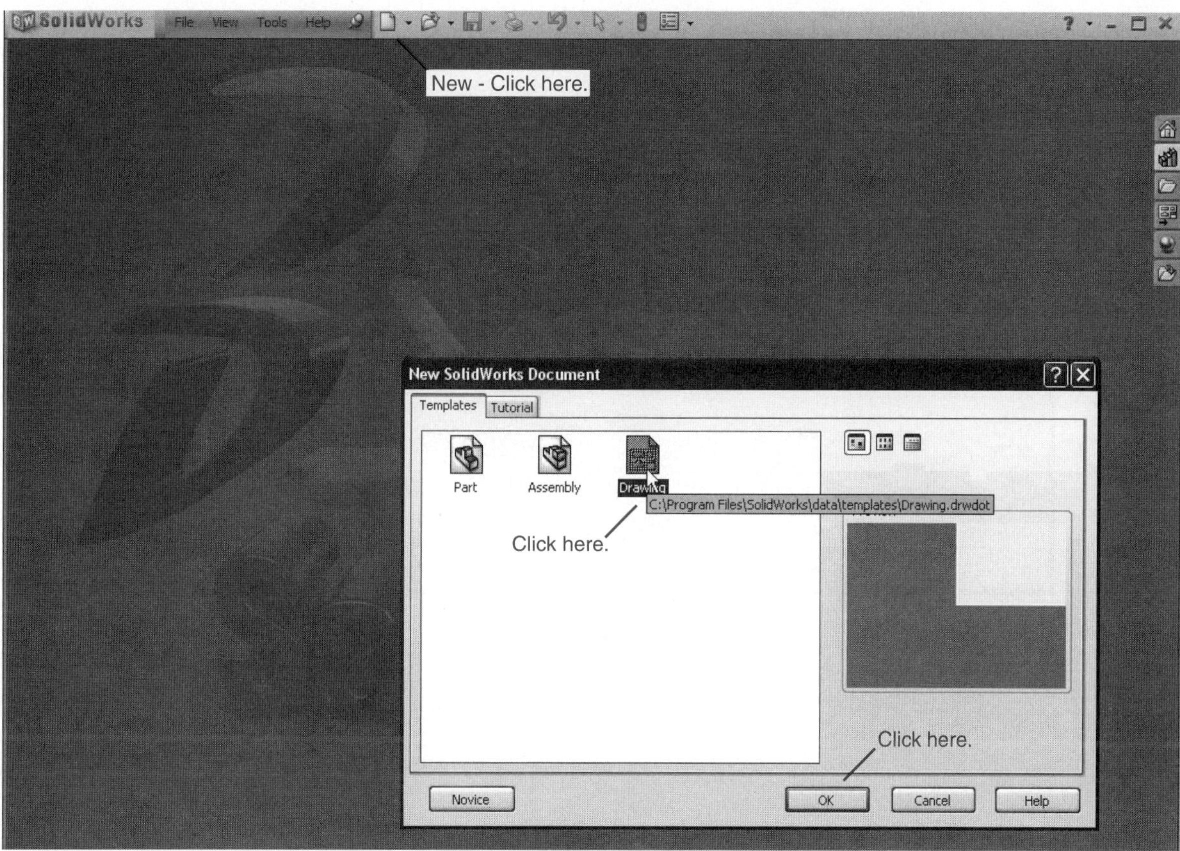

Figure 4-22

1. Start a new drawing by click the **New** tool.
2. Click the **Drawing** icon on the **New SolidWorks Document** box.
3. Click **OK.**

The **Sheet Format/Size** box will appear. See Figure 4-23. Accept the **A-Landscape** format.

TIP

Drawing sheets, that is, the paper drawings are printed on, are manufactured in standard sizes. For example, in the English unit system an A-size drawing sheet is 8.5 × 11 in. In the metric unit system an A0-size drawing sheet is 210 × 297 mm.

A listing of standard sheet sizes is shown in Figure 4-23.

4. Click **OK.**

A drawing template will appear. See Figure 4-24. The template includes a title block, a release block, a tolerance block, and two other blocks. The template format can be customized, but in this example the default template will be used. The title block will be explained in the next section.

5. Click the **X** mark under the **Model View** heading.
6. Move the cursor into the drawing area and right-click the mouse.
7. Select the **Properties** option.

See Figure 4-25.
The **Sheet Properties** box will appear. See Figure 4-26.

8. Click the **Third angle** button.
9. Click **OK.**

Third-angle projection is the format preferred by U.S. companies in compliance with ANSI (American National Standards Institute) standards. First-angle projection is used by countries that are in compliance with ISO (International Standards Organization). Figure 4-27 shows an L-bracket drawn in both first- and third-angle projection. Compare the differences in the projected views.

Figure 4-27 also shows a dimensioned isometric drawing of the L-bracket. The bracket was drawn in Section 3-3. If you have not previously drawn the bracket, do so now and save it as L-bracket.

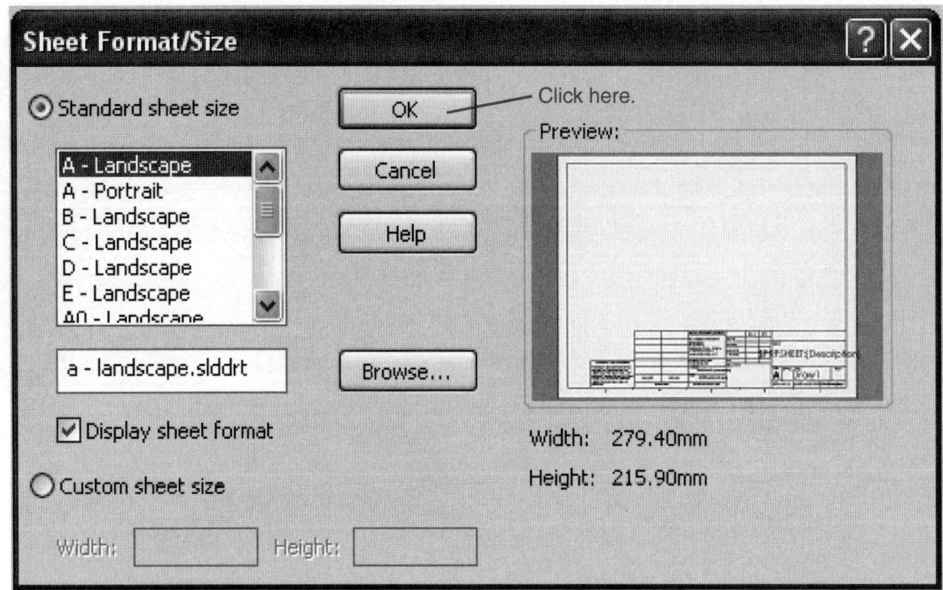

Standard Drawing Sheet Sizes Inches
A = 8.5 × 11
B = 11 × 17
C = 17 × 22
D = 22 × 34
E = 34 × 44

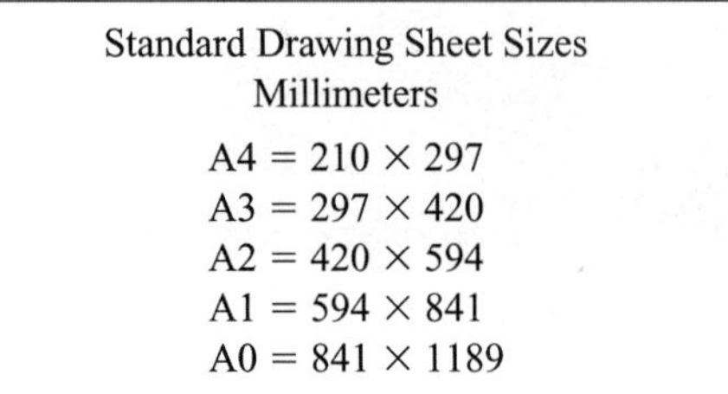

Standard Drawing Sheet Sizes Millimeters
A4 = 210 × 297
A3 = 297 × 420
A2 = 420 × 594
A1 = 594 × 841
A0 = 841 × 1189

Figure 4-23

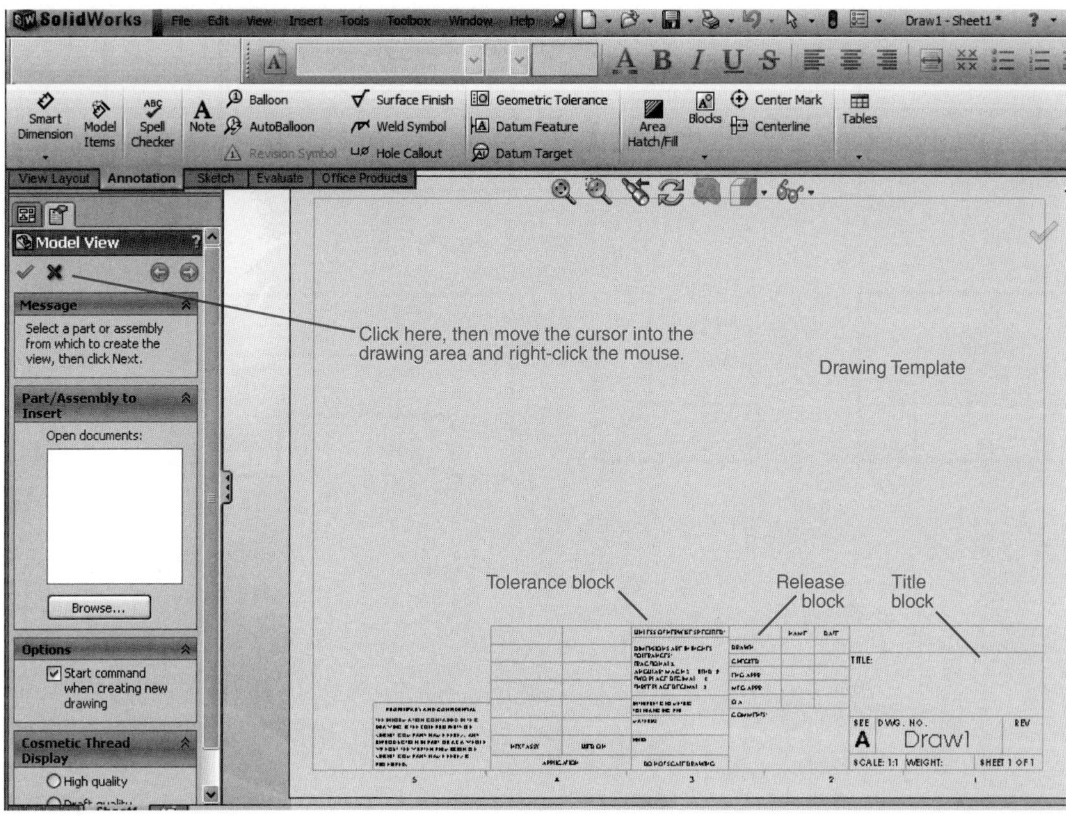

Figure 4-24

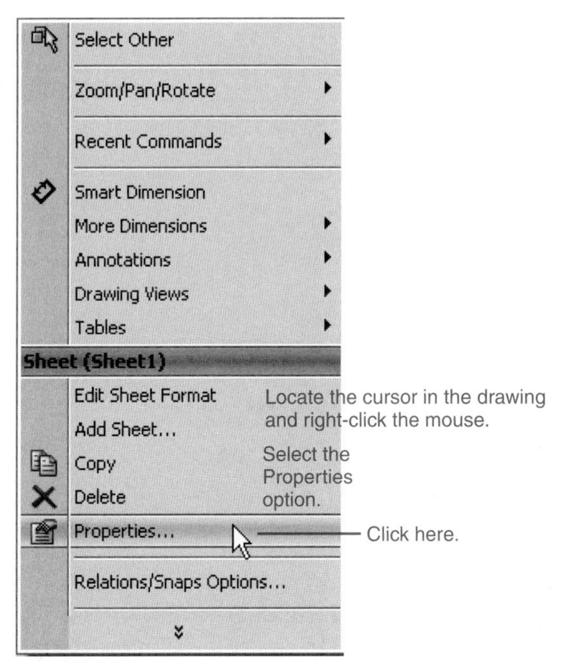

Figure 4-25

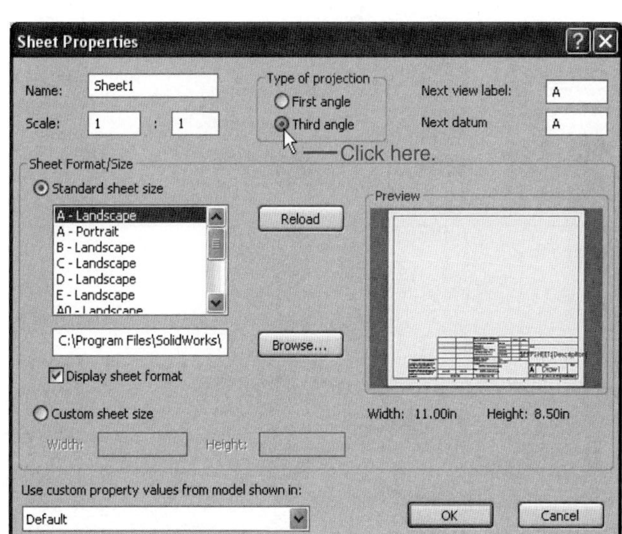

Figure 4-26

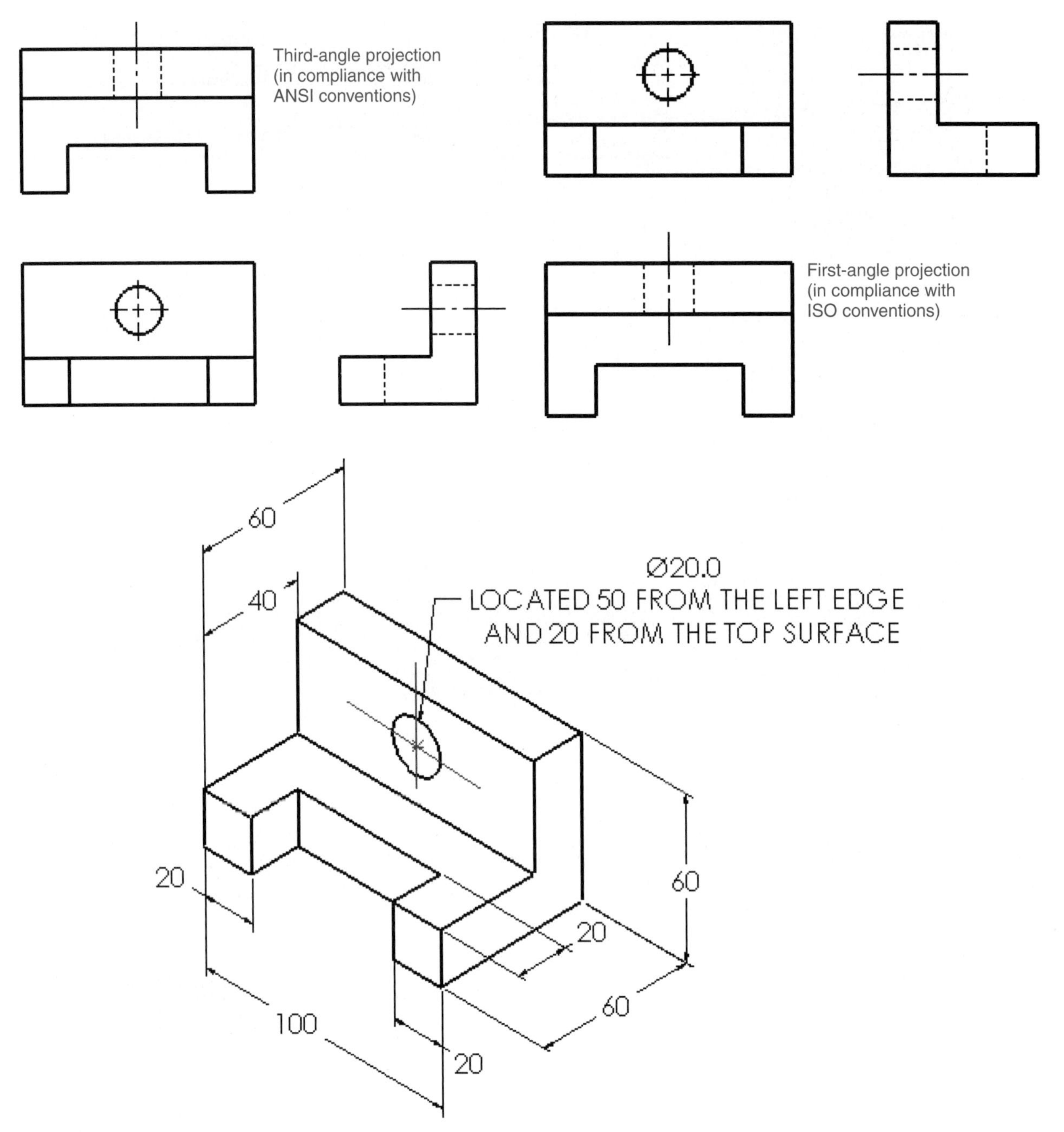

Figure 4-27

10. Click the **Standard 3 View** tool located among the **Drawings** tools.

See Figure 4-28. The **Standard 3 View** box will appear on the left side of the screen.

11. Click the **Browse . . .** box.

The **Open** box will appear. See Figure 4-29.

12. Select the **L-bracket,** and click **Open.**

The orthographic views of the L-bracket will appear on the screen. See Figure 4-30. Notice in the top and right-side views that there are no centerlines for the hole. Centerlines are added using the **Centerline** option found in the **Annotation** tools. See Figure 4-31. The circular view of the hole will automatically generate a set of perpendicular centerlines.

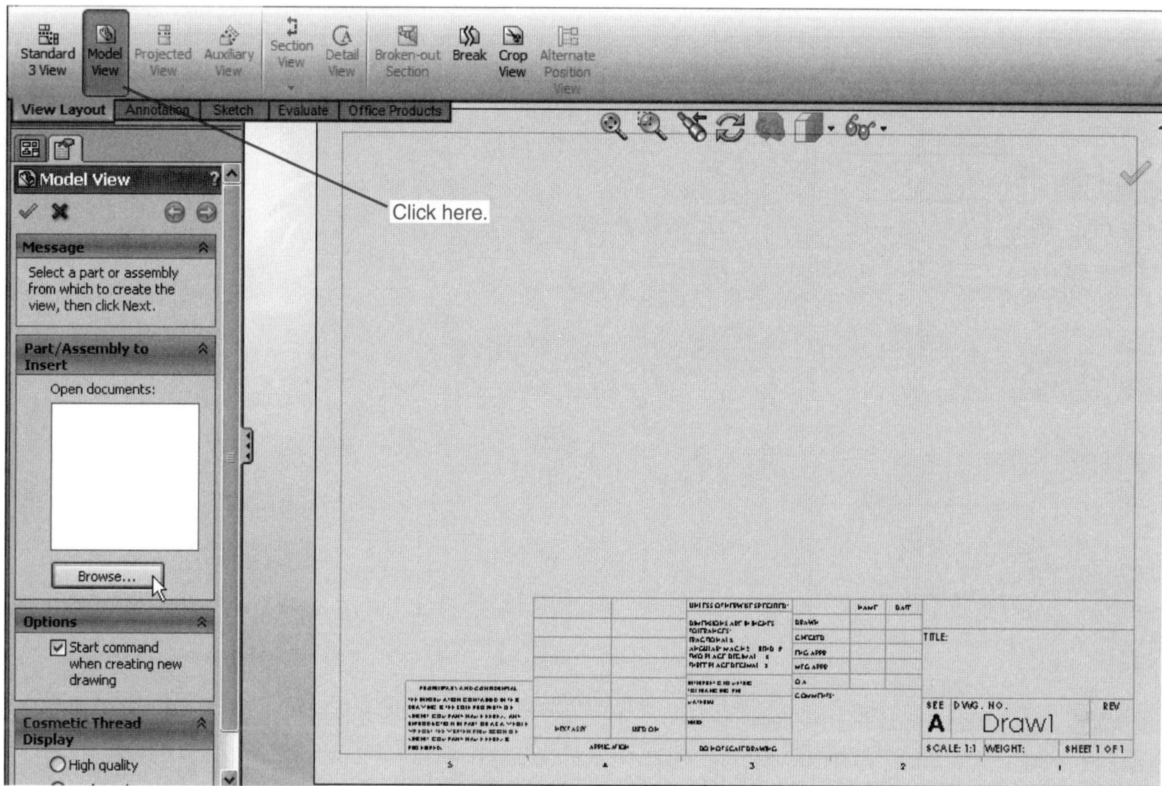

Figure 4-28

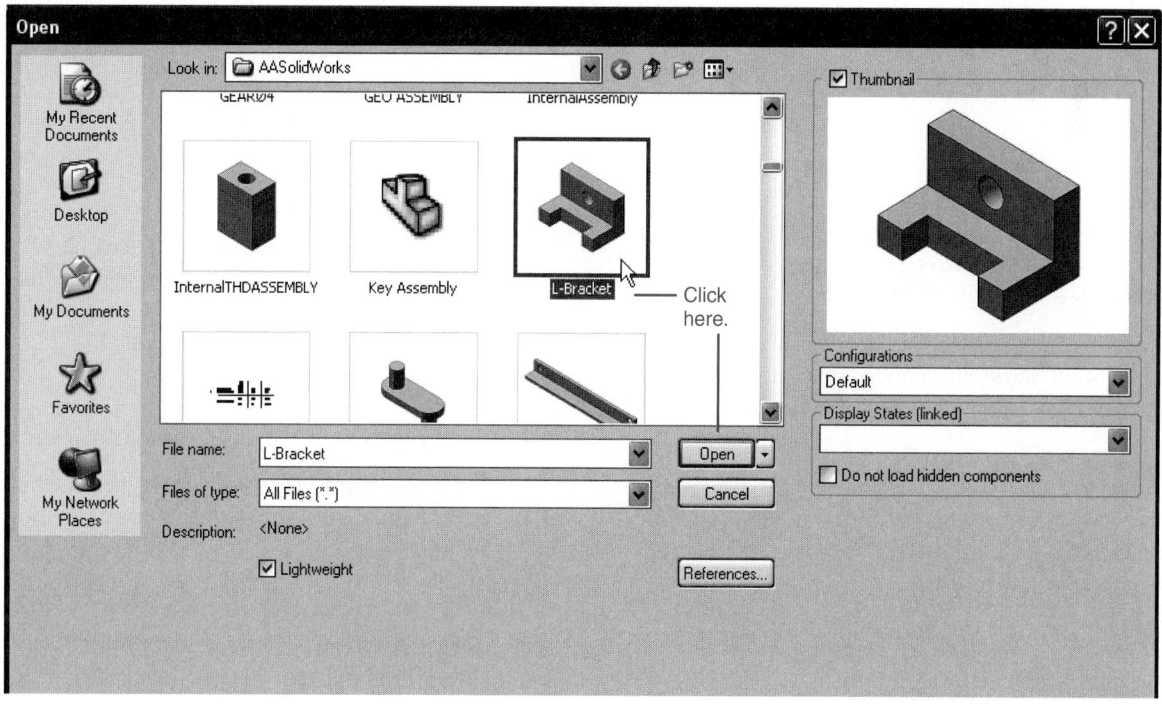

Figure 4-29

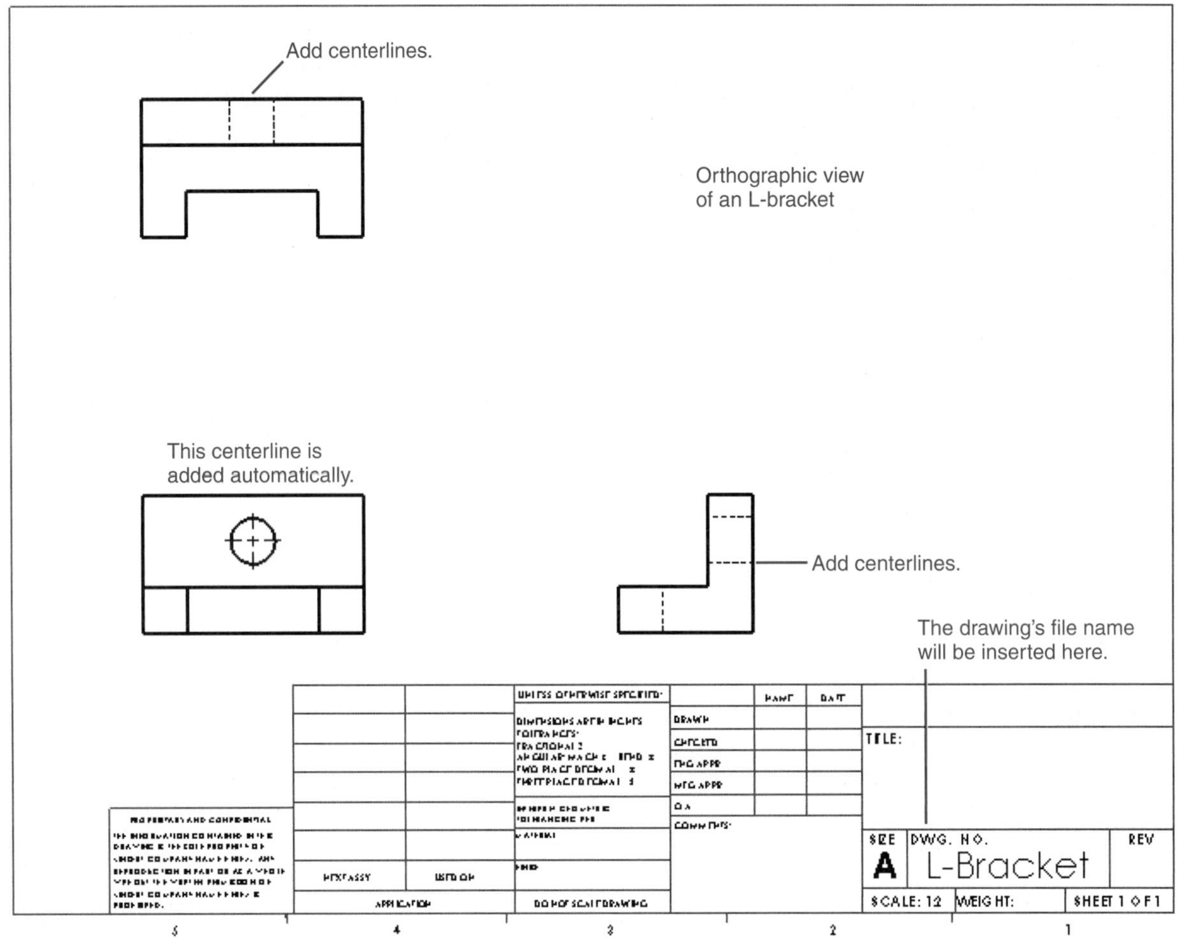

Figure 4-30

13. Click the arrow on the right side of the **Annotation** box and select the **Centerline** option.
14. Click each of the two parallel lines in the top and side views that define the hole.

The centerlines will appear. See Figure 4-32.

Figure 4-33 shows the orthographic views of another object. The dimensions for the object are given in Figure P4-7.

To Move Orthographic Views

Figure 4-34 shows the orthographic views of the L-bracket generated for Figure 4-32. The views can be moved closer together or farther apart

1. Move the cursor into the area of the top view.

   A red boundary line will appear.

2. Click and hold one of the boundary lines.
3. Drag the view to a new location.

To Create Other Views

The **Standard 3 View** tool will generate front, top, and right-side orthographic views of an object. These views are considered the standard three views. Other orthographic views and isometric views can be generated.

1. Click the **Project View** tool.

   The **Project View** tool is one of the **Drawing** tools.

2. Click the front view and move the cursor to the left of the front, creating a new orthographic view.

   In this example a left-side view was created.

3. Click the left view in its new location.
4. Press the <**Esc**> key or click the OK check mark.

   See Figure 4-35.

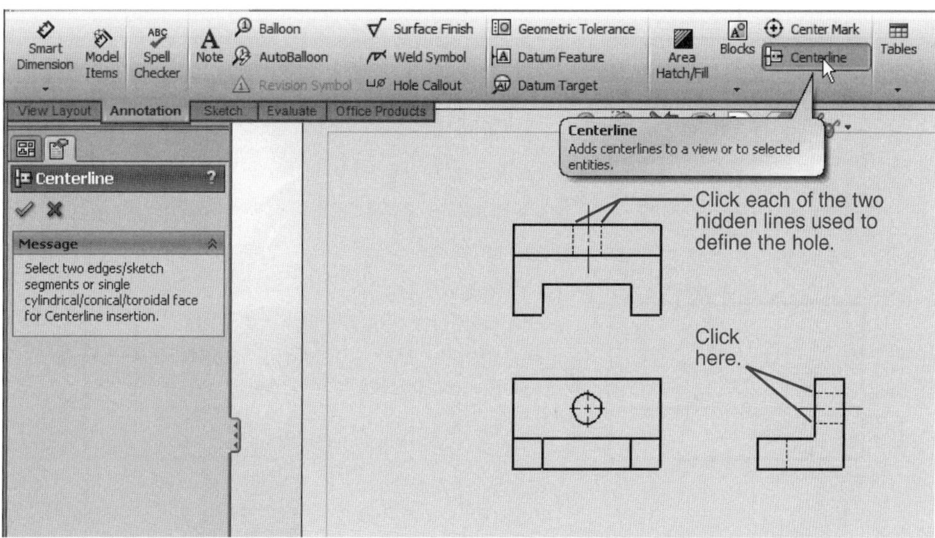

Figure 4-31

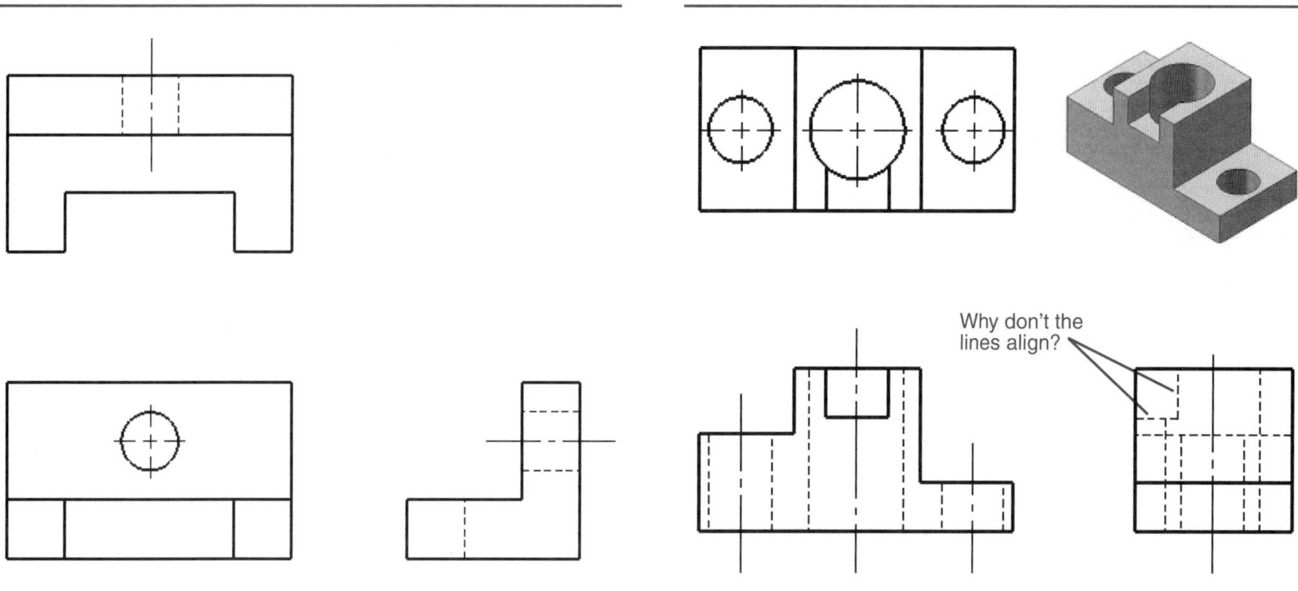

Figure 4-32

Figure 4-33

5. Use the **Centerline** tool to add a centerline to the hole in the left-side view.
6. Click the **Project** tool and click the front view again.
7. Move the cursor to the right and upward.

An isometric view will appear.

8. Click the isometric view in its new location.
9. Press the **<Esc>** key or click the OK check mark.

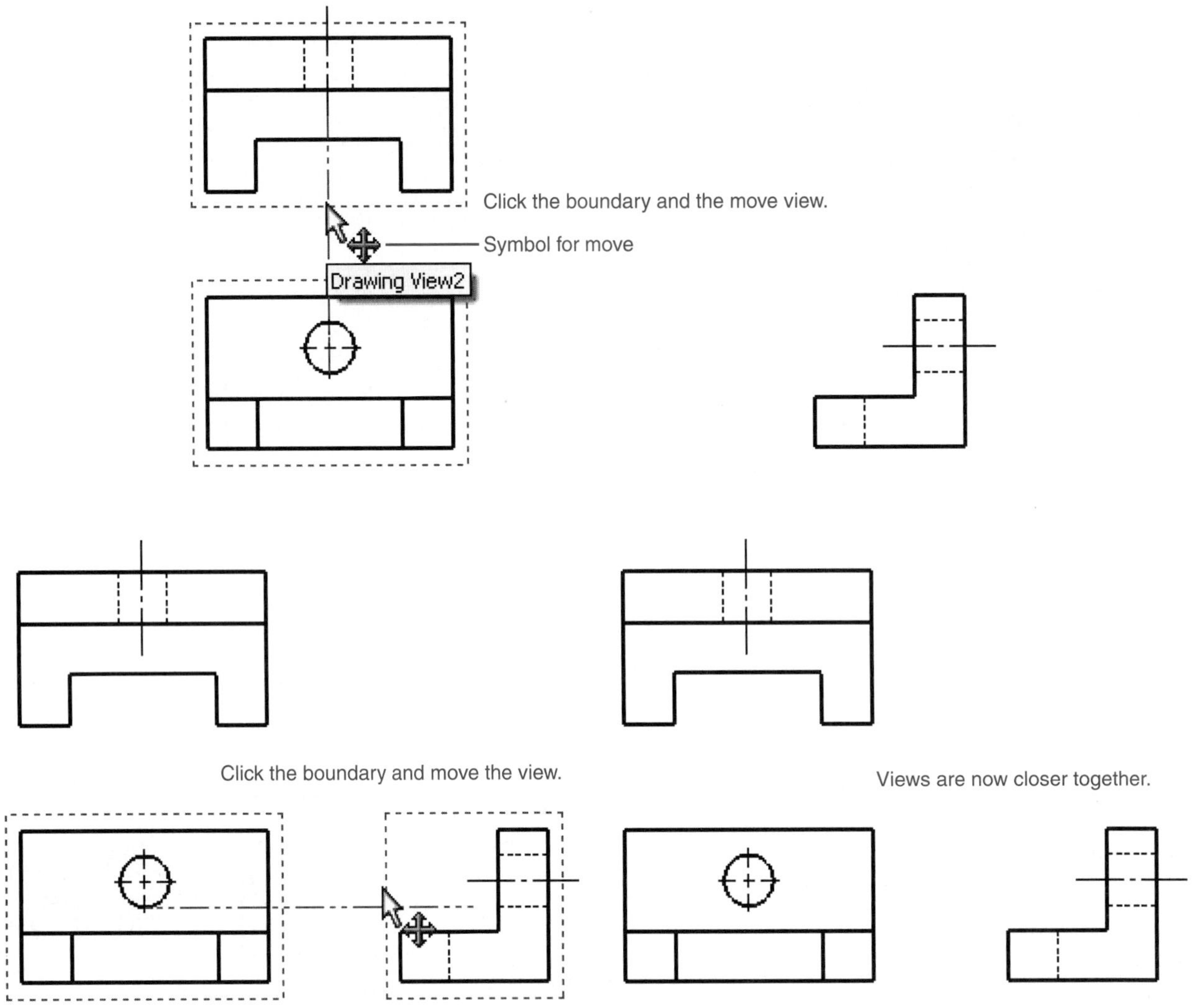

Click the boundary and the move view.
Symbol for move
Drawing View2
Click the boundary and move the view.
Views are now closer together.

Figure 4-34

Isometric view
Left-side view
Click the front view and move the cursor to the left, projecting a left-side view.
Click the front view and move to the right and upward to create an isometric view.

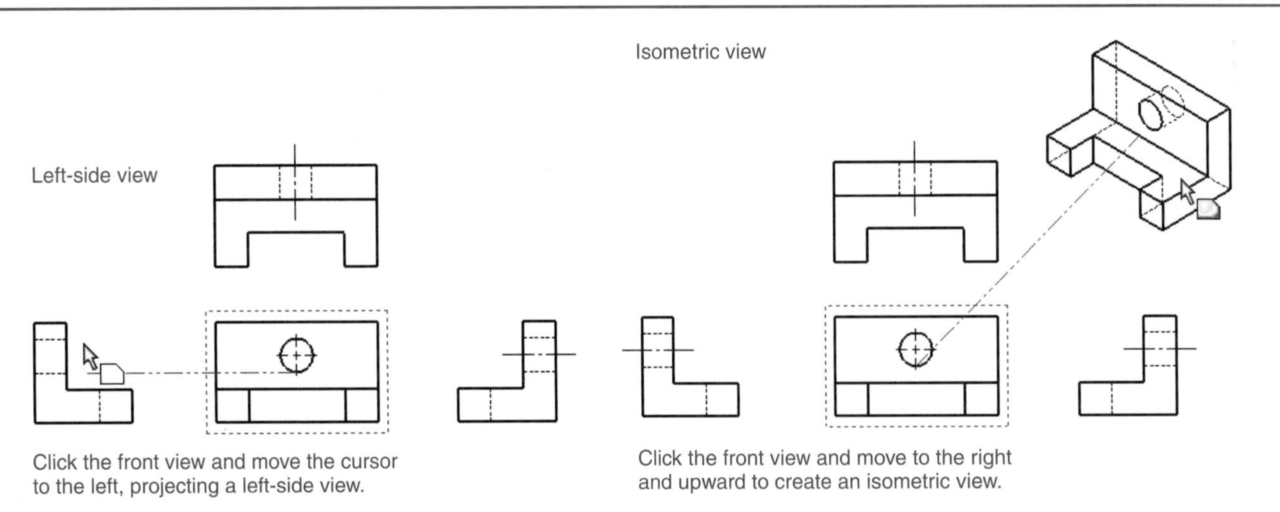

Figure 4-35

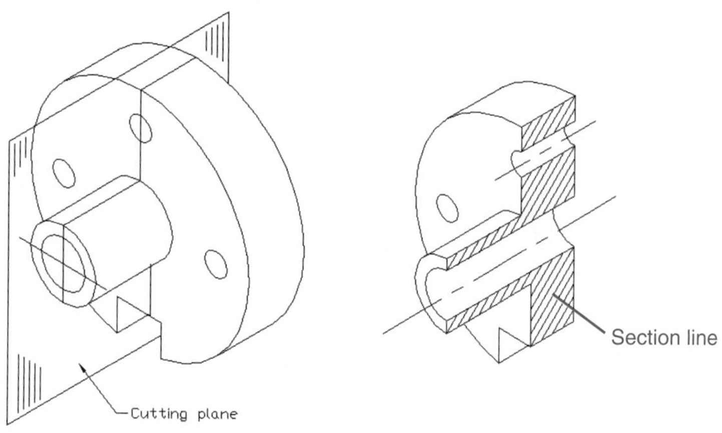

Figure 4-36

4-4 SECTION VIEWS

Some objects have internal surfaces that are not directly visible in normal orthographic views. ***Section views*** are used to expose these surfaces. Section views do not include hidden lines.

Any material cut when a section view is defined is hatched using section lines. There are many different styles of hatching, but the general style is evenly spaced 45° lines. This style is defined as ANSI 31 and will be applied automatically by SolidWorks.

Figure 4-36 shows a three-dimensional view of an object. The object is cut by a cutting plane. ***Cutting planes*** are used to define the location of the section view. Material to one side of the cutting plane is removed, exposing the section view.

Figure 4-37 shows the same object presented using two dimensions. The cutting plane is represented by a cutting plane line. The cutting plane line is defined as A-A, and the section view is defined as view A-A.

All surfaces directly visible must be shown in a section view. In Figure 4-38 the back portion of the object is not affected by the section view and is directly visible from the cutting plane. The section view must include these surfaces. Note how the rectangular section blocks out part of the large hole. No hidden lines are used to show the hidden portion of the large hole.

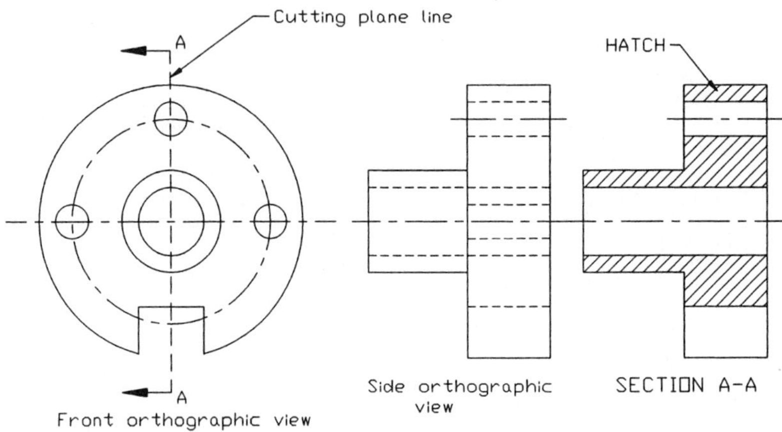

Figure 4-37

4-5 DRAWING A SECTION VIEW USING SOLIDWORKS

This section will show how to draw a section view of an existing model. In this example, the model pictured in Figure 4-33 is used.

1. Start a new drawing using the **Drawing** format.

See the previous section on how to create orthographic views using SolidWorks. Select the **A-Landscape** format and select the third-angle format.

> *Note:*
> See Figures 4-24 to 4-27 for an explanation of how to access the third-angle format.

2. Click the **Model View** tool.

> **TIP**
> The **Model View** tool is similar to the **Standard 3 View** tool but creates only one view rather that three views.

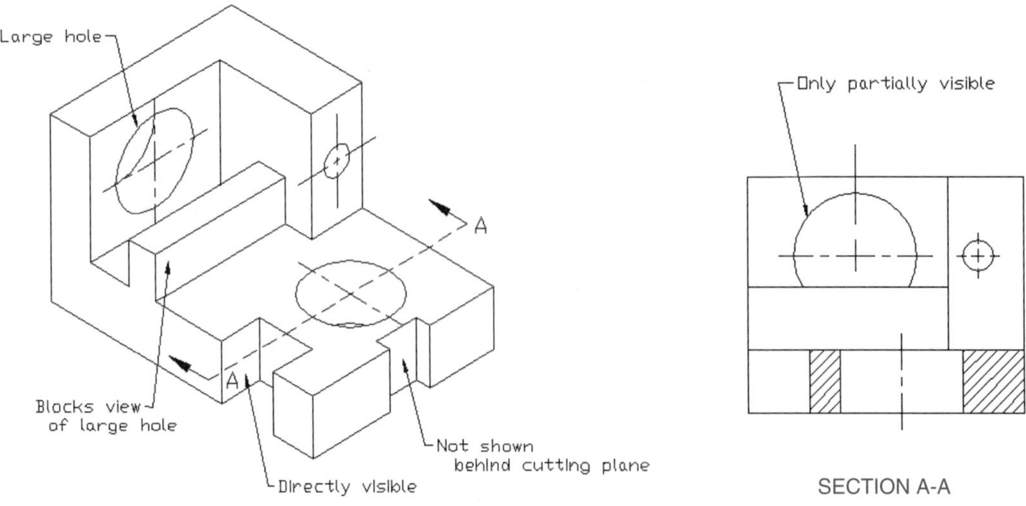

Figure 4-38

3. In the **Part/Assembly to Insert** box click **Browse . . .**

See Figure 4-39. The **Open** box will appear. See Figure 4-40.

4. Click the model to be used to draw orthographic views, and click **Open.**

In this example the model is called **BLOCK, 3 HOLE.** The dimensions for the BLOCK, 3 HOLE can be found in Project P4-7.

A rectangular outline will appear defining the boundaries of the orthographic view. By default, this will be a front view. In this example we want a top view.

5. Click the **Top** view tool.

See Figure 4-41.

6. Locate the top orthographic view on the drawing screen and click the mouse.

See Figure 4-42.

7. Click the **Drawings** tool and click the **Section View** tool.

The orthographic view will be outlined by a dotted line.

> ***Note:***
> If more than one view was present on the screen, you would first have to select which view you wanted to be used to create the section view.

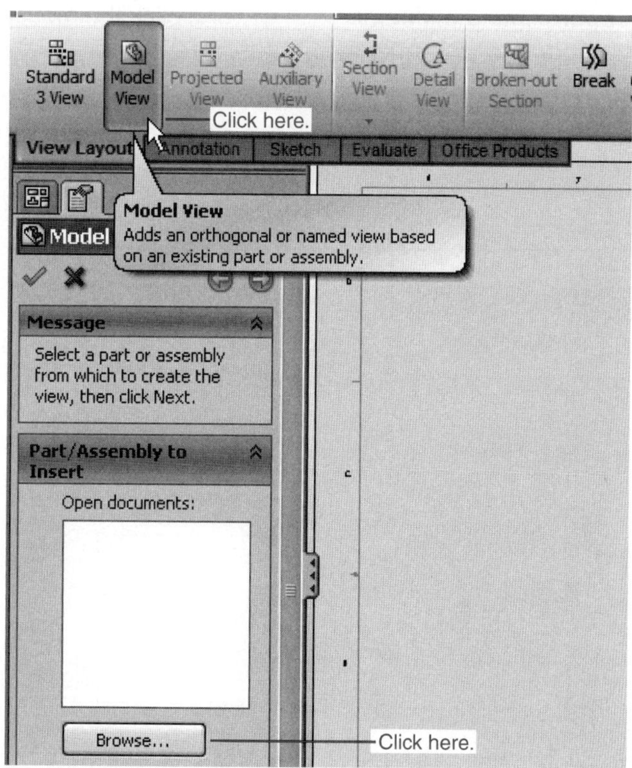

Figure 4-39

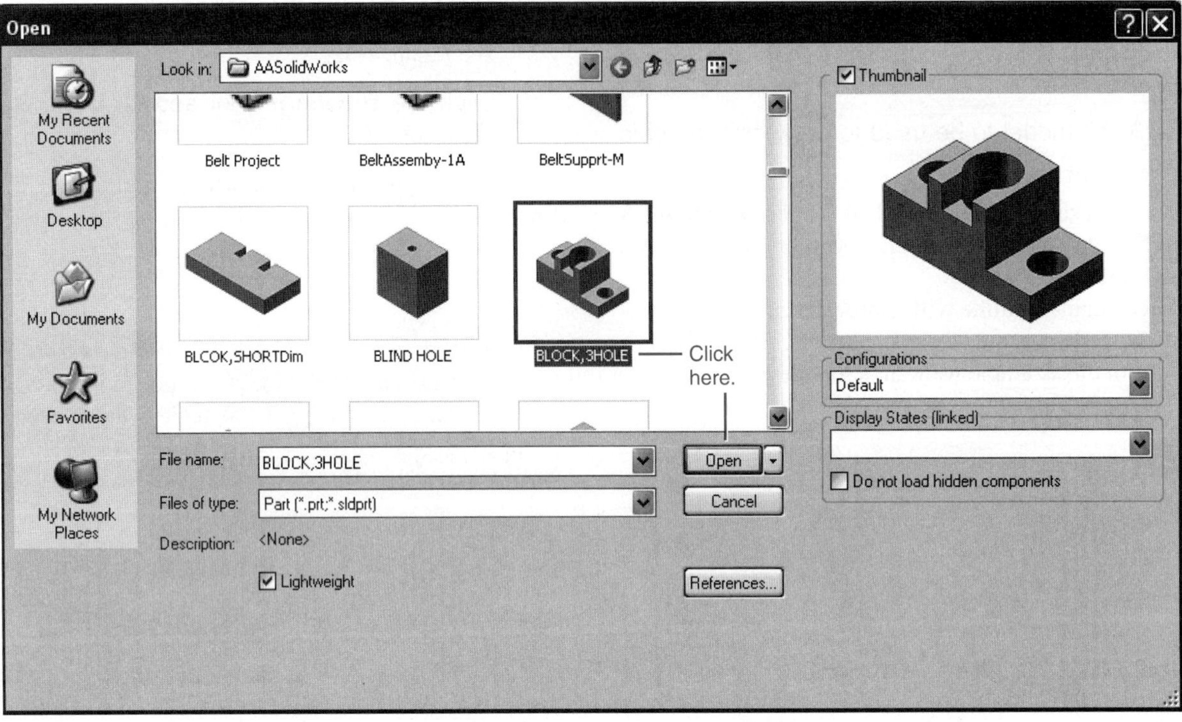

Figure 4-40

8. Define the location of the cutting plane line by moving the cursor to the approximate midpoint of the left vertical line of the orthographic view,

The system will automatically jump to the line's midpoint. A light gray icon will appear.

9. Move the cursor to the left of the view's edge line and click the mouse.

A dotted line will follow the cursor.

10. Move the cursor across the view to a point to the right of the right vertical line.
11. Click the mouse and move the cursor downward.

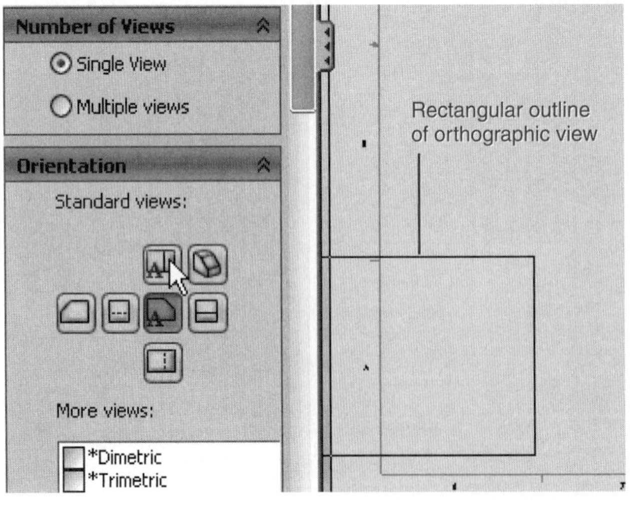

Figure 4-41

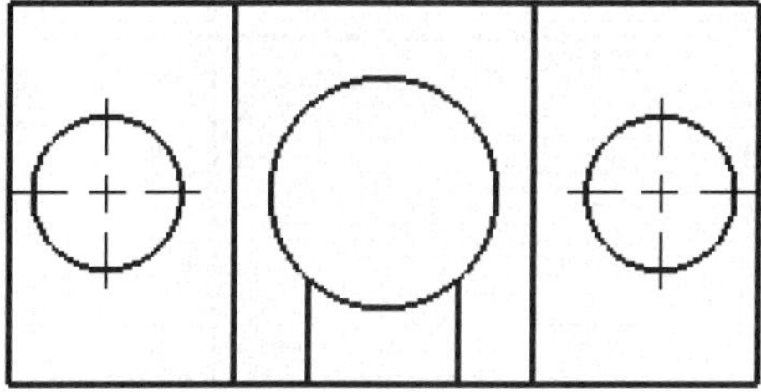

Figure 4-42

The section view will appear and move with the cursor. See Figure 4-43.

12. Select an appropriate location and click the mouse.
13. Click the **Flip direction** box.

    See Figure 4-44.

> ***Note:***
> Section views are always located behind the arrows; that is, the arrows point away from the section view. Think of the arrows as your eyes looking at the section view.

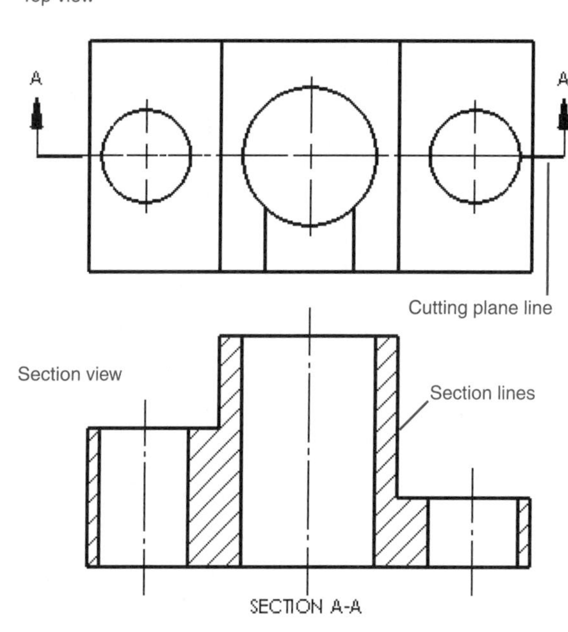

Figure 4-44

14. Click the OK check mark.

More than one section view may be taken from the same model. See Figure 4-45.

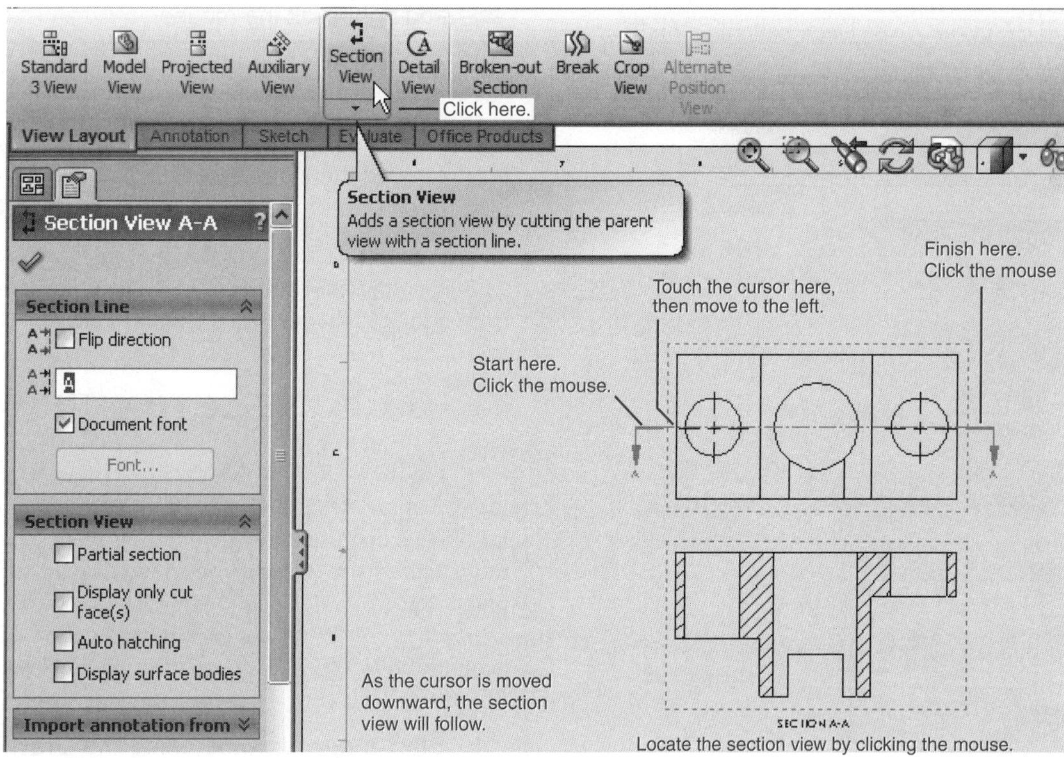

Figure 4-43

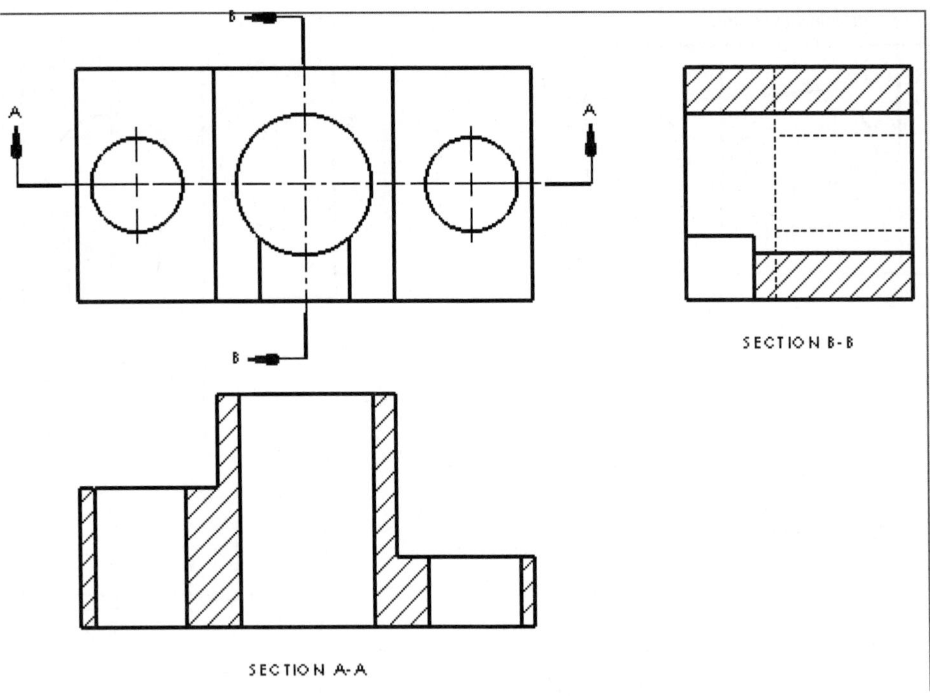

Figure 4-45

The section views shown in Figure 4-45 use a hatching pattern made from evenly spaced 45° lines. This is the most commonly used hatch pattern for section views and is designated as ANSI 31 in the ANSI hatch patterns. SolidWorks can also draw section views using one of five different styles. See Figure 4-46.

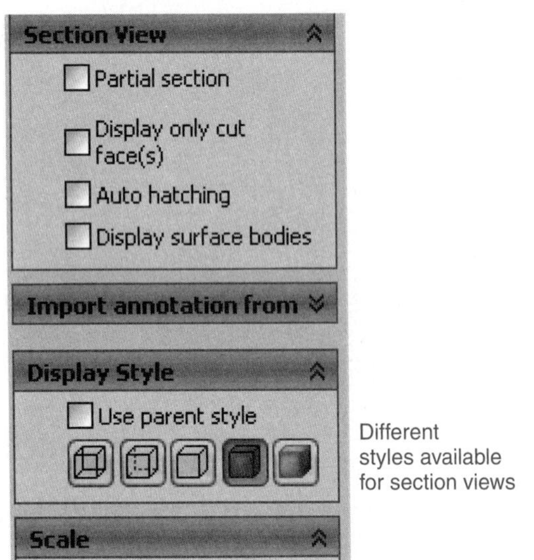

Figure 4-46

To Change the Style of a Section View

1. Move the cursor into the area of the section view and right-click the mouse.

A listing of tools will appear, and the **Display Style** box will appear.

2. Click the mouse again in the section view area to remove the list of tools.
3. Click one of the boxes in the **Display Style** box.

Figure 4-47 shows two of the styles available: shaded with edge lines and shaded. The hidden lines removed style is used for all other illustrations in this chapter.

4-6 ALIGNED SECTION VIEWS

Figure 4-48 shows an example of an aligned section view. Aligned section views are most often used on circular objects and use an angled cutting plane line to include more features in the section view, like an offset cutting plane line.

Figure 4-49 shows an aligned section view created using SolidWorks. The aligned section view was created as follows.

1. Start a new drawing using the **Drawing** format and enter the model for the aligned section view.

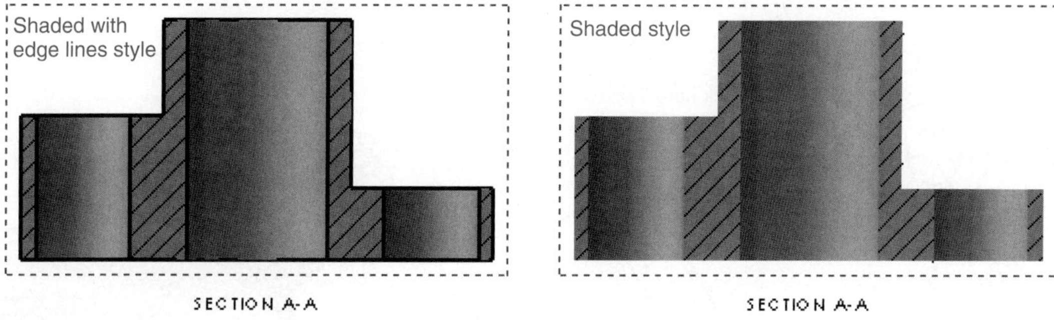

Figure 4-47

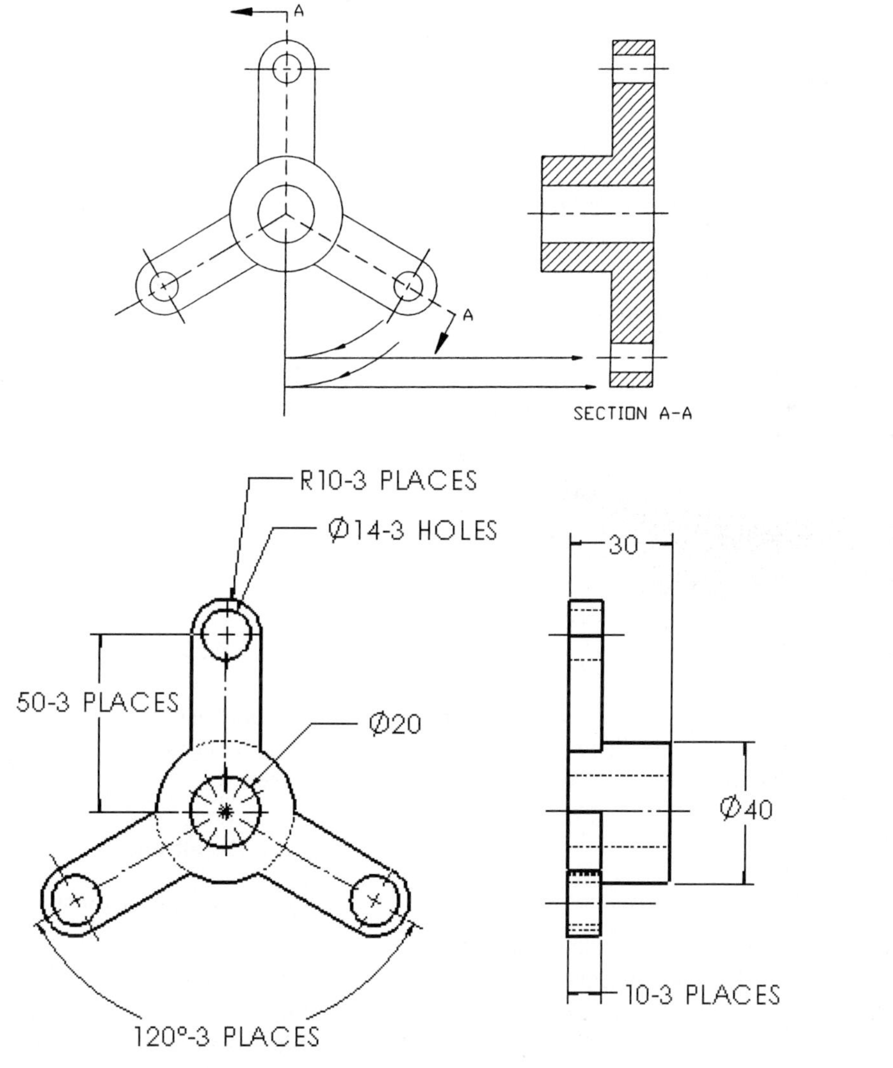

Figure 4-48

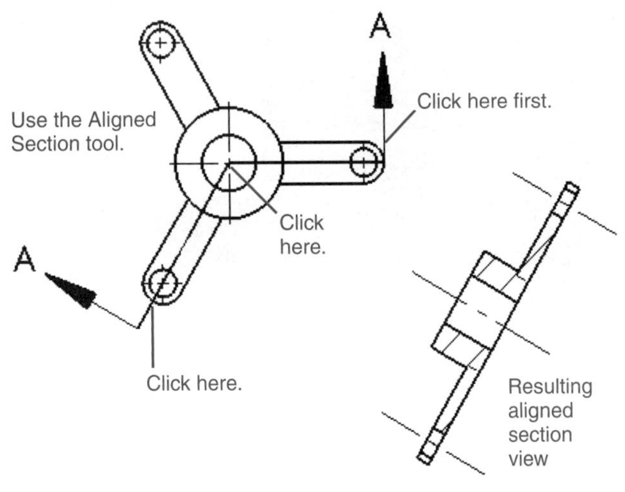

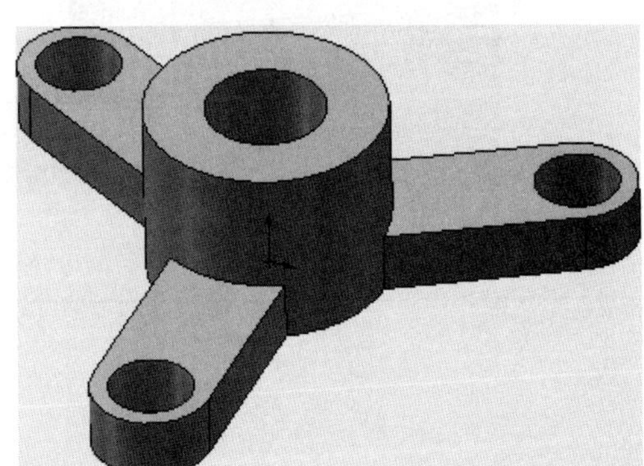

Figure 4-49

The model was drawn previously using the given dimensions.

2. Access the **Aligned Section** tool.
3. Click the edge of the object as shown in Figure 4-49.
4. Click the object's center point.
5. Click the other edge of the object as shown.
6. Move the cursor away from the object.

   The aligned section will appear as the cursor is moved.

7. Change the scale of the object if desired.

4-7 BROKEN VIEWS

It is often convenient to break long continuous shapes so that they take up less drawing space. Figure 4-50 shows a long L-bracket that has a continuous shape; that is, its shape is constant throughout its length.

To Create a Broken View

1. Draw a model of the long L-bracket using the dimension shown in Figure 4-50. Save the model.
2. Start a new drawing using the **Drawing** format and enter the model.
3. Click the **Drawings** tool, and click the **Break** tool.

   See Figure 4-51.

4. Set the **Gap size** for **4mm** and select the **Small Zig Zag Cut** style.
5. Move the cursor onto the long L-bracket and click a location for the first break line.
6. Click a location for the second break line.

   The area between the break lines will be removed.

7. Click the OK check mark.

If the break is not satisfactory, undo the break and insert a new one.

4-8 DETAIL VIEWS

A ***detail view*** is used to clarify specific areas of a drawing. Usually, an area is enlarged so that small details are easier to see.

To Draw a Detail View

In this example, the model shown in Figure P4-7 was used.

1. Create a **Part** drawing for the model shown in Figure P4-7. Save the model.
2. Start a new drawing using the **Drawing** format and create front and top orthographic views of a model. Use third-angle projection.

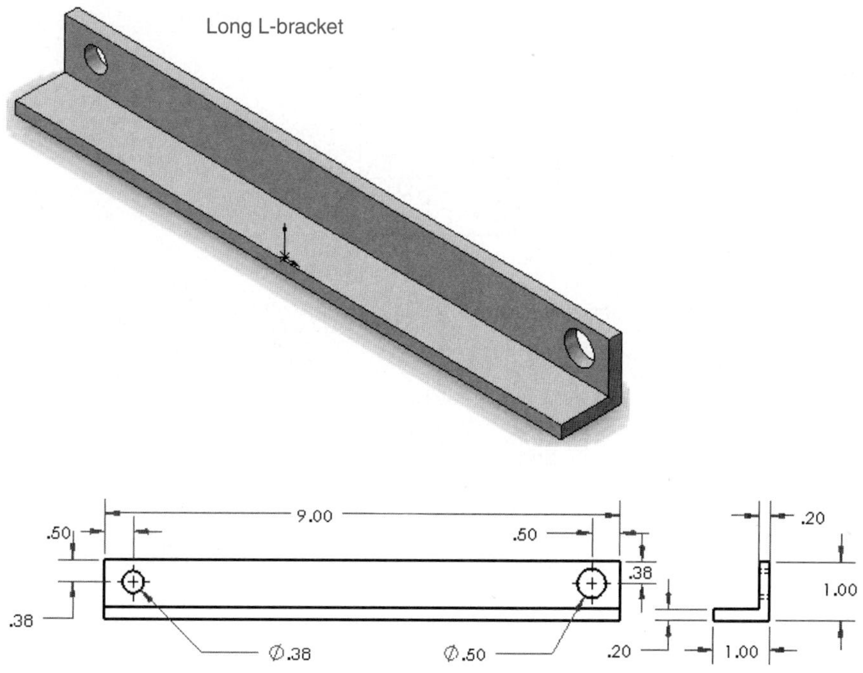

Figure 4-50

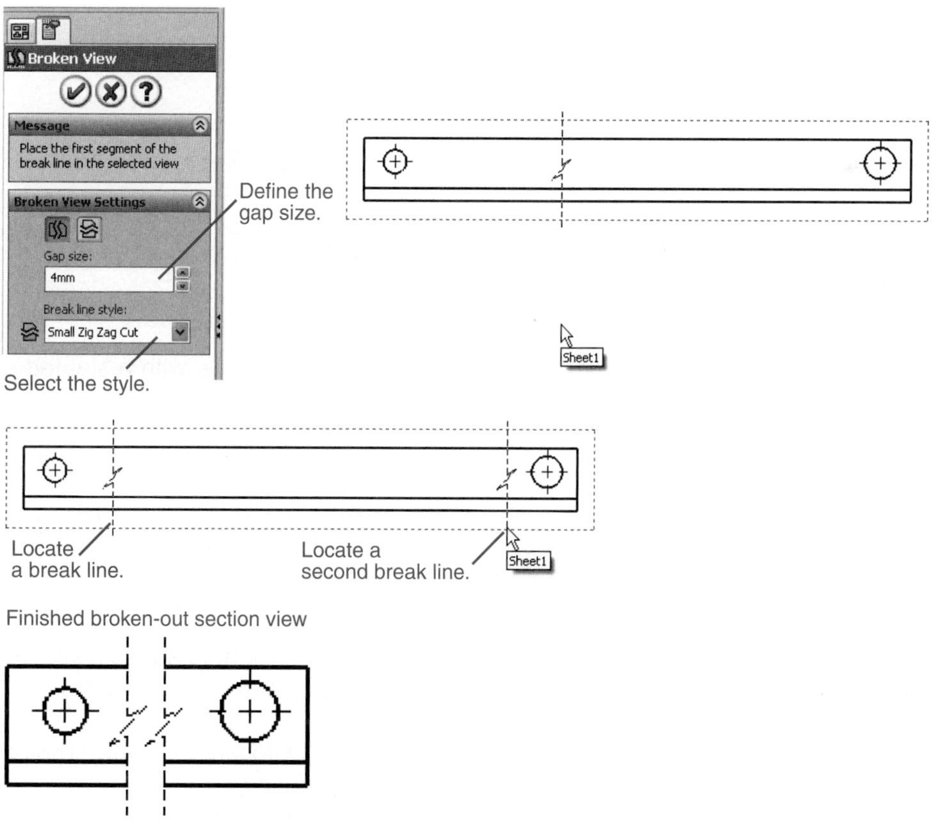

Figure 4-51

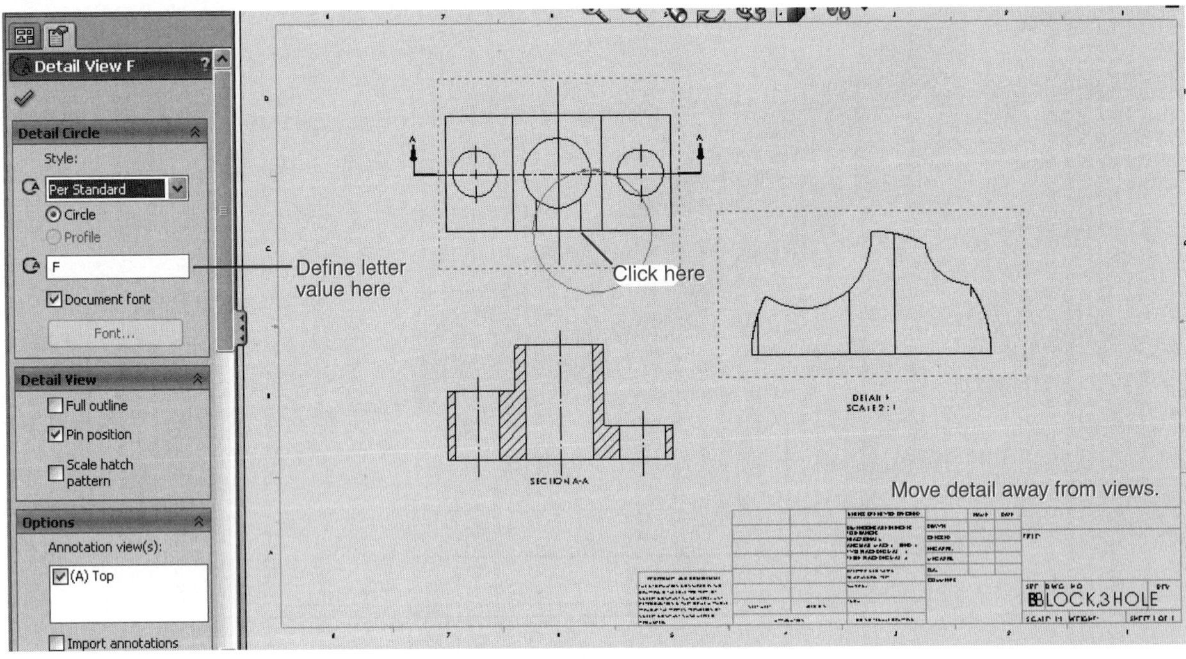

Figure 4-52

3. Click the **Detail View** tool.

See Figure 4-52.

4. Locate the center point for a circle that will be used to define the area for the detail view by clicking a point.

In this example the intersection of the top view's front edge line and the right edge line of the slot were selected.

5. Move the cursor away from the point.

A detail view will appear.

6. When the circle is big enough to enclose all the area you wish to display in the detail view, click the mouse.
7. Move the cursor away from the views.
8. Select a location for the detail view and click the mouse.

The scale of the detail view and the callout letter can be changed by entering values in the **Detail View** box.

4-9 AUXILIARY VIEWS

Auxiliary views are orthographic views used to present true-shaped views of slanted surface.

To Draw an Auxiliary View

1. Draw the model with a slanted surface shown in Figure 4-53.
2. Start a new drawing using the **Drawing** format and create orthographic views of the model.

In this example a front and a right-side view were drawn. See Figure 4-54.

3. Click the **Drawings** tool, then click the **Auxiliary View** tool.
4. Click the slanted edge line in the front view.
5. Move the cursor away from the slanted edge line.
6. Select a location for the auxiliary view and click the mouse.
7. Adjust the cutting plane line as shown.

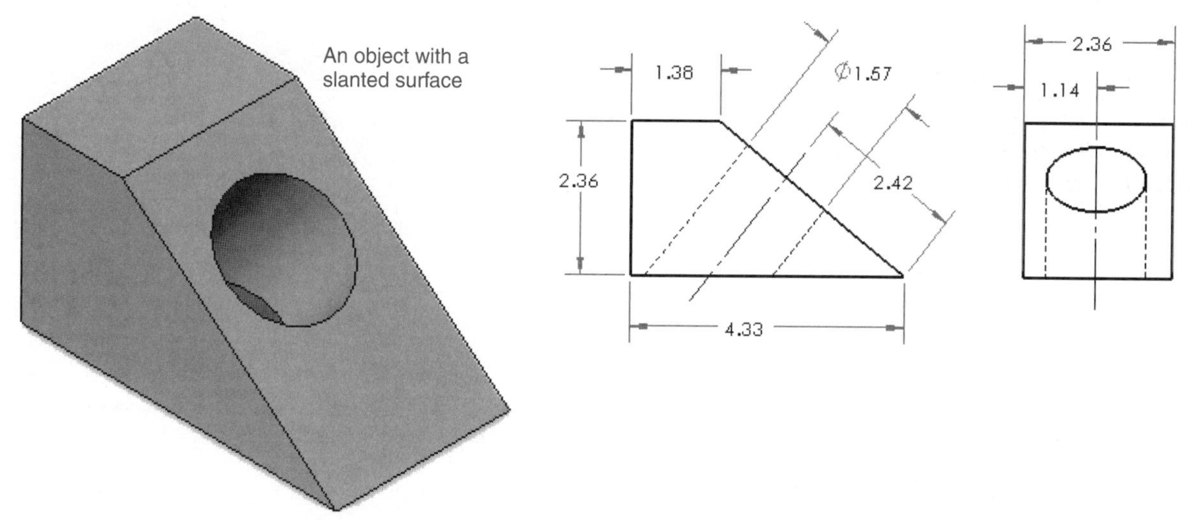

Figure 4-53

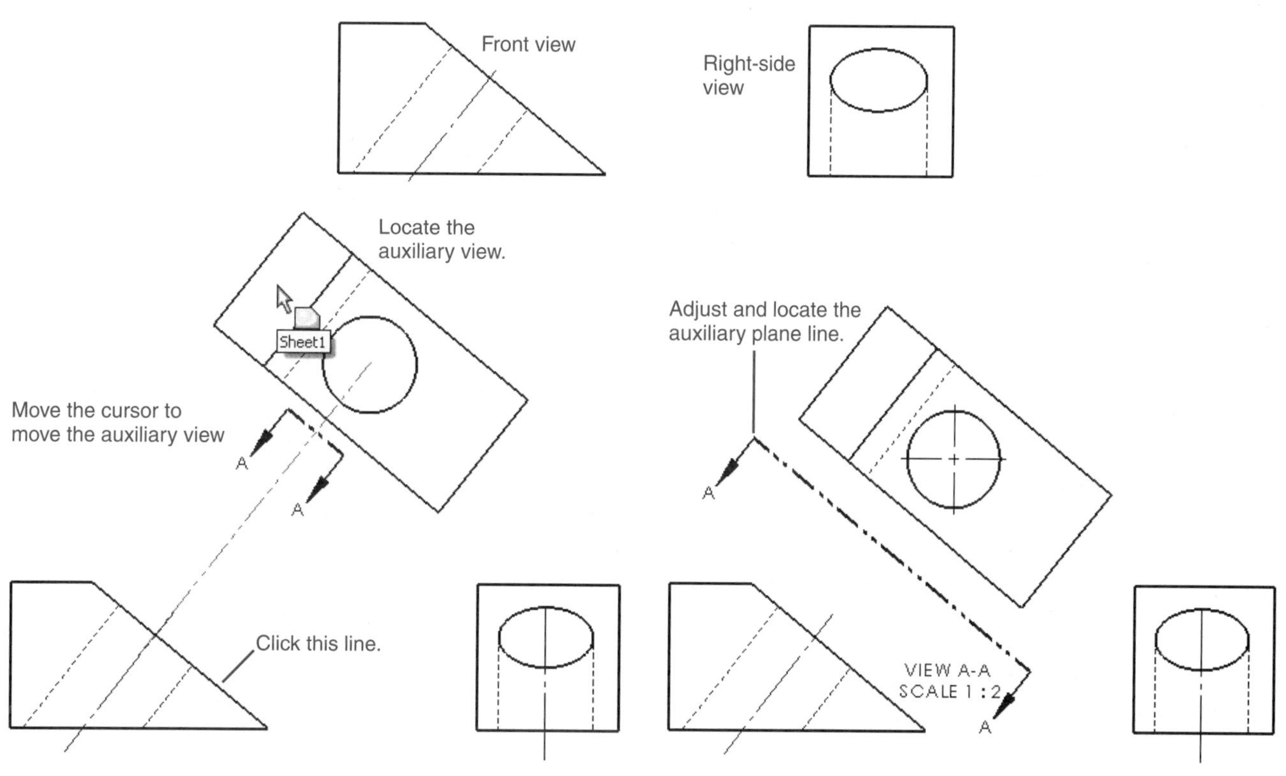

Figure 4-54

4-10 PROJECTS

Project 4-1:

Draw a front, a top, and a right-side orthographic view of each of the objects in Figures P4-1 through P4-24. Make all objects from mild steel.

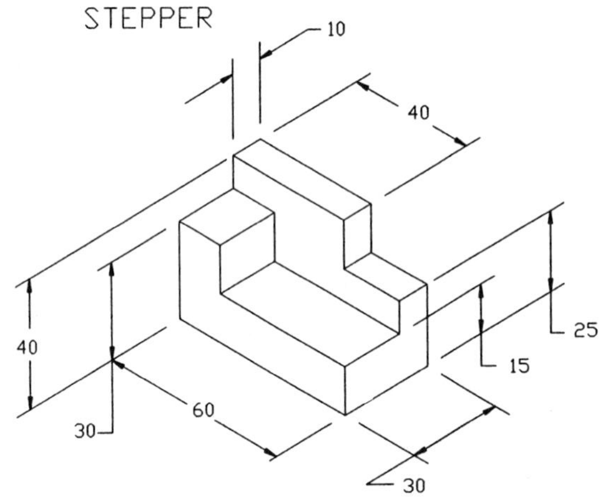

Figure P4-1 MILLIMETERS

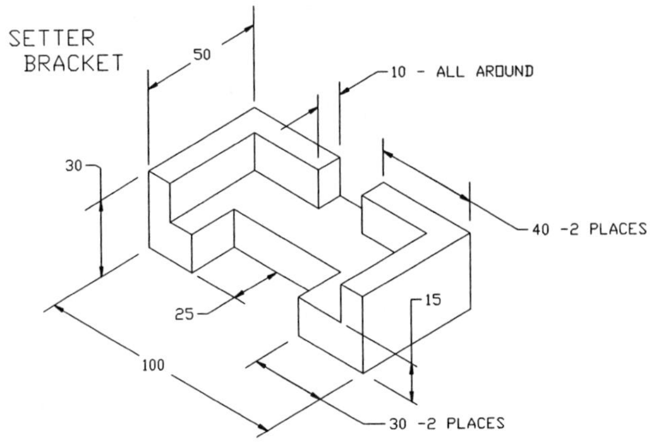

Figure P4-2 MILLIMETERS

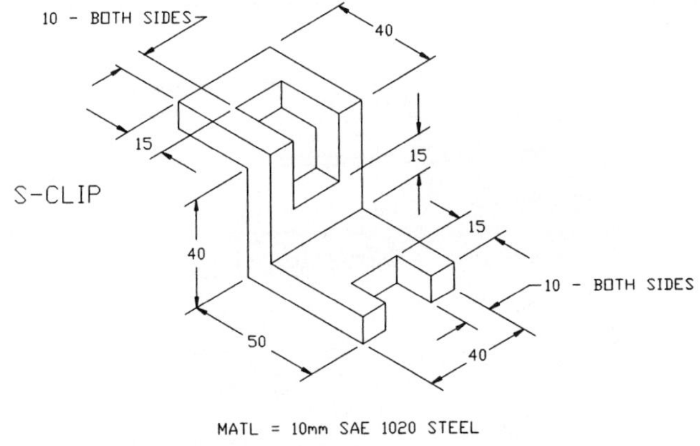

Figure P4-3 MILLIMETERS

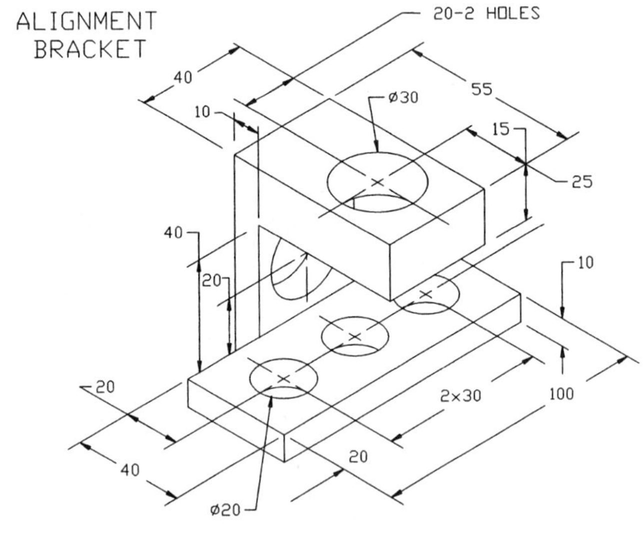

Figure P4-4 MILLIMETERS

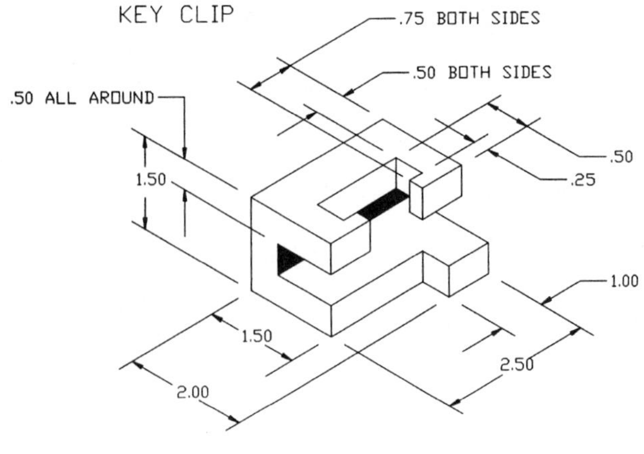

Figure P4-5 INCHES

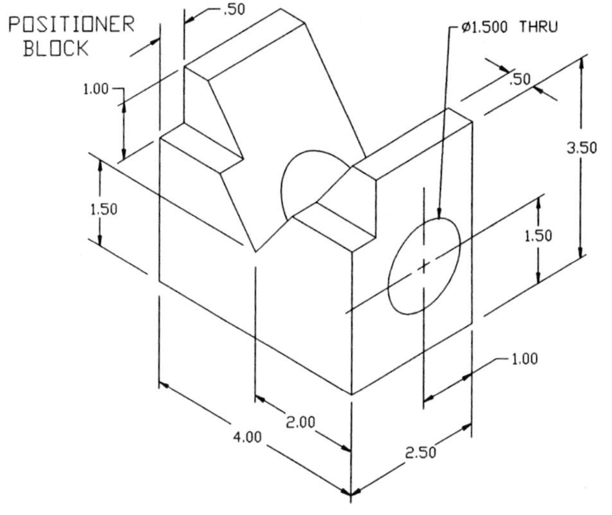

Figure P4-6 INCHES

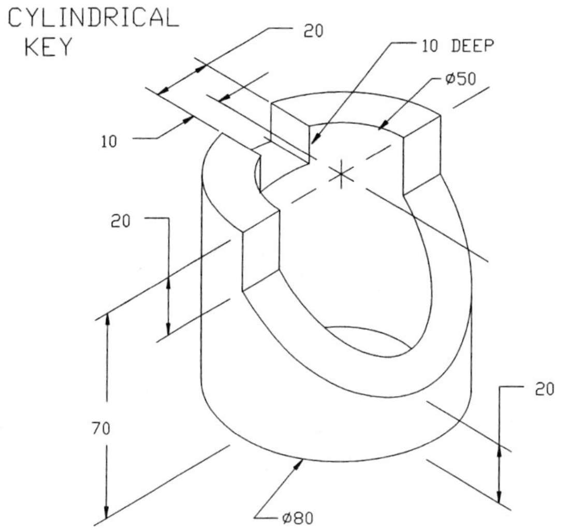

CYLINDRICAL
KEY

Figure P4-8 MILLIMETERS

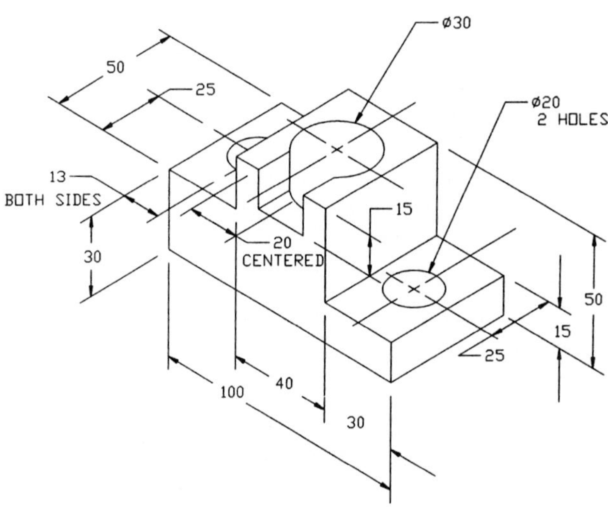

Figure P4-7 MILLIMETERS

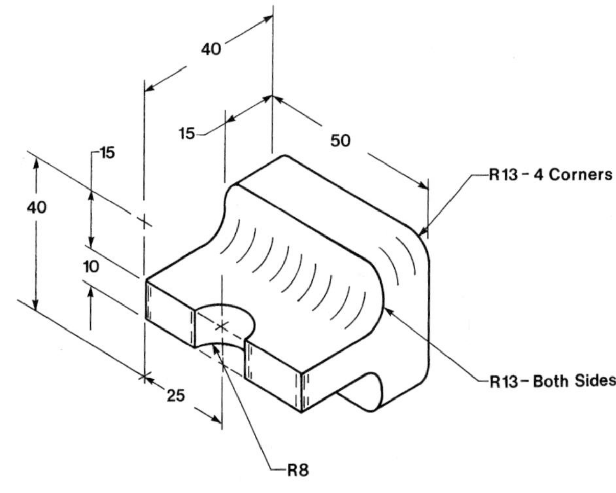

Figure P4-9 MILLIMETERS

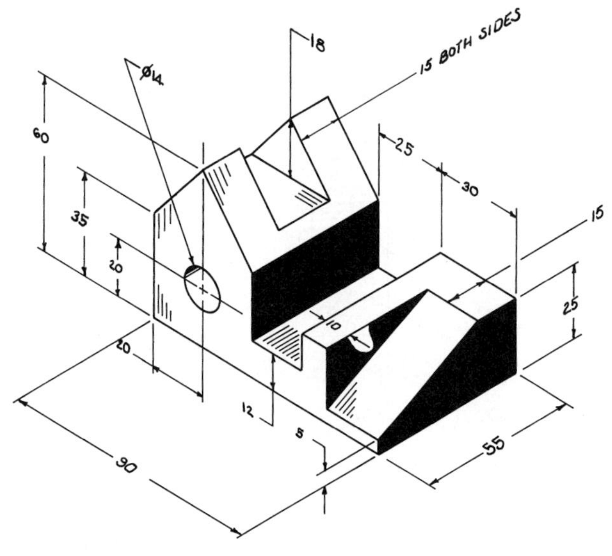

Figure P4-10 MILLIMETERS

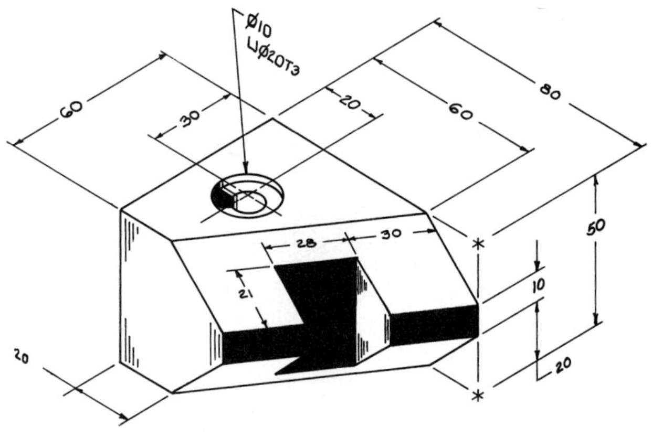

Figure P4-12 MILLIMETERS

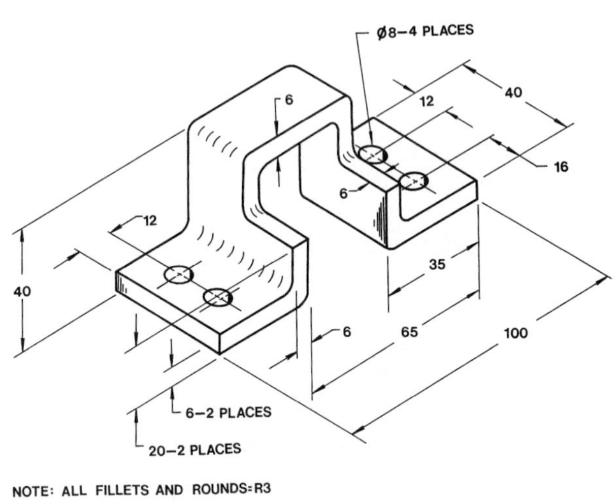

Figure P4-13 MILLIMETERS

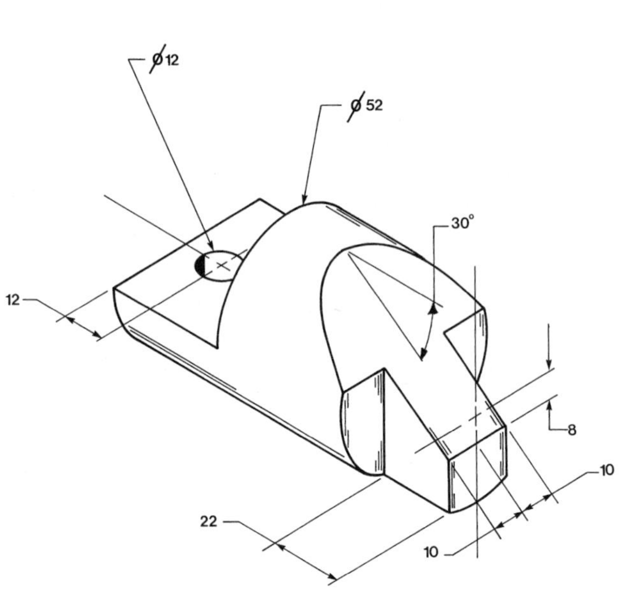

Figure P4-11 MILLIMETERS

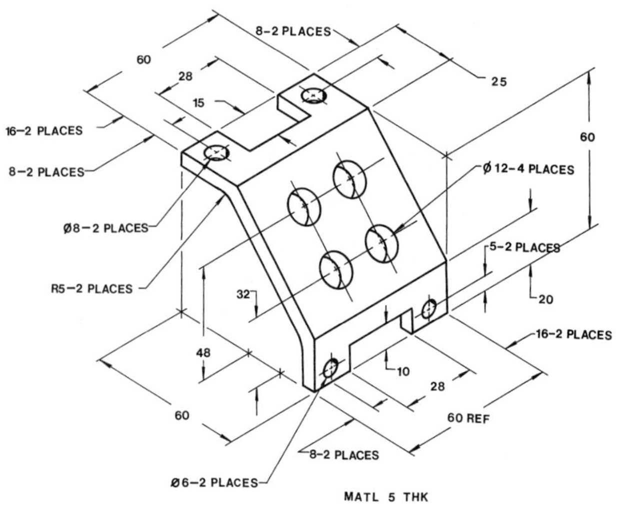

Figure P4-14 MILLIMETERS

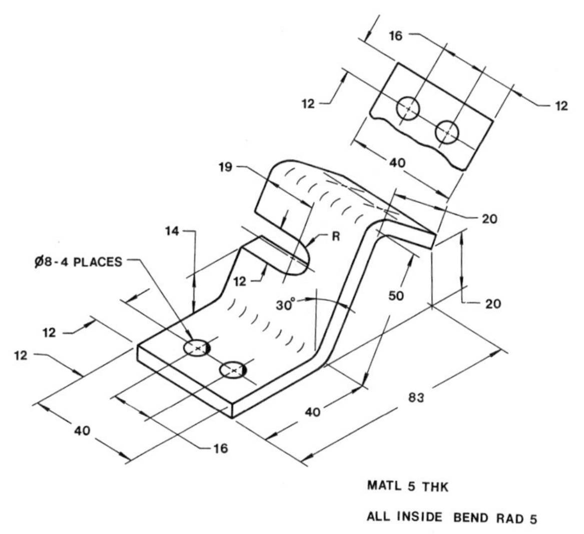

Figure P4-15 MILLIMETERS

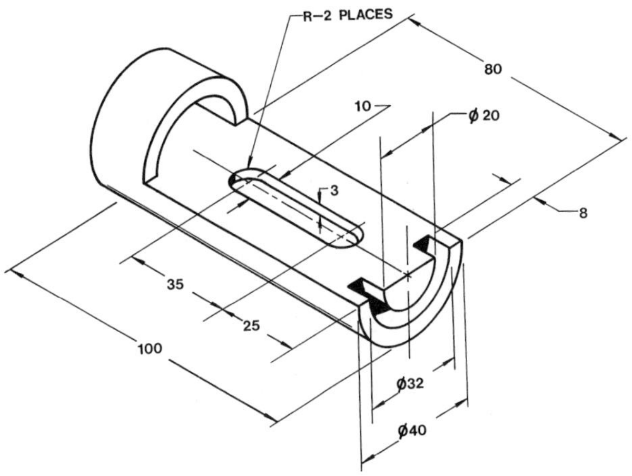

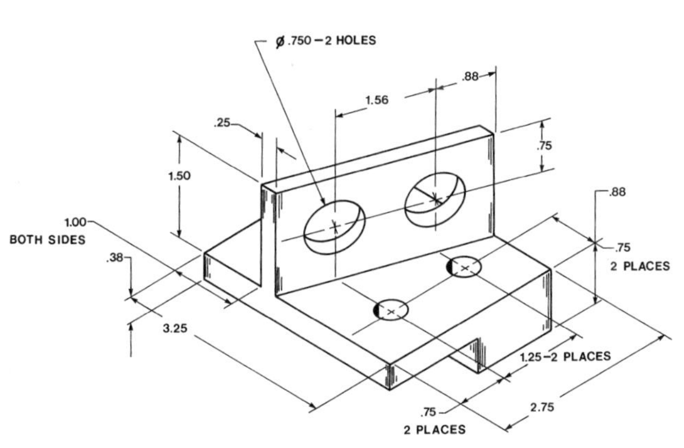

Figure P4-16 INCHES

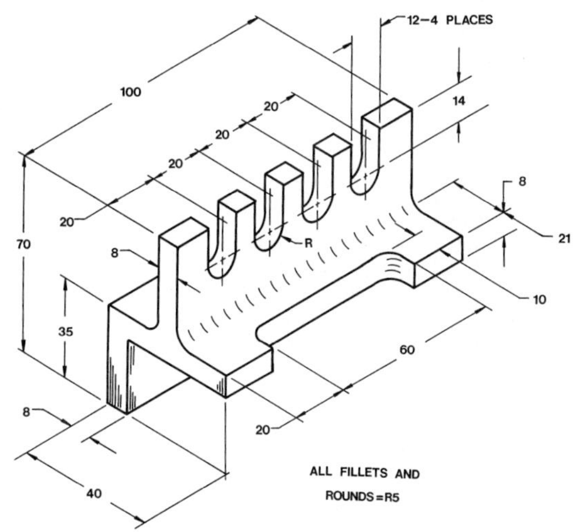

Figure P4-17 MILLIMETERS

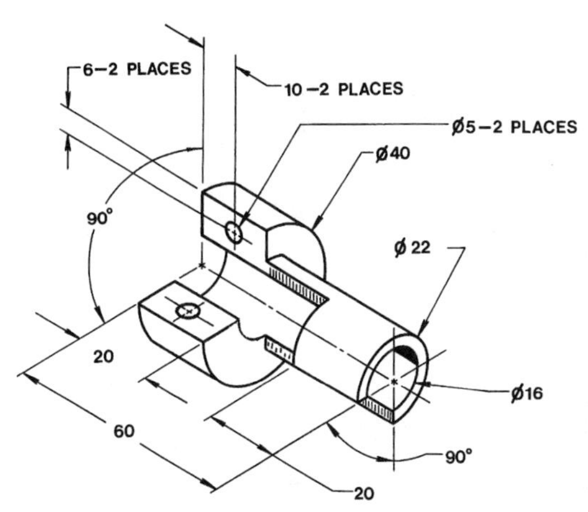

Figure P4-18 MILLIMETERS

Figure P4-19 MILLIMETERS

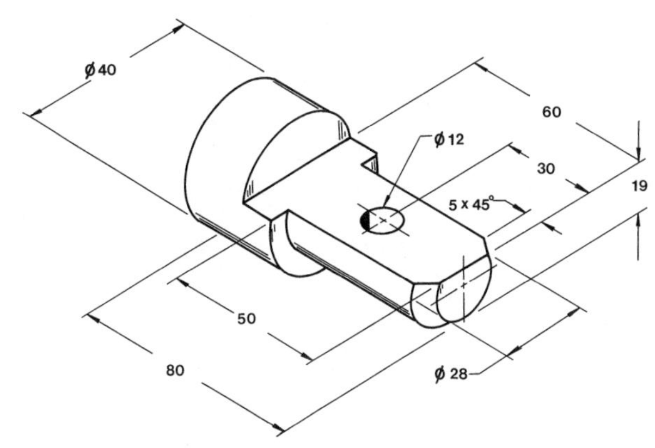

Figure P4-20 MILLIMETERS

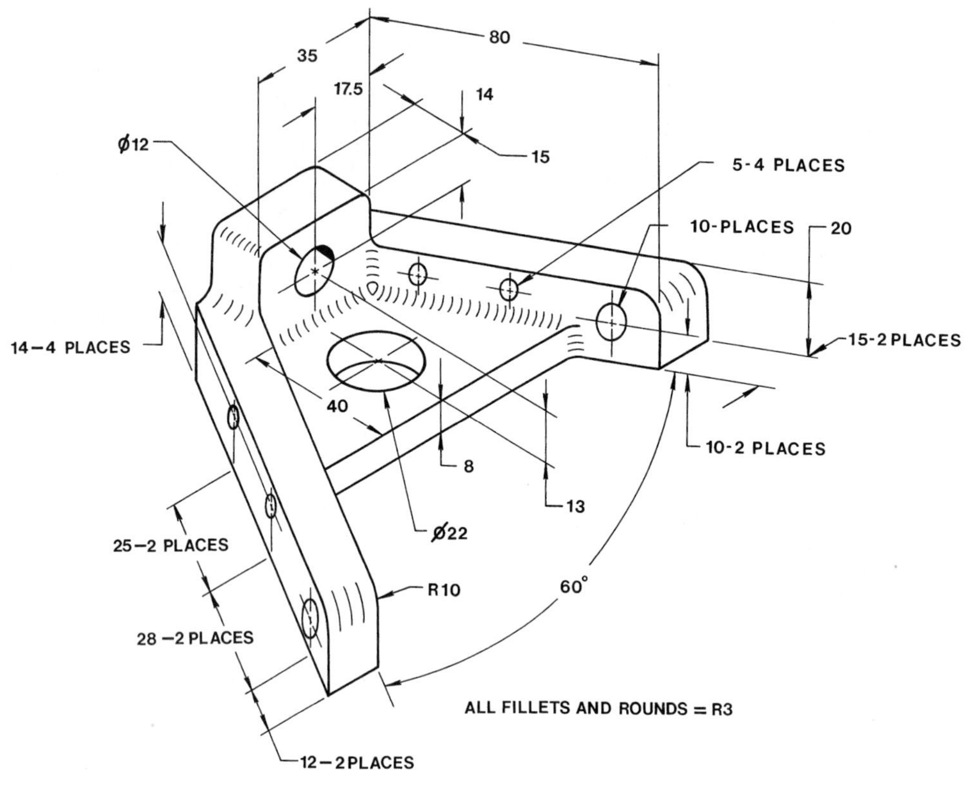

Figure P4-21 MILLIMETERS

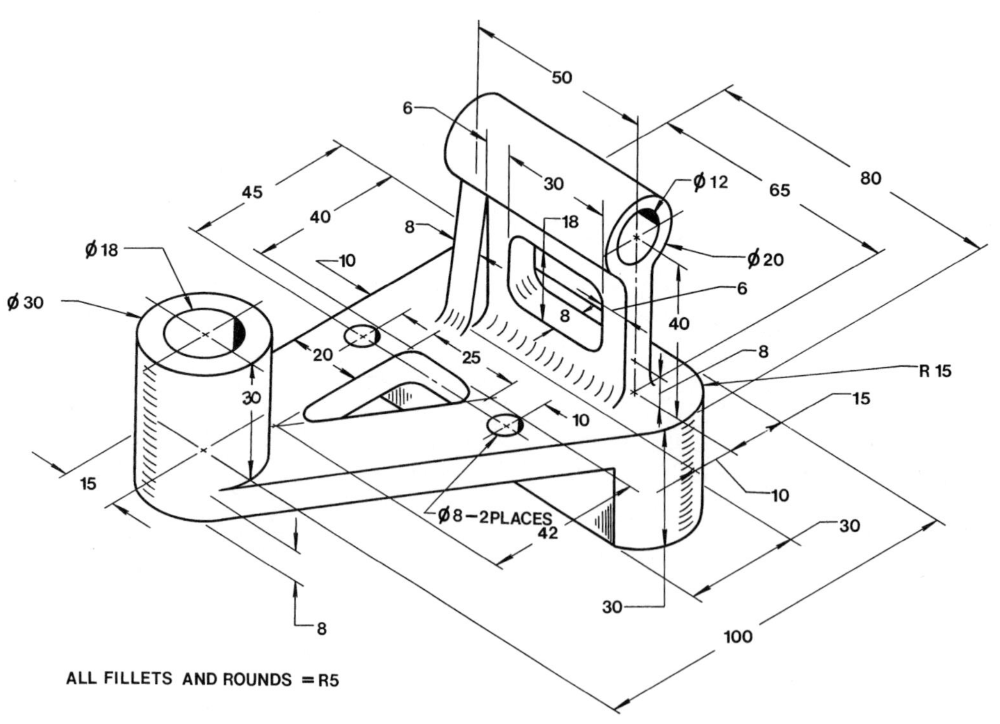

Figure P4-22 MILLIMETERS

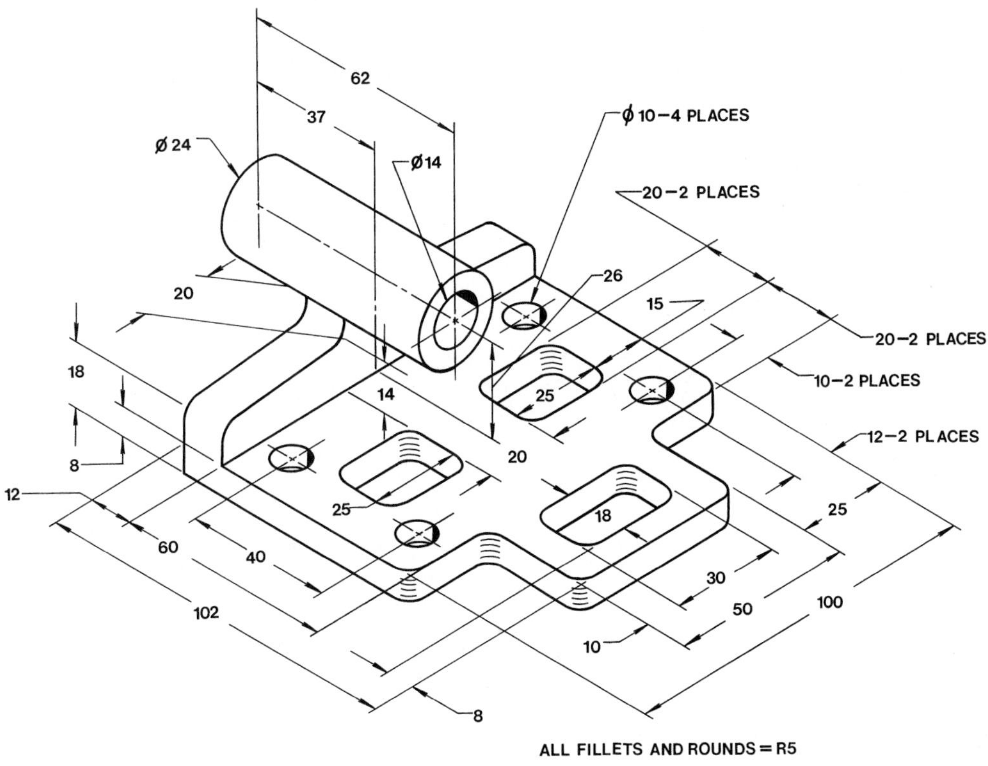

Figure P4-23 MILLIMETERS

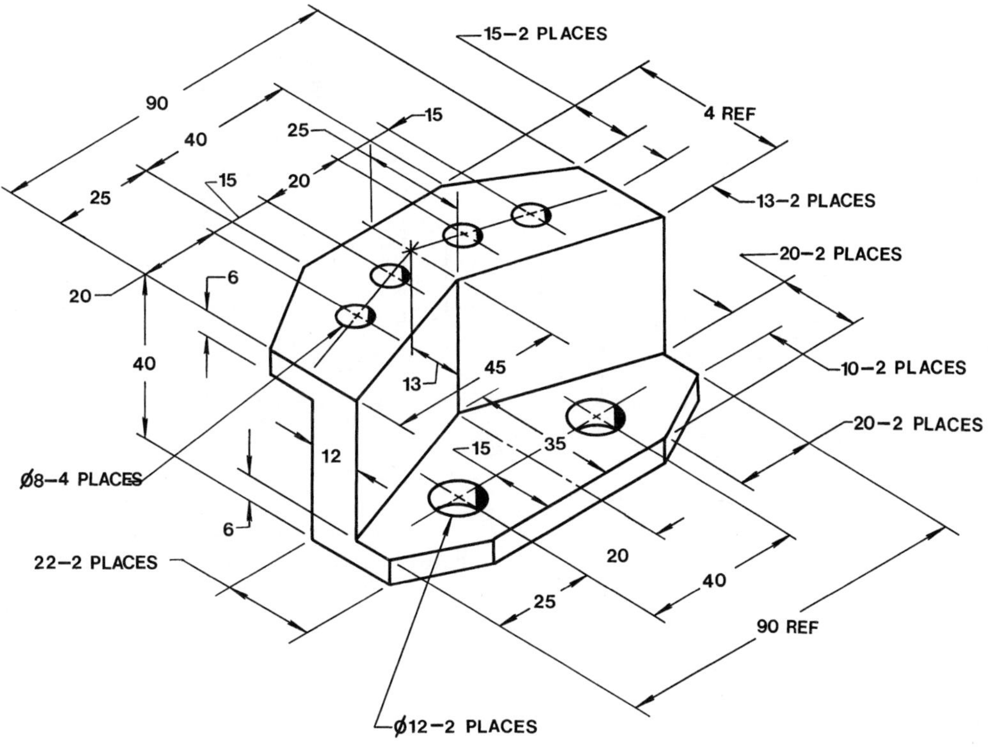

Figure P4-24 MILLIMETERS

Project 4-2:

Draw at least two orthographic views and one auxiliary view of each of the objects in Figures P4-25 through P4-36.

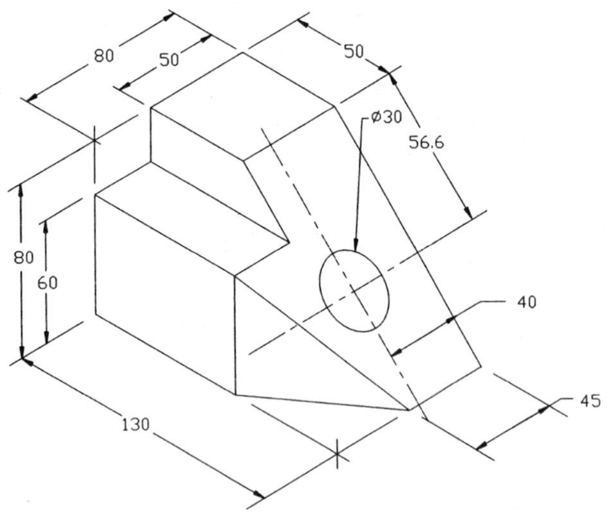

Figure P4-25 MILLIMETERS

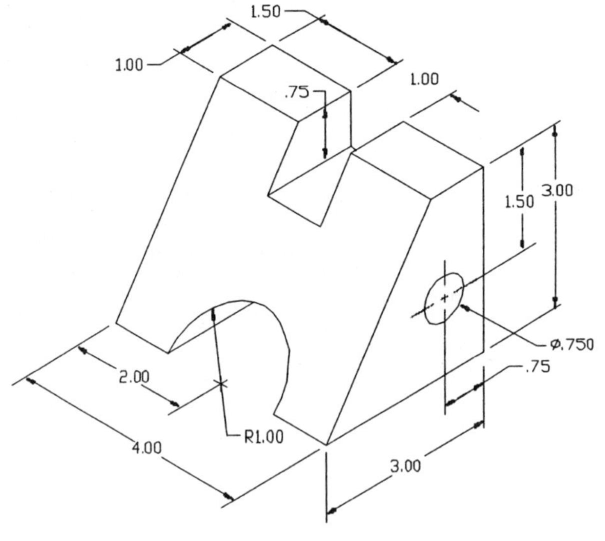

Figure P4-27 INCHES

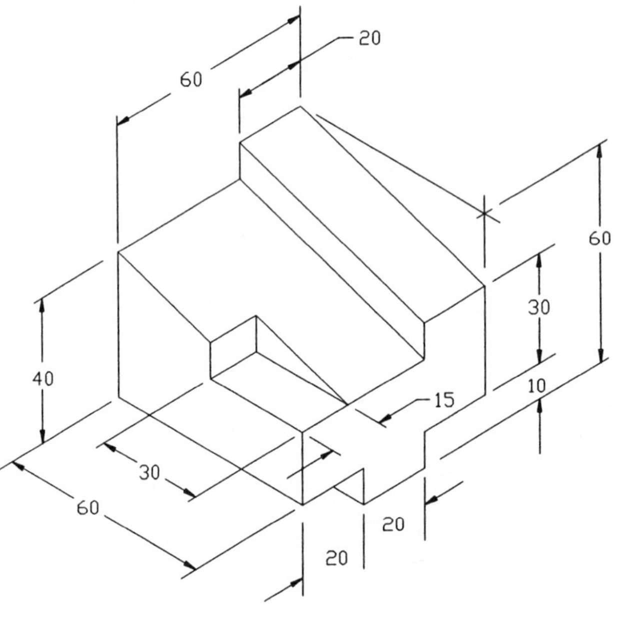

Figure P4-26 MILLIMETERS

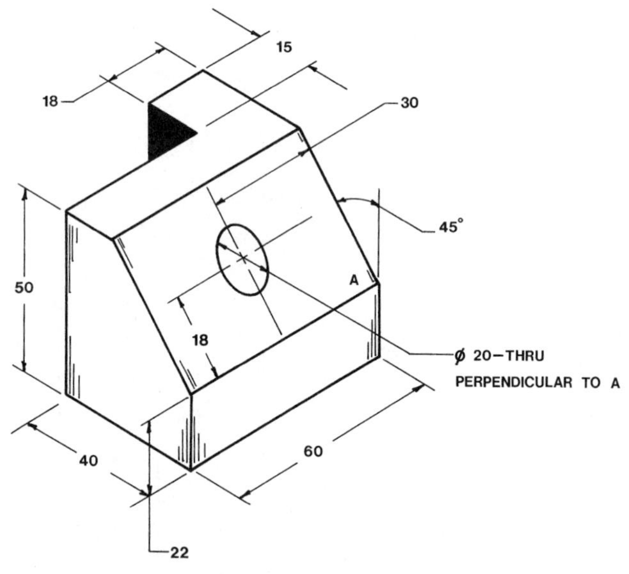

Figure P4-28 MILLIMETERS

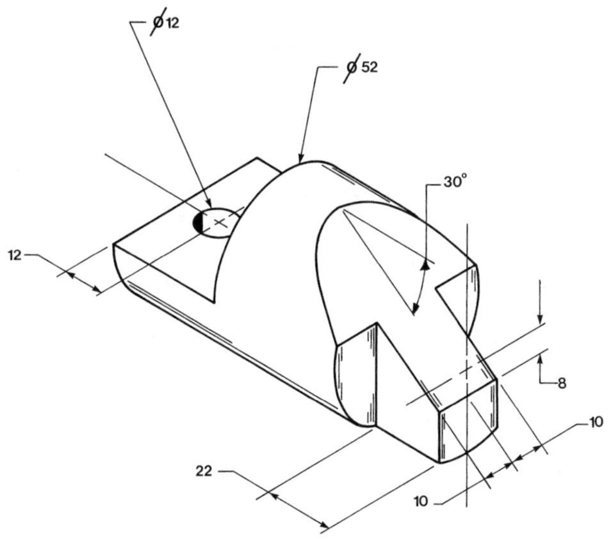

Figure P4-29 MILLIMETERS

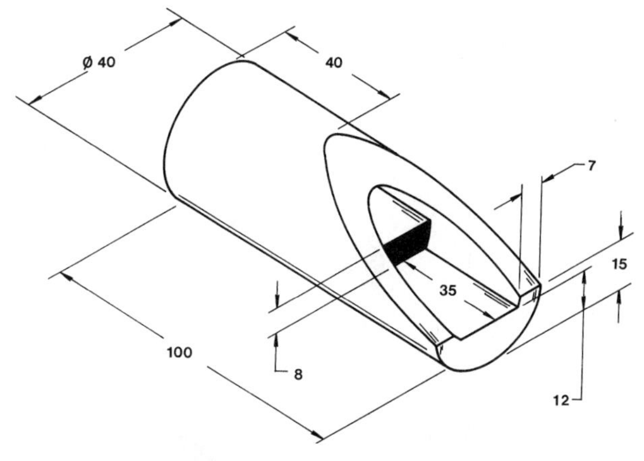

Figure P4-31 MILLIMETERS

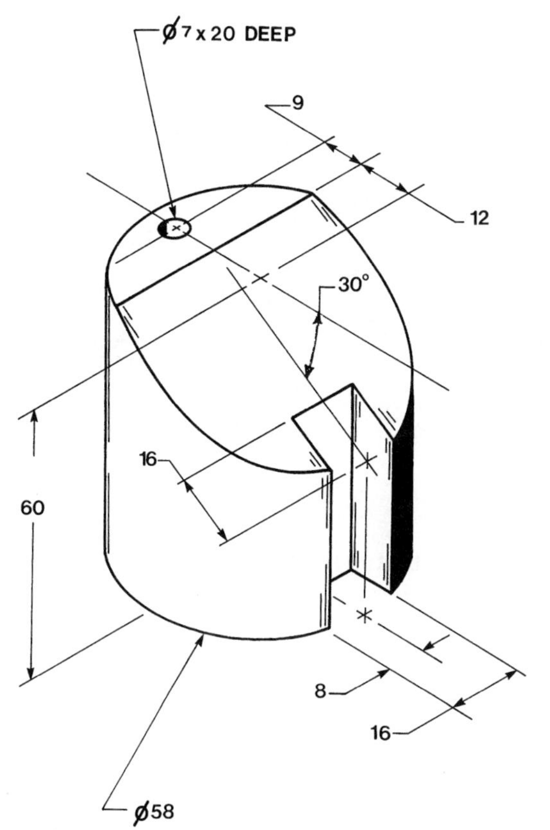

Figure P4-30 MILLIMETERS

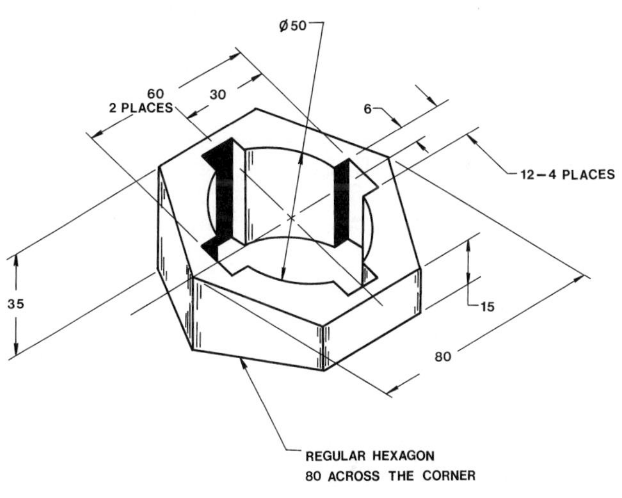

Figure P4-32 MILLIMETERS

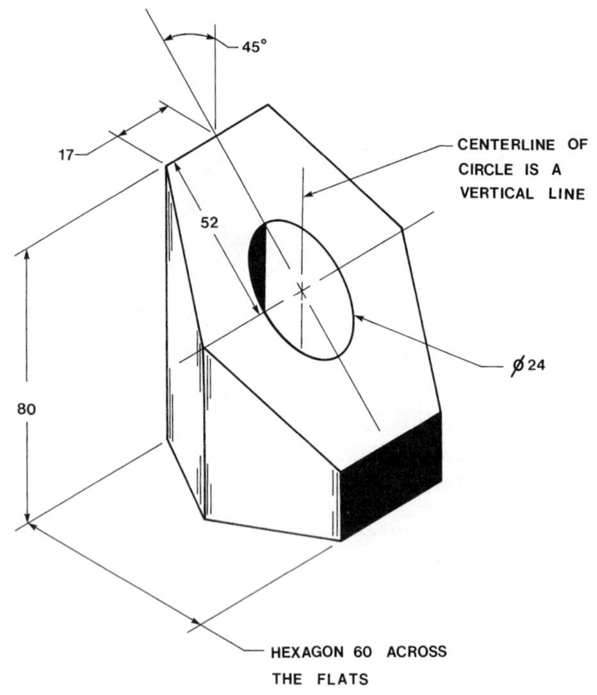

Figure P4-33 MILLIMETERS

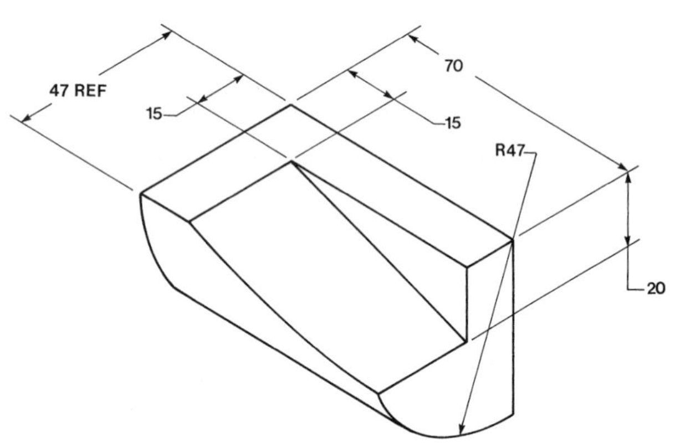

Figure P4-34 MILLIMETERS

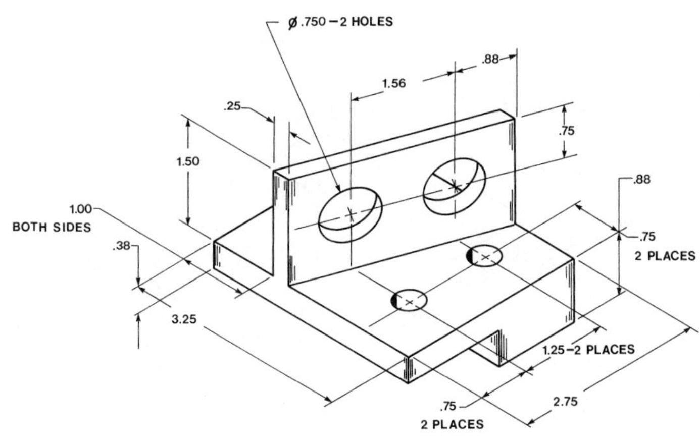

Figure P4-35 INCHES

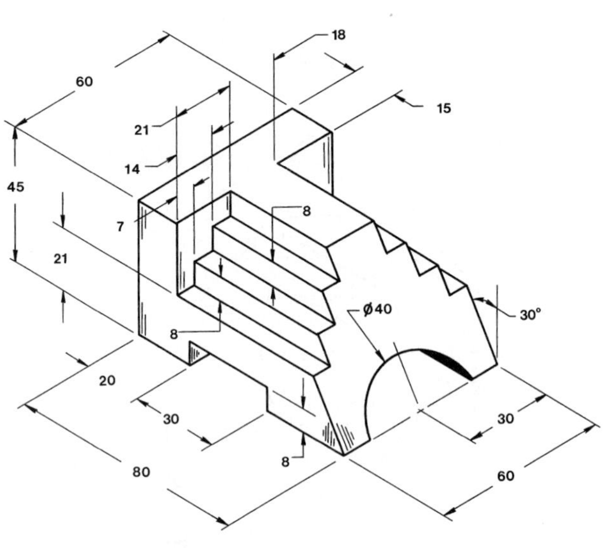

Figure P4-36 MILLIMETERS

Project 4-4:

Define the true shape of the oblique surfaces in each of the objects is Figures P4-37 through P4-40.

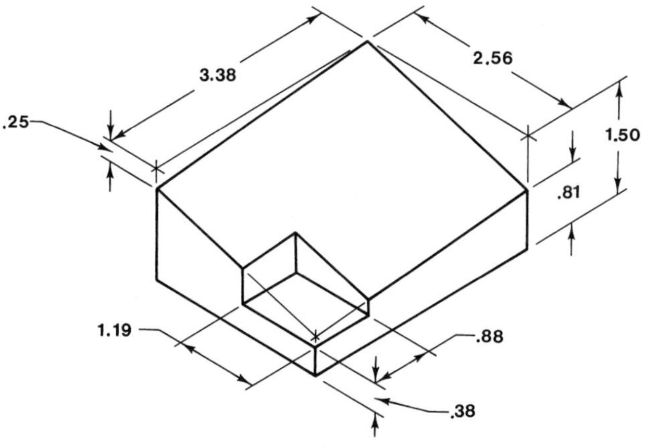

Figure P4-37 INCHES

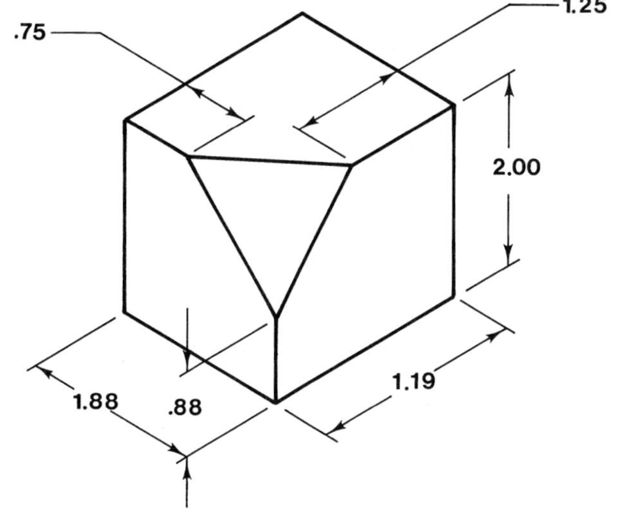

Figure P4-39 INCHES

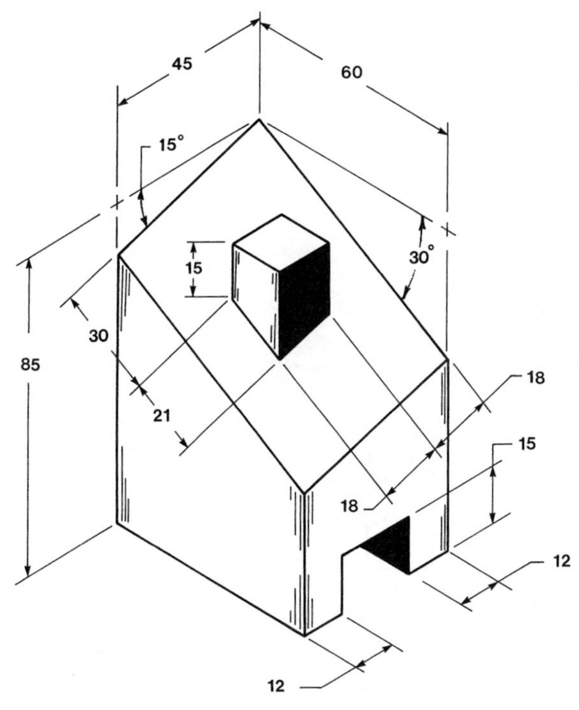

Figure P4-38 MILLIMETERS

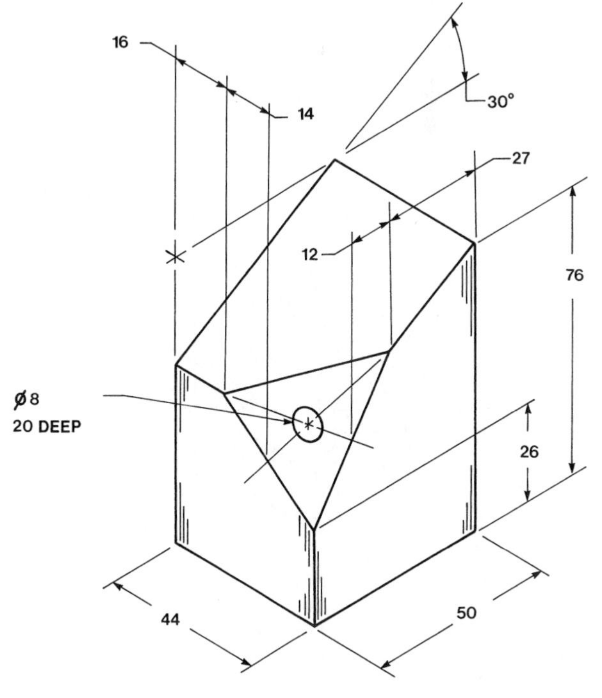

Figure P4-40 MILLIMETERS

Project 4-4:

Draw each of the objects shown in Figures P4-41 through P4-44 as a model, then draw a front view and an appropriate section view of each.

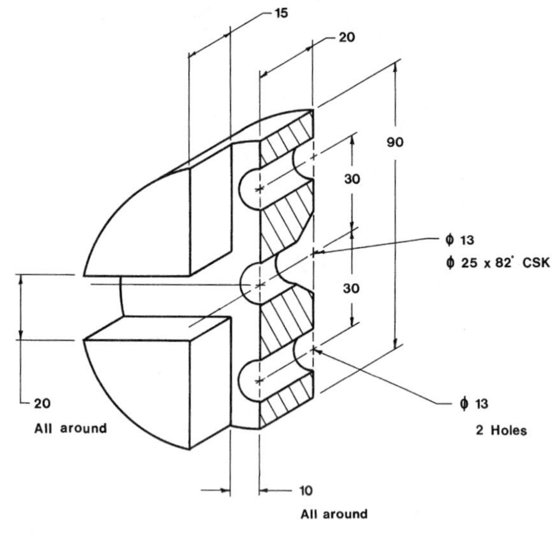

Figure P4-41 MILLIMETERS

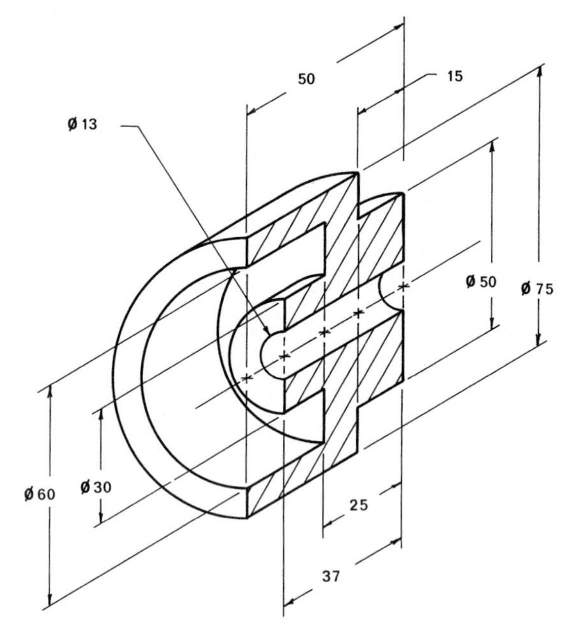

Figure P4-43 MILLIMETERS

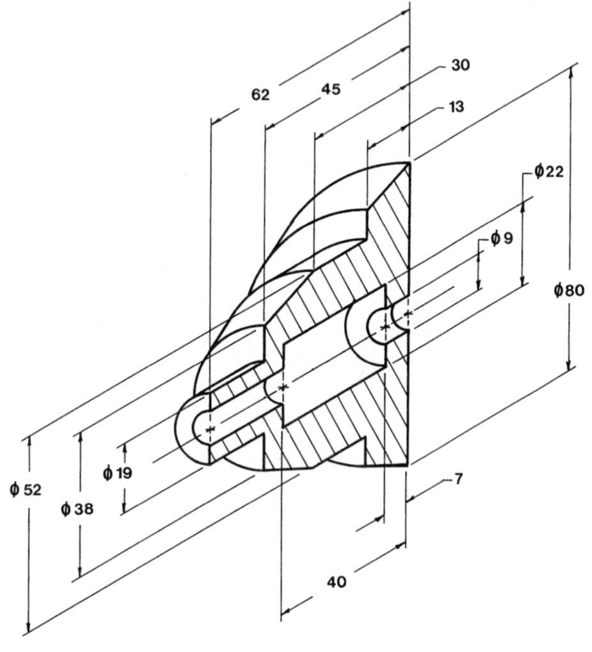

Figure P4-42 MILLIMETERS

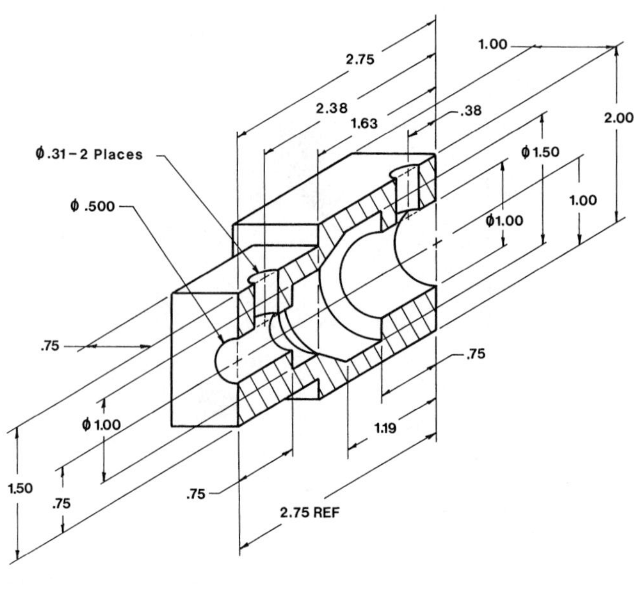

Figure P4-44 INCHES

Project 4-5:

Draw at least one orthographic view and the indicated section view for each object in Figures P4-45 through P4-50.

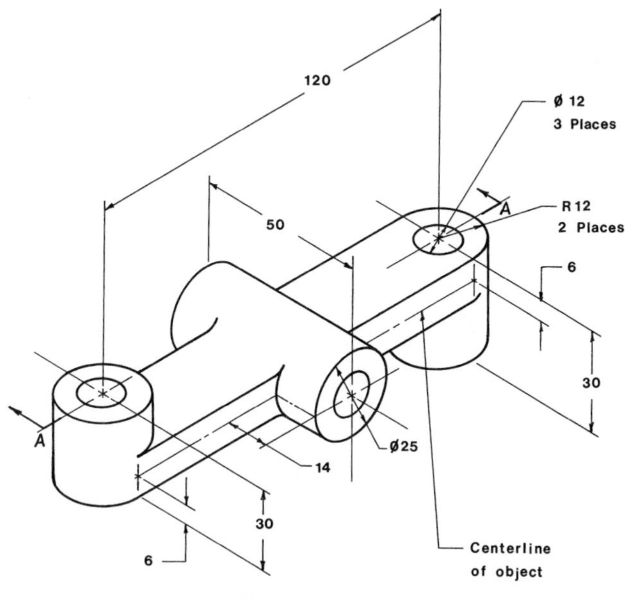

Figure P4-45 MILLIMETERS

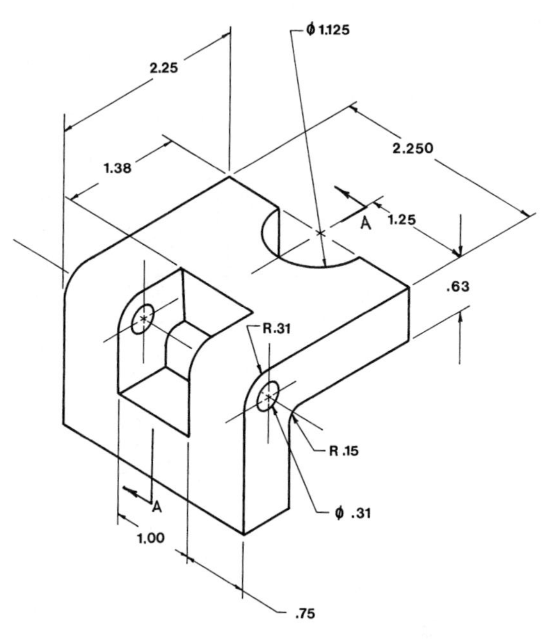

Figure P4-47 INCHES

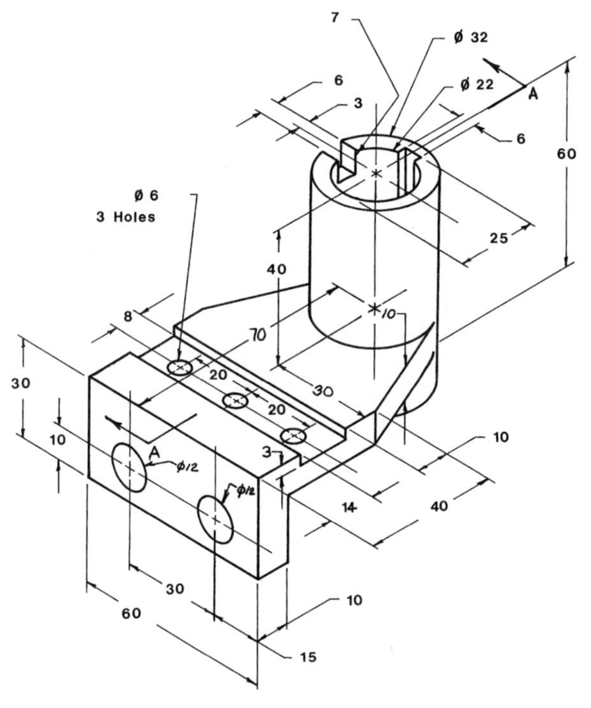

Figure P4-46 MILLIMETERS

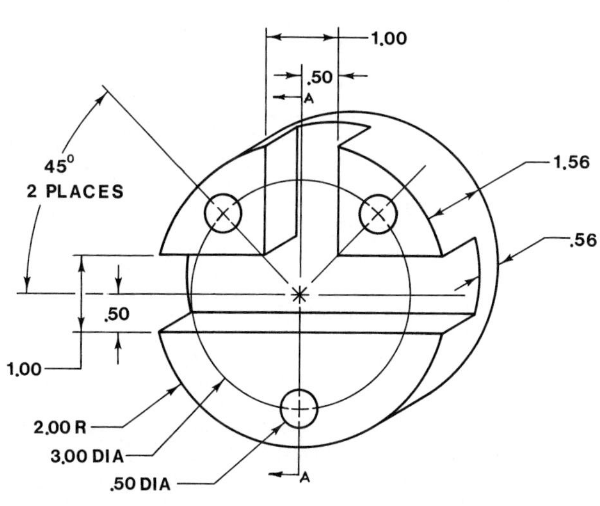

Figure P4-48 INCHES

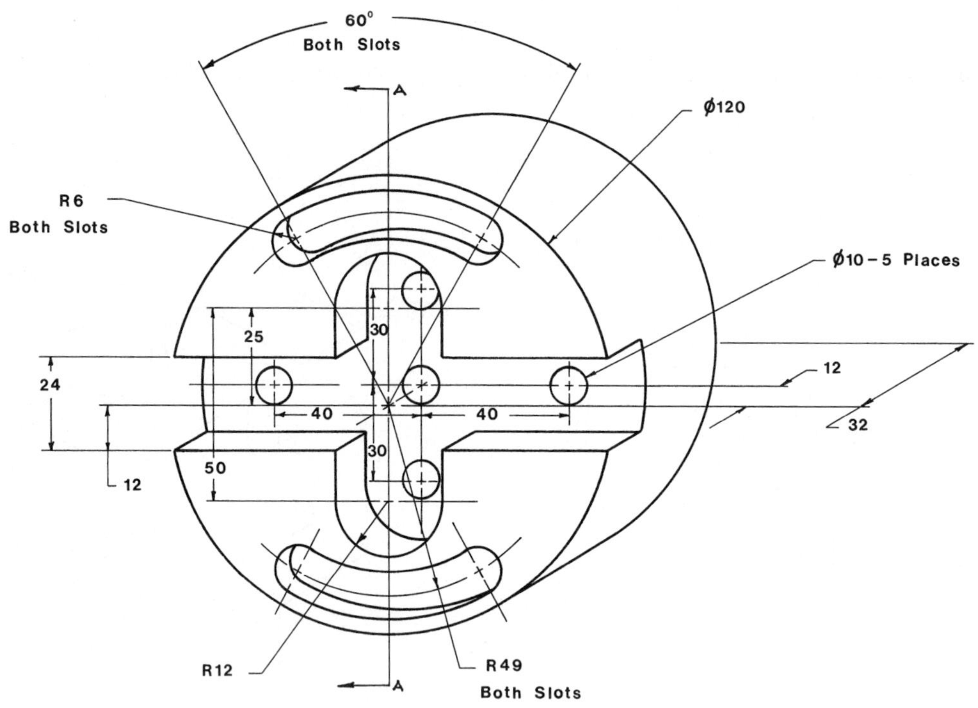

Figure P4-49 MILLIMETERS

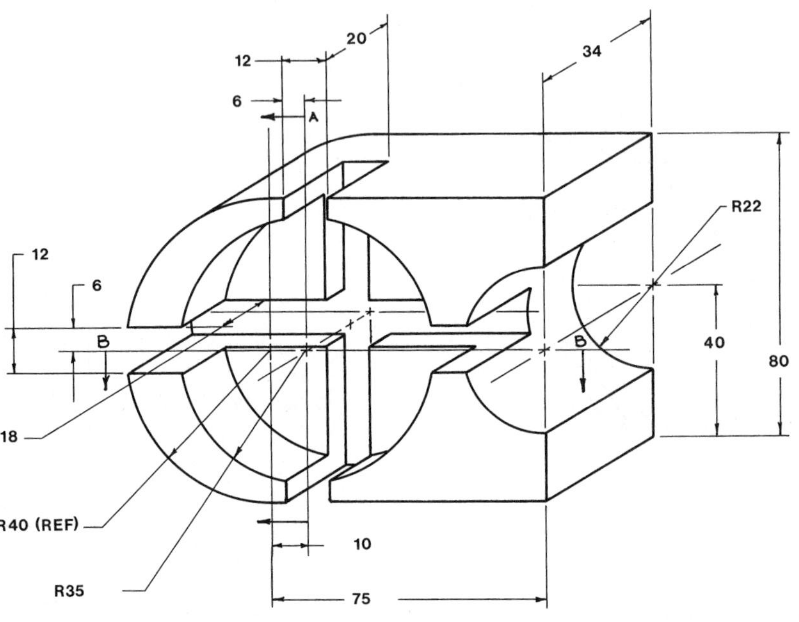

Figure P4-50 MILLIMETERS

Project 4-6:

Given the orthographic views in Figures P4-51 and P4-52, draw a model of each, then draw the given orthographic views and the appropriate section views.

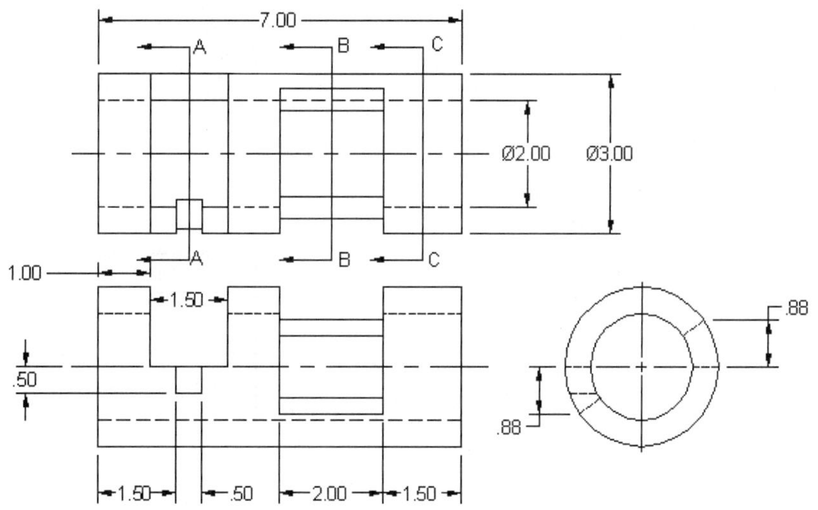

Figure P4-51 INCHES

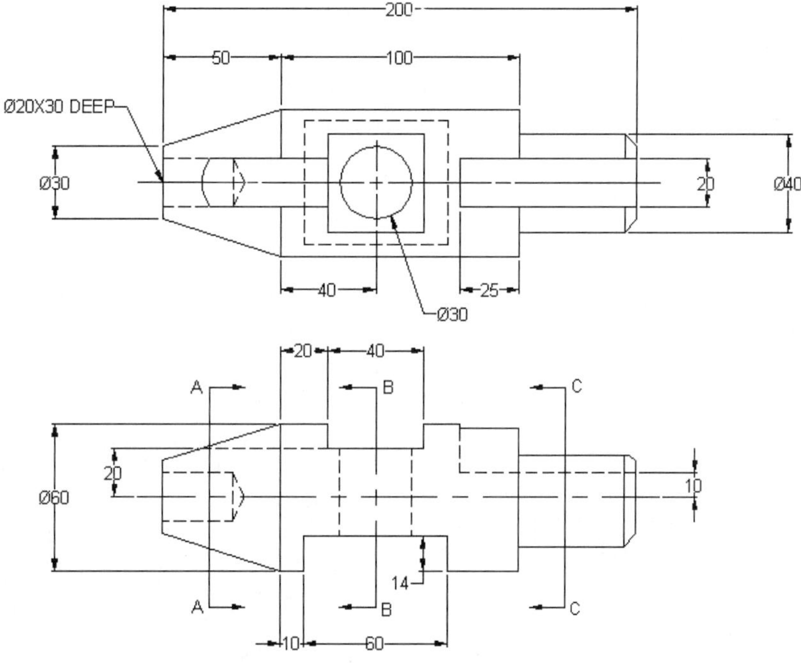

Figure P4-52 MILLIMETERS

Project 4-7:

Draw a 3D model and a set of multiviews for each object shown in Figures P4-53 through P4-60.

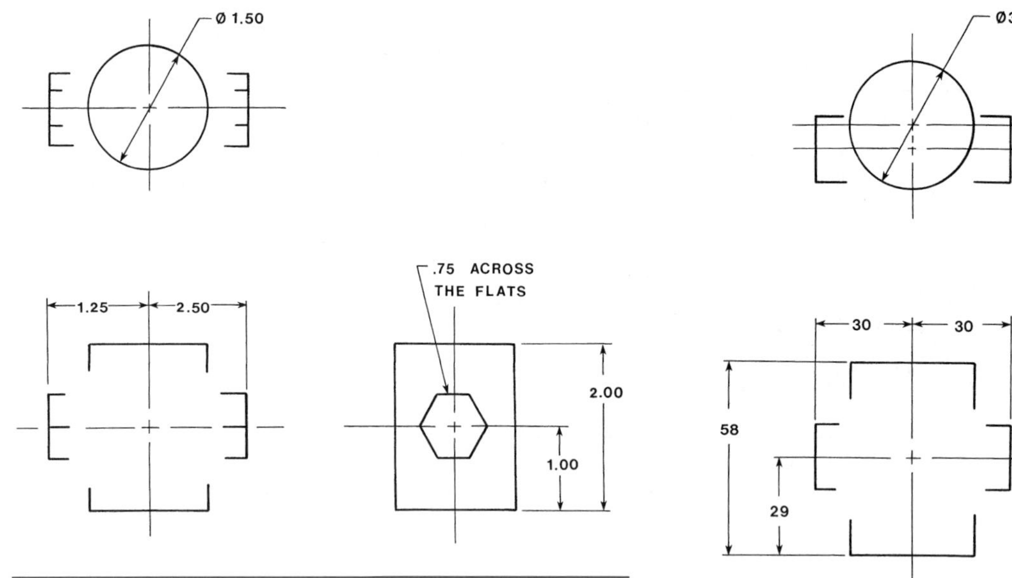

Figure P4-53 INCHES

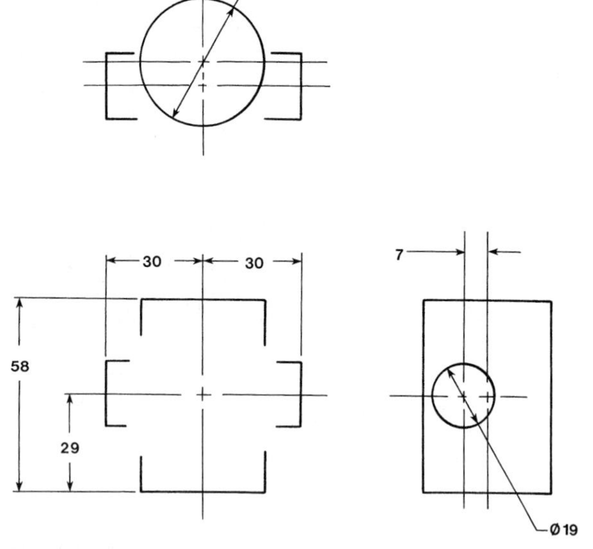

Figure P4-55 MILLIMETERS

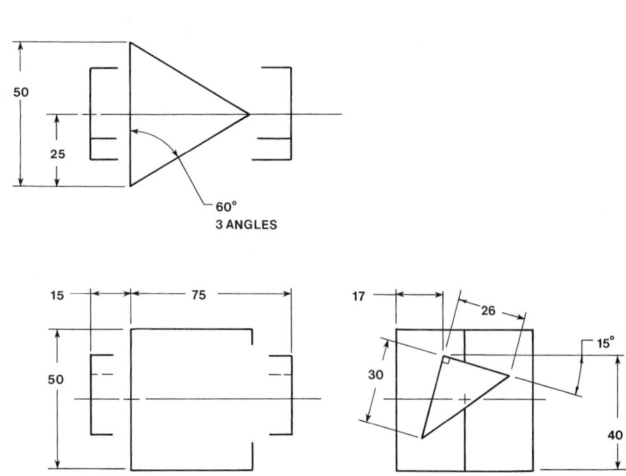

Figure P4-54 MILLIMETERS

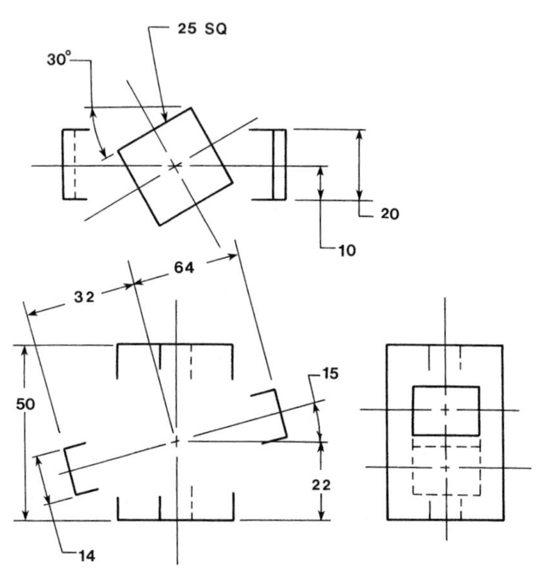

Figure P4-56 MILLIMETERS

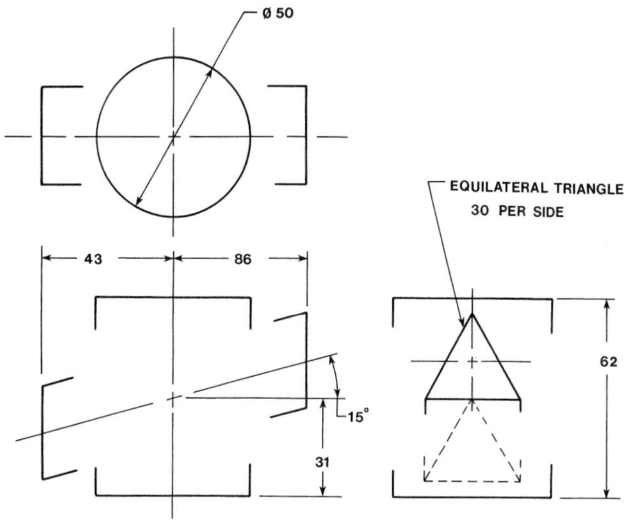

Figure P4-57 MILLIMETERS

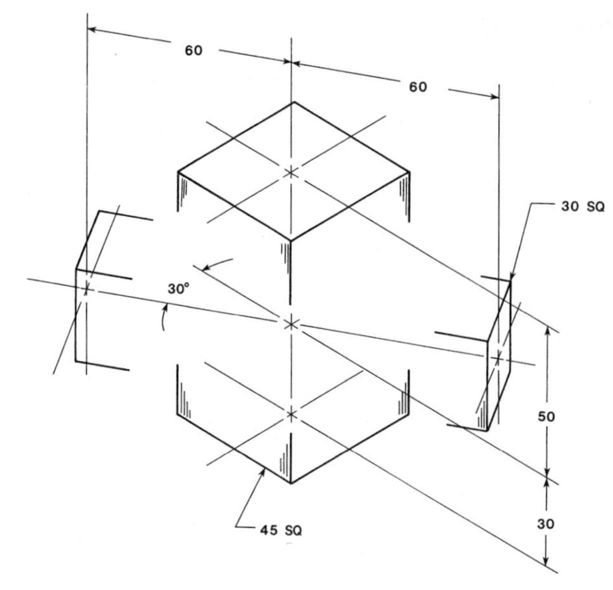

Figure P4-59 MILLIMETERS

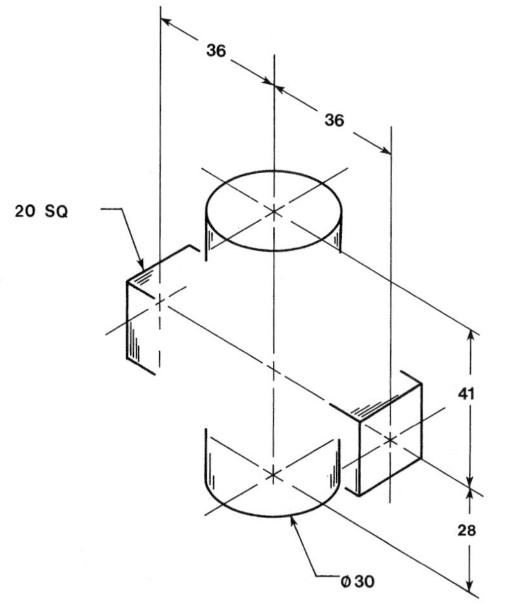

Figure P4-58 MILLIMETERS

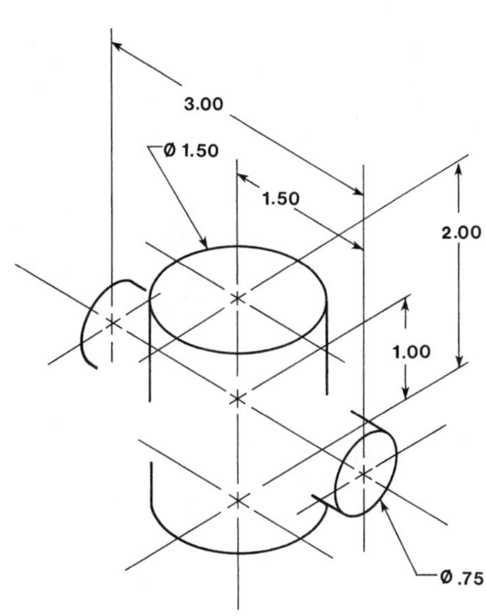

Figure P4-60 INCHES

Project 4-8:

Figures P4-61 through P4-66 are orthographic views. Draw 3D models from the given views. The hole pattern defined in Figure P4-61 also applies to Figure P4-62.

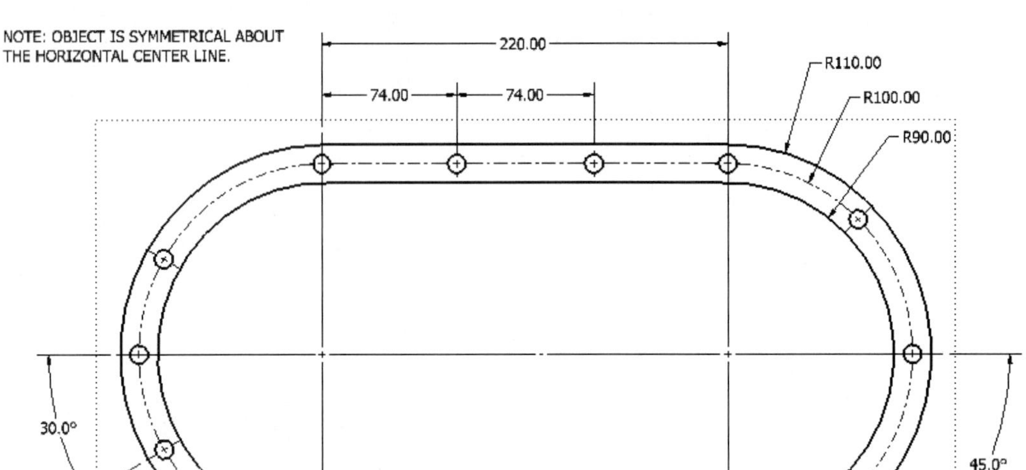

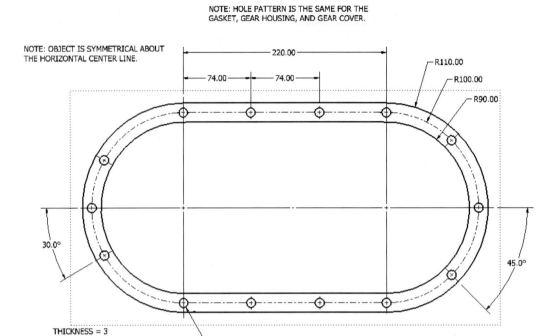

Figure P4-61 MILLIMETERS

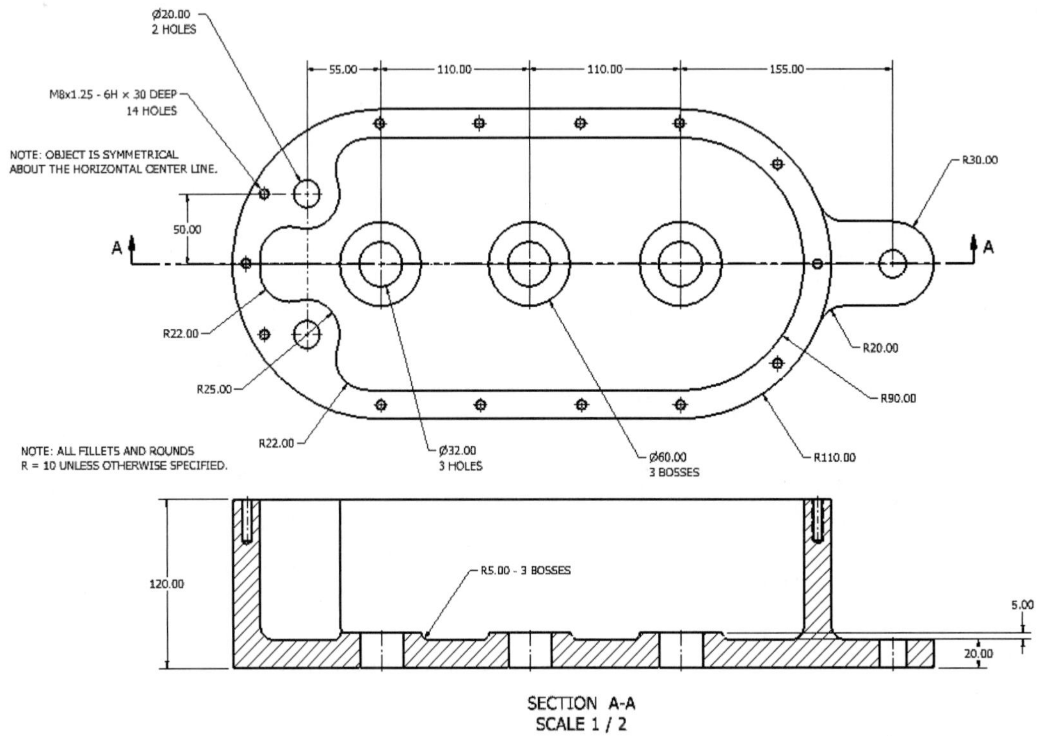

Figure P4-62 MILLIMETERS

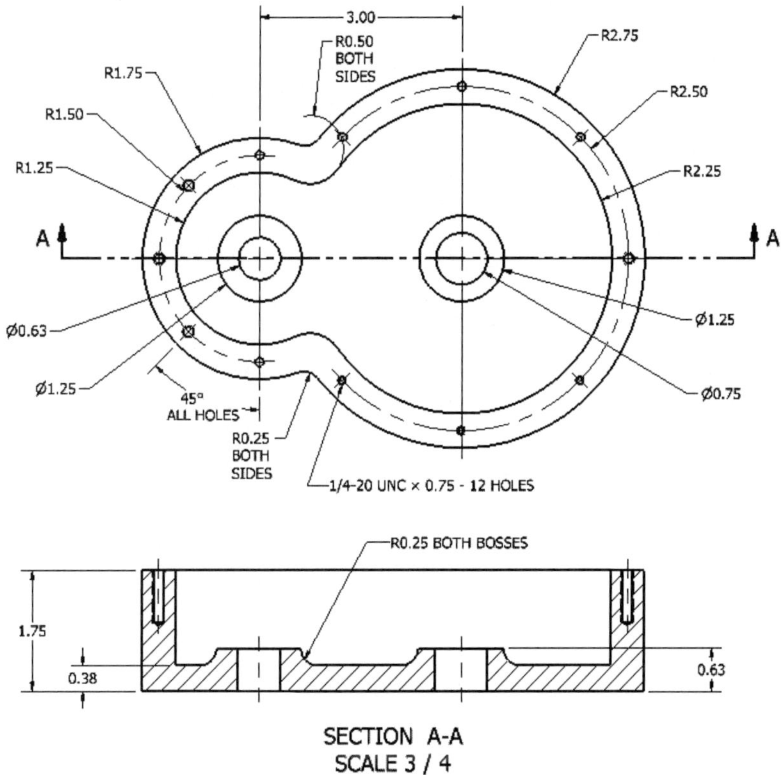

Figure P4-63 INCHES

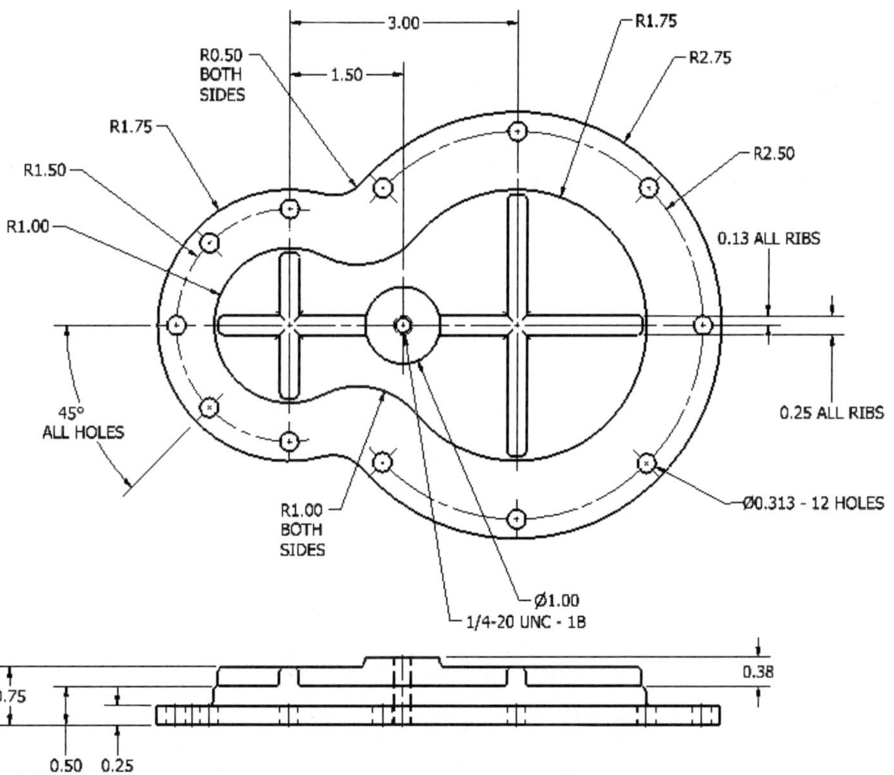

Figure P4-64 INCHES

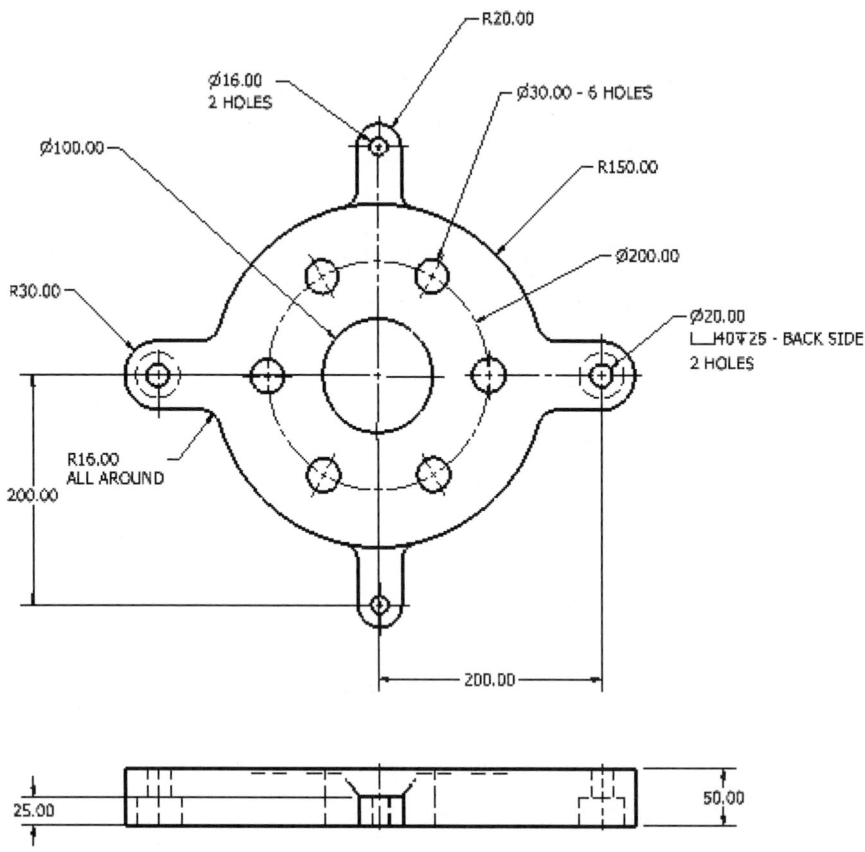

Figure P4-65 MILLIMETERS

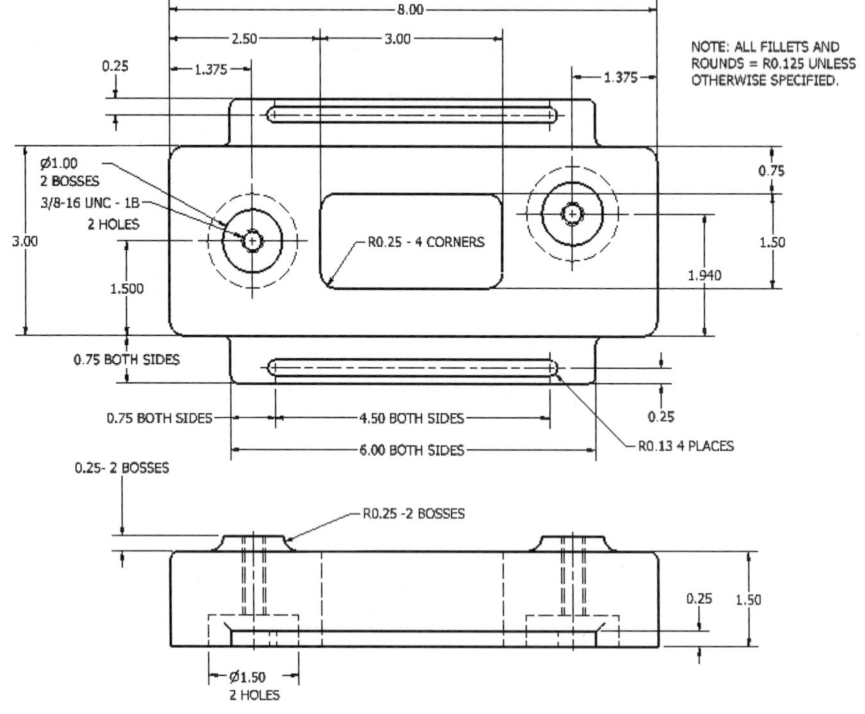

Figure P4-66 INCHES

Project 4-9:

Draw an aligned section view as indicated in Figures P4-67 and P4-68.

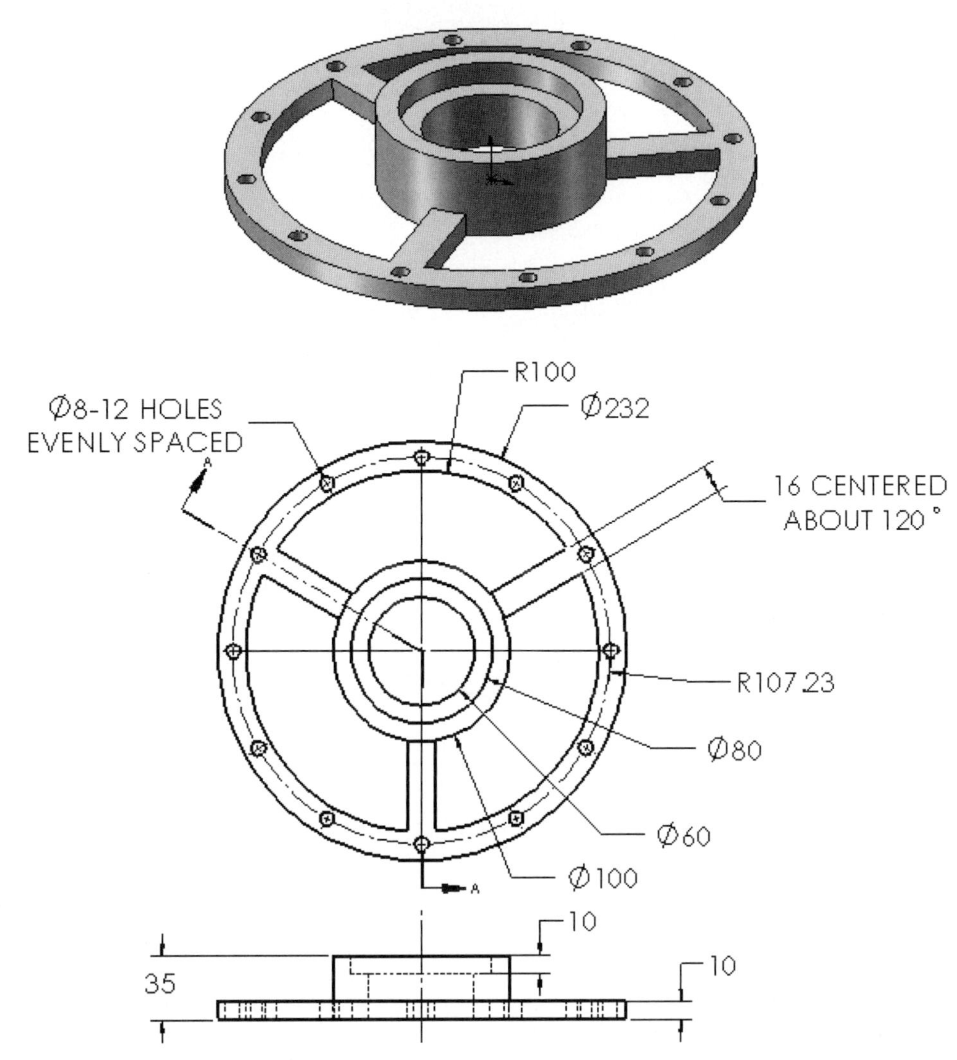

Figure P4-67 MILLIMETERS

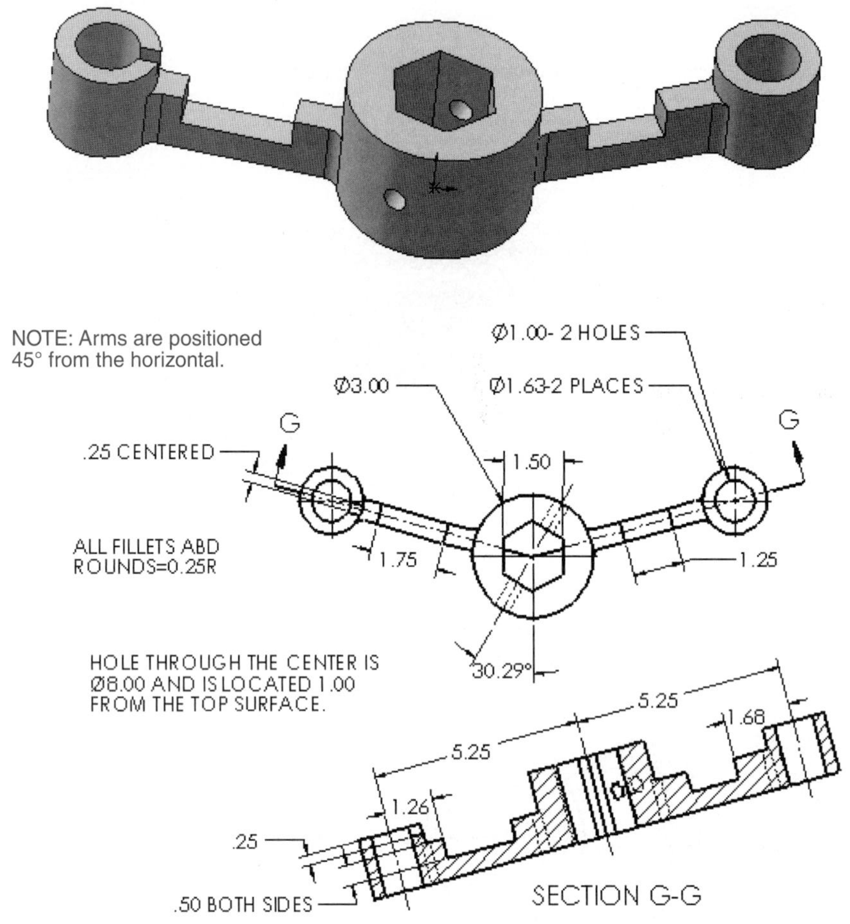

Figure P4-68 INCHES

Project 4-10:

Each of the cross sections shown in Figure P4-69 has been extruded to a very long constant-shaped beam. Draw a front and a right-side orthographic view of the beams. Use the **Break** tool found on the **Drawings** toolbar to shorten the right-side view.

A. L-beam: length = 84
B. Hex beam: length = 102
C. I-beam: length = 96
D. Hollow cylinder beam: length = 120

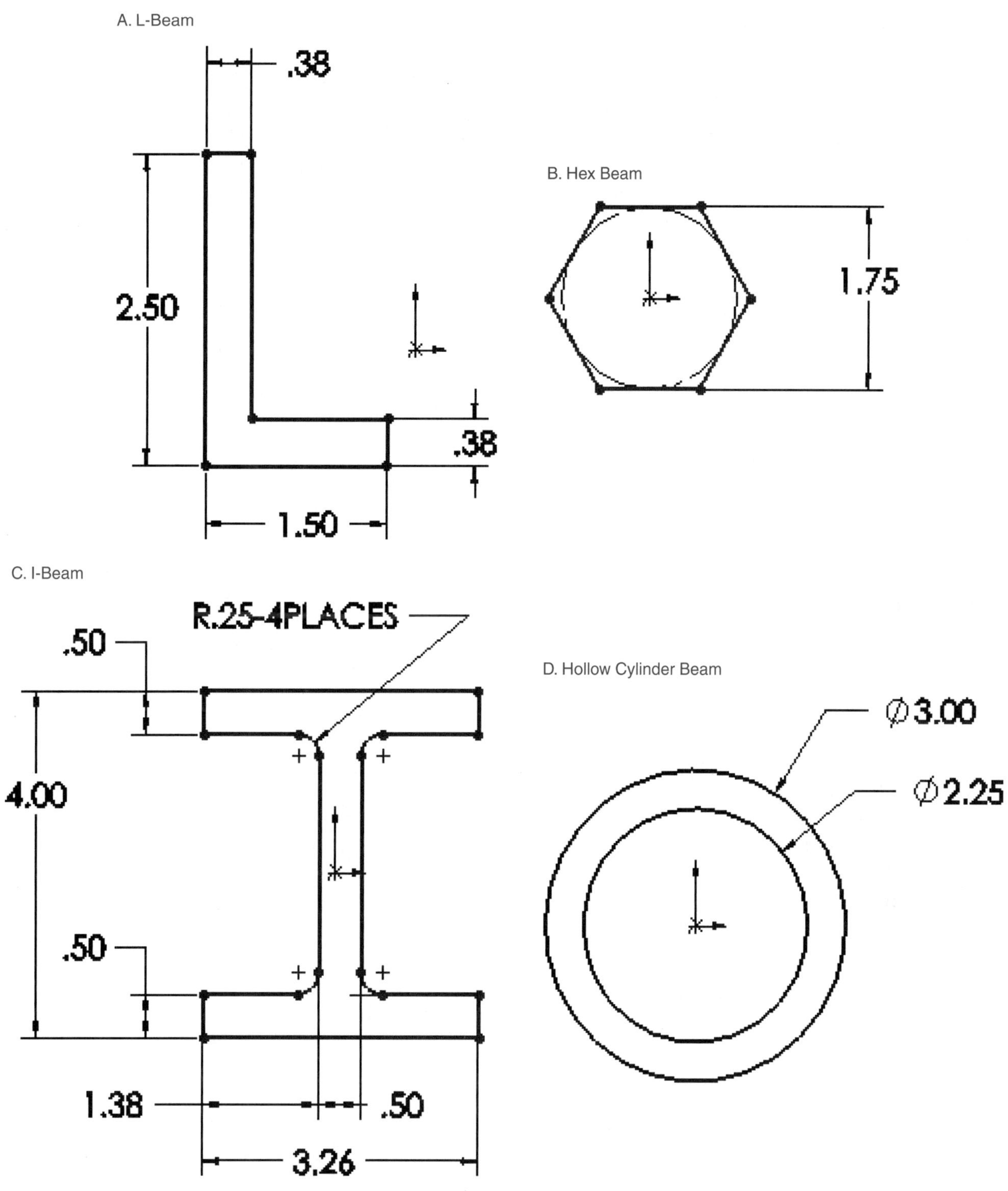

Figure P4-69 INCHES

C H A P T E R 

Assemblies

Objectives

- Learn how to create assembly drawings.
- Learn how to create exploded assembly drawings.
- Learn how to create a parts list.
- Learn how to animate an assembly.
- Learn how to edit a title block.

5-1 INTRODUCTION

This chapter introduces the **Assembly** tools. These tools are used to create assembly drawings. Assembly drawings can be exploded to form isometric assembly drawings that when labeled and accompanied by a parts list become working drawings. Assembly drawings can be animated.

5-2 STARTING AN ASSEMBLY DRAWING

Figure 5-1 shows a test block. The overall dimensions for the block are 80 × 80 × 80 mm. The cutout is 40 × 40 × 80 mm. The test block will be used to help introduce the **Assembly** tools.

1. Start a new drawing.
2. Click the **Assembly** icon.
3. Click **OK.**

   Draw and save as **Block, Test.**

   The **Begin Assembly** box will appear. See Figure 5-2.
5. Click the **Browse . . .** box.

   The **Open** box will appear. See Figure 5-3.
6. Click **Block, Test,** then click **Open.**

   The test block will appear on the screen. See Figure 5-4.
7. Click the **Insert Components** tool and insert a second block.

See Figure 5-5. The first block inserted is fixed in place. In any assembly drawing the first component will automatically be fixed in place. Note the **(f)** notation to the left of **Block, Test <1>.** See Figure 5-6. As the assembly is created, components will move to the fixed first component.

> **TIP**
>
> To remove the fixed condition, locate the cursor on the **(f) Block, Test <1>** callout, right-click the mouse, and click the **Float** option. To return the block to the fixed condition or to fix another component, right-click the component name callout and select the **Fix** option.

5-3 MOVE COMPONENT

See Figure 5-7.

1. Click the **Move Component** tool.
2. Click the second block inserted and hold down the left mouse button.

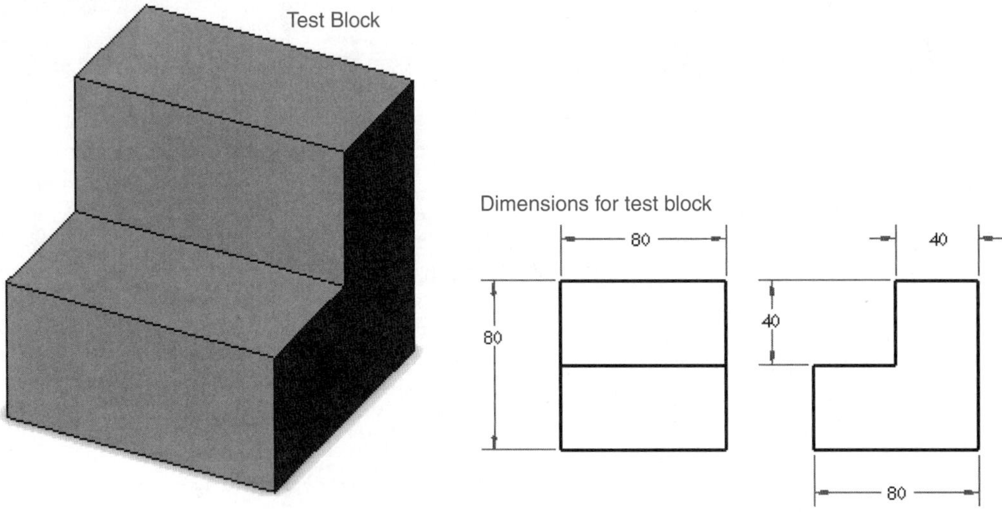

Figure 5-1

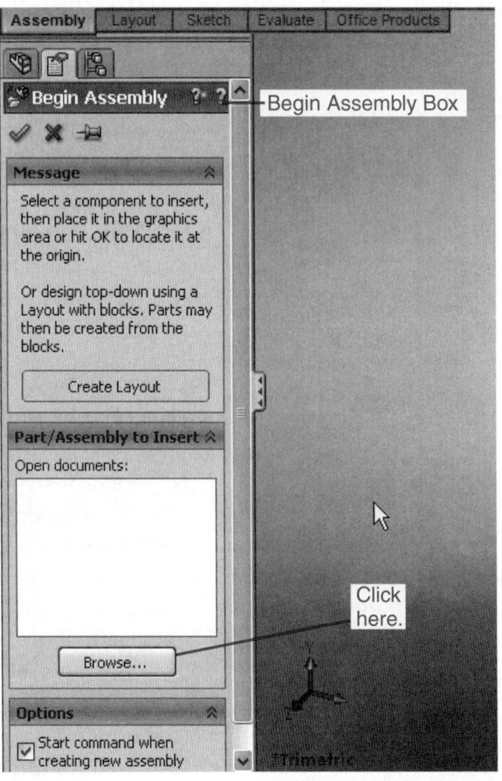

Figure 5-2

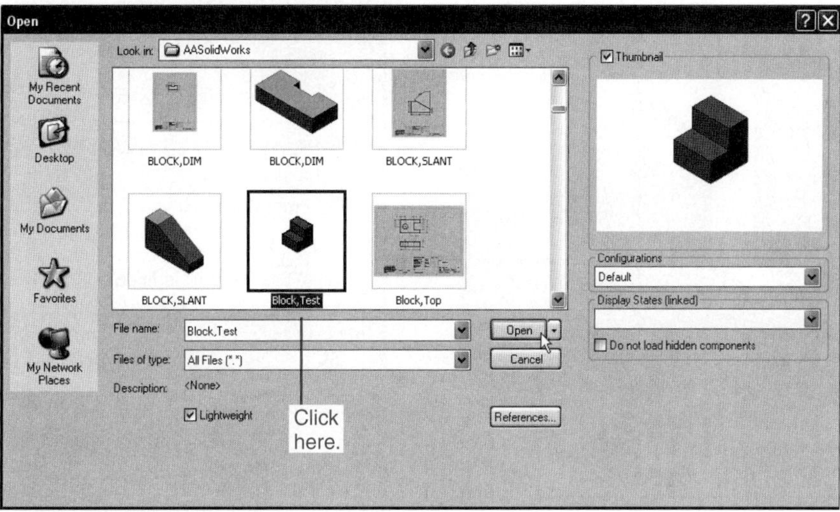

Figure 5-3

3. While holding down the left button, move the block around the screen by moving the mouse.
4. Release the button and click the OK check mark.

5-4 ROTATE COMPONENT

See Figure 5-8.

1. Click the **Rotate Component** tool.
2. Click the second block inserted and hold down the left mouse button.
3. While holding down the left button, rotate the block around the screen by moving the mouse.
4. Release the button and click the OK check mark.
5. Use the **Undo** tool to return the block to its original position.

5-5 MATE

The **Mate** tool is used to align components to create assembly drawings. See Figure 5-9.

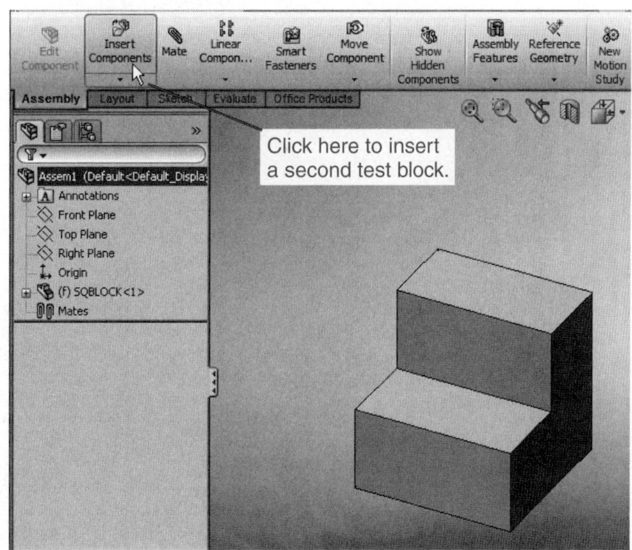

Figure 5-4

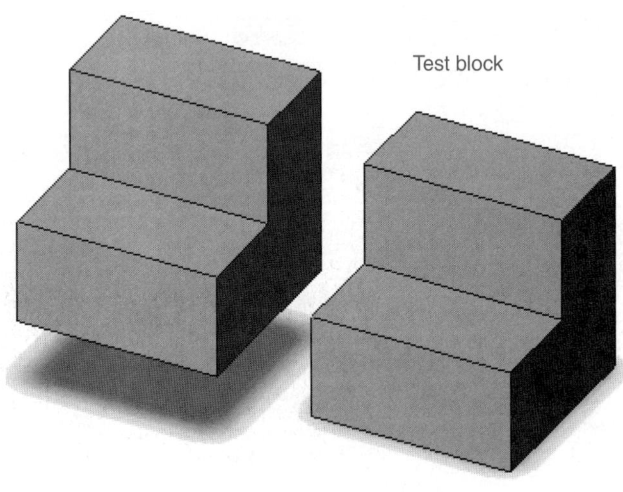

Figure 5-5

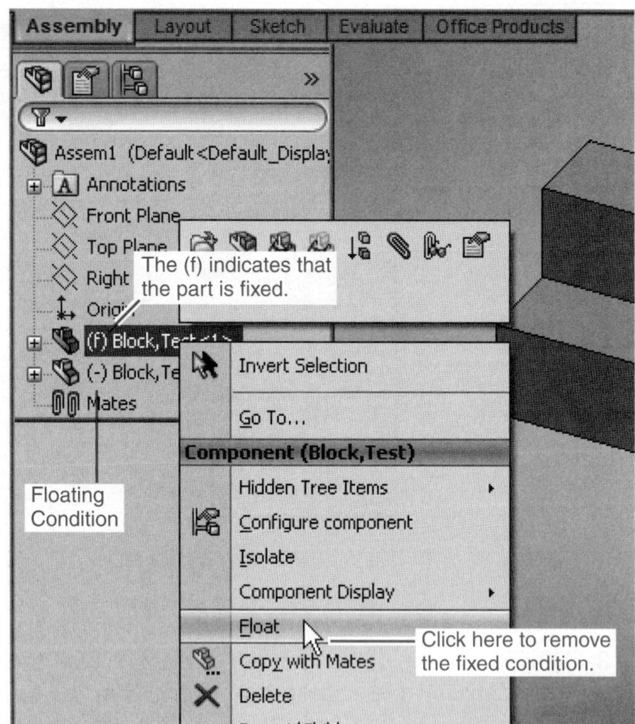

Figure 5-6

First Assembly

Mate the two test blocks side by side.

1. Click the **Mate** tool.
2. Click the upper right edge of the second block inserted.

See Figure 5-10. Note that the second block is listed in the **Mate Selections** box after it is selected.

3. Click the upper left edge on the first block.

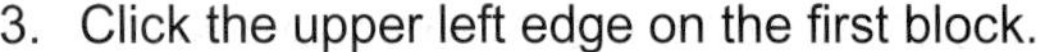

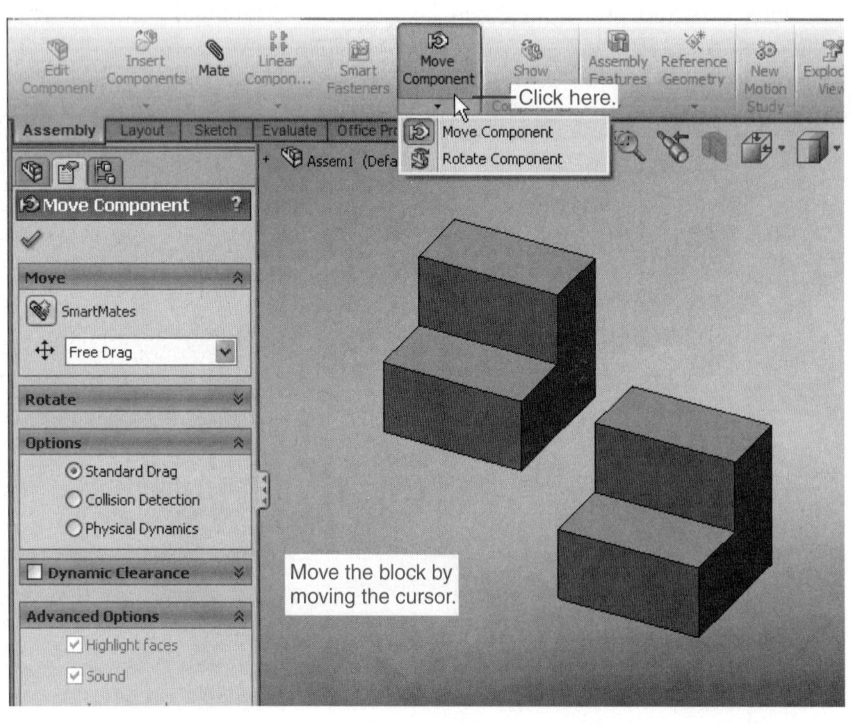

Figure 5-7

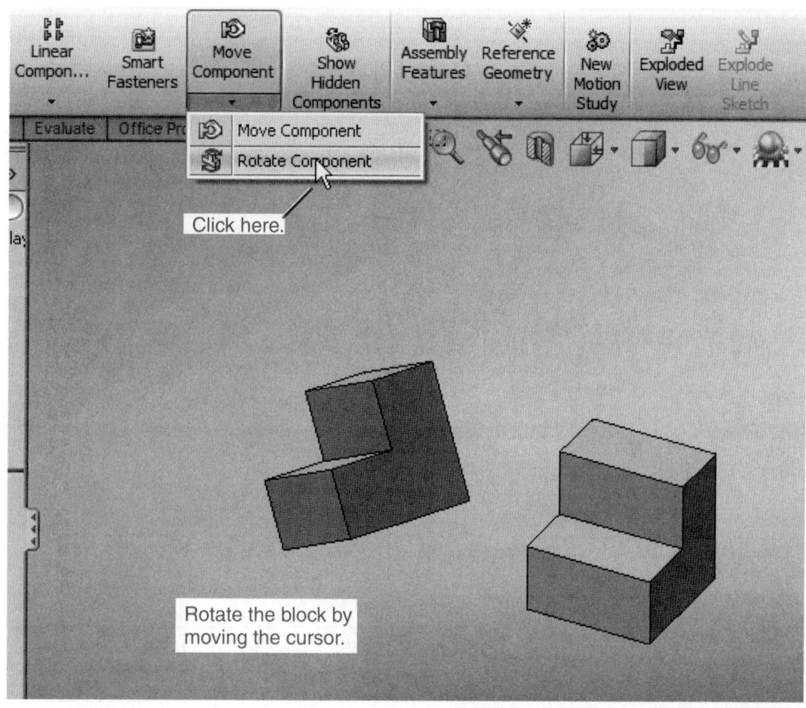

Figure 5-8

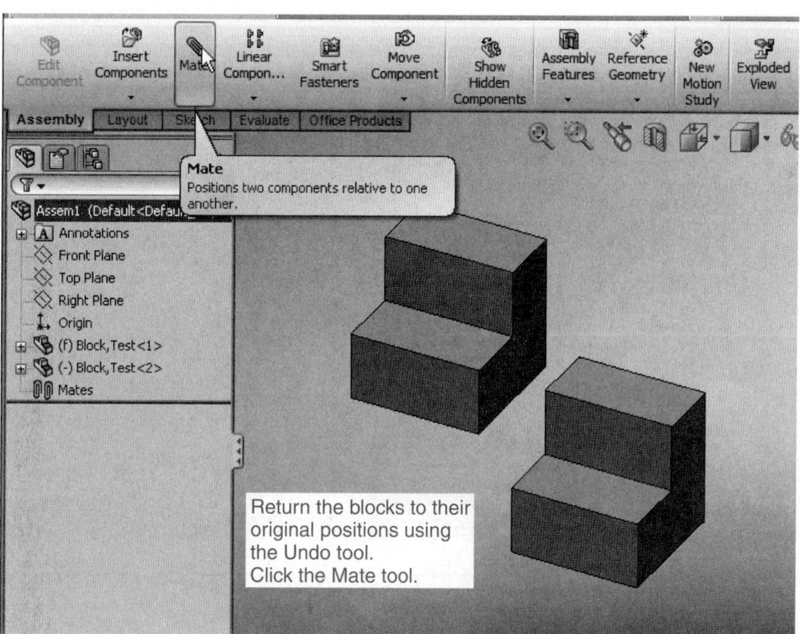

Figure 5-9

The edges will align. See Figure 5-11.

4. Click the OK check mark to clear the tools.

The **Mate Selections** box should be clear.

5. Click the upper front surface of the second block.
6. Click the upper front surface of the first block.

See Figure 5-12. The surfaces will align. See Figure 5-13.

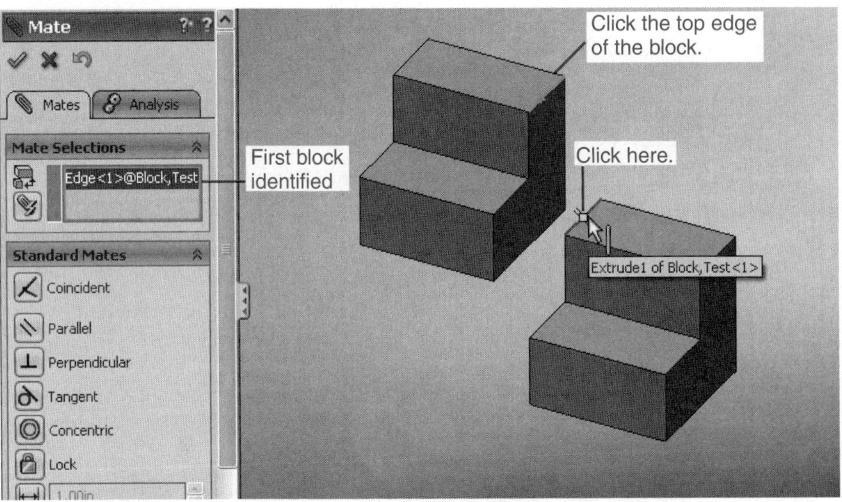

Figure 5-10

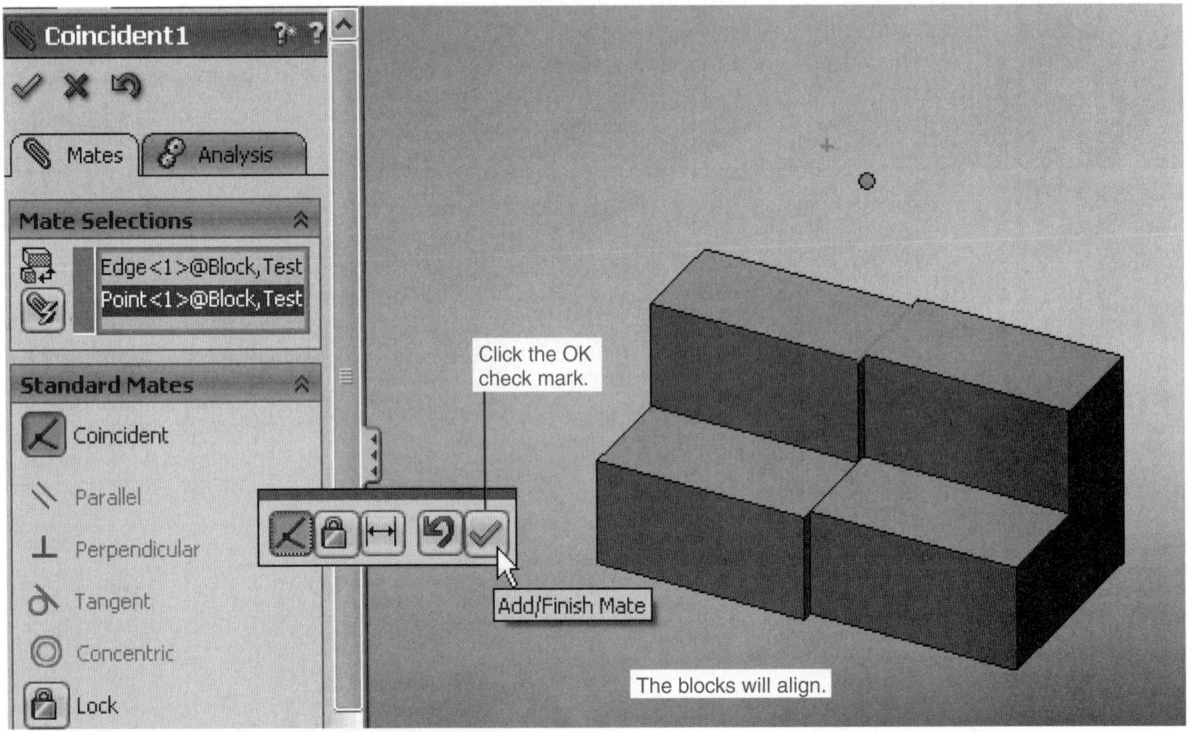

Figure 5-11

Second Assembly

Mate the two test blocks face-to-face.

1. Use the **Undo** tool and return the blocks to their original positions.

See Figure 5-14. The second test block must be rotated into a different position relative to the first test block.

2. Use the **Rotate Component** tool and position the second block as shown.

See Figure 5-15.

3. Use the **Mate** tool and click the lower front face of each block.

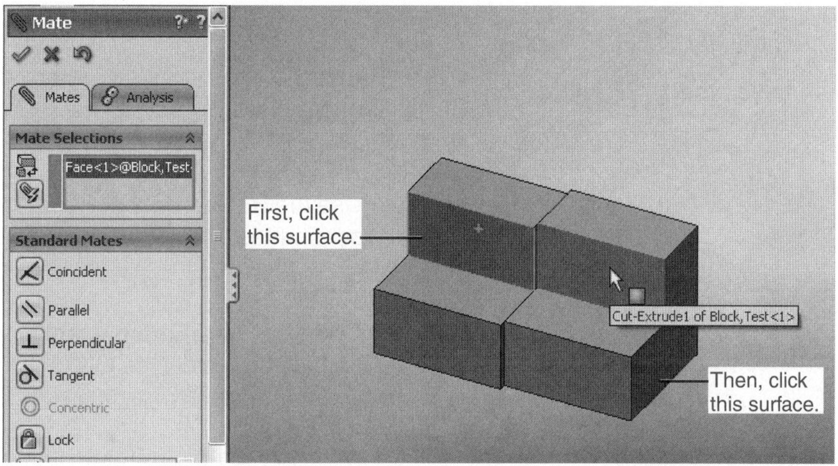

Figure 5-12

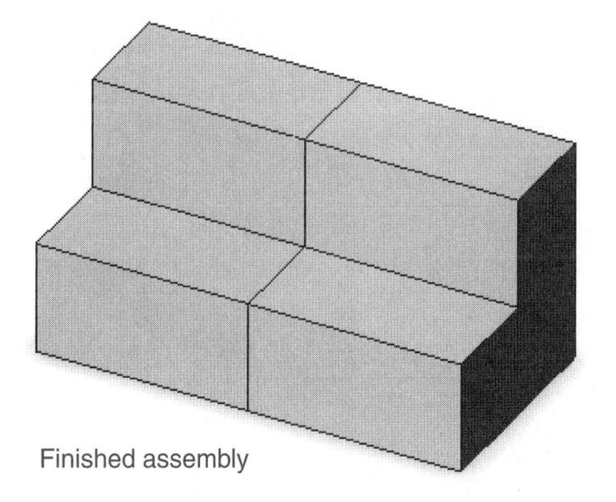

Figure 5-13

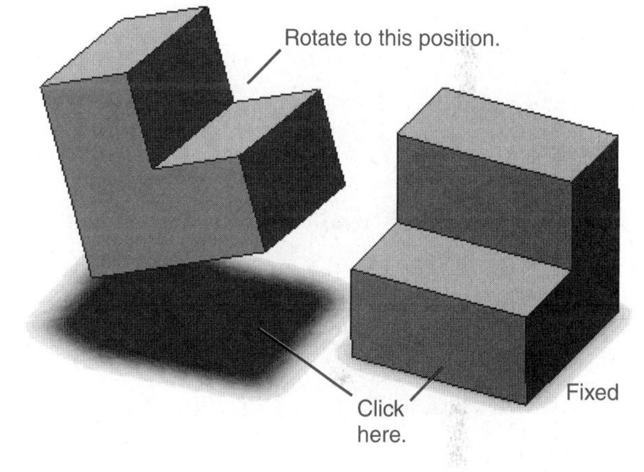

Figure 5-15

Figure 5-14

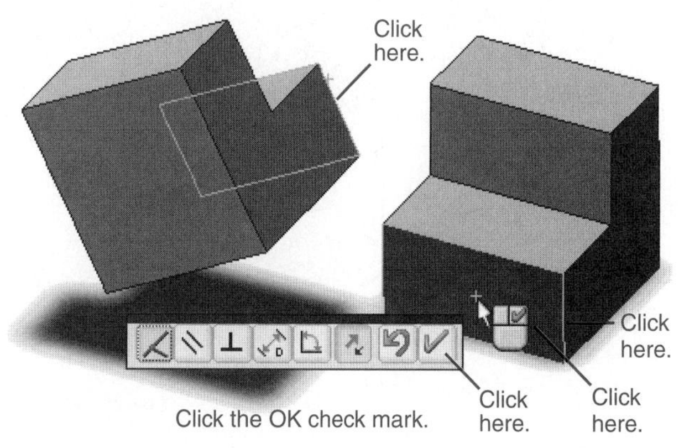

Figure 5-16

The second block will rotate relative to the first block. See Figure 5-16. Recall that the first block is in the fixed condition, and the second block is in the floating condition.

4. Click the **Add/Finish** check mark on the toolbar, then click the OK check mark.
5. Use the Mate tool and click the two faces of the test block as shown.

   See Figure 5-17.

6. Click the **Add/Finish Mate** check mark on the toolbar then click the OK check mark.
7. Use the **Mate** tool and click the two edge lines as shown.

   See Figure 5-18.

8. Click the **Add/Finish Mate** check mark on the toolbar, then click the OK check mark.

Third Assembly

Mate the two test blocks to form a rectangular prism.

1. Use the **Undo** tool and return the blocks to their original positions.

   See Figure 5-14.

2. Use the **Rotate Component** tool and position the second test block as shown.

   See Figure 5-19.

3. Click the **Add/Finish Mate** check mark on the toolbar, then click the OK check mark.
4. Use the **Mate** tool and click the right surfaces of the blocks.
5. Click the **Add/Finish** check mark on the toolbar, then click the OK check mark.

   See Figure 5-20.

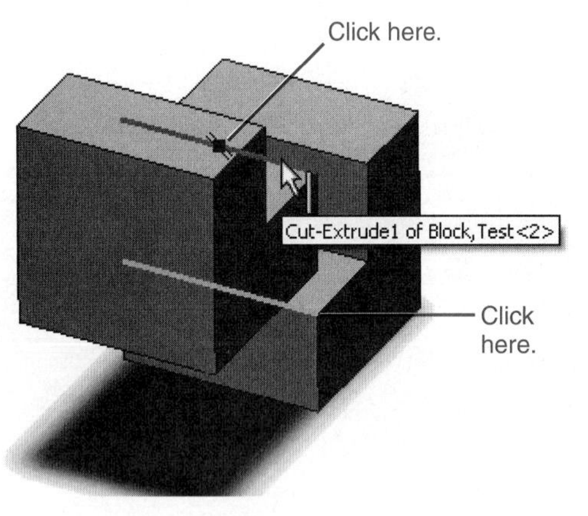
Click here.
Cut-Extrude1 of Block,Test<2>
Click here.

Figure 5-17

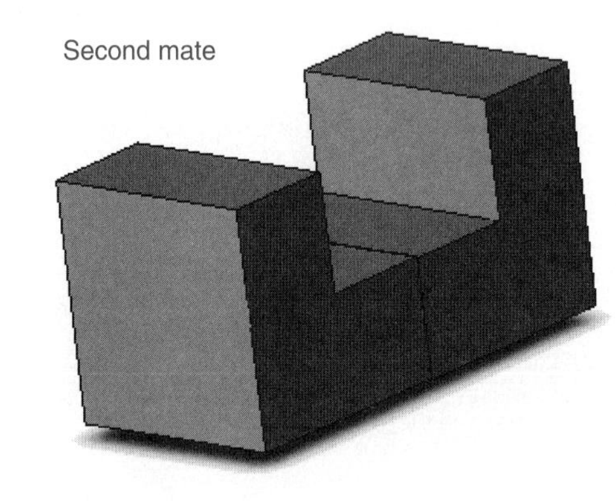
Second mate

Figure 5-18

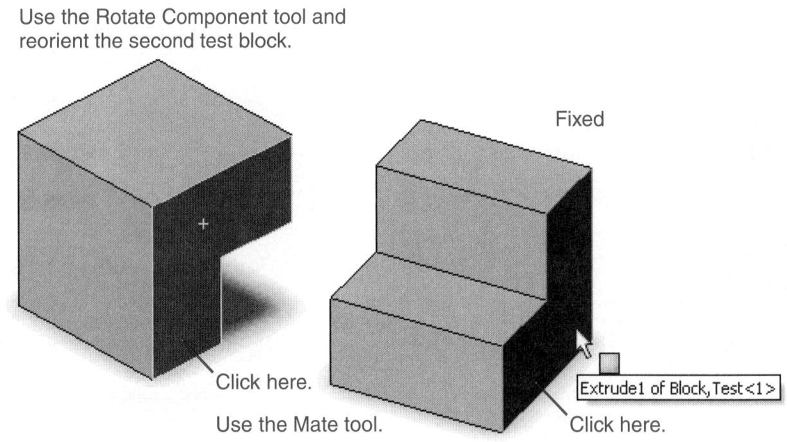
Use the Rotate Component tool and reorient the second test block.
Fixed
Click here.
Use the Mate tool.
Extrude1 of Block,Test<1>
Click here.

Figure 5-19

Then, click the
OK check mark.
Click
here.
Add/Finish Mate

Figure 5-20

6. Click the upper edge of the blocks as shown.

   See Figure 5-21.

7. Click the **Add/Finish Mate** check mark on the toolbar, then click the OK check mark.

   See Figure 5-22.

8. Reorient the blocks so that the bottom surfaces are visible.

   See Figure 5-23.

9. Use the **Mate** tool and click the bottom surfaces of the blocks.

   Figure 5-24 shows the finished assembly.

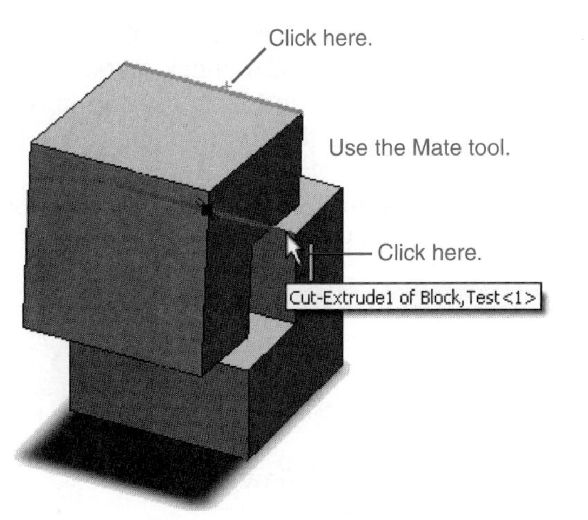
Click here.
Use the Mate tool.
Click here.
Cut-Extrude1 of Block,Test<1>

Figure 5-21

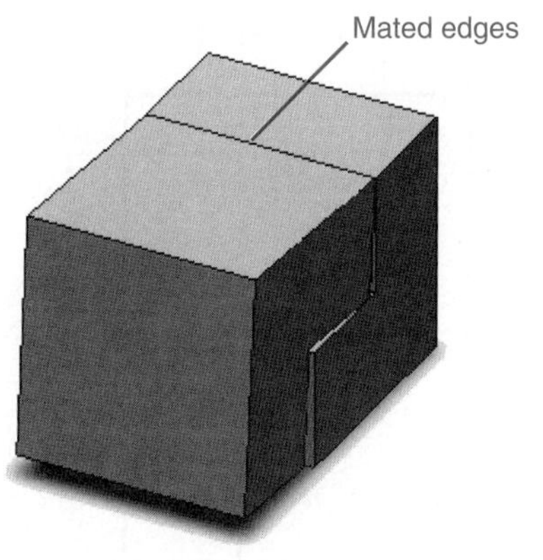
Mated edges

Figure 5-22

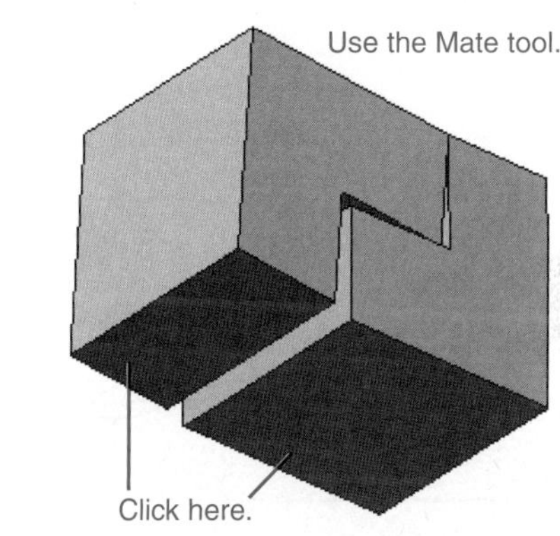
Use the Mate tool.
Click here.

Figure 5-23

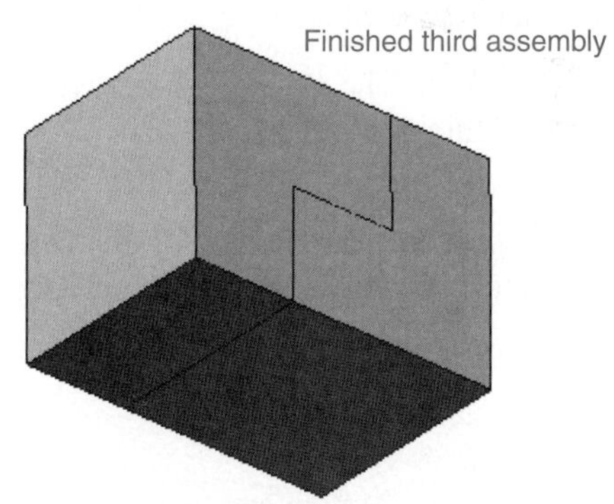
Finished third assembly

Figure 5-24

5-6 BOTTOM-UP ASSEMBLIES

Bottom-up assemblies are assemblies that are created for existing parts; that is, the parts have already been drawn as models. In this example the three parts shown in Figure 5-25 have been drawn and saved.

1. Start a new drawing and select the **Assembly** format.

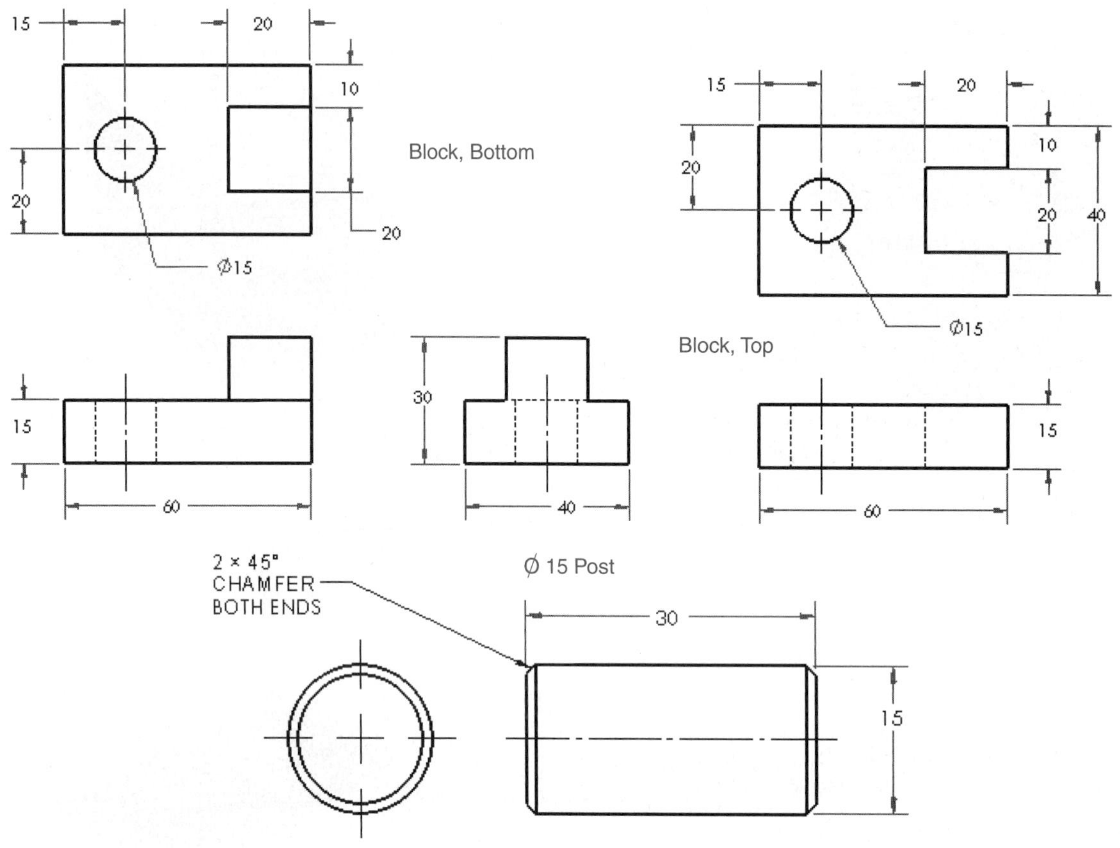

Figure 5-25

2. Click the **Browse . . .** box, then click the **Block, Bottom** component.

See Figure 5-26. The Block, Bottom will appear on the screen. See Figure 5-27.

3. Click the **Insert Component** tool, click the **Browse . . .** box, and select **Block, Top.**
4. Repeat the sequence and select **Ø15 Post.**

See Figure 5-28.

> ***Note:***
> Note that the Block, Bottom was the first part entered and is fixed in its location, as designated by the **(f)** symbol in the Properties Manager box.

5. Use the **Mate** tool and click the center point of the edge line of the Block, Bottom and the Block, Top as shown.

See Figure 5-29. A dot will appear when the cursor is on the center point of the edge. Figure 5-30 shows the resulting mate. If the blocks do not align, use the **Mate** tool again to align the blocks.

6. Click the OK check mark.
7. Click the **Mate** tool and click the **Concentric** option.

See Figure 5-31.

8. Click the side of the Ø15 Post and the inside of the hole in the Block, Top.
9. Click the **Add/Finish Mate** check mark on the toolbar, then click the OK check mark.
10. Use the **Mate** tool and click the top surface of the Ø15 Post and the top surface of the Block, Top.
11. Click the **Add/Finish Mate** check mark on the toolbar, then click the OK check mark.

5-7 CREATING AN EXPLODED ISOMETRIC ASSEMBLY DRAWING

1. Click the **Exploded View** tool.

See Figure 5-32.

2. Click the top surface of the Ø15 Post.

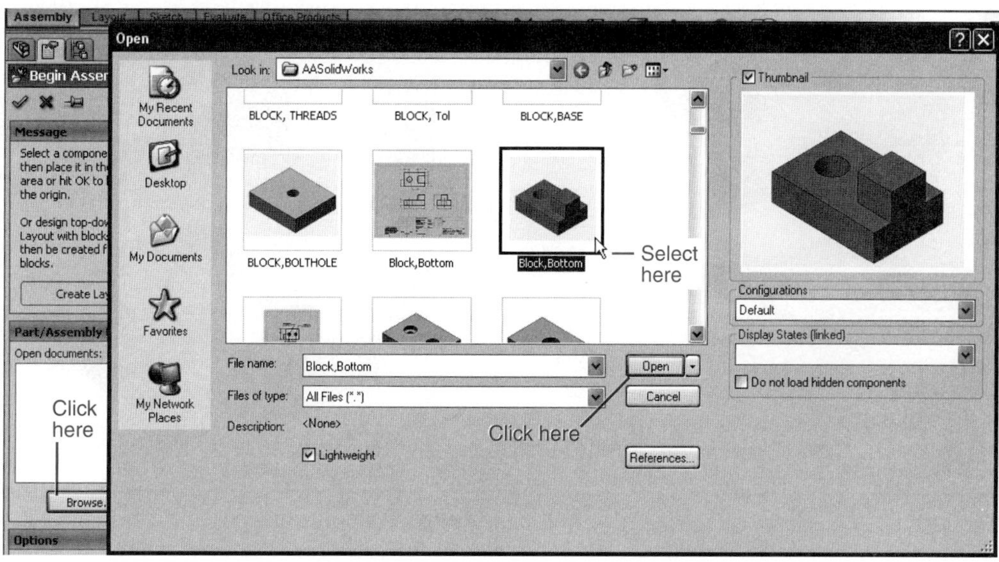

Figure 5-26

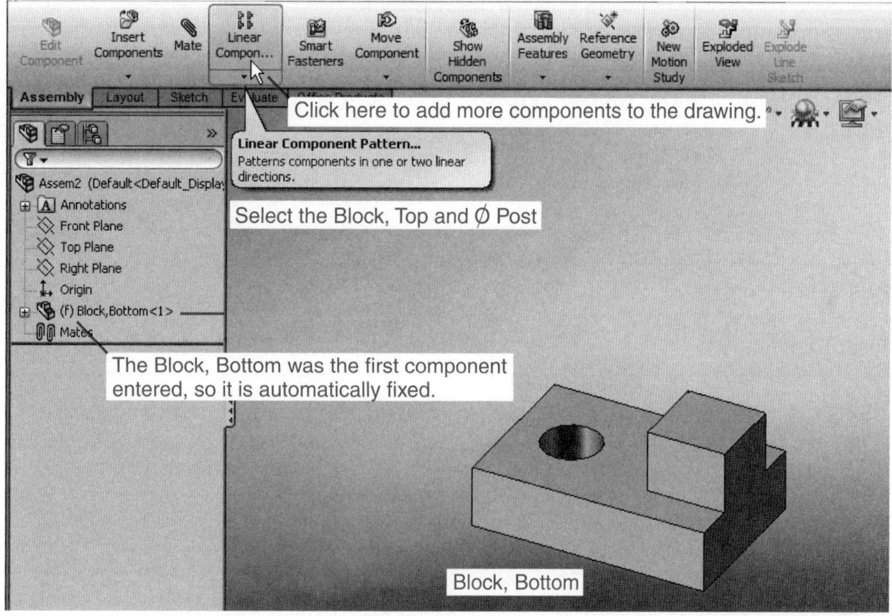

Figure 5-27

An axis system icon will appear. See Figure 5-33. The arrow in the Z-direction (the one pointing vertically) will initially be green.

3. Move the cursor onto the Z-direction arrow and hold down the left mouse button.

   The arrow will turn yellow when selected.

4. Drag the Ø15 Post to a location above the assembly as shown.
5. Click the OK check mark.
6. Repeat the procedure and drag the Block, Top away from the Block, Bottom.
7. Click the OK check mark.
8. Save the assembly.

In this example the assembly was saved as **Block Assembly.** Figure 5-34 shows the final assembly.

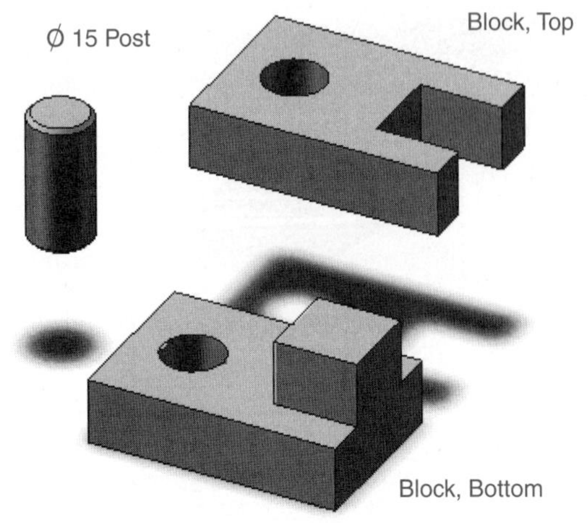

Figure 5-28

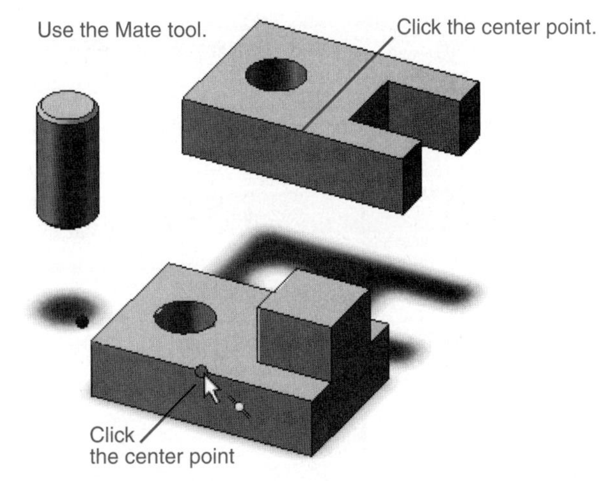

Figure 5-29

5-8 CREATING AN EXPLODED ISOMETRIC DRAWING USING THE DRAWING FORMAT

1. Create a new drawing using the **Drawing** format.
2. Select the **A-Portrait** sheet format.
3. Click the **Browse . . .** box in the **Model View Properties Manager.**

   See Figure 5-35.

4. Select **Block Assembly;** click **Open.**
5. Set the **Orientation** for **Isometric** and the **Display Style** for **Hidden Lines Removed.**

   See Figure 5-36.

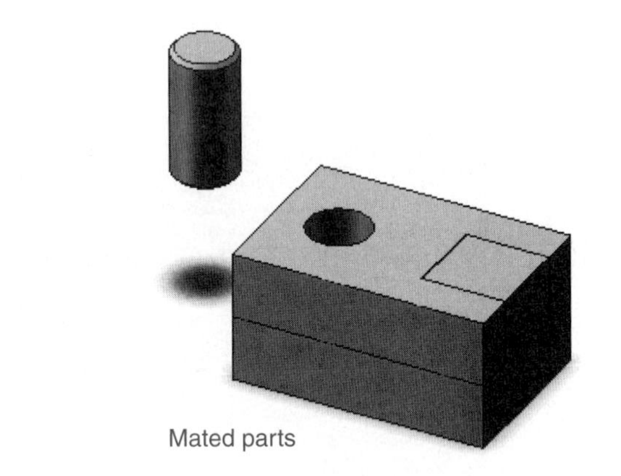

Figure 5-30

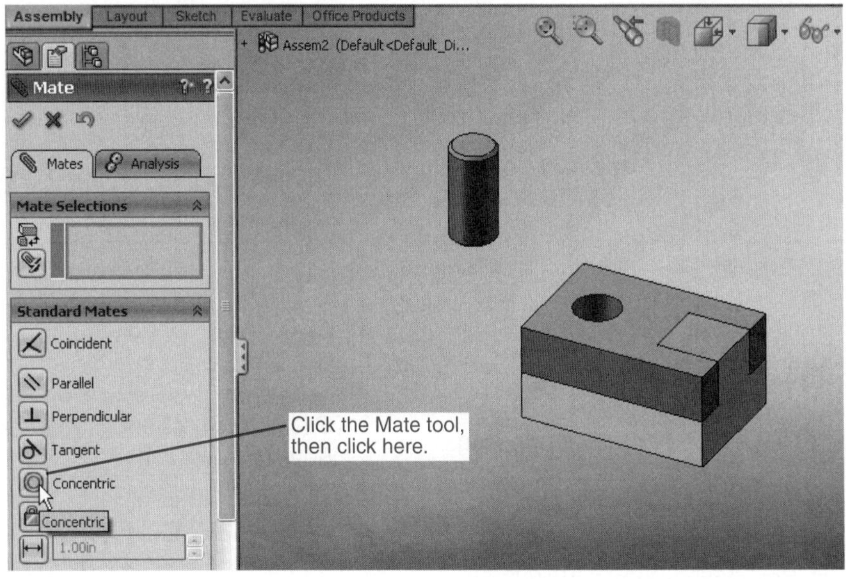

Figure 5-31

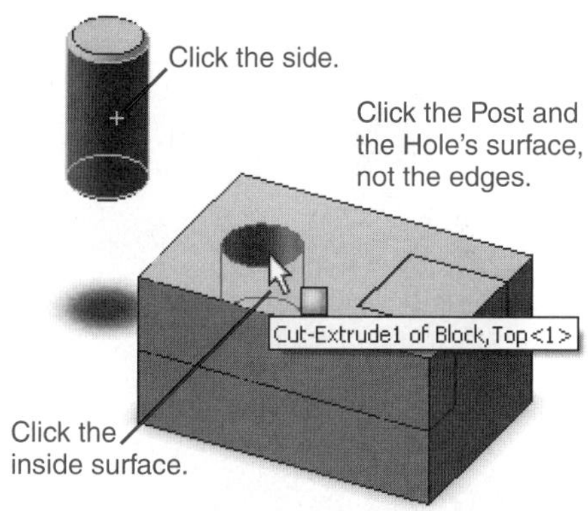
Click the side.
Click the Post and the Hole's surface, not the edges.
Cut-Extrude1 of Block,Top<1>
Click the inside surface.

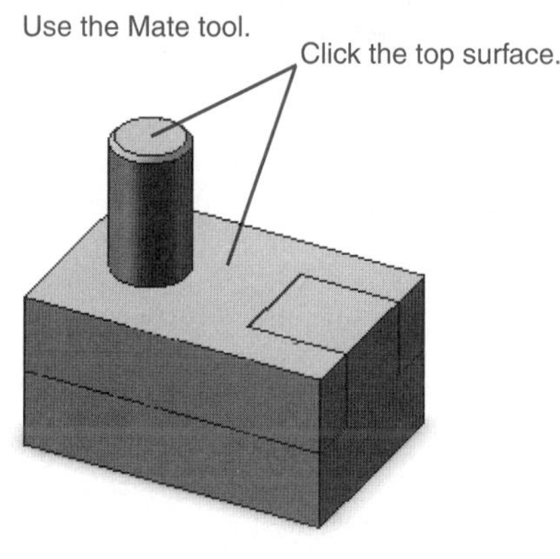
Use the Mate tool.
Click the top surface.

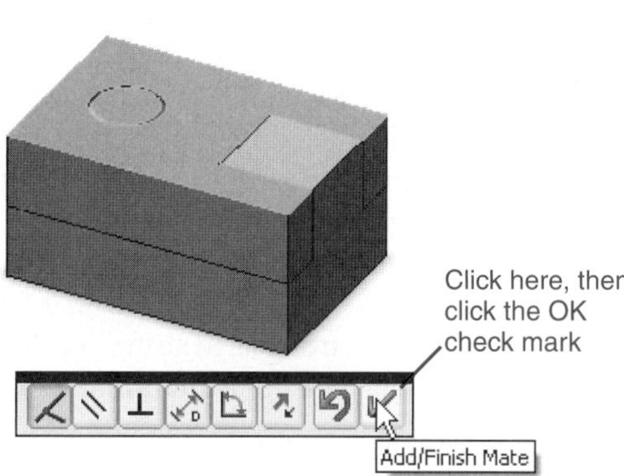
Click here, then click the OK check mark
Add/Finish Mate

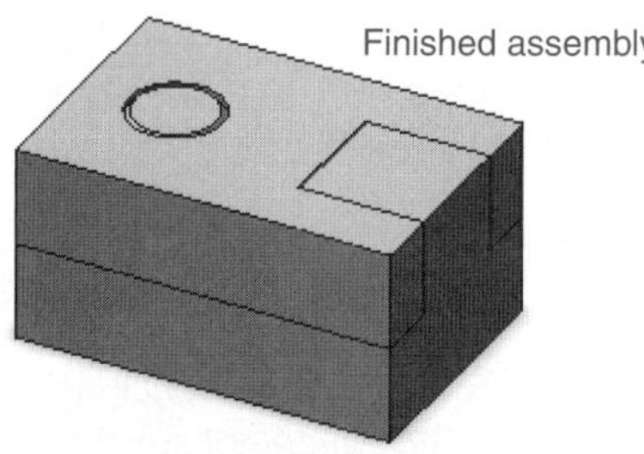
Finished assembly

Figure 5-31 *(continued)*

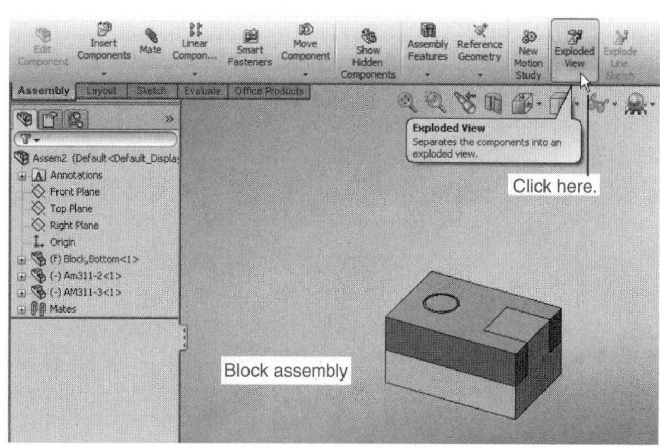
Exploded View
Separates the components into an exploded view.
Click here.
Block assembly

Figure 5-32

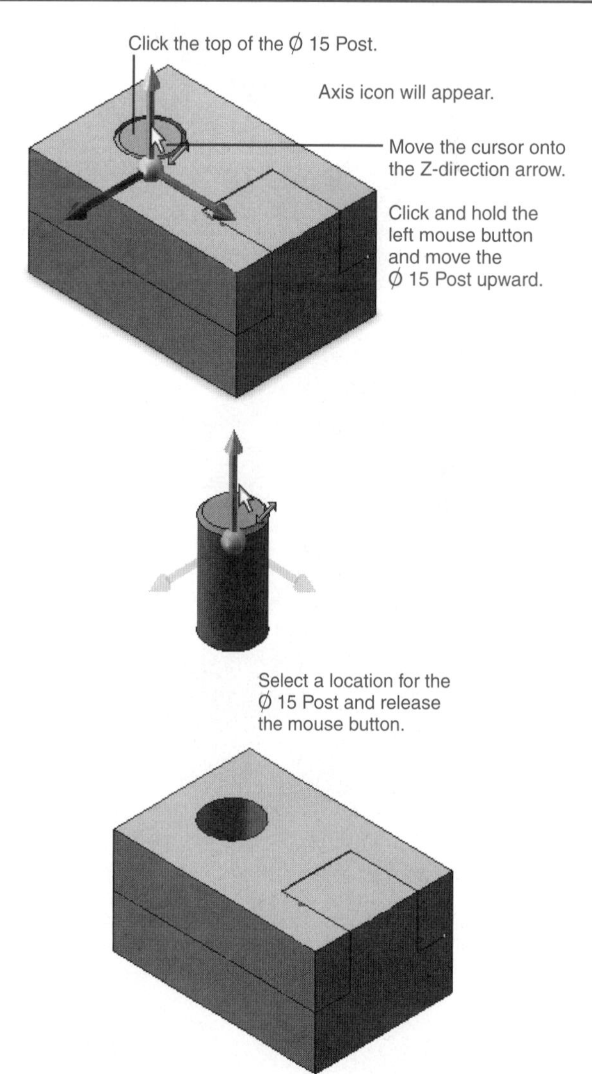
Click the top of the Ø 15 Post.
Axis icon will appear.
Move the cursor onto the Z-direction arrow.
Click and hold the left mouse button and move the Ø 15 Post upward.
Select a location for the Ø 15 Post and release the mouse button.

Figure 5-33

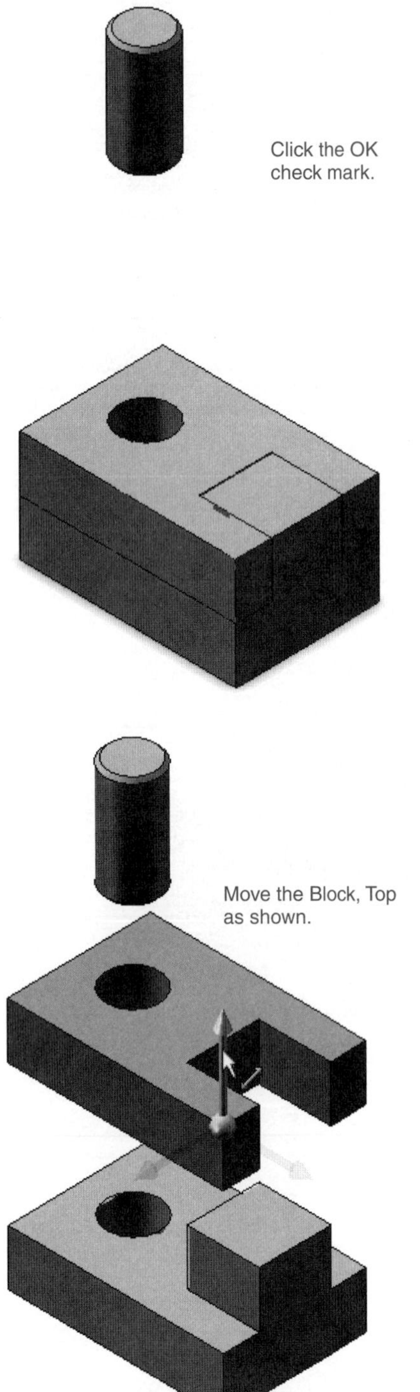
Click the OK
check mark.
Move the Block, Top
as shown.

Figure 5-33 *(continued)*

TIP

As a general rule, hidden lines are not included on isometric drawings.

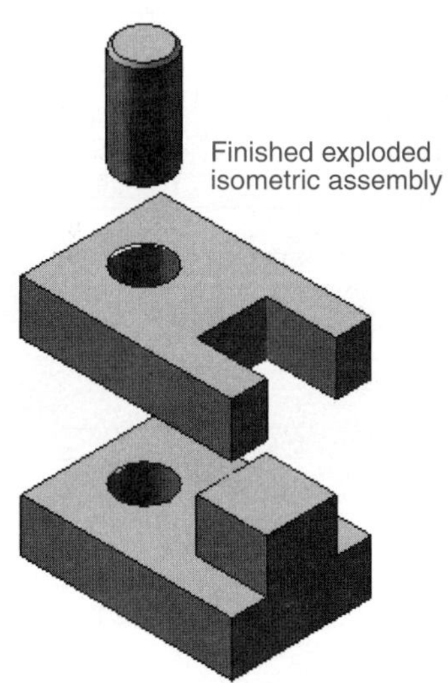
Finished exploded
isometric assembly

Figure 5-34

6. Move the cursor into the drawing area.

   A rectangular outline of the view will appear.

7. Locate the view and click the left mouse button.

   See Figure 5-37.

5-9 ASSEMBLY NUMBERS

Assembly numbers are numbers that identify a part within an assembly. They are different from part numbers. A part number identifies a specific part, and the part number is unique to that part. A part has only one part number but may have different assembly numbers in different assemblies.

Assembly numbers are created using the **Balloon** or **AutoBalloon** tools located on the **Annotation** tool panel.

1. Click the **Annotation** tool.
2. Click the **AutoBalloon** tool.

Figure 5-38 shows the results. The **AutoBalloon** arrangements may not always be the best presentation. Balloons can be applied individually.

TIP

Balloons can be moved by first clicking them. They will change color. Click and hold either the balloon or the box that will appear on the arrow. Either the balloon or the arrow may be dragged to a new location.

3. Undo the auto balloons.
4. Click the **Balloon** tool.

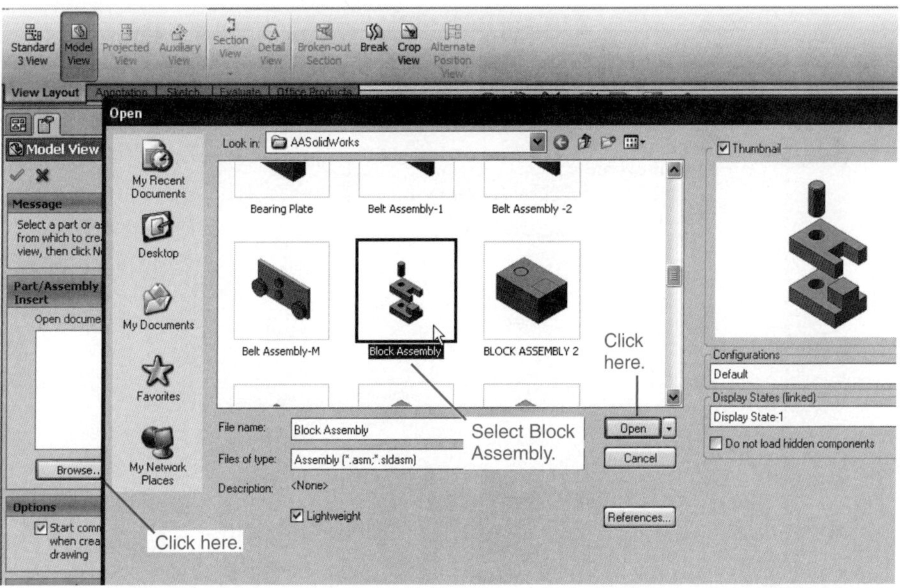

Figure 5-35

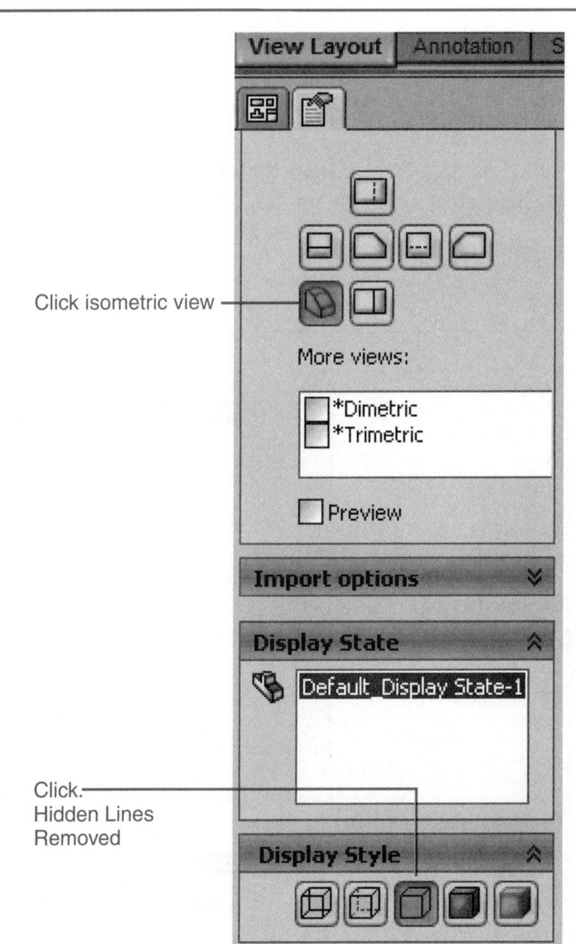

Figure 5-36

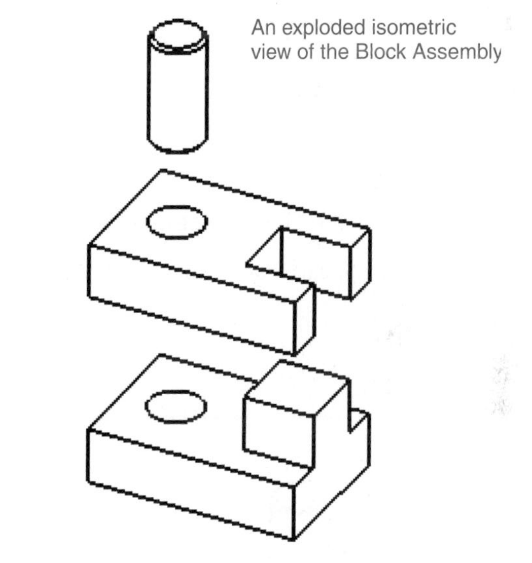

Figure 5-37

5. Click each part and locate the balloon.
6. Click the OK check mark.

See Figure 5-39.

5-10 BILL OF MATERIALS (BOM OR PARTS LIST)

A ***bill of materials*** is a listing of all parts included in an assembly drawing.

1. To access the **Bill of Materials** tool click the **Annotation** toolbox, **Tables,** and **Bill of Materials** tools.

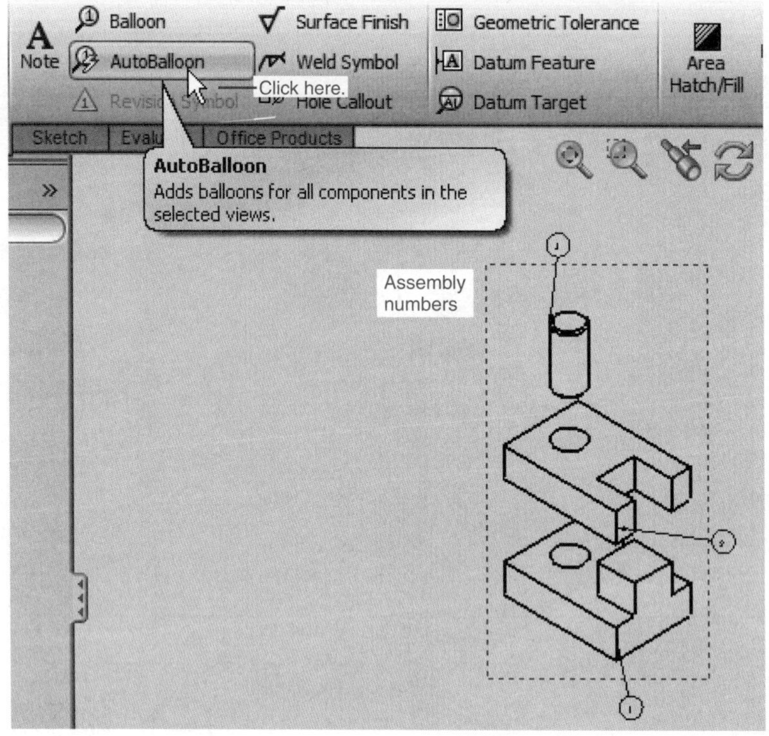

Figure 5-38

See Figure 5-40.

2. Click the area of the Block Assembly.

A red box will appear around the Block Assembly. Click within that box.

3. Click the OK check mark.

Pull the cursor back into the drawing area. The BOM will follow. Select a location for the BOM and click the mouse.

See Figure 5-41.

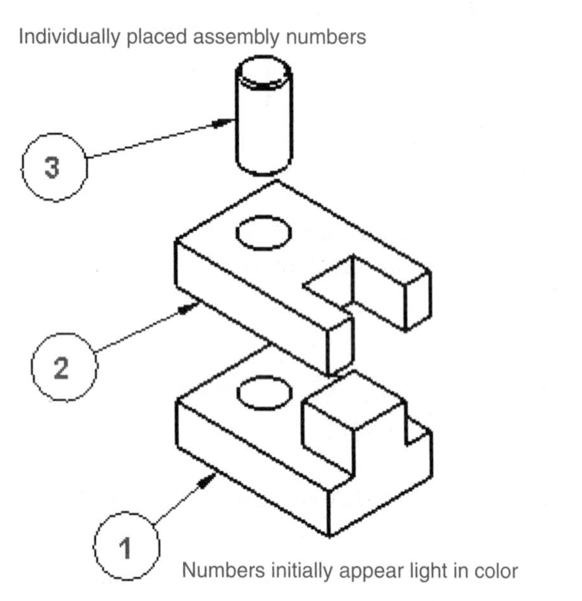

Figure 5-39

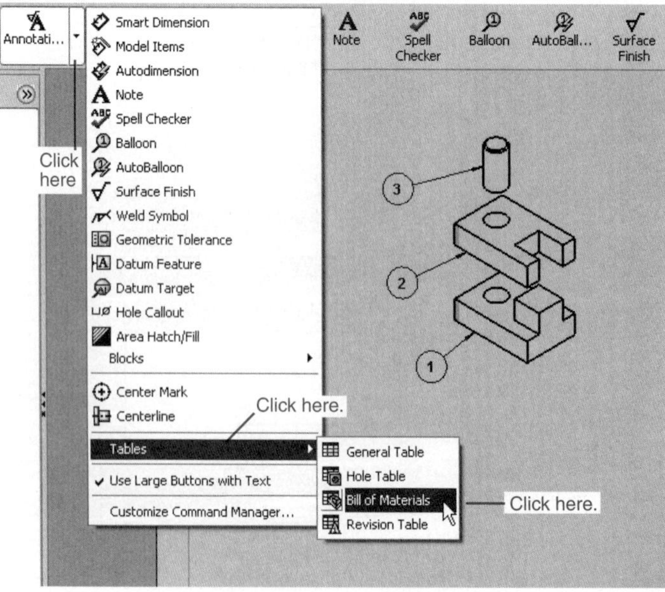

Figure 5-40

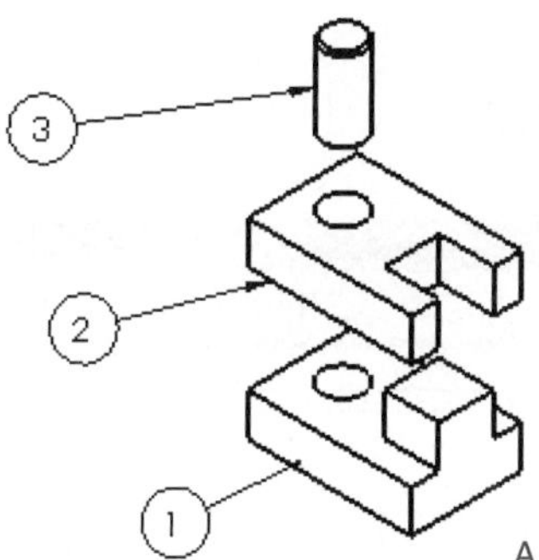

A bill of materials

ITEM NO.	PART NUMBER	DESCRIPTION	QTY.
1	Block,Bottom		1
2	Block,Top		1
3	Ø15 Post		1

These are the parts' file.

Figure 5-41

> ***Note:***
> Note that the information in the **PART NUMBER** column is the parts' file names. These names are directly linked by SolidWorks to the original part drawings. They can be manually edited, but if the assembly is changed and regenerated, the original part names will appear. In this example the original parts were renamed using part numbers as their file names. See Figure 5-42.

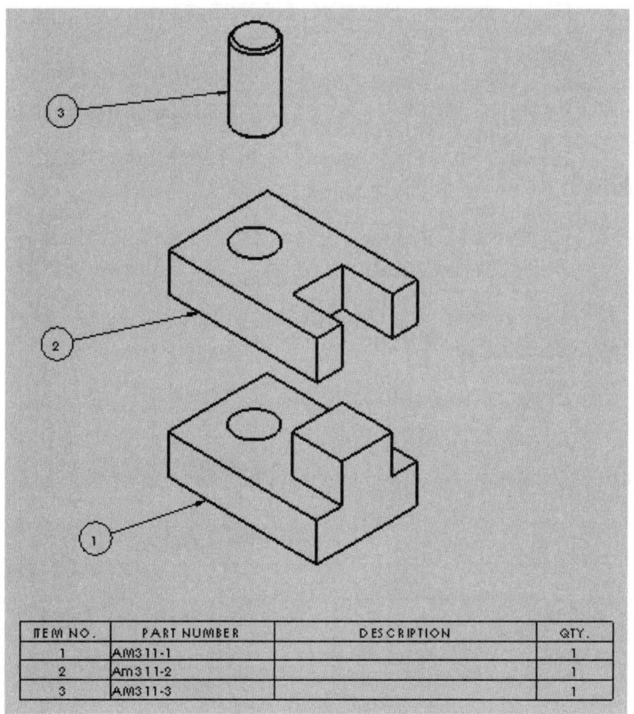

ITEM NO.	PART NUMBER	DESCRIPTION	QTY.
1	AM311-1		1
2	Am311-2		1
3	AM311-3		1

The original part names were changed to part numbers.

Figure 5-42

To Edit the BOM

1. Double-click the box directly under the heading **DESCRIPTION.**

   A warning dialog box will appear.

2. Click the **Keep Link** box.

   The **Formatting** dialog box will appear.

3. Type in a description of the part.

   See Figure 5-43.

4. Click the box below the one just edited.

   A warning box will appear.

5. Click the **Yes** box.

   A second warning box will appear.

6. Click the **Keep Link** box.
7. Edit the remaining boxes as shown.

   See Figure 5-44.

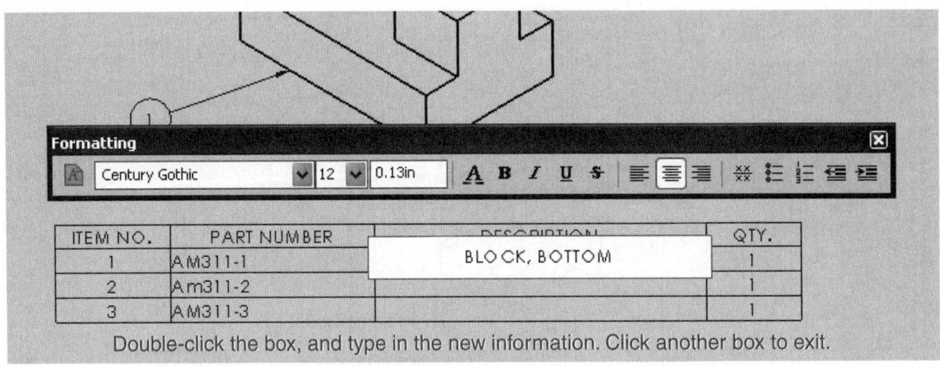

Figure 5-43

ITEM NO.	PART NUMBER	DESCRIPTION	QTY.
1	AM311-1	BLOCK, BOTTOM	1
2	Am311-2	BLOCK,TOP	1
3	AM311-3	Ø15 POST	1

An edited BOM

Figure 5-44

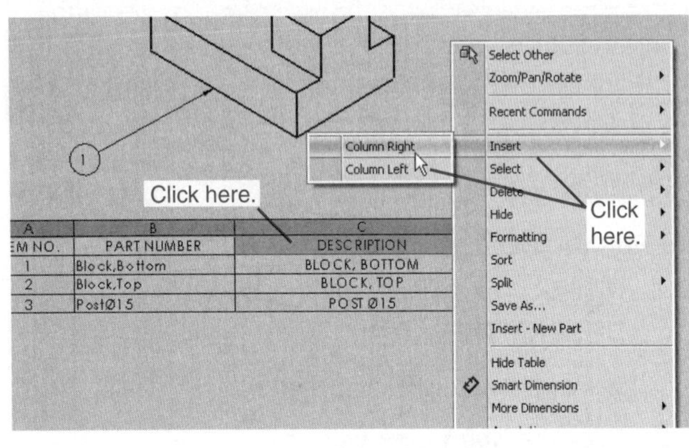

Figure 5-45

To Add Columns to the BOM

1. Right-click the **BLOCK, BOTTOM** box.

   See Figure 5-45.

2. Click the **Insert** option, then click **Column Right.**

   A new column will appear to the right of the BLOCK, BOTTOM box. See Figure 5-46.

3. Right-click one of the boxes in the new column.
4. Select the **Formatting** option; click **Column Width.**

   See Figure 5-47. The **Column Width** dialog box will appear. See Figure 5-48.

5. Enter a new value.

   In this example a value of **1.75 in** was entered. Figure 5-48 shows the new column width.

	DESCRIPTION		QTY.
	BLOCK, BOTTOM		1
	BLOCK,TOP		1
	Ø15 POST		1

A new column has been added.

Figure 5-46

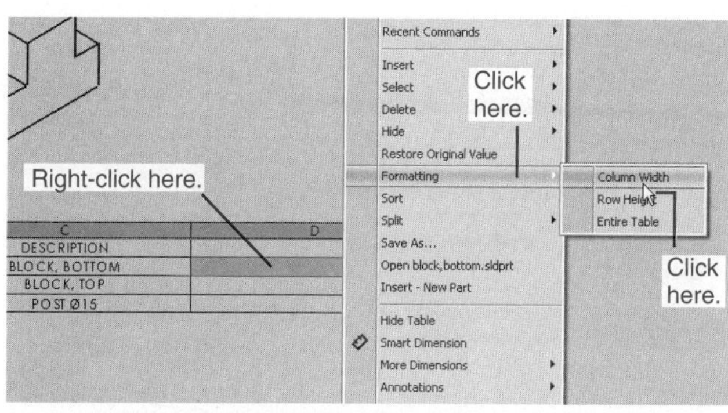

Figure 5-47

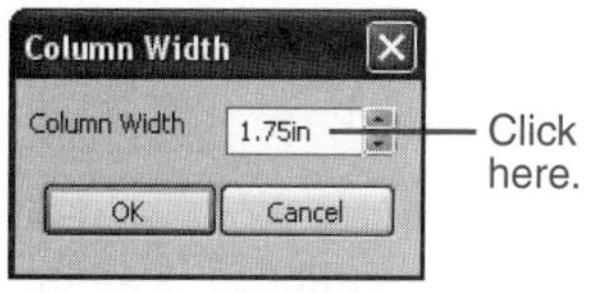

New column width

DESCRIPTION		QTY.
BLOCK, BOTTOM		1
BLOCK,TOP		1
Ø15 POST		1

Figure 5-48

To Edit a BOM

1. Click the top box of the new 1.75-wide column.
2. Type the heading **MATERIALS.**

   See Figure 5-49.

Figure 5-49

3. Add material specifications as shown in Figure 5-50.

   SAE 1020 is a type of mild steel.

4. Add another new column, **NOTES,** to the right of the materials column. Make the column 2.00 wide.

   See Figure 5-51. Notes are included in BOMs to define information about the part that is not visual.

5. Add the notes as shown.

   See Figure 5-52.

6. Edit the BOM so that all columns are justified to the right.

   See Figure 5-53.

5-11 ANIMATE COLLAPSE

Assembly drawings can be animated. In this example the **Animate Collapse** tool will be used.

1. Open the **Block Assembly.**
2. Right-click the **Block Assembly** heading in the **Properties Manager.**

   See Figure 5-54.

3. Click the **Animate Collapse** option.

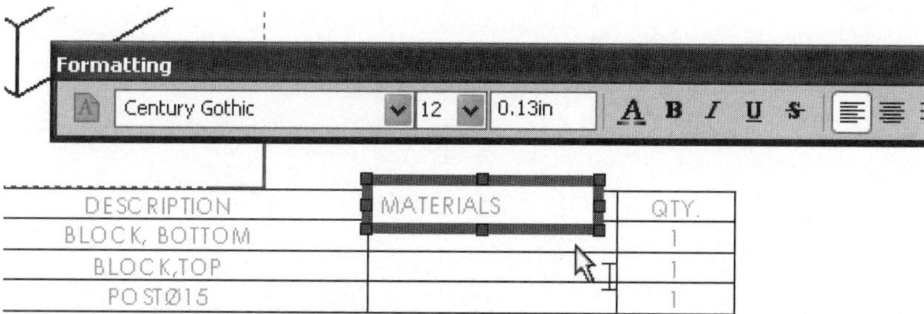

Figure 5-50

New heading

DESCRIPTION	MATERIALS	QTY.
BLOCK, BOTTOM		1
BLOCK,TOP		1
Ø15 POST		1

Figure 5-51

	MATERIALS	QTY.
	SAE1020	1
	SAE1020	1
	MILD STEEL	1

Enter notes

Figure 5-52

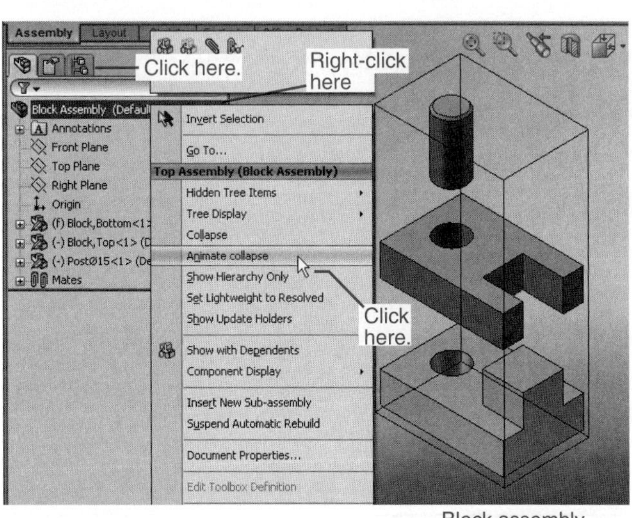

Figure 5-54

The assembly will automatically be animated and start to move. See Figure 5-55.

4. Click the **Start** button to stop the animation and return the assembly to the exploded position.
5. Close the **Animation Controller.**

In this example the **Animate Collapse** tool was used because the assembly was shown in the exploded position. Had the assembly been in a closed assembled position, the **Animate Explode** option would have been used.

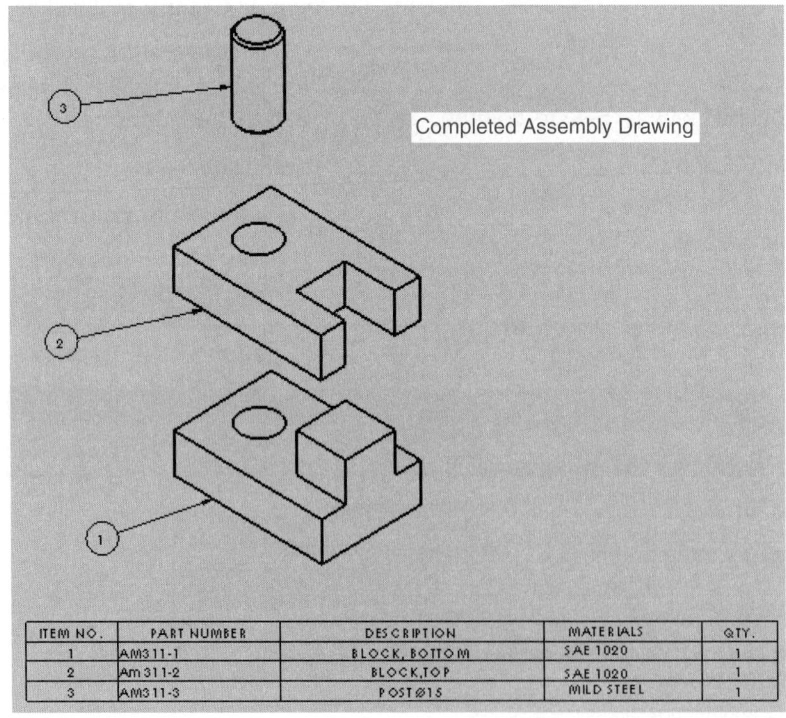

ITEM NO.	PART NUMBER	DESCRIPTION	MATERIALS	QTY.
1	AM311-1	BLOCK, BOTTOM	SAE 1020	1
2	Am311-2	BLOCK,TOP	SAE 1020	1
3	AM311-3	POSTØ15	MILD STEEL	1

Figure 5-53

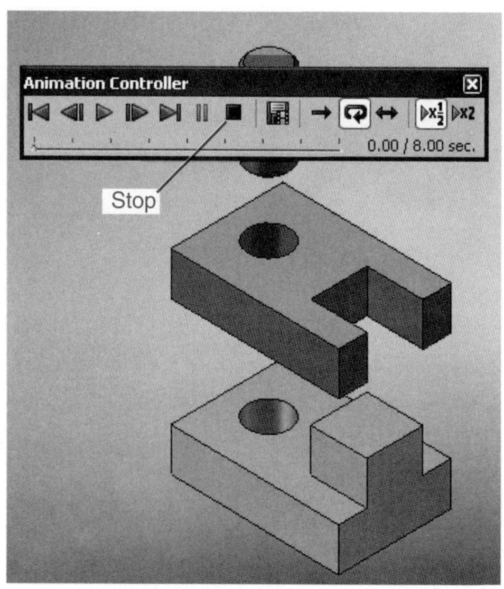

Figure 5-55

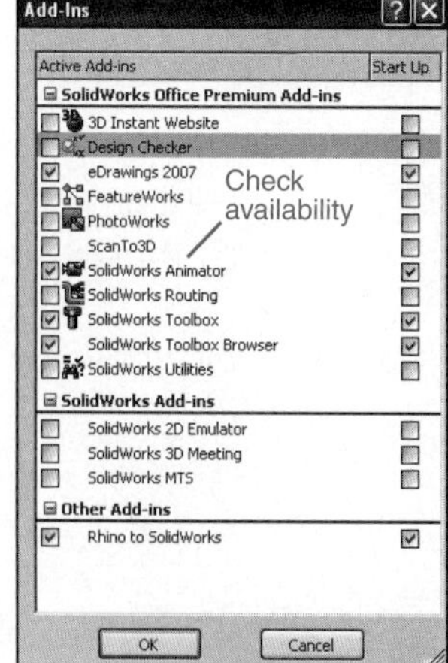

Figure 5-56

5-12 MOTION STUDY

The **Motion Study** tool is used to animate an assembly. Animating an assembly allows the viewer to see and better understand how an assembly moves. The motion study tool will also display any interferences in the motion. There are four types of motion available: motor, spring, contact, and gravity.

Figure 5-56 shows the **Motion Study Manager.** It is accessed by clicking the **Motion Study** tab at the bottom of the screen. Additional motion studies may be added by clicking the **New Motion Study** tool at the top of the screen.

Section 5-12 demonstrates how to apply the **Motion Study** tool to an assembly.

5-13 SAMPLE PROBLEM 5-1: CREATING THE ROTATOR ASSEMBLY

Figure 5-57 shows the components for the Rotator Assembly. The dimensions for the components can be found in Project P5-10 at the end of the chapter. Draw and save the four Rotator Assembly components as **Part** documents.

1. Click the **Mate** tool.
2. Click the **Concentric** tool.
3. Click the side of the bottom post of the Link L&R and the inside of the left hole in the Plate.

See Figure 5-58. The Link L&R and Plate will align.

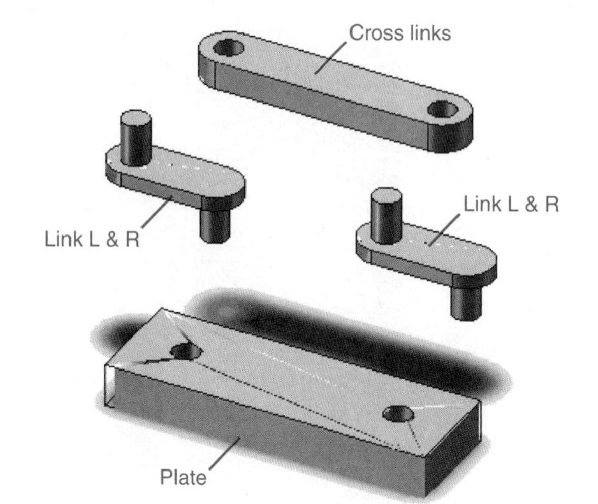

Figure 5-57

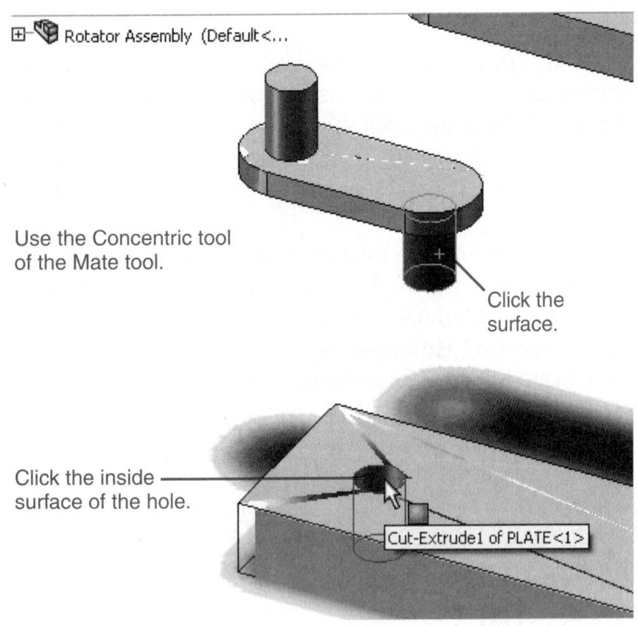

Figure 5-58

TIP

Click the post's and hole's surfaces. Do not click the edge lines.

4. Click the OK check mark.
5. Click the **Mate** tool.
6. Click the top surface of the Plate and the bottom surface of the Link L&R.

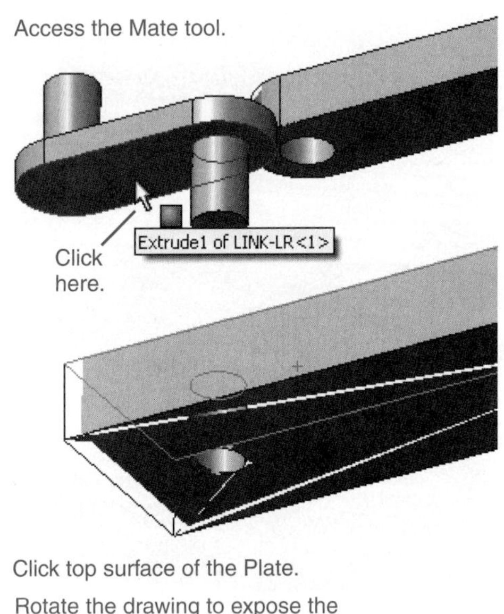

Figure 5-59

See Figure 5-59. Use the **Rotate View** tool to manipulate the view orientation so that the bottom surface of the Link L&R is visible. The part also can be rotated by holding down the mouse wheel and moving the cursor.

7. Click the **Distance** box and enter a value. In this example a value of **2 mm** was entered.

See Figure 5-60. The initial offset values may be in inches. Enter the new values followed by **mm,** and the system will automatically change to metric (millimeter) distances.

8. Click the OK check mark twice.

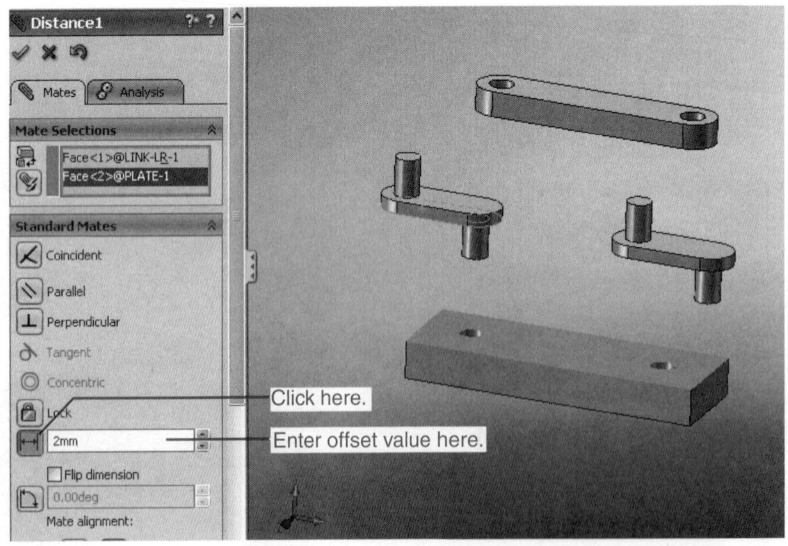

Figure 5-60

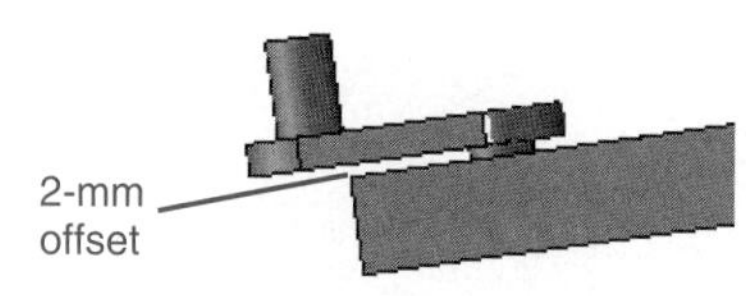

Figure 5-61

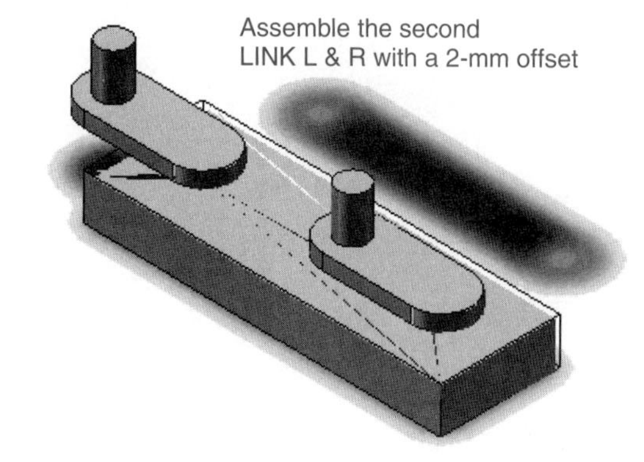

Figure 5-62

Figure 5-61 shows the 2-mm offset between the plate and the link.

9. Return the drawing to the **Isometric** orientation.
10. Repeat the procedure for the other Link L&R.

See Figure 5-62.

11. Access the **Mate** tool and use the **Concentric** tool to align the top post of the left Link L&R with the left hole in the Crosslink.
12. Use the **Mate** tool and click the top surface of the Link L&R's post and the top surface of the Crosslink.
13. Click the **Distance** box and define the offset distance as **2.00 mm**.

See Figure 5-63.

14. Use the **Flip** tool and offset the Crosslink so that the posts protrude 2 mm above the top surface of the Crosslink.
15. Click the OK check mark.

See Figure 5-64.

16. Access the **Mate** tool, click the **Concentric** tool, and align the right hole in the Crosslink with the post on the right Link L&R.

> **TIP**
>
> This is an important step to tie the entire assembly together.

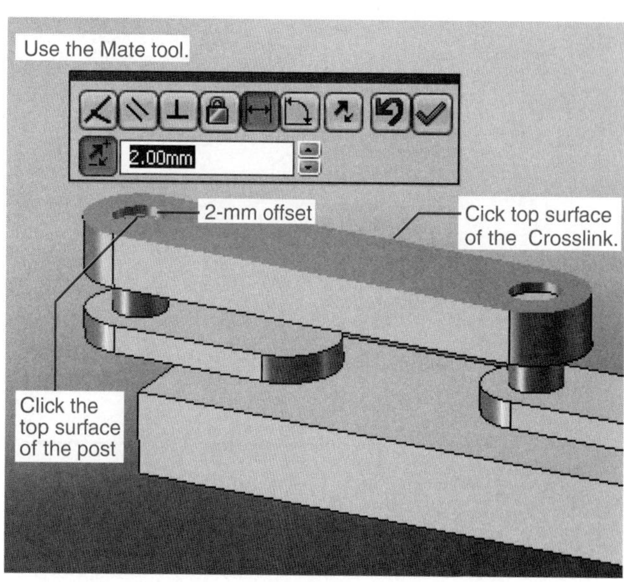

Figure 5-63

17. Locate the cursor on the Crosslink and move it around.

The Crosslink and two Links L&R should rotate about the Plate.

See Figure 5-65.

18. Save the Rotator Assembly.

5-14 USING THE SOLIDWORKS MOTION STUDY TOOL

Figure 5-65 shows the Rotator Assembly created in the last section.

1. Click the **Mate** tool, then click the **Parallel** tool.
2. Make the front surface line of the Crosslink parallel to the front edge of the Plate.

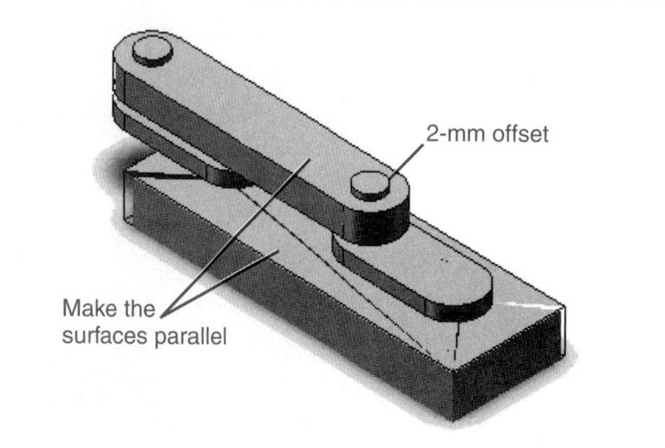

Figure 5-64

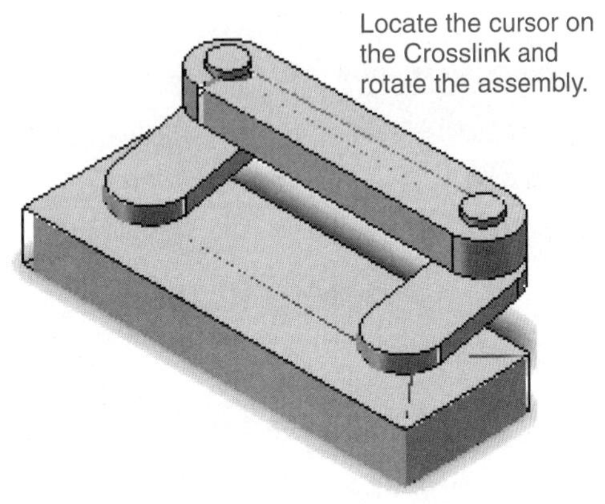

Locate the cursor on
the Crosslink and
rotate the assembly.

Figure 5-65

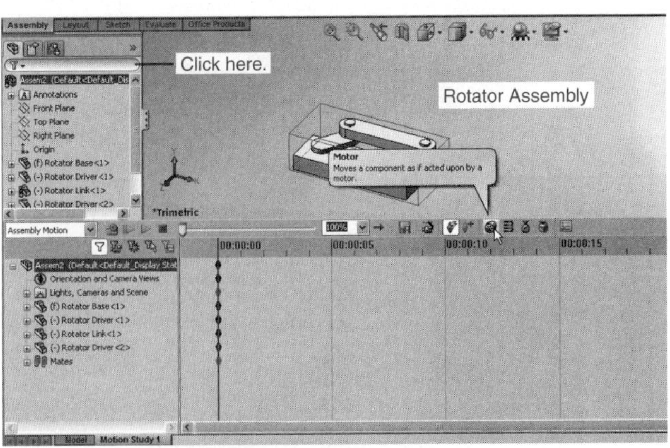

Figure 5-67

This step will assure that the Crosslink rotates in an orientation parallel to the front edge of the Plate. See Figure 5-66.

3. Click the **Motion Study** tab at the bottom of the screen.

See Figure 5-67.

Compare the component listing on the left side of the **Motion Study manager** in Figure 5-67 with the component listing in Figure 5-68. Note that the icons to the left of the components in Figure 5-68 include feathers. The feather indicates that this is a lightweight assembly; that is, only a subset of the model data has been loaded. This is done to save file space and to make the loading faster, particularly for large assemblies. When preparing an assembly for animation use the fully resolved assembly drawing.

To assure that you have a fully resolved assembly when opining a saved assembly make sure the **Lightweight** box is turned off; that is, no check mark appears.

4. Click the **Motor** tool.

The **Motor Manager** box will appear.

See Figure 5-69.

5. Click the **Rotary motion** tool.
6. Click the box under the **Component/Direction** heading, then click the left Link L&R.

The left Link L&R is now the driver link. It will drive the other components.

Motion

1. Go to the **Motion** box and define the assembly's motion.

See Figure 5-70. In this example the default values of **Constant Speed** and **100 RPM** were accepted.

2. Click the OK check mark and return to the **Motion Study Manager.**

See Figure 5-71.

3. Click the **Play** tool.

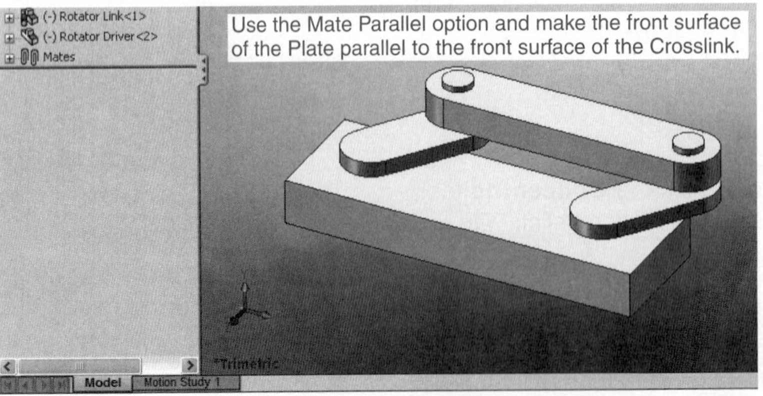

Figure 5-66

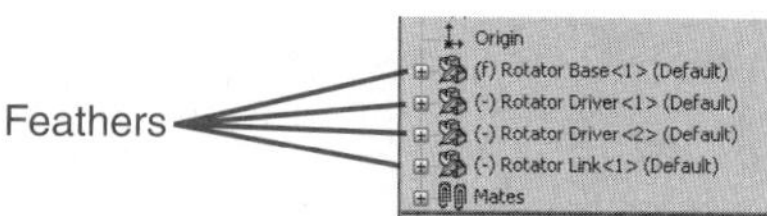

The animator tools

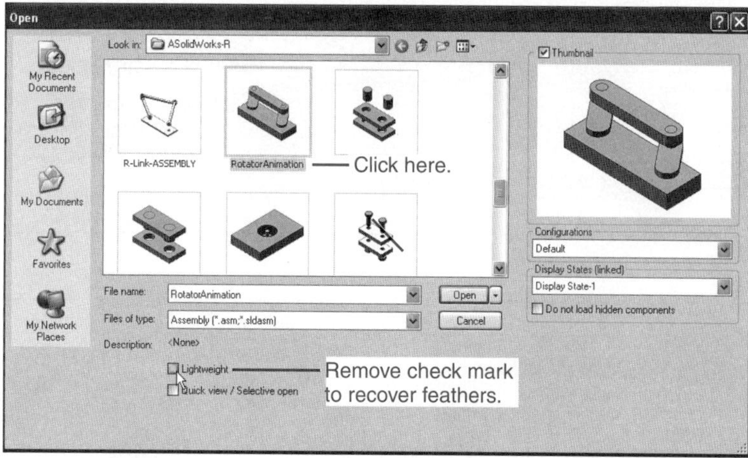

Figure 5-68

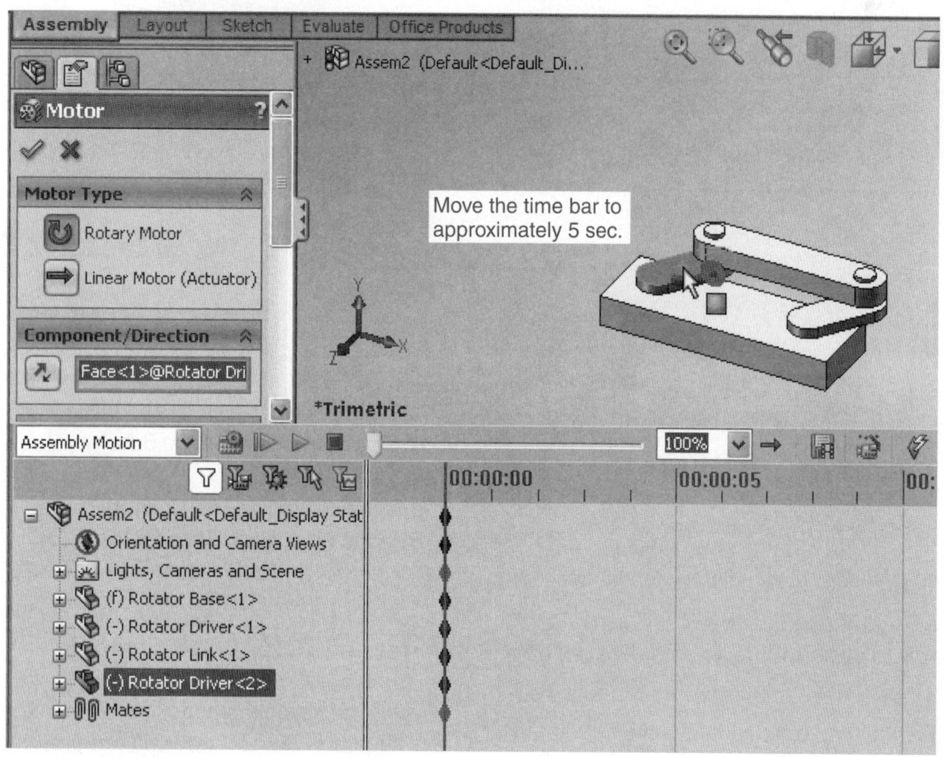

Figure 5-69

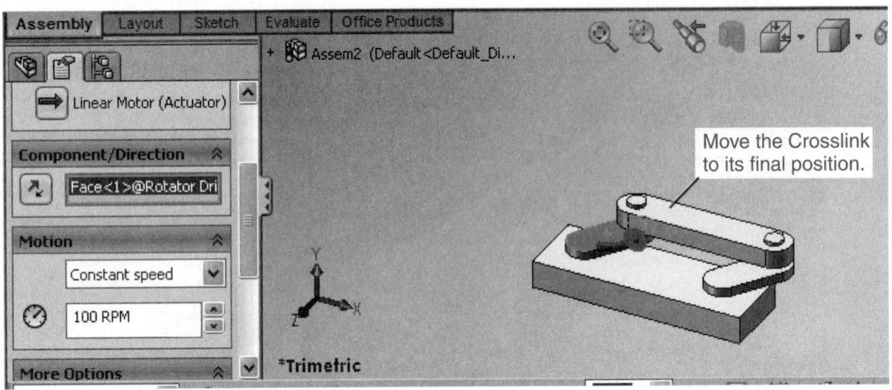

Figure 5-70

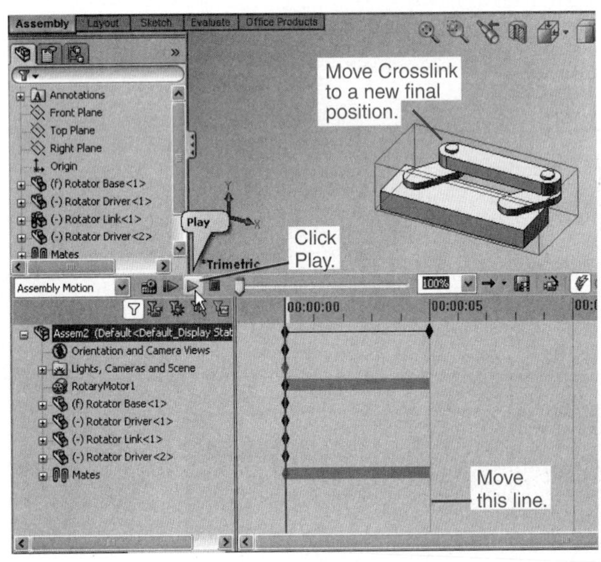

Figure 5-71

5-15 EDITING A PART WITHIN AN ASSEMBLY

Parts already inserted into an assembly drawing can be edited. Figure 5-72 shows the Block Assembly created earlier in the chapter.

1. Right-click the Block, Top.

   Say we wanted to change the hole in the top block.

2. Click the + sign to the left of the **Cut-Extrusion 1** for the **Block, Top** heading in the **Properties Manager.**

   In this example the **Cut-Extrusion 1** is the hole in the top block.

3. Right-click the **Sketch** heading and click the **Edit Sketch** tool.

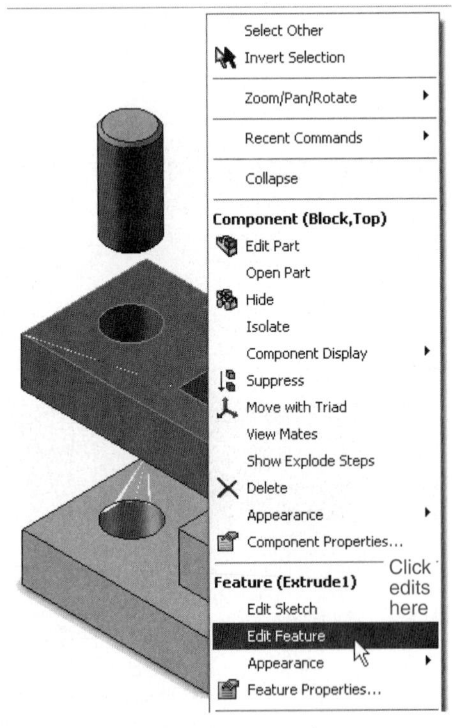

Figure 5-72

4. Double click the **Ø15** hole value and enter a new value.
5. Click the OK check mark.
6. Click the **Exit Sketch** tool.
7. Click the **Edit Component** tool.

5-16 TITLE BLOCKS

A title block contains information about the drawing. See Figure 5-73. The information presented in a title block varies from company to company but usually includes the company's name, the drawing name and part number, the drawing scale, and a revision letter.

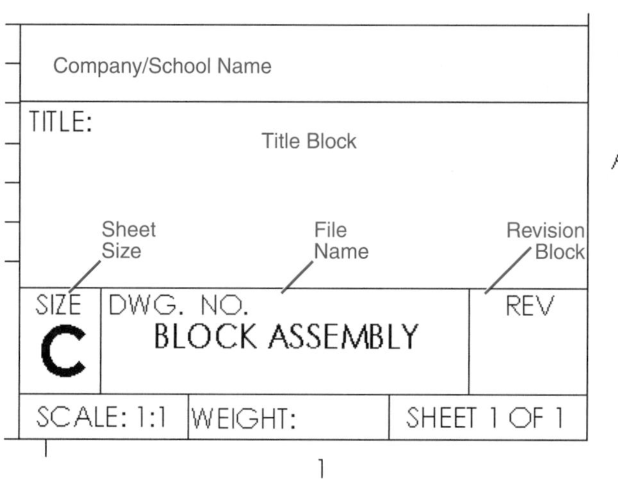

Figure 5-73

Revision Letters

As a drawing goes through its production cycle changes are sometimes made. The changes may be because of errors but they may also be because of the availability of new materials, manufacturing techniques, or new customer requirements. As the changes are incorporated onto the drawing a new revision letter is added to the drawing.

> ***Note:***
> SolidWorks will automatically enter the file name of the document as the part number. In the example shown in Figure 5-73 the drawing number BLOCK ASSEMBLY is not the document's part number. The title block will have to be edited and the correct part number entered.

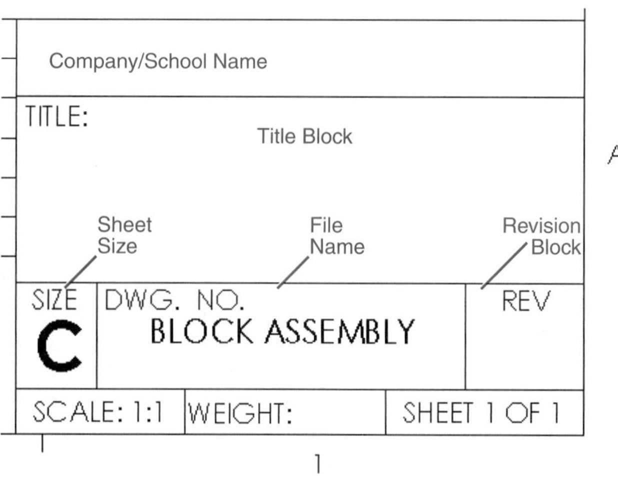

Figure 5-74

To Add Information to a Title Block

Figure 5-74 shows the title block presented in Figure 5-73 . The Block Assembly drawing title has been relocated.

1. Click the **Note** tool located on the **Annotation** toolbar.
2. Locate the **Note** box in the upper portion of the title block as shown.
3. Type the company or school name.
4. Click the check mark.
5. Fill in other information as needed.

To Change Fonts

1. Click the **Tools** heading at the top of the screen.

   See Figure 5-75 .

2. Click the **Options . . .** tool.
3. Click the **Document Properties** tab.
4. Click the **Annotations Font** tool.
5. Click the **Note** tool.
6. Select the **Times New Roman** font.
7. Click **OK** and return to the drawing.

> ***Note:***
> The default font for SolidWorks is Century Gothic. If you change fonts, choose one that is easy to read. Some very stylish fonts are difficult to read and can cause errors.

> **TIP**
> The **Annotations Font** tool can also be used to change the height and style of the font.

Release Blocks

A finished engineering drawing is a legal document that goes through a release process before it becomes final. The release block documents the release process. For example, once you have completed a drawing, you will sign and date the **Drawn by** box located just to the left of the title block. The drawing will then go to a checker, who, after reviewing and incorporating any changes, will sign and date the **Checked** box.

Tolerance Block

The tolerance block will be discussed in Chapter 8, Tolerances.

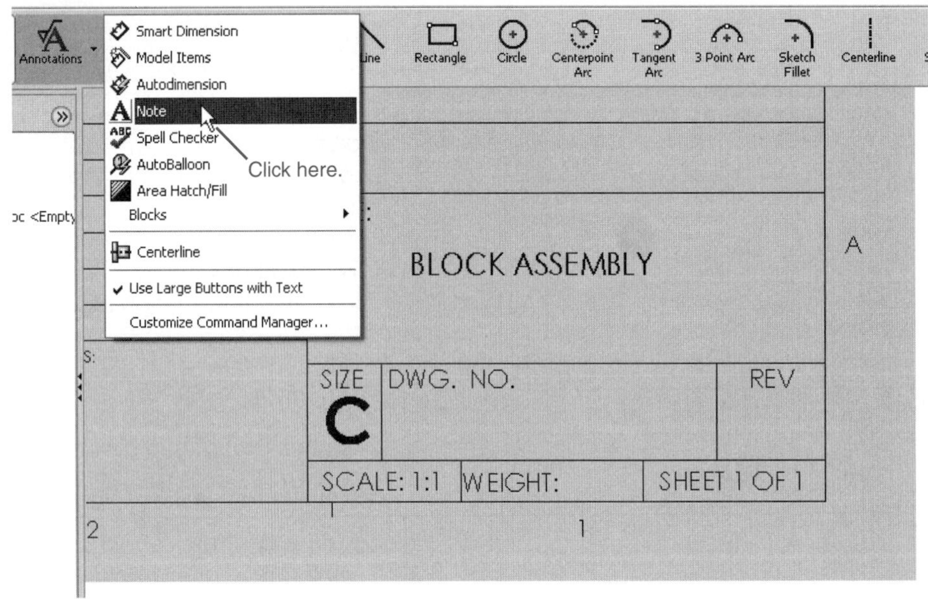

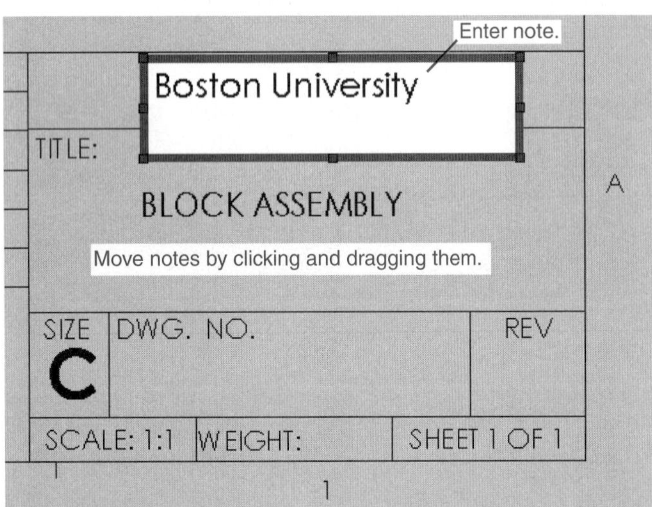

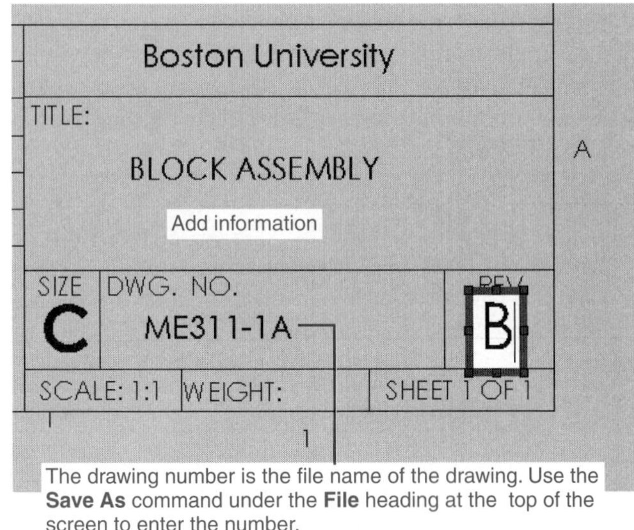

Figure 5-75

Application Block

See Figure 5-76.

This block is used to reference closely related drawings. In this example, we know that the Block assembly will be used on assembly ME-312A and that it was also used on EK131-46. This information makes it easier to access related drawings that can be checked for interfaces.

> ***Note:***
> The note "DO NOT SCALE DRAWING" located at the bottom of the tolerance block is a reminder not to measure the views on the drawing. If a dimension is missing, do not measure the distance on the drawing, because the drawing may not have been reproduced at exactly 100% of the original.

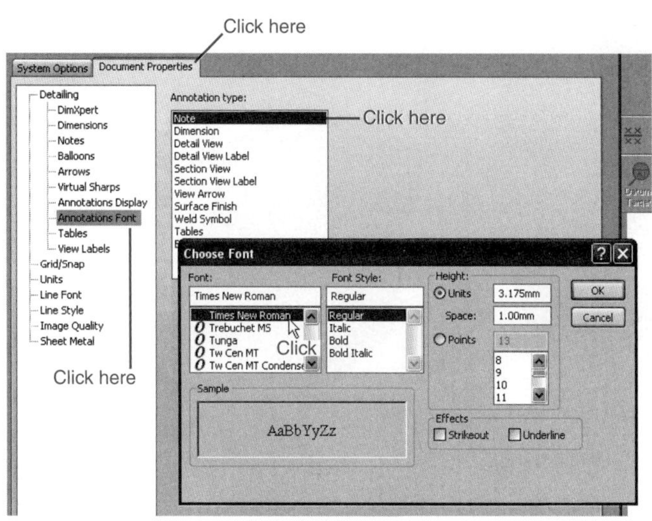

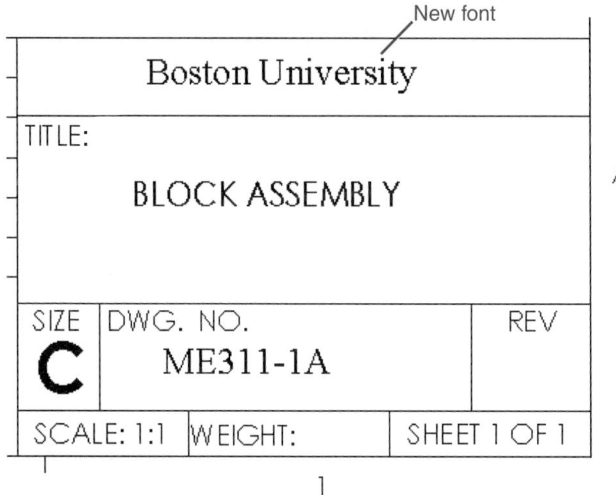

New font
Boston University
TITLE:
BLOCK ASSEMBLY
A
SIZE
C
DWG. NO.
ME311-1A
REV
SCALE: 1:1
WEIGHT:
SHEET 1 OF 1
1

Figure 5-76

Referenced Drawings

See Chapter 8

ME-312A	EK131-46	UNLESS OTHERWISE SPECIFIED:
		DIMENSIONS ARE IN INCHES TOLERANCES: FRACTIONAL ± ANGULAR: MACH ± BEND ± TWO PLACE DECIMAL ± THREE PLACE DECIMAL ±
		INTERPRET GEOMETRIC TOLERANCING PER:
		MATERIAL
NEXT ASSY	USED ON	FINISH
APPLICATION		DO NOT SCALE DRAWING

E

3

Figure 5-77

5-17 PROJECTS

Project 5-1:

Create a **Part** document of the SQBLOCK using the given dimensions. Create assemblies using two SQBLOCKS, positioning the blocks as shown in Figures P5-1A through P5-1G.

Pages 229 through 237 show a group of parts. These parts are used to create the assemblies presented as problems in this section. Use the given descriptions, part numbers, and materials when creating BOMs for the assemblies.

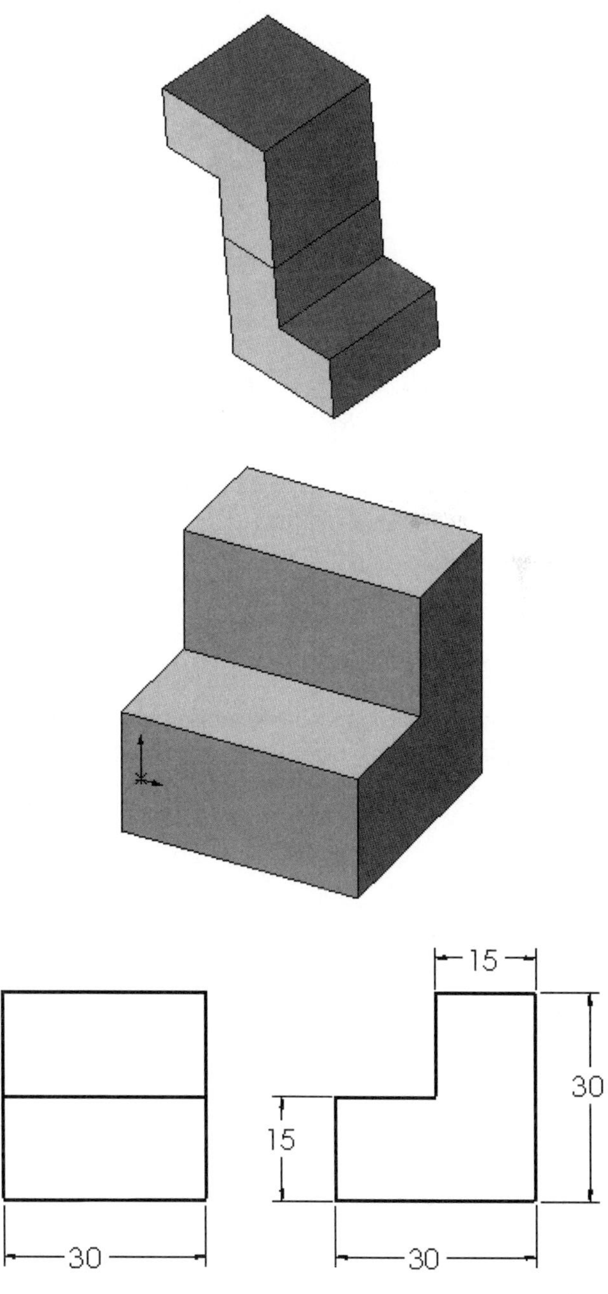

Figure P5-1 MILLIMETERS

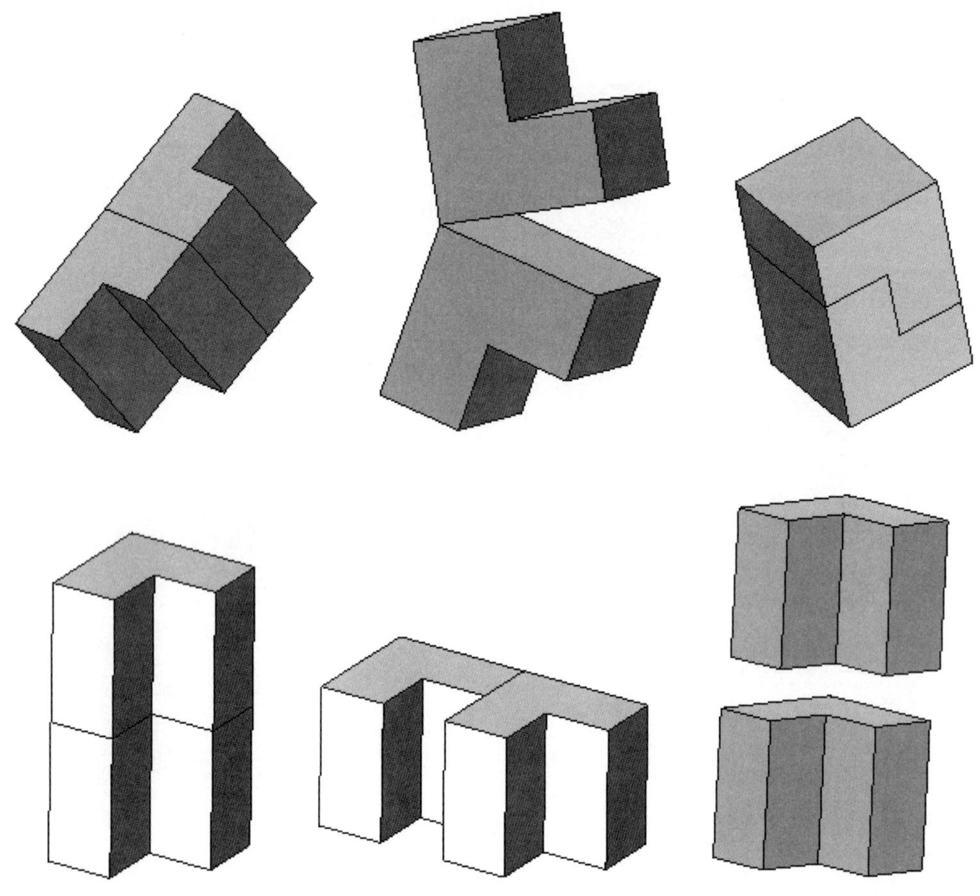

Figure P5-1 *(continued)*

Project 5-2:

Redraw the following models and save them as **Standard (mm).ipn** files. All dimensions are in millimeters.

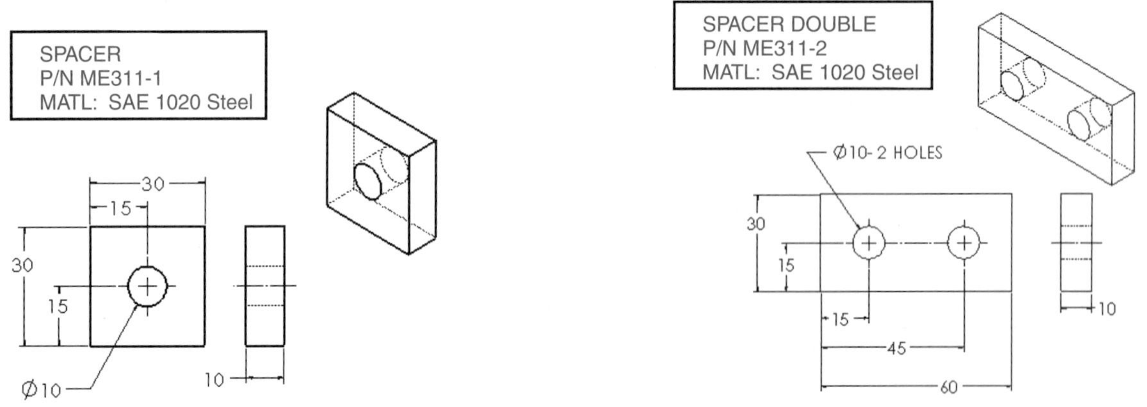

Figure P5-2 MILLIMETERS

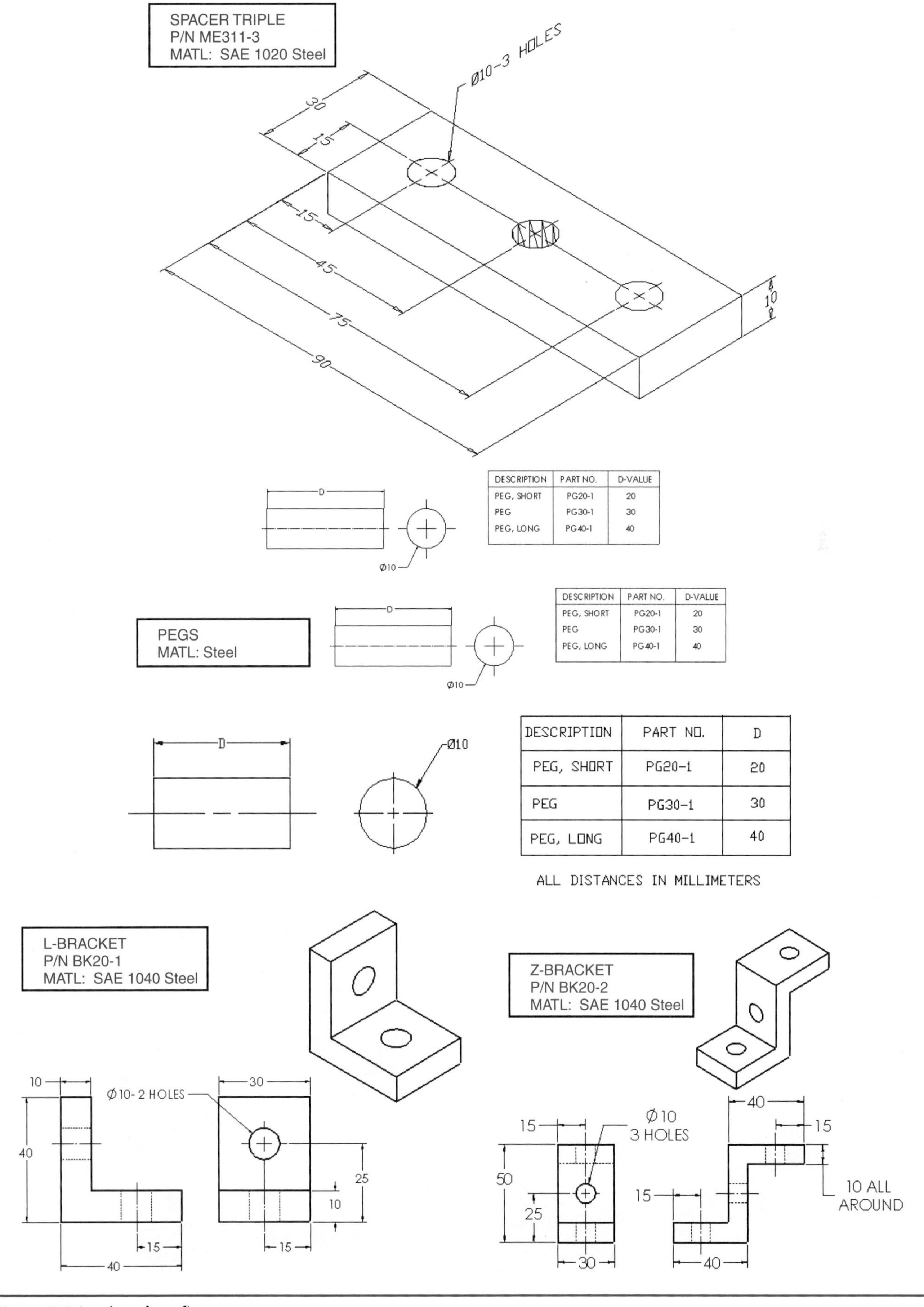

Figure P5-2 ***(continued)***

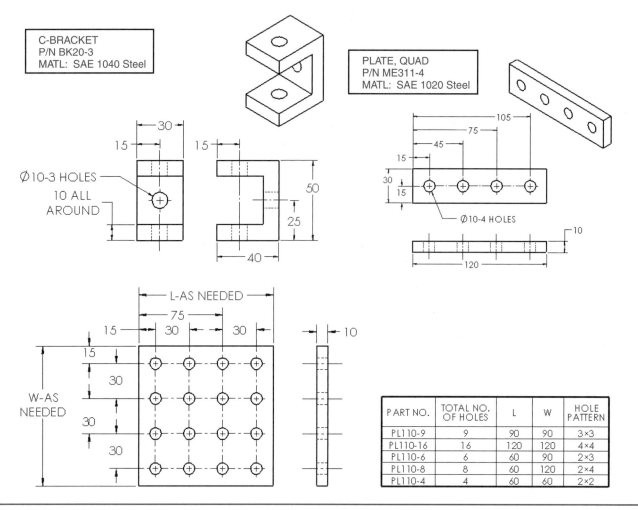

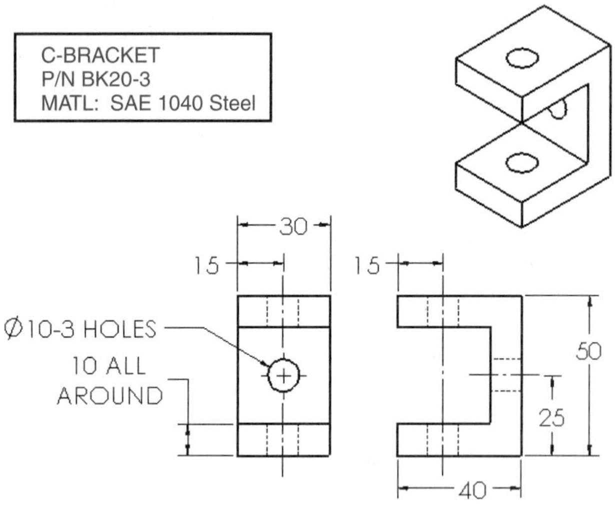

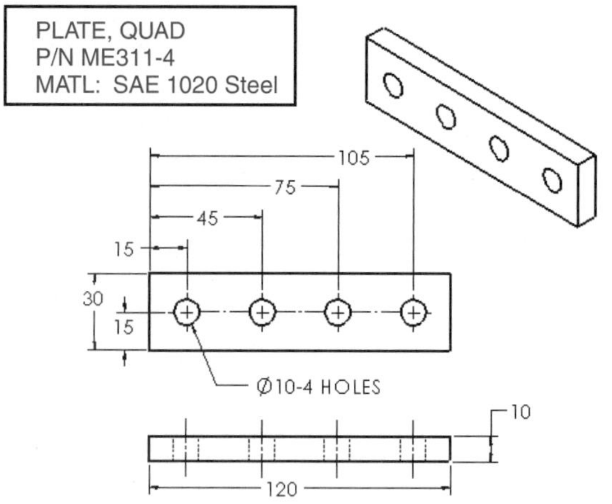

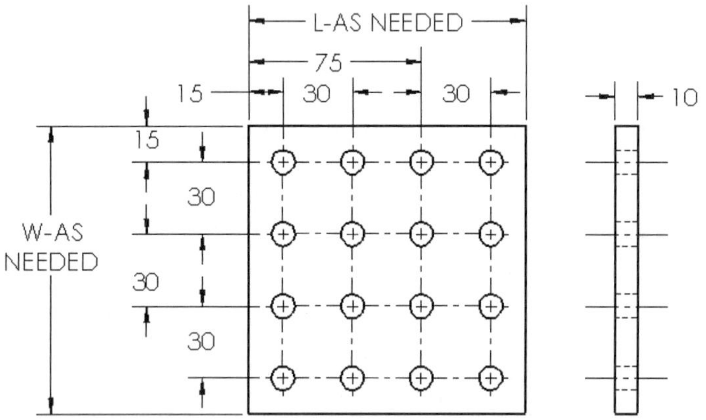

C-BRACKET
P/N BK20-3
MATL: SAE 1040 Steel

PLATE, QUAD
P/N ME311-4
MATL: SAE 1020 Steel

PART NO.	TOTAL NO. OF HOLES	L	W	HOLE PATTERN
PL110-9	9	90	90	3×3
PL110-16	16	120	120	4×4
PL110-6	6	60	90	2×3
PL110-8	8	60	120	2×4
PL110-4	4	60	60	2×2

Figure P5-2 ***(continued)***

Project 5-3:

Draw an exploded isometric assembly drawing of Assembly 1. Create a BOM.

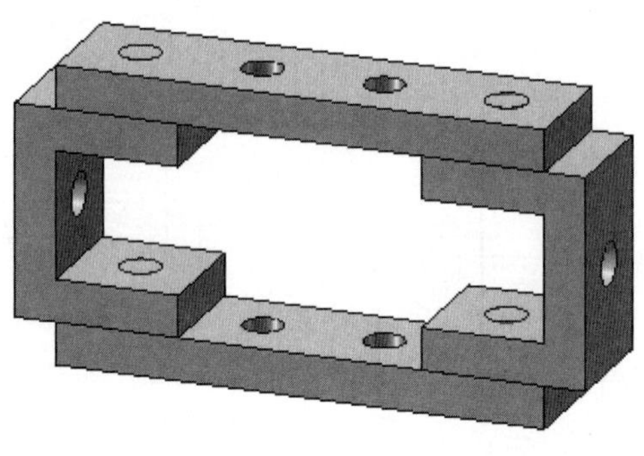

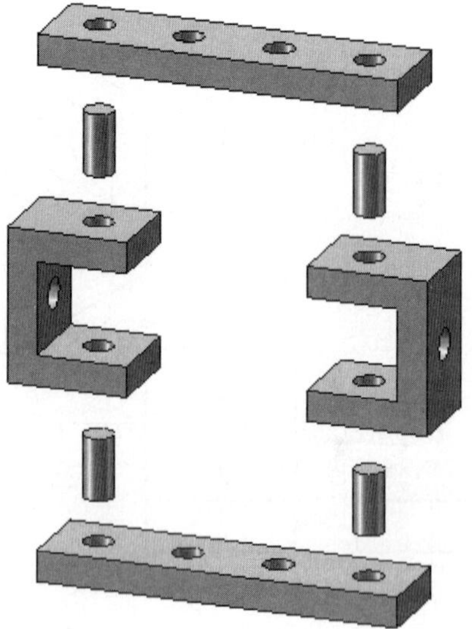

Figure P5-3 MILLIMETERS

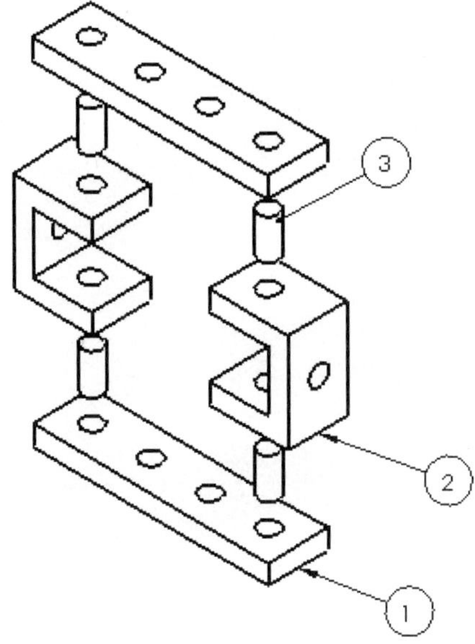

ITEM NO.	PART NUMBER	DESCRIPTION	QTY.
1	ME311-4	PLATE, QUAD	2
2	BK20-3	C-BRACKET	2
3	PG20-1	Ø12×20 PEG	4

Figure P5-3 ***(continued)***

Project 5-4:

Draw an exploded isometric assembly drawing of Assembly 2. Create a BOM.

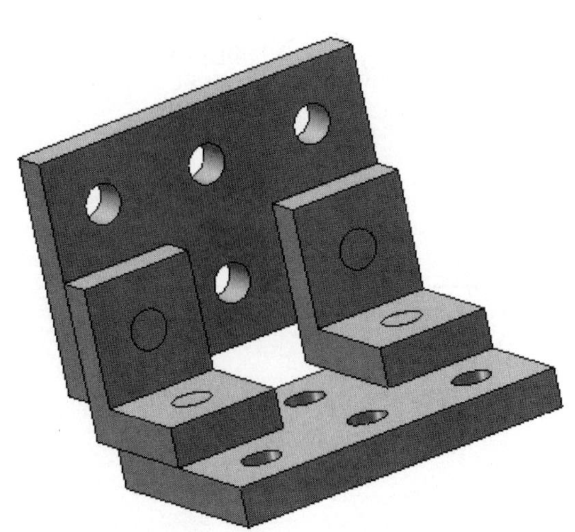

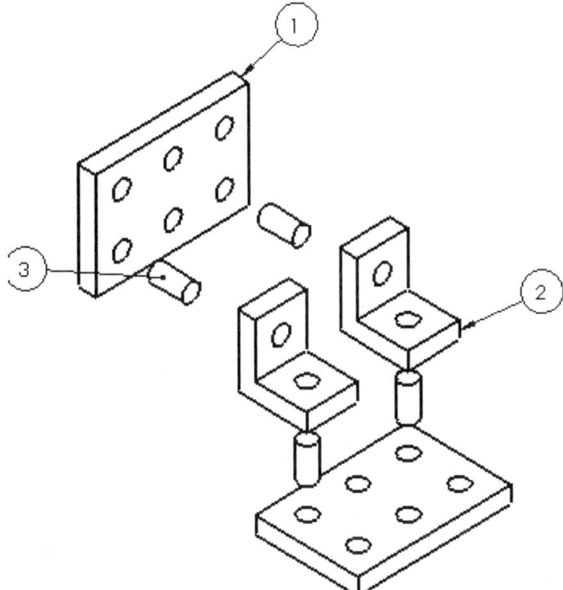

Figure P5-4 MILLIMETERS

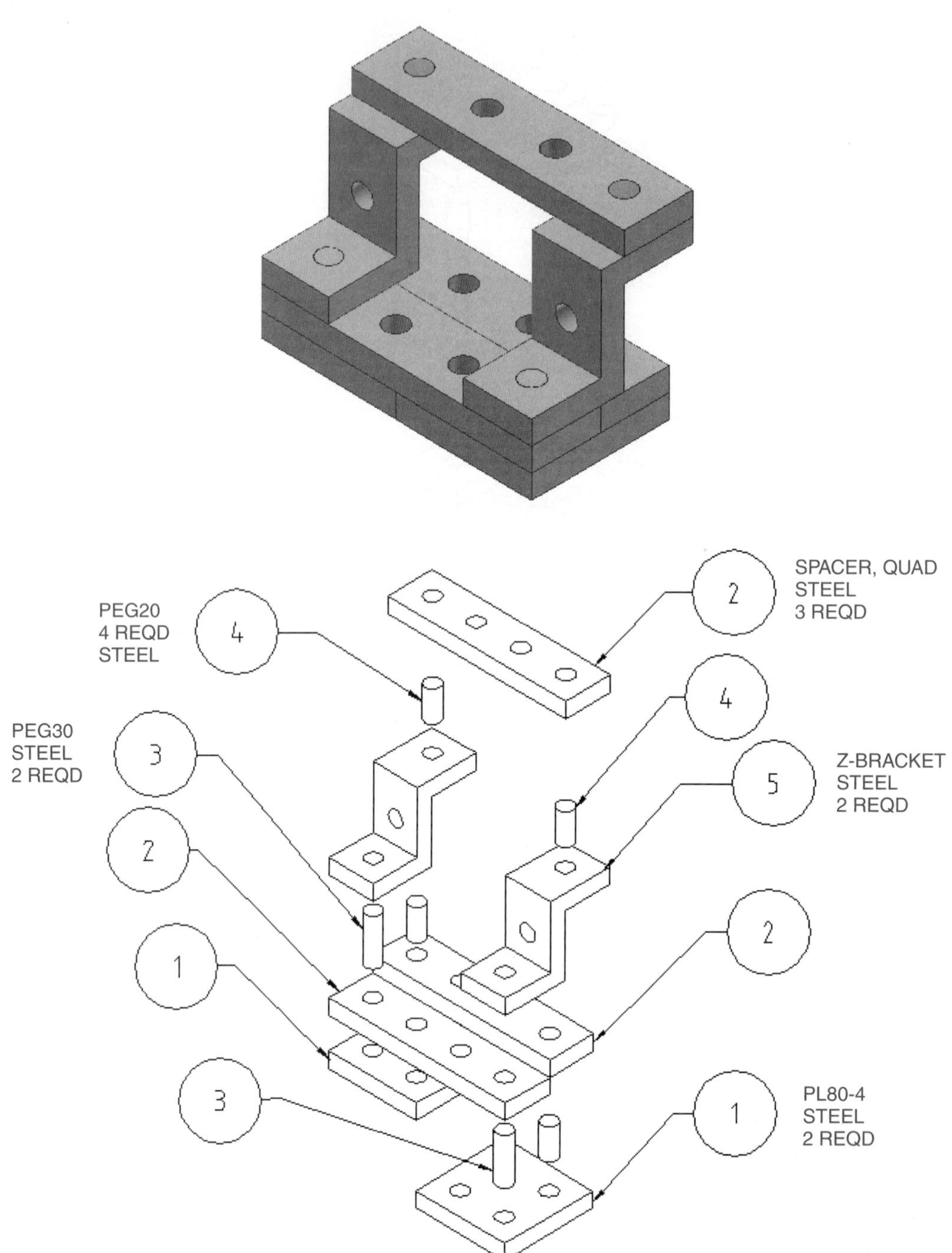

SPACER, QUAD
STEEL
3 REQD
PEG20
4 REQD
STEEL
PEG30
STEEL
2 REQD
Z-BRACKET
STEEL
2 REQD
PL80-4
STEEL
2 REQD
1
2
3
4
5

Figure P5-5

Project 5-6:

Draw an exploded isometric assembly drawing of Assembly 4. Create a BOM.

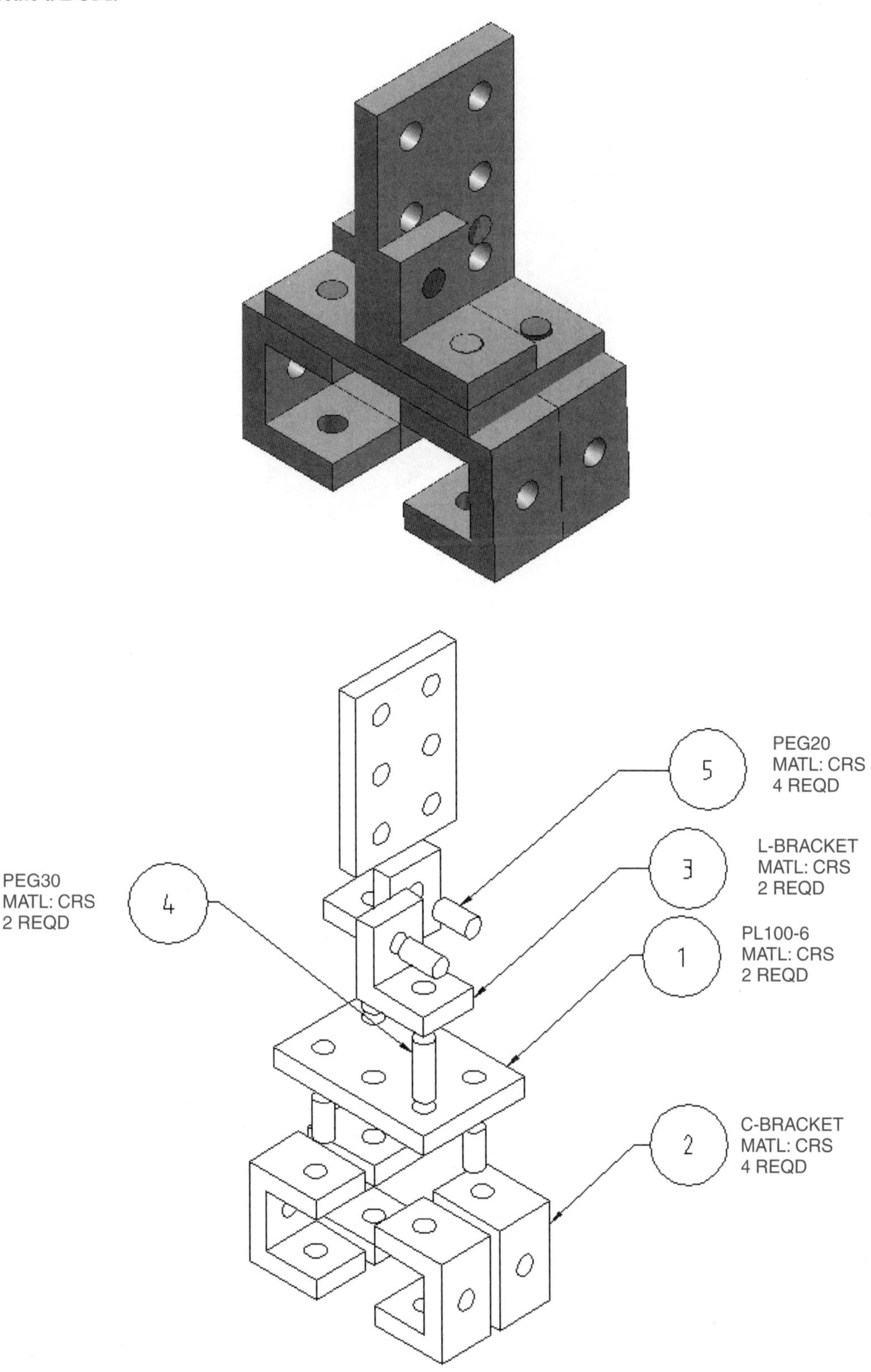

Figure P5-6 MILLIMETERS

Project 5-7:

Draw an exploded isometric assembly drawing of Assembly 5. Create a BOM.

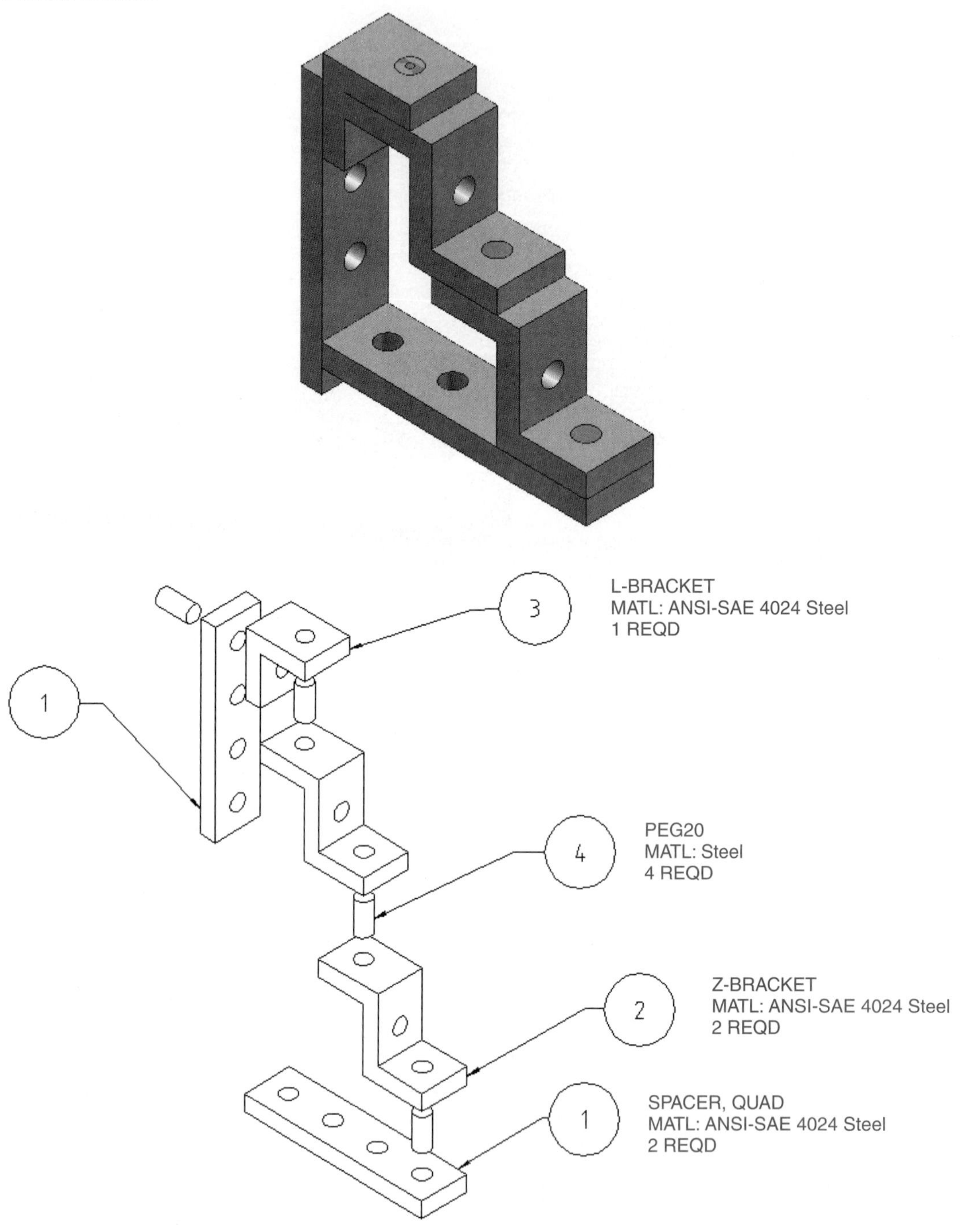

Figure P5-7 MILLIMETERS

Project 5-8:

Draw an exploded isometric assembly drawing of Assembly 6. Create a BOM.

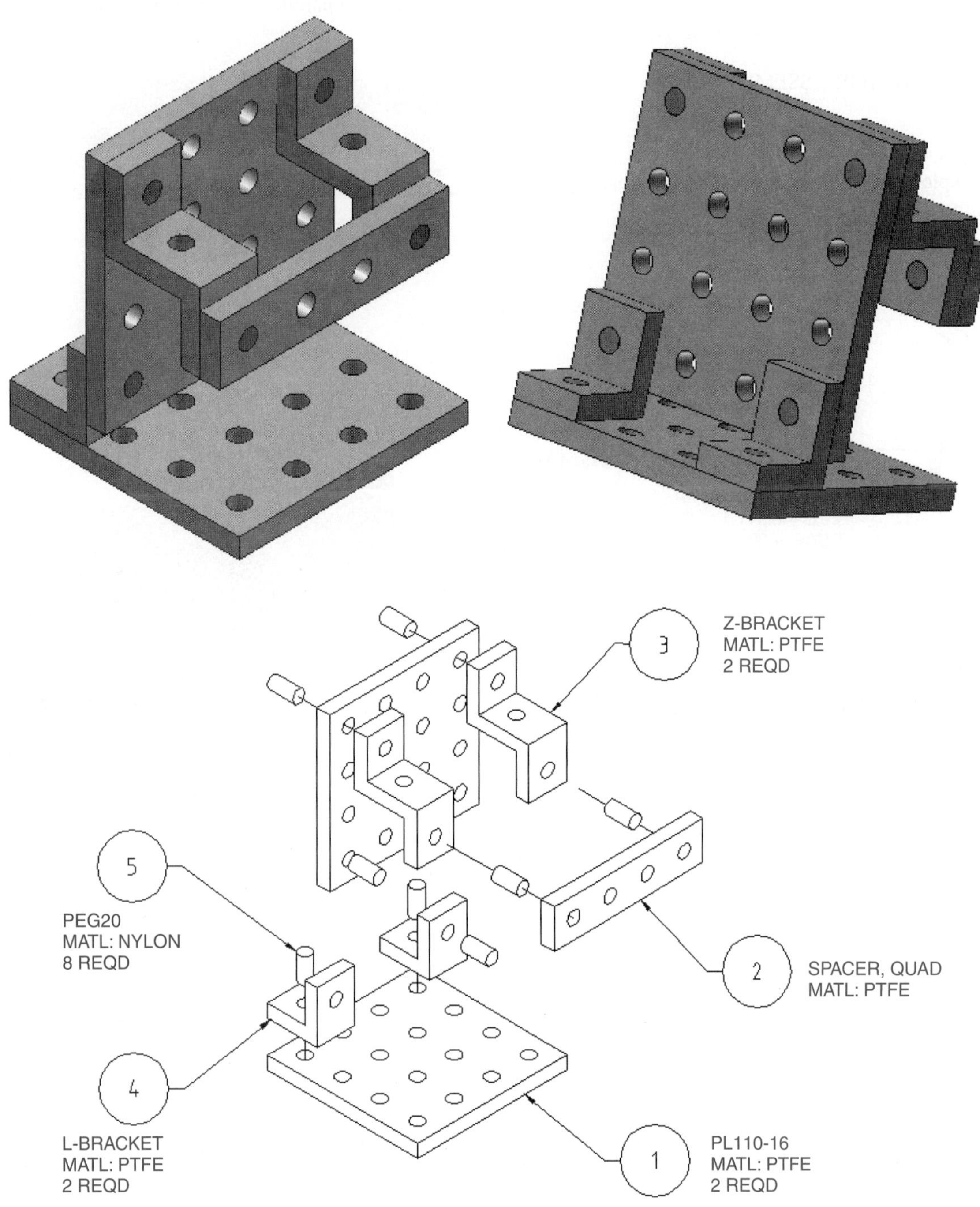

Figure P5-8

Project 5-9:

Create an original assembly based on the parts shown on pages 229–237. Include a scene, an exploded isometric drawing with assembly numbers, and a BOM. Use at least 12 parts.

Project 5-10:

Draw the ROTATOR ASSEMBLY shown. Include the following:

A. An assembly drawing
B. An exploded isometric drawing with assembly numbers
C. A parts list
D. An animated assembly drawing; the LINKs should rotate relative to the PLATE. The LINKs should carry the CROSSLINK. The CROSSLINK should remain parallel during the rotation.

> ***Note:***
> This assembly was used in the section on animating assemblies See page 221.

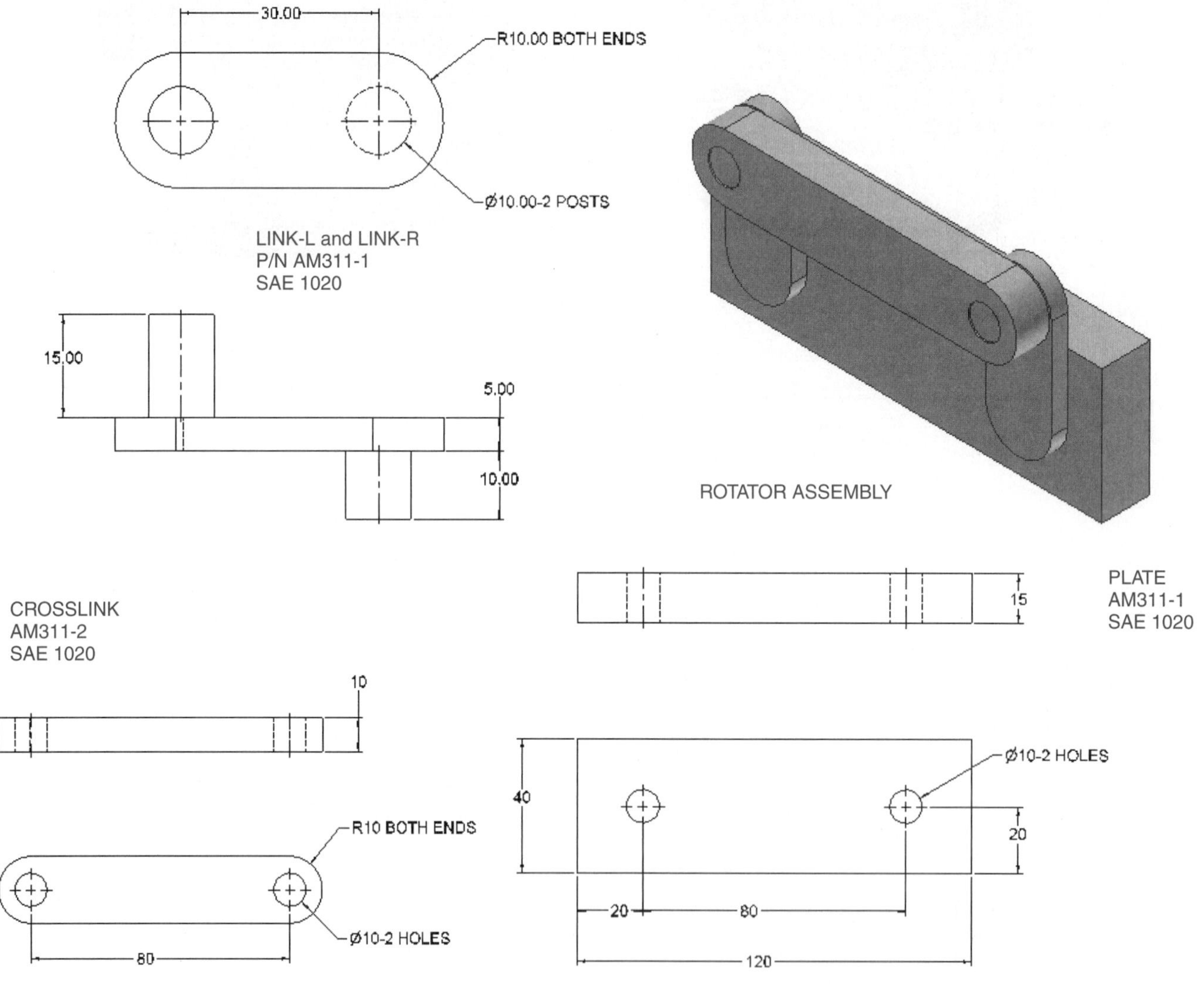

Figure P5-10

Project 5-11:

Draw the FLY ASSEMBLY shown. Include the following:

A. An assembly drawing
B. An exploded isometric drawing with assembly numbers
C. A parts list
D. An animated assembly drawing; the FLYLINK should rotate around the SUPPORT base.

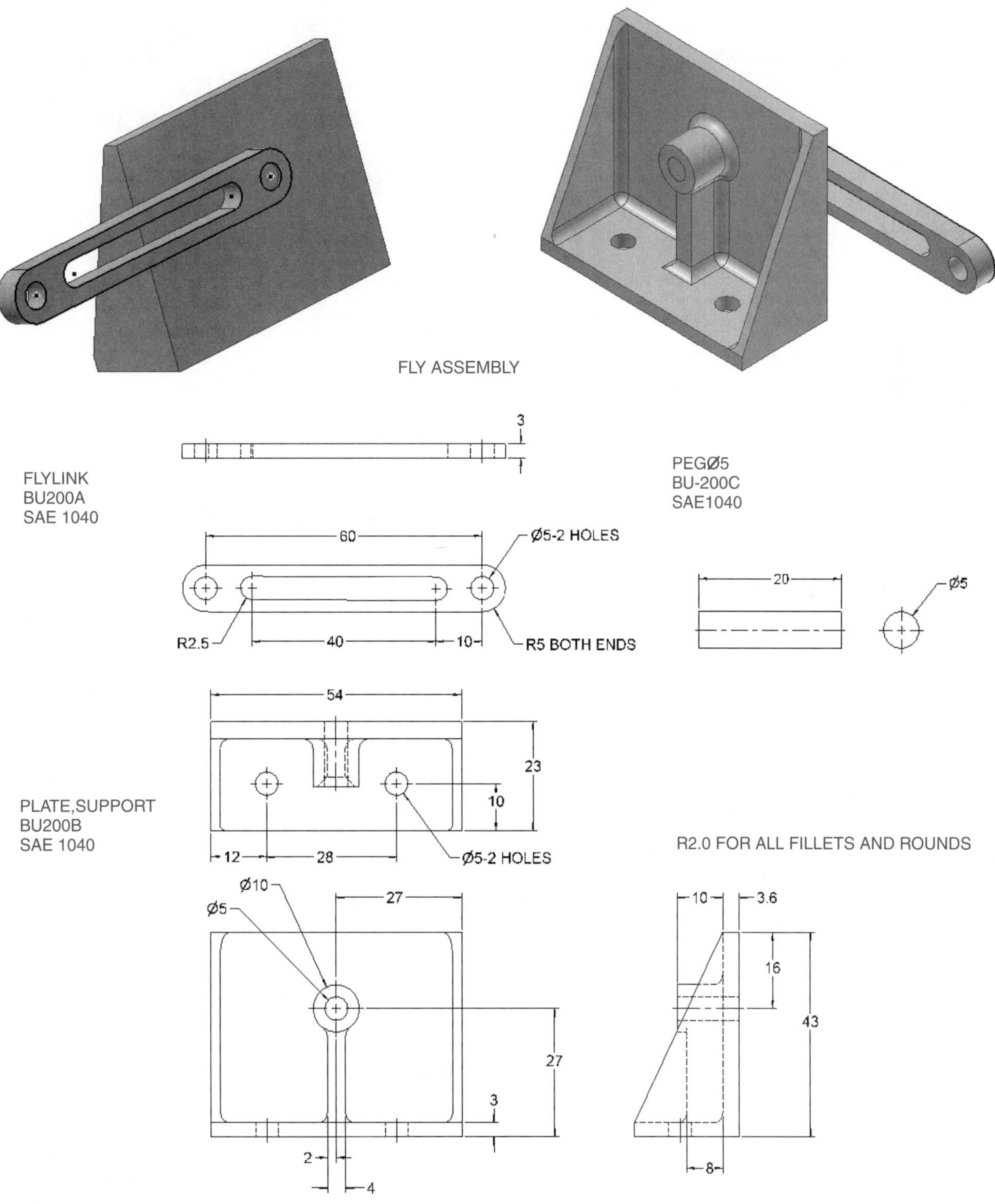

Figure P5-11

Project 5-12:

Draw the ROCKER ASSEMBLY shown. Include the following:

A. An assembly drawing
B. An exploded isometric drawing with assembly numbers
C. A parts list
D. An animated assembly drawing

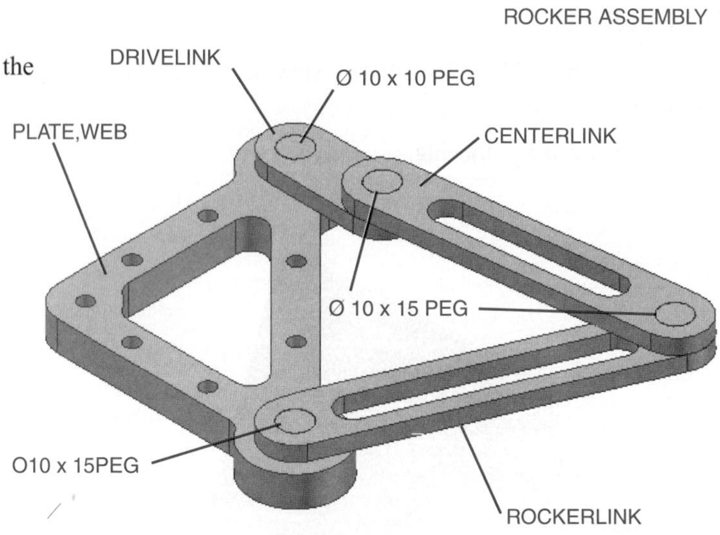

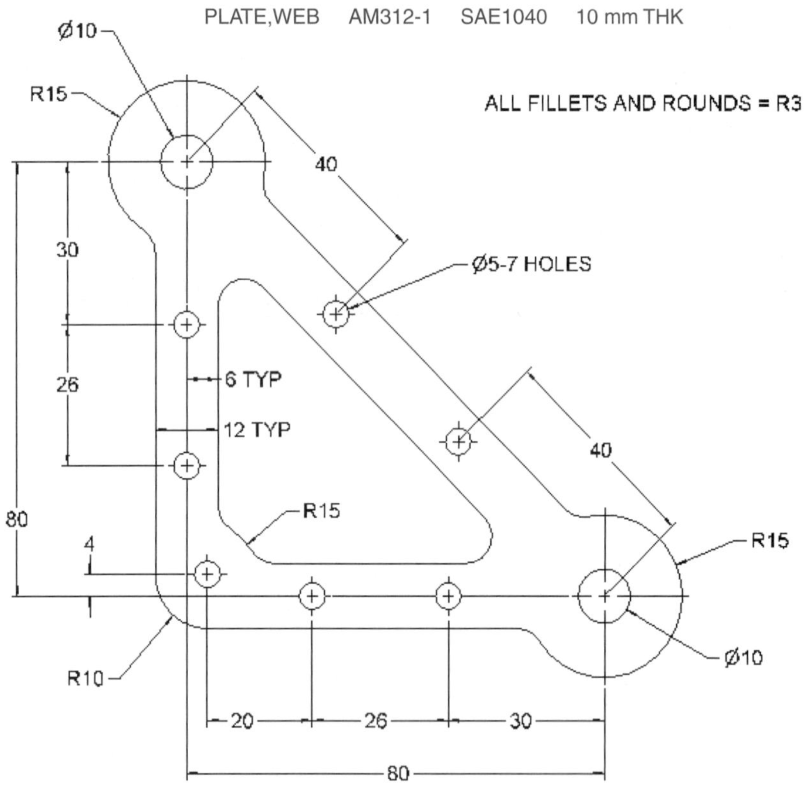

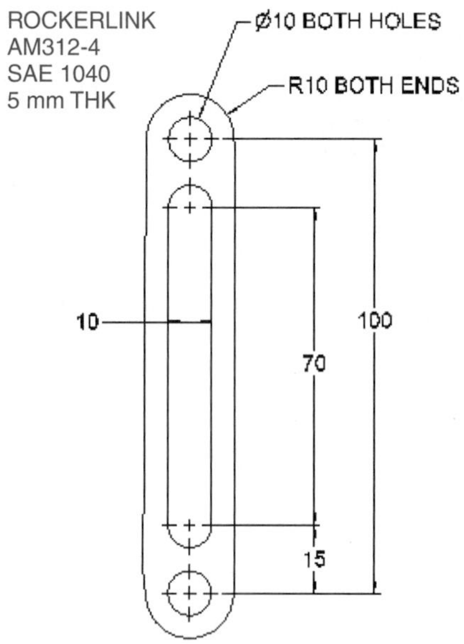

ROCKER ASSEMBLY
DRIVELINK
Ø 10 x 10 PEG
PLATE,WEB
CENTERLINK
Ø 10 x 15 PEG
O10 x 15PEG
ROCKERLINK

DRIVELINK
AM312-2
SAE 1040
5 mm THK
30
R10 BOTH ENDS
Ø10-2 HOLES

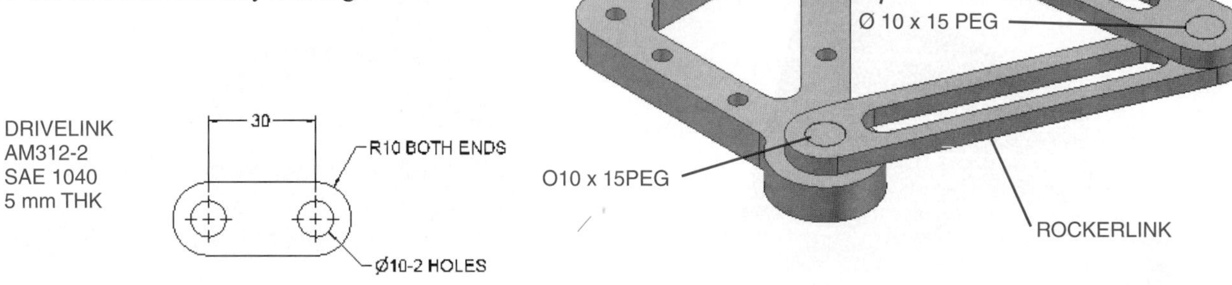

PLATE,WEB AM312-1 SAE1040 10 mm THK
ALL FILLETS AND ROUNDS = R3
Ø10
R15
40
30
Ø5-7 HOLES
26
6 TYP
12 TYP
40
80
R15
4
R15
R10
Ø10
20
26
30
80

ROCKERLINK
AM312-4
SAE 1040
5 mm THK
Ø10 BOTH HOLES
R10 BOTH ENDS
10
100
70
15

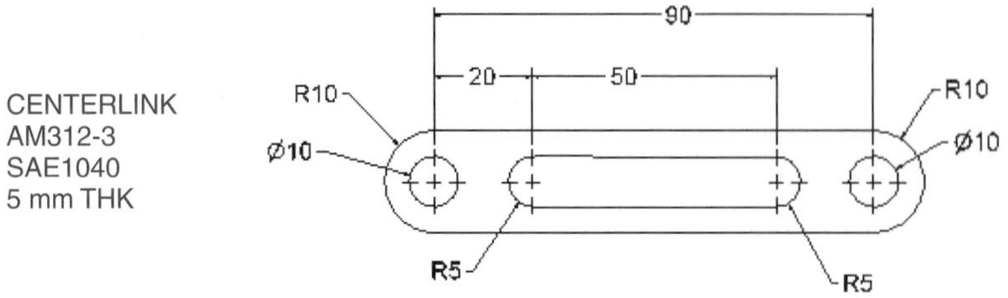

CENTERLINK
AM312-3
SAE1040
5 mm THK
90
20
50
R10
R10
Ø10
Ø10
R5
R5

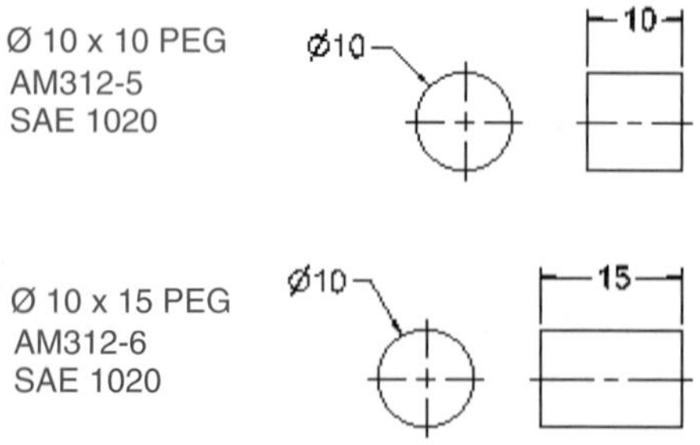

Ø 10 x 10 PEG
AM312-5
SAE 1020
Ø10
10
Ø 10 x 15 PEG
AM312-6
SAE 1020
Ø10
15

Figure P5-12

Project 5-13:

Draw the LINK ASSEMBLY shown. Include the following:

A. An assembly drawing
B. An exploded isometric drawing with assembly numbers
C. A parts list
D. An animated assembly drawing; the HOLDER ARM should rotate between –30° and + 30°.

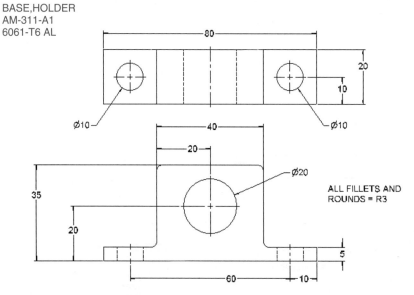

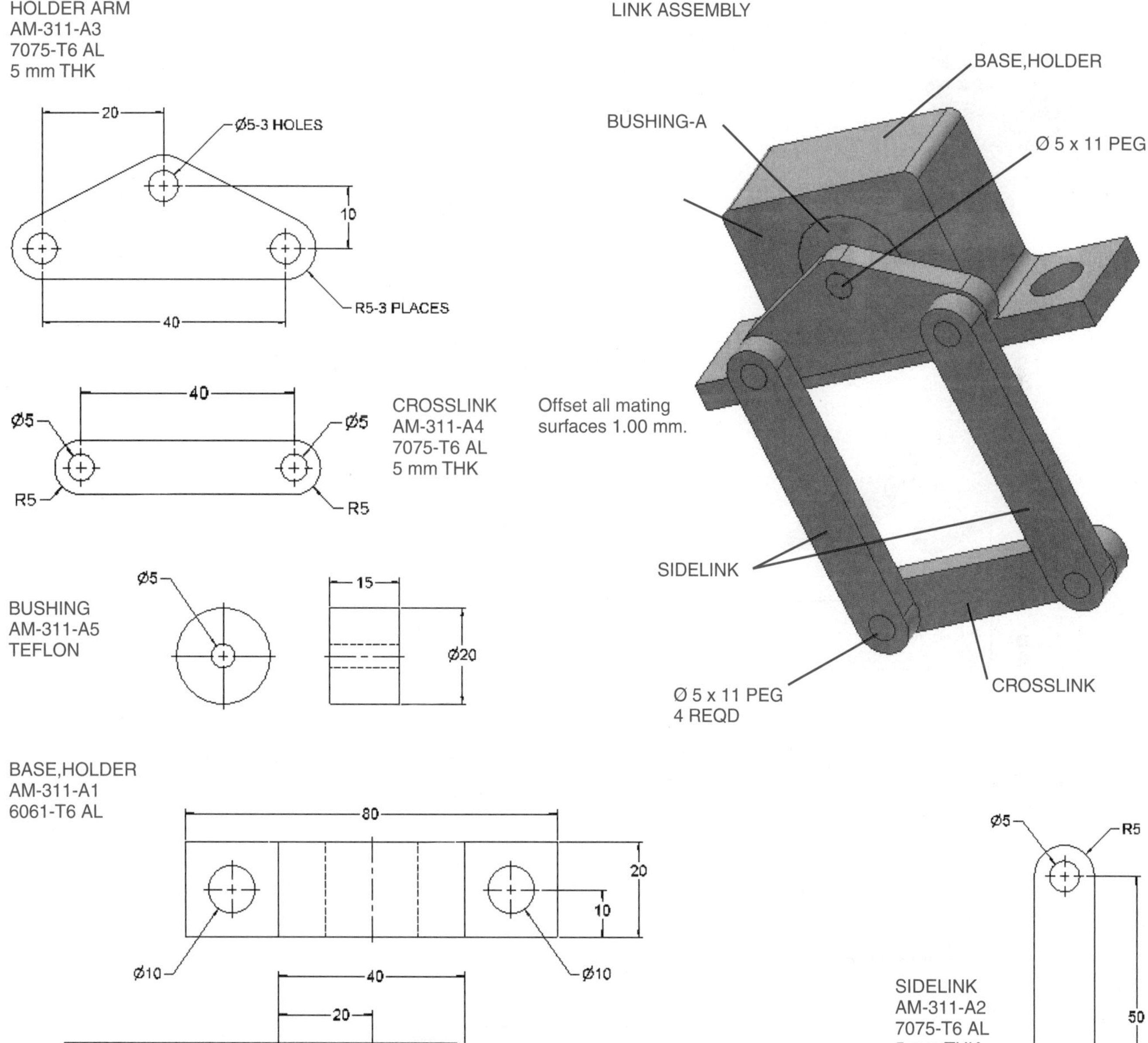

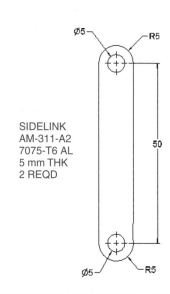

Figure P5-13

Project 5-14:

Draw the PIVOT ASSEMBLY shown using the dimensioned components given. Include the following:

A. A 3D exploded isometric drawing
B. A parts list

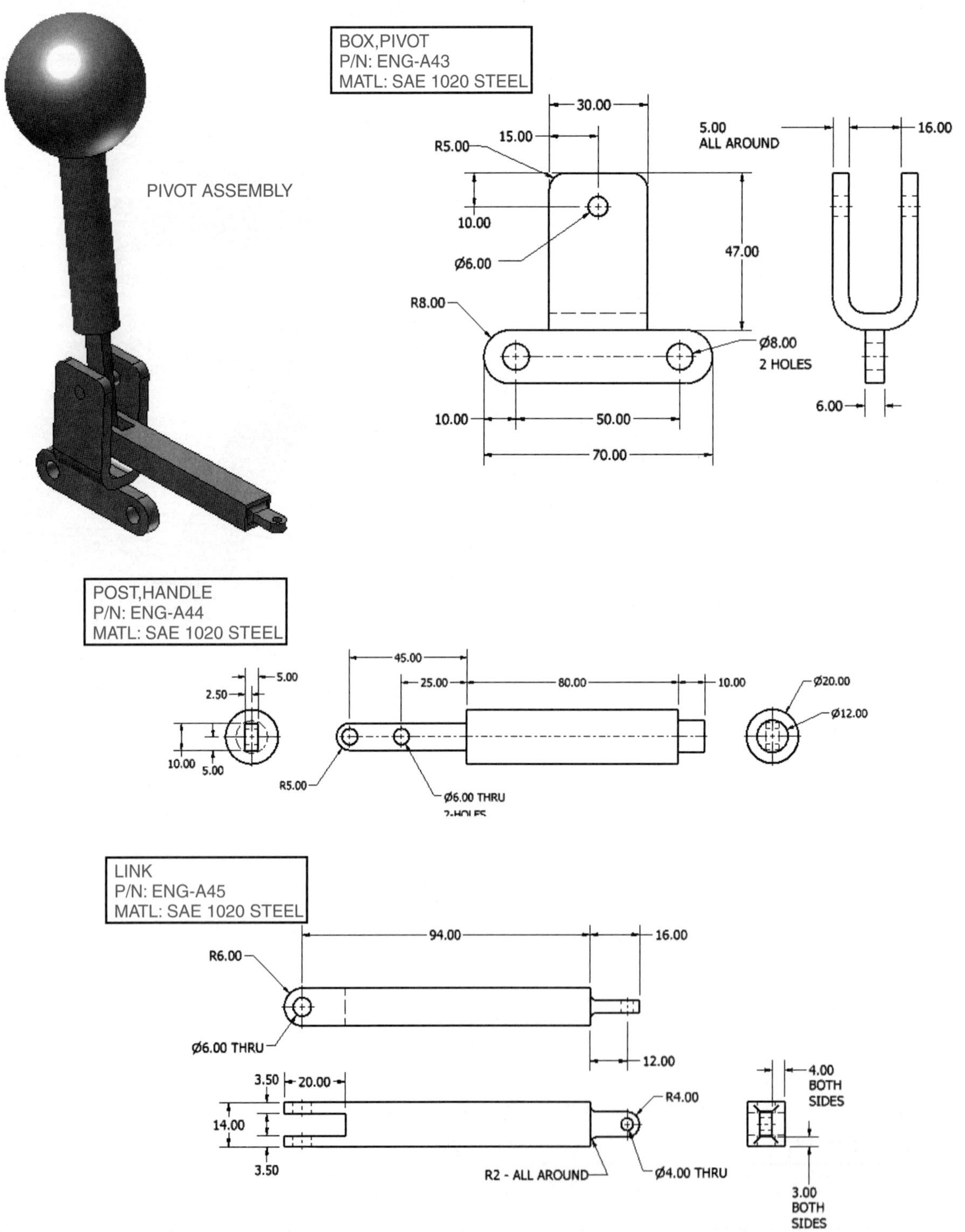

Figure P5-14 MILLIMETERS

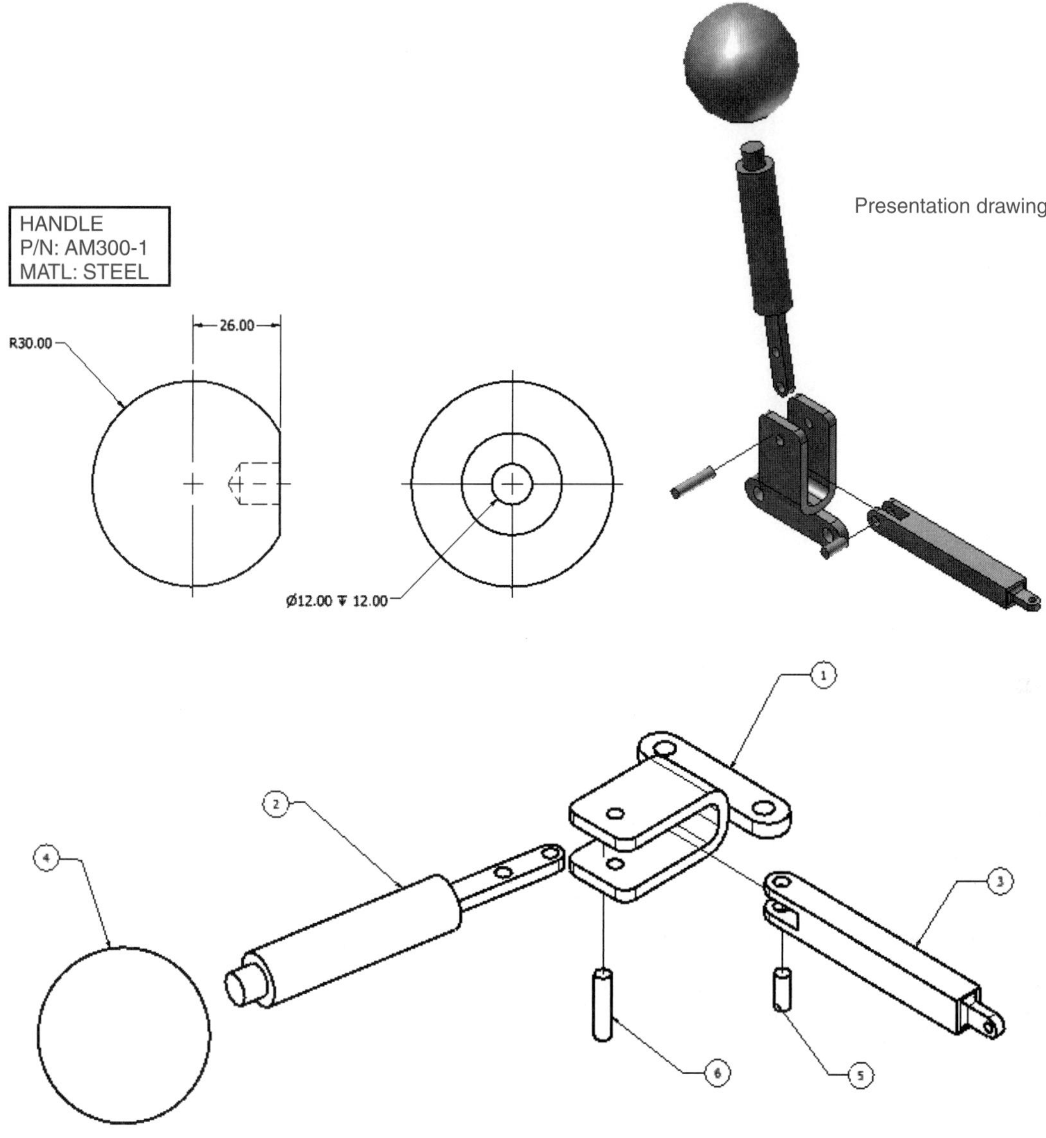

Parts List				
ITEM	PART NUMBER	DESCRIPTION	MATERIAL	QTY
1	ENG-A43	BOX,PIVOT	SAE1020	1
2	ENG-A44	POST,HANDLE	SAE1020	1
3	ENG-A45	LINK	SAE1020	1
4	AM300-1	HANDLE	STEEL	1
5	EK-132	POST-Ø6x14	STEEL	1
6	EK-131	POST-Ø6x26	STEEL	1

Figure P5-14 ***(continued)***

CHAPTER 6

Threads and Fasteners

Objectives

- Explain thread terminology and conventions.
- Learn how to draw threads.
- Learn how to size both internal and external threads.
- Learn how to use standard-sized threads.
- Learn how to use and size washers, nuts, and set screws.

6-1 INTRODUCTION

This chapter explains how to draw threads, washers, and nuts. It also explains how to select fasteners, washers, nuts, and setscrews.

Internal threads are created using the **Hole Wizard** tool, which is located with the **Features** tools. Predrawn fasteners and other standard components may be accessed using the **Design Library.** See Figure 6-1.

> ***Note:***
> The **Design Library** is an add-in accessed through the **Tools** toolbar.

All threads in this book are in compliance with ANSI (American National Standards Institute) standards—ANSI Inch and ANSI Metric threads.

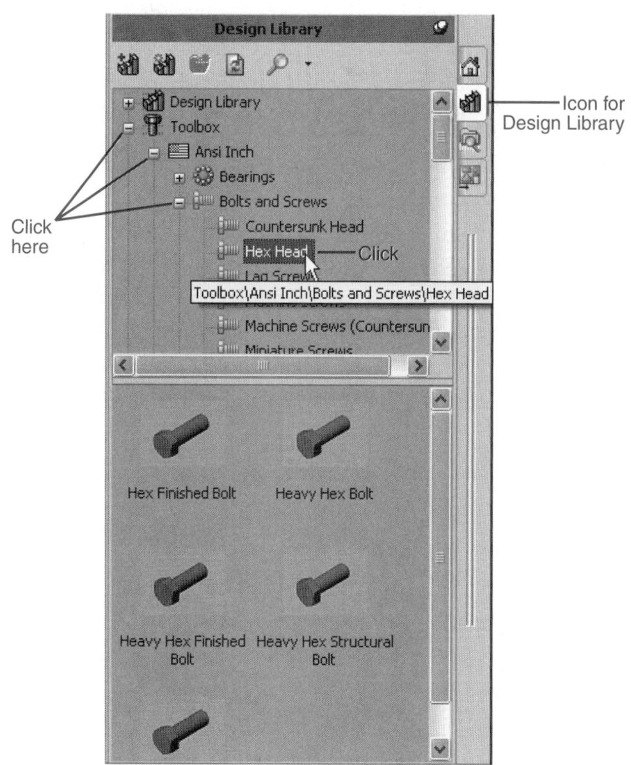

Figure 6-1

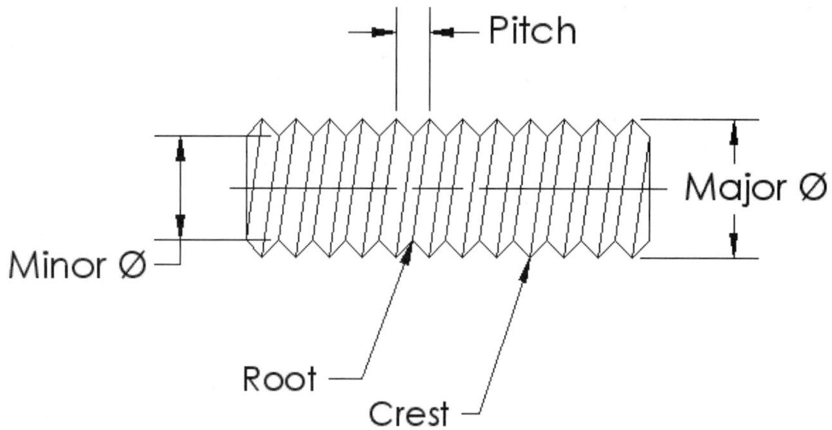

Figure 6-2

6-2 THREAD TERMINOLOGY

Figure 6-2 shows a thread. The peak of a thread is called the ***crest,*** and the valley portion is called the ***root.*** The ***major diameter*** of a thread is the distance across the thread from crest to crest. The ***minor diameter*** is the distance across the thread from root to root.

The ***pitch*** of a thread is the linear distance along the thread from crest to crest. Thread pitch is usually referred to in terms of a unit of length such as 20 threads per inch or 1.6 threads per millimeter.

6-3 THREAD CALLOUTS—METRIC UNITS

Threads are specified on a drawing using drawing callouts. See Figure 6-3. The M at the beginning of a drawing callout specifies that the callout is for a metric thread. Holes that are not threaded use the Ø symbol.

The number following the M is the major diameter of the thread. An M10 thread has a major diameter of 10 mm. The pitch of a metric thread is assumed to be a coarse thread unless otherwise stated. The callout M10 × 30 assumes a coarse thread, or a thread length of 1.5 mm per thread. The number 30 is the thread length in millimeters. The "×" is read as "by," so the thread is called a "ten by thirty."

The callout M10 × 1.25 × 30 specifies a pitch of 1.25 mm per thread. This is not a standard coarse thread size, so the pitch must be specified.

Figure 6-4 shows a listing standard metric thread sizes available in the SolidWorks **Design Library** for one type of hex head bolt. The sizes are in compliance with ANSI Metric specifications.

Whenever possible use preferred thread sizes for designing. Preferred thread sizes are readily available and are usually cheaper than nonstandard sizes. In addition, tooling such as wrenches is also readily available for preferred sizes.

6-4 THREAD CALLOUTS—ANSI UNIFIED SCREW THREADS

ANSI Unified Screw Threads (English units) always include a thread form specification. Thread form specifications

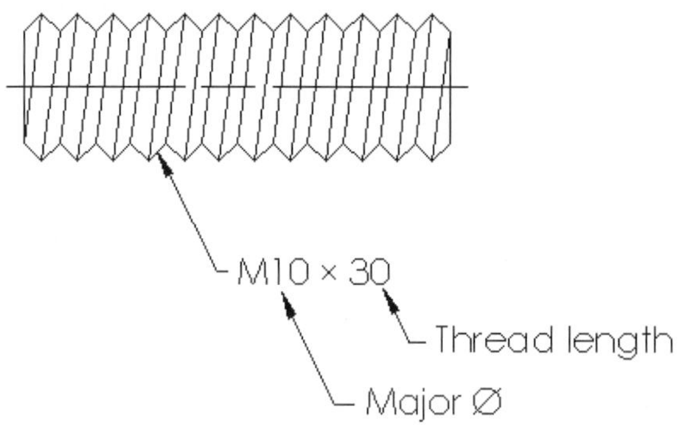

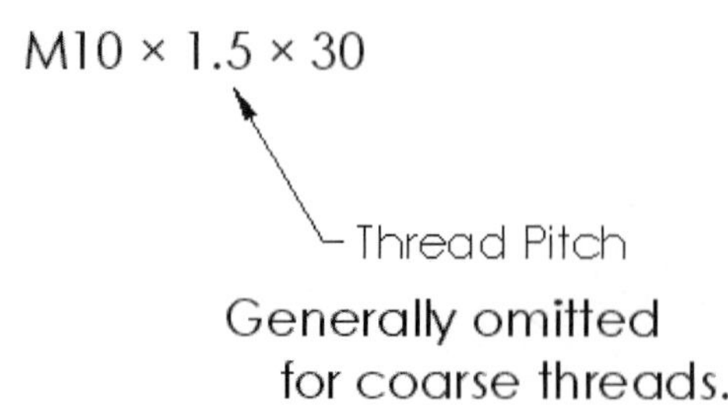

Figure 6-3

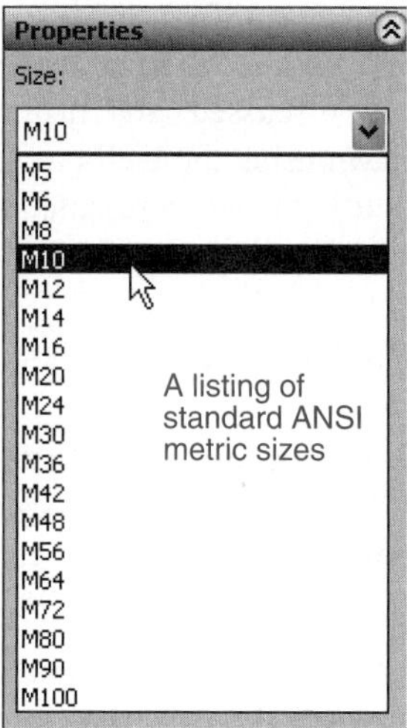

Figure 6-4

are designated by capital letters, as shown in Figure 6-6, and are defined as follows.

UNC—Unified National Coarse
UNF—Unified National Fine
UNEF—Unified National Extra Fine
UN—Unified National, or constant-pitch threads

An ANSI (English units) thread callout starts by defining the major diameter of the thread followed by the pitch specification. The callout .500-13 UNC means a thread whose major diameter is .500 in. with 13 threads per inch. The thread is manufactured to the UNC standards.

There are three possible classes of fit for a thread: 1, 2, and 3. The different class specifications specify a set of manufacturing tolerances. A class 1 thread is the loosest and a class 3 the most exact. A class 2 fit is the most common.

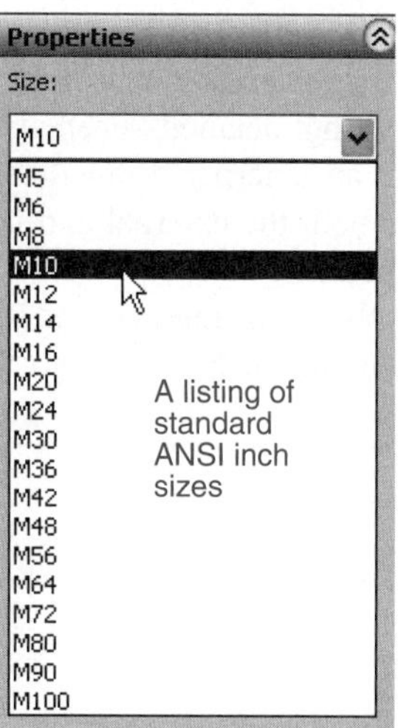

Figure 6-6

The letter A designates an external thread, B an internal thread. The symbol × means "by" as in 2 × 4, "two by four." The thread length (3.00) may be followed by the word LONG to prevent confusion about which value represents the length.

Drawing callouts for ANSI (English unit) threads are sometimes shortened, such as in Figure 6-5. The callout .500-13 UNC-2A × 3.00 LONG is shortened to .500-13 × 3.00. Only a coarse thread has 13 threads per inch, and it should be obvious whether a thread is internal or external, so these specifications may be dropped. Most threads are class 2, so it is tacitly accepted that all threads are class 2 unless otherwise specified. The shortened callout form is not universally accepted. When in doubt, use a complete thread callout.

A listing of standard ANSI (English unit) threads, as presented in SolidWorks, is shown in Figure 6-6. Some of the drill sizes listed use numbers and letters. The decimal equivalents to the numbers are listed in Figure 6-6.

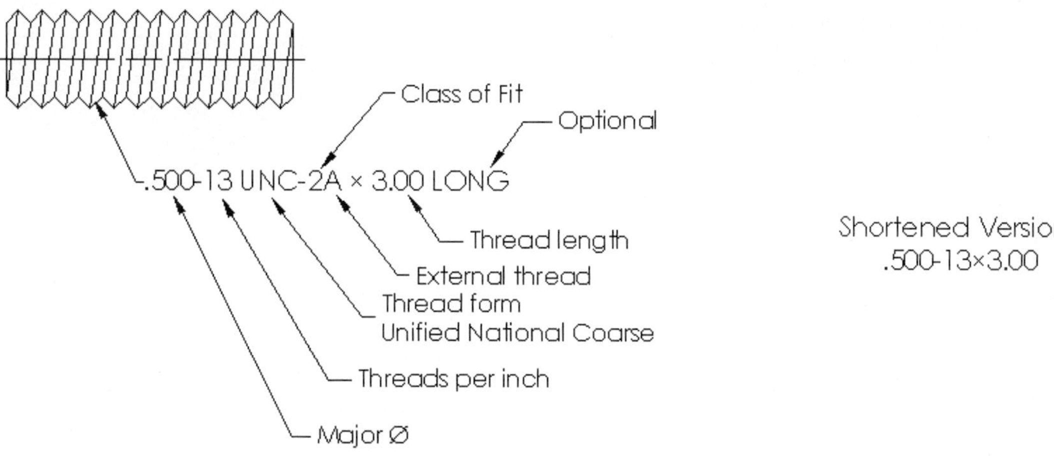

Figure 6-5

6-5 THREAD REPRESENTATIONS

There are three ways to graphically represent threads on a technical drawing: detailed, schematic, and simplified. Figure 6-5 shows an external detailed representation, and Figure 6-7 shows both the external and internal simplified and schematic representations.

Figure 6-8 shows an internal and an external thread created using SolidWorks. Note that no thread representations appear. This is called the **Simplified** representation. SolidWorks uses the **Simplified** thread representation as a way to save file size. Cosmetic thread representations can be created and will be discussed later in the chapter. Actual threads may be drawn using the **Helix** tool. SolidWorks can also draw a **Schematic** thread representation.

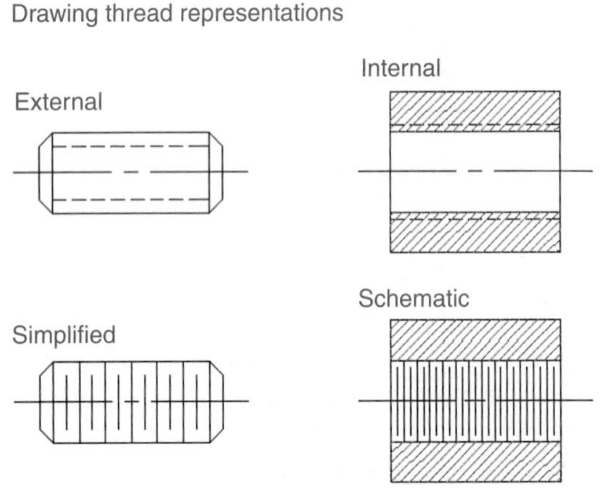

Figure 6-7

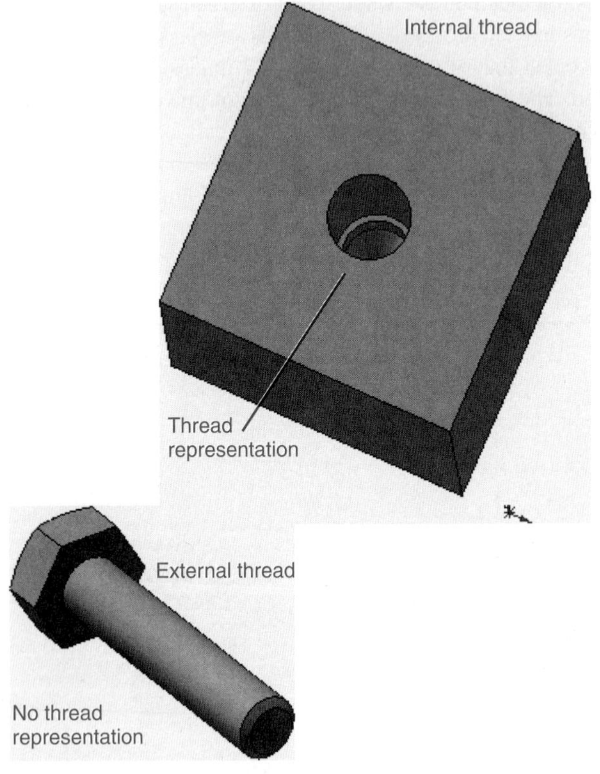

Figure 6-8

6-6 INTERNAL THREADS—INCHES

Internal threads are drawn using the **Hole Wizard.** Figure 6-9 shows a 1.5 × 2.0 × 1.0 block. In this section a 3/8-16 UNC hole will be located in the center of the block.

1. Draw a **1.5 × 2.0 × 1.0** block.
2. Orient the block in the **Isometric** view.
3. Click the **Hole Wizard** tool on the **Features** menu.
4. Define the thread's size and length.

In this example an internal 3/8-16 UNC thread will be created. The thread will go completely through the block. See Figure 6-10.

5. Click the **Cosmetic thread** option.

> *Note:*
> The **Cosmetic thread** option will create a hidden line around the finished hole that serves to indicate that the hole is threaded.

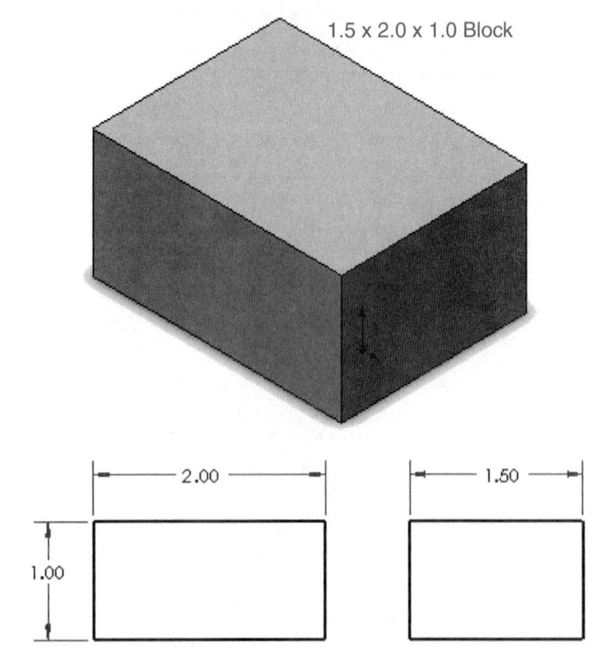

Figure 6-9

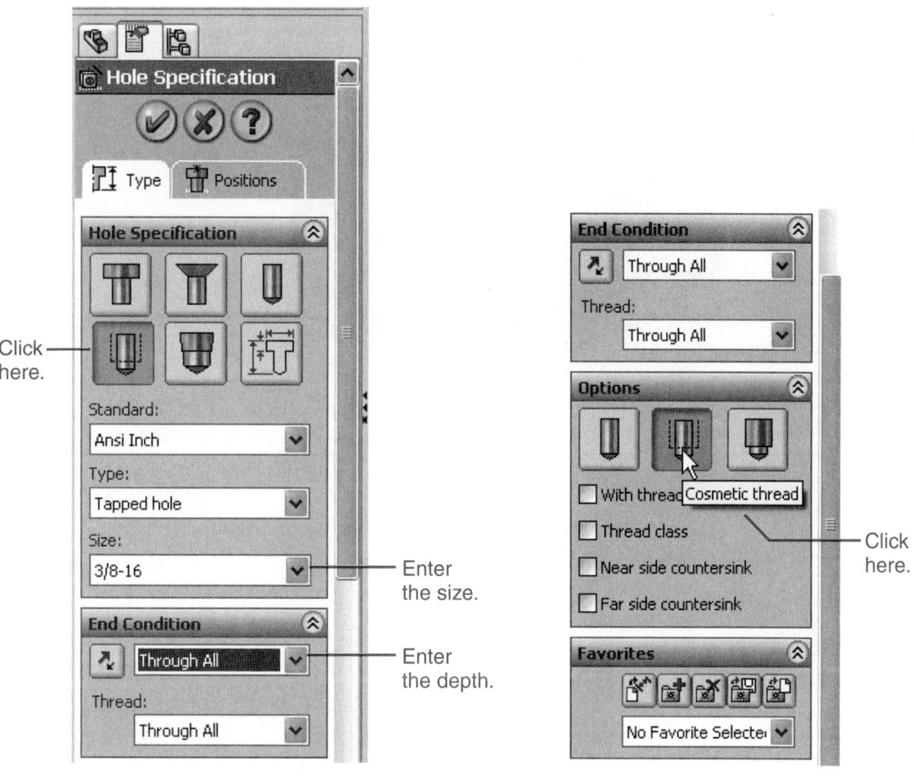

Figure 6-10

6. Click the **Positions** tab in the **Hole Position** box.
7. Click a location near the center of the top surface of the block.

   See Figure 6-11.

8. Use the **Smart Dimension** tool and locate the center point of the hole.
9. Click the OK check mark.

The hidden line surrounding the hole is a cosmetic thread and indicates that the hole is threaded. Note that there are no threads on the inside of the hole.

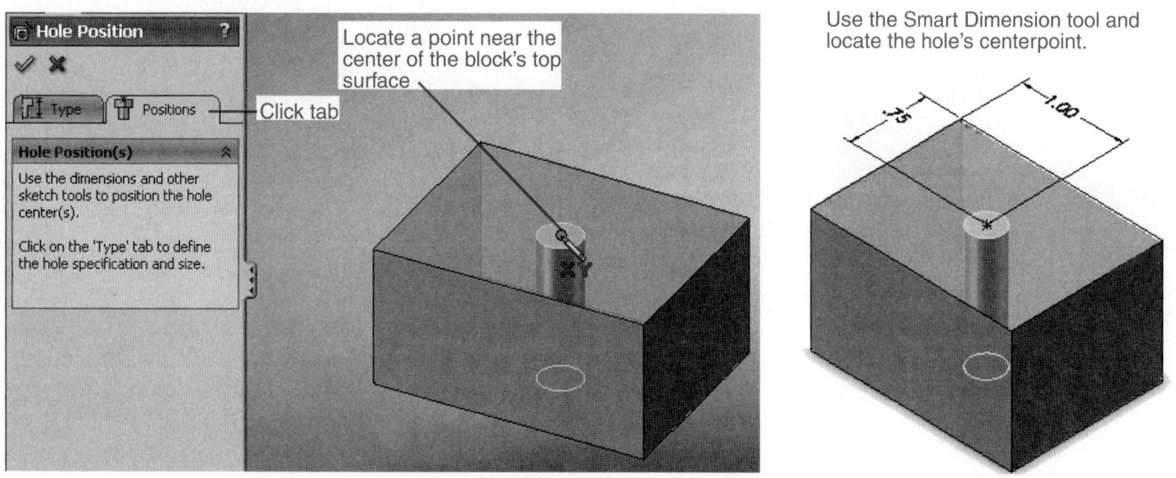

Figure 6-11

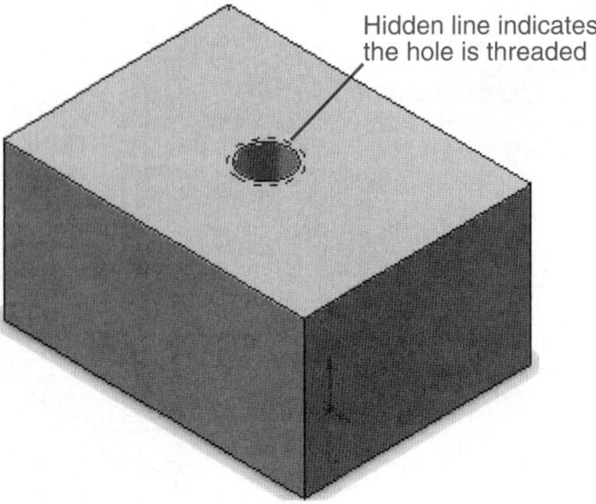

Figure 6-11 *(continued)*

6-7 THREADED BLIND HOLES—INCHES

A ***blind hole*** is one that does not go completely though an object. See Figure 6-12.

1. Use the **Undo** tool and remove the hole added to the 1.5 × 2.0 × 1.0 block.
2. Edit the block so that it is **2.00** thick.
3. Click the **Hole Wizard** tool.
4. Size the hole to **3/8-16** and set the **Blind Thread** depth in the **End Condition** box to **1.25 in.**

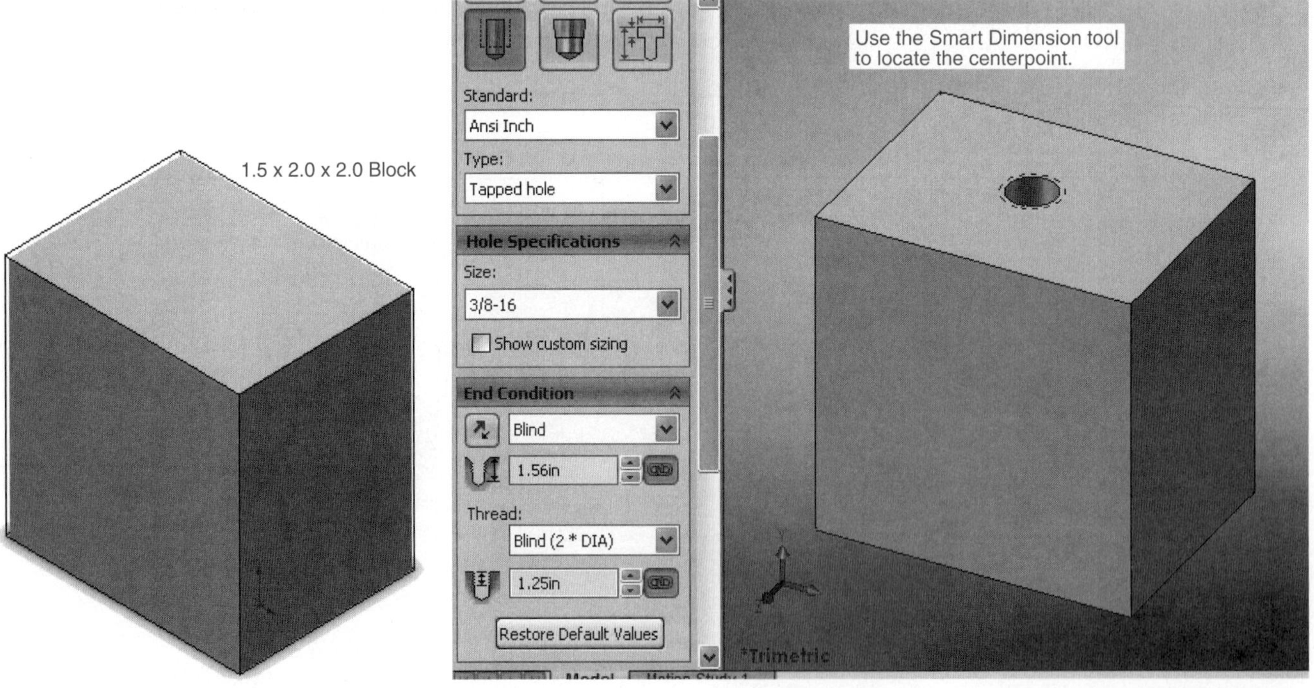

Figure 6-12

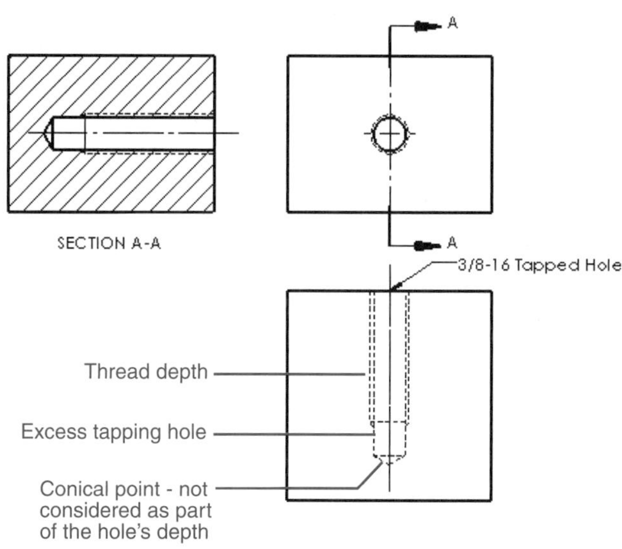

Figure 6-13

> *Note:*
> The tap thread depth is automatically calculated as the hole's thread depth is defined.

5. Click the **Positions** tab and locate a center point near the center of the top surface of the block.
6. Use the **Smart Dimension** tool to locate the center point.
7. Click the OK check mark.

Figure 6-13 shows an orthographic views of the block and a section view. Note that the tapping hole extends beyond the end of the treads and ends with a conical point. The depth of the tapping hole does not include the conical end point.

6-8 INTERNAL THREADS—METRIC

Metric threads are designated by the letter M. For example, M10 × 30 is the callout for a metric thread of diameter 10 and a length of 30. The thread is assumed to be a coarse thread.

> **TIP**
> The symbol **Ø** indicates a hole or cylinder without threads; the symbol **M** indicates metric threads.

1. Draw a **20 × 30 × 15** block.

   See Figure 6-14.

2. Click the **Hole Wizard.**
3. Set the **Standard** for **ANSI Metric,** the hole size for **M10 × 1.0,** and the depth for **Through All.**

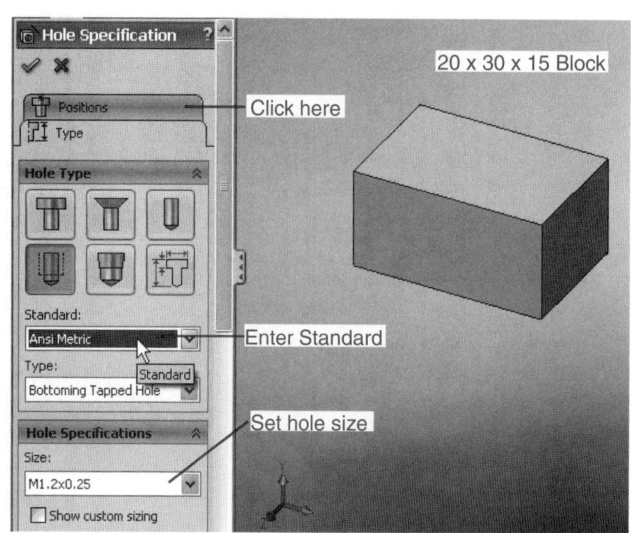

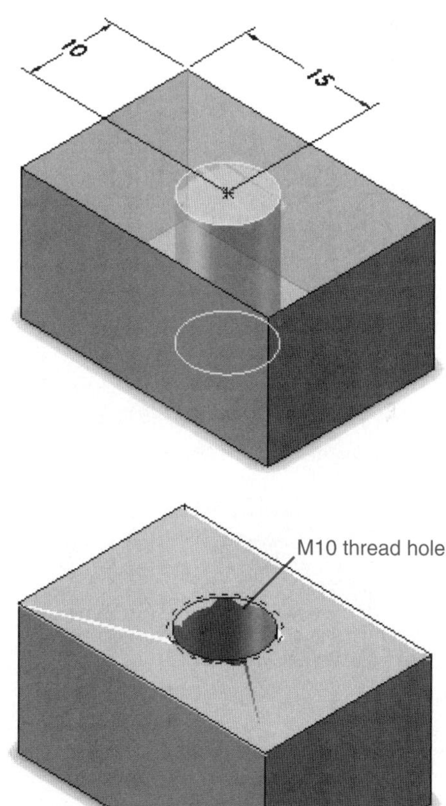

Figure 6-14

4. Click the **Cosmetic thread** option.
5. Click the **Positions** tab and locate the center point near the center of the top surface of the block.

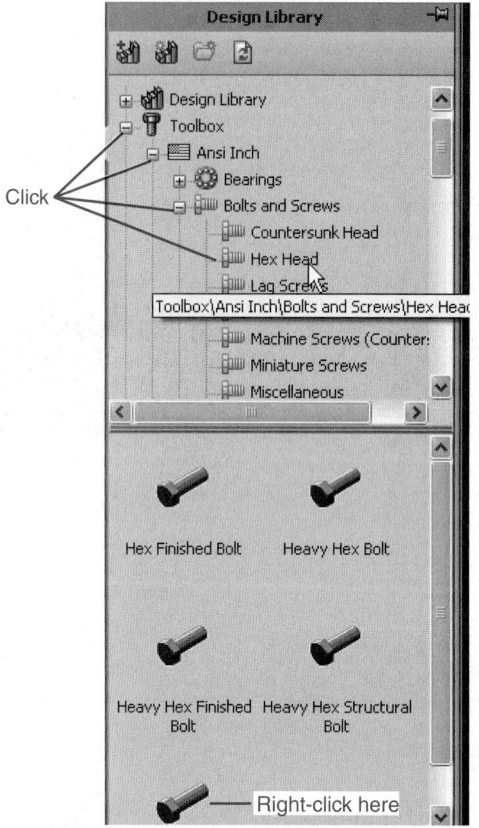
Design Library
Design Library
Toolbox
Ansi Inch
Bearings
Bolts and Screws
Countersunk Head
Hex Head
Lag Screws
Toolbox\Ansi Inch\Bolts and Screws\Hex Head
Machine Screws (Counter:
Miniature Screws
Miscellaneous
Click
Hex Finished Bolt
Heavy Hex Bolt
Heavy Hex Finished Bolt
Heavy Hex Structural Bolt
Right-click here

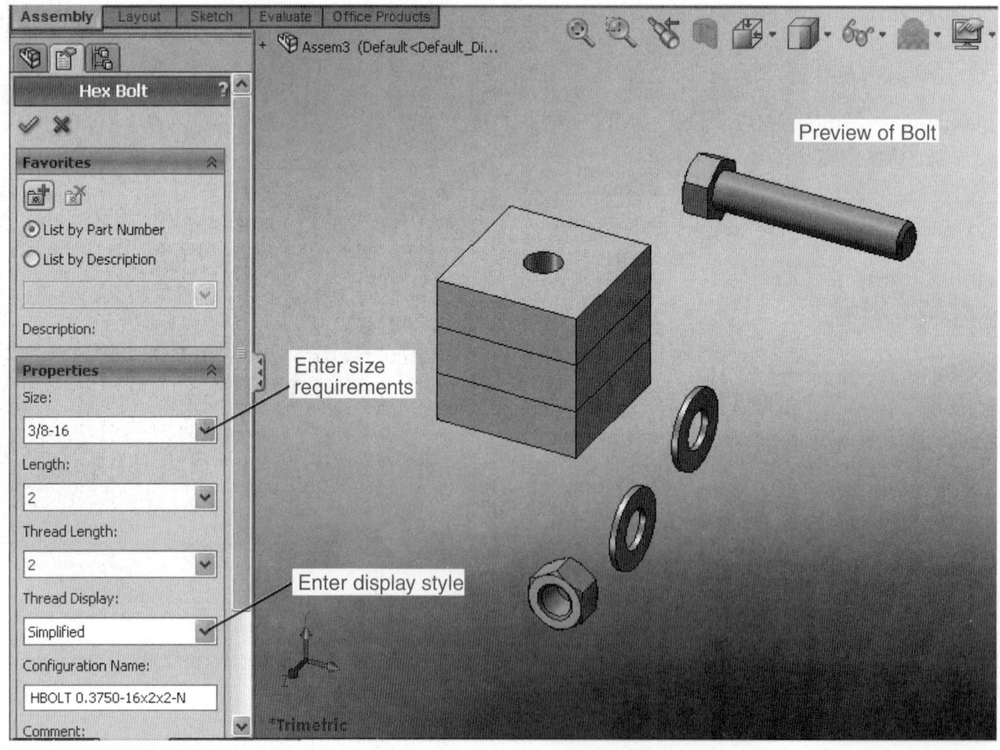
Assembly
Layout
Sketch
Evaluate
Office Products
Assem3 (Default<Default_Di...
Hex Bolt
Favorites
List by Part Number
List by Description
Description:
Properties
Size:
3/8-16
Length:
2
Thread Length:
2
Thread Display:
Simplified
Configuration Name:
HBOLT 0.3750-16x2x2-N
Comment:
Preview of Bolt
Enter size requirements
Enter display style
*Trimetric

Figure 6-15

Figure 6-15 *(continued)*

6. Use the **Smart Dimension** tool to locate the hole's center point.
7. Click the OK check mark.

6-9 ACCESSING THE DESIGN LIBRARY

SolidWorks includes a **Design Library.** The **Design Library** includes a listing of predrawn standard components such as bolts, nuts, and washers. These components may be accessed and inserted into drawings to create assemblies. Figure 6-15 shows how to access hex bolts in the **Design Library.**

> *Note:*
> The **Design Library** is an add-in that can be accessed in the **Tools** menu.

1. Click the **Design Library** tool.
2. Click the **Toolbox** tool.
3. Click the **ANSI Inch** tool.
4. Click the **Bolts and Screws** tool.
5. Click the **Hex Head** tool.

A listing of various types of hex head bolts will appear.

6. Right-click the **Hex Bolt** tool, and click **Create Part.**
7. Define the needed size and length.
8. Define the **Thread Display** style.
9. Click the OK check mark.

> **TIP**
> There are three display styles available for threads. **Schematic, Cosmetic,** and **Simplified.** See Figure 6-15. The **Simplified** style was created to use less file size.

6-10 THREAD PITCH

Thread pitch for and ANSI Inch fastener is defined as

$$P = \frac{1}{N}$$

where

P = pitch
N = number of threads per inch

In ANSI Inch standards a sample bolt callout is ¼-20 UNC × length. The 20 value is the number of threads per inch, so the pitch is 1/20 or 0.05. The pitch for a ¼-28 UNF thread would be 1/28, or 0.036.

A sample thread callout for ANSI Metric is written M10 × 1.0 × 30, where 1.0 is the pitch. No calculation is required to determine the pitch for metric threads. It is included directly in the thread callout.

> **TIP**
> Almost all threads are coarse, so ANSI metric thread callouts omit the pitch designation. A pitch size in included only when a metric thread is not coarse.

Figure 6-16 shows a listing of possible pitch sizes for an M10 thread.

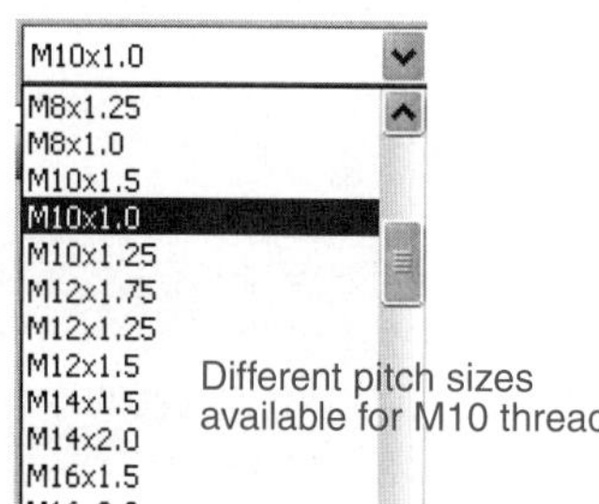

Figure 6-16

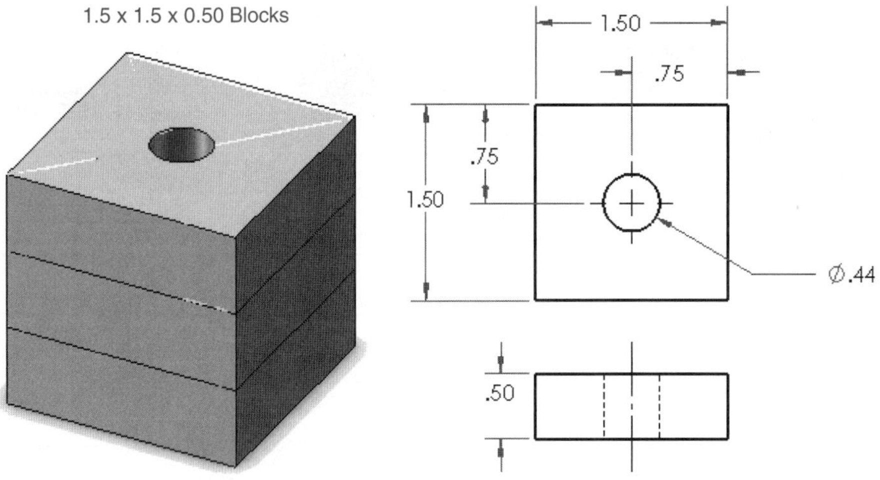

Figure 6-17

Determining an External Thread Length—Inches

Figure 6-17 shows three blocks stacked together. They are to be held together using a hex bolt, two washers, and a nut. The bolt will be a 3/8-16 UNC. What length should be used?

1. Draw a **1.5 × 1.5 × 0.50** block. Draw a **Ø.44** (7/16) hole through the center of the block.

The Ø.438 was selected because it allows for clearance between the bolt and the block.

2. Create an assembly drawing, enter three blocks, and assemble them as shown.
3. Save the assembly as **3-BLOCK ASSEMBLY.**
4. Access the **Design Library, Toolbox, ANSI Inch, Washers,** and **Plain Washers (Type A).**

See Figure 6-18.

5. Click and hold the **Preferred-Narrow Flat Washer Type A.**
6. Click the washer and drag-and-drop it into the field of the drawing.

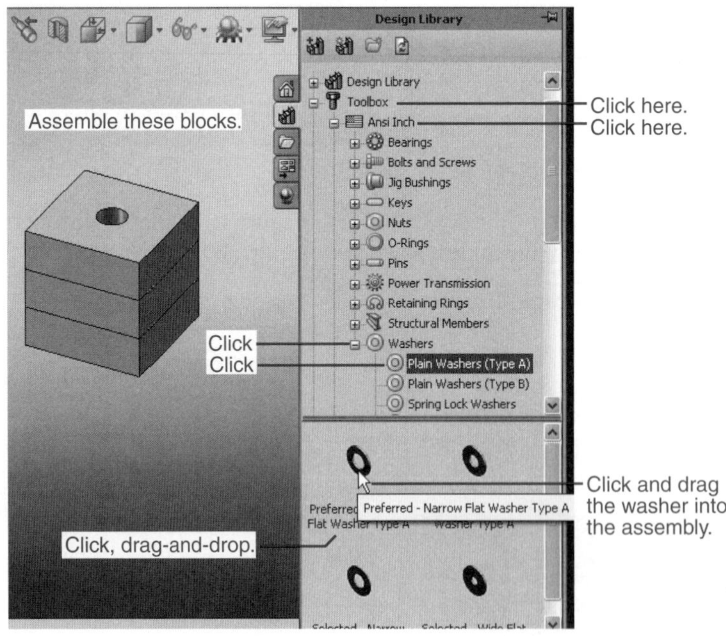

Figure 6-18

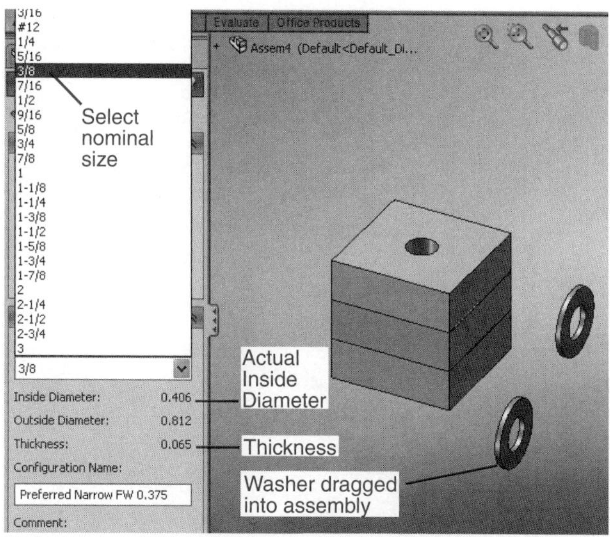

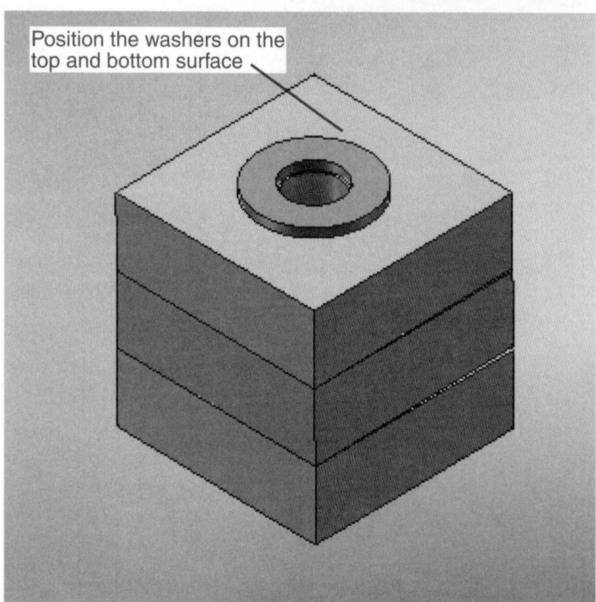

Figure 6-18 ***(continued)***

The washer preview will appear in the drawing area.

7. Size the washer by clicking the arrow to the right of the initial size value and selecting a nominal value.

The term *nominal* refers to a starting value. In this case we are going to use a 3/8-16 UNC thread. The 3/8 value is a nominal value. We select a washer with a specified 3/8 nominal inside diameter. The actual inside diameter of the washer is .406. Clearance between the washer and the bolt is created when the washer is manufactured. The fastener will also not measure .375 but will be slightly smaller. The .375 size is the size of the bolt's shaft before the threads were cut.

Note that the washer thickness is .065 (about 1/16).

8. Click the OK check mark.
9. Add a second washer into the assembly.
10. Use the **Mate** tool to position the washers around the block's holes as shown.
11. Access the **Design Library, Toolbox, ANSI Inch, Nuts, Hex Jam Nut** and drag and drop the nut into the drawing area.

See Figure 6-19.

12. Use the **Mate** tool and position the nut as shown.

The nut thickness is .227. This value was obtained by using the **Edit** tools and determining the extrusion value used to create the nut.

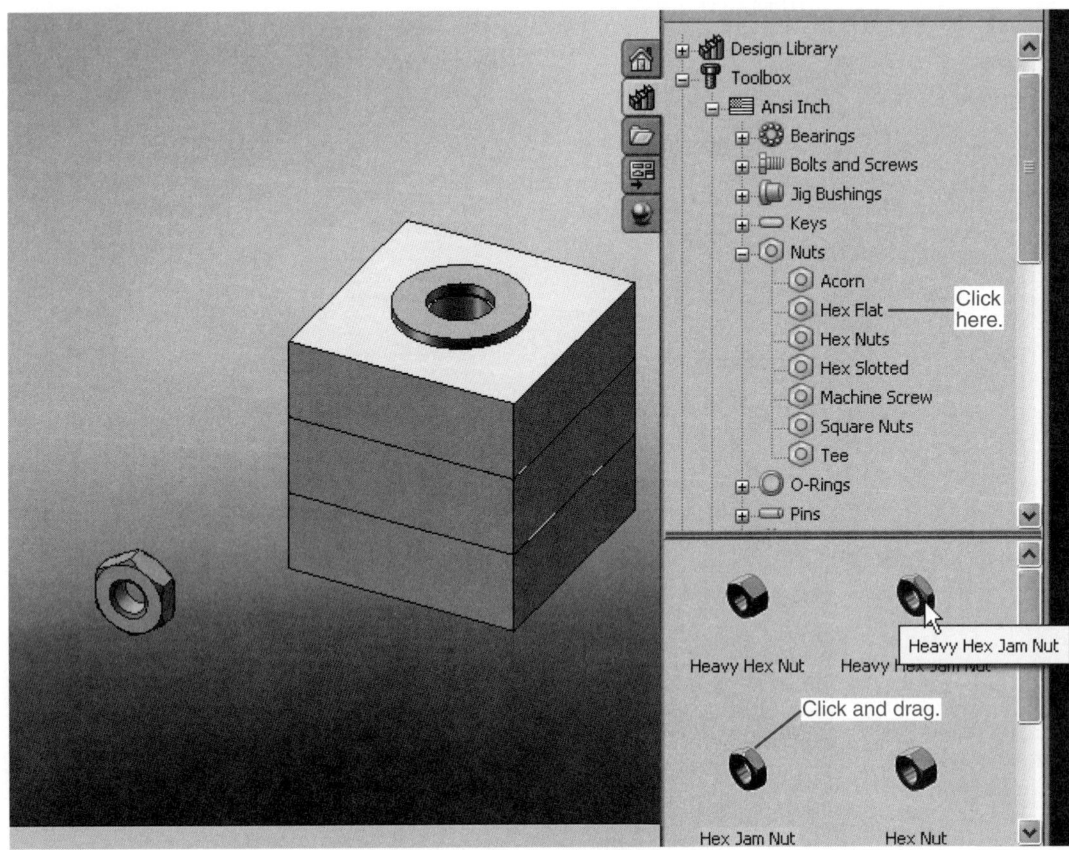
Design Library
Toolbox
Ansi Inch
Bearings
Bolts and Screws
Jig Bushings
Keys
Nuts
Acorn
Hex Flat
Click here.
Hex Nuts
Hex Slotted
Machine Screw
Square Nuts
Tee
O-Rings
Pins
Heavy Hex Jam Nut
Heavy Hex Nut
Click and drag.
Hex Jam Nut
Hex Nut

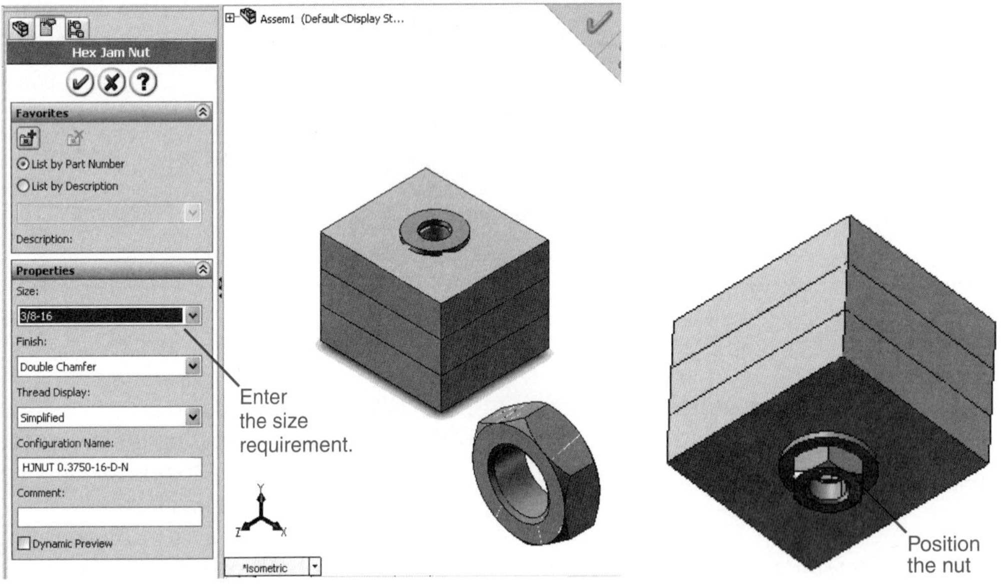
Hex Jam Nut
Favorites
List by Part Number
List by Description
Description:
Properties
Size:
3/8-16
Finish:
Double Chamfer
Thread Display:
Simplified
Configuration Name:
HJNUT 0.3750-16-D-N
Comment:
Dynamic Preview
Enter the size requirement.
*Isometric
Position the nut

Figure 6-19

So far, the bolt must pass through three blocks (.50 × 3 = 1.50), two washers (.065 × 2 = .13), and one nut (.337). Therefore, the initial bolt length is 1.50 + .13 + .227 = 1.857.

> ***Note:***
> Bolt threads must extend beyond the nut to ensure 100% contact with the nut. The extension must be equal to at least two pitches (2*P*).

Calculations used to determine the strength of a bolt/nut combination assume that there is 100% contact between the bolt and the nut; that is, all threads of the nut are in contact with the threads of the nut. However, there is no assurance that the last thread on a bolt is 360°, so at least two threads must extended beyond the nut to ensure 100% contact.

In this example the thread pitch is .0625 (1/16). Two pitches (2*P*) is .125. This value must be added to the initial thread length:

$$1.857 + .125 = 1.982.$$

Therefore the minimum bolt length is 1.982. This value must in turn be rounded up to the nearest standard size. Figure 6-20 shows a listing of standard sizes for a 1 3/8-16 UNC Hex Head bolt.

The final thread length for the given blocks, washers, nut, and 2*P* is 2.00. The bolt callout is

3/8-16 UNC × 2.00 Hex Head Bolt

13. Insert the bolt into the assembly.

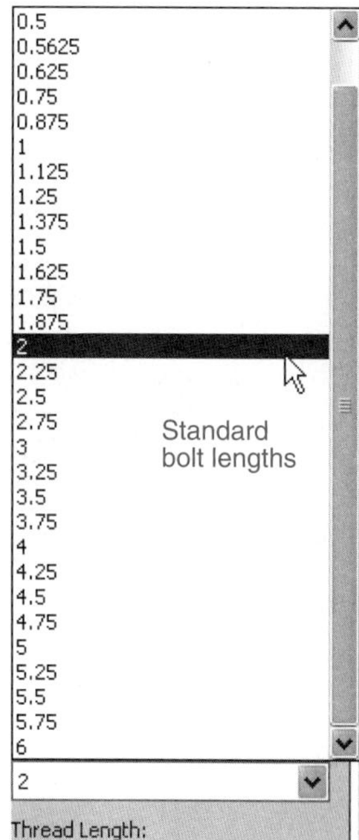

Figure 6-20

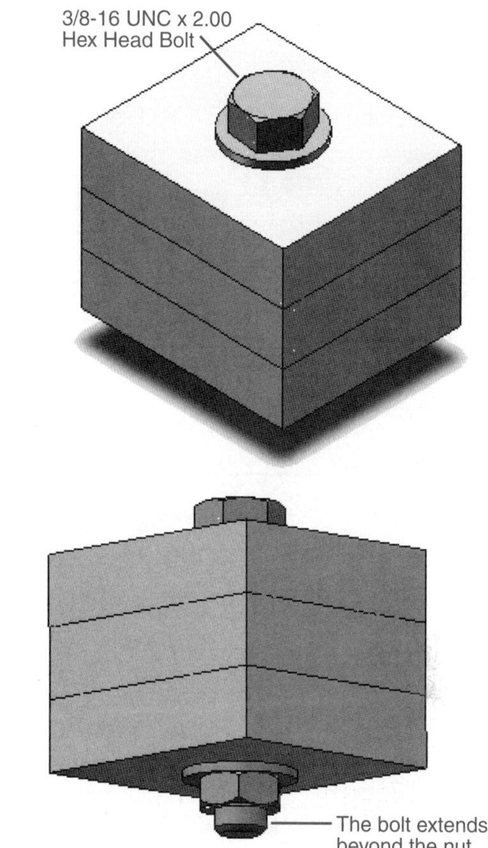

Figure 6-21

See Figure 6-21. Note how the bolt extends beyond the nut.

6-11 SMART FASTENERS

The **Smart Fasteners** tool will automatically create the correct bolt. Given the three blocks, two washers, and nut shown in Figure 6-19, use the **Smart Fasteners** tool to add the appropriate bolt.

1. Click the **Smart Fasteners** tool located on the Assembly toolbar.

   A dialog box will appear. See Figure 6-22.

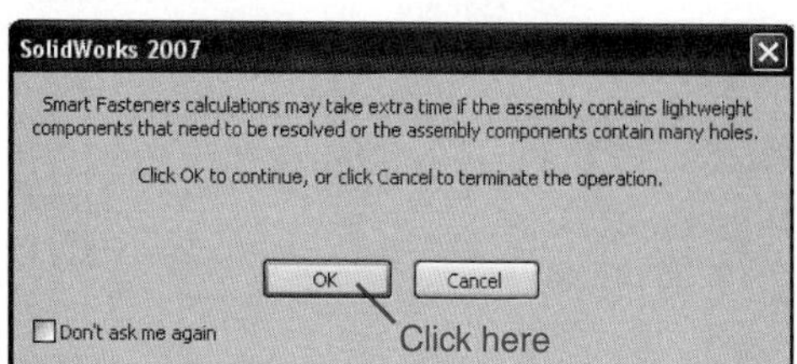

Figure 6-22

2. Click OK.

The **Smart Fasteners Properties Manager** will appear. See Figure 6-23.

3. Click the hole in the top block of the three blocks.

TIP

Click the hole, that is, a cylindrical-shaped section as shown in Figure 6-23, not the hole's edge.

The words **Cut-Extrude 1** will appear in the **Selection** box.

4. Click the **Add** box.

A fastener will appear in the hole. This may take a few seconds. In this example a **Socket Head Cap Screw** appeared in the hole.

5. Right-click the **Socket Head Cap Screw** heading in the **Fasteners** box.
6. Click the **Change fastener type** option.

The **Smart Fasteners** dialog box will appear.

7. Click the arrow to the right of the **Type** box and select a **Hex Head** type.
8. Click **OK.**

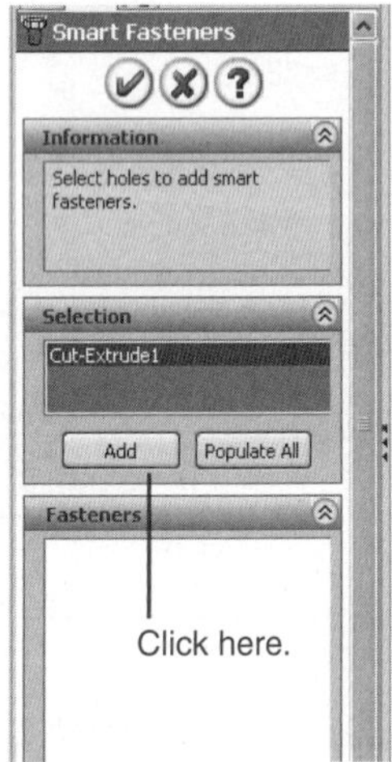

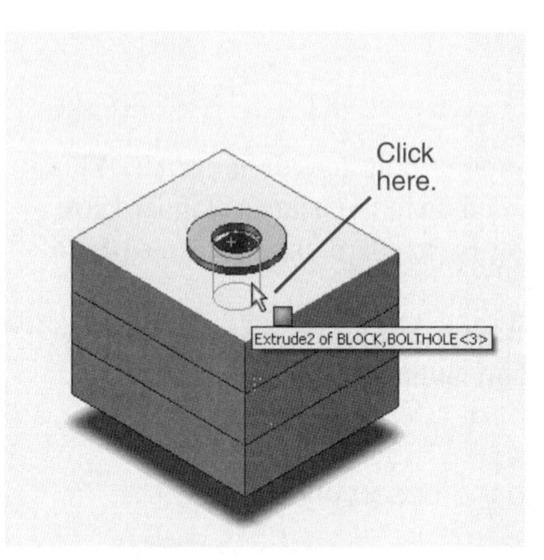

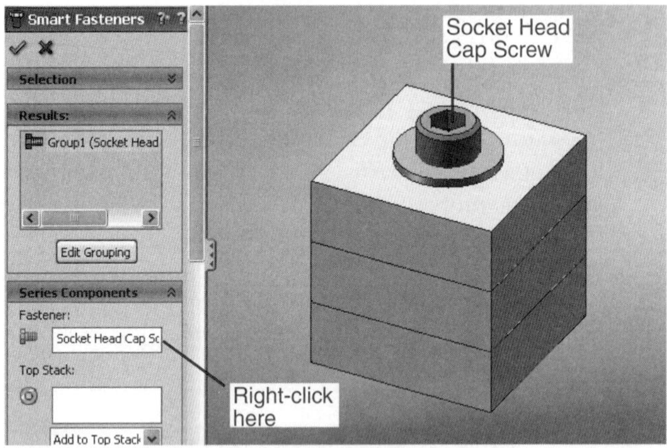

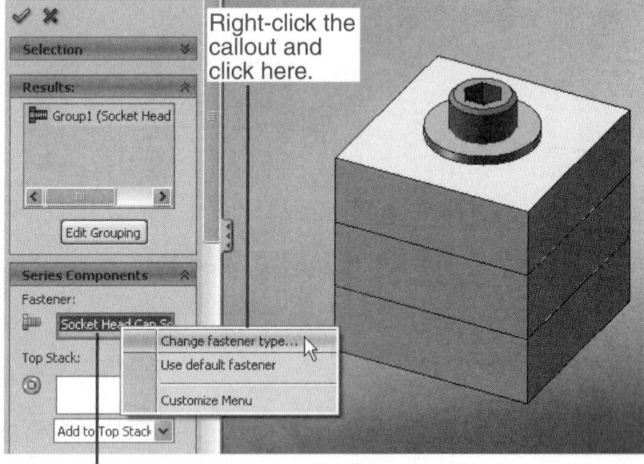

Figure 6-23

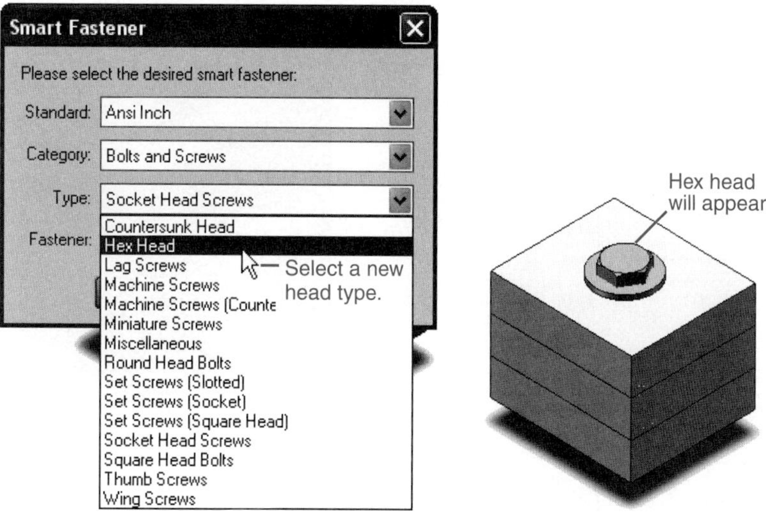

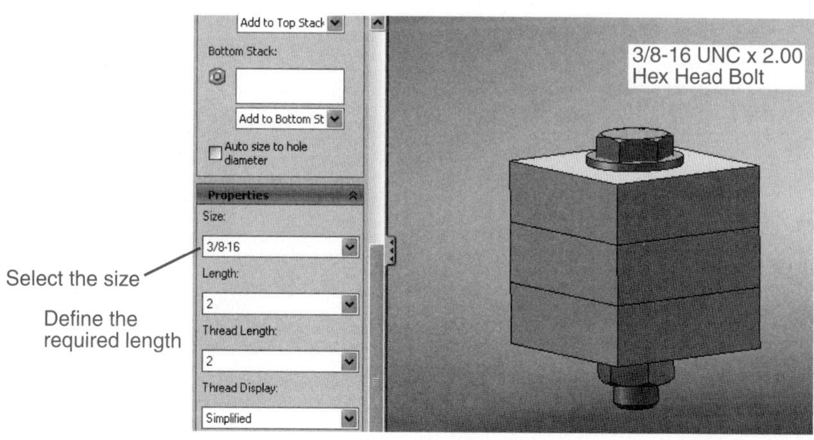

Figure 6-23 *(continued)*

9. Scroll down the Smart Fastener Manager and access The Properties box.
10. Define the thread size and number of threads per inch and the thread length.
11. Click the OK check mark.

Note that the fastener extends beyond the nut.

6-12 DETERMINING AN INTERNAL THREAD LENGTH

Figure 6-27 shows two blocks: Block, Cover and Block, Base. The dimensions for each are given in Figure 6-24. The two blocks are to be assembled and held together using an

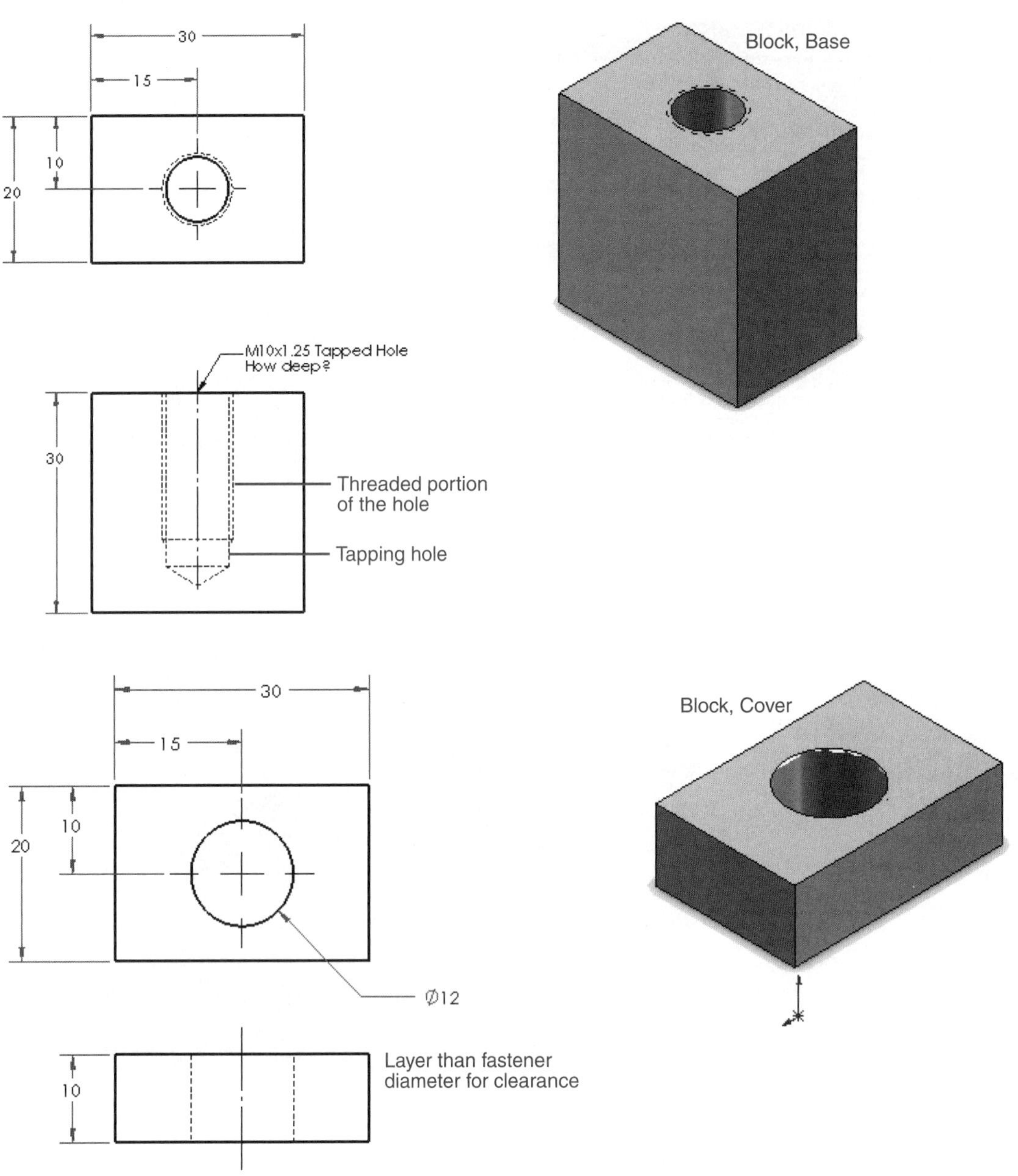

Figure 6-24

M10 × 1.25 × 25 hex head screw. What should be the threaded hole in the Block, Base ?

Note in Figure 6-24 that the tapping hole extends beyond the threads. This to prevent damage to the tapping bit. SolidWorks will automatically calculate the excess length needed, but as a general rule it is at least two pitches (2*P*) beyond the threaded portion of the hole.

The threaded hole should always be longer then the fastener so the fastener doesn't "bottom out," that is, hit the bottom of the threads before the fastener is completely in the hole. Again the general rule is to allow at least two pitches (2*P*) beyond the length of the fastener.

In this example the thread pitch is 1.25.

> **TIP**
>
> Metric thread callouts give the pitch directly.

Two pitches = 2.50. The bolt length is 25, but it must initially pass through the 10-thick Block, Cover, so the length of the bolt in the Block, Base is 15. Adding 2.50 to this value yields a minimum thread length of 17.50. Rounding the value up determines that the threaded hole in the Block, Base should be M10 × 1.25 × 18 deep.

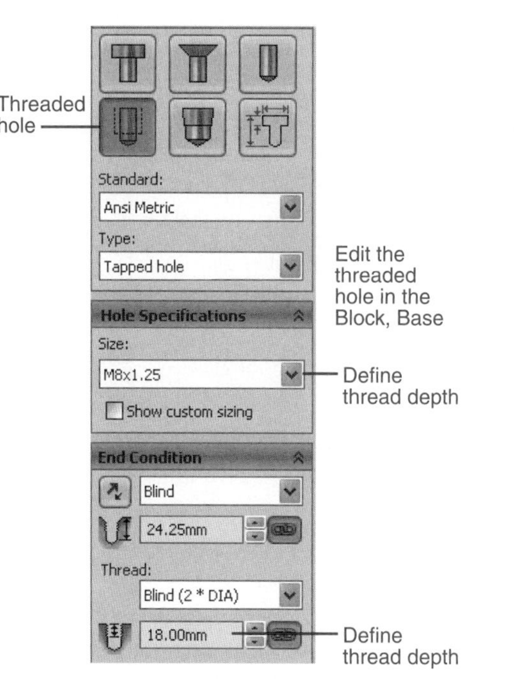

Figure 6-25

1. Draw the parts and assemble them as shown.
2. Use the **Design Library** and add an **ANSI B18.2.3.2M M10 × 1.25 × 25** fastener.
3. Edit the Block, Base to have a threaded hole depth of **18.**

See Figure 6-25.

4. Access the **Design Library** and insert an **ANSI B18.2.3.2M-M10 × 25 HEX HEAD SCREW.**

See Figure 6-26. Figure 6-27 shows the finished Internal Thread Assembly.

5. Save the assembly.

Figure 6-28 shows an isometric view, an orthographic view, and a section view of the Internal Thread Assembly.

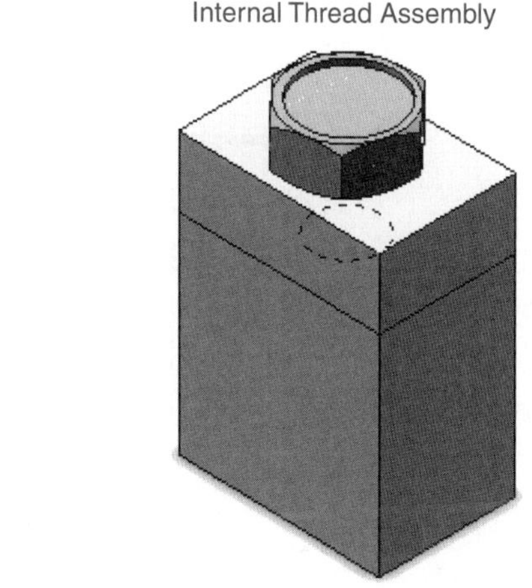

Figure 6-27

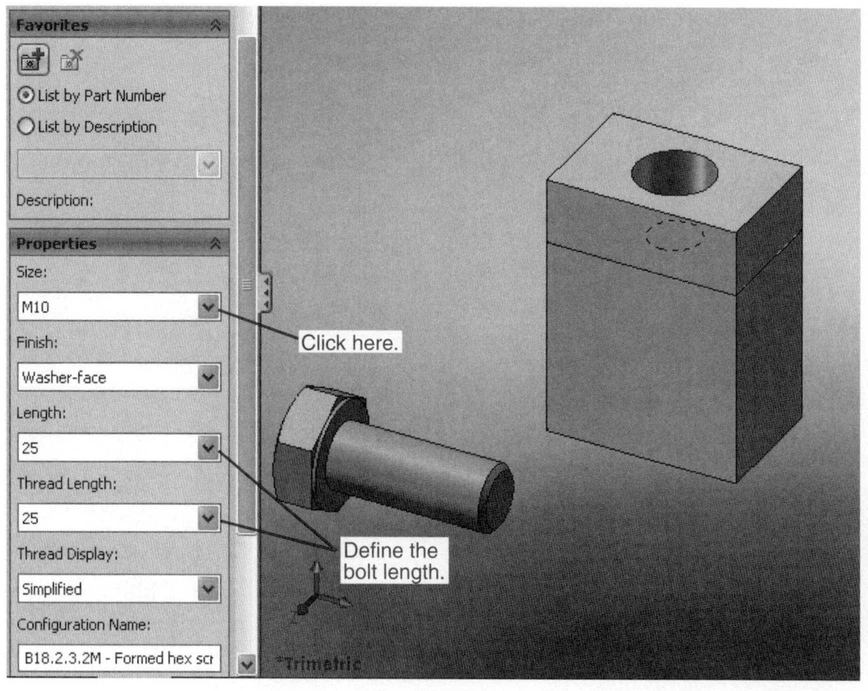

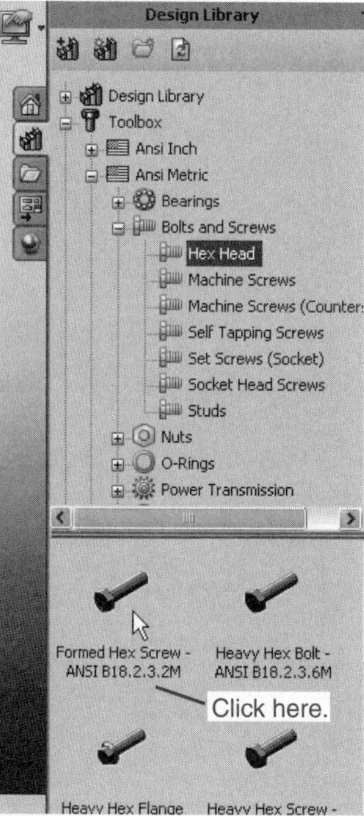

Figure 6-26

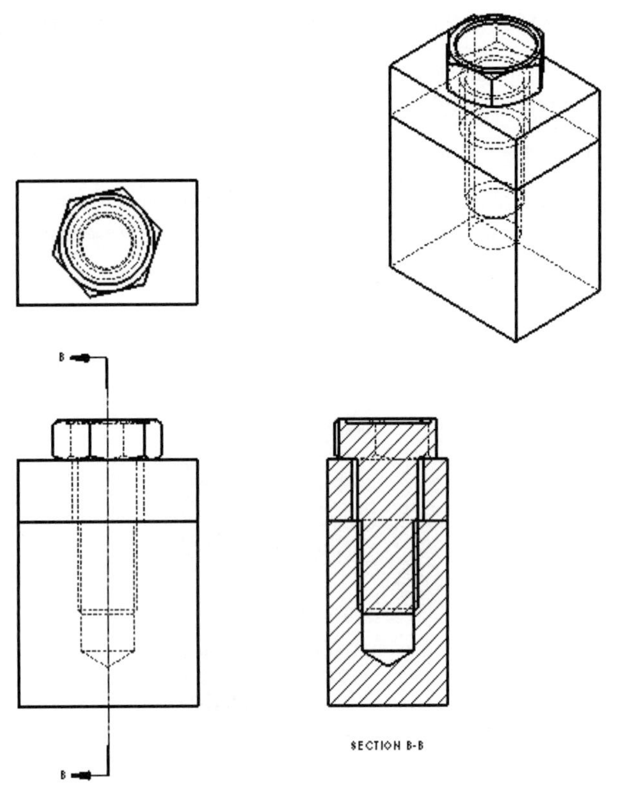

Figure 6-28

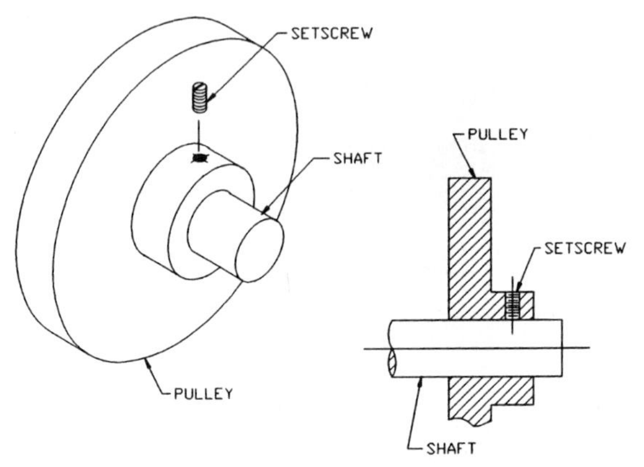

Figure 6-29

6-13 SET SCREWS

Set screws are fasteners used to hold parts like gears and pulleys to rotating shafts or other moving objects to prevent slippage between the two objects. See Figure 6-29.

Most set screws have recessed heads to help prevent interference with other parts.

Many different head styles and point styles are available. See Figure 6-30. The dimensions shown in Figure 6-30 are general sizes for use in this book. For actual sizes, see the manufacturer's specifications.

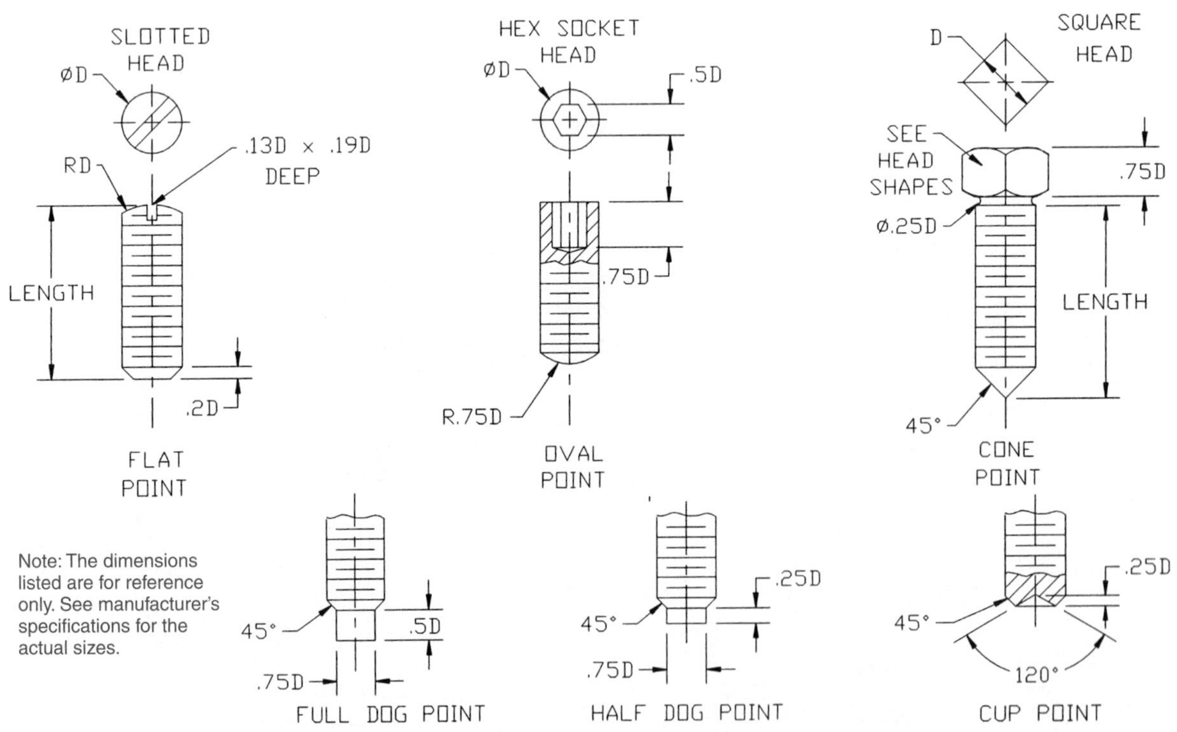

Figure 6-30

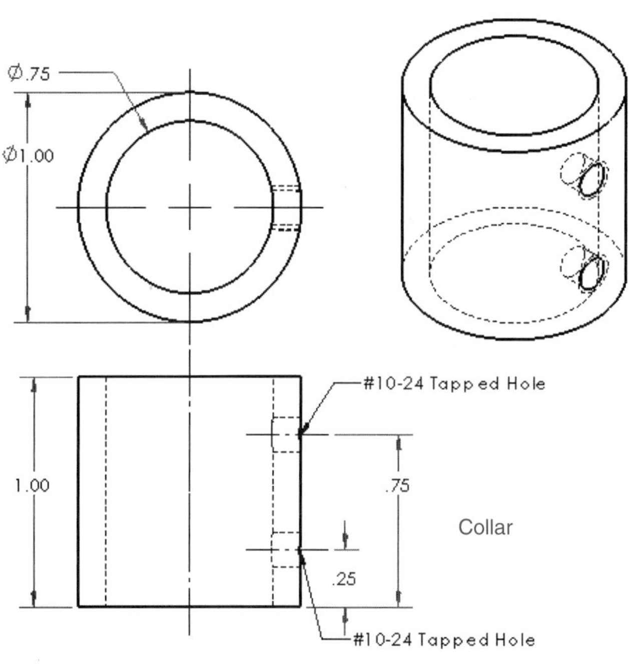

Figure 6-31

6-14 DRAWING A THREADED HOLE IN THE SIDE OF A CYLINDER

Figure 6-31 shows a Ø.75 × Ø1.00 × 1.00 collar with a #10-24 threaded hole. This section will explain how to add a threaded hole through the sides of a cylinder. See Figure 6-32.

1. Draw the collar.
2. Use the **Reference Plane** tool and draw a right plane tangent to the collar.
3. Use the **Reference Plane** tool and draw a top plane aligned with the top of the collar.
4. Use the **Hole Wizard** tool and draw two threaded holes in the side of the cylinder using the given dimensions.
5. Specify an **ANSI Inch #10-24** thread and use the **Smart Dimension** tool to locate the holes on Plane1 relative to Plane2.
6. Use the **Hole Wizard** tool and specify a **#10-24** threaded hole.
7. Select the **Cosmetic thread** representation.

TIP

Do not use the **Through All,** option, as this will create holes on both sides of the collar.

8. Position the holes per the given dimensions.

Use the **Smart Dimension** tool to locate the hole relative to Plane2.

9. Click the OK check mark.
10. Hide the two reference planes.

To Add Set Screws to the Collar

1. Access the **Design Library, Toolbox, ANSI Inch, Bolts and Screws,** and **Set Screws (Slotted).**

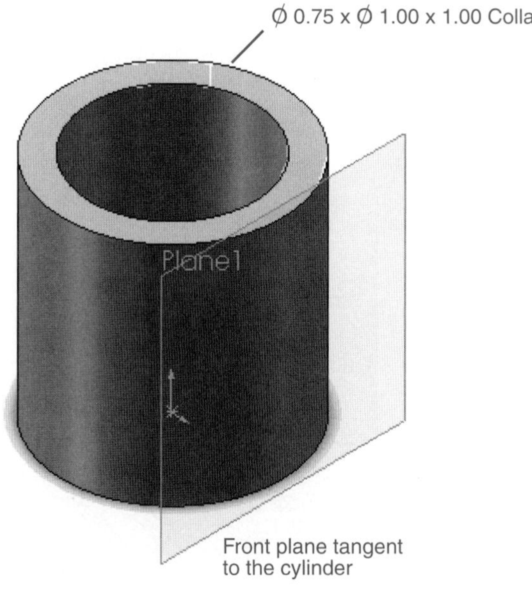

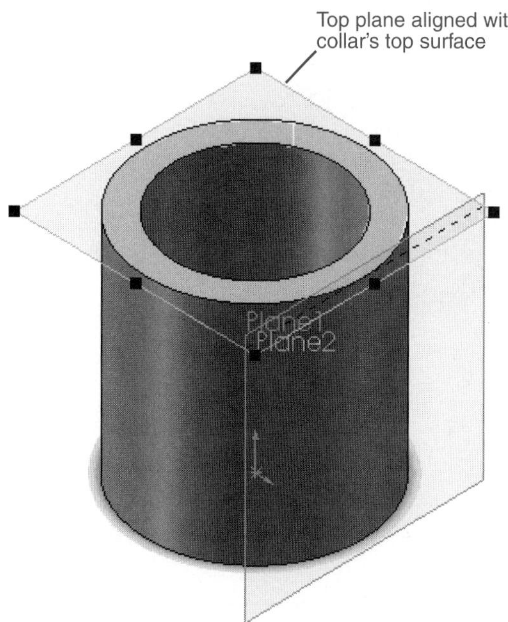

Figure 6-32

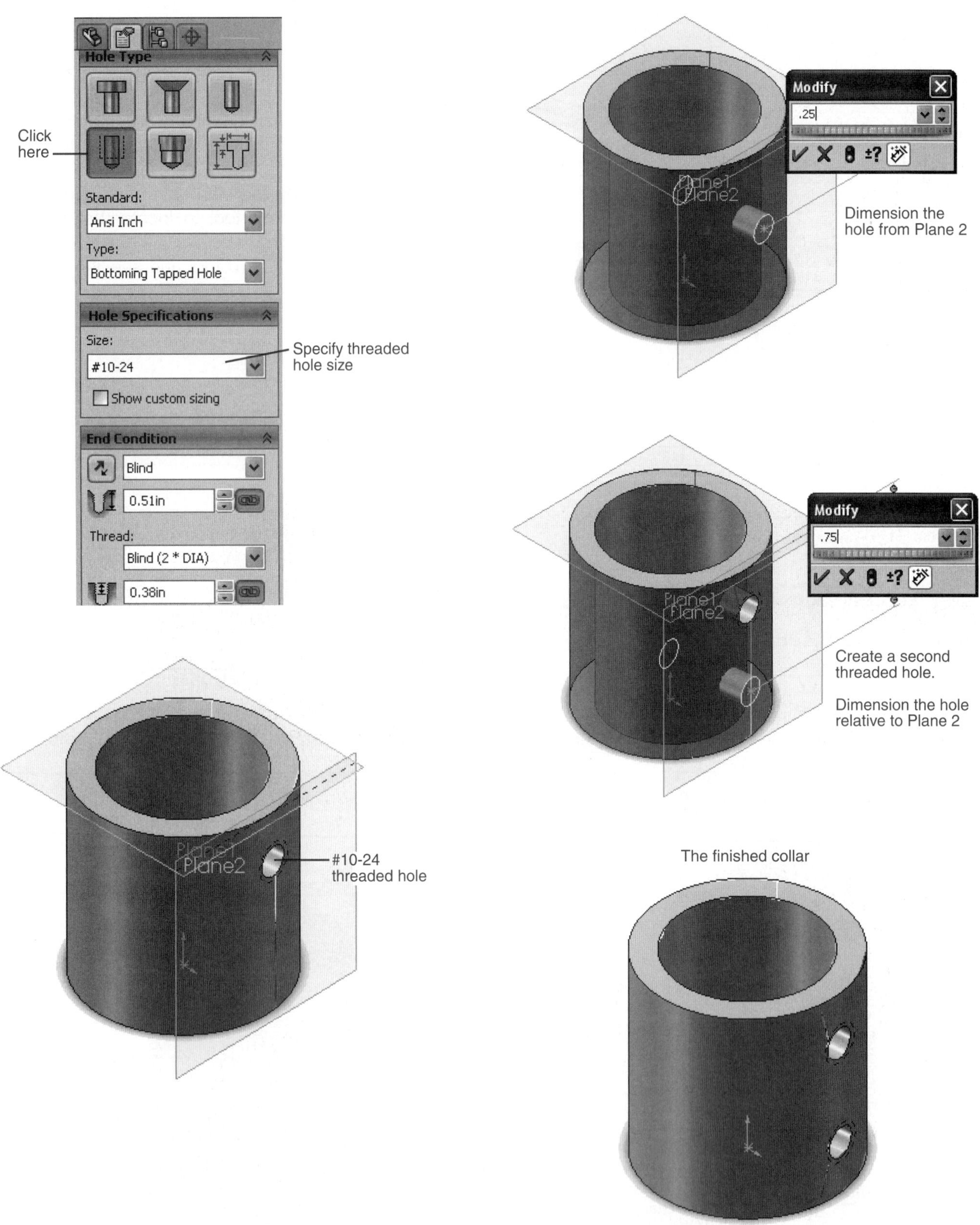

Figure 6-32 ***(continued)***

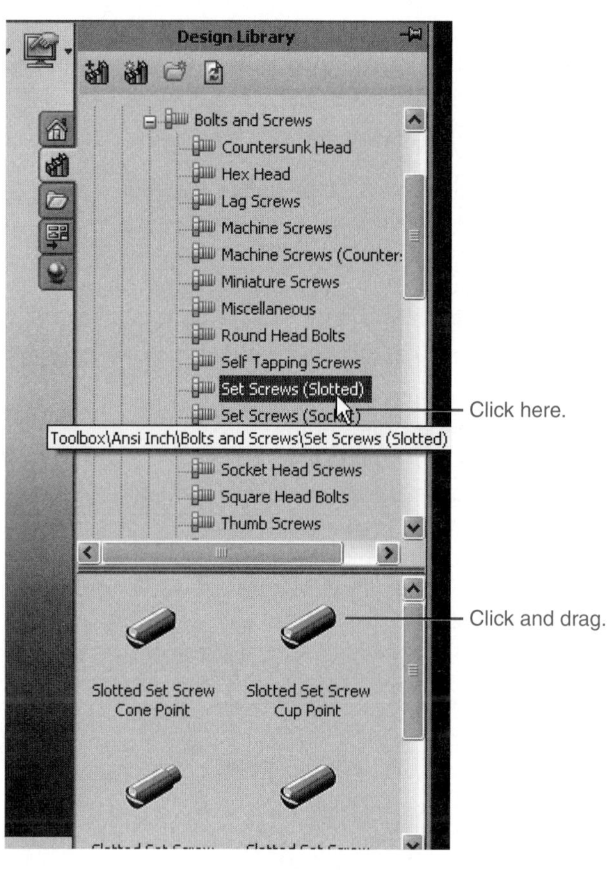

Figure 6-33

See Figure 6-33.

2. Select the **Slotted Set Screw Cup Point** option and click and drag the set screw into the drawing.

See Figure 6-34.

3. Define the size of the set screw as **#10-24** and the length as **0.315.**
4. Click the OK check mark.
5. Use the **Mate** tool and insert the setscrews into the collar.
6. Save the assembly.

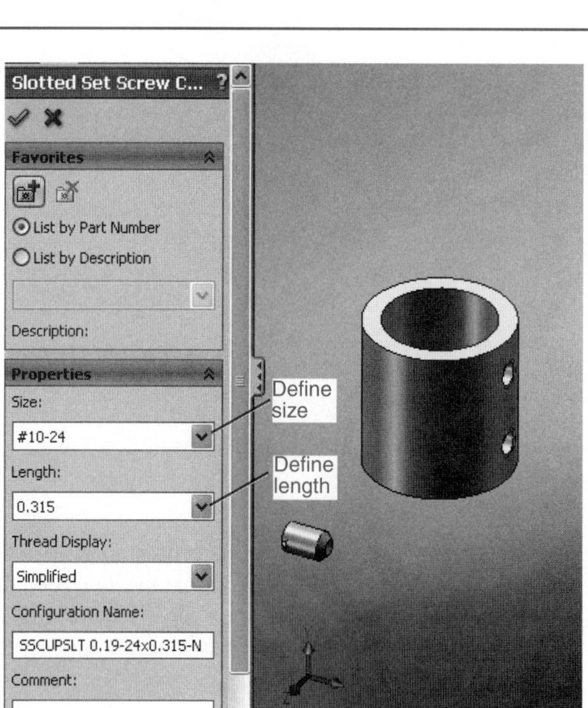

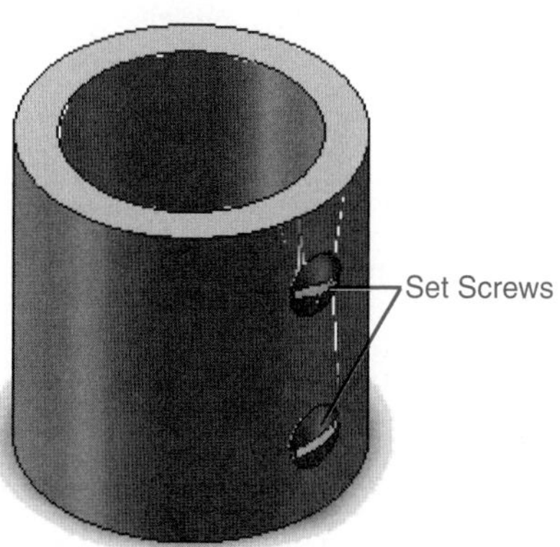

Figure 6-34

Countersunk Holes and Fasteners

Countersunk holes are used in conjunction with flat head screws to assure that the head of the screws are below the top surface of the assembly.

6-15 PROJECTS

Project 6-1: Millimeters

Figure P6-1 shows three blocks. Assume that the blocks are each 30 × 30 × 10 and that the hole is Ø9. Assemble the three blocks so that their holes are aligned and they are held together by a hex head bold secured by an appropriate hex nut. Locate a washer between the bolt head and the top block and between the nut and the bottom block. Create all drawings using either an A4 or A3 drawing sheet, as needed. Include a title block on all drawing sheets.

A. Define the bolt.
B. Define the nut.
C. Define the washers.
D. Draw an assembly drawing including all components.
E. Create a BOM for the assembly.

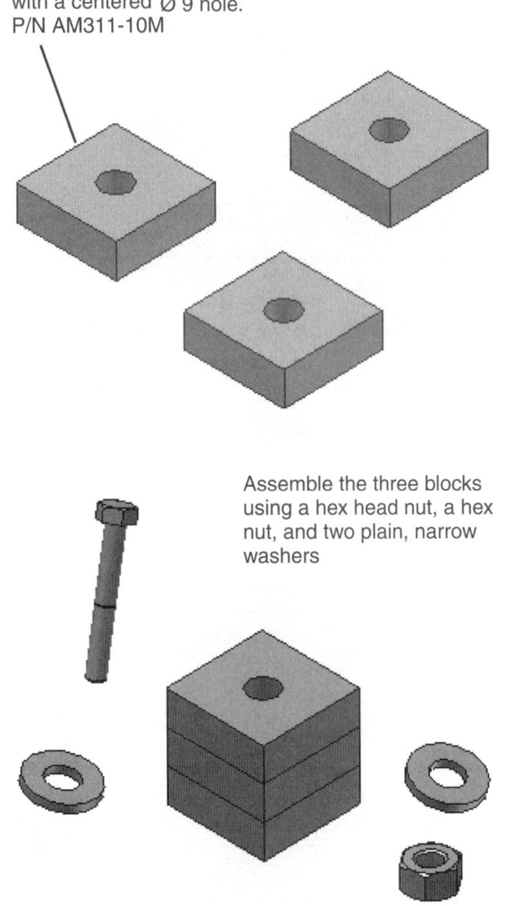
Three blocks, each 30 x 30 x 30
with a centered Ø 9 hole.
P/N AM311-10M
Assemble the three blocks
using a hex head nut, a hex
nut, and two plain, narrow
washers

Figure P6-1

F. Create an isometric exploded drawing of the assembly.
G. Create an animation drawing of the assembly.

Project 6-2: Millimeters

Figure P6-2 shows three blocks, One 30 × 30 × 50 with a centered M8 threaded hole, and two 30 × 30 × 10 blocks with centered Ø9 holes. Join the two 30 × 30 × 10 blocks to the 30 × 30 × 50 block using an M8 hex head bolt. Locate a regular plain washer under the bolt head.

A. Define the bolt.
B. Define the thread depth.
C. Define the hole depth.
D. Define the washers.
E. Draw an assembly drawing including all components.
F. Create a BOM for the assembly.
G. Create an isometric exploded drawing of the assembly.
H. Create an animation drawing of the assembly.

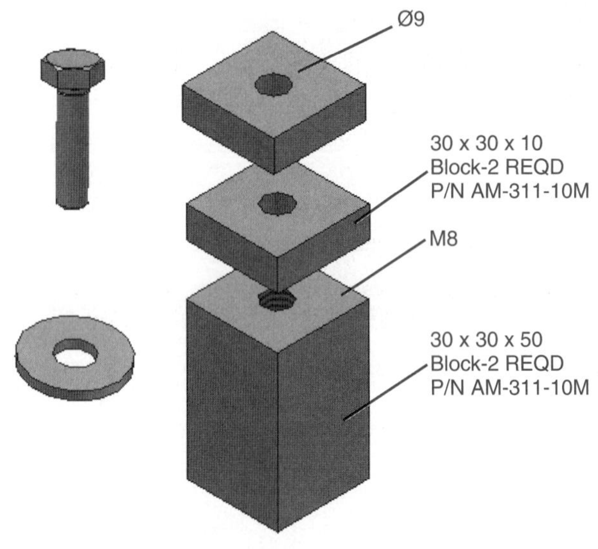
Ø9
30 x 30 x 10
Block-2 REQD
P/N AM-311-10M
M8
30 x 30 x 50
Block-2 REQD
P/N AM-311-10M

Figure P6-2

Project 6-3: Inches

Figure P6-3 shows three blocks. Assume that each block is 1.00 × 1.00 × 0.375 and that the hole is Ø.375. Assemble the three blocks so that their holes are aligned and that they are held together by a 5/16-18 UNC indented regular hex head bolt secured by an appropriate hex nut. Locate a washer between the bolt head and the top block and between

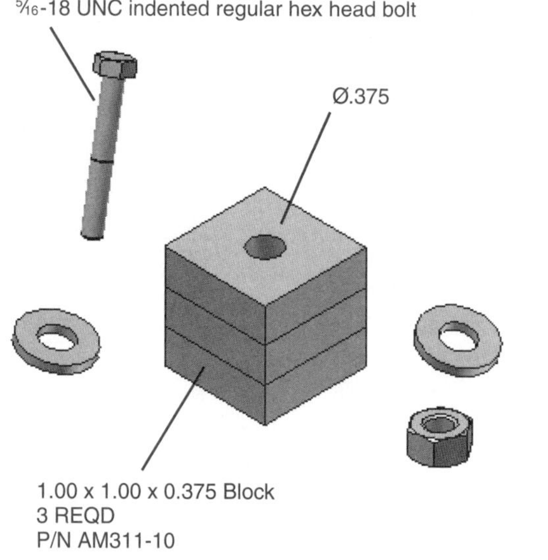

Figure P6-3

the nut and the bottom block. Create all drawings using either an A4 or A3 drawing sheet, as needed. Include a title block on all drawing sheets.

A. Define the bolt.
B. Define the nut.
C. Define the washers.
D. Draw an assembly drawing including all components.
E. Create a BOM for the assembly.
F. Create an isometric exploded drawing of the assembly.
G. Create an animation drawing of the assembly.

Project 6-4: Inches

Figure P6-4 shows three blocks, one 1.00 × 1.00 × 2.00 with a centered threaded hole, and two 1.00 × 1.00 × .375 blocks with centered Ø.375 holes. Join the two 1.00 × 1.00 × .375 blocks to the 1.00 × 1.00 × 2.00 block using a 5/16-18 UNC hex head bolt. Locate a regular plain washer under the bolt head.

A. Define the bolt.
B. Define the thread depth.
C. Define the hole depth.
D. Define the washer.
E. Draw an assembly drawing including all components.
F. Create a BOM for the assembly.

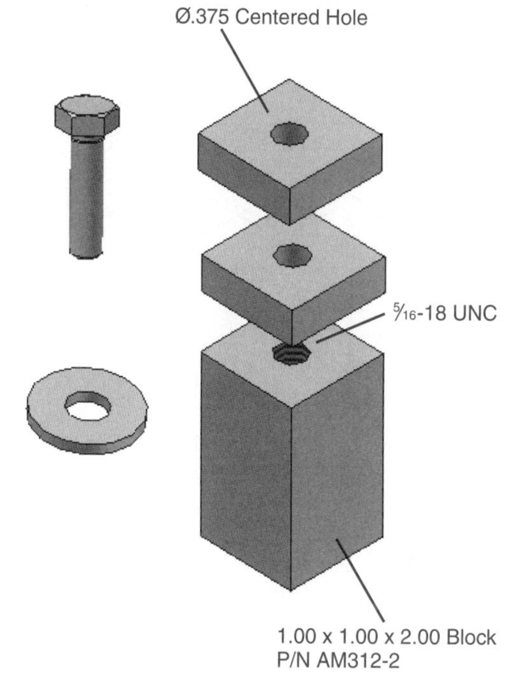

Figure P6-4

G. Create an isometric exploded drawing of the assembly.
H. Create an animation drawing of the assembly.

Project 6-5: Inches or Millimeters

Figure P6-5 shows a centering block. Create an assembly drawing of the block and insert three setscrews into the three threaded holes so that they extend at least .25 in. or 6 mm into the center hole.

A. Use the inch dimensions.
B. Use the millimeter dimensions.
C. Define the setscrews.
D. Draw an assembly drawing including all components.
E. Create a BOM for the assembly.
F. Create an isometric exploded drawing of the assembly.
G. Create an animation drawing of the assembly.

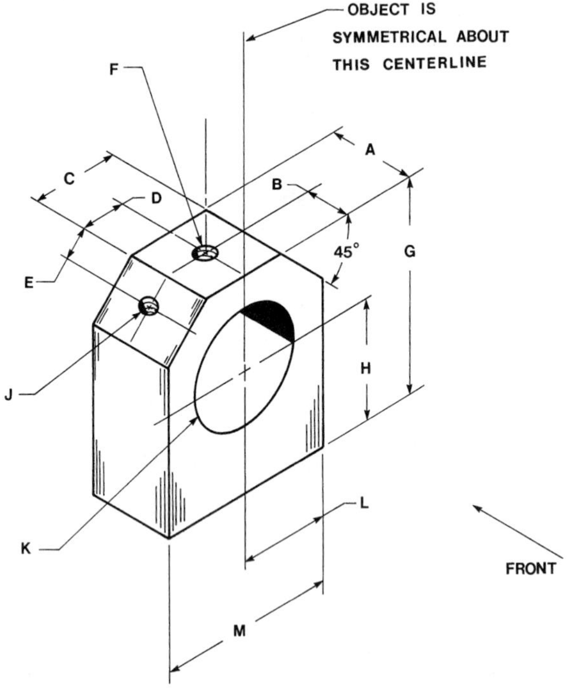

DIMENSION	INCHES	mm
A	1.00	26
B	.50	13
C	1.00	26
D	.50	13
E	.38	10
F	.190-32 UNF	M8X1
G	2.38	60
H	1.38	34
J	.164-36 UNF	M6
K	Ø1.25	Ø30
L	1.00	26
M	2.00	52

Figure P6-5

Project 6-6: Millimeters

Figure P6-6 shows two parts: a head cylinder and a base cylinder. The head cylinder has outside dimensions of Ø40 × 20, and the base cylinder has outside dimensions of Ø40 × 50. The holes in both parts are located on a Ø24 bolt circle. Assemble the two parts using hex head bolts.

A. Define the bolt.
B. Define the holes in the head cylinder, the counterbore diameter and depth, and the clearance hole diameter.
C. Define the thread depth in the base cylinder.
D. Define the hole depth in the base cylinder.
E. Draw an assembly drawing including all components.
F. Create a BOM for the assembly.
G. Create an isometric exploded drawing of the assembly.
H. Create an animation drawing of the assembly.

Project 6-7: Millimeters

Figure P6-7 shows a pressure cylinder assembly.

A. Draw an assembly drawing including all components.
B. Create a BOM for the assembly.
C. Create an isometric exploded drawing of the assembly.
D. Create an animation drawing of the assembly.

Project 6-8: Millimeters

Figure P6-7 shows a pressure cylinder assembly.

A. Revise the assembly so that it uses M10 × 35 hex head bolts.
B. Draw an assembly drawing including all components.
C. Create a BOM for the assembly.
D. Create an isometric exploded drawing of the assembly.
E. Create an animation drawing of the assembly.

Project 6-9: Inches and Millimeters

Figure P6-9 shows a C-block assembly.

Use one of the following fasteners assigned by your instructor.

1. M12 hex head
2. M10 square head
3. ¼-20 UNC hex head
4. ⅜-16 UNC square head

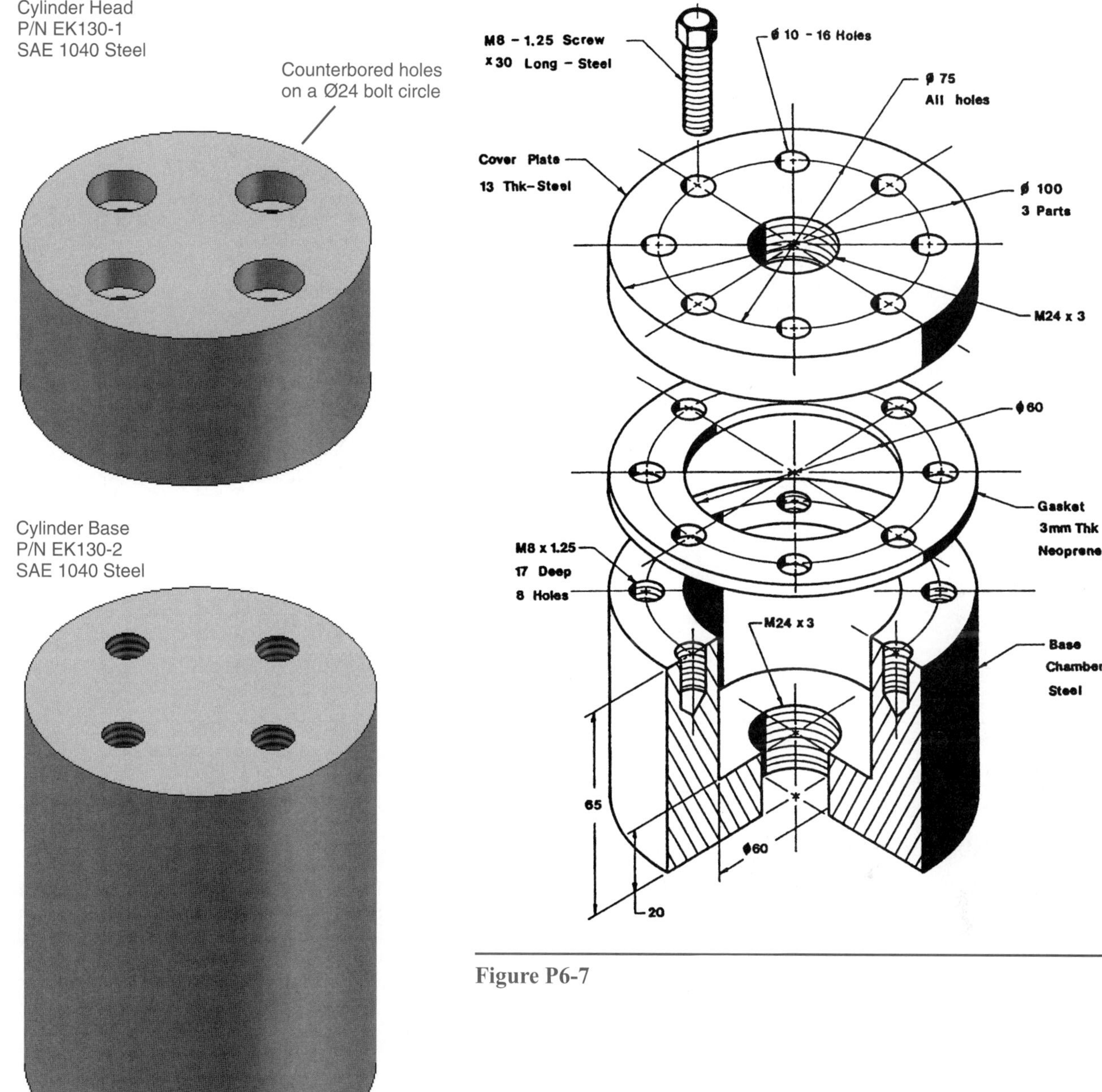

Figure P6-7

Figure P6-6

5. M10 socket head
6. M8 slotted head
7. ¼-20 UNC slotted head
8. ⅜-16 UNC socket head

A. Define the bolt.
B. Define the nut.
C. Define the washers.
D. Draw an assembly drawing including all components.
E. Create a BOM for the assembly.
F. Create an isometric exploded drawing of the assembly.
G. Create an animation drawing of the assembly.

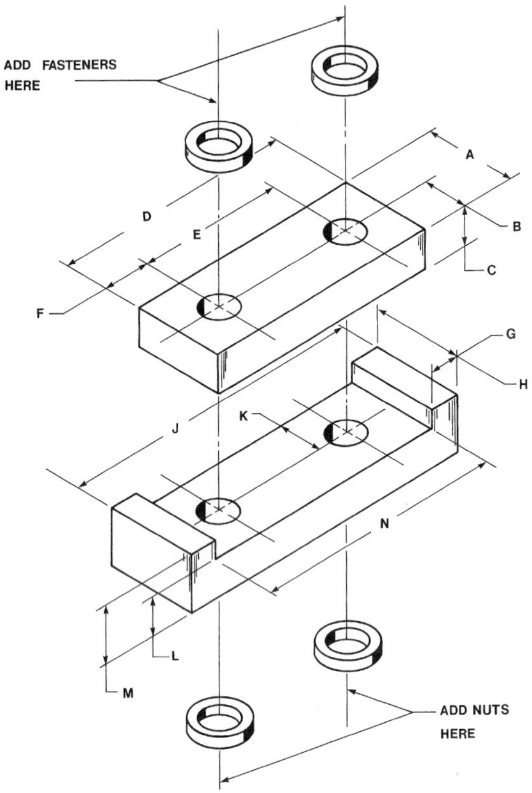

DIMENSION	INCHES	mm
A	1.25	32
B	.63	16
C	.50	13
D	3.25	82
E	2.00	50
F	.63	16
G	.38	10
H	1.25	32
J	4.13	106
K	.63	16
L	.50	13
M	.75	10
N	3.38	86

Figure P6-9

Project 6-10: Millimeters

Figure P6-10 shows an exploded assembly drawing. There are no standard parts, so each part must be drawn individually.

A. Draw an assembly drawing including all components.
B. Create a BOM for the assembly.
C. Create an isometric exploded drawing of the assembly.
D. Create an animation drawing of the assembly.

Project 6-11: Millimeters

Figure P6-11 shows an exploded assembly drawing.

A. Draw an assembly drawing including all components.
B. Create a BOM for the assembly.
C. Create an isometric exploded drawing of the assembly.
D. Create an animation drawing of the assembly.

Project 6-12: Inches or Millimeters

Figure P6-12 shows an exploded assembly drawing. No dimensions are given. If parts 3 and 5 have either M10 or ⅜-16 UNC threads, size parts 1 and 2. Based on these values estimate and create the remaining sizes and dimensions.

A. Draw an assembly drawing including all components.
B. Create a BOM for the assembly.
C. Create an isometric exploded drawing of the assembly.
D. Create an animation drawing of the assembly.

Project 6-13: Inches

Figure P6-13 shows an assembly drawing and detail drawings of a surface guage.

A. Draw an assembly drawing including all components.
B. Create a BOM for the assembly.
C. Create an isometric exploded drawing of the assembly.
D. Create an animation drawing of the assembly.

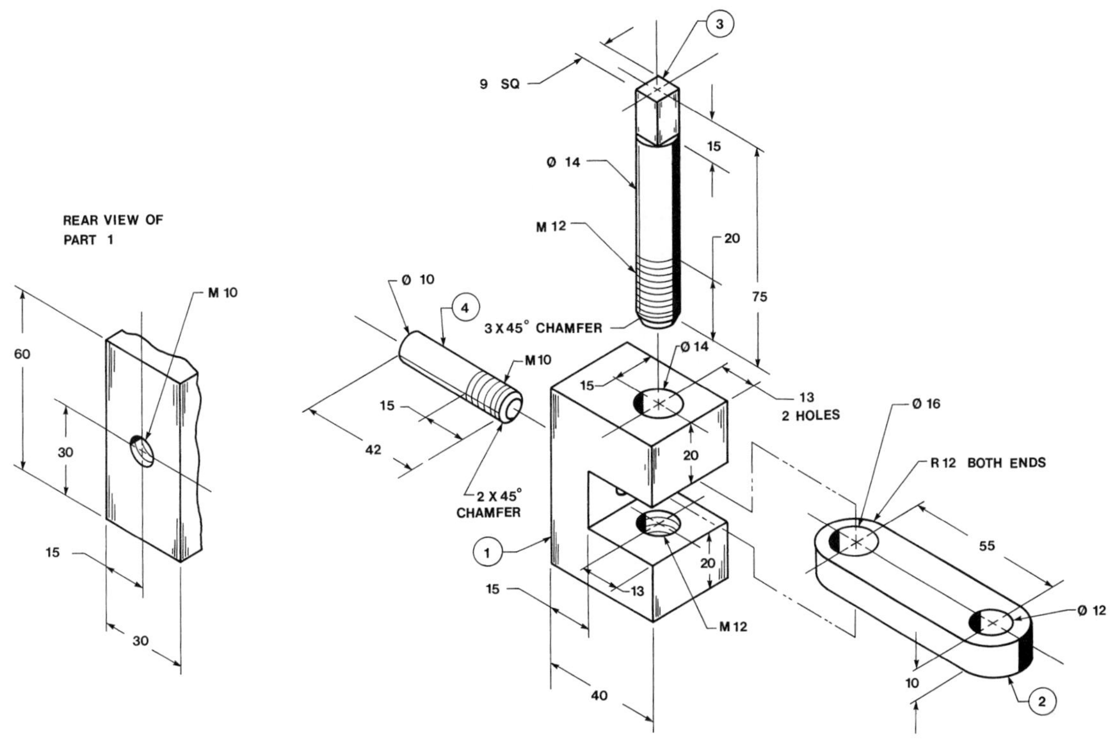

Figure P6-10

Project 6-14: Millimeters

Figure P6-14 shows an assembly made from parts defined on pages 000 through 000. Assemble the parts using M10 threaded fasteners.

A. Define the bolt.
B. Define the nut.
C. Draw an assembly drawing including all components.
D. Create a BOM for the assembly.
E. Create an isometric exploded drawing of the assembly.
F. Create an animation drawing of the assembly.
G. Consider possible interference between the nuts and ends of the fasteners both during and after assembly. Recommend and assembly sequence.

Project 6-15: Millimeters

Figure P6-15 shows an assembly made from parts defined on pages 000 through 000. Assemble the parts using M10 threaded fasteners.

A. Define the bolt.
B. Define the nut.
C. Draw an assembly drawing including all components.
D. Create a BOM for the assembly.
E. Create an isometric exploded drawing of the assembly.
F. Create an animation drawing of the assembly.
G. Consider possible interference between the nuts and ends of the fasteners both during and after assembly. Recommend and assembly sequence.

Project 6-16: Millimeters

Figure P6-16 shows an assembly made from parts defined on pages 000 through 000. Assemble the parts using M10 threaded fasteners.

A. Define the bolt.
B. Define the nut.
C. Draw an assembly drawing including all components.
D. Create a BOM for the assembly.
E. Create an isometric exploded drawing of the assembly.
F. Create an animation drawing of the assembly.

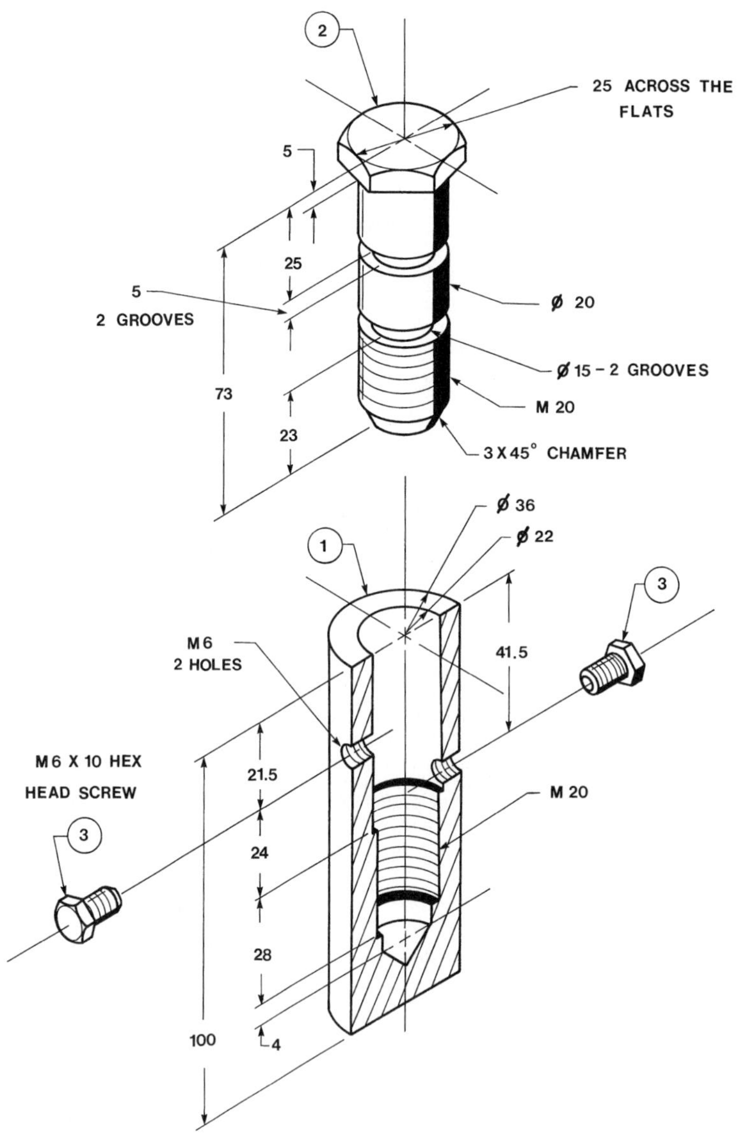

Figure P6-11

G. Consider possible interference between the nuts and ends of the fasteners both during and after assembly. Recommend and assembly sequence.

Project 6-17: Access Controller

Design an access controller based on the information given in Figure P6-17. The controller works by moving an internal cylinder up and down within the base so the cylinder aligns with output holes A and B. Liquids will enter the internal cylinder from the tip, then exit the base through holes A and B. Include as many holes in the internal cylinder as necessary to create the following liquid-exit combinations.

1. A open, B closed
2. A open, B open
3. A closed, B open

The internal cylinder is to be held in place by an alignment key and a stop button. The stop button is to be spring-loaded so that it will always be held in place. The internal cylinder will be moved by pulling out the stop button, repositioning the cylinder, then reinserting the stop button.

Prepare the following drawings.

A. Draw an assembly drawing.
B. Draw detail drawings of each nonstandard part. Include positional tolerances for all holes.
C. Prepare a BOM.

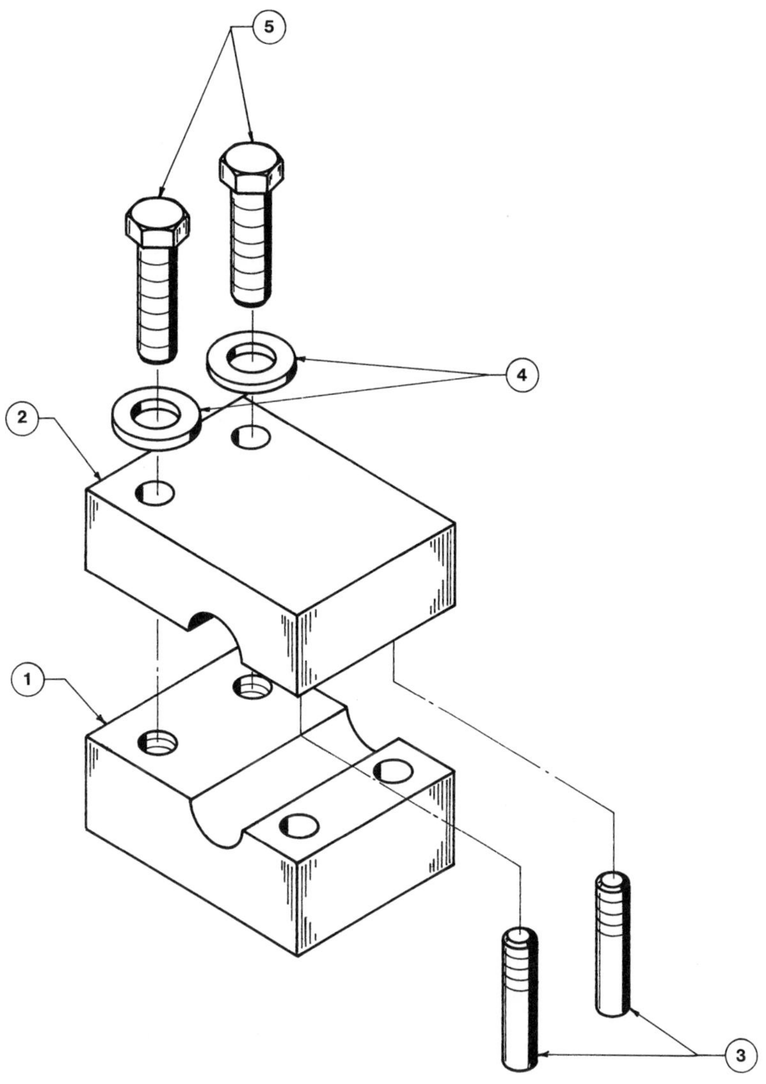

Figure P6-12

Project 6-18: Grinding Wheel

Design a hand-operated grinding wheel as shown in Figure P6-18 specifically for sharpening a chisel. The chisel is to be located on an adjustable rest while it is being sharpened. The mechanism should be able to be clamped to a table during operation using two thumbscrews. A standard grinding wheel is 6.00 in. and ½ in. thick, and has an internal mounting hole with a 50.00±.03 bore.

Prepare the following drawings.

A. Draw an assembly drawings.
B. Draw detail drawings of each nonstandard part. Include positional tolerance for all holes.
C. Prepare a BOM.

Project 6-19: Millimeters

Given the assembly shown in Figure P6-19 on page 000, add the following fasteners.

1. Create an assembly drawings.
2. Create a parts list including assembly numbers.
3. Create a dimensioned drawing of the support block and specify a dimension for each hole including the thread size and the depth required.

Fasteners:

A.

1. M10 × 35 HEX HEAD BOLT
2. M10 × 35 HEX HEAD BOLT
3. M10 × 30 HEX HEAD BOLT
4. M10 × 25 HEX HEAD BOLT

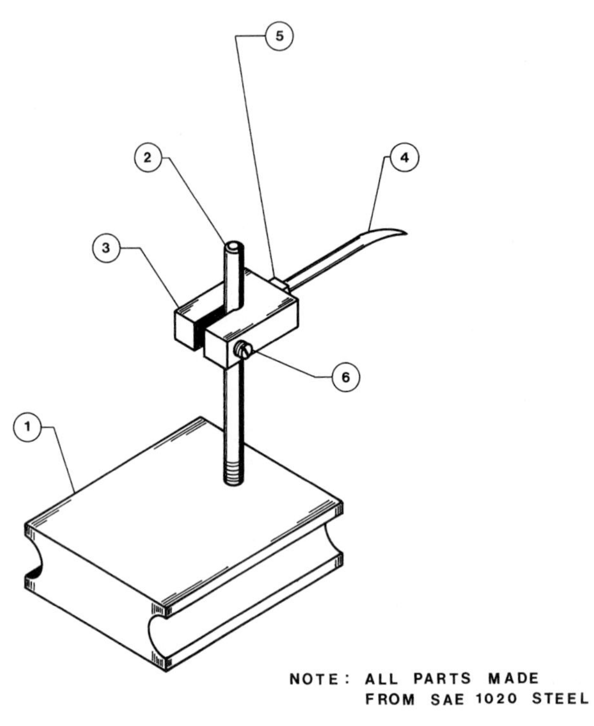
SIMPLIFIED SURFACE GAGE
5
2
4
3
6
1
NOTE: ALL PARTS MADE
FROM SAE 1020 STEEL

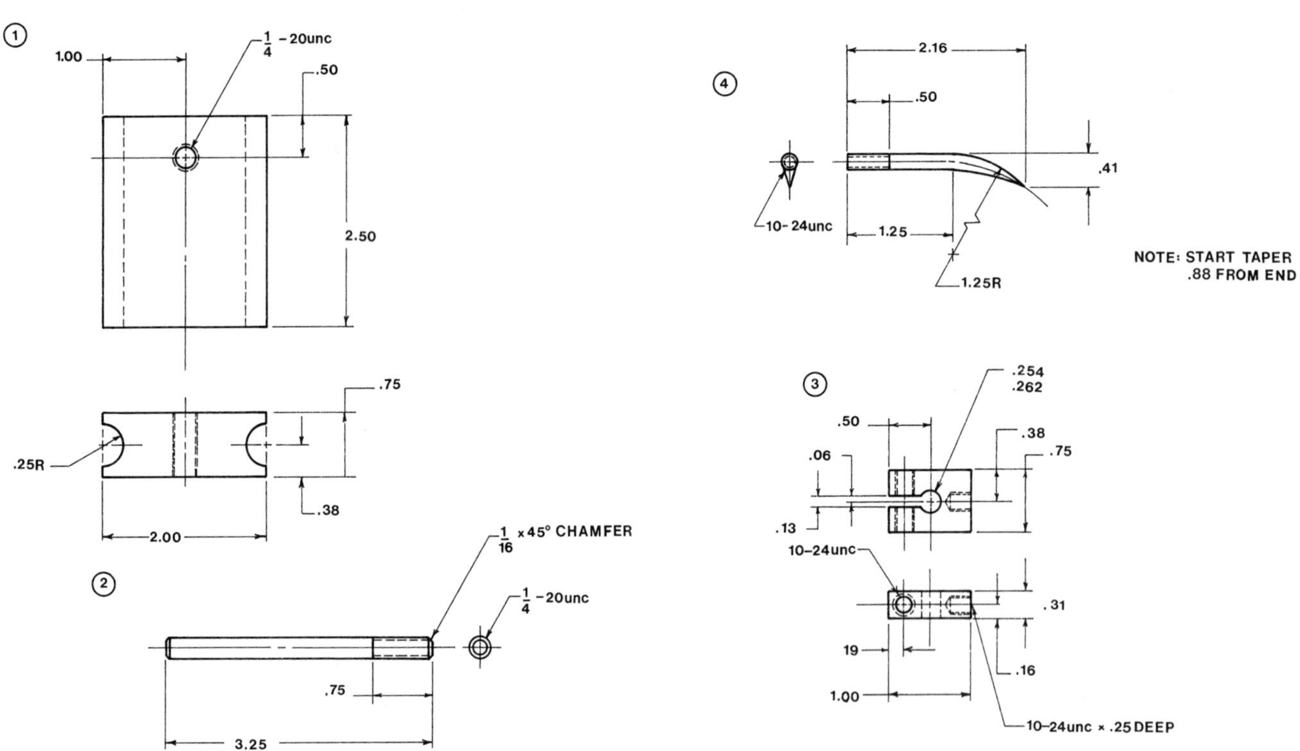
1
1.00
1/4 -20unc
.50
2.50
.75
.25R
.38
2.00
4
2.16
.50
.41
10-24unc
1.25
1.25R
NOTE: START TAPER
.88 FROM END
3
.254
.262
.50
.38
.06
.75
.13
10-24unc
.31
19
.16
1.00
10-24unc × .25 DEEP
2
1/16 ×45° CHAMFER
1/4 -20unc
.75
3.25

Figure P6-13

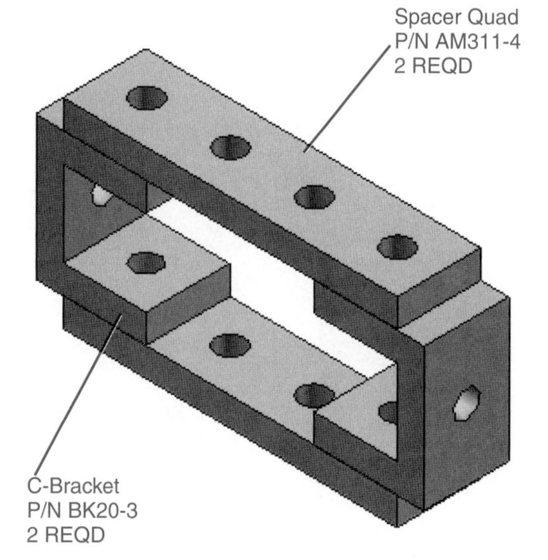

Figure P6-14

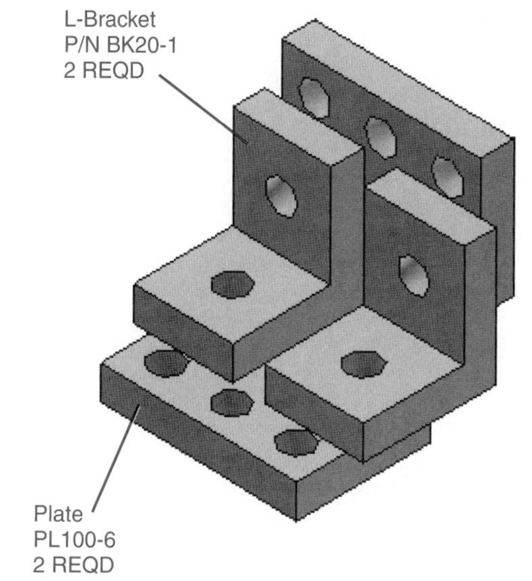

Figure P6-15

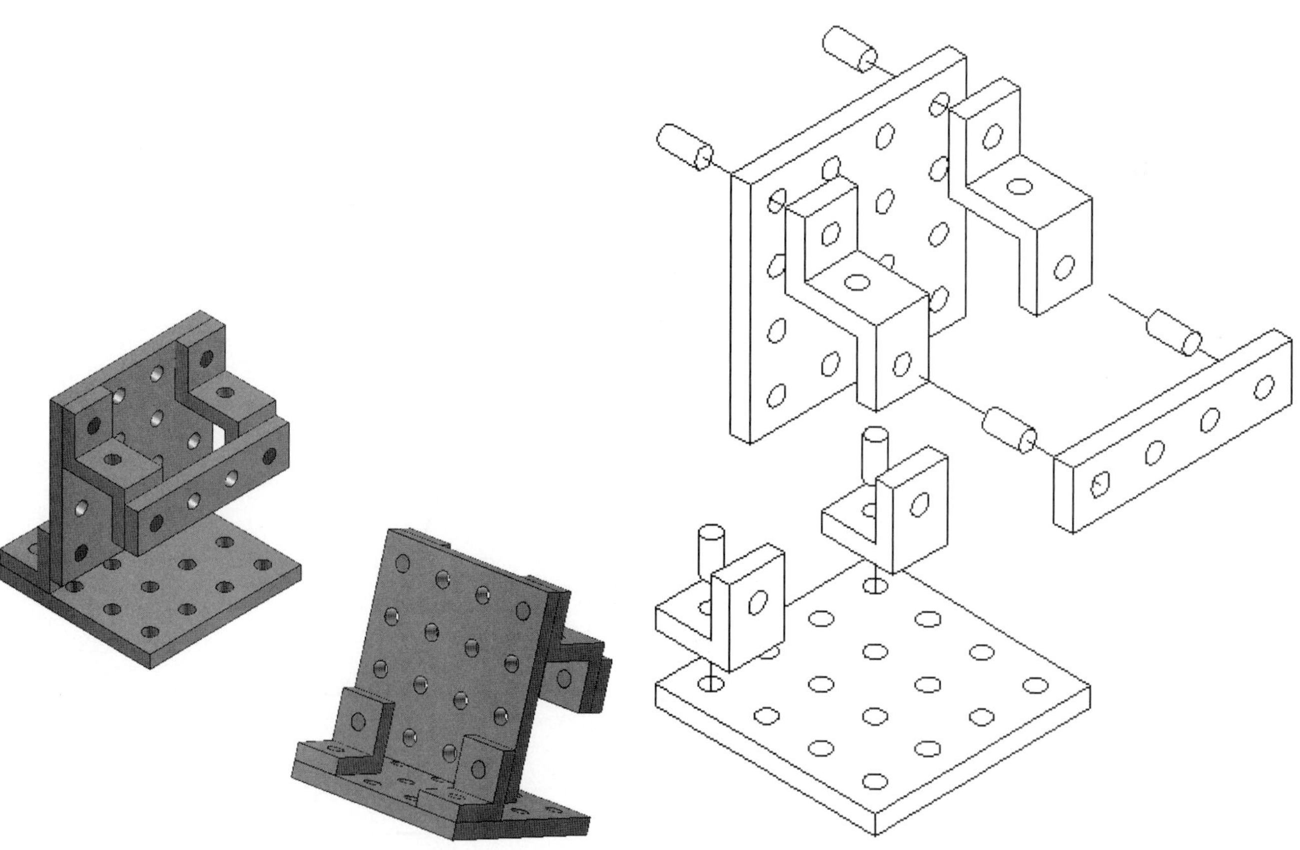

Figure P6-16

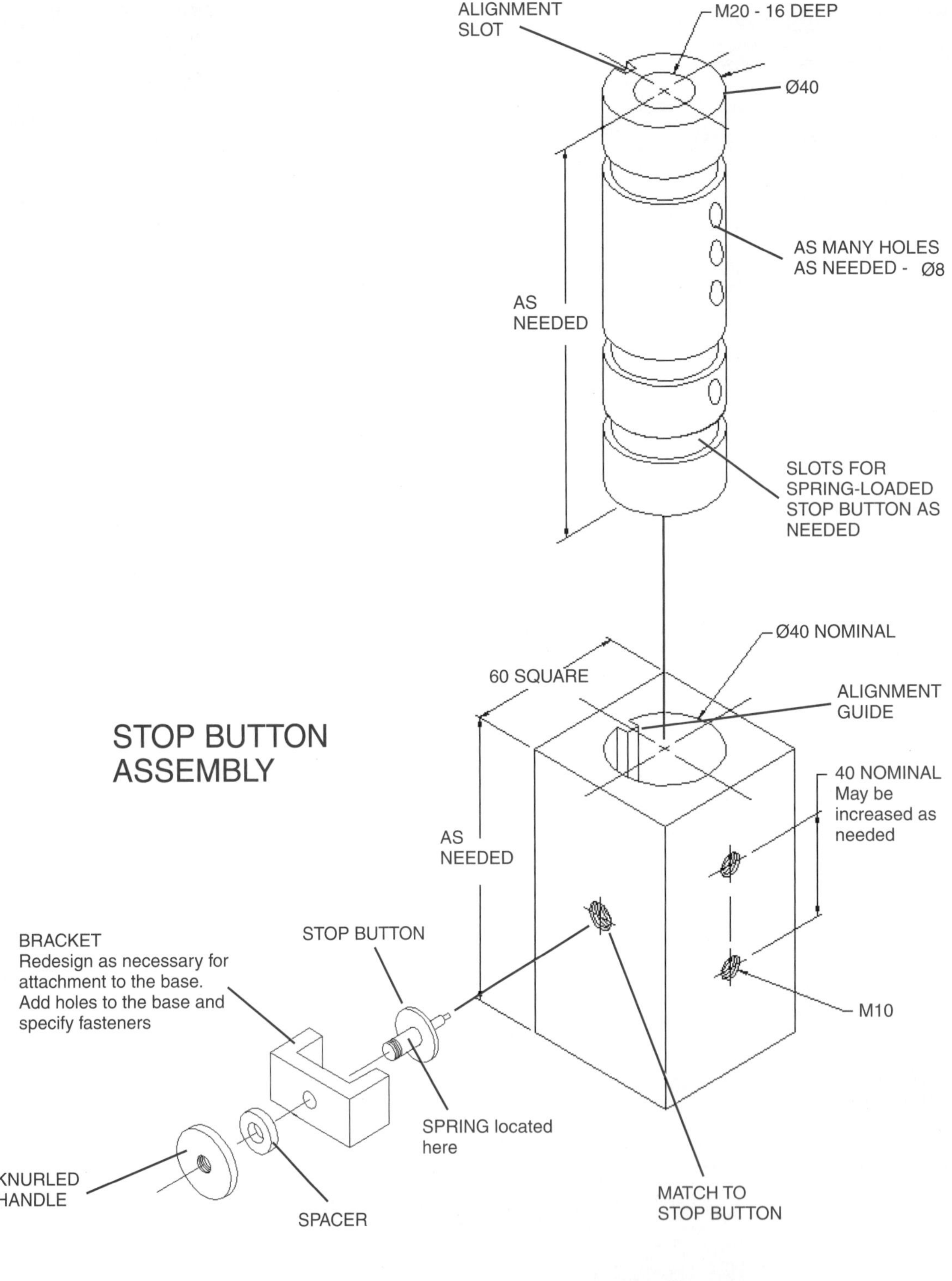
INTERNAL CYLINDER
ALIGNMENT SLOT
M20 - 16 DEEP
Ø40
AS MANY HOLES AS NEEDED - Ø8
AS NEEDED
SLOTS FOR SPRING-LOADED STOP BUTTON AS NEEDED
Ø40 NOMINAL
60 SQUARE
ALIGNMENT GUIDE
STOP BUTTON ASSEMBLY
40 NOMINAL May be increased as needed
AS NEEDED
BRACKET Redesign as necessary for attachment to the base. Add holes to the base and specify fasteners
STOP BUTTON
M10
SPRING located here
KNURLED HANDLE
SPACER
MATCH TO STOP BUTTON
BASE

Figure P6-17

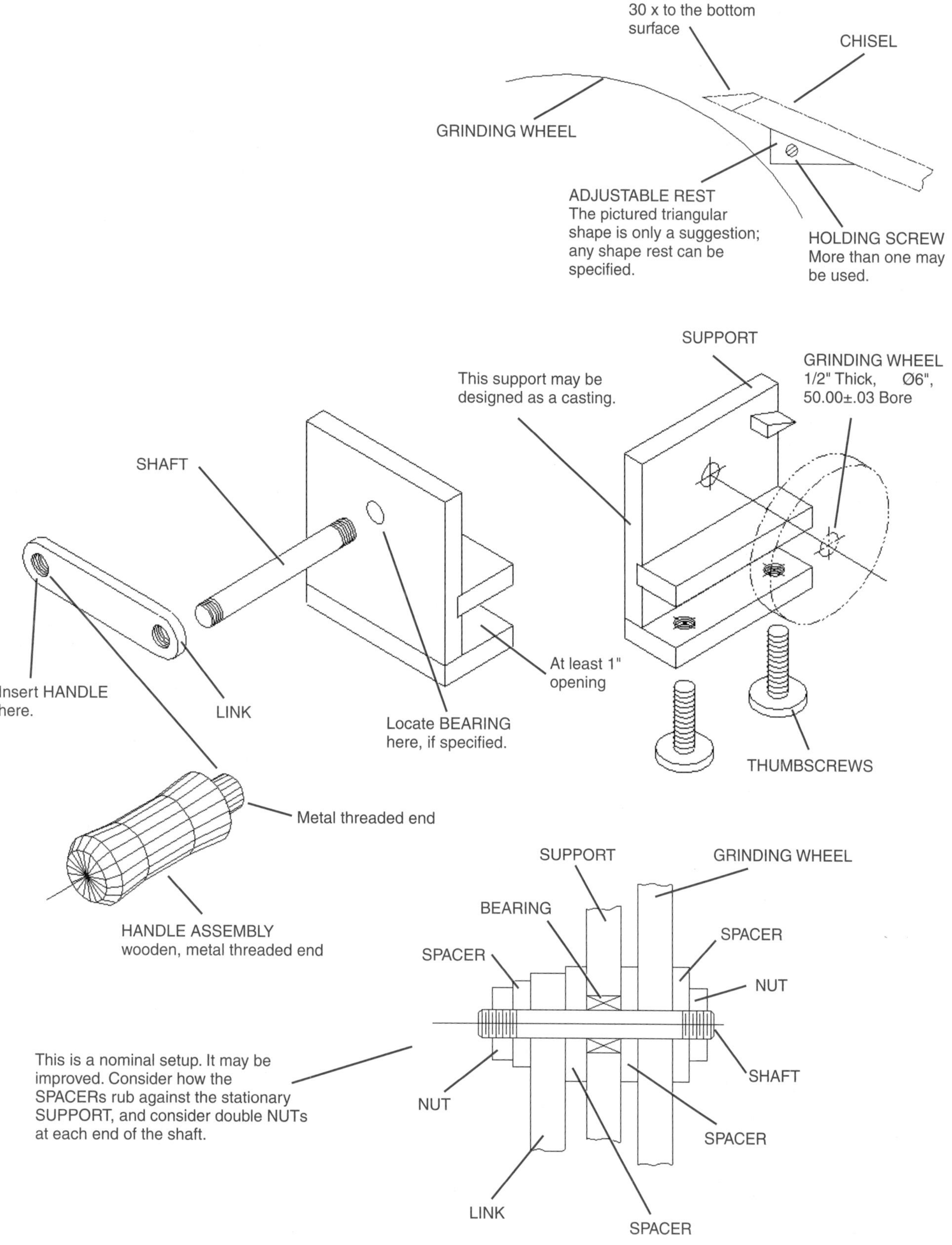
30 x to the bottom
surface
CHISEL
GRINDING WHEEL
ADJUSTABLE REST
The pictured triangular
shape is only a suggestion;
any shape rest can be
specified.
HOLDING SCREW
More than one may
be used.
SUPPORT
GRINDING WHEEL
1/2" Thick, Ø6",
50.00±.03 Bore
This support may be
designed as a casting.
SHAFT
Insert HANDLE
here.
LINK
Locate BEARING
here, if specified.
At least 1"
opening
THUMBSCREWS
Metal threaded end
HANDLE ASSEMBLY
wooden, metal threaded end
SUPPORT
GRINDING WHEEL
BEARING
SPACER
SPACER
NUT
This is a nominal setup. It may be
improved. Consider how the
SPACERs rub against the stationary
SUPPORT, and consider double NUTs
at each end of the shaft.
NUT
SHAFT
SPACER
LINK
SPACER

Figure P6-18

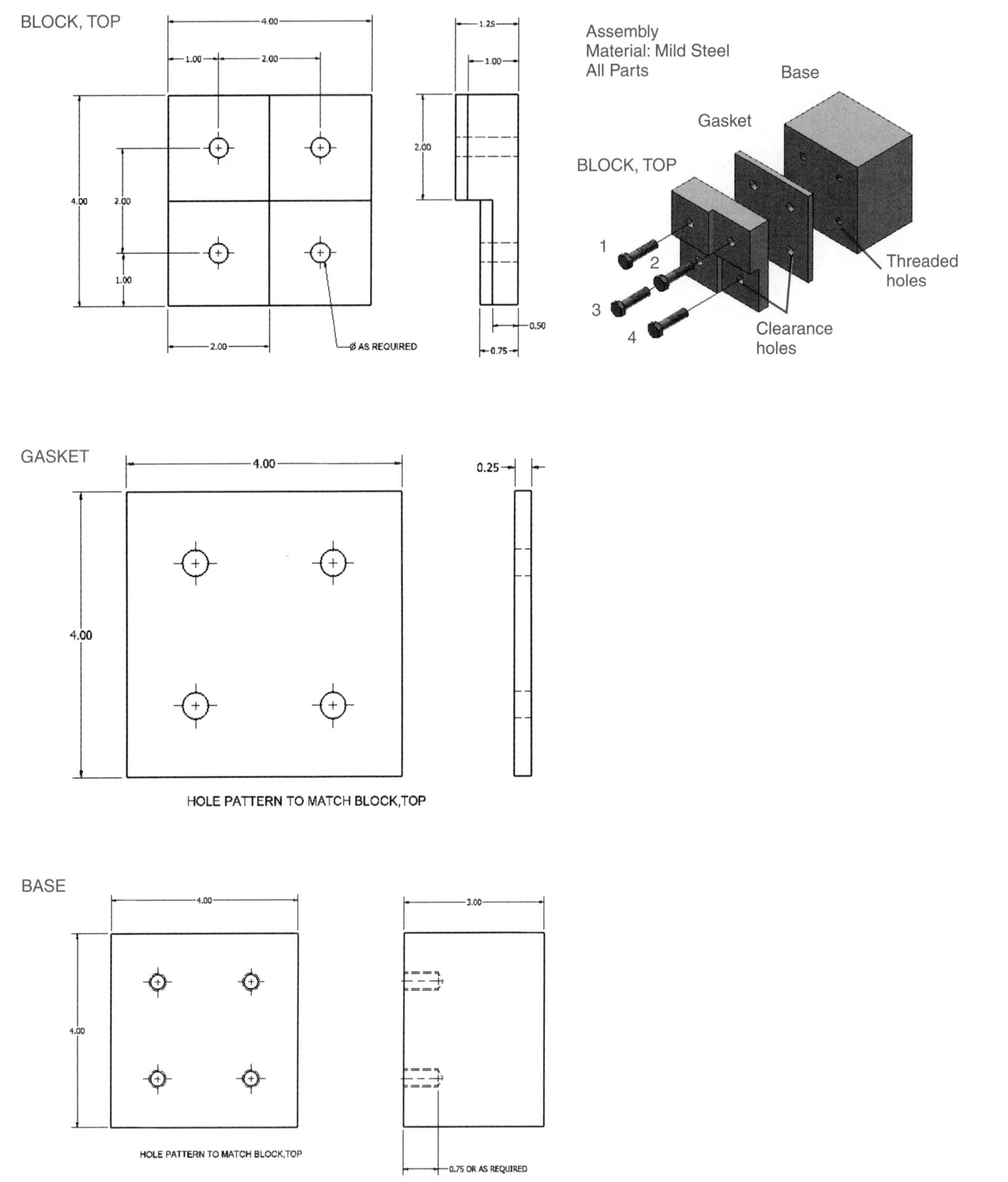
BLOCK, TOP
4.00
1.00
2.00
1.25
1.00
2.00
4.00
2.00
1.00
0.50
2.00
Ø AS REQUIRED
0.75
Assembly
Material: Mild Steel
All Parts
Base
Gasket
BLOCK, TOP
1
2
3
4
Threaded
holes
Clearance
holes
GASKET
4.00
0.25
4.00
HOLE PATTERN TO MATCH BLOCK,TOP
BASE
4.00
3.00
4.00
HOLE PATTERN TO MATCH BLOCK,TOP
0.75 OR AS REQUIRED

Figure P6-19

B.

1. M10 × 1.5 × 35 HEX HEAD BOLT
2. M8 × 35 ROUND HEAD BOLT
3. M10 × 30 HEXAGON SOCKET HEAD CAP SCREW
4. M6 × 30 SQUARE BOLT

Project 6-20: Inches

1. Create an assembly drawing.
2. Create a BOM including assembly numbers.
3. Create a dimensioned drawing of the base and specify a dimension for each hole including the thread size and the depth required.

Fasteners:

A.

1. 3/8-16 UNC × 2.50 HEX HEAD BOLT
2. 1/4-20 UNC × 2.00 HEX HEAD BOLT
3. 7/16-14 UNC × 1.75 HEX HEAD BOLT
4. 5/16-18 UNC × 2.25 HEX HEAD BOLT

B.

1. 1/4-28 UNF × 2.00 HEX HEAD BOLT
2. #8.(.164)-32 UNC × 2.00 HEX HEAD BOLT
3. 3/8-16 UNC × 1.75 PAN HEAD MACHINE BOLT
4. 5/16-18 UNC × 1.75 HEXAGON SOCKET HEAD CAP BOLT

Project 6-21: Millimeters

Given the collar shown in Figure P6-21, add the following set screws.

1. Create an assembly drawing.
2. Create a BOM.
3. Create a dimensioned drawing of the collar. Specify a thread specification for each hole as required by the designated set screw.

A.

1. M4 × 6 ANSI B18.3.5M SOCKET SET SCREW - HALF DOG POINT
2. M3 × 3 SOCKET SET SCREW - OVAL POINT
3. M2.5 × 4 B18.3.6M SOCKET SET SCREW - FLAT POINT
4. M4 × 5 B18.3.1M SOCKET HEAD CAP SCREW

B.

1. M2 × 4 B18.3.4M SOCKET BUTTON HEAD CAP SCREW
2. M3 × 6 B18.3.6M SOCKET SET SCREW - CONE POINT
3. M4 × 5 B18.3.6M SOCKET SET SCREW - FLAT POINT
4. M1.6 × 4 B18.3.6M SOCKET SET SCREW - CUP POINT

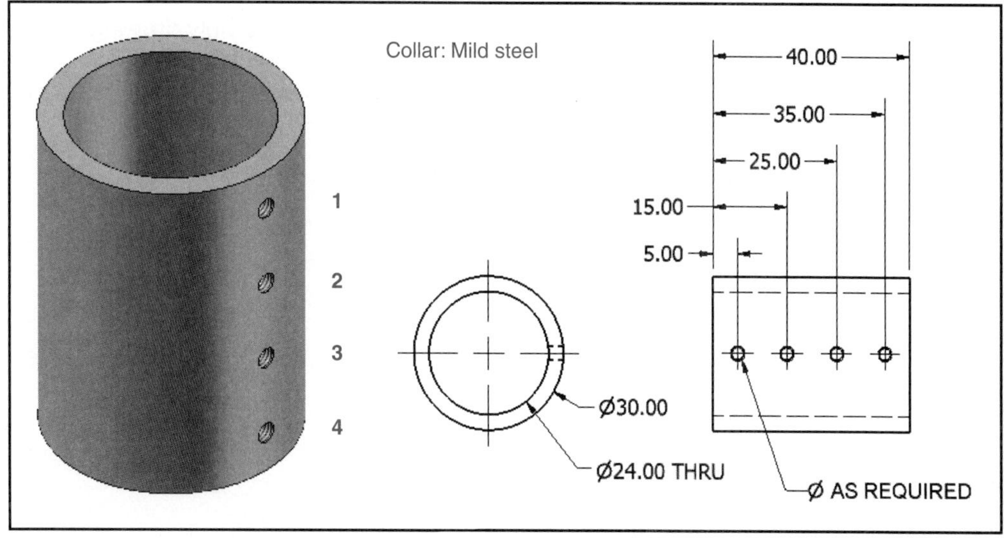

Figure P6-21

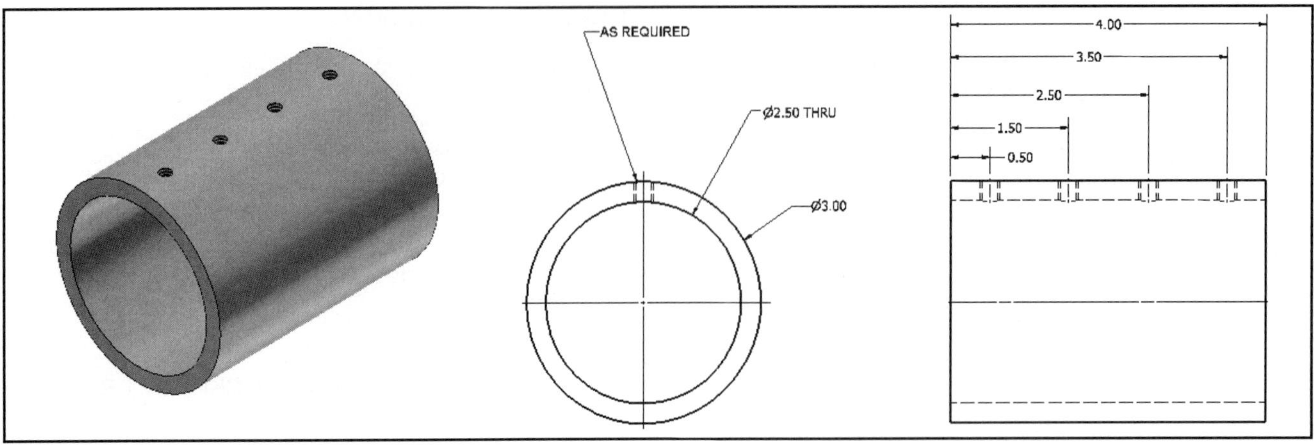

Figure P6-22

Project 6-22: Inches

Given the collar shown in Figure P6-22, add the following set screws.

1. Create an assembly drawing.
2. Create a BOM.
3. Create a dimensioned drawing of the collar. Specify a thread specification for each hole as required by the designated set screw.

Holes:

A.

1. #10 (0.190) × .375 SQUARE HEAD SET SCREW - HALF DOG POINT-INCH
2. #6 (0.138) × .125 SLOTTED HEADLESS SET SCREW-FLAT POINT-INCH
3. #8 (0.164) × 3.75 SOCKET SET SCREW-CUP POINT-INCH
4. #5 (0.126) × .45 HEXAGON SOCKET SET SCREW-CONE POINT-INCH

B.

1. #6 (0.138) × .25 TYPE D-SOCKET SET SCREW-CUP POINT-INCH
2. #8 (0.164) × .1875 SLOTTED HEADLESS SET SCREW-DOG POINT-INCH
3. #10 (0.190) × .58 HEXAGON SOCKET SET SCREW-FLAT POINT-INCH
4. #6 (0.138) × .3125 SOCKET SET SCREW-HALF-DOG POINT-INCH

Project 6-23: Millimeters

Given the components shown in Figure P6-23:

1. Create an assembly drawing.
2. Animate the drawing.
3. Create an exploded isometric drawing.
4. Create a BOM.

Project 6-24: Inches

Given the assembly drawing shown in Figure P6-24:

1. Create an assembly drawing.
2. Animiate the drawing.
3. Create an exploded isometric drawing.
4. Create a BOM.

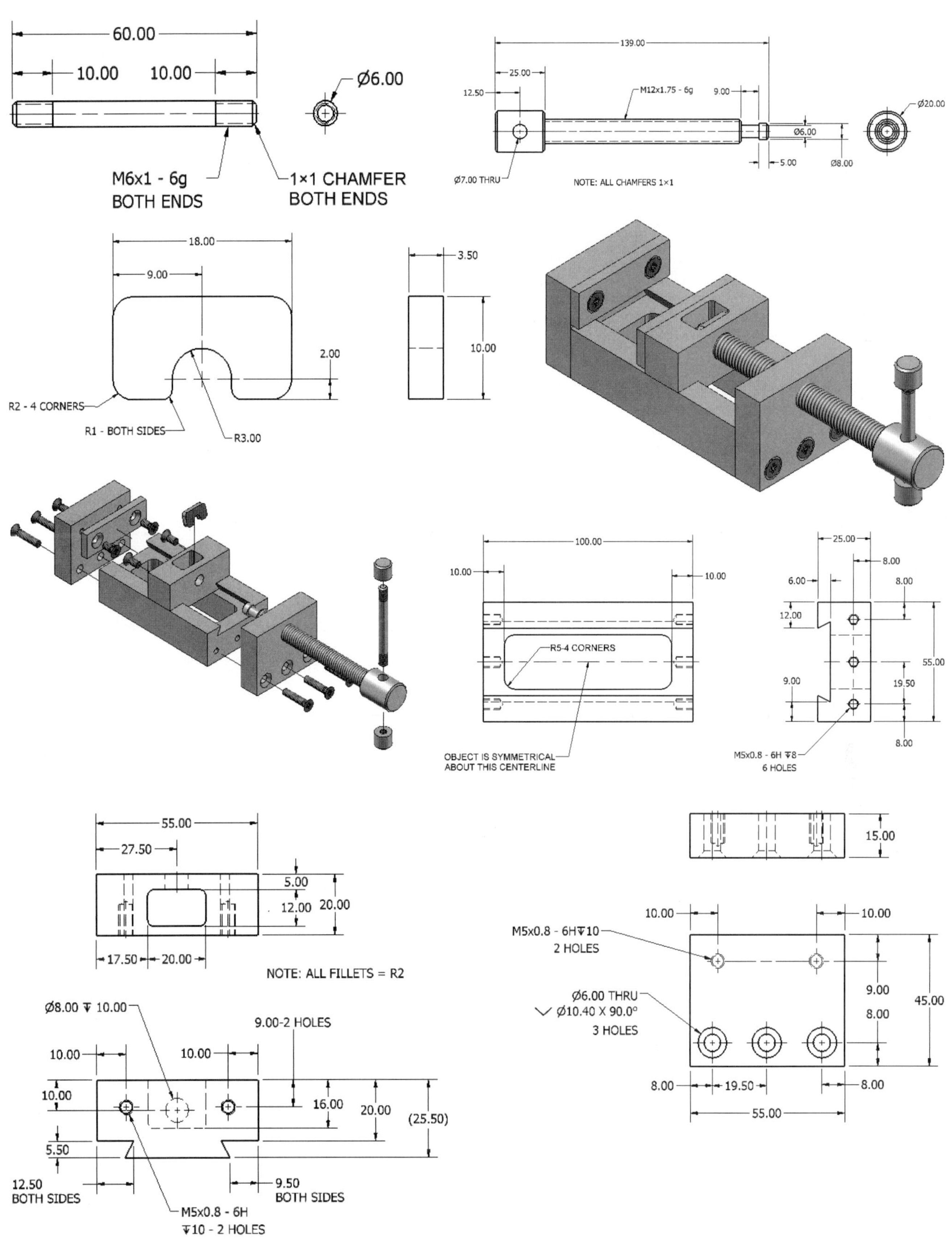
60.00
10.00
10.00
Ø6.00
M6x1 - 6g
BOTH ENDS
1×1 CHAMFER
BOTH ENDS
139.00
25.00
12.50
M12x1.75 - 6g
9.00
Ø20.00
Ø6.00
Ø7.00 THRU
5.00
Ø8.00
NOTE: ALL CHAMFERS 1×1
18.00
9.00
2.00
R2 - 4 CORNERS
R1 - BOTH SIDES
R3.00
3.50
10.00
100.00
10.00
10.00
R5-4 CORNERS
OBJECT IS SYMMETRICAL
ABOUT THIS CENTERLINE
25.00
8.00
6.00
8.00
12.00
55.00
9.00
19.50
8.00
M5x0.8 - 6H ↧8
6 HOLES
55.00
27.50
5.00
12.00
20.00
17.50
20.00
NOTE: ALL FILLETS = R2
15.00
10.00
10.00
M5x0.8 - 6H↧10
2 HOLES
Ø6.00 THRU
⌵ Ø10.40 X 90.0°
3 HOLES
9.00
8.00
45.00
8.00
19.50
8.00
55.00
Ø8.00 ↧ 10.00
9.00-2 HOLES
10.00
10.00
10.00
16.00
20.00
(25.50)
5.50
12.50
BOTH SIDES
9.50
BOTH SIDES
M5x0.8 - 6H
↧10 - 2 HOLES

Figure P6-23

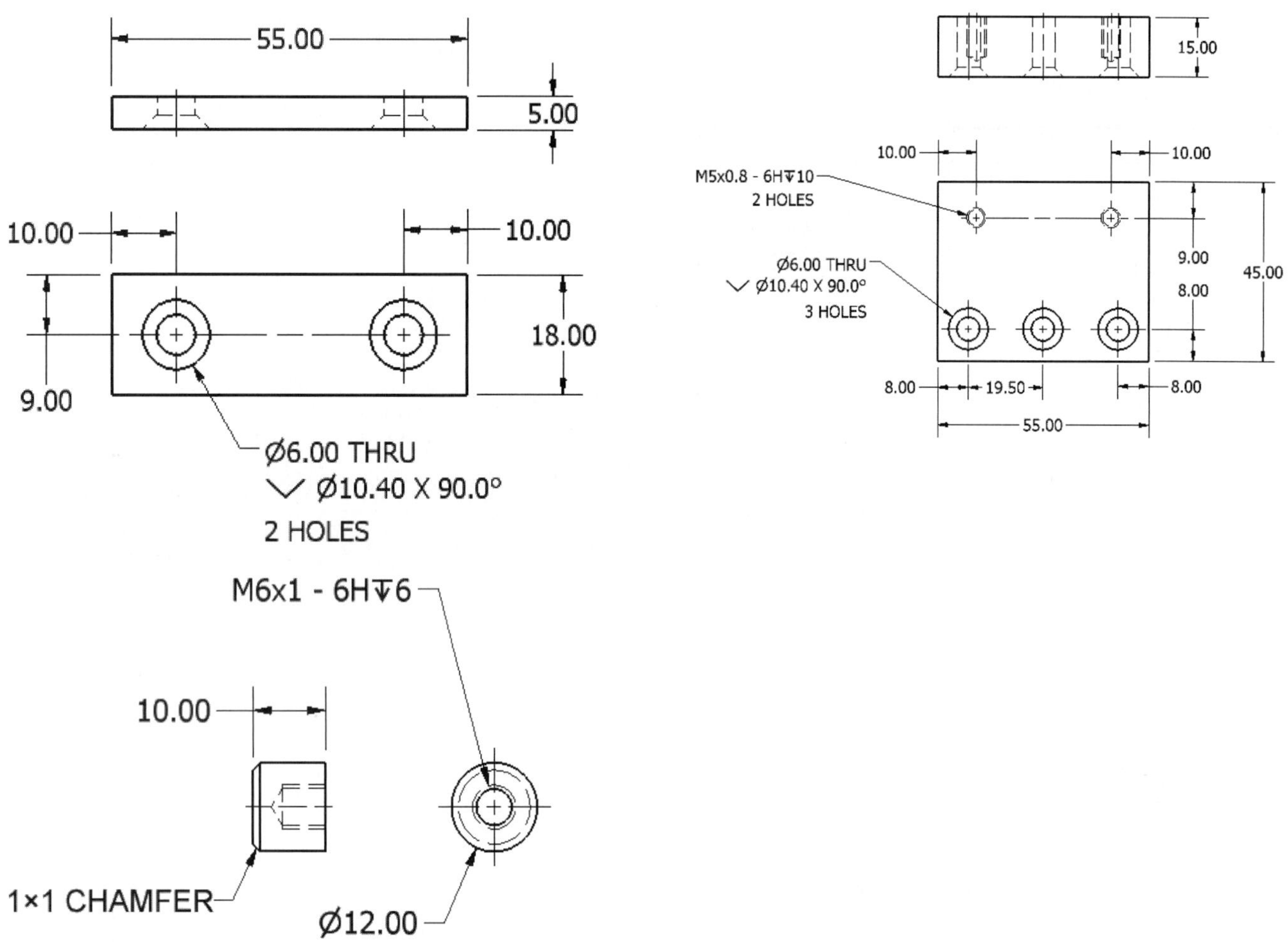

Figure P6-23 *(continued)*

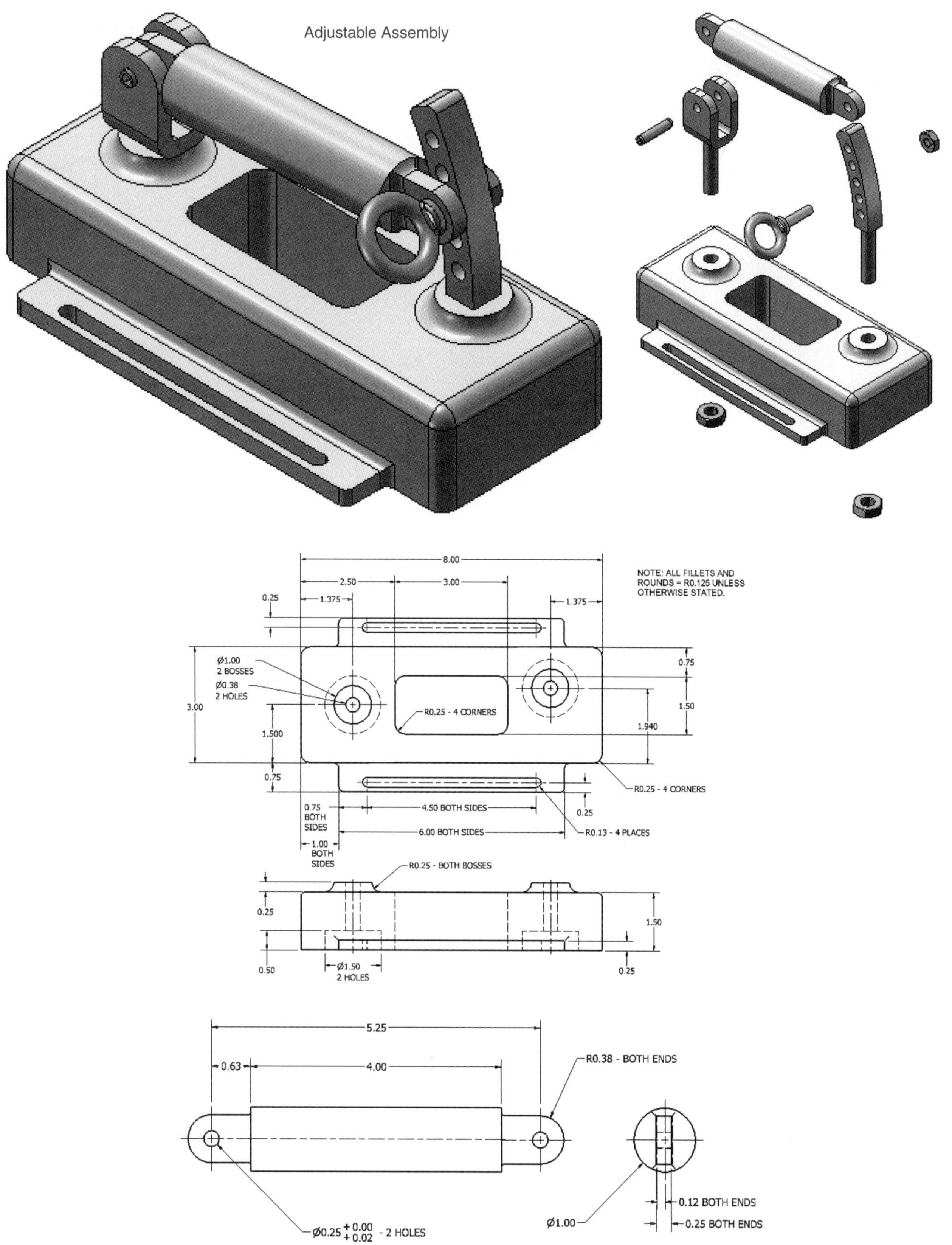
Adjustable Assembly
8.00
2.50
3.00
0.25
1.375
1.375
NOTE: ALL FILLETS AND ROUNDS = R0.125 UNLESS OTHERWISE STATED.
Ø1.00
2 BOSSES
Ø0.38
2 HOLES
3.00
1.500
0.75
R0.25 - 4 CORNERS
0.75
1.50
1.940
R0.25 - 4 CORNERS
0.75 BOTH SIDES
4.50 BOTH SIDES
0.25
6.00 BOTH SIDES
R0.13 - 4 PLACES
1.00 BOTH SIDES
R0.25 - BOTH BOSSES
0.25
1.50
0.50
Ø1.50
2 HOLES
0.25
5.25
0.63
4.00
R0.38 - BOTH ENDS
Ø0.25 +0.00 +0.02 - 2 HOLES
Ø1.00
0.12 BOTH ENDS
0.25 BOTH ENDS
NOTE: ALL FILLETS = R 0.125

Figure P6-24

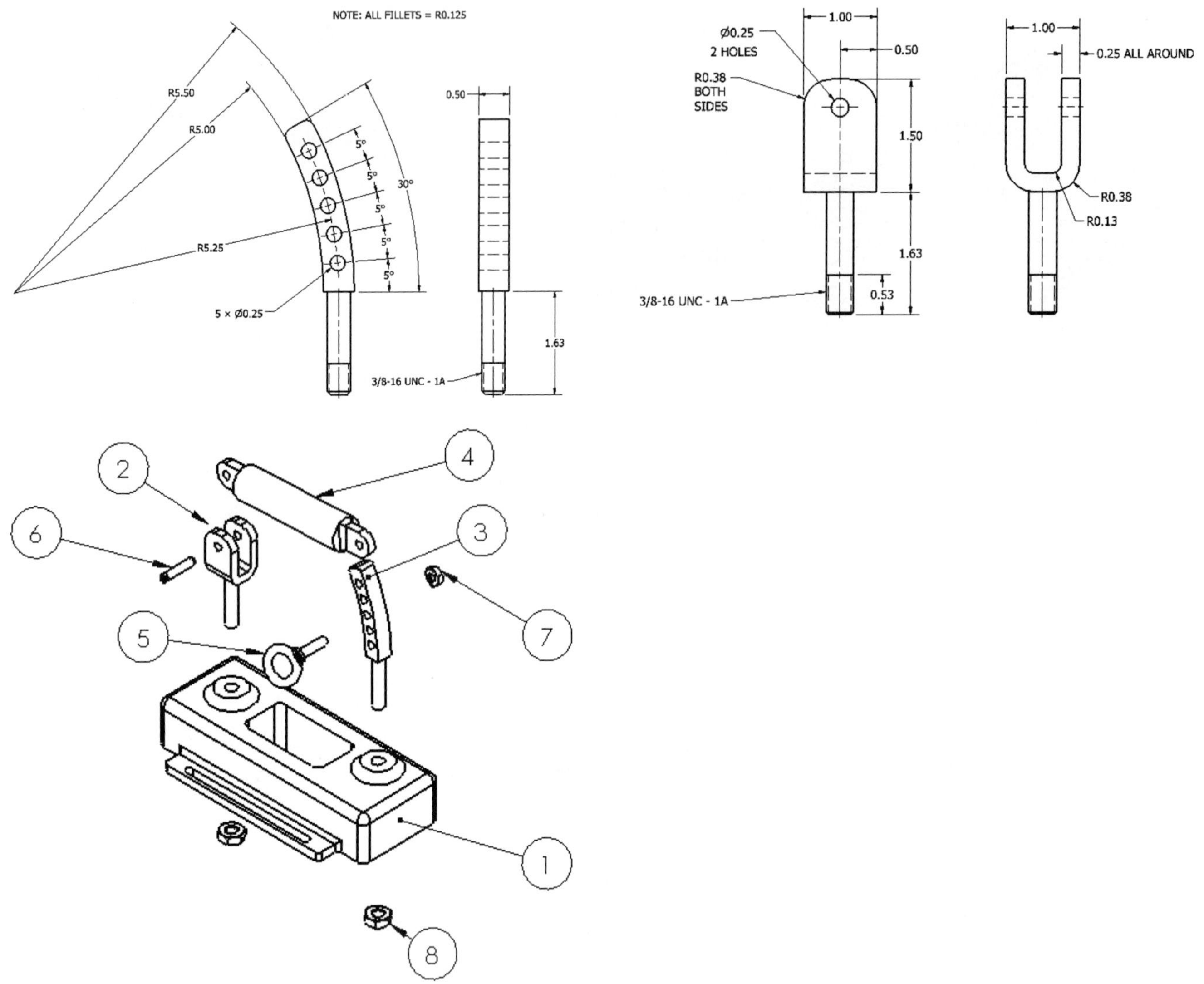

ITEM NO.	PART NUMBER	DESCRIPTION	MATL	QTY.
1	SP6-24a	BASE, CAST #4	CAST IRON	1
2	SP6-24c	SUPPORT, ROUND	SAE 1020	1
3	SP6-24d	POST, ADJUSTABLE	SAE 1020	1
4	SP6-24b	YOKE	SAE 1040	1
5	AI 18.15_type2 0.25x2.22-N-0.75	EYEBOLT, TYPE 2 FORGED	STEEL	1
6	SPS 0.25x1.125	PIN, SPRING, SLOTTED	STEEL	1
7	HHJNUT 0.2500-20-D-N	HEX NUT	STEEL	1
8	HHJNUT 0.3750-16-D-N	HEX NUT	STEEL	2

Figure P6-24 ***(continued)***

CHAPTER 7

Dimensioning

Objectives

- Learn how to dimension objects.
- Learn about ANSI standards and conventions.
- Learn how to dimension different shapes and features.
- Introduce 3D dimensioning.

7-1 INTRODUCTION

Dimensions are added to SolidWorks on **Drawing** documents. Dimensions will appear in **Part** document but these are construction dimensions. These sketch dimensions are used to create a part and are used when a sketch is edited. They may be modified as the part is being created using the **Smart Dimension** tool. They will not appear on the finished model or assembly drawings.

Figure 7-1 shows a dimensioned shape. The upper drawing in Figure 7-1 shows the sketching dimensions that are created as the part is being created. The lower drawing in Figure 7-1 shows dimensions that were created using the **Smart Dimension** tool in a **Drawing** document. These are defining dimensions and will appear on the working drawings. This chapter will show how to apply these types of dimensions.

SolidWorks has ANSI Inch and ANSI Metric dimensions available. Other dimensioning systems are also available such as ISO. This book will be in compliance with ANSI standards.

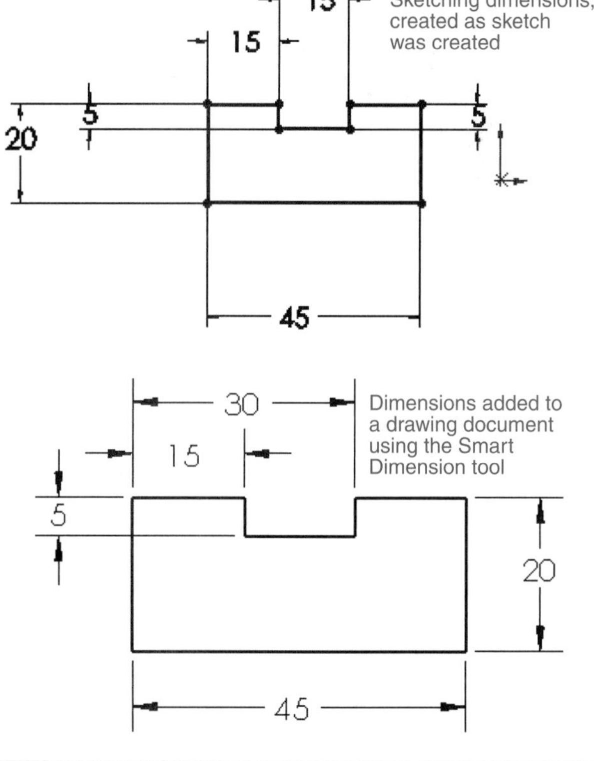

Figure 7-1

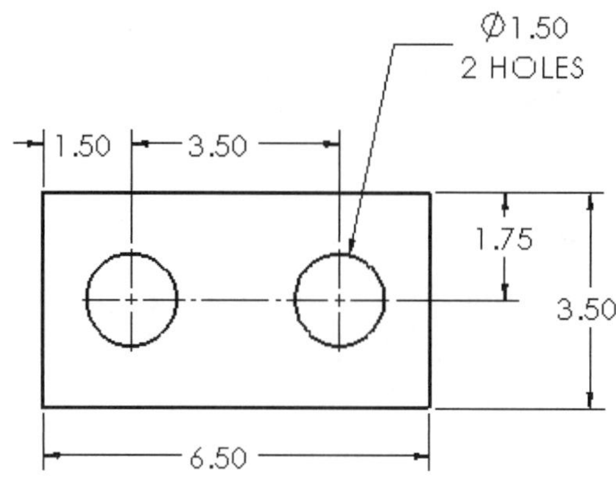

Figure 7-2

7-2 TERMINOLOGY AND CONVENTIONS—ANSI

Some Common Terms

Figure 7-2 shows both ANSI and ISO style dimensions. The terms apply to both styles.

Dimension lines: In mechanical drawings, lines between extension lines that end with an arrowhead and include a numerical dimensional value located within the line.

Extension lines: Lines that extend away from an object and allow dimensions to be located off the surface of an object.

Leader lines: Lines drawn at an angle, not horizontal or vertical, that are used to dimension specific shapes such as holes. The start point of a leader line includes an arrowhead. Numerical values are drawn at the end opposite the arrowhead.

Linear dimensions: Dimensions that define the straight-line distance between two points.

Angular dimensions: Dimensions that define the angular value, measured in degrees, between two straight lines.

Some Dimensioning Conventions

See Figure 7-3.

1. Dimension lines should be drawn evenly spaced; that is, the distance between dimension lines

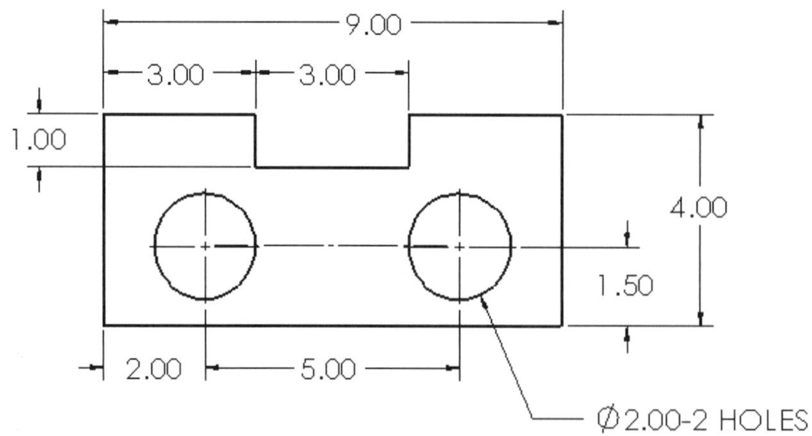

Figure 7-3

should be uniform. A general rule of thumb is to locate dimension lines about 1/2 in. or 15 mm apart.

2. There should a noticeable gap between the edge of a part and the beginning of an extension line. This serves as a visual break between the object and the extension line. The visual difference between the line types can be enhanced by using different colors for the two types of lines.
3. Leader lines are used to define the size of holes and should be positioned so that the arrowhead points toward the center of the hole.
4. Centerlines may be used as extension lines. No gap is used when a centerline is extended beyond the edge lines of an object.
5. Align dimension lines whenever possible to give the drawing a neat, organized appearance.

Some Common Errors to Avoid

See Figure 7-4.

1. Avoid crossing extension lines. Place longer dimensions farther away from the object than shorter dimensions.
2. Do not locate dimensions within cutouts; always use extension lines.
3. Do not locate any dimension close to the object. Dimension lines should be at least 1/2 in. or 15 mm from the edge of the object.
4. Avoid long extension lines. Locate dimensions in the same general area as the feature being defined.

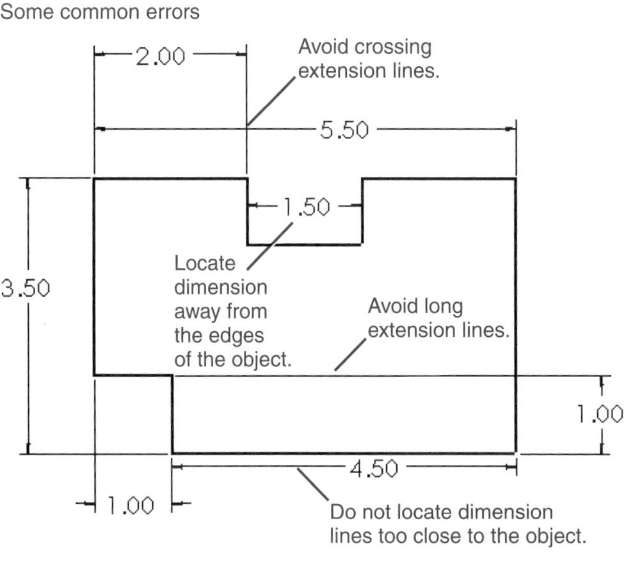

Figure 7-4

7-3 ADDING DIMENSIONS TO A DRAWING

Figure 7-5 shows a part that includes two holes. This section will explain how to add dimension to the part. The part was drawn as a **Part** document and saved as Block, 2 Holes. See Figure 7-9 for the part's dimension. The part is 0.50 thick.

1. Click **New, Drawing, OK** and start a new drawing.
2. Create a top view of the Block, 2 Holes.

   In this example we will work with only one view.

3. Click the **Annotations** tool and select the **Center Mark** option. In the **Center Mark** dialog box, click the **Linear Center Mark** tool.
4. Add a centerline between the two holes by clicking the outside edge of each circle.

The holes now have the same horizontal centerline, so only one vertical dimension can be used to define the hole's location.

> **TIP**
>
> Centerlines can be extended by first clicking them and then dragging an endpoint to a new location.

5. Click the **Smart Dimension** tool, click the top end of the left hole's vertical centerline and the upper left corner of the block. Click the drawing screen to complete the dimension.

   See Figure 7-6.

6. Use the **Smart Dimension** tool and add the horizontal and vertical dimensions as shown.

   See Figure 7-7.

RULE: Keep dimension lines aligned and evenly spaced.

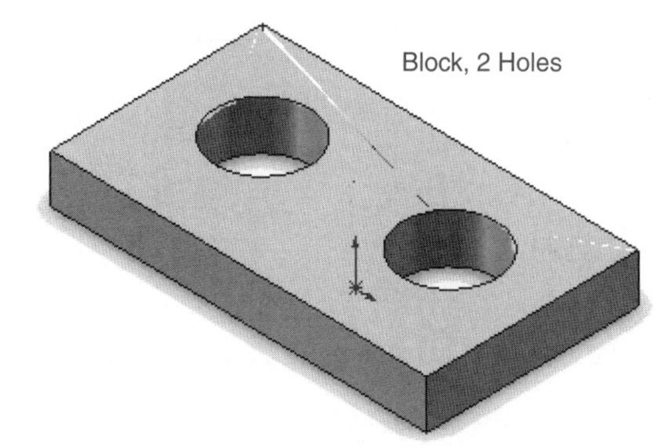

Figure 7-5

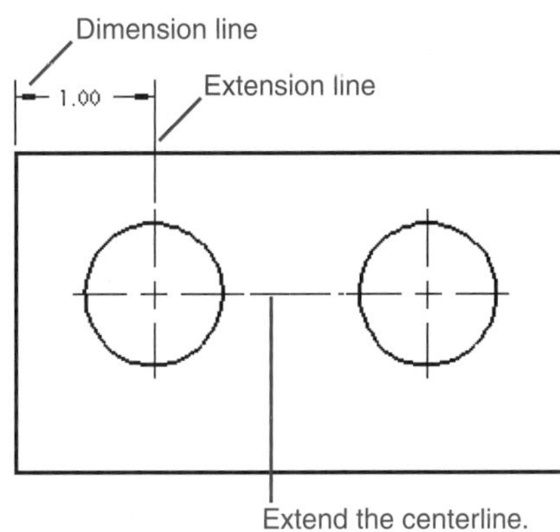

Figure 7-6

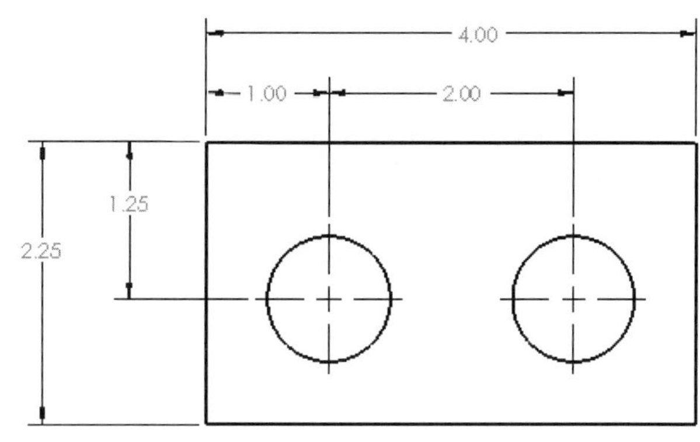

Figure 7-7

7. Click the **Smart Dimension** tool, click the edge of the left hole, and move the cursor away from the hole.

Note that the leader arrow always points at the center of the hole.

8. Select a location off the surface of the part and click the mouse.

RULE: Never locate dimensions on the surface of the part.

9. Go to the **Dimension** dialog box at the left of the screen and locate the cursor in the **Dimension Text** box, and click the mouse.

The text already in the box defines the hole's diameter. See Figure 7-8.

10. Move the cursor to the end of the existing text line, press **<Enter>** to start a new text line, and type **2 HOLES.**
11. Click the OK check mark.
12. Save the drawing.

TIP

Dimensions can be relocated by clicking and dragging the dimension text.

Controlling Dimensions

Various aspects of dimensions can be edited such as text height, arrow location, and text values.

1. Click the **Tools** heading at the top of the screen and select the **Options** option.

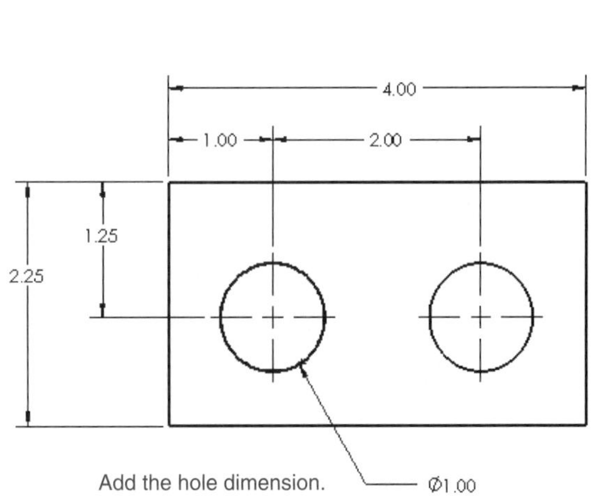

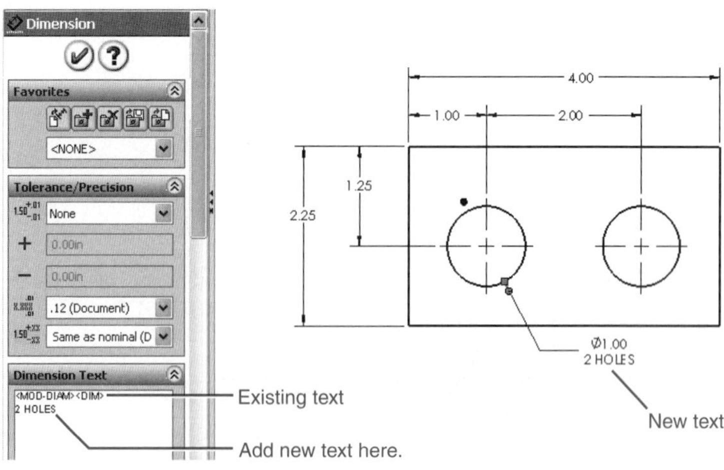

Figure 7-8

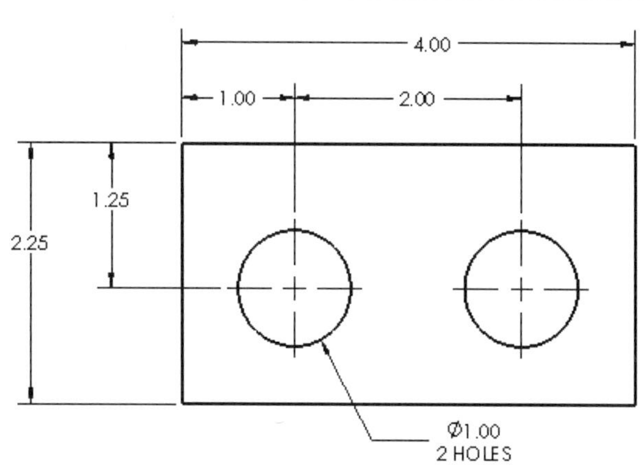

Figure 7-9

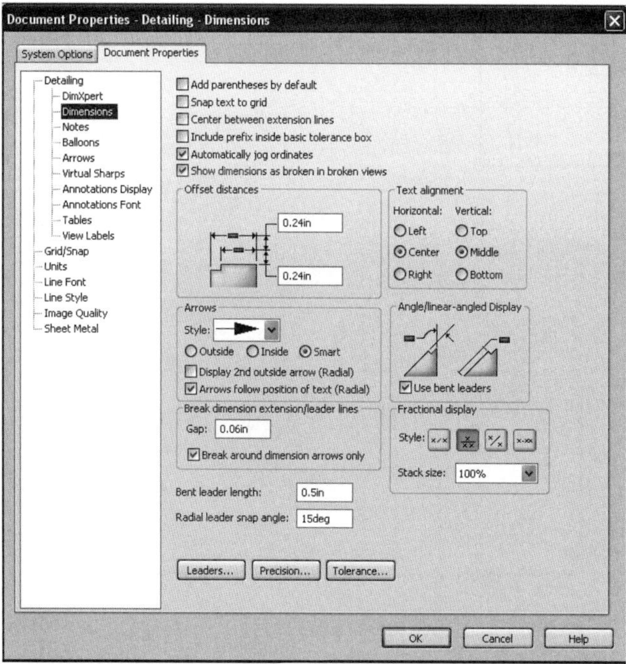

Figure 7-10

The **Document Properties—Detailing—Dimensions** dialog box will appear. See Figure 7-10.

2. Click the **Document Properties** tab.
3. Click the **Dimensions** option.

The **Document Properties—Detailing—Dimensions** dialog box can be used to edit the style and form of dimensions. It can be used to change the way arrows are applied.

4. Click the **Annotations Font,** and select the **Dimension** option.

The **Choose Font** dialog box will appear. See Figure 7-11. This dialog box can be used to change the font, font style, and height of dimension text. The height of text can be measured in inches, millimeters, or points. A point is a printer's term that equals about 1/72 of an inch. (There are 12 points to a pica.)

5. Click the **Height: Units** radio button and change the height to **0.25in.**
6. Click **OK,** then OK.

Figure 7-11 shows the enlarged dimensions.

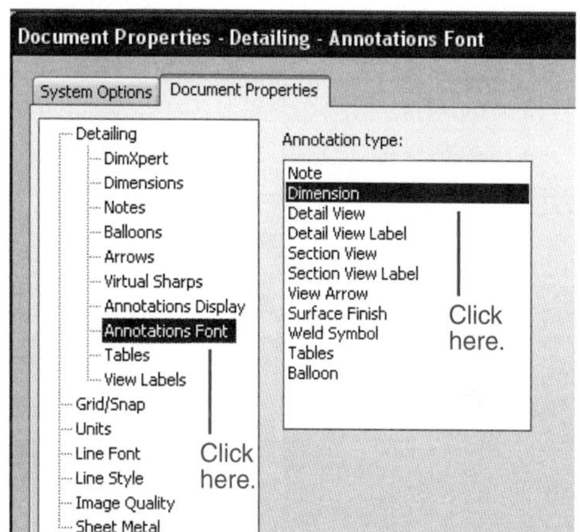

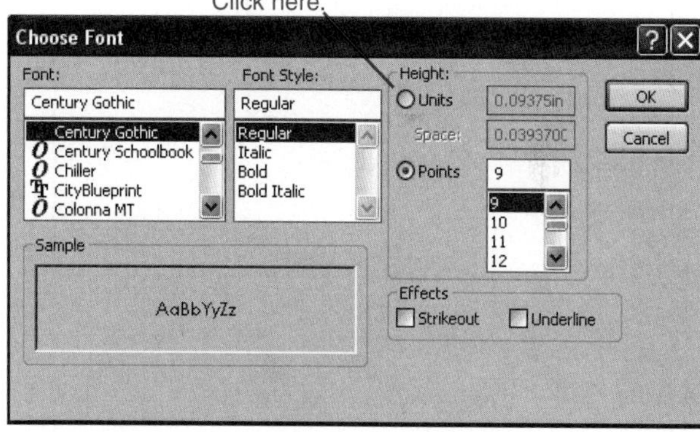

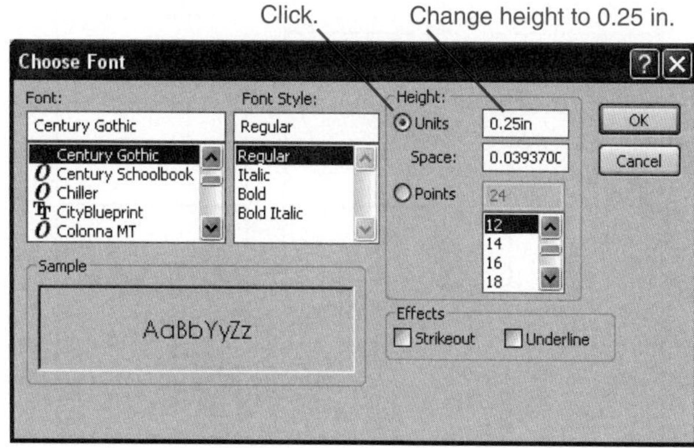

Figure 7-11

0.25 in. high dimensions
4.00
1.00
2.00
1.25
2.25
Ø1.00
2 HOLES

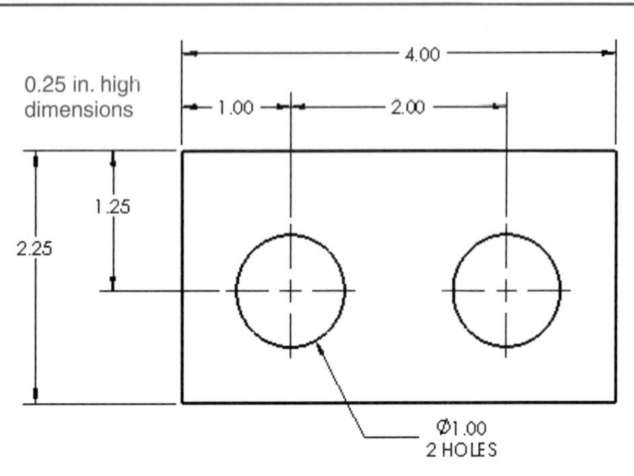

Figure 7-11 ***(continued)***

Dimensioning Short Distances

Figure 7-12 shows an object that includes several short distances. We will start by using the standard dimensions settings and show how to edit them for a particular situation.

1. Use the **Smart Dimension** tool and add dimensions to the drawing.

Note that the arrows for the .50 dimension are aligned with the arrows for the 1.00 dimensions. Dimensions that are aligned in a single row are called ***chain dimensions.*** Note that the .25 dimension is crowded between the two extension lines.

RULE: Never squeeze dimension values. Dimension values should always be presented clearly and should be easy to read.

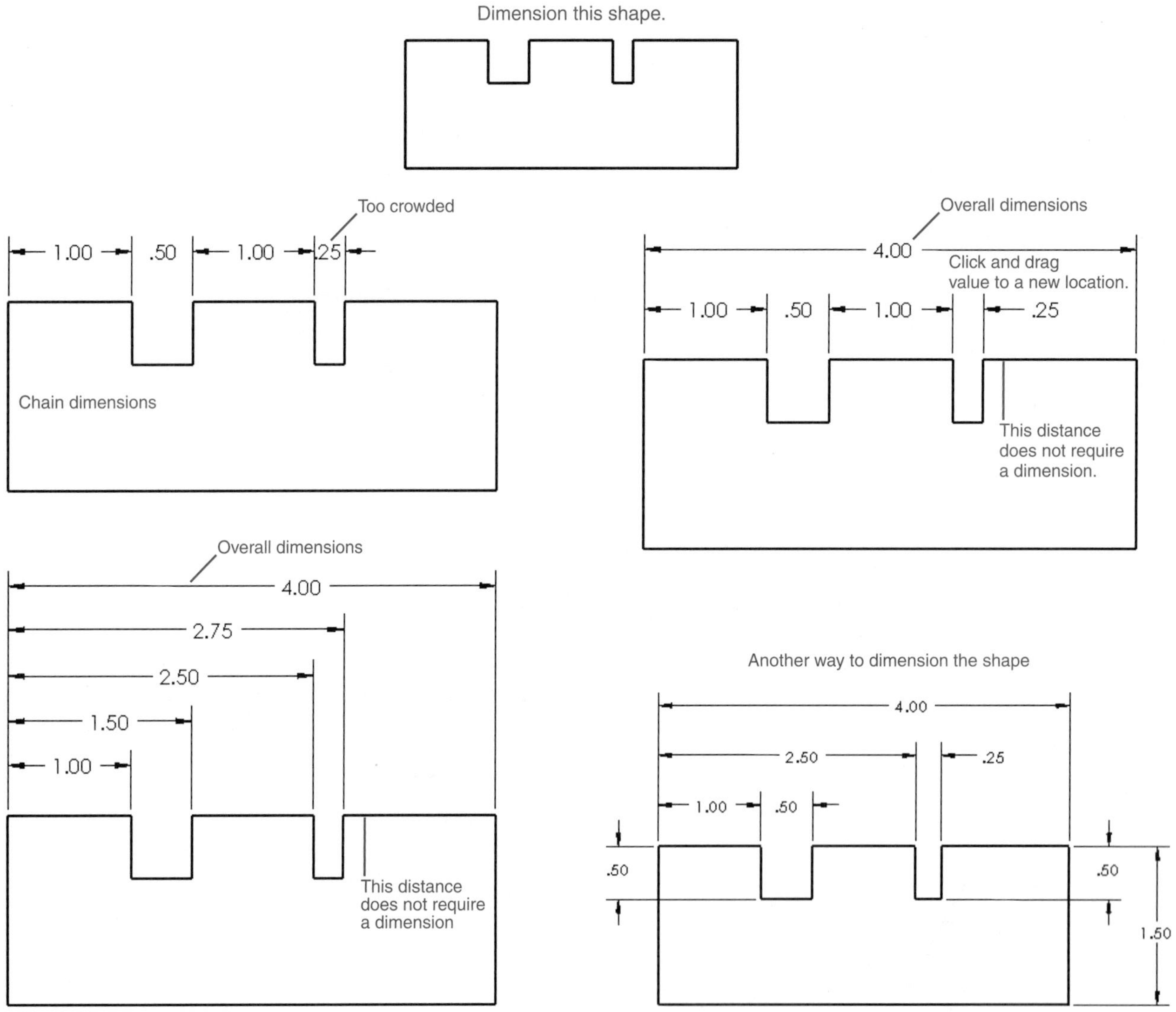

Dimension this shape.
Too crowded
1.00
.50
1.00
.25
Chain dimensions
Overall dimensions
4.00
Click and drag value to a new location.
1.00
.50
1.00
.25
This distance does not require a dimension.
Overall dimensions
4.00
2.75
2.50
1.50
1.00
This distance does not require a dimension
Another way to dimension the shape
4.00
2.50
.25
1.00
.50
.50
.50
1.50

Figure 7-12

There are several possible solutions to the crowded .25 value.

2. Click and drag the .25 dimension to the right outside the extension lines.
3. Add the **4.00** overall dimension.

Dimensions that define the total length and width of an object are called ***overall dimensions.*** In this example the dimension 4.00 defines the total length of the part, so it is an overall dimension. Overall dimensions are located farthest away from the edge of the part.

The right edge of the part, the section below the .25 does not need a dimension. The reason for this will be discussed in the next chapter, on tolerances.

TIP

To delete an existing dimension, click the dimension and press the <**Del**> key.

Figure 7-12 shows two other options for dimensioning. The first is the baseline method, in which all dimensions are taken from the same datum line. The second method is a combination of chain and baseline dimensions.

RULE: Never dimension the same distance twice. This is called double dimensioning.

Figure 7-13 shows an example of double dimensioning. The top edge distance is dimensioned twice: once using the 1.00 + .50 + 1.00 + .25 + 1.25, and a second time using the 4.00 dimension. One of the dimensions must be omitted. Double dimensioning will be explained in more detail in the next chapter.

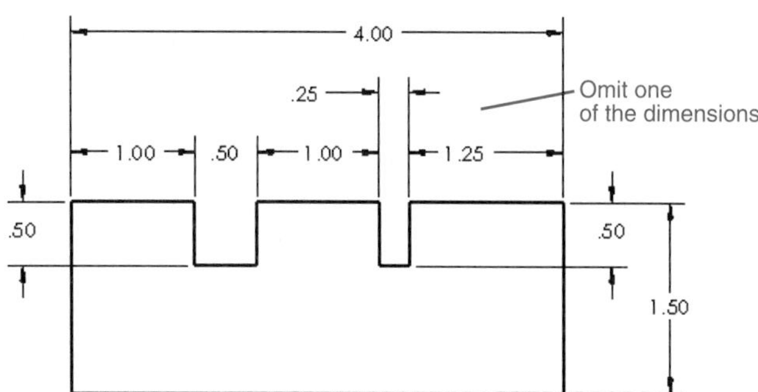

Figure 7-13

Autodimension Tool

The **Autodimension** tool will automatically add dimensions to a drawing.

WARNING: The dimensions created using the **Autodimension** tool are not always in the best locations. The dimensions must be relocated to be in compliance with ANSI conventions.

Figure 7-14 shows a shape to be dimensioned using the **Autodimension** tool.

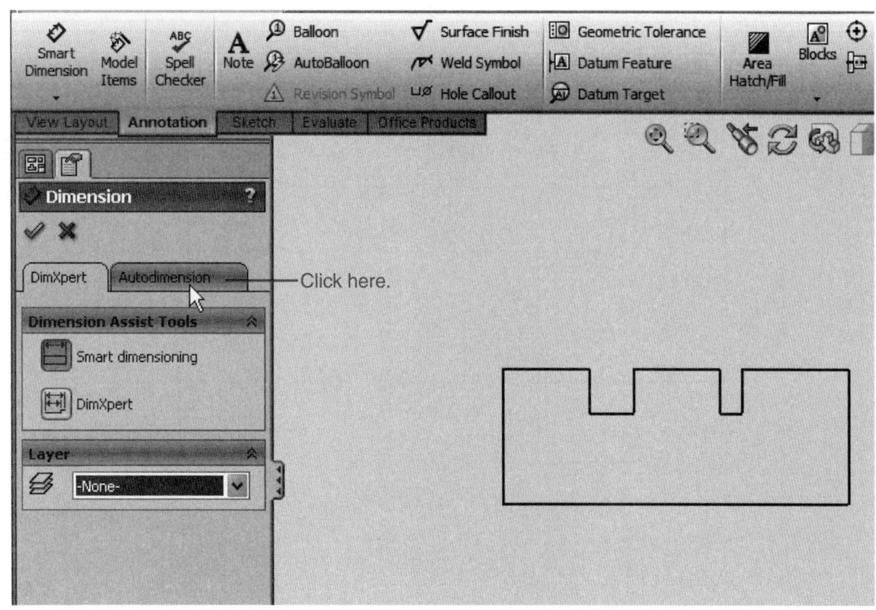

Figure 7-14

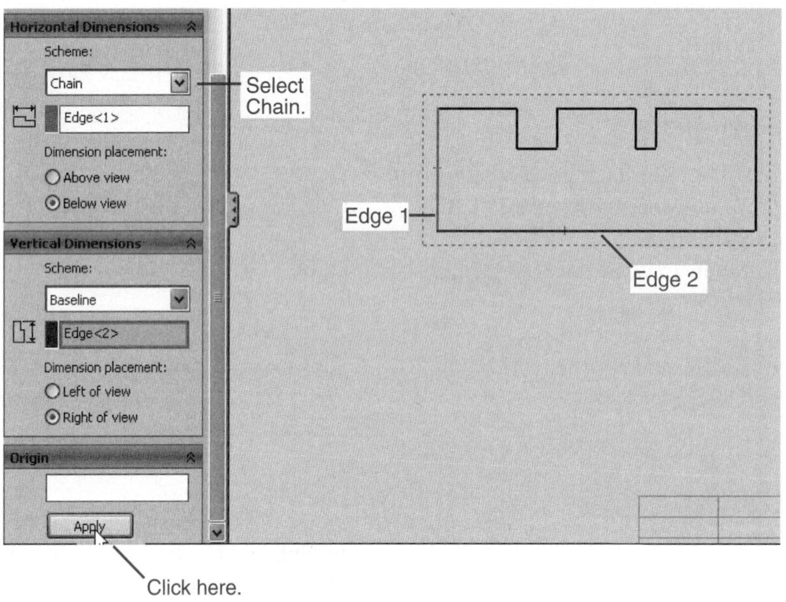

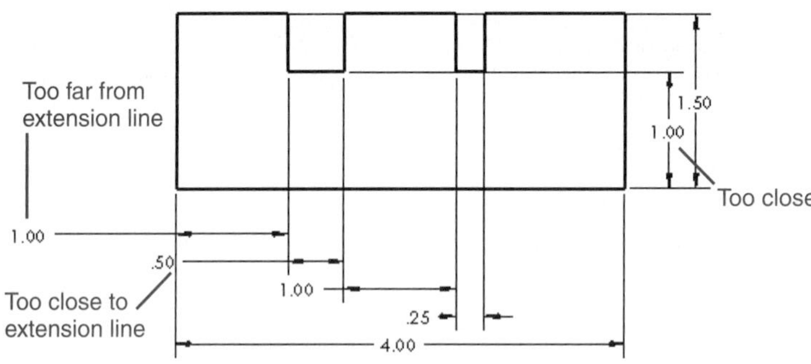

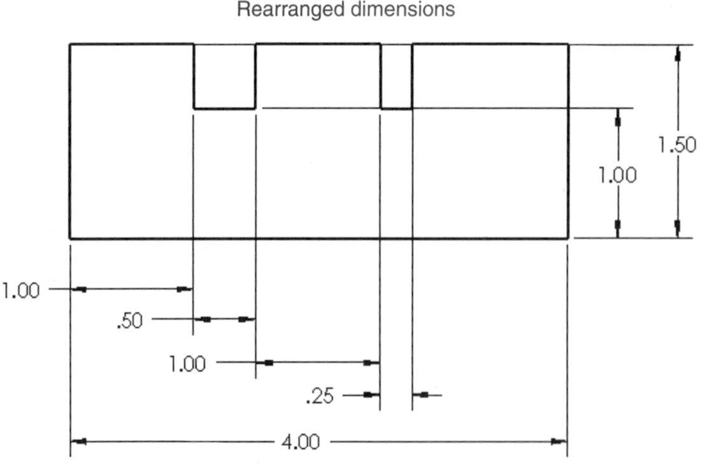

Figure 7-14 *(continued)*

1. Click the arrow on the **Annotation** tool, then click the **Autodimension** tool.

The **Entities to Dimension** dialog box will appear.

2. Select the **Chain Scheme,** define **Edge 1** and **Edge 2,** click the **Apply** box, and click the OK check mark.

Solidworks will automatically pick edges 1 and 2. If it does not, or the edges selected are not the ones you want, click the **Edge** box, then click the edge. The words **Edge <1>** should appear in the box.

Figure 7-14 shows the dimensions applied using the **Autodimension** tool. They are not in acceptable positions.

3. Rearrange the dimensions to comply with standard conventions.

Figure 7-15 shows the shape shown in Figure 7-14 dimensioned using the baseline scheme.

1. Access the **Autodimension** tool and select the **Baseline** scheme.
2. Select **Edge 1** and **Edge 2.**
3. Click **Apply.**
4. Click the OK check mark.

Figure 7-15 shows the dimensions created by the **Autodimension** tool and how the dimensions can be rearranged.

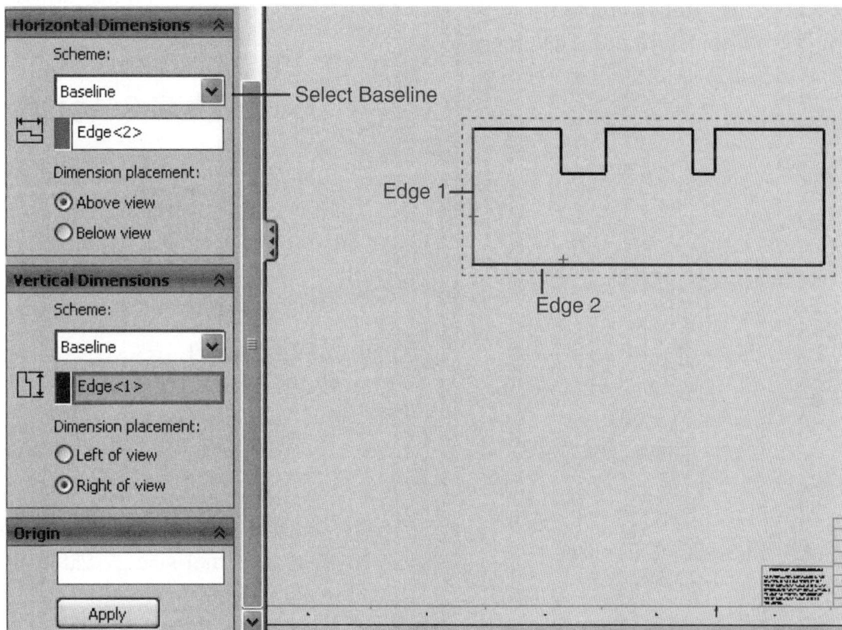

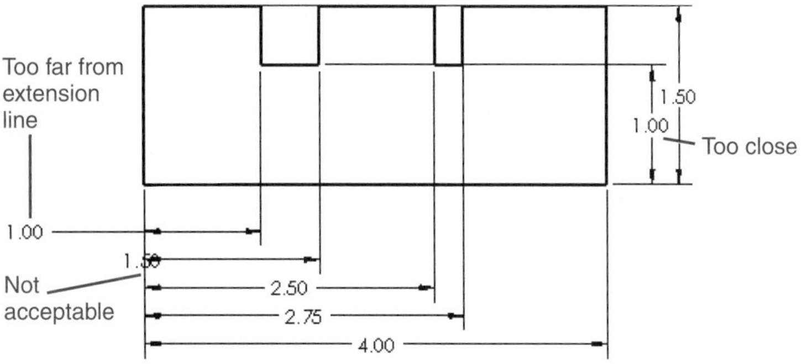

Figure 7-15

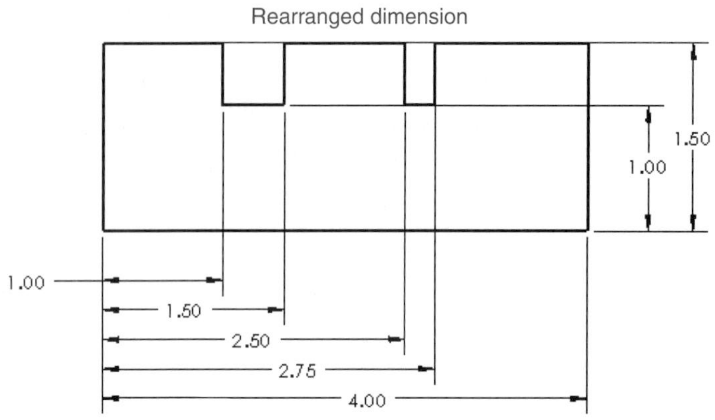

Figure 7-15 ***(continued)***

Ordinate Dimensions

Figure 7-16 shows the object dimensioned using the **Ordinate Scheme** of the **Autodimension** tool. The created dimensions are located on the surface of the part. This is a violation of the convention that states that dimensions should never be located on the surface of the part. Figure 7-16 shows how the ordinate dimensions were rearranged.

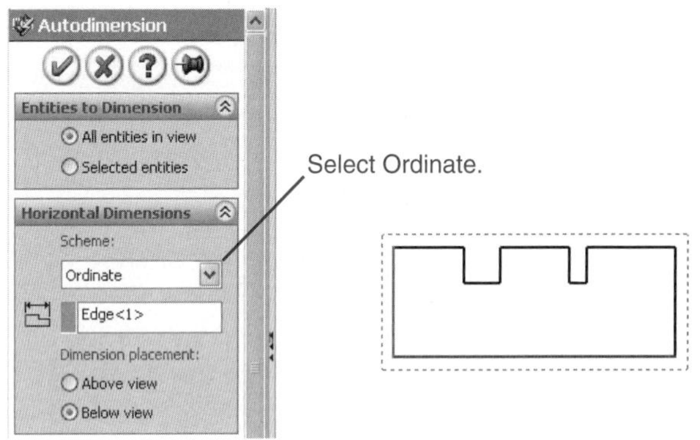

Dimensions created using the Autodimension tool

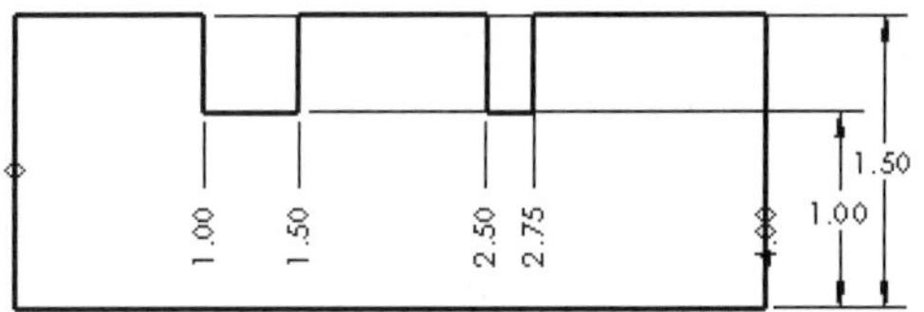

The dimensions are not acceptable.
Dimensions are not allowed on the surface of the part.

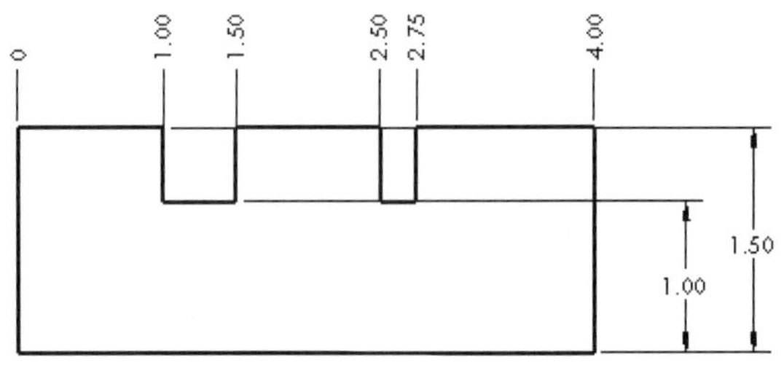

Rearranged dimensions

Figure 7-16

7-4 DRAWING SCALE

Drawings are often drawn "to scale" because the actual part is either too big to fit on a sheet of drawing paper or too small to be seen. For example, a microchip circuit must be drawn at several thousand times its actual size to be seen.

Drawing scales are written using the following formats:

SCALE: 1=1
SCALE: FULL
SCALE: 1000=1
SCALE: .25=1

In each example the value on the left indicates the scale factor. A value greater than 1 indicates that the drawing is larger than actual size. A value smaller than 1 indicates that the drawing is smaller than actual size.

Regardless of the drawing scale selected the dimension values must be true size. Figure 7-17 shows the same rectangle drawn at two different scales. The top rectangle is drawn at a scale of 1 = 1, or its true size. The bottom rectangle is drawn at a scale of 2 = 1, or twice its true size. In both examples the 3.00 dimension remains the same.

7-5 UNITS

It is important to understand that dimensional values are not the same as mathematical units. Dimensional values are manufacturing instructions and always include a tolerance, even if the tolerance value is not stated. Manufacturers use a predefined set of standard dimensions that are applied to any dimensional value that does not include a written tolerance. Standard tolerance values differ from organization to organization. Figure 7-18 shows a chart of standard tolerances.

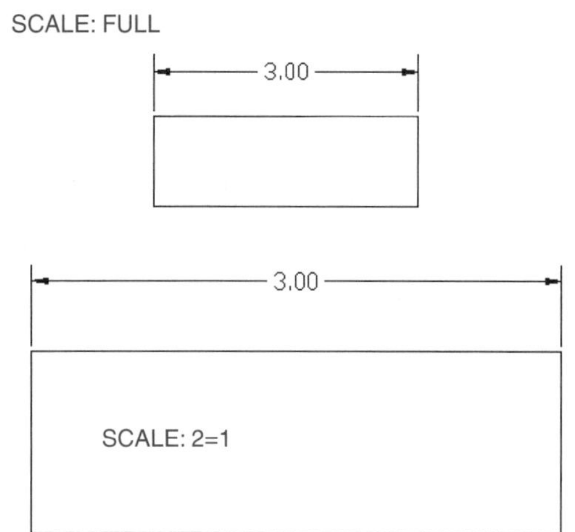

Figure 7-17

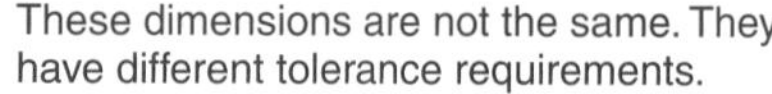

These dimensions are not the same. They have different tolerance requirements.

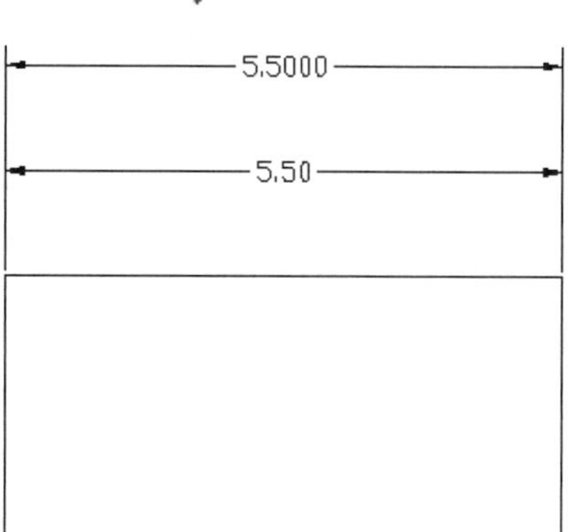

Figure 7-19

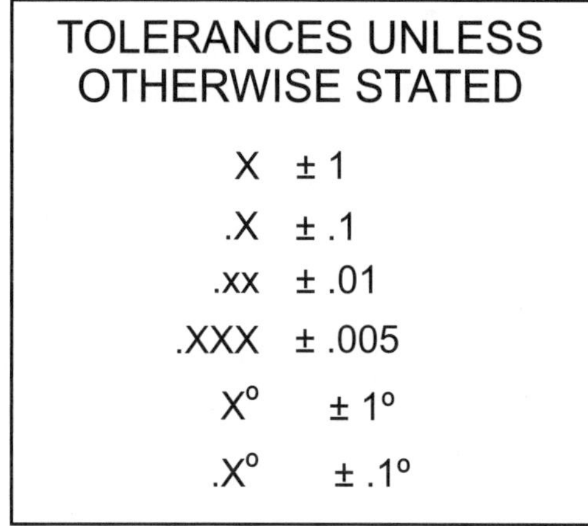

TOLERANCES UNLESS OTHERWISE STATED

X	± 1
.X	± .1
.xx	± .01
.XXX	± .005
X°	± 1°
.X°	± .1°

Figure 7-18

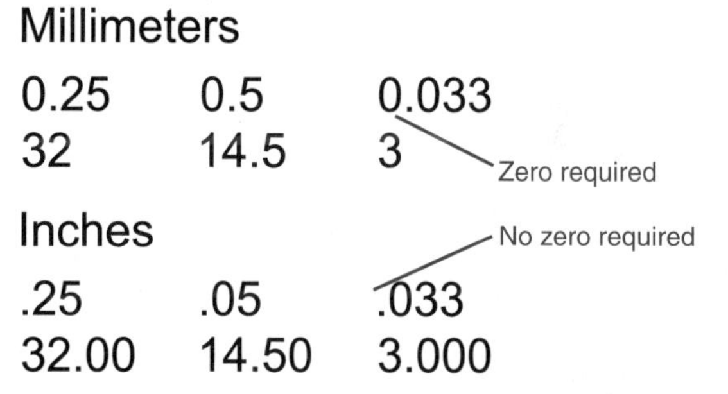

Figure 7-20

In Figure 7-19 a distance is dimensioned twice: once as 5.50 and a second time as 5.5000. Mathematically these two values are equal, but they are not the same manufacturing instruction. The 5.50 value could, for example, have a standard tolerance of ±.01, whereas the 5.5000 value could have a standard tolerance of ±.0005. A tolerance of 6.0005 is more difficult and therefore more expensive to manufacture than a tolerance of ±.01.

Figure 7-20 shows examples of units expressed in millimeters and in decimal inches. A zero is not required to the left of the decimal point for decimal inch values less than one. Millimeter values do not require zeros to the right of the decimal point. Millimeter and decimal inch values never include symbols; the units will be defined in the title block of the drawing.

Aligned Dimensions

Aligned dimensions are dimensions that are parallel to a slanted edge or surface. They are not horizontal or vertical. The units for aligned dimensions should be written horizontally. This is called ***unidirectional dimensioning.***

Figure 7-21 shows the front, right side, and isometric views of an a part with a slanted surface. The dimensions were applied using the **Smart Dimension** tool. Note that the slanted dimension, aligned with the slanted surface, has unidirectional (horizontal) text. The hole dimension was created using the **Note** tool from the **Annotations** toolbox.

Hole Dimensions

Figure 7-22 shows an object that has two holes, one blind, and one completely through. The object has filleted corners. In this section we will add dimensions to the views.

The holes were drawn using the **Hole Wizard** tool. The **Hole Wizard** tool will automatically create a conical point to a hole.

1. Use the **Smart Dimension** tool and locate the two holes.

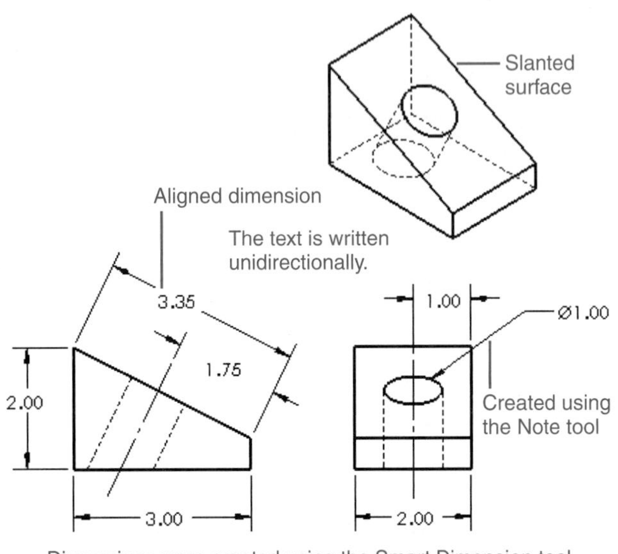

Figure 7-21

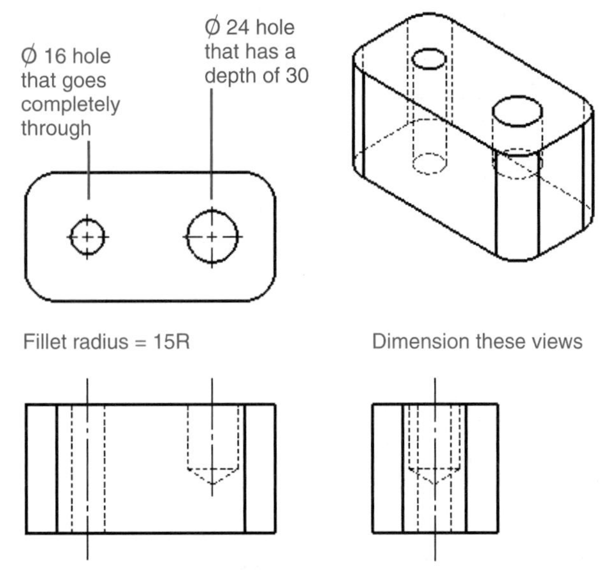

Figure 7-22

See Figure 7-23. In general, dimensions are applied from the inside out, that is, starting with the features in the middle of the part and working out to the overall dimensions. Leader lines are generally applied last, as they have more freedom of location.

2. Use the **Linear Center Mark** tool to draw a centerline between the two holes.

The centerline between the two holes indicates that the vertical 30 dimension applies to both holes.

Change the arrows on the 30 dimensions (both the horizontal and vertical) so that they are inside the extension lines.

3. Click the **Tools** heading at the top of the screen, then click **Options.**
4. Click the **Document Properties** tab, click **Dimensions,** then click the **Inside** button in the **Arrows** box.

See Figure 7-24. The arrows for the 30 dimensions are located within the extension lines. All dimensions

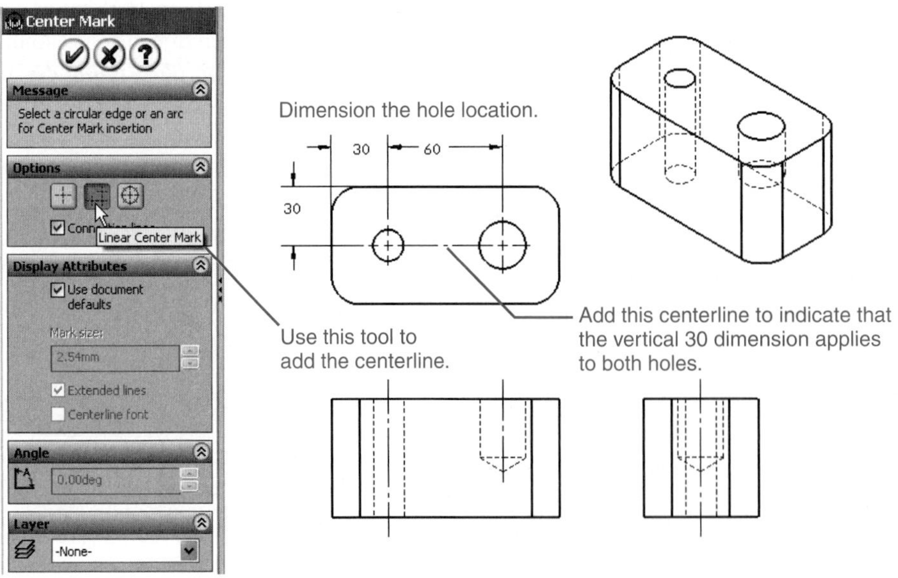

Figure 7-23

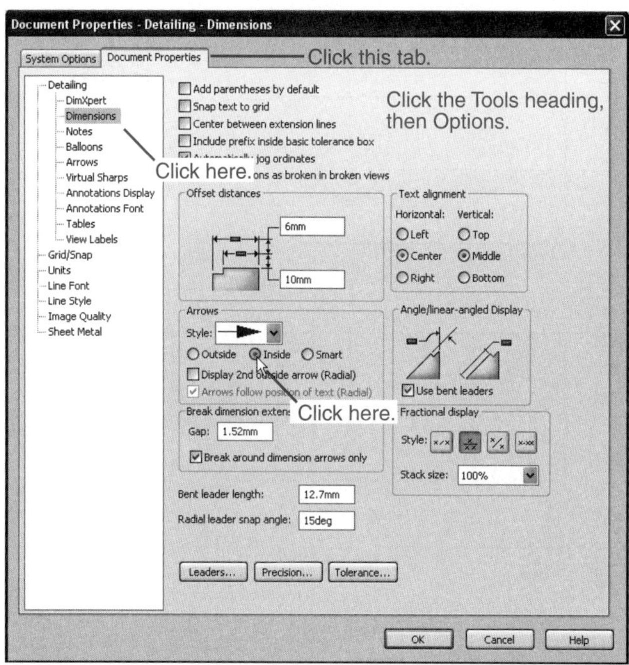

Figure 7-24

will now have their arrows located inside the extension lines.

5. Use the **Smart Dimension** tool and add a dimension to one of the filleted corners.

Note that the arrow is on the outside of the arc. The direction of the arrow that defines the arc can be changed by clicking the arc dimension, clicking the **Leader** tab on the **Dimension Properties Manager,** and clicking the **Dimension to inside of arc** button. See Figure 7-25. The arrow for the radius dimension will be located outside the fillet pointing inward.

> **TIP**
>
> The dimension options found on the **Document Properties Manager** will change all dimension. Clicking a dimension and using the **Dimension Properties Manager** allows you to change just that dimension.

6. Click the fillet dimension again, go to the **Dimension Text** block on the **Dimension Properties Manager,** and type **4 CORNERS** as shown.

See Figure 7-26.

7. Click **OK, Apply,** and OK.
8. Use the **Smart Dimension** tool and dimension the Ø16 hole.

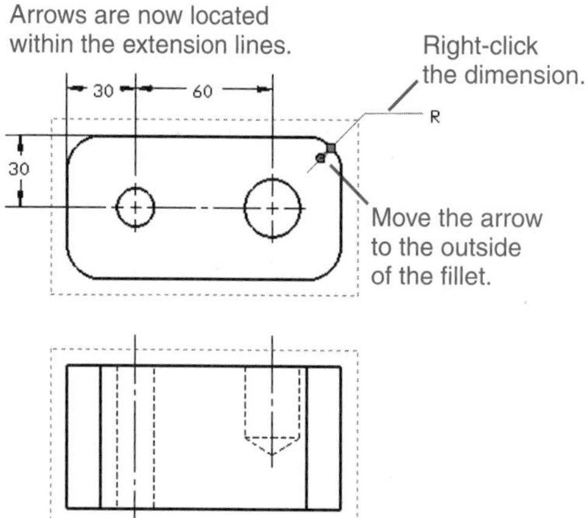

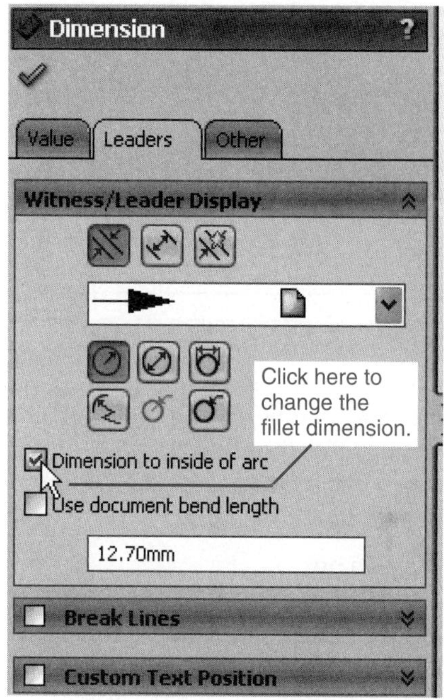

Figure 7-25

The Ø16 hole goes completely through the part, so no depth specification is required.

See Figure 7-27.

9. Dimension the Ø24 hole.

Initially, just the hole's diameter value will appear. The hole does not go completely through the part, so a depth specification is required.

10. Click the Ø14 dimension.

The **Dimension Properties Manager** will appear. See Figure 7-28. Use the **Dimension Text** box to modify the dimension.

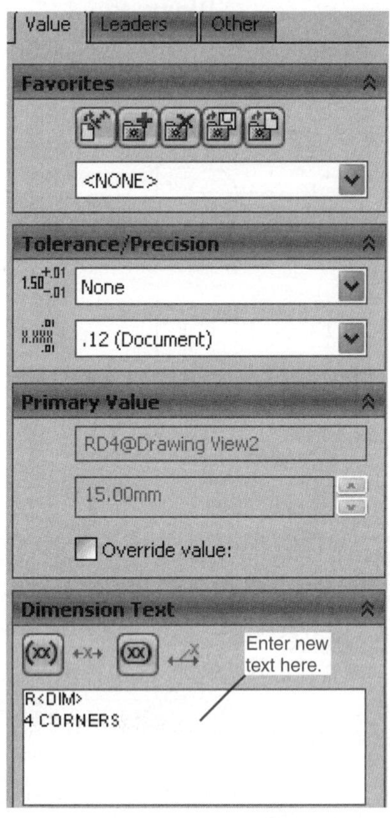

Figure 7-26

11. Locate the cursor to the right of the existing dimension, click the **Hole Depth** symbol, and enter the depth value of **30.** Click the OK check mark.
12. Complete the dimensions.

See Figure 7-29.

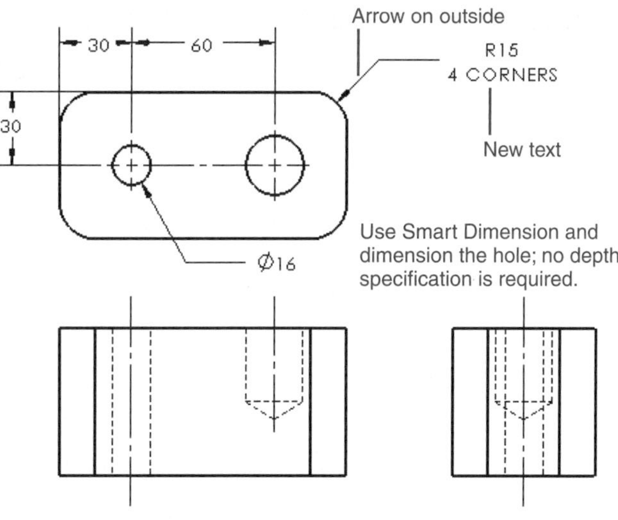

Figure 7-27

> ***Note:***
> If the **Hole Callout** tool had been used, and if this hole had been created using the **Hole Wizard,** the depth dimension would appear automatically.

7-6 DIMENSIONING HOLES AND FILLETS

A ***blind hole*** is a hole that does not go completely through an object. It has a depth requirement. Figure 7-30 shows a 2.00 × 2.00 × 2.00 block with a blind Ø0.50 × 1.18 DEEP hole. It was created as follows.

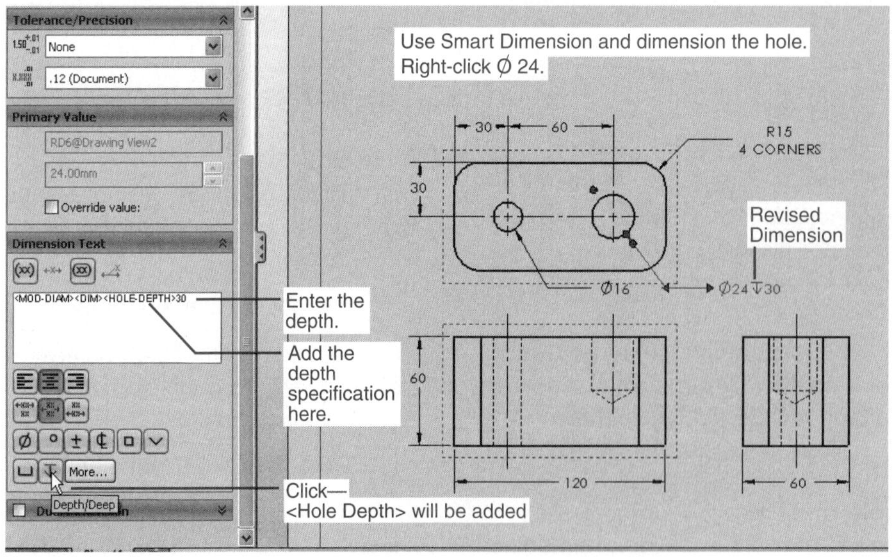

Figure 7-28

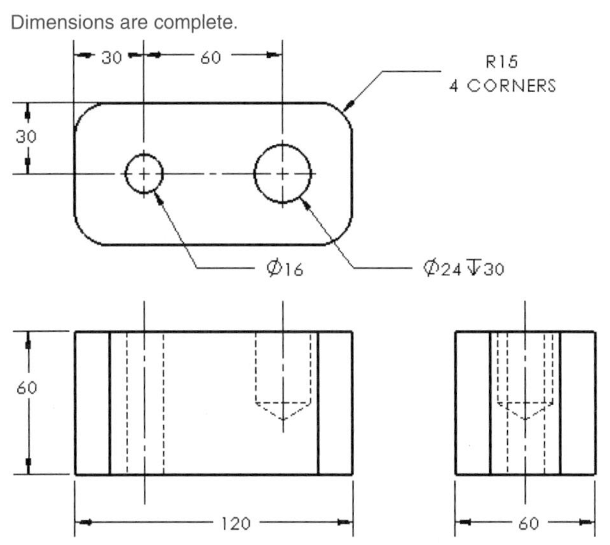

Figure 7-29

Dimensioning a Blind Hole

1. Draw the block.
2. Click the **Hole Wizard** tool.
3. Click the **Hole** tool in the **Hole Specification** box. Define the hole using the **ANSI Inch Standard** with a diameter of **1/2** and a depth of **1.18** in.
4. Click the **Position** tab.
5. Locate the hole as shown.
6. Click the OK check mark.
7. Save the drawing as **Block, Blind.**
8. Start a new **Drawing** document and create a front and a top orthographic view of the block.
9. Add dimensions to the views.
10. Click the **Annotations** toolbox and click the **Hole Callout** option.
11. Click the edge of the hole, move the cursor away from the hole, define a location for the hole callout, and click the mouse. The hole callout dimension will initially appear as a rectangular box.
12. Save the drawing.

Note that the hole includes a conical point. Holes manufactured using twist drills will have conical points. The conical point is not included in the hole's depth dimension. A special drill bit can be used to create a flat-bottomed hole.

Figure 7-31 shows three different methods that can be used to dimension a blind hole.

Figure 7-32 shows three methods of dimensioning holes in sectional views. The single line note version is the preferred method.

Dimensioning Hole Patterns

Figure 7-33 shows two different hole patterns dimensioned. The circular pattern includes the note ∅10-4 HOLES. This note serves to define all four holes within the object.

Figure 7-33 also shows a rectangular object that contains five holes of equal diameter, equally spaced from one another. The notation 5 × ∅10 specifies five holes of 10 diameter. The notation 4 × 20 (=80) means four equal spaces of 20.

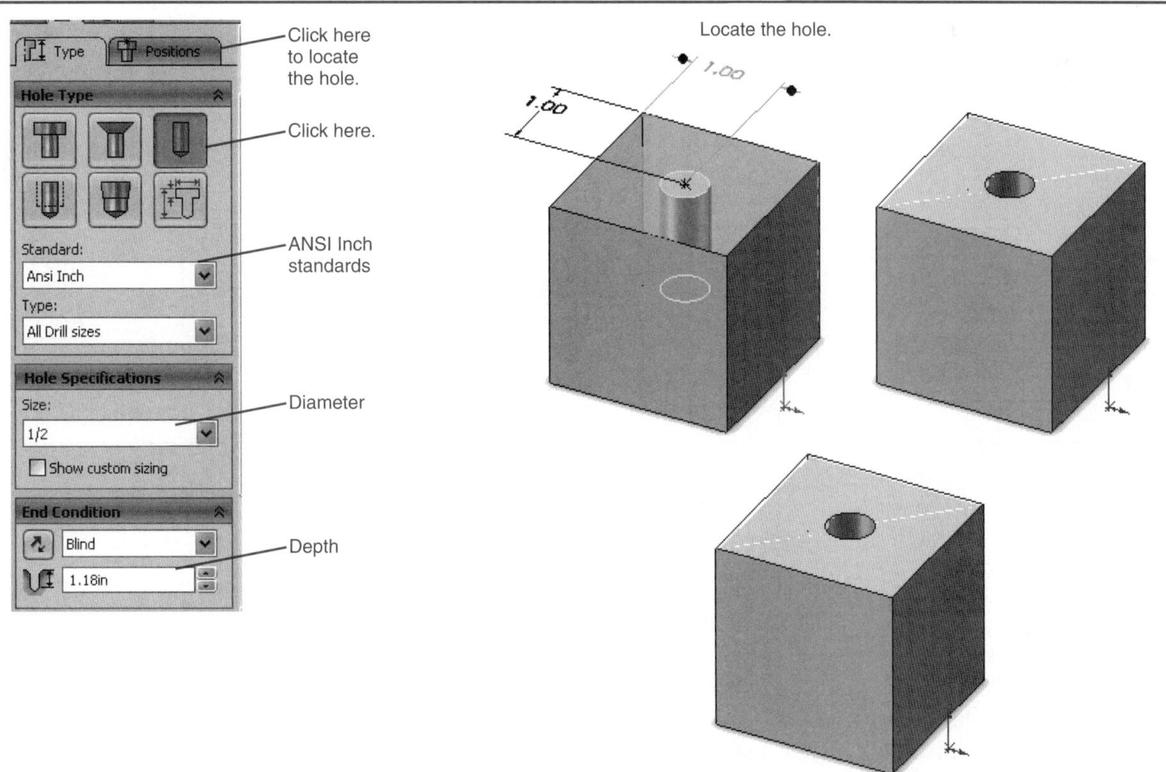

Figure 7-30

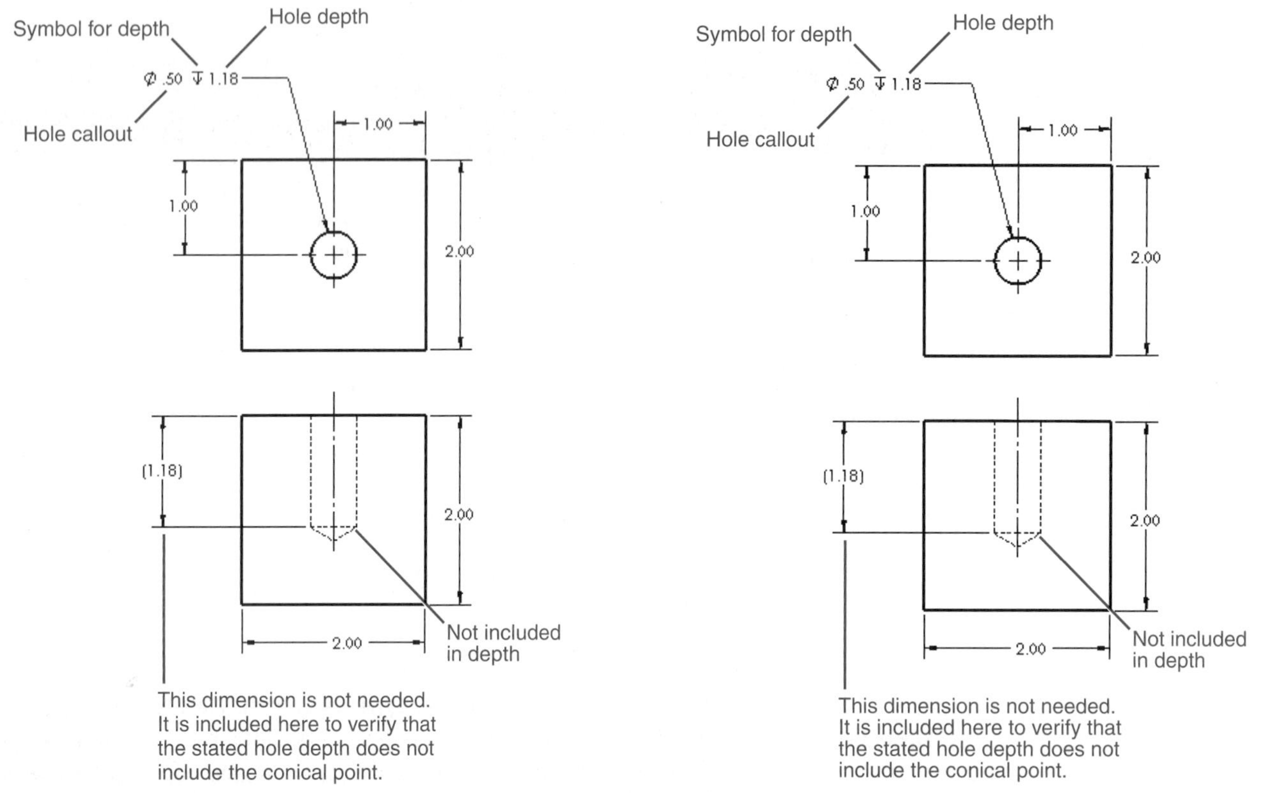

Figure 7-30 *(continued)*

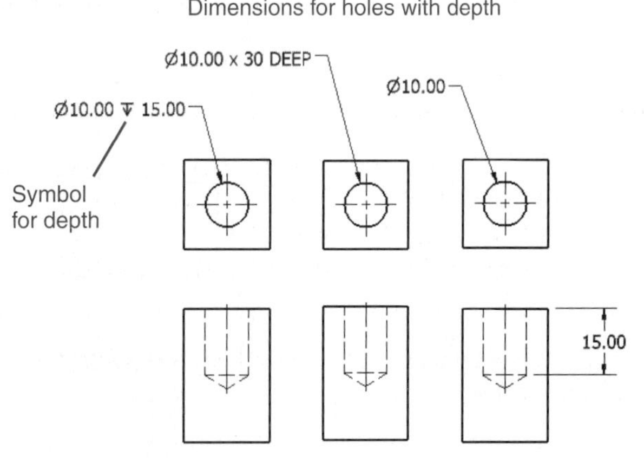

Figure 7-31

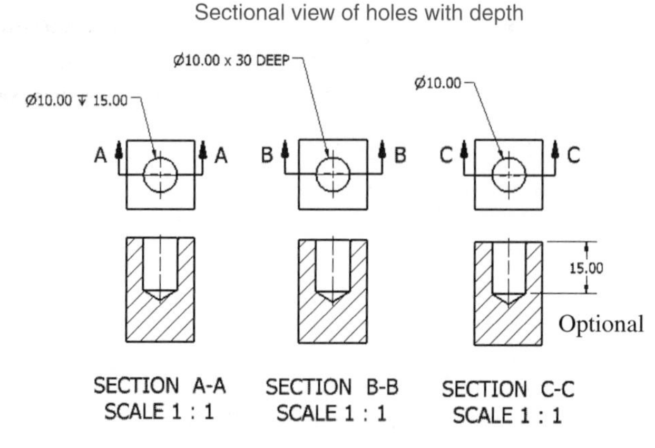

Figure 7-32

The notation (=80) is a reference dimension and is included for convenience. Reference dimensions are explained in Chapter 9.

Figure 7-34 shows two additional methods for dimensioning repeating hole patterns. Figure 7-35 shows a circular hole pattern that includes two different hole diameters. The hole diameters are not noticeably different and could be confused. One group is defined by indicating letter (A); the other is dimensioned in a normal manner.

7-7 DIMENSIONING COUNTERBORED AND COUNTERSUNK HOLES

Counterbored holes are dimensioned in the sequence of their manufacture. First the hole's diameter is given, then the counterbore diameter, then the depth of the counterbore.

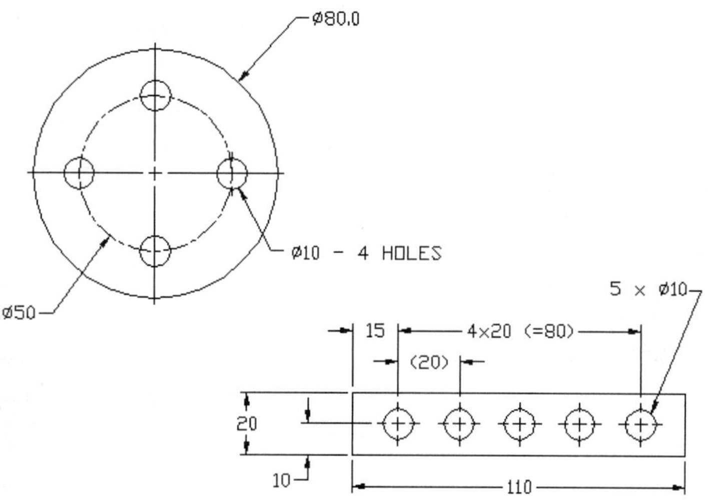

Figure 7-33

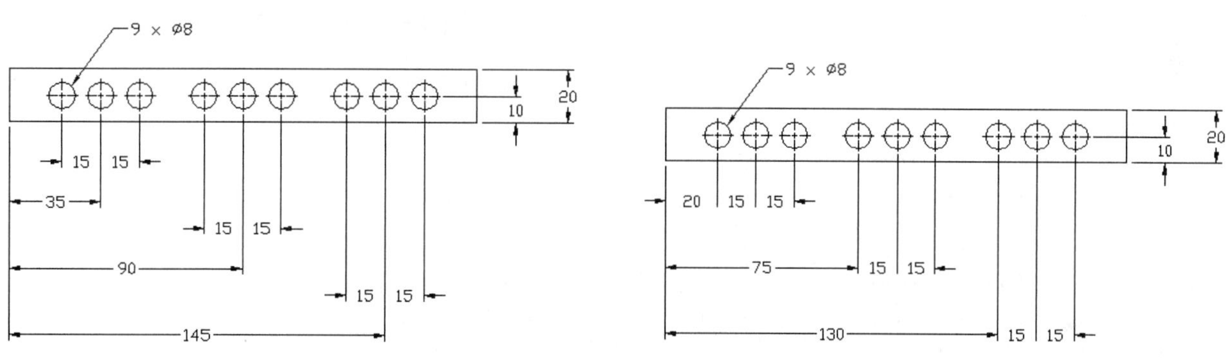

Figure 7-34

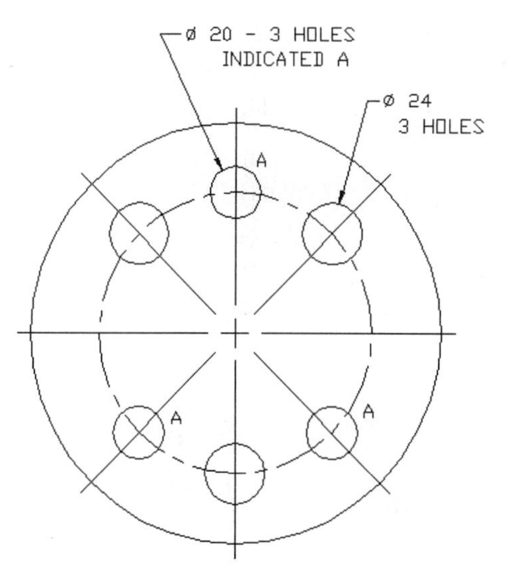

Figure 7-35

Figure 7-36 shows a part that contains two counterbored holes; one goes completely through and the other is blind. Dimensions will applied to both.

1. Draw a **3.00 × 4.00 × 1.75** Block.
2. Use the **Hole Wizard** tool, click the **Counterbore** tool, and draw the counterbored holes.

Remember that one hole goes completely through the block, and the other is blind and has a depth of 1.00.

3. Specify a **3/8 Hex Bolt** for each hole.

See Figure 7-37. SolidWorks will automatically select the diameter for the counterbored hole that will accommodate a Ø3/8 Hex Bolt.

4. Locate the holes using the given dimensions.
5. Save the block as **Block, Cbore.**
6. Start a new **Drawing** document and create a front and a top orthographic view of the **Block, Cbore.**
7. Add all dimensions other than the hole dimensions.
8. Click the **Annotations** tool and select the **Hole Callout** tool.

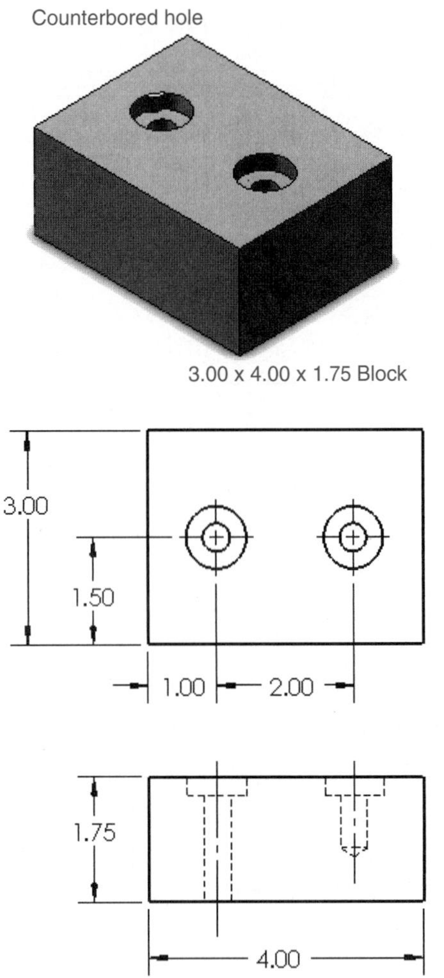

Figure 7-36

See Figure 7-37.

9. Click the edge of each hole, move the cursor away from the hole, and click the mouse when a suitable location is found.

The counterbored hole's dimension note is interpreted as shown in Figure 7-38.

Figure 7-39 shows the Block, Cbore assembled with hex head screws. SolidWorks will automatically generate the correct size counterbored hole for a specified screw. The counterbore depth will align the top of the screw head with the top surface of the part and will define a hole diameter that includes clearance between the fastener and the hole. In this example the Ø.40 is 0.02 larger than the specified 0.38 fastener diameter

If a clearance is required between the top of the screw and the top surface of the part, use the **Head Clearance** tool

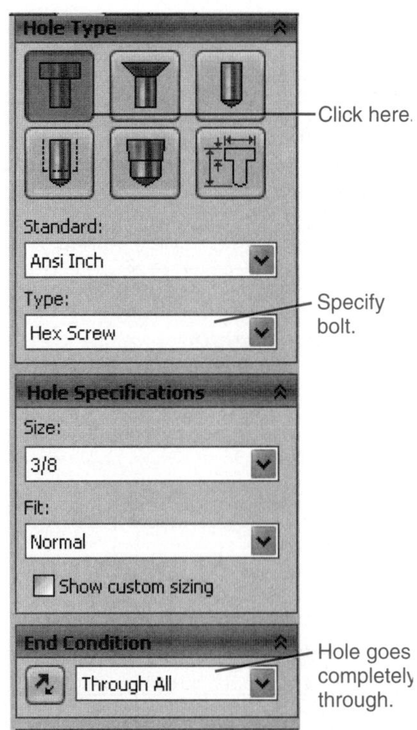

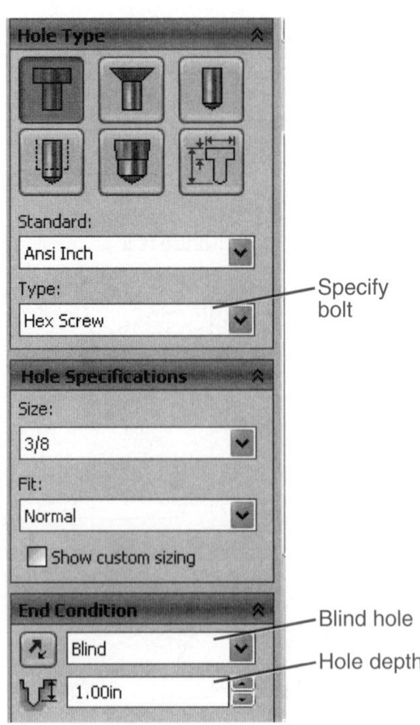

Figure 7-37

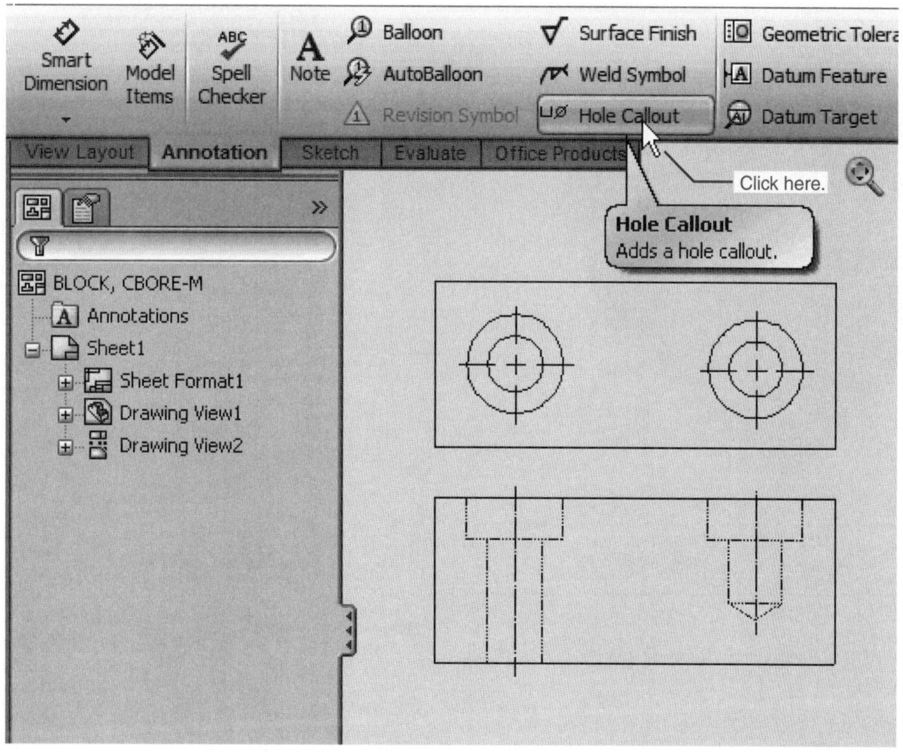

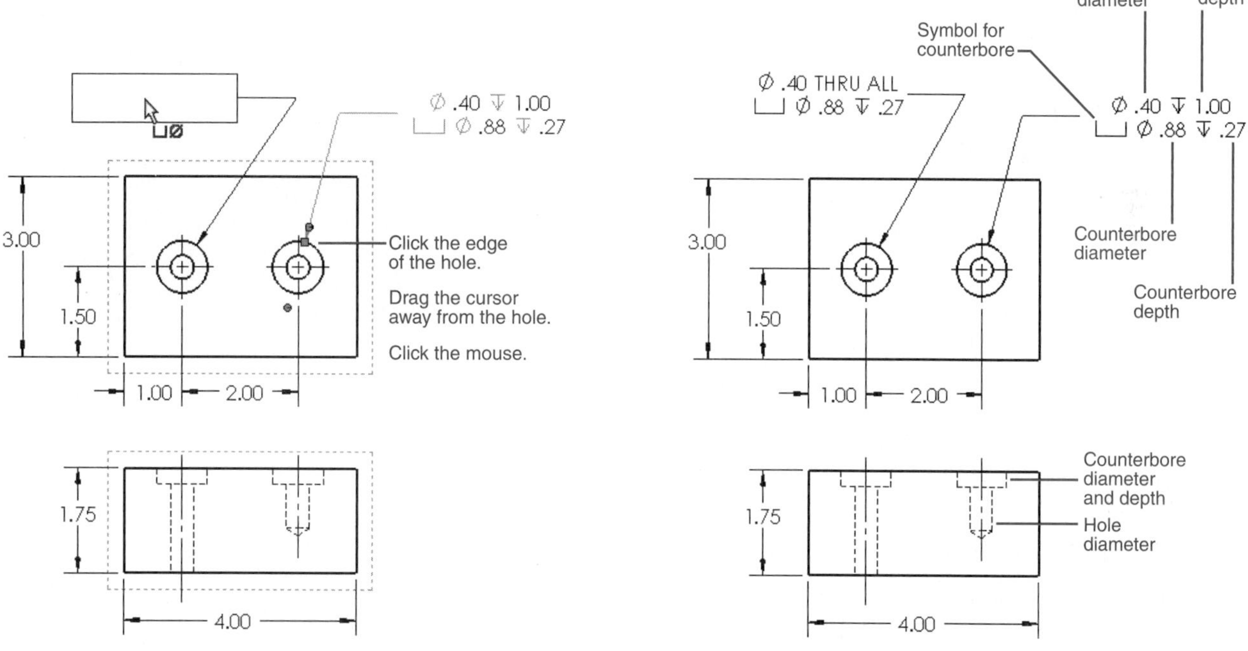

Figure 7-38

in the **Options** box on the **Hole Specification** tab of the **Hole Wizard.** See Figure 7-40.

Note also that the diameter of the counterbored hole is larger than the head of the screw. This is a tool allowance; that is, the hole is large enough to allow a socket wrench to fit over the head of the fastener and still fit within the hole.

Counterbored Hole with Threads

Figure 7-41 shows a 3.00 × 4.00 × 2.00 block with two counterbored holes. Both holes are threaded.

1. Draw the block.
2. Click the **Hole Wizard** and specify a **3/8 -16 UNC** thread that goes completely through.

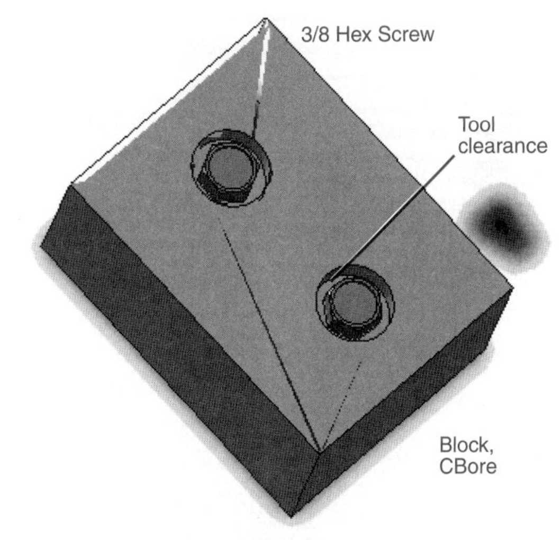

Figure 7-39

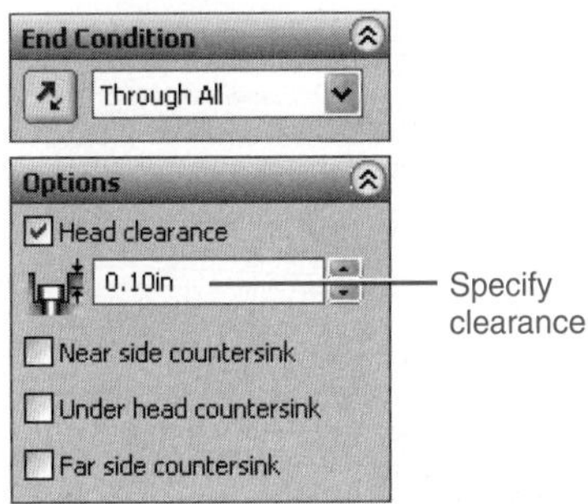

Figure 7-40

3. Click the **Positions** tab and locate the hole.
4. Click the OK check mark.
5. Click the top surface of the block and click the **Sketch** option.
6. Click the **Circle** tool and draw a **Ø0.88** circle to on the top surface centered on the same center point as the Ø3/8-16 hole.

   The dimension for this example came from Figure 7-38.

7. Click the **Features** tool, click the **Extruded Cut** tool, and specify a cut depth of **0.27.**
8. Click the OK check mark.
9. Repeat the procedure adding a second hole with a thread to a depth of **0.85.**

> **TIP**
>
> For an internal thread the thread depth is measured from the top surface of the part.

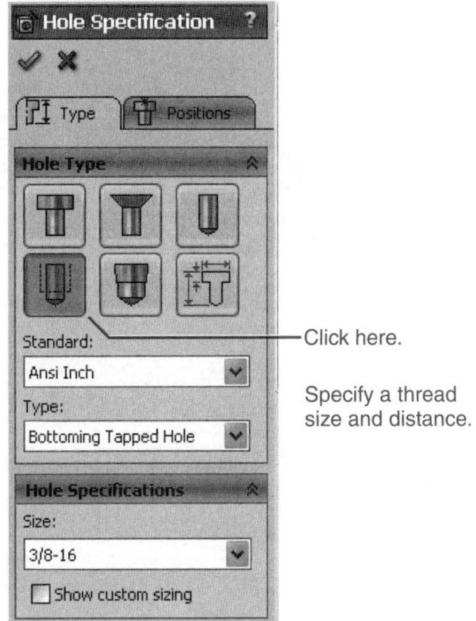

Use the Hole Wizard tool, Positions tab, and locate the hole.

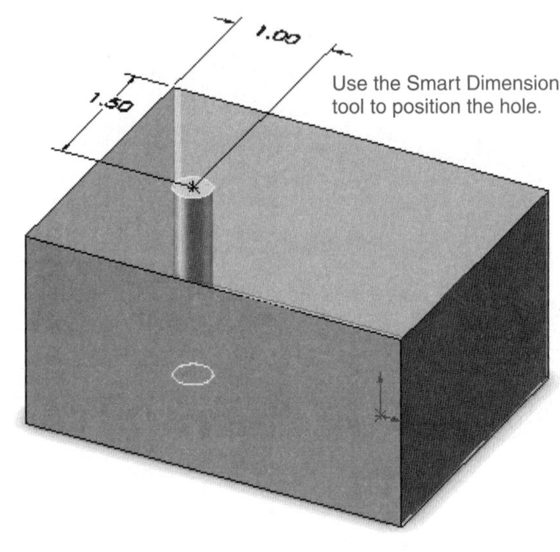

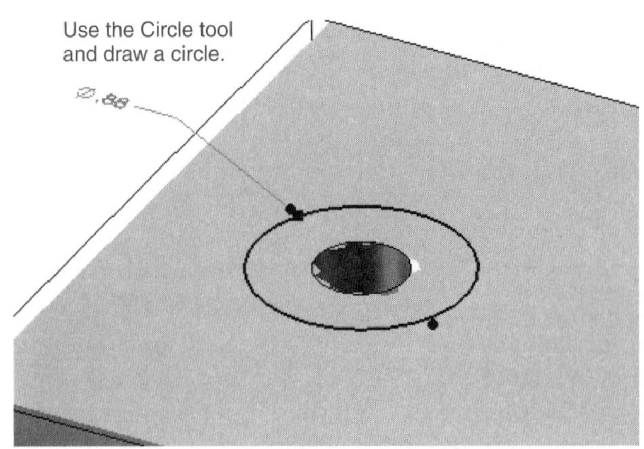

Figure 7-41

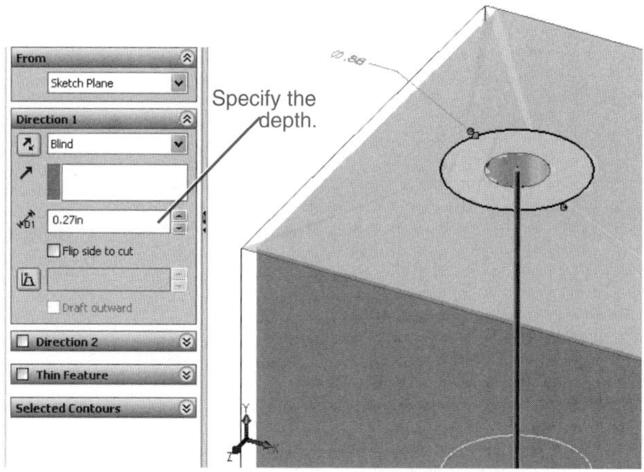

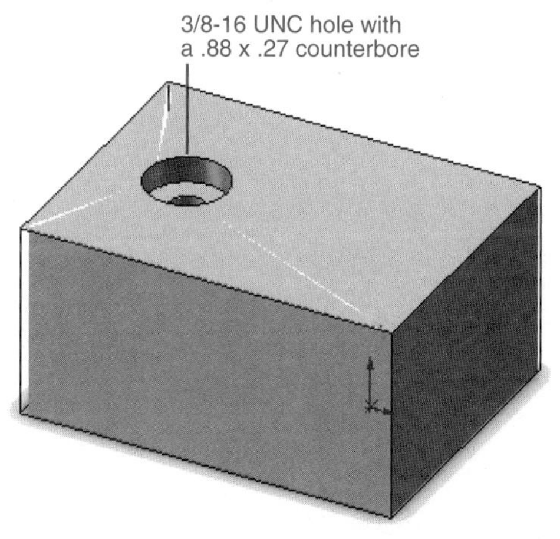

Figure 7-41 *(continued)*

See Figure 7-42.

10. Save the block as **Block, Threads.**
11. Create a new drawing and create front and top orthographic views of the Block, Threads.
12. Add centerlines to the front view and add dimensions as shown.

See Figure 7-43.

13. Use the **Smart Dimension** tool and click the left hole.
14. Locate the text and click the mouse.
15. Click the Ø.88 text and modify the callout to include the thread callout.

The thread callout is modified using the **Dimension Text** box and appropriate symbols.

16. Click the OK check mark.
17. Click the right hole.
18. Locate the text and click the mouse.

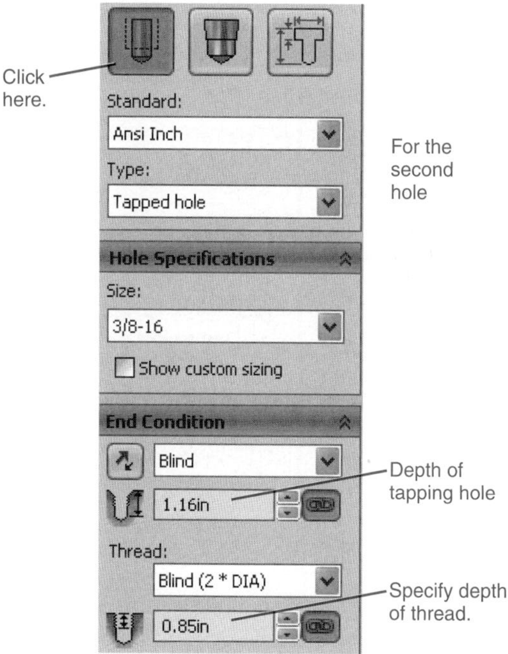

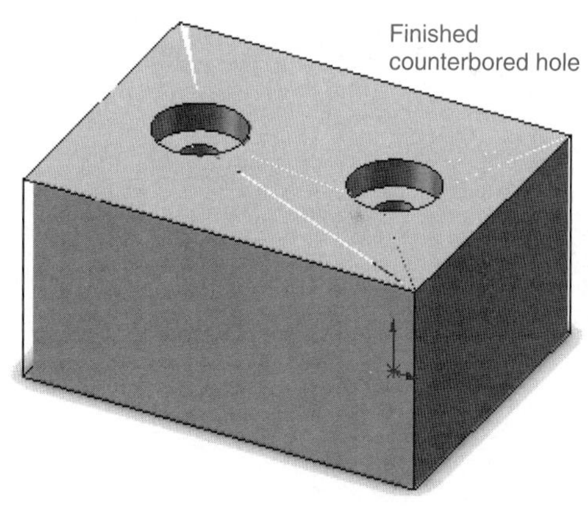

Figure 7-42

19. Click the Ø.88 text and modify the callout to include the thread callout as shown.

Figure 7-44 shows dimensioned counterbored holes using metric units.

To Draw and Dimension Countersunk Holes

Countersunk holes are used with flat head screws to create assemblies where the fasteners do not protrude above the surfaces.

Figure 7-45 shows a part with two countersunk holes; one goes completely through, the other has a depth specification.

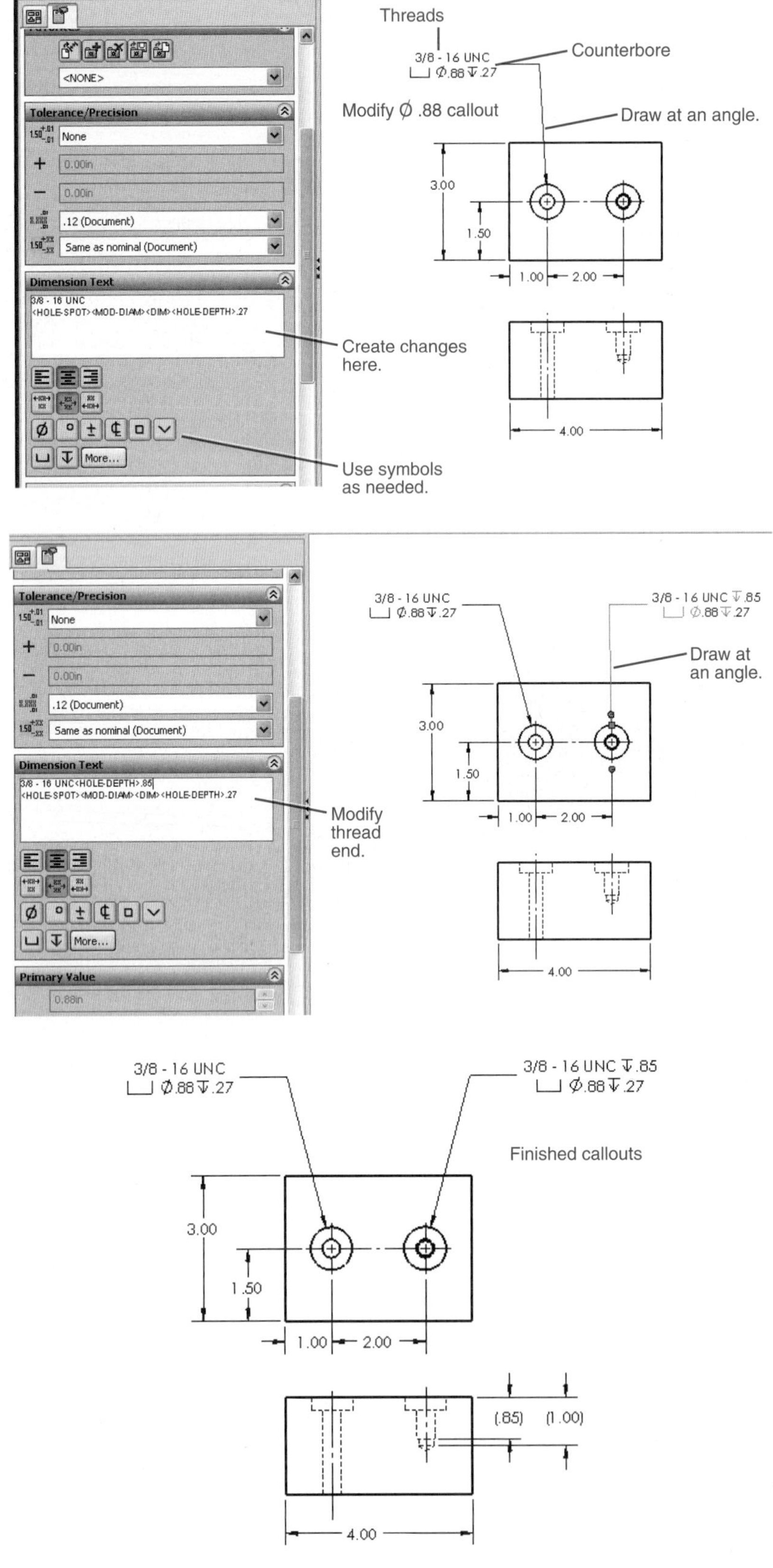
Threads
3/8 - 16 UNC
⌴ Ø.88 ↧.27
Counterbore
Modify Ø .88 callout
Draw at an angle.
3.00
1.50
1.00
2.00
4.00
Tolerance/Precision
None
0.00in
.12 (Document)
Same as nominal (Document)
Dimension Text
3/8 - 16 UNC
<HOLE-SPOT><MOD-DIAM><DIM><HOLE-DEPTH>.27
More...
Create changes here.
Use symbols as needed.
3/8 - 16 UNC ↧.85
⌴ Ø.88 ↧.27
Draw at an angle.
3/8 - 16 UNC<HOLE-DEPTH>.85
<HOLE-SPOT><MOD-DIAM><DIM><HOLE-DEPTH>.27
Modify thread end.
Primary Value
0.88in
Finished callouts
(.85)
(1.00)

Figure 7-43

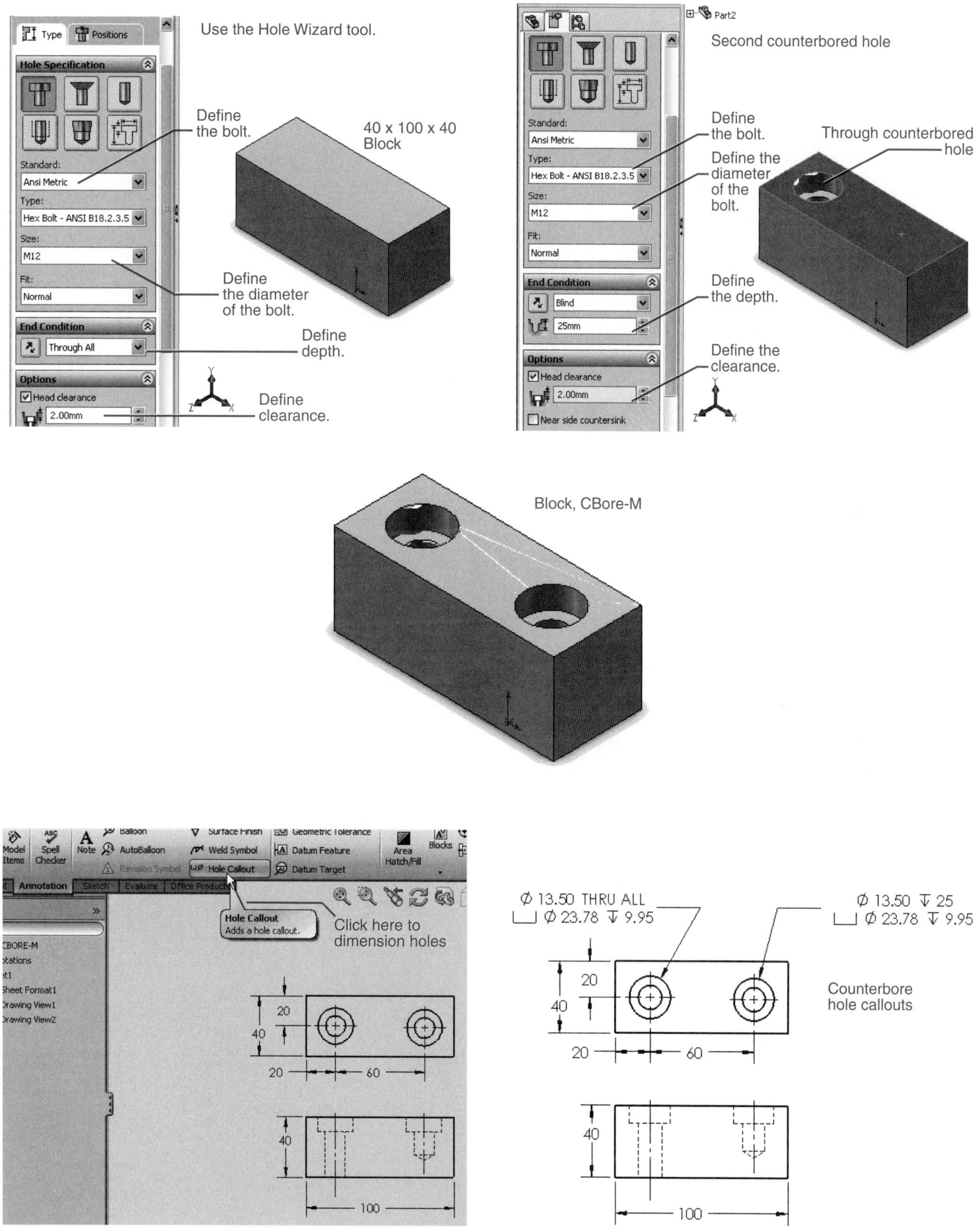

Type Positions
Hole Specification
Standard: Ansi Metric
Type: Hex Bolt - ANSI B18.2.3.5
Size: M12
Fit: Normal
End Condition
Through All
Options
Head clearance
2.00mm

Use the Hole Wizard tool.
Define the bolt.
40 x 100 x 40 Block
Define the diameter of the bolt.
Define depth.
Define clearance.

Part2
Standard: Ansi Metric
Type: Hex Bolt - ANSI B18.2.3.5
Size: M12
Fit: Normal
End Condition
Blind
25mm
Options
Head clearance
2.00mm
Near side countersink

Second counterbored hole
Define the bolt.
Define the diameter of the bolt.
Through counterbored hole
Define the depth.
Define the clearance.

Block, CBore-M

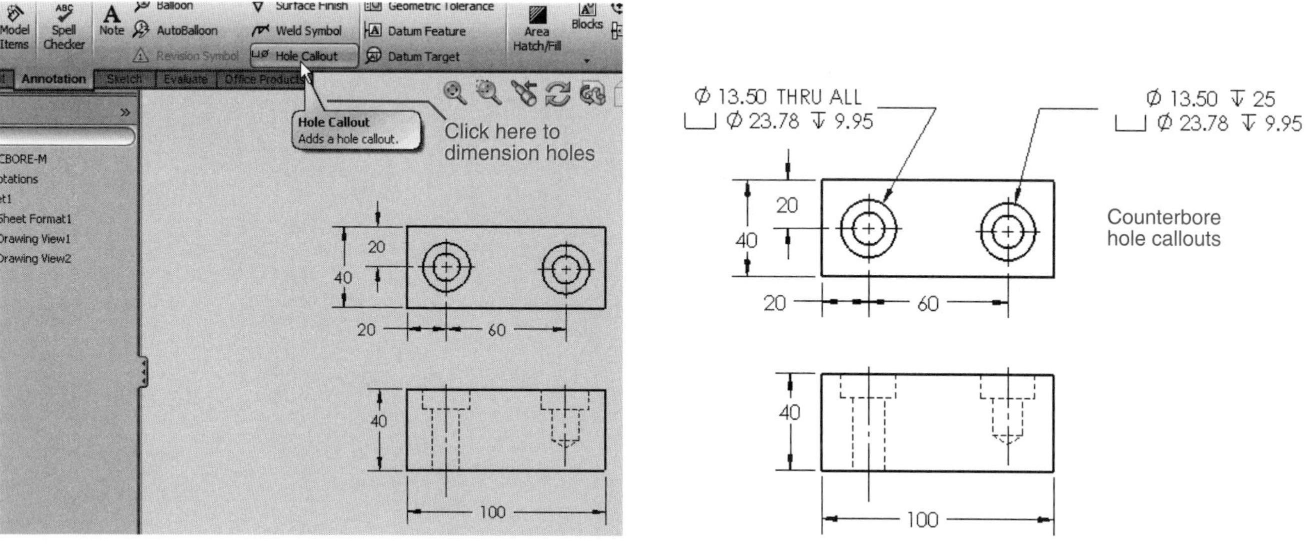

Figure 7-44

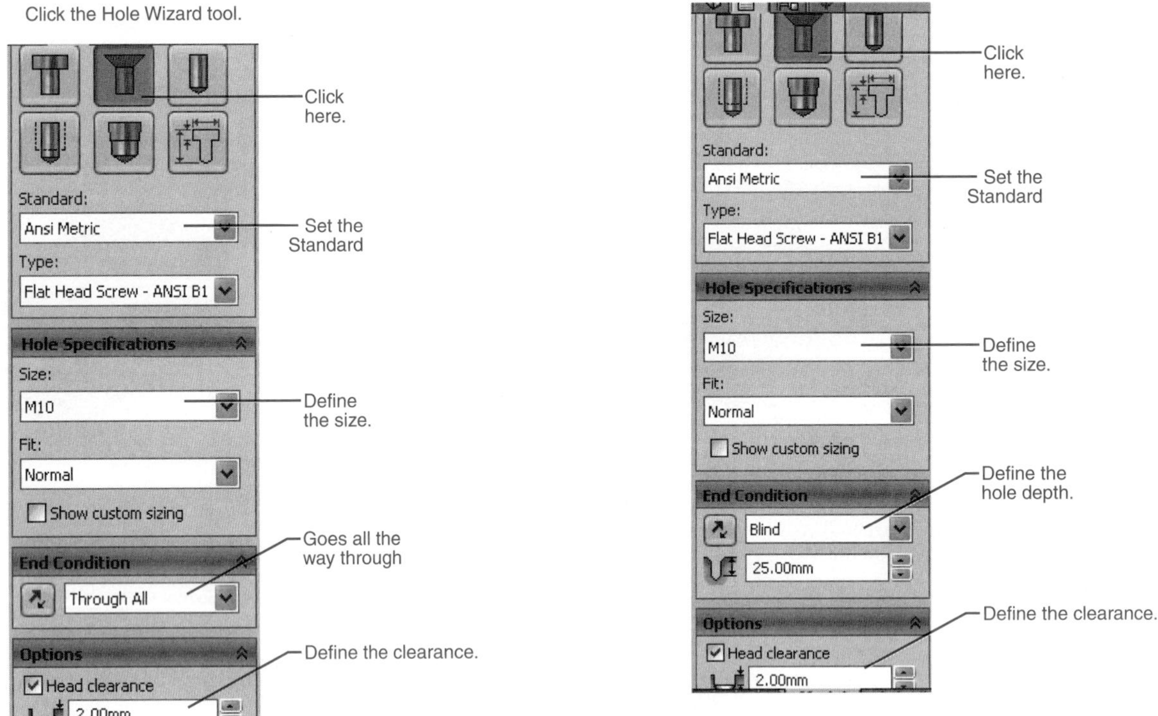
Click the Hole Wizard tool.
Click here.
Standard:
Ansi Metric
Set the Standard
Type:
Flat Head Screw - ANSI B1
Hole Specifications
Size:
M10
Define the size.
Fit:
Normal
Show custom sizing
End Condition
Through All
Goes all the way through
Options
Head clearance
2.00mm
Define the clearance.
Click here.
Standard:
Ansi Metric
Set the Standard
Type:
Flat Head Screw - ANSI B1
Hole Specifications
Size:
M10
Define the size.
Fit:
Normal
Show custom sizing
End Condition
Blind
25.00mm
Define the hole depth.
Options
Head clearance
2.00mm
Define the clearance.

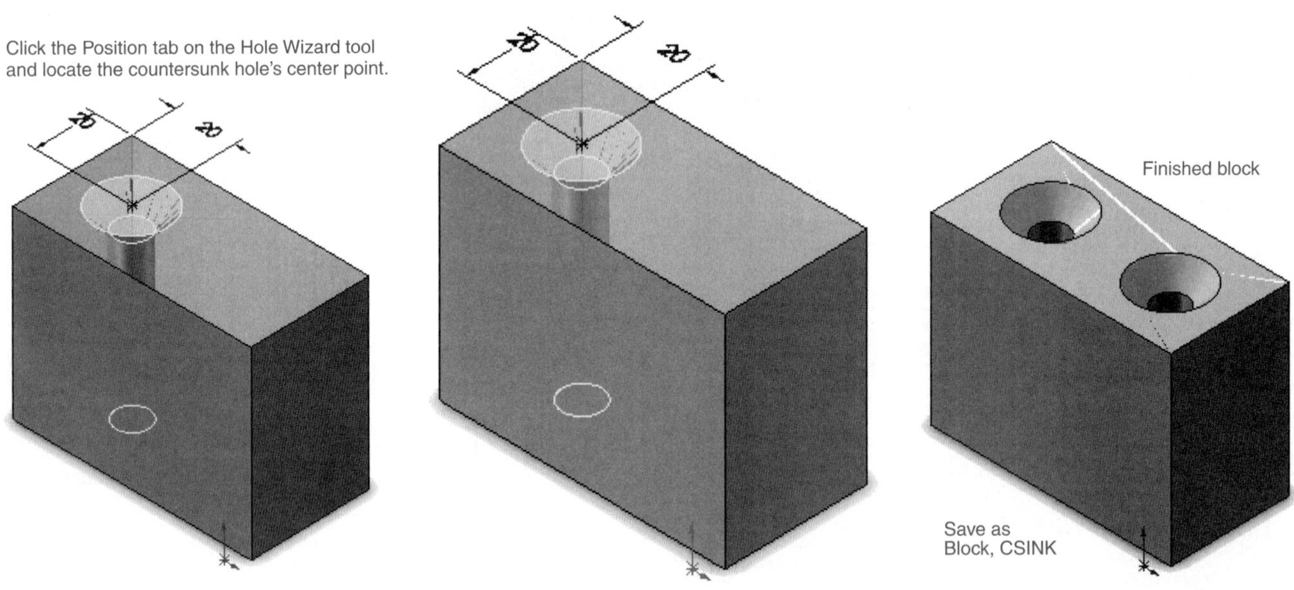
Click the Position tab on the Hole Wizard tool and locate the countersunk hole's center point.
20
20
20
20
Finished block
Save as Block, CSINK

Figure 7-45

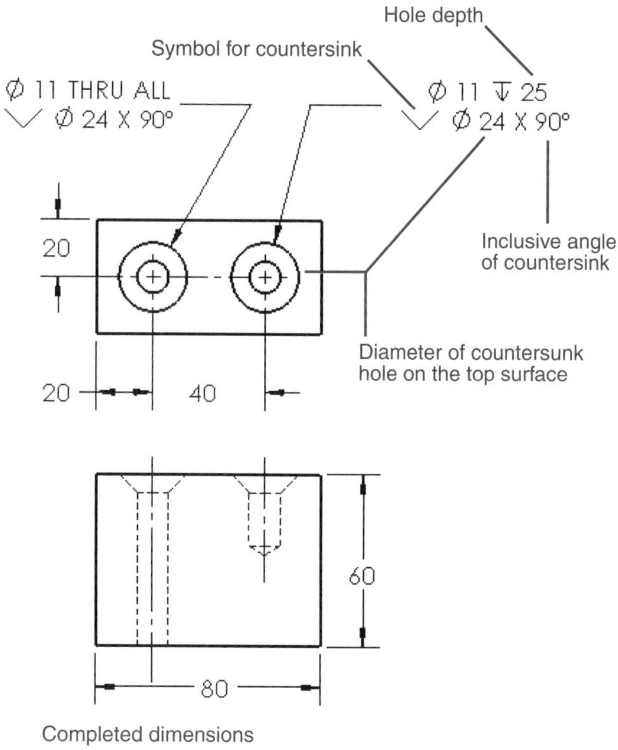

Figure 7-46

1. Draw a 40 × 80 × 60 block.
2. Use the **Hole Wizard** tool, click the **Countersink** tool, specify the **ANSI Metric** standard, select an **M10** size for a flat head screw, and a hole that goes all the way through. Define a head clearance of **2.00.**
3. Click the **Positions** tab and locate the countersunk hole's center point as shown.
4. Click the OK check mark.
5. Click the **Hole Wizard** tool, click the **Countersink** tool, specify the **ANSI Metric** standard, select an **M10** size for a flat head screw, and specify the depth requirement for a blind hole. Define a head clearance of **2.00.**
6. Click the **Positions** tab and locate the hole as shown.
7. Click the OK check mark.
8. Save the drawing as **Block, CSink.**

See Figure 4-46

1. Create a new drawing with a front and top orthographic view of the Block, CSink.
2. Use the **Smart Dimension** tool and add the appropriate dimensions.

Figure 7-49 shows two views of the same object dimensioned in two different ways. In this example only linear dimensions are included.

3. Use the **Center Mark** tool to add a centerline between the two holes indicating they are aligned.
4. Click the **Annotations** tool, click the **Hole Callout** tool, and dimension the two countersunk holes.

7-8 ANGULAR DIMENSIONS

Figure 7-47 shows a model that includes a slanted surface. The dimension value is located beyond the model between two extension lines. Locating dimensions between extension lines is preferred to locating the value between an extension line and the edge of the model.

Avoiding Overdimensioning

Figure 7-48 shows a shape that includes a slanted surface dimensioned in two different ways. The shape on the left uses an angular dimension; the one on the right does not. Both are acceptable.

Figure 7-49 shows an object dimensioned two different ways. The dimensions used in the top example do not include a dimension for the width of the slot. This dimension

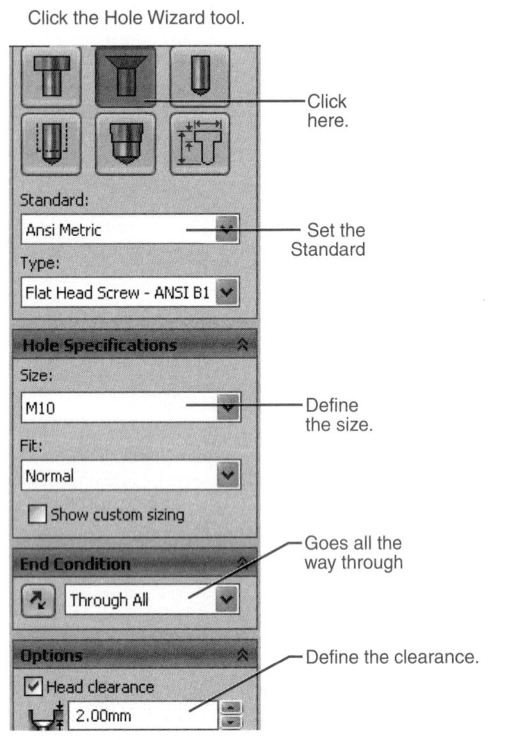

Figure 7-47

is allowed to *float,* that is, allowed to accept any tolerance buildup. The dimensions used in the bottom example dimension the width of the slot but not the upper right edge. In this example the upper right edge is allowed to float or accept any tolerance buildup. The choice of which edge to float depends on the function of the part. If the slot were to interface with a tab on another part, then it would be imperative that it be dimensioned and toleranced to match the interfacing part.

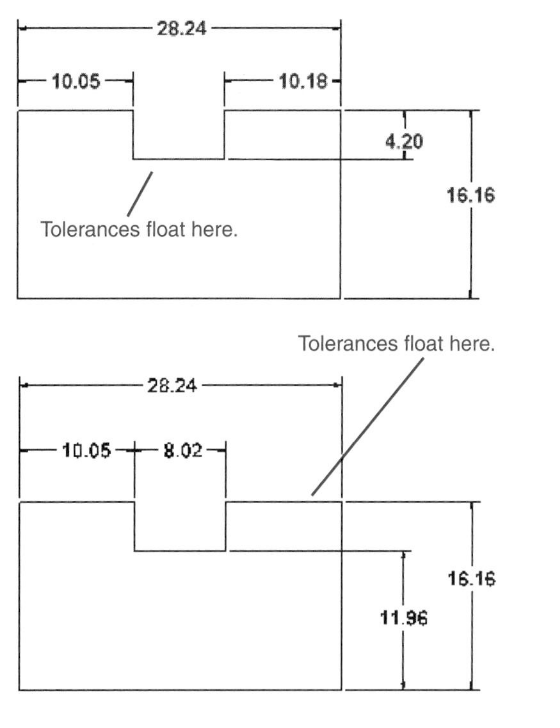

Figure 7-49

7-9 ORDINATE DIMENSIONS

Ordinate dimensions are dimensions based on an X,Y coordinate system. Ordinate dimensions do not include extension lines, dimension lines, or arrowheads but simply horizontal and vertical leader lines drawn directly from the features of the object. Ordinate dimensions are particularly useful when dimensioning an object that includes many small holes.

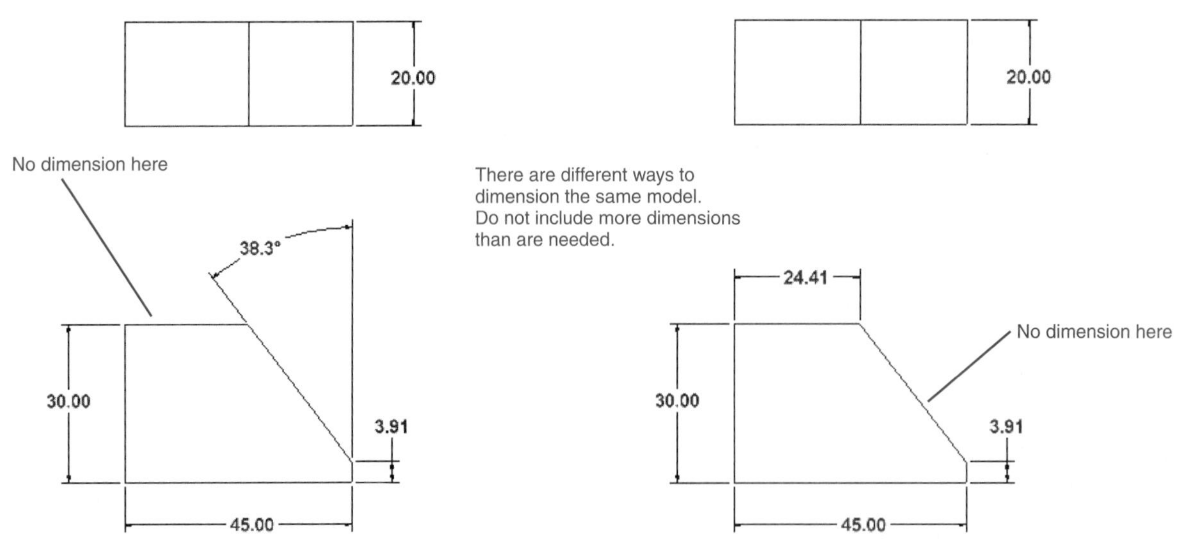

Figure 7-48

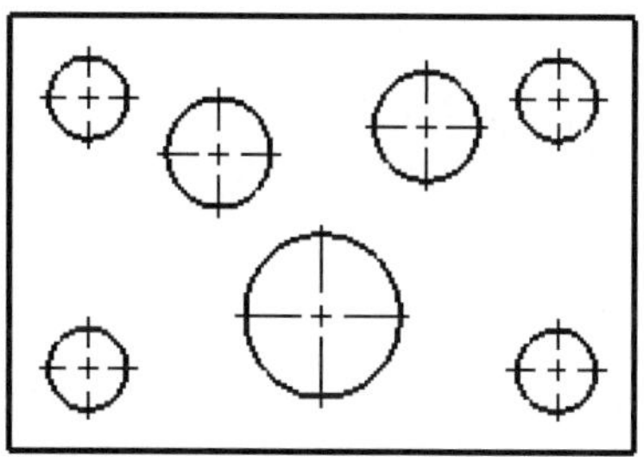

Figure 7-50

Figure 7-50 shows a part that is to be dimensioned using ordinate dimensions. Ordinate dimensions values are calculated from the X,Y origin, which, in this example, is the lower left corner of the front view of the model.

To Create Ordinate Dimensions

See Figure 7-51.

1. Start a new drawing and create a top orthographic view of the part.

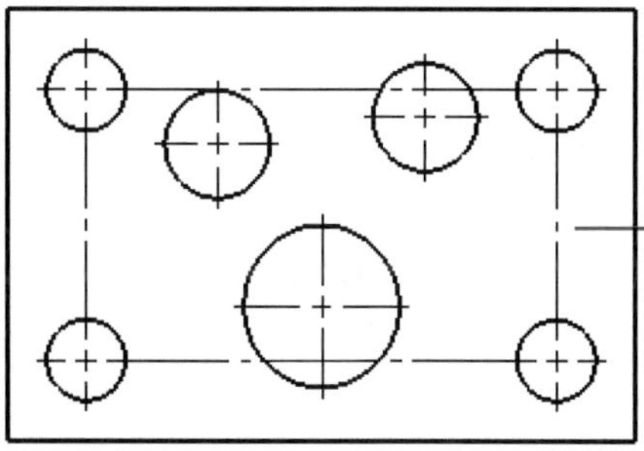

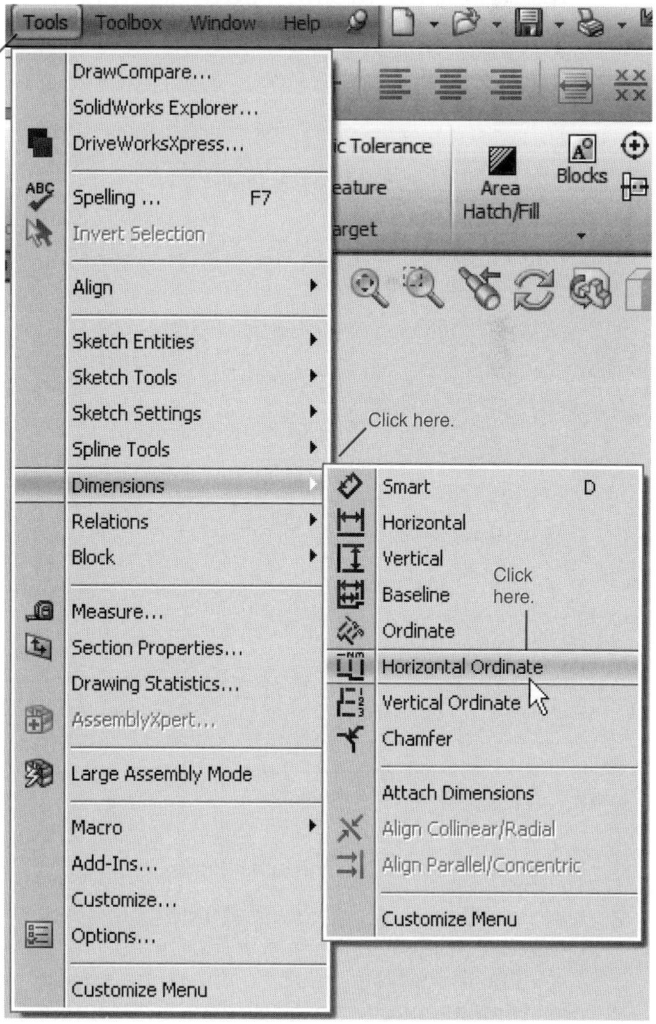

Figure 7-51

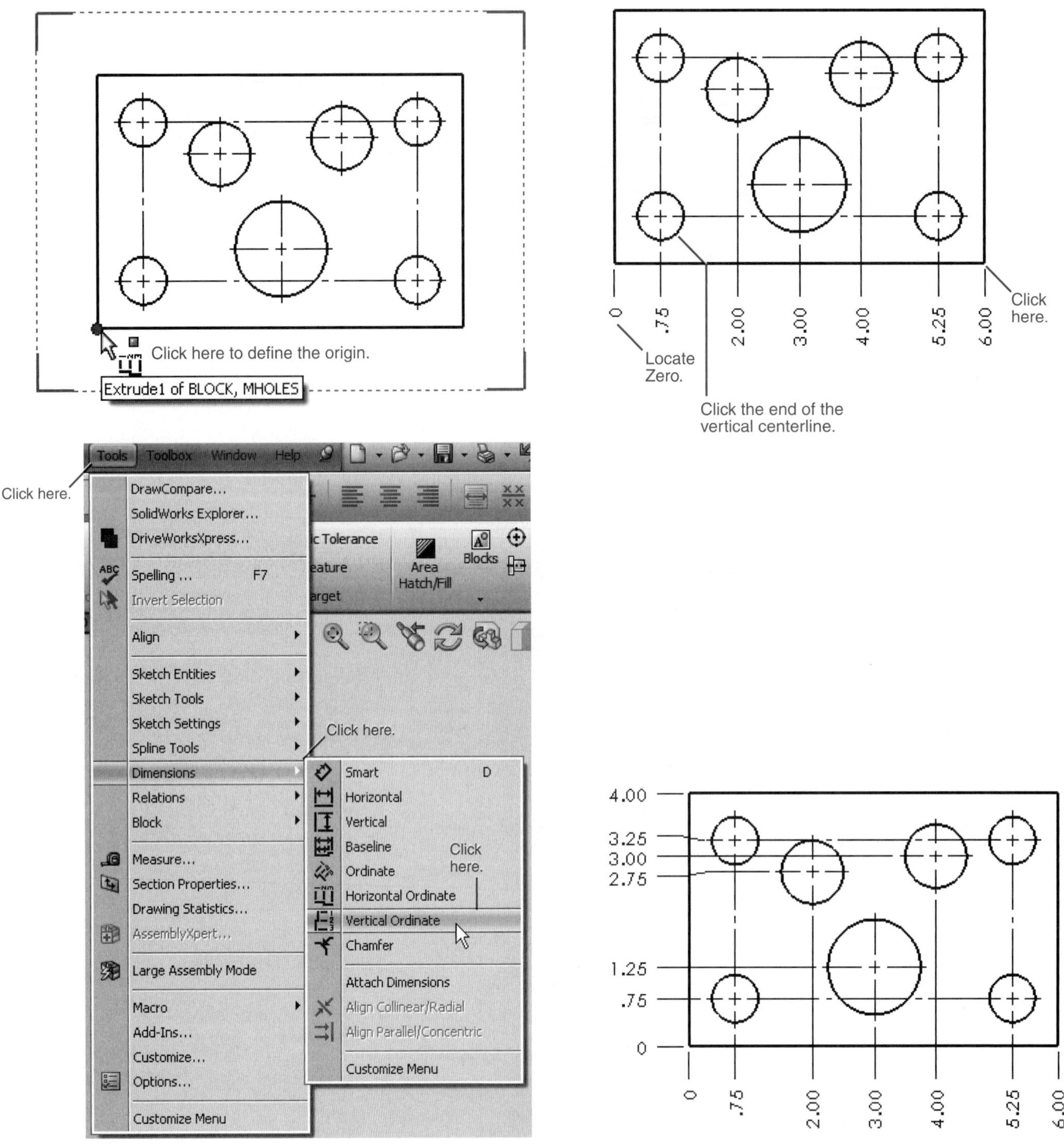

Figure 7-51 ***(continued)***

Use the dimensions shown in either Figure 7-51 or 7-53

2. Use the **Center Mark** tool and add connection centerlines between the four corner holes.
3. Click the **Tools** heading at the top of the screen, click **Dimensions,** and click **Horizontal Ordinate.**
4. Click the lower left corner of the part to establish the origin for the dimensions.
5. Move the cursor away from the origin and define a location for the “0” dimension.

All other horizontal dimensions will align with this location.

6. Click the lower portion of each hole’s vertical centerline and the lower right corner of the part.

7. Click the **Tools** heading again, click **Dimensions,** and click **Vertical Ordinate.**
8. Click the lower left corner of the part to establish the origin for the dimensions.
9. Click the left portion of each holes horizontal centerline and the upper left corner of the part.
10. Add dimensions for the holes.

Figure 7-52 shows the dimensioned part.

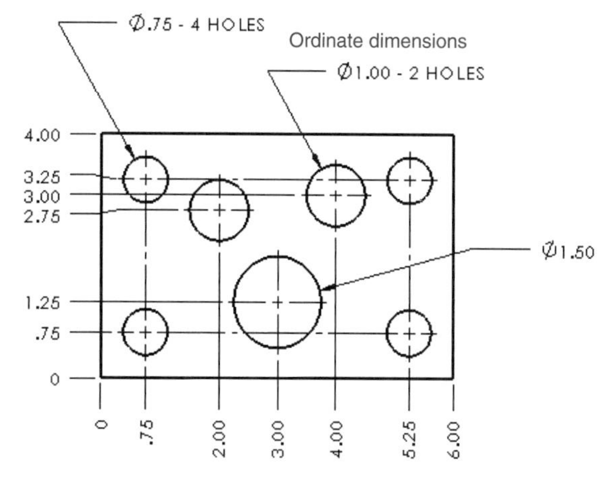

Figure 7-52

7-10 BASELINE DIMENSIONS

Baseline dimensions are a series of dimensions that originate from a common baseline or datum line. Baseline dimensions are very useful because they help eliminate the tolerance buildup that is associated with chain-type dimensions.

To Create Baseline Dimensions

See Figure 7-53.

1. Start a new drawing and create a top orthographic view of the part.
2. Use the **Center Mark** tool and add connection centerlines between the four corner holes.
3. Click the **Tools** heading at the top of the screen, click **Dimensions,** and click **Baseline.**
4. Click the left vertical edge of the part and the lower portion of the first vertical centerline.

This will establish the baseline.

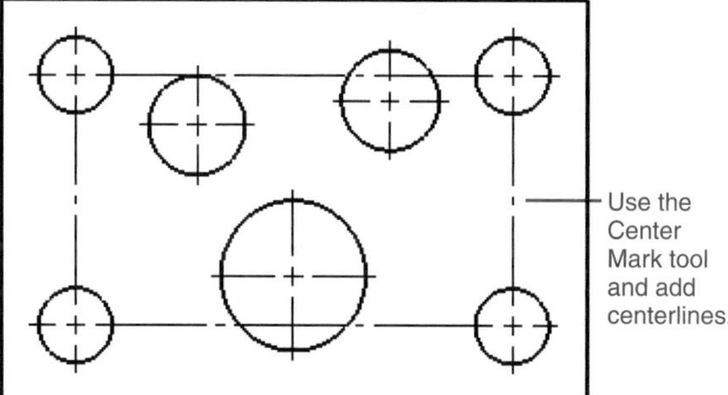

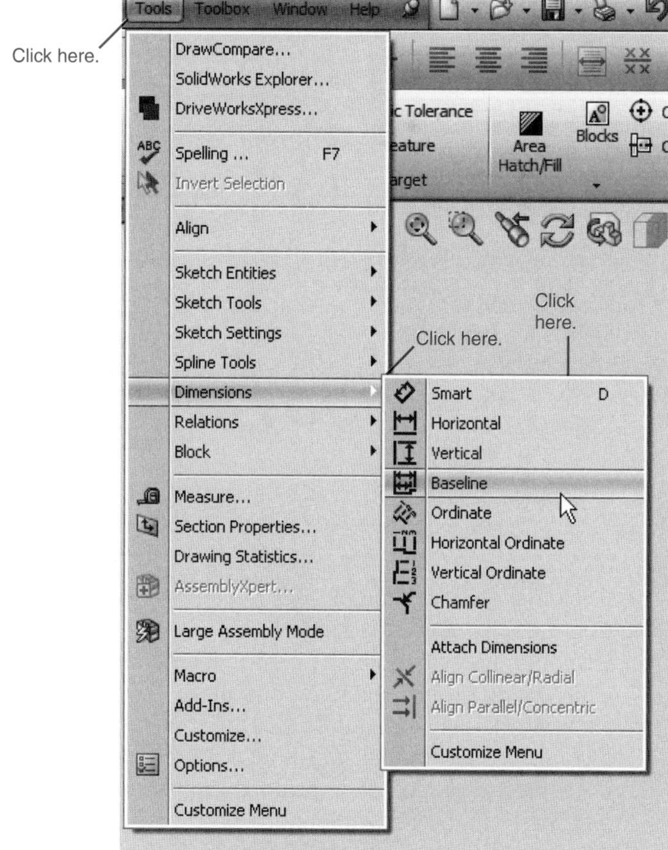

Figure 7-53

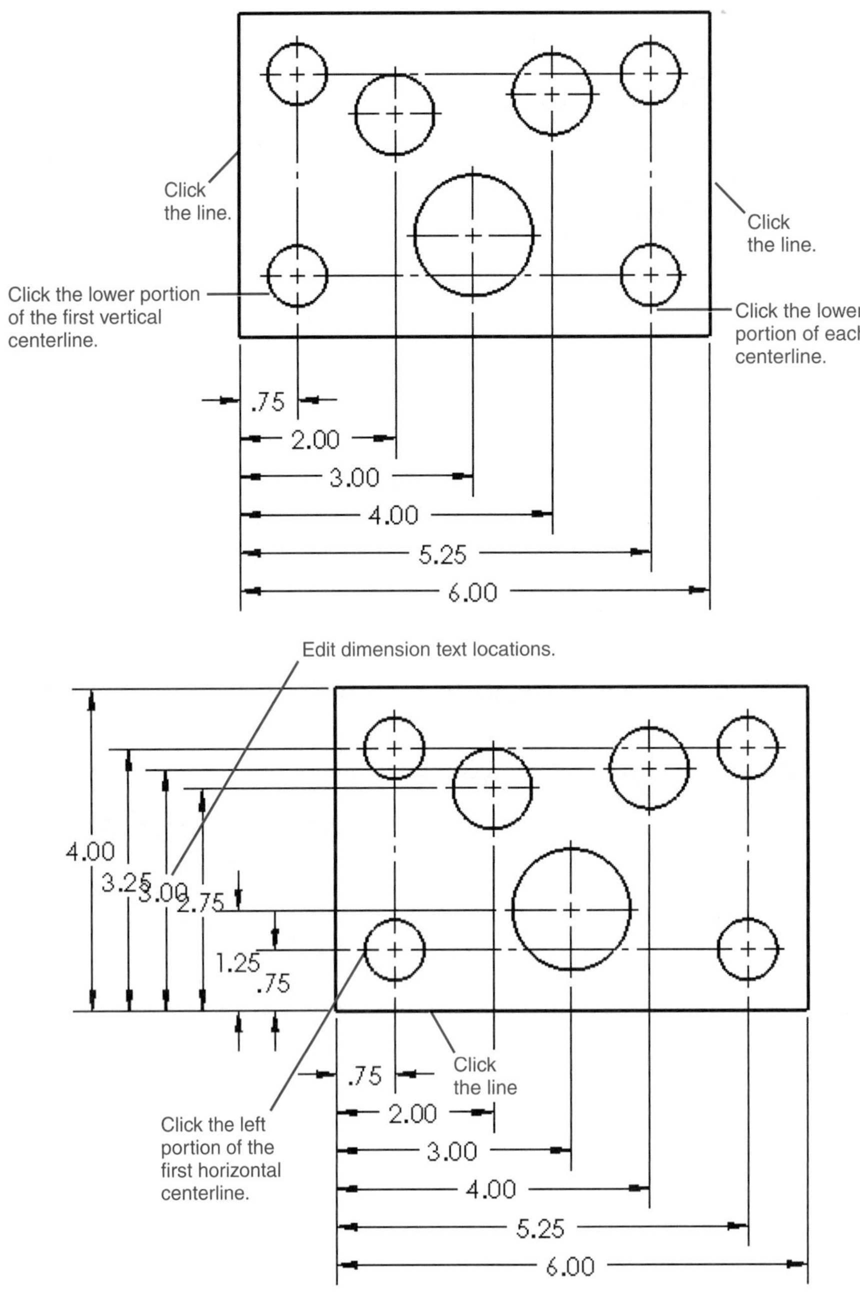

Figure 7-53 ***(continued)***

5. Click the lower portion of each vertical centerline and the right vertical edge line.
6. Click the **Tools** heading at the top of the screen, click **Dimensions,** and click **Baseline.**
7. Click the lower horizontal edge of the part and the left portion of the first horizontal centerline.
8. Click the left portion of each horizontal centerline and the right top horizontal edge line.

The dimension text may overlap as shown. If this happens, edit the text locations.

9. Add the hole dimensions.

Hole Tables

Hole tables are a method for dimensioning parts that have large numbers of holes where standard dimensioning may be cluttered and difficult to read. See Figure 7-54.

1. Start a new drawing and create a top orthographic view of the part.

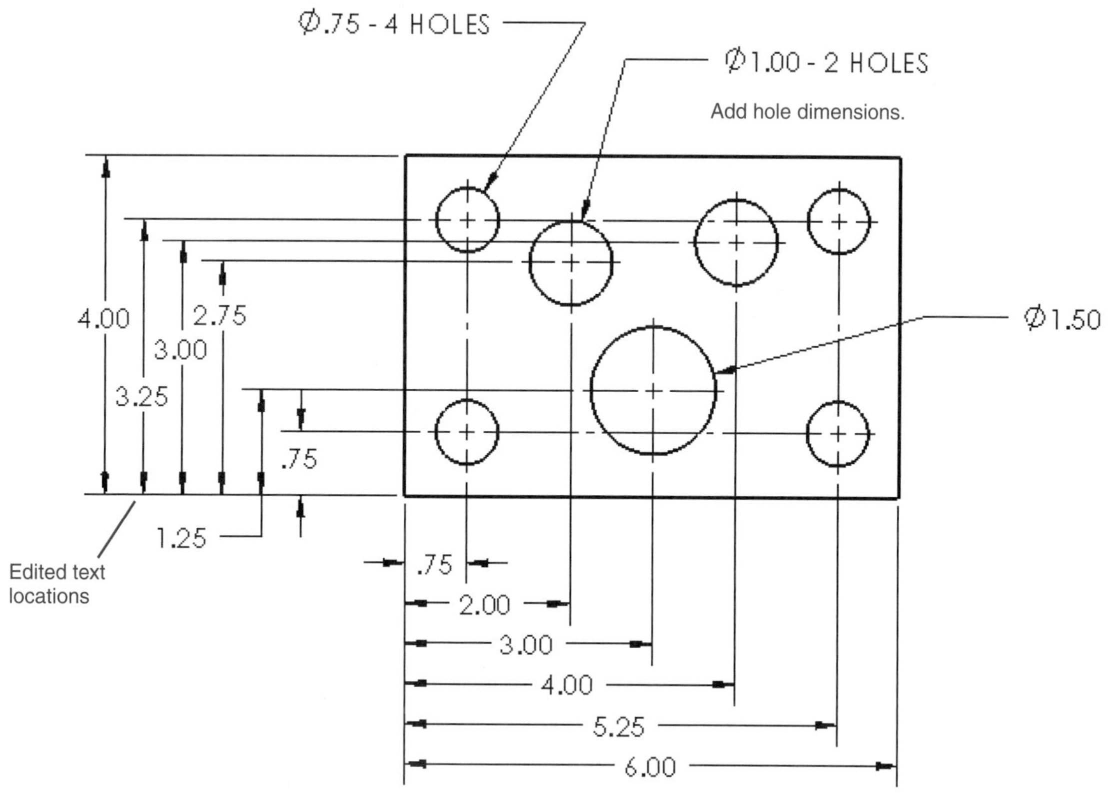

Figure 7-53 *(continued)*

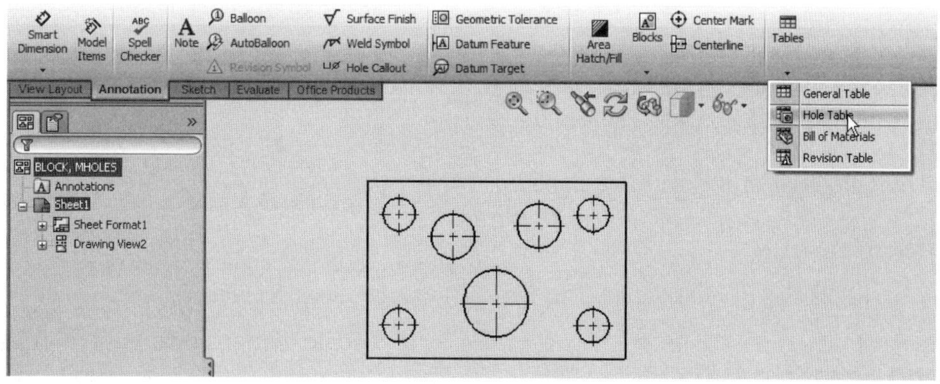

Figure 7-54

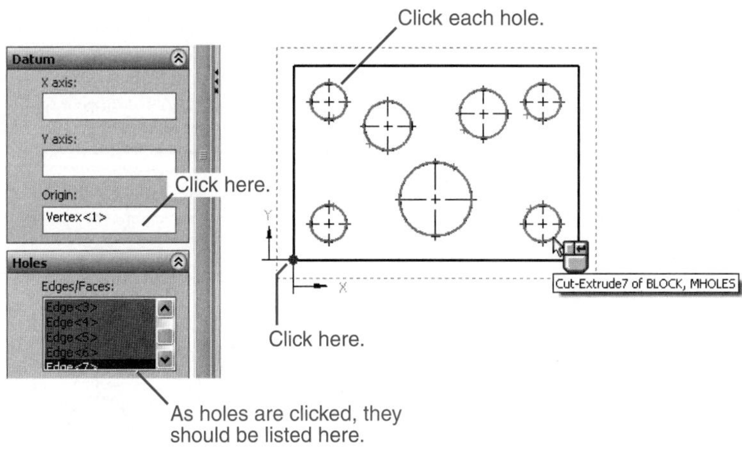

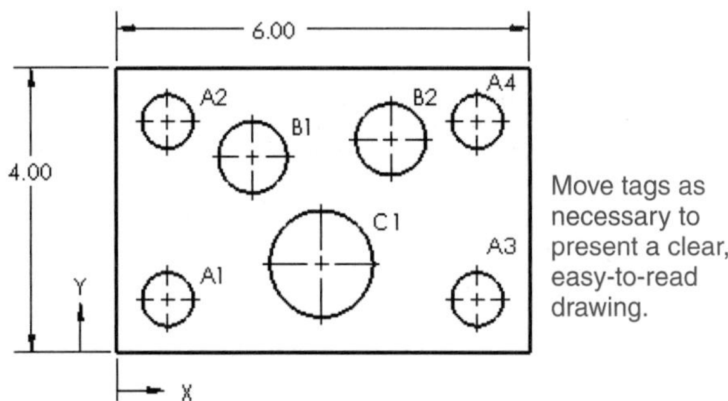

Hole table

TAG	X LOC	Y LOC	SIZE
A1	.75	.75	Ø.75
A2	.75	3.25	Ø.75
A3	5.25	.75	Ø.75
A4	5.25	3.25	Ø.75
B1	2.00	2.75	Ø1.00
B2	4.00	3.00	Ø1.00
C1	3.00	1.25	Ø1.50

Figure 7-54 ***(continued)***

2. Use the **Center Mark** tool and add connection centerlines between the four corner holes.
3. Click the **Annotations** toolbar, click **Tables,** and click **Hole Table.**
4. Click the lower left corner of the part to establish an orign.
5. Click each hole.

As the hole are clicked they should be listed in the **Holes** box.

6. Add the overall dimensions.
7. Move the hole tags to present a clear, easy-to-read drawing.

In this example all tags were located to the upper right of the holes they define.

7-11 LOCATING DIMENSIONS

There are eight general rules concerning the location of dimensions. See Figure 7-55.

1. Locate dimensions near the features they are defining.
2. Do not locate dimensions on the surface of the object.

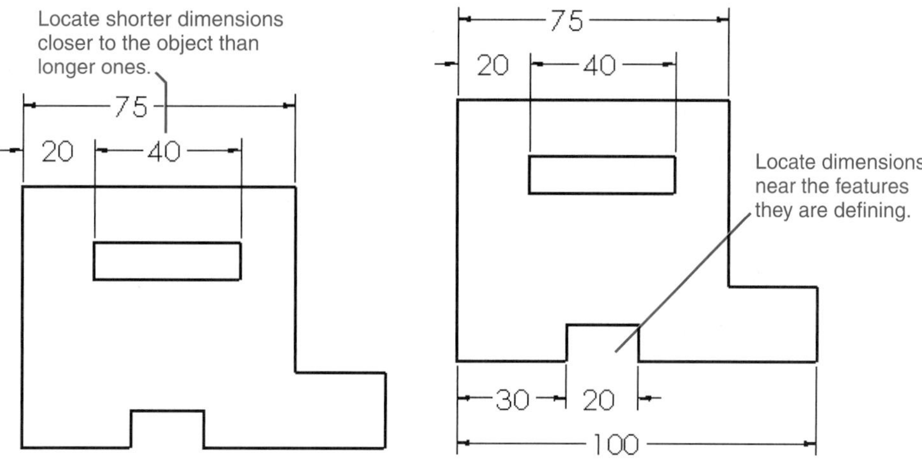

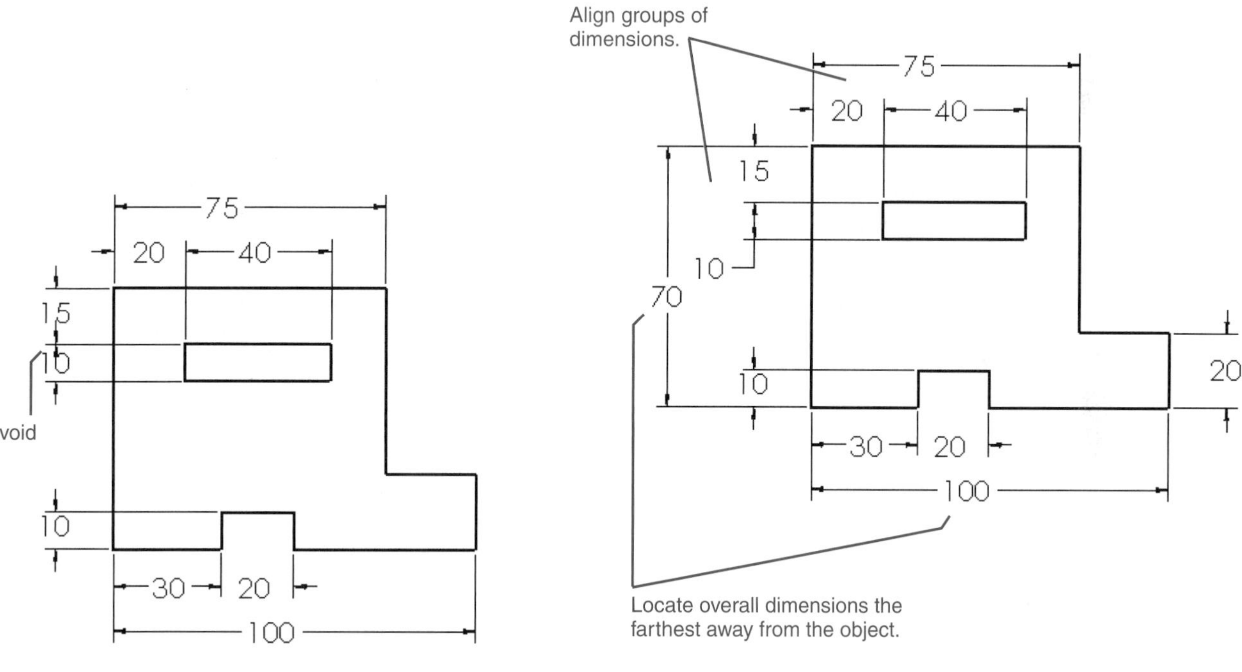

Figure 7-55

3. Align and group dimensions so that they are neat and easy to understand.
4. Avoid crossing extension lines.

Sometimes it is impossible not to cross extension lines because of the complex shape of the object, but whenever possible, avoid crossing extension lines.

5. Do not cross dimension lines.
6. Locate shorter dimensions closer to the object than longer ones.
7. Always locate overall dimensions the farthest away from the object.
8. Do not dimension the same distance twice. This is called double dimensioning and will be discussed in Chapter 8.

7-12 FILLETS AND ROUNDS

Fillets and rounds may be dimensioned individually or by a note. In many design situations all the fillets and rounds are the same size, so a note as shown in Figure 7-56 is used. Any fillets or rounds that have a different radius from that specified by the note are dimensioned individually.

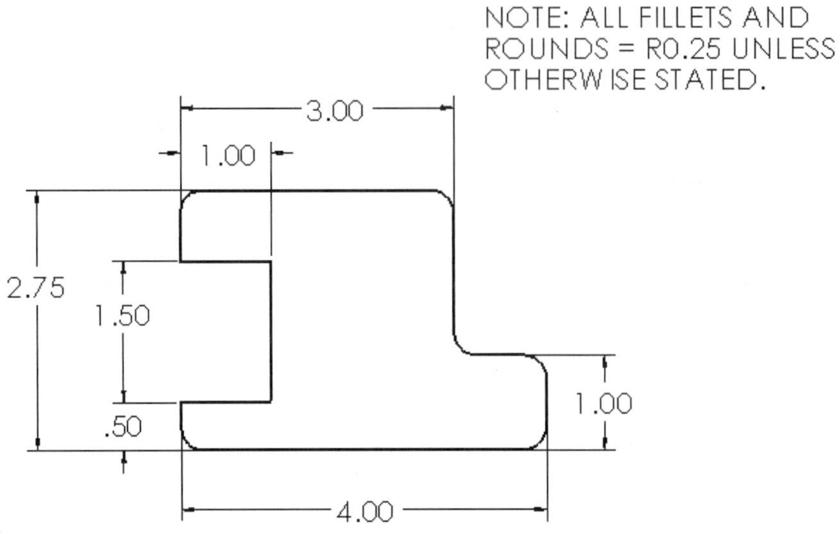

Figure 7-56

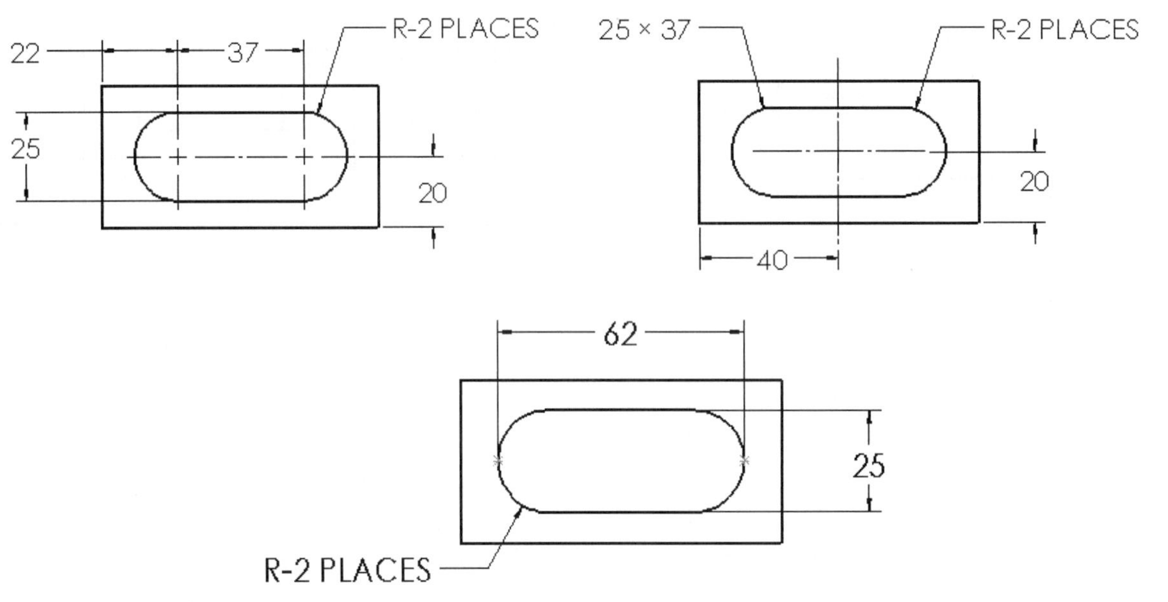

Figure 7-57

7-13 ROUNDED SHAPES—INTERNAL

Internal rounded shapes are called ***slots.*** Figure 7-57 shows three different methods for dimensioning slots. The end radii are indicated by the note R - 2 PLACES, but no numerical value is given. The width of the slot is dimensioned, and it is assumed that the radius of the rounded ends is exactly half of the stated width.

7-14 ROUNDED SHAPES—EXTERNAL

Figure 7-58 shows two shapes with external rounded ends. As with internal rounded shapes, the end radii are indicated but no value is given. The width of the object is given, and the radius of the rounded end is assumed to be exactly half of the stated width.

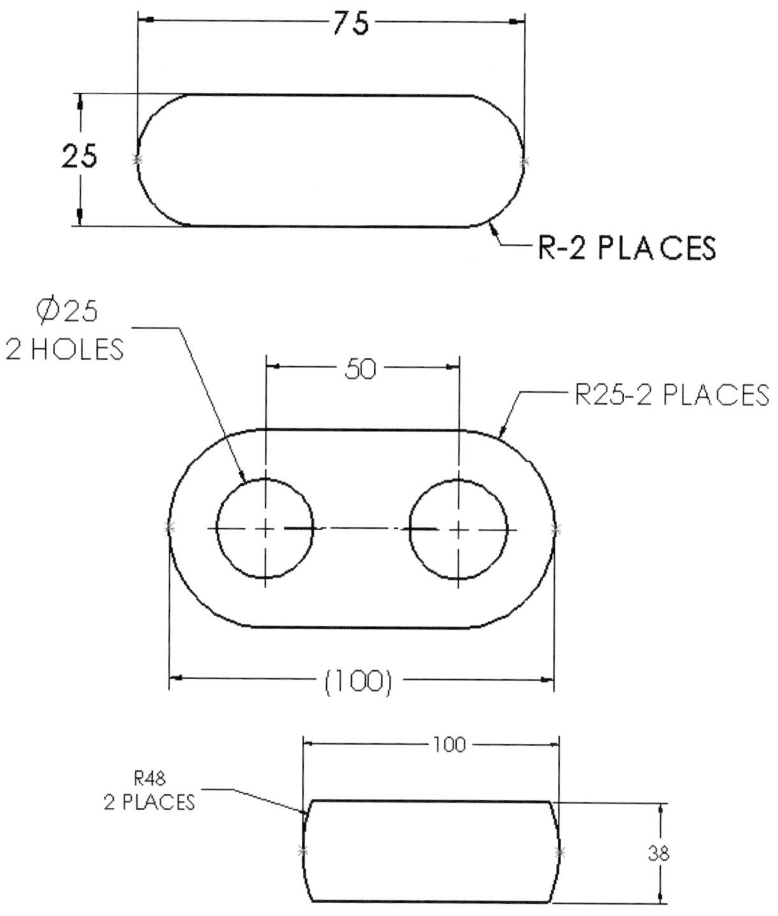

Figure 7-58

The second example shown in Figure 7-58 shows an object dimensioned using the object's centerline. This type of dimensioning is done when the distance between the holes is more important than the overall length of the object; that is, the tolerance for the distance between the holes is more exact than the tolerance for the overall length of the object.

The overall length of the object is given as a reference dimension (100). This means the object will be manufactured based on the other dimensions, and the 100 value will be used only for reference.

Objects with partially rounded edges should be dimensioned as shown in Figure 7-58. The radii of the end features are dimensioned. The center point of the radii is implied to be on the object centerline. The overall dimension is given; it is not referenced unless specific radii values are included.

7-15 IRREGULAR SURFACES

There are three different methods for dimensioning irregular surfaces: tabular, baseline, and baseline with oblique extension lines. Figure 7-59 shows an irregular surface dimensioned using the tabular method. An XY axis is defined using the edges of the object. Points are then defined relative to the XY axis. The points are assigned reference numbers, and the reference numbers and XY coordinate values are listed in chart form as shown.

Figure 7-60 shows an irregular curve dimensioned using baseline dimensions. The baseline method references all dimensions to specified baselines. Usually there are two baselines, one horizontal and one vertical.

It is considered poor practice to use a centerline as a baseline. Centerlines are imaginary lines that do not exist on the object and would make it more difficult to manufacture and inspect the finished objects.

Baseline dimensioning is very common because it helps eliminate tolerance buildup and is easily adaptable to many manufacturing processes.

7-16 POLAR DIMENSIONS

Polar dimensions are similar to polar coordinates. A location is defined by a radius (distance) and an angle. Figure 7-61 shows an object that includes polar dimensions.

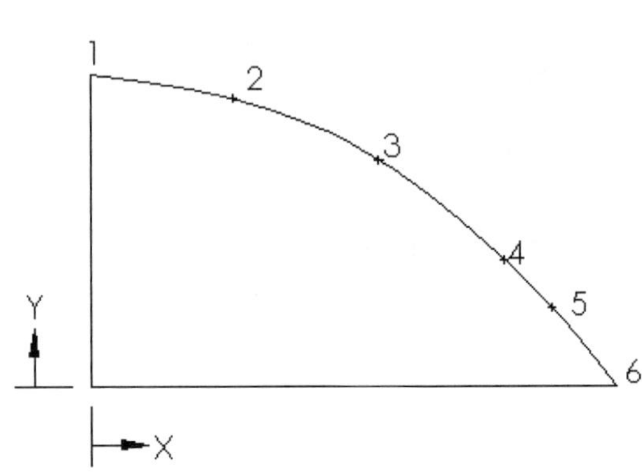

STATION	1	2	3	4	5	6
X	0	20	40	55	62	70
Y	40	38	30	16	10	0

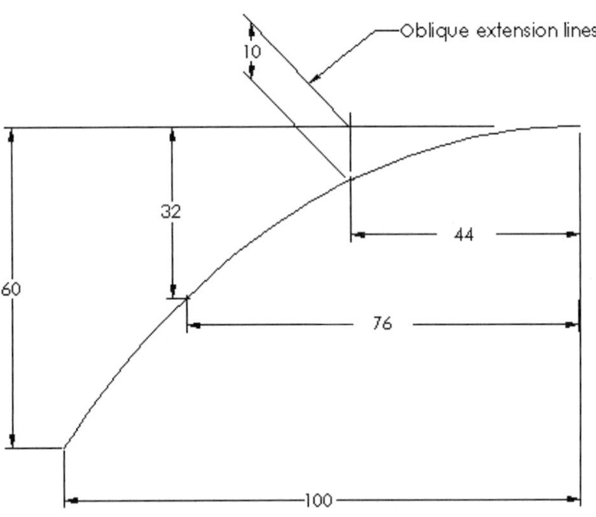

Figure 7-59

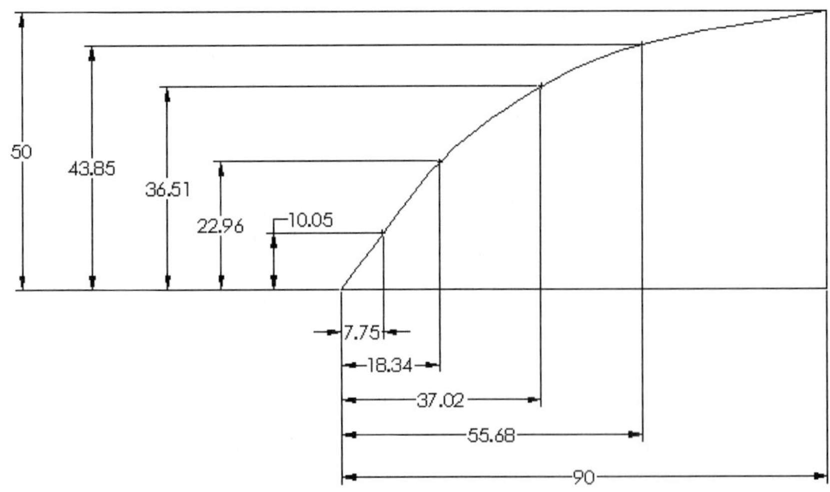

Figure 7-60

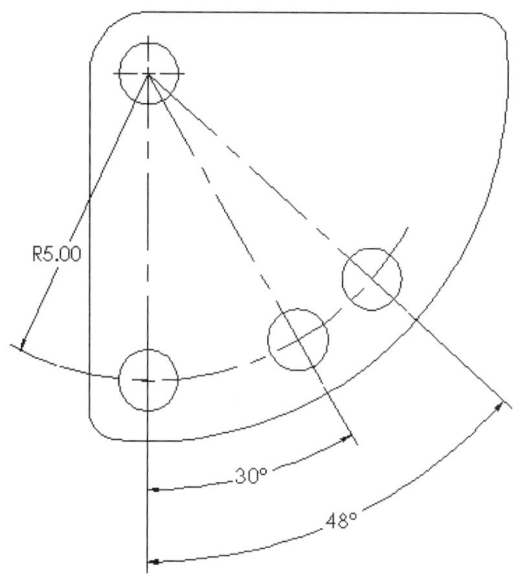

Figure 7-61

The holes are located on a circular centerline, and their positions from the vertical centerline are specified using angles.

Figure 7-62 shows an example of a hole pattern dimensioned using polar dimensions.

7-17 CHAMFERS

Chamfers are angular cuts made on the edges of objects. They are usually used to make it easier to fit two parts together. They are most often made at 45° angles but may be made at any angle. Figure 7-63 shows two objects with chamfers between surfaces 90° apart and two examples between surfaces that are not 90° apart. Either of the two types of dimensions shown for the 45° dimension may be used. If an angle other than 45° is used, the angle and setback distance must be specified.

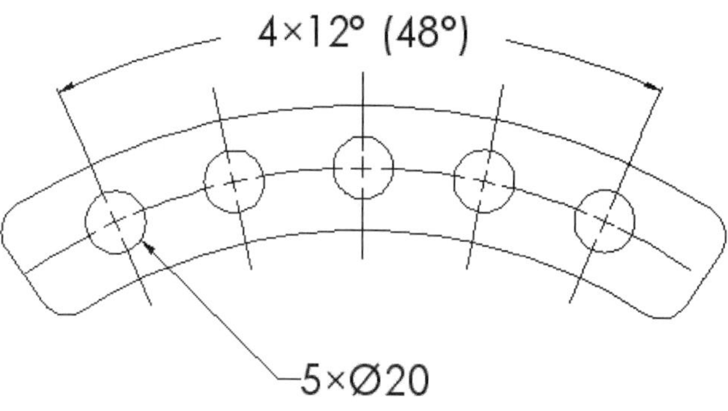

Figure 7-62

Figure 7-64 shows two examples of internal chamfers. Both define the chamfer using an angle and diameter. Internal chamfers are very similar to countersunk holes.

7-18 SYMBOLS AND ABBREVIATIONS

Symbols are used in dimensioning to help accurately display the meaning of the dimension. Symbols also help eliminate language barriers when reading drawings.

Abbreviations should be used very carefully on drawings. Whenever possible, write out the full word including

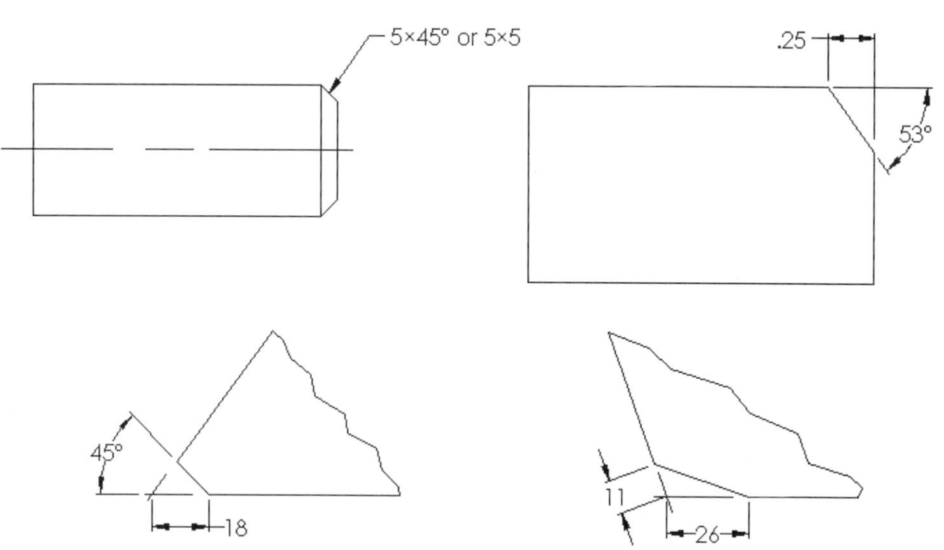

Figure 7-63

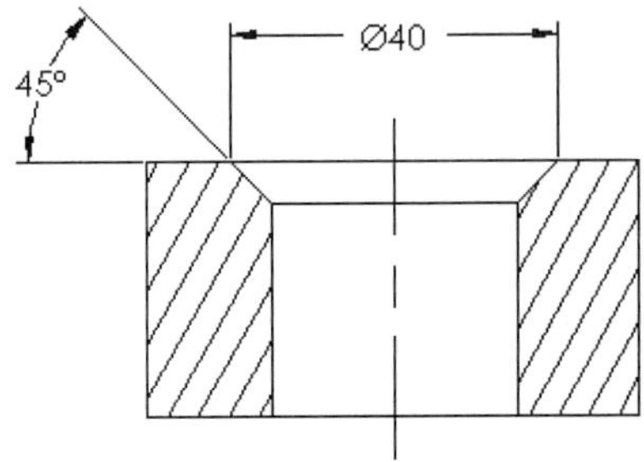

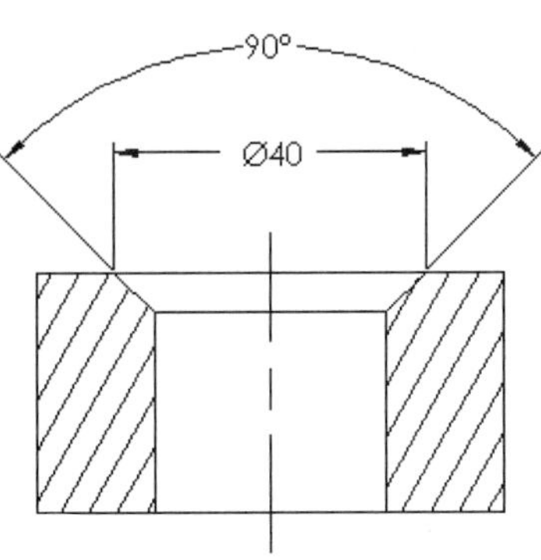

Figure 7-64

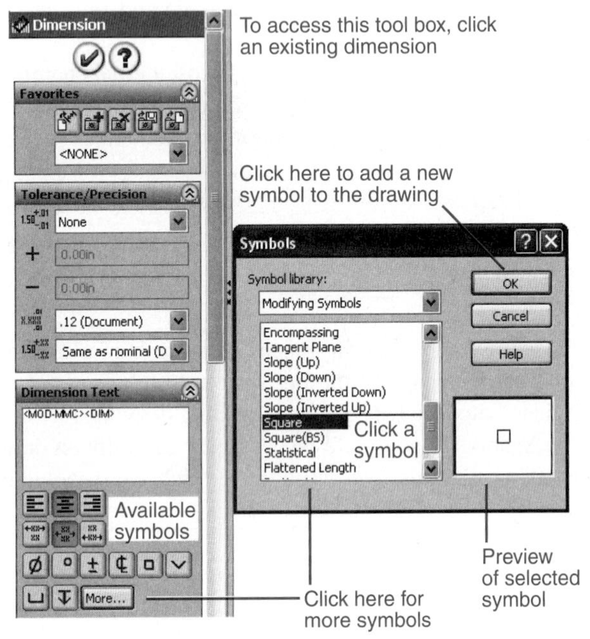

Figure 7-65

AL	=	Aluminum
C'BORE	=	Counterbore
CRS	=	Cold Rolled Steel
CSK	=	Countersink
DIA	=	Diameter
EQ	=	Equal
HEX	=	Hexagon
MAT'L	=	Material
R	=	Radius
SAE	=	Society of Automotive Engineers
SFACE	=	Spotface
ST	=	Steel
SQ	=	Square
REQD	=	Required

Figure 7-66

correct punctuation. Figure 7-66 shows several standard abbreviations used on technical drawings.

Figure 7-66 shows a list of symbols available on the dimension toolbar.

> **TIP**
>
> To access the **Dimension** toolbox, click an existing dimension.

More symbols are available by clicking the **More** box. A list of available symbols will appear. Click a new symbol. A preview will appear of the selected symbol. Click **OK** and the symbol will appear on the drawing next to the existing symbol.

7-19 SYMMETRICAL AND CENTERLINE SYMBOLS

An object is symmetrical about an axis when one side is an exact mirror image of the other. Figure 7-67 shows a symmetrical object. The two short parallel lines symbol or

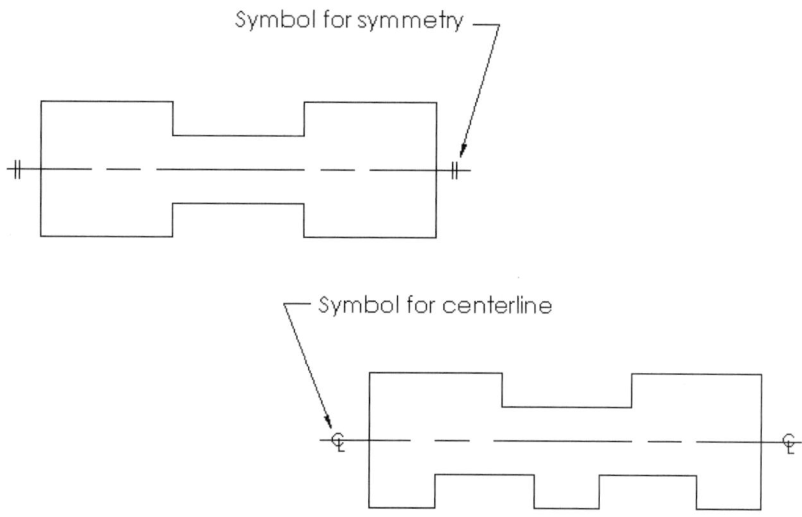

Figure 7-67

the note OBJECT IS SYMMETRICAL ABOUT THIS AXIS (centerline) may be used to designate symmetry.

If an object is symmetrical, only half the object need be dimensioned. The other dimensions are implied by the symmetry note or symbol.

Centerlines are slightly different from the axis of symmetry. An object may or may not be symmetrical about its centerline. See Figure 7-67. Centerlines are used to define the center of both individual features and entire objects. Use the centerline symbol when a line is a centerline, but do not use it in place of the symmetry symbol.

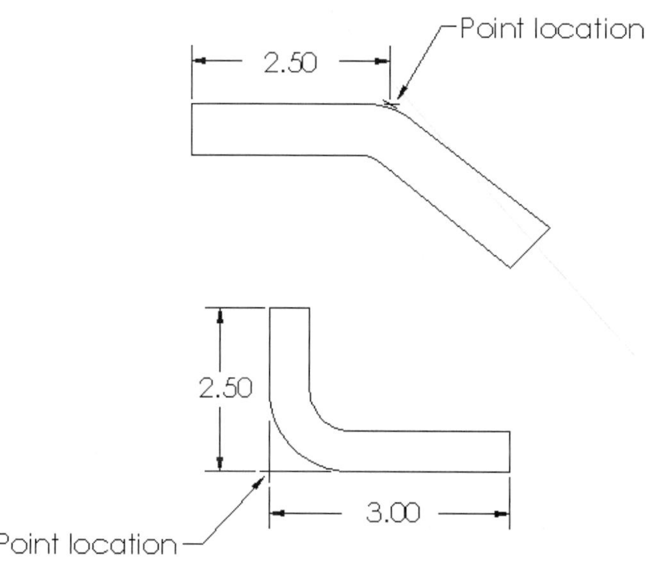

Figure 7-68

7-20 DIMENSIONING TO A POINT

Curved surfaces can be dimensioned using theoretical points. See Figure 7-68. There should be a small gap between the surface of the object and the lines used to define the theoretical point. The point should be defined by the intersection of at least two lines.

There should also be a small gap between the extension lines and the theoretical point used to locate the point.

7-21 DIMENSIONING SECTION VIEWS

Section views are dimensioned, as are orthographic views. See Figure 7-69. The section lines should be drawn at

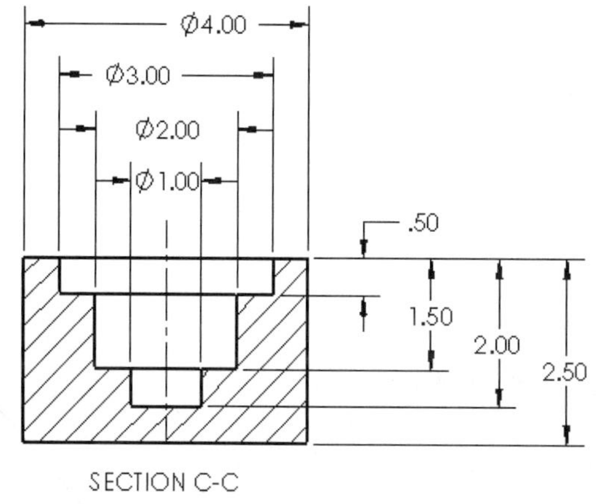

Figure 7-69

an angle that allows the viewer to clearly distinguish between the section lines and the extension lines.

7-22 DIMENSIONING ORTHOGRAPHIC VIEWS

Dimensions should be added to orthographic views where the features appear in contour. Holes should be dimensioned in their circular views. Figure 7-70 shows three views of an object that has been dimensioned.

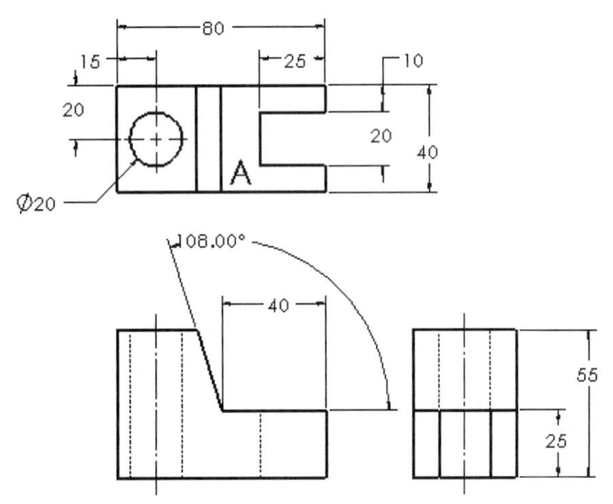

Figure 7-70

The hole dimensions are added to the top view, where the hole appears circular. The slot is also dimensioned in the top view because it appears in contour. The slanted surface is dimensioned in the front view.

The height of surface A is given in the side view rather than run along extension lines across the front view. The length of surface A is given in the front view. This is a contour view of the surface.

It is considered good practice to keep dimensions in groups. This makes it easier for the viewer to find dimensions.

Be careful not to double-dimension a distance. A distance should be dimensioned only once. If a 30 dimension were added above the 25 dimension on the right-side view, it would be an error. The distance would be double-dimensioned: once with the 25 + 30 dimension and again with the 55 overall dimension. The 25 + 30 dimensions are mathematically equal to the 55 overall dimension, but there is a distinct difference in how they affect the manufacturing tolerances. Double dimensions are explained more fully in Chapter 8.

Dimensions Using Centerlines

Figure 7-71 shows an object dimensioned from its centerline. This type of dimensioning is used when the distance between the holes relative to each other is critical.

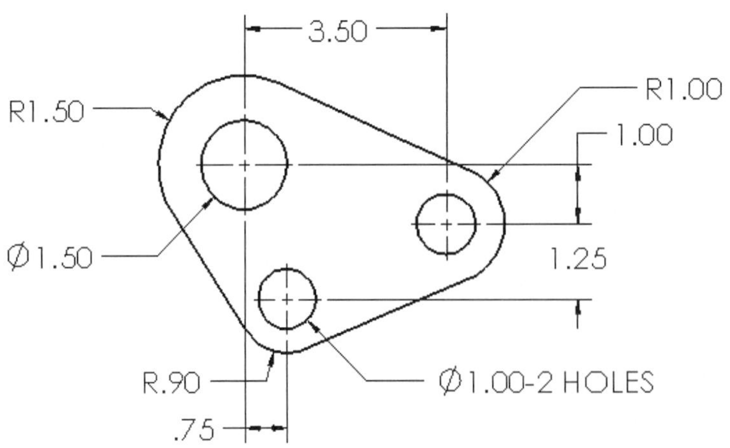

Figure 7-71

7-23 PROJECTS

Project 7-1:

Measure and redraw the shapes in Figures P7-1 through P7-24. The dotted grid background has either .50-in. or 10-mm spacing. All holes are through holes. Specify the units and scale of the drawing. Use the **Part** template to create a model. Use the grid background pattern to determine the dimensions. Use the **Drawing** template to create the orthographic view shown. Use the **Smart Dimension** tool to dimension the view.

A. Measure using millimeters.
B. Measure using inches.

All dimensions are within either .25 in. or 5 mm. All fillets and rounds are R.50 in., R.25 in. or R10 mm, R5 mm.

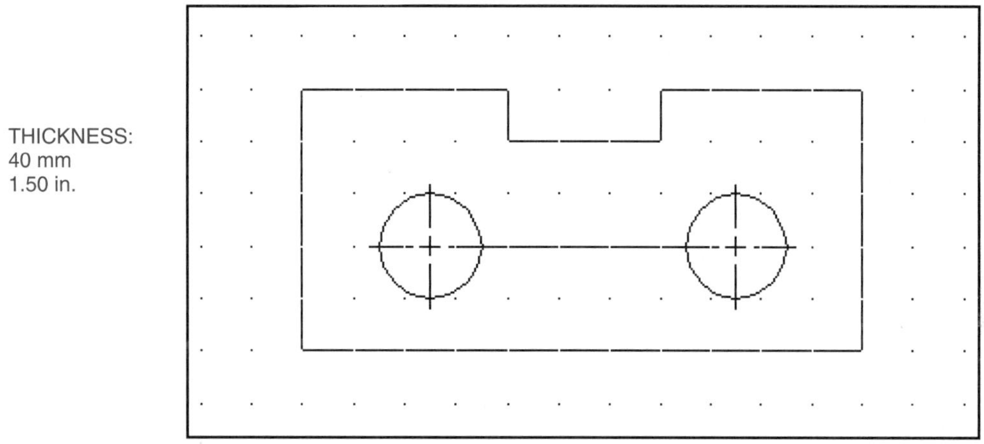

THICKNESS:
40 mm
1.50 in.

Figure P7-1

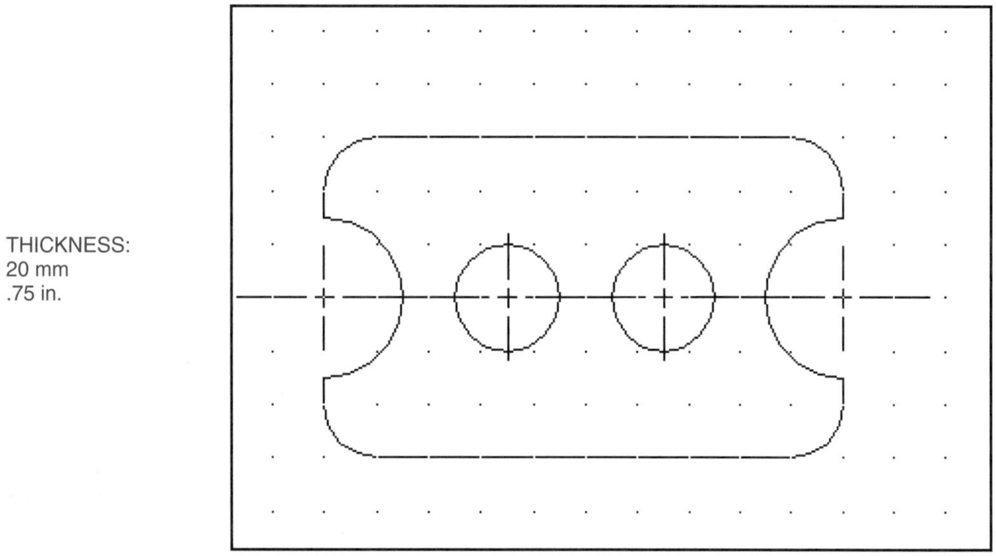

THICKNESS:
20 mm
.75 in.

Figure P7-2

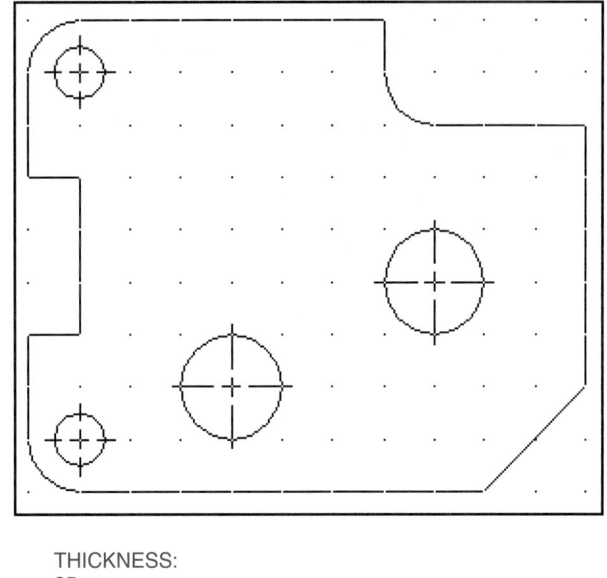

Figure P7-3

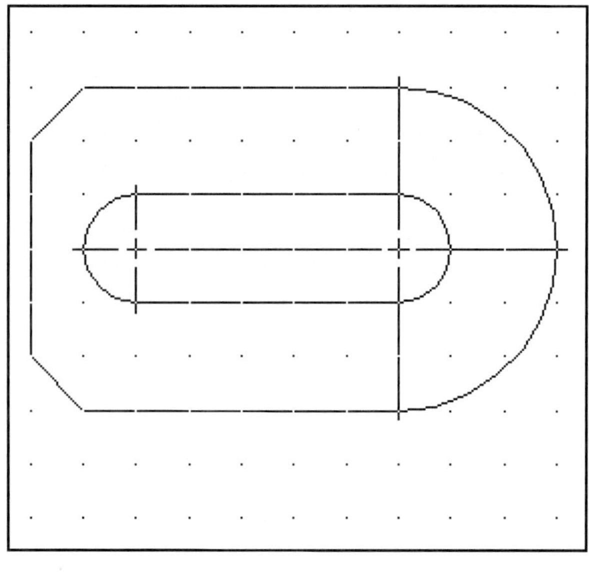

Figure P7-5

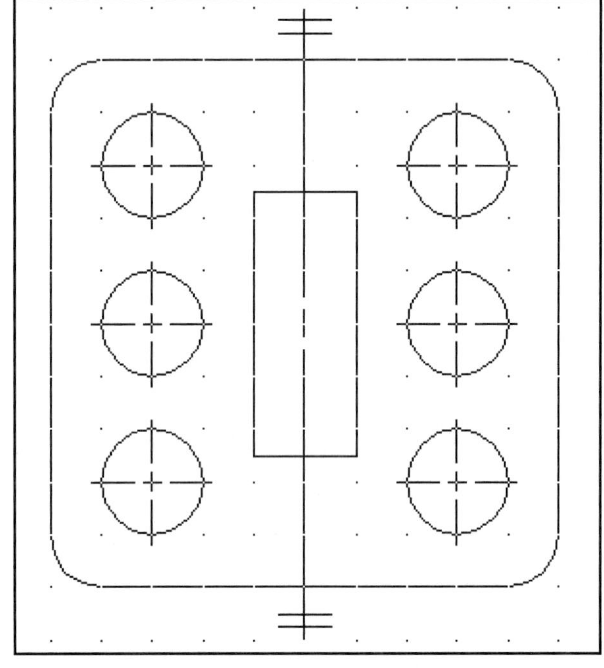

Figure P7-4

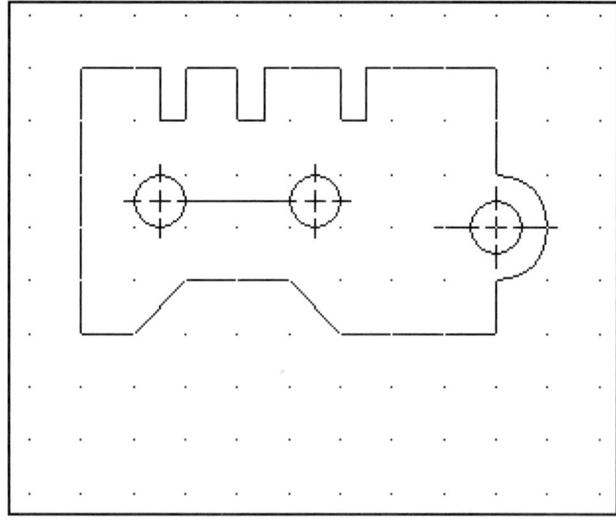

Figure P7-6

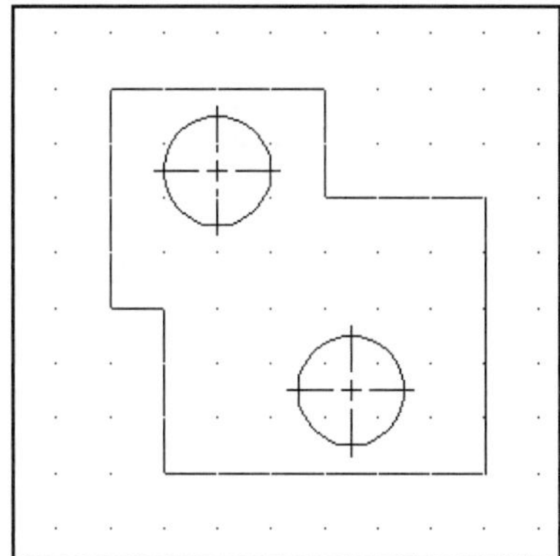

THICKNESS:
12 mm
.50 in.

Figure P7-7

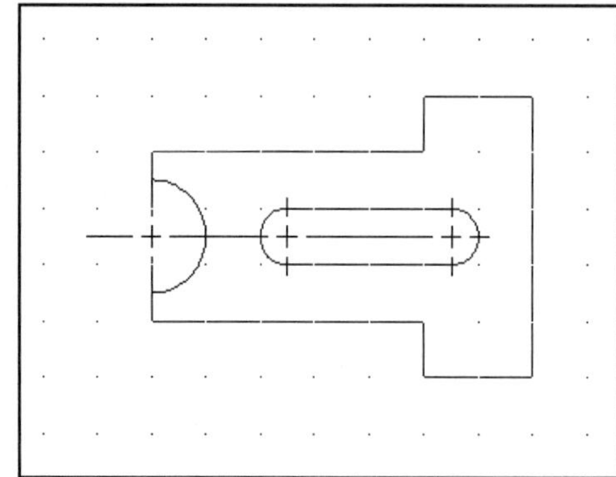

THICKNESS:
25 mm
1.00 in.

Figure P7-8

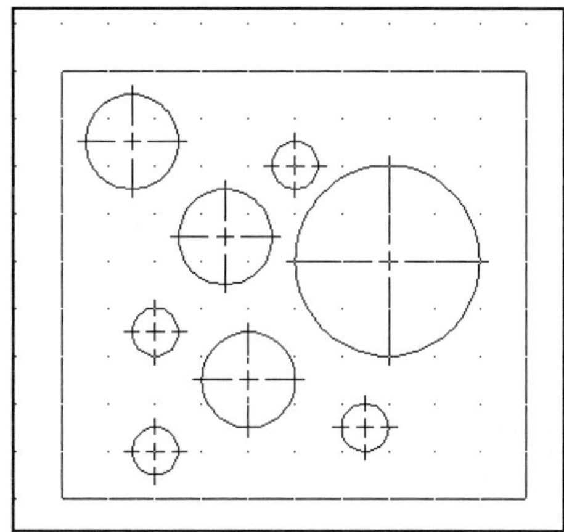

THICKNESS:
5 mm
.25 in.

Figure P7-9

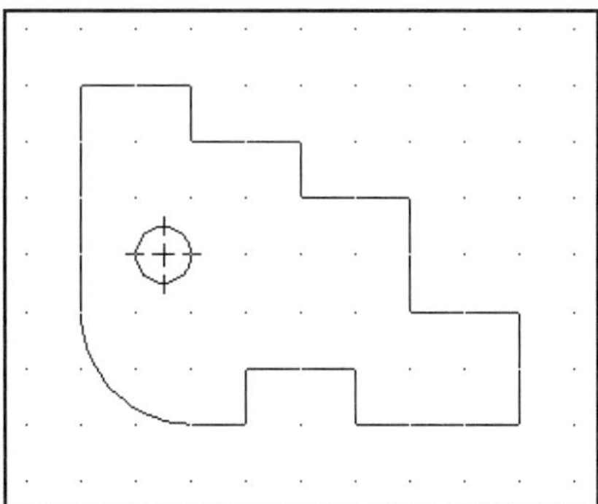

THICKNESS:
20 mm
.75 in.

Figure P7-10

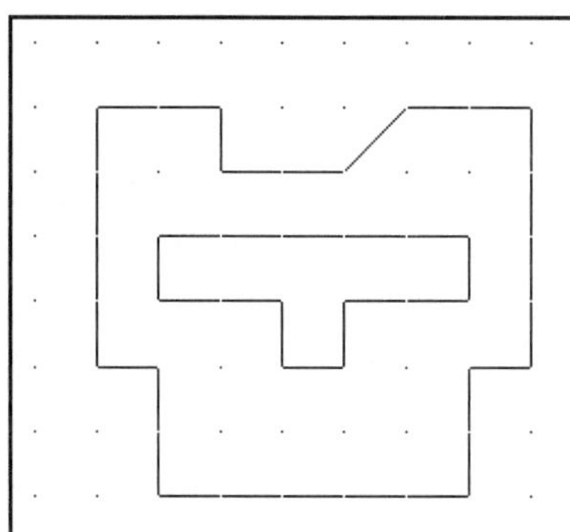

THICKNESS:
18 mm
.625 in.

Figure P7-11

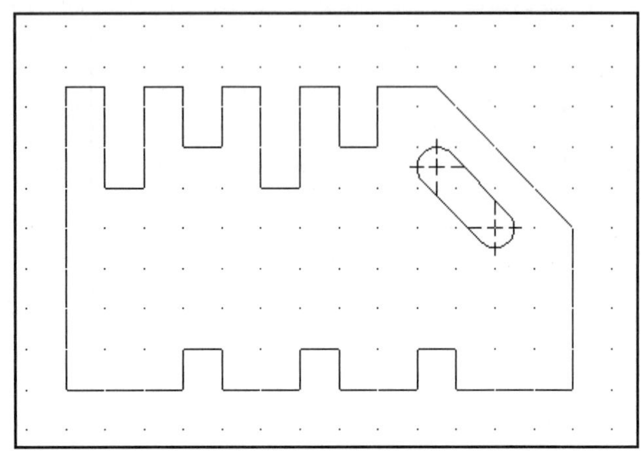

THICKNESS:
24 mm
1.00 in.

Figure P7-12

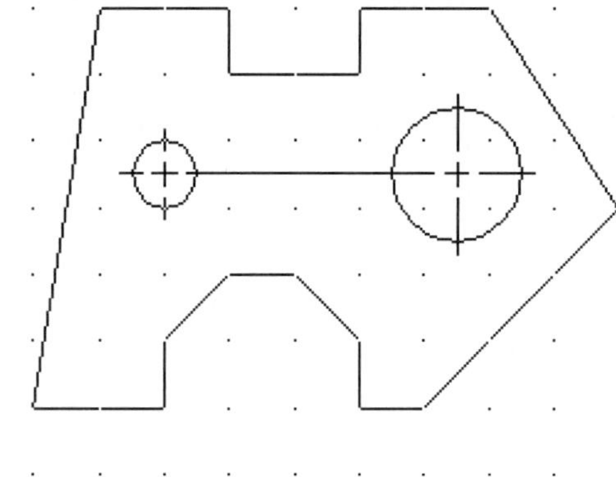

THICKNESS:
10 mm
.25 in.

Figure P7-13

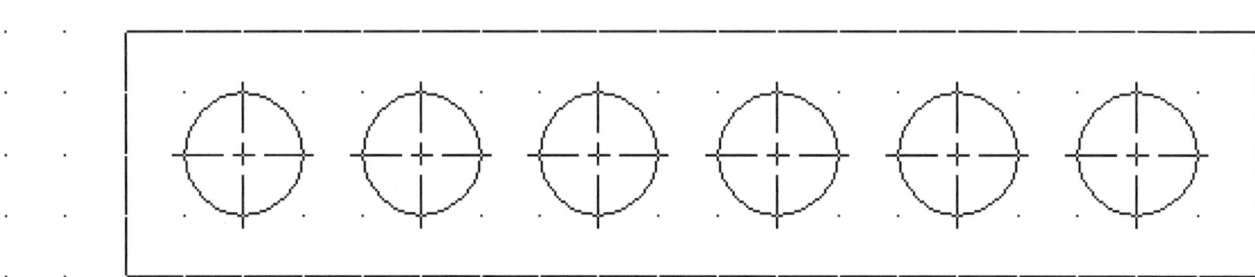

THICKNESS:
8 mm
.25 in.

Figure P7-14

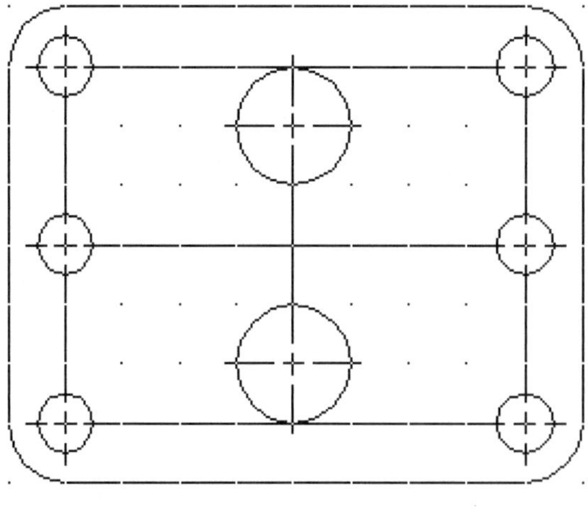

THICKNESS:
20 mm
.75 in.

Figure P7-15

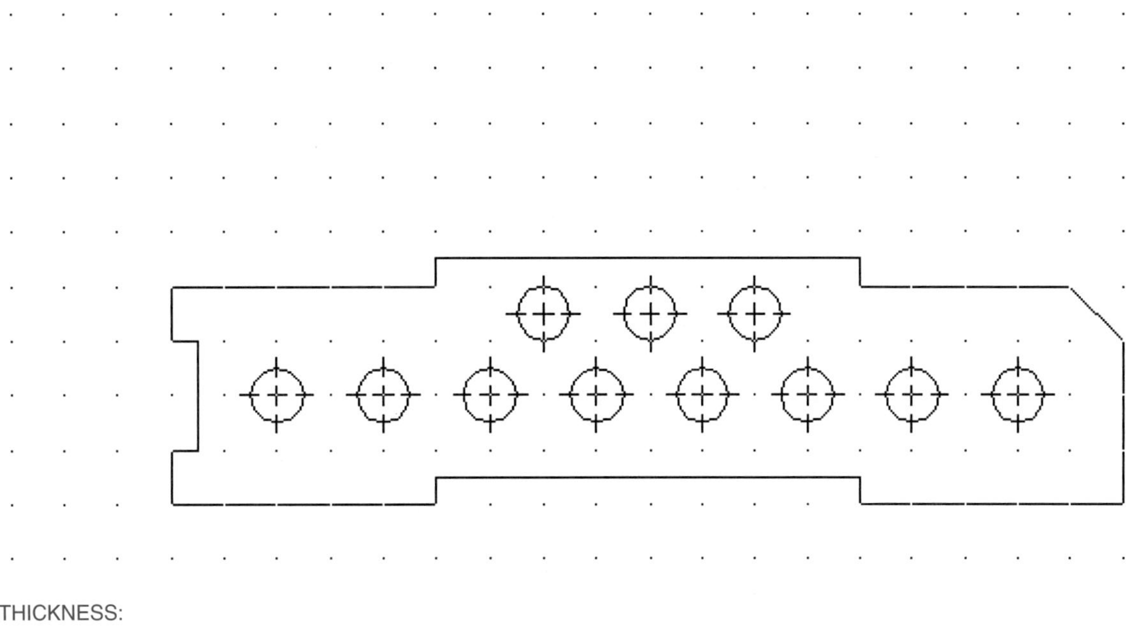

Figure P7-16

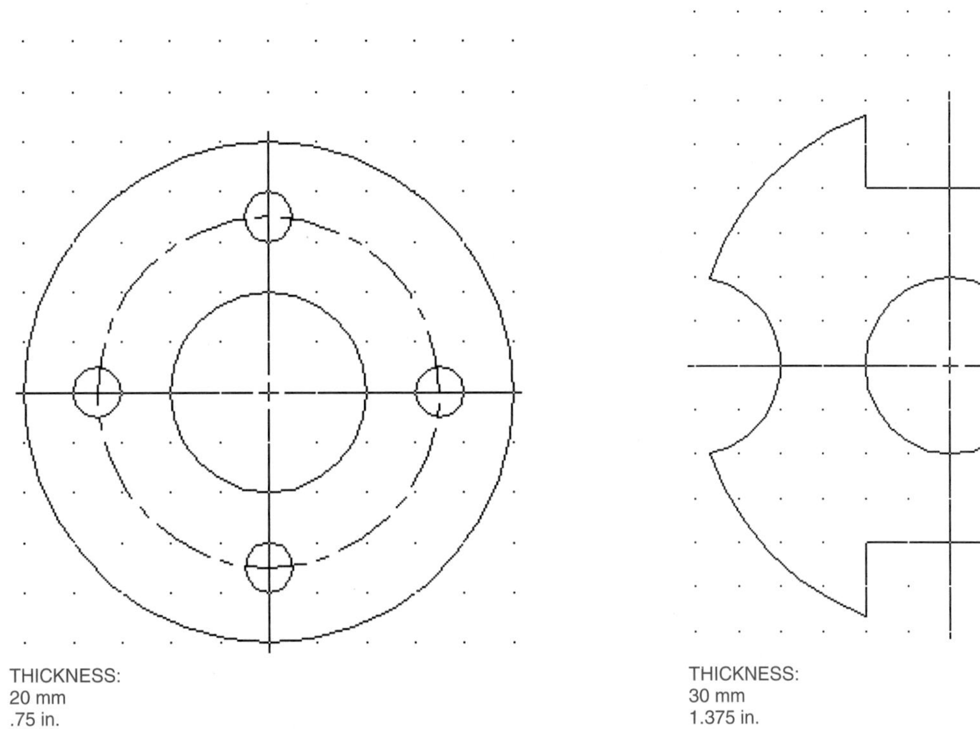

Figure P7-17

Figure P7-18

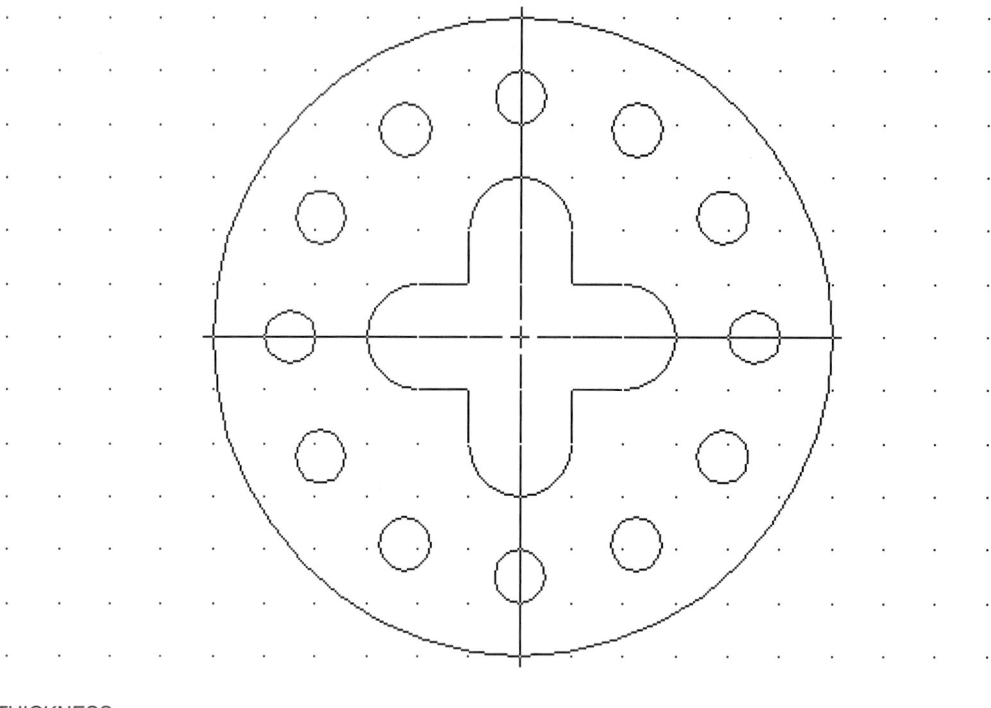

THICKNESS:
12 mm
.30 in.

Figure P7-19

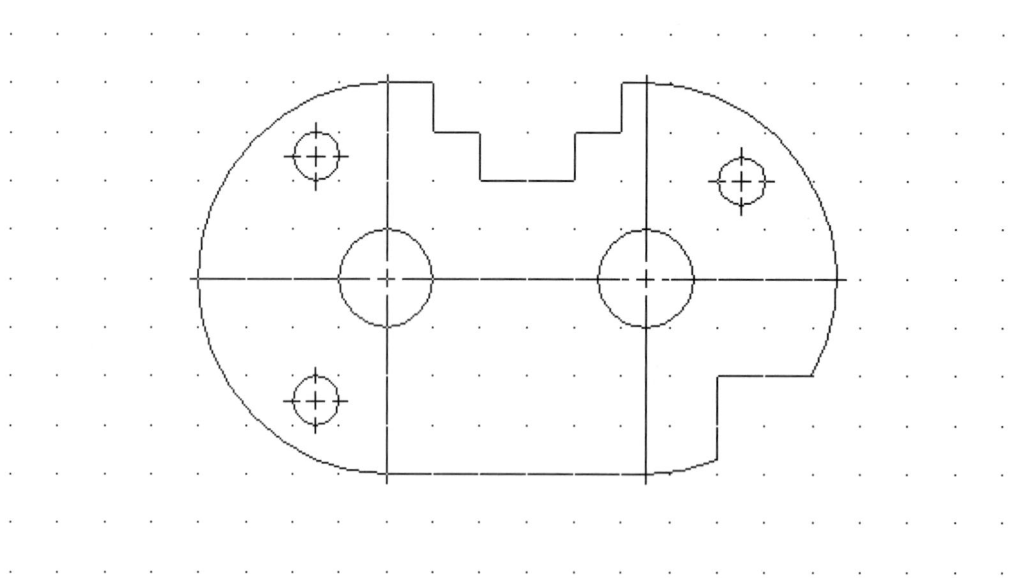

THICKNESS:
5 mm
.125 in.

Figure P7-20

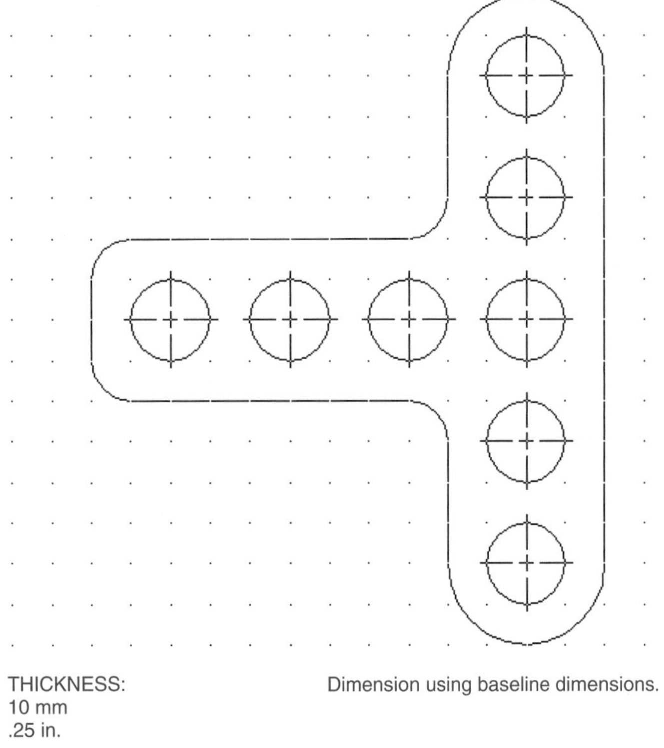

THICKNESS:
10 mm
.25 in.

Dimension using baseline dimensions.

Figure P7-21

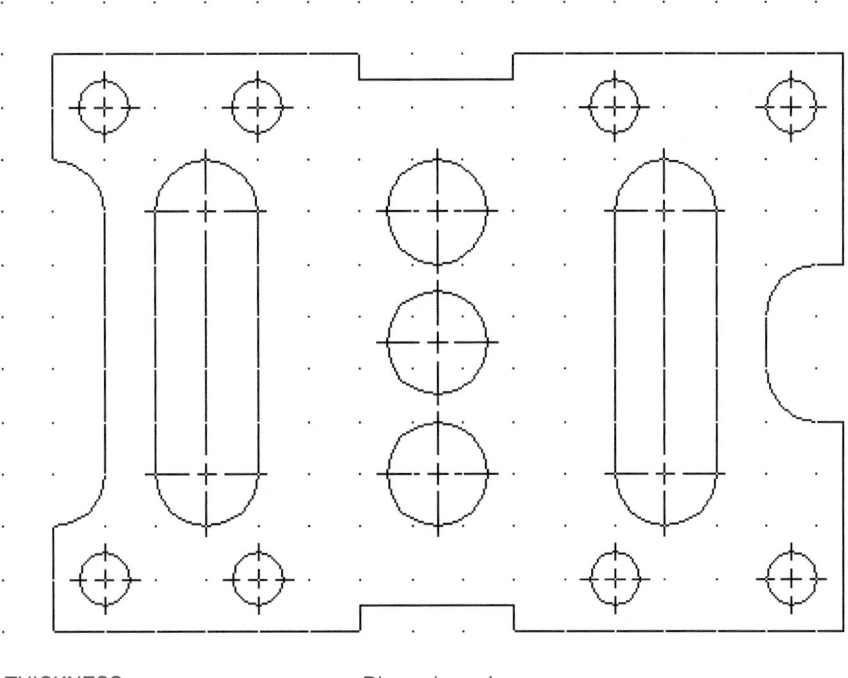

THICKNESS:
15 mm
.50 in.

Dimension using
A. Baseline dimensions.
B. Ordinate dimensions.
C. Chain dimensions.
D. Hole table.

Figure P7-22

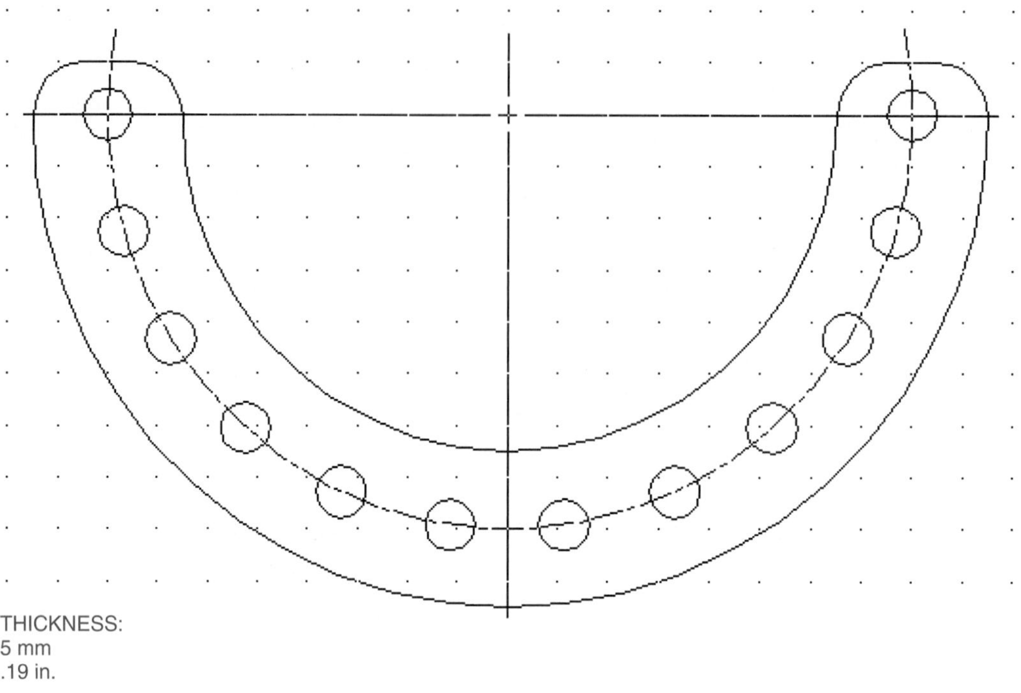

Figure P7-23

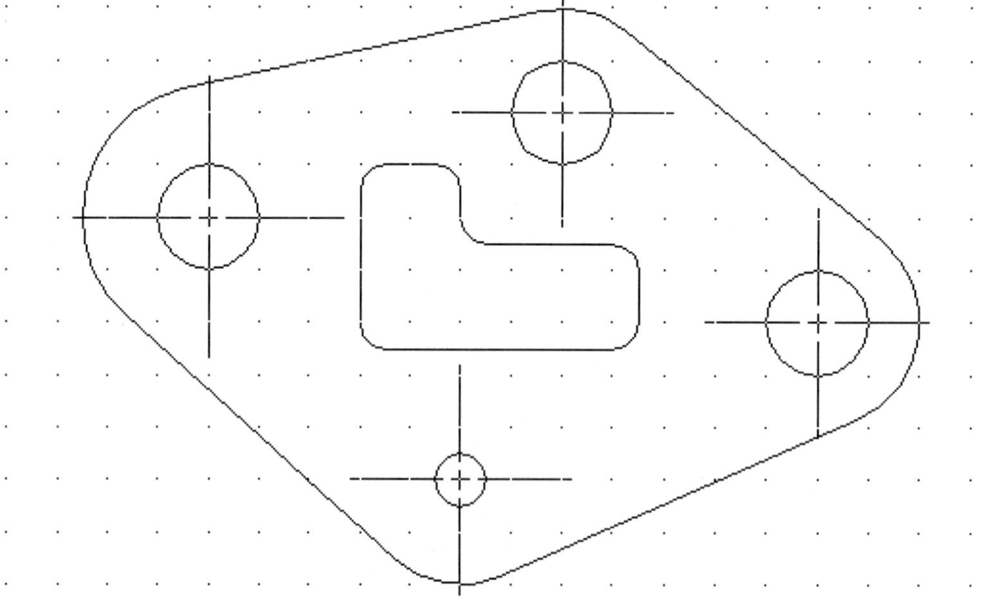

Figure P7-24

Project 7-2:

Use the **Part** template to draw models of the objects shown in Figures P7-25 through P7-42.

1. Create orthographic views of the objects. Dimension the orthographic view.
2. Create 3D models of the objects. Dimension the 3D models.

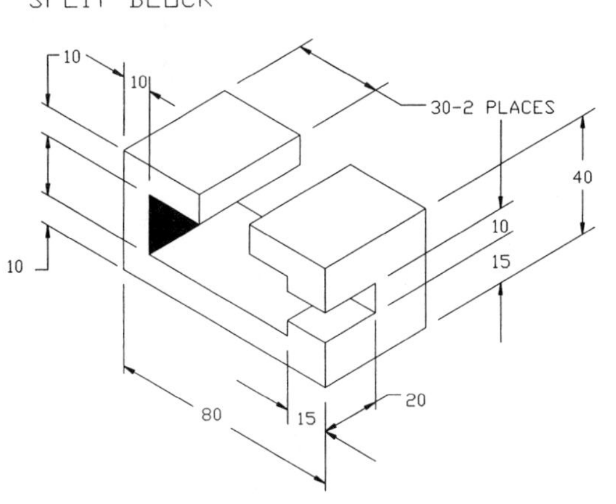

Figure P7-25 MILLIMETERS

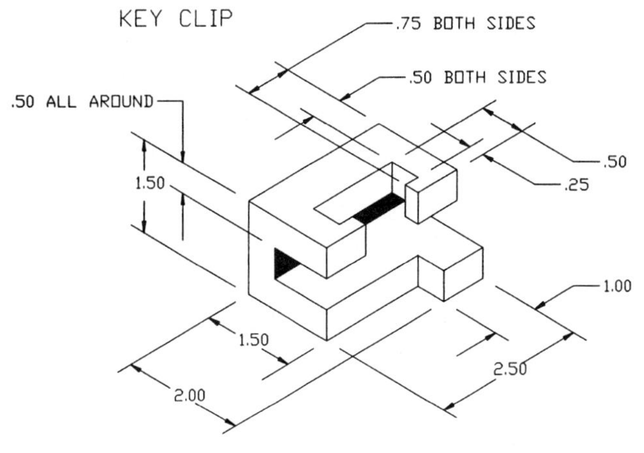

Figure P7-27 INCHES

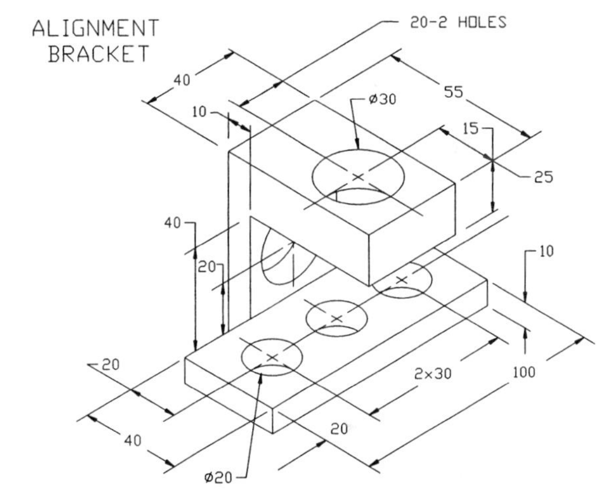

Figure P7-28 MILLIMETERS

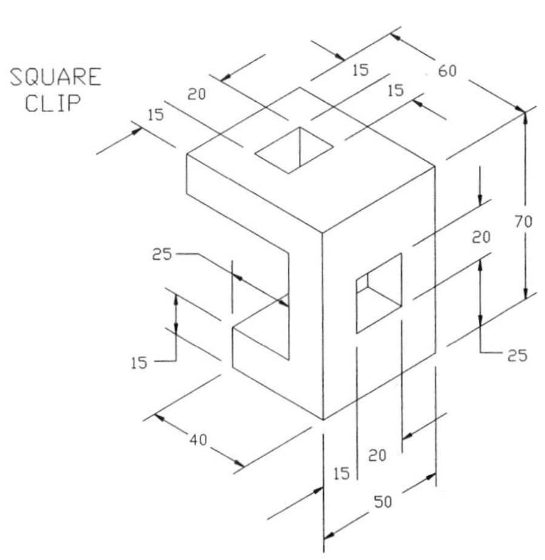

Figure P7-26 MILLIMETERS

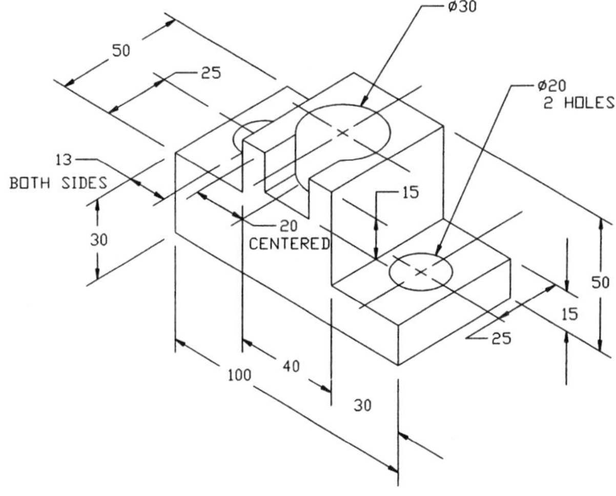

Figure P7-29 MILLIMETERS

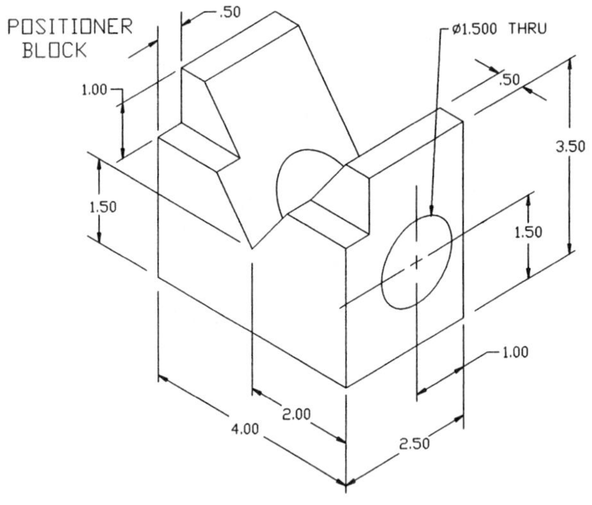

Figure P7-30 INCHES

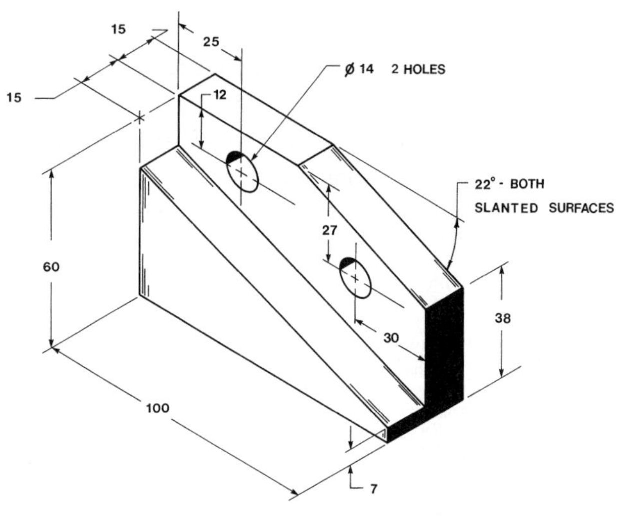

Figure P7-33 MILLIMETERS

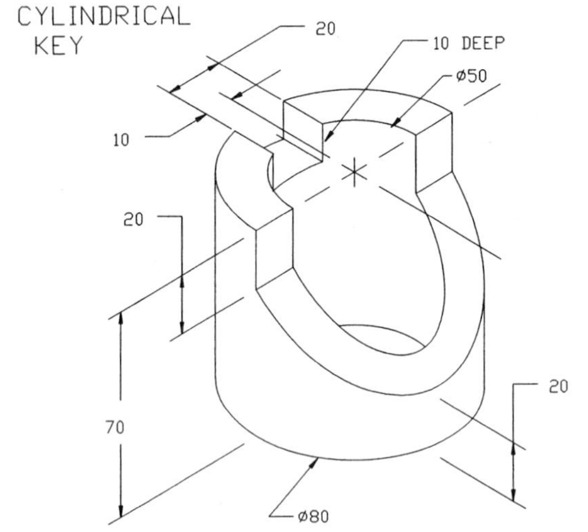

Figure P7-31 MILLIMETERS

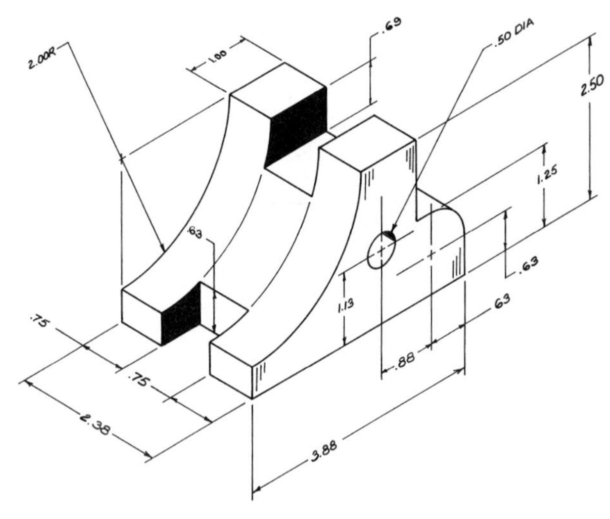

Figure P7-34 INCHES

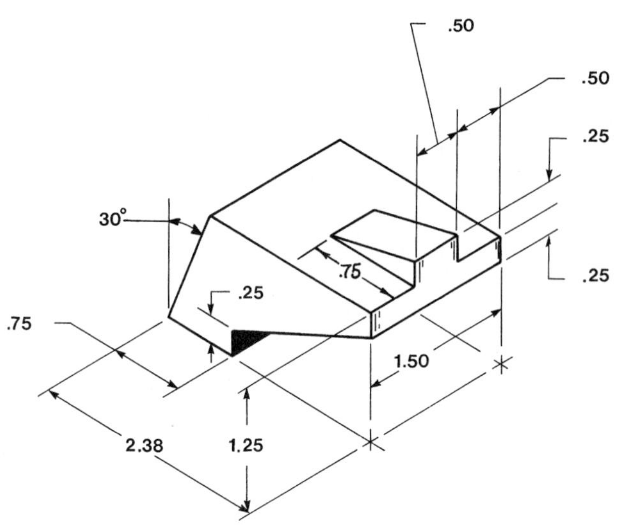

Figure P7-32 INCHES

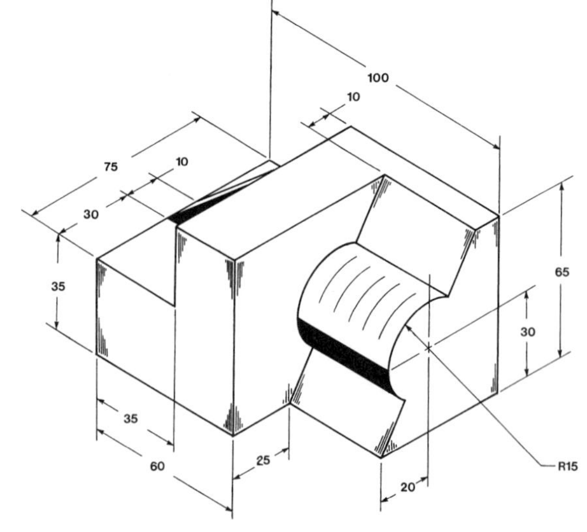

Figure P7-35 MILLIMETERS

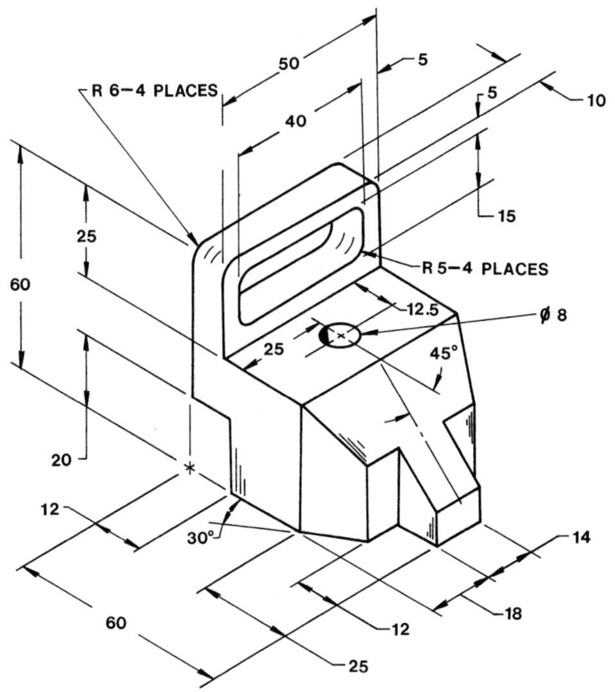

Figure P7-36 MILLIMETERS

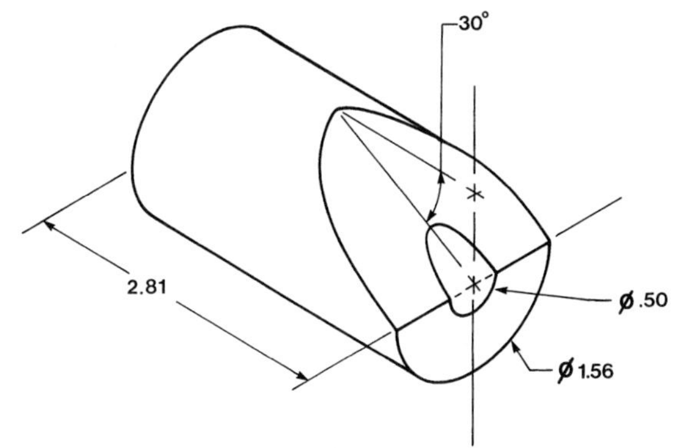

Figure P7-37 INCHES

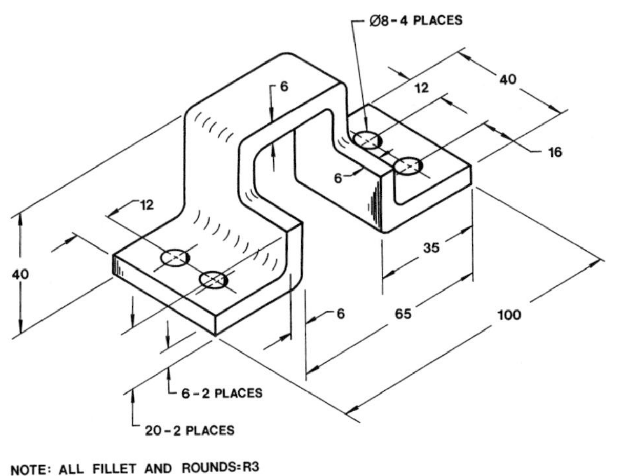

Figure P7-38 MILLIMETERS

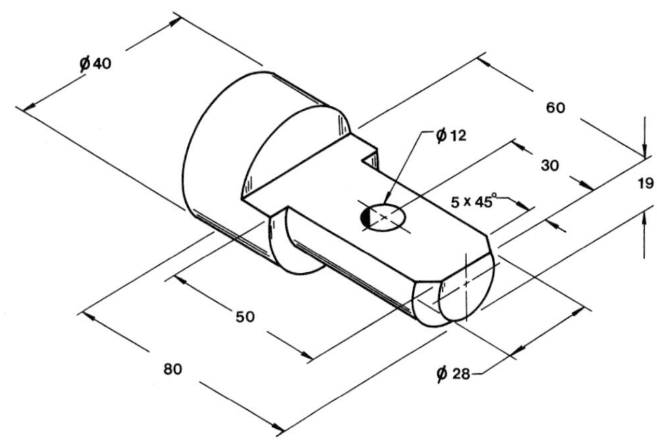

Figure P7-39 MILLIMETERS

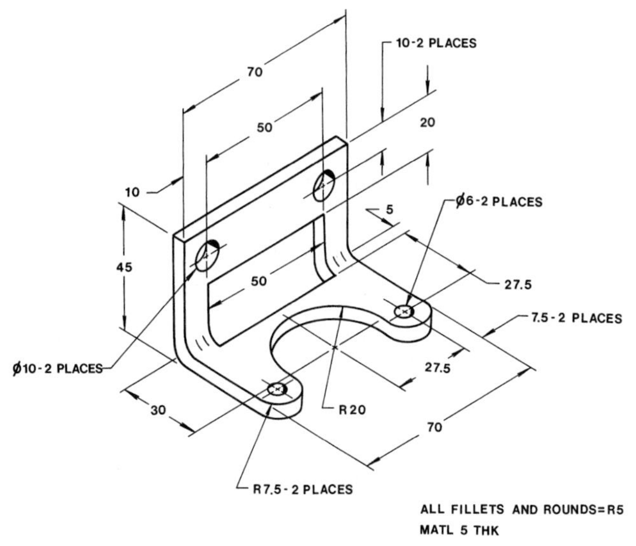

Figure P7-40 MILLIMETERS

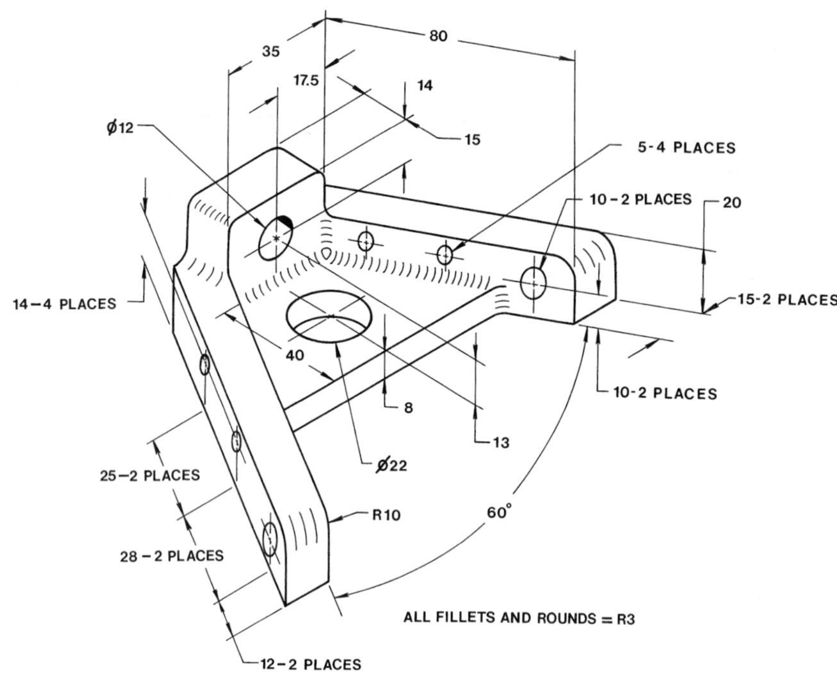

Figure P7-41 MILLIMETERS

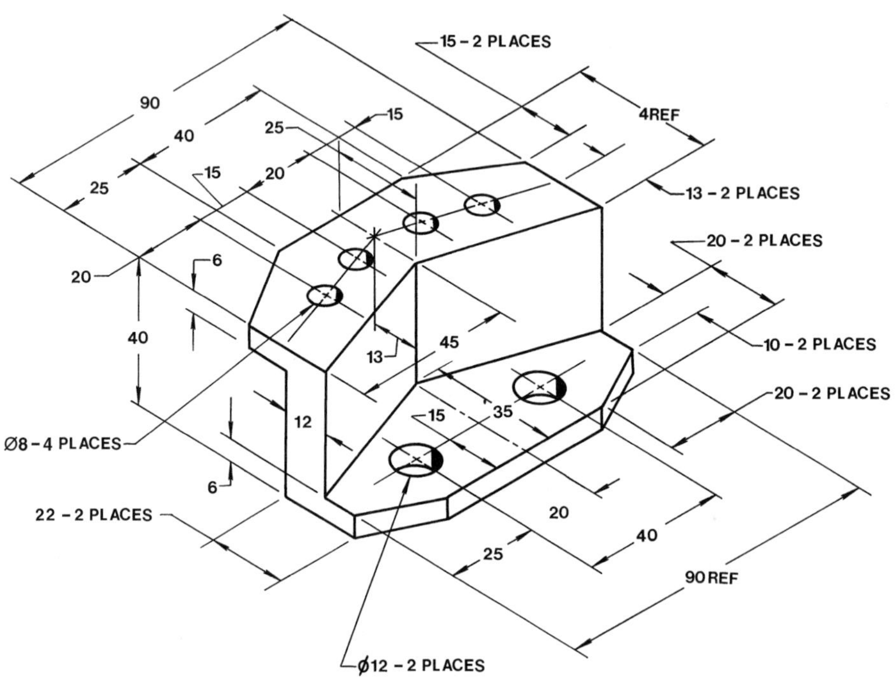

Figure P7-42 MILLIMETERS

Project 7-3:

1. Draw a 3D model from the given top orthographic and sectional views in Figure P7-43.
2. Draw a top orthographic view and a sectional view of the object and add dimensions.

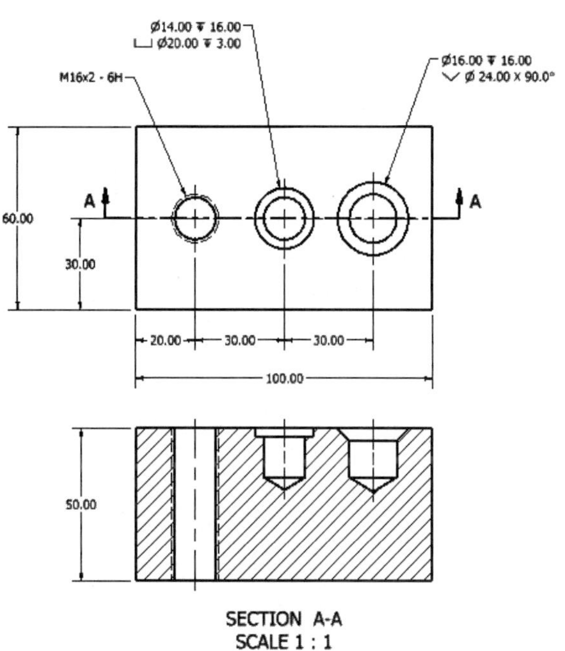

Figure P7-43 MILLIMETERS

Project 7-4:

1. Draw a 3D model from the given top orthographic and sectional views in Figure P7-44.
2. Draw a top orthographic view and a sectional view of the object and add dimensions.

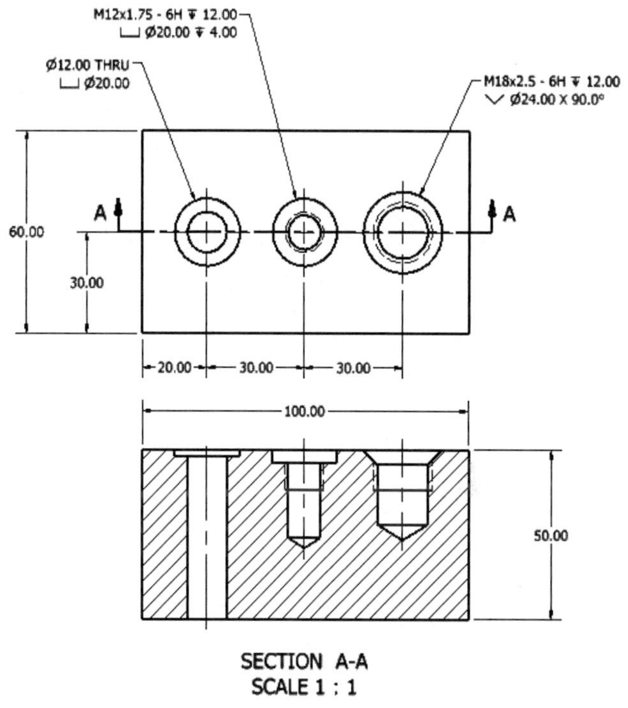

Figure P7-44 MILLIMETERS

Project 7-5:

1. Draw a 3D model from the given top orthographic and sectional views in Figure P7-45.
2. Draw a top orthographic view and a sectional view of the object and add dimensions.

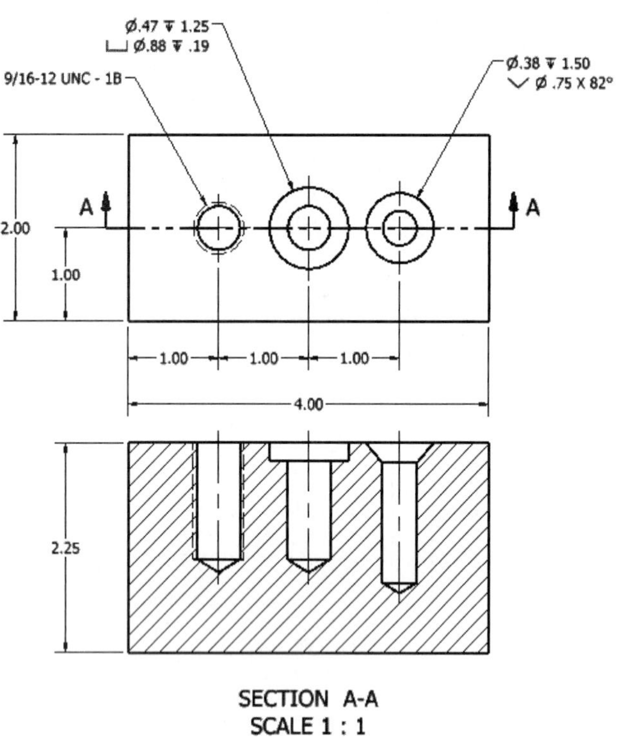

Figure P7-45 INCHES

Project 7-6:

1. Draw a 3D model from the given top orthographic and sectional views in Figure P7-46.
2. Draw a top orthographic view and a sectional view of the object and add dimensions.

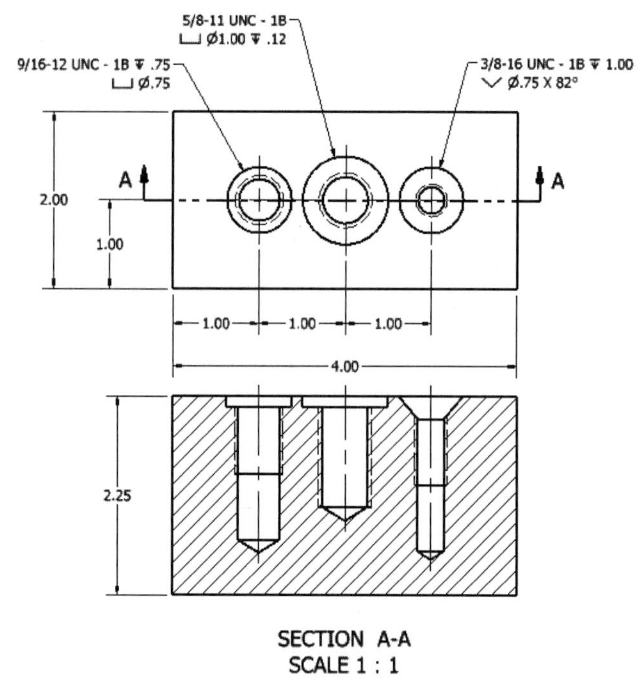

Figure P7-46 INCHES

CHAPTER 8

Tolerancing

Objectives

- Understand tolerance conventions.
- Understand the meaning of tolerances.
- Learn how to apply tolerances.
- Understand geometric tolerances.
- Understand positional tolerances.

8-1 INTRODUCTION

Tolerances define the manufacturing limits for dimensions. All dimensions have tolerances either written directly on the drawing as part of the dimension or implied by a predefined set of standard tolerances that apply to any dimension that does not have a stated tolerance.

This chapter explains general tolerance conventions and how they are applied using SolidWorks. It includes a sample tolerance study and an explanation of standard fits and surface finishes.

8-2 DIRECT TOLERANCE METHODS

There are two methods used to include tolerances as part of a dimension: *plus and minus,* and *limits.* Plus and minus tolerances can be expressed in either bilateral (deviation) or unilateral (symmetric) form.

A ***bilateral tolerance*** has both a plus and a minus value, whereas a ***unilateral tolerance*** has either the plus or the minus value equal to 0. Figure 8-1 shows a horizontal dimension of 60 mm that includes a bilateral tolerance of plus or minus 1 and another dimension of 60.00 mm that includes a bilateral tolerance of plus 0.20 or minus 0.10. Figure 8-1 also shows a dimension of 65 mm that includes a unilateral tolerance of plus 1 or minus 0.

> *Note:*
> Bilateral tolerance are called ***symmetric*** in SolidWorks Unilateral tolerances are called ***deviation.***

Plus or minus tolerances define a range for manufacturing. If inspection shows that all dimensioned distances on an object fall within their specified tolerance range, the object is considered acceptable; that is, it has been manufactured correctly.

The dimension and tolerance of 60 ± 0.1 means that the part must be manufactured within a range no greater than 60.1 nor less than 59.9. The dimension and tolerance $65 + 1, -0$ defines the tolerance range as 65 to 66.

Figure 8-2 shows some bilateral and unilateral tolerances applied using decimal inch values. Inch dimensions and tolerances are written using a slightly different format than millimeter dimensions and tolerances, but they also define

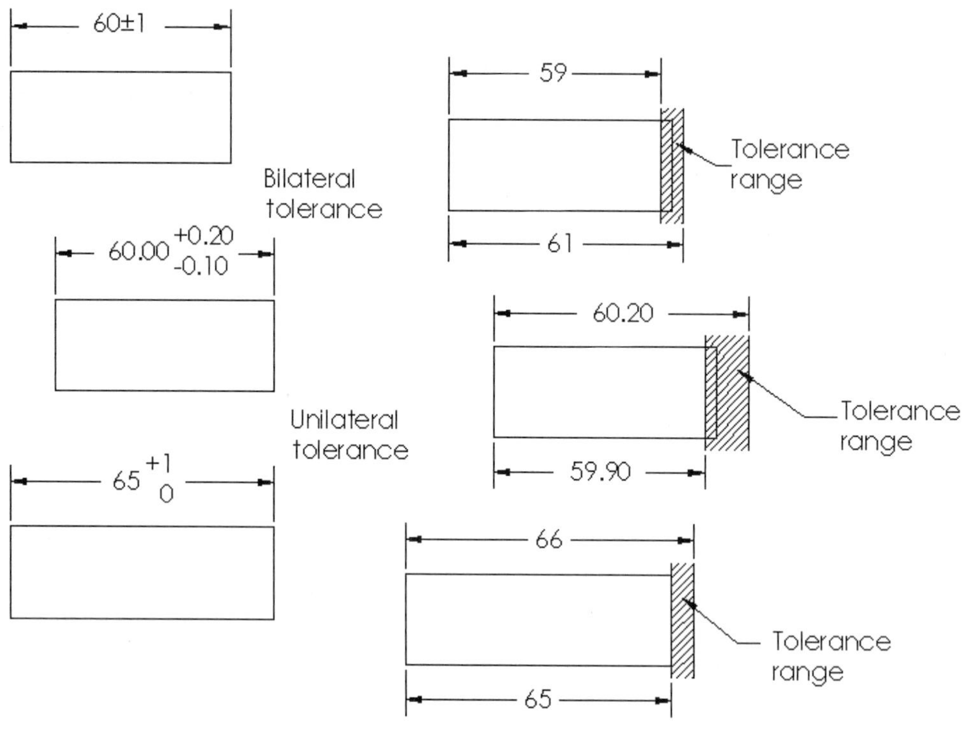

Figure 8-1

manufacturing ranges for dimension values. The horizontal bilateral dimension and tolerance 2.50 ± .02 defines the longest acceptable distance as 2.52 in. and the shortest as 2.48. The unilateral dimension 2.50 + .02 −.00 defines the longest acceptable distance as 2.52 and the shortest as 2.50.

8-3 TOLERANCE EXPRESSIONS

Dimension and tolerance values are written differently for inch and millimeter values. See Figure 8-3. Unilateral dimensions for millimeter values specify a zero limit with a

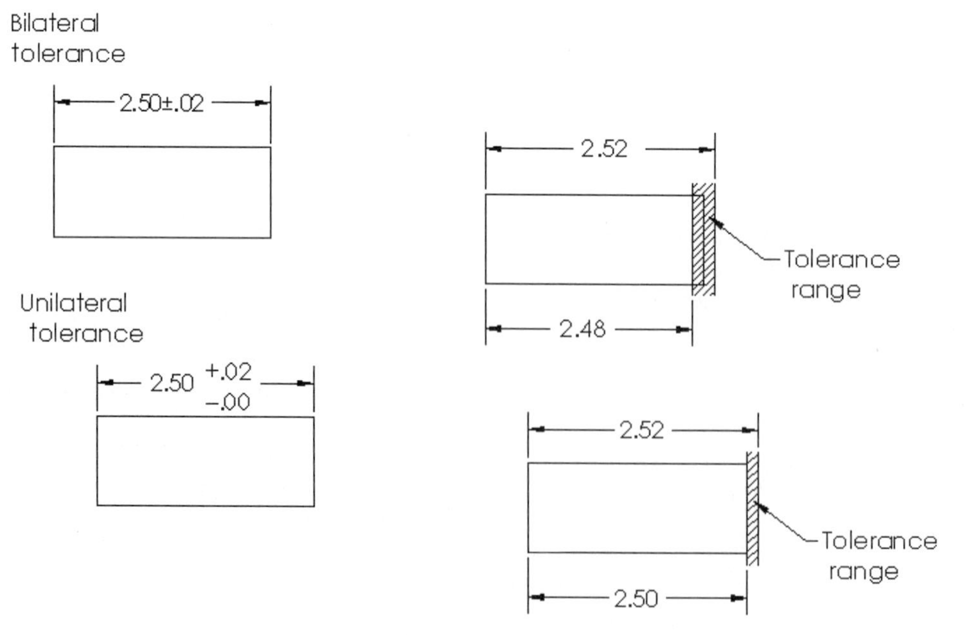

Figure 8-2

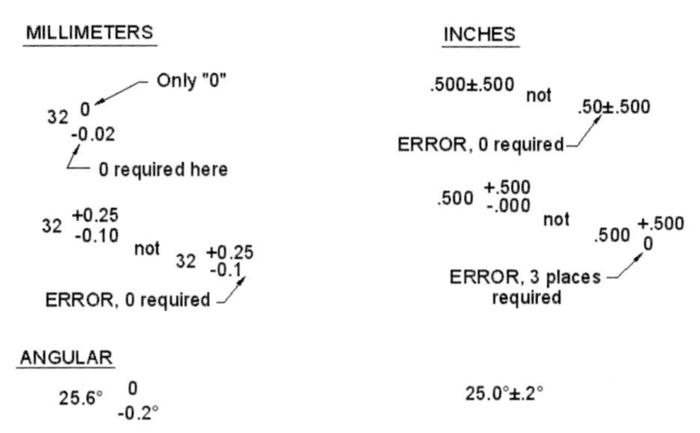

Figure 8-3

GIVEN (mm):

$12^{+0.2}_{-0.1}$

MEANS:
TOL MAX = 12.2
TOL MIN = 11.9
TOTAL TOL = 0.3

OBJECT	AS MEASURED	ACCEPTABLE ?
1	12.160	OK
2	12.020	OK
3	12.203	Too Long
4	11.920	OK
5	11.895	Too Short

Figure 8-4

GIVEN (inches):

2.50±.02

MEANS:
TOL MAX = 3.52
TOL MIN = 3.48
TOTAL TOL = .04

OBJECT	AS MEASURED	ACCEPTABLE ?
1	3.520	OK
2	3.486	OK
3	3.470	Too Short
4	3.521	Too Long
5	3.515	OK

Figure 8-5

single 0. A zero limit for inch values must include the same number of decimal places given for the dimension value. In the example shown in Figure 8-3, the dimension value .500 has a unilateral tolerance with minus zero tolerance. The zero limit is written as .000, three decimal places for both the dimension and the tolerance.

Both values in a bilateral tolerance for inch values must contain the same number of decimal places; for millimeter values the tolerance values need not include the same number of decimal places as the dimension value. In Figure 8-3 the dimension value 32 is accompanied by tolerances of +0.25 and −0.10. This form is not acceptable for inch dimensions and tolerances. An equivalent inch dimension and tolerance would be written $32.00^{+.25}_{-.10}$.

Degree values must include the same number of decimal places in both the dimension value and the tolerance values for bilateral tolerances. A single 0 may be used for unilateral tolerances.

8-4 UNDERSTANDING PLUS AND MINUS TOLERANCES

A millimeter dimension and tolerance of 12.0 + 0.2/−0.1 means the longest acceptable distance is 12.2000 . . . 0, and the shortest is 11.9000 . . . 0. The total range is 0.3000 . . . 0.

After an object is manufactured, it is inspected to ensure that the object has been manufactured correctly. Each dimensioned distance is measured, and if it is within the specified tolerance, is accepted. If the measured distance is not within the specified tolerance, the part is rejected. Some rejected objects may be reworked to bring them into the specified tolerance range, whereas others are simply scrapped.

Figure 8-4 shows a dimension with a tolerance. Assume that five objects were manufactured using the same 12.0 +0.2/−0.1 dimension and tolerance. The objects were then inspected and the results were as listed. Inspected measurements are usually expressed to at least one more decimal place than that specified in the tolerance. Which objects are acceptable and which are not? Object 3 is too long, and object 5 is too short because their measured distances are not within the specified tolerances.

Figure 8-5 shows a dimension and tolerance of 3.50 +.02 in. Object 3 is not acceptable because it is too short, and object 4 is too long.

8-5 CREATING PLUS AND MINUS TOLERANCES

Figure 8-6 shows a dimensioned view. This section will show how to add plus and minus to the existing dimensions.

1. Create a part using the dimensions shown.
2. Save the part as **BLOCK, TOL.**

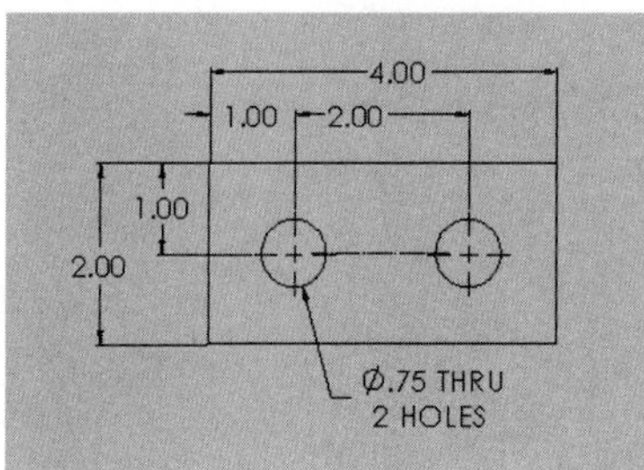

Figure 8-6

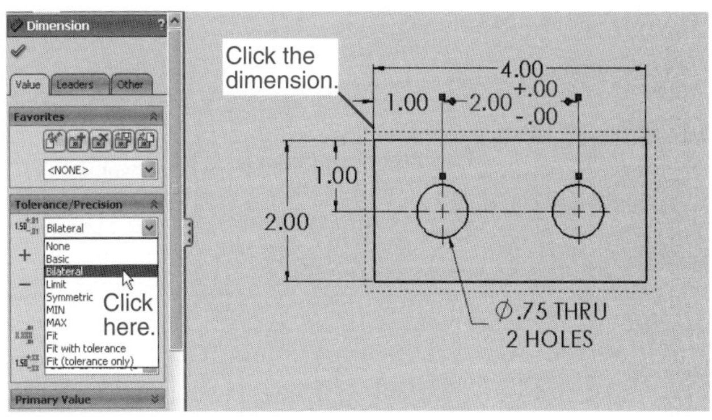

Figure 8-7

3. Create a drawing of the BLOCK, TOL and create an orthographic view as shown.
4. Add dimensions as shown.

See Figure 8-7.

5. Click the horizontal **2.00** dimension.

Click the arrow in the **Tolerance/Precision** box as shown.

6. Select the **Bilateral** option.
7. Enter a plus tolerance of **0.02** and a minus tolerance of **0.01.**

See Figure 8-8.

8. Click the OK check mark.

To Add Plus and Minus Symmetric Tolerances Using the Dimension Text Box

See Figure 8-9.

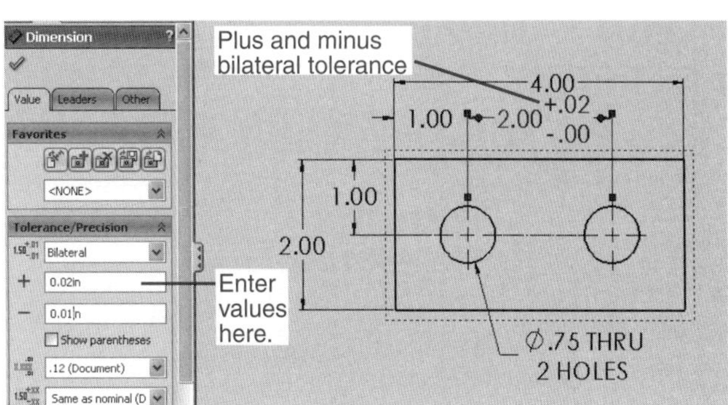

Figure 8-8

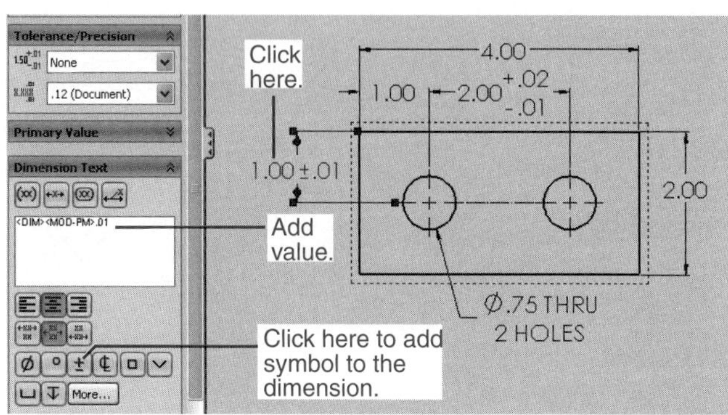

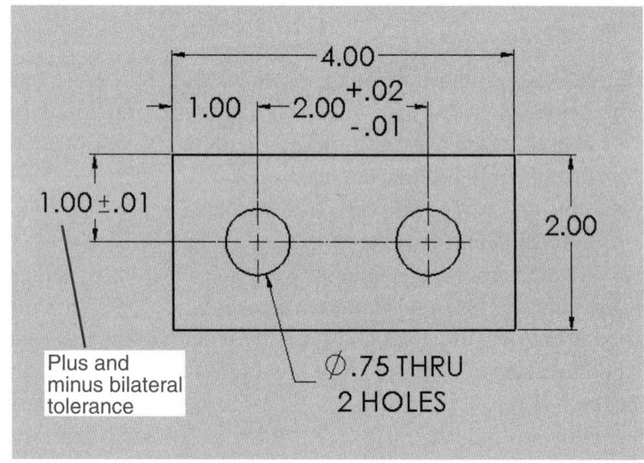

Figure 8-9

1. Click the vertical **1.00** dimension.

Note the entry in the **Dimension Text** box: **<DIM>.** This represents the existing text value taken from the part's construction dimensions.

2. Move the cursor into the **Dimension Text** box and click the **±** symbol.

Note that the entry in the **Dimension Text** box now reads **<DIM><MOD-PM>**. This indicates that the ± symbol has been added to the dimension text.

3. Type **.01** after <MOD-PM>.
4. Click the OK check mark.
5. Save the BLOCK, TOL drawing.

> **TIP**
>
> A symmetric tolerance can also be created using the **Symmetric** option in the **Tolerance/Precision** box.

LIMIT TOLERANCES (millimeters)

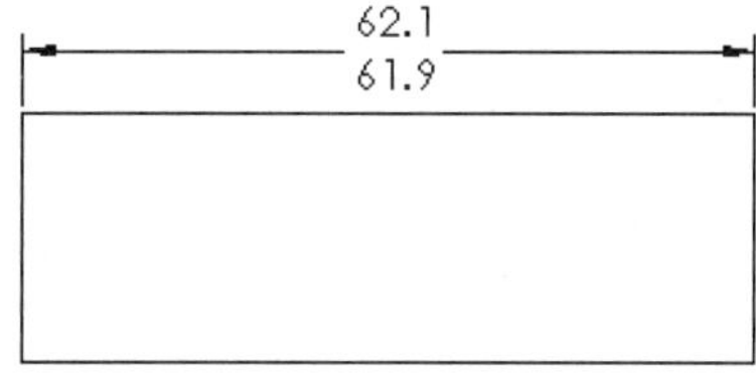

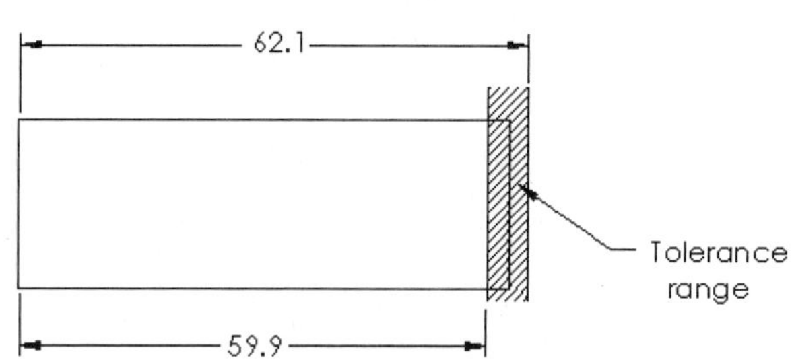

LIMIT TOLERANCES (inches)

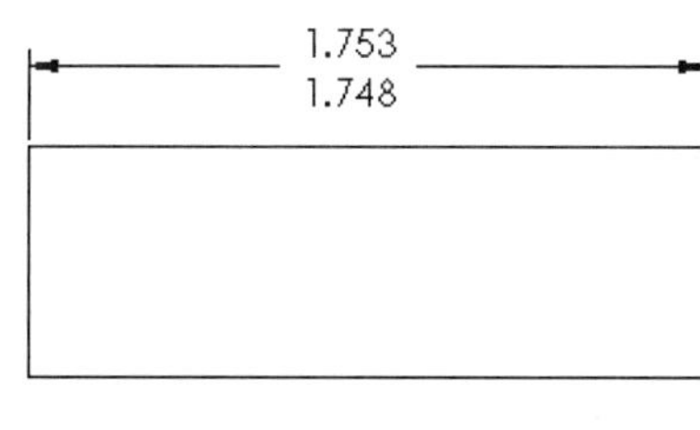

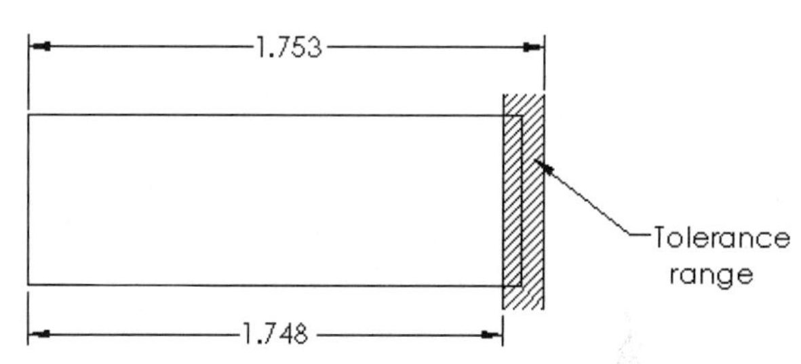

Figure 8-10

8-6 CREATING LIMIT TOLERANCES

Figure 8-10 shows examples of limit tolerances. Limit tolerances replace dimension values. Two values are given: the upper and lower limits for the dimension value. The limit tolerance 62.1 and 61.9 is mathematically equal to 62 ± 0.1, but the stated limit tolerance is considered easier to read and understand.

Limit tolerances define a range for manufacture. Final distances on an object must fall within the specified range to be acceptable.

This section uses the BLOCK, TOL drawing created in the last section. See Figure 8-11.

1. Click the vertical **2.00** dimension
2. Select the **Limit** option as shown.
3. Set the upper limit for **0.02** and the lower limit for **0.01.**
4. Click the OK check mark.

8-7 CREATING ANGULAR TOLERANCES

Figure 8-12 shows an example of an angular dimension with a symmetric tolerance. The procedures explained for applying different types of tolerances to linear dimensions also apply to angular dimensions.

See Figure 8-12.

1. Draw the part shown in Figure 8-12. Extrude the part to a thickness of **0.50.**
2. Save the part as **BLOCK, ANGLE**
3. Create a drawing of the BLOCK, ANGLE and create an orthographic view as shown.
4. Dimension the view.
5. Click the **45.00°** dimension.
6. Select the **Symmetric** option.
7. Enter a value of **0.20.**
8. Click the OK check mark
9. Save the drawing.

8-8 STANDARD TOLERANCES

Most manufacturers establish a set of standard tolerances that are applied to any dimension that does not include a specific tolerance. Figure 8-13 shows some possible standard tolerances. Standard tolerances vary from company to company. Standard tolerances are usually listed on the first page of a drawing to the left of the title block, but this location may vary.

The X value used when specifying standard tolerances means any X stated in that format. A dimension value of 52.00 would have an implied tolerance of ±.01 because the stated standard tolerance is .XX ±.01, so any dimension value with two decimal places has a standard implied tolerance of ±.01. A dimension value of 52.000 would have an implied tolerance of ±.001.

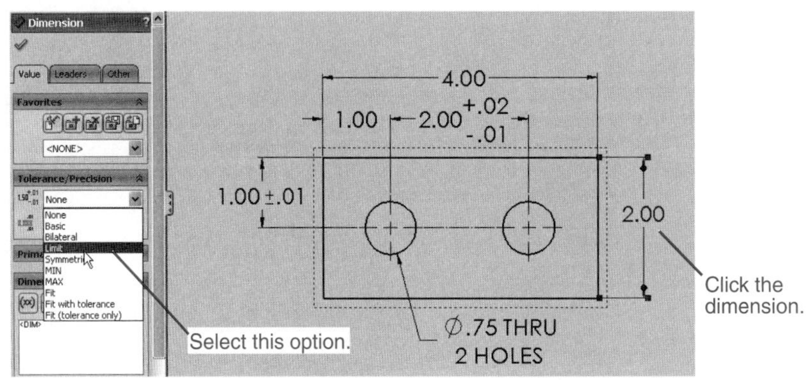

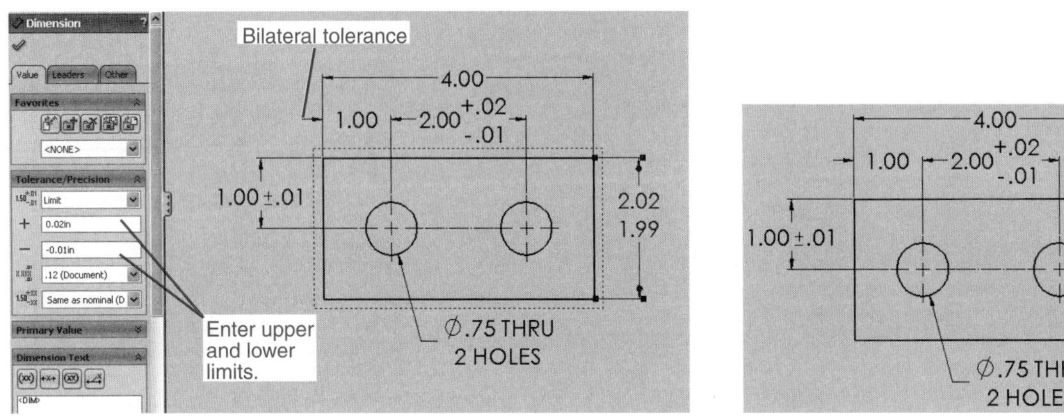

Figure 8-11

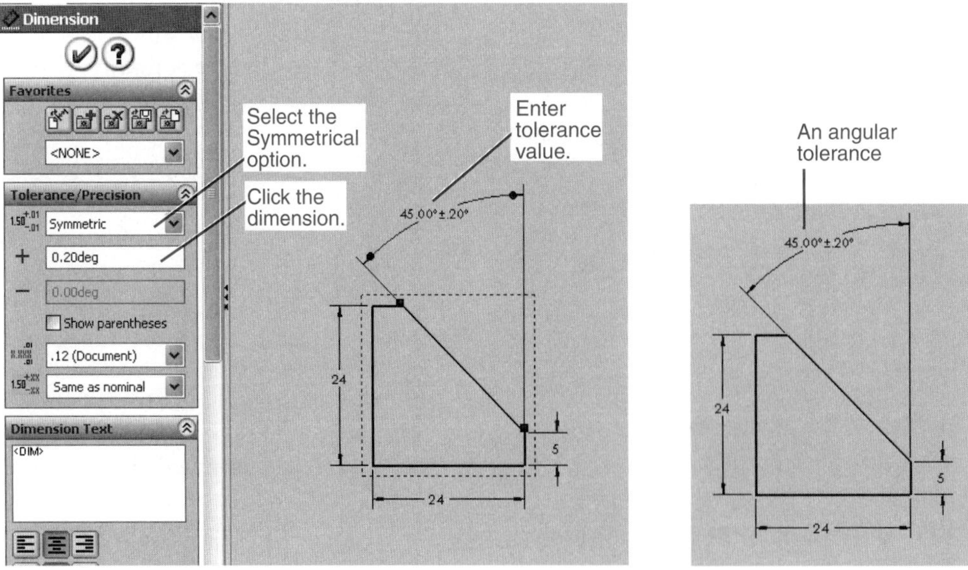

Figure 8-12

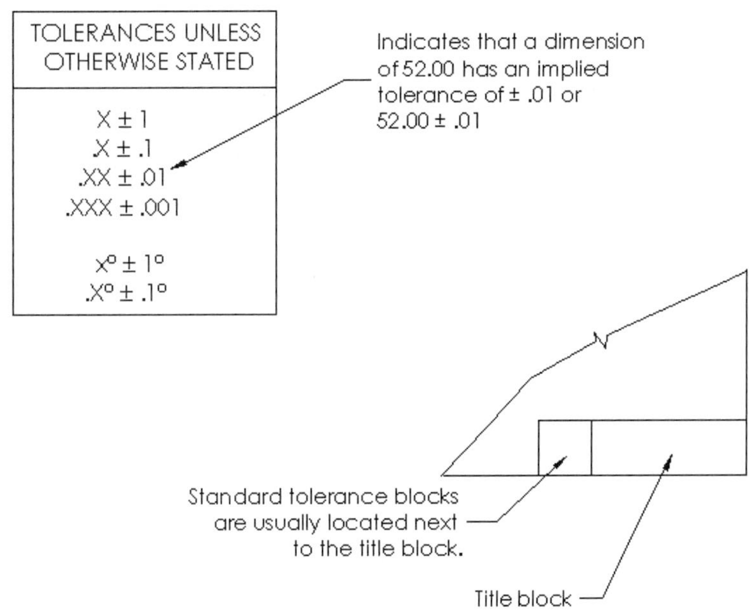

Figure 8-13

8-9 DOUBLE DIMENSIONING

It is an error to dimension the same distance twice. This mistake is called ***double dimensioning.*** Double dimensioning is an error because it does not allow for tolerance buildup across a distance.

Figure 8-14 shows an object that has been dimensioned twice across its horizontal length, once using three 30-mm dimensions and a second time using the 90-mm overall dimension. The two dimensions are mathematically equal but are not equal when tolerances are considered. Assume that each dimension has a standard tolerance of ±1 mm. The three 30-mm dimensions could create an acceptable distance of 90 ± 3 mm, or a maximum distance of 93 and a minimum distance of 87. The overall dimension of 90 mm allows a maximum distance of 91 and a minimum distance of 89. The two dimensions yield different results when tolerances are considered.

> ***Note:***
> Never dimension the same distance twice.

The size and location of a tolerance depends on the design objectives of the object, how it will be manufactured, and how it will be inspected. Even objects that have similar shapes may be dimensioned and toleranced very differently.

One possible solution to the double dimensioning shown in Figure 8–14 is to remove one of the 30-mm dimensions and allow that distance to "float," that is, absorb the cumulated tolerances. The choice of which 30-mm dimension to eliminate depends on the design objectives of the part. For this example the far-right dimension was eliminated to remove the double-dimensioning error.

Another possible solution to the double-dimensioning error is to retain the three 30-mm dimensions and to change the 90-mm overall dimension to a reference dimension. A reference dimension is used only for mathematical convenience. It is not used during the manufacturing or inspection process. A reference dimension is designated on a drawing using parentheses: (90).

If the 90-mm dimension was referenced, then only the three 30-mm dimensions would be used to manufacture and inspect the object. This would eliminate the double-dimensioning error.

8-10 CHAIN DIMENSIONS AND BASELINE DIMENSIONS

There are two systems for applying dimensions and tolerances to a drawing: chain and baseline. Figure 8-15 shows examples of both systems. ***Chain dimensions*** dimension each feature to the feature next to it. ***Baseline dimensions*** dimension all features from a single baseline or datum.

Chain and baseline dimensions may be used together. Figure 8-15 also shows two objects with repetitive features; one object includes two slots, and the other, three sets of three holes. In each example, the center of the repetitive feature is dimensioned to the left side of the object, which serves as a baseline. The sizes of the individual features are dimensioned using chain dimensions referenced to centerlines.

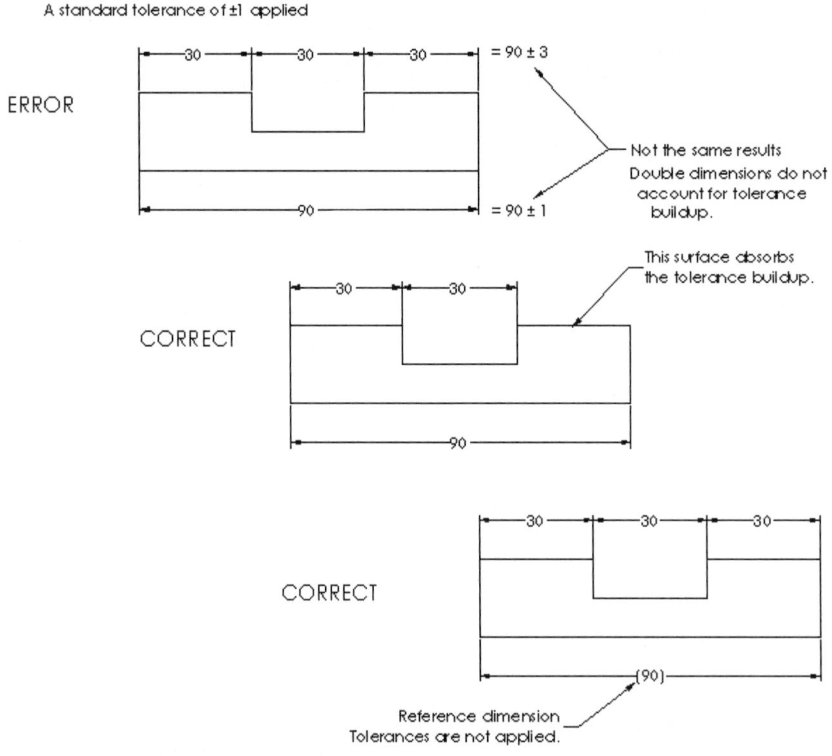

Figure 8-14

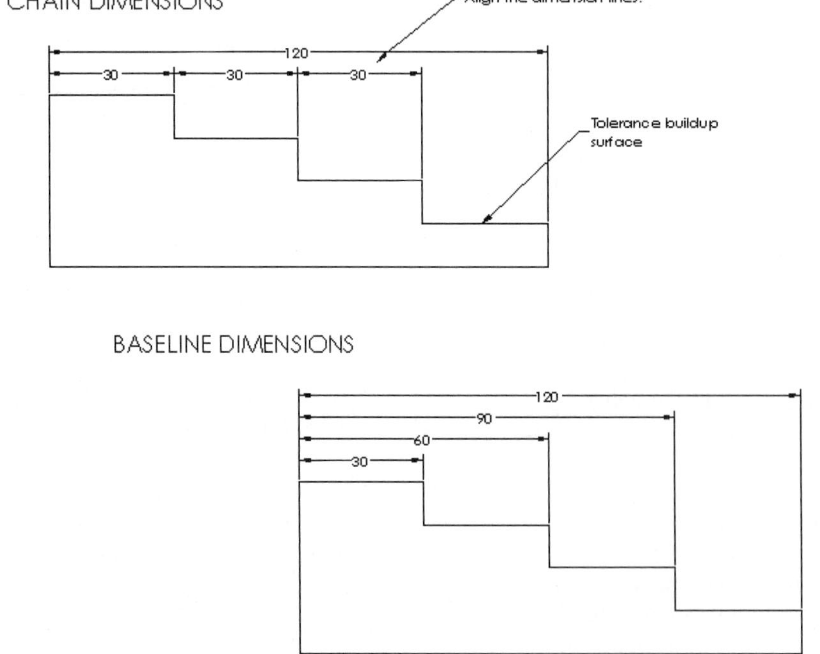

Figure 8-15

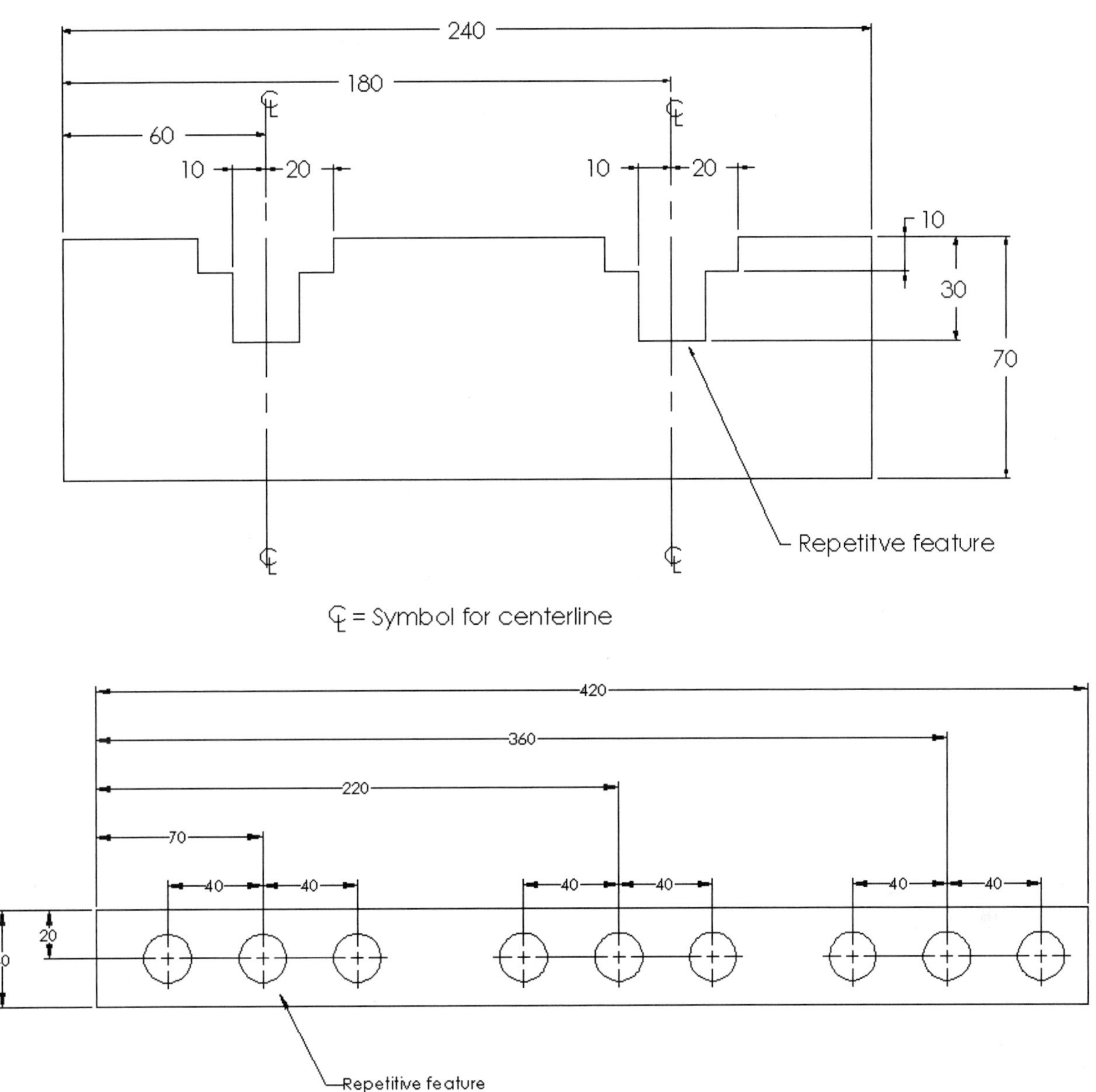

Figure 8-15 ***(continued)***

Baseline dimensions eliminate tolerance buildup and can be related directly to the reference axis of many machines. They tend to take up much more area on a drawing than do chain dimensions.

Chain dimensions are useful in relating one feature to another, such as the repetitive hole pattern shown in Figure 8-15. In this example the distance between the holes is more important than the individual hole's distance from the baseline.

Figure 8-16 shows the same object dimensioned twice, once using chain dimensions and once using baseline dimensions. All distances are assigned a tolerance range of 2 mm, stated using limit tolerances. The maximum distance for surface A is 28 mm using the chain system and 27 mm using the baseline system. The 1-mm difference comes from the elimination of the first 26–24 limit dimension found on the chain example but not on the baseline.

The total tolerance difference is 6 mm for the chain and 4 mm for the baseline. The baseline reduces the tolerance variations for the object simply because it applies the tolerances and dimensions differently. So why not always use baseline dimensions? For most applications, the baseline system is probably better, but if the distance between the individual features is more critical than the distance from the feature to the baseline, use the chain system.

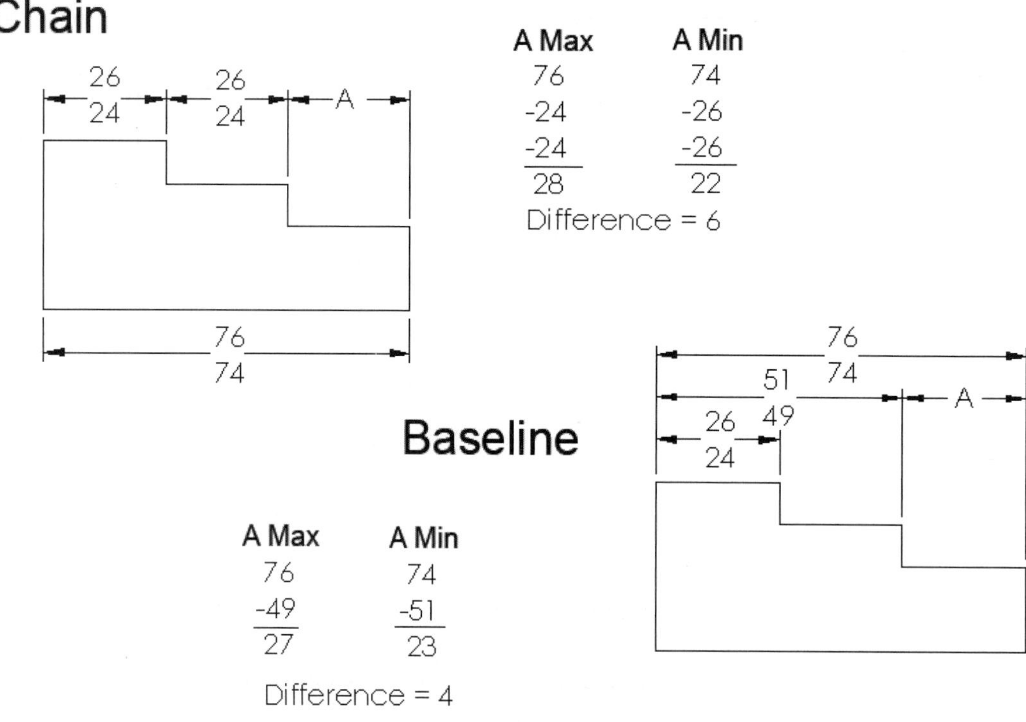

Figure 8-16

Baseline Dimensions Created Using SolidWorks

See Figure 8-17. See also Chapter 7.

Note in the example of baseline dimensioning shown in Figure 8-17 that each dimension is independent of the other. This means that if one of the dimensions is manufactured incorrectly, it will not affect the other dimensions.

8-11 TOLERANCE STUDIES

The term ***tolerance study*** is used when analyzing the effects of a group of tolerances on one another and on an object. Figure 8-18 shows an object with two horizontal dimensions. The horizontal distance A is not dimensioned. Its length depends on the tolerances of the two horizontal dimensions.

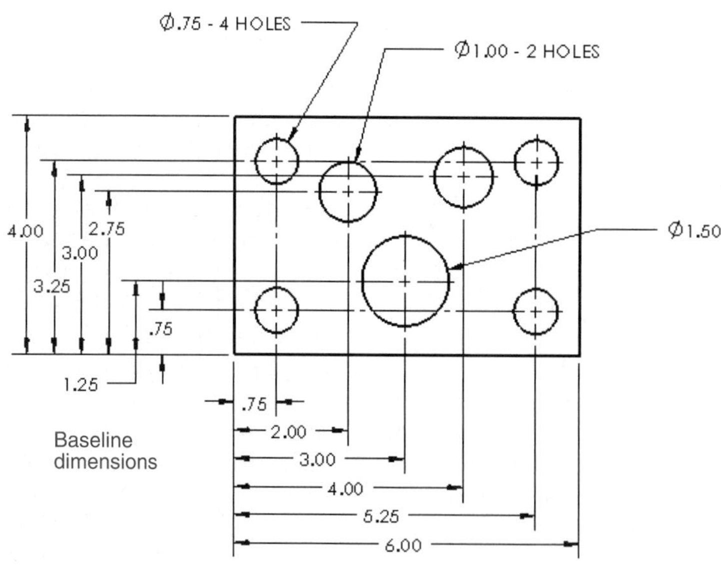

Figure 8-17

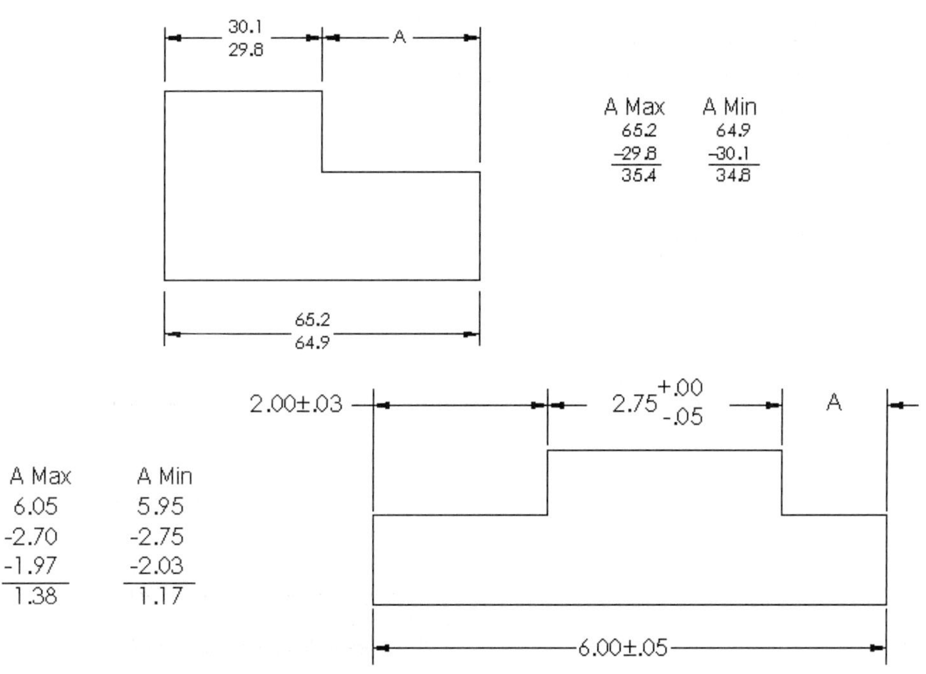

Figure 8-18

Calculating the Maximum Length of A

Distance A will be longest when the overall distance is at its longest and the other distance is at its shortest.

$$\begin{array}{r} 65.2 \\ -29.8 \\ \hline 35.4 \end{array}$$

Calculating the Minimum Length of A

Distance A will be shortest when the overall length is at its shortest and the other length is at its longest.

$$\begin{array}{r} 64.9 \\ -30.1 \\ \hline 34.8 \end{array}$$

> ***Note:***
> The hole locations can also be defined using polar dimensions.

8-12 RECTANGULAR DIMENSIONS

Figure 8-19 shows an example of rectangular dimensions referenced to baselines. Figure 8-20 shows a circular object on which dimensions are referenced to a circle's centerlines. Dimensioning to a circle's centerline is critical to accurate hole location.

8-13 HOLE LOCATIONS

When rectangular dimensions are used, the location of a hole's center point is defined by two linear dimensions. The result is a rectangular tolerance zone whose size is based on the linear dimension's tolerances. The shape of the center point's tolerance zone may be changed to circular using positioning tolerancing as described later in the chapter.

Figure 8-21 shows the location and size dimensions for a hole. Also shown are the resulting tolerance zone and the overall possible hole shape. The center point's tolerance is .2 by .3 based on the given linear locating tolerances.

The hole diameter has a tolerance of ±.05. This value must be added to the center point location tolerances to define the maximum overall possible shape of the hole. The maximum possible hole shape is determined by drawing the maximum radius from the four corner points of the tolerance zone.

This means that the left edge of the hole could be as close to the vertical baseline as 12.75 or as far as 13.25. The 12.75 value was derived by subtracting the maximum hole diameter value 12.05 from the minimum linear distance 24.80 (24.80 − 12.05 = 12.75). The 13.25 value was derived by subtracting the minimum hole diameter 11.95 from the maximum linear distance 25.20 (25.20 − 11.95 = 13.25).

Figure 8-22 shows a hole's tolerance zone based on polar dimensions. The zone has a sector shape, and the possible hole shape is determined by locating the maximum radius at the four corner points of the tolerance zone.

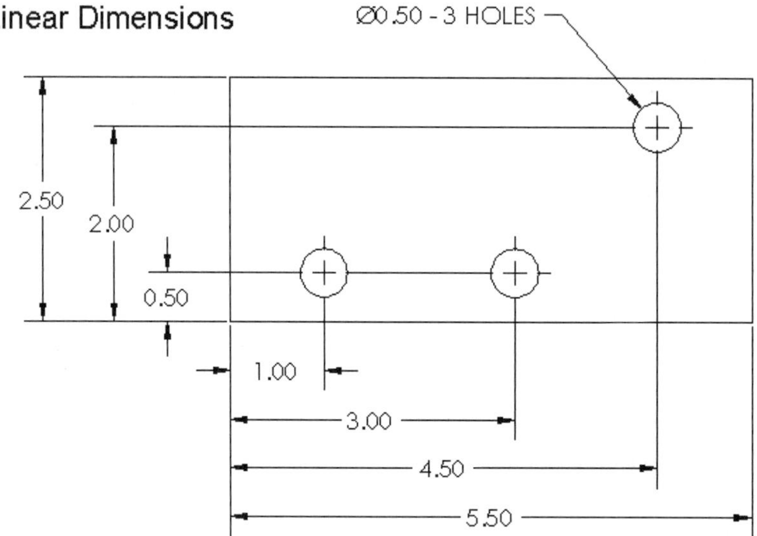

Figure 8-19

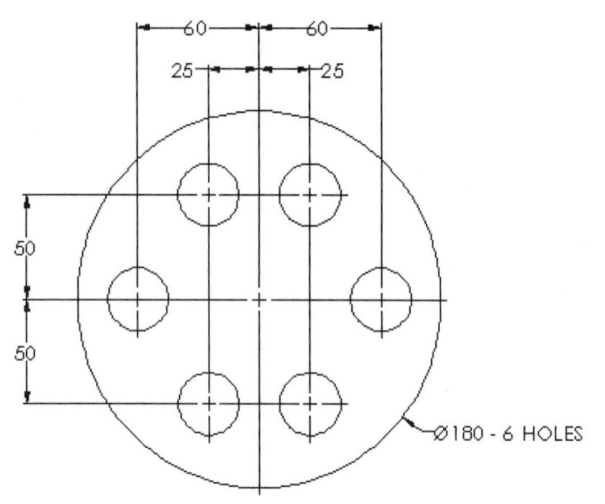

Figure 8-20

8-14 CHOOSING A SHAFT FOR A TOLERANCED HOLE

Given the hole location and size shown in Figure 8–21, what is the largest diameter shaft that will always fit into the hole?

Figure 8-23 shows the hole's center point tolerance zone based on the given linear locating tolerances. Four circles have been drawn centered at the four corners on the linear tolerance zone that represents the smallest possible hole diameter. The circles define an area that represents the maximum shaft size that will always fit into the hole, regardless of how the given dimensions are applied.

The diameter size of this circular area can be calculated by subtracting the maximum diagonal distance across the linear tolerance zone (corner to corner) from the minimum hole diameter.

The results can be expressed as a formula.

For Linear Dimensions and Tolerances

$$S_{max} = H_{min} - DTZ$$

where

S_{max} = maximum shaft diameter
H_{min} = minimum hole diamter
DTZ = diagonal distance across the tolerance zone

In the example shown the diagonal distance is determined using the Pythagorean theorem:

$$DTZ = \sqrt{(.4)^2 + (.6)^2}$$
$$= \sqrt{.16 + .36}$$
$$DTZ = .72$$

This means that the maximum shaft diameter that will always fit into the given hole is 11.23:

$$S_{max} = H_{min} - DTZ$$
$$= 11.95 - .72$$
$$S_{max} = 11.23$$

This procedure represents a restricted application of the general formula presented later in the chapter for positioning tolerances.

Note:
Linear tolerances generate a square or rectangular tolerance zone.

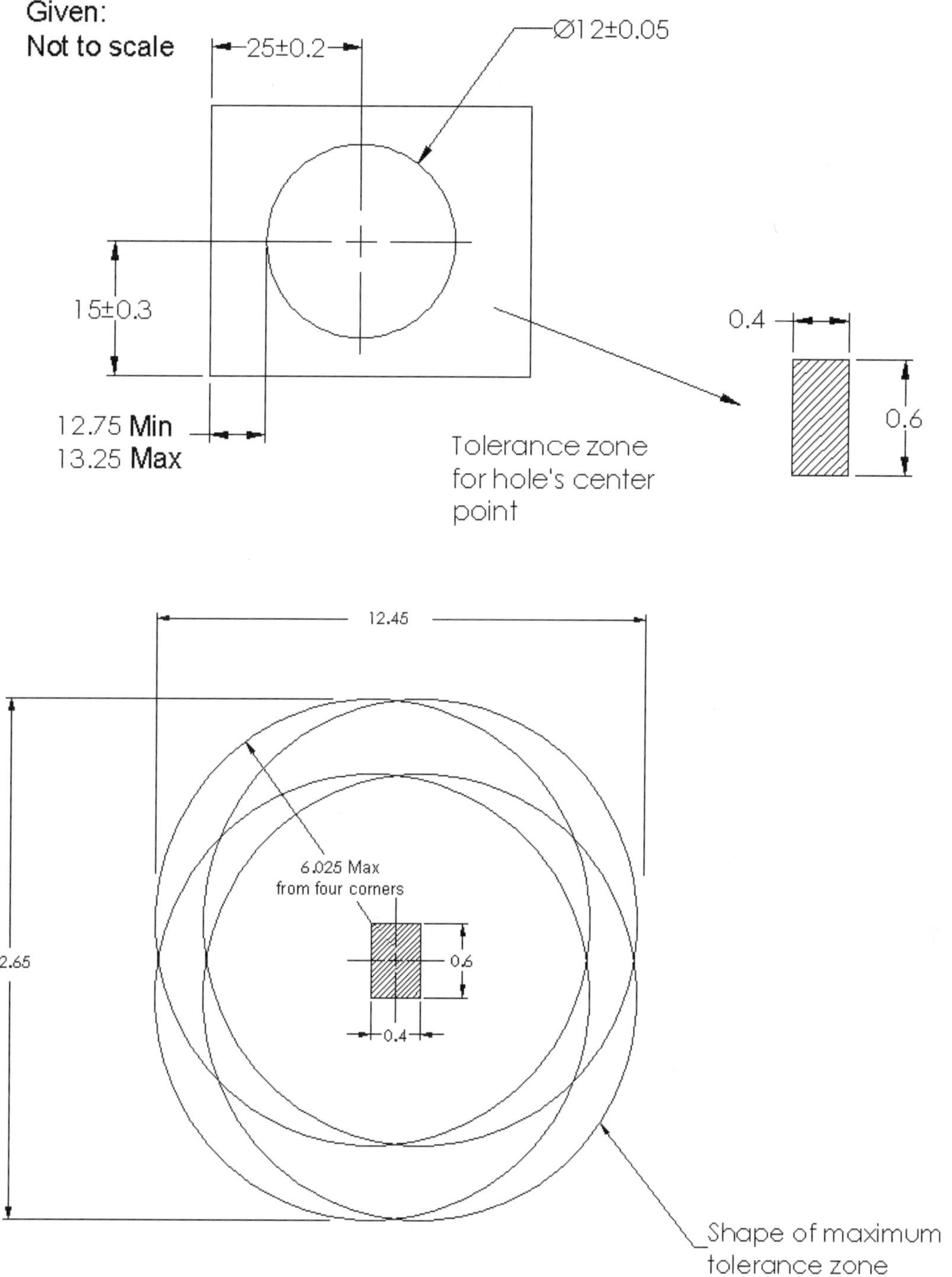

Figure 8-21

Once the maximum shaft size has been established, a tolerance can be applied to the shaft. If the shaft had a total tolerance of .25, the minimum shaft diameter would be 11.23 − .25, or 10.98. Figure 8-23 shows a shaft dimensioned and toleranced using these values.

The formula presented is based on the assumption that the shaft is perfectly placed on the hole's center point. This assumption is reasonable if two objects are joined by a fastener and both objects are free to move. When both objects are free to move about a common fastener, they are called ***floating objects.***

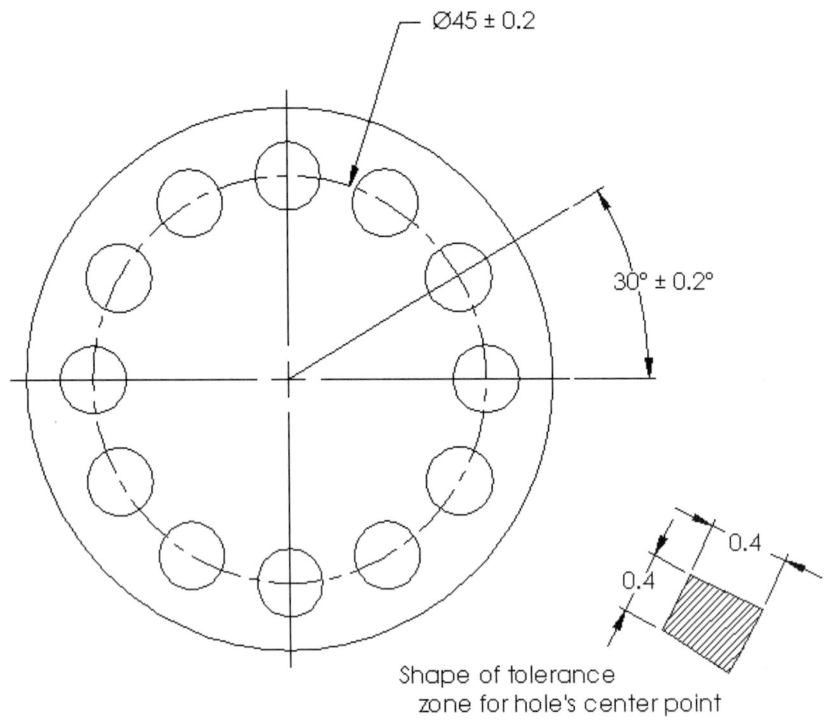

Figure 8-22

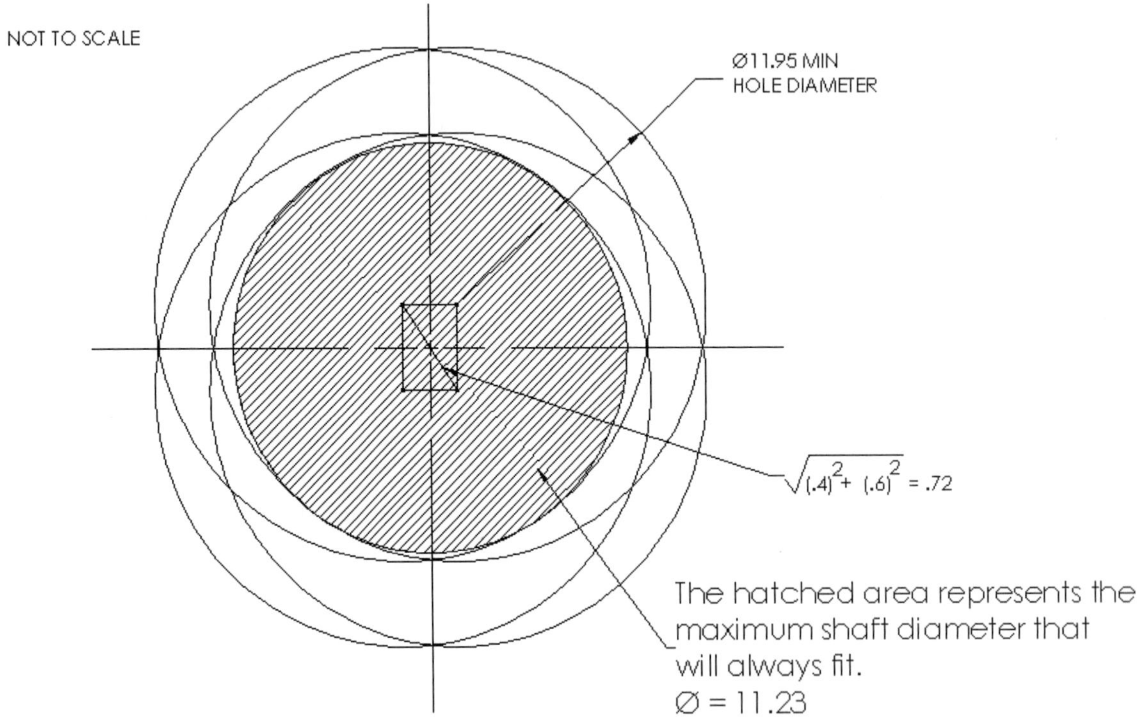

Figure 8-23

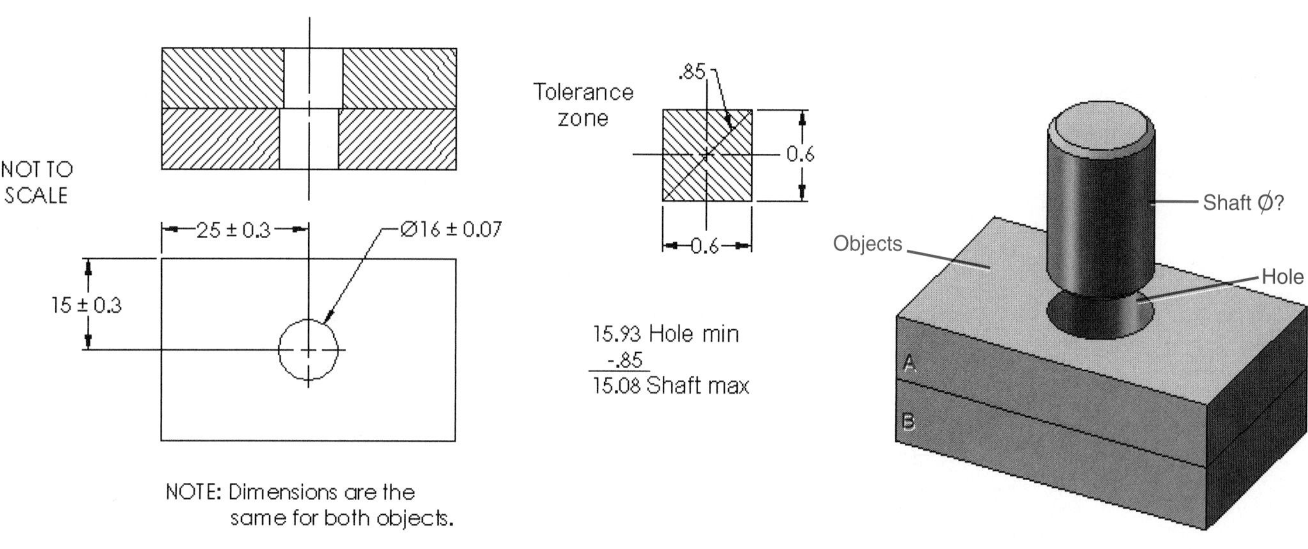

Figure 8-24

8-15 SAMPLE PROBLEM SP8-1

Parts A and B in Figure 8-24 are to be joined by a common shaft. The total tolerance for the shaft is to be .05. What are the maximum and minimum shaft diameters?

Both objects have the same dimensions and tolerances and are floating relative to each other.

$$S_{max} = H_{min} - DTZ$$
$$= 15.93 - .85$$
$$S_{max} = 15.08$$

The shaft's minimum diameter is found by subtracting the total tolerance requirement from the calculated maximum diameter:

$$15.80 - .05 = 15.03$$

Therefore,

Shaft max = 5.08
Shaft min = 5.03

8-16 SAMPLE PROBLEM SP8-2

The procedure presented in Sample Problem SP8-1 can be worked in reverse to determine the maximum and minimum hole size based on a given shaft size.

Objects AA and BB as shown in Figure 8-25 are to be joined using a bolt whose maximum diameter is .248. What is the minimum hole size for objects that will always accept the bolt? What is the maximum hole size if the total hole tolerance is .005?

$$S_{max} = H_{min} - DTZ$$

In this example H_{min} is the unknown factor, so the equation is rewritten as

$$H_{min} = S_{max} + DTZ$$
$$= .248 + .010$$
$$H_{min} = .258$$

This is the minimum hole diameter, so the total tolerance requirement is added to this value:

$$.258 + .005 = .263$$

Therefore,

Hole max = .263
Hole min = .258

8-17 NOMINAL SIZES

The term ***nominal*** refers to the approximate size of an object that matches a common fraction or whole number. A shaft with a dimension of 1.500 + .003 is said to have a nominal size of "one and a half inches." A dimension of 1.500 + .000/−.005 is still said to have a nominal size of one and a half inches. In both examples 1.5 is the closest common fraction.

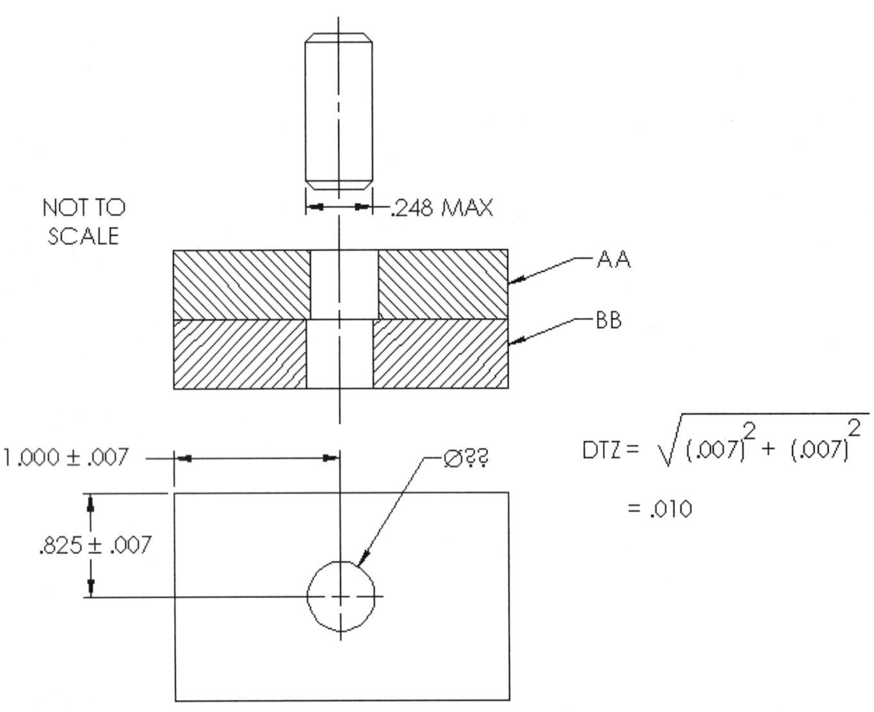

Figure 8-25

8-18 STANDARD FITS (METRIC VALUES)

Calculating tolerances between holes and shafts that fit together is so common in engineering design that a group of standard values and notations has been established. These values may be calculated using the **Limits and Fits** option of the **Design Library** tool.

There are three possible types of fits between a shaft and a hole: clearance, transitional, and interference. There are several subclassifications within each of these categories.

A ***clearance fit*** always defines the maximum shaft diameter as smaller than the minimum hole diameter. The difference between the two diameters is the amount of clearance. It is possible for a clearance fit to be defined with zero clearance; that is, the maximum shaft diameter is equal to the minimum hole diameter.

An ***interference fit*** always defines the minimum shaft diameter as larger than the maximum hole diameter; that is, the shaft is always bigger than the hole. This definition means that an interference fit is the converse of a clearance fit. The difference between the diameter of the shaft and the hole is the amount of interference.

An interference fit is primarily used to assemble objects together. Interference fits eliminate the need for threads, welds, or other joining methods. Using an interference for joining two objects is generally limited to light load applications.

It is sometimes difficult to visualize how a shaft can be assembled into a hole with a diameter smaller than that of the shaft. It is sometimes done using a hydraulic press that slowly forces the two parts together. The joining process can be augmented by the use of lubricants or heat. The hole is heated, causing it to expand, the shaft is inserted, and the hole is allowed to cool and shrink around the shaft.

A ***transition fit*** may be either a clearance or an interference fit. It may have a clearance between the shaft and the hole or an interference.

The notations are based on Standard International Tolerance values. A specific description for each category of fit follows.

Clearance Fits

H11/c11or C11/h11 = loose running fit
H8/d8 or D8/h8 = free running fit
H8/f7 or F8/h7 = close running fit
H7/g6 or G7/h6 = sliding fit
H7/h6 = locational clearance fit

Transitional Fits

H7/k6 or K7/h6 = locational transition fit
H7/n6 or N7/h6 = locational transition fit

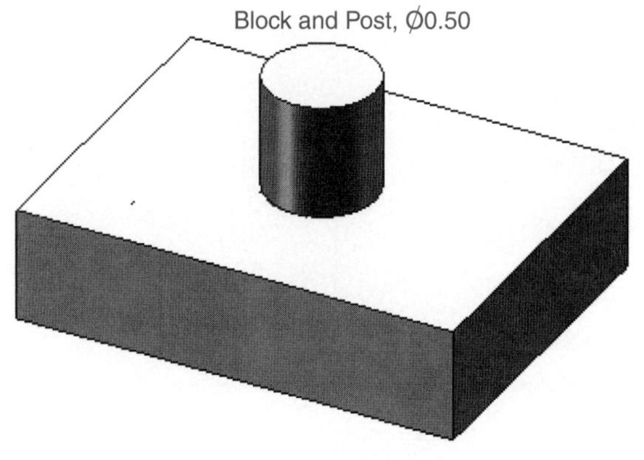

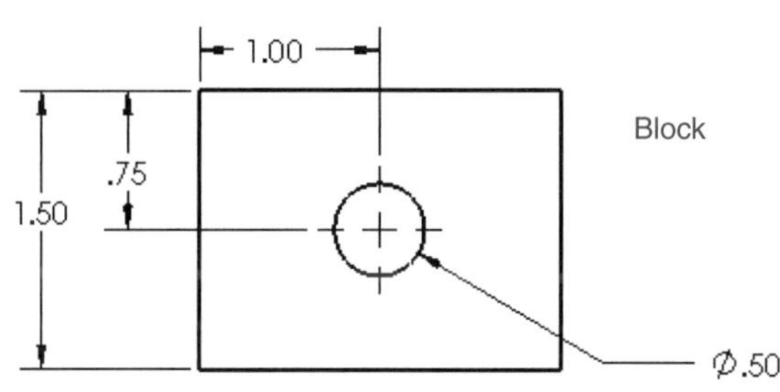

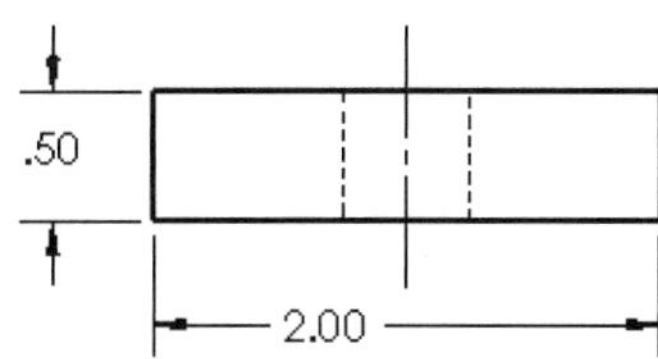

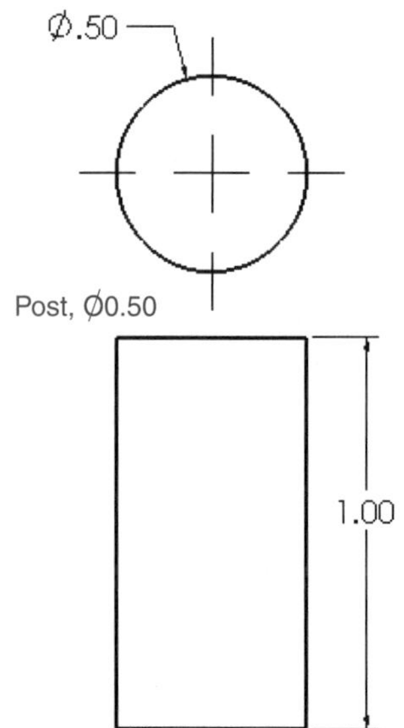

Figure 8-26

Interference Fits

H7/p6 or P7/h6 = locational transition fit
H7/s6 or S7/h6 = medium drive fit
H7/u6 or U7/h6 = force fit

8-19 STANDARD FITS (INCH VALUES)

Inch values are accessed in the **Design Library** tool by selecting the ANSI-Inch standards.

Fits defined using inch values are classified as follows:

RC = running and sliding fits
LC = clearance locational fits
LT = transitional locational fits
LN = interference fits
FN = force fits

Each of these general categories has several subclassifications within it defined by a number, for example, Class RC1, Class RC2, through Class RC8. The letter designations are based on International Tolerance Standards, as are metric designations.

> **TIP**
>
> Charts of tolerance values can be found in the appendix.

To Add a Fit Callout to a Drawing

Figure 8-26 shows a block and post. Figure 8-27 shows a drawing containing a front and a top orthographic view of the block and post assembly.

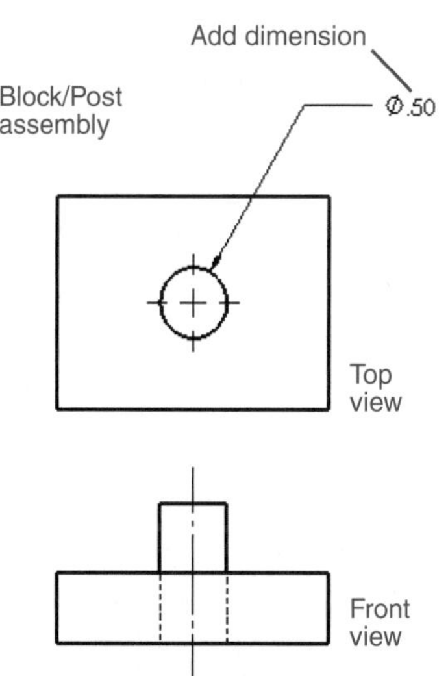

Figure 8-27

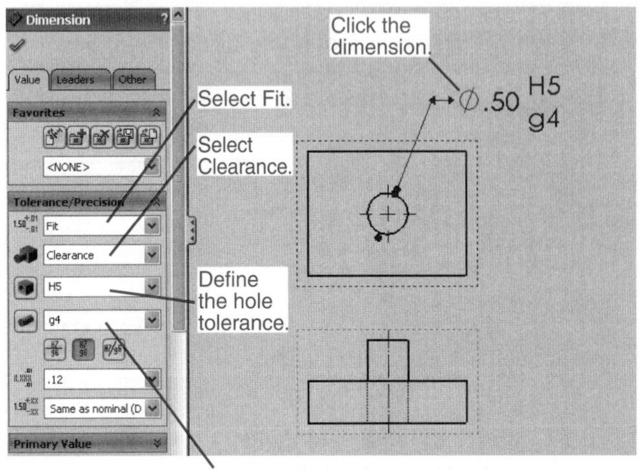

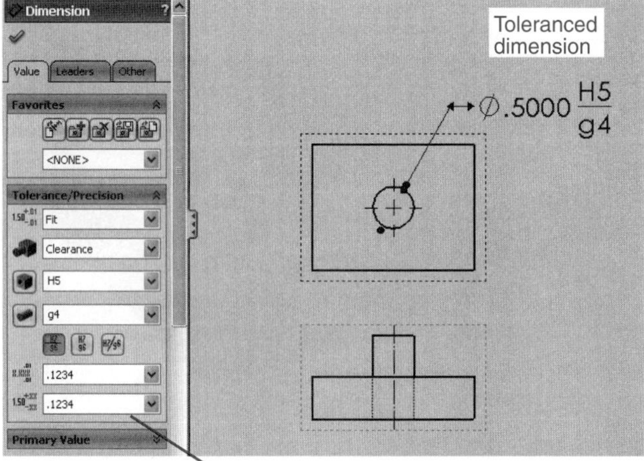

Figure 8-28

1. Draw the block and post and create an assembly drawing as shown in Figure 8-26.
2. Draw a front and a top orthographic view of the assembly as shown.
3. Add a **Ø.50** dimension to the top view.
4. Click the **Ø.50** dimension.

The **Dimension** toolbox will appear. See Figure 8-28.

5. Select the **Fit** option from the **Tolerance/Precision** box as shown.
6. Select a **Clearance** fit.
7. Select an **H5** tolerance for the hole.

> **TIP**
>
> SolidWorks will automatically select a matching shaft tolerance.

8. Accept the **g4** tolerance for the shaft.
9. Change the number of decimal places in the Ø.50 dimension to four places, **Ø.5000.**
10. Click the OK check mark.

Reading Fit Tables

There are several fit tables in the appendix both for English units and metric units. The metric tables can be read directly, as they state hole and shaft dimension. For example, the tolerance for a Preferred Clearance Fit for a 10mm nominal hole using a loose running fit is 10.090/10.000 for the hole and 9.920/9.830 for the shaft. The tolerance callout would be H11/c11. English unit tables require interpretation.

Figure 8-29 shows the table values for a .5000 nominal hole using an H5/g4 tolerance. The tolerance values are in thousands of an inch; that is, a listed value of 0.25 equals 0.0025 in. The ∅0.5000 nominal value is in the 0.40–0.71 size range, so the tolerance values are as shown. These values can be applied to the detail drawings of the block and shaft. See Figure 8-30.

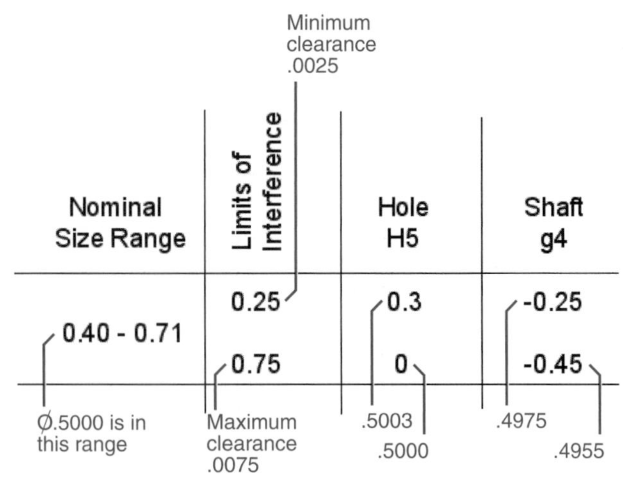

Figure 8-29

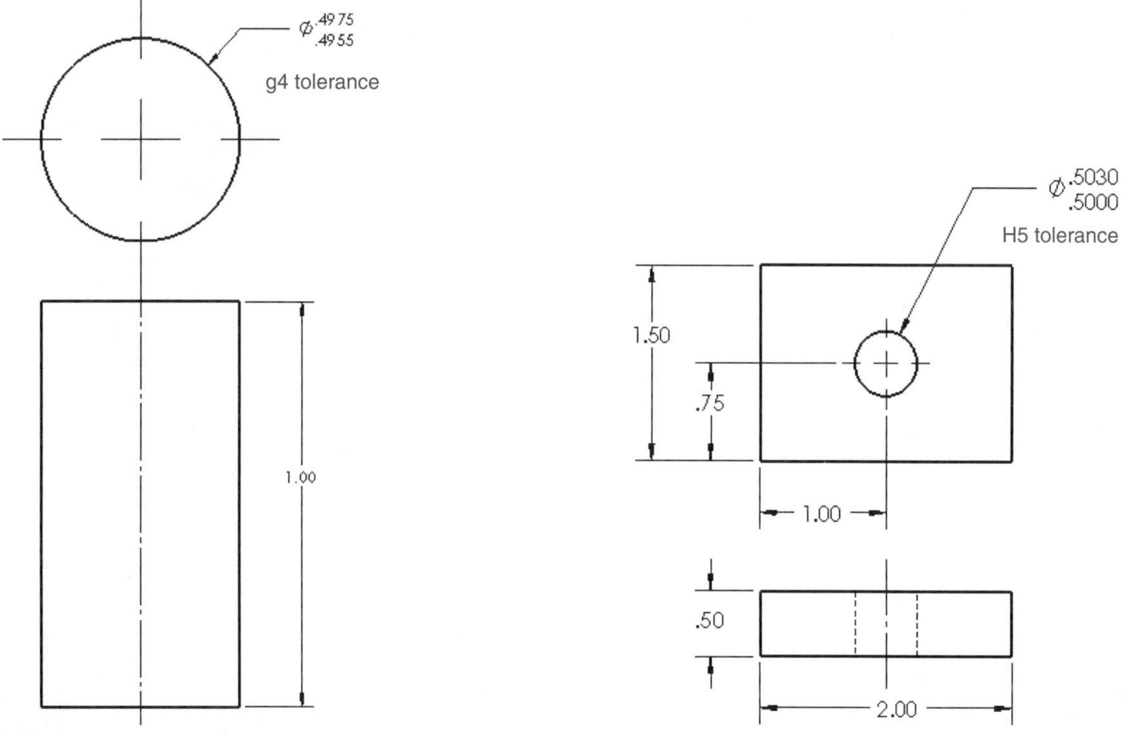

Figure 8-30

8-20 PREFERRED AND STANDARD SIZES

It is important that designers always consider preferred and standard sizes when selecting sizes for designs. Most tooling is set up to match these sizes, so manufacturing is greatly simplified when preferred and standard sizes are specified. Figure 8-31 shows a listing of preferred sizes for metric values.

PREFERRED SIZES			
1	1.1	12	14
1.2	1.4	16	18
1.6	1.8	20	22
2	2.2	25	28
2.5	2.8	30	35
3	3.5	40	45
4	4.5	50	55
5	5.5	60	70
6	7	80	90
8	9	100	110
10	11	120	140

Figure 8-31

Consider the case of design calculations that call for a 42-mm-diameter hole. A 42-mm-diameter hole is not a preferred size. A diameter of 40 mm is the closest preferred size, and a 45-mm diameter is a second choice. A 42-mm hole could be manufactured but would require an unusual drill size that may not be available. It would be wise to reconsider the design to see if a 40-mm-diameter hole could be used, and if not, possibly a 45-mm-diameter hole.

A production run of a very large quantity could possibly justify the cost of special tooling, but for smaller runs it is probably better to use preferred sizes. Machinists will have the required drills, and maintenance people will have the appropriate tools for these sizes.

Figure 8-32 shows a listing of standard fractional drill sizes. Most companies now specify metric units or decimal inches; however, many standard items are still available in fractional sizes, and many older objects may still require fractional-sized tools and replacement parts. A more complete listing is available in the appendix.

8-21 SURFACE FINISHES

The term ***surface finish*** refers to the accuracy (flatness) of a surface. Metric values are measured using micrometers (μm), and inch values are measured in microinches (μin.).

STANDARD TWIST DRILL SIZES					
Fraction	Decimal Equivalent	Fraction	Decimal Equivalent	Fraction	Decimal Equivalent
7/16	0.1094	21/64	0.3281	11/16	0.6875
1/8	0.1250	11/64	0.3438	3/4	0.7500
9/64	0.1406	23/64	0.3594	13/16	0.8125
5/32	0.1562	3/8	0.3750	7/8	0.8750
11/64	0.1719	25/64	0.3906	15/16	0.9375
3/16	0.1875	13/32	0.4062	1	1.0000
13/64	0.2031	27/64	0.4219		
7/32	0.2188	7/16	0.4375		
1/4	0.2500	29/64	0.4531		
17/64	0.2656	15/32	0.4688		
9/32	0.2812	1/2	0.5000		
19/64	0.2969	9/16	0.5625		
5/16	0.3125	5/8	0.6250		

Figure 8-32

The accuracy of a surface depends on the manufacturing process used to produce the surface. Figure 8-33 shows a listing of manufacturing processes and the quality of the surface finish they can be expected to produce.

Surface finishes have several design applications. ***Datum surfaces,*** or surfaces used for baseline dimensioning, should have fairly accurate surface finishes to help assure accurate measurements. Bearing surfaces should have good-quality surface finishes for better load distribution, and parts that operate at high speeds should have smooth finishes to help reduce friction. Figure 8-34 shows a screw head sitting on a very wavy surface. Note that the head of the screw is actually in contact with only two wave peaks, meaning all the bearing load is concentrated on the two peaks. This situation could cause stress cracks and greatly weaken the surface. A better-quality surface finish would increase the bearing contact area.

Surface Roughness Average Obtained by Common Production Methods

Process	Roughness Height Rating - microinches, micromillimeters										
μmm	50	25	12.5	6.3	3.2	1.6	0.8	0.4	0.2	0.1	0.05
μin	2000	1000	500	250	125	63	32	16	8	4	2
Flame Cutting											
Snagging											
Sawing											
Planing & Shaping											
Drilling											
Chemical Milling											
Electric Discharge											
Milling											
Broaching											
Reaming											
Electron Beam											
Laser											

Surface Roughness Average Obtained by Common Production Methods

Process	Roughness Height Rating - microinches, micromillimeters										
μmm	50	25	12.5	6.3	3.2	1.6	0.8	0.4	0.2	0.1	0.05
μin	2000	1000	500	250	125	63	32	16	8	4	2
Electrochemical											
Boring, Turning											
Barrel Finishing											
Electronic Grinding											
Grinding											
Honing											
Electropolishing											
Polishing											
Lapping											
Reaming											

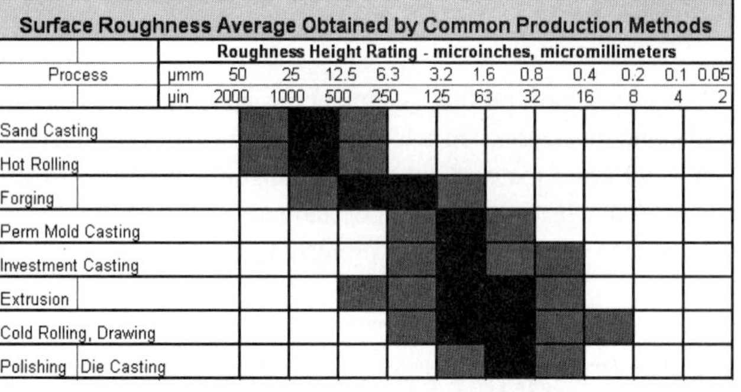

Surface Roughness Average Obtained by Common Production Methods

Process	Roughness Height Rating - microinches, micromillimeters										
μmm	50	25	12.5	6.3	3.2	1.6	0.8	0.4	0.2	0.1	0.05
μin	2000	1000	500	250	125	63	32	16	8	4	2
Sand Casting											
Hot Rolling											
Forging											
Perm Mold Casting											
Investment Casting											
Extrusion											
Cold Rolling, Drawing											
Polishing Die Casting											

Figure 8-33

Bearing Load

Force

Surface

Resultant

Resultant

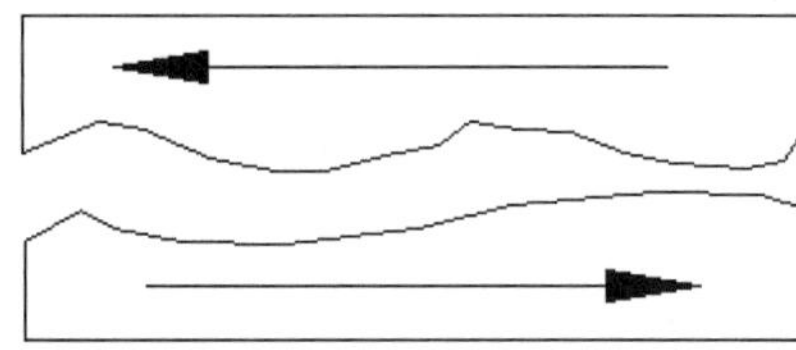

Figure 8-34

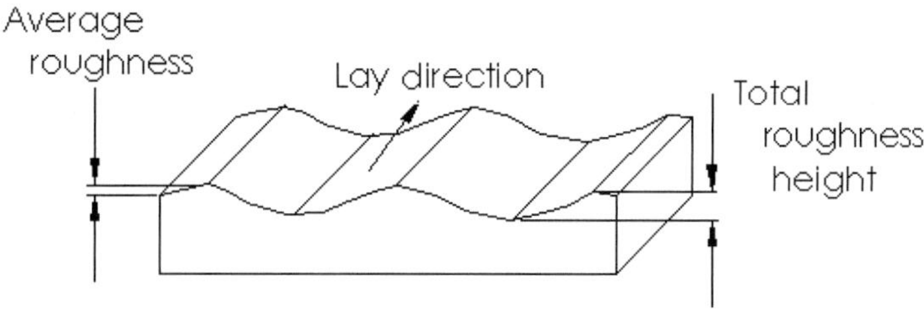

Figure 8-35

Figure 8-34 also shows two very rough surfaces moving in contact with each other. The result will be excess wear to both surfaces because the surfaces touch only on the peaks, and these peaks will tend to wear faster than flatter areas. Excess vibration can also result when interfacing surfaces are too rough.

Surface finishes are classified into three categories: surface texture, roughness, and lay. ***Surface texture*** is a general term that refers to the overall quality and accuracy of a surface.

Roughness is a measure of the average deviation of a surface's peaks and valleys. See Figure 8-35.

Lay refers to the direction of machine marks on a surface. See Figure 8-36. The lay of a surface is particularly important when two moving objects are in contact with each other, especially at high speeds.

8-22 SURFACE CONTROL SYMBOLS

Surface finishes are indicated on a drawing using surface control symbols. See Figure 8-37. The general surface control symbol looks like a check mark. Roughness values may be included with the symbol to specify the required accuracy. Surface control symbols can also be used to specify the manufacturing process that may or may not be used to produce a surface.

Figure 8–37 shows two applications of surface control symbols. In the first example, a 0.8-μm (32 μin.) surface finish is specified on the surface that serves as a datum for several horizontal dimensions. A 0.8-μm surface finish is generally considered the minimum acceptable finish for datums.

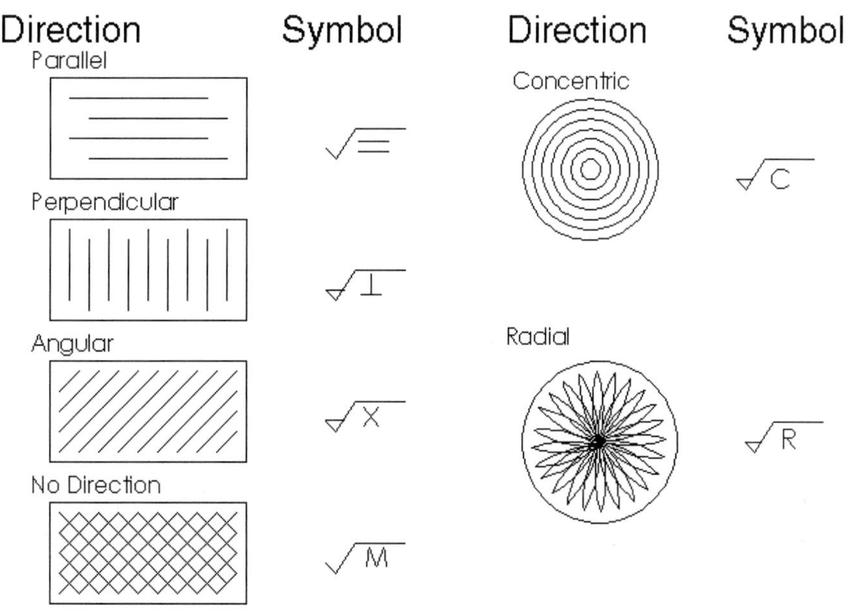

Figure 8-36

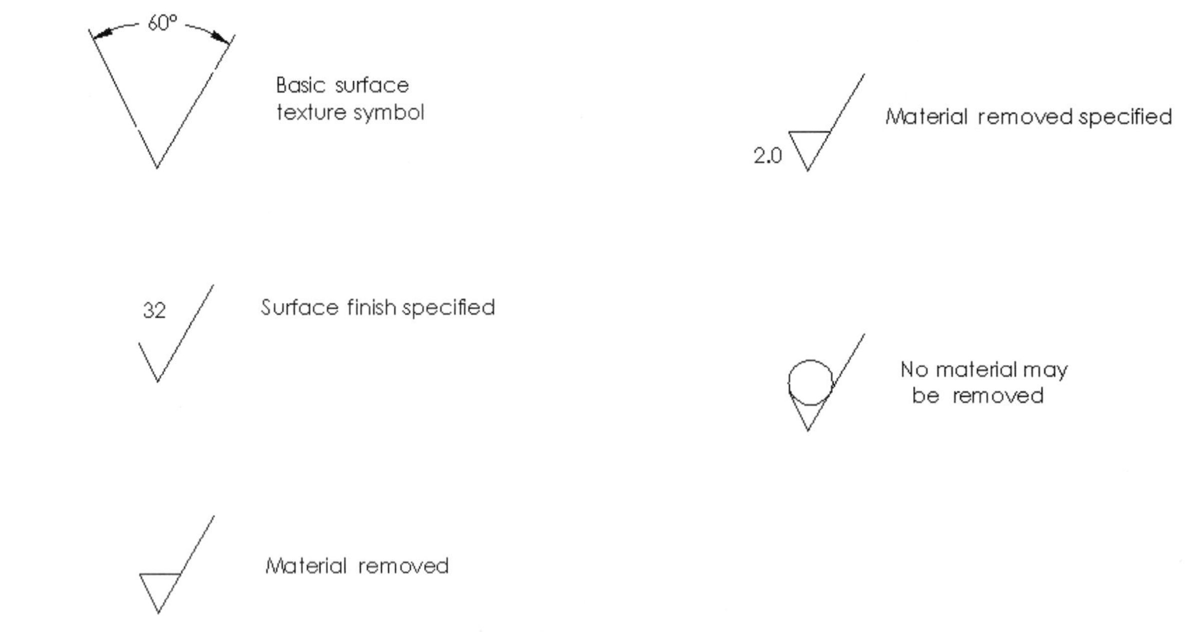

Figure 8-36 ***(continued)***

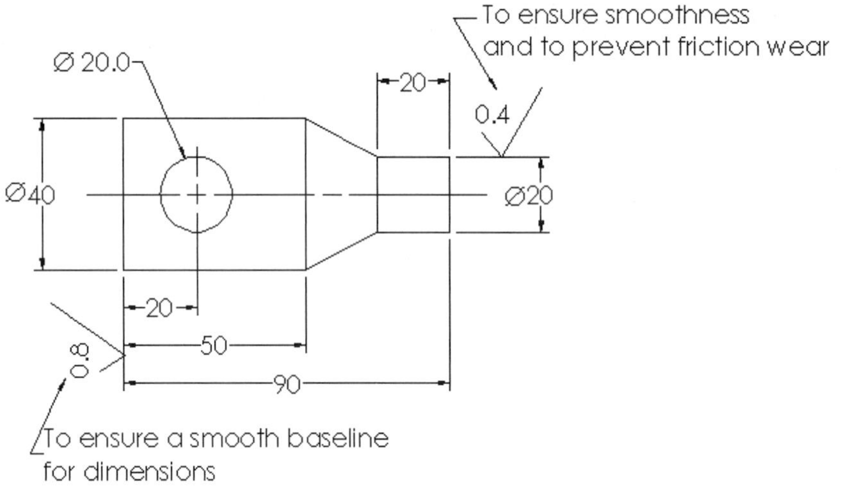

Figure 8-37

A second finish mark with a value of 0.4 μm is located on an extension line that refers to a surface that will be in contact with a moving object. The extra flatness will help prevent wear between the two surfaces.

8-23 APPLYING SURFACE CONTROL SYMBOLS

Figure 8-38 shows a dimensioned orthographic view. Surface symbols will be added to this view.

1. Click the **Annotations** tool and select the **Surface Finish** tool.

See Figure 8-39.

2. Select the **Basic** symbol and enter a value of **32.**
3. Move the cursor into the drawing area and locate the surface control symbol on an extension line as shown.
4. Click the **<Esc>** key.
5. Click the OK check mark
6. Save the drawing.

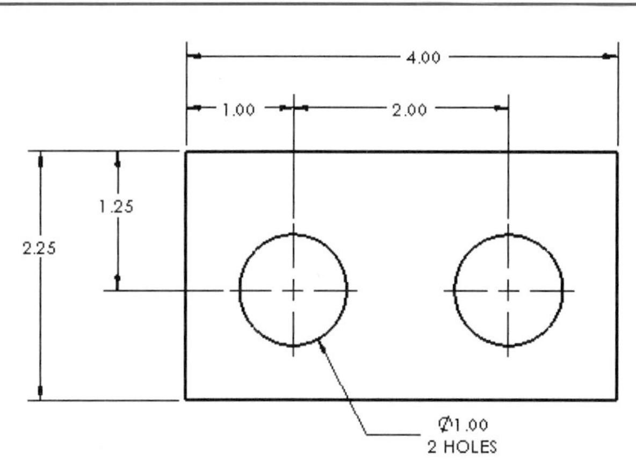

Figure 8-38

To Add a Lay Symbol to a Drawing

Use the same drawing as in Figure 8-39.

1. Click the **Annotations** tool and select the **Surface Finish** tool.

See Figure 8-40.

2. Click the **Lay Direction** box and select the **Multi-Directional** symbol.
3. Click the **Machine Required** symbol box.
4. Move the cursor into the drawing area and locate the surface control symbol on an extension line as shown.
5. Click the **<Esc>** key.
6. Click the OK check mark.

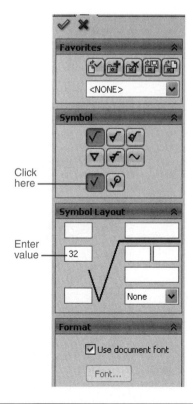

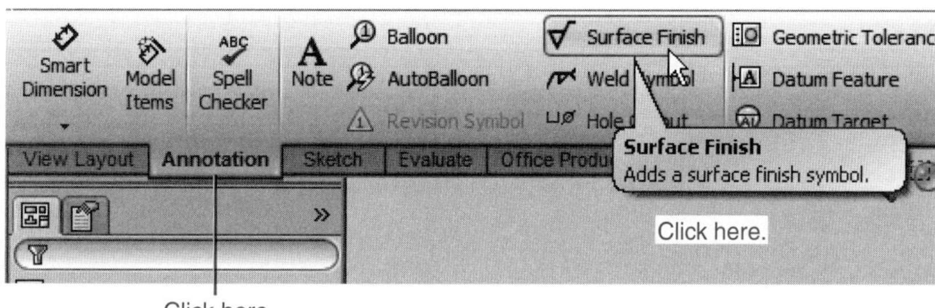

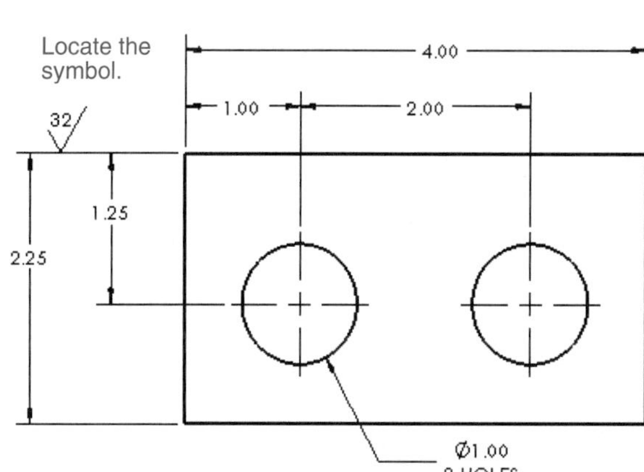

Figure 8-39

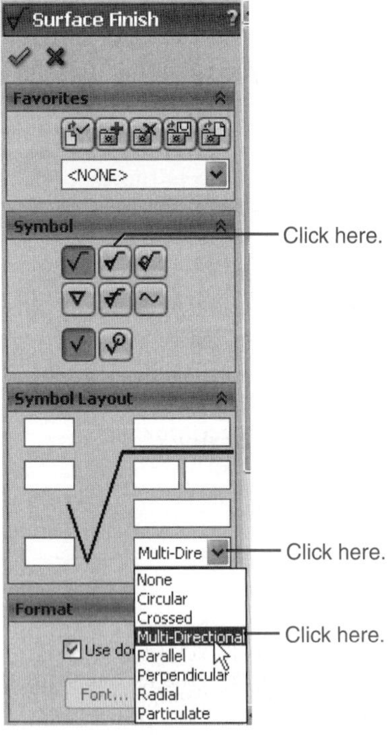

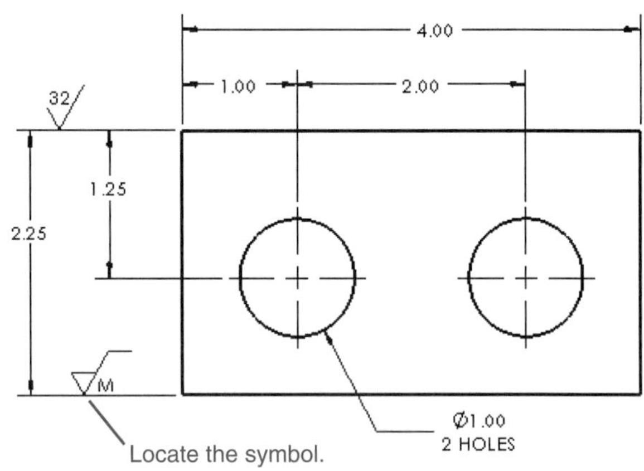

Figure 8-40

8-24 DESIGN PROBLEMS

Figure 8-41 shows two objects that are to be fitted together using a fastener such as a screw-and-nut combination. For this example a cylinder will be used to represent a fastener. Only two nominal dimensions are given. The dimensions and tolerances were derived as follows.

The distance between the centers of the holes is given as 50 nominal. The term *nominal* means that the stated value is only a starting point. The final dimensions will be close to the given value but do not have to equal it.

Assigning tolerances is an iteration process; that is, a tolerance is selected and other tolerance values are calculated from the selected initial values. If the results are not satisfactory, go back and modify the initial value and calculate the other values again. As your experience grows you will become better at selecting realistic initial values.

In the example shown in Figure 8-41, start by assigning a tolerance of $\pm$ .01 to both the top and bottom parts for both the horizontal and vertical dimensions used to locate the holes. This means that there is a possible center point variation of .02 for both parts. The parts must always fit together, so tolerances must be assigned based on the worst-case condition, or when the parts are made at the extreme ends of the assigned tolerances.

Figure 8-42 shows a greatly enlarged picture of the worst-case condition created by a tolerance of $\pm$.01. The center points of the holes could be as much as .028 apart if the two center points were located at opposite corners of the tolerance zones. This means that the minimum hole diameter must always be at least .028 larger than the maximum stud diameter. In addition, there should be a clearance tolerance assigned so that the hole and stud are never exactly the same size. Figure 8-43 shows the resulting tolerances.

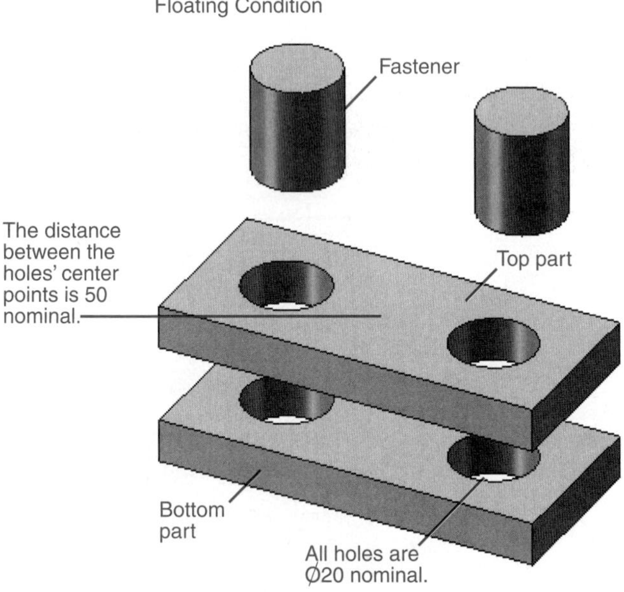

Figure 8-41

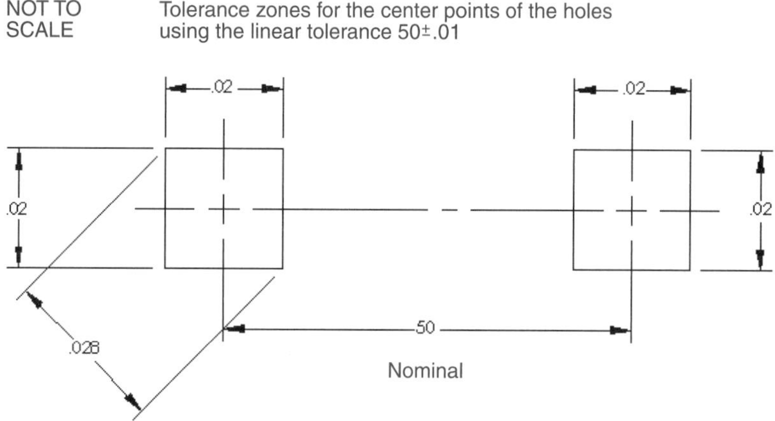

Figure 8-42

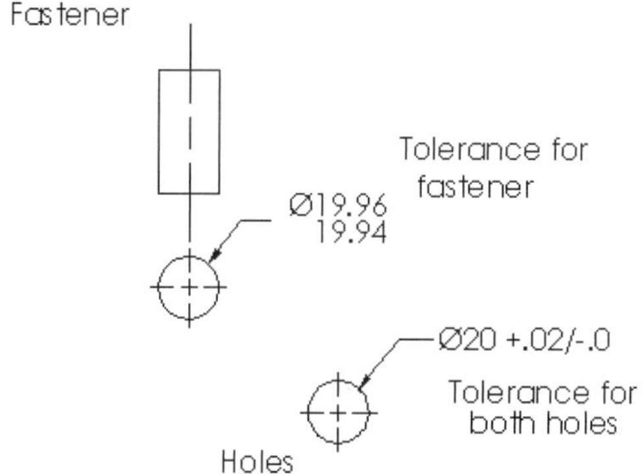

The 19.96 value includes a .01 clearance allowance, and the 19.94 value is the result of an assigned feature tolerance of .02.

Figure 8-43

TIP

The tolerance zones in this section are created by line dimensions that generated square tolerance zones.

Floating Condition

The top and bottom parts shown in Figure 8-41 are to be joined by two independent fasteners; that is, the location of one fastener does not depend on the location of the other. This situation is called a ***floating condition.***

This means that the tolerance zones for both the top and bottom parts can be assigned the same values and that a fastener diameter selected to fit one part will also fit the other part.

The final tolerances were developed by first defining a minimum hole size of 20.00. An arbitrary tolerance of .02 was assigned to the hole and was expressed as 20.00 + .02/−0; so that the hole can never be any smaller than 20.00.

The 20.00 minimum hole diameter dictates that the maximum fastener diameter can be no greater than 19.97, or .03 (the rounded-off diagonal distance across the tolerance zone—.028) less than the minimum hole diameter. A .01 clearance was assigned. The clearance ensures that the hole and fastener are never exactly the same diameter. The resulting maximum allowable diameter for the fastener is 19.96. Again, an arbitrary tolerance of .02 was assigned to the fastener. The final fastener dimensions are therefore 19.96 to 19.94.

The assigned tolerances ensure that there will always be at least .01 clearance between the fastener and the hole. The other extreme condition occurs when the hole is at its largest possible size (20.02) and the fastener is at its smallest (19.94). This means that there could be as much as .08 clearance between the parts. If this much clearance is not acceptable, then the assigned tolerances will have to be reevaluated.

Figure 8-44 shows the top and bottom parts dimensioned and toleranced. Any dimensions that do not have assigned tolerances are assumed to have standard tolerances.

Note, in Figure 8-44, that the top edge of each part has been assigned a surface finish. This was done to help ensure the accuracy of the 20 ± .01 dimension. If this edge surface was rough, it could affect the tolerance measurements.

This example will be done later in the chapter using geometric tolerances. Geometric tolerance zones are circular rather than rectangular.

Fixed Condition

Figure 8-45 shows the same nominal conditions presented in Figure 8-41, but the fasteners are now fixed to the top part. This situation is called the ***fixed condition.***

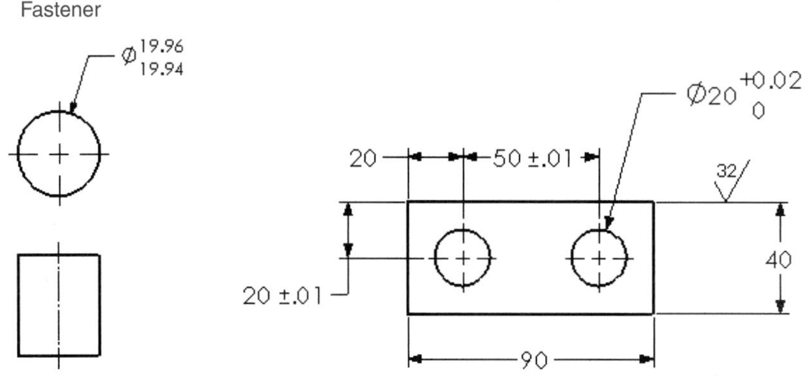

Figure 8-44

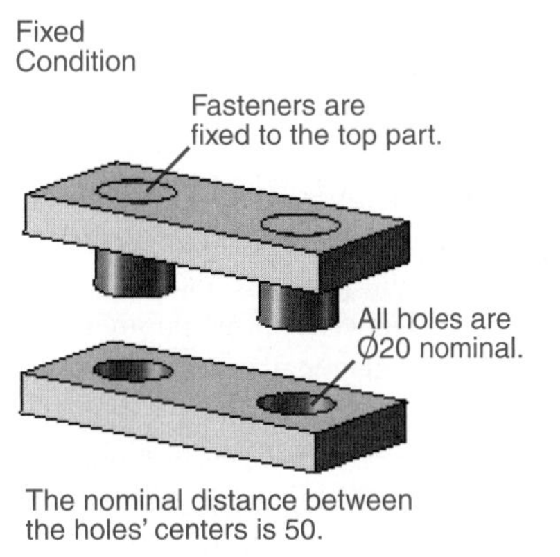

Figure 8-45

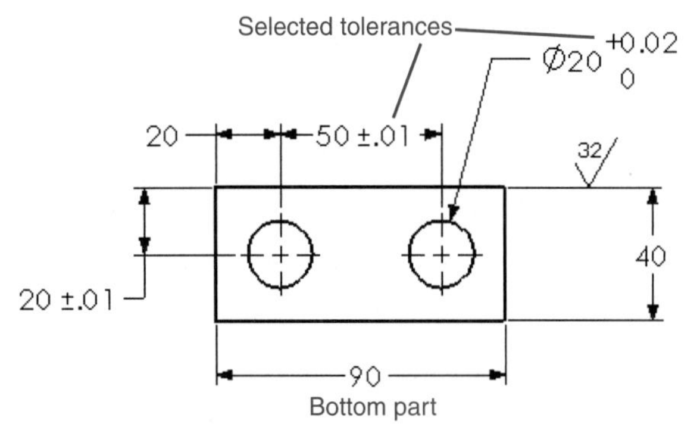

Figure 8-46

In analyzing the tolerance zones for the fixed condition, two position tolerances must be considered: the positional tolerances for the holes in the bottom part, and the positional tolerances for the fixed fasteners in the top part. This relationship may be expressed in an equation as follows:

$$S_{max} + DTSZ = H_{min} - DTZ$$

where

S_{max} = maximum shaft (fastener) diameter
H_{min} = minimum hole diameter
DTSZ = diagonal distance across the shaft's center point tolerance zone
DTZ = diagonal distance across the hole's center point tolerance zone

If a dimension and tolerance of 50 ± .01 is assigned to both the center distance between the holes and the center distance between the fixed fasteners, the values for DTSZ and DTZ will be equal. The formula can then be simplified as follows.

$$S_{max} = H_{min} - 2(DTZ)$$

where DTZ equals the diagonal distance across the tolerance zone. If a hole tolerance of 20.00 + .02/−0 is also defined, the resulting maximum shaft size can be determined, assuming that the calculated distance of .028 is rounded off to .03. See Figure 8-46.

$$S_{max} = 20.00 - 2(0.03)$$
$$= 19.94$$

This means that 19.94 is the largest possible shaft diameter that will just fit. If a clearance tolerance of .01 is assumed to ensure that the shaft and hole are never exactly the same size, the maximum shaft diameter becomes 19.93. See Figure 8-47.

A feature tolerance of .02 on the shaft will result in a minimum shaft diameter of 19.91. Note that the .01 clearance tolerance and the .02 feature tolerance were arbitrarily chosen. Other values could have been used.

Designing a Hole Given a Fastener Size

The previous two examples started by selecting a minimum hole diameter and then calculating the resulting fastener size. Figure 8-48 shows a situation in which the fastener size is defined, and the problem is to determine the

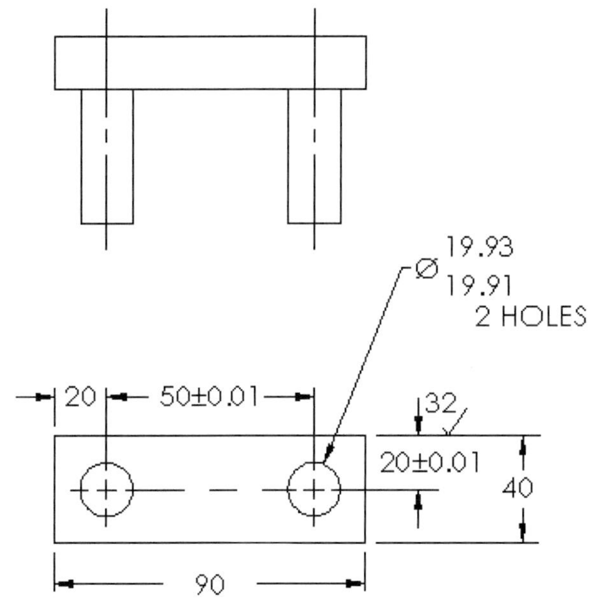

Figure 8-47

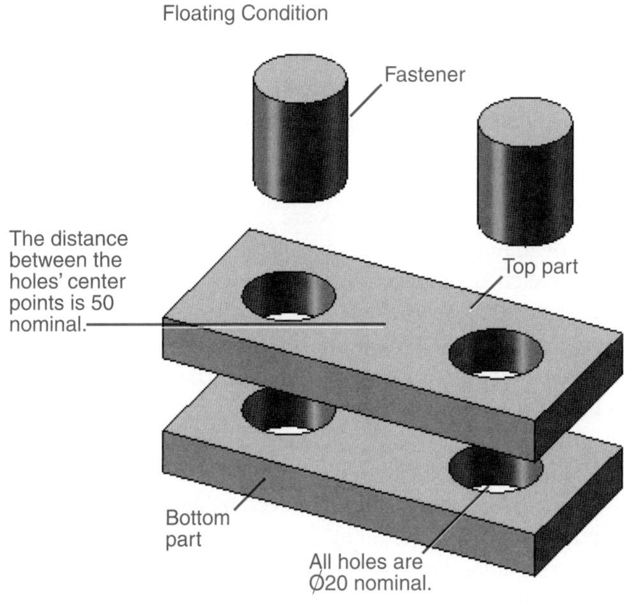

Figure 8-48

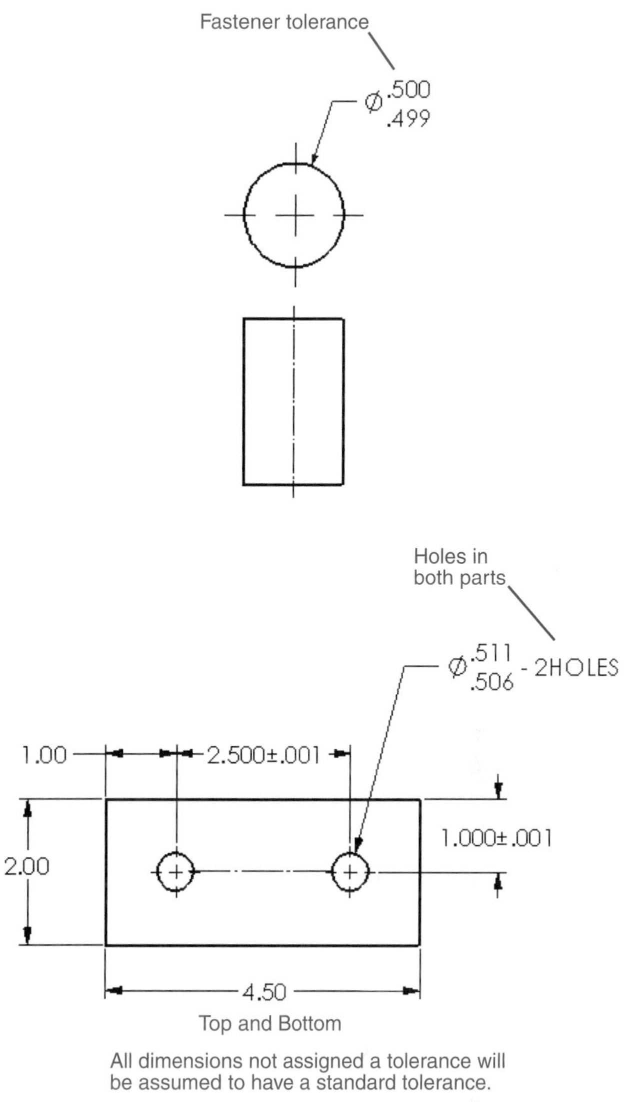

Figure 8-49

appropriate hole sizes. Figure 8-49 shows the dimensions and tolerances for both top and bottom parts.

Requirements:

Clearance, minimum = .003
Hole tolerances =.005
Positional tolerance = .002

8-25 GEOMETRIC TOLERANCES

Geometric tolerancing is a dimensioning and tolerancing system based on the geometric shape of an object. Surfaces may be defined in terms of their flatness or roundness, or in terms of how perpendicular or parallel they are to other surfaces.

Geometric tolerances allow a more exact definition of the shape of an object than do conventional coordinate-type tolerances. Objects can be toleranced in a manner more closely related to their design function or so that their features and surfaces are more directly related to each other.

8-26 TOLERANCES OF FORM

Tolerances of form are used to define the shape of a surface relative to itself. There are four classifications: flatness, straightness, roundness, and cylindricity. Tolerances of form are not related to other surfaces but apply only to an individual surface.

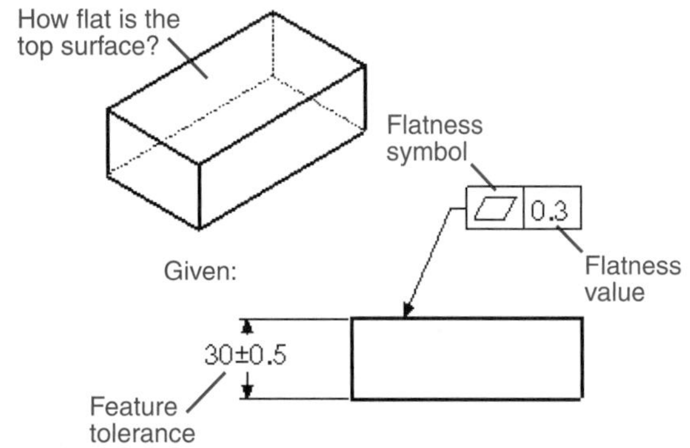

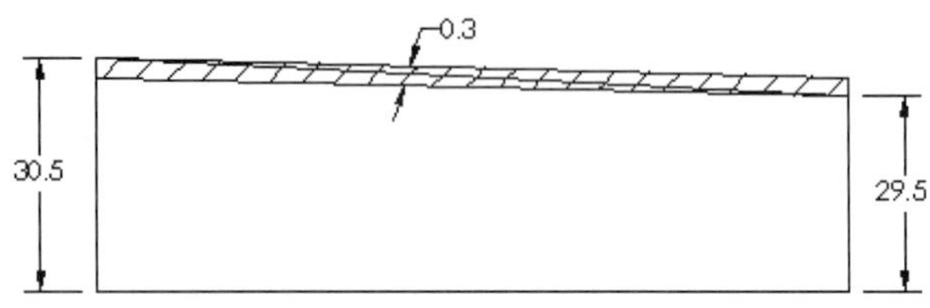

Figure 8-50

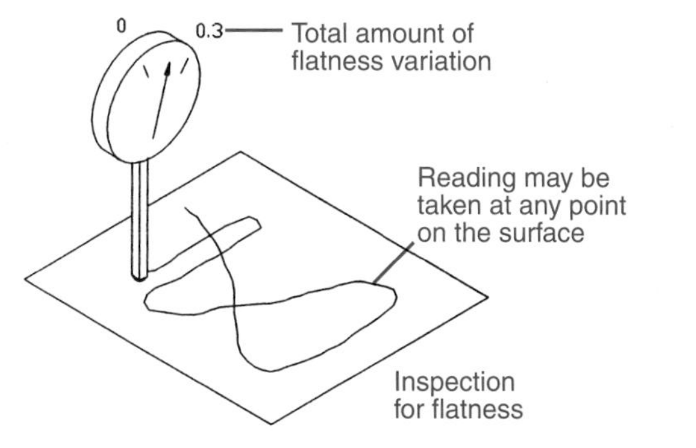

Figure 8-51

8-27 FLATNESS

Flatness tolerances are used to define the amount of variation permitted in an individual surface. The surface is thought of as a plane not related to the rest of the object.

Figure 8-50 shows a rectangular object. How flat is the top surface? The given plus or minus tolerances allow a variation of (± 0.5) across the surface. Without additional tolerances the surface could look like a series of waves varying between 30.5 and 29.5.

If the example in Figure 8-50 was assigned a flatness tolerance of 0.3, the height of the object—the feature tolerance—could continue to vary based on the 30 ± 0.5 tolerance, but the surface itself could not vary by more than 0.3. In the most extreme condition, one end of the surface could be 30.5 above the bottom surface and the other end 29.5, but the surface would still be limited to within two parallel planes 0.3 apart as shown.

To better understand the meaning of flatness, consider how the surface would be inspected. The surface would be acceptable if a gauge could be moved all around the surface and never vary by more than 0.3. See Figure 8-51. Every point in the plane must be within the specified tolerance.

8-28 STRAIGHTNESS

Straightness tolerances are used to measure the variation of an individual feature along a straight line in a specified direction. Figure 8-52 shows an object with a straightness tolerance applied to its top surface. Straightness differs from flatness because straightness measurements are checked by moving a gauge directly across the surface in a single direction. The gauge is not moved randomly about the surface, as is required by flatness.

Straightness tolerances are most often applied to circular or matching objects to help ensure that the parts are not barreled or warped within the given feature tolerance range and, therefore, do not fit together well. Figure 8-53 shows a cylindrical object dimensioned and toleranced using a standard feature tolerance. The surface of the cylinder may vary within the specified tolerance range as shown.

Figure 8-54 shows the same object shown in Figure 8-53 dimensioned and toleranced using the same feature tolerance but also including a 0.05 straightness tolerance. The straightness tolerance limits the surface variation to 0.05 as shown.

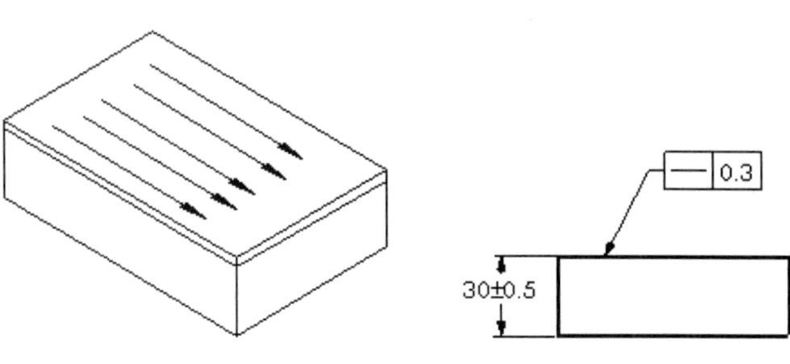

Figure 8-52

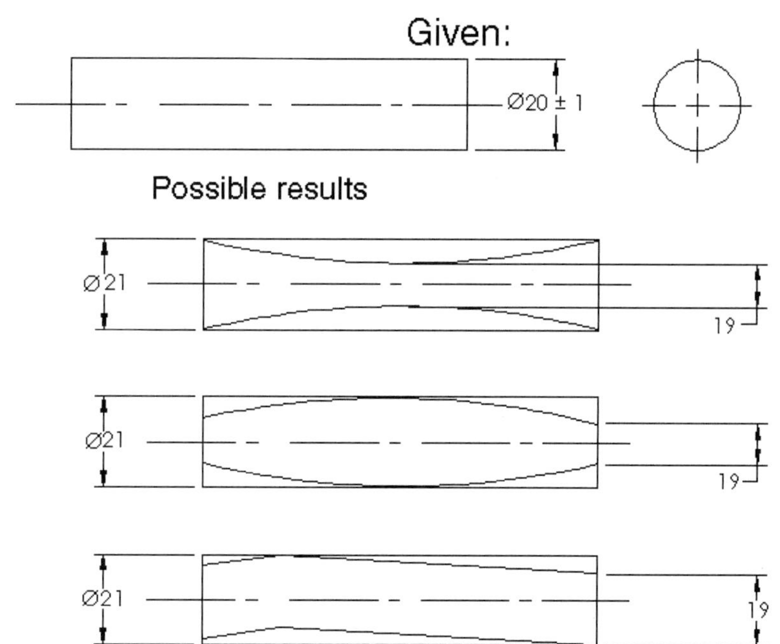

Figure 8-53

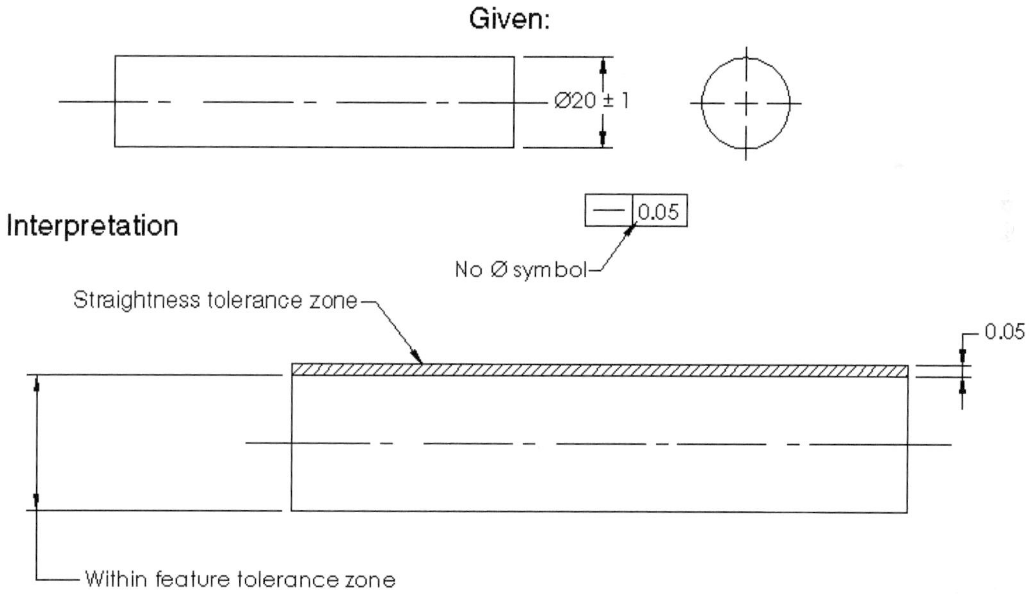

Figure 8-54

8-29 STRAIGHTNESS (RFS AND MMC)

Figure 8-55 again shows the same cylinder shown in Figures 8-53 and 8-54. This time the straightness tolerance is applied about the cylinder's centerline. This type of tolerance permits the feature tolerance and geometric tolerance to be used together to define a *virtual condition.* A virtual condition is used to determine the maximum possible size variation of the cylinder or the smallest diameter hole that will always accept the cylinder.

The geometric tolerance specified in Figure 8-55 is applied to any circular segment along the cylinder, regardless

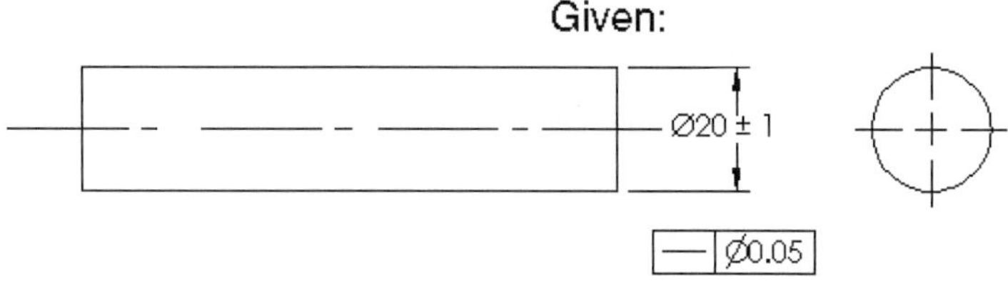

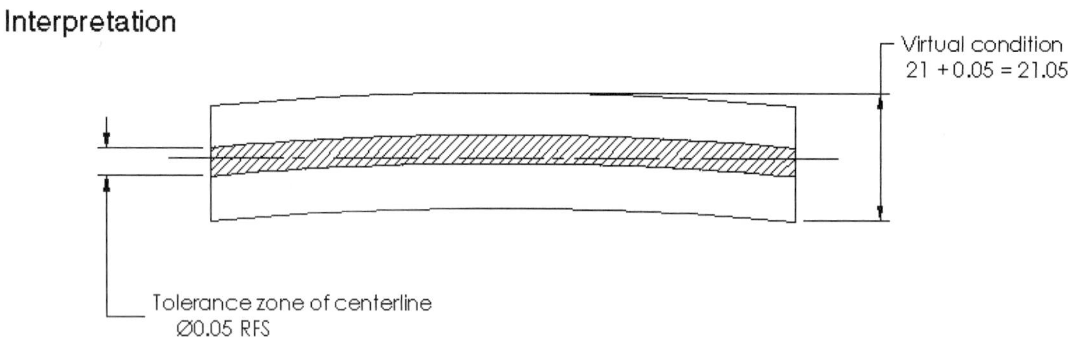

Figure 8-55

of the cylinder's diameter. This means that the 0.05 tolerance is applied equally when the cylinder's diameter measures 19 or when it measures 21. This application is called RFS, *regardless of feature size.* This application is called RFS, *regardless of feature size*. RFS condition applies if no material condition is specified. In Figure 8-55 no symbol is listed after the 0.05 value, so it is assumed to be applied RFS.

Figure 8-56 shows the cylinder dimensioned with an MMC condition applied to the straightness tolerance. MMC stands for *maximum material condition* and means that the specified straightness tolerance (0.05) is applied only at the MMC condition or when the cylinder is at its maximum diameter size (21).

A shaft is an external feature, so its largest possible size or MMC occurs when it is at its maximum diameter. A hole is an internal feature. A hole's MMC condition occurs when it is at its smallest diameter. The MMC condition for holes will be discussed later in the chapter along with positional tolerances.

Applying a straightness tolerance at MMC allows for a variation in the resulting tolerance zone. Because the 0.05

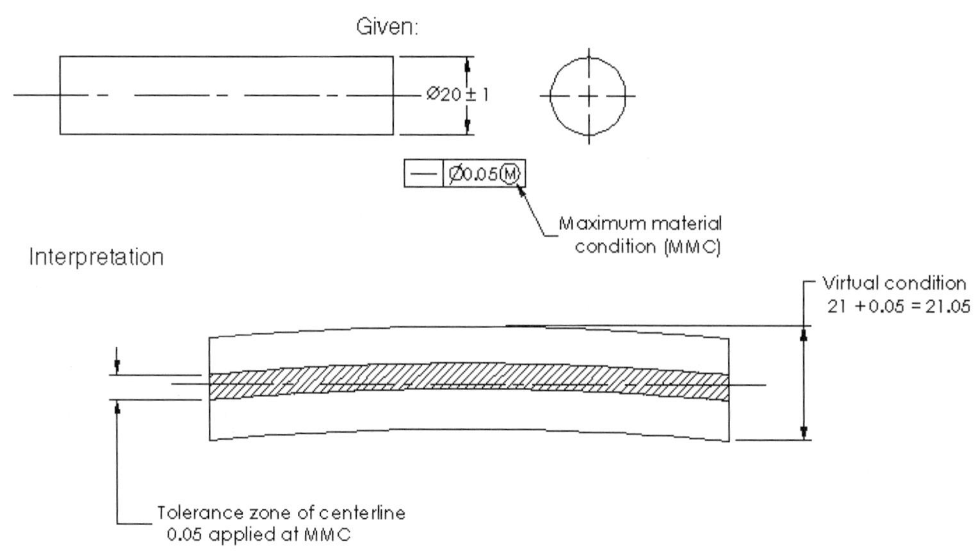

Figure 8-56

Measured Size	Allowable Tolerance Zone	Virtual Condition
21.0	0.05	21.05
20.9	0.15	21.15
20.8	0.25	21.25
.	.	.
.	.	.
.	.	.
20.0	1.05	22.05
.	.	.
.	.	.
.	.	.
19.0	2.05	23.05

Figure 8-56 ***(continued)***

flatness tolerance is applied at MMC, the virtual condition is still 21.05, the same as with the RFS condition; however, the tolerance is applied only at MMC. As the cylinder's diameter varies within the specified feature tolerance range the acceptable tolerance zone may vary to maintain the same virtual condition.

The table in Figure 8-56 shows how the tolerance zone varies as the cylinder's diameter varies. When the cylinder is at its largest size or MMC, the tolerance zone equals 0.05, or the specified flatness variation. When the cylinder is at its smallest diameter, the tolerance zone equals 2.05, or the total feature size plus the total flatness size. In all variations the virtual size remains the same, so at any given cylinder diameter value, the size of the tolerance zone can be determined by subtracting the cylinder's diameter value from the virtual condition.

> ***Note:***
> Geometric tolerance applied at MMC allow the tolerance zone to grow.

Figure 8-57 shows a comparison between different methods used to dimension and tolerance a .750 shaft. The first example uses only a feature tolerance. This tolerance sets an upper limit of .755 and a lower limit of .745. Any variations within that range are acceptable.

The second example in Figure 8-57 sets a straightness tolerance of .003 about the cylinder's centerline. No conditions are defined, so the tolerance is applied RFS. This limits the variations in straightness to .003 at all feature sizes. For example, when the shaft is at its smallest possible feature size of .745, the .003 still applies. This means that a shaft measuring .745 that had a straightness variation greater than .003 would be rejected. If the tolerance had been applied at MMC, the

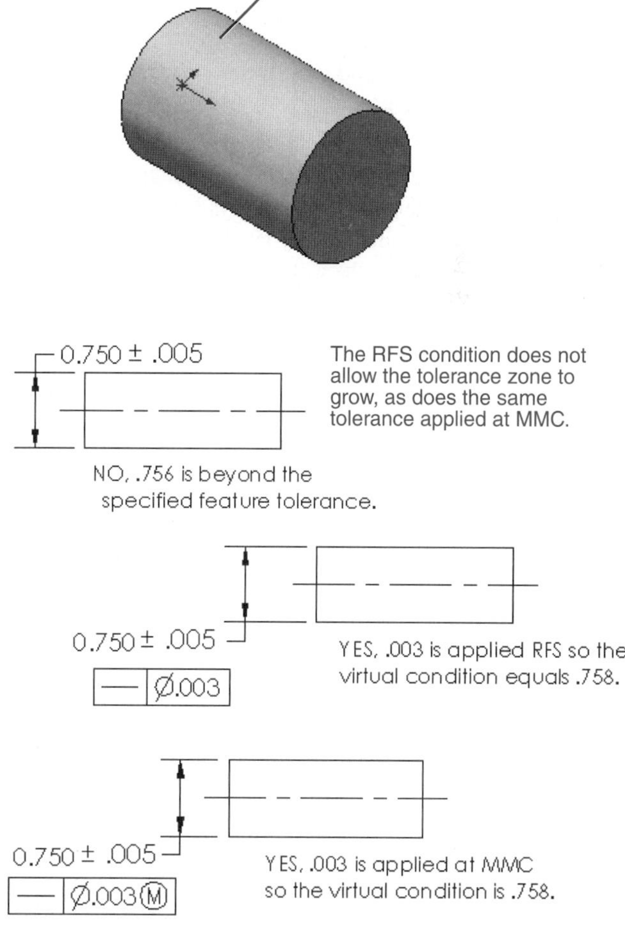
If the cylinder measures Ø.756, is it within tolerance given the following tolerance conditions?
0.750 ± .005
The RFS condition does not allow the tolerance zone to grow, as does the same tolerance applied at MMC.
NO, .756 is beyond the specified feature tolerance.
0.750 ± .005
— Ø.003
YES, .003 is applied RFS so the virtual condition equals .758.
0.750 ± .005
— Ø.003 Ⓜ
YES, .003 is applied at MMC so the virtual condition is .758.

Figure 8-57

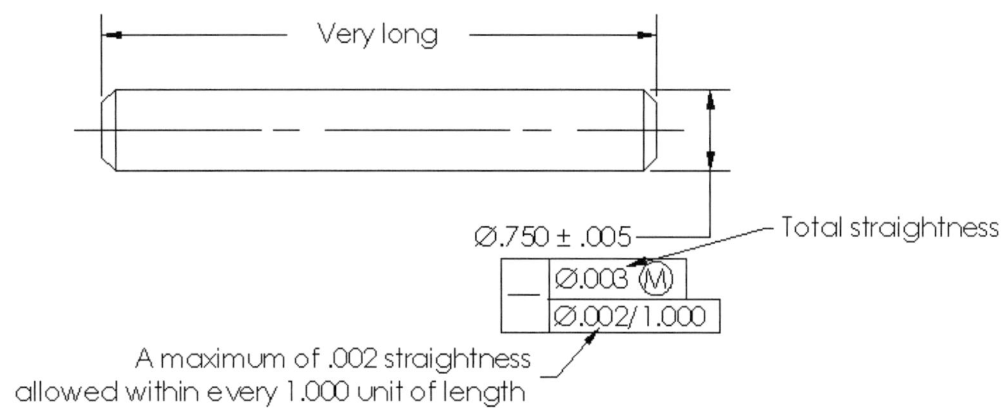

Figure 8-58

part would be accepted. This does not mean that straightness tolerances should always be applied at MMC. If straightness is critical to the design integrity or function of the part, then straightness should be applied in the RFS condition.

The third example in Figure 8-57 applies the straightness tolerance about the centerline at MMC. This tolerance creates a virtual condition of .758. The MMC condition allows the tolerance to vary as the feature tolerance varies, so when the shaft is at its smallest feature size, .745, a straightness tolerance of .003 is acceptable (.005 feature tolerance + .003 straightness tolerance).

If the tolerance specification for the cylinder shown in Figure 8-57 was 0.000 applied at MMC, it would mean that the shaft would have to be perfectly straight at MMC or when the shaft was at its maximum value (.755); however, the straightness tolerance can vary as the feature size varies, as discussed for the other tolerance conditions. A 0.000 tolerance means that the MMC and the virtual conditions are equal.

Figure 8-58 shows a very long .750 diameter shaft. Its straightness tolerance includes a length qualifier that serves to limit the straightness variations over each inch of the shaft length and to prevent excess waviness over the full length. The tolerance .002/1.000 means that the total straightness may vary over the entire length of the shaft by .003 but that the variation is limited to .002 per 1.000 of shaft length.

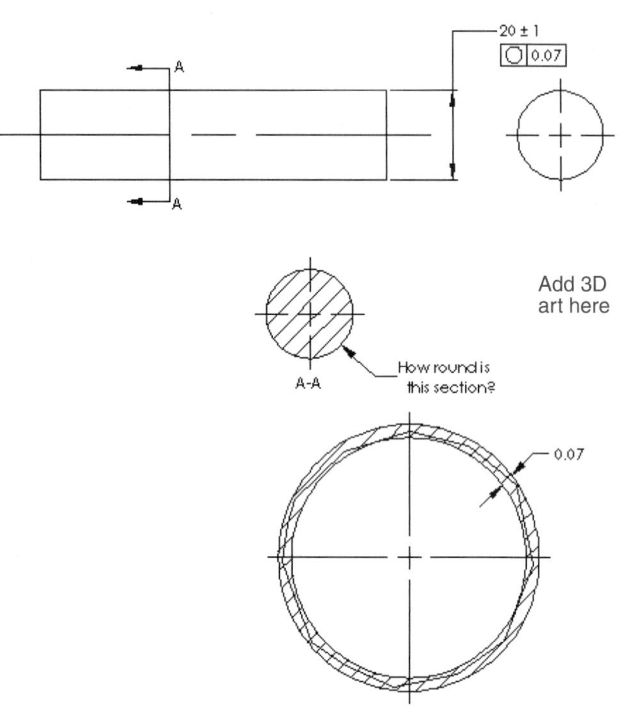

Figure 8-59

8-30 CIRCULARITY

A ***circularity tolerance*** is used to limit the amount of variation in the roundness of a surface of revolution. It is measured at individual cross sections along the length of the object. The measurements are limited to the individual cross sections and are not related to other cross sections. This means that in extreme conditions the shaft shown in Figure 8-59 could actually taper from a diameter of 21 to a diameter of 19 and never violate the circularity requirement. It also means that qualifications such as MMC cannot be applied.

Figure 8-59 shows a shaft that includes a feature tolerance and a circularity tolerance of 0.07. To understand circularity tolerances, consider an individual cross section or slice of the cylinder. The actual shape of the outside edge of the slice varies around the slice. The difference between the maximum diameter and the minimum diameter of the slice can never exceed the stated circularity tolerance.

Circularity tolerances can be applied to tapered sections and spheres, as shown in Figure 8-60. In both applications, circularity is measured around individual cross sections, as it was for the shaft shown in Figure 8-59.

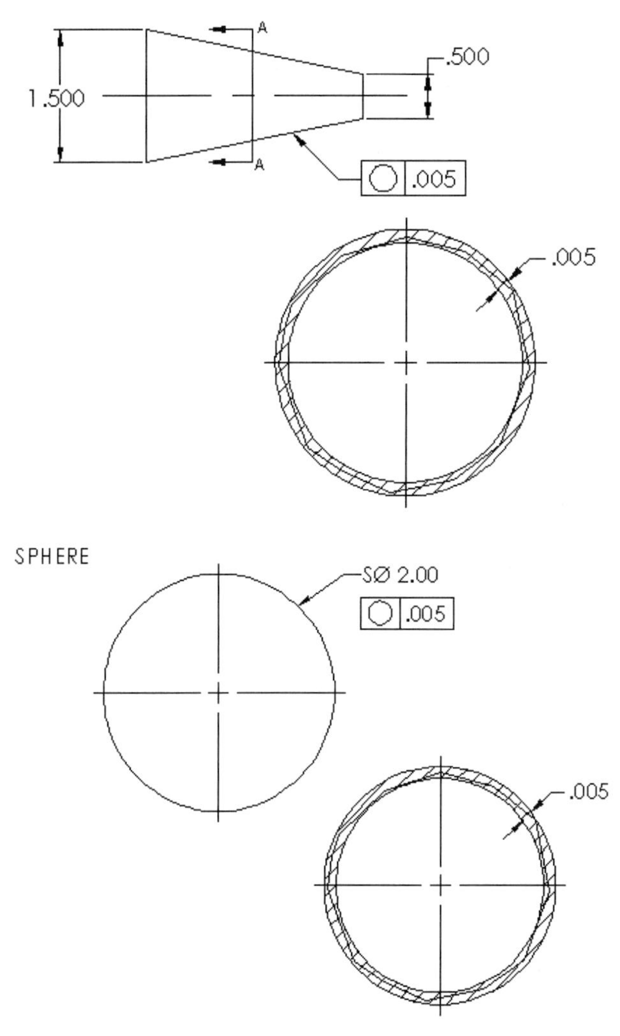

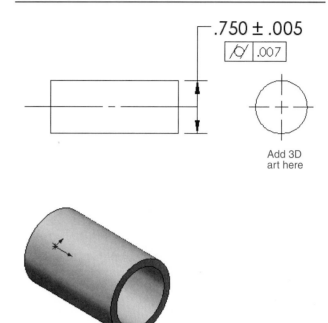

Figure 8-60

8-31 CYLINDRICITY

Cylindricity tolerances are used to define a tolerance zone both around individual circular cross sections of an object and also along its length. The resulting tolerance zone looks like two concentric cylinders.

Figure 8-61 shows a shaft that includes a cylindricity tolerance that establishes a tolerance zone of .007. This means that if the maximum measured diameter is determined to be .755, the minimum diameter cannot be less than .748 anywhere on the cylindrical surface. Cylindricity and circularity are somewhat analogous to flatness and straightness. Flatness and cylindricity are concerned with variations across an entire surface or plane. In the case of cylindricity, the plane is shaped like a cylinder. Straightness and circularity are concerned with variations of a single element of a surface: a straight line across the plane in a specified direction for straightness, and a path around a single cross section for circularity.

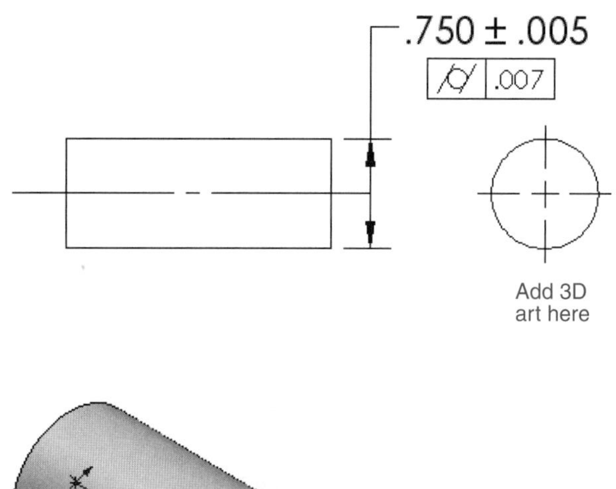

Figure 8-61

8-32 GEOMETRIC TOLERANCES USING SOLIDWORKS

Geometric tolerances are tolerances that limit dimensional variations based on the geometric properties. Figure 8-62 shows three different ways geometric tolerance boxes can be added to a drawing.

Figure 8-63 shows lists of geometric tolerance symbols.

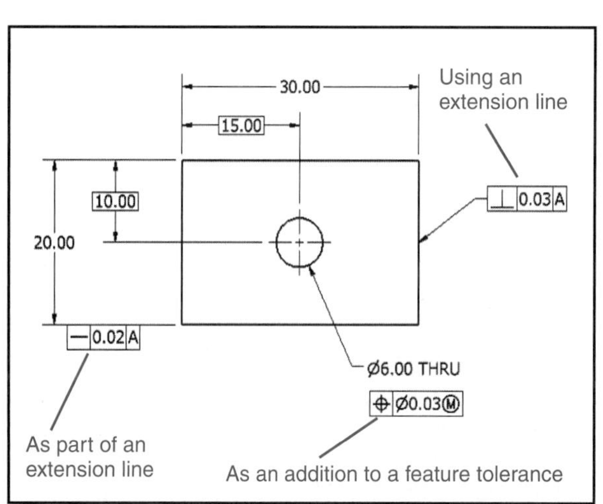

Figure 8-62

	TYPE OF TOLERANCE	CHARACTERISTIC	SYMBOL
FOR INDIVIDUAL FEATURES	FORM	STRAIGHTNESS	—
		FLATNESS	▱
		CIRCULARITY	○
		CYLINDRICITY	⌭
INDIVIDUAL OR RELATED FEATURES	PROFILE	PROFILE OF A LINE	⌒
		PROFILE OF A SURFACE	⌓
RELATED FEATURES	ORIENTATION	ANGULARITY	∠
		PERPENDICULARITY	⊥
		PARALLELISM	//
	LOCATION	POSITION	⌖
		CONCENTRICITY	◎
	RUNOUT	CIRCULAR RUNOUT	↗
		TOTAL RUNOUT	⌰

TERM	SYMBOL
AT MAXIMUM MATERIAL CONDITION	Ⓜ
REGARDLESS OF FEATURE SIZE	Ⓢ
AT LEAST MATERIAL CONDITION	Ⓛ
PROJECTED TOLERANCE ZONE	Ⓟ
DIAMETER	Ø
SPHERICAL DIAMETER	SØ
RADIUS	R
SPHERICAL RADIUS	SR
REFERENCE	( )
ARC LENGTH	⌒

Figure 8-63

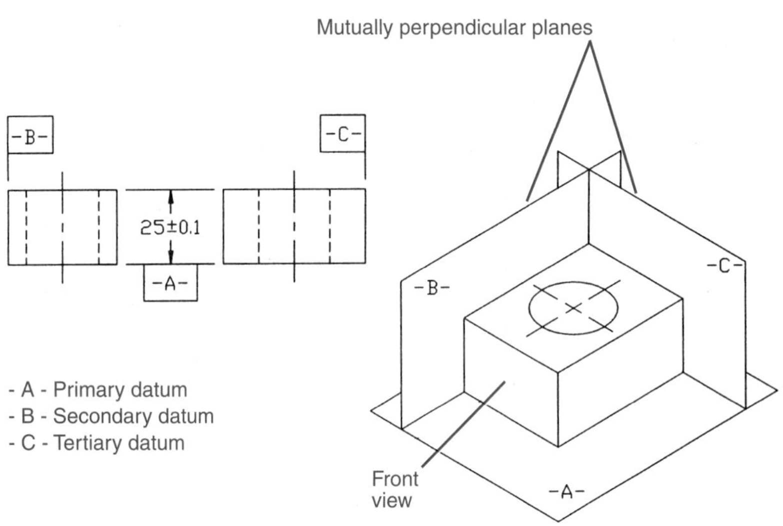

Figure 8-64

8-33 DATUMS

A ***datum*** is a point, axis, or surface used as a starting reference point for dimensions and tolerances. Figure 8-64 and Figure 8-65 show a rectangular object with three datum planes labeled –A–, –B–, and –C–. The three datum planes are called the primary, secondary, and tertiary datums, respectively. The three datum planes are, by definition, exactly 90° to one another.

Figure 8-66 shows a cylindrical datum frame that includes three datum planes. The X and Y planes are perpendicular to each other, and the base A plane is perpendicular to the datum axis between the X and Y planes.

Datum planes are assumed to be perfectly flat. When assigning a datum status to a surface, be sure that the surface is reasonably flat. This means that datum surfaces should be toleranced using surface finishes, or created using machine techniques that produce flat surfaces.

To Add a Datum Indicator

Figure 8-67 shows a dimensioned orthographic view. This section shows how to define the lower surface as a datum feature, datum A. Note that a surface finish of 16 has been added to the lower surface. Datum surfaces are assumed to be flat and smooth.

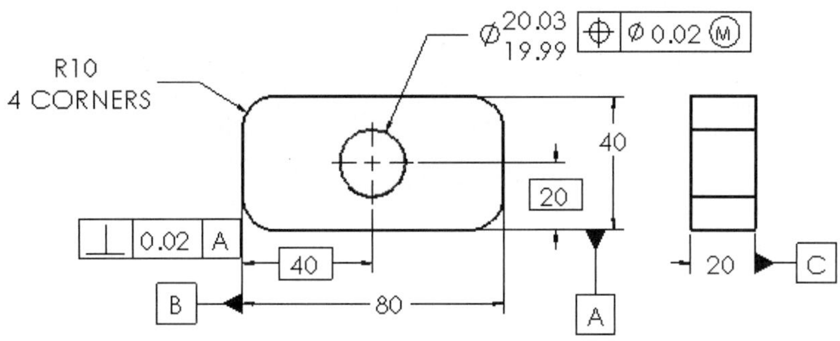

Figure 8-65

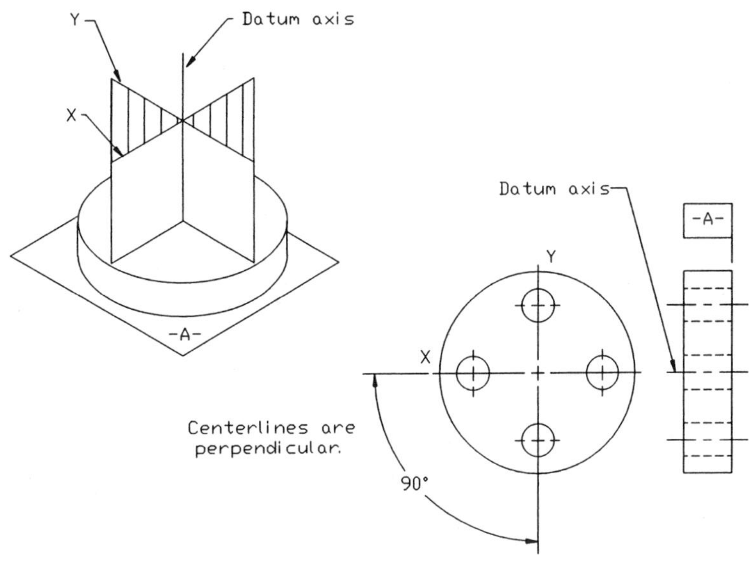

Figure 8-66

1. Click the **Annotations** tool and select the **Datum Feature** tool.

The **Datum Feature** toolbox will appear.

2. Enter the letter **A** and select the **Filled Triangle with Shoulder** option.
3. Locate the datum symbol on the drawing as shown.
4. Click the **<ESC>** key.
5. Click the OK check mark.

> **TIP**
>
> Once in place, a datum symbol can be repositioned by clicking and dragging the symbol.

To Define a Perpendicular Tolerance

Define the right vertical edge of the part as datum B and perpendicular to datum A within a tolerance of .001.

1. Click the **Annotations** tool and click the **Datum Feature** tool and define the left vertical surface as **datum B.**
2. Click the **Annotations** tool and click the **Geometric Tolerance** tool.

See Figure 8-68. The **Properties/Geometric Tolerance** dialog box will appear.

3. Click the arrow to the right of the **Symbol** box and select the perpendicular symbol.
4. Enter the **Tolerance** and **Primary** datum information.
5. Click **OK.**

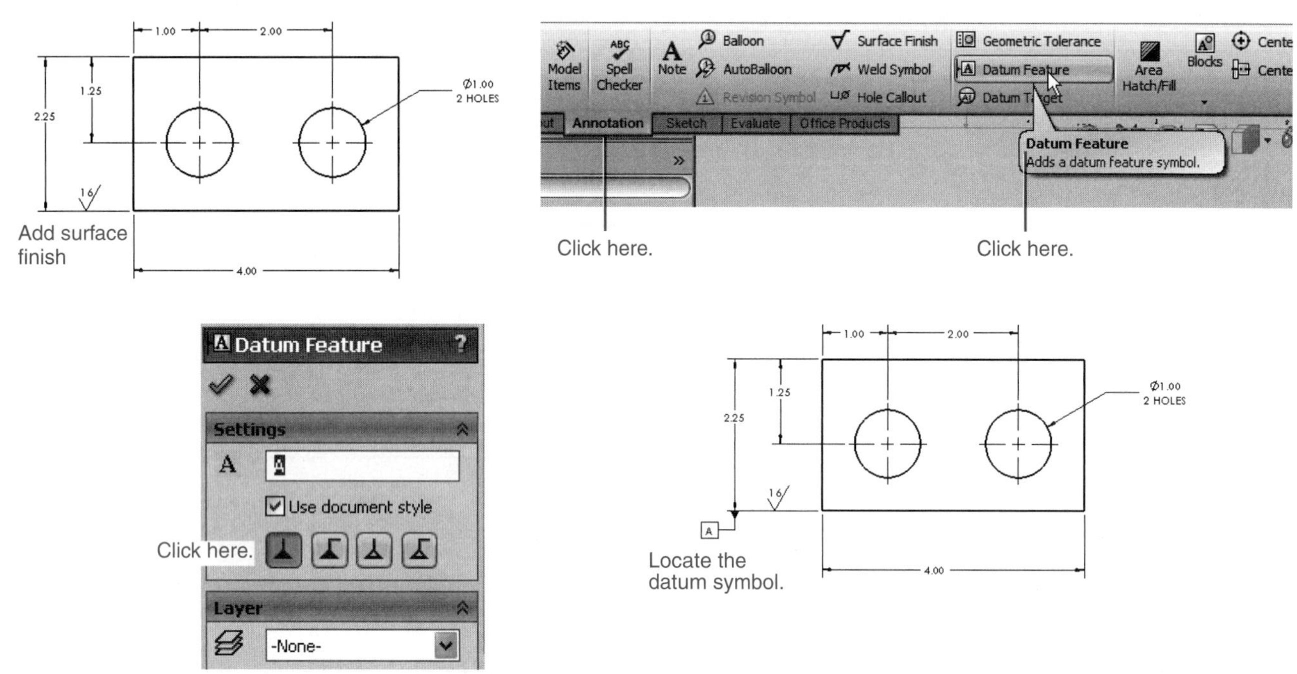
Add surface finish
Click here.
Click here.
Datum Feature
Adds a datum feature symbol.
Click here.
Locate the datum symbol.

Figure 8-67

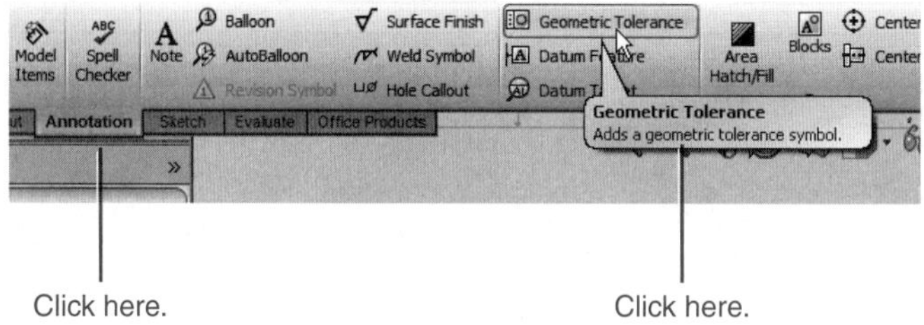
Geometric Tolerance
Adds a geometric tolerance symbol.
Click here.
Click here.

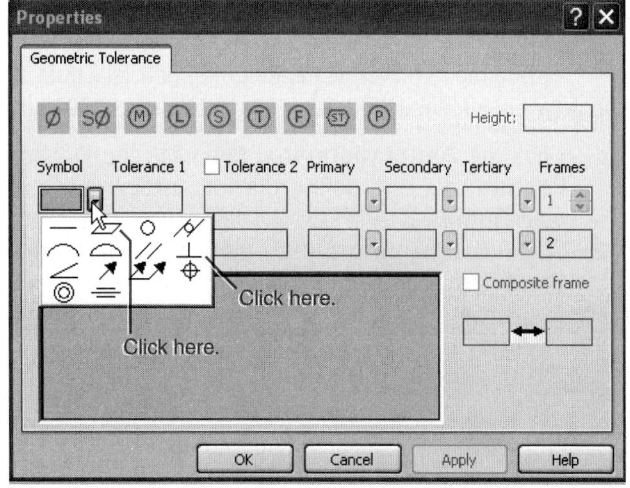
Click here.
Click here.

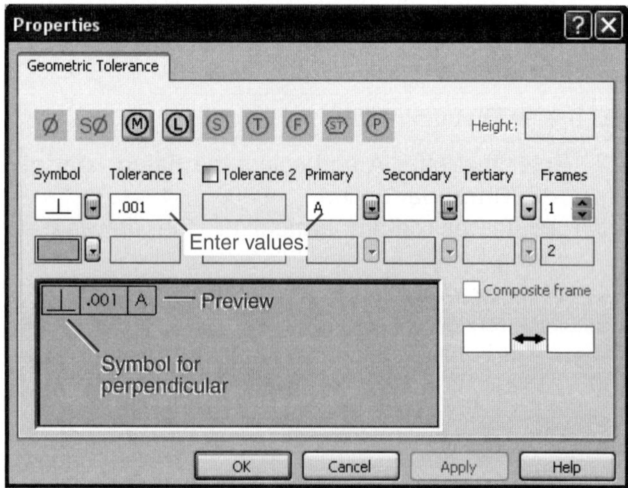
Enter values.
Preview
Symbol for perpendicular

Figure 8-68

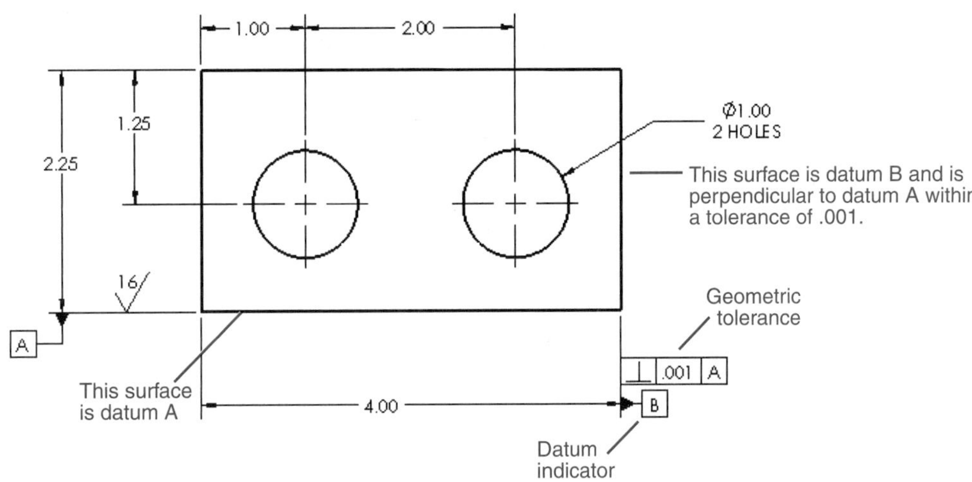

Figure 8-68 *(continued)*

6. Locate the geometric symbol on the extension line as shown.
7. Click the OK check mark.

To Define a Straightness Value for Datum Surface A

The surface finish value of 16 defines the smoothness of the surface but not the straightness. Think of surface finish as waves, and straightness as an angle. A straightness value of .002 indicates that there is a band of width .002 located .001 on either side of a theoretically perfectly straight line. The surface may vary but must always be within the .002 boundary. See Figure 8-69.

1. Click the **Annotations** tool and select the **Geometric Tolerance** tool.
2. Enter the **Straightness** symbol, and define the tolerance as **.002.**
3. Click **OK.**
4. Locate the symbol under the datum A symbol as shown.
5. Click the OK check mark.

8-34 TOLERANCES OF ORIENTATION

Tolerances of orientation are used to relate a feature or surface to another feature or surface. Tolerances of orientation include perpendicularity, parallelism, and angularity. They may be applied using RFS or MMC conditions, but they cannot be applied to individual features by themselves. To define a surface as parallel to another surface is very much like assigning a flatness value to the surface. The difference is that flatness applies only within the surface; every point on the surface is related to a defined set of limiting parallel planes. Parallelism defines every point in the surface relative to another surface. The two surfaces are therefore directly related to each other, and the condition of one affects the other.

Orientation tolerances are used with locational tolerances. A feature is first located, then it is oriented within the locational tolerances. This means that the orientation tolerance must always be less than the locational tolerances. The next four sections will further explain this requirement.

8-35 PERPENDICULARITY

Perpendicularity tolerances are used to limit the amount of variation for a surface or feature within two planes perpendicular to a specified datum. Figure 8-70 shows a rectangular object. The bottom surface is assigned as datum A, and the right vertical edge is toleranced so that it must be perpendicular within a limit of 0.05 to datum A. The perpendicularity tolerance defines a tolerance zone 0.05 wide between two parallel planes that are perpendicular to datum A.

The object also includes a horizontal dimension and tolerance of 40±1. This tolerance is called a *locational tolerance* because it serves to locate the right edge of the object. As with rectangular coordinate tolerances, discussed earlier in the chapter, the 40±1 controls the location of the edge—how far away or how close it can be to the left edge—but does not directly control the shape of the edge. Any shape that falls within the specified tolerance range is acceptable. This may in fact be sufficient for a given design, but if a more controlled shape is required, a perpendicularity tolerance must be added. The perpendicularity tolerance works within the locational tolerance to ensure that the edge is not only within the locational tolerance but is also perpendicular to datum A.

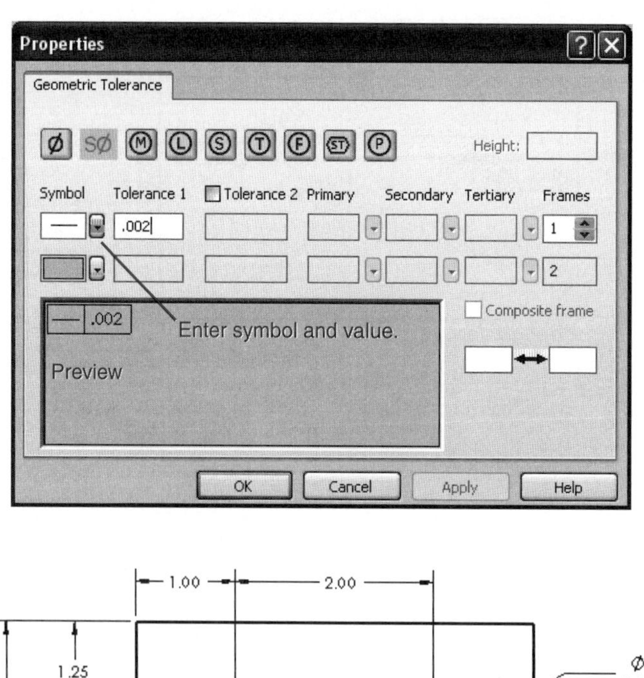

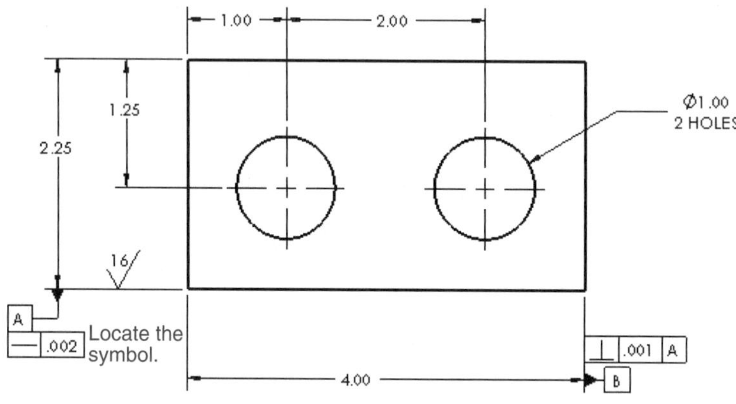

Figure 8-69

Figure 8-70 shows the two extreme conditions for the 40±1 locational tolerance. The perpendicularity tolerance is applied by first measuring the surface and determining its maximum and minimum lengths. The difference between these two measurements must be less than 0.05. So if the measured maximum distance is 41, then no other part of the surface may be less then 41 − 0.05 = 40.95.

Tolerances of perpendicularity serve to complement locational tolerances, to make the shape more exact, so tolerances of perpendicularity must always be smaller than tolerances of location. It would be of little use, for example, to assign a perpendicularity tolerance of 1.5 for the object shown in Figure 8-71. The locational tolerance would prevent the variation from ever reaching the limits specified by such a large perpendicularity tolerance.

Figure 8-72 shows a perpendicularity tolerance applied to cylindrical features: a shaft and a hole. The figure includes examples of both RFS and MMC applications. As with straightness tolerances applied at MMC, perpendicularity tolerances applied about a hole or shaft's centerline allow the tolerance zone to vary as the feature size varies.

The inclusion of the ∅ symbol in a geometric tolerance is critical to its interpretation. See Figure 8-73. If the ∅ symbol is not included, the tolerance applies only to the view in which it is written. This means that the tolerance zone is shaped like a rectangular slice, not a cylinder, as would be the case if the ø symbol were included. In general it is better to always include the ∅ symbol for cylindrical features because it generates a tolerance zone more like that used in positional tolerancing.

Figure 8-73 shows a perpendicularity tolerance applied to a slot, a noncylindrical feature. Again, the MMC specification is always for variations in the tolerance zone.

8-36 PARALLELISM

Parallelism tolerances are used to ensure that all points within a plane are within two parallel planes that are parallel to a referenced datum plane. Figure 8-74 shows a rectangular object that is toleranced so that its top surface is parallel to the bottom surface within 0.02. This means that

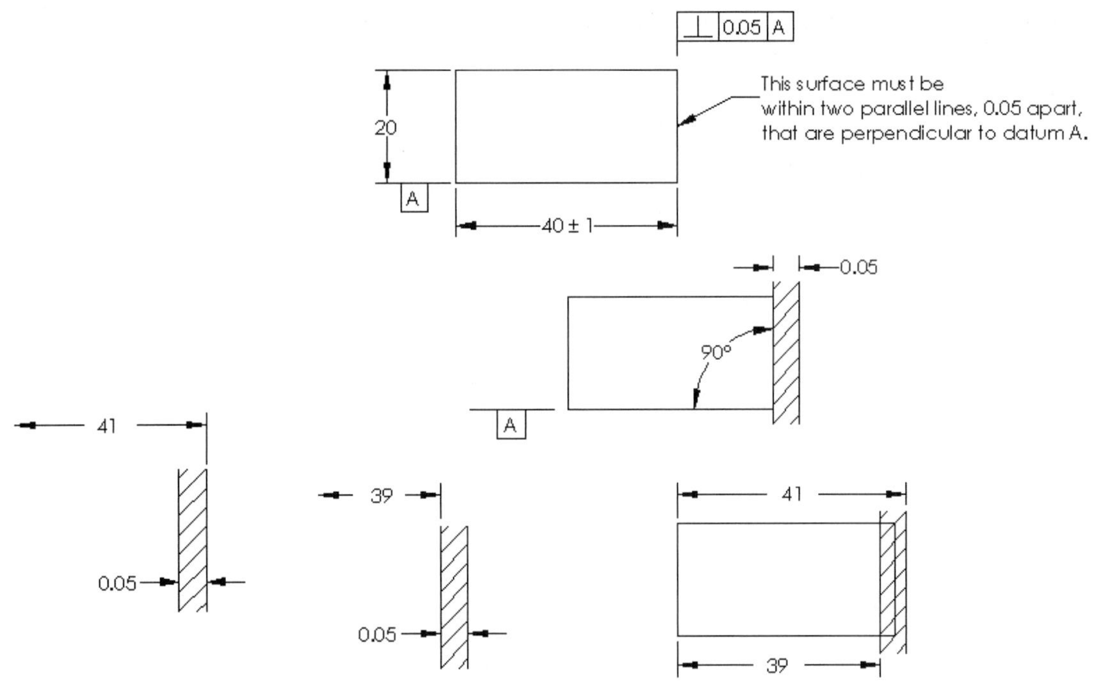

Figure 8-70

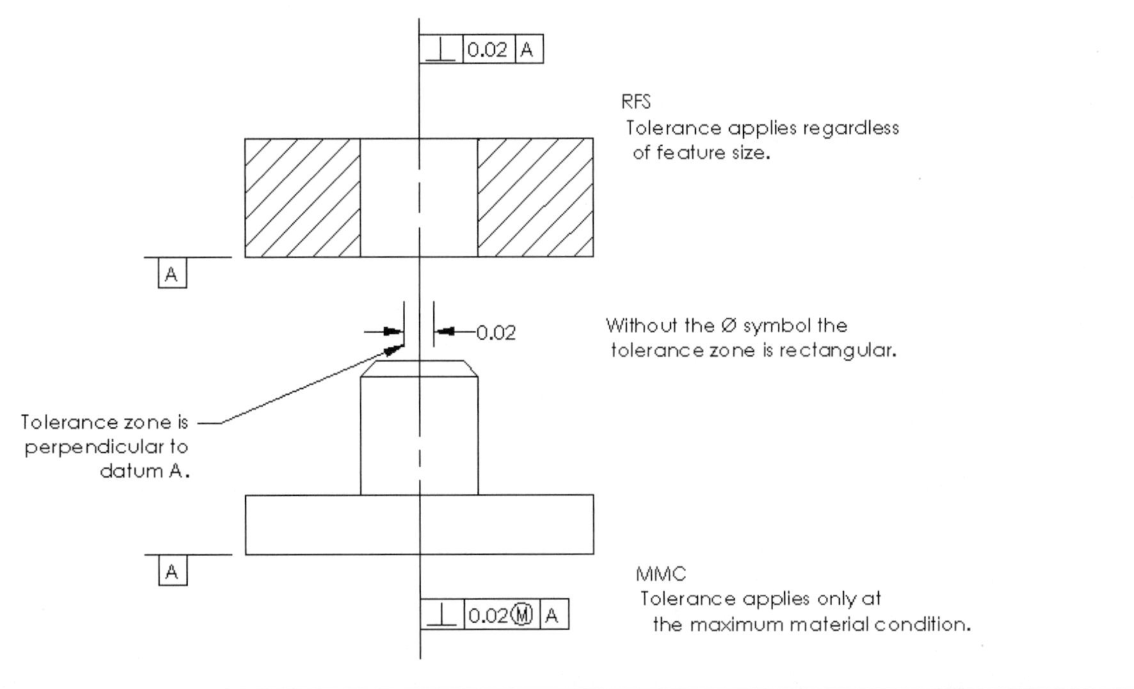

Figure 8-71

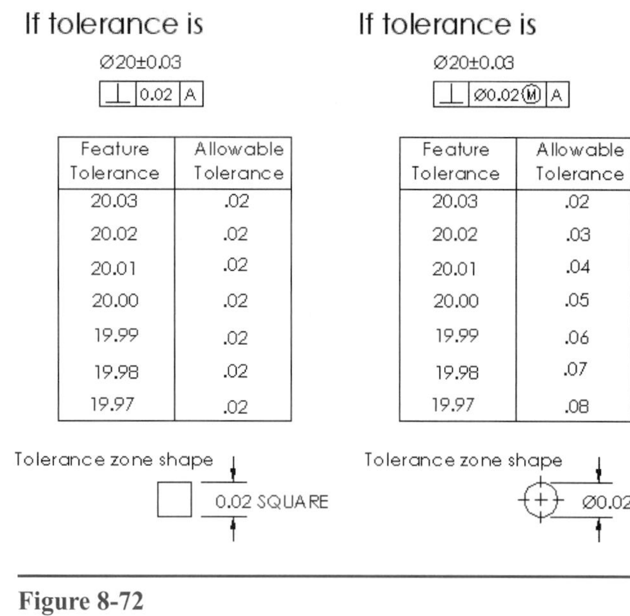

Feature Tolerance	Allowable Tolerance
20.03	.02
20.02	.02
20.01	.02
20.00	.02
19.99	.02
19.98	.02
19.97	.02

Feature Tolerance	Allowable Tolerance
20.03	.02
20.02	.03
20.01	.04
20.00	.05
19.99	.06
19.98	.07
19.97	.08

Figure 8-72

every point on the top surface must be within a set of parallel planes 0.02 apart. These parallel tolerancing planes are located by determining the maximum and minimum distances from the datum surface. The difference between the maximum and minimum values may not exceed the stated 0.02 tolerance.

In the extreme condition of maximum feature size, the top surface is located 40.5 above the datum plane. The parallelism tolerance is then applied, meaning that no point on the surface may be closer than 40.3 to the datum. This is an RFS condition. The MMC condition may also be applied, thereby allowing the tolerance zone to vary as the feature size varies.

8-37 ANGULARITY

Angularity tolerances are used to limit the variance of surfaces and axes that are at an angle relative to a datum. Angularity tolerances are applied like perpendicularity and parallelism tolerances as a way to better control the shape of locational tolerances.

Figure 8-75 shows an angularity tolerance and several ways it is interpreted at extreme conditions.

8-38 PROFILES

Profile tolerances are used to limit the variations of irregular surfaces. They may be assigned as either bilateral or unilateral tolerances. There are two types of profile tolerances: surface and line. *Surface* profile tolerances limit the variation of an entire surface, whereas a *line* profile tolerance limits the variations along a single line across a surface.

Figure 8-77 shows an object that includes a surface profile tolerance referenced to an irregular surface. The tolerance is considered a bilateral tolerance because no other specification is given. This means that all points on the surface must be located between two parallel planes 0.08 apart that are centered about the irregular surface. The measurements are taken perpendicular to the surface.

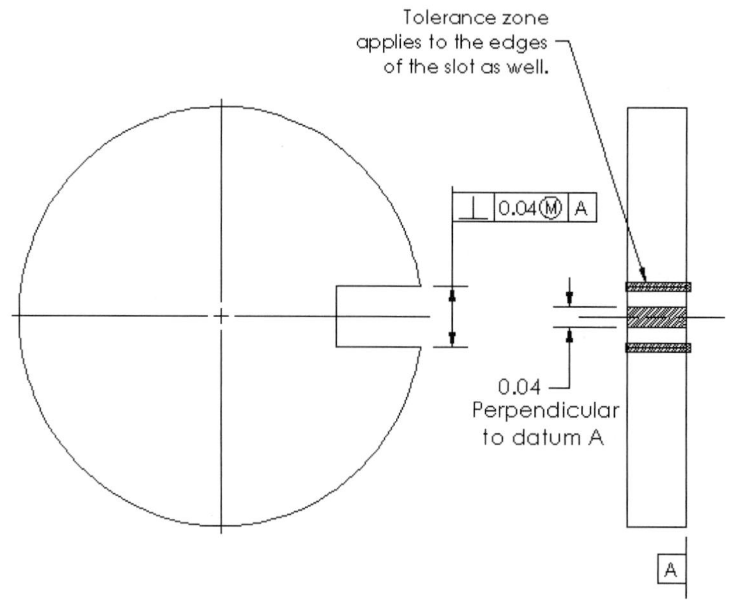

Figure 8-73

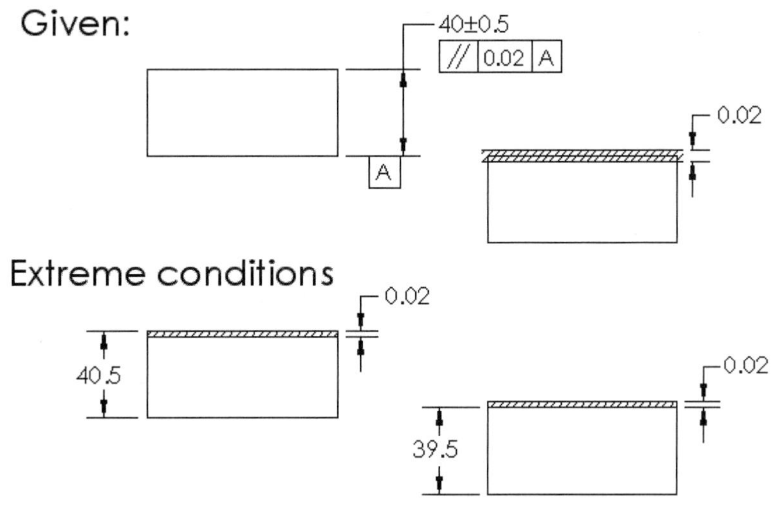

Figure 8-74

Unilateral applications of surface profile tolerances must be indicated on the drawing using phantom lines. The phantom line indicates the side of the true profile line of the irregular surface on which the tolerance is to be applied. A phantom line above the irregular surface indicates that the tolerance is to be applied using the true profile line as 0, and then the specified tolerance range is to be added above that line. See Figures 8-76 to 8-78.

Profiles of line tolerances are applied to irregular surfaces, as shown in Figure 8-78. Profiles of line tolerances are particularly helpful when tolerancing an irregular surface that is constantly changing, such as the surface of an airplane wing.

Surface and line profile tolerances are somewhat analogous to flatness and straightness tolerances. Flatness and surface profile tolerances are applied across an entire surface,

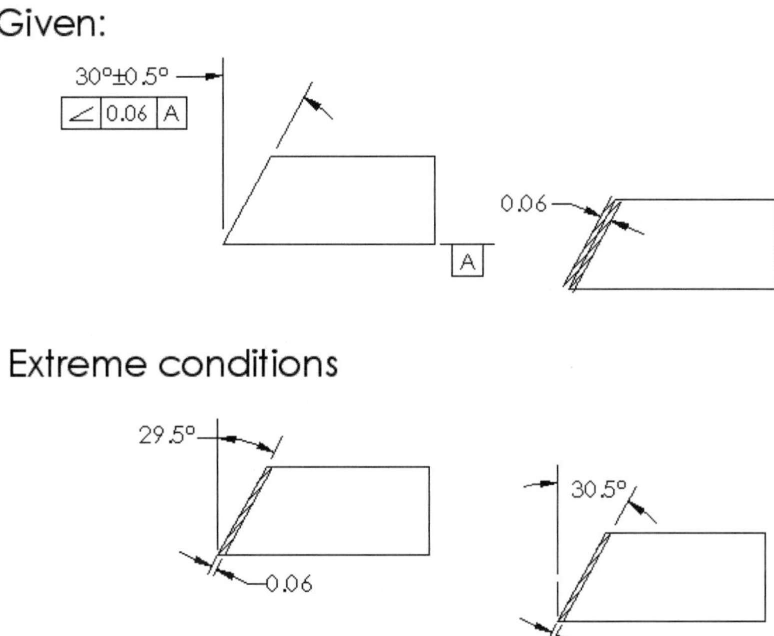

Figure 8-75

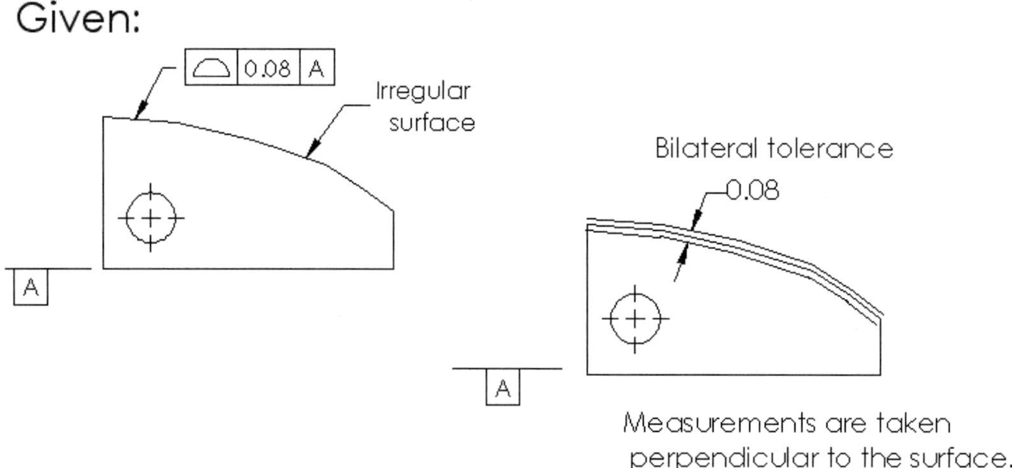

Figure 8-76

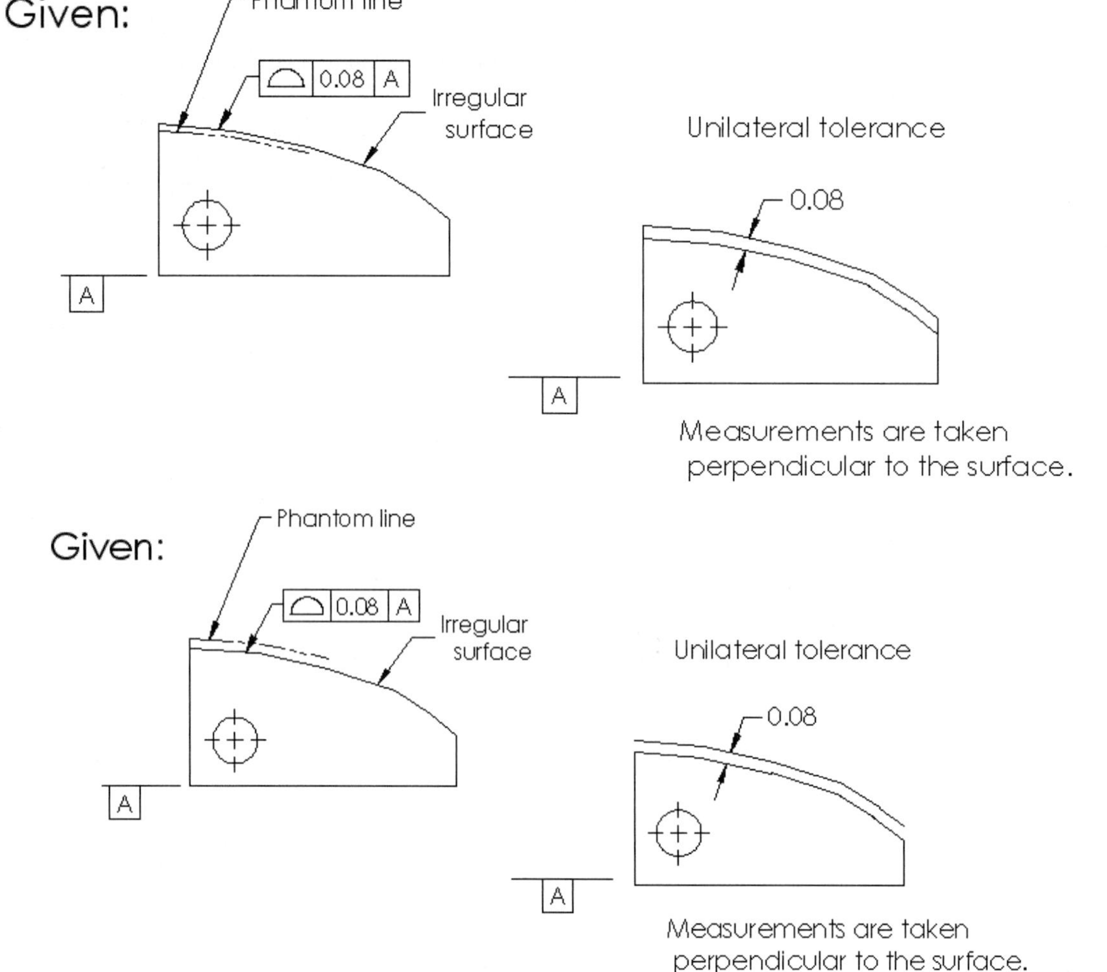

Figure 8-77

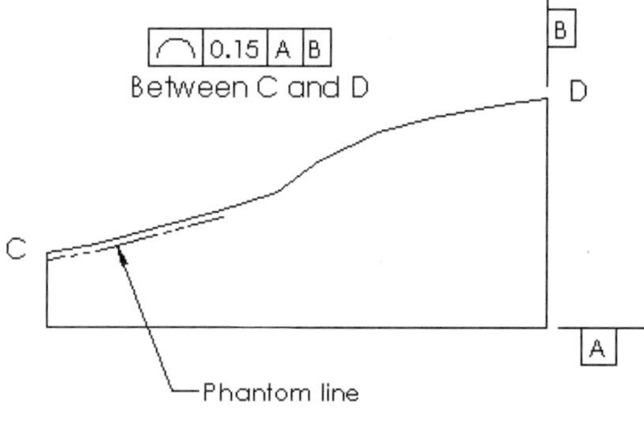

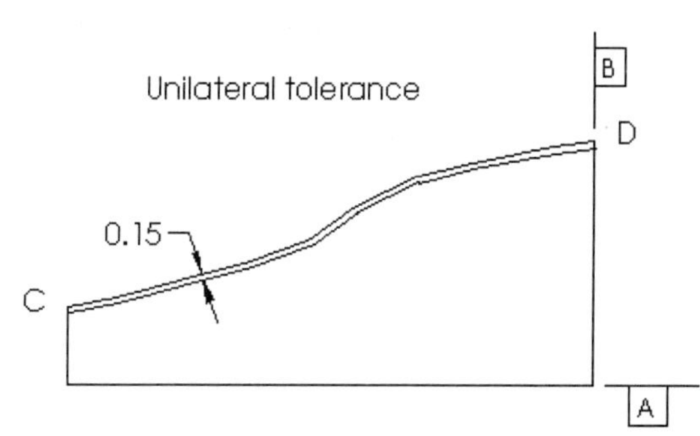

Figure 8-78

whereas straightness and line profile tolerances are applied only along a single line across the surface.

8-39 RUNOUTS

A ***runout tolerance*** is used to limit the variations between features of an object and a datum. More specifically, they are applied to surfaces around a datum axis such as a cylinder or to a surface constructed perpendicular to a datum axis. There are two types of runout tolerances: circular and total.

Figure 8-79 shows a cylinder that includes a circular runout tolerance. The runout requirements are checked by rotating the object about its longitudinal axis or datum axis while holding an indicator gauge in a fixed position on the object's surface.

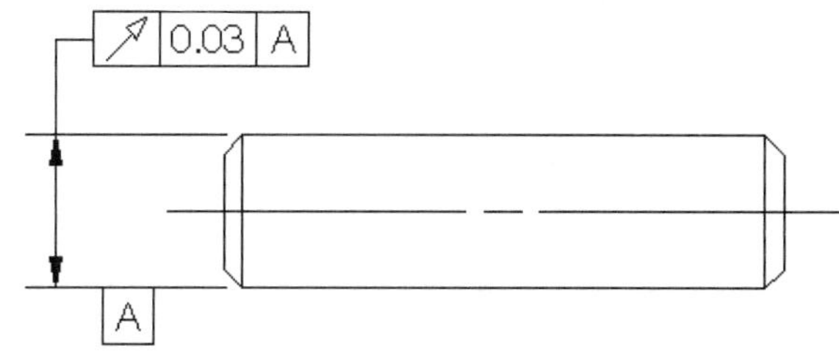

Figure 8-79

Runout tolerances may be either bilateral or unilateral. A runout tolerance is assumed to be bilateral unless otherwise indicated. If a runout tolerance is to be unilateral, a phantom line is used to indicate the side of the object's true surface to which the tolerance is to be applied. See Figure 8-80.

Runout tolerances may be applied to tapered areas of cylindrical objects, as shown in Figure 8-81. The tolerance is checked by rotating the object about a datum axis while holding an indicator gauge in place.

A total runout tolerance limits the variation across an entire surface. See Figure 8-82. An indicator gauge is not held in place while the object is rotated, as it is for circular runout tolerances, but is moved about the rotating surface.

Figure 8-83 shows a circular runout tolerance that references two datums. The two datums serve as one datum. The object can then be rotated about both datums simultaneously as the runout tolerances are checked.

8-40 POSITIONAL TOLERANCES

As defined earlier, *positional tolerances* are used to locate and tolerance holes. Positional tolerances create a circular tolerance zone for hole center point locations, in contrast with the rectangular tolerance zone created by linear coordinate dimensions. See Figure 8-84. The circular tolerance zone allows for an increase in acceptable tolerance variation without compromising the design integrity of the object. Note how some of the possible hole center points fall in an area outside the rectangular tolerance zone but are still within the circular tolerance zone. If the hole had been located using linear coordinate dimensions, center points located

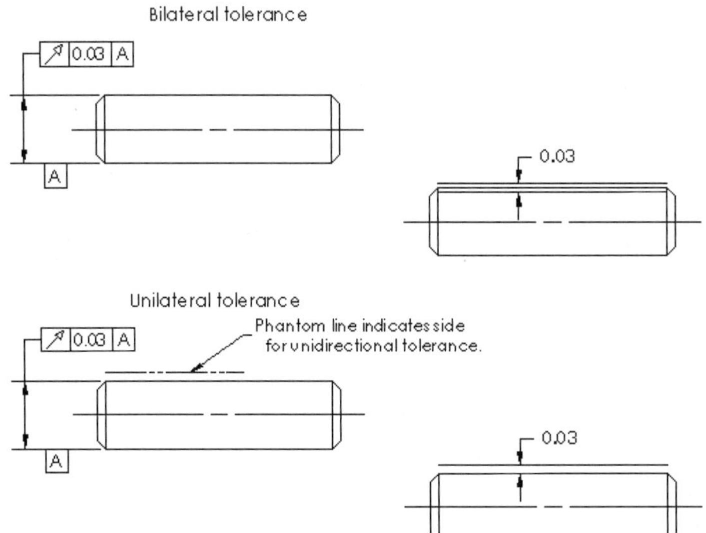

Figure 8-80

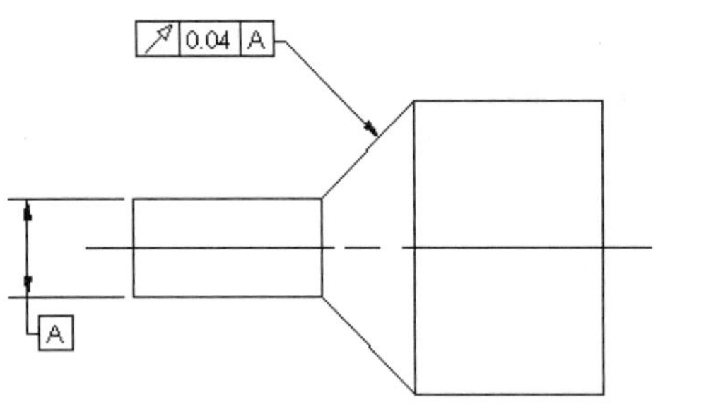

Figure 8-81

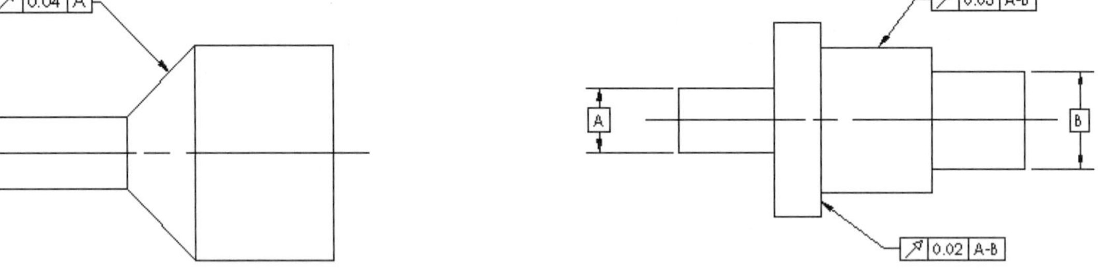

Figure 8-83

RUNOUT tolerance

0.03 A

A

Figure 8-82

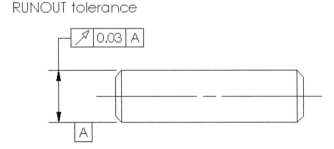

beyond the rectangular tolerance zone would have been rejected as beyond tolerance, and yet holes produced using these locations would function correctly from a design standpoint. The center point locations would be acceptable if positional tolerances had been specified. The finished hole is round, so a round tolerance zone is appropriate. The rectangular tolerance zone rejects some holes unnecessarily.

Holes are dimensioned and toleranced using geometric tolerances by a combination of locating dimensions, feature dimensions and tolerances, and positional tolerances. See Figure 8-85. The locating dimensions are enclosed in rectangular boxes and are called ***basic dimensions.*** Basic dimensions are assumed to be exact.

The feature tolerances for the hole are as presented earlier in the chapter. They can be presented using plus or minus or limit-type tolerances. In the example shown in Figure 8-85 the diameter of the hole is toleranced using a plus and minus 0.05 tolerance.

The basic locating dimensions of 45 and 50 are assumed to be exact. The tolerances that would normally accompany linear locational dimensions are replaced by the positional tolerance. The positional tolerance also specifies that the tolerance be applied at the centerline at maximum material condition. The resulting tolerance zones are as shown in Figure 8-85.

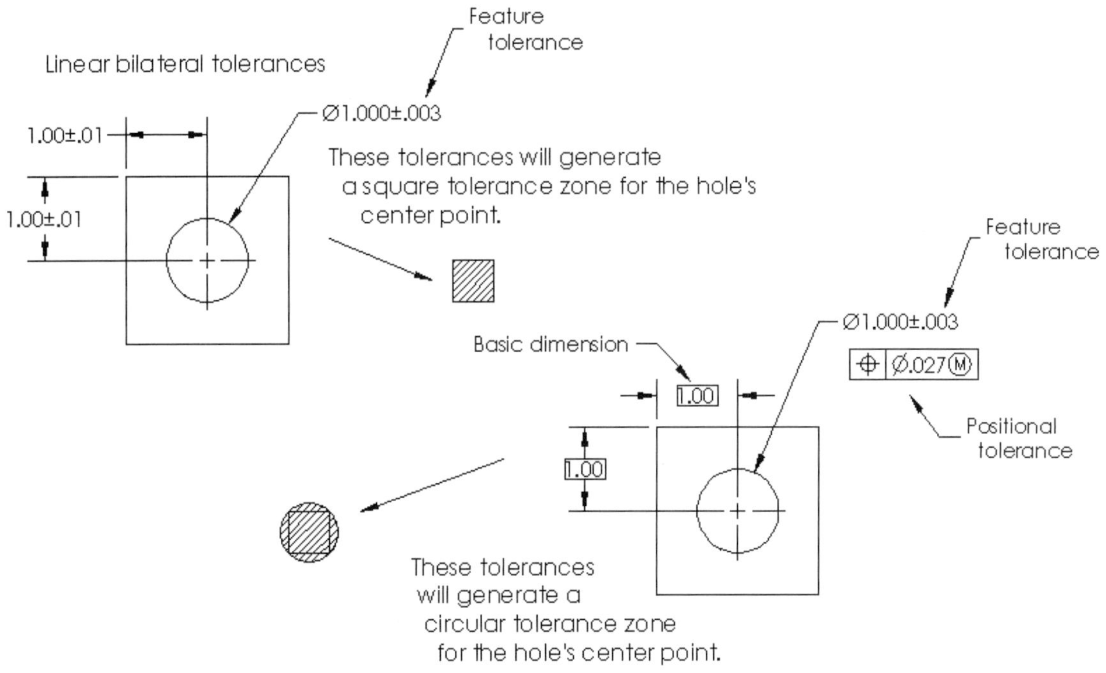
Linear bilateral tolerances
Feature tolerance
Ø1.000±.003
1.00±.01
1.00±.01
These tolerances will generate a square tolerance zone for the hole's center point.
Feature tolerance
Ø1.000±.003
Ø.027Ⓜ
Basic dimension
1.00
1.00
Positional tolerance
These tolerances will generate a circular tolerance zone for the hole's center point.

Figure 8-84

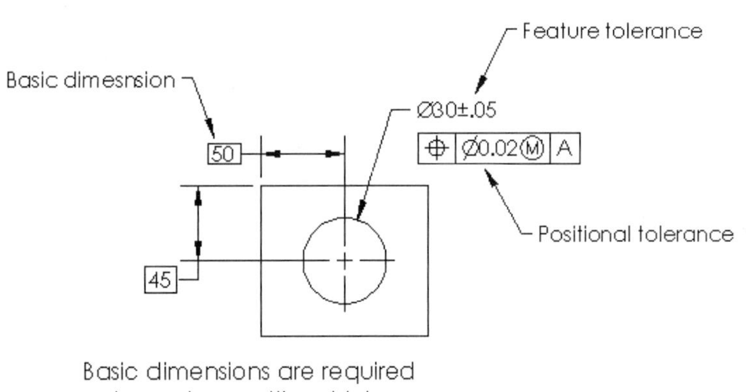
Feature tolerance
Basic dimesnsion
Ø30±.05
50
Ø0.02Ⓜ A
Positional tolerance
45
Basic dimensions are required when using positional tolerances.

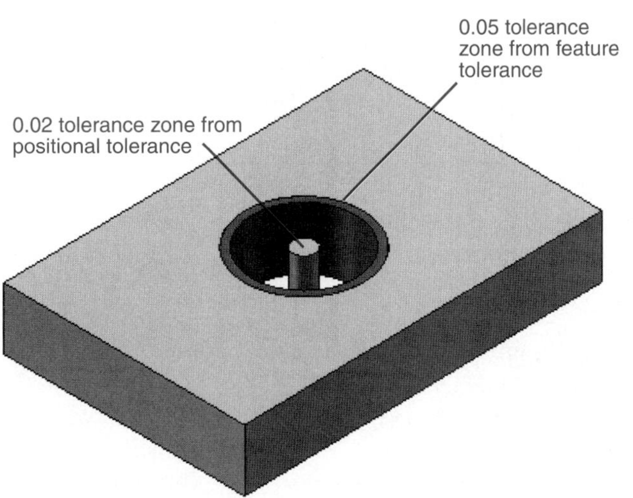
0.05 tolerance zone from feature tolerance
0.02 tolerance zone from positional tolerance

Figure 8-85

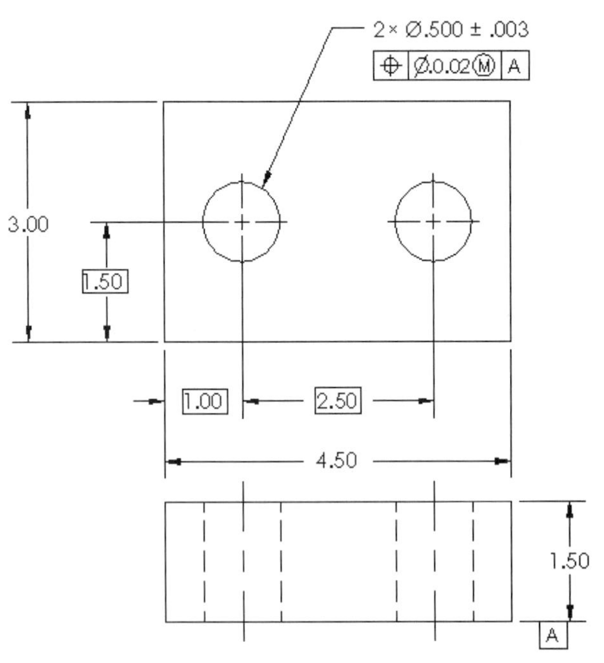

Figure 8-86

Figure 8-86 shows an object containing two holes that are dimensioned and toleranced using positional tolerances. There are two consecutive horizontal basic dimensions. Because basic dimensions are exact, they do not have tolerances that accumulate; that is, there is no tolerance buildup.

8-41 CREATING POSITIONAL TOLERANCES USING SOLIDWORKS

Figure 8-87 shows an orthographic view that has been dimensioned. Note that the hole has a dimension and tolerance of ∅1.000±.001. This is the hole's feature tolerance. It deals only with the hole's diameter variation. It does not tolerance the hole's location.

To Create the Positional Tolerance

1. Click the **Annotations** tool and click the **Geometric Tolerance** tool.
2. Enter the symbol for positional tolerance, the symbol for diameter, the tolerance value, and the symbol for maximum material condition.

The collective symbol would read "Apply a .001 positional tolerance about the hole's center point at the maximum material condition."

3. Locate the symbol on the drawing under the feature tolerance as shown.

Create basic dimensions to accompany the geometric positional tolerance. See Figure 8-88.

4. Click on the **2.00** dimension.

The **Dimension Properties Manager** will appear.

5. Click the **Basic** tool in the **Tolerance/Precision** box.

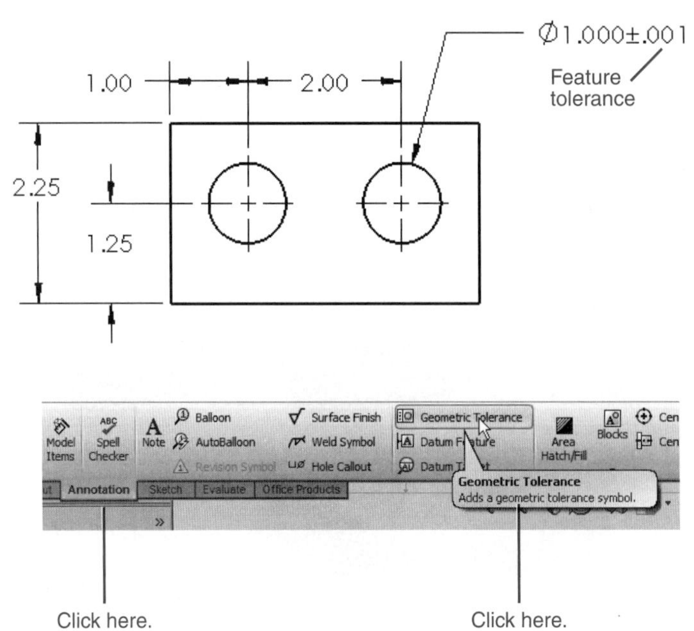

Figure 8-87

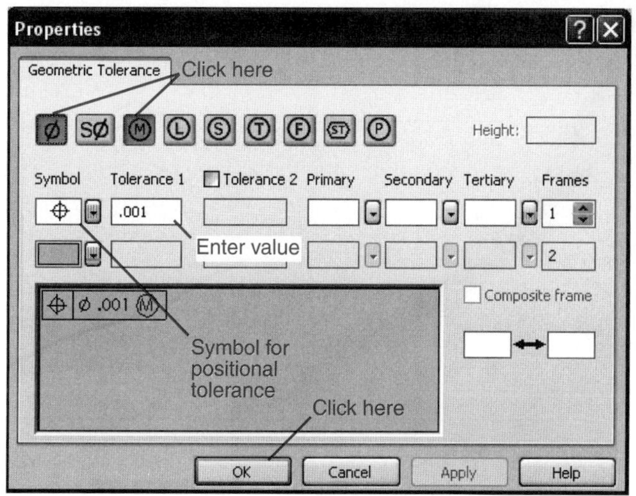

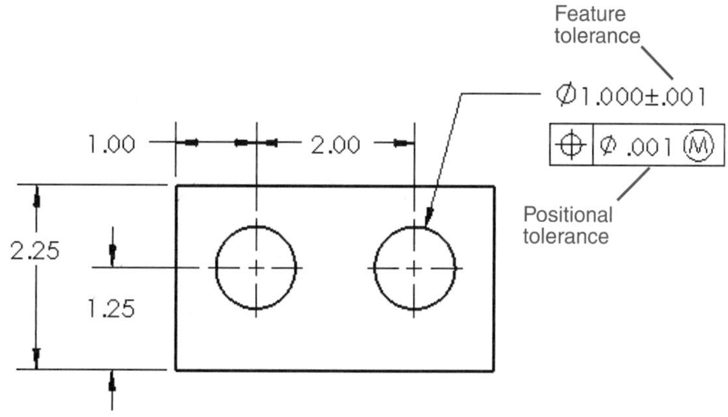

Figure 8-87 *(continued)*

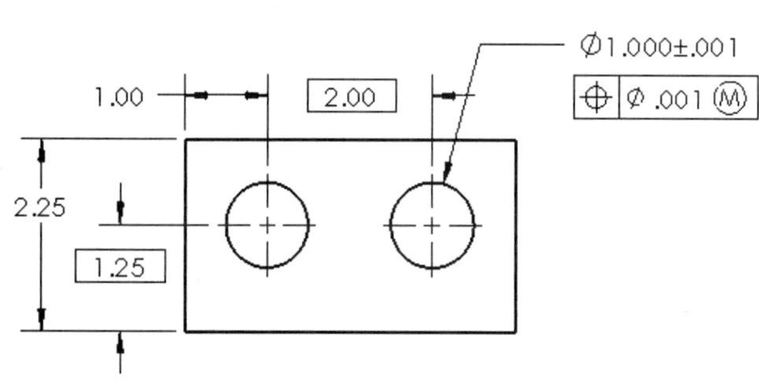

Figure 8-88

6. Click the **1.25** dimension and make it a basic dimension.
7. Save the drawing.
8. Click the OK check mark.

TIP

Geometric positional tolerances must include basic dimensions. Basic dimensions are assumed to be perfect. The locational tolerance associated with locating dimensions has been moved to the geometric positional tolerance.

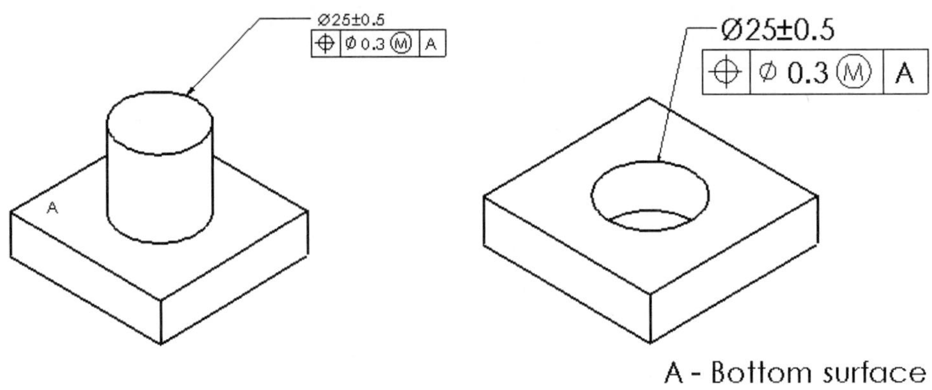

Figure 8-89

8-42 VIRTUAL CONDITION

Virtual condition is a combination of a feature's MMC and its geometric tolerance. For external features (shafts) it is the MMC plus the geometric tolerance; for internal features (holes) it is the MMC minus the geometric tolerance.

The following calculations are based on the dimensions shown in Figure 8-89.

Calculating the Virtual Condition for a Shaft

25.5 MMC for shaft—maximum diameter
+0.3 Geometric tolerance
25.8 Virtual condition

Calculating the Virtual Condition for a Hole

24.5 MMC for hole—minimum diameter
−0.3 Geometric tolerance
24.2 Virtual condition

8-43 FLOATING FASTENERS

Positional tolerances are particularly helpful when dimensioning matching parts. Because basic locating dimensions are considered exact, the sizing of mating parts is dependent only on the hole and shaft's MMC and the geometric tolerance between them.

The relationship for floating fasteners and holes in objects may be expressed as a formula:

$$H - T = F$$

where:

H = hole at MMC
T = geometric tolerance
F = shaft at MMC

A ***floating fastener*** is one that passes through two or more objects, and all parts have clearance holes for the tolerance. It is not attached to either object and it does not screw into either object. Figure 8-90 shows two objects that are to be joined by a common floating shaft, such as a bolt or screw. The feature size and tolerance and the positional geometric tolerance are both given. The minimum size hole that will always just fit is determined using the preceding formula.

$$H - T = F$$
$$11.97 - .02 = 11.95$$

Therefore, the shaft's diameter at MMC, the shaft's maximum diameter, equals 11.95. Any required tolerance would have to be subtracted from this shaft size.

The .02 geometric tolerance is applied at the hole's MMC, so as the hole's size expands within its feature tolerance, the tolerance zone for the acceptable matching parts also expands.

8-44 SAMPLE PROBLEM SP8-3

The situation presented in Figure 8-90 can be worked in reverse; that is, hole sizes can be derived from given shaft sizes.

The two objects shown in Figure 8-91 are to be joined by a .250-in. bolt. The parts are floating; that is, they are both free to move, and the fastener is not joined to either object. What is the MMC of the holes if the positional tolerance is to be .030?

A manufacturer's catalog specifies that the tolerance for .250 bolts is .2500 to .2600.

Rewriting the formula

$$H - T = F$$

to isolate the H yields

$$\begin{aligned} H &= F + T \\ &= .260 + .030 \\ &= .290 \end{aligned}$$

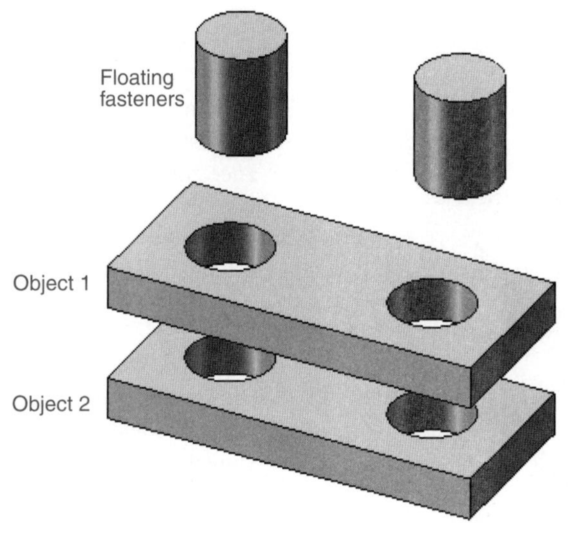

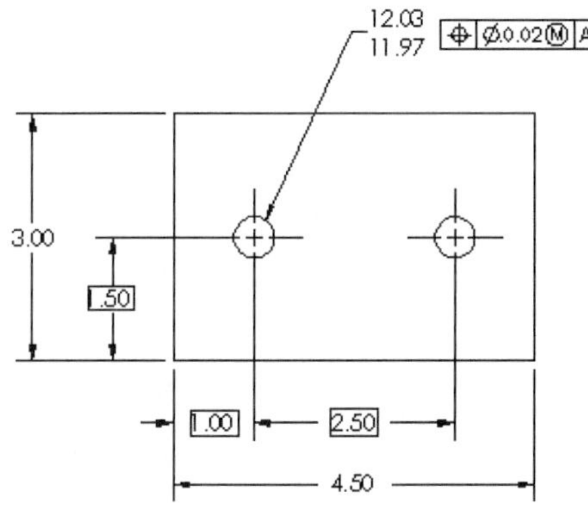

SIZE	TOLERANCE ZONE
11.97 MMC	.02
11.98	.03
11.99	.04
12.00	.05
12.01	.06
12.02	.07
12.03 LMC	.08

11.97 MMC
-0.02
11.95 virtual condition

Maximum possible fastener diameter= 11.95

Figure 8-90

The .290 value represents the minimum hole diameter, MMC, for all four holes that will always accept the .250 bolt. Figure 8-92 shows the resulting drawing callout.

Any clearance requirements or tolerances for the hole would have to be added to the .290 value.

8-45 SAMPLE PROBLEM SP8-4

Repeat the problem presented in SP8-3 but be sure that there is always a minimum clearance of .002 between the hole and the shaft, and assign a hole tolerance of .008.

Sample problem SP8-3 determined that the maximum hole diameter that will always accept the .250 bolt was .290 based on the .030 positioning tolerance. If the minimum clearance is to be .002, the maximum hole diameter is found as follows:

.290 Minimum hole diameter that will always accept the bolt (0 clearance at MMC)
+.002 Minimum clearance
.292 Minimum hole diameter including clearance

Now, assign the tolerance to the hole:

.292 Minimum hole diameter
+.001 Tolerance
.293 Maximum hole diameter

See Figure 8-93 for the appropriate drawing callout. The choice of clearance size and hole tolerance varies with the design requirements for the objects.

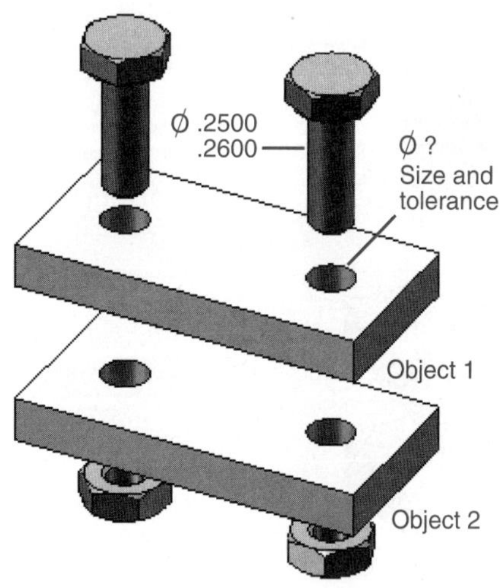

Figure 8-91

8-46 FIXED FASTENERS

A ***fixed fastener*** is a fastener that is restrained in one of the parts. For example, one end of the fastener is screwed into one of the parts using threads. See Figure 8-94. Because the fastener is fixed to one of the objects, the geometric tolerance zone must be smaller than that used for floating fasteners. The fixed fastener cannot move without moving the object it is attached to. The relationship between fixed fasteners and holes in mating objects is defined by the formula

$$H - 2T = F$$

The tolerance zone is cut in half for each part. This can be demonstrated by the objects shown in Figure 8-95. The same feature sizes that were used in Figure 8-91 are assigned, but in this example the fasteners are fixed. Solving for the geometric tolerance yields a value as follows:

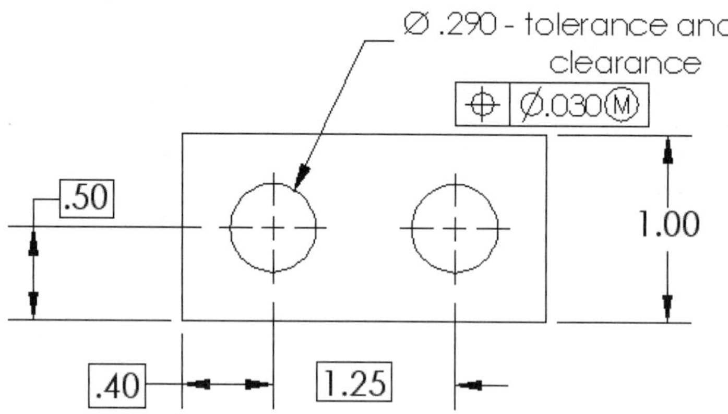

Figure 8-92

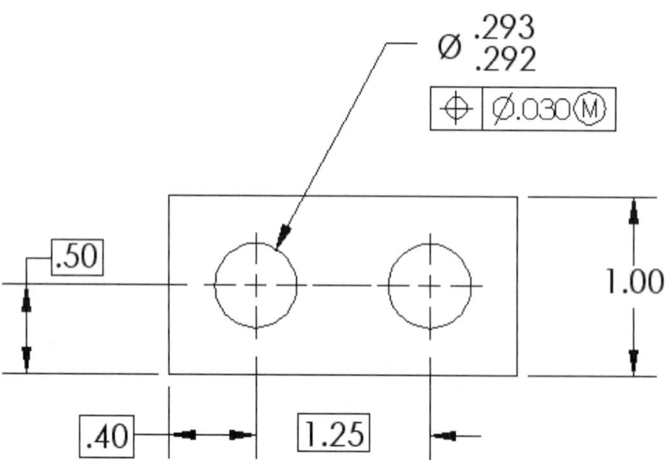

Figure 8-93

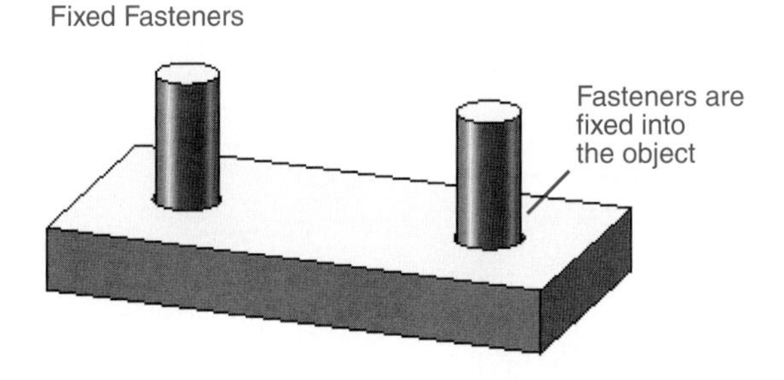

Figure 8-94

$$H - F = 2T$$
$$11.97 - 11.95 = 2T$$
$$.02 = 2T$$
$$.01 = T$$

The resulting positional tolerance is half that obtained for floating fasteners.

8-47 SAMPLE PROBLEM SP8-5

This problem is similar to sample problem SP8-3, but the given conditions are applied to fixed fasteners rather than floating fasteners. Compare the resulting shaft diameters for the two problems. See Figure 8-96.

A. What is the minimum diameter hole that will always accept the fixed fasteners?
B. If the minimum clearance is .005 and the hole is to have a tolerance of .002, what are the maximum and minimum diameters of the hole?

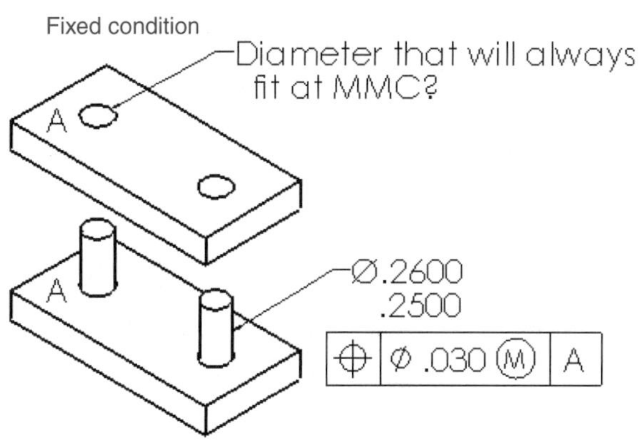

Figure 8-95

$$H - 2T = F$$
$$H = F + 2T$$
$$= .260 + 2(.030)$$
$$= .260 + .060$$
$= .320$ Minimum diameter that will always accept the fastener

If the minimum clearance is .005 and the hole tolerance is .002,

.320	Virtual condition
+.005	Clearance
.325	Minimum hole diameter

.325	Minimum hole diameter
+.002	Tolerance
.327	Maximum hole diameter

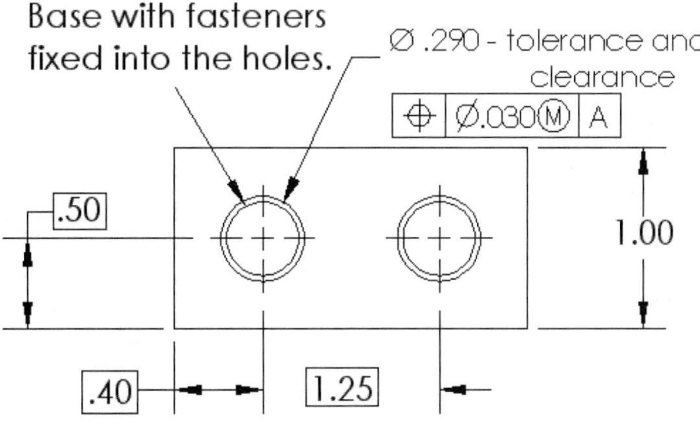

Figure 8-96

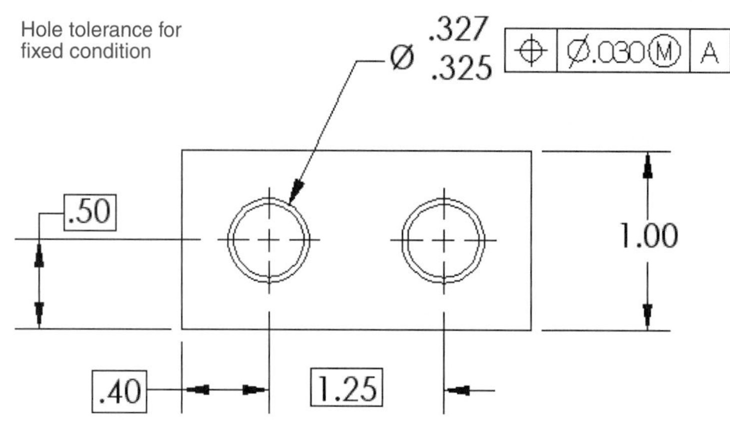

Figure 8-97

The maximum and minimum values for the hole's diameter can then be added to the drawing of the object that fits over the fixed fasteners. See Figure 8-97.

8-48 DESIGN PROBLEMS

This problem was originally done on p. 362 using rectangular tolerances. It is done in this section using positional geometric tolerances so that the two systems can be compared. It is suggested that the previous problem be reviewed before reading this section.

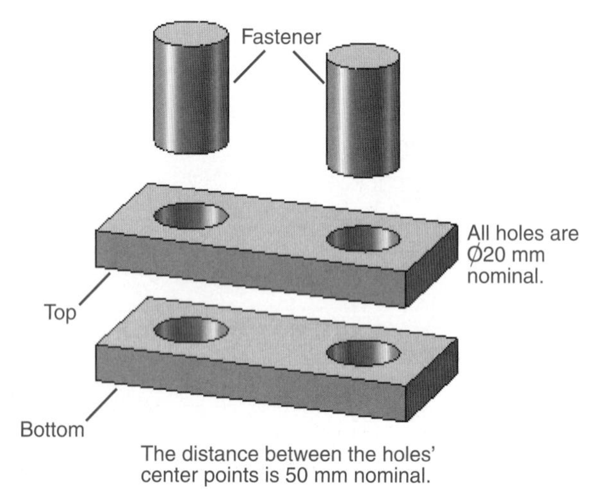

Figure 8-98

Figure 8-98 shows top and bottom parts that are to be joined in the floating condition. A nominal distance of 50 between hole centers and 20 for the holes has been assigned. In the previous solution a rectangular tolerance of ±.01 was selected, and there was a minimum hole diameter of 20.00. Figure 8-99 shows the resulting tolerance zones.

The diagonal distance across the rectangular tolerance zone is .028 and was rounded off to .03 to yield a maximum possible fastener diameter of 19.97. If the same .03 value is used to calculate the fastener diameter using positional tolerance, the results are as follows:

$$H - T = F$$
$$20.00 - .03 = 19.97$$

The results seem to be the same, but because of the circular shape of the positional tolerance zone, the manufactured results are not the same. The minimum distance between the inside edges of the rectangular zones is 49.98, or .01 from the center point of each hole. The minimum distance from the innermost points of the circular tolerance zones is 49.97, or .015 (half the rounded-off .03 value) from the center point of each hole. The same value difference also occurs for the maximum distance between center points, where 50.02 is the maximum distance for the rectangular tolerances, and 50.03 is the maximum distance for the circular tolerances. The size of the circular tolerance zone is larger because the hole tolerances are assigned at MMC. Figure 8-99 shows a comparison between the tolerance zones, and Figure 8-100 shows how the positional tolerances would be presented on a drawing of either the top or bottom part.

Figure 8-101 shows the same top and bottom parts joined together in the fixed condition. The initial nominal

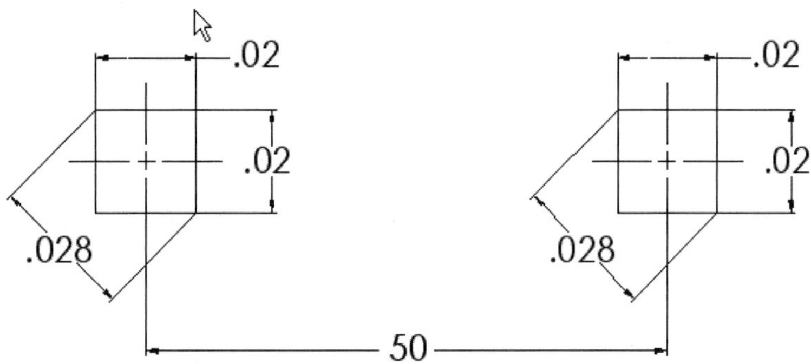
Linear tolerance zones based on ± tolerances.
.02
.02
.028
.02
.02
.028
50
NOT TO SCALE
Rectangular range: 49.98 to 50.02

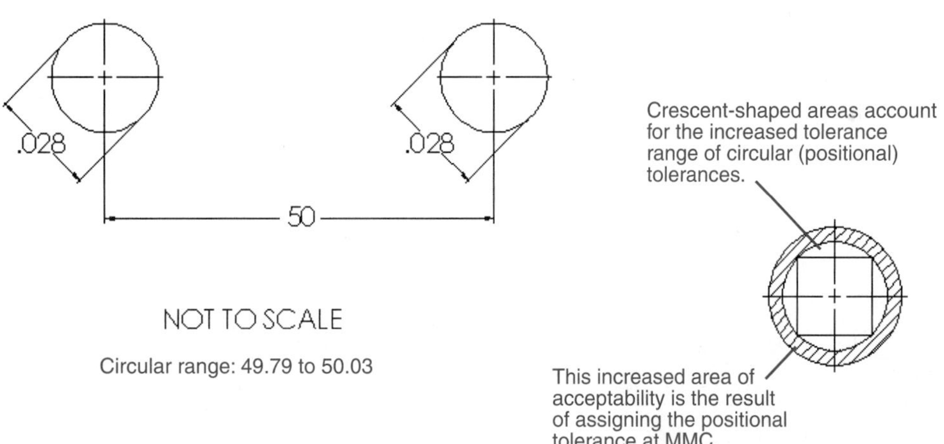
Tolerance zones based on positional (⌖) tolerances.
.028
.028
50
NOT TO SCALE
Circular range: 49.79 to 50.03
Crescent-shaped areas account for the increased tolerance range of circular (positional) tolerances.
This increased area of acceptability is the result of assigning the positional tolerance at MMC.

Figure 8-99

values are the same. If the same .03 diagonal value is assigned as a positional tolerance, the results are as follows:

$$H - T = F$$
$$20.00 - .06 = 19.94$$

These results appear to be the same as those generated by the rectangular tolerance zone, but the circular tolerance zone allows a greater variance in acceptable manufactured parts. Figure 8-102 shows how the positional tolerance would be presented on a drawing.

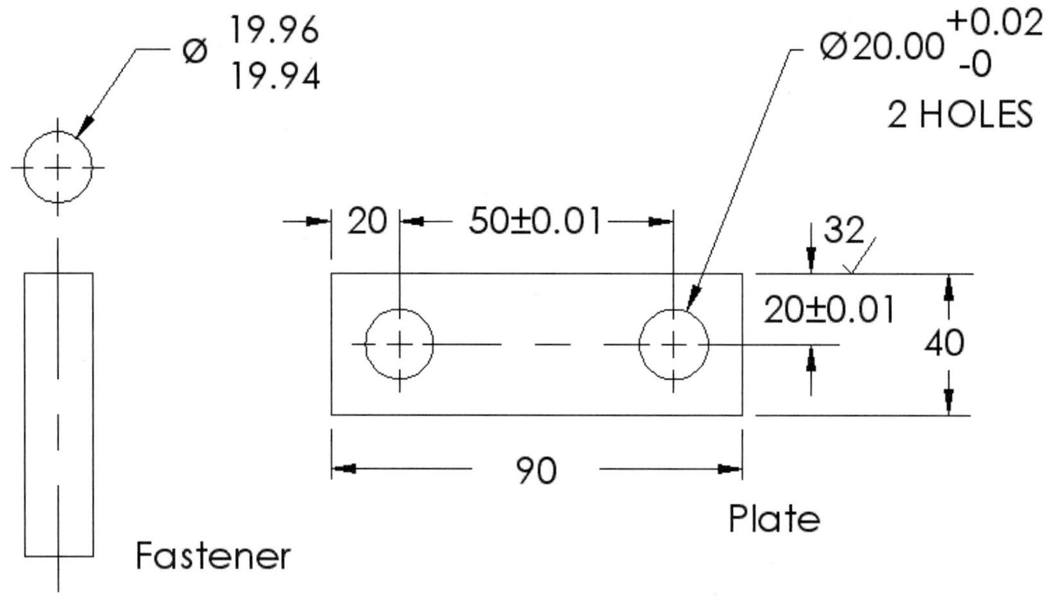

Figure 8-100

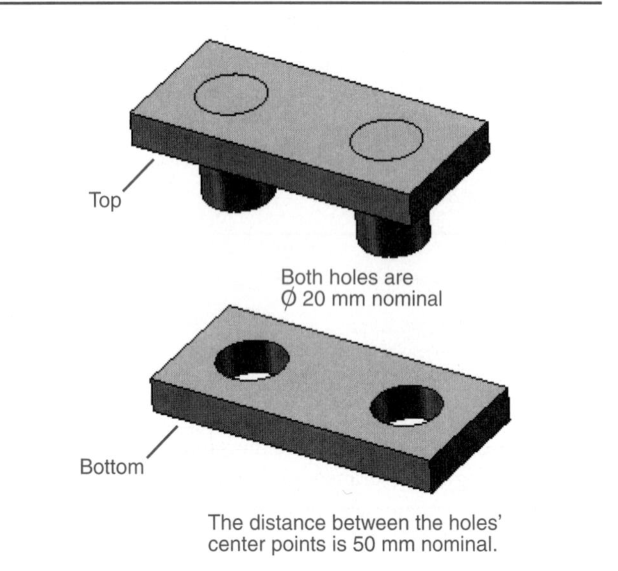

Figure 8-101

H – 2T = F
20.00 – .06 = 19.94

Subtracting .01 for clearance results in a maximum shaft diameter of 19.93.

Ø 19.93
19.91
2 HOLES

20
50±0.01
32
20±0.01
40
90

Assigning a shaft tolerance of .02 results in a maximum shaft diameter of 19.91.

Figure 8-102

8-49 PROJECTS

Project 8-1:

Draw a model of the objects shown in Figures P8-1A through P8-1D using the given dimensions and tolerances. Create a drawing layout with a view of the model as shown. Add the specified dimensions and tolerances.

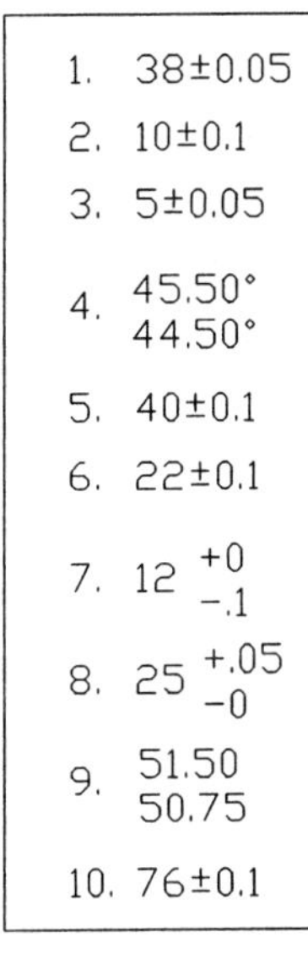

1. 38±0.05
2. 10±0.1
3. 5±0.05
4. 45.50° / 44.50°
5. 40±0.1
6. 22±0.1
7. 12 +0 / −.1
8. 25 +.05 / −0
9. 51.50 / 50.75
10. 76±0.1

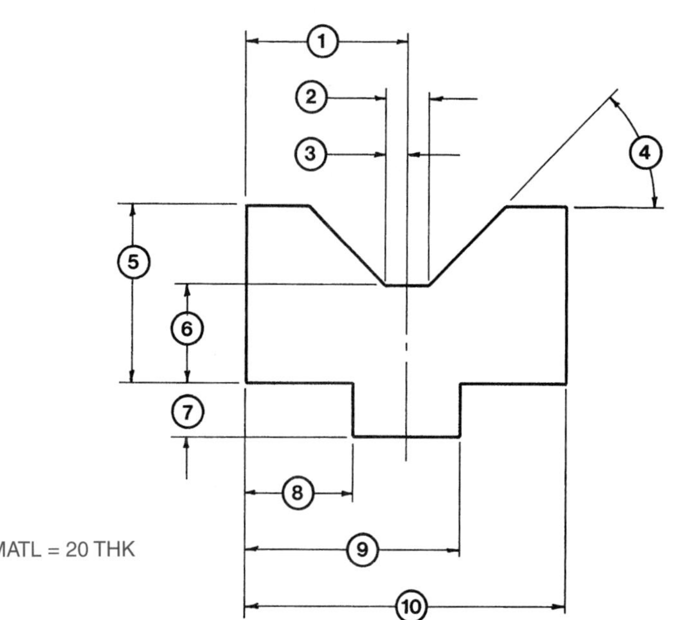

Figure P8-1A MILLIMETERS

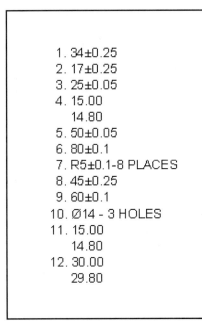

1. 34±0.25
2. 17±0.25
3. 25±0.05
4. 15.00 / 14.80
5. 50±0.05
6. 80±0.1
7. R5±0.1-8 PLACES
8. 45±0.25
9. 60±0.1
10. Ø14 - 3 HOLES
11. 15.00 / 14.80
12. 30.00 / 29.80

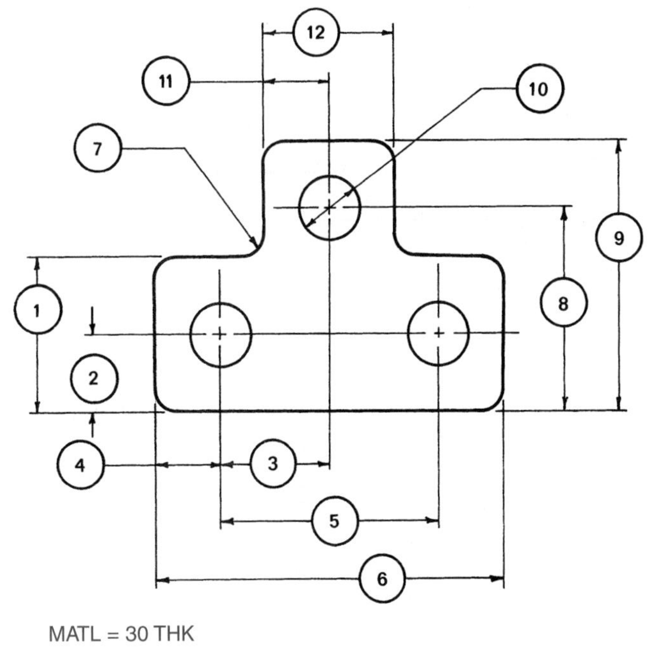

Figure P8-1B MILLIMETERS

1. 3.00±.01
2. 1.56±.01
3. 46.50°
   45.50°
4. .750±.005
5. 2.75
   2.70
6. 3.625±.010
7. 45°±.5°
8. 2.250±.005

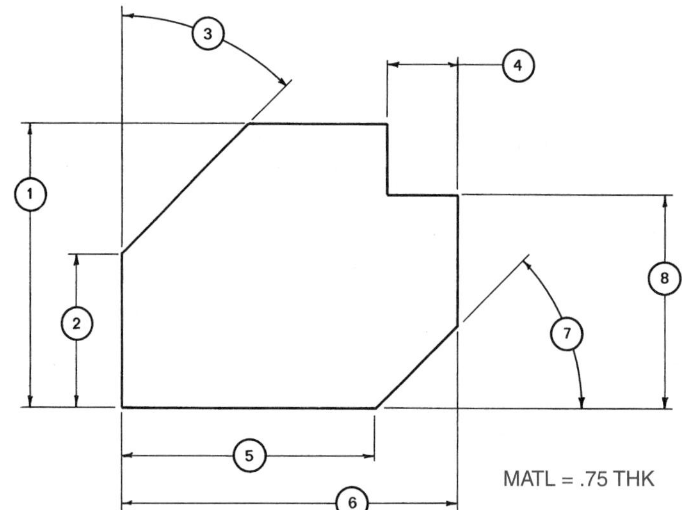

Figure P8-1C INCHES

1. 50 $^{+.2}_{0}$
2. R45±.1 - 2 PLACES
3. 63.5 $^{0}_{-.2}$
4. 76±.1
5. 38±.1
6. ⌀12.00 $^{+.05}_{0}$ - 3 HOLES
7. 30±.03
8. 30±.03
9. 100 $^{+.4}_{0}$

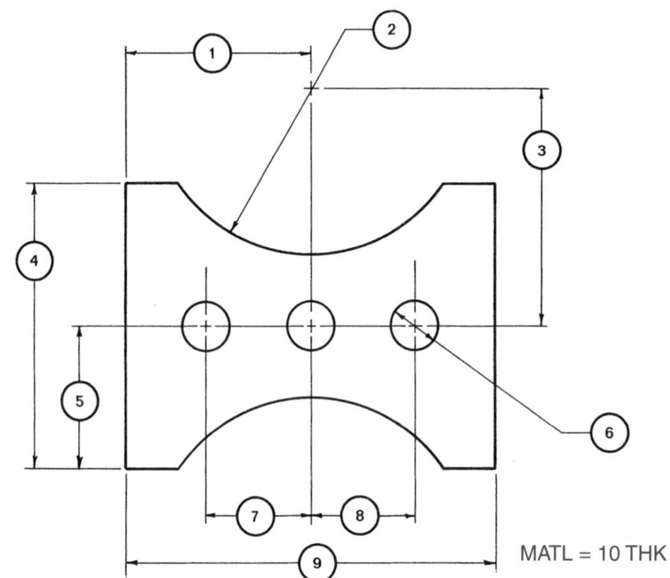

Figure P8-1D MILLIMETERS

Project 8-2:

Redraw the following object, including the given dimensions and tolerances. Calculate and list the maximum and minimum distances for surface A.

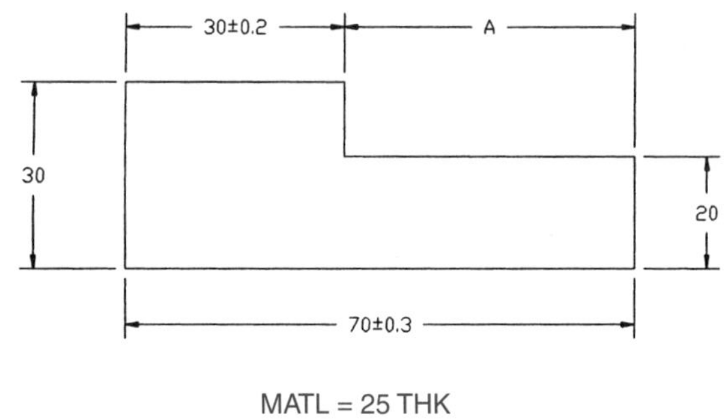

Figure P8-2 MILLIMETERS

Project 8-3:

A. Redraw the following object, including the dimensions and tolerances. Calculate and list the maximum and minimum distances for surface A.
B. Redraw the given object and dimension it using baseline dimensions. Calculate and list the maximum and minimum distances for surface A.

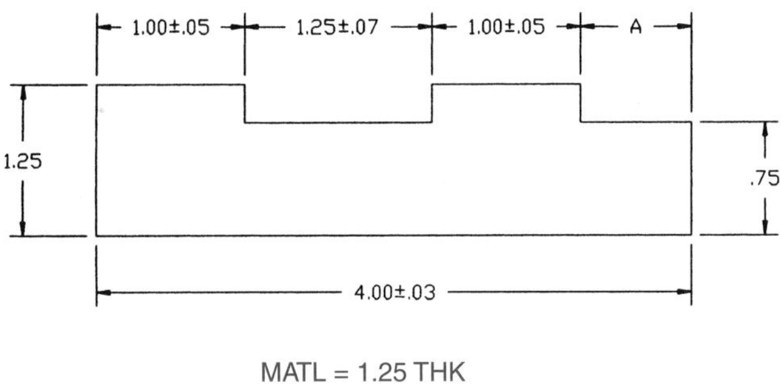

Figure P8-3 INCHES

Project 8-4:

Redraw the following object, including the dimensions and tolerances. Calculate and list the maximum and minimum distances for surfaces D and E.

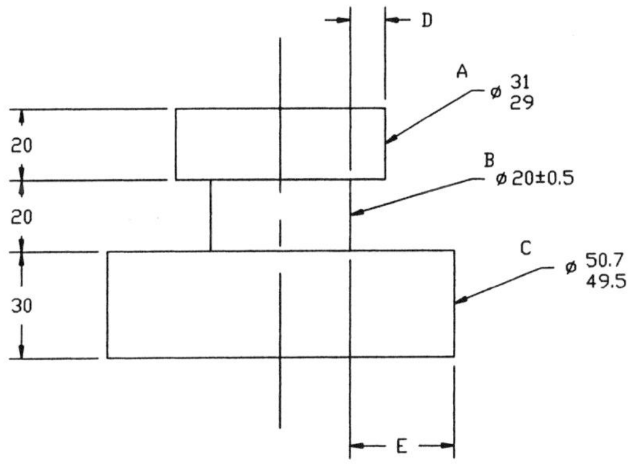

Figure P8-4 MILLIMETERS

Project 8-5:

Dimension the following object twice, once using chain dimensions and once using baseline dimensions. Calculate and list the maximum and minimum distances for surface D for both chain and baseline dimensions. Compare the results.

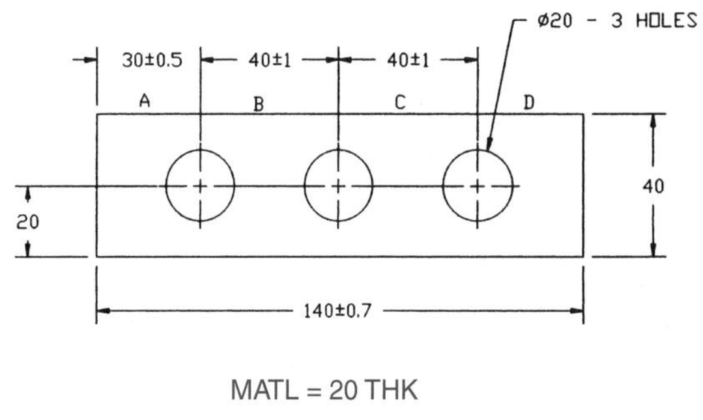

Figure P8-5 MILLIMETERS

Project 8-6:

Redraw the following shapes, including the dimensions and tolerances. Also list the required minimum and maximum values for the specified distances.

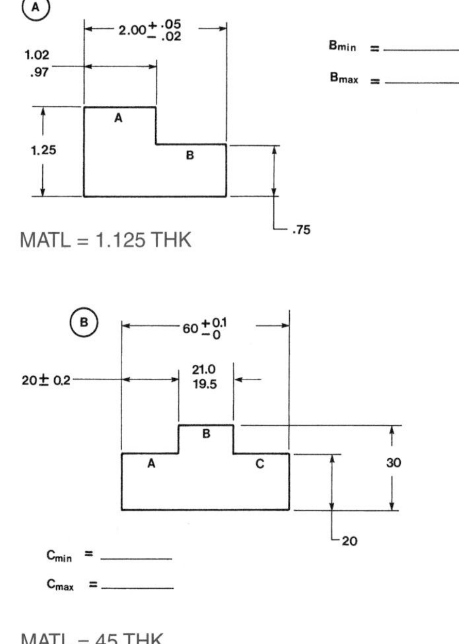

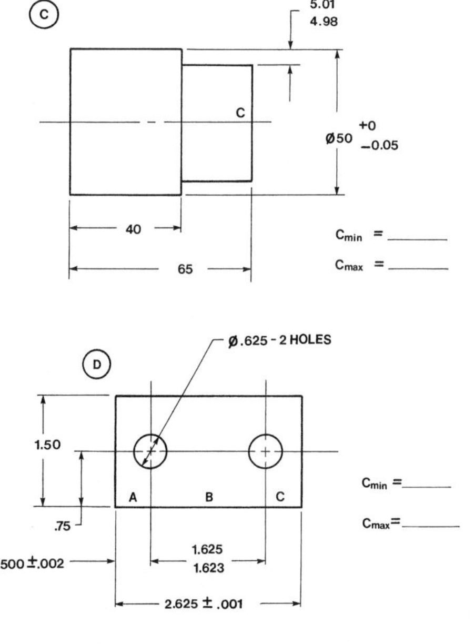

Figure P8-6 INCHES

Project 8-7:

Redraw and complete the following inspection report. Under the Results column classify each "AS MEASURED" value as OK if the value is within the stated tolerances, REWORK if the value indicates that the measured value is beyond the stated tolerance but can be reworked to bring it into the acceptable range, or SCRAP if the value is not within the tolerance range and cannot be reworked to make it acceptable.

INSPECTION REPORT

PART NAME AND NO: 10755002

INSPECTOR:

DATE:

BASE DIMENSION	TOLERANCES		AS MEASURED	RESULTS
	MAX	MIN		
(1) 100 ± 0.5			99.8	
(2) $\phi\, \begin{matrix}57\\56\end{matrix}$			57.01	
(3) 22 ± 0.3			21.72	
(4) $\begin{matrix}40.05\\39.95\end{matrix}$			39.98	
(5) 22 ± 0.3			21.68	
(6) $R52^{+0}_{-0.2}$			51.99	
(7) $35^{+0.2}_{-0.3}$			35.20	
(8) $30^{+0.4}_{0}$			30.27	
(9) $6.0^{+.1}_{-.2}$			5.85	
(10) 12.0 ± 0.2			11.90	

1.00 3 PLACES

.50 —10 PLACES

Figure P8-7 MILLIMETERS

Project 8-8:

Redraw the following charts and complete them based on the following information. All values are in millimeters.

A. Nominal = 16, Fit = H8/d8
B. Nominal = 30, Fit = H11/c11
C. Nominal = 22, Fit = H7/g6
D. Nominal = 10, Fit = C11/h11
E. Nominal = 25, Fit = F8/h7
F. Nominal = 12, Fit = H7/k6
G. Nominal = 3, Fit = H7/p6
H. Nominal = 18, Fit = H7/s6
I. Nominal = 27, Fit = H7/u6
J. Nominal = 30, Fit = N7/h6

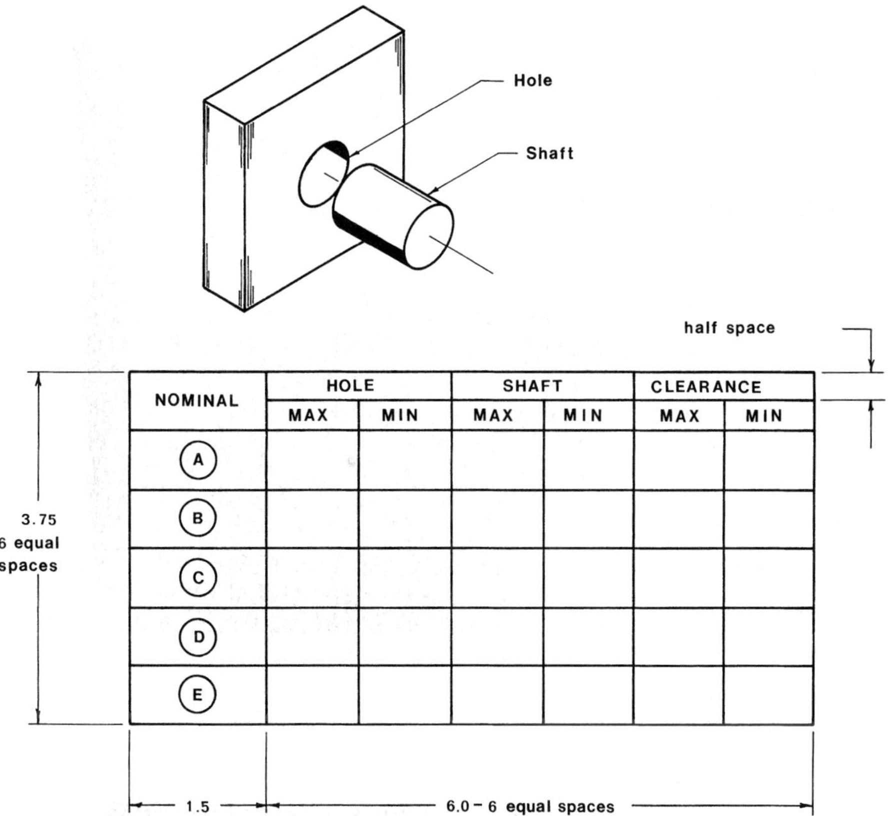

NOMINAL	HOLE		SHAFT		INTERFERENCE	
	MAX	MIN	MAX	MIN	MAX	MIN
(F)						
(G)						
(H)						
(I)						
(J)						

Use the same dimensions given above

Figure P8-8 MILLIMETERS

Project 8-9:

Redraw the following charts and complete them based on the following information. All values are in inches.

A. Nominal = 0.25, Fit = Class LC5, H7/g6
B. Nominal = 1.00, Fit = Class LC7, H10/e9
C. Nominal = 1.50, Fit = Class LC9, F11/h11
D. Nominal = 0.75, Fit = Class RC3, H7/f6
E. Nominal = 1.75, Fit = Class RC6, H9/e8
F. Nominal = .500, Fit = Class LT2, H8/js7
G. Nominal = 1.25, Fit = Class LT5, H7/n6
H. Nominal = 1.38, Fit = Class LN3, J7/h6
I. Nominal = 1.625, Fit = Class FN, H7/s6
J. Nominal = 2.00, Fit = Class FN4, H7/u6

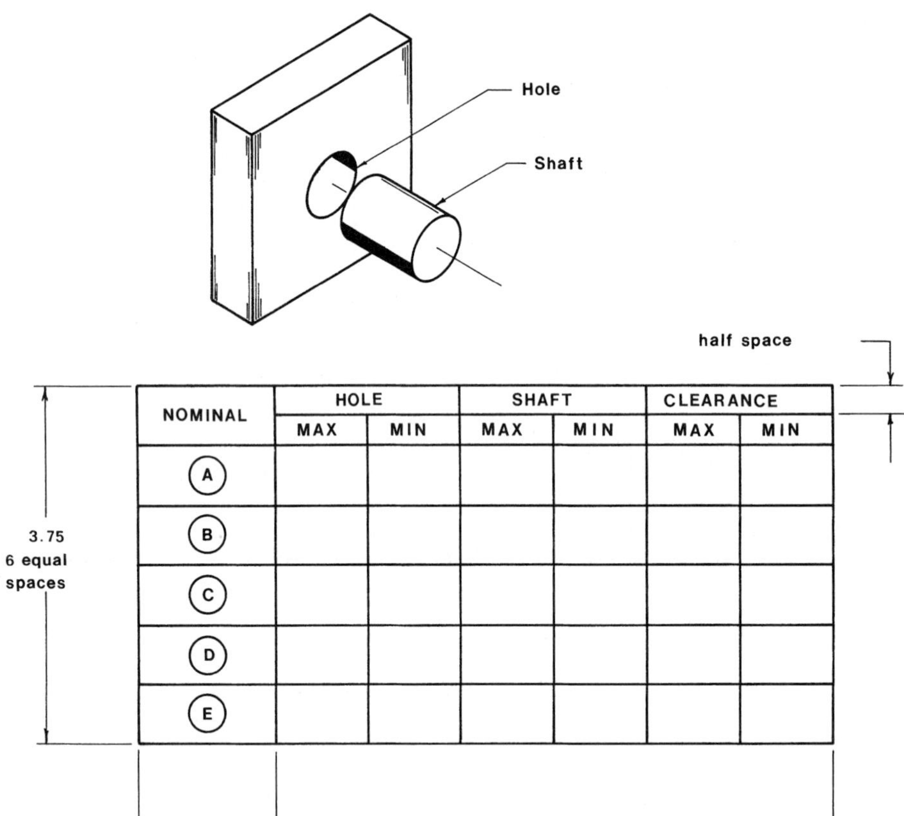

NOMINAL	HOLE		SHAFT		INTERFERENCE	
	MAX	MIN	MAX	MIN	MAX	MIN
F						
G						
H						
I						
J						

Use the same dimensions given above

Figure P8-9 INCHES

Project 8-10:

Draw the chart shown and add the appropriate values based on the dimensions and tolerances given in Figures P8-10A through P8-10D.

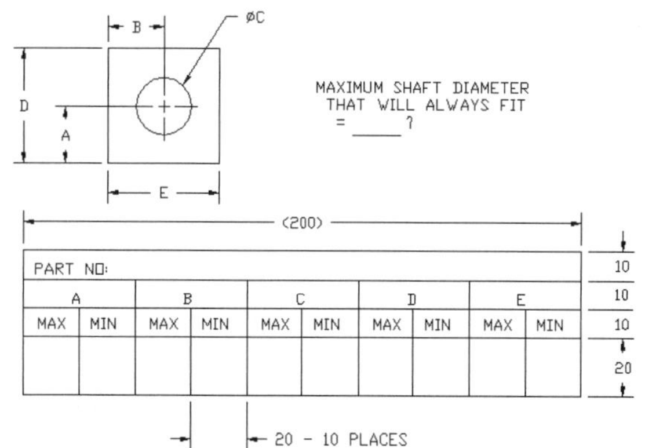

PART NO: 9-M53A

A. 20±0.1

B. 30±0.2

C. Ø20±0.05

D. 40

E. 60

Figure P8-10A MILLIMETERS

PART NO: 9-M53B

A. 32.02
31.97

B. 47.52
47.50

C. Ø$18^{+0.05}_{0}$

D. 64±0.05

E. 100±0.05

Figure P8-10B MILLIMETERS

PART NO: 9-E47A

A. 2.00±.02

B. 1.75±.03

C. Ø.750±.005

D. 4.00±.05

E. 3.50±.05

Figure P8-10C MILLIMETERS

PART NO: 9-E47B

A. $18^{+0}_{-0.02}$

B. $26^{+0}_{-0.04}$

C. Ø 24.03
23.99

D. 52±0.04

E. 36±0.02

Figure P8-10D MILLIMETERS

Project 8-11:

Prepare front and top views of parts 4A and 4B based on the given dimensions. Add tolerances to produce the stated clearances.

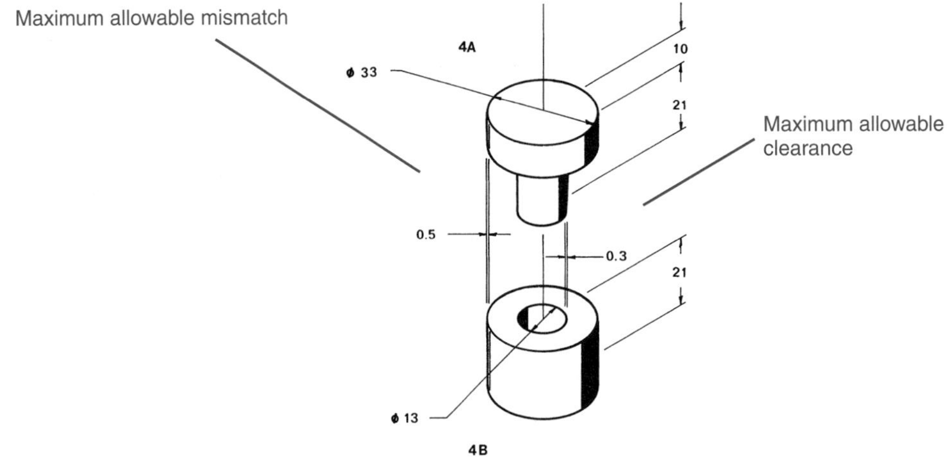

Figure P8-11 MILLIMETERS

Project 8-12:

Redraw parts A and B and dimensions and tolerances to meet the "UPON ASSEMBLY" requirements.

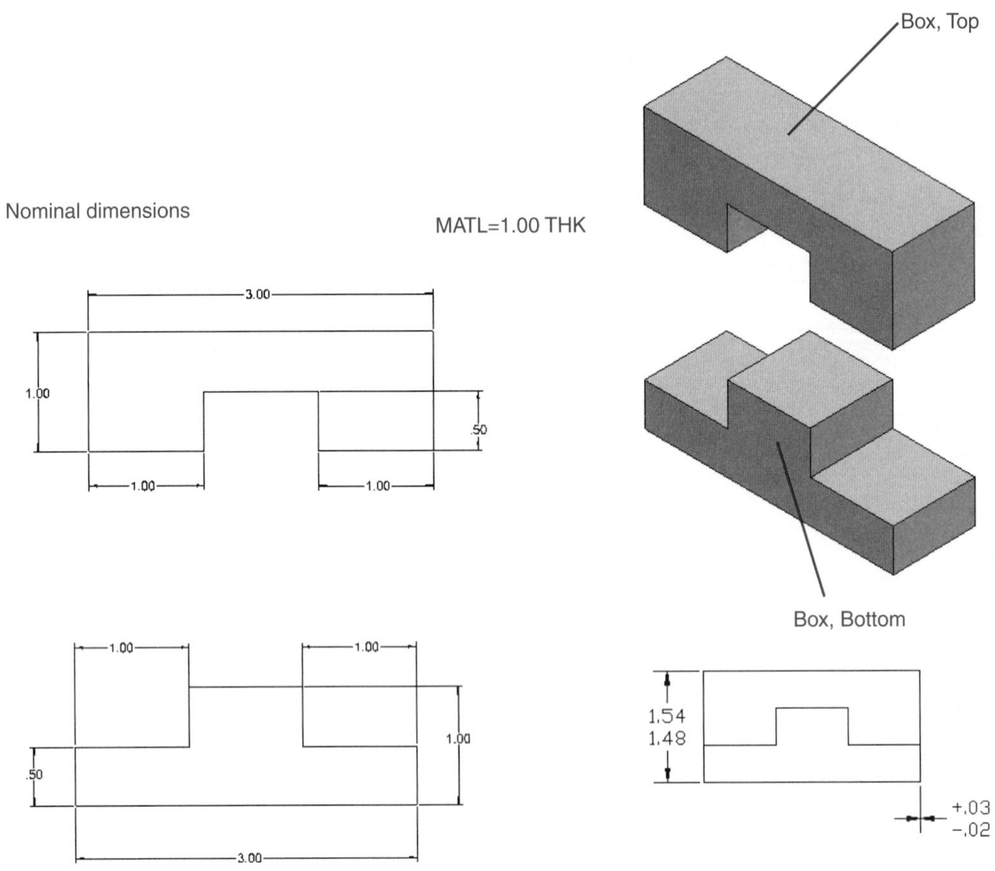

Figure P8-12 INCHES

Project 8-13:

Draw a front and top view of both given objects. Add dimensions and tolerances to meet the "FINAL CONDITION" requirements.

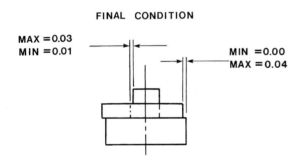

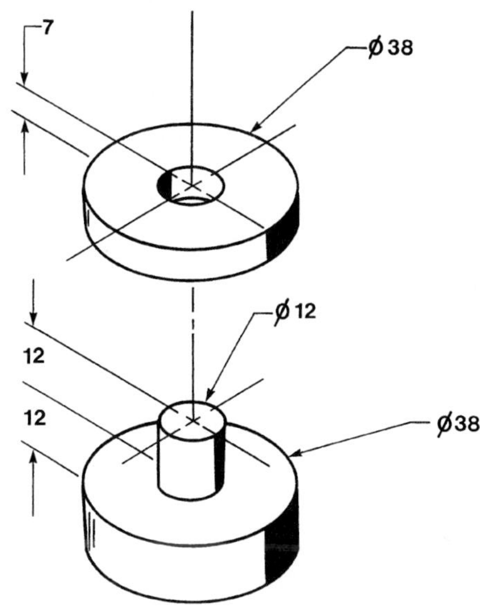

Figure P8-13 MILLIMETERS

Project 8-14:

Given the following nominal sizes, dimension and tolerance parts AM311 and AM312 so that they always fit together regardless of orientation. Further, dimension the overall lengths of each part so that in the assembled condition they will always pass through a clearance gauge with an opening of 80.00±0.02.

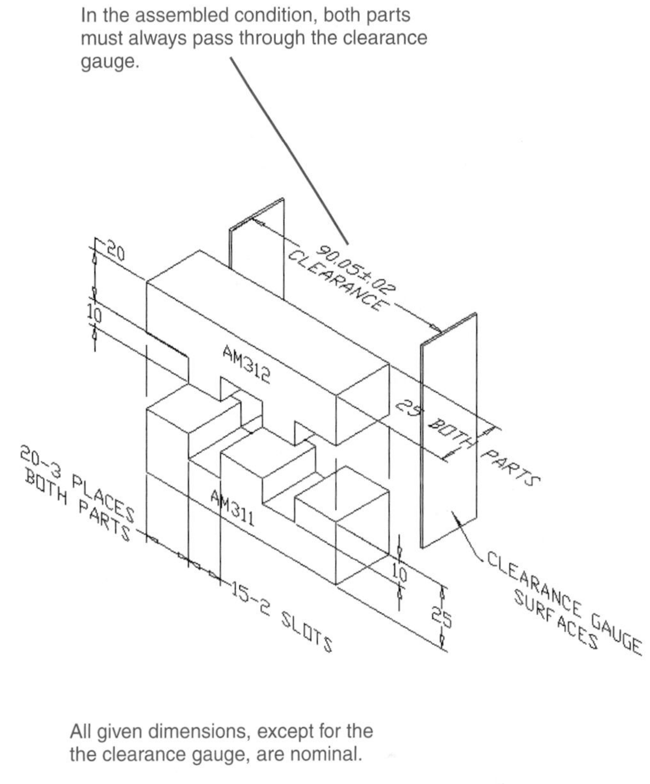

Figure P8-14 MILLIMETERS

Project 8-15:

Given the following rail assembly, add dimensions and tolerances so that the parts always fit together as shown in the assembled position.

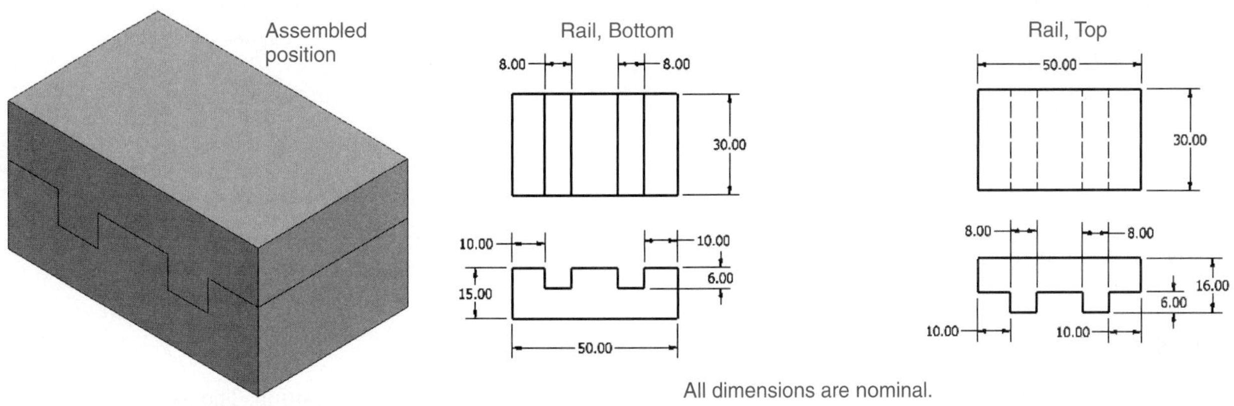

Figure P8-15 MILLIMETERS

Project 8-16:

Given the following peg assembly, add dimensions and tolerances so that the parts always fit together as shown in the assembled position.

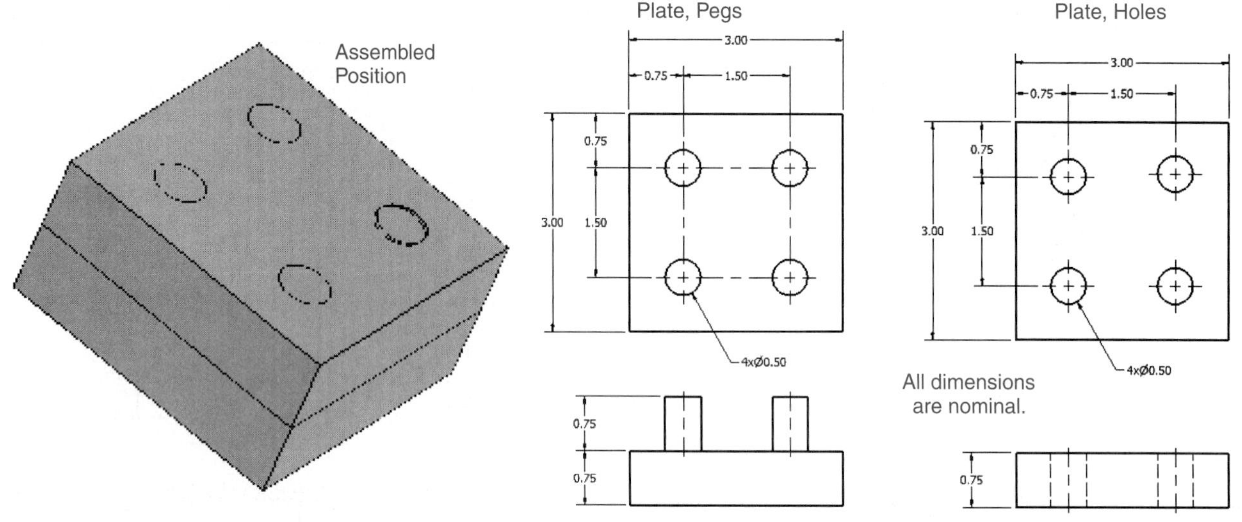

Figure P8-16 INCHES

Project 8-17:

Given the following collar assembly, add dimensions and tolerances so that the parts always fit together as shown in the assembled position.

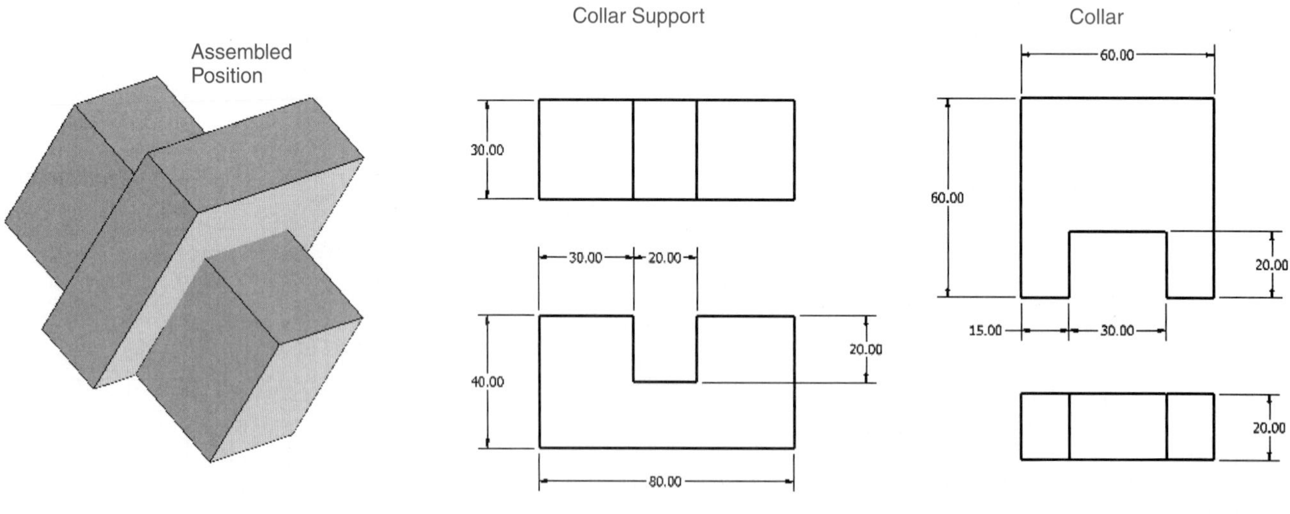

Figure P8-17 MILLIMETERS

Project 8-18:

Given the following vee-block assembly, add dimensions and tolerances so that the parts always fit together as shown in the assembled position. The total height of the assembled blocks must be between 4.45 and 4.55 in.

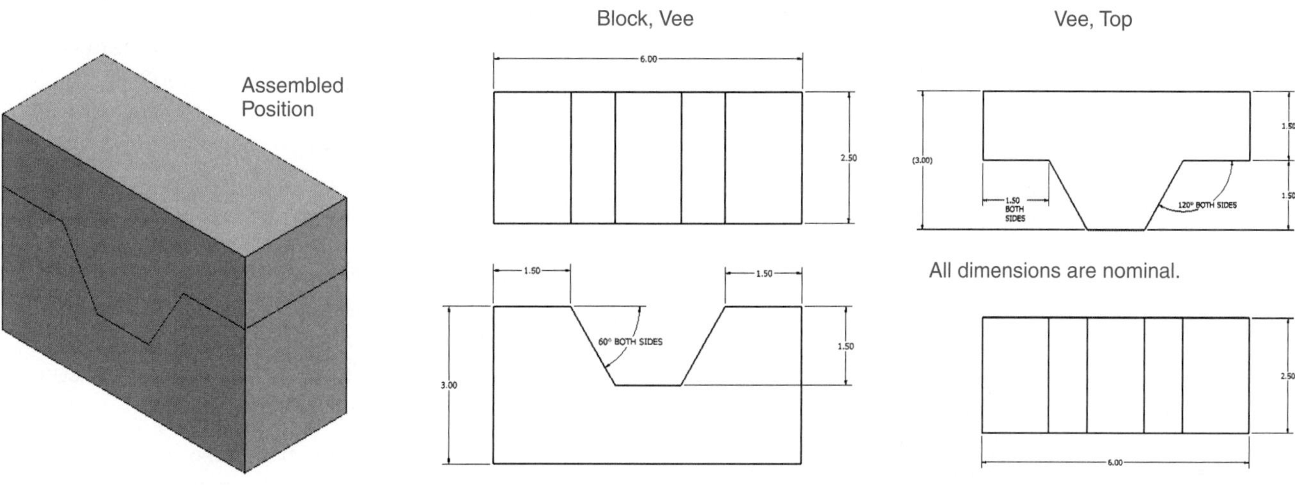

Figure P8-18 INCHES

Project 8-19:

Design a bracket that will support the three ∅100 wheels shown. The wheels will utilize three ∅5.00 ± 0.01 shafts attached to the bracket. The bottom of the bracket must have a minimum of 10 mm from the ground. The wall thickness of the bracket must always be at least 5 mm, and the minimum bracket opening must be at least 15 mm.

1. Prepare a front and a side view of the bracket.
2. Draw the wheels in their relative positions using phantom lines.
3. Add all appropriate dimensions and tolerances.

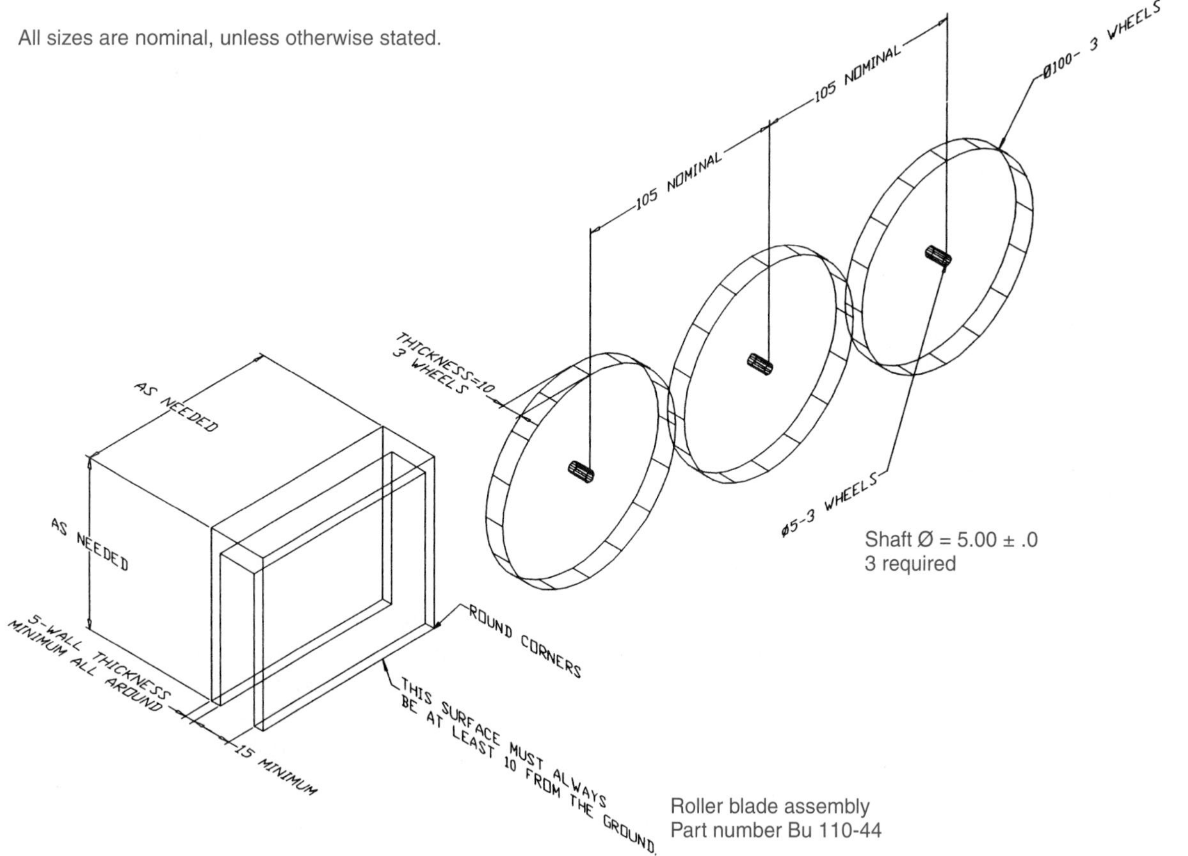

Figure P8-19A MILLIMETERS

Given a TOP and a BOTTOM part in the floating condition as shown in Figure P8-19B, satisfy the requirements given in projects P8-20 through P8-23 so that the parts always fit together regardless of orientation. Prepare drawings of each part including dimensions and tolerances.

A. Use linear tolerances.
B. Use positional tolerances.

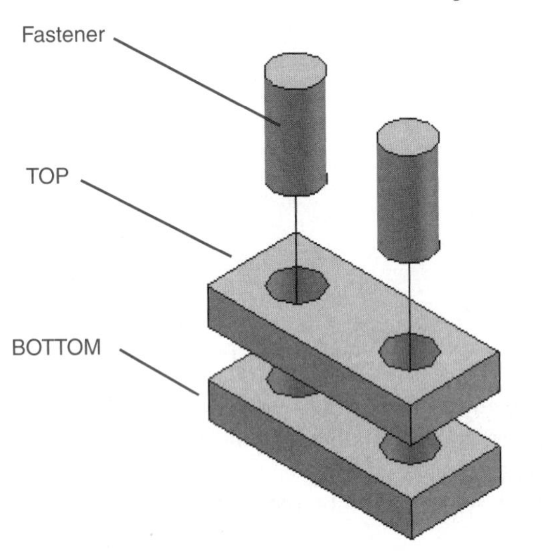

Figure P8-19B

Project 8-20: Inches

A. The distance between the holes' center points is 2.00 nominal.
B. The holes are Ø.375 nominal.
C. The fasteners have a tolerance of .001.
D. The holes have a tolerance of .002.
E. The minimum allowable clearance between the fasteners and the holes is .003.

Project 8-21: Millimeters

A. The distance between the holes' center points is 80 nominal.
B. The holes are Ø12 nominal.
C. The fasteners have a tolerance of 0.05.
D. The holes have a tolerance of 0.03.
E. The minimum allowable clearance between the fasteners and the holes is 0.02.

Project 8-22: Inches

A. The distance between the holes' center points is 3.50 nominal.
B. The holes are Ø.625 nominal.
C. The fasteners have a tolerance of .005.
D. The holes have a tolerance of .003.
E. The minimum allowable clearance between the fasteners and the holes is .002.

Project 8-23: Millimeters

A. The distance between the holes' center points is 65 nominal.
B. The holes are Ø16 nominal.
C. The fasteners have a tolerance of 0.03.
D. The holes have a tolerance of 0.04.
E. The minimum allowable clearance between the fasteners and the holes is 0.03.

Given a top and a bottom part in the fixed condition as shown in Figure P8-23, satisfy the requirements given in projects P8-24 through P8-27 so that the parts fit together regardless of orientation. Prepare drawings of each part including dimensions and tolerances.

A. Use linear tolerances
B. Use positional tolerances.

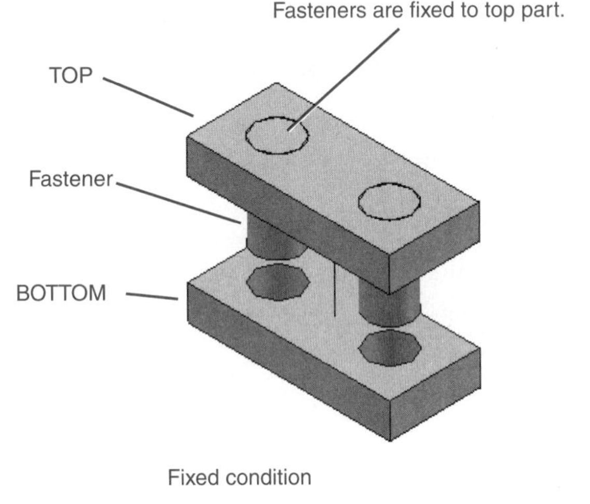

Figure P8-23

Project 8-24: Millimeters

A. The distance between the holes' center points is 60 nominal.
B. The holes are Ø10 nominal.
C. The fasteners have a tolerance of 0.04.
D. The holes have a tolerance of 0.02.
E. The minimum allowable clearance between the fasteners and the holes is 0.02.

Project 8-25: Inches

A. The distance between the holes' center points is 3.50 nominal.

B. The holes are Ø.563 nominal.
C. The fasteners have a tolerance of .005.
D. The holes have a tolerance of .003.
E. The minimum allowable clearance between the fasteners and the holes is .002.

Project 8-26: Millimeters

A. The distance between the holes' center points is 100 nominal.
B. The holes are Ø18 nominal.
C. The fasteners have a tolerance of 0.02.
D. The holes have a tolerance of 0.01.
E. The minimum allowable clearance between the fasteners and the holes is 0.03

Project 8-27: Inches

A. The distance between the holes' center points is 1.75 nominal.
B. The holes are Ø.250 nominal.
C. The fasteners have a tolerance of .002.
D. The holes have a tolerance of .003.
E. The minimum allowable clearance between the fasteners and the holes is .001.

Project 8-28: Millimeters

Dimension and tolerance the rotator assembly shown in Figure P8-28. Use the given dimensions as nominal and add sleeve bearings between the LINKs and both the CROSS-LINK and the PLATE. Create drawings of each part. Modify the dimensions as needed and add the appropriate tolerances. Specify the selected sleeve bearing.

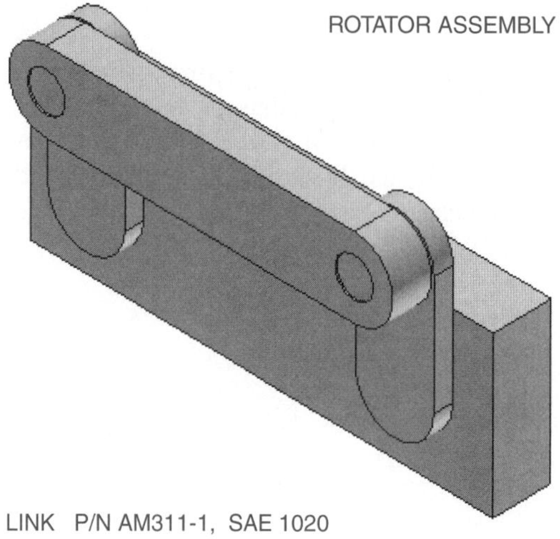

LINK P/N AM311-1, SAE 1020

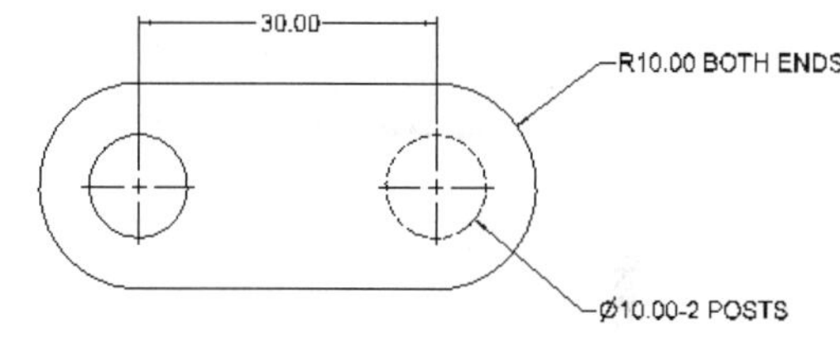

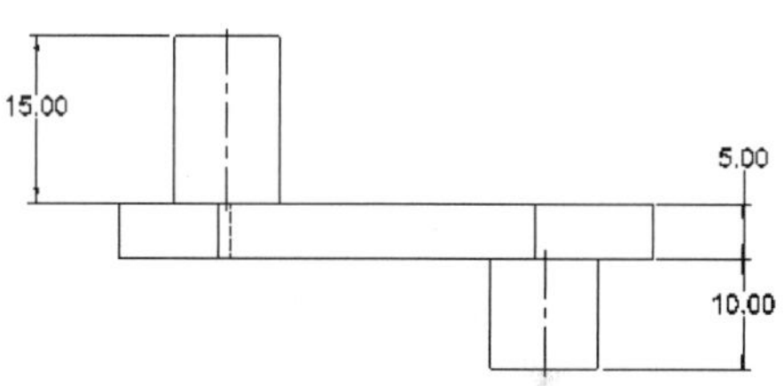

CROSS-LINK P/N AM311-2, SAE 1020

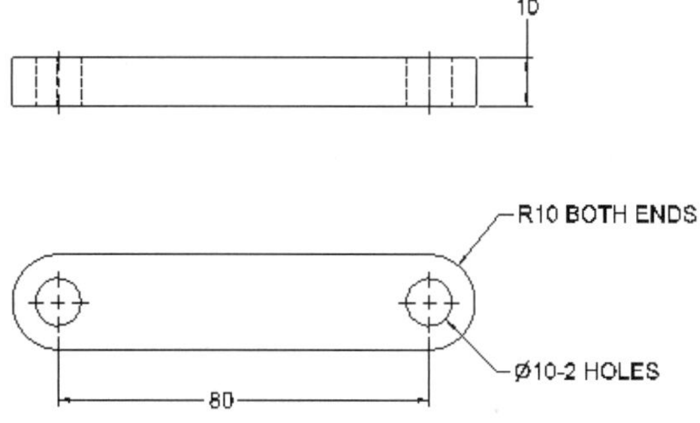

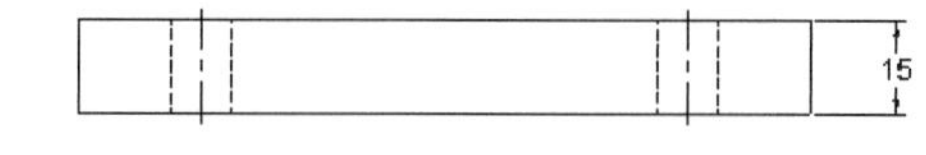

PLATE P/N AM311-3, SAE 1020

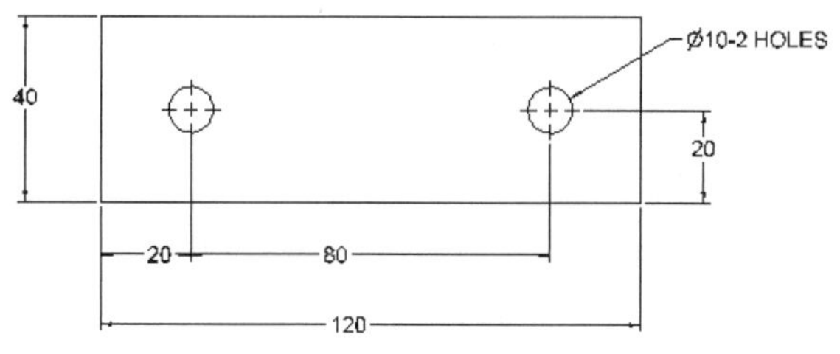

Figure P8-28

Project 8-29:

Dimension and tolerance the rocker assembly shown in Figure P8-29. Use the given dimensions as nominal, and add sleeve bearings between all moving parts. Create drawings of each part. Modify the dimensions as needed and add the appropriate tolerances. Specify the selected sleeve bearing.

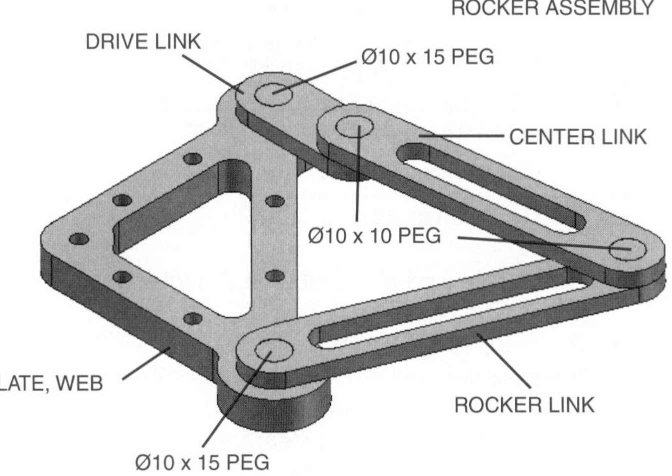

DRIVE LINK
AM312-2
SAE 1040
5 mm THK

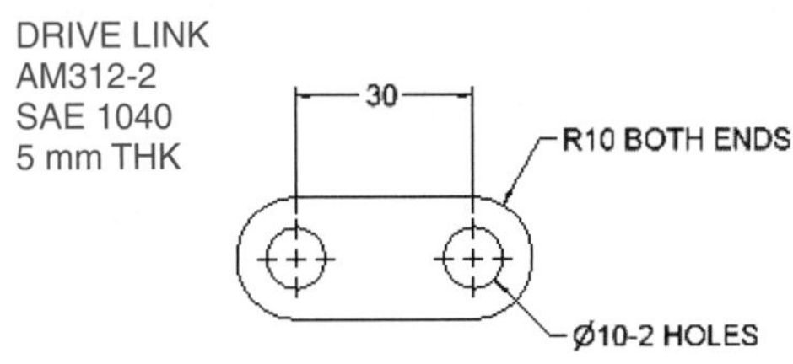

PLATE, WEB AM312-1, SAE 1040, 10 mm THK

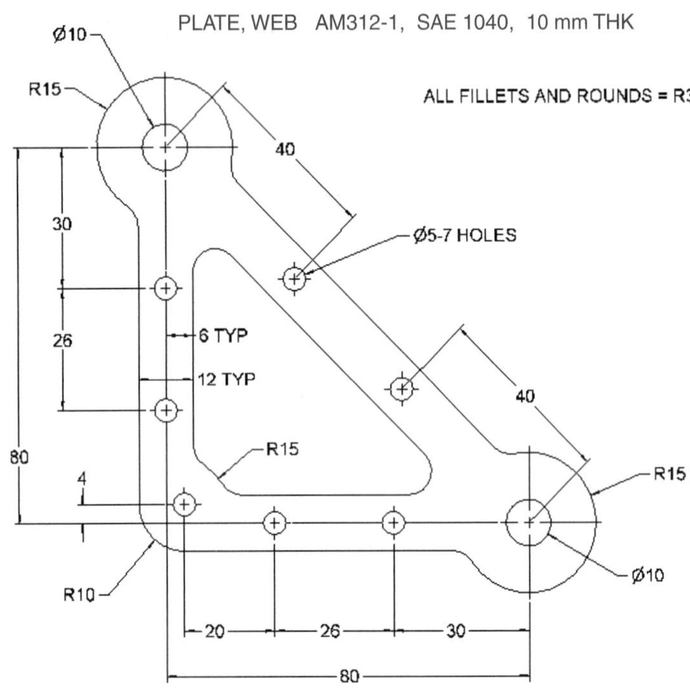

ROCKER LINK
AM312-4
SAE 1040
5 mm THK

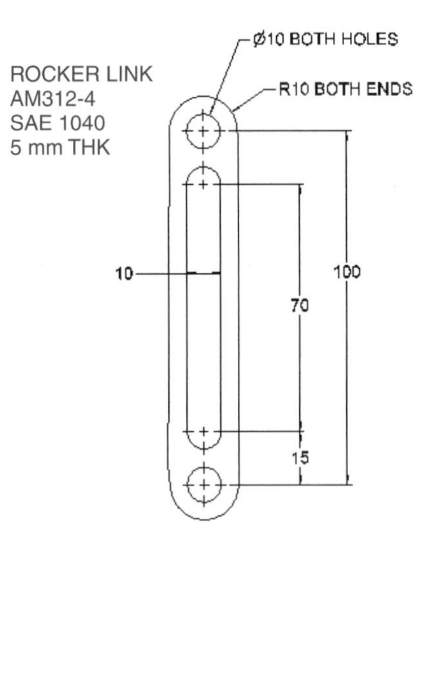

Ø10 x 10 PEG AM 312-5
SAE 1020

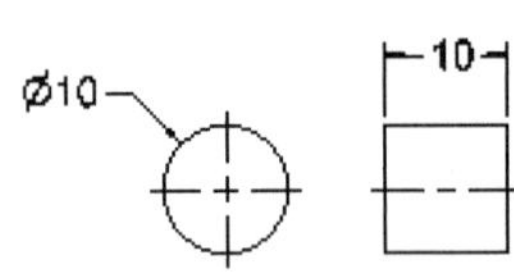

CENTER LINK AM312-3, SAE 1040, 5 mm THK

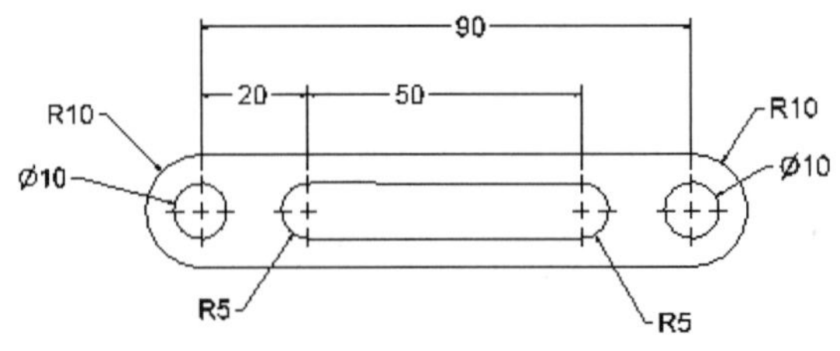

Ø10 x 15 PEG AM 312-6
SAE 1020

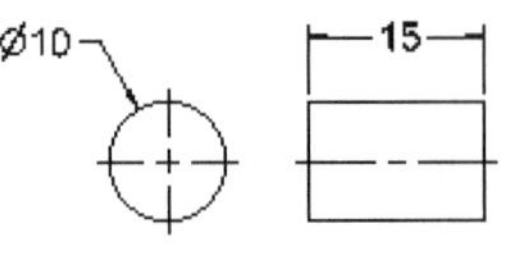

Figure P8-29

Project 8-30:

Draw the model shown in Figure P8-30, create a drawing layout with the appropriate views, and add the specified dimensions and tolerances.

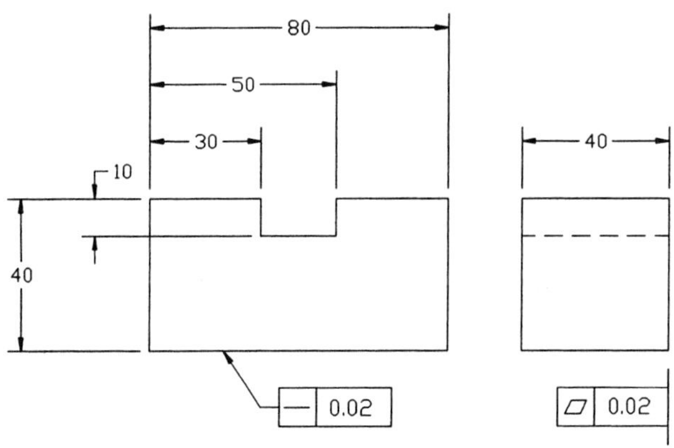

Figure P8-30

Project 8-31:

Redraw the shaft shown in Figure P8-31, create a drawing layout with the appropriate views, and add a feature dimension and tolerance of 36 ± 0.1 and a straightness tolerance of 0.07 about the centerline at MMC.

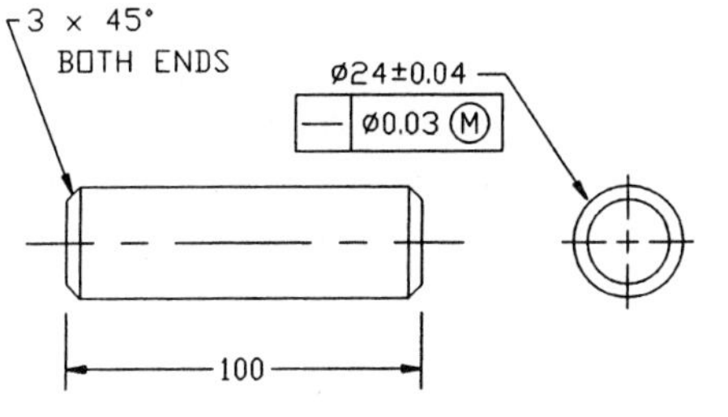

Figure P8-31

Project 8-32:

A. Given the shaft shown in Figure P8-32, what is the minimum hole diameter that will always accept the shaft?

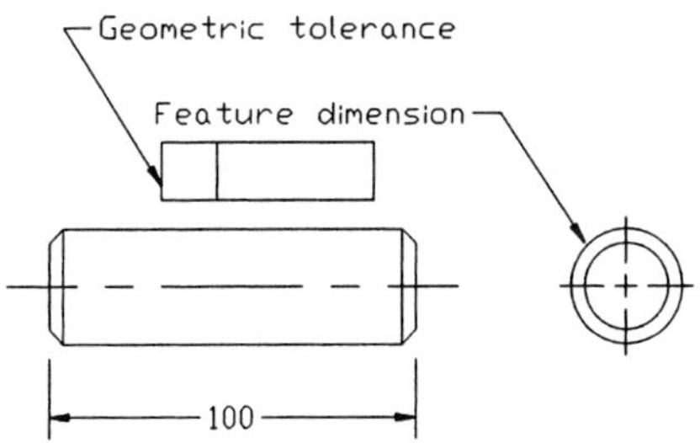

Figure P8-32

B. If the minimum clearance between the shaft and a hole is equal to 0.02, and the tolerance on the hole is to be 0.6, what are the maximum and minimum diameters for the hole?

Project 8-33:

A. Given the shaft shown in Figure P8-33, what is the minimum hole diameter that will always accept the shaft?
B. If the minimum clearance between the shaft and a hole is equal to .005, and the tolerance on the hole is to be .007, what are the maximum and minimum diameters for the hole?

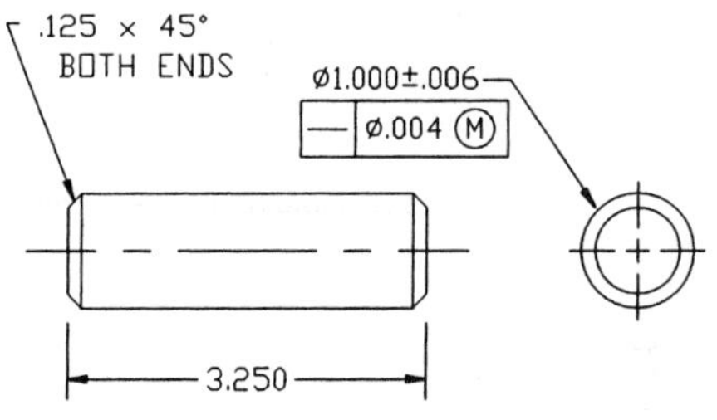

Figure P8-33

Project 8-34:

Draw a front and a right-side view of the object shown in Figure P8-34 and add the appropriate dimensions and tolerances based on the following information. Numbers located next to an edge line indicate the length of the edge.

A. Define surfaces A, B, and C as primary, secondary, and tertiary datums, respectively.
B. Assign a tolerance of ±0.5 to all linear dimensions.
C. Assign a feature tolerance of 12.07 − 12.00 to the protruding shaft.

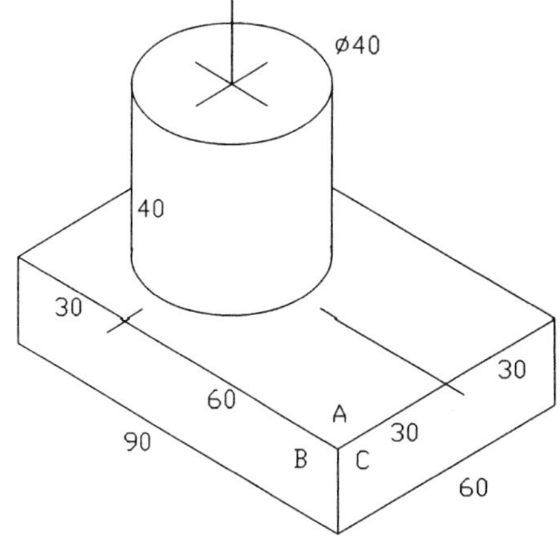

Figure P8-34

D. Assign a flatness tolerance of 0.01 to surface A.
E. Assign a straightness tolerance of 0.03 to the protruding shaft.
F. Assign a perpendicularity tolerance to the centerline of the protruding shaft of 0.02 at MMC relative to datum A.

Project 8-35:

Draw a front and a right-side view of the object shown in Figure P8-35 and add the following dimensions and tolerances.

A. Define the bottom surface as datum A.
B. Assign a perpendicularity tolerance of 0.4 to both sides of the slot relative to datum A.
C. Assign a perpendicularity tolerance of 0.2 to the centerline of the 30 diameter hole at MMC relative to datum A.
D. Assign a feature tolerance of ±0.8 to all three holes.
E. Assign a parallelism tolerance of 0.2 to the common centerline between the two 20 diameter holes relative to datum A.
F. Assign a tolerance of ±0.5 to all linear dimensions.

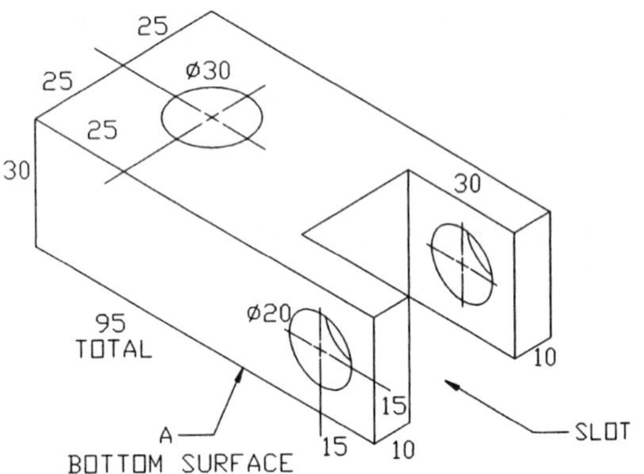

Figure P8-35

Project 8-36:

Draw a circular front and the appropriate right-side view of the object shown in Figure P8-36 and add the following dimensions and tolerances.

A. Assign datum A as indicated.
B. Assign the object's longitudinal axis as datum B.
C. Assign the object's centerline through the slot as datum C.
D. Assign a tolerance of ±0.5 to all linear tolerances.

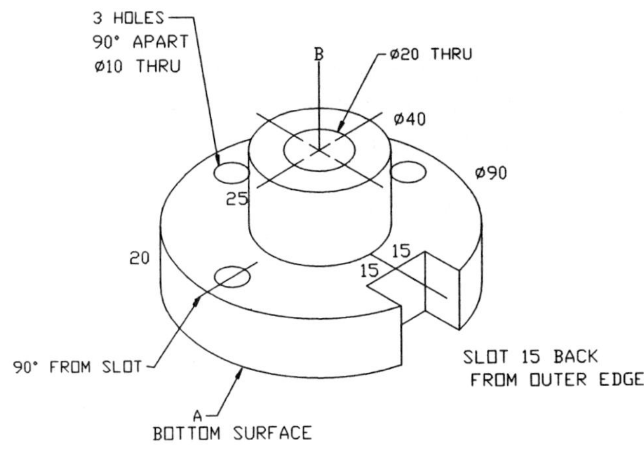

Figure P8-36

E. Assign a tolerance of ±0.5 to all circular features.
F. Assign a parallelism tolerance of 0.01 to both edges of the slot.
G. Assign a perpendicularity tolerance of 0.01 to the outside edge of the protruding shaft.

Project 8-37:

Given the two objects shown in Figure P8-37, draw a front and a side view of each. Assign a tolerance of ±0.5 to all linear dimensions. Assign a feature tolerance of ±0.4 to the shaft, and also assign a straightness tolerance of 0.2 to the shaft's centerline at MMC.

Tolerance the hole so that it will always accept the shaft with a minimum clearance of 0.1 and a feature tolerance of 0.2. Assign a perpendicularity tolerance of 0.05 to the centerline of the hole at MMC.

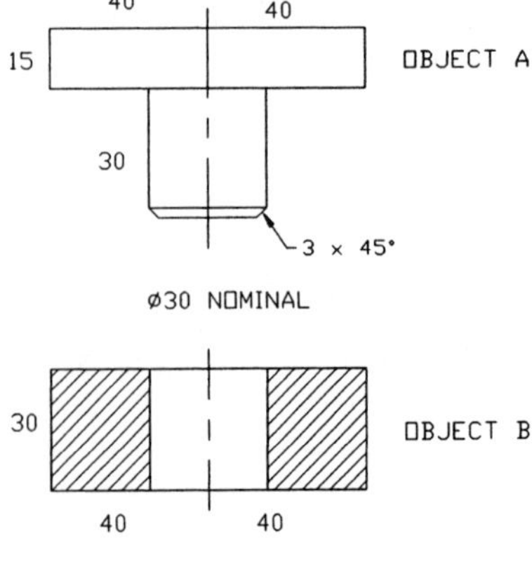

Figure P8-37

Project 8-38:

Given the two objects shown in Figure P8-38, draw a front and a side view of each. Assign a tolerance of ±0.005 to all linear dimensions. Assign a feature tolerance of ±0.004 to the shaft, and also assign a straightness tolerance of 0.002 to the shaft's centerline at MMC.

Tolerance the hole so that it will always accept the shaft with a minimum clearance of 0.001 and a feature tolerance of 0.002.

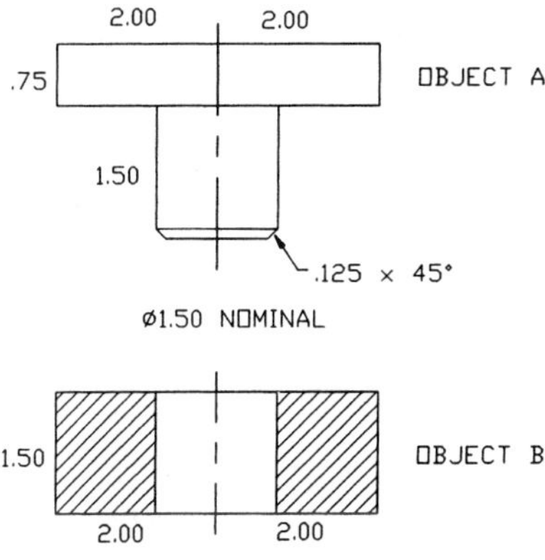

Figure P8-38

Project 8-39:

Draw a model of the object shown in Figure P8-39, then create a drawing layout including the specified dimensions. Add the following tolerances and specifications to the drawing.

A. Surface 1 is datum A.
B. Surface 2 is datum B and is perpendicular to datum A within 0.1 mm.

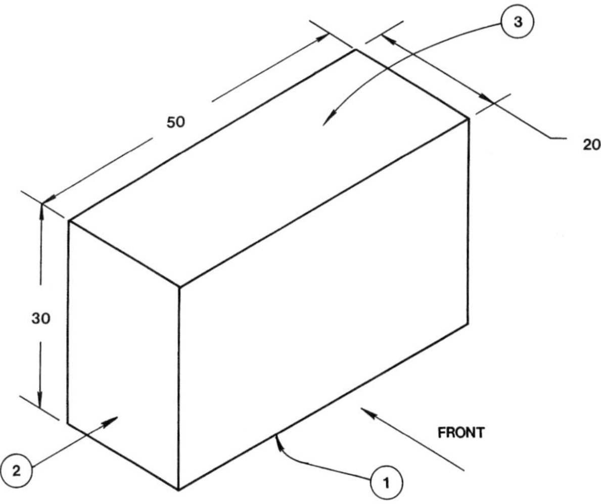

Figure P8-39

C. Surface 3 is datum C and is parallel to datum A within 0.3 mm.
D. Locate a 16-mm diameter hole in the center of the front surface that goes completely through the object. Use positional tolerances to locate the hole. Assign a positional tolerance of 0.02 at MMC perpendicular to datum A.

Project 8-40:

Draw a model of the object shown in Figure P8-40, then create a drawing layout including the specified dimensions. Add the following tolerances and specifications to the drawing.

A. Surface 1 is datum A.
B. Surface 2 is datum B and is perpendicular to datum A within .003 in.
C. Surface 3 is parallel to datum A within .005 in.
D. The cylinder's longitudinal centerline is to be straight within .001 in. at MMC.
E. Surface 2 is to have circular accuracy within .002 in.

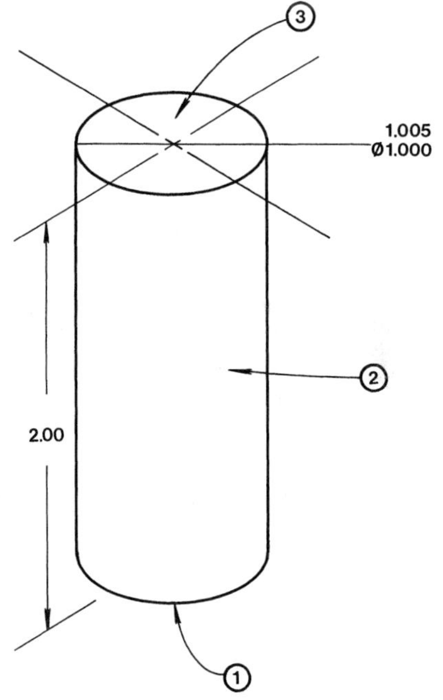

Figure P8-40

Project 8-41:

Draw a model of the object shown in Figure P8-41, then create a drawing layout including the specified dimensions. Add the following tolerances and specifications to the drawing.

A. Surface 1 is datum A.
B. Surface 4 is datum B and is perpendicular to datum A within 0.08 mm.

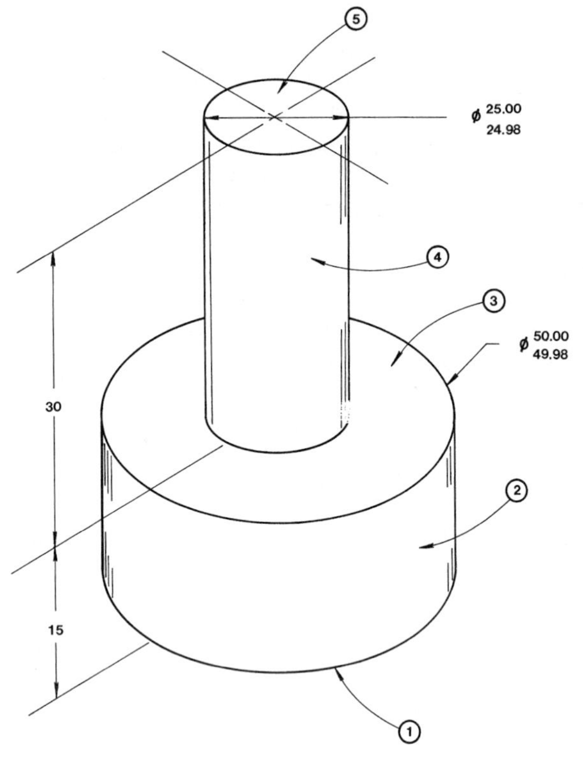

Figure P8-41

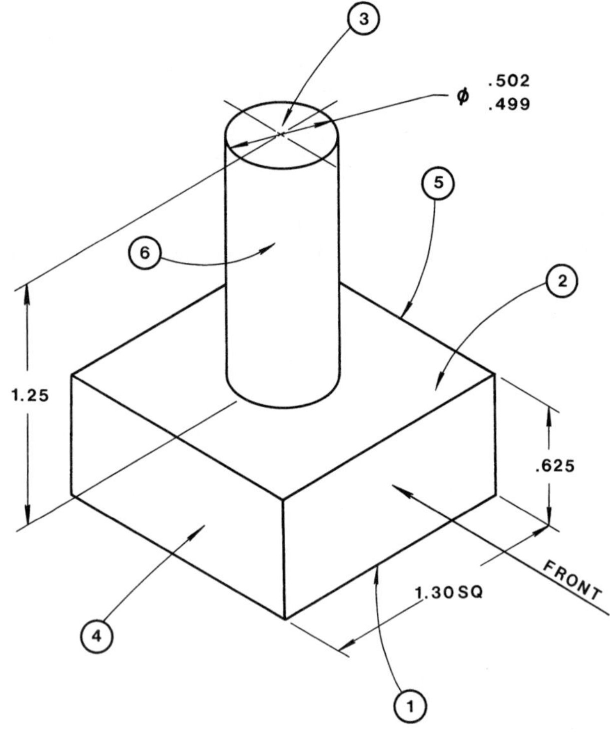

Figure P8-42

C. Surface 3 is flat within 0.03 mm.
D. Surface 5 is parallel to datum A within 0.01 mm.
E. Surface 2 has a runout tolerance of 0.2 mm relative to surface 4.
F. Surface 1 is flat within 0.02 mm.
G. The longitudinal centerline is to be straight within 0.02 at MMC and perpendicular to datum A.

Project 8-42:

Draw a model of the object shown in Figure P8-42, then create a drawing layout including the specified dimensions. Add the following tolerances and specifications to the drawing.

A. Surface 2 is datum A.
B. Surface 6 is perpendicular to datum A with .000 allowable variance at MMC but with a .002 in. MAX variance limit beyond MMC.
C. Surface 1 is parallel to datum A within .005.
D. Surface 4 is perpendicular to datum A within .004 in.

Project 8-43:

Draw a model of the object shown in Figure P8-43, then create a drawing layout including the specified dimensions. Add the following tolerances and specifications to the drawing.

A. Surface 1 is datum A.
B. Surface 2 is datum B.

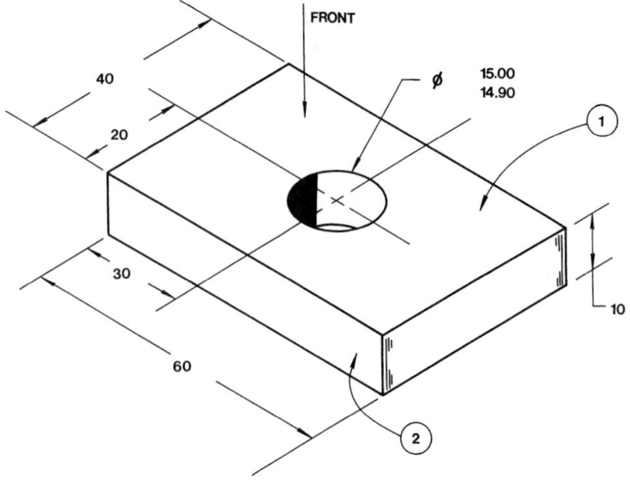

Figure P8-43

C. The hole is located using a true position tolerance value of 0.13 mm at MMC. The true position tolerance is referenced to datums A and B.
D. Surface 1 is to be straight within 0.02 mm.
E. The bottom surface is to be parallel to datum A within 0.03 mm.

Project 8-44:

Draw a model of the object shown in Figure P8-44, then create a drawing layout including the specified dimensions. Add the following tolerances and specifications to the drawing.

A. Surface 1 is datum A.
B. Surface 2 is datum B.
C. Surface 3 is perpendicular to surface 2 within 0.02 mm.
D. The four holes are to be located using a positional tolerance of 0.07 mm at MMC referenced to datums A and B.
E. The centerlines of the holes are to be straight within 0.01 mm at MMC.

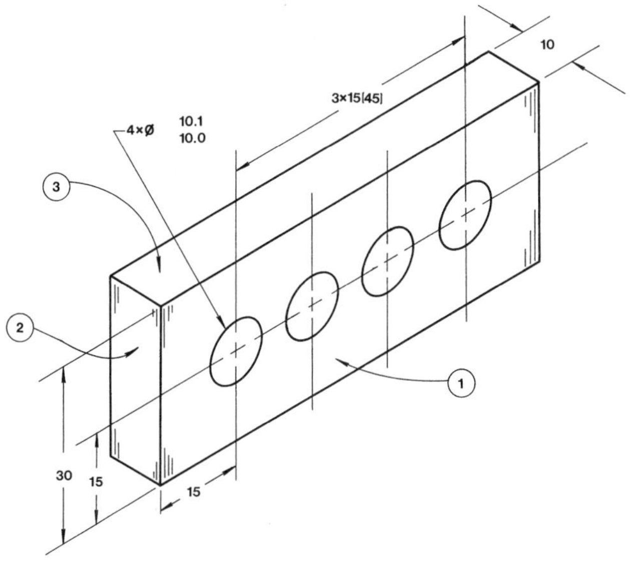

Figure P8-44

Project 8-45:

Draw a model of the object shown in Figure P8-45, then create a drawing layout including the specified dimensions. Add the following tolerances and specifications to the drawing.

A. Surface 1 has a dimension of .378−.375 in. and is datum A. The surface has a dual primary runout with datum B to within .005 in. The runout is total.
B. Surface 2 has a dimension of 1.505−1.495 in. Its runout relative to the dual primary datums A and B is .008 in. The runout is total.
C. Surface 3 has a dimension of 1.000 ± .005 and has no geometric tolerance.
D. Surface 4 has no circular dimension but has a total runout tolerance of .006 in. relative to the dual datums A and B.
E. Surface 5 has a dimension of .500−.495 in. and is datum B. It has a dual primary runout with datum A within .005 in. The runout is total.

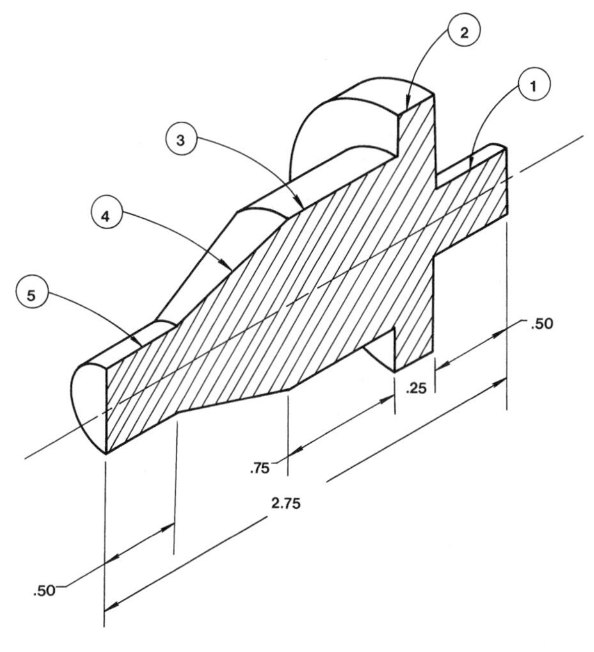

Figure P8-45

Project 8-46:

Draw a model of the object shown in Figure P8-46, then create a drawing layout including the specified dimensions. Add the following tolerances and specifications to the drawing.

A. Hole 1 is datum A.
B. Hole 2 is to have its circular centerline parallel to datum A within 0.2 mm at MMC when datum A is at MMC.
C. Assign a positional tolerance of 0.01 to each hole's centerline at MMC.

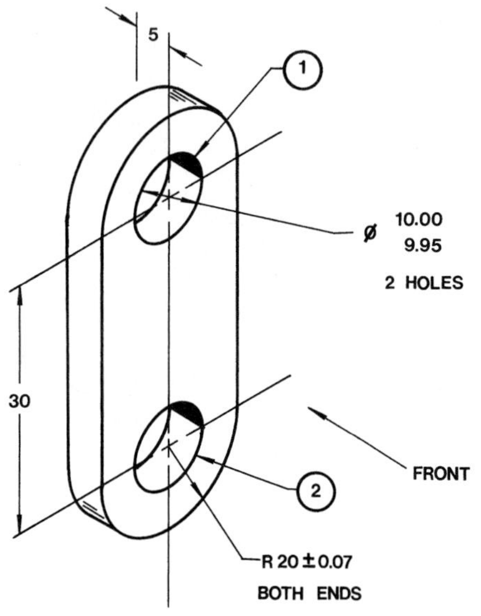

Figure P8-46

Project 8-47:

Draw a model of the object shown in Figure P8-47, then create a drawing layout including the specified dimensions. Add the following tolerances and specifications to the drawing.

A. Surface 1 is datum A.
B. Surface 2 is datum B.
C. The six holes have a diameter range of .502–.499 in. and are to be located using positional tolerances so that their centerlines are within .005 in. at MMC relative to datums A and B.
D. The back surface is to be parallel to datum A within .002 in.

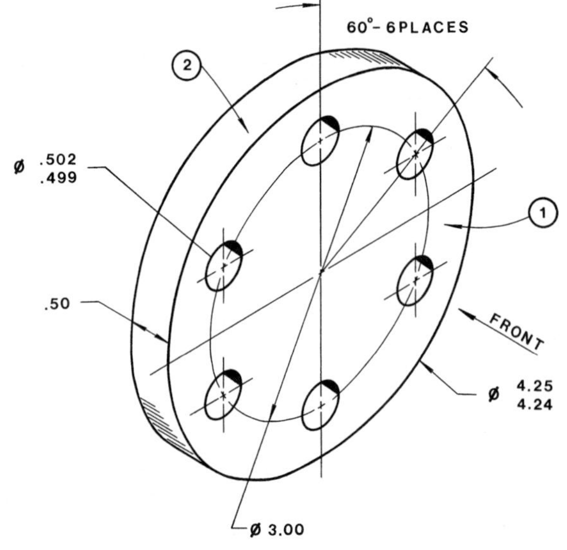

Figure P8-47

Project 8-48:

Draw a model of the object shown in Figure P8-48, then create a drawing layout including the specified dimensions. Add the following tolerances and specifications to the drawing.

A. Surface 1 is datum A.
B. Hole 2 is datum B.
C. The eight holes labeled 3 have diameters of 8.4−8.3 mm with a positional tolerance of 0.15 mm at MMC relative to datums A and B. Also, the eight holes are to be counterbored to a diameter of 14.6−14.4 mm and to a depth of 5.0 mm.
D. The large center hole is to have a straightness tolerance of 0.2 at MMC about its centerline.

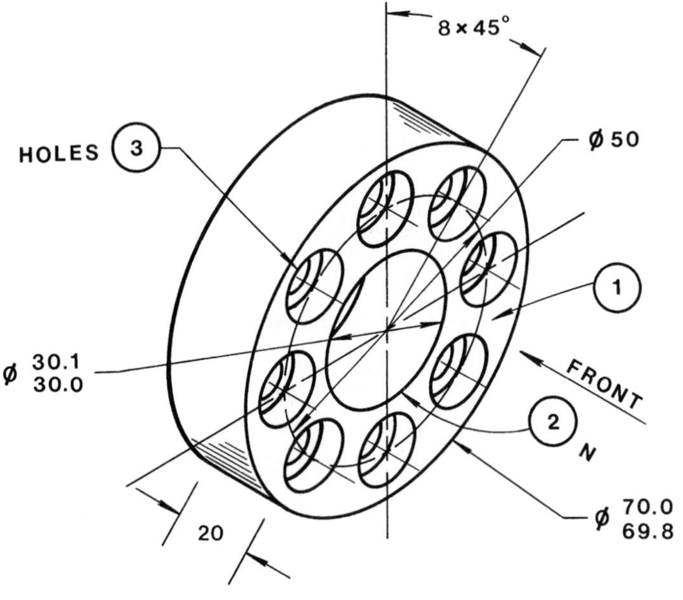

Figure P8-48

Project 8-49:

Draw a model of the object shown in Figure P8-49, then create a drawing layout including the specified dimensions. Add the following tolerances and specifications to the drawing.

A. Surface 1 is datum A.
B. Surface 2 is datum B.
C. Surface 3 is datum C.
D. The four holes labeled 4 have a dimension and tolerance of 8 + 0.3, −0 mm. The holes are to be located using a positional tolerance of 0.05 mm at MMC relative to datums A, B, and C .

E. The six holes labeled 5 have a dimension and tolerance of 6 +0.2, −0 mm. The holes are to be located using a positional tolerance of 0.01 mm at MMC relative to datums A, B, and C .

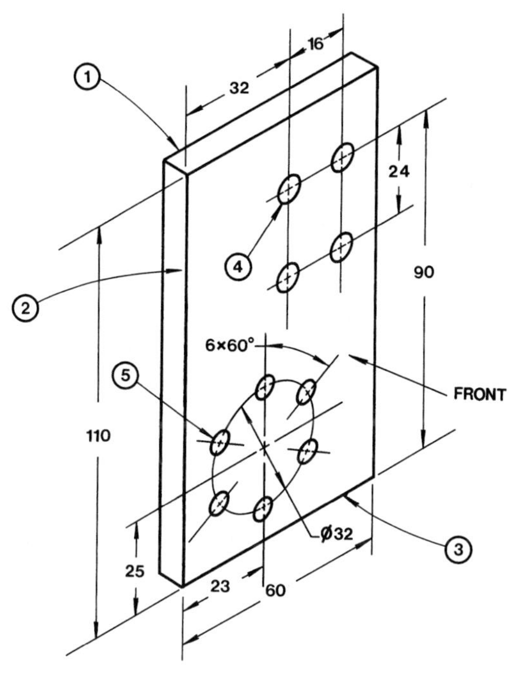

Figure P8-49

Project 8-50:

The objects in Figure P8-50A and P8-50B labeled A and B are to be toleranced using four different tolerances as shown. Redraw the charts shown in Figure P8-50 and list the appropriate allowable tolerance for "as measured" increments of 0.1 mm or .001 in. Also include the appropriate geometric tolerance drawing called out above each chart.

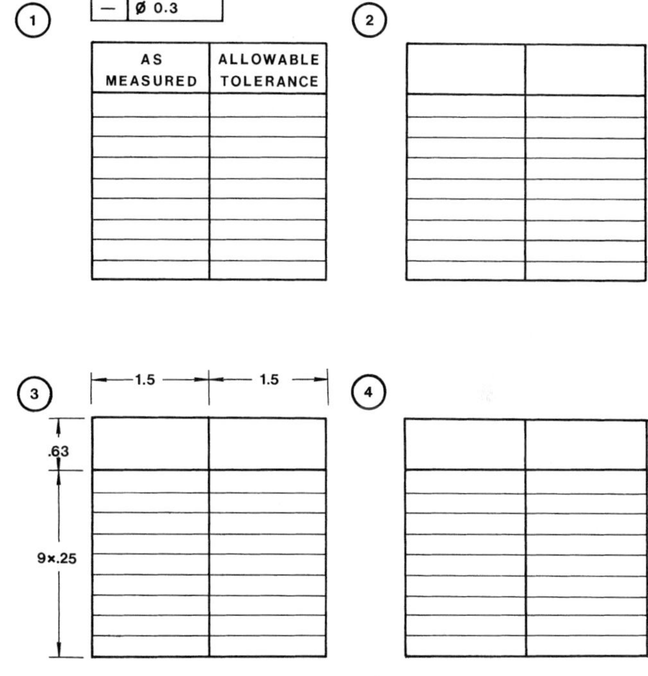

Figure P8-50A

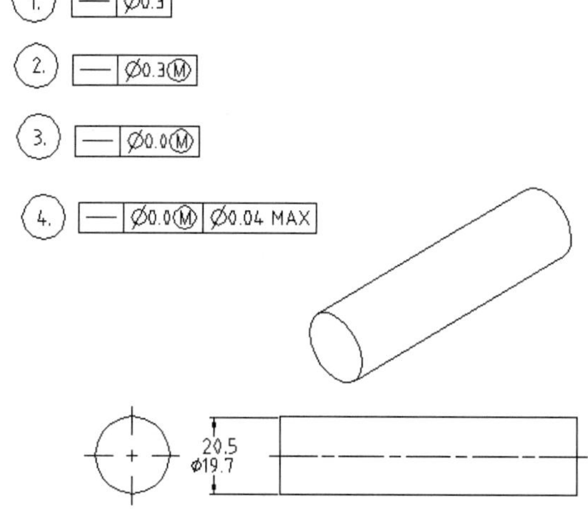

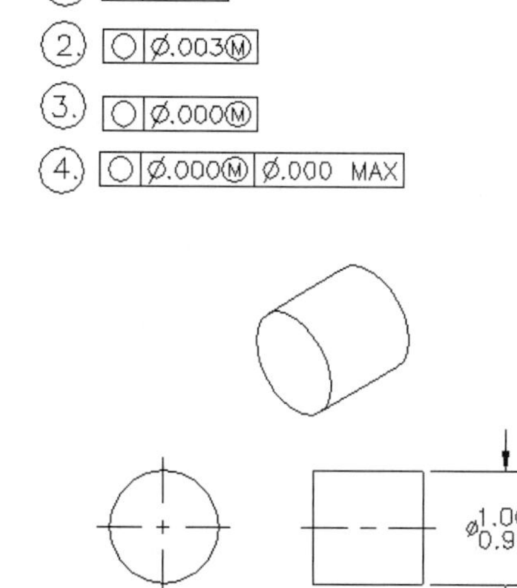

Figure P8-50B (A)(MILLIMETERS) (B) INCHES

Project 8-51:

Assume that there are two copies of the part in Figure P8-51 and that these parts are to be joined together using four fasteners in the floating condition. Draw front and top views of the object, including dimensions and tolerances. Add the following tolerances and specifications to the drawing, then draw front and top views of a shaft that can be used to join the two objects. The shaft should be able to fit into any of the four holes.

A. Surface 1 is datum A .
B. Surface 2 is datum B .
C. Surface 3 is perpendicular to surface 2 within 0.02 mm.
D. Specify the positional tolerance for the four holes applied at MMC.
E. The centerlines of the holes are to be straight within 0.01 mm at MMC.
F. The clearance between the shafts and the holes is to be 0.05 minimum and 0.10 maximum.

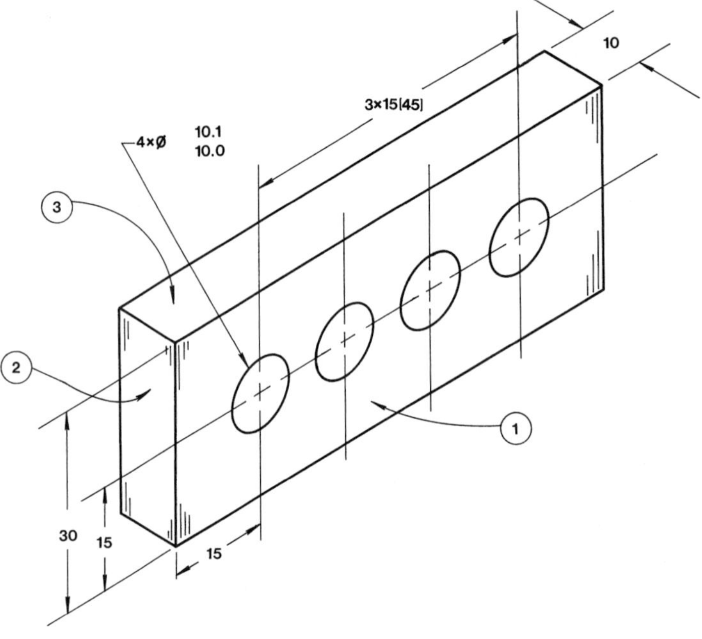

Figure P8-51 MILLIMETERS

Project 8-52:

Dimension and tolerance parts 1 and 2 of Figure P8-52 so that part 1 always fits into part 2 with a minimum clearance of .005 in. The tolerance for part 1's outer matching surface is .006 in.

Project 8-53:

Dimension and tolerance parts 1 and 2 of Figure P8-53 so that part 1 always fits into part 2 with a minimum clearance of 0.03 mm. The tolerance for part 1's diameter is 0.05 mm. Take into account the fact that the interface is long relative to the diameters.

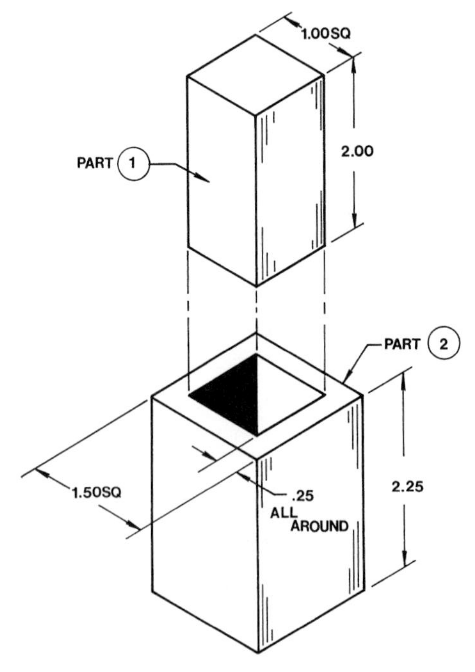

Figure P8-52 INCHES

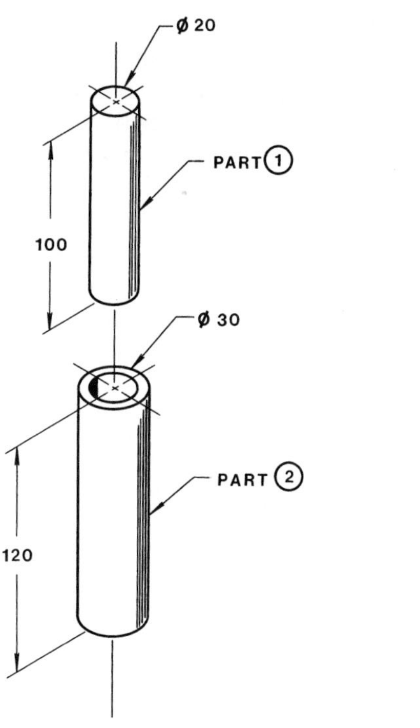

Figure P8-53 MILLIMETERS

Project 8-54:

Assume that there are two copies of the part in Figure P8-54 and that these parts are to be joined together using six fasteners in the floating condition. Draw front and top views of the object, including dimensions and tolerances. Add the following tolerances and specifications to the drawing, then draw front and top views of a shaft that can be used to join the two objects. The shaft should be able to fit into any of the six holes.

A. Surface 1 is datum A .
B. Surface 2 is round within .003.
C. Specify the positional tolerance for the six holes applied at MMC.
D. The clearance between the shafts and the holes is to be .001 minimum and .003 maximum.

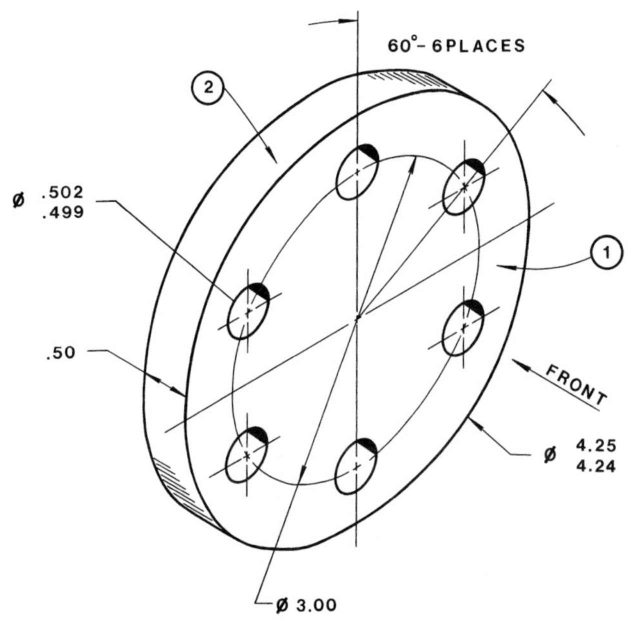

Figure P8-54 INCHES

Project 8-55:

The assembly shown in Figure P8-55 is made from parts defined in Chapter 5.

A. Draw an exploded assembly drawing.
B. Draw a BOM.
C. Use the drawing layout mode and draw orthographic views of each part. Include dimensions and geometric tolerances. The pegs should have a minimum clearance of 0.02. Select appropriate tolerances

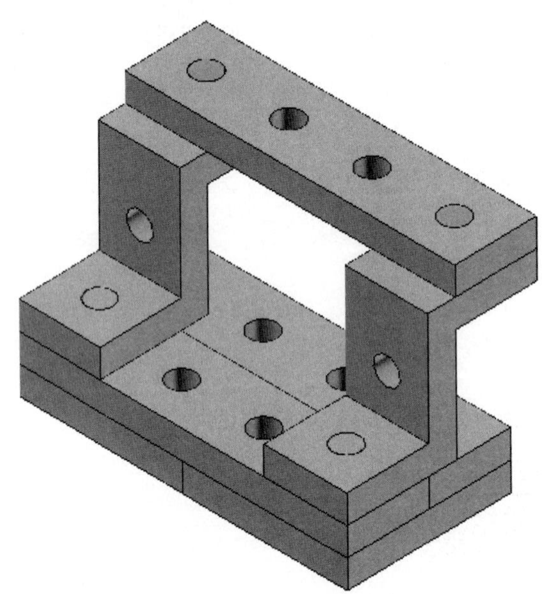

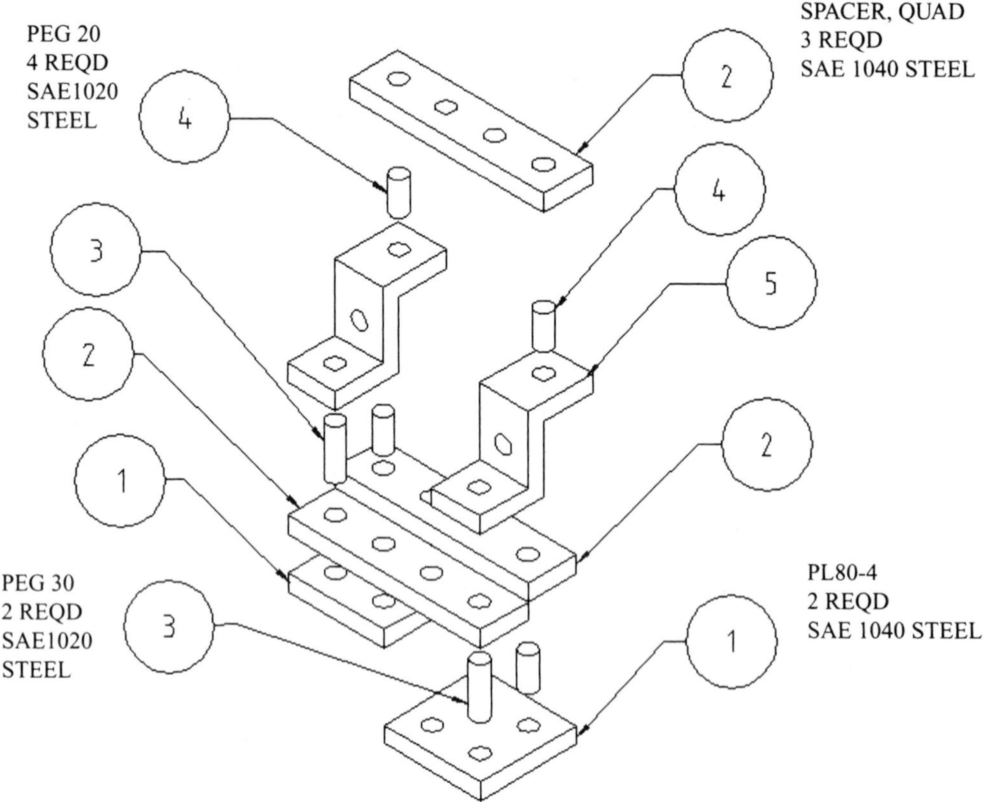

Figure P8-55 MILLIMETERS

CHAPTER 9

Gears, Pulleys, and Chains

Objectives

- To learn the concept of power transmission
- To learn the fundamentals of gears
- To learn the fundamentals of pulleys
- To learn the fundamentals of chains
- To learn how to draw and animate gears, pulleys, and chains

9-1 INTRODUCTION

Gears, pulleys, and chains are part of a broader category called ***power transmission.*** Power comes from a source such as an engine, motor, or windmill. The power is then transferred to a mechanism that performs some function. For example an automobile engine transmits power from the engine to the wheels via a gear box. Bicyclists transmit the power of their legs to wheels via a chain and sprocket.

This section explains how gears, pulleys, and chains are drawn using SolidWorks and how the finished drawings can be animated. There is also a discussion of how speed is transferred and changed using gears, pulleys, and chains. Figure 9-1 shows a spur gear drawn using SolidWorks.

9-2 GEAR TERMINOLOGY

Pitch Diameter (*D*): The diameter used to define the spacing of gears. Ideally, gears are exactly tangent to each other along their pitch diameters.

Diametral Pitch (*P*): The number of teeth per inch. Meshing gears must have the same diametral pitch. Manufacturers' gear charts list gears with the same diametral pitch.

Module (*M*): The pitch diameter divided by the number of teeth. The metric equivalent of diametral pitch.

Number of Teeth (*N*): The number of teeth of a gear.

Circular Pitch (*CP*): The circular distance from a fixed point on one tooth to the same position on the next tooth as measured along the pitch circle. The circumference of the pitch circle divided by the number of teeth.

Preferred Pitches: The standard sizes available from gear manufacturers. Whenever possible, use preferred gear sizes.

Center Distance (*CD*): The distance between the center points of two meshing gears.

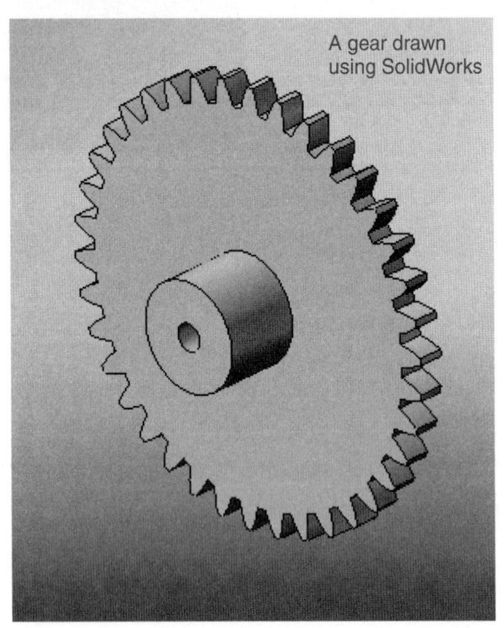

Figure 9-1

Backlash: The difference between a tooth width and the engaging space on a meshing gear.
Addendum (*a*): The height of a tooth above the pitch diameter.
Dedendum (*d*): The depth of a tooth below the pitch diameter.
Whole Depth: The total depth of a tooth. The addendum plus the dedendum.
Working Depth: The depth of engagement of one gear into another. Equal to the sum of the two gears' addendeums.
Circular Thickness: The distance across a tooth as measured along the pitch circle.
Face Width (*F*): The distance from front to back along a tooth as measured perpendicular to the pitch circle.
Outside Diameter: The largest diameter of the gear. Equal to the pitch diameter plus the addendum.
Root Diameter: The diameter of the base of the teeth. The pitch diameter minus the dedendum.
Clearance: The distance between the addendum of the meshing gear and the dedendum of the mating gear.
Pressure Angle: The angle between the line of action and a line tangent to the pitch circle. Most gears have pressure angles of either 14.5° or 20°

See Figure 9-2.

9-3 GEAR FORMULAS

Figure 9-3 shows a chart of formulas commonly associated with gears. The formulas are for spur gears.

9-4 CREATING GEARS USING SOLIDWORKS

In this section we will create two gears and then create an assembly that includes a support plate and two posts to hold the gears in place. The specifications for the two gears are as follows. See Figure 9-4.

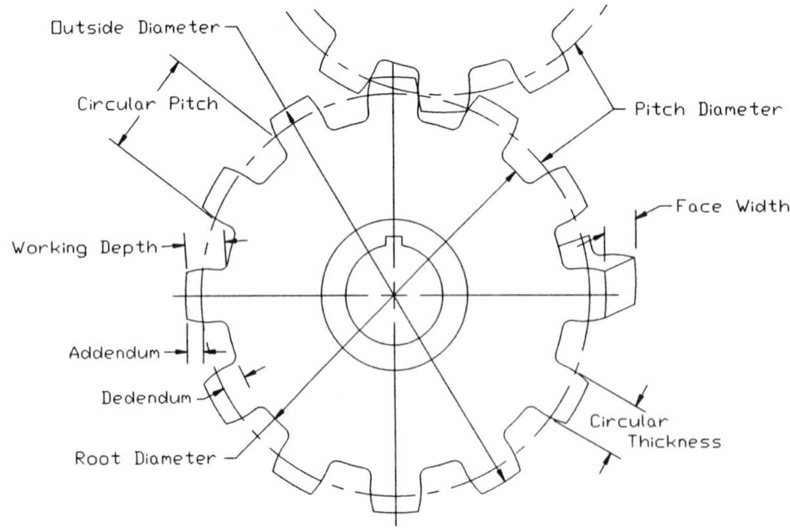

Figure 9-2

Diametral pitch (P)	$P = \frac{N}{D}$
Pitch diameter (D)	$D = \frac{N}{P}$
Number of teeth (N)	$N = DP$
Addendum (a)	$a = \frac{1}{P}$
Metric	
Module (M)	$M = \frac{D}{N}$

Figure 9-3

Gear 1: Diametral pitch = 24
- Number of teeth = 30
- Face thickness = 0.50
- Bore = Ø0.50
- Hub Ø = 1.00
- Hub height = 0.50
- Pressure angle = 20

Gear 2: Diametral pitch = 24
- Number of teeth = 60
- Face thickness = 0.50
- Bore = Ø0.50
- Hub Ø = 1.00
- Hub height = 0.50
- Pressure angle = 20

> **TIP**
>
> Gears must have the same diametral pitch to mesh properly.

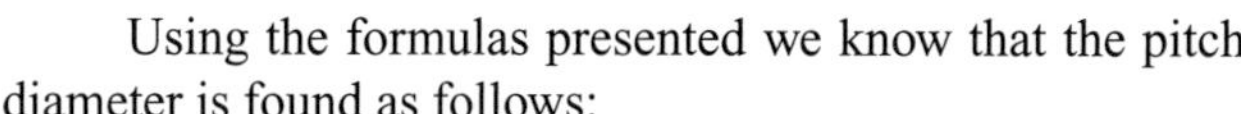

Using the formulas presented we know that the pitch diameter is found as follows:

$$D = N/P$$

So

$$D1 = 30/24 = 1.25 \text{ in.}$$
$$D2 = 60/24 = 2.50 \text{ in.}$$

The center distance between gears is found from the relation $(D1 + D2)/2$:

$$\frac{1.25 + 2.50}{2} = 1.875 \text{ in.}$$

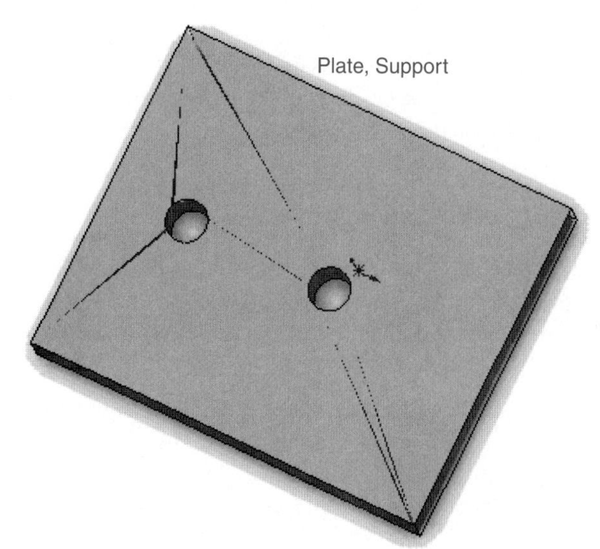

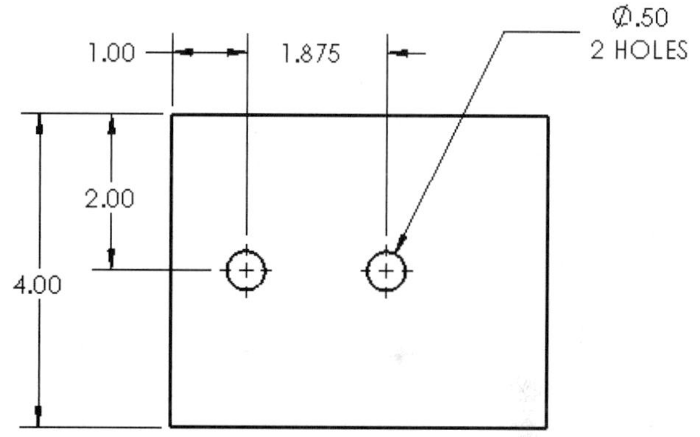

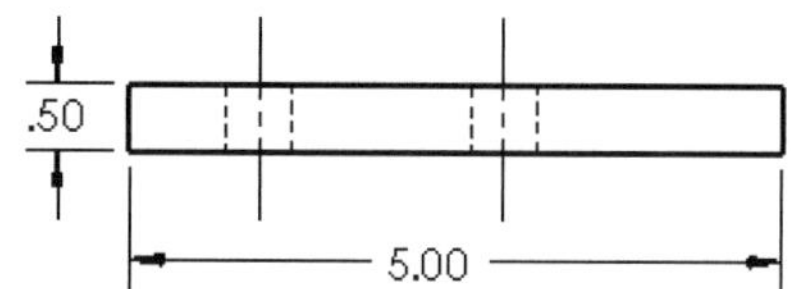

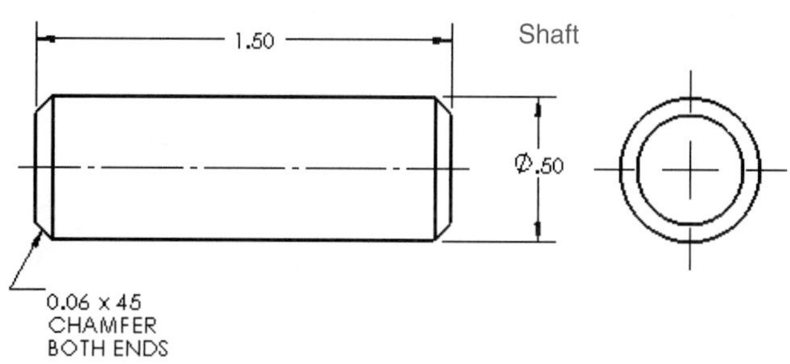

Figure 9-4

This center distance data was used to create the Plate, Support shown in Figure 9-4.

The bore for the gears is defined as 0.50, so shafts that hold the gears will be Ø0.50, and the holes in the Plate, Support will also be 0.50.

> ***Note:***
> Tolerances for gears, shafts, and support plates will be discussed in Chapter 10, Bearings and Fit Tolerances.

The shafts will have a nominal diameter of Ø0.50 and a length of 1.50. The length was derived by allowing 0.50 for the gear thickness, 0.50 for the Plate, Support thickness, and 0.50 clearance between the gear and the plate. See Figure 9-4. In this example 0.06 × 45° chamfers were added to both ends of the shafts.

To Create a Gear Assembly

1. Draw the Plate, Support and Shaft shown in Figure 9-4.
2. Start a new **Assembly** drawing.
3. Assemble the plate and shafts as shown.

See Figure 9-5. The top surface of the shafts is offset 1.00 from the surface of the plate.

Create the gears using the **Design Library.** See Figure 9-6.

4. Click the **Design Library** tool, click **Toolbox, ANSI Inch, Power Transmission,** and **Gears.**
5. Click the **Spur Gear** tool and drag the icon into the drawing area.

The **Spur Gear Properties Manager** will appear. See Figure 9-7.

6. Enter the gear values as presented earlier for Gears 1 and 2 and create the two gears.

See Figure 9-8.

7. Use the **Mate** tool and assemble the gears onto the shafts so that they mesh. First, use the **Mate/Concentric** tool to align the gears' bores with the shafts, then use the **Mate/Parallel** tool to align the top surface of the shafts with the top surfaces of the gears.

See Figure 9-9.

8. Zoom in on the gear teeth and align them so they mesh.

> **TIP**
> Gears can meshed by rotating one of the gears using the cursor.

9. Click the **Mate** tool.
10. Click **Mechanical Mates.**
11. Select the **Gear** option.

See Figure 9-10.

12. Define the gear mate by clicking the inside bore of the two gears.

See Figure 9-11.

13. Define the ratio between the gears.

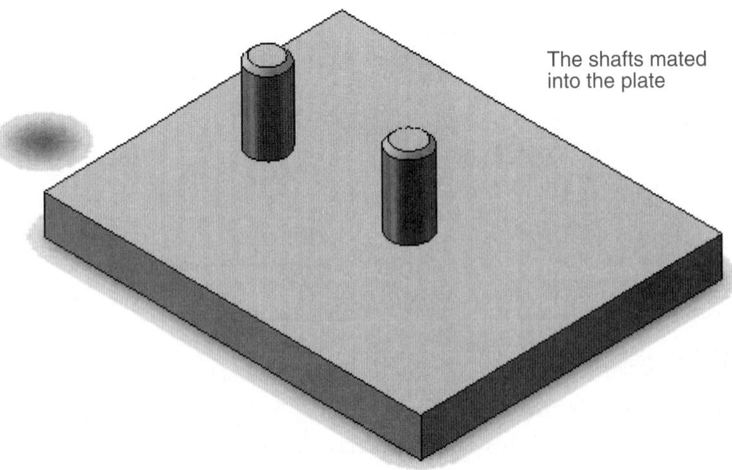

Figure 9-5

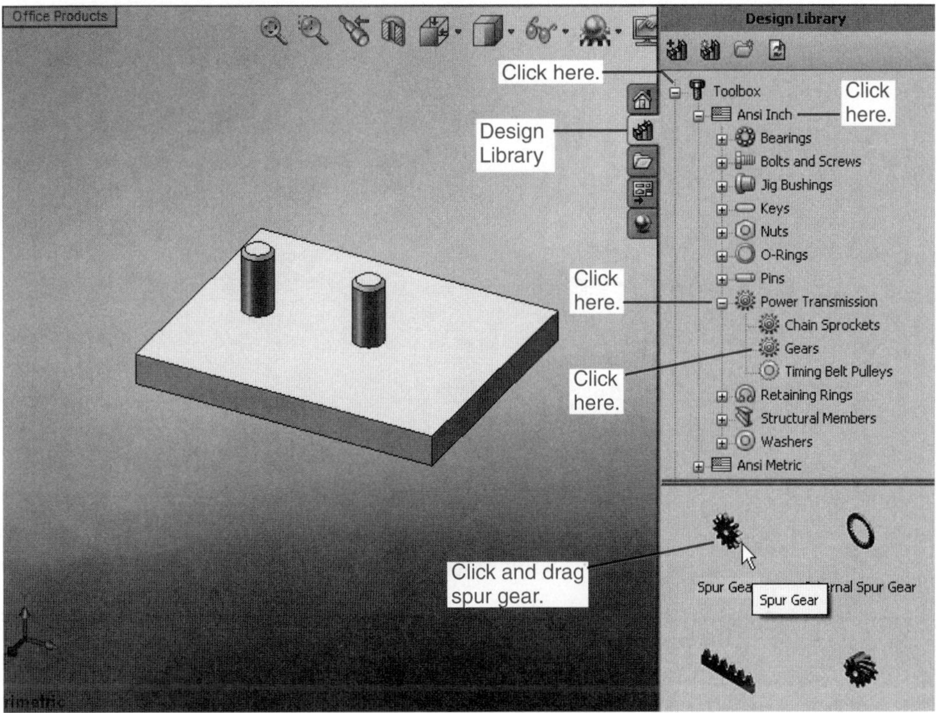

Figure 9-6

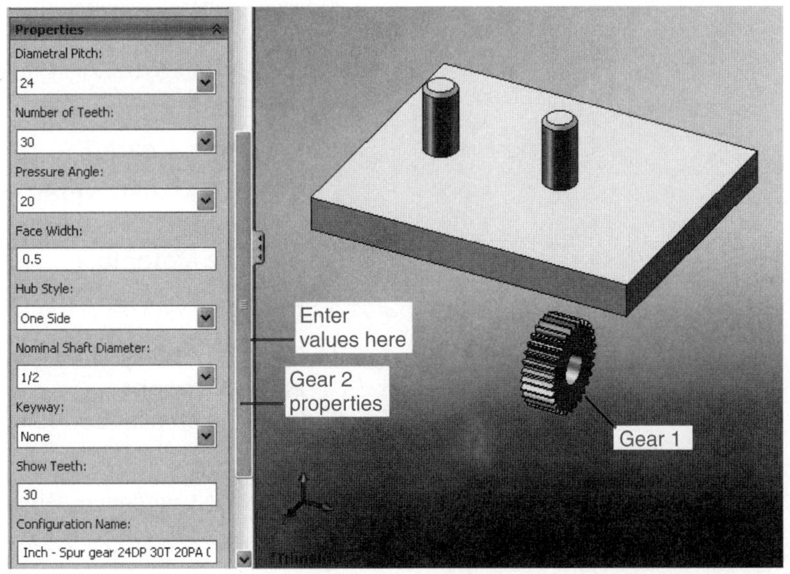

Figure 9-7

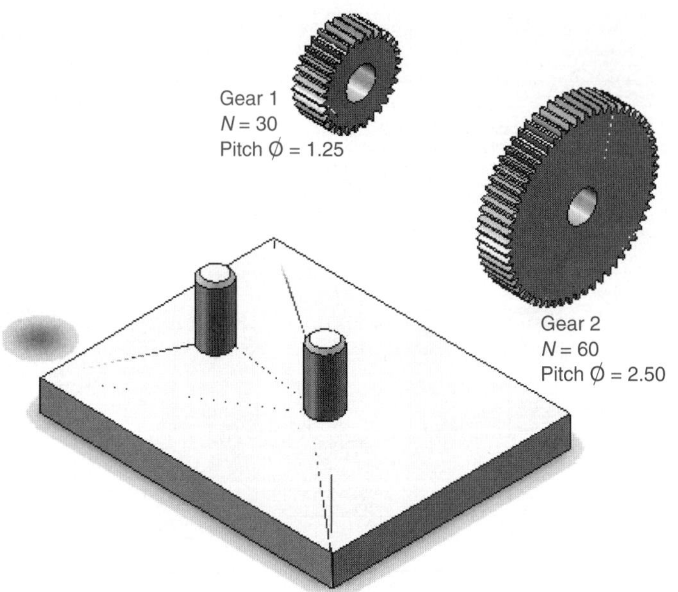

Figure 9-8

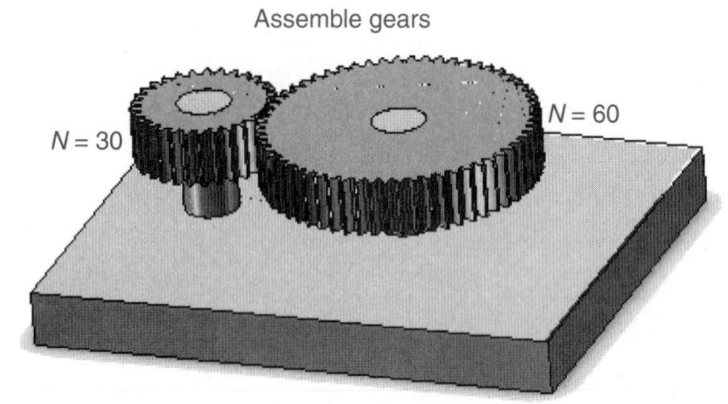

Figure 9-9

See Figure 9-12. In this example the ratio between the two gears is 2:1; that is, the smaller 30-tooth gear goes around twice for every revolution of the 60-tooth larger gear.

14. Click the OK check mark.
15. Locate the cursor on the smaller gear and rotate the gears.

TIP

If the gears were not aligned, step 8, an error message will appear stating that the gears interfere with each other. The gears will turn relative to each other even if they interfere, but it is better to go back and align the gears.

To Animate the Gears

1. Click the **Motion Study** tab at the bottom of the screen.
2. Click the **Motor** tool.

See Figure 9-13.

3. Click the **Rotary Motor** option in the **Motor Properties Manager.**
4. Click the smaller 30-tooth gear.

A red arrow will appear on the gear, and the gear will be identified in the **Component/Direction** box. See Figure 9-14.

5. Click the OK check mark.

The gears will animate. See Figure 9-15. The time for the animation can be increased by dragging the upper right diamond to the right as shown in Figure 9-16.

Figure 9-10

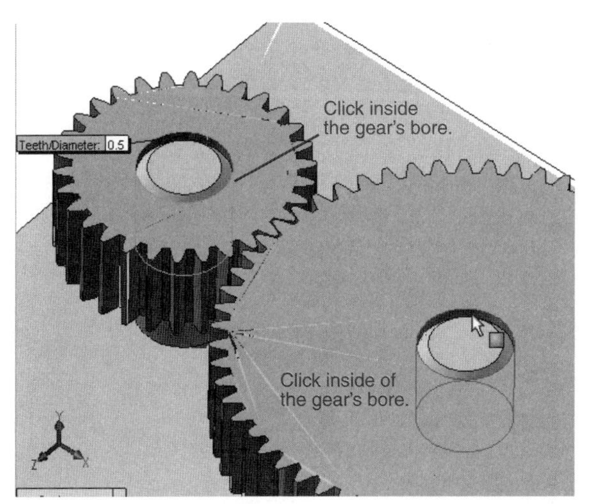

Figure 9-11

9-5 GEAR RATIOS

Gear ratios are determined by the number of teeth of each gear. In the previous example a gear with 30 teeth was meshed with a gear that had 60 teeth. Their gear ratio is 2:1, that is, the smaller gear turns twice for every one revolution of the larger gear. Figure 9-17 shows a group of four gears. A grouping of gears is called a ***gear train.*** The gear train shown contains two gears with 30 teeth and two gears with 90 teeth. One the 30-tooth gears is mounted on the same shaft as one of the 90-tooth gears. The gear ratio for the gear train is found as follows:

$$\left(\frac{3}{1}\right)\left(\frac{3}{1}\right) = \frac{9}{1}$$

Thus, if the leftmost 30-tooth gear is turning at 1750 RPM, the rightmost 90-tooth gear turns at

$$\frac{1750}{9} = 199.4 \text{ RPM}$$

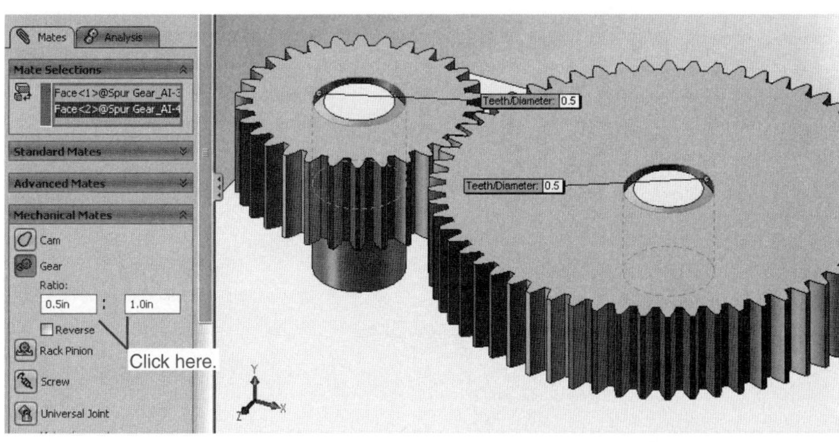

Figure 9-12

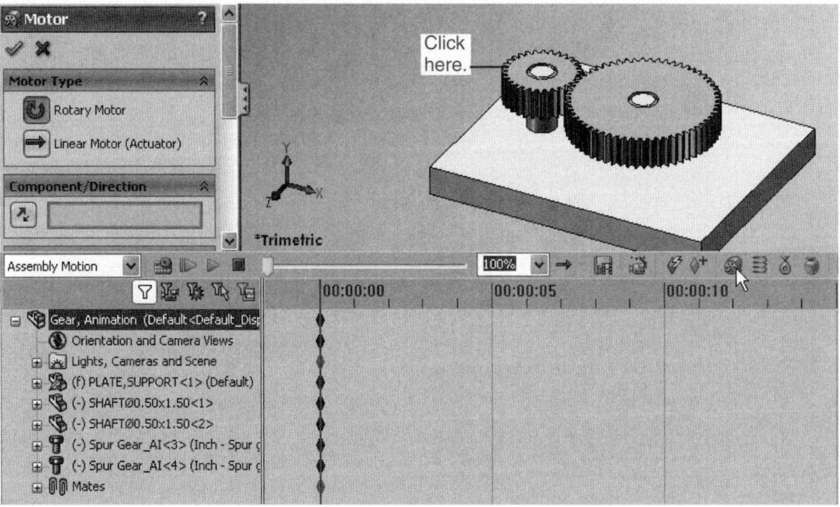

Figure 9-13

9-6 POWER TRANSMISSION—SHAFT TO GEAR

When a gear is mounted on a shaft there must be a way to transfer the power from the shaft to the gear and from the gear to the shaft. Three common ways to achieve this transfer are to use set screws, keys, and splines. This section shows how to add set screws and keyways to gears. Splines will not be included.

9-7 SET SCREWS AND GEAR HUBS

This section shows how add a hub to a gear and then how to create a threaded hole in the hub that will accept a set screw.

1. Start a new **Part** drawing and create the **Ø0.50 × 2.25** shaft shown in Figure 9-18. Save the part.
2. Start a new **Assembly** drawing.
3. Use the **Insert Component** tool and add the Ø0.50 × 2.25 shaft to the drawing.
4. Access the **Design Library** and click **Toolbox, Ansi Inch, Power Transmission,** and **Gears.**
5. Select the **Spur Gear** option and click and drag a gear onto the drawing screen.

   See Figure 9-19.

6. Set the gear's properties as follows. See Figure 9-20.

   Diametral pitch: **24**
   Number of teeth: **36**
   Pressure angle: **14.5**
   Face width: **0.5**
   Hub style: **One Side**
   Hub Diameter: **1.00**
   Overall length: **1.00**

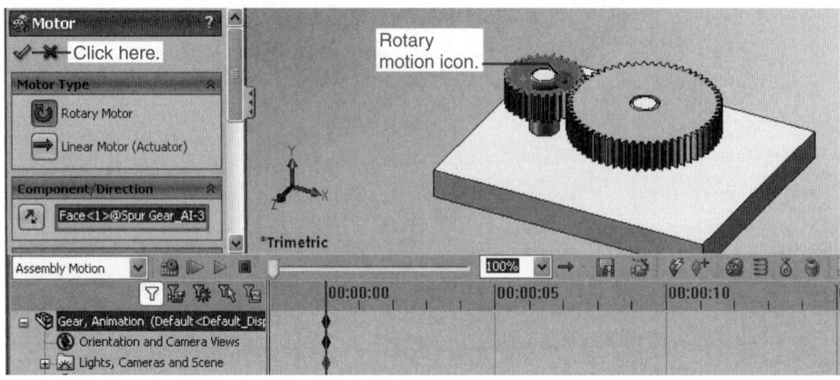

Figure 9-14

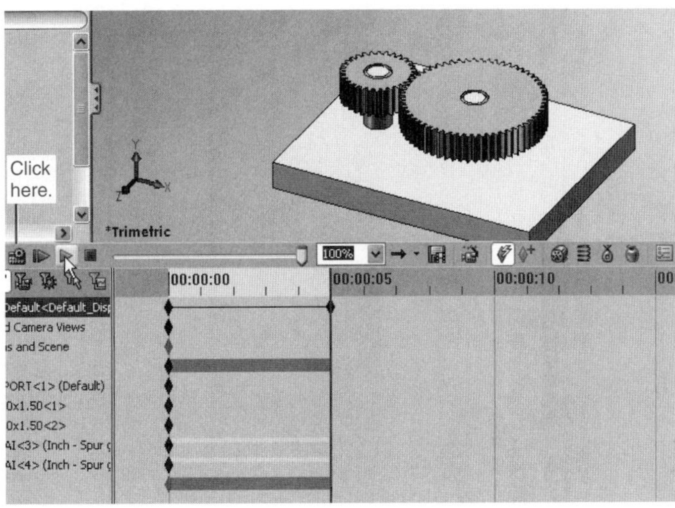

Figure 9-15

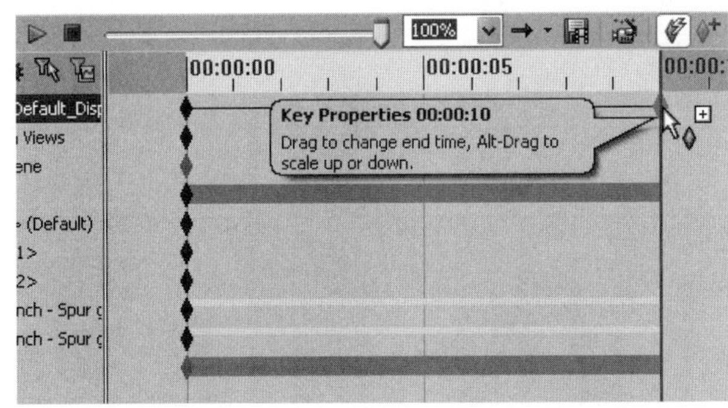

Figure 9-16

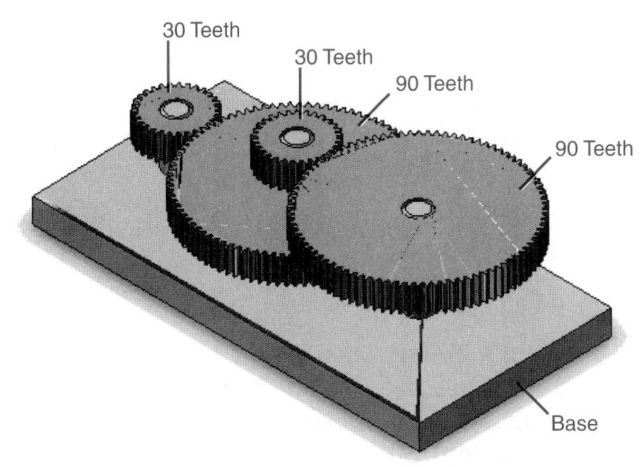

Figure 9-17

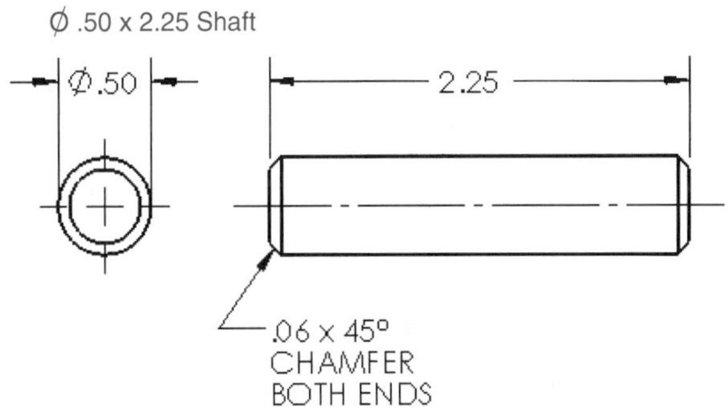

Figure 9-18

TIP

The overall length is the face width plus the hub height. In this example the face width is .5, and the overall length is 1.00, so the hub height is .5.

7. Click the Ok check mark.

   See Figure 9-21.

To Add a Threaded Hole to the Gear's Hub

1. Access the **Hole Wizard** tool located in the **Assembly Features** toolbox at the top of the screen.
2. Define the **Type** of hole.

See Figure 9-22. In this example a #6-32 thread was selected for the hole. The depth of the hole must exceed the

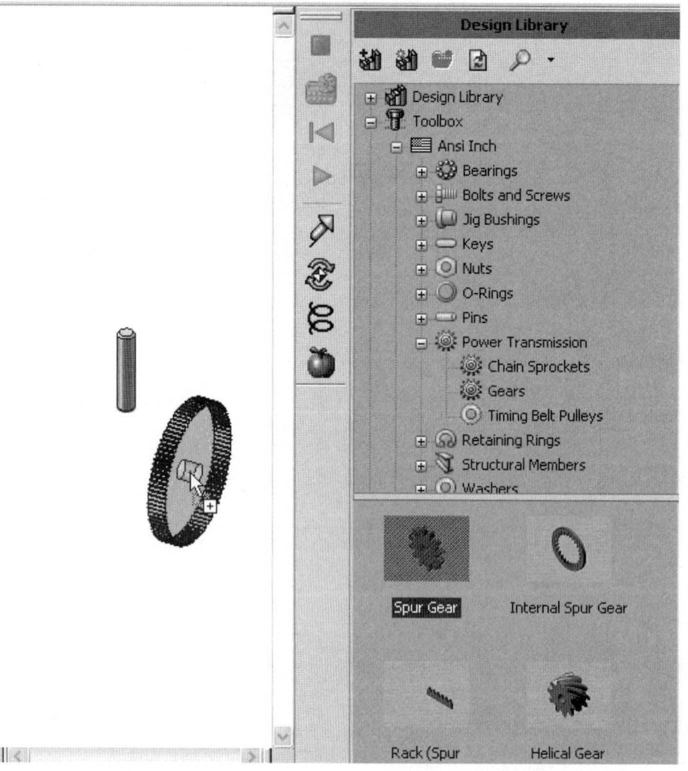

Figure 9-19

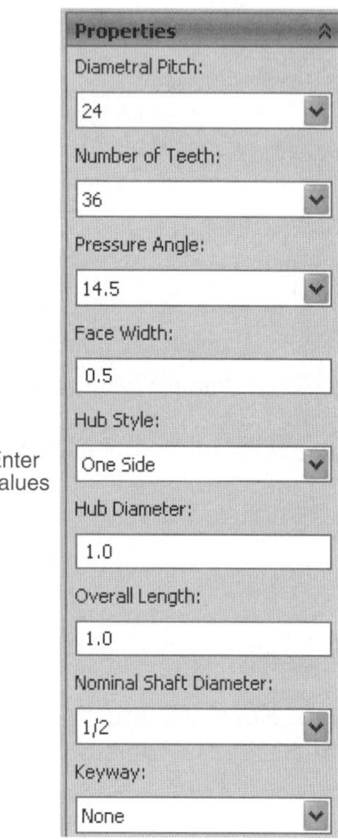

Figure 9-20

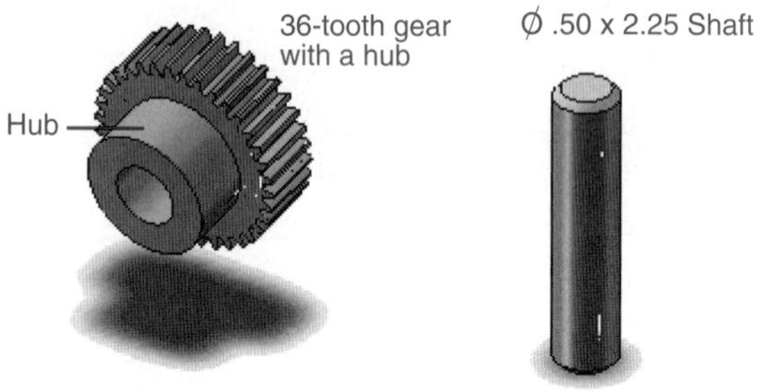

36-tooth gear with a hub

Hub

Ø .50 x 2.25 Shaft

Figure 9-21

wall thickness of the hub, which is 0.25. In this example a depth of 0.50 was selected.

3. Click the **Hole Position** tab and locate the threaded hole on the outside surface of the hub.

   See Figure 9-23.

4. Click the **Smart Dimension** tool and create a **0.25** dimension between the center point of the hole and the top surface of the hub.
5. Access the **Design Library,** click **Toolbox, Ansi Inch, Bolts and Screws,** and **Set Screws (Slotted).**

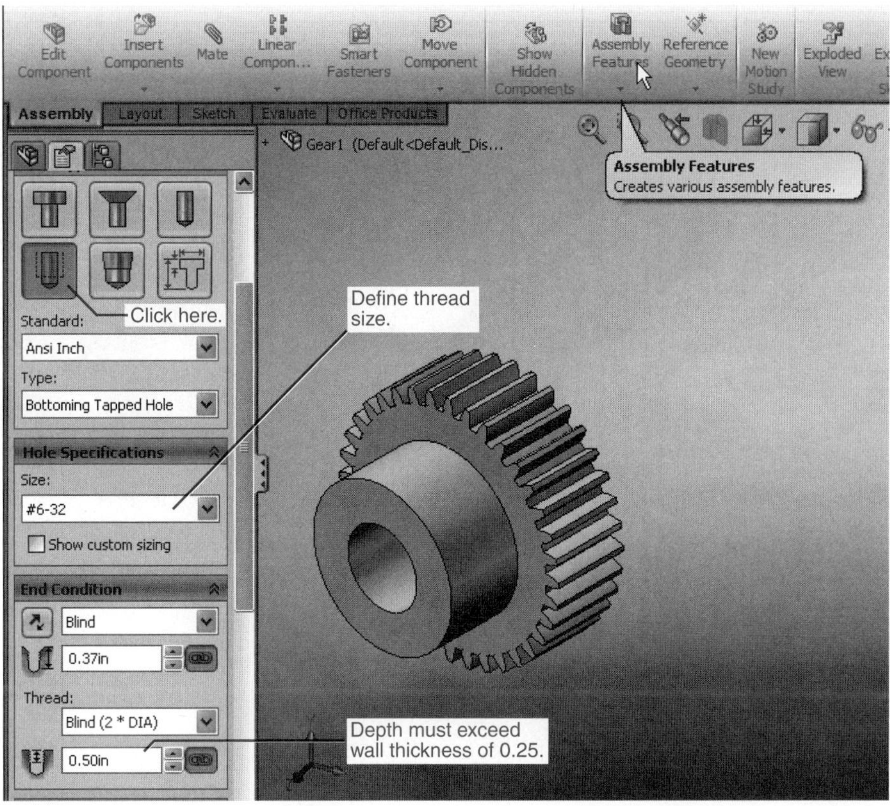

Figure 9-22

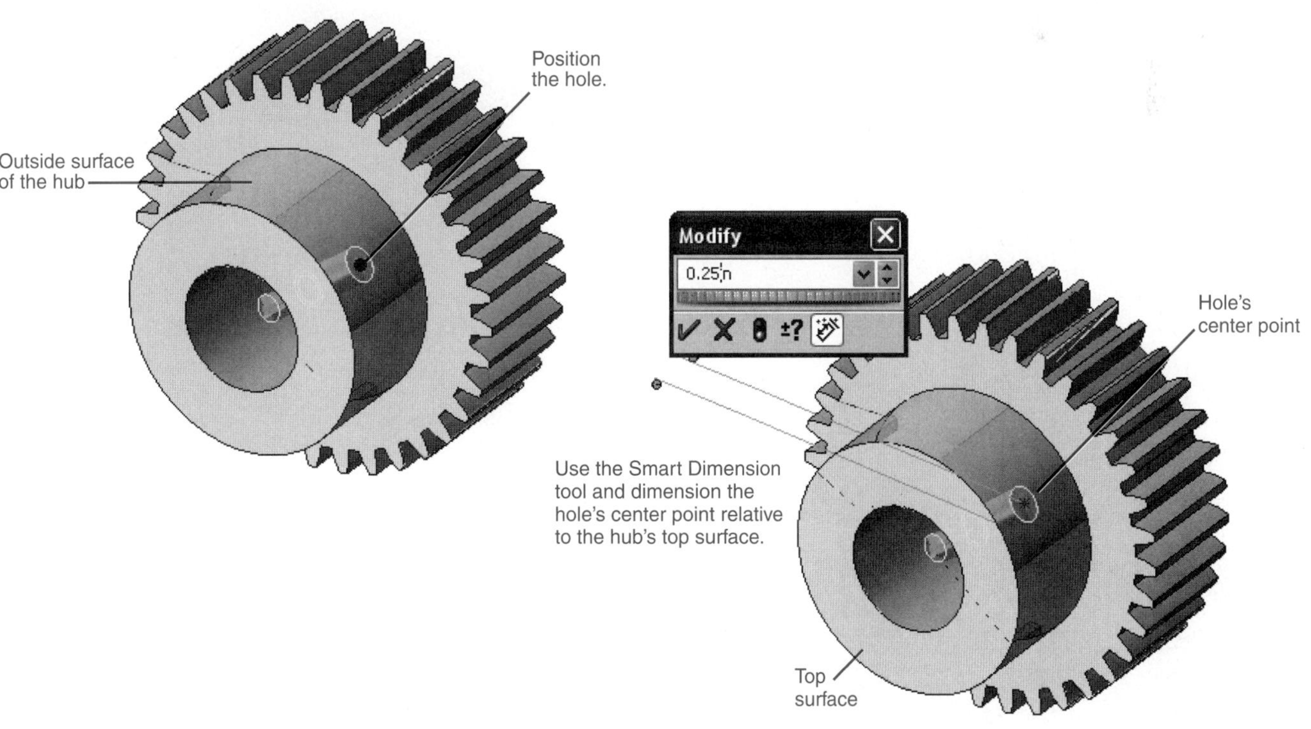

Figure 9-23

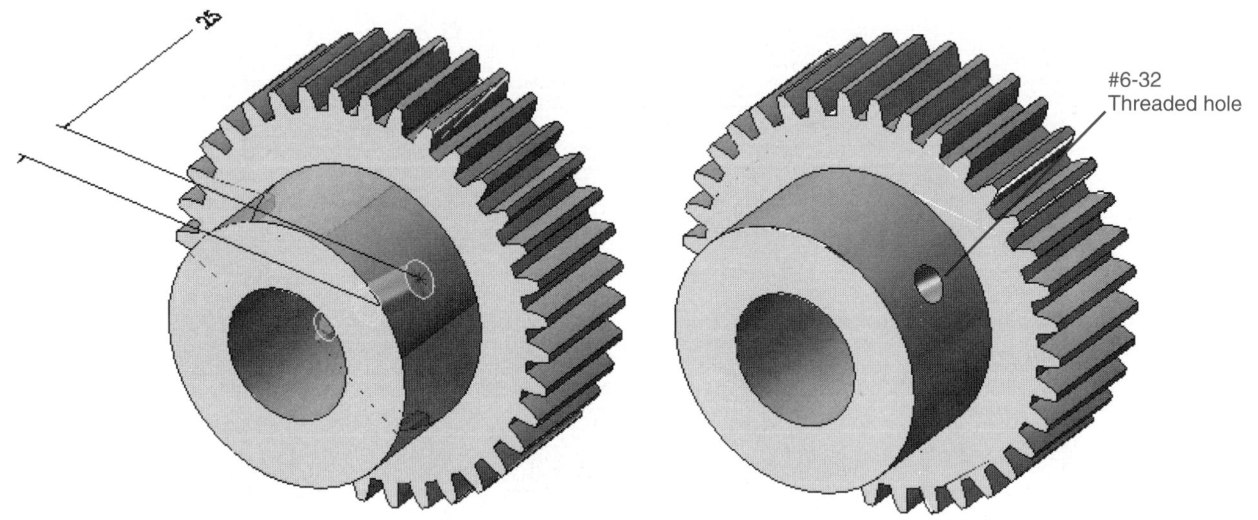

Figure 9-23 *(continued)*

6. Select a **Slotted Set Screw Oval Point** and drag it onto the drawing screen.
7. Define the **Properties** of the set screw as **#6-32, 0.263** long; click the OK check mark.

   See Figure 9-24.

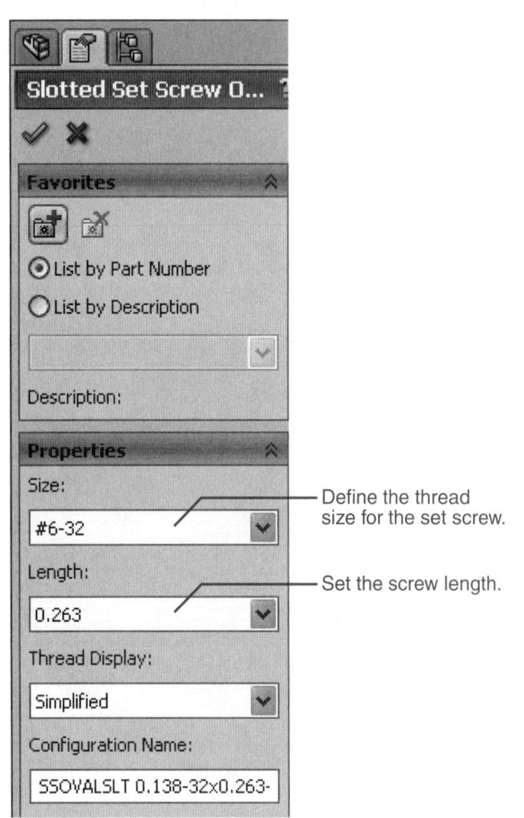

Figure 9-24

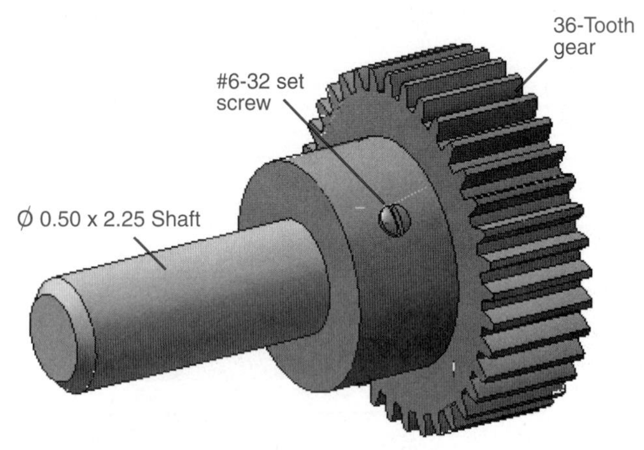

Figure 9-25

8. Use the **Mate** tool and assemble the shaft and set screw into the gear as shown.

   See Figure 9-25.

9-8 KEYS, KEYSEATS, AND GEARS

Keys are used to transfer power from a drive shaft to an entity such as a gear or pulley. A ***keyseat*** is cut into both the shaft and the gear, and the key is inserted between them. See Figure 9-26. The SolidWorks **Design Library** contains two types of keys: parallel and Woodruff.

In this section we will insert a parallel key between a Ø0.50 × 3.00 shaft to a gear. Both the shaft and gear will have keyseats.

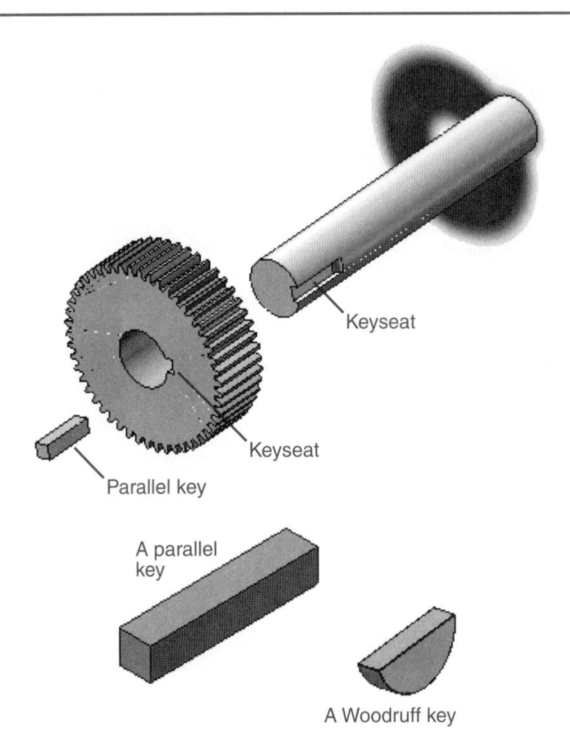

Figure 9-26

To Define and Create Keyseats in Gears

1. Draw a **Ø0.50 × 3.00** shaft and save the shaft as **Ø0.50 × 3.00 SHAFT.**
2. Start a new **Assembly** drawing and insert the shaft into the drawing.
3. Access the **Design Library, Toolbox, Ansi Inch, Power Transmission,** and **Gears** folders.
4. Click and drag a spur gear into the drawing area.
5. Define the gear's properties as shown.

See Figure 9-27. This gear will not have a hub. Define a **Square(1)** keyway.

6. Click the OK check mark.

> *Note:*
> The gear will automatically have a keyseat cut into it. The size of the keyseat is based on the gear's bore diameter.

The key will also be sized according to the gear's bore diameter, but say we wish to determine the exact keyway size. See Figure 9-28.

1. Right-click the gear and select the **Open Part** option.

A warning dialog box will appear.

2. Click **OK.**
3. Click the **Make Drawing from Part/Assembly** tool.

The **New SolidWorks Document** dialog box will appear.

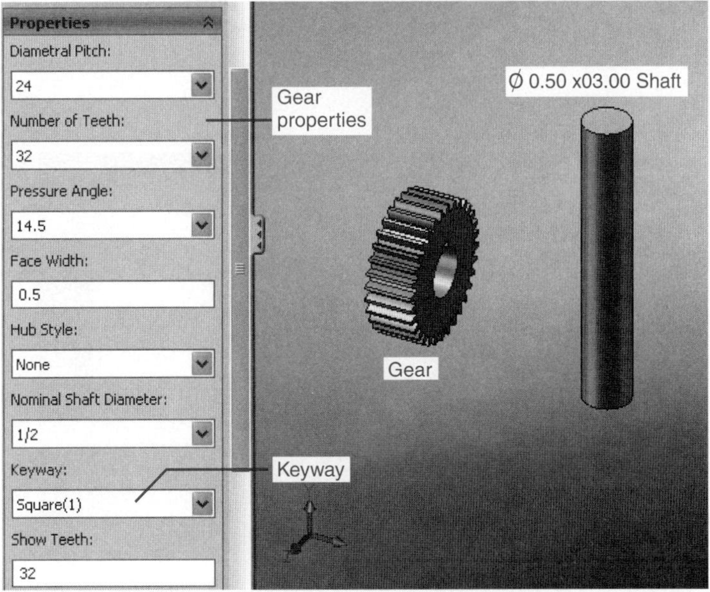

Figure 9-27

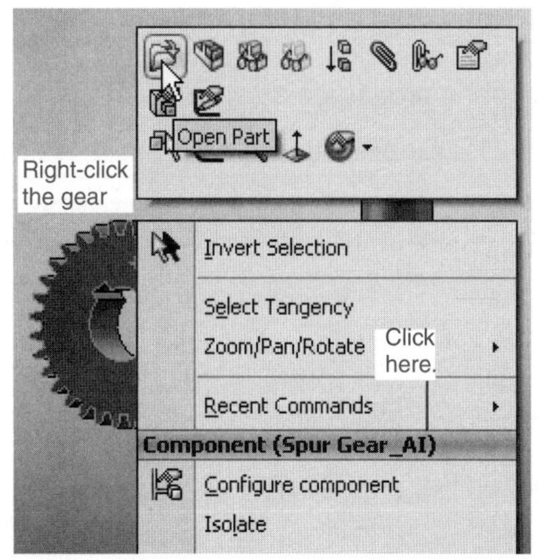
Open Part
Right-click the gear
Invert Selection
Select Tangency
Zoom/Pan/Rotate
Click here.
Recent Commands
Component (Spur Gear_AI)
Configure component
Isolate

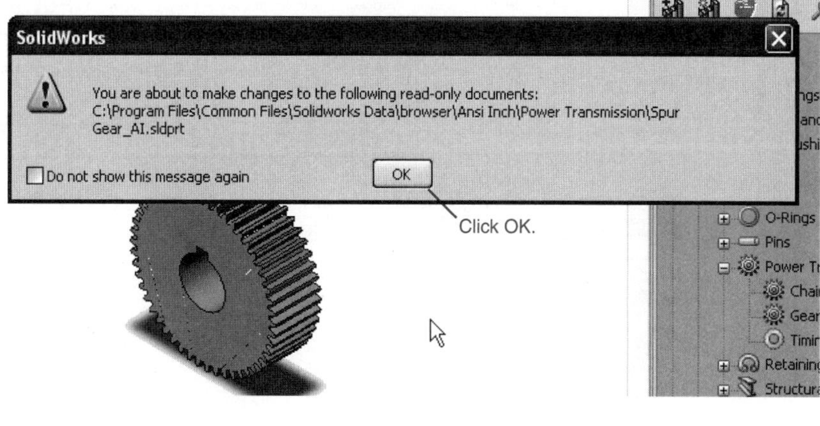
SolidWorks
You are about to make changes to the following read-only documents:
C:\Program Files\Common Files\Solidworks Data\browser\Ansi Inch\Power Transmission\Spur Gear_AI.sldprt
Do not show this message again
OK
Click OK.
O-Rings
Pins

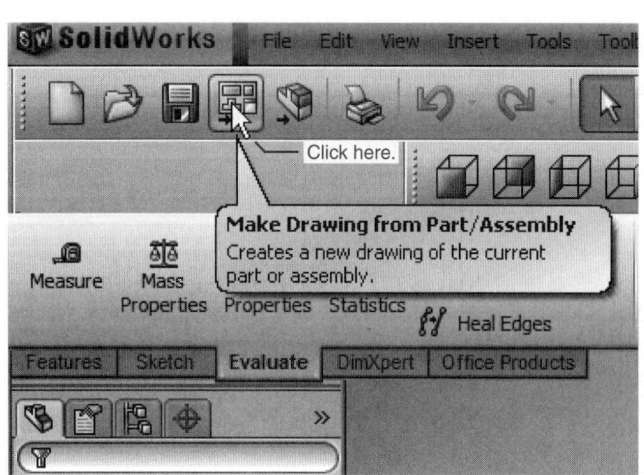
SolidWorks
File Edit View Insert Tools
Click here.
Make Drawing from Part/Assembly
Creates a new drawing of the current part or assembly.
Measure
Mass Properties
Properties
Statistics
Heal Edges
Features Sketch Evaluate DimXpert Office Products

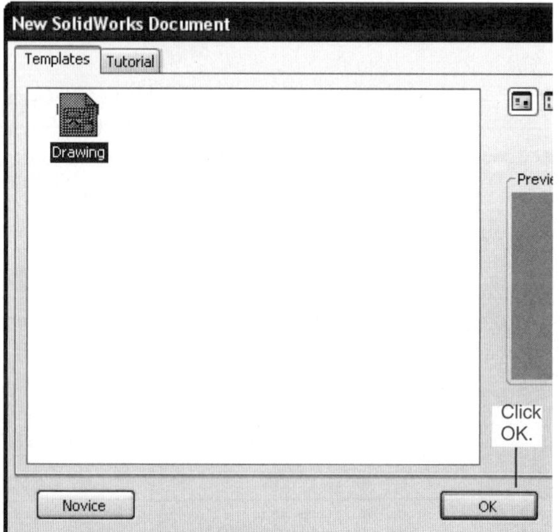
New SolidWorks Document
Templates
Tutorial
Drawing
Click OK.
Novice
OK

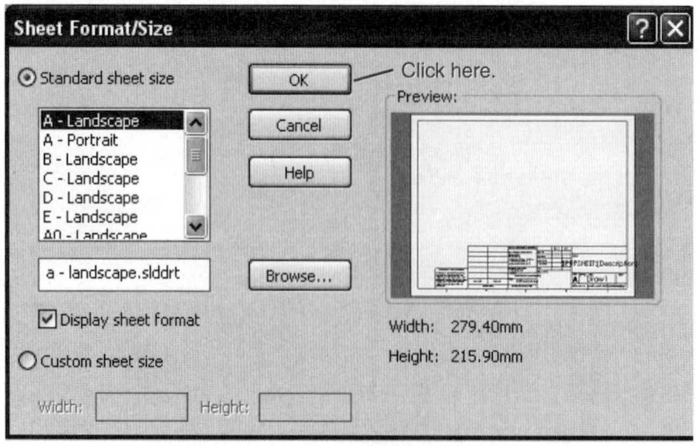
Sheet Format/Size
Standard sheet size
OK
Click here.
Cancel
Help
Preview:
A - Landscape
A - Portrait
B - Landscape
C - Landscape
D - Landscape
E - Landscape
a - landscape.slddrt
Browse...
Display sheet format
Custom sheet size
Width: 279.40mm
Height: 215.90mm
Width:
Height:

Figure 9-28

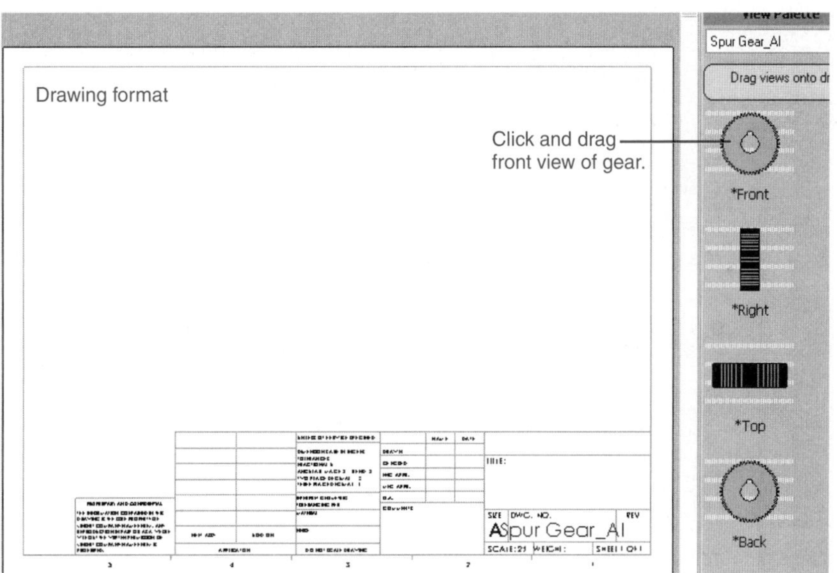

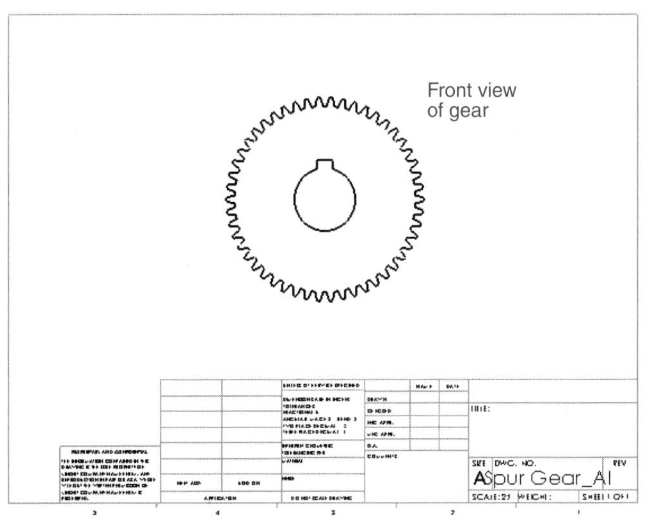

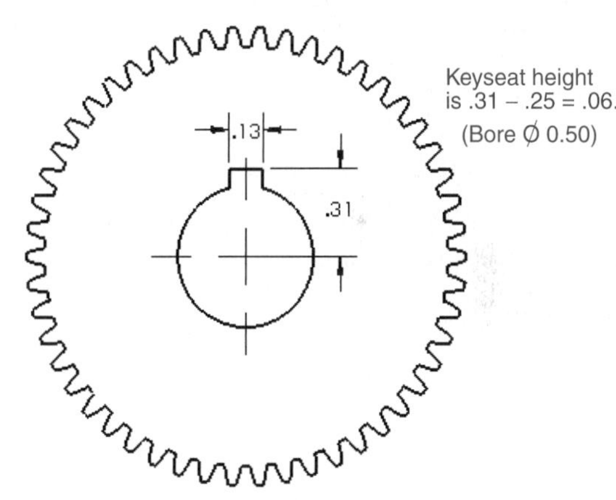

Figure 9-29

4. Click **OK.**

   The **Sheet Format/Size** dialog box will appear.

5. Click **OK.**

The system will switch to the **Drawing** format. See Figure 9-29.

6. Click and drag a front view of the gear into the drawing area.
7. Use the **Smart Dimension** tool and dimension the keyseat.

Notice that the keyseat's width is .13, or a little more than 125. The height of the keyseat is measured from the bore's center point. The height is defined as .31. Therefore, the height of the keyseat is .31 − .25 (the radius of the bore) = .06, or about half the width.

To Return to the Assembly Drawing

1. Click the **File** heading at the top of the screen, and select the **Close** option.

   Do not save the gear drawing.

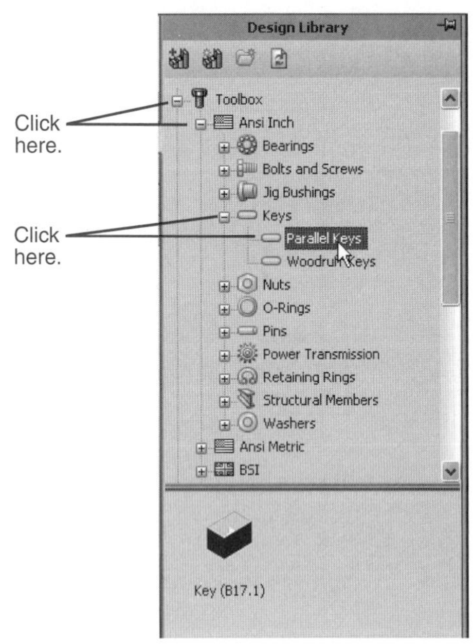

Figure 9-30

2. Again, click the **File** heading at the top of the screen, and select the **Close** option.

   The drawing will return to the assembly drawing.

To Define and Create a Parallel Key

1. Access the **Design Library, Toolbox, Ansi Inch, Keys,** and **Parallel Keys.**

   See Figure 9-30.

2. Click and drag the parallel key icon into the drawing screen.
3. Enter the shaft diameter value.

In this example the shaft diameter is 0.50 or ½ inch (8/16). This value is between 7/16 and 9/16.

Note that key dimensions are also given as .125 × .125 and a keyseat depth of .0625. Define the key length as 0.50. The key size automatically matches the keyway in the gear. The width of the gear's keyseat was .13, or .005 larger than the key. A rule of thumb is to make the height of the keyseat in both the shaft and the gear equal to a little more than the key's height. The height of the keyseat in the gear was .06, so the depth of the keyway in the shaft will be .07, for a total keyway height of .06 + .07 = .13. The calculation does not take into account the tolerances between the shaft and the gear or the tolerances between the key and the keyseat. For exact tolerance values refer to *Machinery's Handbook* or some equivalent source.

4. Click the OK check mark.

To Create a Keyseat in the Shaft

The keyway for the shaft will be .13 × .07.

1. Click the top surface of the Ø0.50 × 3.00 shaft.
2. Click the **Normal To** tool.

See Figure 9-31. The top surface of the shaft will become normal to the drawing screen.

3. Right-click the normal surface again and select the **Sketch** option.
4. Access the **Sketch Tools** and draw a vertical line from the center point of the shaft as shown.

   See Figure 9-32.

5. Access the **Sketch Tools** and draw a rectangle as shown.

Draw the rectangle so that the top horizontal line is above the edge of the shaft.

6. Use the **Smart Dimension** tool to locate the left vertical line of the rectangle 0.065 from the vertical construction line.

> **TIP**
>
> If the vertical centerline moves rather than the left vertical line, left-click the vertical construction line and select the **Fix** option.

7. Use the **Smart Dimension** tool and dimension the rectangle as shown.

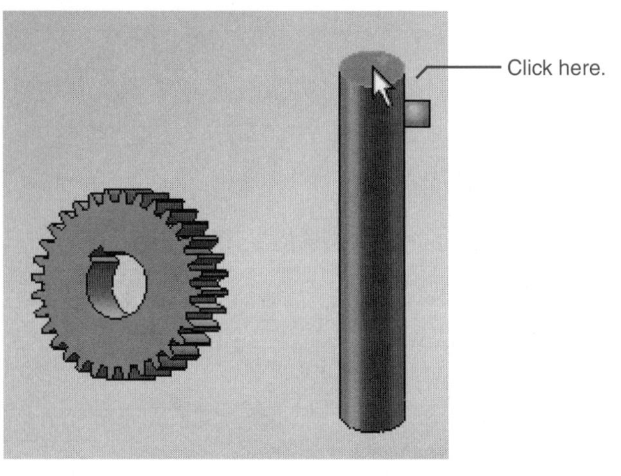

Figure 9-31

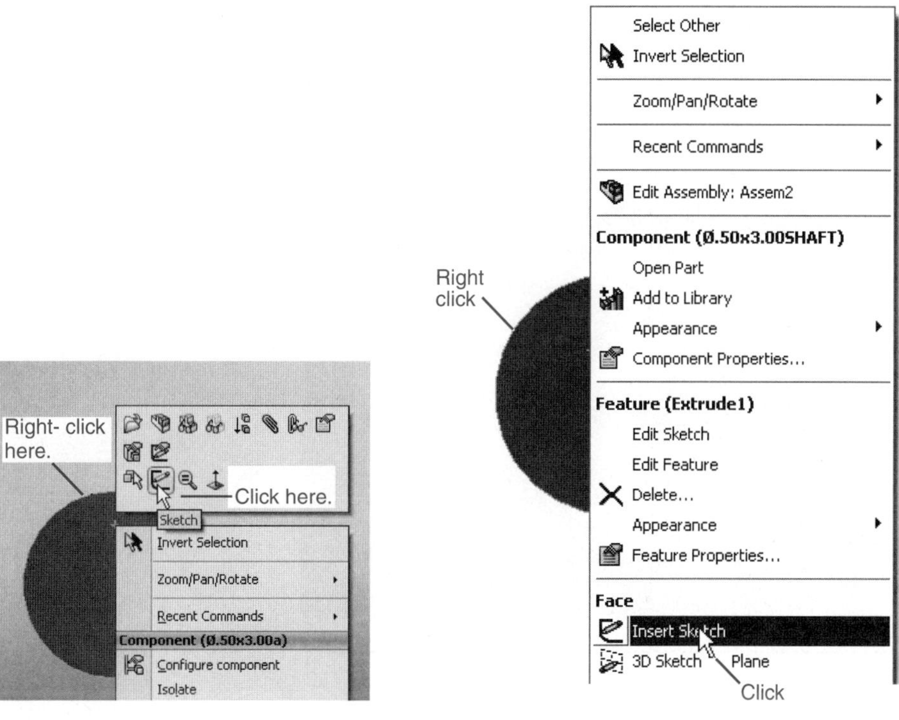

Figure 9-31 *(continued)*

To Create the Keyseat

1. Access the **Extruded Cut** tool on the **Assembly Features** toolbox on the **Assembly** toolbar and click the dimensioned rectangle.

   See Figure 9-33.

2. Define the cut length for **0.50 in;** click the OK check mark.

The keyseat will end with an arc-shaped cut. The radius of the arc is equal to the depth of the keyseat. The arc shape is generated by the cutting tool used to create the keyseat.

To Create the Arc-Shaped End of a Keyseat

1. Right-click the inside vertical surface of the keyseat and click the **Sketch** tool.

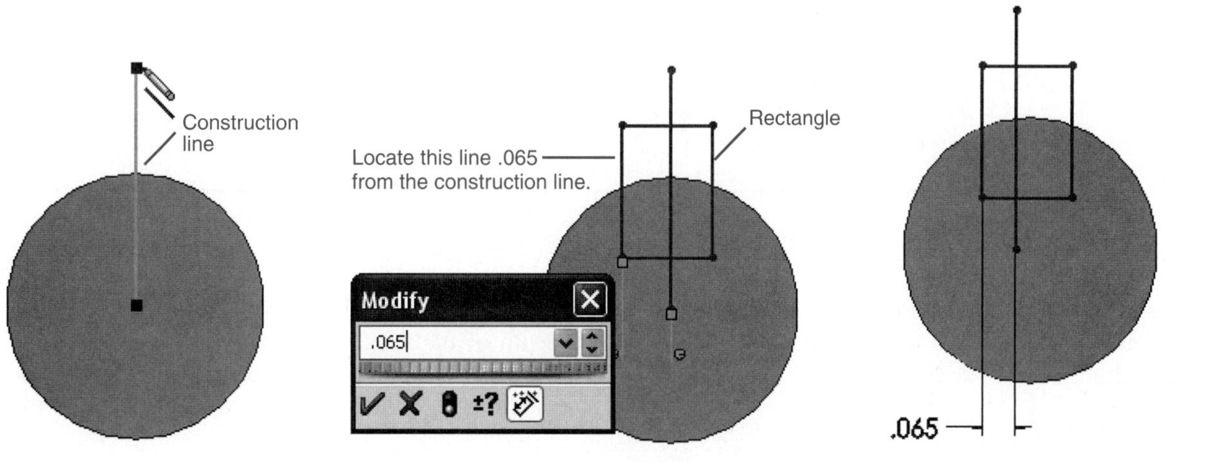

Figure 9-32

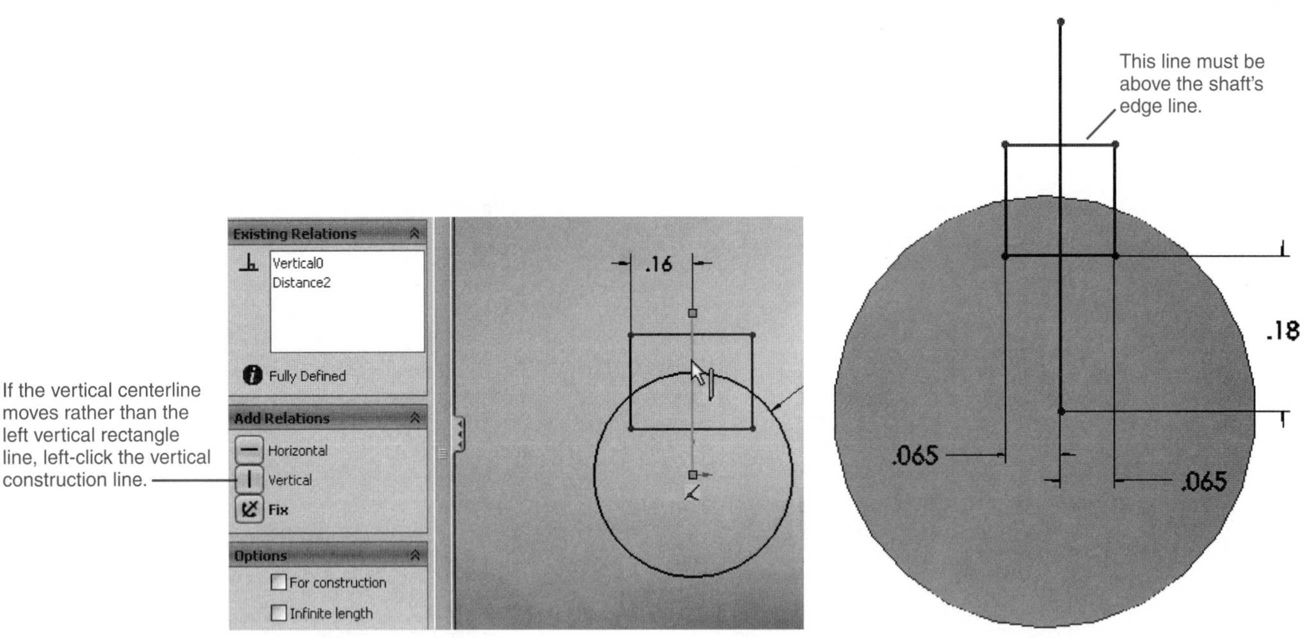

Figure 9-32 ***(continued)***

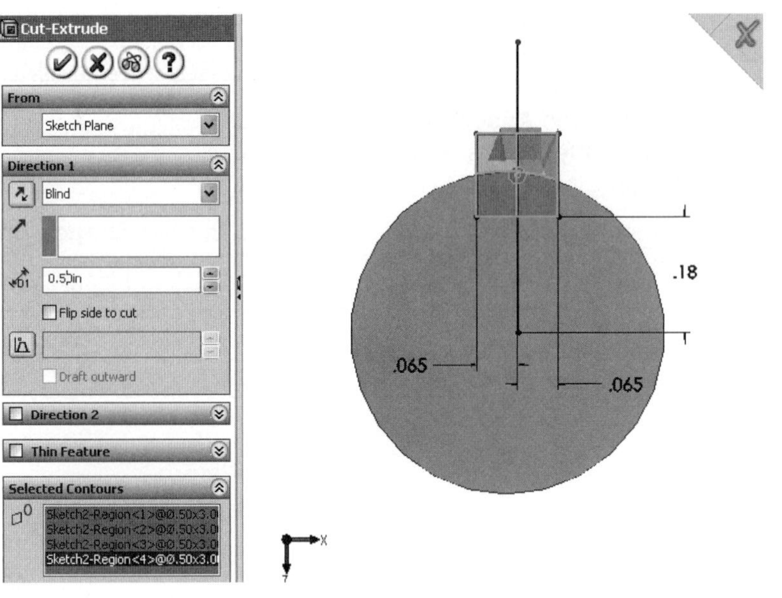

Figure 9-33

2. Use the **Circle** tool and draw a circle centered about the end of the keyseat on the surface of the shaft.

   See Figure 9-34.

3. Use the **Smart Dimension** tool and create an arc at the end of the keyseat.

   In this example a radius value of 0.06 was used. The depth of the keyseat is 0.07, but the edge surface is off center, so it will be slightly less than the depth value. There should be a smooth transition from the keyseat to the arc.

4. Use the **Extruded Cut** tool to cut the arc-shaped end surface.

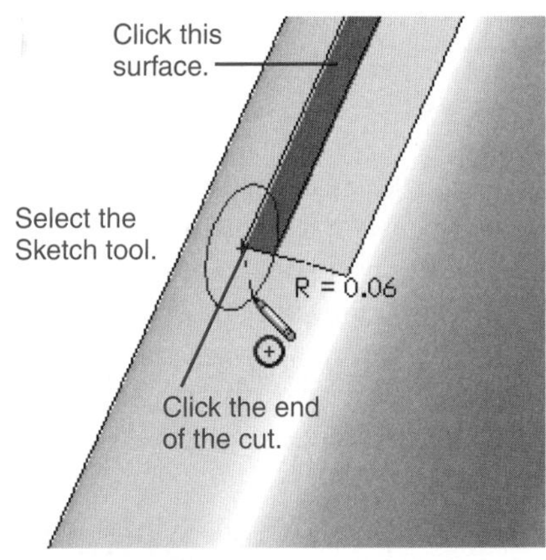

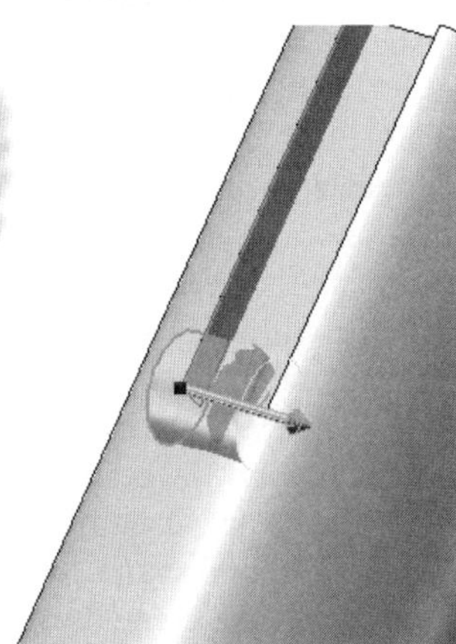

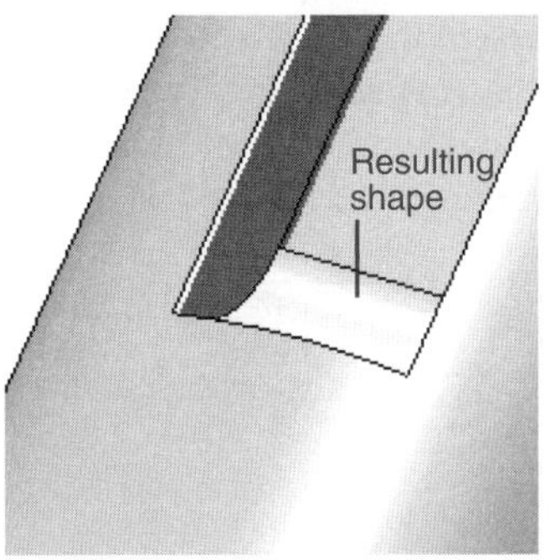

Figure 9-34

9-9 SAMPLE PROBLEM 9-1—SUPPORT PLATES

This exercise explains how to determine the size of plates used to support spur gears and their shafts.

Say we wish to design a support plate that will support four spur gears. The gear specifications are as follows. See Figure 9-35.

Gear 1
- Diametral Pitch = **24**
- Number of Teeth = **20**

Figure 9-35

- Pressure Angle = **14.5°**
- Face Width = **0.375**
- Hub Style = **One Side**
- Hub Diameter = **0.75**
- Overall Length = **.875**
- Nominal Shaft Diameter = **1/2**
- Keyway = **None**

Gear 2
- Diametral Pitch = **24**
- Number of Teeth = **60**
- Pressure Angle = **14.5°**
- Face Width = **0.375**
- Hub Style = **One Side**
- Hub Diameter = **0.75**
- Overall Length = **.875**
- Nominal Shaft Diameter = **1/2**
- Keyway = **None**

To Determine the Pitch Diameter

The pitch diameter of the gears is determined by

$$D = \left(\frac{N}{P}\right)$$

where

D = pitch diameter
N = number of teeth
P = diametral pitch

Therefore, for Gear 1

$$D = \left(\frac{20}{24}\right) = .83$$

For Gear 2

$$D = \left(\frac{60}{24}\right) = 2.50$$

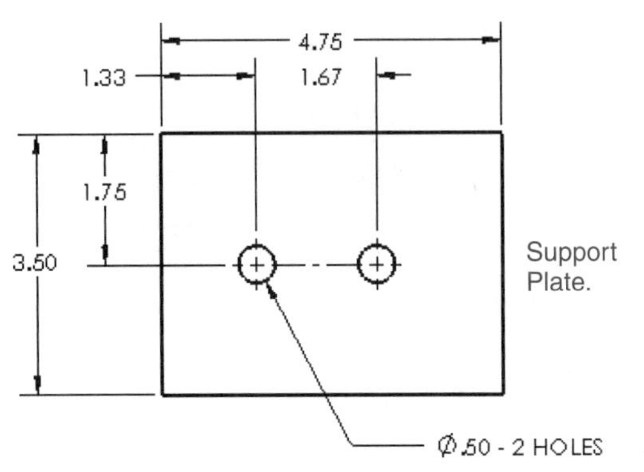

Figure 9-36

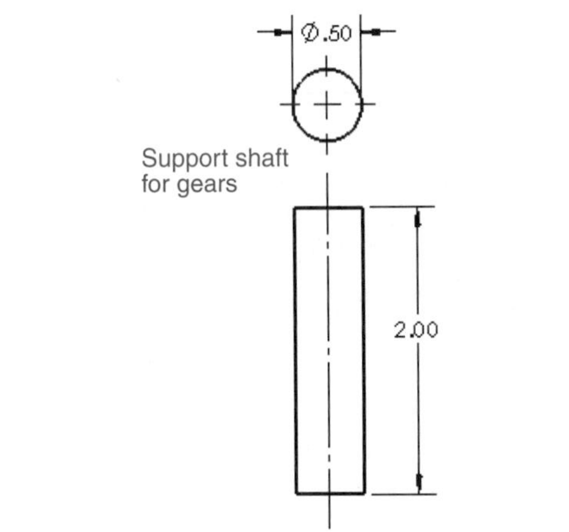

Figure 9-37

The center distance (CD) between the gears is calculated as follows.

$$CD = \frac{.83 + 2.50}{2} = 1.67$$

The radius of the gears is .46 and 1.25, respectively.

Figure 9-36 shows a support plate for the gears. The dimensions for the support plate were derived from the gear pitch diameters and an allowance of about 0.50 between the gear pitch diameters and the edge of the support plate. For example, the pitch diameter of the larger gear is 2.50. Allowing 0.50 between the top edge and the bottom edge gives 0.50 + 2.50 + 0.50 = 3.50.

The pitch diameter for the smaller gear is .83. Adding the .50 edge distance gives a distance of 1.33 from the smaller gear's center point. The center distance between the gears is 1.67. Therefore, the total length of the support plate is 1.33 + 1.67 + 1.75 = 4.75. The height will be 3.50.

Each of the gears has a ½ nominal shaft diameter. For this example a value of 0.50 will be assigned to both the gear bores and the holes in the support plate. In Chapter 10 this example will be presented again using bearings that will include tolerances.

Figure 9-37 shows a Ø.50 × 2.00 shaft that will be used to support the gears.

Create an **Assembly** drawing using the support plate, two Ø.50 × 2.00 shafts, and the two gears. See Figure 9-38. The gears were created using the given information. Figure 9-38 also shows the components in their assembled position. Save the assembly as **Two Gear Assembly.**

Create a drawing using the Two Gear Assembly in the **Isometric** orientation with no hidden lines. See Figure 9-39. Access the **Annotations** menu, click the **Tables** tool, and

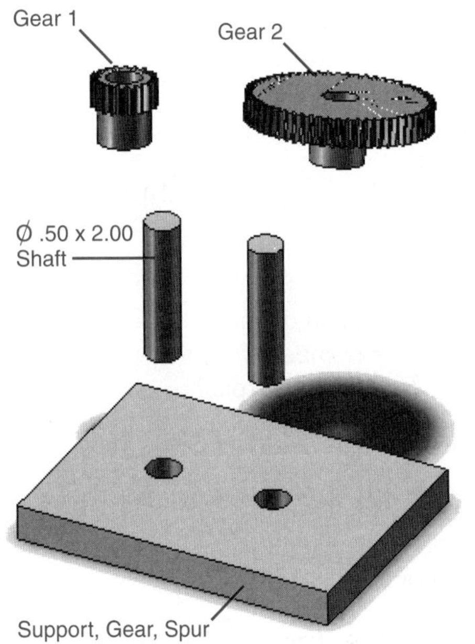

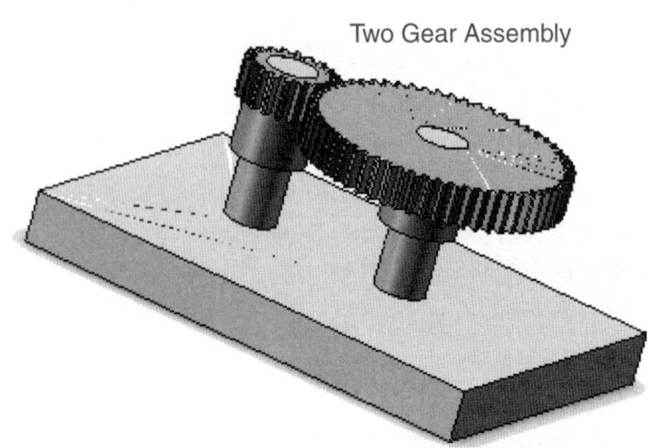

Figure 9-38

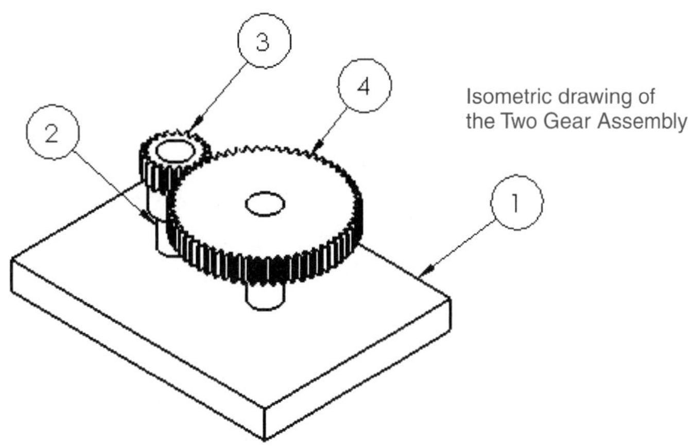

BOM

ITEM NO.	PART NUMBER	DESCRIPTION	QTY.
1	Support, Gear, Spur		1
2	Ø.50x2.00		2
3	Inch - Spur gear 24DP 20T 14.5PA 0.375FW --- S20O0.75H.875L0.5N		1
4	Inch - Spur gear 24DP 60T 14.5PA 0.375FW --- S60O0.75H.875L0.5N		1

These are not part numbers

Figure 9-39

select the **Bill of Materials** tool. Locate the bill of materials (BOM) as shown in Figure 9-39.

The PART NUMBER column does not show part numbers but lists the file names assigned to each part and in the case of the gears, a listing of gear parameters.

To Edit the Bill of Materials

See Figure 9-40.

1. Double-click the first cell under the heading DESCRIPTION.

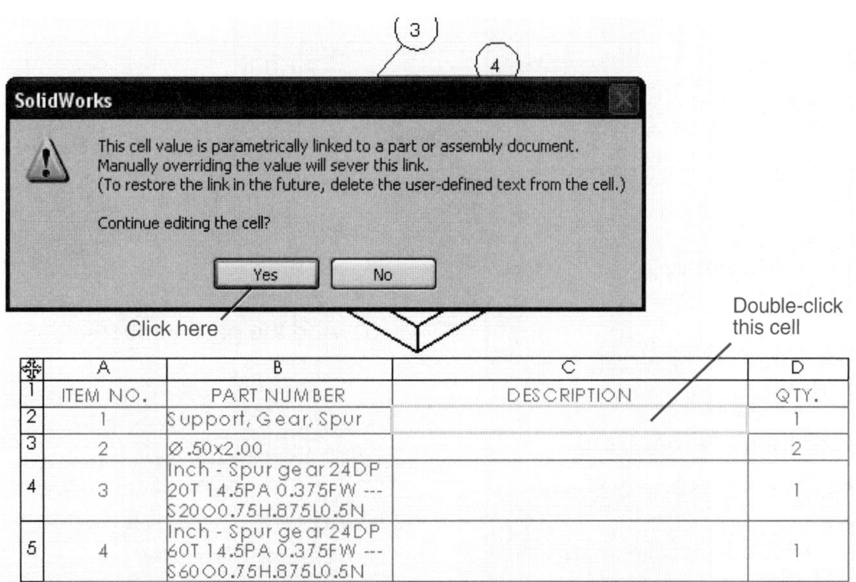

	A	B	C	D
1	ITEM NO.	PART NUMBER	DESCRIPTION	QTY.
2	1	Support, Gear, Spur		1
3	2	Ø.50x2.00		2
4	3	Inch - Spur gear 24DP 20T 14.5PA 0.375FW --- S20O0.75H.875L0.5N		1
5	4	Inch - Spur gear 24DP 60T 14.5PA 0.375FW --- S60O0.75H.875L0.5N		1

Figure 9-40

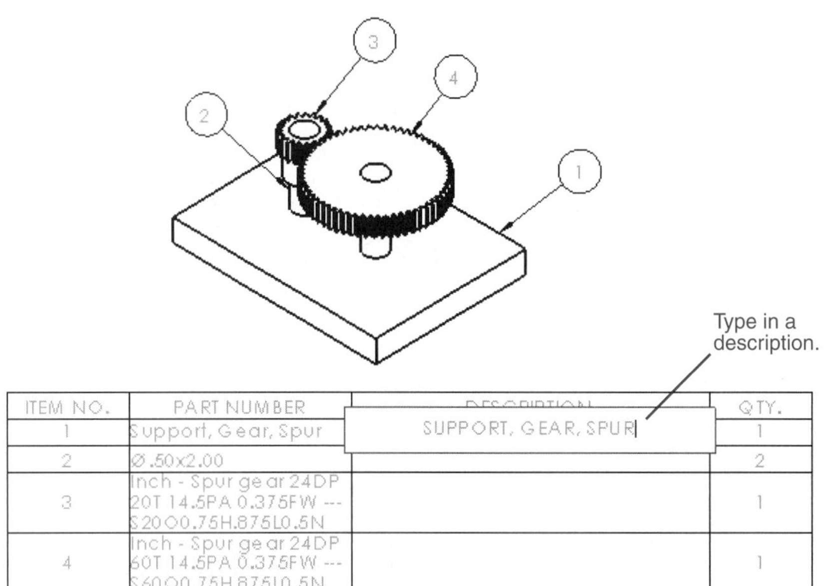

ITEM NO.	PART NUMBER	DESCRIPTION	QTY.
1	Support, Gear, Spur	SUPPORT, GEAR, SPUR	1
2	Ø.50x2.00		2
3	Inch - Spur gear 24DP 20T 14.5PA 0.375FW --- S20O0.75H.875L0.5N		1
4	Inch - Spur gear 24DP 60T 14.5PA 0.375FW --- S60O0.75H.875L0.5N		1

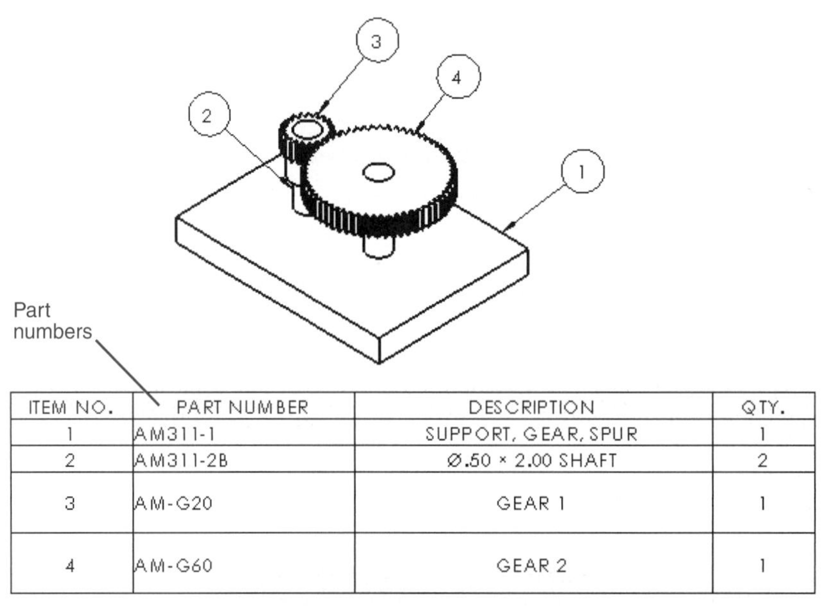

ITEM NO.	PART NUMBER	DESCRIPTION	QTY.
1	AM311-1	SUPPORT, GEAR, SPUR	1
2	AM311-2B	Ø.50 × 2.00 SHAFT	2
3	AM-G20	GEAR 1	1
4	AM-G60	GEAR 2	1

Edit the BOM.

Figure 9-40 ***(continued)***

A warning dialog box will appear.

2. Click **Yes.**

An editing text box will appear in the cell.

3. Type in the part description.
4. In this example the file name was used.

> ***Note:***
> The description was typed using only uppercase letters. Uppercase letters are the preferred convention.

5. Complete the editing of the DESCRIPTION column.
6. Add the part numbers.

> ***Note:***
> Part numbers differ from item numbers (assembly numbers). The support plate is item number 1 and has a part number of AM311-1. If the plate were to be used in another assembly, it might have a different item number, but it will always have the same AM311-1 part number.

9-10 RACK AND PINION GEARS

Figure 9-41 shows a rack and pinion gear setup. It was created using the **Assembly** format starting with a Ø.50 × 2.25 shaft and with rack and pinion gear from the **Design Library.**

1. Start a new **Assembly** drawing.
2. Insert a Ø.50 × 2.25 shaft.

The shaft will serve as a base for the gears and a reference for animation.

3. Access the **Design Library, Toolbox, ANSI inches, Power Transmission, Gears,** and click and drag a **Rack (Spur Rectangular)** into the drawing area.
4. Set the rack's properties as shown in Figure 9-42.
5. Click and drag a spur gear into the drawing area.

The spur gear will become the pinion.

6. Set the pinion's properties as shown in Figure 9-43.
7. Reorient the components and use the **Mate** tool to insert the pinion onto the shaft.

See Figure 9-44.

8. Use the **Mate** tool to make the top surface of the pinion parallel with the front flat surface of the rack.
9. Use the **Mate** tool and align the top surface (not an edge) of one of the pinion's teeth with the bottom surface of one of the rack's teeth.

See Figure 9-44.

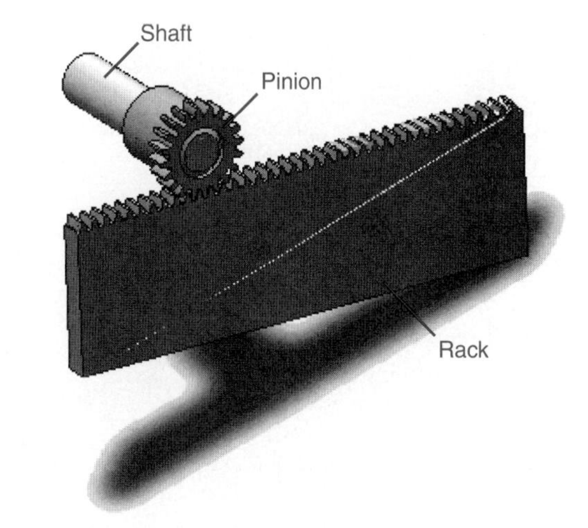

Figure 9-41

10. Adjust the pinion as needed to create a proper fit between the pinion and the rack by locating the cursor on the pinion and rotating the pinion.

To Animate the Rack and Pinion

See Figure 9-45. This animation is based on the rack and pinion setup created in the previous section.

1. Click the **Mate** tool.
2. Click **Mechanical Mates.**
3. Click the **Rack Pinion** option.
4. Click the front edge of the rack's teeth.

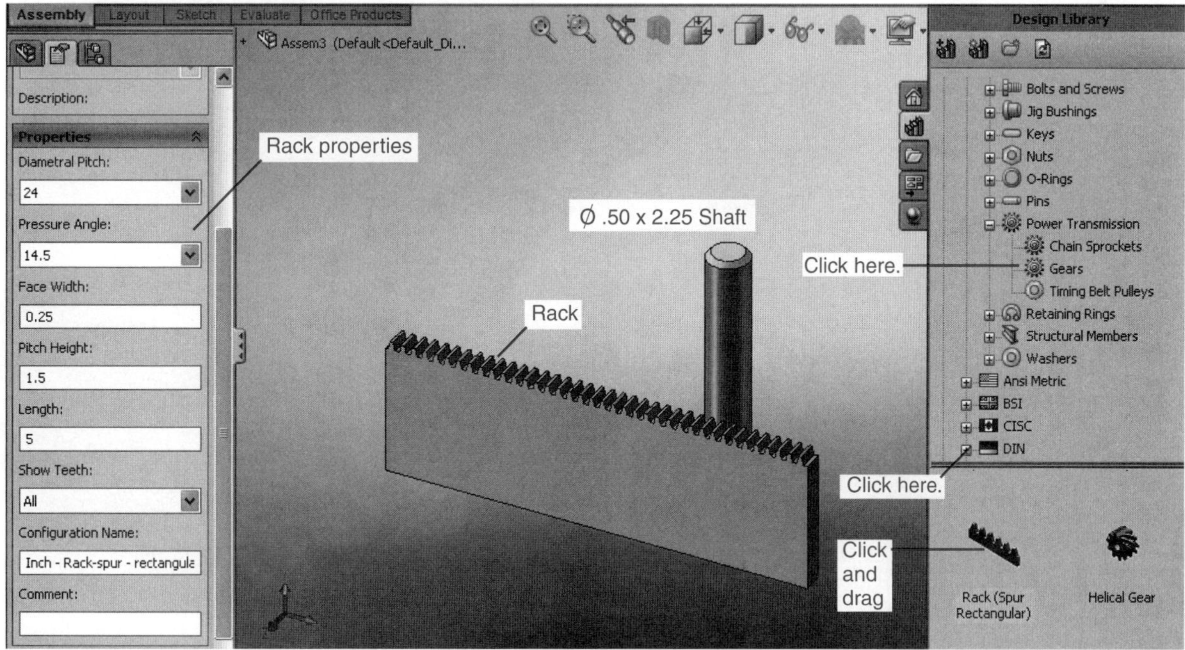

Figure 9-42

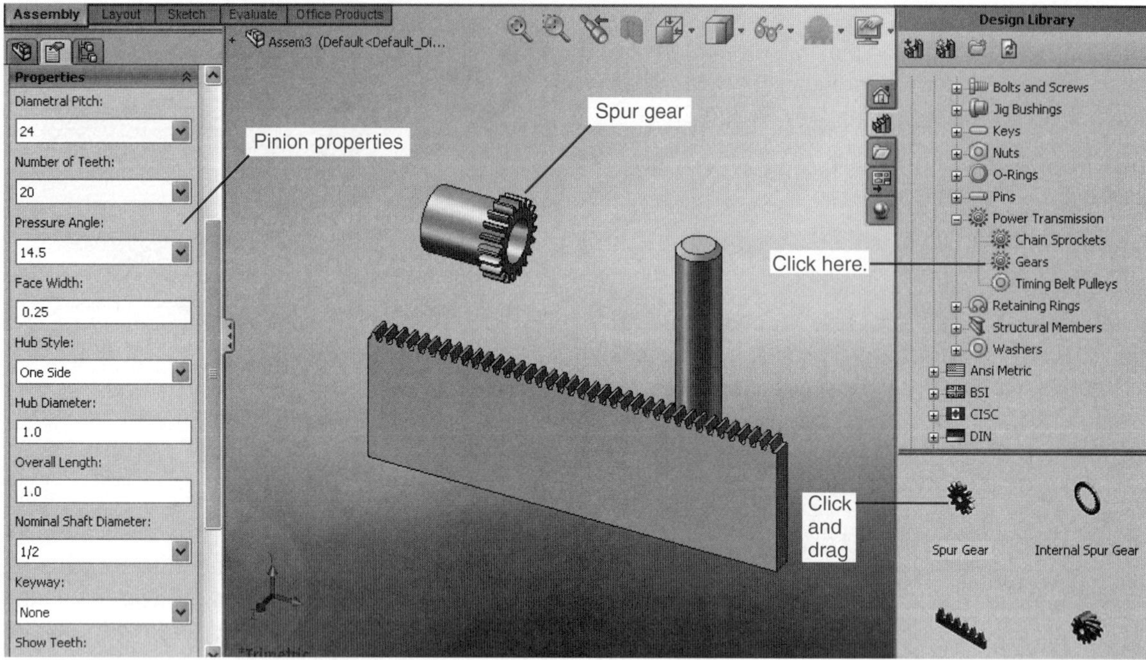

Figure 9-43

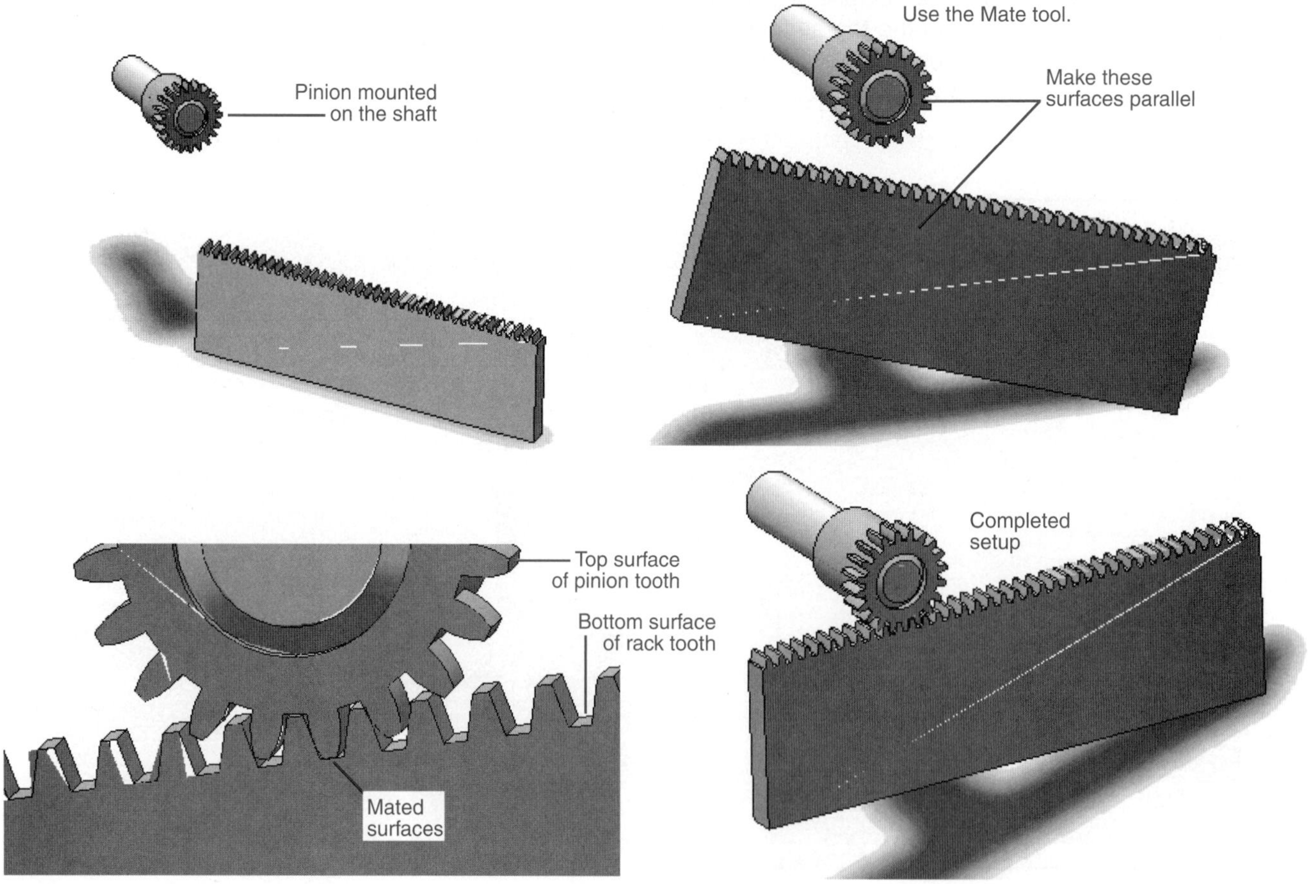

Pinion mounted on the shaft

Use the Mate tool.

Make these surfaces parallel

Top surface of pinion tooth

Bottom surface of rack tooth

Mated surfaces

Completed setup

Figure 9-44

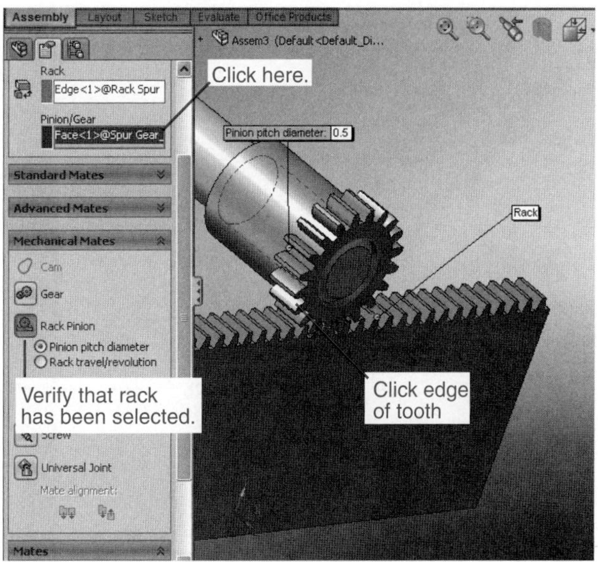

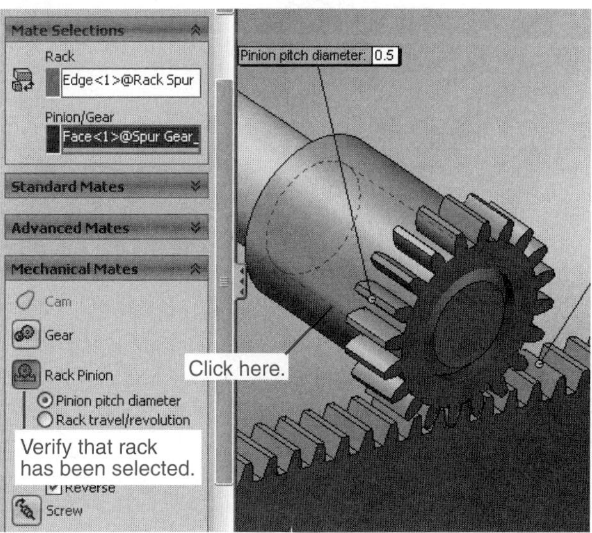

Figure 9-45

5. Click the pinion gear (not an edge).
6. Click the **Reverse** box so that a check mark appears.
7. Use the cursor to rotate the pinion.

   The rack will slide back and forth as the pinion is moved.

9-11 METRIC GEARS

Gears created using the metric system are very similar to gears created using English units with one major exception. Gears in the English system use the term *pitch* to refer

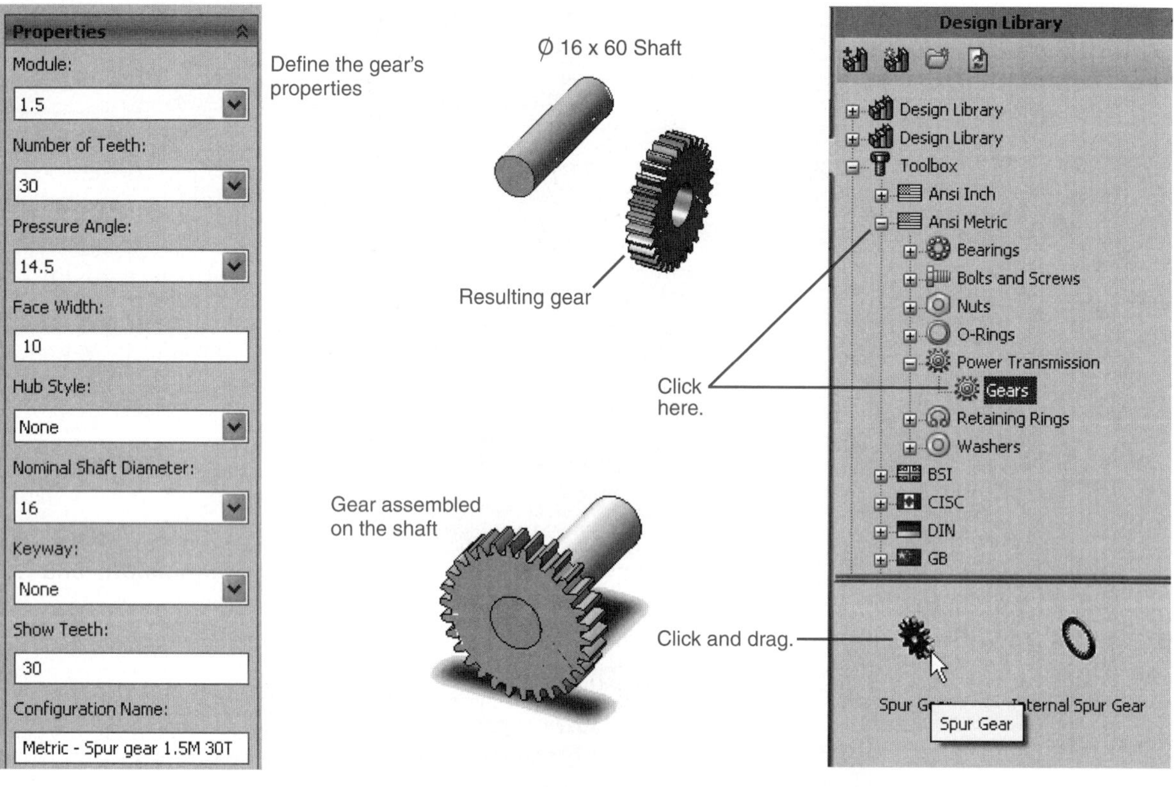

Figure 9-46

to the number of teeth per inch. Gears in the metric system use the term ***module*** to refer to the pitch diameter divided by the number of teeth. As meshing gears in the English system must have the same pitch, so meshing gears in the metric system must have the same module.

To Create a Metric Gear

See Figure 9-46

1. Start a new **Part** drawing and set the units for **MMGS.**
2. Draw a Ø16 × 60 millimeter shaft. Save the shaft as **Ø16 × 60.**
3. Start a new **Assembly** drawing and insert the Ø16 shaft.
4. Access the **Design Library.**
5. Click **Toolbox, ANSI Metric, Power Transmission,** and **Gears.**
6. Click and drag a spur gear into the drawing area.
7. Define the gear's properties as follows:
   a. Module = **1.5**
   b. Number of Teeth = **30**
   c. Pressure Angle = **14.5**
   d. Face Width = **10**
   e. Hub Style = **None**
   f. Nominal Shaft Diameter = **16**
   g. Keyway = **None**
8. Use the **Mate** tool and assemble the gear onto the shaft.

9-12 BELTS AND PULLEYS

Belts and pulleys are another form of power transmission. They are cheaper than gears, require less stringent tolerances, can be used to cover greater distances, and can absorb shock better. However, belts cannot take as much load as gears and can slip or creep, and operate at slower speeds.

9-13 BELT AND PULLEY STANDARD SIZES

There are many different-sized belts and pulleys. Listed here are belt designations, belt overall thicknesses, belt widths, and pulley widths that can be used to create assemblies within the context of this text. For other belt and pulley properties see manufacturers' specifications

Standard Belt Sizes—Single-Sided Belt Thickness
Mini Extra Light: MXL (0.080)—0.045
Extra Light: XL (0.200)—0.09
Light: L (0.375)—0.14
Heavy: H (0.500)—0.16
Extra Heavy: XL (0.875)—0.44
Double Extra Heavy: XXL (1.250)—0.62

Standard Pulley Widths
MXL: 0.25
XL: 0.38
L: 0.50, 0.75, 1.00
H: 1.00, 1.50, 2.00, 3.00
XH: 2.00, 3.00, 4.00
XXH: 2.00, 3.00, 4.00, 5.00

Standard Belt Widths
XXL—0.12, 0.19, 0.25
XL—0.25, 0.38
L— 0.50, 0.75, 1.00
H— 0.75, 1.00, 1.50, 2.00, 3.00,
XH—2.00, 3.00, 4.00
XXH — 2.00, 3.00, 4.00, 5.00

To Draw a Belt and Pulley Assembly

Figure 9-47 shows dimensioned drawings of the support plate and shaft.

1. Create **Part** documents of the support plate and the shaft
2. Assemble two shafts into the support plate. The shafts should extend 1.25 beyond the support plate.

See Figure 9-48.

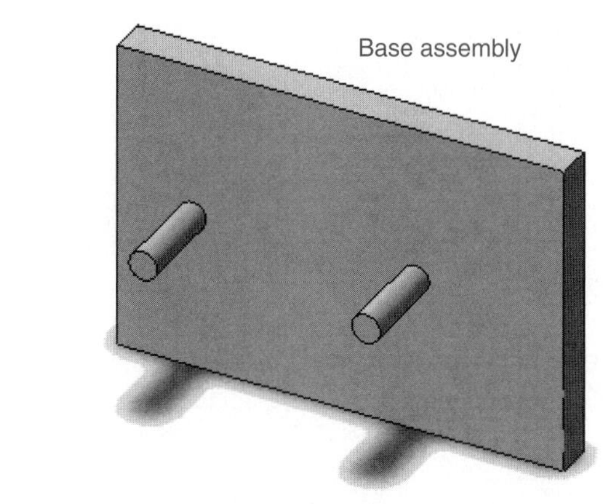

Figure 9-48

3. Access the **Design Library** and click **Toolbox, Ansi Inch, Power Transmission,** and **Timing Belts.**
4. Click and drag a **Timing Belt Pulley** into the drawing area.
5. Set the properties as follows: Belt Pitch = **(0.200) = XL,** Belt Width = **0.38,** Pulley Style = **Flanged,** Number of grooves = **20,** Hub Diameter = **.375,** Overall length = **.500,** Keyway = **None.**

See Figure 9-49.

6. Create two pulleys.

> *Note:*
> If a warning box appears, accept the error and click the **Close** box.

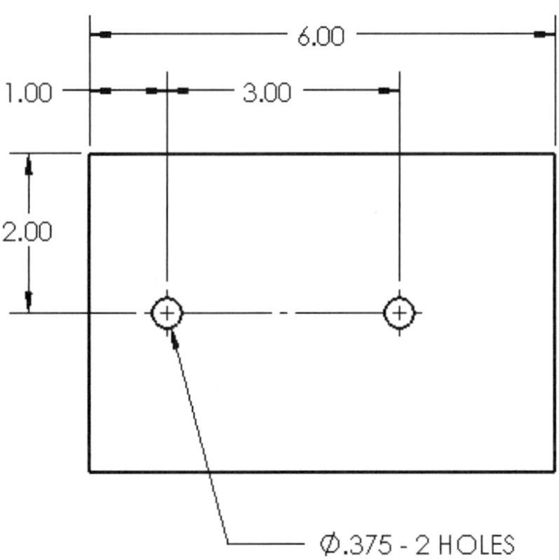

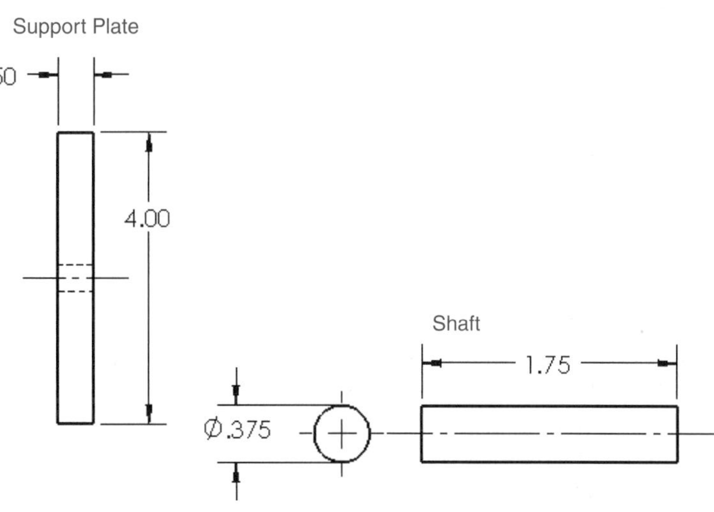

Figure 9-47

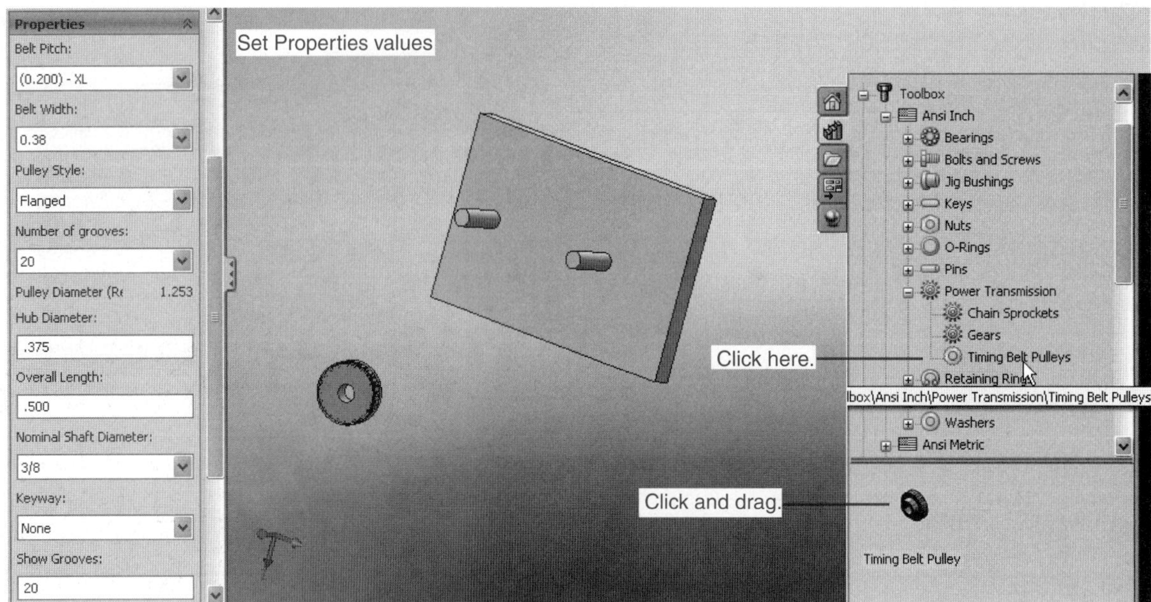

Figure 9-49

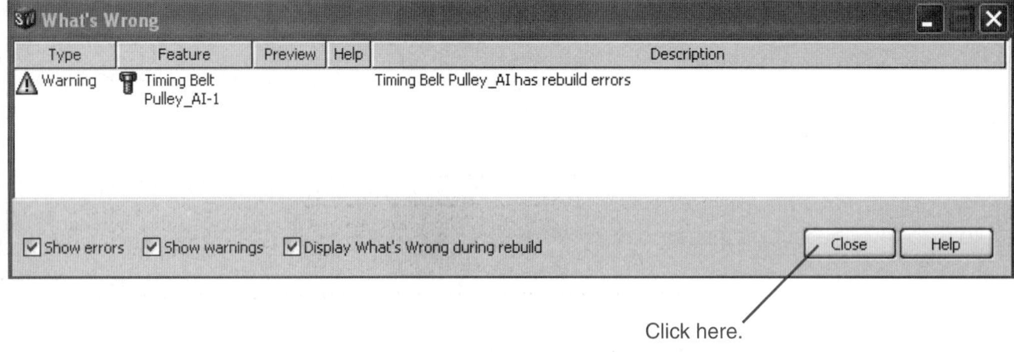

Figure 9-50

See Figure 9-50.

7. Assemble the pulleys onto the ends of the shafts.

See Figure 9-51.

8. Click the **Insert** tool at the top of the screen, click **Assembly Feature,** then **Belt/Chain.**

See Figure 9-52.

9. Select the **Belt Members** by clicking the top surfaces on the pulleys' teeth as shown.

See Figure 9-53.

10. Scroll down the **Belt/Chain** box, click the **Use belt thickness** box, and set the thickness for **0.14 in.**
11. Click the **Engage belt** box.

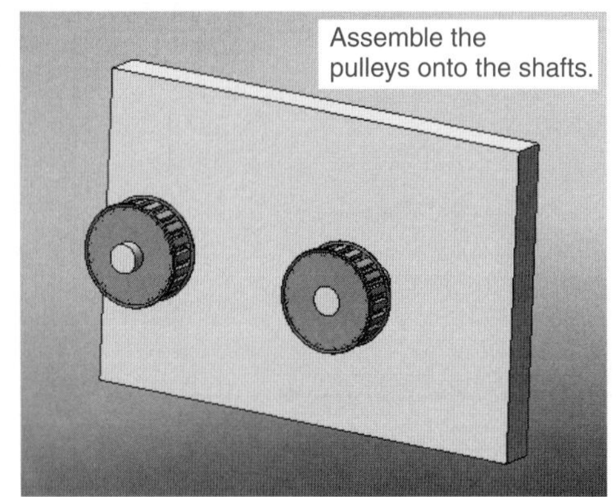

Figure 9-51

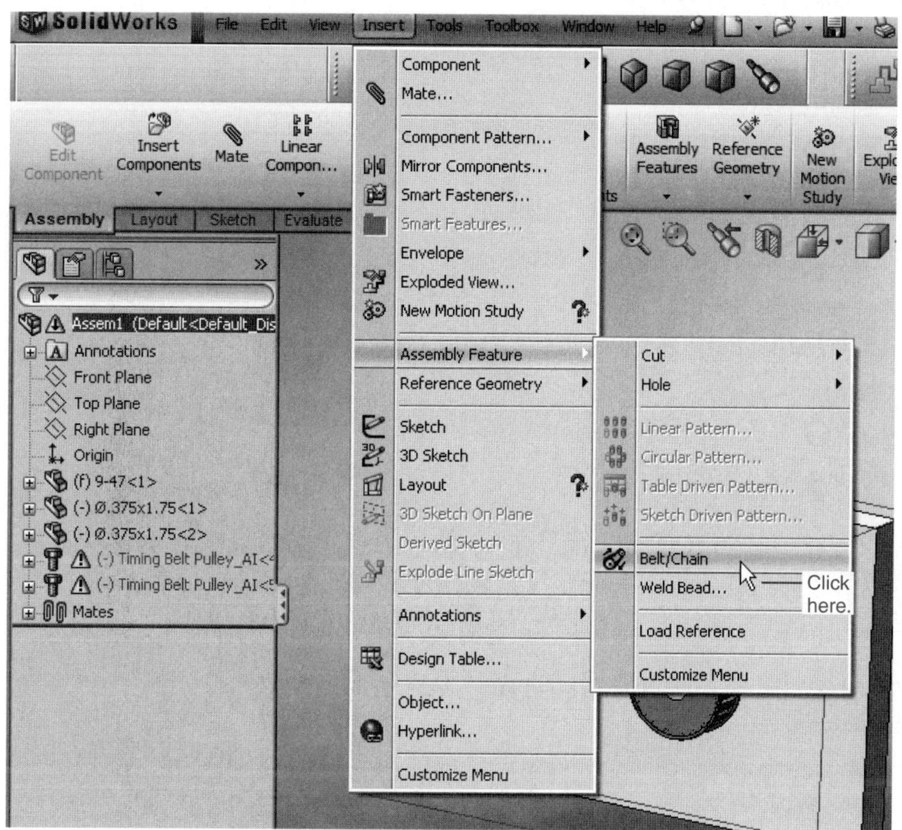
Click here.

Figure 9-52

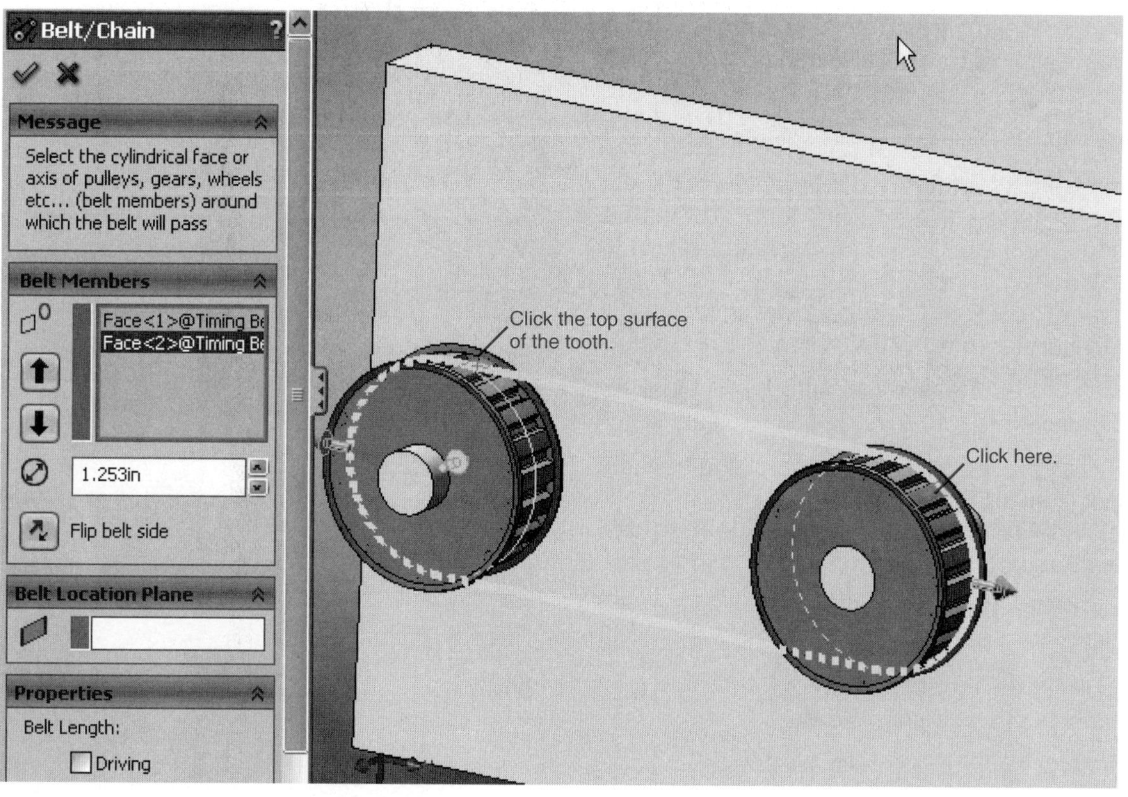
Click the top surface of the tooth.
Click here.

Figure 9-53

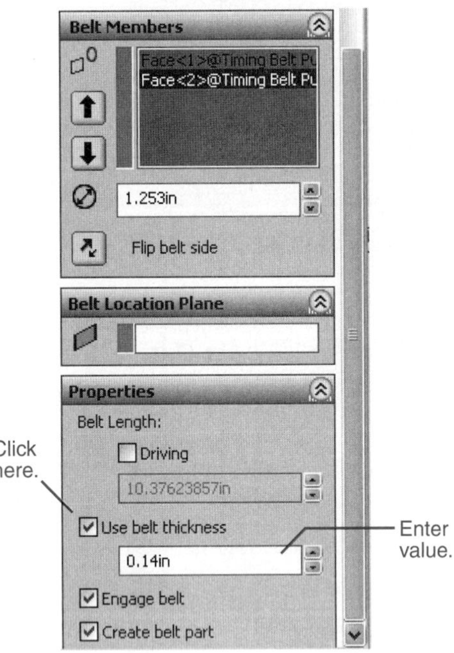

Figure 9-54

12. Click the OK check mark.

See Figure 9-54. The thickness value came from the data listed in step 5.

13. Save the Assembly as **Belt Assembly - 1.**
14. Save the belt as **Belt1** (This will be the default file name.)

If a warning box appears, click the **Close** option.

15. Open **Belt Assembly - 1,** then right-click **Belt1** in the **Browse . . .** box. Click the **Edit Feature** option. Click the OK check mark and return to the **Browse . . .** box.
16. Right-click the **Belt1** heading, then right-click the **[Belt<Belt Assembly-1]<1>** heading and select the **Edit Part** option.

See Figure 9-55.

17. Left-click the top straight section of the belt and select the **Edit Sketch** option.
18. Click the **Features** tool and select the **Extruded Boss/Base** option.

The **Extrude Properties Manager** will appear. See Figure 9-56.

19. Set **Direction 1** for **Mid Plane.**
20. Set the **Depth** value for **0.42 in.**

This width keeps the belt inside the flanges.

21. Click the **Thin Feature** option and set the thickness for **0.14in.**

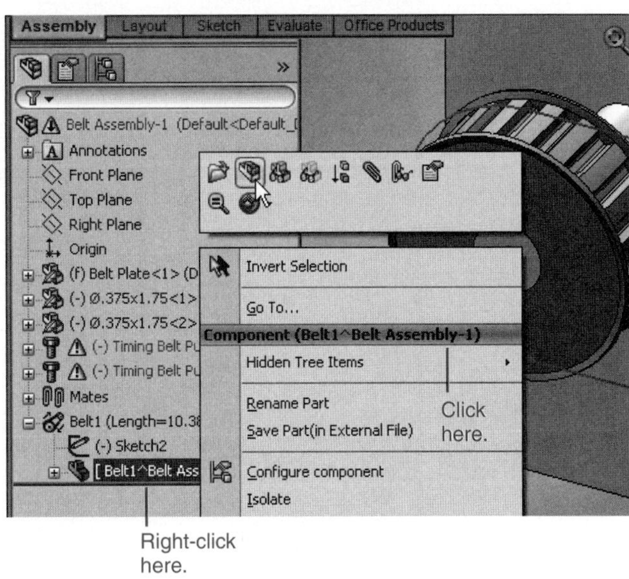

Figure 9-55

22. Click the OK check mark.

See Figure 9-57.

9-14 PULLEYS AND KEYS

Figure 9-58 shows an assembly made from the support plate and two shafts. Figure 9-59 shows a dimensioned drawing of the support plate and a shaft. The shaft includes a keyway defined to accept a 0.125 × 0.125 × 0.250 square key.

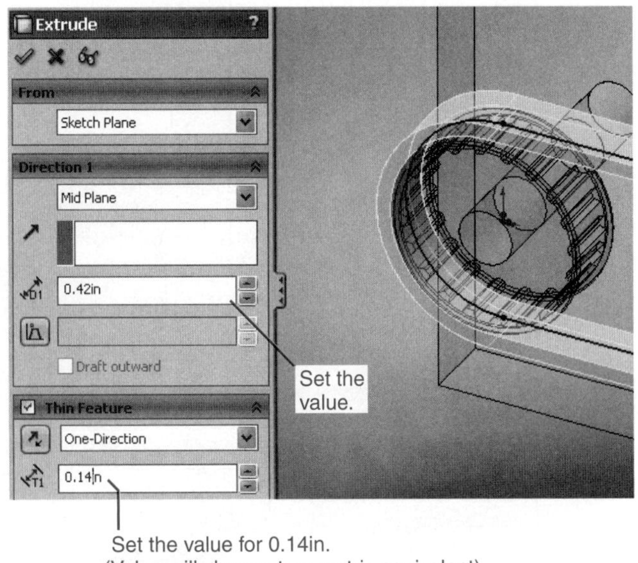

Figure 9-56

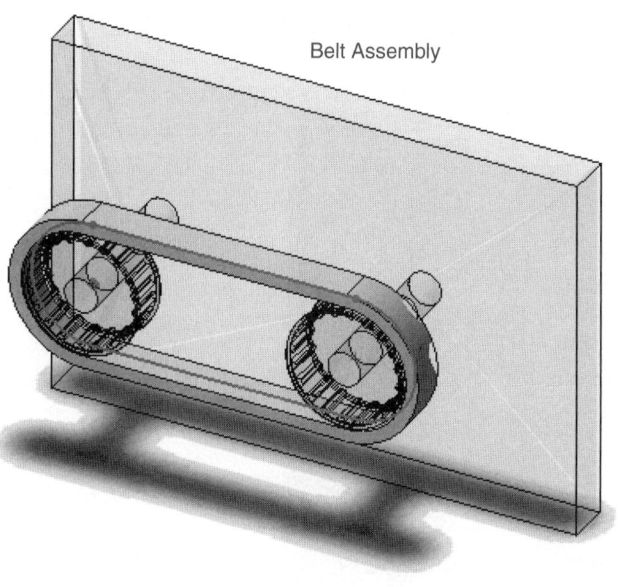

Figure 9-57

To Add a Keyway to a Pulley

1. Access the **Design Library,** click **Toolbox, Ansi Inches, Power Transmission,** and **Timing Belt Pulley.**
2. Click and drag a pulley into the drawing area.
3. Set the values as shown in Figure 9-60. Set the **Keyway** for **Square 1.**

See Figure 9-60.

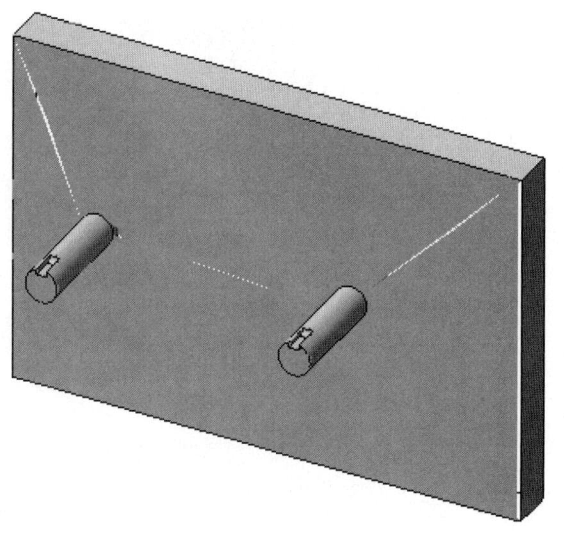

Figure 9-58

4. Click the OK check mark.
5. Assemble the pulleys onto the shafts.

See Figure 9-61.

1. Access the **Design Library,** click **Toolbox, Ansi Inches, Keys,** and **Parallel Keys.**
2. Click and drag a key into the drawing area.
3. Set the key's **Properties** values for a shaft diameter of **7/16 - 9/16.** Set the **Length** for **0.25.**

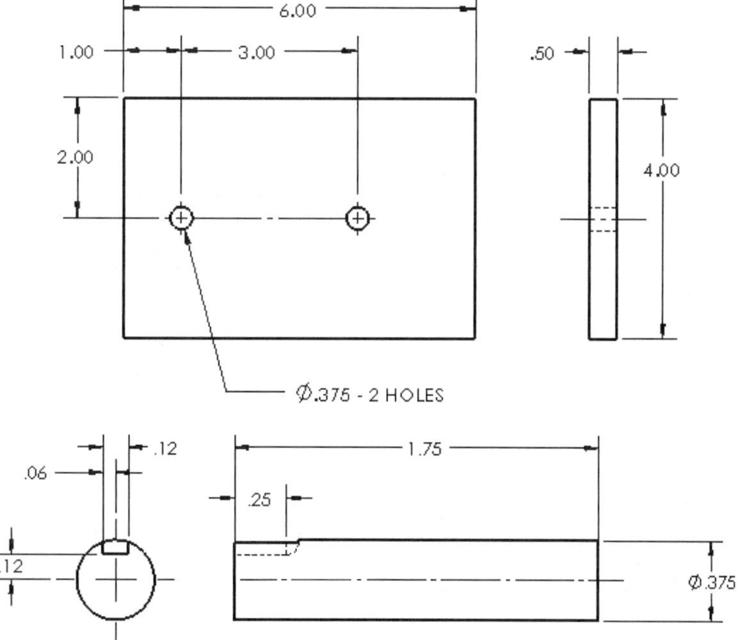

Figure 9-59

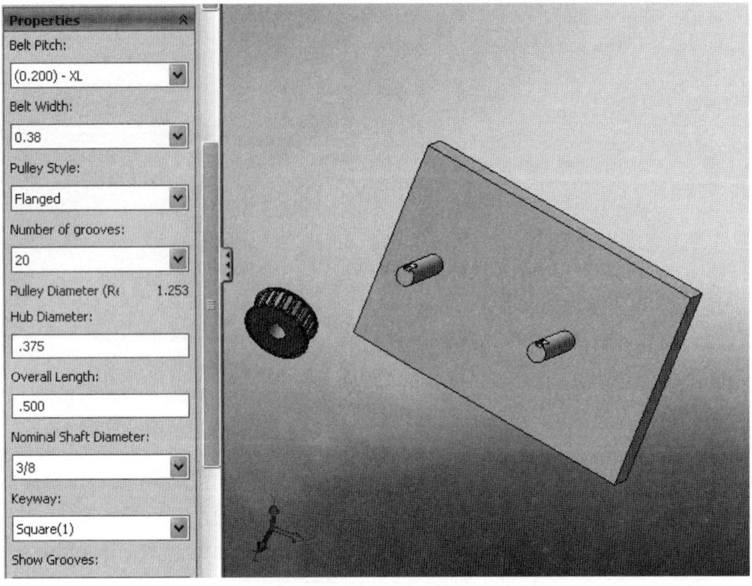

Figure 9-60

4. Click the OK check mark.

   See Figure 9-62.

5. Assemble the keys into the keyways and add a timing belt.

   See Figure 9-63.

Figure 9-61

9-15 MULTIPLE PULLEYS

More than one pulley can be included in an assembly. Figure 9-64 shows drawings for a support plate and shaft.

To Create a Multi-Pulley Assembly

1. Create an **Assembly** drawing of the support plate and shafts with the shafts inserted into the support plate so that the shafts extend 1.00 beyond the surface of the support plate.

   See Figure 9-65.

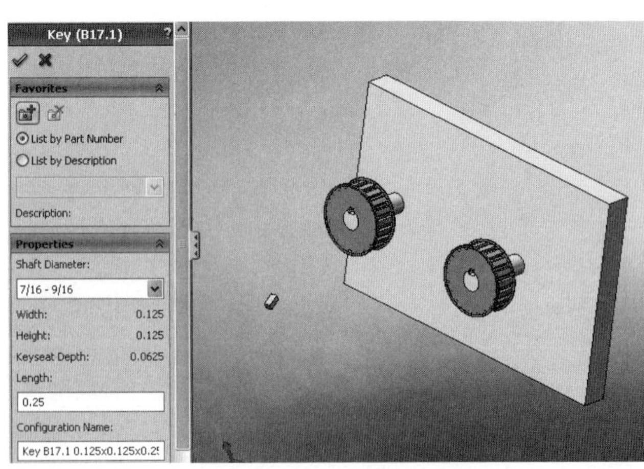

Figure 9-62

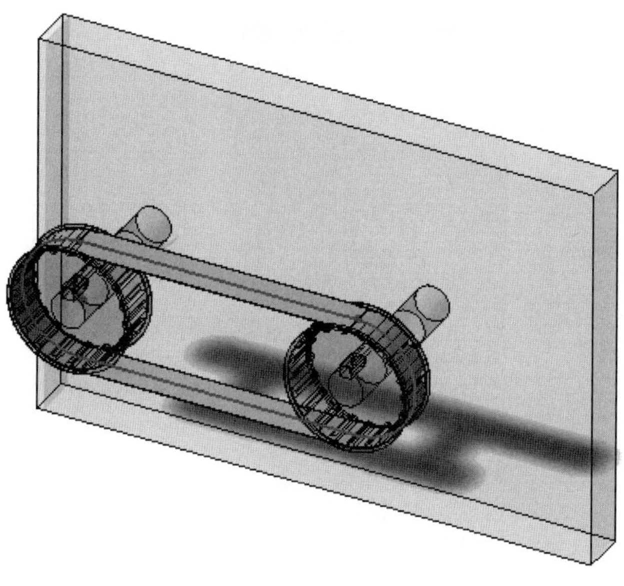

Figure 9-63

2. Create two XL pulleys with the properties specified in Figure 9-66.
3. Create two L pulleys with the properties specified in Figure 9-67.
4. Assemble the pulleys onto the shafts as shown.

   See Figure 9-68.

5. Click **Insert, Assembly Feature,** and **Belt/Chain.**
6. Click the top surface of the pulley's teeth to identify the belt location. Use the **Flip belt side** tool if necessary.

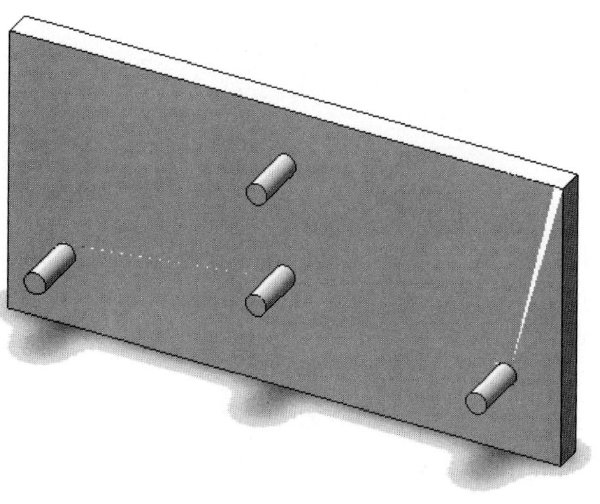

Figure 9-65

Figure 9-69 shows the assembly with a belt profile. Width and thickness may be added to belt, as explained in the previous section.

> ***Note:***
> If you use the cursor to rotate one of the pulleys, they will all rotate.

9-16 CHAINS AND SPROCKETS

SolidWorks creates chains and sprockets in a manner similar to that used to create belts and pulleys. The resulting chain is a representation of a chain but looks like a belt representation.

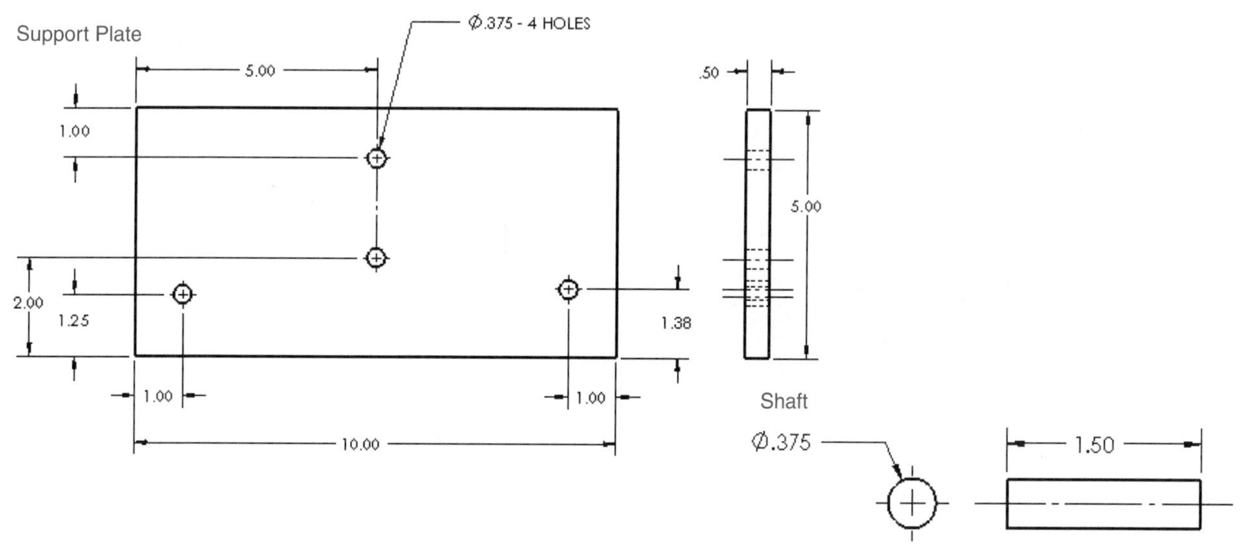

Figure 9-64

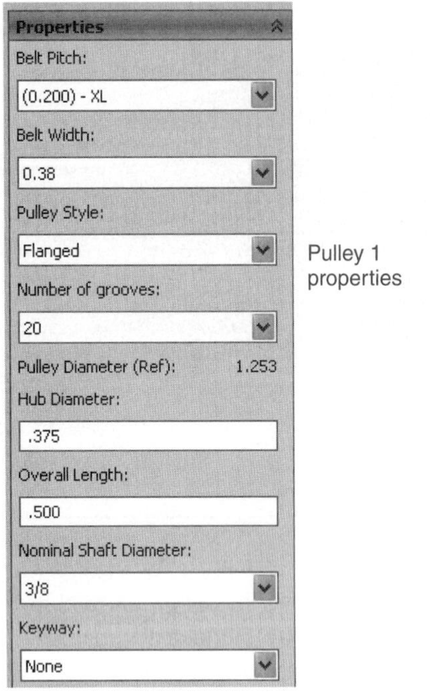

Figure 9-66

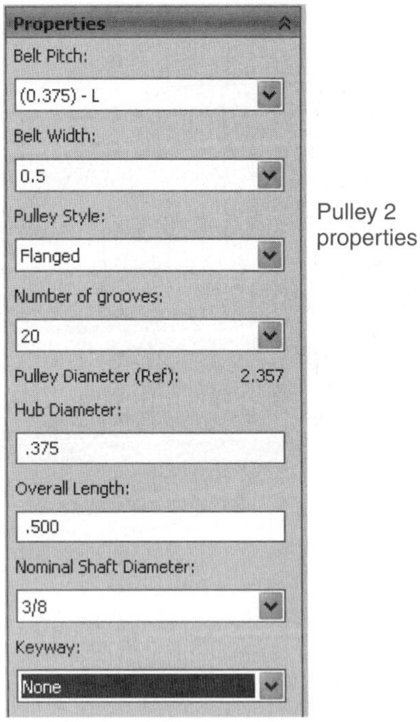

Properties
Belt Pitch:
(0.375) - L
Belt Width:
0.5
Pulley Style:
Flanged
Number of grooves:
20
Pulley Diameter (Ref): 2.357
Hub Diameter:
.375
Overall Length:
.500
Nominal Shaft Diameter:
3/8
Keyway:
None

Pulley 2 properties

Figure 9-67

Figure 9-70 shows a support plate and a shaft that will be used to create a chain and sprocket assembly.

To Create a Chain and Sprocket Assembly

1. Draw the support plate and shaft shown in Figure 9-70 and create an **Assembly** drawing. The shafts should extend 3.00 beyond the top surface of the support plate.

   See Figure 9-71.

2. Access the **Design Library** and click **Toolbox, Ansi Inch, Power Transmission,** and **Chain Sprockets.**

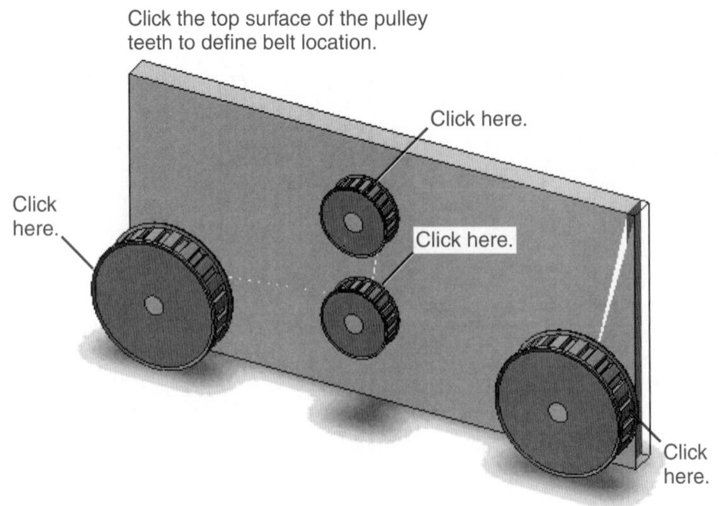

Figure 9-68

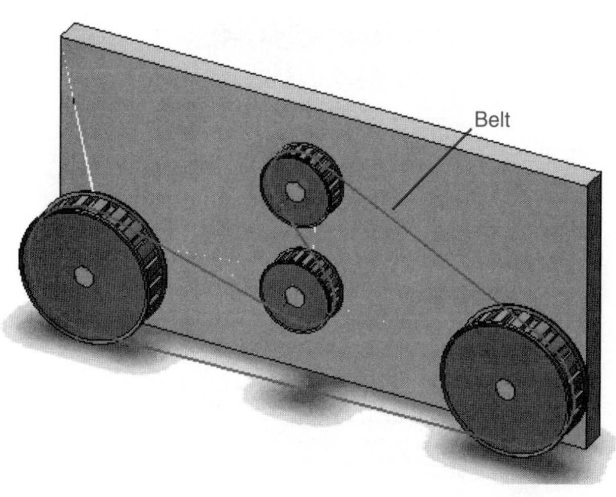

Figure 9-69

3. Click **Silent Larger Sprocket** and drag the icon into the field of the drawing.
4. Set the following chain property values:

   Chain Number = **SC610**
   Number of Teeth = **24**
   Hub Style = **None**
   Nominal Shaft Diameter = **1**
   Keyway = **None**

5. Assemble the sprockets onto the shafts.

   See Figure 9-72.

6. Click **Insert** at the top of the screen, then **Assembly Feature,** and **Belt/Chain.**

   See Figure 9-73.

7. Click the bottom surface of a sprocket tooth as shown on both sprockets.

   See Figure 9-74.

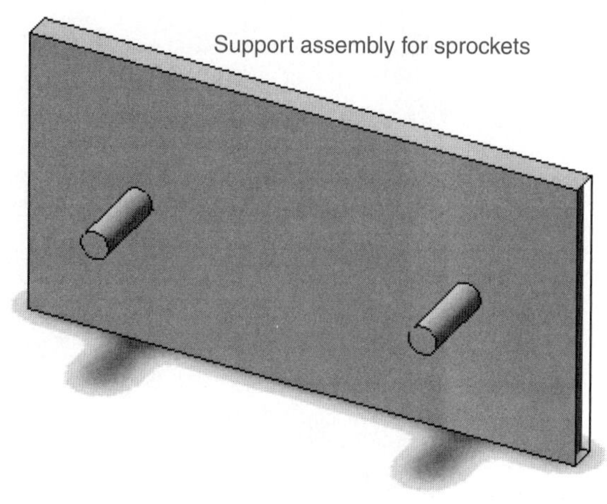

Figure 9-71

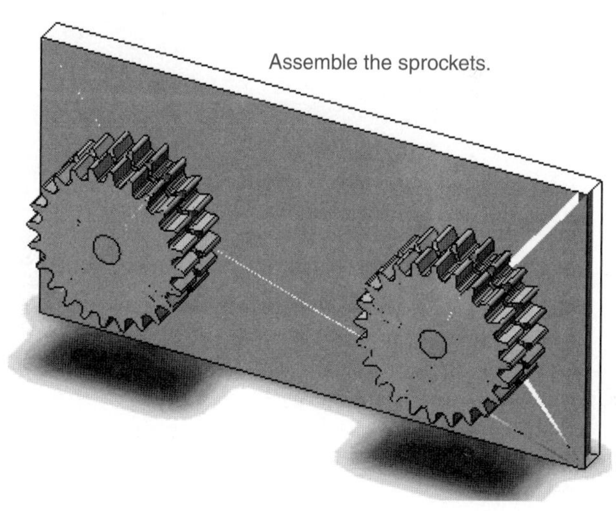

Figure 9-72

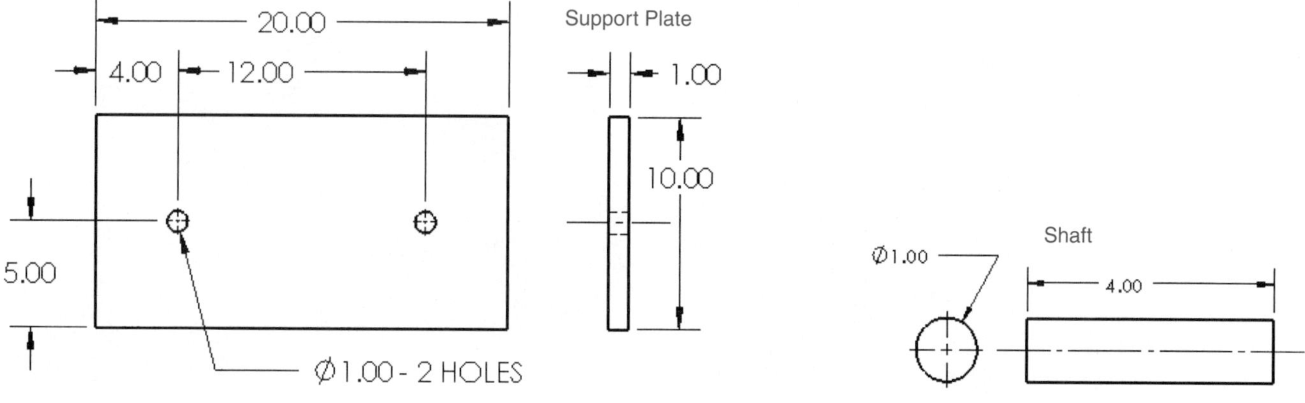

Figure 9-70

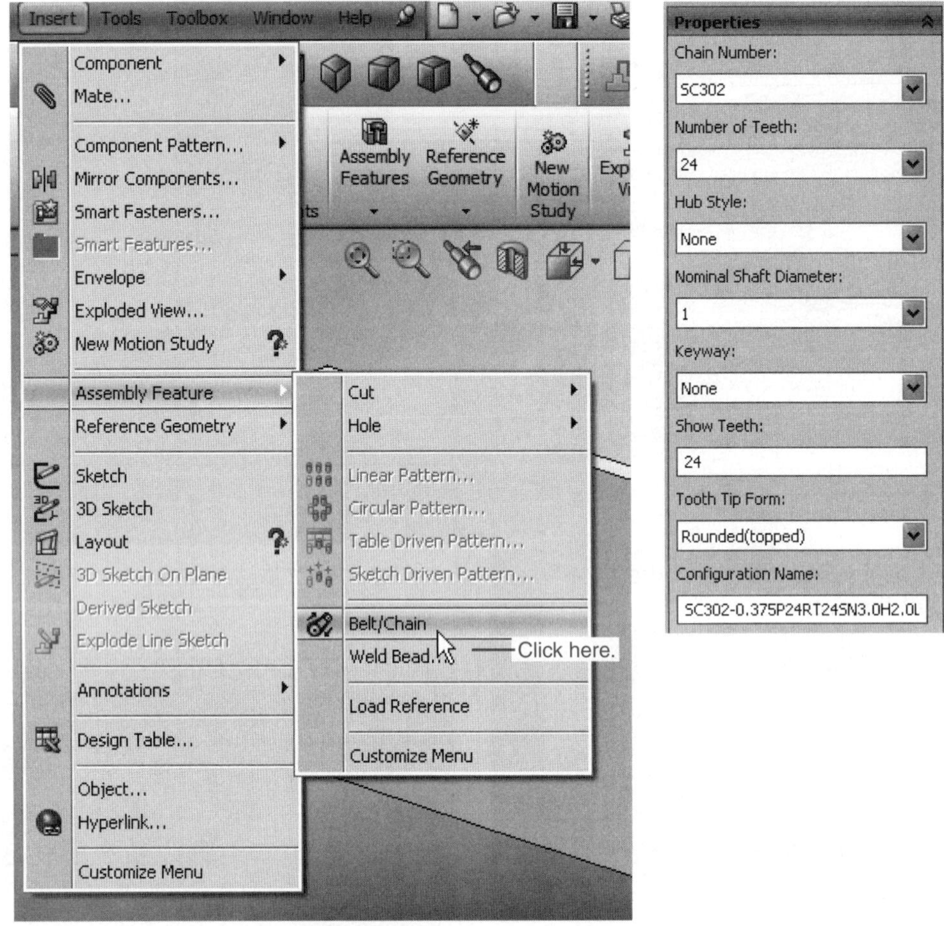

Figure 9-73

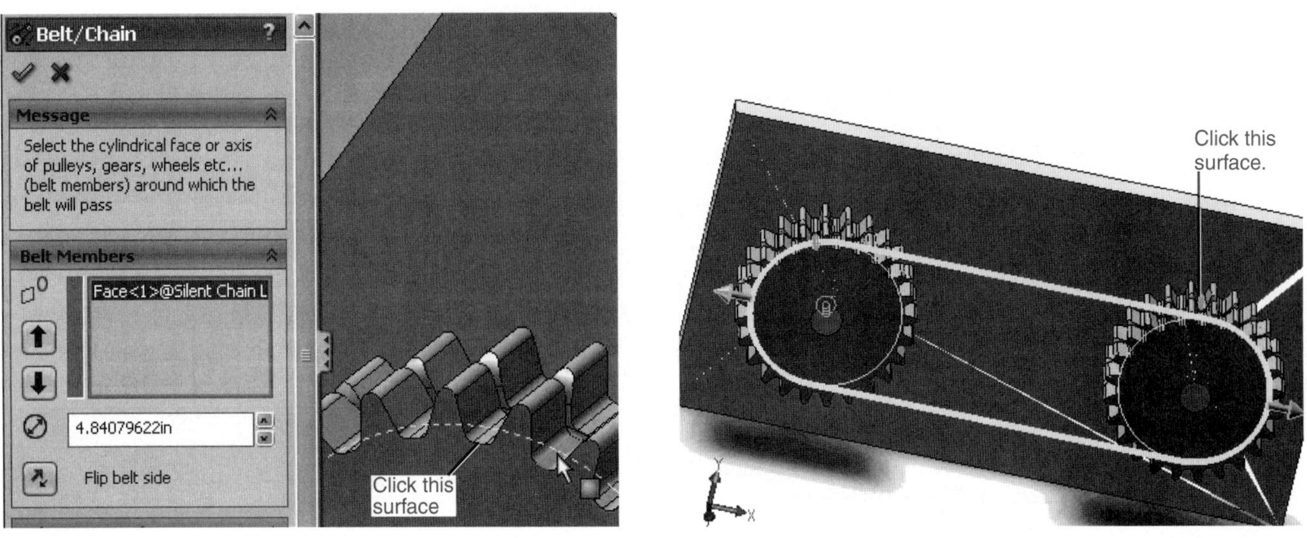

Figure 9-74

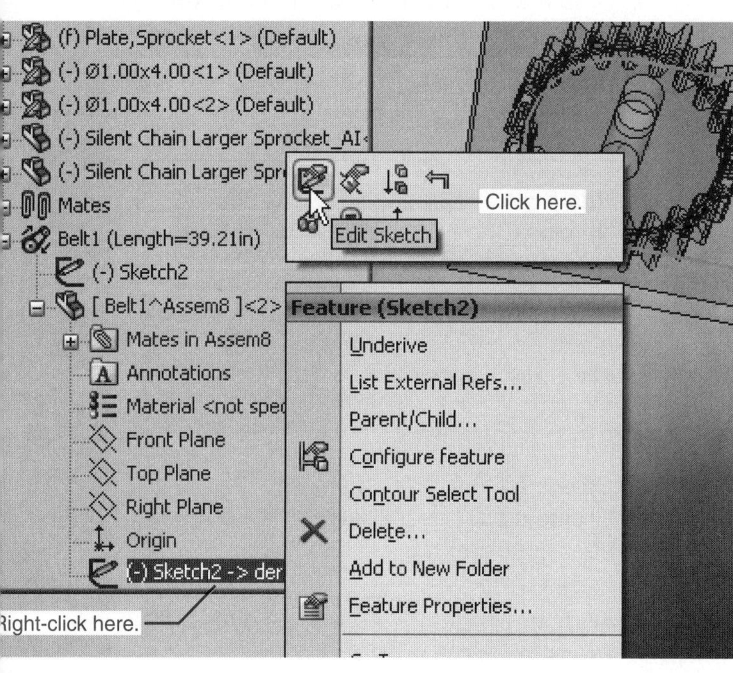

Figure 9-75

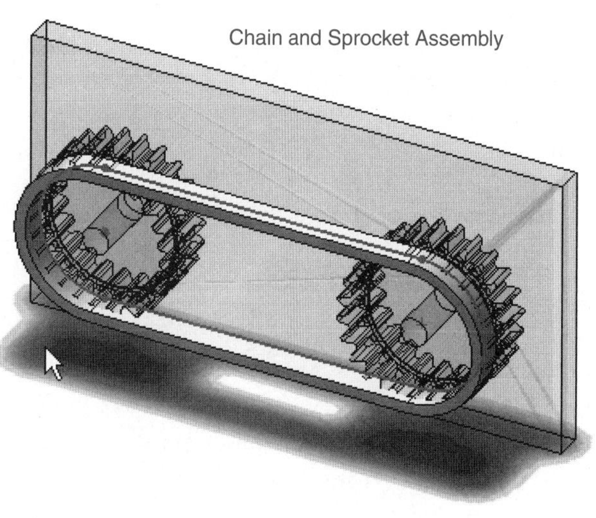

Figure 9-77

To Add Thickness and Width to the Chain

1. Right-click **Belt1** in the **Browse . . .** box and select the **Edit Feature** option.

   See Figure 9-75.

2. In the **Belt1** box scroll down and click the **Create belt part** box.
3. Click the OK check mark.
4. Save the assembly and the belt.
5. Click the + sign to the left of the **Belt1** heading in the **Browse . . .** box. Click the + sign to the left of the **[Belt1, Assem . .]** heading, right-click the **Sketch 2** heading, and select the **Edit Part** option.
6. Left-click the upper horizontal segment of the belt (chain) and select the **Edit Sketch** option. Click the **Extrude Boss/Base** tool on the **Features** toolbar.
7. Set **Direction 1** for **Mid Plane,** D1 for **25mm,** and **Thin Feature** value for **10.00mm.**

   See Figures 9-76 and Figure 9-77.

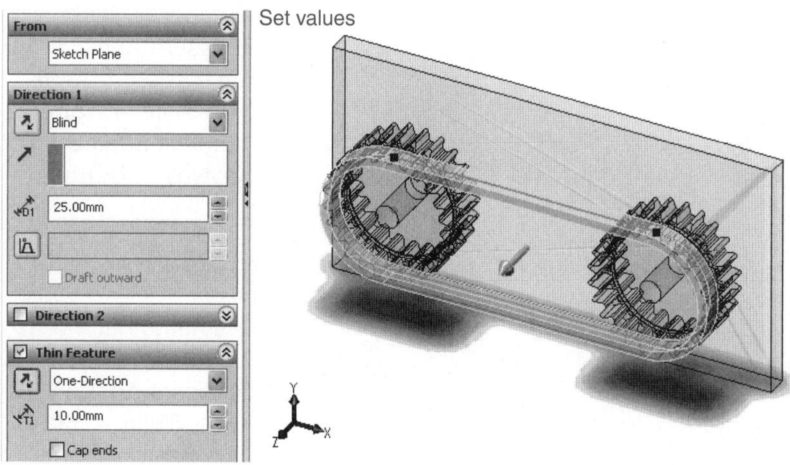

Figure 9-76

9-17 PROJECTS

Project 9-1: Inches

See Figure P9-1.

1. Create a Ø.375 × 1.75 shaft.
   A. Create a spur gear based on the following specifications:
      Diametral Pitch = **32**
      Number of Teeth = **36**
      Pressure Angle = **14.5**
      Face Width = **.250**
      Hub Style = **None**
      Nominal Shaft Diameter = **3/8**
      Keyway = **None**
   B. Assemble the gear onto the shaft with a 0.25 offset from the end of the shaft.

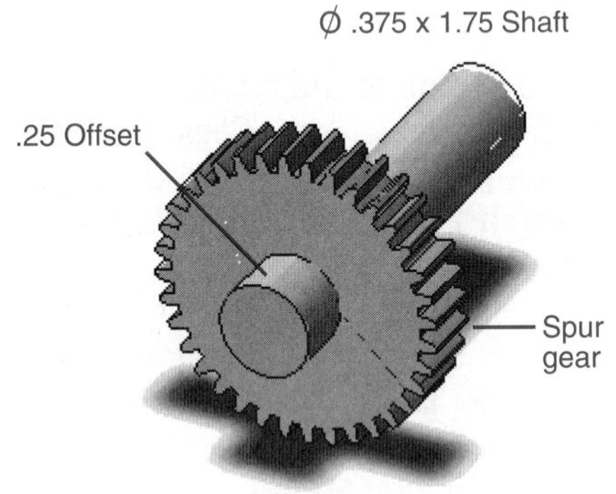

Figure P9-1

Project 9-2: Inches

A. Create a Ø.250 × 1.50 shaft.
B. Create a spur gear based on the following specifications:
   Diametral Pitch = **40**
   Number of Teeth = **56**
   Pressure Angle = **14.5**
   Face Width = **.125**
   Hub Style = **None**
   Nominal Shaft Diameter = **1/4**
   Keyway = **None**
C. Assemble the gear onto the shaft with a 0.125 offset from the end of the shaft.

Project 9-3: Inches

A. Create a Ø1.00 × 4.00 shaft.
B. Create a spur gear based on the following specifications:
   Diametral Pitch = **8**
   Number of Teeth = **66**
   Pressure Angle = **14.5**
   Face Width = **.625**
   Hub Style = **None**
   Nominal Shaft Diameter = **1**
   Keyway = **None**
C. Assemble the gear onto the shaft with a 0.00 offset from the end of the shaft.

Project 9-4: Millimeters

A. Create a Ø8.0 × 30 shaft.
B. Create a spur gear based on the following specifications:
   Module = **2**
   Number of Teeth = **40**
   Pressure Angle = **14.5**
   Face Width = **12**
   Hub Style = **None**
   Nominal Shaft Diameter = **8**
   Keyway = **None**
C. Assemble the gear onto the shaft with a 5.0 offset from the end of the shaft.

Project 9-5: Inches

See Figure P9-5.

A. Create a Ø.625 × 4.00 shaft.
B. Create a spur gear based on the following specifications:
   Gear 1:
      Diametral Pitch = **10**
      Number of Teeth = **42**
      Pressure Angle = **14.5**
      Face Width = **.375**
      Hub Style = **None**
      Nominal Shaft Diameter = **5/8**
      Keyway = **None**
C. Create a second gear based on the following specifications:
   Gear 2:
      Diametral Pitch = **10**
      Number of Teeth = **68**
      Pressure Angle = **14.5**
      Face Width = **.500**
      Hub Style = **None**
      Nominal Shaft Diameter = **5/8**
      Keyway = **None**

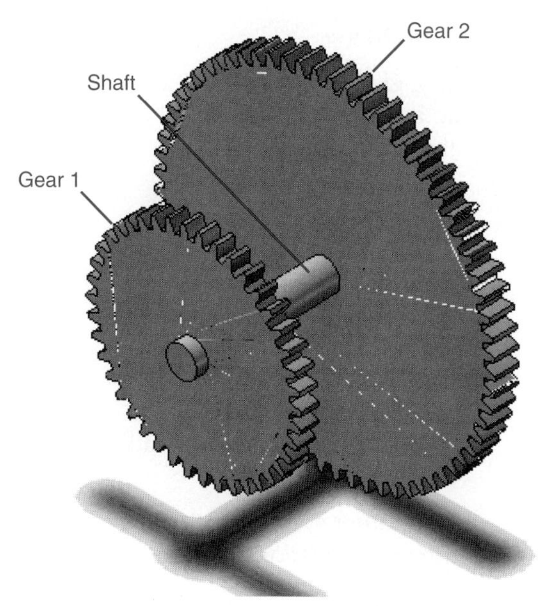

Figure P9-5

D. Assemble the gears onto the shaft with Gear 1 offset 0.25 from the front end of the shaft and Gear 2 offset 3.00 from the front end of the shaft.

Project 9-6: Inches

A. Create a Ø.25 × 2.75 shaft.
B. Create a spur gear based on the following specifications:

Gear 1:
- Diametral Pitch = **40**
- Number of Teeth = **18**
- Pressure Angle = **14.5**
- Face Width = **.125**
- Hub Style = **None**
- Nominal Shaft Diameter = **1/4**
- Keyway = **None**

C. Create a second gear based on the following specifications:

Gear 2:
- Diametral Pitch = **40**
- Number of Teeth = **54**
- Pressure Angle = **14.5**
- Face Width = **.125**
- Hub Style = **None**
- Nominal Shaft Diameter = **1/4**
- Keyway = **None**

D. Assemble the gears onto the shaft with Gear 1 offset .125 from the front end of the shaft and Gear 2 offset 2.00 from the front end of the shaft.

Project 9-7: Millimeters

A. Create a Ø12 × 80 shaft.
B. Create a spur gear based on the following specifications:

Gear 1:
- Module = **1.0**
- Number of Teeth = **16**
- Pressure Angle = **14.5**
- Face Width = **8**
- Hub Style = **None**
- Nominal Shaft Diameter = **12**
- Keyway = **None**

C. Create a second gear based on the following specifications:

Gear 2:
- Module = **1.0**
- Number of Teeth = **48**
- Pressure Angle = **14.5**
- Face Width = **10**
- Hub Style = **None**
- Nominal Shaft Diameter = **12**
- Keyway = **None**

D. Assemble the gears onto the shaft with Gear 1 offset 5 from the front end of the shaft and Gear 2 offset 50 from the front end of the shaft.

Project 9-8: Inches

See Figure P9-8.

A. Create a Ø.375 × 2.75 shaft. Save the shaft.
B. Create a spur gear based on the following specifications:

Gear 1:
- Diametral Pitch = **10**
- Number of Teeth = **22**
- Pressure Angle = **14.5**
- Face Width = **.375**
- Hub Style = **One Side**
- Hub Diameter = **.75**
- Overall Length = **.75**
- Nominal Shaft Diameter = **3/8**
- Keyway = **None**

C. Create another spur gear based on the following specifications:

Gear 2:
- Diametral Pitch = **10**
- Number of Teeth = **44**
- Pressure Angle = **14.5**
- Face Width = **.375**
- Hub Style = **One Side**

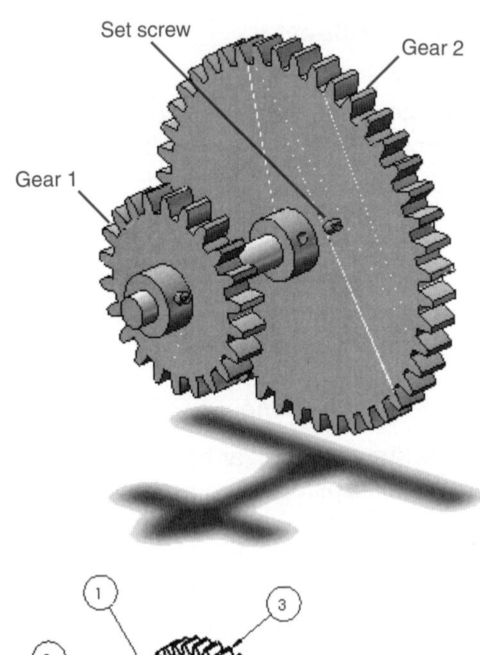

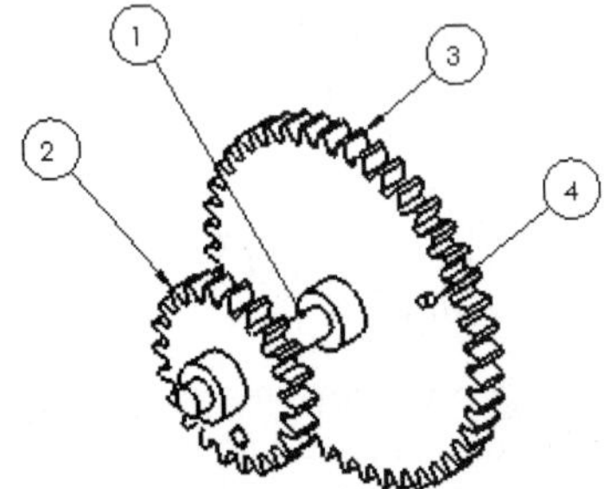

ITEM NO.	PART NUMBER	DESCRIPTION	QTY.
1	AM-311-A1	Ø.375 × 2.75 SHAFT	1
2	AM311-A2	GEAR 1 - N22	1
3	AM311-A3	GEAR 2 - N44	1
4	#6-32 UNC	SET SCREW	2

Figure P9-8

Hub Diameter = **.75**
Overall Length = **.75**
Nominal Shaft Diameter = **3/8**
Keyway = **None**

D. Add #6-32 threaded holes to each gear hub .19 from the top hub surface.
E. Assemble the gears onto the shaft with Gear 1 offset .25 from the front end of the shaft and Gear 2 offset 2.25 from the front end of the shaft.
F. Insert a #6-32 Slotted Set Screw with an Oval Point into each hole.
G. Create an exploded assembly drawing.
H. Create a bill of materials.
I. Animate the assembly.

Project 9-9: Inches

A. Create a Ø.375 × 3.25 shaft. Save the shaft.
B. Create a spur gear based on the following specifications:

Gear 1:
Diametral Pitch = **20**
Number of Teeth = **18**
Pressure Angle = **14.5**
Face Width = **.25**
Hub Style = **One Side**
Hub Diameter = **.50**
Overall Length = **.50**
Nominal Shaft Diameter = **3/8**
Keyway = **None**

C. Create another spur gear based on the following specifications:

Gear 2:
Diametral Pitch = **20**
Number of Teeth = **63**
Pressure Angle = **14.5**
Face Width = **.25**
Hub Style = **One Side**
Hub Diameter = **.50**
Overall Length = **.50**
Nominal Shaft Diameter = **3/8**
Keyway = **None**

D. Add #4-40 threaded holes to each gear hub .19 from the top hub surface.
E. Assemble the gears onto the shaft with Gear 1 offset .25 from the front end of the shaft and Gear 2 offset 2.63 from the front end of the shaft.

Project 9-10: Millimeters

A. Create a 24 × 120 shaft. Save the shaft.
B. Create a spur gear based on the following specifications:

Gear 1:
Module = **1.5**
Number of Teeth = **18**
Pressure Angle = **14.5**
Face Width = **12**
Hub Style = **One Side**
Hub Diameter = **32**
Overall Length = **30**
Nominal Shaft Diameter = **16**
Keyway = **None**

C. Create another spur gear based on the following specifications:

Gear 2:
Module = **1.5**
Number of Teeth = **70**

Pressure Angle = **14.5**
Face Width = **12**
Hub Style = **One Side**
Hub Diameter = **40**
Overall Length = **30**
Nominal Shaft Diameter = **16**
Keyway = **None**

D. Add M3.0 threaded holes to each gear hub 10 from the top hub surface.
E. Assemble the gears onto the shaft with Gear 1 offset 4.0 from the front end of the shaft and Gear 2 offset 80.0 from the front end of the shaft.
F. Insert an M3 Socket Set Screw with a Cup Point into each hole.
G. Create an exploded assembly drawing.
H. Create a bill of materials.
I. Animate the assembly.

Project 9-11: Inches

See Figure P9-11.

A. Draw three Ø.375 × 3.00 shafts.
B. Draw the support plate shown in Figure P9-11.
C. Access the **Design Library** and create two Gear 1s and two Gear 2s.

The gears are defined as follows:

Gear 1:
Diametral Pitch = **16**
Number of Teeth = **24**
Pressure Angle = **14.5**
Face Width = **.25**
Hub Style = **One Side**
Hub Diameter = **.50**
Overall Length = **.50**
Nominal Shaft Diameter = **3/8**
Keyway = **None**

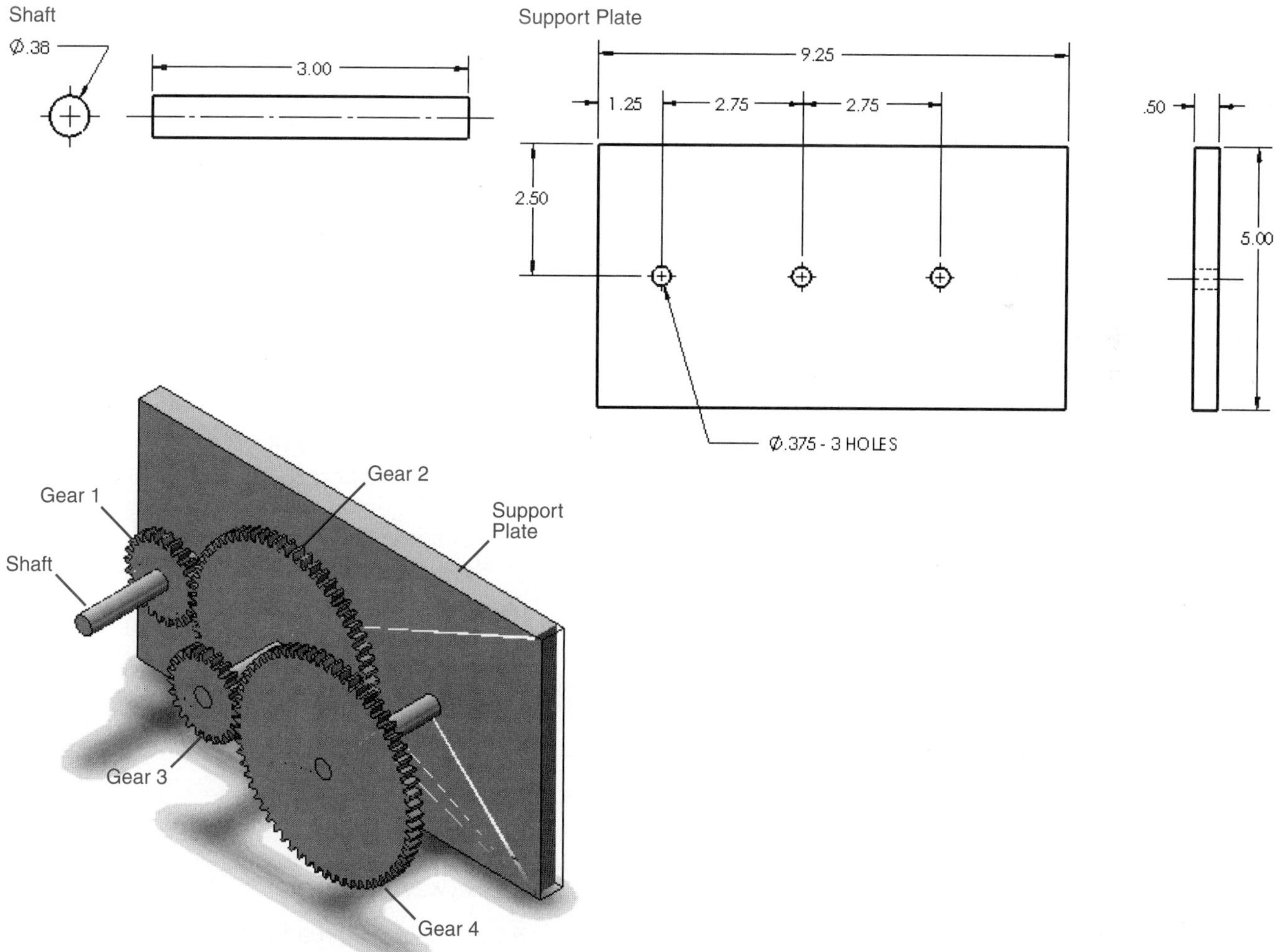

Figure P9-11

Gear 2:

Diametral Pitch = **16**
Number of Teeth = **64**
Pressure Angle = **14.5**
Face Width = **.25**
Hub Style = **One Side**
Hub Diameter = **.50**
Overall Length = **.50**
Nominal Shaft Diameter = **3/8**
Keyway = **None**

D. Add #6-32 threaded holes to each gear hub .19 from the top hub surface.
E. Assemble the gears onto the shafts so that Gear 1 and Gear 2 are offset .50 from the support plate, and Gear 3 and Gear 4 are parallel to the ends of the shafts.
F. Insert a #6-32 Slotted Set Screw with an Oval Point into each hole.
G. Create an exploded assembly drawing.
H. Create a bill of materials.
I. Animate the assembly.

Project 9-12: Inches—Design Problem

Based on Figure P9-11 define a support plate and shafts that support the following gears. Use two of each gear.

Parameters:

Plate: .50 thick, a distance of at least .50 beyond the other edge of the gears to the edge of the plate.

Shafts: Diameters that match the gear's bore diameter; minimum offset between the plate and the gear is .50 or greater.

Gear 1:

Diametral Pitch = **10**
Number of Teeth = **24**
Pressure Angle = **14.5**
Face Width = **.375**
Hub Style = **One Side**
Hub Diameter = **1.00**
Overall Length = **.875**
Nominal Shaft Diameter = **7/16**
Keyway = **None**

A. Create another spur gear based on the following specifications:

Gear 2:

Diametral Pitch = **10**
Number of Teeth = **96**
Pressure Angle = **14.5**
Face Width = **.375**
Hub Style = **One Side**
Hub Diameter = **1.00**
Overall Length = **.875**
Nominal Shaft Diameter = **7/16**
Keyway = **None**

B. Add #6-32 threaded holes to each gear hub 0.19 from the top hub surface.
C. Assemble the gears onto the shafts so that Gear 1 and Gear 2 are offset .50 from the support plate, and Gear 3 and Gear 4 are parallel to the ends of the shafts.
D. Insert a #6-32 Slotted Set Screw with an Oval Point into each hole.
E. Create an exploded assembly drawing.
F. Create a bill of materials.
G. Animate the assembly.

Project 9-13: Inches—Design Problem

Based on Figure P9-11 define a support plate and shafts that support the following gears. Use two of each gear.

Parameters:

Plate: .50 thick, a distance of at least .50 beyond the other edge of the gears to the edge of the plate.

Shafts: Diameters that match the gear's bore diameter: minimum offset between the plate and the gear is .50 or greater.

Gear 1:

Diametral Pitch = **6**
Number of Teeth = **22**
Pressure Angle = **14.5**
Face Width = **.500**
Hub Style = **One Side**
Hub Diameter = **1.50**
Overall Length = **1.25**
Nominal Shaft Diameter = **.75**
Keyway = **None**

Gear 2:

Diametral Pitch = **6**
Number of Teeth = **77**
Pressure Angle = **14.5**
Face Width = **.50**
Hub Style = **One Side**
Hub Diameter = **1.50**
Overall Length = **1.25**
Nominal Shaft Diameter = **.75**
Keyway = **None**

A. Add ¼-20 UNC threaded holes to each gear hub 0.25 from the top hub surface.
B. Assemble the gears onto the shafts so that Gear 1 and Gear 2 are offset 0.50 from the

support plate, and Gear 3 and Gear 4 are parallel to the ends of the shafts.

C. Insert a ¼-20 UNC Slotted Set Screw with an Oval Point into each hole.
D. Create an exploded assembly drawing.
E. Create a bill of materials.
F. Animate the assembly.

Project 9-14: Millimeters—Design Problem

Based on Figure P9-11 define a support plate and shafts that support the following gears. Use two of each gear.

Parameters:

Plate: 20 thick, a distance of at least 25 beyond the other edge of the gears to the edge of the plate.

Shafts: Diameters that match the gear's bore diameter; minimum offset between the plate and the gear is 20 or greater.

Gear 1:

Module = **2.5**
Number of Teeth = **20**
Pressure Angle = **14.5**
Face Width = **16**
Hub Style = **One Side**
Hub Diameter = **26**
Overall Length = **30**
Nominal Shaft Diameter = **20**
Keyway = **None**

Gear 2:

Module = **2.5**
Number of Teeth = **50**
Pressure Angle = **14.5**
Face Width = **16**
Hub Style = **One Side**
Hub Diameter = **30**
Overall Length = **30**
Nominal Shaft Diameter = **20**
Keyway = **None**

A. Add M4 threaded holes to each gear hub 12 from the top hub surface.
B. Assemble the gears onto the shafts so that Gear 1 and Gear 2 are offset 10 from the support plate, and Gear 3 and Gear 4 are parallel to the ends of the shafts.
C. Insert an M4 Slotted Set Screw with an Oval Point into each hole.
D. Create an exploded assembly drawing.
E. Create a bill of materials.
F. Animate the assembly.

Project 9-15: Inches

See Figure P9-15.

A. Draw four Ø.375 × 3.00 shafts.
B. Draw the support plate shown in Figure P9-15.
C. Access the **Design Library** and create three Gear 1s and three Gear 2s.

The gears are defined as follows:

Gear 1:

Diametral Pitch = **16**
Number of Teeth = **24**
Pressure Angle = **14.5**
Face Width = **.25**
Hub Style = **One Side**
Hub Diameter = **.50**
Overall Length = **.50**
Nominal Shaft Diameter = **3/8**
Keyway = **None**

Gear 2:

Diametral Pitch = **16**
Number of Teeth = **64**
Pressure Angle = **14.5**
Face Width = **.25**
Hub Style = **One Side**
Hub Diameter = **.50**
Overall Length = **.50**
Nominal Shaft Diameter = **3/8**
Keyway = **None**

D. Add #6-32 threaded holes to each gear hub 0.19 from the top hub surface.
E. Assemble the gears onto the shafts so that the offset between the support plate and the gears is as defined in Figure P9-15.
F. Insert a #6-32 Slotted Set Screw with an Oval Point into each hole.
G. Create an exploded assembly drawing.
H. Create a bill of materials.
I. Animate the assembly.

Project 9-16: Inches—Design Problem

Based on Figure P9-15 define a support plate and shafts that support the following gears. Use two of each gear.

Parameters:

Plate: .50 thick, a distance of at least .50 beyond the other edge of the gears to the edge of the plate.

Shafts: Diameters that match the gear's bore diameter; minimum offset between the plate and the gear is .50 or greater.

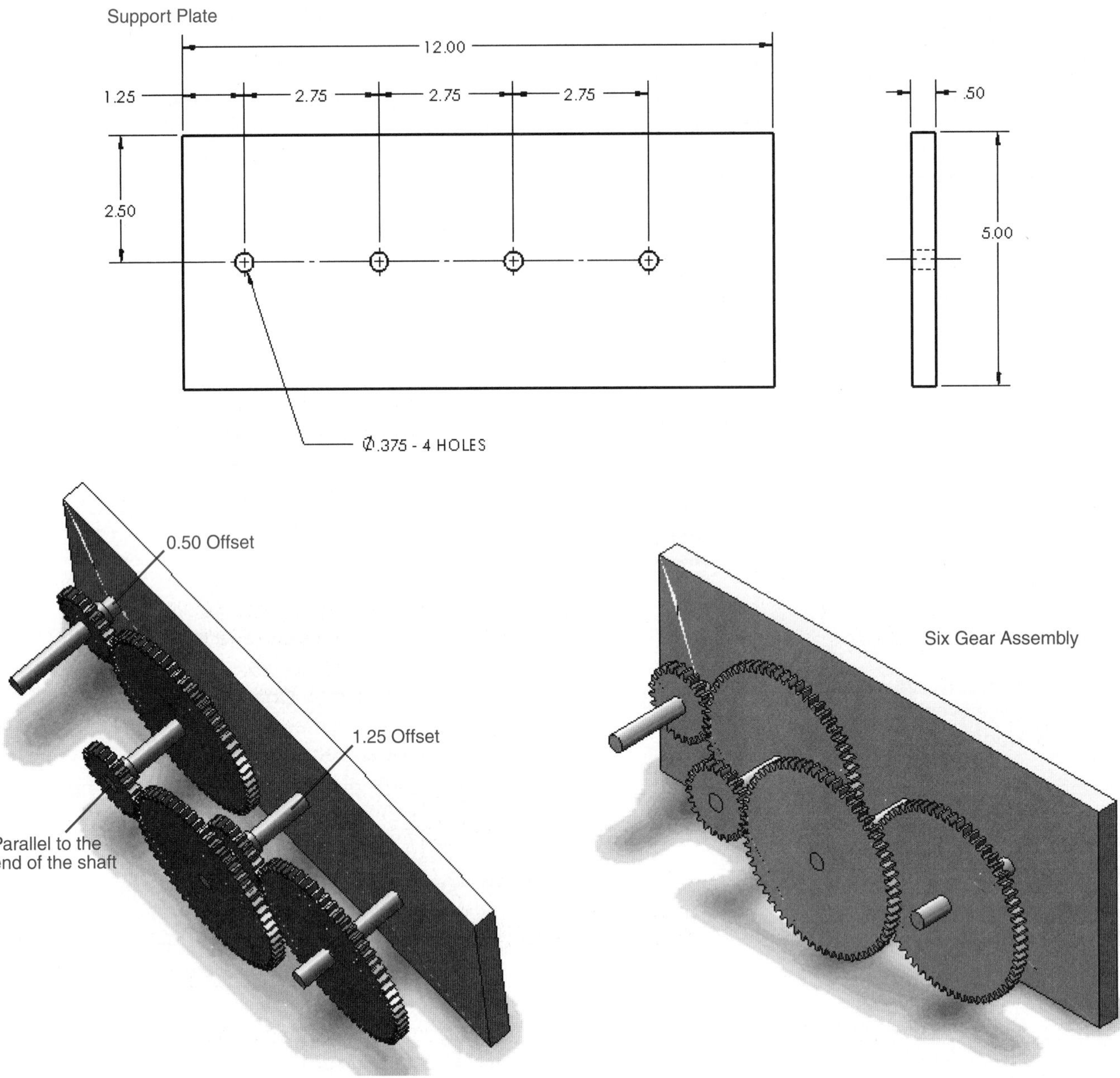

Figure P9-15

Gear 1:
- Diametral Pitch = **6**
- Number of Teeth = **22**
- Pressure Angle = **14.5**
- Face Width = **.500**
- Hub Style = **One Side**
- Hub Diameter = **1.50**
- Overall Length = **1.25**
- Nominal Shaft Diameter = **.75**
- Keyway = **None**

Gear 2:
- Diametral Pitch = **6**
- Number of Teeth = **77**
- Pressure Angle = **14.5**
- Face Width = **.50**
- Hub Style = **One Side**
- Hub Diameter = **1.50**
- Overall Length = **1.25**
- Nominal Shaft Diameter = **.75**
- Keyway = **None**

A. Add ¼-20 UNC threaded holes to each gear hub 0.25 from the top hub surface.

B. Assemble the gears onto the shafts so that Gear 1 and Gear 2 are offset .50 from the support plate, and Gear 3 and Gear 4 are parallel to the ends of the shafts.

C. Insert a ¼-20 UNC Slotted Set Screw with an Oval Point into each hole.

D. Create an exploded assembly drawing.
E. Create a bill of materials.
F. Animate the assembly.

Project 9-17: Millimeters—Design Problem

Based on Figure P9-15 define a support plate and shafts that support the following gears. Use two of each gear.

Parameters:

Plate: 20 thick, a distance of at least 25 beyond the other edge of the gears to the edge of the plate.

Shafts: Diameters that match the gear's bore diameter; minimum offset between the plate and the gear is 20 or greater.

Gear 1:
- Module = **2.5**
- Number of Teeth = **20**
- Pressure Angle = **14.5**
- Face Width = **16**
- Hub Style = **One Side**
- Hub Diameter = **26**
- Overall Length = **30**
- Nominal Shaft Diameter = **20**
- Keyway = **None**

Gear 2:
- Module = **2.5**
- Number of Teeth = **50**
- Pressure Angle = **14.5**
- Face Width = **16**
- Hub Style = **One Side**
- Hub Diameter = **30**
- Overall Length = **30**
- Nominal Shaft Diameter = **20**
- Keyway = **None**

A. Add M4 threaded holes to each gear hub 12 from the top hub surface.
B. Assemble the gears onto the shafts so that Gear 1 and Gear 2 are offset 10 from the support plate, and Gear 3 and Gear 4 are parallel to the ends of the shafts.
C. Insert an M4 Slotted Set Screw with an Oval Point into each hole.
D. Create an exploded assembly drawing.
E. Create a bill of materials.
F. Animate the assembly.

Project 9-18: Inches

See Figure P9-18.

A. Create a Ø.375 × 2.00 shaft.
B. Create the support plate shown in Figure P9-18.
C. Access the **Design Library** and create two pulleys.

The pulleys are defined as follows:

Pulley 1:
- Belt Pitch = **(.375)–L**
- Belt Width = **.5**
- Pulley Style = **Flanged**
- Number of Grooves = **20**
- Hub Diameter = **.375**
- Overall Length = **.500**
- Nominal Shaft Diameter = **3/8**
- Keyway = **None**

Pulley 2:
- Belt Pitch = **(.375)–L**
- Belt Width = **.5**
- Pulley Style = **Flanged**
- Number of Grooves = **32**
- Hub Diameter = **.375**
- Overall Length = **.500**
- Nominal Shaft Diameter = **3/8**
- Keyway = **None**

D. Assemble the shafts into the support plate.
E. Assemble the pulleys onto the shafts.
F. Add a timing belt between the pulleys. Make the belt a thin feature with a .14 thickness. Make the width of the belt .42in.

Project 9-19: Inches—Design Problem

A. Create a Ø.500 × 3.50 shaft.
B. Create a support plate so that the center distance between the pulleys' center points is 5.52 and that the distance between the outside edge of the pulleys and the edge of the support plate is at least .50 but less than 1.00.
C. Access the **Design Library** and create two pulleys.

The pulleys are defined as follows:

Pulley 1:
- Belt Pitch = **(.500)–H**
- Belt Width = **1.5**
- Pulley Style = **Unflanged**
- Number of Grooves = **26**
- Hub Diameter = **.500**
- Hub Length = **.500**
- Nominal Shaft Diameter = **1/2**
- Keyway = **None**

Pulley 2:
- Belt Pitch = **(.500)–H**
- Belt Width = **1.5**
- Pulley Style = **Unflanged**
- Number of Grooves = **44**
- Hub Diameter = **.75**
- Overall Length = **1.00**
- Nominal Shaft Diameter = **1/2**
- Keyway = **None**

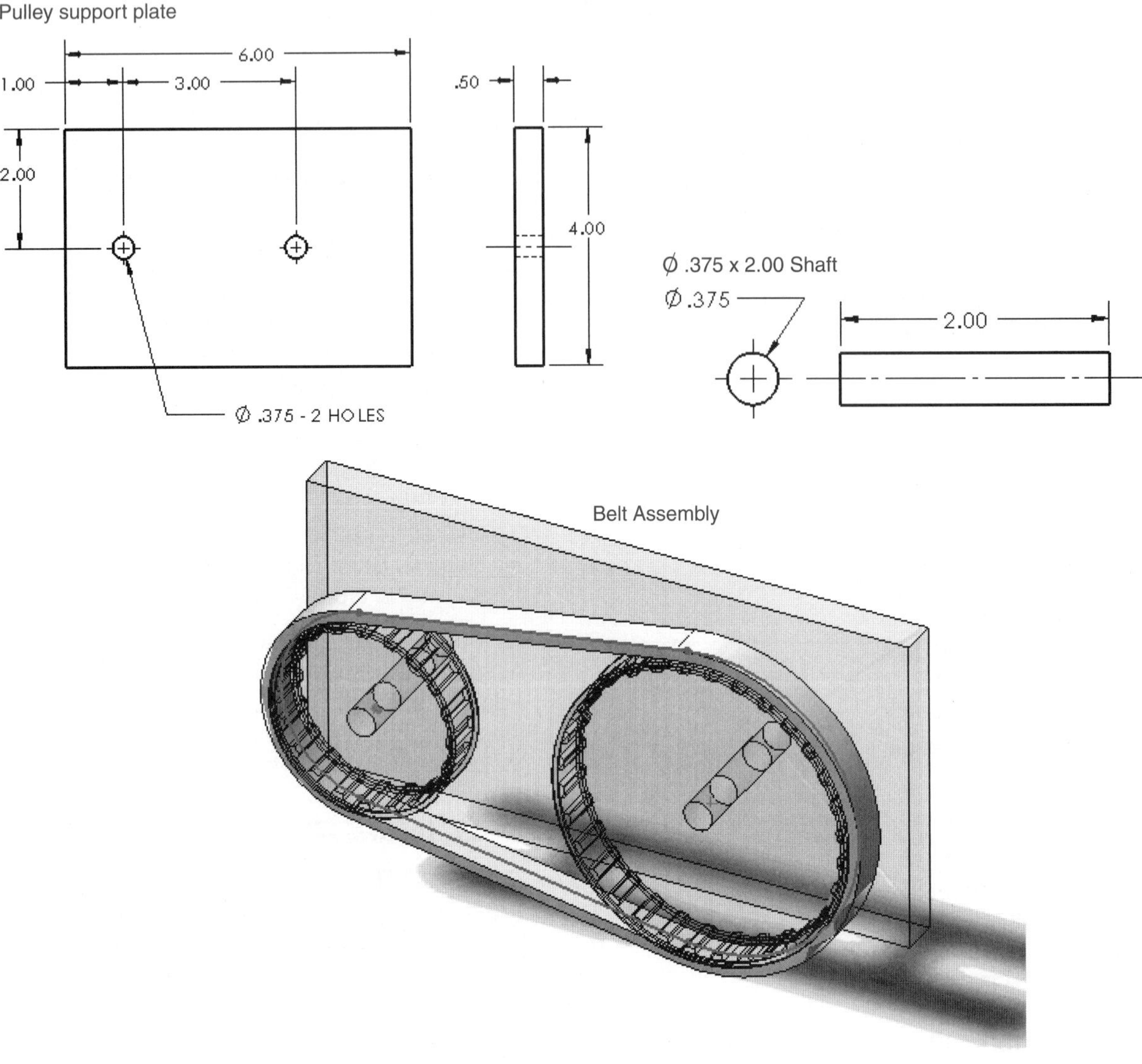

Figure P9-18

D. Assemble the shafts into the support plate.
E. Assemble the pulleys onto the shafts.
F. Add a timing belt between the pulleys. Make the belt a thin feature with a .16 thickness. Make the width of the belt 1.50 in.

Project 9-20: Inches—Design Problem

A. Create a Ø.500 × 4.50 shaft.
B. Create a support plate so that the center distance between the pulleys' center points is 21.50 and that the distance between the outside edge of the pulleys and the edge of the support plate is at least .50 but less than 1.00.
C. Access the **Design Library** and create two pulleys.

The pulleys are defined as follows:

Pulley 1:
- Belt Pitch = **(.875)–XH**
- Belt Width = **2**
- Pulley Style = **Unflanged**
- Number of Grooves = **30**
- Hub Diameter = **1.00**
- Overall Length = **4.00**
- Nominal Shaft Diameter = **1/2**
- Keyway = **None**

Pulley 2:
- Belt Pitch = **(.875)–XH**
- Belt Width = **2.0**
- Pulley Style = **Unflanged**
- Number of Grooves = **48**
- Hub Diameter = **1.00**

Overall Length = **4.00**
Nominal Shaft Diameter = **1/2**
Keyway = **None**

D. Assemble the shafts into the support plate.
E. Assemble the pulleys onto the shafts.
F. Add a #10-24 threaded hole to each pulley hub and insert a #10-24 UNC Slotted Set Screw Dog Point into each threaded hole.
G. Add a timing belt between the pulleys. Make the belt a thin feature with a .44 thickness. Make the width of the belt 2.00 in.

Project 9-21: Inches

Create a support plate and shaft as defined in Figure P9-21.

A. Create three Ø.375 × 3.00 shafts.
B. Create three identical pulleys as defined below.
C. Assemble the shafts into the support plate.
D. Assemble the pulleys onto the shafts.
E. Add a timing belt between the pulleys in the pattern shown. Make the belt a thin feature with a .14 thickness. Make the width of the belt .42in.

Pulley Properties:
Belt Pitch = **(.375)–L**
Belt Width = **.5**
Pulley Style = **Flanged**
Number of Grooves = **32**
Hub Diameter = **.375**
Overall Length = **.500**
Nominal Shaft Diameter = **3/8**
Keyway = **None**

Project 9-22: Inches

A. Create a support plate and shaft as defined in Figure P9-22.
B. Create four Ø.375 × 3.00 shafts.
C. Create three identical pulleys as defined below.
D. Assemble the shafts into the support plate.
E. Assemble the pulleys onto the shafts.
F. Add a timing belt between the pulleys in the pattern shown. Make the belt a thin feature with a .14 thickness. Make the width of the belt .42 in.

Pulley Properties:
Belt Pitch = **(0.375)–L**
Belt Width = **0.5**
Pulley Style = **Flanged**
Number of Grooves = **32**
Hub Diameter = **.375**
Overall Length = **.500**
Nominal Shaft Diameter = **3/8**
Keyway = **None**

Project 9-23: Inches

A. Create a support plate and shaft as defined in Figure P9-23. Holes labeled A are Ø.375, and holes labeled B are Ø.500.
B. Create three Ø.375 × 3.00 shafts and two Ø.500 × 3.00 shafts.

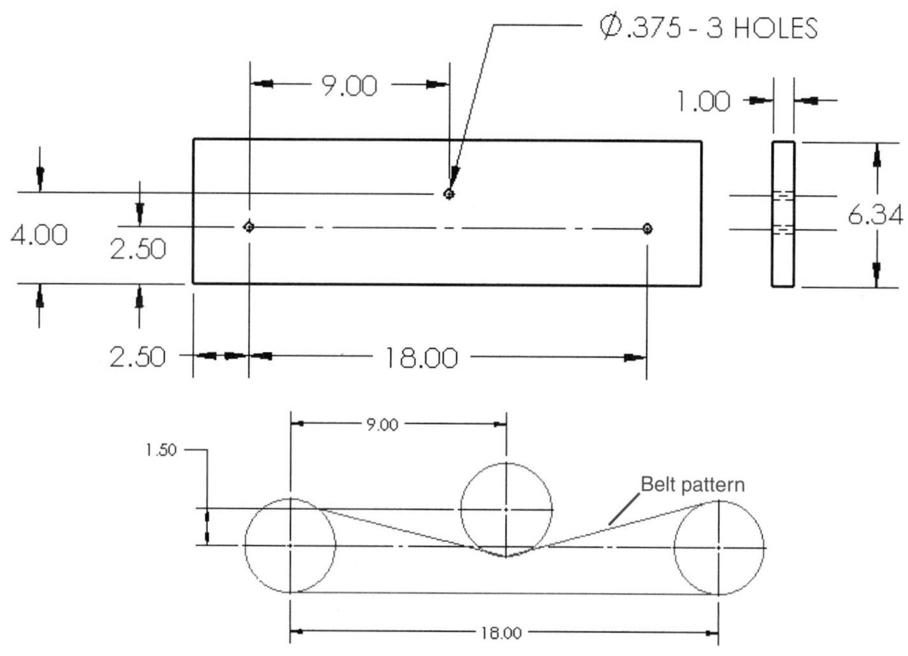

Figure P9-21

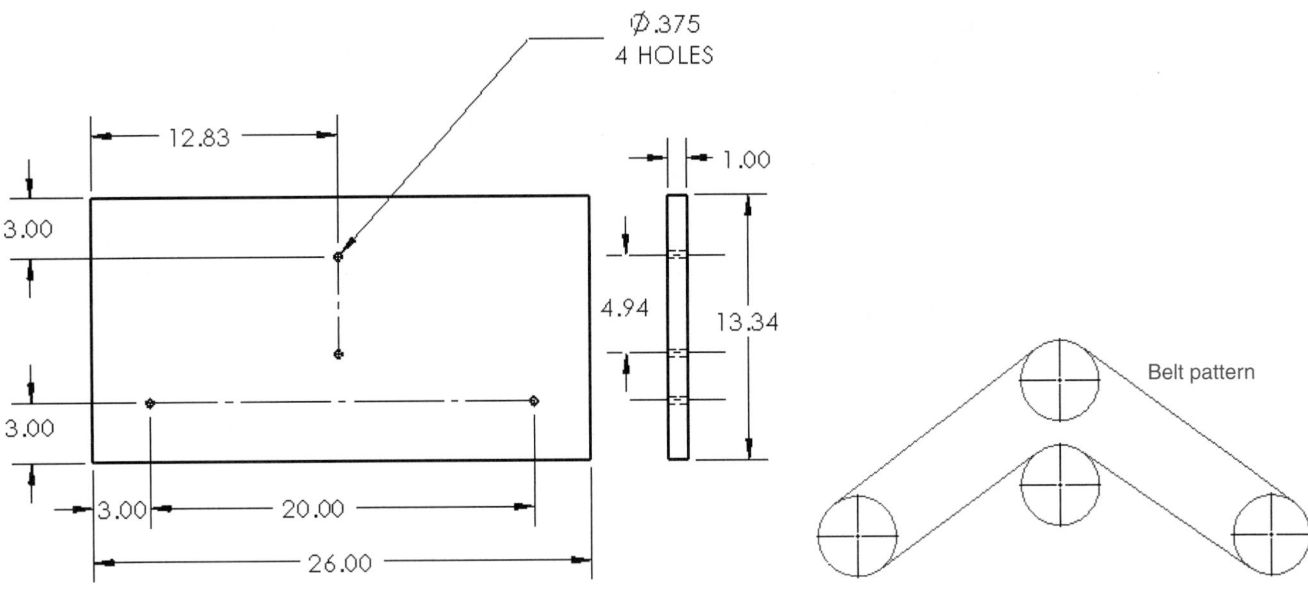

Figure P9-22

C. Create three small pulleys and two large pulleys as defined below.
D. Assemble the shafts into the support plate.
E. Assemble the pulleys onto the shafts.
F. Add a timing belt between the pulleys in the pattern shown. Make the belt a thin feature with a .16 thickness. Make the width of the belt .92 in.

Pulley 1 Properties:
- Belt Pitch = **(.375)–L**
- Belt Width = **1.00**
- Pulley Style = **Flanged**
- Number of Grooves = **24**
- Hub Diameter = **.375**
- Overall Length = **.500**
- Nominal Shaft Diameter = **3/8**
- Keyway = **None**

Pulley 2 Properties:
- Belt Pitch = **(.500)–H**
- Belt Width = **1.00**
- Pulley Style = **Flanged**
- Number of Grooves = **48**
- Hub Diameter = **.500**
- Overall Length = **.500**
- Nominal Shaft Diameter = **1/2**
- Keyway = **None**

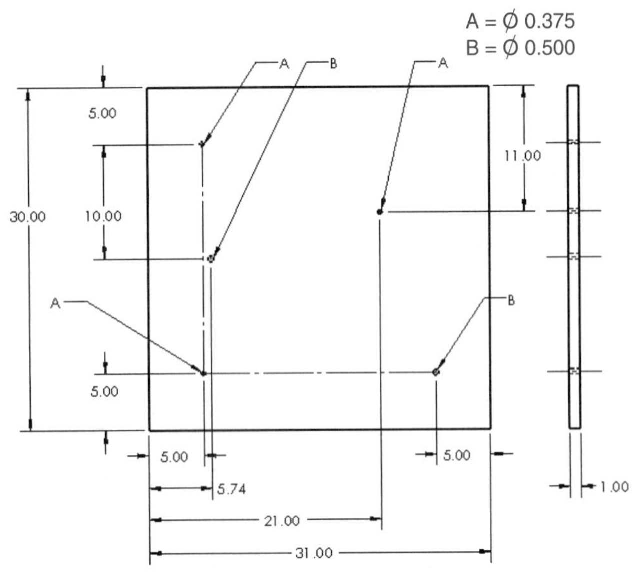

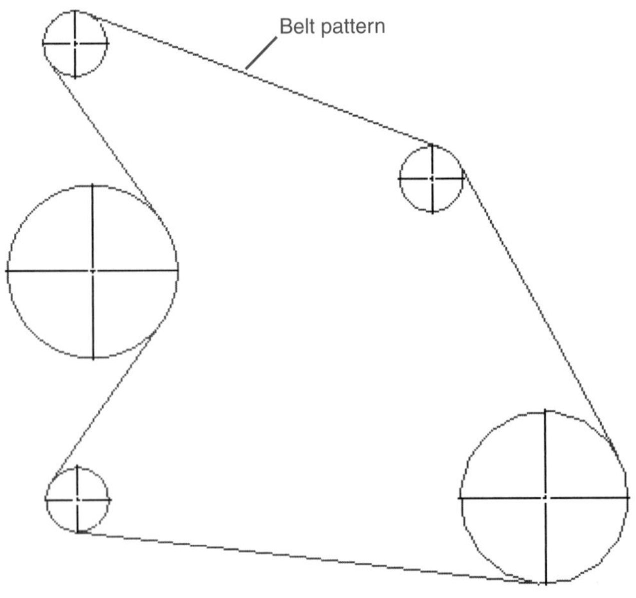

Figure P9-23

CHAPTER 10

Bearings and Fit Tolerances

Objectives

- Learn about sleeve and ball bearings
- Learn about fits
- Learn how fits are applied to bearings and shafts
- Learn about tolerances for bearings

10-1 INTRODUCTION

This text deals with two types of bearings: sleeve bearings or *bushings* and ball bearings. ***Sleeve bearings*** are hollow cylinders made from a low-friction material such as Teflon or impregnated bronze. Sleeve bearings may have flanges. See Figure 10-1. ***Ball bearings*** include spherical bearings in an internal race that greatly reduce friction. In general, sleeve bearings are cheaper than ball bearings, but ball bearings can take heavier loads at faster speeds. A listing of ball bearings is included in the **Design Library**.

10-2 SLEEVE BEARINGS

Sleeve bearings are identified by the following callout format:

Inside diameter × Outside Diameter × Thickness

For example,

.375 × .750 × .500 or 3/8 × ¾ × ½

To Draw a Sleeve Bearing

Draw a .500 × 1.000 × 1.000 sleeve bearing. See Figure 10-2

1. Start a new **Part** drawing.
2. Select the **Front Plane** orientation.
3. Click the **Sketch** group, then **click** the **Circle** tool.
4. Draw a **Ø1.000** circle. Use the **Smart Dimension** tool to size the circle.
5. Click the **Features** group, then click the **Extruded Boss/Base** tool.
6. Define the thickness of the extrusion as **1.00 in**.
7. Click the OK check mark.
8. Right-click the front surface of the cylinder and select the **Sketch** tool.
9. Use the **Circle** tool and the **Smart Dimension** tool to draw a **Ø.5000** circle on the front surface of the cylinder.
10. Click the **Features** group and select the **Extruded Cut** tool.
11. Define the Ø.500 to be cut and click the OK check mark.

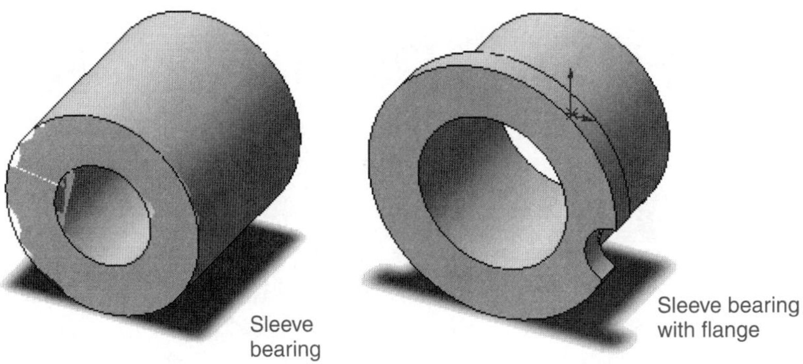

Figure 10-1

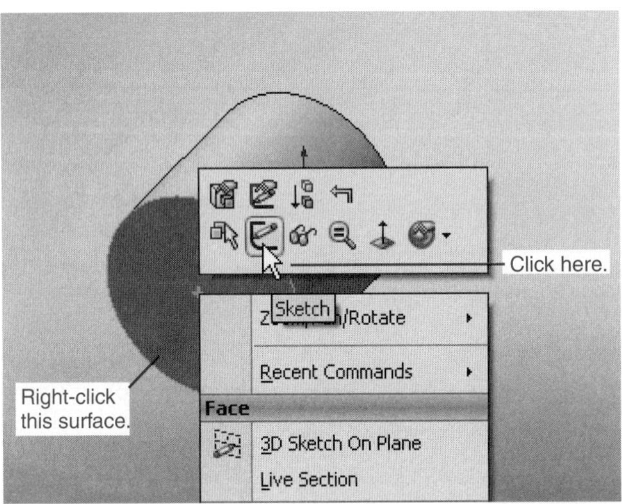

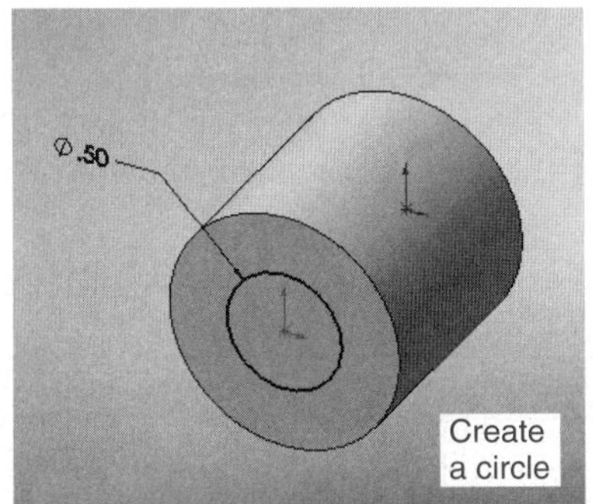

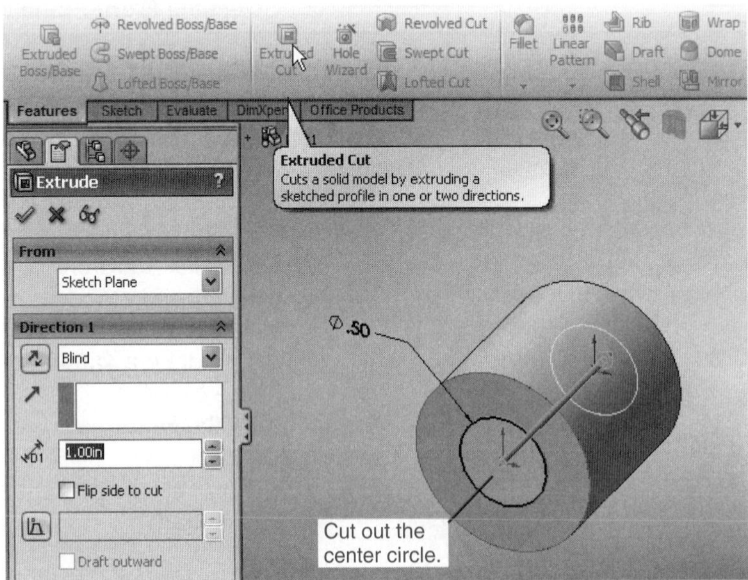

Figure 10-2

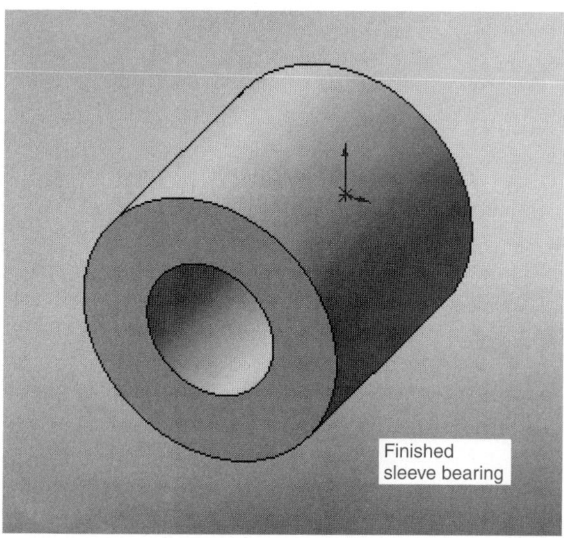

Figure 10-2 *(continued)*

To Use a Sleeve Bearing in an Assembly Drawing

See Figures 10-3 and 10-4.

1. Draw the support plate and Ø.500 × 2.500 shaft defined in Figure 10-3. Save the drawings.
2. Create a new **Assembly** drawing.
3. Add the support plate, shaft, and sleeve bearing (created in the last section) to the assembly drawing.

See Figure 10-4.

4. Use the **Mate** tool and assemble the sleeve bearing into the support plate and the shaft into the sleeve bearing. The front surface of the shaft should be 1.50 offset from the front surface of the support plate.
5. Save the assembly as **Sleeve Assembly**.
6. Use the **Exploded View** tool. Select a direction and pull the shaft out of the assembly.

See Figure 5-33 for instructions on how to use the **Exploded View** tool.

7. Use the **Exploded View** tool to pull the bearing away from the support plate.
8. Save the exploded drawing as **Sleeve Assembly**.

Replace the old **Sleeve Assembly** drawing.

9. Start a new drawing.
10. Click the **Annotations** tool, click the **Balloon** tool, and add the assembly numbers as shown.
11. Click the **Annotations** tool, click the **Tables** tool, click the **Bill of Materials** tool, and add a BOM to the drawing.

> ***Note:***
> The descriptions are written in only uppercase letters.

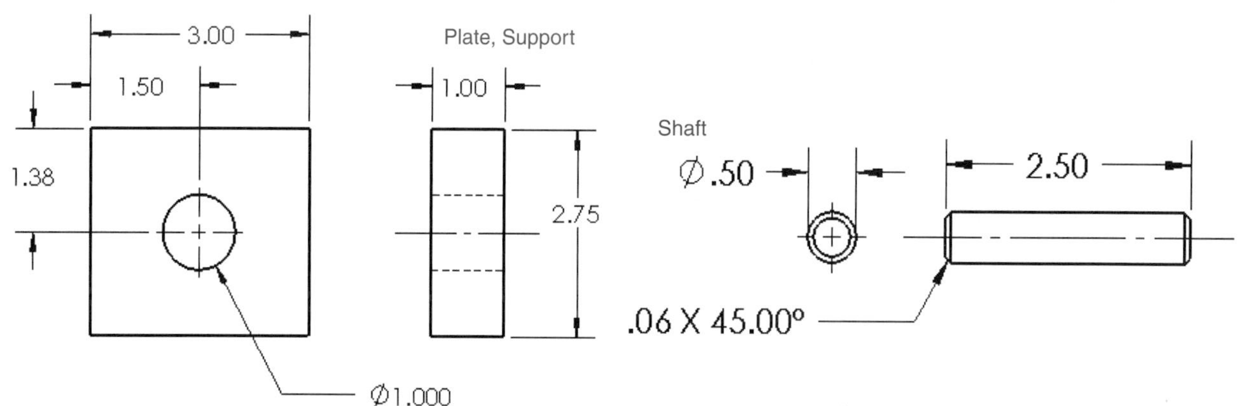

Figure 10-3

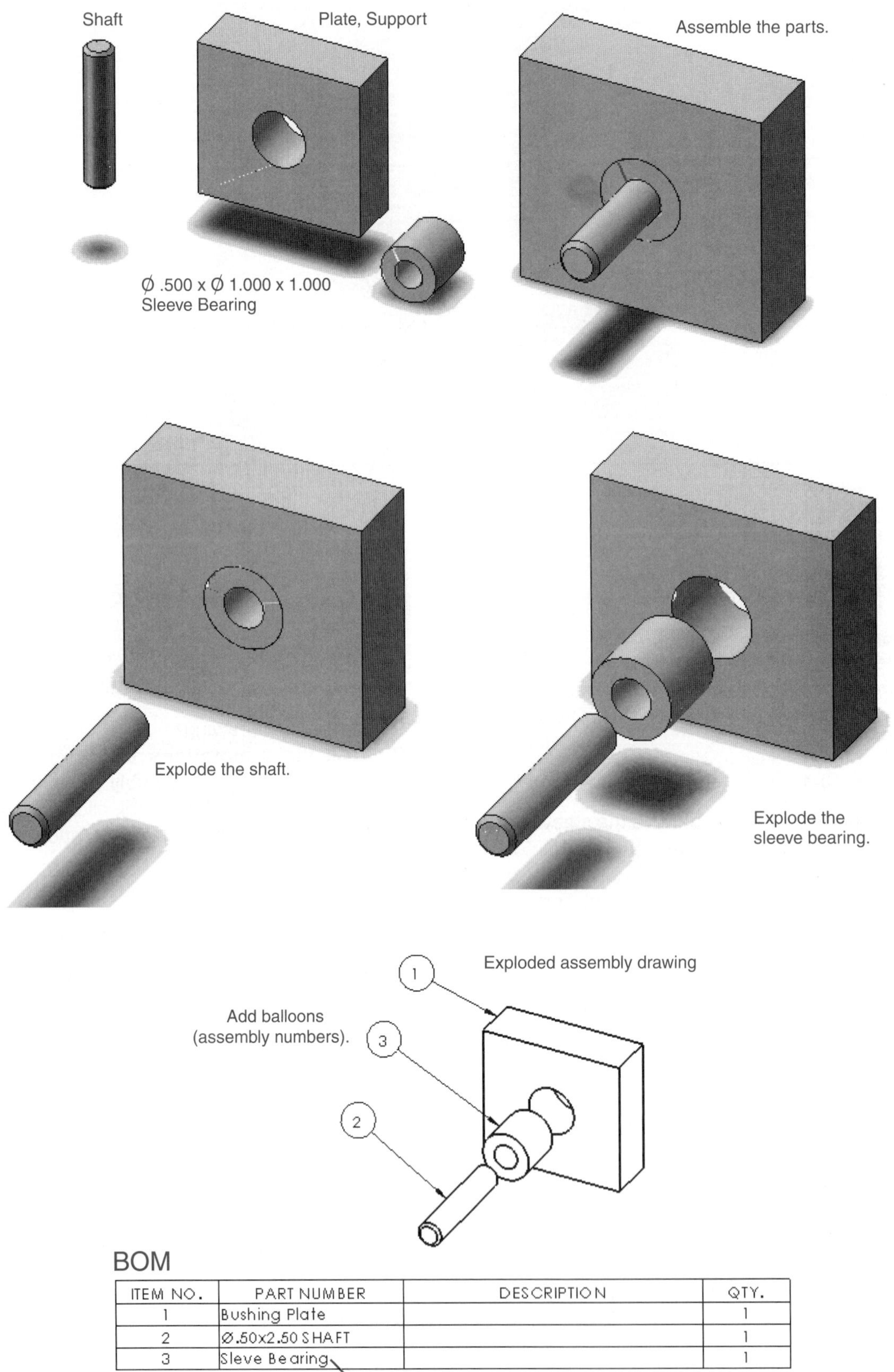

ITEM NO.	PART NUMBER	DESCRIPTION	QTY.
1	Bushing Plate		1
2	Ø.50x2.50 SHAFT		1
3	Sleve Bearing		1

Figure 10-4

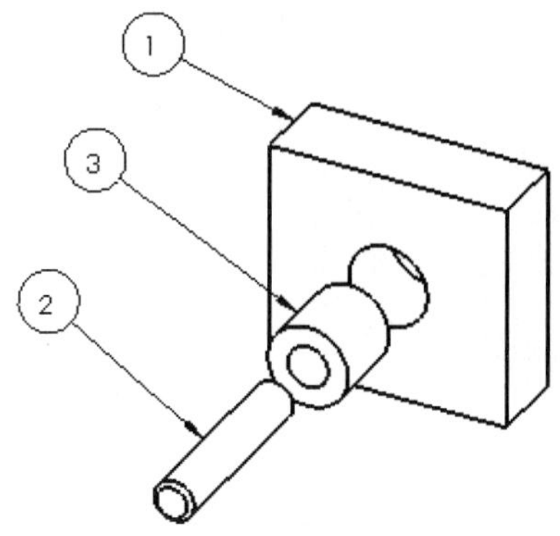

Edit the BOM.

ITEM NO.	PART NUMBER	DESCRIPTION	QTY.
1	BU-2009A	PLATE, SUPPORT	1
2	BU2008-.50	Ø.50 × 2.50 SHAFT	1
3	BU-2009B	.50×1.00×.50 SLEEVE BEARING	1

Figure 10-4 ***(continued)***

10-3 SLEEVE BEARINGS WITH FLANGES

Sleeve bearings may also include flanges. See Figure 10-5. Flanges are defined by their outside diameter and thickness. The sleeve bearing shown in Figure 10-5 is defined as follows:

Ø.75 × Ø1.00 × .75 with a Ø1.25 × .13 FLANGE

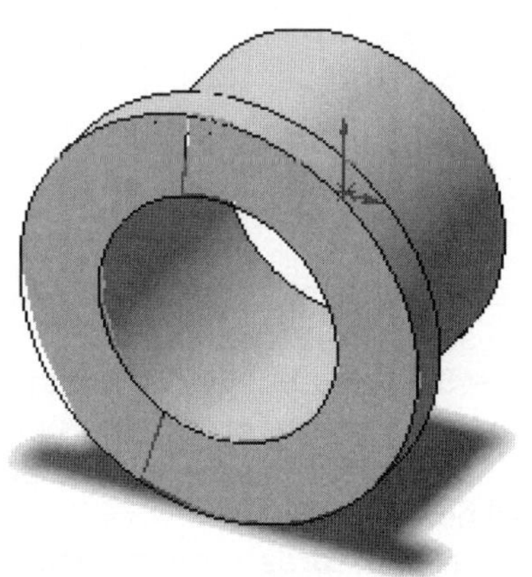

Figure 10-5

To Add a Flange to an Existing Sleeve Bearing Drawing

Figure 10-6 shows a drawing of a Ø.75 × Ø1.00 × .75 sleeve bearing.

1. Right-click the front face of the bearing and select the **Sketch** tool.
2. Use the **Circle** tool and draw a **Ø1.25** circle.
3. Click the **Features** group and the **Extruded Boss/Base** tool and extrude the Ø1.25 circle a depth of **0.13 in**.
4. Right-click the front face of the bearing and select the **Sketch** tool.
5. Use the **Circle** tool and draw a **Ø.75** circle.
6. Click the **Features** group and the **Extruded Boss/Base** tool and extrude the Ø.75 circle a depth of **.13**.

10-4 FLANGE CUTOUTS

Figure 10-7 shows a flanged sleeve bearing with a circular cutout in the flange. When the bearing is assembled a socket head screw can be inserted into the cut to prevent the bearing from rotating with a rotating shaft that is inserted into it.

To Draw a Cutout on a Flange

1. Draw a flanged sleeve bearing as defined in the previous section.

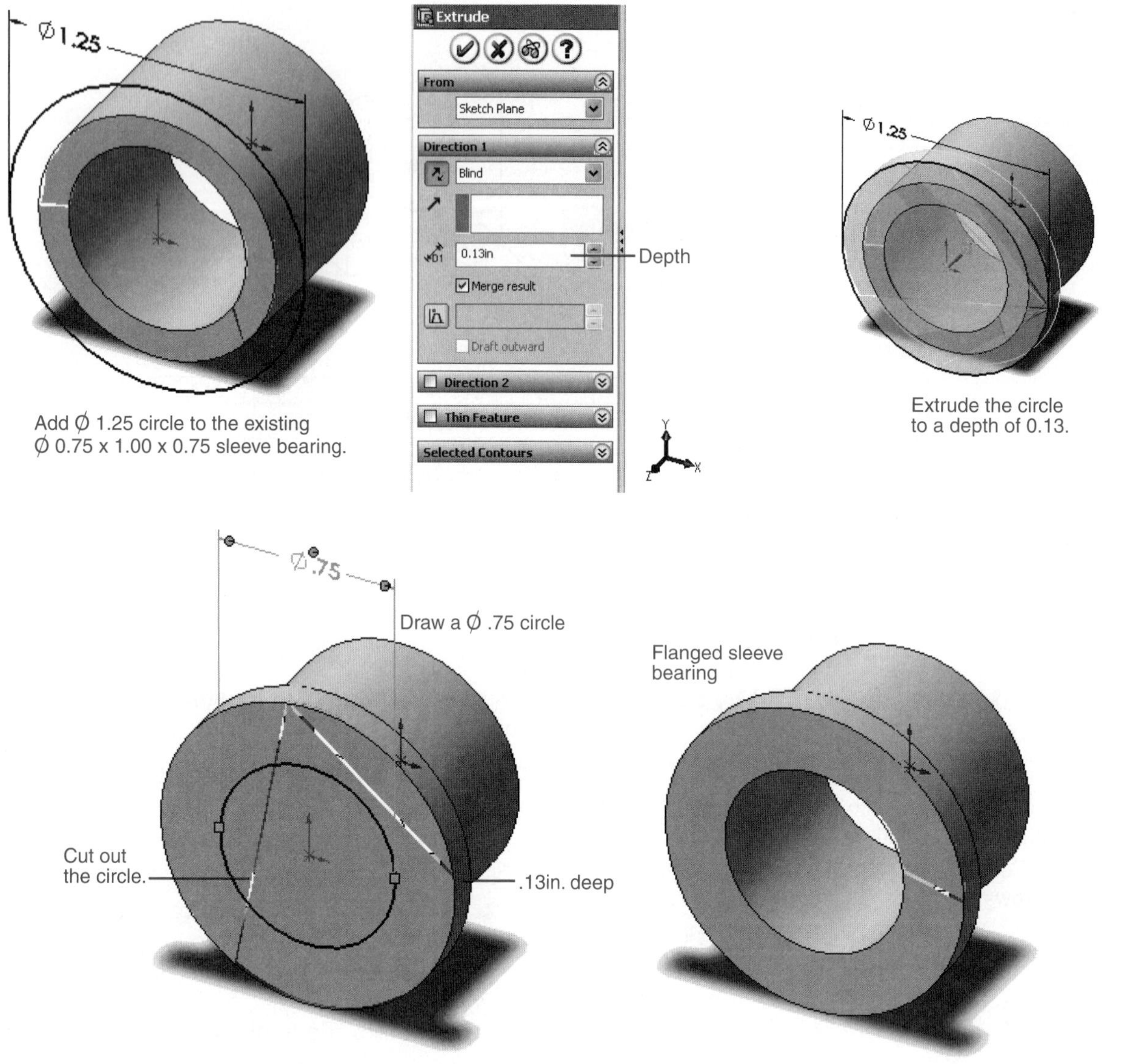

Ø1.25
Add Ø 1.25 circle to the existing Ø 0.75 x 1.00 x 0.75 sleeve bearing.
Extrude
From
Sketch Plane
Direction 1
Blind
0.13in
Merge result
Draft outward
Direction 2
Thin Feature
Selected Contours
Depth
Ø1.25
Extrude the circle to a depth of 0.13.
Ø.75
Draw a Ø .75 circle
Cut out the circle.
.13in. deep
Flanged sleeve bearing

Figure 10-6

Cutout in bearing's flange

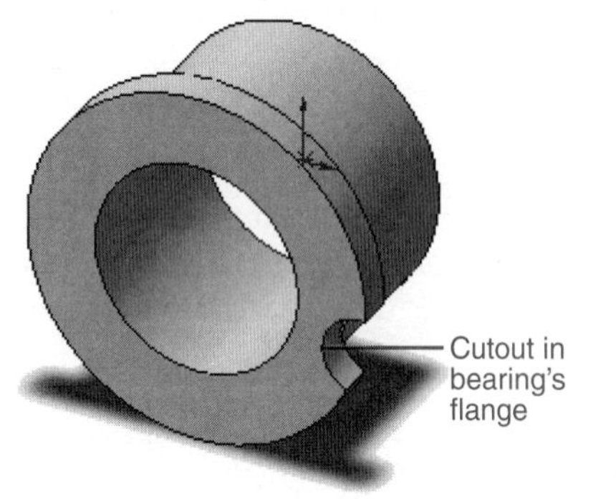

Figure 10-7

See Figure 10-8.

2. Right-click the front surface of the flanged bearing and select the **Sketch** option.
3. Click the **Sketch** group and select the **Circle** tool.
4. Draw a **Ø.25** circle whose center point is located on the outside edge of the flanged portion of the flanged bearing.
5. Click the **Features** group and select the **Extruded Cut** tool and cut the circle out of the flange.

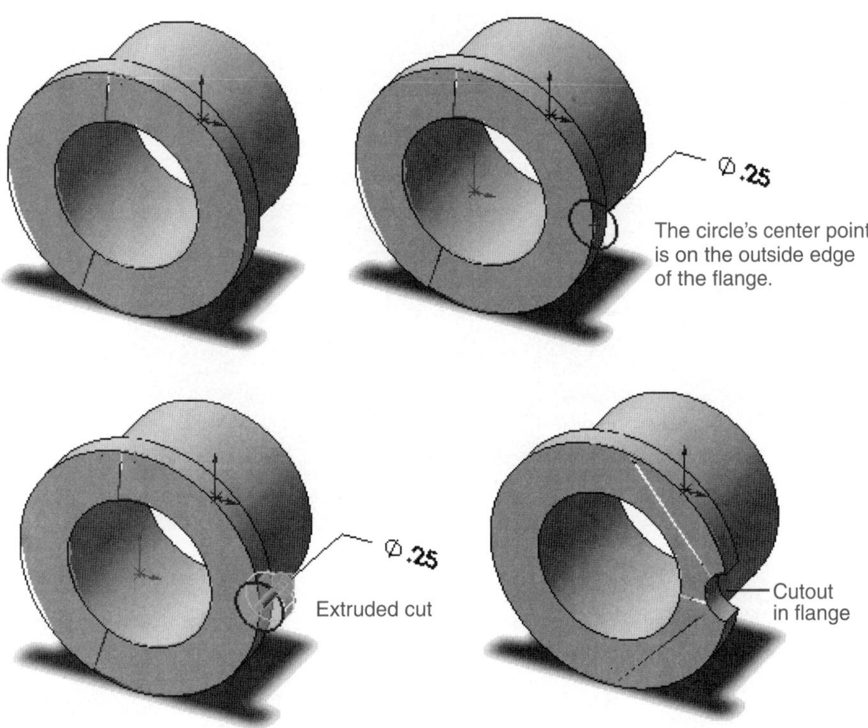

Figure 10-8

10-5 SAMPLE PROBLEM SP10-1

Figure 10-9 shows an assembly drawing that includes a flanged bearing and a socket screw. It was created as follows.

The flanged bearing with a cutout was created in the last section. See Figure 10-8. Figure 10-3 defines the support plate. The shaft is Ø.75 × 3.00.

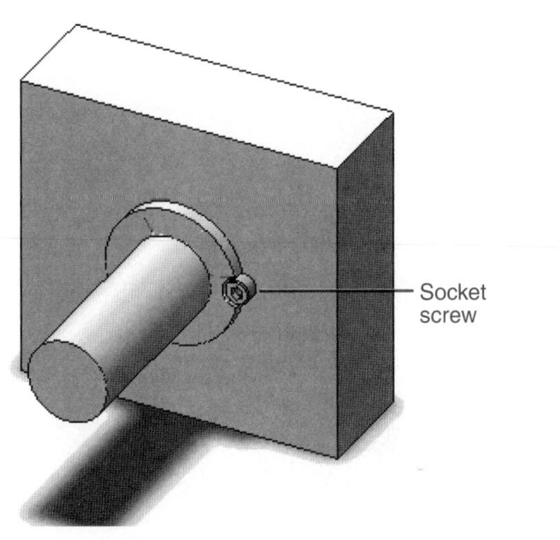

Figure 10-9

Modify the existing support plate to accept the socket screw.

In this example a #6-32 × .50 Socket Head Cap Screw will be used, so a #6-32 threaded hole must be added to the support plate. The center point for the hole is located on the outside edge of the flange or .625 (Ø = 1.25) from the center point of the flange. In this example a through hole will be added. This hole may also be located .88 and 1.38 from the edges as shown.

Figure 10-10 shows a front view of the support plate.

1. Click the **Features** group and click the **Hole Wizard** tool.
2. Set the hole type for a **#6-32** threaded hole that goes **Through All**.
3. Click the **Positions** tab and add the threaded hole just to the right of the existing Ø1.00 hole.
4. Use the **Smart Dimension** tool and locate the center point of the existing Ø1.00 hole.
5. Save the support plate as **Bearing Support Plate**.

Create an Assembly Drawing

See Figure 10-11.

1. Start a new **Assembly** drawing.
2. Add the bearing support plate, flanged bearing with a cutout, and Ø.750 × 3.00 shaft to the drawing.

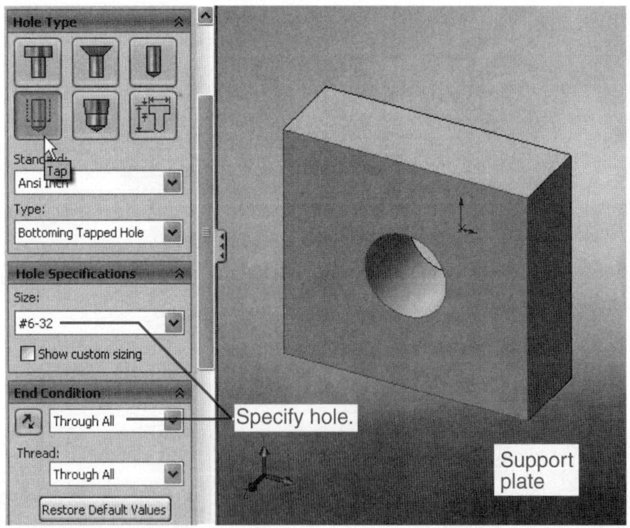

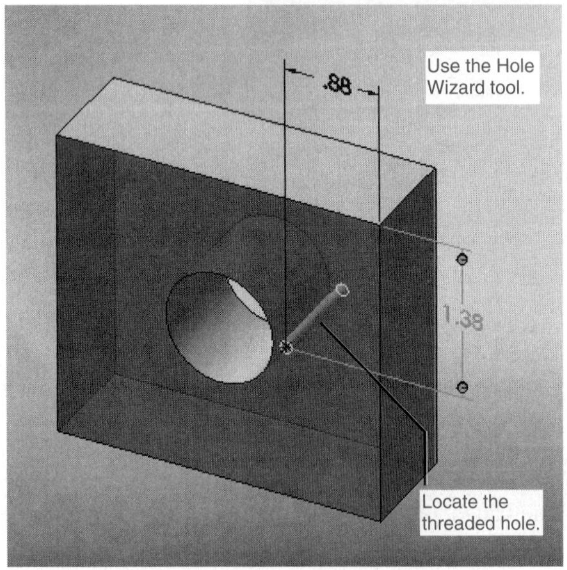

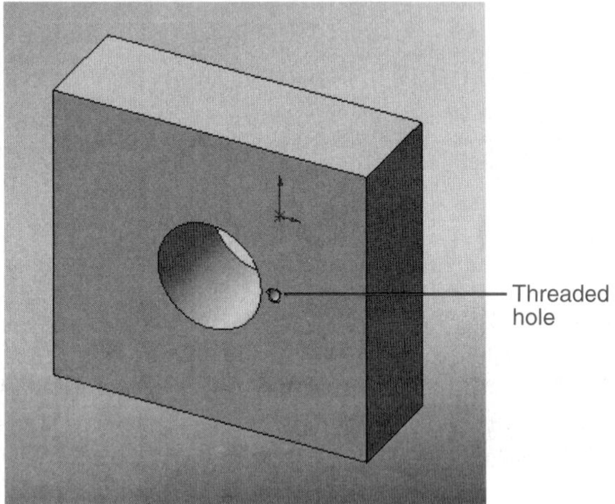

Figure 10-10

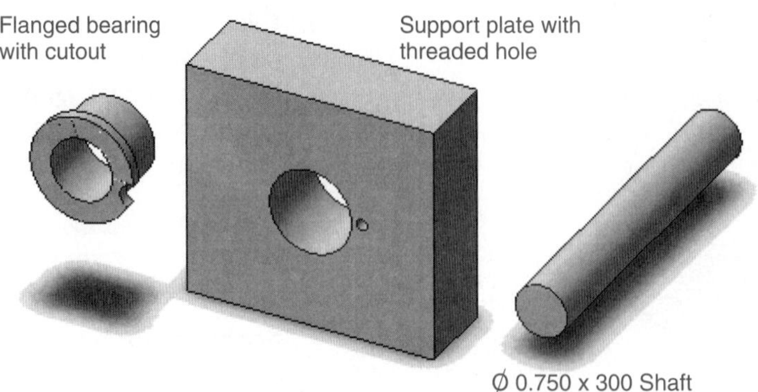

Figure 10-11

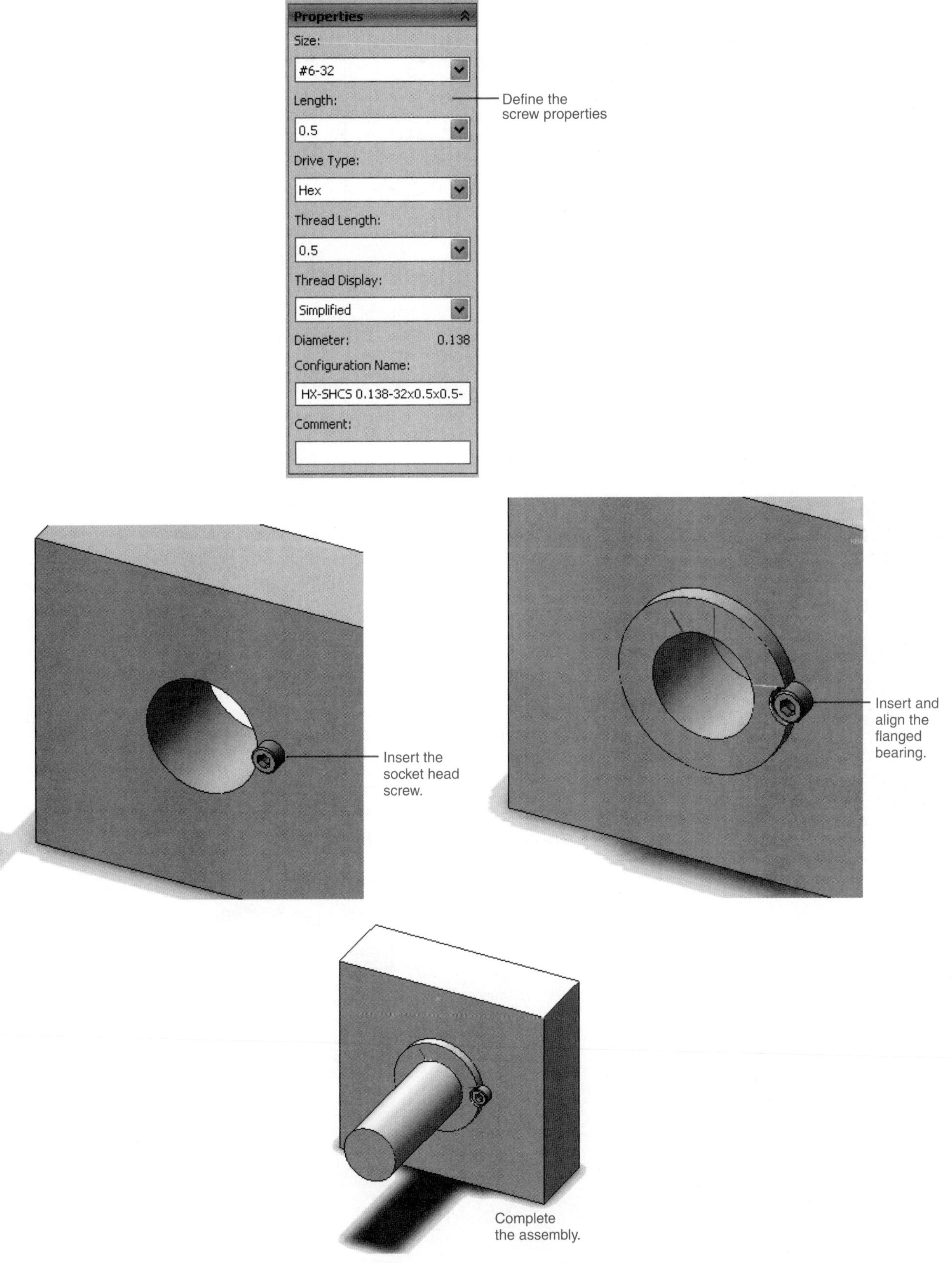

Figure 10-11 ***(continued)***

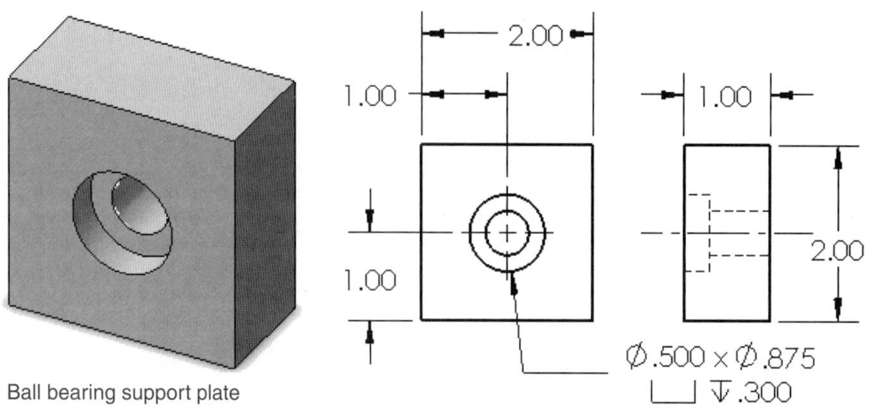

Figure 10-12

3. Access the **Design Library, Toolbox, Ansi Inch, Bolts and Screws,** and select **Socket Head Screw**.
4. Click and drag socket head screws into the drawing area.
5. Set the screw properties to **#6-32 × 0.500 LONG**.
6. Use the **Mate** tool and assemble the socket screw into the support plate.
7. Assemble the flanged bearing into the support plate.
8. Align the cut in the flange with the head of the socket head screw.
9. Complete the assembly.

10-6 BALL BEARINGS

Ball bearings are identified by the following callout format:

Inside Diameter × Outside Diameter × Thickness

For example,

.375 × .750 × .500 or 3/8 × ¾ × ½

A listing of standard ball bearing sizes can be found in the **Design Library**. For this example a .5000 × .8750 × .2188 instrument ball bearing will be used and will be inserted into a counterbored hole. Only nominal dimensions will be considered. Tolerances will be defined later in the chapter.

Figure 10-12 shows a ball bearing support plate.

1. Draw and save the ball bearing support plate.
2. Draw and save a Ø.500 × 2.50 shaft with .03 chamfers at each end.
3. Start a new **Assembly** drawing and insert the ball bearing support plate and Ø.500 × 2.50 shaft.

See Figure 10-13.

4. Access the **Design Library, Toolbox, Ansi Inch, Bearings, Ball Bearings,** and select the **Instrument Ball Bearing – AFB** option.

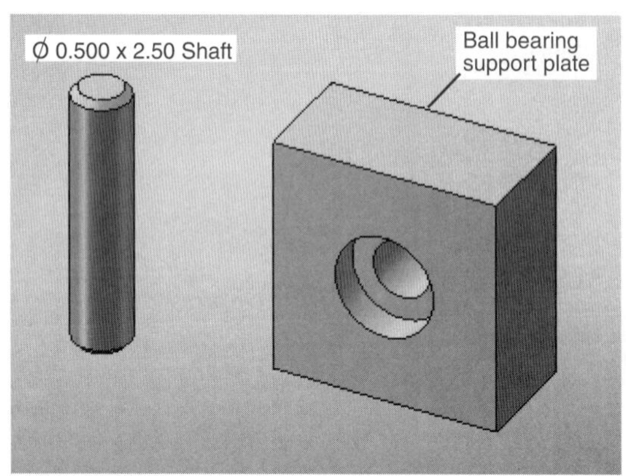

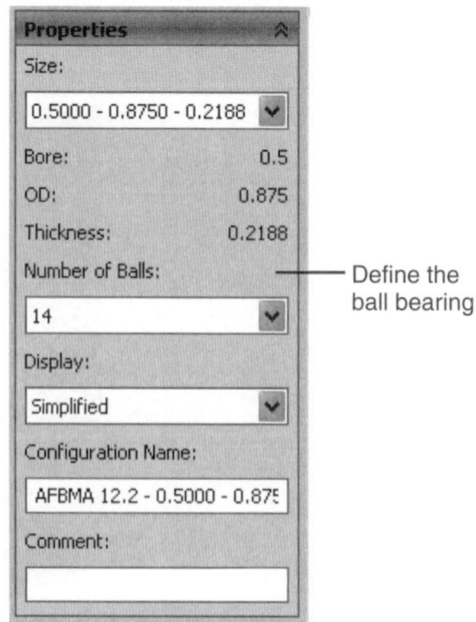

Figure 10-13

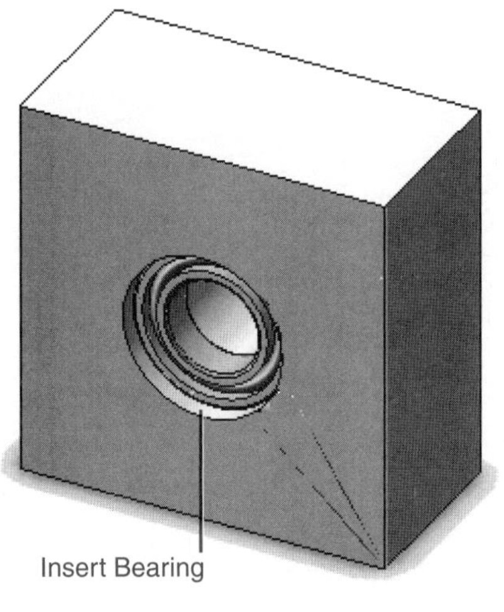

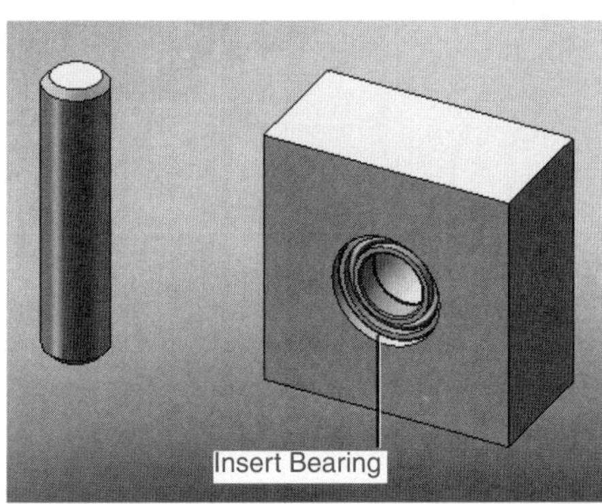

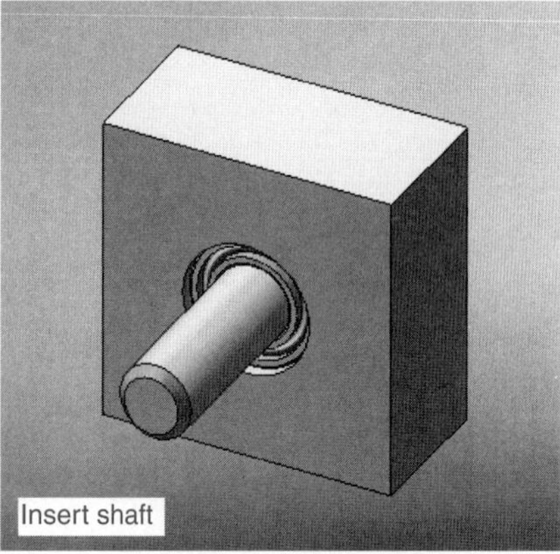

Figure 10-13 *(continued)*

5. Click and drag the bearing into the drawing screen and set the properties as shown.

   In this example a 0.5000 − 0.8750 − 0.2188 was used.

6. Insert the ball bearing into the counterbored hole.
7. Insert the shaft into the bearing.

> **Note:**
> The term *nominal* refers to a starting value for the shaft and hole. It is not the final dimension.

10-7 FITS AND TOLERANCES FOR BEARINGS

The tolerance between a shaft and a bearing and between a bearing and a support part is critical. Incorrect tolerances can cause excessive wear or vibration and affect the performance of the assembly.

In general, a clearance fit is used between the shaft and the inside diameter of the bearing, and an interference fit is used between the outside diameter of the bearing and the support structure. A listing of standard tolerances is included in the appendix.

10-8 FITS—INCHES

Tolerances for shafts and holes have been standardized and are called ***fits***. An example of a fit callout is H7/g6. The hole tolerance is always given first using an uppercase letter, and the shaft tolerance is given second using a lowercase letter.

10-9 CLEARANCE FITS

Say a Ø0.500 nominal shaft is to be inserted into a Ø0.500 nominal hole using an H7/g6 clearance fit, which is also referred to as a Class LC5 Clearance fit.

The following data are given in a table in the appendix. See Figure 10-14. The values are given in thousandths of an inch. The nominal value for the hole is 0.5000, so the +0.7 table value means .5007 in. The −0.25 table value for the 0.5000 nominal shaft means 0.49975 in. The limits of clearance values are the differences between the hole minimum value and the shaft maximum value, 0.00 and −0.25, or 0.25 absolute, and between the maximum hole value and the minimum shaft value, +0.7 and −0.65, or 1.35.

Class LC5			
Nominal Size Range	Limits of Clearance	Standard Limits	
		Hole H7	Shaft g6
0.40 - 0.71	0.25 1.35	+0.7 0	−0.25 −0.65

Figure 10-14

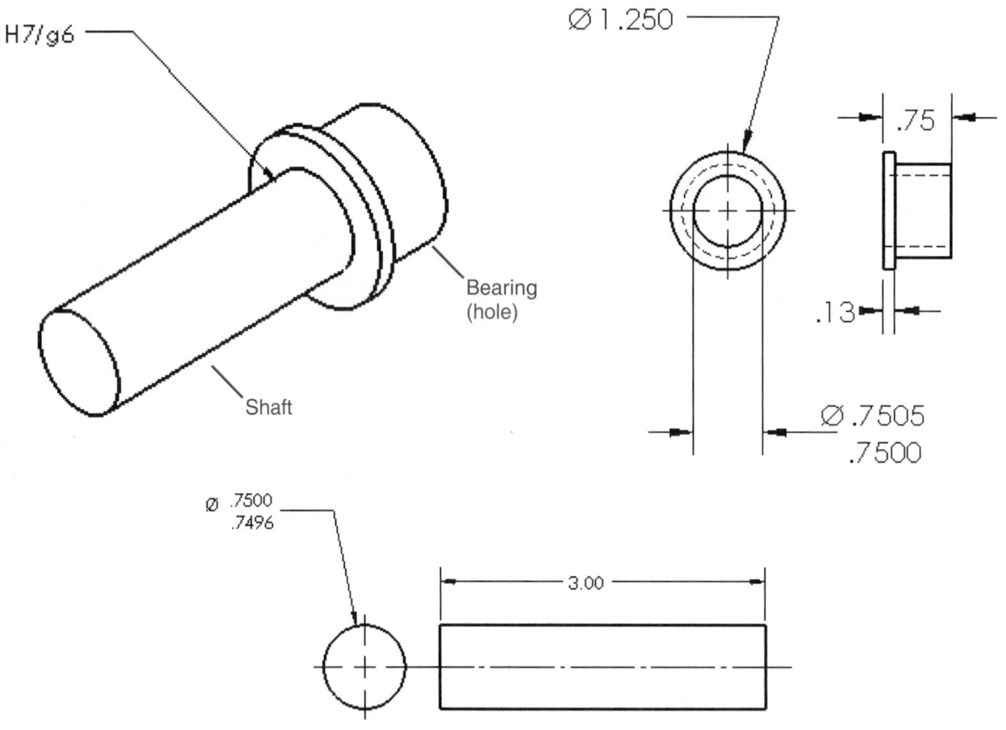

Figure 10-15

10-10 HOLE BASIS

The 0 value for the hole's minimum indicates that the tolerances were derived using ***hole basis*** calculations; that is, the tolerances were applied starting with the minimum hole value. Tolerances applied starting with the shaft are called ***shaft basis***.

10-11 SHAFT BASIS

The limits of clearance values would be applied starting with the minimum shaft diameter. If the H7/g6 tolerances were applied using the shaft basis, the resulting tolerance values for the shaft would be 0.50000 − 0.50040, and for the hole would be 0.50065 (.50040 + .00025)−0.50135. These values maintain the limits of tolerance, 0.50135 − 0.00135, and the individual tolerances for the hole (0.50135 − 0.50065 = 0.0007) and the shaft (0.50040 − 0.50000 = .00040).

10-12 SAMPLE PROBLEM SP10-2

Say a shaft with nominal values of Ø.750 × 3.00 is to be fitted into a bearing with an inside diameter bore, nominal, of 0.7500 using Class LC5 fit, hole basis. What are the final dimensions for the shaft and bearing's bore? The table values for the hole are 0/+0.5, yielding a hole tolerance of .7500−.7505, and the shaft values for the hole are 0/−0.4, yielding a shaft tolerance of .7500−.7496.

> ***Note:***
> The fact that both the hole and the shaft could be .7500 is called ***locational fit***.

See Figure 10-15.

10-13 INTERFERENCE FITS

When the shaft is equal to or larger in diameter than the hole, the fit is called an ***interference fit***. Interference fits are sometimes used to secure a shaft into a hole rather than use a fastener or adhesive. For example, an aluminum shaft with a nominal diameter of .250 in. inserted into a hole in a steel housing with a Ø.250 nominal hole using .0006 in. interference would require approximately 123 in.-lbs of torque to turn the shaft.

Class LN1			
Nominal Size Range	Limits of Interference	Standard Limits	
		Hole	Shaft
0.71 - 1.19	0 1.0	+0.5 0	+1.0 +0.5

Hole basis

Figure 10-16

In this example a sleeve bearing with a nominal outside diameter (O.D.) of .875 is to be inserted into a Ø.875 nominal hole using an LN1 Interface Locational fit. The hole and shaft (bearing O.D.) specifications are H6/n5. The following values were derived from a table in the appendix. See Figure 10-16.

All stated values are in thousandths of an inch. The 0 in the column for the hole indicates that it is a hole basis calculation (see an explanation in the previous section). Given the .875 nominal value for both the hole and the shaft, the hole and shaft tolerances are as follows. See Figure 10-17.

Hole: Ø.8755/ .875 Shaft: Ø.8760/.8755

10-14 MANUFACTURED BEARINGS

Most companies do not manufacture their own bearings but, rather, purchase them from a bearing manufacturer. This means that tolerances must be assigned to assemblies based on existing given tolerances for the purchased bearings.

> ***Note:***
> Companies that manufacture bearings usually also manufacture shafts that match the bearings; that is, the tolerances for the bearings and shafts are coordinated.

Figure 10-18 shows a typical manufactured sleeve bearing. The dimensions and tolerances are included. The inside diameter (bore or I.D.) of the bearing is matched to the shaft using a clearance fit, and the O.D. is to be matched to the support using an interference fit. The procedure is to find standard fits that are closest to the bearing's manufactured dimensions and apply the limits of tolerance to create the needed tolerances.

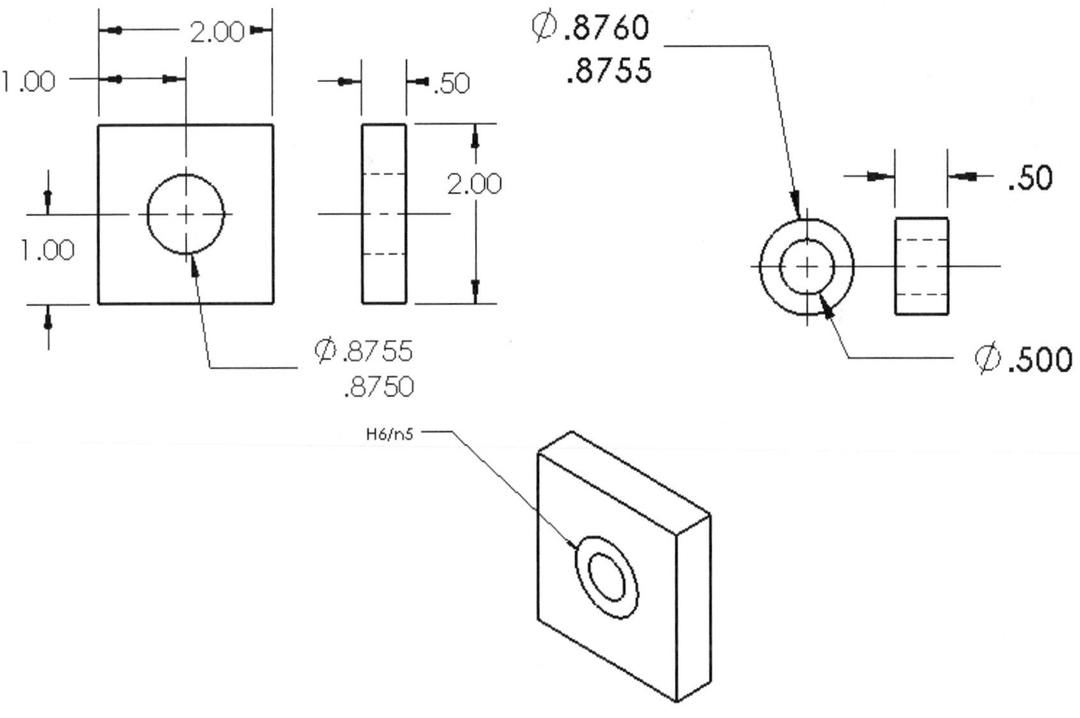

Figure 10-17

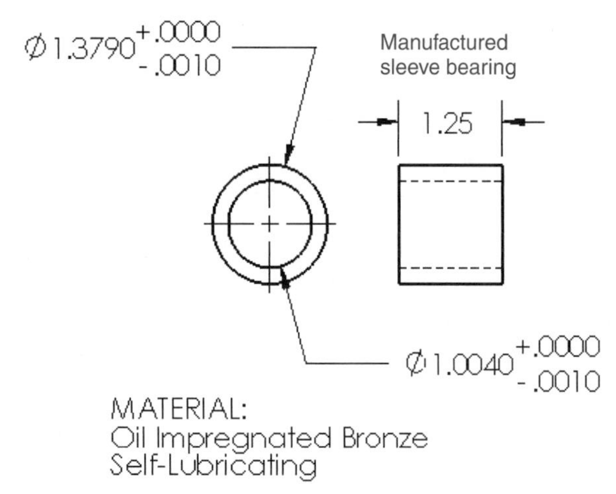

Figure 10-18

Clearance for a Manufactured Bearing

Refer to the standard fit tables in the appendix and find a tolerance range for a hole that matches or comes close to the bearing's I.D. tolerance of .001 (the +.000/−.001 creates a tolerance range of .001). The given I.D. is 1.0040, so it falls within the 0.71−1.19 nominal size range. An LC2 Clearance fit (H8/h7) has a hole tolerance specification of 0.0 to 0.0008, 0.0002 smaller than the bearing's manufactured tolerance of .0010. The given tolerance is Ø1.0040/1.0030.

The limits of clearance for the LC2 standard fit are 0.0 to 0.0013. If these limits are maintained, the smallest hole diameter is equal to the largest shaft diameter (1.0030 − 0.0 = 1.0030), and the smallest shaft diameter is .0013 less than the largest hole diameter (1.0040 − .0013 = 1.0027).

Therefore, the shaft tolerances are

Shaft: Ø1.0030/1.0027

These tolerances give a tolerance range for the shaft of .0003, or .0002 less than the stated .0005 found in the table. This difference makes up for the .0002 difference between the actual hole diameter's tolerance range of 0.0010 and the standard H8 tolerance of 0.0008.

To Apply a Clearance Fit Tolerance Using SolidWorks

Figure 10-19 shows a shaft with a nominal diameter of 1.0040. Enter the required 1.0030/1.0027 tolerance.

1. Click the **Limits** option in the **Tolerance/Precision** box.
2. Set the upper limit for **−0.0010** and the lower limit for **−0.0013**.
3. Click the OK check mark.

Interference for a Manufactured Bearing

The O.D. for the manufactured bearing is 1.379 + .000/ −.001. Written as a limit tolerance, it is 1.3790/1.3780. The tolerance range for the O.D. is 0.001. An interference tolerance is required between the O.D. of the bearing and the hole in the support.

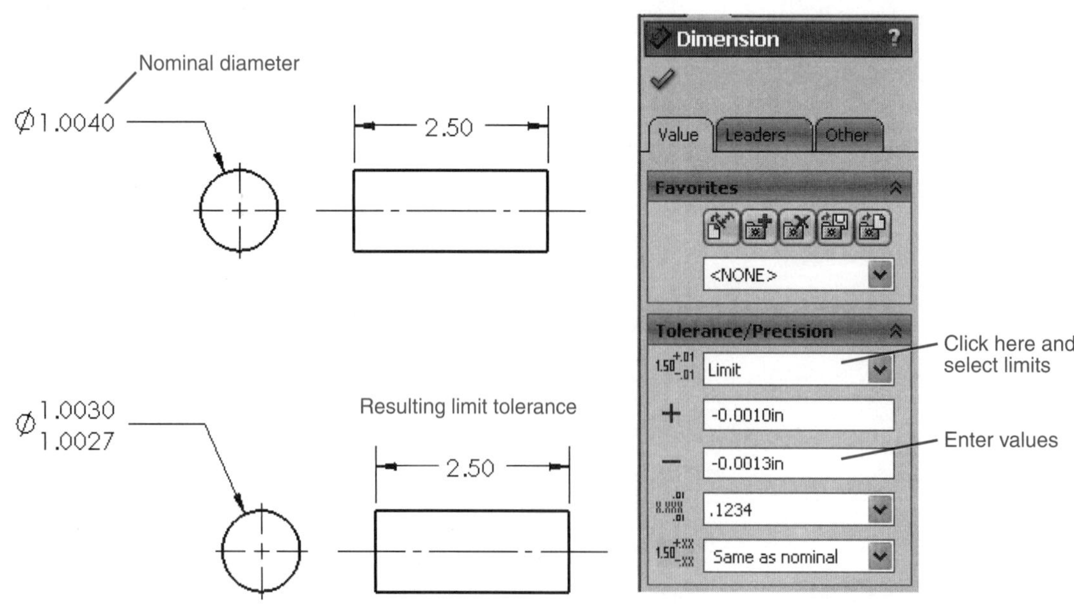

Figure 10-19

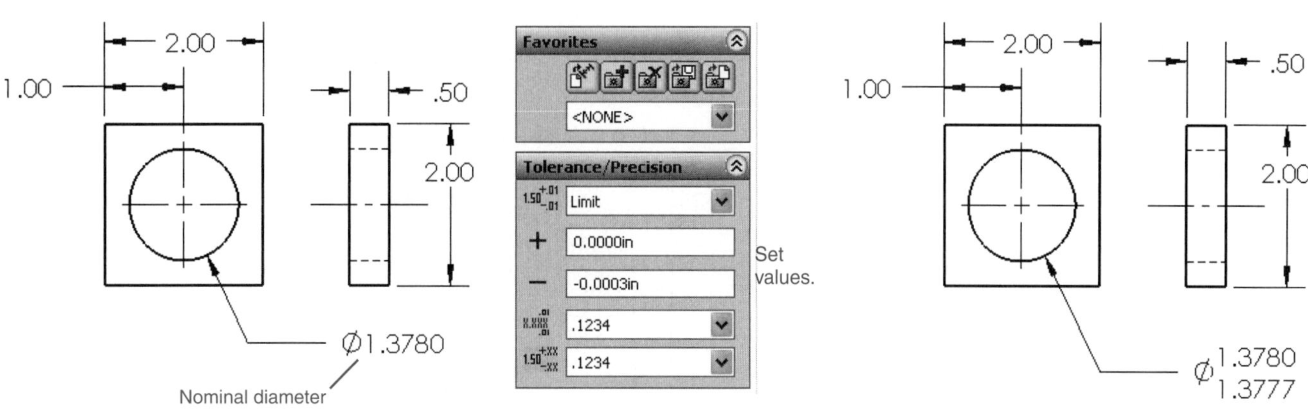

Figure 10-20

> **Note:**
> An interference fit is also called a ***press fit***.

A search of the Standard Fit tables in the appendix for a shaft (the O.D. of the bearing acts like a shaft in this condition) tolerance range of 0.001 finds that an LN2 (H7/p6) shaft range is .0008, or .0002 less than manufactured tolerance.

The limits of interference for the LN2 standard fit are 0.0 to 0.0013. If these limits are maintained, the smallest shaft diameter is equal to the largest hole diameter (1.3780 + 0.0 = 1.3780), and the largest shaft diameter is .0013 greater than the smallest hole diameter (1.3790 − .0013 = 1.3777).

Therefore, the shaft tolerances are

Hole: Ø1.3780/1.3777

These tolerances give a tolerance range for the shaft of .0003, or .0002 less than the stated .0005 found in the table. This difference makes up for the .0002 difference between the actual hole diameter's tolerance range of 0.0010 and the standard H7 tolerance of 0.0008.

To Apply an Interference Fit Tolerance Using SolidWorks

Figure 10-20 shows a support with a nominal diameter of 1.3780. Enter the required 1.3780/1.3777 tolerance. See Chapter 8 for further explanation on how to apply tolerances.

1. Click the **Limits** option in the **Tolerance/Precision** box.
2. Set the upper limit for **-0.0000** and the lower limit for **-0.0003**.
3. Click the OK check mark.

Using SolidWorks to Apply Standard Fit Tolerances to an Assembly Drawing

Figure 10-21 shows the assembly of the shaft and support toleranced in the previous section with the manufactured bearing. The standard tolerance callouts are added as follows.

1. Use the **Smart Dimension** tool and dimension the O.D. of the bearing.
2. Access the **Tolerance/Precision** box and select the **Fit** option.
3. Set the hole fit tolerance for **H8** and the shaft fit tolerance for **H7**.
4. Click the OK check mark.
5. Use the **Smart Dimension** tool and dimension the I.D. of the bearing.
6. Access the **Tolerance/Precision** box and select the **Fit** option.
7. Set the hole fit tolerance for **H6** and the shaft fit tolerance for **p6**.

10-15 FIT TOLERANCES—MILLIMETERS

The appendix also includes tables for preferred fits using metric values. These tables are read directly. For example, the values for a Close Running Preferred Clearance fit H8/f7 for a nominal shaft diameter of 16 is as follows:

Hole: Ø16.027/16.000 Shaft: Ø15.984/15.966
Fit (limits of fits): 0.016

The value 16.000 indicates that the hole basis condition was used to calculate the tolerances. Metric fits are applied in the same manner as English unit values.

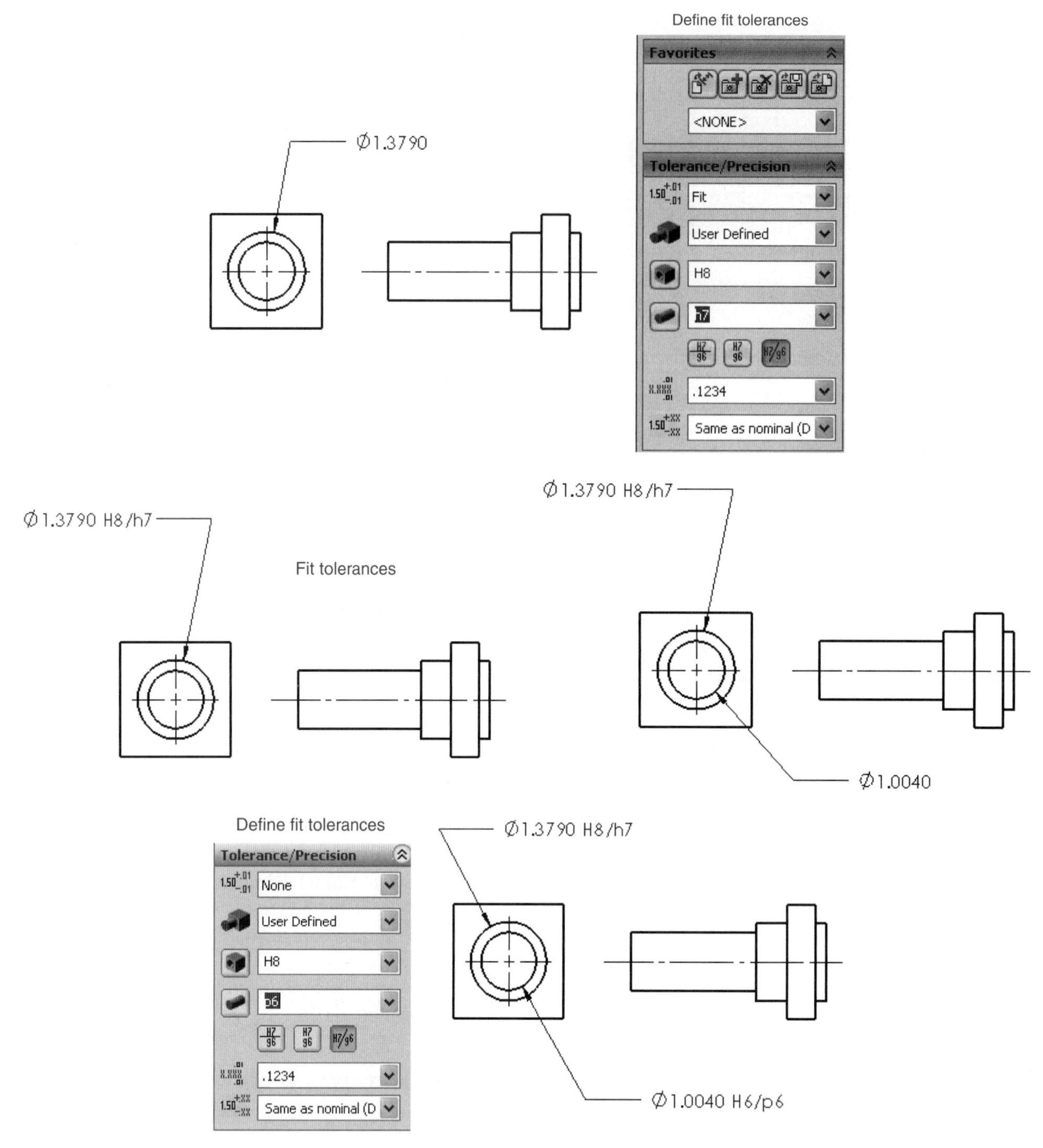

Figure 10-21

10-16 PROJECTS

Figure P10-1 shows a support plate with three holes. A dimensioned drawing of the support plate is included. The holes are lettered. Three shafts are also shown. All shafts are 3.00 long. For Projects 10-1 to P10-8:

A. Create dimensioned and tolerances drawings for the support plate and shafts.
B. Specify tolerances for both the support plate holes and the shaft's diameters based on the given fit information. All shafts are 3.00 long.

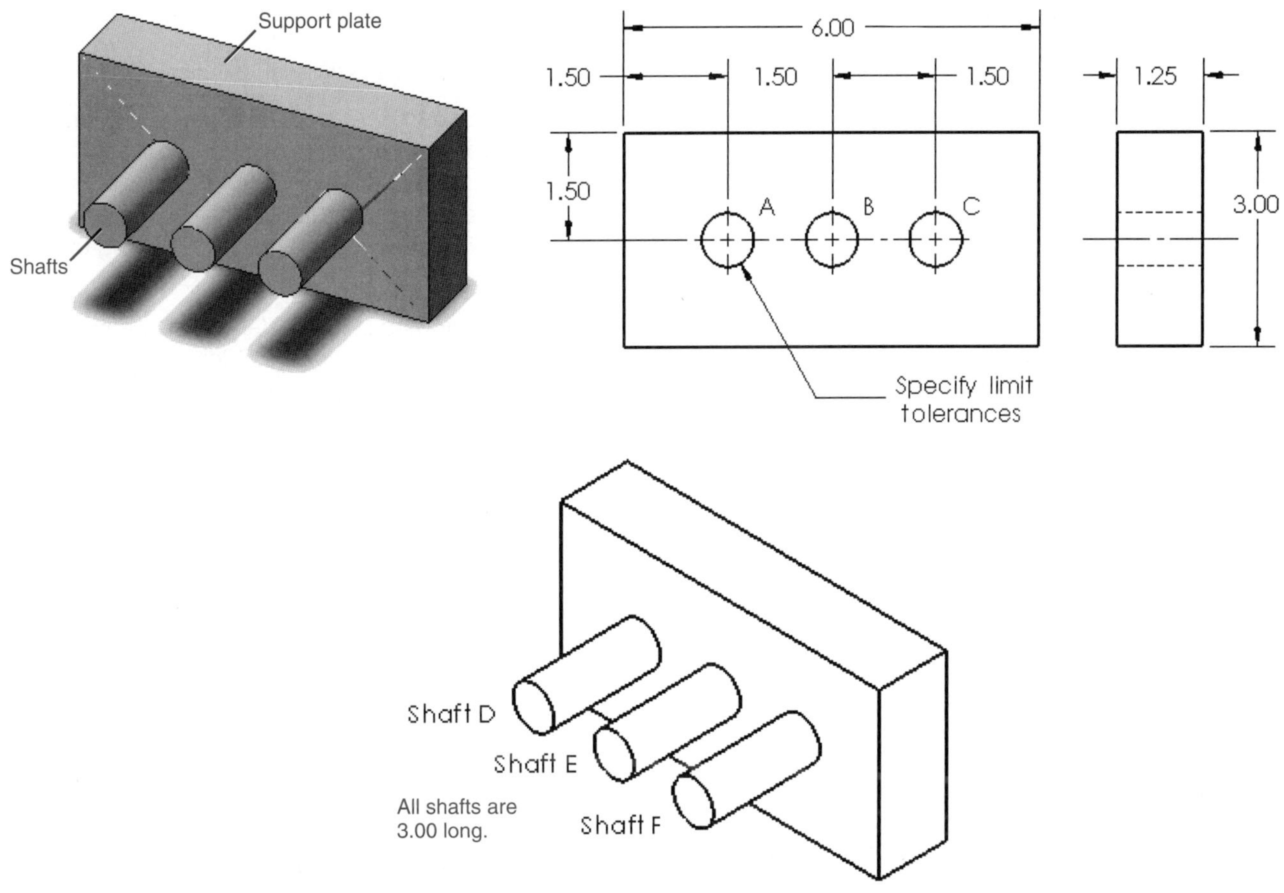

Figure P10-1

Project 10-1: Clearance Fits—Inches

Hole A/Shaft D: H7/h6, Ø.125 nominal
Hole B/Shaft E: H6/h5, Ø.750 nominal
Hole C/Shaft F: H9/f8, Ø.250 nominal

Project 10-2: Clearance Fits—Inches

Hole A/Shaft D: H10/d9, Ø1.123 nominal
Hole B/Shaft E: H7/h6, Ø.500 nominal
Hole C/Shaft F: H5/g4, Ø.625 nominal

Project 10-3: Clearance Fits—Inches

Hole A/Shaft D: H9/f8, Ø.500 nominal
Hole B/Shaft E: H8/e7, Ø.635 nominal
Hole C/Shaft F: H7/f6, Ø1.000 nominal

Project 10-4: Clearance Fits—Millimeters

Hole A/Shaft D: D9/h9, Ø10.0 nominal
Hole B/Shaft E: H7/h6, Ø16.0 nominal
Hole C/Shaft F: C11/h11. Ø20.0 nominal

Project 10-5: Interference Fits—Inches

Hole A/Shaft D: H6/n5, Ø.250 nominal
Hole B/Shaft E: H7/p6, Ø.750 nominal
Hole C/Shaft F: H7/r6, Ø.250 nominal

Project 10-6: Interference Fits—Inches

Hole A/Shaft D: FN2, Ø.375 nominal
Hole B/Shaft E: FN3, Ø1.500 nominal
Hole C/Shaft F: FN4, Ø.250 nominal

Project 10-7: Locational Fits—Inches

Hole A/Shaft D: H8/k7, Ø.4375 nominal
Hole B/Shaft E: H7/k6, Ø.7075 nominal
Hole C/Shaft F: H8/js7, Ø1.155 nominal

Project 10-8: Interference Fits—Millimeters

Hole A/Shaft D: H7/k6, Ø12.0 nominal
Hole B/Shaft E: H7/p6, Ø25.0 nominal
Hole C/Shaft F: N7/h6, Ø8.0 nominal

Figure P10-2 Shows a U-bracket, four sleeve bearings, and two shafts. A dimensioned drawing of the U-bracket is also included. For Projects 10-9 to 10-12:

A. Create dimensioned and toleranced drawings for the U-bracket, sleeve bearings, and shafts. All shafts are 5.00 long.
B. Specify tolerances for the shaft's diameter and the outside diameter of the sleeve bearings based on the given interference fits.

C. Specify tolerances for the holes in the U-bracket and the outside diameter of the sleeve bearings based on the sizes given in the appendix.
D. Create new links for parts 7, 8, and 9, and note the changes in motion created.

Project 10-9: Inches

Clearance between shaft and bearing: H9/f8, Ø.875 nominal
Interference between the hole in the U-bracket and the bearing: H7/p6. Ø.375 nominal

Project 10-10: Inches

Clearance between the shaft and the bearing: H9/f8, Ø.875 nominal
Interference between the hole in the U-bracket and the bearing: Class FN2, Ø1.125 nominal

Project 10-11: Inches

Clearance between the shaft and the bearing: H10/h9, Ø.500 nominal
Interference between the hole in the U-bracket and the bearing: H7/r6, Ø.750 nominal

Project 10-12: Millimeters

Clearance between the shaft and the bearing: H9/d9, Ø10.0 nominal
Interference between the hole in the U-bracket and the bearing: H7/p6, Ø16.0 nominal

Project 10-13: Inches

A 4-bar assembly is defined in Figure P10-13.

1. Create a three-dimensional assembly drawing of the 4-bar assembly.
2. Animate the links using LINK-1 as the driver.
3. Redraw the individual parts, add the appropriate dimensions, and add the following tolerances:

   A. Assign an LN1 interference fit between the links and the needle roller bearing.
   B. Assign an LC2 clearance between the holder posts, both regular and long posts, and the inside diameter of the needle roller bearing.
   C. Assign an LC3 clearance between the holder posts, both regular and long posts, and the spacers.

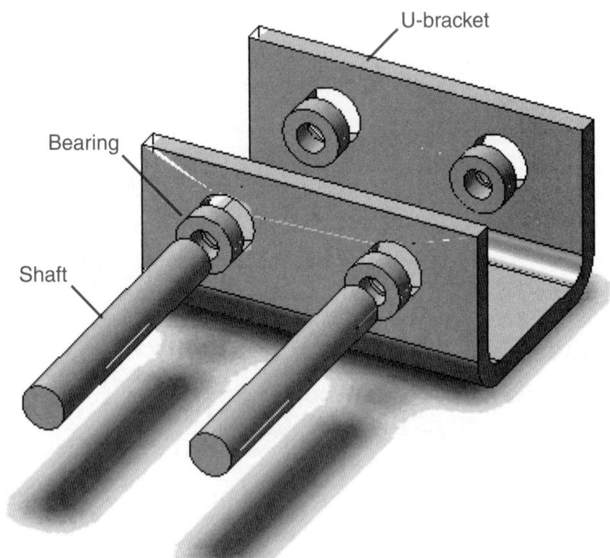

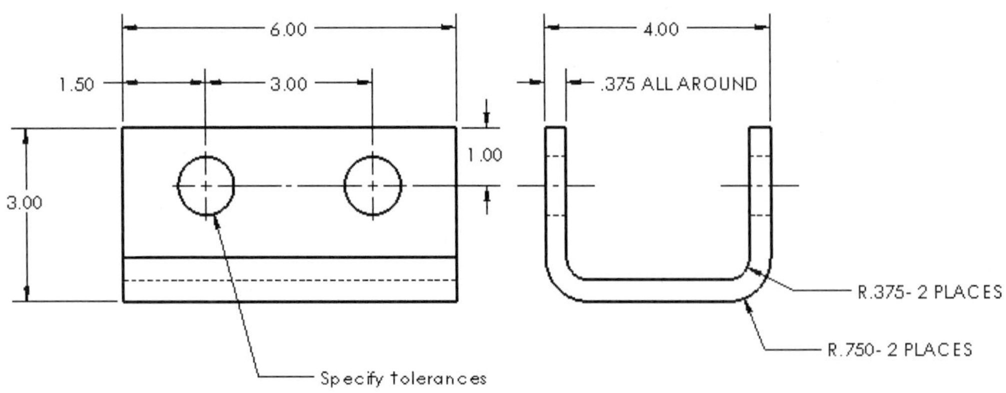

Figure P10-2

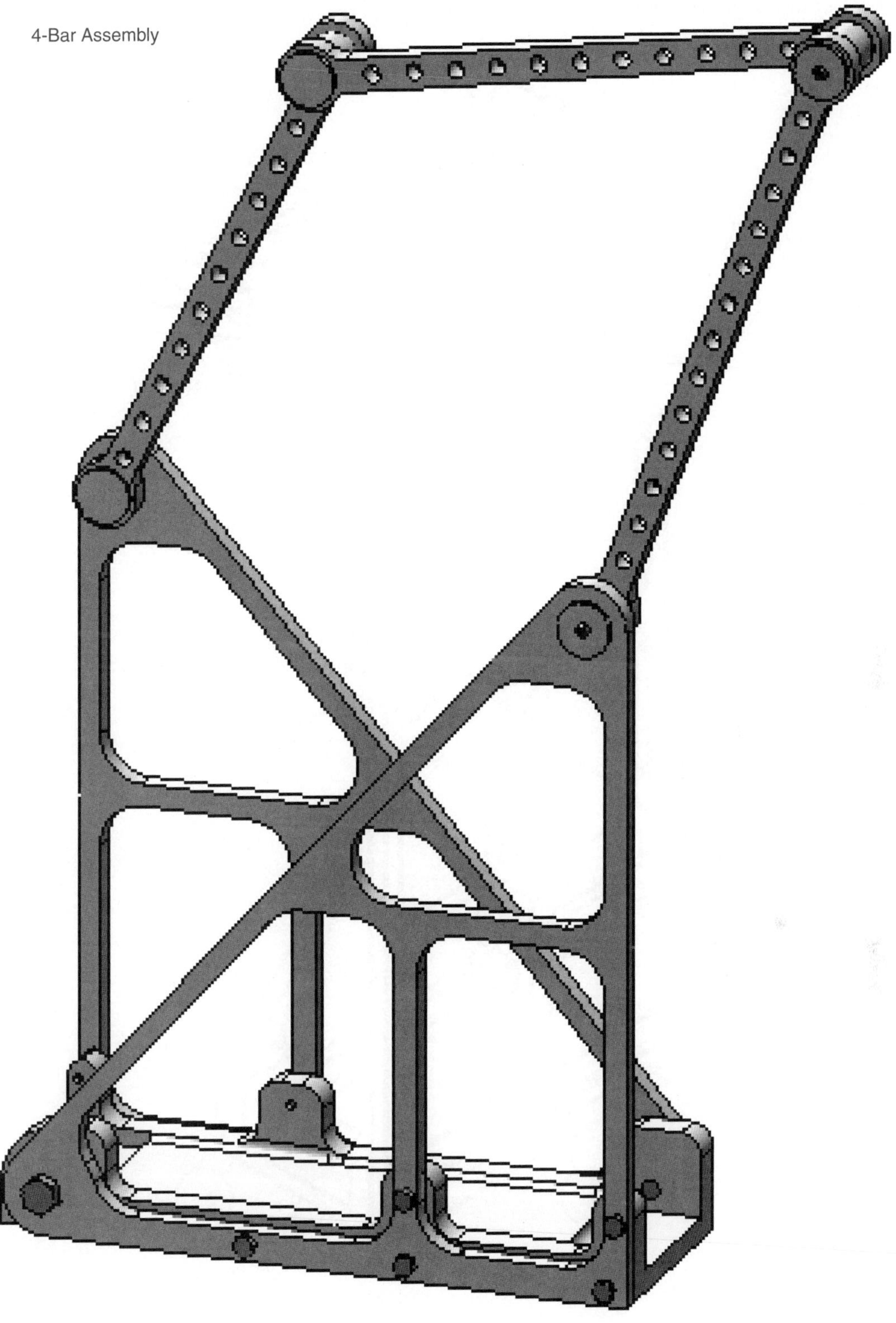

Figure P10-13

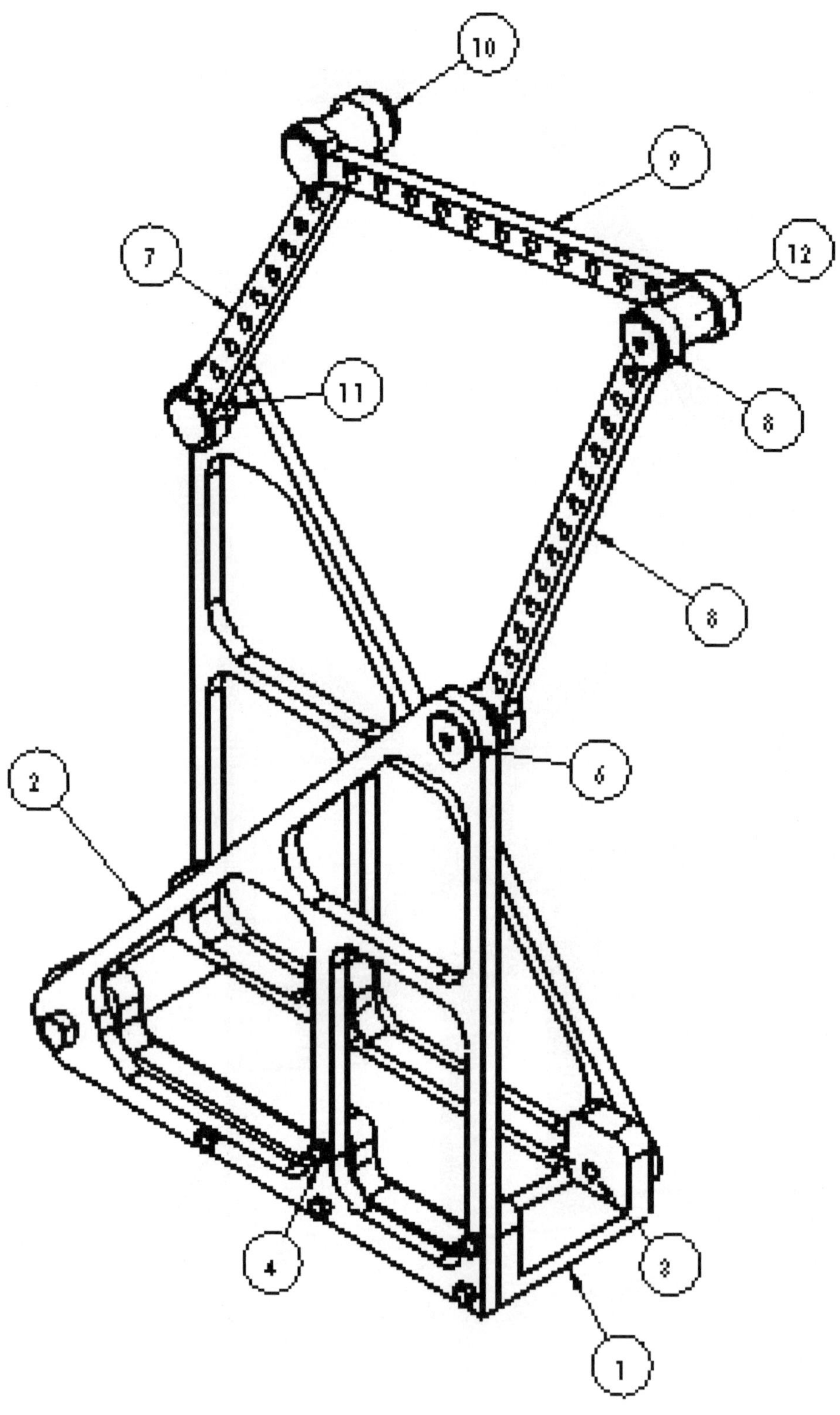

Figure P10-13 *(continued)*

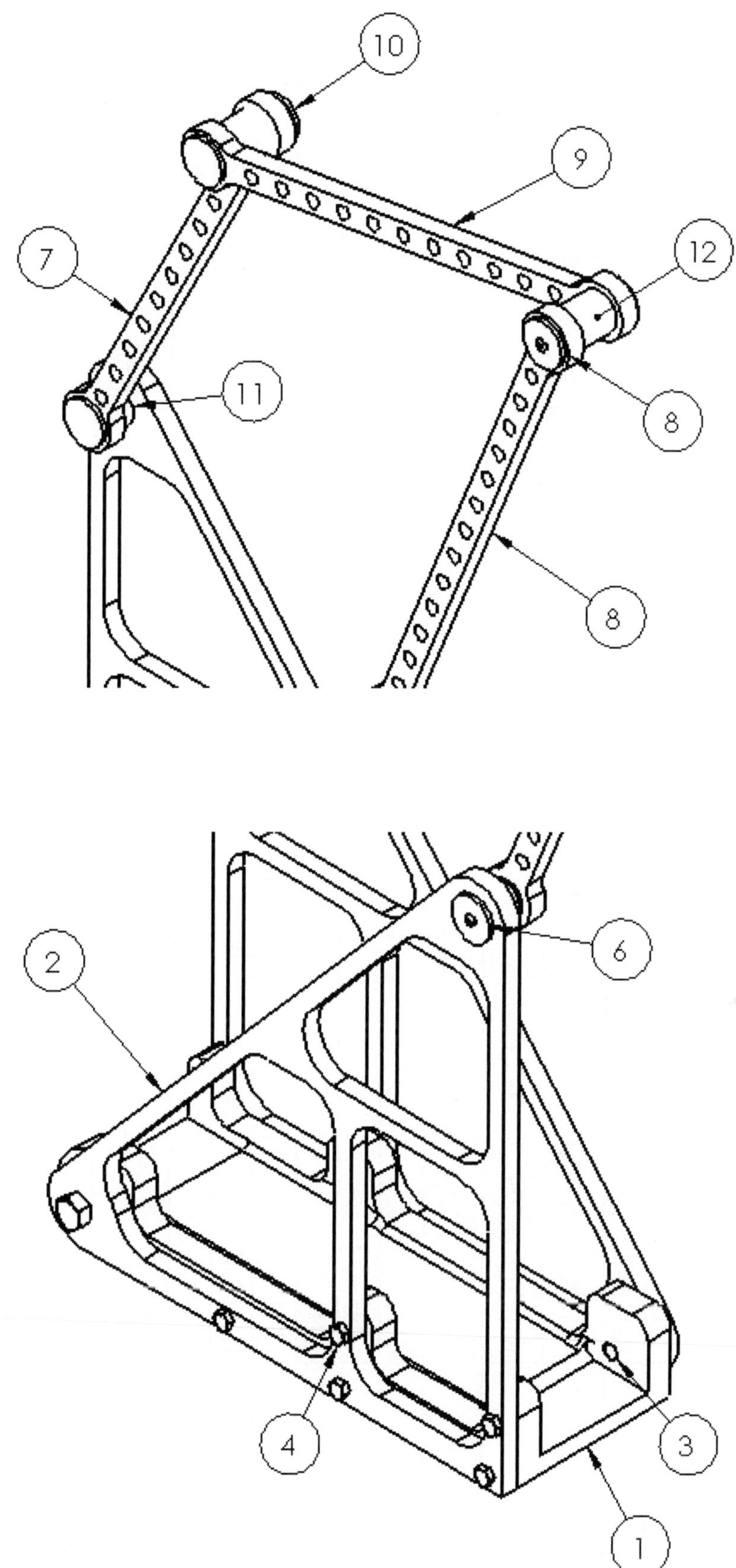

Figure P10-13 *(continued)*

ITEM NO.	PART NUMBER	DESCRIPTION	QTY.
1	BU09-ME1	HOLDER, BASE	1
2	BU09-ME2	HOLDER, SIDE	2
3	HBOLT 0.5000-13x1.25x1.25-N		2
4	HBOLT 0.2500-20x1x1-N		11
5	HBOLT 0.2500-20x1.25x1.25-N		1
6	BU09-P1	POST, PIVOT, SHORT	2
7	LINK-01	LINK1, ASSEMBLY	1
8	LINK-03	LINK3, ASSEMBLY	1
9	LINK-02	LINK 2, ASSEMBLY	1
10	BU09-P2	POST, PIVOT, LONG	2
11	BU09-S1	SPACER, SHORT	2
12	BU09-S2	SPACER, LONG	2

Figure P10-13 ***(continued)***

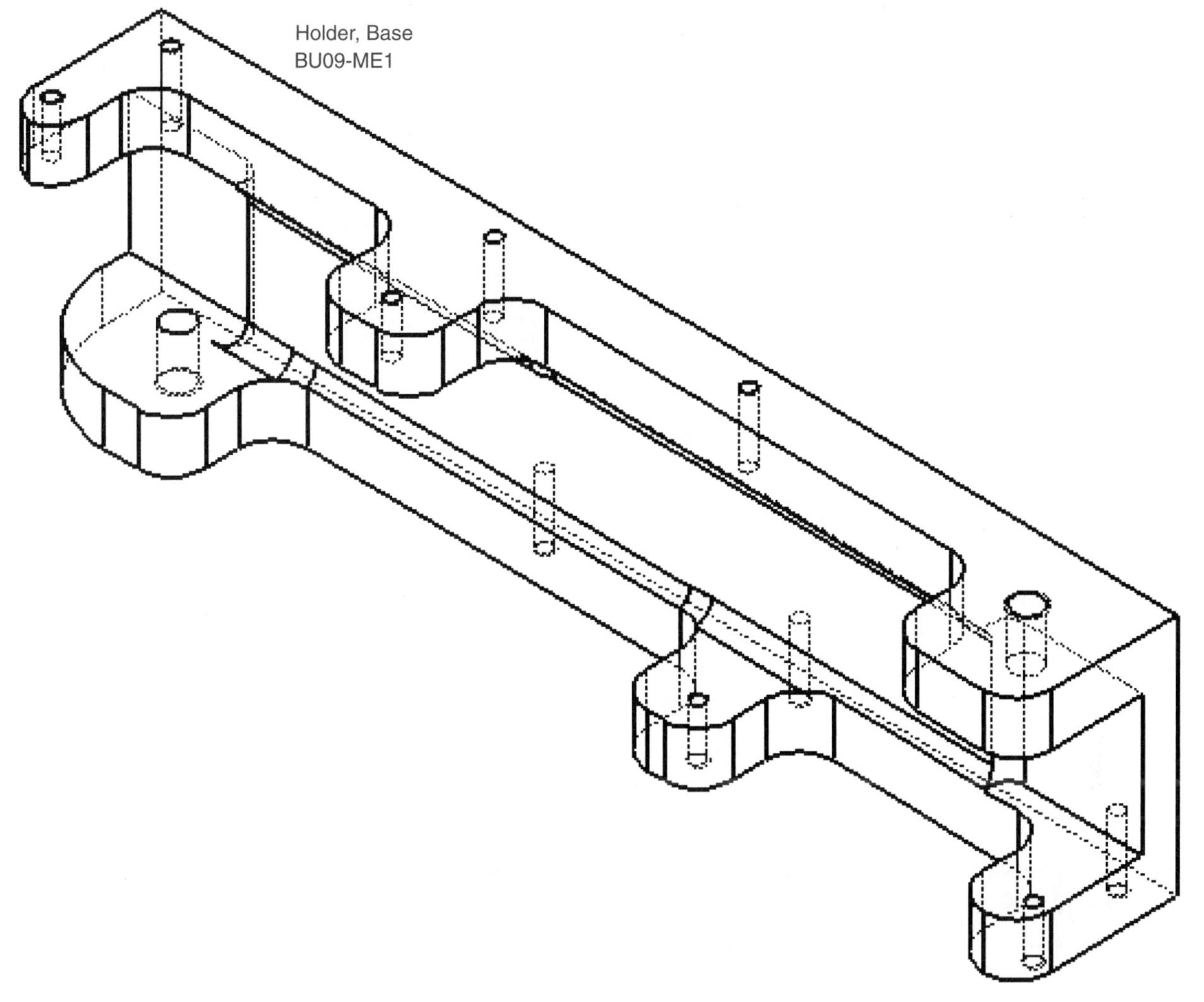

Figure P10-13 *(continued)*

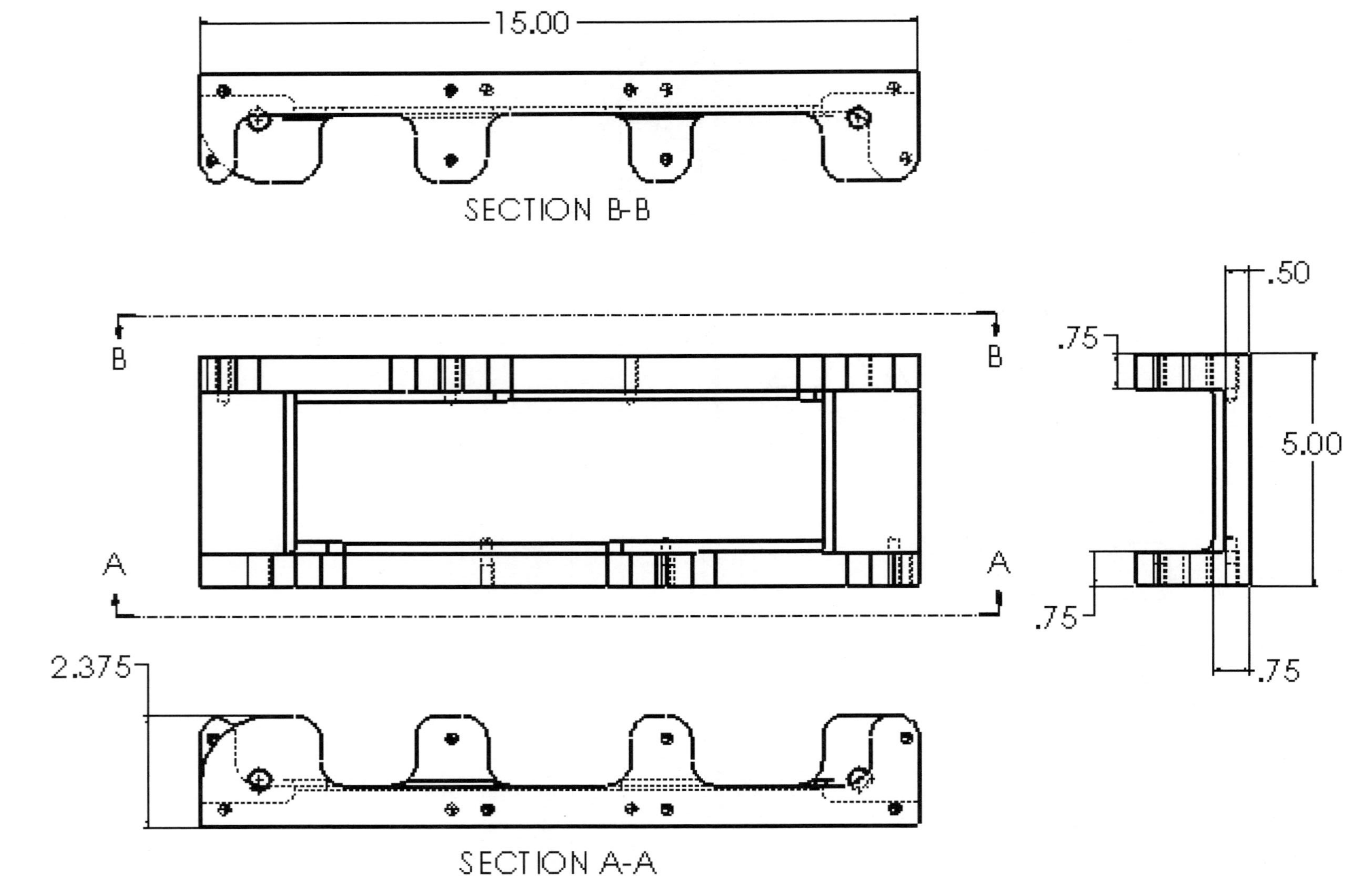

Figure P10-13 ***(continued)***

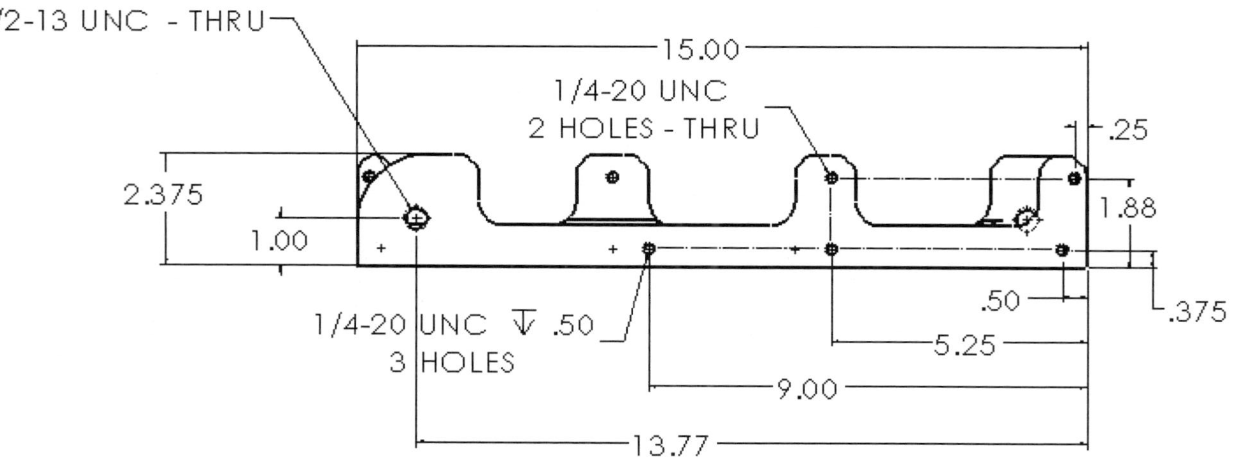

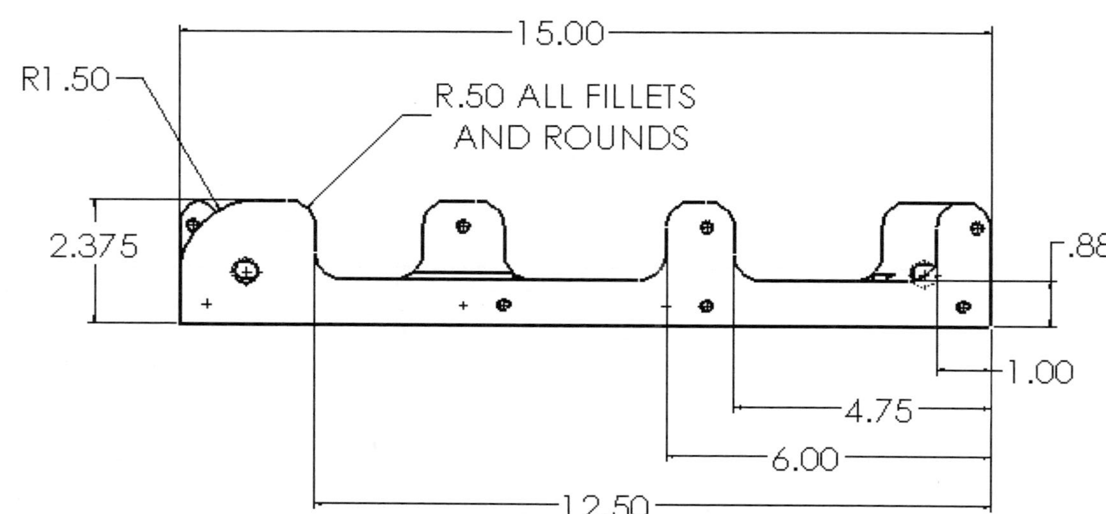

Figure P10-13 ***(continued)***

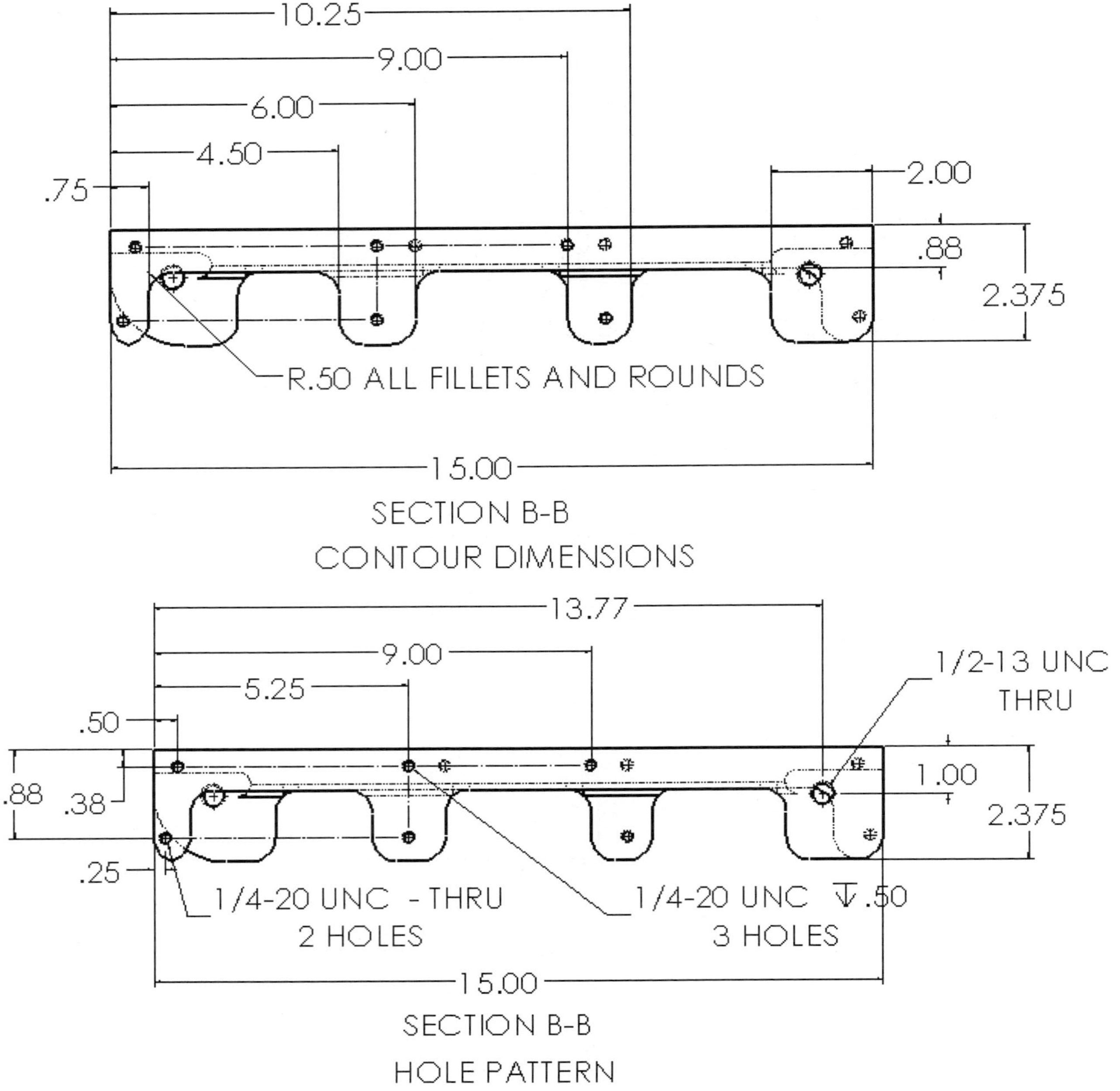

Figure P10-13 ***(continued)***

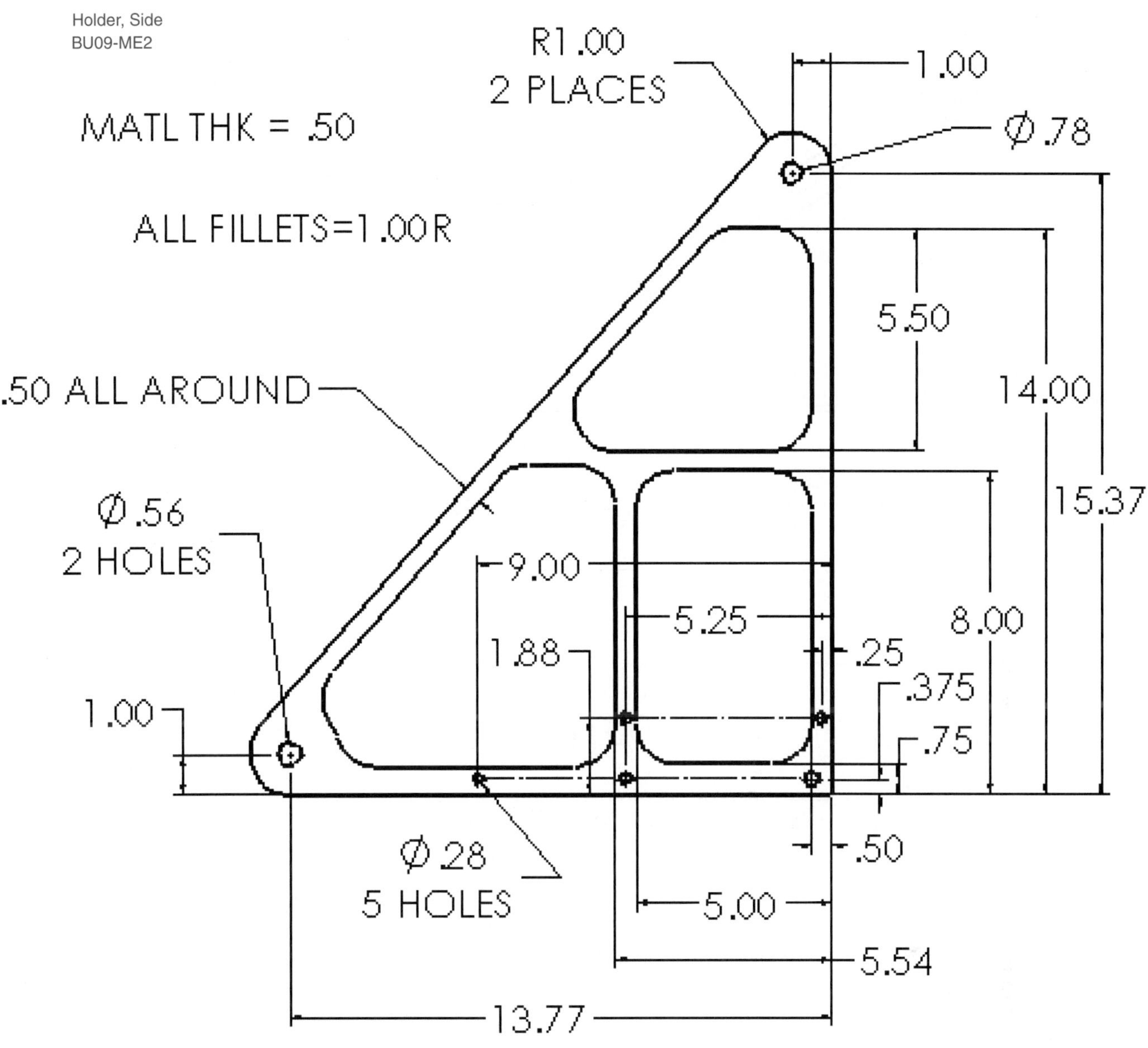

Figure P10-13 ***(continued)***

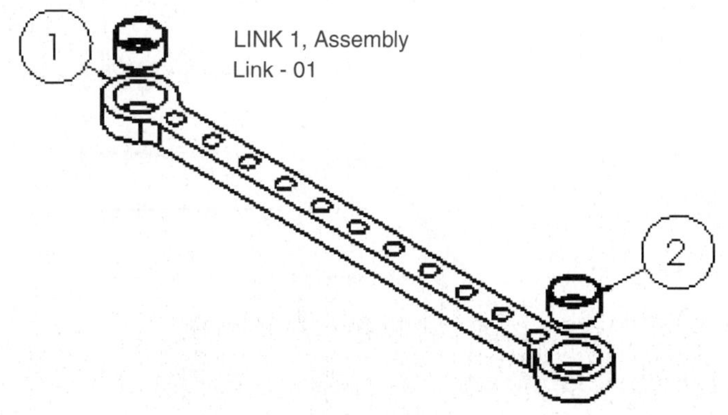

ITEM NO.	PART NUMBER	DESCRIPTION	QTY.
1	BU09-L1	LINK-1	1
2	AFBMA 18.2.3.1 - 12NIH135 - 20,SI,NC,20	NEEDLE ROLLER BEARING	2

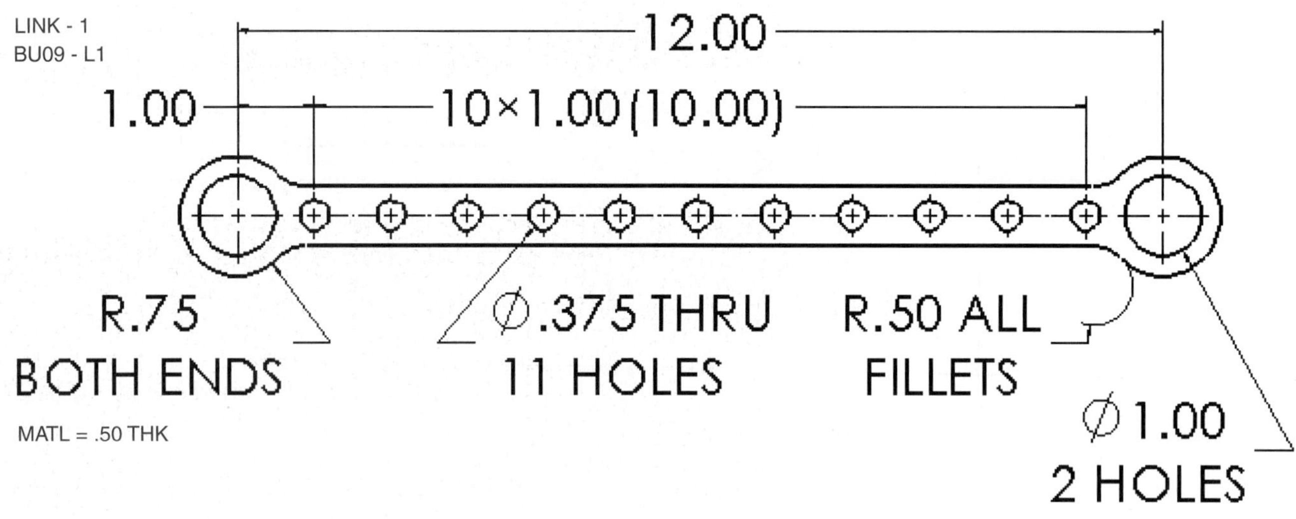

Figure P10-13 ***(continued)***

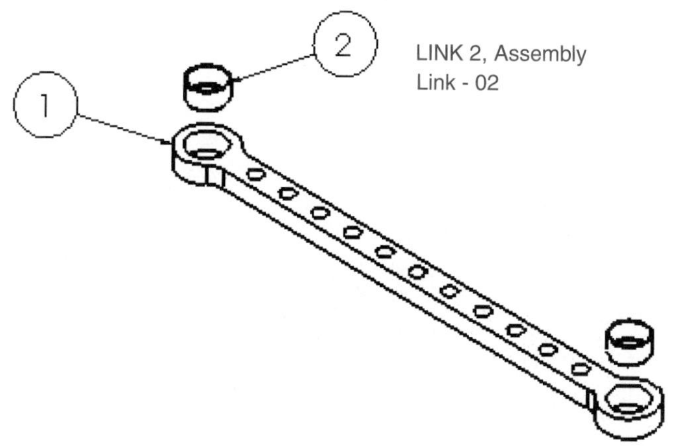

ITEM NO.	PART NUMBER	DESCRIPTION	QTY.
1	BU09-L2	LINK - 2	1
2	AFBMA 18.2.3.1 - 12NIHB5 - 20,SI,NC,20	NEEDLE ROLLER BEARING	2

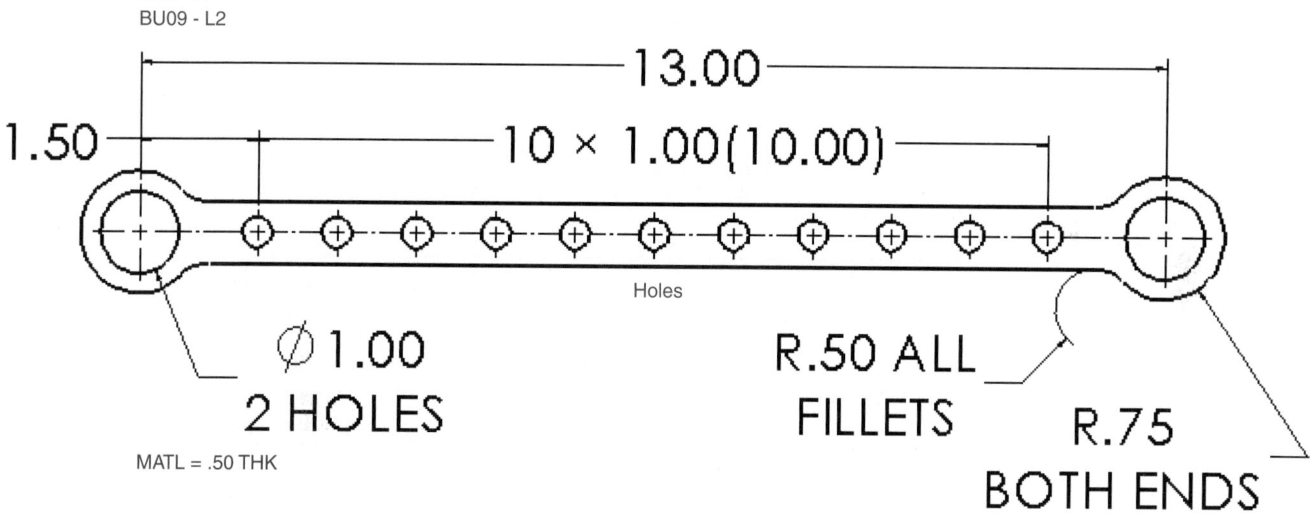

Figure P10-13 *(continued)*

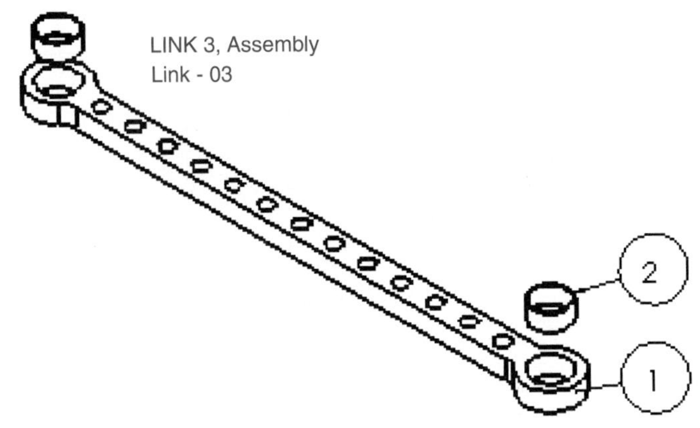

ITEM NO.	PART NUMBER	DESCRIPTION	QTY.
1	BU09-L3	LINK-3	1
2	AFBMA 18.2.3.1 - 12NIHI35 - 20,SI,NC,20	NEEDLE ROLLER BEARING	2

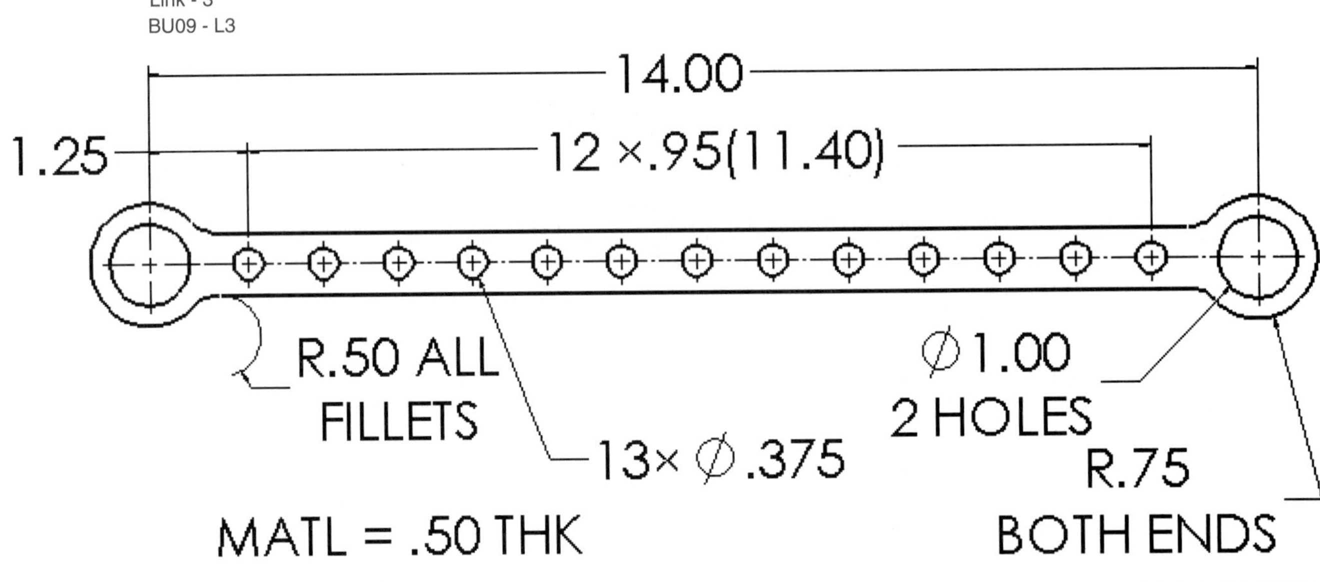

Figure P10-13 ***(continued)***

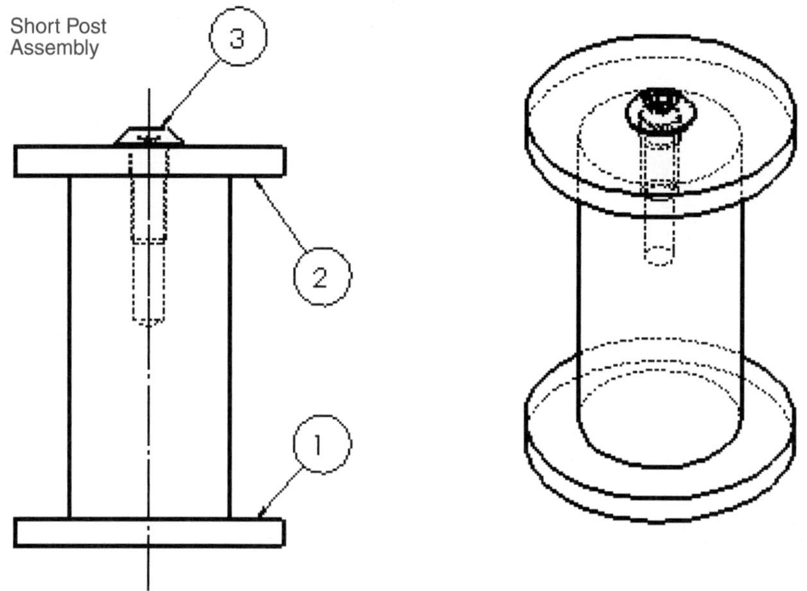

ITEM NO.	PART NUMBER	DESCRIPTION	QTY.
1	BU09-07	POST,HOLDER	1
2	BU09--10	DISK, TOP	1
3	SBHCSCREW0.164-32x0.4375-HX-N	SOCKET BUTTON HEAD CAP SCREW	1

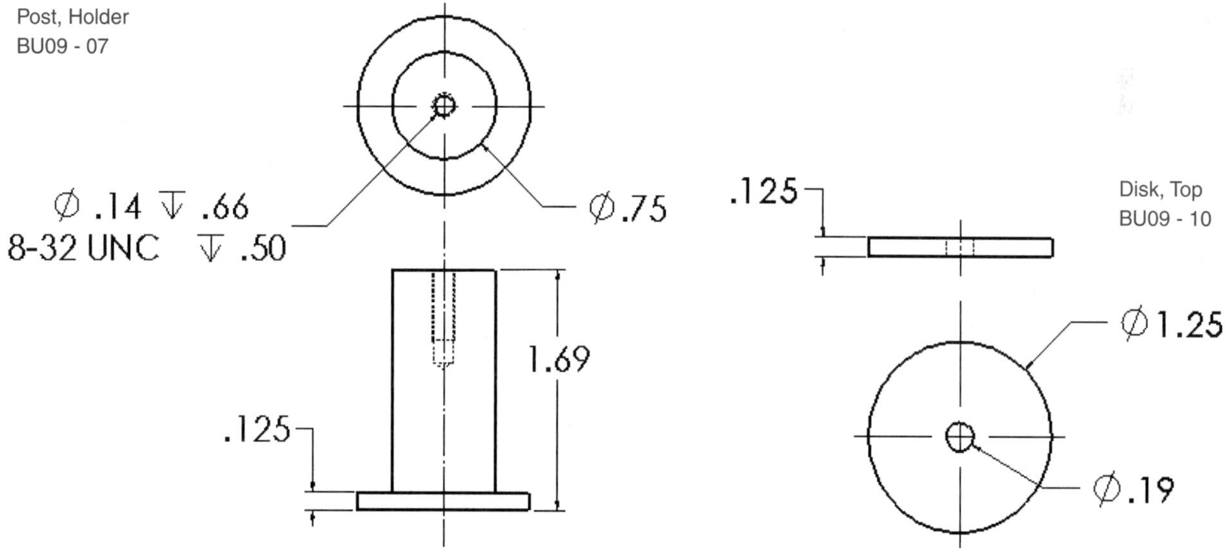

Figure P10-13 *(continued)*

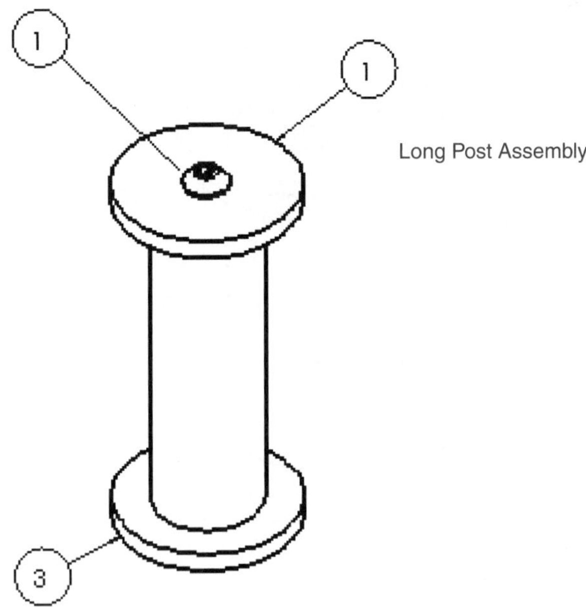

ITEM NO.	PART NUMBER	DESCRIPTION	QTY.
1	BU09-10	DISK, TOP	1
2	SBHCSCREW 0.164-32x0.4375-HX-N	SOCKET BUTTON HEAD CAP SCREW	1
3	BU09-08	POST, HOLDER, LONG	1

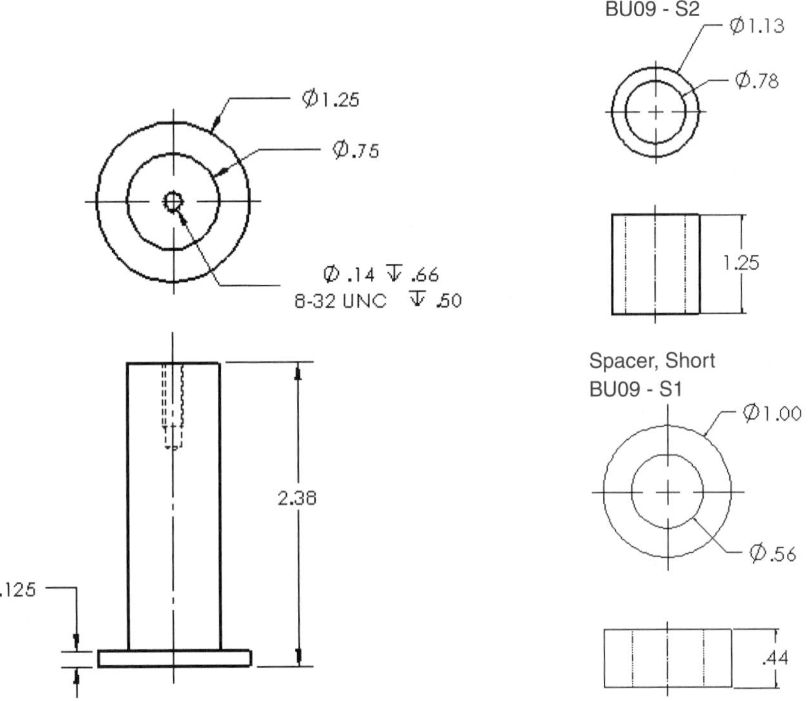

Figure P10-13 *(continued)*

C H A P T E R 

Cams and Springs

Objectives

- Learn how to draw cams using SolidWorks
- Learn how to draw displacement diagrams
- Understand the relationship between cams and followers
- Learn how to draw springs

11-1 INTRODUCTION

Cams are mechanical devices used to translate rotary motion into linear motion. Traditionally, cam profiles are designed by first defining a displacement diagram and then transferring the displacement diagram information to a base circle. Figure 11-1 shows a cam and a displacement diagram.

11-2 BASE CIRCLE

Cam profiles are defined starting with a base circle. The diameter of the base circle will vary according to the design situation. The edge of the base circle is assumed to be the 0.0 displacement line on the displacement diagram.

11-3 TRACE POINT

The trace point is the center point of the roller follower. SolidWorks defines the shape of the cam profile by defining the path of the trace point.

11-4 DWELL, RISE, AND FALL

In the displacement diagram shown in Figure 11-1, the displacement line rises .500 in. in the first 90°. This type of motion is call *rise*.

The displacement line then remains at .500 from 90° to 270°. This type of motion is called *dwell*.

> **TIP**
>
> A circle is a shape of constant radius. If a circle was used as a cam, the follower would not go up or down but would remain in the same position, because the circle's radius is constant.

The displacement line falls 0.500 from 270° to 315°. This type of motion is called a *fall*. The displacement line dwells between 315° and 360°.

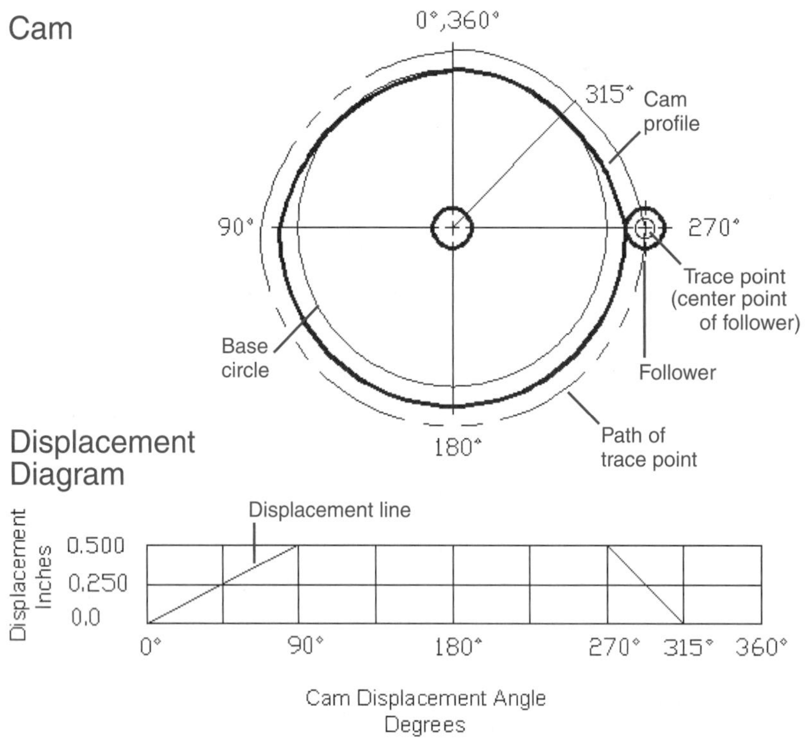

Figure 11-1

Shape of the Rise and Fall Lines

The shape of the cam's surface during either a rise or a fall is an important design consideration. The shape of the profile will affect the acceleration and deceleration of the follower, and that will in turn affect the forces in both the cam and the follower. SolidWorks includes 13 different types of motions.

Cam Direction

Note that the 90° reference is located on the left side of the cam. This indicates clockwise direction.

11-5 CREATING CAMS IN SOLIDWORKS

SolidWorks creates cams by working from existing templates. There are templates for circular and linear cams and for internal and external cams. The templates allow you to work directly on the cam profile and eliminate the need for a displacement diagram. In the following example a circular cam with a 4.00-in. base circle and a profile that rises 0.5 in. in 90° using harmonic motion, dwells for 180°, falls 0.50 in. in 45° using harmonic motions, and dwells for 45°. See the approximate shape of the cam presented in Figure 11-1.

To Access the Cam Tools

1. Create a new **Part** document.
2. Select a **Front Plane** orientation.
3. Click the **Toolbox** heading at the top of the screen.
4. Click the **Cams** tool.

See Figure 11-2. The **Cam - Circular** toolbox will appear. See Figure 11-3.

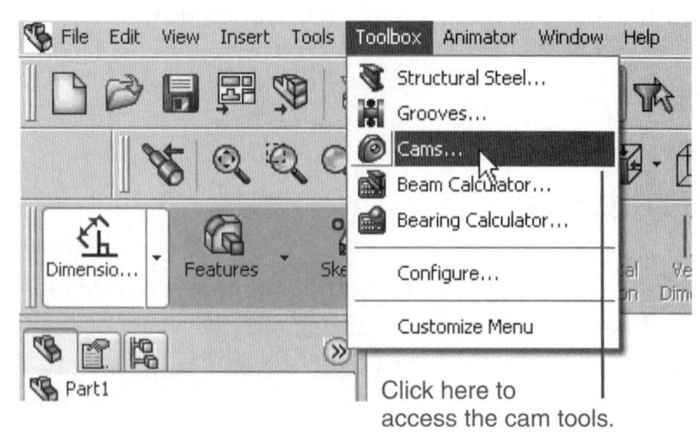

Figure 11-2

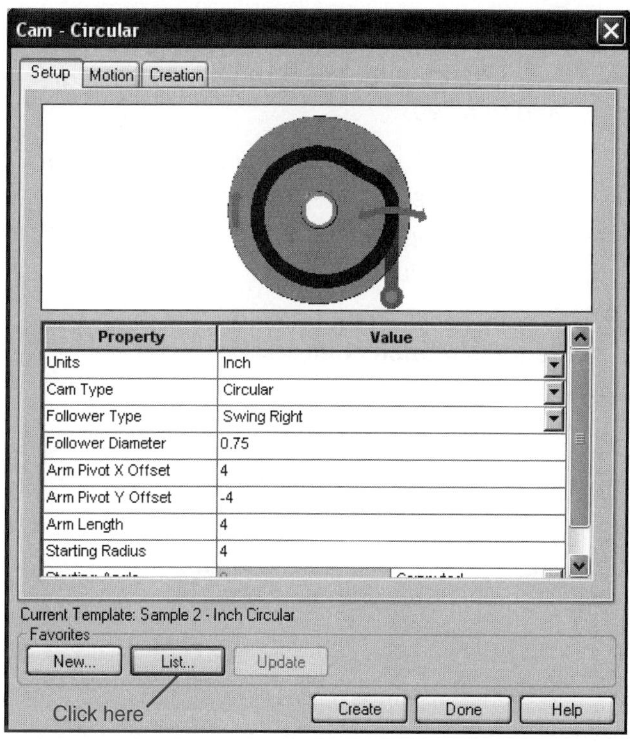

Figure 11-3

11-6 CAM - CIRCULAR SETUP TAB

1. Click the **List** option on the **Setup** tab of the **Cam - Circular** toolbox.

   The **Favorites** dialog box will appear. See Figure 11-4. This box includes a listing of cam templates that can be modified to create a different cam.

2. Click the **Sample 2 - Inch Circular** option.
3. Click the **Load** box, then click the **Done** box.
4. Define the properties needed for the cam's setup.

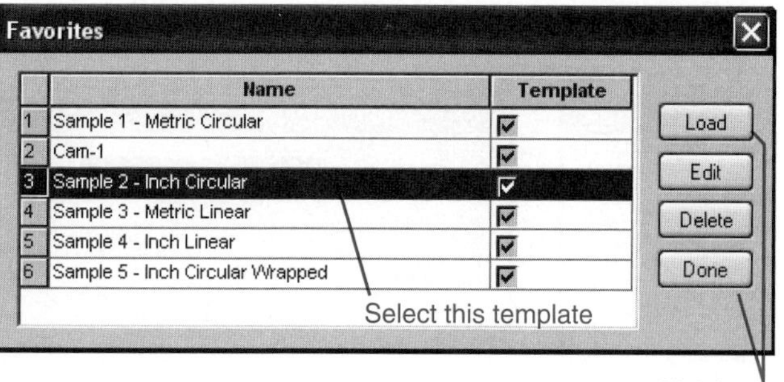

Figure 11-4

See Figure 11-5. The properties for the example cam are as follows:

Units: Inch
Cam Type: Circular
Follower Type: Translating

This follower type will locate the follower directly in-line with a ray from the cam's center point.

Follower Diameter: 0.50
Starting Radius: 2.25

This property defines a Ø4.00 base circle with a radius of 2.00 plus an additional 0.25 radius value to reach the center point of the follower. The follower has a diameter of 0.5.

> ***Note:***
> The cam profile is defined by the *path of the trace point*. The trace point is the center point of the circular follower. In this example the trace point at the 0.0° point on the cam is located 2.00 + 0.25 from the center point of the cam.

Starting Angle: 0

This property defines the ray between the cam's center point and the follower's center point as 0.0°.

Rotation Direction: Clockwise

See Figure 11-5.

> **TIP**
> Some of the **Value** boxes include other options. SolidWorks will generate real-time previews as these options are clicked. Those interested are encouraged to click and study the various options available.

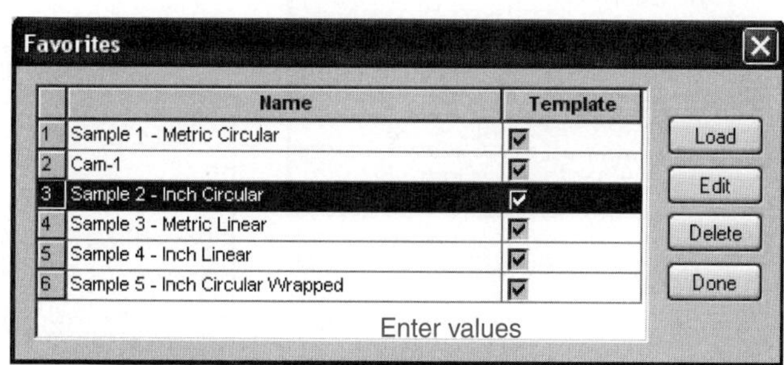

Figure 11-5

11-7 CAM - CIRCULAR MOTION TAB

1. Click the **Motion** tab on the **Cam - Circular** dialog box.

   See Figure 11-6.

2. Click the **Remove All** box.

This step will remove all existing motion types and enable you to define a new cam.

3. Click the **Add** box.

   The **Motion Creation Details** dialog box will appear.

4. Click the arrowhead to the right of the **Motion Type** box.
5. Define the **Motion Type** as **Harmonic**.
6. Define the **End Radius** as **2.75** and the **Degrees Motion** as **90**.

These values define the follower rise as 0.50 in. over a distance of 90° using harmonic motion.

7. Click the **Add** box again.
8. Define the following details:

   Motion Type: Dwell
   Degrees Motion: 180.

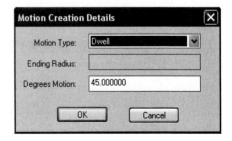

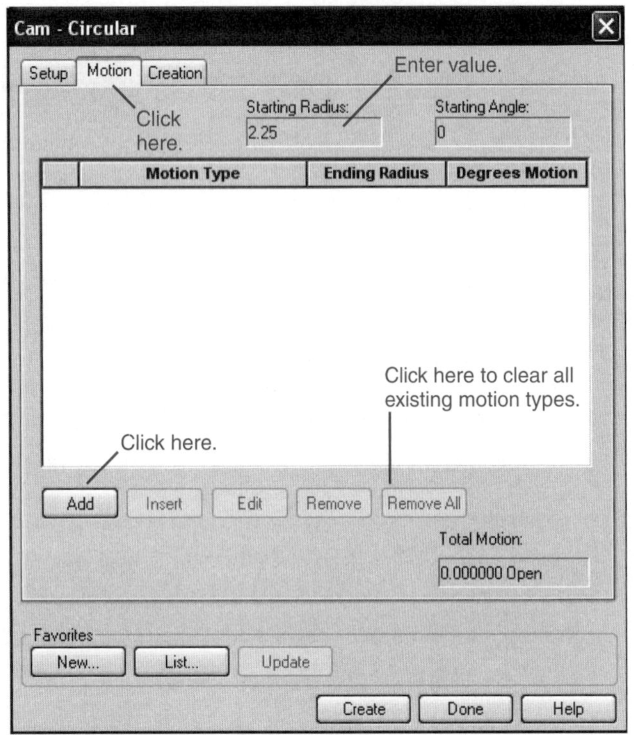

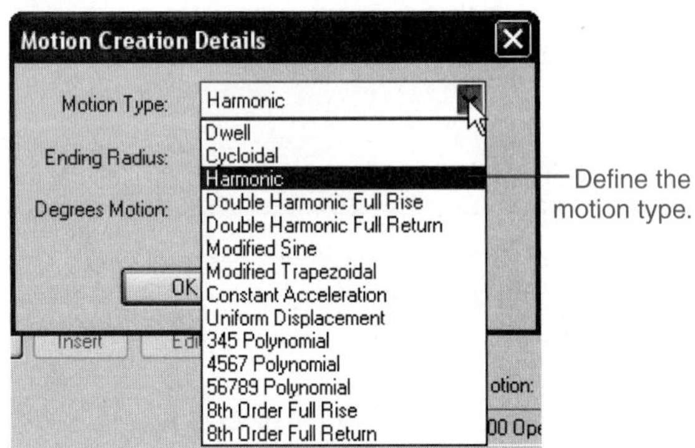

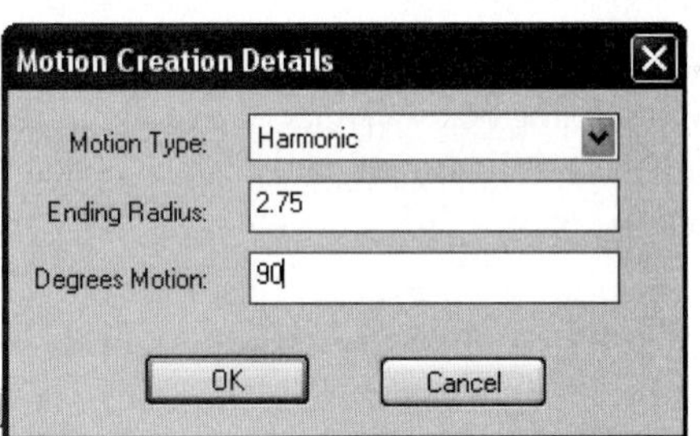

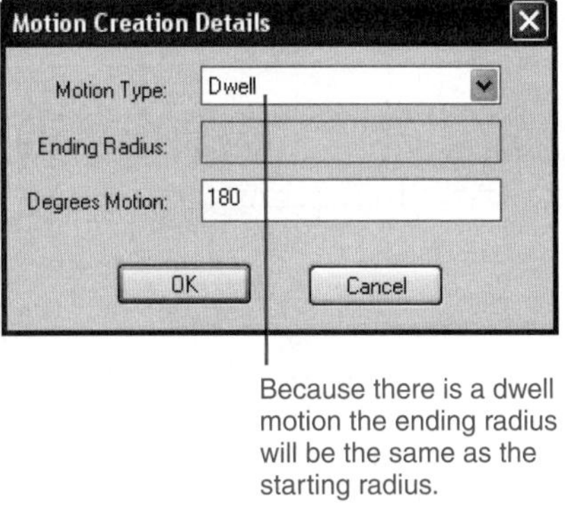

Figure 11-6

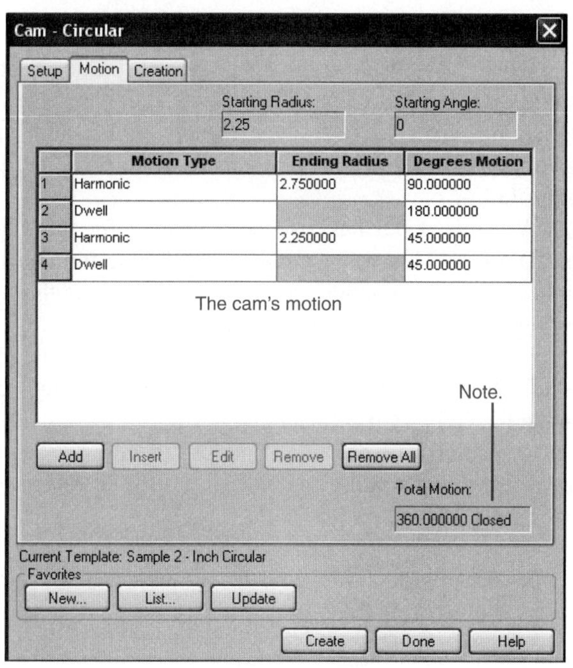

Figure 11-7

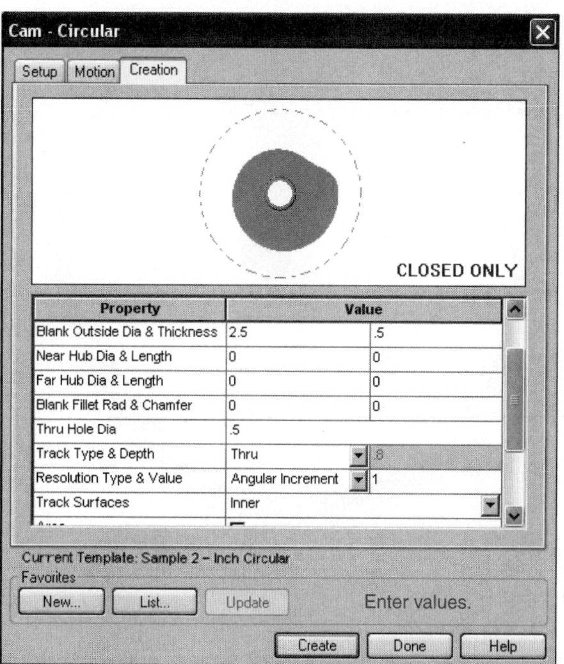

Figure 11-8

Because the dwell motion type was selected, the ending radius will automatically be the same as the starting radius.

9. Click **OK**.
10. Click the **Add** box again.
11. Set the motion as follows:

    Motion Type: Harmonic
    Ending Radius: 2.25
    Degrees Motion: 45.00

    This will return the follower to the base circle.

12. Click the **Add** box again.
13. Select a **Motion Type** of **Dwell** and **Degrees Motion** of **45**.

Note that the **Total Motion** is 360.00. The cam profile has now returned to the original starting point of 0.0°. This is called the ***closed condition***. If the total number of degrees of motion is less than 360°, it is called an ***open condition***. If the number of degrees of motion is greater that 360° it is called the ***wrapped condition***.

Figure 11-7 shows the finished **Motion** tab box.

11-8 CAM - CIRCULAR CREATION TAB

1. Click the **Creation** tab on the **Cam - Circular** dialog box.

   Enter the appropriate values as shown in Figure 11-8.

2. Define the cam's **Blank Outside Dia** as **6** and the **Thickness** as .50 in.

   This cam will not have a hub.

3. Define both the **Near** and **Far Hub Dia & Length** as **0**.
4. Define the **Blank Fillet Rad & Chamfer** as **0.**
5. Define the **Thru Hole Dia** as **0.5**.
6. Define the **Track Type & Depth** as **Thru**.
7. Click the **Arcs** box so that a check mark appears.
8. Set the **Track Surfaces** for **Inner**.

   Accept all the other default values.

9. Click the **Create** box.
10. Click the **Done** box.
11. Click the **Top Plane** orientation.

Accept all other defaul values. Figure 11-9 shows the finished cam. Figure 11-10 shows a top view of the cam. It also shows the cam with the original Ø4.00 base circle superposed onto the surface. Note how the cam profile rises, dwells, falls, and dwells. Figure 11-10 also shows the relationship between the cam profile and the path of the trace point.

11-9 HUBS ON CAMS

There are two methods for creating hubs on cams: add the hub directly using the **Cam - Circular** dialog box, or create a hub on an existing cam using the **Sketch** and **Features** tools.

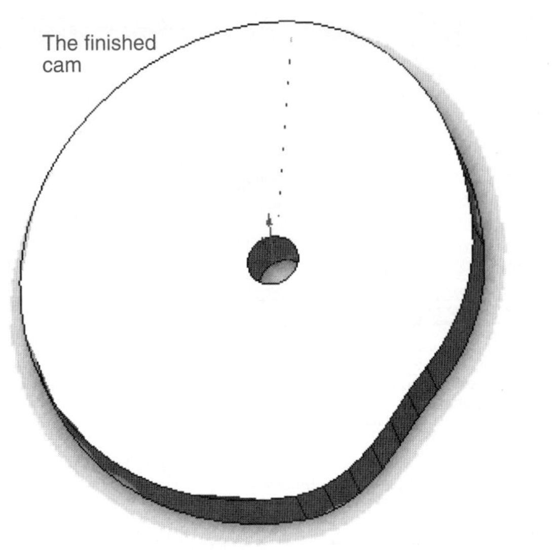

Figure 11-9

Using the Cam - Circular Dialog Box to Create a Hub

Figure 11-11 shows the **Creation** tab portion of the **Cam – Circular** dialog box that was originally presented in Figure 11-8. The values shown in Figure 11-11 include values for the **Near Hub**. The diameter is to be **Ø1.0** and the length **.75**.

A value of **0.5** has also been entered for the **Thru Hole Dia** box. This will generate a Ø0.5 hole through the hub diameter. The hole will go through the hub and through the cam. All other values are the same.

Figure 11-12 shows the modified cam that includes the hub. Note that the dimensions match those values entered in the **Cam - Circular** dialog box.

A second, far-side, hub could also be added by entering the appropriate values in the **Far Hub Dia & Length** box on the **Cam - Circular** dialog box.

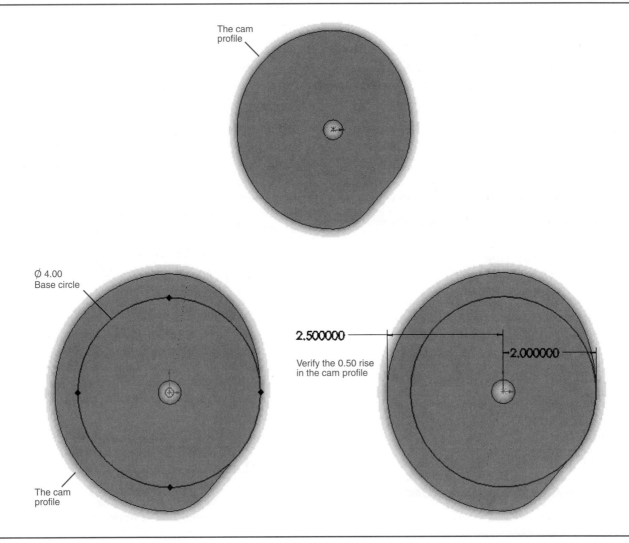

Figure 11-10

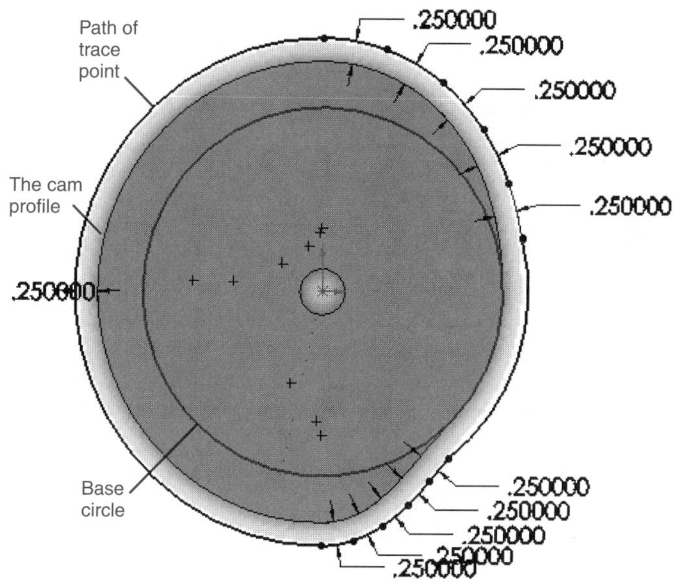

Figure 11-10 ***(continued)***

Using the Sketch and Features Tools to Create a Hub

Figure 11-13 shows the cam created in the first part of this chapter. A hub can be added as follows.

1. Right-click the mouse and select the **Sketch** tool.
2. Use the **Circle** tool and add a circle on the sketch plan centered on the cam's center point.

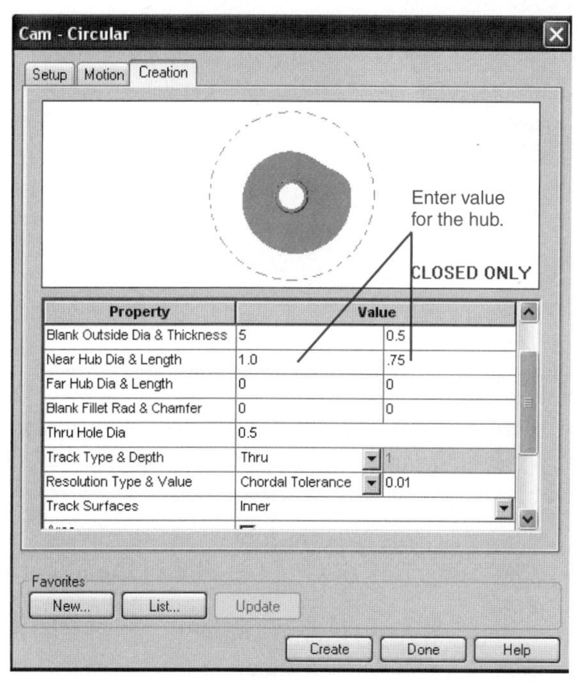

Figure 11-11

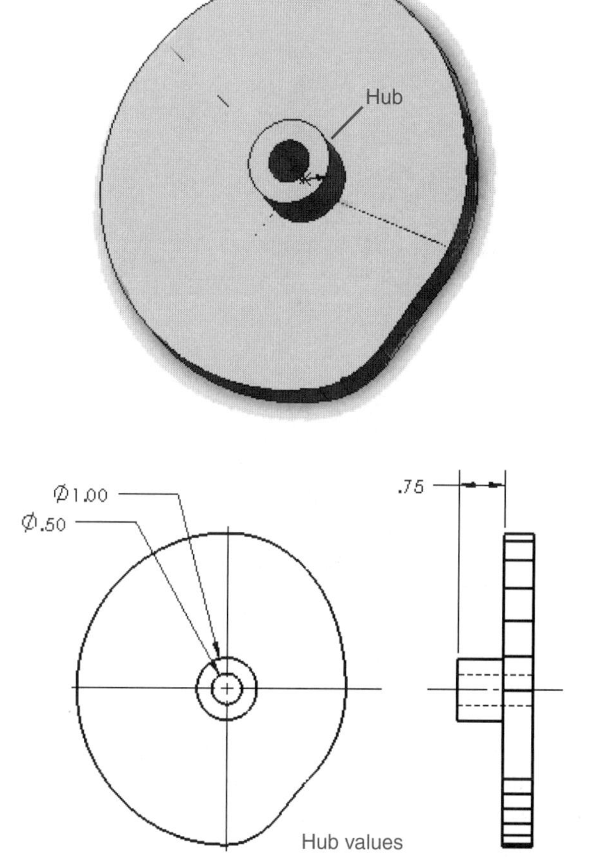

Figure 11-12

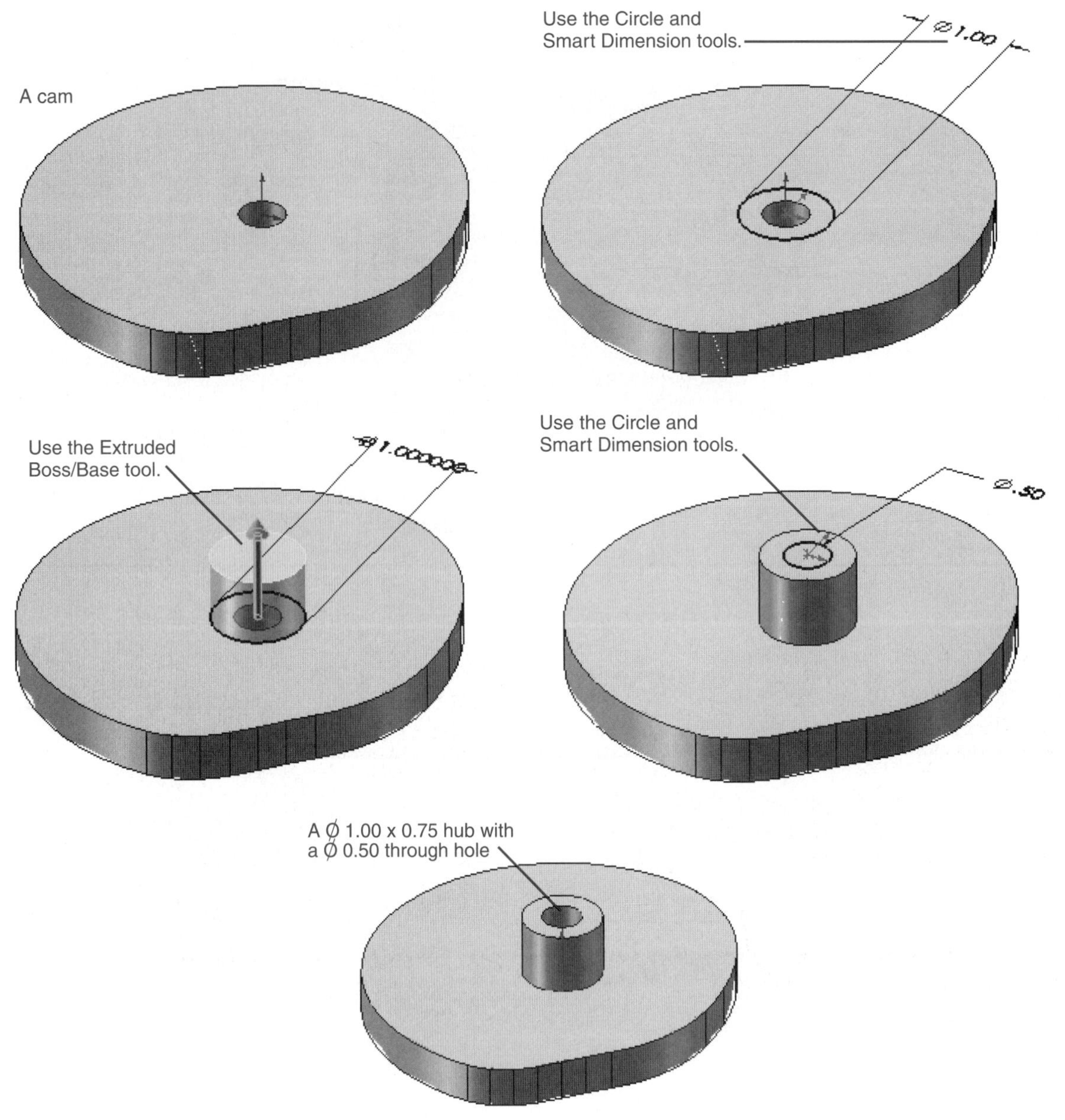
Use the Circle and
Smart Dimension tools.
Ø1.00
A cam
Use the Extruded
Boss/Base tool.
Ø1.000000
Use the Circle and
Smart Dimension tools.
Ø.50
A Ø 1.00 x 0.75 hub with
a Ø 0.50 through hole

Figure 11-13

3. Use the **Smart Dimension** tool and size the circle to **Ø1.00**.
4. Use the **Extruded Boss/Base** tool to extrude the Ø1.00 circle **0.75**.
5. Right-click the mouse and add a new sketch to the top surface of the hub.
6. Use the **Sketch** and **Features** tools to create a **Ø0.50** circle on the top surface of the hub.
7. Use the **Extruded Cut** tool and cut the circle through both the hub and the cam a distance of **1.25 in**.

To Add a Threaded Hole to a Cam's Hub

Threaded holes are added to a cam's hub to accept set screws that hold a cam in place against a rotating shaft. See Figure 11-14.

1. Click the **Hole Wizard** tool.
2. Click the **Tap** box in the **Hole Specification** box.
3. Select the **ANSI Inch** standards.
4. Select a $\frac{1}{4}$**-20 UNC** thread.
5. Define the threaded hole's depth as **0.25**.

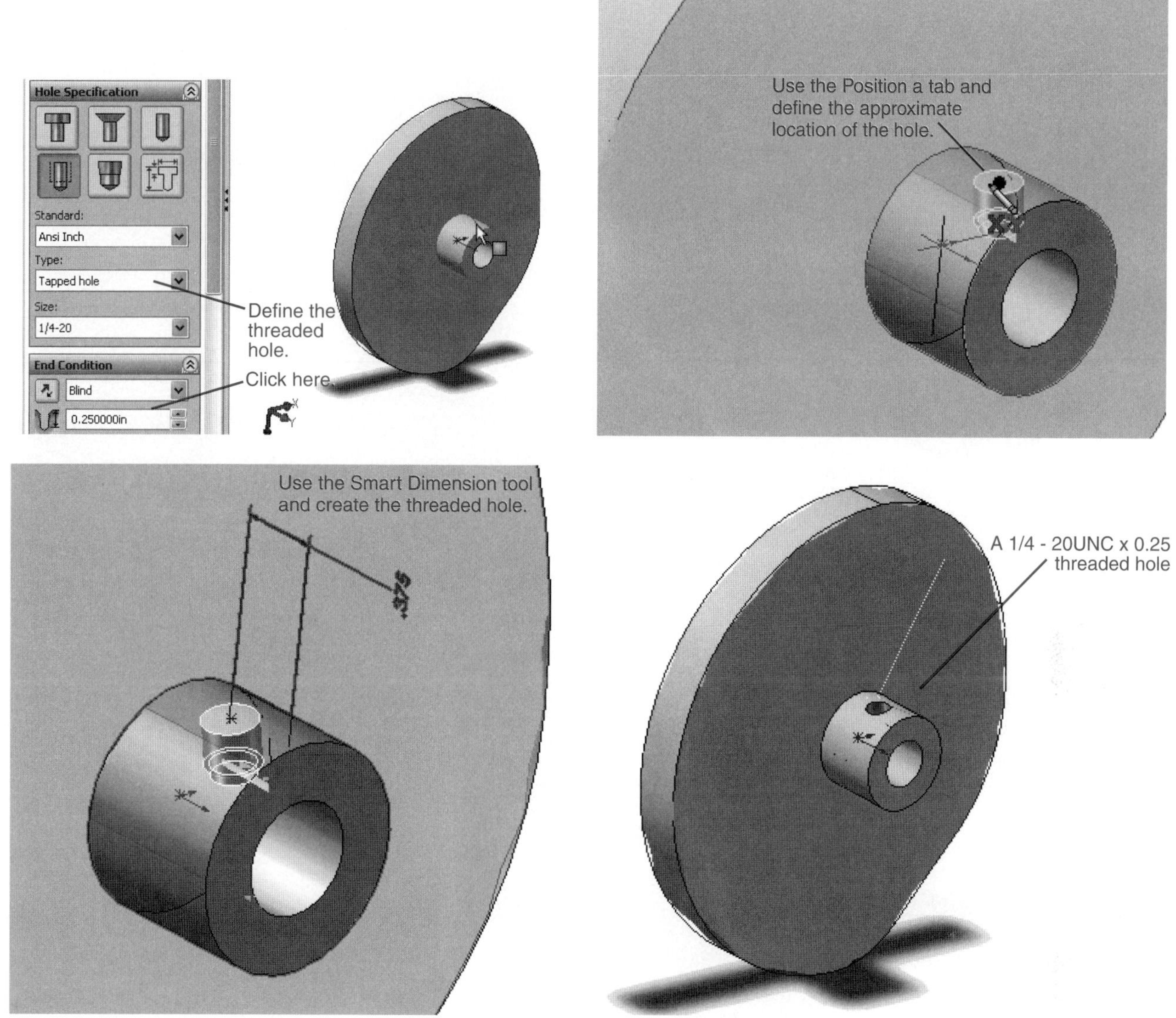

Figure 11-14

The diameter of the hub is 1.00 and that of the through hole is 0.50. Therefore, the wall thickness of the hub is 0.25. The threaded hole will pass through only one side.

6. Click the outside surface of the hub.
7. Click the **Positions** tab in the **Hole Specification** box.
8. Select a point approximately **.375** from the top surface of the hub (about halfway).
9. Use the **Smart Dimension** tool and locate the hole's center point exactly **.375** from the hub's top surface.
10. Click the OK check mark.

See Figure 11-15.

To Add a Keyway to Cam

Keys can also be used to hold a cam in place against a drive shaft. Keyways may be cut through the cam hub or just through the cam.

Figure 11-15 shows the cam created earlier in the chapter. A keyway for a $\frac{1}{4} \times \frac{1}{4}$-in. square key is created as follows.

1. Right-click the front surface of the cam, and click the **Sketch** tool.
2. Change the orientation to a view looking directly at the front surface.
3. Draw two construction lines from the cam's center point, one vertical and one horizontal.
4. Use the **Rectangle** tool and draw a rectangle as shown.

Cam
Click the front surface and select the Sketch tool.

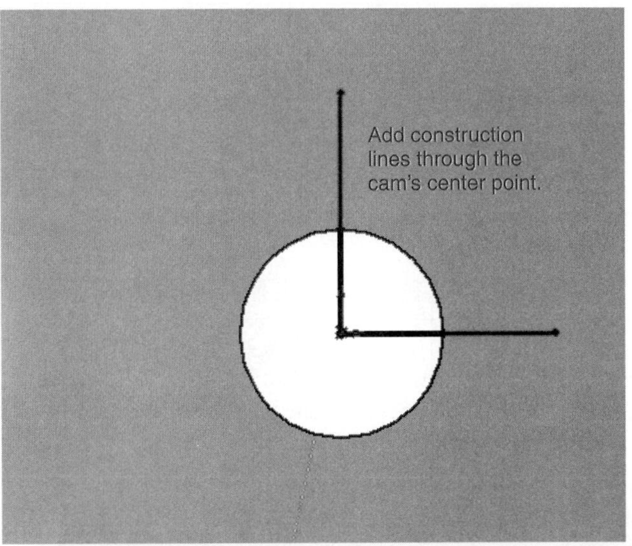
Add construction lines through the cam's center point.

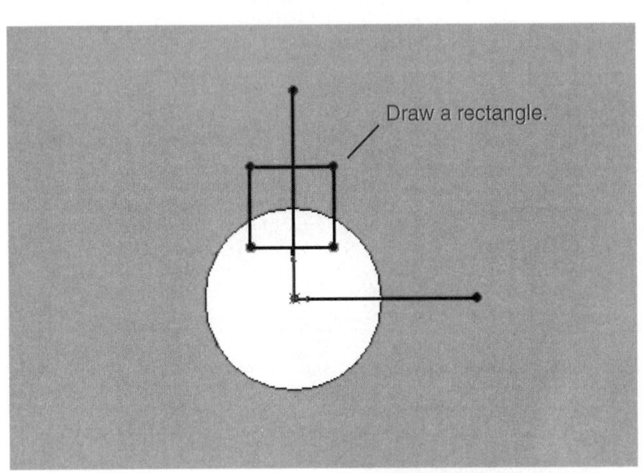
Draw a rectangle.

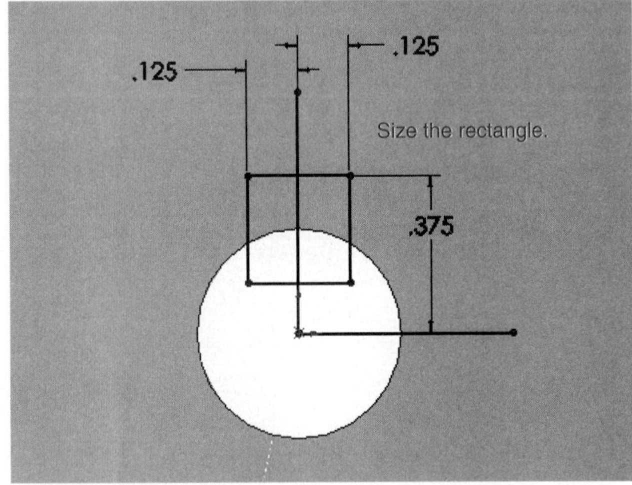
.125
.125
Size the rectangle.
.375

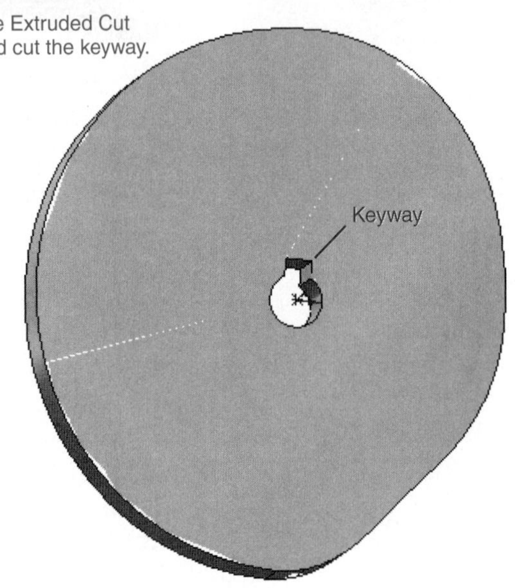
Use the Extruded Cut tool and cut the keyway.
Keyway

Figure 11-15

5. Use the **Smart Dimension** tool and size the rectangle to accept a $\frac{1}{4} \times \frac{1}{4}$-in. square key.

Tolerances for keys and keyways can be found in Chapter 9.

6. Use the **Extruded Cut** tool and cut the keyway into the cam.

11-10 SPRINGS

To Draw a Spring

This section shows how to draw a spring that will be used in the next section as part of the cam assembly. See Figure 11-16.

1. Start a new **Drawing** document.
2. Select the top plane and draw a Ø0.500 circle.

The value Ø0.500 will define the centerline of the helix. A Ø0.125 circle will be swept along the helical path to form the spring. This generates an inside diameter for the spring of Ø0.437 (0.500 − 0.063 = 0.437) and an outside diameter of Ø0.563.

3. Select the **Diametric** orientation from the axis orientation icon menu.
4. Click the **Insert** heading at the top of the screen, click **Curve**, and select the **Helix/Spiral** tool.

The **Helix Spiral** dialog box will appear.

5. Select the **Height and Revolution** option in the **Defined By** box.
6. Set the **Parameters** values for **Height = 1.75 in. 6 Revolutions,** and a **Start angle** of 0.00°.
7. Click the OK check mark.
8. Click the **Right Plane** option.
9. Right-click the plane and click the **Sketch** option.
10. Draw a **Ø0.125** circle with its center point on the end of the helix.
11. Click the **Exit Sketch** tool.
12. Click the **Features** tool and select the **Swept Boss/Base** tool.

The **Sweep** dialog box will appear.

13. Define the circle as the **Profile** and the helix as the **Path**.

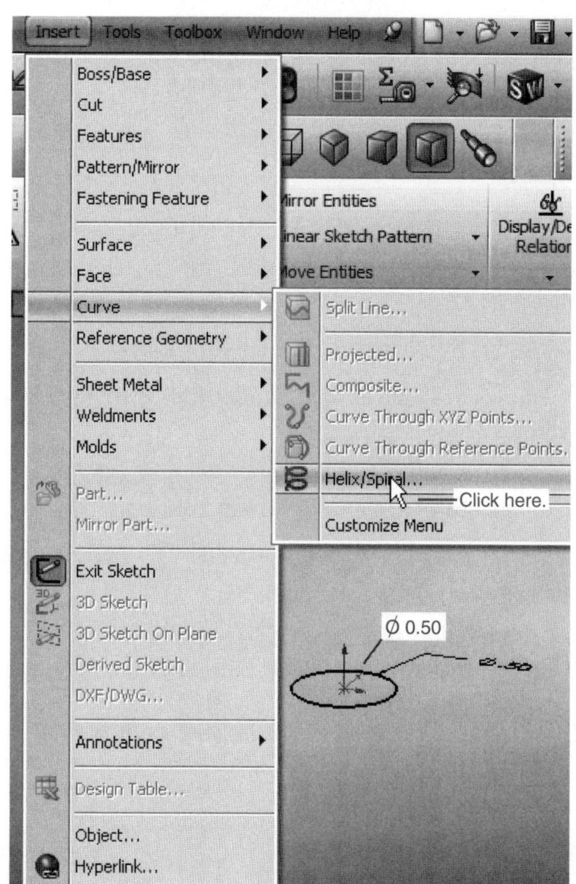

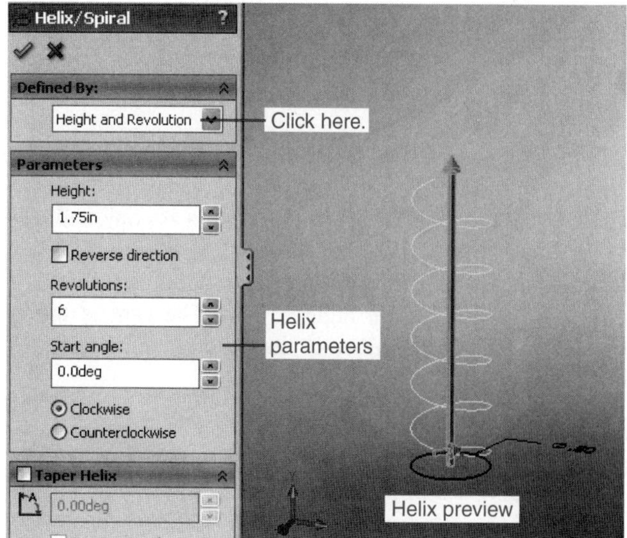

Figure 11-16

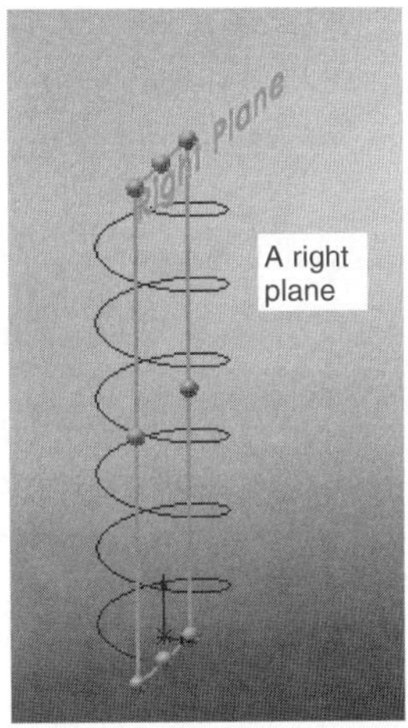

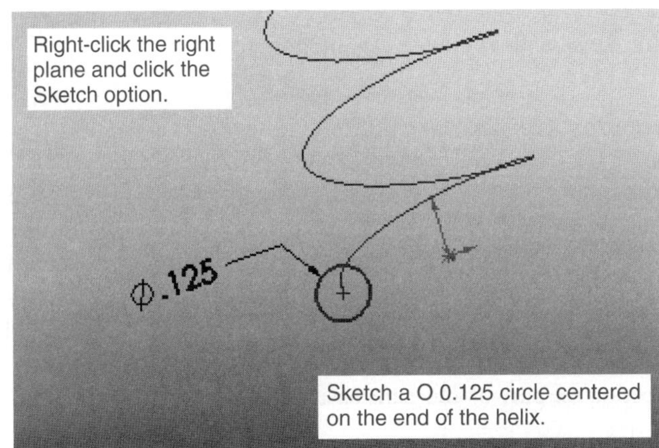

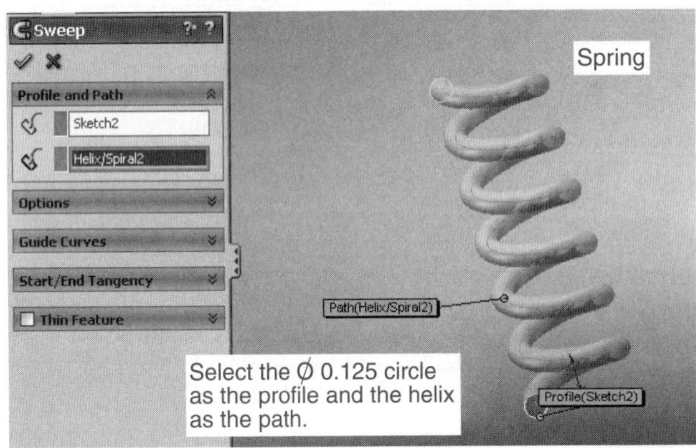

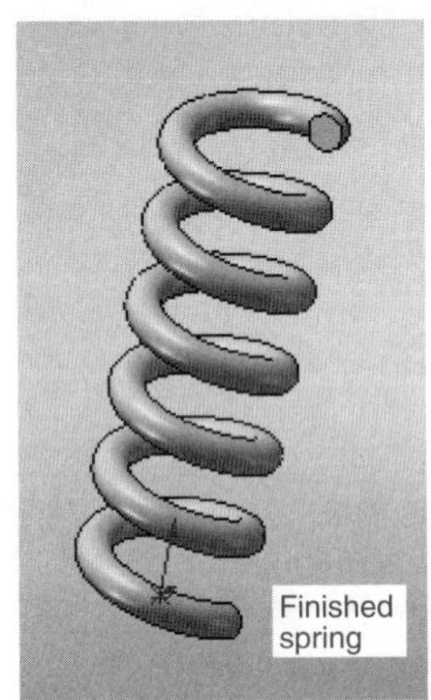

Figure 11-16 ***(continued)***

14. Click the OK check mark.
15. Save the spring as **Cam Spring**.

11-11 SAMPLE PROBLEM SP11-1—CAMS IN ASSEMBLIES

In this section we will create an assembly drawing that includes a cam. The cam will include a keyway. See Figure 11-15. The support shaft will also include a keyway, and a $\frac{1}{4} \times \frac{1}{4} \times \frac{1}{2}$-in. square key will be inserted between the shaft and cam. Dimensioned drawings for the components used in the assembly are shown in Figure 11-17. The cam is the same as was developed earlier in the chapter. See Figures 11-6 to 11-9.

1. Start a new **Assembly** document.
2. Use the **Insert Component Browse**... option and insert the appropriate components.

In this example the first component entered into the assembly drawing screen is the cam bracket. The cam bracket will automatically be fixed in place so that all additional components will move to the bracket. See Figure 11-18.

3. Add a bearing from the **Design Library**.

In this example an **Instrument Ball Bearing 0.5000-1.1250-0.2500** was selected.

4. Insert the bearing into the cam bracket.
5. Insert the cam shaft into the bearing.

Insert the shaft so that it extends 1.50 from the front surface of the bracket.

6. Assemble the cam onto the shaft.
7. Align the keyway in the cam with the keyway in the shaft.
8. Create a $\frac{1}{4} \times \frac{1}{4} \times \frac{1}{2}$ square key from the **Design Library**.

> ***Note:***
> A $\frac{1}{4} \times \frac{1}{4} \times \frac{1}{2}$ key can be drawn as an individual component.

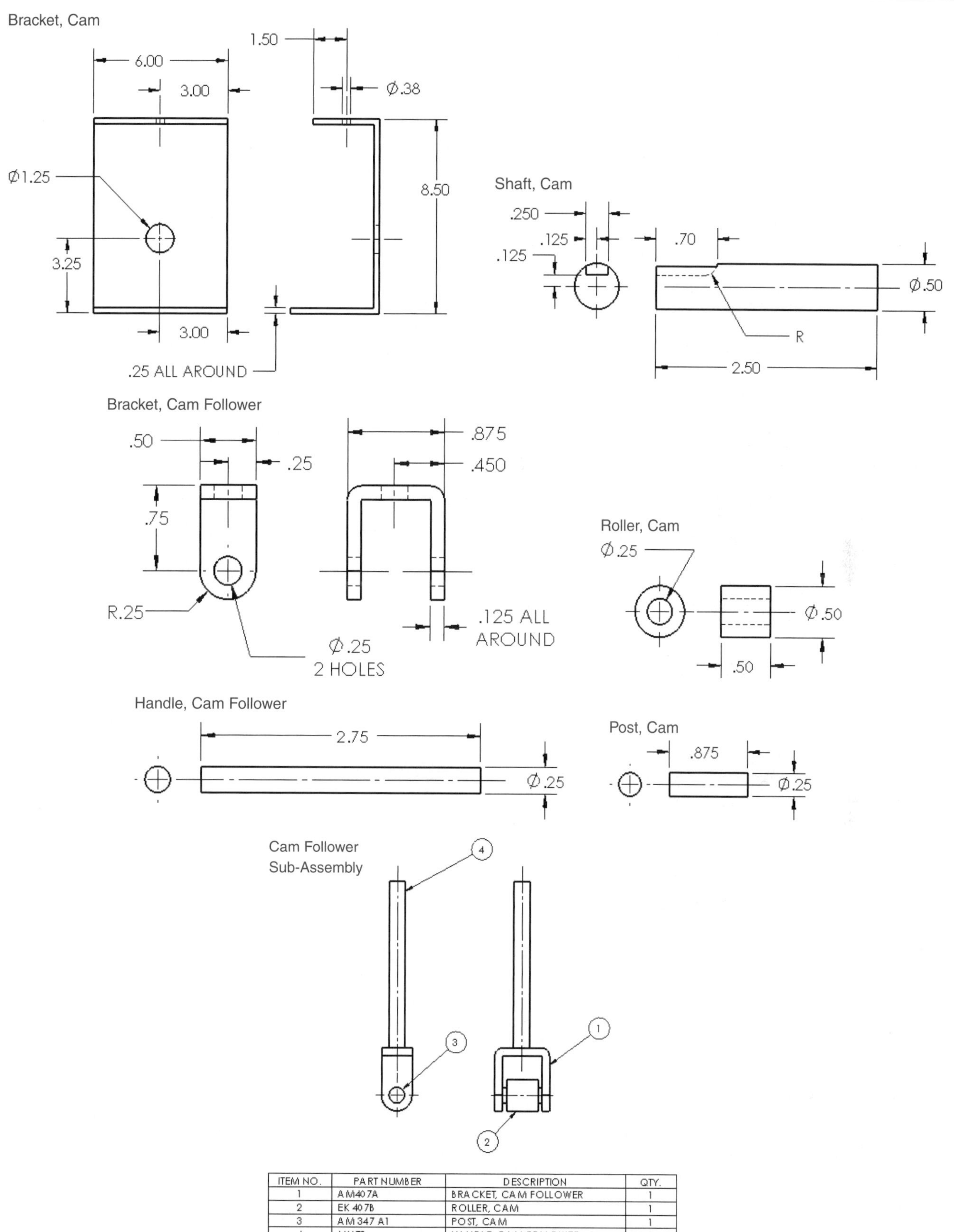

ITEM NO.	PART NUMBER	DESCRIPTION	QTY.
1	AM407A	BRACKET, CAM FOLLOWER	1
2	EK 407B	ROLLER, CAM	1
3	AM347 A1	POST, CAM	1
4	MN78	HANDLE, CAM FOLLOWER	1

Figure 11-17

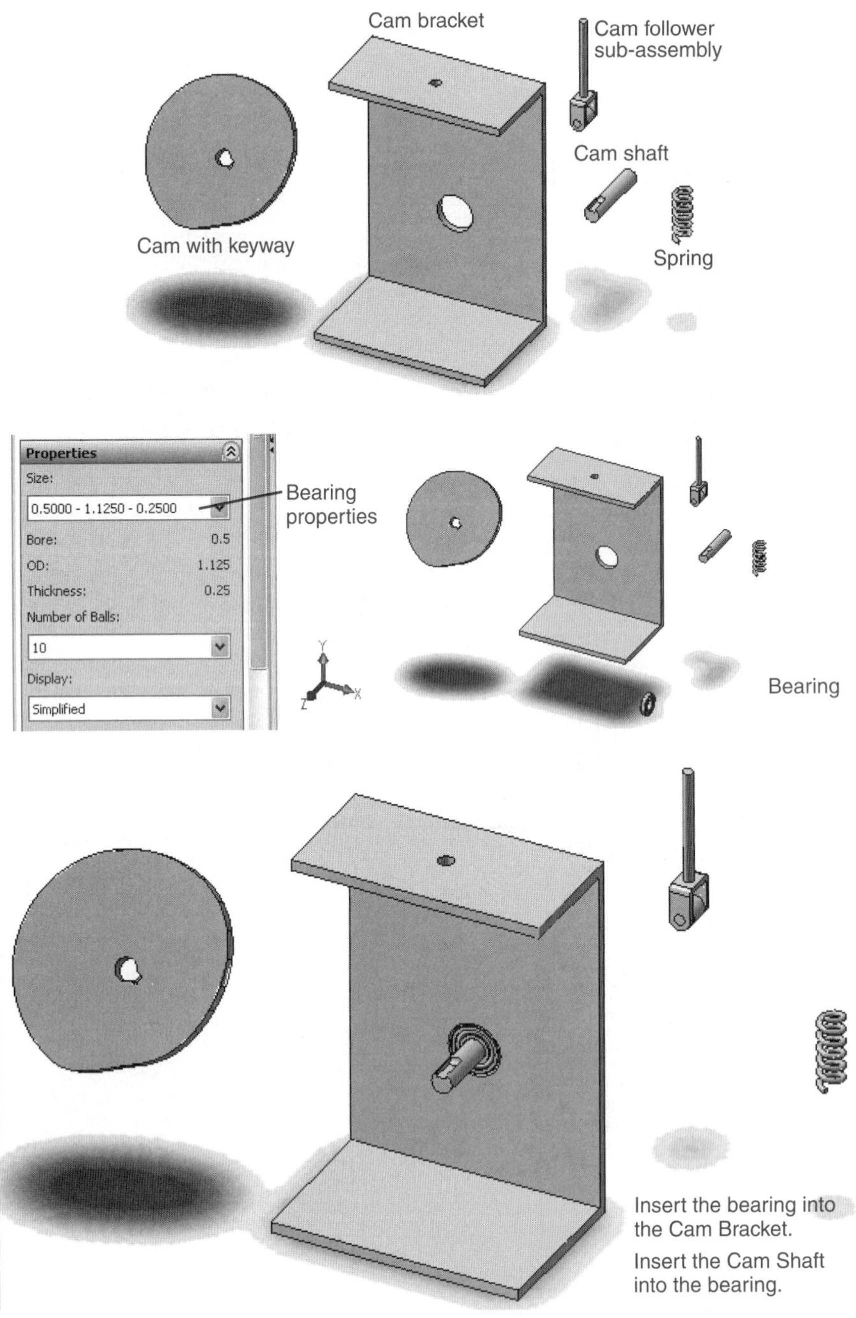

Figure 11-18

9. Insert the key between the shaft and the cam.
10. Insert the cam follower subassembly.
11. Align the roller cam follower with the profile of the cam.
12. Locate the spring around the shaft of the cam follower subassembly
13. Save the assembly as **Cam Assembly**.

Creating an Orthographic Drawing and a Bill of Materials

1. Start a new **Drawing** document.
2. Use third-angle projection and create a front and a right-side orthographic view of the cam assembly.
3. Click on the **Annotations** tool and add the appropriate centerlines.

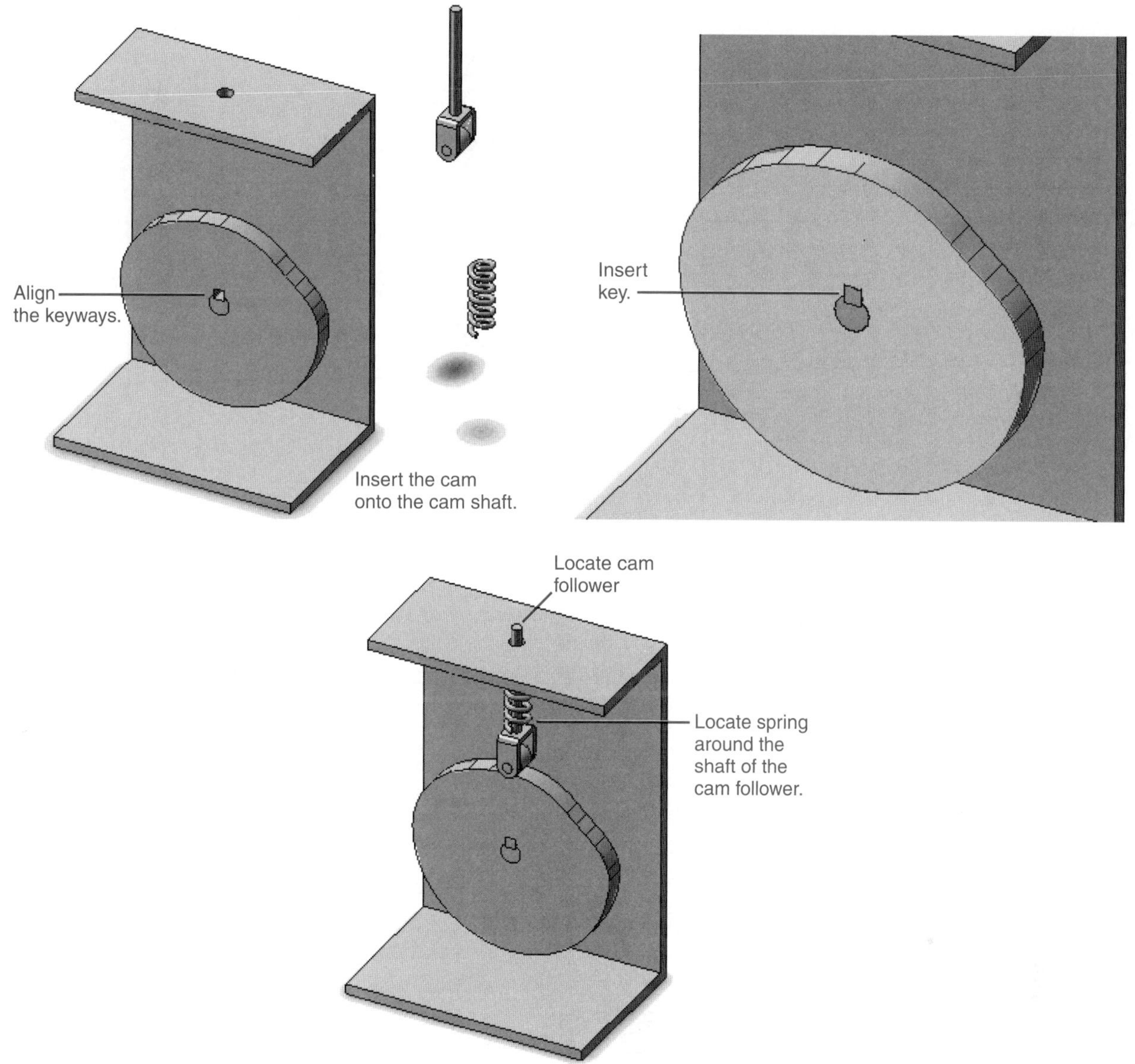
Align
the keyways.
Insert the cam
onto the cam shaft.
Insert
key.
Locate cam
follower
Locate spring
around the
shaft of the
cam follower.

Figure 11-18 ***(continued)***

See Figure 11-19.

4. Click on the **Annotations** tool and select the **AutoBalloon** tool.

Note that balloon numbers (assembly numbers) have been added to all parts including the parts of the cam follower subassembly.

5. Click on the **Annotations** tool, then **Tables,** and add the bill of materials to the drawing.

Note that the balloon numbers have changed, so that the cam follower subassembly is now identified as item number 5. All components of the subassembly are labeled as 5.

Note also that the part names are listed under the part number heading, because the BOM lists file names as part numbers. The BOM must be edited.

6. Edit the BOM by double-clicking a cell and either entering new information or modifying the existing information.

Use the format noun, modifier when entering part names. Use uppercase letters. Justify the cell inputs to the left.

> ***Note:***
> The part number of the bearing selected from the **Design Library** will automatically be inserted into the BOM.

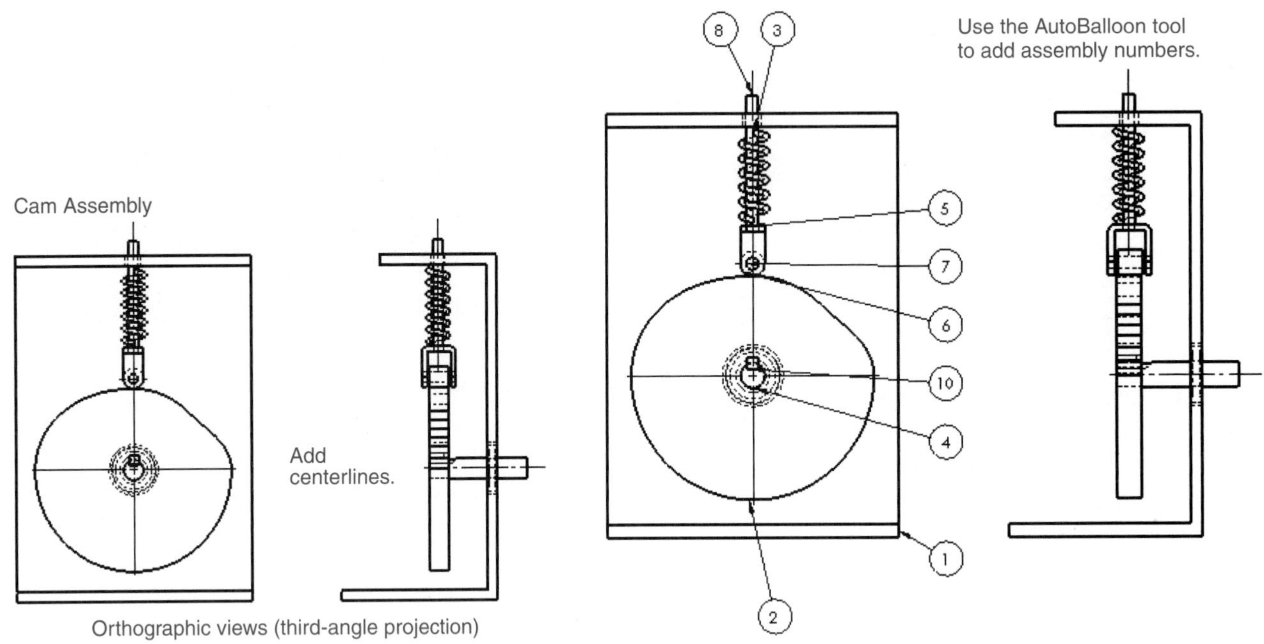

An edited BOM

ITEM NO.	PART NUMBER	DESCRIPTION	QTY.
1	EK-407A	BRACKET, CAM	1
2	EK-407B	CAM - KEYWAY	1
3	AM311-A2	SPRING, CAM	1
4	MN402-1	SHAFT, CAM	1
5	BU-2009S	FOLLOWER, CAM SUB-ASSEMBLY	1
6	AFBMA 12.2 - 0.5000 - 1.1250 - 0.2500 - 10,SI,NC,10		1
7	DR42	KEY, CAM	1

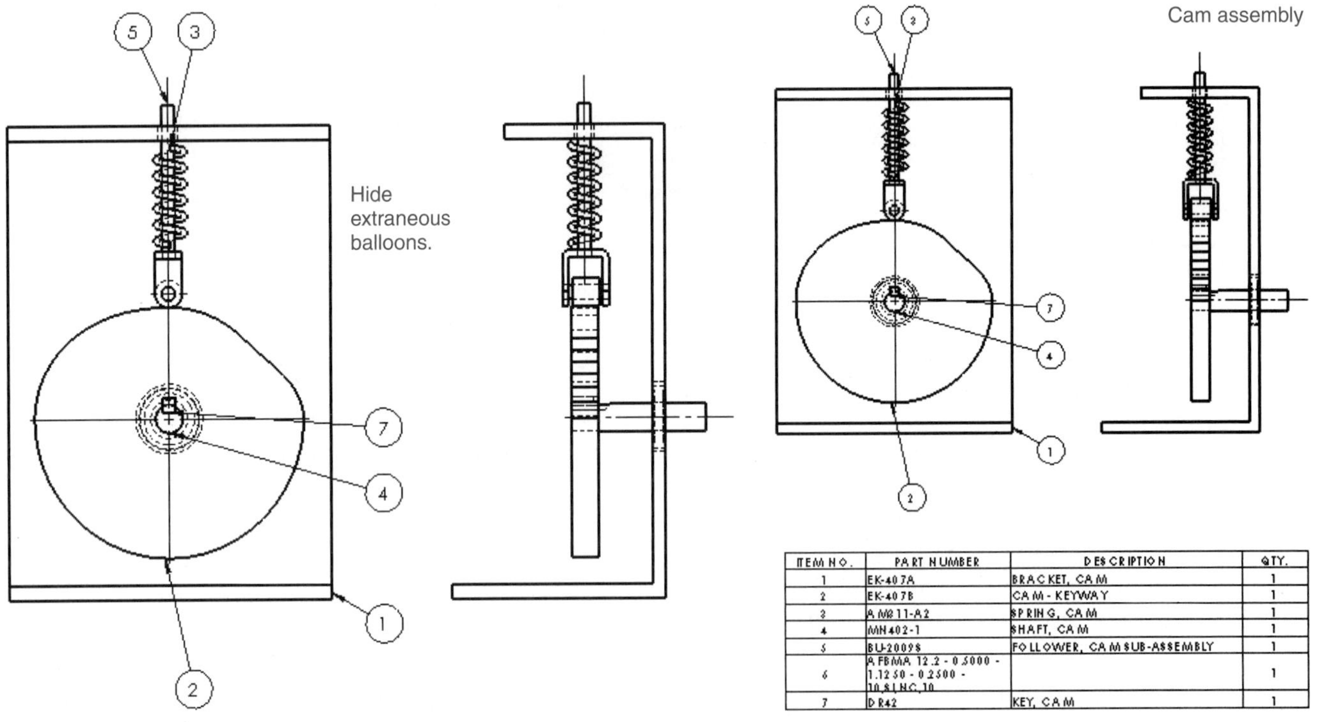

ITEM NO.	PART NUMBER	DESCRIPTION	QTY.
1	EK-407A	BRACKET, CAM	1
2	EK-407B	CAM - KEYWAY	1
3	AM311-A2	SPRING, CAM	1
4	MN402-1	SHAFT, CAM	1
5	BU-2009S	FOLLOWER, CAM SUB-ASSEMBLY	1
6	AFBMA 12.2 - 0.5000 - 1.1250 - 0.2500 - 10,SI,NC,10		1
7	DR42	KEY, CAM	1

Figure 11-19

7. Hide the extraneous number 5 balloons. Only one is needed.
8. Save the drawing as **Cam Assembly.**

11-12 PROJECTS

Draw the cams as specified in Projects 11-1 through 11-6.

Project 11-1: Inches

See Figure P11-1.

Units = Inches
Cam Type = Circular
Follower Type = Translating
Follower Diameter = .375
Starting Radius = 1.4375
Starting Angle = 0°
Rotation Direction = Clockwise

Starting Radius = 1.4375
Dwell = 45°
Rise 0.375, Harmonic Motion, 135°
Dwell = 90°
Fall 0.375, Harmonic Motion, 90°

Blank Outside Dia = 2.8675
Thickness = .375
No Hub
Thru Hole Dia = 0.625

Project 11-2: Inches

See Figure P11-2

Units = Inches
Cam Type = Circular

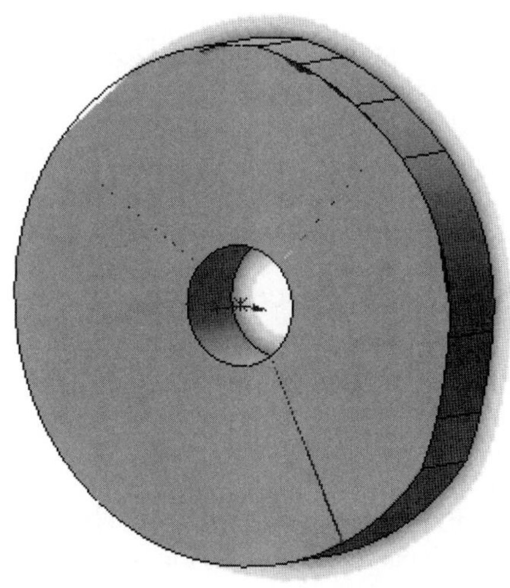

Figure P11-1

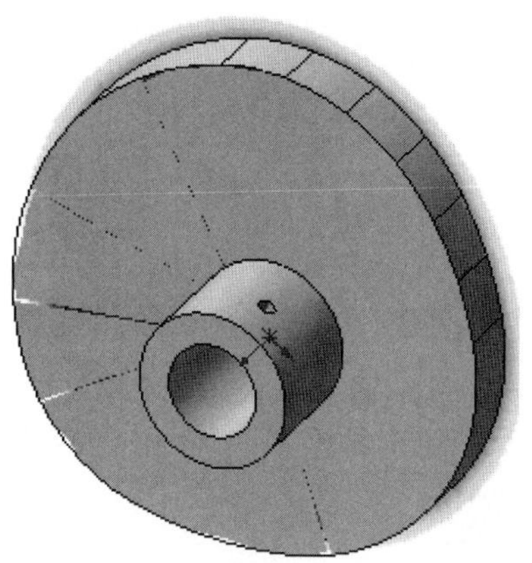

Figure P11-2

Follower Type = Translating
Follower Diameter = .50
Starting Radius = 2.00
Starting Angle = 0°
Rotation Direction = Clockwise

Starting Radius = 2.00
Dwell = 45°
Rise 0.438, Modified Trapezoidal Motion, 90°
Dwell = 90°
Fall 0.375, Modified Trapezoidal Motion, 90°
Dwell = 45°

Blank Outside Dia = 4.876
Thickness = 0.500
Near Hub Dia & Length = 1.25, 1.00
Thru Hole Dia = 0.75

Add a #6-32 threaded hole 0.50 from the top of the hub.

Project 11-3: Design Problem

Use a base circle of Ø4.00 in.
The follower has a Ø0.50 in.
Cam motion:
- Dwell 45°
- Rise 0.25 in. using Uniform Displacement for 45°
- Dwell 45°
- Rise 0.25 in. using Uniform Displacement for 45°
- Dwell 45°
- Fall 0.25 in. using Uniform Displacement for 45°
- Dwell 45°
- Fall 0.25 in. using Uniform Displacement for 45°

The hub has a diameter of 1.50 in. and extends 1.50 in. from the surface of the cam.
The cam bore is Ø0.75 in.
The hub includes a #10-32 threaded hole.

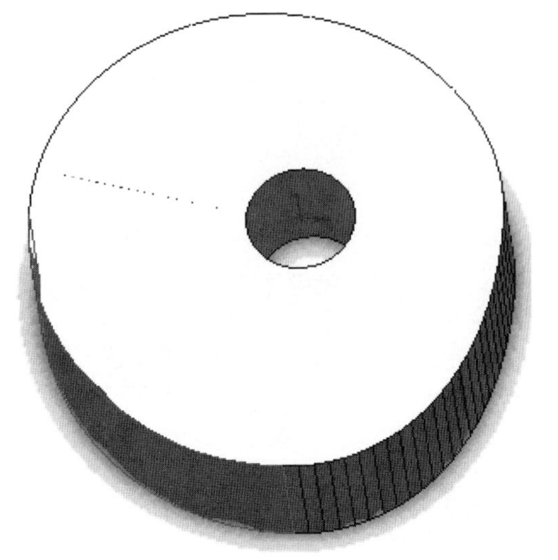

Figure P11-4

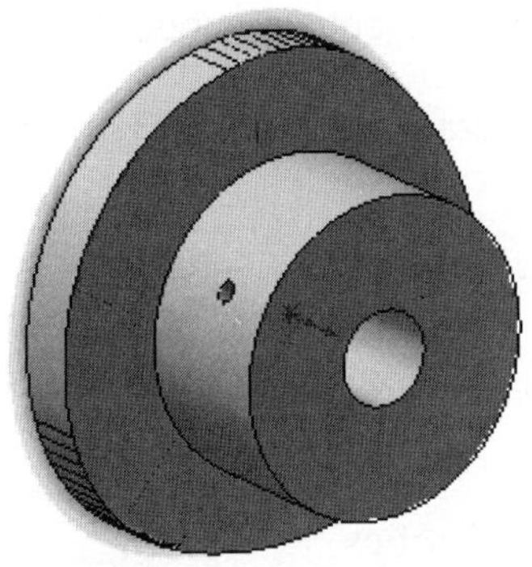

Figure P11-5

Project 11-4: Millimeters

See Figure P11-4

Units = Metric
Cam Type = Circular
Follower Type = Translating
Follower Diameter = 20
Starting Radius = 40
Starting Angle = 0°
Rotation Direction = Clockwise

Starting Radius = 40
Dwell = 45°
Rise 10, Harmonic Motion, 135°
Dwell = 90°
Fall 10, Harmonic Motion, 90°

Blank Outside Dia = 100
Thickness = 20
No Hub
Thru Hole Dia = 16.0

Project 11-5:

See Figure P11-5.

Units = Metric
Cam Type = Circular
Follower Type = Translating
Follower Diameter = 16
Starting Radius = 50.0
Starting Angle = 0°
Rotation Direction = Clockwise

Starting Radius = 50.0
Dwell = 45°
Rise 8.0, Modified Trapezoidal Motion, 90°
Dwell = 90°
Fall 8.0, Modified Trapezoidal Motion, 90°
Dwell = 45°

Blank Outside Dia = 108
Thickness = 12.0
Near Hub Dia & Length = 60, 30
Thru Hole Dia = 18.00

Add an M4 threaded hole 15 from the top of the hub.

Project 11-6: Design Problem

Use a base circle of Ø80.0 mm.
The follower has a Ø12.0 mm.
Cam motion:
- Dwell 45°
- Rise 10.0 mm using Uniform Displacement for 45°
- Dwell 45°
- Rise 5.0 mm using Uniform Displacement for 45°
- Dwell 45°
- Fall 5.0 mm using Uniform Displacement for 45°
- Dwell 45°
- Fall 10.0 mm using Uniform Displacement for 45°

The hub has a diameter of 30.0 mm and extends 26.0 mm from the surface of the cam.
The cam bore is Ø16.0 mm.
The hub includes an M6 threaded hole.

Project 11-7: Design Problem

Figure P11-7 shows a cam assembly. Dimensioned drawings of each part are shown in Figure 11-17.

1. Draw the assembly.
2. Insert the following cam:

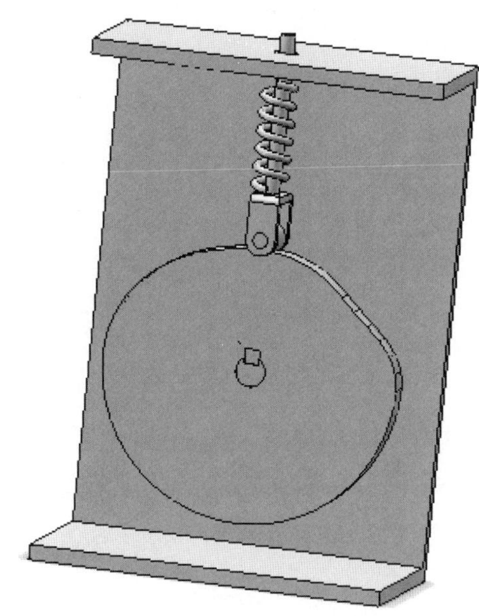

Figure P11-7

Cam parameters:
Base Circle = Ø5.00 in.
Follower Diameter = 0.50 in.
Select a bearing from the **Design Library**.

Cam motion:
Dwell 45°
Rise 0.250 in. using Uniform Displacement for 45°
Dwell 45°
Rise 0.250 in. using Uniform Displacement for 45°
Dwell 45°
Fall 0.250 in. using Uniform Displacement for 45°
Dwell 45°
Fall 0.250 in. using Uniform Displacement for 45°

3. Create a keyway in both the cam and the cam shaft that will accept a 0.375 × 0.375 × 0.500-in. square key.
4. Calculate the distance between the top surface of the cam follower bracket and the underside of the top flange on the cam bracket, and create a spring to fit into the space.

Appendix

Wire and Sheet Metal Gauges

Gauge	Thickness	Gauge	Thickness
000 000	0.5800	18	0.0403
00 000	0.5165	19	0.0359
0 000	0.4600	20	0.0320
000	0.4096	21	0.0285
00	0.3648	22	0.0253
0	0.3249	23	0.0226
1	0.2893	24	0.0201
2	0.2576	25	0.0179
3	0.2294	26	0.0159
4	0.2043	27	0.0142
5	0.1819	28	0.0126
6	0.1620	29	0.0113
7	0.1443	30	0.0100
8	0.1285	31	0.0089
9	0.1144	32	0.0080
10	0.1019	33	0.0071
11	0.0907	34	0.0063
12	0.0808	35	0.0056
13	0.0720	36	0.0050
14	0.0641	37	0.0045
15	0.0571	38	0.0040
16	0.0508	39	0.0035
17	0.0453	40	0.0031

Figure A-1

American Standard Clearance Locational Fits

Nominal Size Range Inches	Class LC1			Class LC2			Class LC3			Class LC4		
	Limits of Clearance	Standard Limits		Limits of Clearance	Standard Limits		Limits of Clearance	Standard Limits		Limits of Clearance	Standard Limits	
Over To		Hole H6	Shaft h5		Hole H7	Shaft h6		Hole H8	Shaft h7		Hole H10	Shaft h9
0 - 0.12	0	+0.25	0	0	+0.4	0	0	+0.6	0	0	+1.6	0
	0.45	0	-0.2	0.65	0	-0.25	1	0	-0.4	2.6	0	-1.0
0.12 - 0.24	0	+0.3	0	0	+0.5	0	0	+0.7	0	0	+1.8	0
	0.5	0	-0.2	0.8	0	-0.3	1.2	0	-0.5	3.0	0	-1.2
0.24 - 0.40	0	+0.4	0	0	+0.6	0	0	+0.9	0	0	+2.2	0
	0.65	0	-0.25	1.0	0	-0.4	1.5	0	-0.6	3.6	0	-1.4
0.40 - 0.71	0	+0.4	0	0	+0.7	0	0	+1.0	0	0	+2.8	0
	0.7	0	-0.3	1.1	0	-0.4	1.7	0	-0.7	4.4	0	-1.6
0.71 - 1.19	0	+0.5	0	0	+0.8	0	0	+1.2	0	0	+3.5	0
	0.9	0	-0.4	1.3	0	-0.5	2	0	-0.8	5.5	0	-2.0
1.19 - 1.97	0	+0.6	0	0	+1.0	0	0	+1.6	0	0	+4.0	0
	1.0	0	-0.4	1.6	0	-0.6	2.6	0	-1.0	6.5	0	-2.5

Figure A-2A

Nominal Size Range Inches	Class LC5			Class LC6			Class LC7			Class LC8		
	Limits of Clearance	Standard Limits		Limits of Clearance	Standard Limits		Limits of Clearance	Standard Limits		Limits of Clearance	Standard Limits	
Over To		Hole H7	Shaft g6		Hole H9	Shaft f8		Hole H10	Shaft e9		Hole H10	Shaft d9
0 - 0.12	0.1	+0..4	-0.1	0.3	+1.0	-0.3	0.6	+1.6	-0.6	1.0	+1.6	-1.0
	0.75	0	-0.35	1.9	0	-0.9	3.2	0	-1.6	3.6	0	-2.0
0.12 - 0.24	0.15	+0.5	-0.15	0.4	+1.2	-0.4	0.8	+1.8	-0.8	1.2	+1.8	-1.2
	0.95	0	-0.45	2.3	0	-1.1	3.8	0	-2.0	4.2	0	-2.4
0.24 - 0.40	0.2	+0.6	-0.2	0.5	+1.4	-0.5	1.0	+2.2	-1.0	1.6	+2.2	-1.6
	1.2	0	-0.6	2.8	0	-1.4	4.6	0	-2.4	5.2	0	-3.0
0.40 - 0.71	0.25	+0.7	-0.25	0.6	+1.6	-0.6	1.2	+2.8	-1.2	2.0	+2.8	-2.0
	1.35	0	-0.65	3.2	0	-1.6	5.6	0	-2.8	6.4	0	-3.6
0.71 - 1.19	0.3	+0.8	-0.3	0.8	+2.0	-0.8	1.6	+3.5	-1.6	2.5	+3.5	-2.5
	1.6	0	-0.8	4.0	0	-2.0	7.1	0	-3.6	8.0	0	-4.5
1.19 - 1.97	0.4	+1.0	-0.4	1.0	+2.5	-1.0	2.0	+4.0	-2.0	3.0	+4.0	-3.0
	2.0	0	-1.0	5.1	0	-2.6	8.5	0	-4.5	9.5	0	-5.5

Figure A-2B

American Standard Running and Sliding Fits

(Hole Basis)

Nominal Size Range Inches		Class RC1			Class RC2			Class RC3			Class RC4	
	Limits of Clearance	Standard Limits		Limits of Clearance	Standard Limits		Limits of Clearance	Standard Limits		Limits of Clearance	Standard Limits	
Over To		Hole H5	Shaft g4		Hole H6	Shaft g5		Hole H7	Shaft f6		Hole H8	Shaft f7
0 - 0.12	0.1 0.45	+0.2 0	-0.1 -0.25	0.1 0.55	+0.25 0	-0.1 -0.3	0.3 0.95	+0.4 0	-0.3 -0.55	0.3 1.3	+0.6 0	-0.3 -0.7
0.12 - 0.24	0.15 0.5	+0.2 0	-0.15 -0.3	0.15 0.65	+0.3 0	-0.15 -0.35	0.4 1.12	+0.5 0	-0.4 -0.7	0.4 1.5	+0.7 0	-0.4 -0.0
0.24 - 0.40	0.2 0.6	+0.25 0	-0.2 -0.35	0.2 0.85	+0.4 0	-0.2 -0.45	0.5 1.5	+0.6 0	-0.5 -0.9	0.5 2.0	+0.9 0	-0.5 -1.1
0.40 - 0.71	0.25 0.75	+0.3 0	-0.25 -0.45	0.25 0.95	+0.4 0	-0.25 -0.55	0.6 1.7	+0.7 0	-0.6 -1.0	0.6 2.3	+1.0 0	-0.6 -1.3
0.71 - 1.19	0.3 0.95	+0.4 0	-0.3 -0.55	0.3 1.2	+0.5 0	-0.3 -0.7	0.8 2.1	+0.8 0	-0.8 -1.3	0.8 2.8	+1.2 0	-0.8 -1.6
1.19 - 1.97	0.4 1.1	+0.4 0	-0.4 -0.7	0.4 1.4	+0.6 0	-0.4 -0.8	1.0 2.6	+1.0 0	-1.0 -1.6	1.0 3.6	+1.6 0	-1.0 -2.0

Figure A-3A

Nominal Size Range Inches		Class RC5			Class RC6			Class RC7			Class RC8	
	Limits of Clearance	Standard Limits		Limits of Clearance	Standard Limits		Limits of Clearance	Standard Limits		Limits of Clearance	Standard Limits	
Over To		Hole H8	Shaft e7		Hole H9	Shaft e8		Hole H9	Shaft d8		Hole H10	Shaft c9
0 - 0.12	0.6 1.6	+0.6 0	-0.6 -1.0	0.6 2.2	+1.0 0	-0.6 -1.2	1.0 2.6	+1.0 0	-1.0 -1.6	2.5 5.1	+1.6 0	-2.5 -3.5
0.12 - 0.24	0.8 2.0	+0.7 0	-0.8 -1.3	0.8 2.7	+1.2 0	-0.8 -1.5	1.2 3.1	+1.2 0	-1.2 -1.9	2.8 5.8	+1.8 0	-2.8 -4.0
0.24 - 0.40	1.0 2.5	+0.9 0	-1.0 -1.6	1.0 3.3	+1.4 0	-1.0 -1.9	1.6 3.9	+1.4 0	-1.6 -2.5	3.0 6.6	+2.2 0	-3.0 -4.4
0.40 - 0.71	1.2 2.9	+1.0 0	-1.2 -1.9	1.2 3.8	+1.6 0	-1.2 -2.2	2.0 4.6	+1.6 0	-2.0 -3.0	3.5 7.9	+2.8 0	-3.5 -5.1
0.71 - 1.19	1.6 3.6	+1.2 0	-1.6 -2.4	1.6 4.8	+2.0 0	-1.6 -2.8	2.5 5.7	+2.0 0	-2.5 -3.7	4.5 10.0	+3.5 0	-4.5 -6.5
1.19 - 1.97	2.0 4.6	+1.6 0	-2.0 -3.0	2.0 6.1	+2.5 0	-2.0 -3.6	3.0 7.1	+2.5 0	-3.0 -4.6	5.0 11.5	+4.0 0	-5.0 -7.5

Figure A-3B

American Standard Transition Locational Fits

Nominal Size Range Inches Over – To	Class LT1 Fit	Class LT1 Standard Limits Hole H7	Class LT1 Standard Limits Shaft js6	Class LT2 Fit	Class LT2 Standard Limits Hole H8	Class LT2 Standard Limits Shaft js7	Class LT3 Fit	Class LT3 Standard Limits Hole H7	Class LT3 Standard Limits Shaft k6
0 - 0.12	-0.10 +0.50	+0.4 0	+0.10 -0.10	-0.2 +0.8	+0.6 0	+0.2 -0.2			
0.12 - 0.24	-0.15 -0.65	+0.5 0	+0.15 -0.15	-0.25 +0.95	+0.7 0	+0.25 -0.25			
0.24 - 0.40	-0.2 +0.5	+0.6 0	+0.2 -0.2	-0.3 +1.2	+0.9 0	+0.3 -0.3	-0.5 +0.5	+0.6 0	+0.5 +0.1
0.40 - 0.71	-0.2 +0.9	+0.7 0	+0.2 -0.2	-0.35 +1.35	+1.0 0	+0.35 -0.35	-0.5 +0.6	+0.7 0	+0.5 +0.1
0.71 - 1.19	-0.25 +1.05	+0.8 0	+0.25 -0.25	-0.4 +1.6	+1.2 0	+0.4 -0.4	-0.6 +0.7	+0.8 0	+0.6 +0.1
1.19 - 1.97	-0.3 +1.3	+1.0 0	+0.3 -0.3	-0.5 +2.1	+1.6 0	+0.5 -0.5	+0.7 +0.1	+1.0 0	+0.7 +0.1

Figure A-4A

Nominal Size Range Inches Over – To	Class LT4 Fit	Class LT4 Standard Limits Hole H8	Class LT4 Standard Limits Shaft k7	Class LT5 Fit	Class LT5 Standard Limits Hole H7	Class LT5 Standard Limits Shaft n6	Class LT6 Fit	Class LT6 Standard Limits Hole H7	Class LT6 Standard Limits Shaft n7
0 - 0.12				-0.5 +0.15	+0.4 0	+0.5 +0.25	-0.65 +0.15	+0.4 0	+0.65 +0.25
0.12 - 0.24				-0.6 +0.2	+0.5 0	+0.6 +0.3	-0.8 +0.2	+0.5 0	+0.8 +0.3
0.24 - 0.40	-0.7 +0.8	+0.9 0	+0.7 +0.1	-0.8 +0.2	+0.6 0	+0.8 +0.4	-1.0 +0.2	+0.6 0	+1.0 +0.4
0.40 - 0.71	-0.8 +0.9	+1.0 0	+0.8 +0.1	-0.9 +0.2	+0.7 0	+0.9 +0.5	-1.2 +0.2	+0.7 0	+1.2 +0.5
0.71 - 1.19	-0.9 +1.1	+1.2 0	+0.9 +0.1	-1.1 +0.2	+0.8 0	+1.1 +0.6	-1.4 +0.2	+0.8 0	+1.4 +0.6
1.19 - 1.97	-1.1 +1.5	+1.6 0	+1.1 +0.1	-1.3 +0.3	+1.0 0	+1.3 +0.7	-1.7 +0.3	+1.0 0	+1.7 +0.7

Figure A-4B

American Standard Interference Locational Fits

Nominal Size Range Inches Over	To	Limits of Interference	Class LN1 Standard Limits Hole H6	Shaft n5	Limits of Interference	Class LN2 Standard Limits Hole H7	Shaft p6	Limits of Interference	Class LN3 Standard Limits Hole H7	Shaft r6
0	0.12	0	+0.25	+0.45	0	+0.4	+0.63	0.1	+0.4	+0.75
		0.45	0	+0.25	0.65	0	+0.4	0.75	0	+0.5
0.12	0.24	0	+0.3	+0.5	0	+0.5	+0.8	0.1	+0.5	+0.9
		0.5	0	+0.3	0.8	0	+0.5	0.9	0	+0.6
0.24	0.40	0	+0.4	+0.65	0	+0.6	+1.0	0.2	+0.6	+1.2
		0.65	0	+0.4	1.0	0	+0.6	1.2	0	+0.8
0.40	0.71	0	+0.4	+0.8	0	+0.7	+1.1	0.3	+0.7	+1.4
		0.8	0	+0.4	1.1	0	+0.7	1.4	0	+1.0
0.71	1.19	0	+0.5	+1.0	0	+0.8	+1.3	0.4	+0.8	+1.7
		1.0	0	+0.5	1.3	0	+0.8	1.7	0	+1.2
1.19	1.97	0	+0.6	+1.1	0	+1.0	+1.6	0.4	+1.0	+2.0
		1.1	0	+0.6	1.6	0	+1.0	2.0	0	+1.4

Figure A-5

American Standard Force and Shrink Fits

Nominal Size Range Inches Over	To	Limits of Interference	Class FN 1 Standard Limits Hole	Shaft	Limits of Interference	Class FN 2 Standard Limits Hole	Shaft	Limits of Interference	Class FN 3 Standard Limits Hole	Shaft	Limits of Interference	Class FN 4 Standard Limits Hole	Shaft
0	0.12	0.05	+0.25	+0.5	0.2	+0.4	+0.85				0.3	+0.4	+0.95
		0.5	0	+0.3	0.85	0	+0.6				0.95	0	+0.7
0.12	0.24	0.1	+0.3	+0.6	0.2	+0.5	+1.0				0.4	+0.5	+1.2
		0.6	0	+0.4	1.0	0	+0.7				1.2	0	+0.9
0.24	0.40	0.1	+0.4	+0.75	0.4	+0.6	+1.4				0.6	+0.6	+1.6
		0.75	0	+0.5	1.4	0	+1.0				1.6	0	+1.2
0.40	0.56	0.1	+0.4	+0.8	0.5	+0.7	+1.6				0.7	+0.7	+1.8
		0.8	0	+0.5	1.6	0	+1.2				1.8	0	+1.4
0.56	0.71	0.2	+0.4	+0.9	0.5	+0.7	+1.6				0.7	+0.7	+1.8
		0.9	0	+0.6	1.6	0	+1.2				1.8	0	+1.4
0.71	0.95	0.2	+0.5	+1.1	0.6	+0.8	+1.9				0.8	+0.8	+2.1
		1.1	0	+0.7	1.9	0	+1.4				2.1	0	+1.6
0.95	1.19	0.3	+0.5	+1.2	0.6	+0.8	+1.9	0.8	+0.8	+2.1	1.0	+0.8	+2.1
		1.2	0	+0.8	1.9	0	+1.4	2.1	0	+1.6	2.3	0	+1.8
1.19	1.58	0.3	+0.6	+1.3	0.8	+1.0	+2.4	1.0	+1.0	+2.6	1.5	+1.0	+3.1
		1.3	0	+0.9	2.4	0	+1.8	2.6	0	+2.0	3.1	0	+2.5
1.58	1.97	0.4	+0.6	+1.4	0.8	+1.0	+2.4	1.2	+1.0	+2.8	1.8	+1.0	+3.4
		1.4	0	+1.0	2.4	0	+1.8	2.8	0	+2.2	3.4	0	+2.8

Figure A-6

Preferred Clearance Fits — Cylindrical Fits
(Hole Basis; ANSI B4.2)

Basic Size		Loose Running			Free Running			Close Running			Sliding			Locational Clear.		
		Hole H11	Shaft c11	Fit	Hole H9	Shaft d9	Fit	Hole H8	Shaft f7	Fit	Hole H7	Shaft g6	Fit	Hole H7	Shaft h6	Fit
4	Max	4.075	3.930	0.220	4.030	3.970	0.090	4.018	3.990	0.040	4.012	3.996	0.024	4.012	4.000	0.020
	Min	4.000	3.855	0.070	4.000	3.940	0.030	4.000	3.978	0.010	4.000	3.988	0.004	4.000	3.992	0.000
5	Max	5.075	4.930	0.220	5.030	4.970	0.090	5.018	4.990	0.040	5.012	4.996	0.024	5.012	5.000	0.020
	Min	5.000	4.855	0.070	5.000	4.940	0.030	5.000	4.978	0.010	5.000	4.988	0.004	5.000	4.992	0.000
6	Max	6.075	5.930	0.220	6.030	5.970	0.090	6.018	5.990	0.040	6.012	5.996	0.024	6.012	6.000	0.020
	Min	6.000	5.885	0.070	6.000	5.940	0.030	6.000	5.978	0.010	6.000	5.988	0.004	6.000	5.992	0.000
8	Max	8.090	7.920	0.260	8.036	7.960	0.112	8.022	7.987	0.050	8.015	7.995	0.029	8.015	8.000	0.024
	Min	8.000	7.830	0.080	8.000	7.924	0.040	8.000	7.972	0.013	8.000	7.986	0.005	8.000	7.991	0.000
10	Max	10.090	9.920	0.026	10.036	9.960	0.112	10.022	9.987	0.050	10.015	9.995	0.029	10.015	10.000	0.024
	Min	10.000	9.830	0.080	10.000	9.924	0.040	10.000	9.972	0.013	10.000	9.986	0.005	10.000	9.991	0.000
12	Max	12.112	11.905	0.315	12.043	11.950	0.136	12.027	11.984	0.061	12.018	11.994	0.035	12.018	12.000	0.029
	Min	12.000	11.795	0.095	12.000	11.907	0.050	12.000	11.966	0.016	12.000	11.983	0.006	12.000	11.989	0.000
16	Max	16.110	15.905	0.315	16.043	15.950	0.136	16.027	15.984	0.061	16.018	15.994	0.035	16.018	16.000	0.029
	Min	16.000	15.795	0.095	16.000	15.907	0.050	16.000	15.966	0.016	16.000	19.983	0.006	16.000	15.989	0.000
20	Max	20.130	19.890	0.370	20.052	19.935	0.169	20.033	19.980	0.074	20.021	19.993	0.041	20.021	20.000	0.034
	Min	20.000	19.760	0.110	20.000	19.883	0.065	20.000	19.959	0.020	20.000	19.980	0.007	20.000	19.987	0.000
25	Max	25.130	24.890	0.370	25.052	24.935	0.169	25.033	24.980	0.074	25.021	24.993	0.041	25.021	25.000	0.034
	Min	25.000	24.760	0.110	25.000	24.883	0.065	25.000	24.959	0.020	25.000	24.980	0.007	25.000	24.987	0.000
30	Max	30.130	29.890	0.370	30.052	29.935	0.169	30.033	29.980	0.074	30.021	29.993	0.041	30.021	30.000	0.034
	Min	30.000	29.760	0.110	30.000	29.883	0.065	30.000	29.959	0.020	30.000	29.980	0.007	30.000	29.987	0.000

Figure A-7

Preferred Transition and Interference Fits — Cylindrical Fits
(Hole Basis; ANSI B4.2)

Basic Size		Locational Trans.			Locational Trans.			Locational Inter.			Medium Drive			Force		
		Hole H7	Shaft k6	Fit	Hole H7	Shaft n6	Fit	Hole H7	Shaft p6	Fit	Hole H7	Shaft s6	Fit	Hole H7	Shaft u6	Fit
4	Max	4.012	4.009	0.011	4.012	4.016	0.004	4.012	4.020	0.000	4.012	4.027	-0.007	4.012	4.031	-0.011
	Min	4.000	4.001	-0.009	4.000	4.008	-0.016	4.000	4.012	-0.020	4.000	4.019	-0.027	4.000	4.023	-0.031
5	Max	5.012	5.009	0.011	5.012	5.016	0.004	5.012	5.020	0.000	5.012	5.027	-0.007	5.012	5.031	-0.011
	Min	5.000	5.001	-0.009	5.000	5.008	-0.016	5.000	5.012	-0.020	5.000	5.019	-0.027	5.000	5.023	-0.031
6	Max	6.012	6.009	0.011	6.012	6.016	0.004	6.012	6.020	0.000	6.012	6.027	-0.007	6.012	6.031	-0.011
	Min	6.000	6.001	-0.009	6.000	6.008	-0.016	6.000	6.012	-0.020	6.000	6.019	-0.027	6.000	6.023	-0.031
8	Max	8.015	8.010	0.014	8.015	8.019	0.005	8.015	8.024	0.000	8.015	8.032	-0.008	8.015	8.037	-0.013
	Min	8.000	8.001	-0.010	8.000	8.010	-0.019	8.000	8.015	-0.024	8.000	8.023	-0.032	8.000	8.028	-0.037
10	Max	10.015	10.010	0.014	10.015	10.019	0.005	10.015	10.024	0.000	10.015	10.032	-0.008	10.015	10.037	-0.013
	Min	10.000	10.001	-0.010	10.000	10.010	-0.019	10.000	10.015	-0.024	10.000	10.023	-0.032	10.000	10.028	-0.037
12	Max	12.018	12.012	0.017	12.018	12.023	0.006	12.018	12.029	0.000	12.018	12.039	-0.010	12.018	12.044	-0.015
	Min	12.000	12.001	-0.012	12.000	12.012	-0.023	12.000	12.018	-0.029	12.000	12.028	-0.039	12.000	12.033	-0.044
16	Max	16.018	16.012	0.017	16.018	16.023	0.006	16.018	16.029	0.000	16.018	16.039	-0.010	16.018	16.044	-0.015
	Min	16.000	16.001	-0.012	16.000	16.012	-0.023	16.000	16.018	-0.029	16.000	16.028	-0.039	16.000	16.033	-0.044
20	Max	20.021	20.015	0.019	20.021	20.028	0.006	20.021	20.035	-0.001	20.021	20.048	-0.014	20.021	20.054	-0.020
	Min	20.000	20.002	-0.015	20.000	20.015	-0.028	20.000	20.022	-0.035	20.000	20.035	-0.048	20.000	20.041	-0.054
25	Max	25.021	25.015	0.019	25.021	25.028	0.006	25.021	25.035	-0.001	25.021	25.048	-0.014	25.021	25.061	-0.027
	Min	25.000	25.002	-0.015	25.000	25.015	-0.028	25.000	25.022	-0.035	25.000	25.035	-0.048	25.000	25.048	-0.061
30	Max	30.021	30.015	0.019	30.021	30.028	0.006	30.021	30.035	-0.001	30.021	30.048	-0.014	30.021	30.061	-0.027
	Min	30.000	30.002	-0.015	30.000	30.015	-0.028	30.000	30.022	-0.035	30.000	30.035	-0.048	30.000	30.048	-0.061

Figure A-8

Preferred Clearance Fits — Cylindrical Fits
(Shaft Basis; ANSI B4.2)

Basic Size		Loose Running			Free Running			Close Running			Sliding			Locational Clear.		
		Hole C11	Shaft h11	Fit	Hole D9	Shaft h9	Fit	Hole F8	Shaft h7	Fit	Hole G7	Shaft h6	Fit	Hole H7	Shaft h6	Fit
4	Max	4.145	4.000	0.220	4.060	4.000	0.090	4.028	4.000	0.040	4.016	4.000	0.024	4.012	4.000	0.020
	Min	4.070	3.925	0.070	4.030	3.970	0.030	4.010	3.988	0.010	4.004	3.992	0.004	4.000	3.992	0.000
5	Max	5.145	5.000	0.220	5.060	5.000	0.090	5.028	5.000	0.040	5.016	5.000	0.024	5.012	5.000	0.020
	Min	5.070	4.925	0.070	5.030	4.970	0.030	5.010	4.988	0.010	5.004	4.992	0.004	5.000	4.992	0.000
6	Max	6.145	6.000	0.220	6.060	6.000	0.090	6.028	6.000	0.040	6.016	6.000	0.024	6.012	6.000	0.020
	Min	6.070	5.925	0.070	6.030	5.970	0.030	6.010	5.988	0.010	6.004	5.992	0.004	6.000	5.992	0.000
8	Max	8.170	8.000	0.260	8.076	8.000	0.112	8.035	8.000	0.050	8.020	8.000	0.029	8.015	8.000	0.024
	Min	8.080	7.910	0.080	8.040	7.964	0.040	8.013	7.985	0.013	8.005	7.991	0.005	8.000	7.991	0.000
10	Max	10.170	10.000	0.260	10.076	10.000	0.112	10.035	10.000	0.050	10.020	10.000	0.029	10.015	10.000	0.024
	Min	10.080	9.910	0.080	10.040	9.964	0.040	10.013	9.985	0.013	10.005	9.991	0.005	10.000	9.991	0.000
12	Max	12.205	12.000	0.315	12.093	12.000	0.136	12.043	12.000	0.061	12.024	12.000	0.035	12.018	12.000	0.029
	Min	12.095	11.890	0.095	12.050	11.957	0.050	12.016	11.982	0.016	12.006	11.989	0.006	12.000	11.989	0.000
16	Max	16.205	16.000	0.315	16.093	16.000	0.136	16.043	16.000	0.061	16.024	16.000	0.035	16.018	16.000	0.029
	Min	16.095	15.890	0.095	16.050	15.957	0.050	16.016	15.982	0.016	06.006	15.989	0.006	16.000	15.989	0.000
20	Max	20.240	20.000	0.370	20.117	20.000	0.169	20.053	20.000	0.074	20.028	20.000	0.041	20.021	20.000	0.034
	Min	20.110	19.870	0.110	20.065	19.948	0.065	20.020	19.979	0.020	20.007	19.987	0.007	20.000	19.987	0.000
25	Max	25.240	25.000	0.370	25.117	25.000	0.169	25.053	25.000	0.074	25.028	25.000	0.041	25.021	25.000	0.034
	Min	25.110	24.870	0.110	25.065	24.948	0.065	25.020	24.979	0.020	25.007	24.987	0.007	25.000	24.987	0.000
30	Max	30.240	30.000	0.370	30.117	30.000	0.169	30.053	30.000	0.074	30.028	30.000	0.041	30.021	30.000	0.034
	Min	30.110	29.870	0.110	30.065	29.948	0.065	29.979	29.979	0.020	30.007	29.987	0.007	30.000	29.987	0.000

Figure A-9

Preferred Transition and Interference Fits — Cylindrical Fits (Shaft Basis; ANSI B4.2)

Basic Size		Locational Trans.			Locational Trans.			Locational Inter.			Medium Drive			Force		
		Hole K7	Shaft h6	Fit	Hole N7	Shaft h6	Fit	Hole F7	Shaft h6	Fit	Hole S7	Shaft h6	Fit	Hole U7	Shaft h6	Fit
4	Max	4.003	4.000	0.011	3.996	4.000	0.004	3.992	4.000	0.000	3.985	4.000	-0.007	3.981	4.000	-0.011
	Min	3.991	3.992	-0.009	3.984	3.992	-0.016	3.980	3.992	-0.020	3.973	3.992	-0.027	3.969	3.992	-0.031
5	Max	5.003	5.000	0.011	4.996	5.000	0.004	4.992	5.000	0.000	4.985	5.000	-0.007	4.981	5.000	-0.011
	Min	4.991	4.992	-0.009	4.984	4.992	-0.016	4.980	4.992	-0.020	4.973	4.992	-0.027	4.969	4.992	-0.031
6	Max	6.003	6.000	0.011	5.996	6.000	0.004	5.992	6.000	0.000	5.985	6.000	-0.007	5.981	6.000	-0.011
	Min	5.991	5.991	-0.009	5.984	5.992	-0.016	5.980	5.992	-0.020	5.973	5.992	-0.027	5.969	5.992	-0.031
8	Max	8.005	8.000	0.014	7.996	8.000	0.005	7.991	8.000	0.000	7.983	8.000	-0.008	7.978	8.000	-0.013
	Min	7.990	7.991	-0.010	7.981	7.991	-0.019	7.976	7.991	-0.024	7.968	7.991	-0.032	7.963	7.991	-0.037
10	Max	10.005	10.000	0.014	9.996	10.000	0.005	9.991	10.000	0.000	9.983	10.000	-0.008	9.978	10.000	-0.013
	Min	9.990	9.991	-0.010	9.981	9.991	-0.019	9.976	9.991	-0.024	9.968	9.991	-0.032	9.963	9.991	-0.037
12	Max	12.006	12.000	0.017	11.995	12.000	0.006	11.989	12.000	0.000	11.979	12.000	-0.010	11.974	12.000	-0.015
	Min	11.988	11.989	-0.012	11.977	11.989	-0.023	11.971	11.989	-0.029	11.961	11.989	-0.039	11.956	11.989	-0.044
16	Max	16.006	16.000	0.017	15.995	16.000	0.006	15.989	16.000	0.000	15.979	16.000	-0.010	15.974	16.000	-0.015
	Min	15.988	15.989	-0.012	15.977	15.989	-0.023	15.971	15.989	-0.029	15.961	15.989	-0.039	15.956	15.989	-0.044
20	Max	20.006	20.000	0.019	19.993	20.000	0.006	19.986	20.000	-0.001	19.973	20.000	-0.014	19.967	20.000	-0.020
	Min	19.985	19.987	-0.015	19.972	19.987	-0.028	19.965	19.987	-0.035	19.952	19.987	-0.048	19.946	19.987	-0.054
25	Max	25.006	25.000	0.019	24.993	25.000	0.006	24.986	25.000	-0.001	24.973	25.000	-0.014	24.960	25.000	-0.027
	Min	24.985	24.987	-0.015	24.972	24.987	-0.028	24.965	24.987	-0.035	24.952	24.987	-0.048	24.939	24.987	-0.061
30	Max	30.006	30.000	0.019	29.993	30.000	0.006	29.986	30.000	-0.001	29.973	30.000	-0.014	29.960	30.000	-0.027
	Min	29.985	29.987	-0.015	29.972	29.987	-0.028	29.987	29.987	-0.035	29.952	29.987	-0.048	29.939	29.987	-0.061

Figure A-10

Metric Threads—Preferred Sizes			
First Choice	**Second Choice**	**First Choice**	**Second Choice**
1	1.1	12	14
1.2	1.4	16	18
1.6	1.8	20	22
2	2.2	25	28
2.5	2.8	30	35
3	3.5	40	45
4	4.5	50	55
5	5.5	60	70
6	7	80	90
8	9	100	110
10	11	120	140

Figure A-11

Standard Thread Lengths—Inches														
	3/16	**1/4**	**3/8**	**1/2**	**5/8**	**3/4**	**7/8**	**1**	**1 1/4**	**1 1/2**	**1 3/4**	**2**	**2 1/2**	**3**
#2 - 5	√	√	√	√	√	√	√	√						
#4 - 40		√	√	√	√	√	√	√	√	√				
#6 - 32		√	√	√	√	√		√	√	√	√	√	√	√
#8 - 32		√	√	√	√	√		√	√	√	√	√	√	√
#10 - 24		√	√	√	√	√		√	√	√	√	√	√	√
#10 - 32		√	√	√		√		√	√	√	√	√	√	√
#12 - 24			√	√	√	√		√	√	√	√	√	√	√
1/4 20				√	√	√	√	√	√	√	√	√	√	√
5/16 18				√	√	√	√	√	√	√	√	√	√	√
3/8 16				√	√	√	√	√	√	√	√	√	√	√
1/2 13						√	√	√	√	√	√	√	√	√
5/8 11							√	√	√	√	√	√	√	√
3/4 10										√		√		√

Figure A-12

American National Standard Plain Washers					
Nominal Washer Size		Series	Inside Diameter	Outside Diameter	Thickness
No. 0	0.060	N R W	0.068 0.068 0.068	0.125 0.188 0.250	0.025 0.025 0.025
No. 1	0.073	N R W	0.084 0.084 0.084	0.156 0.219 0.281	0.025 0.025 0.032
No. 2	0.086	N R W	0.094 0.094 0.094	0.188 0.250 0.344	0.025 0.032 0.032
No. 3	0.099	N R W	0.109 0.109 0.109	0.219 0.312 0.406	0.025 0.032 0.040
No. 4	0.112	N R W	0.125 0.125 0.125	0.250 0.375 0.438	0.032 0.040 0.040
No. 5	0.125	N R W	0.141 0.141 0.141	0.281 0.406 0.500	0.032 0.040 0.040
No. 6	1.380	N R W	0.156 0.156 0.156	0.312 0.438 0.562	0.032 0.040 0.040
No. 8	0.164	N R W	0.188 0.188 0.183	0.375 0.500 0.633	0.040 0.040 0.063
No. 10	0.190	N R W	0.203 0.203 0.203	0.406 0.562 0.734	0.040 0.040 0.063
No. 12	0.216	N R W	0.234 0.234 0.234	0.438 0.625 0.875	0.040 0.063 0.063
1/4	0.250	N R W	0.281 0.281 0.281	0.500 0.734 1.000	0.063 0.063 0.063
5/16	0.312	N R W	0.344 0.344 0.344	0.625 0.875 1.125	0.063 0.063 0.063
3/8	0.375	N R W	0.406 0.406 0.406	0.734 1.000 1.250	0.063 0.063 0.100
7/16	0.438	N R W	0.469 0.469 0.469	0.875 1.125 1.469	0.063 0.063 0.100
1/2	0.500	N R W	0.531 0.531 0.531	1.000 1.2.5 1.125	0.063 0.100 0.100

Figure A-13

American National Standard Plain Washers					
Nominal Washer Size		Series	Inside Diameter	Outside Diameter	Thickness
9/16	0.562	N R W	0.594 0.594 0.594	1.125 1.469 2.000	0.063 0.100 0.100
5/8	0.625	N R W	0.656 0.656 0.656	1.250 1.750 2.250	0.100 0.100 0.160
3/4	0.750	N R W	0.812 0.812 0.812	1.375 2.000 2.500	0.100 0.100 0.160
7/8	0.875	N R W	0.938 0.938 0.938	1.469 2.250 2.750	0.100 0.160 0.160
1	1.000	N R W	1.062 1.062 1.062	1.750 2.500 3.000	0.100 0.160 0.160

Figure A-13 *(continued)*

Index

A

B

C

D

E

F

G

H

I

K

L

M

N

O

P

R

S

T

U

V